# THE VIRGIN ENCYCLOPEDIA OF
# 80s
## MUSIC

**third edition**

**compiled and edited by**
### COLIN LARKIN

In Association with
MUZE UK Ltd

*Dedicated to the Compact Disc*

First published in Great Britain in 2003 by
Virgin Books Ltd
Thames Wharf Studios
Rainville Road
London W6 9HA

A catalogue record for this book is available
from the British Library.

ISBN 1 85227 969 9

# muze

Written, edited and produced by
MUZE UK Ltd
All editorial enquiries and justified complaints
should be sent to:
Suite 16, Arcade Chambers, 28 High Street,
Brentwood, Essex, CM14 4AH.
**www.muze.com**

Editor-In-Chief: Colin Larkin
Assistant Editor: Nic Oliver
Production Editor: Susan Pipe
Typographic Design: Roger Kohn
Design Assistant: Aku Young
Special thanks to Paul Zullo
and Tom Goldsworthy of Muze Inc., and to
KT Forster and Carolyn Thorne of Virgin Books.

Typeset by Roland Flanger Studio
Printed and bound in Great Britain by
Mackays of Chatham Ltd, Chatham, Kent

# INTRODUCTION

My criticism of the 80s has probably been overdone. My problem has always been with music that is not natural. For me, those watery flanged guitars, boing-boing syn drum, and goddam awful electric pianos that merely diddled, were as bad as the government in power (on both sides of the Atlantic). The favoured record production of the decade was so crisp and so up-front it hurt. Nevertheless, I thought I hated it all. Guess what, I was talking out of my backside once again. Checking over the selections for this book made me realise how much excellent stuff there was hidden under the massive pile of dross.

I had forgotten that the decade gave us the Police, the Cure in their prime, those fantastic Madness videos, the Fall, two priceless Blue Nile albums which I only discovered in the 90s along with Talk Talk's *Spirit Of Eden*. Then there was the uplifting pop of Nik Kershaw, Altered Images and Haircut 100, the slightly weird but excellent Immaculate Fools and the wholesome rock of the Pretenders.

The Rain Parade, Bangles, Smithereens, R.E.M. and Green On Red fed my 60s withdrawal symptoms. In fact, I purchased more albums in the 80s than any other decade so far. So I hope this book will surprise you as much as it did me. As terrible as the 80s were, there was a ton of great music. There *were* real musicians playing real instruments without the aid of a synloopdigitizer. There *were* many classic songs that which will endure. Your duty is to flick through and decide for yourself, I ain't saying nothing. The book covers the artists that I think represent the decade, good and bad.

*The Virgin Encyclopedia Of Eighties Music* is one of a major ongoing series of books taken from the multi-volume *Encyclopedia Of Popular Music*. Other titles always available are:

## ENTRY STYLE

All albums, EPs (extended-play 45s), newspapers, magazines, television programmes, films and stage musicals are referred to in italics. All song titles appear in single quotes. We spell rock 'n' roll like this. There are two main reasons for spelling rock 'n' roll with 'n' as opposed to 'n'. First, historical precedent: when the term was first coined in the 50s, the popular spelling was 'n'. Second, the 'n' is not simply an abbreviation of 'and' (in which case 'n' would apply) but as a phonetic representation of n as a sound. The ' ', therefore, serve as inverted commas rather than as apostrophes. The further reading section at the end of each entry has been expanded to give the reader a much wider choice of available books. These are not necessarily recommended titles but we have attempted to leave out any publication that has little or no merit.

We have also started to add videos at the end of the entries, but have decided not to list DVDs, simply because there is not enough time. Again, this is an area that is expanding faster than we can easily cope with, but there are many items in the videography and the filmography. Release dates in keeping with albums attempt to show the release date in the country of origin. We have also tried to include both US and UK titles in the case of a title change.

## DATES OF BIRTH

Occasionally we hear from an artist or manager asking us to change the date of birth, usually upwards, to make the artist younger. We have to reluctantly comply with this unless we have sighted birth registration details. We are constantly seeking accurate birth data, and confirmed corrections would be gratefully received.

## DISCOGRAPHY

In attempting to put the record label with albums I am very aware that most labels listed are either from the USA or the UK. These will continue to be our prime sources. We have attempted to list the label (and country) where the release was first issued. Because of the continuing CD revolution and the constant repackaging we have listed the most recent reissues. What we have not done is to list the latest label. That would be too much of a task. Once again please refer to the website www.muze.com for both US and UK labels and catalogue numbers as well as track listings. This book is not meant to be a discographical tool; we are more concerned with the artist's music and career. For the majority of artists in this work, complete discographies have been compiled. However, on occasion, the discography section at the end of an entry is incomplete. This is not due to lack of effort on our behalf but simply to the fact that some artists have had such extensive careers that it is impossible to go back over numerous decades of files. From our experience, most record companies do not retain this detailed information. The aim of the discography is to allow the reader to investigate further the work of a particular artist. We have included, where possible, the regular albums together with the first year of release date in the known country of origin, which is generally in the USA or the UK. In many cases the delay in releasing the record in another country can be years. Some Latin, African, Caribbean and other Third World recordings have been assigned approximate release dates as the labels often do not carry any release date. We do not list bootlegs but one or two may have accidentally crept in.

In the case of recordings made before the general availability of the LP (album), approximately 1950, we have aimed to inform the reader of the date of recordings and the year of release. Since the advent of the compact disc in 1982, and its subsequent popularity, the reissue market has expanded enormously. There are outstanding reissue programmes going ahead, usually with bonus tracks or alternative takes. Companies such as Collectables and Rhino in the USA and Ace and Castle in the UK are just two labels putting two-on-one, a fantastic bonus taking advantage of the CD over short-timed vinyl albums from the 50s and 60s. Our MUZE online database contains every CD release since day one.

## Album Ratings

Due to many requests from librarians and readers we continue to rate all albums. All new releases are reviewed either by myself or by our team of contributors. We also take into serious consideration the review ratings of the leading music journals and critics' opinions.

Our system is slightly different to most 5-Star ratings in that we rate according to the artist in question's work. Therefore, a 4-Star album from Pat Metheny may have the overall edge over a 4-Star album by Bucks Fizz. Sorry Bucks.

The ratings are carefully made, and consequently you will find we are very sparing with 5-Star and 1-Star albums.

★★★★★
Outstanding in every way.
A classic and therefore strongly recommended. No comprehensive record collection should be without this album.

Excellent.
A high-standard album from this artist and therefore highly recommended.

Good.
By the artist's usual standards and therefore recommended.

Disappointing.
Flawed or lacking in some way.

★
Poor.
An album to avoid unless you are a completist.

## Plagiarism

In maintaining the largest text database of popular music in the world, we are naturally protective of its content. We license to approved licensees only. It is both flattering and irritating to see our work reproduced without credit. Time and time again over the past few years I have read a newspaper obituary, knowing that I wrote that line or phrase. Secondly, it has come to our notice that other companies attempting to produce their own rock or pop encyclopedias use our material as a core. Flattering this might also be, but highly illegal. We have been making sure over the past two years that the publishers of these maverick music guides will be stopped once and for all for plagiarizing work that has taken us a lifetime to assemble. Having spent many hours with our lawyers taking action, I do know a bit about copyright law. Be careful and mostly, be warned, we usually know who you are. Our text appears on hundreds of websites, mostly unofficial ones. Once again, thanks for the compliment but make sure that you always credit and acknowledge us as your source (copyright MUZE UK or Encyclopedia Of Popular Music), otherwise we will have to shut you down.

## Chart Positions & Record Sales

The aim of this book is not to document chart positions and record sales. Many are discussed in passing but are ultimately left to the main books available. The reference books we have used were those formerly edited by Gambaccini, Rice and Rice, but now we use the new bible *The Complete Book Of The British Charts, Singles And Albums*, edited by Brown, Kutner and Warwick for the UK. Joel Whitburn's *(Top Pop Singles, Top Pop Albums, Country Singles, R&B Singles and Pop Memories)* for the USA are published by Record Research and are absolutely indispensable. Our chart information from 1952 to 1960 was originally taken from the *New Musical Express*, and from 1960 to 1968 was gleaned from the *Record Retailer*. While we have adhered to the BMRB in the main we feel that the *New Musical Express* and the recently departed *Melody Maker* charts were accepted more than the dreary *Record Retailer*, as the latter published its chart before the weekly sales were recorded. If we were to have stuck religiously to the *Record Retailer*, then the Beatles would have only had one record entering the chart at number 1. And cor blimey, we can't have that! It is generally known that most of their records reached number 1 on the week of release in the UK, and this was reflected in the main weekly music papers. This aberration fortunately does not occur in the USA, thanks to the longevity and accuracy of *Billboard* and Joel Whitburn's efforts. We now use the UK chart published by *Music Week*.

For the USA, when we refer to a gold disc for singles it signifies sales of 1,000,000 copies pre-1989 and 500,000 thereafter. The RIAA (Record Industry Association Of America) made this change in 1989, and *Billboard* followed suit. Similarly, when platinum awards were introduced, they initially signified sales of 2,000,000 copies and post-1989 of 1,000,000. For albums from 1958 to 1974, the term gold refers to LPs that sold $1 million worth of units at manufacturers' wholesale prices. Recognizing that due to rising prices the number of units necessary to gain gold status was dropping, the RIAA as of 1 January 1975 added the further proviso that to be gold an LP had to have sold at least 500,000 copies. A platinum LP has to have sold 1,000,000 copies. In the UK the BPI determines – singles: platinum 600,000 units, gold 400,000 and silver 200,000. For albums: platinum 300,000, gold 100,000, silver 60,000. For the recent introduction of CD box sets, a four-CD box has to sell 250,000 copies to go platinum, although this does not apply to two-disc sets at the present time.

## CRITICAL OPINION

The aim was always to strike a balance between being highly opinionated and bland, with a sprinkle of humour. We have attempted to express the generally accepted opinion and have not set out to be controversial (except in some cases where we hope our entries on certain lesser-known artists will lead to a reappraisal of their work).

## ACKNOWLEDGEMENTS

Still first and foremost, Johnny Rogan, who continues to be a fair critic and a good chum. He was the first person to hear of my proposal for the original *Encyclopedia* and agreed to be involved.

His great attention to detail shaped the original editorial style-sheet, and he was instrumental in approaching some early contributors. Additionally there is occasionally at the end of a phone the free advice of Pete Frame, Peter Doggett, Johnny Black and Fred Dellar. And if I fancy an earbashingly opinionated ten minutes about the current state of music, Stuart Batsford is top of the list. Chris Charlesworth is still a most agreeable and experienced Bayko construction engineer. Continuing praise for the efforts of Pete 'the hound' Bassett and his Quite Great company, Anita, Louise and Nige. Appreciation again and again to production editor Susan Pipe; efficient, trustworthy and loyal as ever, a rare thing in this day and age. Similarly invaluable is my extremely talkative assistant editor Nic Oliver. Michael Kaye continues as our database/software developer, his determination to fix bugs is admirable.

Our contributors are further reduced in number, as we now update and amend all our existing text and write most of the new stuff. Our team over the past year has included: Daryl Easlea, Greg Prato, Ian Bell, Dominic Chadwick, Tony Clayton-Lea, Jurgen Funk, Karen Glossop, David Hemingway, Joel McIver, Jake Kennedy, Sam Hendricks, Ben Hogwood, Ed Houghton, Mark Keresman, Siobhan Long, Dan Nosworthy, Alex Ogg, Jon Staines, Richard Wilson. Alongside, Spencer Leigh and Salsri Nyah continue to supply their specialist knowledge. The 'very necessary' Bruce Crowther continues to produce anything we throw at him, providing it is jazz. And to Carl Newsum and Dennis of Slipped Disc II in Chelmsford. Support your local independent record shop.

Past contributors' work may still appear in this volume, so just in case, I acknowledge with thanks once again: Simon Adams, David Ades, Mike Atherton, Gavin Badderley, Alan Balfour, Michael Barnett, John Bauldie, Johnny Black, Chris Blackford, Pamela Boniface, Keith Briggs, Michael Ian Burgess, Paul M. Brown, Tony Burke, John Child, Linton Chiswick, Rick Christian, Alan Clayson, Paul Cross, Norman Darwen, Roy Davenport, Peter Doggett, Kevin Eden, John Eley, Lars Fahlin, Tim Footman, John Fordham, Per Gardin, Ian Garlinge, Mike Gavin, Andy Hamilton, Mark Hodkinson, Brian Hogg, Mike Hughes, Arthur Jackson, Mark Jones, Max Jones, Simon Jones, Ian Kenyon, Dave Laing, Steve Lake, Paul Lewis, Graham Lock, John Martland, Bernd Matheja, Chris May, Dave McAleer, David McDonald, York Membery, Toru Mitsui, Greg Moffitt, Michael Newman, Pete Nickols, Lyndon Noon, Zbigniew Nowara, James Nye, Ken Orton, Ian Peel, Dave Penny, Alan Plater, Barry Ralph, John Reed, Emma Rees, Jamie Renton, Lionel

Robinson, Johnny Rogan, Alan Rowett, Dave Sissons, Neil Slaven, Chris Smith, Steve Smith, Mitch Solomons, Christopher Spencer, Mike Stephenson, Sam Sutherland, Jeff Tamarkin, Ray Templeton, Christen Thomsen, Liz Thompson, Gerard Tierney, John Tobler, Adrian T'Vell, Pete Wadeson, Frank Warren, Ben Watson, Pete Watson, Simon Williams, Val Wilmer, Dave Wilson and Barry Witherden. Others that have been missed are either through my own sloppy error or deliberate intention.

Record Company Press Offices. These invaluable people are often bombarded with my requests for biogs and review copies. Only a few actually respond, and those that do are very important to us. It always amazes me how some major record companies completely ignore our numerous requests and others of similar stature are right on the button. Thanks this time especially to Matt Wheeler at Polydor, Alan Robinson at Indiscreet, Dorothy Howe and Matt Sweeting at Sanctuary, Erik James, Florence Halfon, Rick Conrad and Carlos Anaia at Warners, Sue and Dave Williams at Frontier Promotions, Tones Sansom and Vanessa Cotton at Triad Publicity, Joe Foster, Andrew Lauder at Evangeline, Bob, Tom at Snapper, Neil Scaplehorn at Ace, Murray Chalmers, Chris Latham and the team at Parlophone/Capitol, Mike Gott at BGO, Tim Wright and Ian McNay at Cherry Red/RPM, Mick Houghton at Brassneck, Zoe Stafford at RCA, Shane O'Neill at Universal, Ted Cummings at MCA, Jonathan Gill at Demon, Paul at Big Moon, Mal Smith at Delta, Darren Crisp at Crisp Productions and Pat Tynan at Koch International.

To the few friends who you can trust, colleagues and family who play no direct part in producing these books but make my life more tolerable: Nils von Veh, Fred Nelson, Mark T., Stuart Batsford, Danny Sperling, Bob Harris, Johnnie Walker, Mark Simpson, Kathleen Dougherty, Chris Braham, David Gould, Roger Kohn, Roy Sheridan, Kip Trevor, Alan Lynch, John Burton, David Larkin, Sabra Larkin, Kay and Kevin, Sally Decibelle and the four long lost London cousins, Danny, Peter, Michael and John.

To all our colleagues in the USA at Muze Inc., and at the head office of MUZE UK, who oil the smooth running of our EPM unit. And especially, but in no order whatsoever to Gary Geller, Scott Lehr, Catherine Hamilton, Justin Sedgmond, Ian Bell, Karien de Witt, Jennifer Rose, Paul Parrierra (and the Raiders), Jim Allen, Paul Brennan, Jean-Pierre Zephir, Sean Sullivan, Kristin Zirkel, Amanda Denhoff, Isaac Morales, Phil Antman, Bill Schmitt, Holly Lehr, Simon 'blesshislittle' Hart, Jeanne Petras, Stephanie Jones, Ed Moore, Michael Lupitkin, Michael Kennedy, Mike Doustan, Tom Goldsworthy, and of course Marc 'night of fear' Miller and my new boss Paul 'nightfall of diamonds' Zullo. Finally, love to Jennie and the tins, Nad, Mot and Nemrac.

*Colin Larkin, October 2002*

## A CERTAIN RATIO

No UK act crystallized independent, punk-influenced funk more than Manchester's A Certain Ratio. The original line-up comprised Jeremy Kerr (bass), Simon Topping (vocals, trumpet), Peter Terrell (guitar), Martin Moscrop (guitar, trumpet), Martha Tilson (vocals, ex-Occult Chemistry), who joined a little later, although she had left by 1982, and Donald Johnson (drums) who replaced a drum machine. They signed to Factory Records in 1979 for the cassette-only release, *The Graveyard And The Ballroom*. One side was recorded at Graveyard Studios, the other live, supporting Talking Heads at London's Electric Ballroom. After releasing 'All Night Party' in May 1979, there was a hiatus before 'Flight', a UK Independent Top 10 hit over a year later. In the meantime, the band had teamed up with Factory's European sister company Benelux, for a cover version of Banbarra's mid-70s funk classic 'Shack Up', in July 1980. This edgy but rhythmic version offered an excellent snapshot of the band's innovative studio technique. *To Each ...*, the band's official debut album, attracted BBC disc jockey John Peel in 1981, a year that also yielded 'Do The Du' (officially intended for release in the USA), and in December 'Waterline' also fared well. The following year saw a move from the independent to the national charts as *Sextet* further established the band's reputation. Like *To Each ...*, *Sextet* housed an intriguing, mostly instrumental collection hinged around funk rhythms. A 12-inch single for Benelux, 'Guess Who', surfaced in July, followed by the *Knife Slits Water* EP in October, coinciding with the release of *I'd Like To See You Again*. The band also issued an obscure 12-inch single on the Rock Steady label, 'Abracadabra', under the guise of Sir Horatio, in September 1982. A year later, 'I Need Someone Tonight' was released, reaching the UK Independent Top 10. Topping and Terrell had departed, the former resurfacing in 1987 with Mike Pickering as acid house innovators T-Coy. They duo were replaced by Andy Connell, and 'Brazilia' became the band's first project of 1985. 'Wild Party', in June, featured new saxophonist Tony Quigley. Those anticipating a new album had to wait until the end of 1986 for *Force*, although a compilation, *The Old & The New*, had provided some consolation earlier in the year. 'Mickey Way' promoted *Force* and continued ACR's run of independent hits.

By 1987, the band had outgrown the confines of mere cult status and, looking to branch out, signed with A&M Records. To bridge the gap, the Dojo label issued *A Certain Ratio – Live In America* in February, alongside 'Greetings Four', for the European label Materiali Sonari. It was not until the summer of 1989 that new ACR product arrived, and both 'The Big E' and 'Backs To The Wall' revealed a shift towards a more accessible sound. However, neither of these, nor 'Your Blue Eyes' in October, the *Four For The Floor* EP in February 1990, nor 'Won't Stop Loving You' in May, could provide that elusive hit. As a result *Good Together* and *ACR:MCR* made little impact and A Certain Ratio left A&M soon afterwards. The band then moved to New Order manager Rob Gretton's Rob's Records, although Creation Records reissued their back catalogue and also unveiled a sampler album of remixes from their vast discography (including contributions from Electronic and 808 State). Their experimental work and love of collage material has ensured their status as one of the most uncompromisingly original acts working in the post-punk era. *Change The Station* was the first album of new material in seven years.

● ALBUMS: *The Graveyard And The Ballroom* cassette only (Factory 1980) ★★, *To Each ...* (Factory 1981) ★★★★, *Sextet* (Factory 1982) ★★★, *I'd Like To See You Again* (Factory 1982) ★★★, *Force* (Factory 1986) ★★★, *A Certain Ratio – Live In America* (Dojo 1987) ★★, *Good Together* (A&M 1989) ★★★, *ACR:MCR* (A&M 1990) ★★★, *Up In Downsville* (Rob's 1992) ★★★, *Looking For A Certain Ratio* remixes (Creation 1994) ★★★, *Change The Station* (Rob's 1997) ★★★.

● COMPILATIONS: *The Old & The New* (Factory 1986) ★★★, *Early* (Soul Jazz 2002) ★★★★.

## A FLOCK OF SEAGULLS

This new-wave electro-pop act from Liverpool, England, had remarkable success in the USA before finding a large following in Britain. The band comprised Mike Score (b. 5 November 1957; keyboards, vocals), Ali Score (drum machine, vocals), Paul Reynolds (b. 4 August 1962; guitar) and Frank Maudsley (b. 10 November 1959; bass). Following an adventurous EP on Bill Nelson's Cocteau label the band made their album debut with *A Flock Of Seagulls*, a splendid example of futurist pop that contained a number of notable tracks including 'I Ran (So Far Away)', which made the US Top 10 in July 1982. Ex-hairdresser Mike Score received numerous press jibes for his 'silly haircut'; he had cultivated his none-too-natural blond locks to hang irritatingly over his keyboards. Although *Listen* was another infectious collection of songs, they were unable to find any lasting popularity in their homeland to back up the success of 'Wishing (If I Had A Photograph Of You)', which reached number 10 in November 1982. Paul Reynolds departed after the release of *The Story Of A Young Heart*. That album and *Dream Come True* (made as a trio) were way below par and the band subsequently disintegrated. Score organized a new version of the band in 1989, touring the USA and issuing a single 'Magic', of which commodity this band had little. They, too, broke up. Score resurfaced once more in 1995 minus the haircut but with *The Light At The End Of The World*, and has carried the band name into the new millennium.

● ALBUMS: *A Flock Of Seagulls* (Jive 1982) ★★★, *Listen* (Jive 1983) ★★★, *The Story Of A Young Heart* (Jive 1984) ★★, *Dream Come True* (Jive 1986) ★★,

*The Light At The End Of The World* (Sava 1995) ★★.
● COMPILATIONS: *The Best Of A Flock Of Seagulls* (Jive 1987) ★★★, *20 Classics Of The '80s* (Emporio 1995) ★★★, *Greatest Hits Remixed* (Cleopatra 1999) ★★★.

## A WITNESS

Formed in Manchester, England, A Witness shared the distinctive sound adopted by the Ron Johnson label acts: fast, quirky songs bearing an obvious debt to both Captain Beefheart and Pere Ubu. The band was formed by Keith Curtis (vocals), Rick Aitken (b. 18 August 1956, d. October 1989; guitar) and Vince Hunt (bass). An EP, *Loudhailer Songs*, in 1985, attracted the *New Musical Express*, who included the band on their seminal *C86* sampler tape. An album, *I Am John Pancreas*, followed in 1986, featuring manic, awkward guitar riffs and offbeat lyrics. Alan Brown was subsequently recruited to replace the band's drum machine. After the release of another EP, *One Foot In The Groove*, in 1988, the Ron Johnson label folded, prompting a short-lived period at Fundamental Records who issued A Witness' second album, *Sacred Cow Heart*. The Membranes' Vinyl Drip label was responsible for the band's next and possibly finest single, 'I Love You, Mr. Disposable Razors', in 1989. Sadly, Aitken died in a climbing accident the same year and the band subsequently folded. Strange Fruit Records released a mini-album compiling A Witness' two 1988 sessions for BBC disc jockey John Peel. The band also covered the Doors' 'Break On Through' on a tribute album to the music of 1967, *Through The Looking Glass*. Curtis went on to play with the Membranes and Gold Blade, while Hunt and Brown reunited in Marshall Smith in the late 90s.
● ALBUMS: *I Am John Pancreas* (Ron Johnson 1986) ★★★, *Sacred Cow Heart* (Fundamental/Communion 1988) ★★★, *Double Peel Sessions* mini-album (Strange Fruit 1989) ★★★.
● COMPILATIONS: *Threaphurst Lane* (Overground 2000) ★★★.

## A-HA

Formed in early 1983 this Norwegian rock trio comprises Morten Harket (b. 14 September 1959, Kongsberg, Norway; lead vocals), Magne Furuholmen (b. 1 November 1962, Manglerud, Oslo, Norway; vocals, keyboards) and Pål Waaktaar (b. Pål Garnst, 6 September 1961, Manglerud, Oslo, Norway; vocals, guitar). After several years spent playing in various Scandinavian bands, including Spider Empire, Soldier Blue and Bridges, they finally found the perfect pop combination and set about selling their image to the international market. Warner Brothers Records signed them, but the debut single, 'Take On Me', produced by Tony Mansfield, sold poorly. Undeterred, A-Ha's management elected to re-record the song with Alan Tarney at the helm. With the assistance of a brilliant promotional video, utilizing animated pencil sketches, the single reached number 1 in the USA and number 2 in the UK. The timing could not have been better, and during 1985 the trio neatly assumed the teenage pin-up pop idolatry previously bestowed on Duran

and Wham!. With their chiselled good looks and exotic Scandinavian accents, the band could seemingly do no wrong. The expertly enunciated 'The Sun Always Shines On TV' took them to the top of the UK charts and reached the US Top 20. This was followed by a world tour and a further series of UK Top 10 hits, including 'Train Of Thought', 'Hunting High And Low', 'I've Been Losing You' and 'Cry Wolf'.

In 1987, Pål Waaktaar was commissioned to compose the theme for the James Bond movie *The Living Daylights*, with John Barry. After two essentially pop albums and acutely aware of the ephemeral power of the pin-up pop star, the band carefully attempted to make the uneasy transition to long-term success with 1988's sombre *Stay On These Roads*. In 1989, Harket appeared in the Norwegian film *Kamilla Og Tyven*, in addition to recording a one-off single with Bjorn Eidsvag. The band's solid musicianship continued to serve them well, and their mannered vocal style brought further UK chart success in 1990 with a revival of the Everly Brothers' 'Crying In The Rain' and *East Of The Sun, West Of The Moon*. The follow-up *Memorial Beach* included the minor hits 'Move To Memphis' and 'Dark Is The Night', but failed to capture the hearts of the critics.

Harket subsequently embarked on a solo career, Furuholmen formed Timbersound with Kjetil Bjerkestrand, while Waaktaar formed the New York-based Savoy with his wife Lauren. The trio re-formed A-Ha in the late 90s and returned to the studio to record the well-received albums *Minor Earth/Major Sky* and *Lifelines*.
● ALBUMS: *Hunting High And Low* (Warners 1985) ★★★, *Scoundrel Days* (Warners 1986) ★★, *Stay On These Roads* (Warners 1988) ★★★, *East Of The Sun, West Of The Moon* (Warners 1990) ★★★, *Memorial Beach* (Warners 1993) ★★, *Minor Earth/Major Sky* (Warners 2000) ★★★, *Lifelines* (Warners 2002) ★★★.
● COMPILATIONS: *Headlines And Deadlines: The Hits Of A-Ha* (Warners 1991) ★★★.
● VIDEOS: *Headlines And Deadlines: The Hits Of A-Ha* (Warner Music Video 1991), *Live In South America* (Warner Music Video 1993), *Homecoming: Live At Vallhall* (Warner Music Vision 2002).

## ABBOTT, GREGORY

b. 2 April 1954, Harlem, New York City, New York, USA. This R&B singer-songwriter began pursuing a musical career while working for his doctorate at the University of California at Berkeley. He soon moved to Los Angeles and married famed songstress Freda Payne, who recorded four of his songs. He returned to his home in New York and began working as a researcher in a stockbroking firm. Associates at the firm took an interest in Abbott's musical career and financed a studio and label, Gramercy Park Records. Abbott recorded a few acts for the label before trying to record himself. In 1986, he signed with Columbia Records, and enjoyed a huge hit with 'Shake You Down' (number 1 R&B, number 1 pop), which became the fastest song in US music history to reach one million airplays. In the UK, the song went to number 6 on the singles chart. Abbott continued his success in the R&B field with 'I Got The Feelin' (It's

Over)' (number 5 R&B) in 1987, and 'I'll Prove It To You' (number 5 R&B) in 1988. He has since balanced songwriting interests with his solo career, and while never enjoying the heady commercial success of his debut he continues to produce pleasant collections of easy-listening R&B.

● ALBUMS: *Shake You Down* (Columbia 1986) ★★★★, *I'll Prove It To You* (Columbia 1988) ★★★, *One World* (Musik 1994) ★★★, *Eyes, Whispers, Rhythm, Sex ...* (Musik 2000) ★★★.

● COMPILATIONS: *Super Hits* (Sony 1998) ★★★★.

## ABC

Purveyors of 'perfect pop' in the early 80s, ABC's sound has always been dominated by the stunning vocal range and lyrical songwriting skills of lead singer Martin Fry (b. 9 March 1958, Manchester, England). The band was formed after Fry had interviewed Mark White (b. 1 April 1961, Sheffield, Yorkshire, England; guitar) and Stephen Singleton (b. 17 April 1959, Sheffield, Yorkshire, England; saxophone), two members of Sheffield-based electronic outfit Vice Versa, for his fanzine *Modern Drugs*. Accepting the invitation to join as vocalist, Fry took artistic control of the act, changing the name to ABC, as well as altering the musical direction towards a more pop-orientated course. The band was completed by the arrival of temporary bass player Mark Lickley and drummer David Robinson, although the latter was soon replaced by David Palmer (b. 29 May 1961, Chesterfield, Derbyshire, England). The band's debut single 'Tears Are Not Enough', featuring Robinson, was released on their Neutron label. The song made the UK Top 20 in late 1981, but it was the following year that cemented ABC's reputation, with three UK Top 10 hits in a seven-month period: 'Poison Arrow', 'The Look Of Love' and 'All Of My Heart'.

Their pristine pop songs were nowhere better showcased than on the superb *The Lexicon Of Love*. This Trevor Horn-produced album remains a benchmark of 80s pop, and a formidable collection of melodramatic love songs assembled in one neat package. The album reached number 1 and stayed in the UK charts for a year, and broke into the US Top 30. The follow-up *Beauty Stab* was recorded as a trio following Palmer's defection to the Yellow Magic Orchestra. The relative failure of the album to emulate the debut's success resulted in further personnel upheaval, and by 1984, only Fry and White remained from the original line-up. They continued as ABC, using session musicians and undergoing a change of image for the promotion of *How To Be A ... Zillionaire!*, almost to the extent of becoming caricatures. This image, particularly in videos, gave the band some success in the USA with 'Be Near Me' reaching the Top 10 in 1985 and '(How To Be A) Millionaire' peaking at number 20 the following January.

Fry became seriously ill in 1986 and was absent for over a year while he received treatment for Hodgkin's disease. He teamed up with White once more for 1987's memorable UK Top 20/US Top 5 hit, 'When Smokey Sings', although the attendant *Alphabet City* failed to match the success of their debut album. A move to Parlophone Records at the start of the 90s failed to revive their fortunes. By the middle of the decade, only Fry remained from the original line-up. His voice remained intact but in desperate need of songs of the standard of ABC's 80s heyday. *Skyscraping* was a good attempt at recreating the 'classic' ABC sound, but sounded dated in an era dominated by urban music. Since the album's release Fry has continued to lead ABC on the 80s revival circuit.

● ALBUMS: *The Lexicon Of Love* (Neutron/Mercury 1982) ★★★★★, *Beauty Stab* (Neutron/Mercury 1983) ★★★, *How To Be A ... Zillionaire!* (Neutron/Mercury 1985) ★★★, *Alphabet City* (Neutron/Mercury 1987) ★★★, *Up* (Neutron/Mercury 1989) ★★★, *Abracadabra* (Parlophone/MCA 1991) ★★, *Skyscraping* (Blatant/Deconstruction 1997) ★★★, *Lexicon Of Live* (Blatant 1999) ★★★.

● COMPILATIONS: *Absolutely* (Neutron/Mercury 1990) ★★★, *The Remix Collection* (Connoisseur 1993) ★★★, *The Best Of ABC: The Millennium Collection* (Mercury 2000) ★★★, *Hello! An Introduction To ABC* (Mercury 2001) ★★★, *Look Of Love: The Very Best Of ABC* (Mercury 2001) ★★★★, *Poison Arrow* (Spectrum 2002) ★★.

● VIDEOS: *Mantrap* (Hendring Music Video 1983), *Absolutely* (PolyGram Music Video 1990).

## ABDUL, PAULA

b. 19 June 1962, San Fernando, California, USA. After spending much of her childhood in dance schools and troupes, Paula Abdul secured a role in the L.A. Lakers basketball cheerleaders team and at 17 became their choreographer. Spotted by the Jacksons, she was employed to assist them on dance routines for their live dates on the *Victory* tour. Abdul's big break came when she landed a job choreographing a young Janet Jackson's videos for *Control*. Their immediate success focused attention on Abdul's dance talents and she quickly found herself much in demand from a string of other artists (including ZZ Top, Duran Duran and the Pointer Sisters) seeking a high MTV profile. The inevitable move to her own singing career brought immediate fame. Stylistically in the mould of her former pupil, Janet Jackson, her third single, 'Straight Up', went to number 1 in the US in 1988, and was followed by three other chart-topping singles: 'Forever Your Girl', 'Cold Hearted' and 'Opposites Attract'. The latter's popularity was enhanced by the video's depiction of the singer duetting with a cartoon character, MC Skat Cat.

Abdul's debut, *Forever Your Girl*, triumphed on both sides of the Atlantic, reaching number 1 in the USA, staying there for 10 weeks, and peaking at number 3 in the UK. A follow-up collection of remixes, *Shut Up And Dance*, issued in early 1990, marked time until *Spellbound* was released in 1991. The latter gave Abdul another US chart-topping album and spawned two US number 1 singles in 'Rush, Rush' and 'The Promise Of A New Day'. Her popularity in Europe, although quite substantial ('Straight Up', 'Opposites Attract' and 'Rush, Rush' were all UK Top 10 singles), was nonetheless no match for her image in the USA, being every young girl's role model as the all-singing, all-dancing trouper. Abdul's choreography work in the movies and her marriage to actor Emilio Estevez also helped maintain her high profile, although the couple were divorced in May 1994. She returned in 1995 (after a long absence owing to a lawsuit filed by a former backing singer) with the minor hit single 'My Love Is For Real', which preceded *Head Over Heels*. Abdul made her adult acting debut in January 1997 with the television movie, *Touched By Evil*. She subsequently signed an abortive recording contract with Mercury Records, while continuing to work as a top-ranked choreographer. In 2000, she co-wrote Kylie Minogue's UK chart-topping single 'Spinning Around'. Two years later, she resurfaced as a judge on *American Idol*, the US version of the phenomenally successful UK series *Pop Idol*.

● ALBUMS: *Forever Your Girl* (Virgin 1988) ★★★, *Spellhound* (Virgin 1991) ★★★, *Head Over Heels* (Virgin 1995) ★★.
● COMPILATIONS: *Shut Up And Dance* remixes (Virgin 1990) ★★, *Greatest Hits* (Virgin 2000) ★★★★.
● VIDEOS: *Straight Up* (Virgin Vision 1988), *Captivated '92: The Video Collection* (Virgin Vision 1991), *Under My Spell Live* (Virgin Vision 1993).
● FILMS: *Junior High School* (1981).

### ABSOLUTE BEGINNERS

Based on Colin MacInnes' 1958 cult novel, which foresaw the rise of the Mod movement and much of the youth explosion of the 60s, Julien Temple, once part of the Sex Pistols/Malcolm McLaren entourage, directed this stylized 1986 film adaptation. However, rather than focus on the novel's dramatic tension – part of the action revolves around the Notting Hill Race riots – he transformed the narrative into a gaudy musical. The result was not generally considered a success. In the screenplay, by Richard Burridge, Don Macpherson and Christopher Wicking, aspiring photographer Colin (Eddie O'Connell) and embryonic fashion designer Suzette (Patsy Kensit) are a definite item before haughty couturier Henley of Mayfair (James Fox) muscles in and slips a ring on the lady's engagement finger. Colin loses his cool, and embarks on a trip which brings him into contact with an assortment of low-lifes who populate the 'arty' London area of Soho, such as pimps, hustlers, jazzers, and a promoter of young boy singers who bears a remarkable likeness to the infamous Larry Parnes. David Bowie plays advertising executive Vendice Partners, and also cast were Ray Davies, Mandy Rice-Davies, Eve Ferret, Lionel Blair, Tony Hippolyte, Graham Fletcher-Cook, Joe McKenna, Steven Berkoff, Sade, Bruce Payne and Alan Freeman, portraying a character called Call-Me-Cobber. Sylvia Syms, who featured in a bona fide 50s screen musical, *Expresso Bongo*, was also on hand, along with future television *Cracker* star Robbie Coltrane. Musical highlights included Ray Davies' 'Quiet Life' and Slim Gaillard's 'Selling Out', as well as Bowie's own compositions 'Absolute Beginners' and 'That's Motivation'. With those on the soundtrack were 'Killer Blow' (Sade), 'Have You Ever Had It Blue?' (Style Council), 'Ted Ain't Dead' (Tenpole Tudor), 'Rodrigo Bay' (Working Week),

'Having It All' (Eighth Wonder), 'Bongo Rock' (Jet Streams), 'Hey, Little Schoolgirl' (Paragons), 'So What' (Smiley Culture), 'Rock, Baby, Rock' (Bertice Reading) and 'Riot City' (Jerry Dammers). *Absolute Beginners*, filmed in Super Techniscope and Rank colour, was co-financed by leading UK company, Goldcrest Films. They were involved in highly acclaimed movies such as *Chariots Of Fire*, *Ghandi*, and *Local Hero*, but *Absolute Beginners* prefaced a decline in fortunes that eventually resulted in them being acquired by Brent Walker in 1987. The *Absolute Beginners* tagline was 'Welcome to the world of your dreams' – more like a nightmare in many respects.

### AC/DC

This theatrical Australian hard rock band was formed in November 1973 by Malcolm Young (b. 6 January 1953, Glasgow, Scotland; rhythm guitar) after the demise of his previous outfit, the Velvet Underground (no relation to the US group). Young, whose elder brother George had already achieved stardom in Australia as a member of the Easybeats, also enlisted his younger brother, Angus Young (b. 31 March 1955, Glasgow, Scotland; guitar). Their sister later suggested that Angus wear his school uniform on stage, a gimmick that rapidly became their trademark. The two brothers made their debut appearance in a bar in Sydney on 31 December 1973, along with Dave Evans (vocals), Larry Van Kriedt (bass) and Colin Burgess (drums). In late 1974, the Young brothers and Evans moved to Melbourne. Another immigrant from the UK, Bon Scott (b. Ronald Belford Scott, 9 July 1946, Forfar, Scotland, d. 19 February 1980, London, England; vocals), graduated from being the band's chauffeur to becoming their vocalist when Dave Evans refused to go on stage one night. (Evans went on to form Rabbit, releasing two albums for CBS Records in Australia, before joining Hot Cockerel in 1984 and releasing *David Evans And Thunder Down Under* in 1986.) Scott had previously recorded with two Australian outfits, pop group the Valentines (1966–68) and rockers Fraternity (1970–74). Indeed, after he emigrated from Scotland in 1951, he had also spent five consecutive years as drum champion (under-17 section) with the Perth Pipe Band. After such a wholesome start, a prison conviction for assault and battery indicated a more volatile side to his nature, and resulted in him being refused admission to the army. In 1965, he joined the Spectors, before the aforementioned periods with the Valentines and Fraternity.

The AC/DC line-up that welcomed Scott had already recorded a solitary single, 'Can I Sit Next To You Girl', but it was his voice that graced their first two albums, *High Voltage* and *T.N.T.*. The latter album also introduced two new members, Mark Evans (b. 2 March 1956, Melbourne, Australia; bass) and Phil Rudd (b. Phillip Hugh Norman Witschke, 19 May 1954, Melbourne, Australia; drums). Both sets were produced by George Young and his writing partner, another former Easybeat, Harry Vanda. Neither set was issued outside Australia, though Atlantic Records in Britain did offer a selection of material from both records under the title *High Voltage* in 1976. These albums established AC/DC as a major draw in their native territory, and brought them to the attention of Atlantic, who promptly relocated the band to London in January 1976. However, Evans was replaced by Cliff Williams (b. 14 December 1949, Romford, Essex, England; ex-Home) in June 1977 after the former tired of touring. He went on to Finch/Contraband, then a variety of bands including Swanee, Heaven, Best and Party Boys.

Once AC/DC began to tour outside Australia, the band quickly amassed a cult following, as much for the unashamed gimmickry of its live show as for its furious, frequently risqué brand of hard rock. *Let There Be Rock* broke them as a chart act in the UK, with its contents including the perennial crowd-pleaser, 'Whole Lotta Rosie'. The live *If You Want Blood You've Got It* consolidated their position, but 1979's *Highway To Hell* established them as international stars. This, the band's first album with producer Mutt Lange, also proved to be their last with Bon Scott. On 19 February 1980, after a night of heavy drinking, he was left unconscious in a friend's car, and was later found to be dead, having choked on his own vomit. The coroner recorded a verdict of death by misadventure.

Scott's death threatened the band's future, but his replacement, former Geordie lead singer Brian Johnson (b. 5 October 1947, Dunston, England), proved more than equal to the task. His first album with the band, *Back In Black*, reached number 1 in the UK and Australia, number 4 in the USA, and spawned the UK number 15 single 'Rock 'n' Roll Ain't Noise Pollution'. The album was certified as having sold 12 million copies in the USA by March 1996. In 1981, *For Those About To Rock (We Salute You)* topped the American charts for three weeks, the band headlined at the Donington Festival and also achieved two Top 20 UK singles ('Let's Get It Up' and 'For Those About To Rock (We Salute You)'). After *Flick Of The Switch* in 1983, drummer Phil Rudd left the band to become a helicopter pilot in New Zealand, and was replaced by Simon Wright (b. 19 June 1963; ex-A II Z and Tytan) – who in turn departed to join Dio in 1989. His replacement was Chris Slade (b. 30 October 1946; ex-Manfred Mann's Earth Band).

In keeping with their superstar status, AC/DC maintained an increasingly relaxed schedule through the 80s, touring to support each carefully spaced album release. Two UK Top 20 singles, 'Who Made Who' (1986) and 'Heatseeker' (1988), confirmed their enduring popularity. There were further 'casualties', however. When Malcolm Young was unfit to tour in 1988 his cousin, Stevie Young (ex-Starfighters), temporarily deputized. Paul Greg also stepped in for Cliff Williams on the US leg of their 1991 tour. A year earlier, *The Razors Edge* had been one of the more successful albums of their later career, producing a Top 20 UK hit, 'Thunderstruck' and reaching number 2 on the album chart in America. In 1992, they issued a live album, while the attendant single, 'Highway To Hell', made the UK Top 20. With Brian Johnson long having buried the ghost of Bon Scott, the band showed no signs of

varying its winning musical formula, and in 1994 were buoyed by the return of Rudd to the line-up. The following year's *Ballbreaker* marked a powerful return after a lengthy break from recording. The ensuing *Bonfire* box set, meanwhile, served as a fitting memorial to Bon Scott. The band greeted the new millennium in typical style with the 'business as usual' recording, *Stiff Upper Lip*.

● ALBUMS: *High Voltage* Australia only (Albert 1975) ★★, *T.N.T.* Australia only (Albert 1976) ★★, *Dirty Deeds Done Dirt Cheap* (Atlantic 1976) ★★★, *Let There Be Rock* (Atlantic 1977) ★★★★, *Powerage* (Atlantic 1978) ★★★, *If You Want Blood You've Got It* (Atlantic 1978) ★★★, *Highway To Hell* (Atlantic 1979) ★★★★, *Back In Black* (Atlantic 1980) ★★★★, *For Those About To Rock (We Salute You)* (Atlantic 1981) ★★★★, *Flick Of The Switch* (Atlantic 1983) ★★, *'74 Jailbreak* mini-album (Atlantic 1984) ★★, *Fly On The Wall* (Atlantic 1985) ★★, *Who Made Who* (Atco 1986) ★★★, *Blow Up Your Video* (Atlantic 1988) ★★, *The Razors Edge* (Atco 1990) ★★★, *Live* (Atco 1992) ★★, *Ballbreaker* (Atlantic 1995) ★★★, *Stiff Upper Lip* (EMI 2000) ★★★.
● COMPILATIONS: *High Voltage* (Atlantic 1976) ★★, *Box Set 1* (EMI 1981) ★★★, *Box Set 2* (EMI 1987) ★★★, *Bonfire* 4-CD box set (EMI 1997) ★★★★.
● VIDEOS: *Let There Be Rock* (Warner Home Video 1985), *Fly On The Wall* (Atlantic Video 1985), *Who Made Who* (Atlantic Video 1986), *Clipped* (AVision 1991), *Live At Donington* (AVision 1992), *No Bull* (Warner Music Vision 1996), *Stiff Upper Lip Live* (Warner Music Vision 2001).
● FURTHER READING: *The AC/DC Story*, Paul Ezra. *AC/DC*, Malcolm Dome. *AC/DC: Hell Ain't No Bad Place To Be*, Richard Bunton. *AC/DC: An Illustrated Collectors Guide Volumes 1 & 2*, Chris Tesch. *AC/DC Illustrated Biography*, Mark Putterford. *Shock To The System*, Mark Putterford. *HM Photo Book*, no author listed. *The World's Most Electrifying Rock 'n' Roll Band*, Malcolm Dome (ed.). *Highway To Hell: The Life & Times Of AC/DC Legend Bon Scott*, Clinton Walker. *AC/DC: The World's Heaviest Rock*, Martin Huxley. *Get Your Jumbo Jet Out Of My Airport: Random Notes For AC/DC Obsessives*, Howard Johnson. *AC/DC: The Definitive History*, The Kerrang! Files.

## ACCELERATORS

From North Carolina, USA, and unconnected to the New Jersey and Los Angeles bands of the same name (and several others in different territories), these Accelerators were led by singer, guitarist and songwriter Gerald Duncan. It was he who largely orchestrated the band's competent but unenthralling mid-80s career. He had help, however, in the shape of renowned producer and musician Don Dixon, and local star Mitch Easter of Let's Active, who both appeared on the band's appealing 1983 debut, *Leave My Heart*. However, only Duncan and drummer Doug Welchel survived the transition to the Accelerators' second line-up, which also featured guitarist Brad Rice. *The Accelerators* featured two songs produced by Dixon; among the strongest tracks on the album was, significantly, a remake of the debut album's track 'Two Girls In Love'. Another highlight was the cover version of the Box Tops' 'The

Letter'. Given the four-year interval between recordings, it did not bode well for their future, a suspicion confirmed when the band effectively disappeared from view once more, only re-emerging in 1991 for the perfunctory *Dream Train*. Duncan re-emerged at the end of the decade with Ron Bartholomew (bass), Dave Bartholomew (guitar) and Chris Henderson (drums). This new line-up recorded the Accelerators' fourth album, *Nearer*.

● ALBUMS: *Leave My Heart* (Dolphin 1983) ★★★, *The Accelerators* (Profile 1987) ★★, *Dream Train* (Profile 1991) ★★★, *Nearer* (DES 2000) ★★★.

## ACCEPT

This German heavy rock quintet originally comprised Udo Dirkschneider (vocals), Gerhard Wahl (guitar) and Wolf Hoffman (b. 10 December 1959, Mainz, Germany; guitar), Frank Friedrich (drums) and Peter Baltes (bass). Formed in 1976 in their hometown of Solingen, Jorg Fischer replaced Wahl in 1978. The band's power metal sound was characterized by Dirkschneider's guttural howl and the speed drumming of Stefan Kaufmann, who replaced Friedrich after their 1979 debut. Fischer left in 1982 following a tour supporting Judas Priest (although he did return briefly in 1983). *Restless & Wild*, from 1983, epitomized their blitzing style, which had an undeniable influence on the thrash movement that developed during the late 80s. *Metal Heart* adopted a more melodic approach, but, unhappy with this style, Dirkschneider left and formed his own outfit, Udo. A series of replacement vocalists came and went, including Rob Armitage (ex-Baby Tuckoo), David Reece and Jim Stacey (Stacey stepped in to complete tracks on *Eat The Heat* after Reece and Baltes had a physical confrontation on tour in the USA). Several lacklustre albums were released during these years that received little critical acclaim or commercial reward. Internal problems persisted, with Kaufmann contracting a muscular disease and being replaced by Ken Mary (House Of Lords). However, the band eventually disintegrated in 1989. Reece went on to form Bangalore Choir while old sparring partner Baltes contributed to Dokken. The band reunited in the 90s with a revised line-up including Dirkschneider, Hoffman, Baltes and Kaufmann, releasing several low-key albums before they disbanded once more.

● ALBUMS: *Accept* (Brain 1979) ★★★, *I'm A Rebel* (Logo 1980) ★★★, *Breaker* (Brain 1981) ★★★, *Restless & Wild* (Heavy Metal 1983) ★★★, *Balls To The Wall* (Portrait 1984) ★★★★, *Metal Heart* (Portrait 1985) ★★★, *Kaizoku-Ban* (Portrait 1986) ★★, *Russian Roulette* (Portrait 1986) ★★★, *Eat The Heat* (RCA 1989) ★★, *Staying A Life: Live In Japan* (Epic 1990) ★★★, *Objection Overruled* (RCA 1993) ★★★, *Death Row* (Pavement 1995) ★★★, *Steel Glove* (Castle 1996) ★★, *Predator* (Sweat Shop 1997) ★★★, *The Final Chapter* (CMC International 1998) ★★★

● COMPILATIONS: *Best Of Accept* (Metronome 1983) ★★★, *Accept* (Portrait 1986) ★★★, *Hungry Years* (Razor 1991) ★★★, *The Collection* (Castle 1991) ★★★, *Steel Glove: The Collection* (Castle 1995) ★★★, *All Areas Worldwide* (GUN 1998) ★★.

## ACID HOUSE

DJ Pierre was the man, alongside his partner Spanky, who was largely heralded as the figurehead of this musical movement. The sound was developed in a Chicago, Illinois, USA basement in 1986, where the duo had just purchased and installed a bass machine, the Roland TB 303: 'We'd got the 303 and we were trying to figure out what knobs do what. The machine already had acid in it. At first I thought it was some kind of shit we gotta erase out of it before we programme it. Spanky had a 15-minute beat track he'd programmed a couple of days earlier . . . and I kept turning the knobs to see what kind of effect they had on the bassline.' That session was recorded and passed to DJ Ron Hardy, who mixed it into his sets at Chicago's Warehouse club. Soon this new sound was being much discussed and became known as Hardy's *Acid Tracks* (an alternative theory has been advanced that Marshall Jefferson developed the 'sound' of acid, but Pierre's version has generally been given more credence). Ironically, the 303 was a budget bass synthesizer that was designed for use with the 606 drum machine, but flopped commercially. The 'acid' element came about due to the five hand-tuned filters that could manipulate and 'squelch' or stress the bass notes, as they were being played back. Originally the 'acid' prefix was bereft of drug connotations. While Pierre released the influential *Acid Trax* series on Phuture, the sound gripped the UK club scene in 1988, and bands such as D-Mob took up the mantle with a bastardized version. Records such as 'Acid Man' by Jolly Roger (actually Eddie Richards, later DJ to the Shamen) started to feature in the charts. Ably represented by the 'Smiley' logo and the warehouse party culture, the acid phenomenon of 1988 rivalled the punk scene of the previous decade for its notoriety within the establishment and UK press. This time, the connection between Ecstasy, the scene's drug of choice, and the music was made more explicit. Eventually, the style went underground once more as it was superseded by techno and other dance music forms. Notable archivists such as Richie Hawtin and Ege Bam Yasi did much to revive the style, or 'the 303 sound', in the 90s, as did Hardfloor, Laurent Garnier and Cosmic Baby in Europe.

## ACOUSTIC ALCHEMY

Formed in the mid-80s, Acoustic Alchemy was essentially Greg Carmichael (b. 1953, London, England; nylon string guitar) and Nick Webb (b. 1954, Manchester, England, d. 5 February 1998; steel string guitar). Their blend of instrumental music was neither jazz nor pop, but contained elements of both, together with flamenco, reggae and folk. Webb was a child actor who studied at the London Academy Of Music And Dramatic Art, and was originally musically influenced by John Martyn and Pentangle, running a folk club in Berkhamsted. After studying jazz at Leeds College Of Music, Webb spent a couple of years attempting to become a pop songwriter. Increasingly drawn towards jazz, he founded Acoustic Alchemy with classical guitarist Simon James in the early 80s before linking up with

Carmichael in 1986. Carmichael had studied classical guitar at the London College of Music and gained experience playing with jazz groups. Their break came, when frustrated by the apathy for their music in England, they took a Virgin Atlantic Airlines in-flight gig and literally played their way to America. They were signed to MCA Records as part of their Master Series, and debuted with the excellent *Red Dust And Spanish Lace*, which contained one of their finest compositions 'Mr Chow', an example of Chinese Reggae! Following *Blue Chip* they joined GRP Records, although their debut for the label, *Reference Point*, lacked the life and sparkle of their MCA work. They redressed the balance with *Back On The Case* in 1991, although subsequent albums sounded workmanlike. By this time, however, the group had built up a substantial following in America thanks to their popularity on 'adult contemporary radio' stations. They were also successful in Japan and mainland Europe. Webb died of pancreatic cancer in February 1998. Carmichael continues to record under the name.

● ALBUMS: *Red Dust And Spanish Lace* (MCA 1987) ★★★★, *Natural Elements* (MCA 1988) ★★★, *Blue Chip* (MCA 1989) ★★★, *Reference Point* (GRP 1990) ★★, *Back On The Case* (GRP 1991) ★★★, *The New Edge* (GRP 1993) ★★, *Arcanum* (GRP 1996) ★★, *Positive Thinking* (GRP 1998) ★★★, *The Beautiful Game* (Higher Octave 2000) ★★★, *Aart* (Higher Octave 2001) ★★★.

● COMPILATIONS: *Early Alchemy* (GRP 1992) ★★★, *The Very Best Of Acoustic Alchemy* (Universal 2002) ★★★.

## ADAM AND THE ANTS

Formed from the ashes of the short-lived B-Sides in April 1977, the original line-up of this UK band comprised Adam Ant (b. Stuart Leslie Goddard, 3 November 1954, London, England; vocals, guitar), backed by Lester Square (guitar), Andy Warren (vocals, bass) and Paul Flanagan (drums). The line-up was relatively *ad hoc* between 1977 and 1979 with Mark Ryan (b. Mark Gaumont, England) replacing Lester Square (who joined the Monochrome Set – as Andy Warren later did) and the colourful Jordan (b. Pamela Rooke) occasionally taking vocals. Other members included drummers Kenny Morris and Dave Barbe (b. David Barbarossa, Mauritius), guitarists Johnny Bivouac and Matthew Ashman (b. London, England, d. 21 November 1995), and bass player Leigh Gorman. Heavily influenced by the Sex Pistols, the band incorporated bondage gear and sado-masochistic imagery into their live act and repertoire. Adam Ant appeared with Toyah in Derek Jarman's controversial *Jubilee*, where he seemed more convincing than onstage. Although the first-generation line-up comprising Ant, Ashman, Warren and Barbarossa recorded one studio set, *Dirk Wears White Sox*, their critical reputation among new wave writers was poor.

At the end of the decade, Ant sought the advice of Sex Pistols manager Malcolm McLaren, who took on the role of image consultant for a £1,000 fee. His advice prompted a radical shift in musical policy and a daring new look combining Native American (Apache) imagery and piratical garb. In January 1980, however, the Ants fell victim to McLaren's charisma and Barbarossa, Ashman and Gorman abandoned their leader to form the newsworthy Bow Wow Wow. At this point, most observers assumed that Ant's career was over; in fact, it was just beginning. With an entirely fresh set of Ants consisting of Marco Pirroni (b. 27 April 1959, London, England; vocals, guitar), Kevin Mooney (vocals, bass) and two drummers, Terry Lee Miall (b. Terry Day, 8 November 1958, London, England) and Merrick (b. Christopher Hughes, 3 March 1954, London, England), Ant effectively reinvented himself. Out went the punk riffs and bondage to be replaced by a sound heavily influenced by the Burundi Black drummers. With his Red Indian war paint and colourful costume, the new look Adam And The Ants enjoyed three UK hits in 1980, culminating in the number 2 'Ant Music', in which Ant boldly dismissed his rivals and proclaimed his sound to be of the moment. His prognosis was correct: 1981 was the year of Adam And The Ants, and their pop prescience was captured in a series of excellently produced videos. With his striking looks and clever use of costume, Adam Ant was a natural pin-up. His portrayal of a highwayman ('Stand And Deliver') and pantomime hero ('Prince Charming') brought two UK number 1 hits and ushered in an era of 'New Pop', where fancy dressing-up and catchy, melodic songs without a message became the norm. At the start of the year, Mooney was replaced by ex-Roxy Music associate Gary Tibbs (b. 21 January 1958, London, England). Following January 1982's number 3 hit 'Ant Rap', it came as little surprise when Adam announced that he was dissolving the unit in early 1982 to pursue a solo career as Adam Ant, retaining Pirroni as his writing partner. Hughes, who had produced all of the band's hit singles, went on to enjoy a successful production career, most notably with Tears For Fears.

● ALBUMS: *Dirk Wears White Sox* (Do It 1979) ★★, *Kings Of The Wild Frontier* (CBS/Epic 1980) ★★★, *Prince Charming* (CBS/Epic 1981) ★★, *Peel Sessions* (Strange Fruit 1990) ★★.

● COMPILATIONS: *Hits* (CBS 1986) ★★★, *Antics In The Forbidden Zone* (Columbia 1990) ★★★, *The Collection* (Castle 1991) ★★★, *Antmusic: The Very Best Of Adam Ant* (Arcade 1993) ★★★★, *B-Side Babies* (Epic/Legacy 1994) ★★★, *Super Hits* (Epic/Legacy 1998) ★★★, *The Very Best Of Adam And The Ants* (Columbia 1999) ★★★★, *Antbox* 3-CD box set (Columbia 2000) ★★★, *Live At The BBC* (Fuel 2000 2001) ★★.

● VIDEOS: *Prince Charming Revue* (CBS Video 1982), *Live In Japan* aka *Live In Tokyo* (CBS Video/Arcade 1982), *Hits* (CBS/Fox Video 1986), *Antmusic: The Very Best Of Adam Ant* (Arcade Video 1993), *AntVideo* (Columbia 2000).

● FURTHER READING: *Adam And The Ants*, Mike West. *Adam And The Ants*, Chris Welch. *Adam And The Ants*, Fred and Judy Vermorel. *Adam Ant Tribal Rock Special*, Martha Rodriguez (design). *The Official Adam Ant Story*, James Maw. *Adam And The Ants Kings: The Official Adam And The Ants Song Book*, Stephen Lavers.

## ADAM ANT

b. Stuart Leslie Goddard, 3 November 1954, London, England. After an initially chequered, then immensely successful career leading Adam And The Ants, Goddard went solo in early 1982. For support, he retained old musical partner Marco Pirroni and relaunched himself with the frantic 'Goody Two Shoes', which hit number 1 in the UK in May. The average 'Friend Or Foe' followed at number 9, but thereafter the spell was broken. Phil Collins was recruited as producer to halt Adam's sudden decline and the pantomime-influenced 'Puss In Boots' duly made the Top 5. The revival was only temporary, however, and by the end of 1983, Adam's chart career was practically non-existent. The original god of the 'New Pop' seemed commercially bankrupt, his place taken by new idols such as Duran Duran, Culture Club and Wham!. Even an appearance at Live Aid in 1985 with 'Vive Le Rock' could only produce a number 50 UK chart entry and Goddard switched adroitly to acting. A surprise chart comeback (number 13) in 1990 with 'Room At The Top' appeared a lucky strike and did not seriously distract the singer from his thespian pursuits. A new album in 1995, promoted by concert appearances in West London, provoked further media saturation and good reviews, but little in terms of record sales. The next time Ant made the news was in a distressing series of incidents in the London area in January 2002, following which he was legally confined at the Royal Free Hospital under the 1983 Mental Health Act. He pleaded guilty to affray charges in August.

● ALBUMS: *Friend Or Foe* (CBS/Epic 1982) ★★★, *Strip* (CBS/Epic 1983) ★★, *Vive Le Rock* (CBS/Epic 1985) ★★, *Manners & Physique* (MCA 1990) ★★, *Wonderful* (EMI/Capitol 1995) ★★★.

● COMPILATIONS: *Hits* (CBS 1986) ★★★, *Antics In The Forbidden Zone* (Columbia 1990) ★★★, *The Collection* (Castle 1991) ★★★, *Antmusic: The Very Best Of Adam Ant* (Arcade 1993) ★★★, *B-Side Babies* (Epic/Legacy 1994) ★★★, *Super Hits* (Epic/Legacy 1998) ★★★, *The Very Best Of Adam And The Ants* (Columbia 1999) ★★★, *Antbox* 3-CD box set (Columbia 2000) ★★★.

● VIDEOS: *Prince Charming Revue* (CBS Video 1982), *Live In Japan* aka *Live In Tokyo* (CBS Video/Arcade 1982), *Hits* (CBS/Fox Video 1986), *Antmusic: The Very Best Of Adam Ant* (Arcade Video 1993), *AntVideo* (Columbia 2000).

● FURTHER READING: *Adam And The Ants*, Mike West. *Adam And The Ants*, Chris Welch. *Adam And The Ants*, Fred and Judy Vermorel. *Adam Ant Tribal Rock Special*, Martha Rodriguez (design). *The Official Adam Ant Story*, James Maw. *Adam And The Ants Kings: The Official Adam And The Ants Song Book*, Stephen Lavers.

● FILMS: *Jubilee* (1977), *Nomads* (1986), *Slamdance* (1987), *Cold Steel* (1987), *World Gone Wild* (1988), *Spellcaster* (1988), *Trust Me* (1989), *Sunset Heat* aka *Midnight Heat* (1991), *Love Bites* (1993), *Acting On Impulse* aka *Eyes Of A Stranger* (1993), *Drop Dead Rock* (1995), *Desert Winds* (1995), *Cyber Bandits* (1995), *Lover's Knot* (1996), *Sweetwater* (1999).

## ADICTS

The Adicts can be singled out from the host of other UK punk hopefuls of the early 80s largely due to their image. The adoption of black bowler hats and face make-up showed more than a passing resemblance to the unruly characters in Stanley Kubrick's controversial film *A Clockwork Orange*, and reflected the Adicts' brand of boot-boy, new wave music. The band was originally based in Ipswich, Suffolk, England, and comprised lead singer Monkey (b. Keith Warren), who had grotesquely perfected Malcolm McDowell's Alex grin, plus Kid Dee (b. Michael Davison; drums), Pete Davidson (guitar) and Mel Ellis (bass). Their debut EP, *Lunch With The Adicts*, was the first release on the Dining Out label in 1981. This was followed by *Songs Of Praise* for DWED in October, which has subsequently become something of a cult classic in punk record-collecting circles. The band then moved to the Fall Out label for 'Viva La Revolution', before they again changed labels, settling at the appropriately named Razor Records. There they achieved two UK Independent Top 10 singles, 'Chinese Takeaway' (1982) and 'Bad Boy' (1983). The ensuing album, *Sound Of Music*, even managed to scrape into the lower reaches of the UK chart for one week, which was only 380 weeks less than Julie Andrews' collection of the same name. All was then quiet for two years, until the Adicts popped up in 1985, back at Fall Out, with a new EP, *Bar Room Bop*. In the late 80s, there was a trickle of albums of limited interest outside of hardened punk audiences in Europe and the USA. The band, which re-formed in 1993, have continued to play to loyal audiences around the world.

● ALBUMS: *Songs Of Praise* (DWED 1981) ★★★, *Sound Of Music* (Razor 1982) ★★★, *Smart Alex* (Razor 1985) ★★★, *Fifth Overture* (RCA 1986) ★★, *Live And Loud!* (Dojo 1987) ★★, *Rockers In Rags (Live In Alabama)* (Fallout 1990) ★★, *27* (Hard Slug 1993) ★★★, *Joker In The Pack* (Harry May 2000) ★★, *Rise And Shine* (Captain Oi! 2002) ★★.

● COMPILATIONS: *This Is Your Life (1978-80)* (Fallout 1985) ★★★, *The Complete Adicts Singles Collection* (Anagram 1995) ★★★★, *Ultimate Addiction: The Best Of* (Cleopatra 1997) ★★★, *The Very Best Of The Adicts* (Anagram 1999) ★★★, *Rockers Into Orbit* (Fallout 2002) ★★.

● VIDEOS: *Live At The Manhattan Club* (Jettisoundz 1983), *Let's Go* (Visionary 1994).

## ADOLESCENTS

The first line-up of the early 80s hardcore band the Adolescents, from Fullerton, Orange County, California, USA, comprised Frank Agnew (rhythm guitar), Rikk Agnew (lead guitar), Casey Royer (drums, vocals), Tony 'Montana' Brandenburg (vocals) and Steve 'Soto' Rodgers (bass, vocals). Brandenburg formed the band, enlisting the Agnews and Royer, who were all formerly members of Social Distortion. Rikk Agnew had, in addition, formerly played with several Los Angeles bands including the Detours, while Rodgers had been part of Agent Orange. Following a flirtation with Posh Boy Records (the 'Amoeba' single, of which only 15 copies were pressed), the band's debut emerged on Frontier

Records in 1981. Immediately afterwards, the band collapsed. Rikk Agnew went on to release a solo album (*All By Myself*) for Frontier the following year, which largely consisted of songs written for the intended second Adolescents album. Afterwards, he played with both Christian Death and TSOL. The Adolescents re-formed for reunion gigs in 1986 and effectively became an active unit once more. *Brats In Battalions*, released on the band's own label, included guitarist Alfie Agnew deputizing for brother Frank on a powerful punk/metal hybrid. The line-up switched for *Balboa Fun\*Zone*, but the songwriting of the remaining original members, Rikk Agnew and Steve 'Soto' Rodgers, was seen to its best advantage. It was followed by a live album drawn from concerts recorded five years apart. Agnew's second solo effort, credited to Rikk Agnew's Yard Sale, featured his returning two brothers, Alfie and Frank. The Adolescents disbanded in 1989, though further reunions are probably not out of the question given the band's previous record.

● ALBUMS: *Adolescents* (Frontier 1981) ★★★, *Brats In Battalions* (SOS 1987) ★★★, *Balboa Fun\*Zone* (Triple X 1988) ★★★★, *Live 1981 And 1986* (Triple X 1989) ★★★, *Return To The Black Hole* 1989 recording (Triple X 1997) ★★★.

## ADRENALIN OD

Formed in October 1981 in New Jersey, USA, the hardcore band Adrenalin OD originally comprised Paul Richard (vocals), Jack Steeples (bass), Dave Scott (drums), and Jim Foster (guitar). Following their 1983 debut (the six-track *Let's Barbeque With Adrenalin OD* EP, for their own Buy Our Records label), Foster was replaced by Bruce Wingate. *The Wacky Hi-Jinks Of Adrenalin OD* delighted in song titles such as 'A.O.D. Vs Godzilla' and 'Middle Aged Whore', and featured rousing three-minute punk pop songs. The logical progression was to tackle 'A.O.D. Vs Son Of Godzilla' on the follow-up collection, 1986's *Humungousfungusamongus*, and that is exactly what the band did, this time with the aid of hugely improved studio technique. The Ramones' producer Daniel Rey joined the band in time for *Cruisin' With Elvis In Bigfoot's UFO*, which continued their preoccupation with monster movies and other offbeat subjects, notably 'Bulimic Food Fight' and 'Something About ... Amy Carter'. By this point the band had slowed down their sound, now relying on a more conventional, yet still energized, rock 'n' roll platform. Produced by Andy Shernoff (Dictators/Wild Kingdom), *Ishtar* did not advance on previous gains, despite the band tackling Queen's 'Sheer Heart Attack' (they had previously covered the same band's 'We Will Rock You' on a 1985 split EP with Bedlam). Though the band has now wound down operations, they occasionally reunite for live shows.

● ALBUMS: *Let's Barbeque With Adrenalin OD* mini-album (Buy Our Records 1983) ★★, *The Wacky Hi-Jinks Of Adrenalin OD* (Buy Our Records 1984) ★★, *Humungousfungusamongus* (Buy Our Records 1986) ★★★, *Cruising With Elvis In Bigfoot's UFO* (Buy Our Records 1988) ★★★, *Ishtar* (Restless 1989) ★★.

● COMPILATIONS: *Sittin' Pretty* (Grand Theft Audio 1995) ★★★.

## ADVENTURES

Formed in early 1984, the Adventures' story can be traced back six years to the Belfast, Northern Ireland power-pop/punk act the Starjets, which featured vocalist Terry Sharpe and guitarist Pat Gribben. The duo eventually sought their fortune on the London pub circuit and put together the Adventures with Pat Gribben's wife Eileen on vocals, aided by Gerard 'Spud' Murphy (guitar), Tony Ayre (bass) and Paul Crowder (drums). A contract with Chrysalis Records brought minimal chart success during 1984 and 1985, prompting the band to take a sabbatical in order to rethink their approach. A new contract with Elektra Records saw them achieve modest acclaim for *The Sea Of Love*, while the single 'Broken Land' entered the UK Top 20 in April 1988. Although they attempted to consolidate their position, 'Down In The Sea Of Love' failed to reach the Top 40 and the band's subsequent career proved less than eventful. Pat Gribben subsequently worked as a songwriter.

● ALBUMS: *Theodore And Friends* (UK) *The Adventures* (US) (Chrysalis 1985) ★★, *The Sea Of Love* (Elektra 1988) ★★★, *Trading Secrets With The Moon* (Elektra 1989) ★★★, *Lions & Tigers & Bears* (Polydor 1993) ★★★.

## AEROSMITH

One of the USA's most popular of all hard-rock acts, Aerosmith was formed in 1970 when vocalist Steven Tyler (b. Steven Victor Tallarico, 26 March 1948, Yonkers, New York City, New York, USA; vocals) met Joe Perry (b. Anthony Joseph Perry, 10 September 1950, Lawrence, Massachusetts, USA; guitar) while the latter was working in a Sunapee, New Hampshire ice cream parlour, the Anchorage. Tyler was in the area visiting the family-owned holiday resort, Trow-Rico. Perry, then playing in the Jam Band, invited Tyler (who had previously released one single, 'When I Needed You', with his own band Chain Reaction, and another, 'You Should Have Been Here Yesterday', with William Proud And The Strangeurs) to join him in a Cream-styled rock combo. Together with fellow Jam Band member Tom Hamilton (b. 31 December 1951, Colorado Springs, Colorado, USA; bass) and new recruits Joey Kramer (b. 21 June 1950, the Bronx, New York City, New York, USA; drums) and Ray Tabano (guitar), the band's founding line-up was complete. However, Tabano was quickly replaced by the former member of Justin Tyme, Earth Inc., Teapot Dome and Cymbals Of Resistance, Brad Whitford (b. 23 February 1952, Winchester, Massachusetts, USA). After playing their first gig at the Nipmuc Regional High School, the band took the name Aerosmith (rejecting other early monikers including Hookers). Their popularity throughout the Boston area grew rapidly, and a triumphant gig at Max's Kansas City, witnessed by Clive Davis, led to a recording contract with Columbia Records. In 1973, Aerosmith secured a minor chart placing with their self-titled debut album. Although its attendant single, 'Dream On', initially peaked at number 59, it became a Top 10 hit in April 1976. *Get Your Wings* inaugurated a fruitful working relationship with producer Jack Douglas. Nationwide tours established the quintet as a major attraction, a position consolidated by the highly successful *Toys In The Attic*, which has now sold in excess of six million copies worldwide. A fourth album, *Rocks*, achieved platinum status within months of its release. Aerosmith maintained their pre-eminent position with *Draw The Line* and the powerful *Live! Bootleg*, but despite popular acclaim, they failed to gain the approbation of many critics who dubbed the band 'derivative', particularly of Led Zeppelin. Tyler's physical resemblance to Mick Jagger, and his foil-like relationship with guitarist Perry, also inspired comparisons with the Rolling Stones, with whom they shared several musical reference points.

In 1978, the band undertook a US tour of smaller, more intimate venues in an attempt to decelerate their rigorous schedule. They appeared in the ill-fated *Sgt. Pepper's Lonely Hearts Club Band* movie (as the Future Villain band), and although their rousing version of 'Come Together' reached the US Top 30, tension between Tyler and Perry proved irreconcilable. The guitarist left the band following the release of the disappointing *Night In The Ruts* and subsequently founded the Joe Perry Project. Jimmy Crespo joined Aerosmith in 1980, but the following year Brad Whitford left to pursue a new career with former Ted Nugent band member, guitarist Derek St. Holmes. Newcomer Rick Dufay debuted on *Rock In A Hard Place*, but this lacklustre set failed to capture the fire of the band's classic recordings.

Contact between the band and Perry and Whitford was re-established during a 1984 tour. Antagonisms were set aside and, the following year, the quintet's most enduring line-up was performing together again. The first fruits of a lucrative new contract with Geffen Records, the Ted Templeman-produced *Done With Mirrors* was a tentative first step, after which Tyler and Perry underwent a successful rehabilitation programme to rid themselves of drug and alcohol dependency, synonymous with the band's hedonistic lifestyle. In 1986, they accompanied rappers Run-DMC on 'Walk This Way', an Aerosmith song from *Toys In The Attic* and a former US Top 10 entry in its own right. The collaboration was an international hit, rekindling interest in Aerosmith's career, with the following year's 'Dude (Looks Like A Lady)' reaching number 14 in the US charts. Recorded with producer Bruce Fairbairn, *Permanent Vacation* became one of their bestselling albums, and the first to make an impression in the UK, while the highly acclaimed *Pump* and *Get A Grip* (also produced by Fairbairn) emphasized their revitalization.

Fêted by a new generation of acts, the quintet are now seen as elder statesmen, but recent recordings show them leading by example. *Big Ones* was a well-chosen compilation, satisfying long-term fans, but more importantly, it introduced a younger audience to a dinosaur band who still sound fresh and exciting, refuse to compromise and certainly have not 'gone soft'. Those wishing to immerse themselves should invest in the impressive 13-CD box set *Box Of Fire*, which comes complete with rare bonus tracks and a free, ready-to-strike match!

The band returned to Columbia Records in the mid-90s and spent an age recording *Nine Lives*. In Tyler's words, 'This album has taken me as far as I've ever wanted to go and gotten me back again.' It was worth the wait, bearing all the usual trademarks, and yet sounding strangely fresh. The hit single 'Falling In Love (Is Hard On The Knees)' preceded its release in February 1997. Although Tyler has reached his half-century, he still seems ageless on stage – even Jagger and Bruce Springsteen seem jaded compared to this rock 'n' roll ballet-dancer, apparently still in his prime. In September 1998, the band achieved their first ever US number 1 with the Diane Warren-penned ballad 'I Don't Want To Miss A Thing', taken from the soundtrack of the movie *Armageddon*. The song stayed at the top for four weeks, and provided the band with their first UK Top 10 single, eventually climbing to number 4 in October. The new century saw the band as sharp as ever, with *Just Push Play* proving to be another strong album in a career that now spans four decades.

● ALBUMS: *Aerosmith* (Columbia 1973) ★★★, *Get Your Wings* (Columbia 1974) ★★★, *Toys In The Attic* (Columbia 1975) ★★★★, *Rocks* (Columbia 1976) ★★★★, *Draw The Line* (Columbia 1977) ★★★, *Live! Bootleg* (Columbia 1978) ★★★, *Night In The Ruts* (Columbia 1979) ★★, *Rock In A Hard Place* (Columbia 1982) ★★, *Done With Mirrors* (Geffen 1985) ★★★, *Permanent Vacation* (Geffen 1987) ★★★, *Pump* (Geffen 1989) ★★★★, *Get A Grip* (Geffen 1993) ★★★★, *Nine Lives* (Columbia 1997) ★★★★, *A Little South Of Sanity* (Geffen 1998) ★★★★, *Just Push Play* (Columbia 2001) ★★★.

● COMPILATIONS: *Aerosmith's Greatest Hits* (Columbia 1980) ★★★★, *Classics Live!* (Columbia 1986) ★★, *Classics Live II* (Columbia 1987) ★★★, *Gems* (Columbia 1988) ★★★, *Anthology* (Raw Power/Castle 1988) ★★, *Pandora's Box* 3-CD box set (Columbia 1991) ★★★, *Big Ones* (Geffen 1994) ★★★★, *Box Of Fire* 13-CD box set (Columbia 1994) ★★★★, *Classics Live! Complete* (Columbia 1998) ★★★, *Young Lust: The Aerosmith Anthology* (Geffen 2001) ★★★★, *O Yeah! Ultimate Aerosmith Hits* (Columbia 2002) ★★★★.

● VIDEOS: *Video Scrapbook* (CBS/Fox Video 1987), *Live Texxas Jam '78* (CBS Music Video Enterprises 1988), *Permanent Vacation 3x5* (Geffen Home Video 1988), *Things That Go Pump In The Night* (Geffen Home Video 1990), *The Making Of Pump* (CBS Music Video Enterprises 1990), *Big Ones You Can Look At* (Geffen Home Video 1994).

● FURTHER READING: *The Fall And Rise Of Aerosmith*, Mark Putterford. *Live!*, Mark Putterford. *Toys In The Attic: The Rise, Fall And Rise Of Aerosmith*, Martin Huxley. *What It Takes*, Dave Bowler and Brian Dray. *Dream On: Living On The Edge With Steven Tyler*, Cyrinda Foxe-Tyler and Danny Fields. *Walk This Way: The Autobiography Of Aerosmith*, Aerosmith with Stephen Davis.

## AFRAID OF MICE

Previously known variously as Beano, the Press and the Jones, Liverpool, England's Afraid Of Mice was formed in early 1979 by ex-Next member Philip Franz Jones (guitar, vocals), who for six years struggled with continuously fluctuating personnel to find a suitable, permanent line-up. With the emergence of bands such as Echo And The Bunnymen, the Teardrop Explodes and OMD, there was a great deal of interest in the second 'Liverpool Scene'. Consequently, the band's appearance on a local compilation, *A Trip To The Dentist*, initiated a contract with Charisma Records. Following two well-received singles, 'I'm On Fire' and 'Intercontinental', *Afraid Of Mice* was released in 1982, with one-time David Bowie producer Tony Visconti at the controls. Described as 'power-pop with an edge', its mixture of punchy guitars, angry lyrics and simple, classic pop achieved considerable critical acclaim. Even so, commercial success proved much more elusive. After one final single, 'At The Club', and a give-away flexi-disc, 'Transparents', they parted company with Charisma. Although they continued to play live under various names including the Lumberjack Ballet, Afraid Of Mice's final vinyl appearances were the live *Official Bootleg* in 1983 and a solitary track, 'Don't Take Your Love Away', on the *Jobs For The Boys* compilation in 1985. Afraid Of Mice were finally laid to rest in 1986 when Phil Jones teamed up with Alex McKechnie (ex-Passage; Modern Eon) in Two's A Crowd. They eventually became Up And Running, releasing the *Live At Lime Street* album. There was a one-off reunion gig at Liverpool's Royal Court Theatre in 1994.

● ALBUMS: *Afraid Of Mice* (Charisma 1982) ★★★, *Afraid Of Mice: The Official Bootleg* (Own Label 1983) ★★.

## AFRIKA BAMBAATAA

b. Kevin Donovan, 10 April 1960, the Bronx, New York City, New York, USA. His name deriving from that of a nineteenth-century Zulu chief, translating as 'Chief Affection', Bambaataa was the founding father of New York's Zulu Nation. The name was inspired by the movie *Zulu*, starring Michael Caine, and the code of honour and bravery of its black participants. A loose community of mainly black street youths, Zulu Nation and its leader, more than any other element, helped to transform the gangs of the late 70s into the hip-hop crews of the early 80s. Bambaataa himself had been a member of the notorious Black Spades, among other sects, and from 1977-85 he had a social importance to match his towering MC and DJ profiles, organizing breakdance competitions and musical events promoting the ethos of peace and racial tolerance.

By 1980, Afrika Bambaataa was the pre-eminent hip-hop DJ in New York, commanding massive followings and eclipsing even Grandmaster Flash in popularity. He made his recording debut the same year, producing two versions of 'Zulu Nation Throwdown' for two rap groups associated with the Zulu Nation – Cosmic Force and Soul Sonic Force. Signing to the independent label Tommy Boy Records, he made his first own-name release in 1982, as Afrika Bambaataa And The Jazzy Five, with 'Jazzy Sensation' (based on Gwen Guthrie's 'Funky Sensation'). It was followed by the seminal 'Planet Rock', a wholly synthesized record this time based on Kraftwerk's 'Trans-Europe Express'. In one leap, it

took hip-hop music far beyond its existing street rhyme and percussion break format. The contribution of Arthur Baker and John Robie in programming its beats was also highly significant, for in turn they gave birth to the electro rap movement that dominated the mid-80s and paved the way for the popularization of dance music. 'Planet Rock' also gave its name to the record label Bambaataa established in the Bronx. 'Looking For The Perfect Beat' continued the marriage of raw lyrics and synthesized electro-boogie, and was another major milestone for the genre. The follow-up album, *Beware (The Funk Is Everywhere)*, even included a take on the MC5's 'Kick Out The Jams' (produced by Bill Laswell). Bambaataa also recorded an album as part of Shango, backed by Material members Laswell and Michael Beinhorn, in a party dance vein that accommodated a cover version of Sly Stone's 'Thank You'. Never one to stay in one place for long, he went on to record two vastly different and unexpected singles – 'World Destruction' with ex-Sex Pistols vocalist John Lydon and 'Unity' with the funk godfather James Brown.

Afrika Bambaataa fell out of the limelight in the latter half of the 80s, as new generations of disc jockeys and rappers stepped forward with their own innovations and fresh beats. However, *The Light* included an enterprising cast (UB40, Nona Hendryx, Boy George, Bootsy Collins, Yellowman and George Clinton – the latter a huge early musical and visual influence on Bambaataa). *The Decade Of Darkness (1990-2000)* also went some way towards redressing the balance, including an update of James Brown's 'Say It Loud – I'm Black And I'm Proud'. In March 1994, Bambaataa cropped up on Profile Records with the disappointing 'What's The Name Of This Nation?'. Two years later, he re-formed Soul Sonic Force to record *Lost Generation*, and continues to DJ and record new material on a regular basis.

Afrika Bambaataa's influence on rap's development is pivotal, and is felt in many more subtle ways than, for example, the direct sampling of his work on 90s crossover hits such as 95 South's 'Whoot! There It Is' or Duice's 'Dazey Duks'. The Tommy Boy anthology *Looking For The Perfect Beat* is a perfect introduction to this seminal artist.

● ALBUMS: with Shango *Funk Theology* (Celluloid 1984) ★★★, with Soul Sonic Force *Planet Rock – The Album* (Tommy Boy 1986) ★★★★, *Beware (The Funk Is Everywhere)* (Tommy Boy 1986) ★★★ *Death Mix Throwdown* (Blatant 1987) ★★★★, *The Light* (Capitol 1988) ★★★, *The Decade Of Darkness (1990-2000)* (EMI 1991) ★★★, *Don't Stop – Planet Rock Remix* (ZTT 1992) ★★★, with Soul Sonic Force *Lost Generation* (Hot 1996) ★★, *Hydraulic Funk* (Strictly Hype 2000) ★★★★.

● COMPILATIONS: *Looking For The Perfect Beat 1980–1985* (Tommy Boy 2001) ★★★★.

## AGE OF CHANCE

Hard, guitar-fuelled indie pop raiders from Leeds, Yorkshire, England, who at one point looked likely to translate Gang Of Four's vision to a mass audience: 'We're part experimental, part bop and we look pretty good as well.' With a line-up boasting Steve

Elvidge (vocals), Neil Howbs (guitar), Geoff Taylor (bass) and Jan Penny (percussion, stand-up drums), their first single was 'Motorcity' on their own label, which proved a big hit with BBC disc jockey John Peel. A follow-up, 'Bible Of The Beats', pushed them further in the direction of caustic dance. Although their early live sets rarely extended beyond 20 minutes, they proved attractive to a media that could make photogenic capital out of their lavish costumes (such as designer cyclist garb). Their metallic treatment of Prince's 'Kiss' was a mutant dance mini-classic, while a reading of the Trammps' 'Disco Inferno' brought them to within sniffing distance of the UK Top 40. Signing to Virgin Records, a succession of anonymous singles failed to nudge them any closer. Only the Public Enemy-remixed 'Take It' (featuring embryonic rapping) was of much interest, before Steve E left in the midst of considerable acrimony. Despite enlisting a replacement, Charles Hutchinson, the band was soon dropped by Virgin. When he, in turn, deserted, Perry briefly handled vocals before the band finally gave up the ghost in 1991. Elvidge persevered with his love of samples and loops by working with Mad Love, who went nowhere. Elvidge worked as a DJ in Leeds and York, while Howson publishes a listings magazine, *View*. Perry works for Leeds Council, and Taylor for the Grand Theatre in the same city.
● ALBUMS: *One Thousand Years Of Trouble* (Virgin 1987) ★★, *Mecca* (Charisma 1990) ★★★.
● VIDEOS: *Crush TV* (Virgin Vision 1988).

### AGENT ORANGE

Named after the chemical defoliant so chillingly used by the USA in the Vietnam War, Agent Orange were one of a number of bands formed in the highly active 'So-Cal' hardcore scene of Fullerton, Orange County, Los Angeles. The original line-up comprised Mike Palm (vocals, guitar), Steve 'Soto' Rodgers (bass) and Scott Miller (drums). However, Rodgers left early in their development to form another local punk attraction, the Adolescents. His replacement was James Levesque.
The band's first important supporter was KROQ disc jockey Rodney Bingenheimer, who was fundamental to the promotion of many similar outfits. Their debut release, the *Bloodstains* EP, was the only one to feature Rodgers, and its title track was the first song the fledgling band wrote. Afterwards, they signed to prominent local label Posh Boy Records, run by Robbie Fields. The subsequent debut album showed the band rising above the usual three-chord bluster of hardcore with a melodic approach that recalled 60s surf instrumental bands (the Ventures being the most obvious influence). However, the band stormed out of the studio near to the album's completion, complaining about being 'produced' and Fields' behaviour in general, leaving engineer David Hines and Jay Lansford (of Simpletones, Stepmothers and Channel 3 fame) to finish off the recordings. The *Bitchin' Summer* EP was one of the first skate/surf punk crossover items, with three energized surf guitar instrumentals establishing the band's future direction. Various problems delayed the next release until the trio signed with Enigma

Records for 1984's *When You Least Expect It ...* EP, which saw a conscious and largely unsuccessful attempt to accommodate a more disciplined, polished sound, a mistake compounded by a pointless cover version of Jefferson Airplane's 'Somebody To Love'. However, all the elements came together for 1986's *This Is The Voice* – the overdriven guitar mesh now allied to first-rate songwriting and delivery. This time the cover of 'Dangerman' was fine, but subordinate to the Agent Orange originals. Levesque had been replaced by Brent Liles (ex-Social Distortion) the previous year.
Agent Orange remained largely quiet during the early part of the 90s save for a live album. Palm returned in 1996 with two new members and a studio album, *Virtually Indestructible*. Their 2000 release was a mixture of new recordings and re-recordings.
● ALBUMS: *Living In Darkness* (Posh Boy 1981) ★★, *This Is The Voice* (Enigma 1986) ★★★, *Real Live Sound* (Restless 1990) ★★, *Virtually Indestructible* (Gunka 1996) ★★, *Greatest & Latest: This, That-N-The Other Thing* (Cleopatra 2000) ★★★.

### AGENT STEEL

This heavy metal unit was formed in Los Angeles, California, USA, and had existed in various guises since the early 80s. The most popular line-up consisted of John Cyriis (b. John Camps, Brazil; vocals, ex-Abattoir), Juan Garcia (guitar, ex-Abattoir), Kurt Colfelt (guitar), George Robb (bass) and Chuck Profus (drums). Signing to Combat Records, the band released their 1985 debut *Skeptics Apocalypse*. However, they experienced difficulty with their record label and internal wrangles owing to Cyriis' reputed eccentricity. With label problems resolved, the band (featuring new guitarist Bernie Versye/Versailles) released an EP entitled *Mad Locust Rising*. A further line-up change saw Michael Zaputil replacing Robb on the band's finest recording, the trash-fixated *Unstoppable Force*. However, they experienced further disruption when Cyriis decided he wanted to relocate the band to Florida. The rest of the band was less than delighted with the provisional change in locale and left (or rather, stayed). Cyriis continued with various musicians in the new location, but was never able to match previous standards. Disillusioned, he dissolved the band in 1988, and, after a brief tenure alongside Profus in Pontius Prophet, left the music business. Garcia joined Evil Dead.
Garcia, Profus and Versailles returned at the end of the 90s with a new line-up of Agent Steel, featuring Bruce Hall (vocals) and Karlos Medina (bass). They recorded a well-received new studio album, *Omega Conspiracy*, released on the Candlelight label in 1999. Due to pressure from original vocalist Cyriis, the band was temporarily forced to change their name to Order Of The Illuminati.
● ALBUMS: *Skeptics Apocalypse* (Combat/Roadrunner 1985) ★★★, *Unstoppable Force* (Combat/Music For Nations 1987) ★★★, *Omega Conspiracy* (Candlelight 1999) ★★★.
● VIDEOS: *Mad Locust Rising* (Jettisoundz 1989).

## AGNOSTIC FRONT

Originally comprising Roger Miret (vocals), Vinnie Stigma (guitar), Adam Moochie (bass) and Dave Jones (drums), Agnostic Front were the epitome of New York hardcore bands of the mid-80s. Growing up onstage at CBGB's, like many of that scene's participants, as their career progressed they adopted elements that instead identified them more with the heavy metal scene. Politically not the most circumspect of bands, even by hard rock's standards, their avowed right-wing stance and staunch nationalism served to set them apart from other punk and hardcore bands. With new members Rob Kabula (bass) and Jim Colletti (drums) completing the formidable early line-up, Miret spat out the lyrics on their classic debut with quite remarkable ferocity (he apparently spent his spare time breeding pit-bull terriers). Several break-ups disrupted the recording of *Cause For Alarm*, which featured new members Alex Kinon (guitar) and Louie Beatto (drums), and shortly afterwards Kinon, Beatto and Kabula all departed. The core duo of Miret and Stigma were joined by guitarist Steve Martin, bass player Alan Peters and drummer Will Shepler, although shortly before the release of *Liberty & Justice For ...* Peters was replaced by Craig Setari. Guitarist Matt Henderson replaced Martin on *One Voice*, an album that featured lyrics written by Miret during an 18-month prison sentence on drugs charges. Although their reputation grew over the years, little changed in Agnostic Front's musical formula, their principal strength always remaining the live arena. They played their last live show together at CBGB's on 20 December 1992. Miret's younger brother, Freddy Cricien, meanwhile, formed Madball with other former members of Agnostic Front. The band reunited in the late-90s with the returning Kabula and a new drummer, Jimmy Collette, touring to support their new album *Something's Gotta Give*.

● ALBUMS: *Victim In Pain* (Rat Cage 1984) ★★★, *Cause For Alarm* (Combat Core 1986) ★★, *Liberty & Justice For ...* (Combat 1987) ★★★, *Live At CBGB* (In-Effect/Relativity 1989) ★★, *One Voice* (Relativity 1992) ★★★, *Last Warning* (Relativity 1993) ★★★, *Raw Unleashed* (Grand Theft Audio 1995) ★★, *Something's Gotta Give* (Epitaph 1997) ★★★, *Riot, Riot Upstart* (Epitaph 1999) ★★★, *Dead Yuppies* (Epitaph 2001) ★★★.

## AIR SUPPLY

Formed around the partnership of Russell Hitchcock (b. 15 June 1949, Melbourne, Australia; vocals) and Graham Russell (b. 1 June 1950, Sherwood, Nottingham, England; guitar, vocals), soft-rockers Air Supply turned out a solid string of seven US Top 5 singles between 1980 and 1982. The duo first came together in Sydney, Australia, during 1975 while performing in a production of the Tim Rice and Andrew Lloyd Webber musical *Jesus Christ Superstar*. They formed Air Supply with Chrissie Hammond (vocals), who was soon replaced by bass player Jeremy Paul. After signing a recording contract with CBS Records, the band recorded their debut album with a line-up comprising Hitchcock, Russell, Paul,

Mark McEntee (lead guitar), Adrian Scott (keyboards) and Jeff Browne (drums). The single 'Love And Other Bruises' reached the Australian Top 10. Nigel Macara and Rex Goh (b. 5 May 1951, Singapore) replaced Browne and McEntee on 1977's *The Whole Thing Started*. The band undertook a North American tour supporting Rod Stewart, gaining important international exposure, but this coincided with the departure of Paul who went on to form Divinyls with McEntee. Hitchcock and Russell were joined by David Moyse (b. 5 November 1957, Adelaide, Australia; guitar), Brian Hamilton (bass, vocals) and Ralph Cooper (b. 6 April 1951, Coffs Harbour, Australia; drums) on 1978's *Life Support*, which also featured contributions from Frank Esler-Smith (b. 5 June 1948, London, England, d. 1991; keyboards).

Air Supply's international breakthrough came about after they signed an American distribution deal with Arista Records in 1980. The band's debut for the label, which featured new bass player Criston Barker, included three US Top 5 hits with the title track, 'All Out Of Love' (their only substantial UK success, reaching number 11) and 'Every Woman In The World'. The US number 10 album *The One That You Love* yielded three more major American Top 5 singles, with the number 1 title track, 'Here I Am (Just When I Thought I Was Over You)' and 'Sweet Dreams'. By now the line-up had stabilized around Hitchcock, Russell, Moyse, Cooper, Goh, Esler-Smith and David Green (b. 30 October 1949, Melbourne, Australia; bass). 'Even The Nights Are Better' reached US number 5 in 1982, but the attendant *Now And Forever* was a poor collection. In 1983, they achieved their second US number 2 with 'Making Love Out Of Nothing At All', taken from their hugely popular *Greatest Hits* album. The line-up on 1985's self-titled set featured Hitchcock, Russell, Esler-Smith, Cooper, Ken Rarick (keyboards), Wally Stocker (b. Walter Stocker, 17 March 1954, London, England; guitar, ex-Babys) and Don Cromwell (bass). Towards the end of the decade the popularity of Air Supply declined although they continued to tour regularly. They disbanded in 1988 but Hitchcock and Russell re-formed the unit in 1991. Subsequent releases failed to reach the charts in most overseas markets, but were remarkably popular in Asia. The two mainstays continue to play the US and Asian concert circuit with a varying line-up of musicians. Out of their occasional studio forays 1997's *The Book Of Love* is the strongest since the band's early 80s heyday.

● ALBUMS: *Air Supply* aka *Love And Other Bruises* (CBS 1976) ★★★, *The Whole Thing's Started* (CBS 1977) ★★★, *Life Support* (Wizard 1979) ★★, *Lost In Love* (Wizard/Arista 1980) ★★, *The One That You Love* (Big Time/Arista 1981) ★★★, *Now And Forever* (Arista 1982) ★★, *Air Supply* (Arista 1985) ★★, *Hearts In Motion* (Arista 1986) ★★, *The Christmas Album* (Arista 1987) ★★, *The Earth Is ...* (Giant 1991) ★★, *The Vanishing Race* (Giant 1993) ★★, *News From Nowhere* (Giant 1995) ★★, *Now And Forever: Greatest Hits Live* (Giant 1996) ★★★, *The Book Of Love* (Giant 1997) ★★★, *Yours Truly* (Giant 2001) ★★.

● COMPILATIONS: *Greatest Hits* (Big Time/Arista

1983) ★★★, *Making Love: The Very Best Of Air Supply* (Arista 1983) ★★★, *The Definitive Collection* (Arista 1999) ★★★, *The Ultimate Collection* (Giant 1999) ★★★.
● VIDEOS: *The Definitive DVD Collection* (Arista 1999).

## AKKERMAN, JAN

b. 24 December 1946, Amsterdam, Netherlands. When Akkerman surfaced in 1973 as Best Guitarist in a *Melody Maker* poll, it was the public zenith of a professional career that started in Amsterdam in 1958 as one of Johnny And The Cellar Rockers. Their drummer, Pierre Van Der Linden, later played with Akkerman in the Hunters – who owed much artistically to the Shadows – during the guitarist's five years of study at the city's Music Lyceum, from which he graduated with a catholic taste that embraced mainstream pop, Latin, medieval and the music of Frank Zappa, among leading preferences. With Van Der Linden, Bert Ruiter (bass) and Kaz Lux (vocals) Akkerman formed Brainbox, a hard rock outfit whose only album (featuring the single 'Down Man') was issued on Parlophone Records in 1969. Owing to Akkerman's keen participation in rehearsals with the nascent Focus, Brainbox dismissed him. In 1971, after the release of the Focus album *In And Out Of Focus*, Akkerman asked Van Der Linden to join him in a new band, and having also recruited Thijs Van Leer and Cyril Havermans from Focus, they retained the latter name. Among the major factors in the band's success over the next few years were Akkerman's powers of improvization on his trademark Les Paul guitar and his skill as an arranger. Furthermore, his solo albums were widely acclaimed, although the first, *Profile*, was simply an accumulation of tracks taped during the interval between Brainbox and Focus. Orchestrated by Columbia University professor of music George Flynn, *Tabernakel* was a more ambitious affair, featuring Akkerman's developing dexterity on the lute, and guest appearances by Tim Bogert and Carmine Appice.
Suddenly unhappy with their overall musical drift and tired of the treadmill of the road, Akkerman left Focus in March 1976 to begin sessions with Lux for what became *Eli*. Several more fusion collections followed, including the lushly orchestrated *Aranjuez* and a 1978 live set. Akkerman also recorded with pianist Joachim Kühn and clarinettist Tony Scott during this period. During the 80s, many Akkerman albums reached only Dutch shops until re-released by Charly Records for the UK market. Although his periodic reunions with Focus have attracted most attention, he also recorded the albums *The Talisman* (1988) and *To Oz And Back* (1989) on President Records as part of Forcefield with Ray Fenwick (ex-Spencer Davis Group) and Cozy Powell, before retracing a solo path with the comparatively high-profile *The Noise Of Art* for Miles Copeland's I.R.S. Records label. Akkerman has continued to produce quality low-key recordings into the new millennium, which he actively promotes on his excellent Akkernet website.
● ALBUMS: *Talent For Sale* (Imperial 1968) ★★★,

*Profile* 1969 recordings (Harvest 1972) ★★★, *Guitar For Sale* (Emidisc 1973) ★★★, *Tabernakel* (Atlantic 1974) ★★★★, with Kaz Lux *Eli* (Atlantic 1977) ★★★, *Jan Akkerman* (Atlantic 1978) ★★★, with Claus Ogerman *Aranjuez* (Columbia 1978) ★★★★, *Live: Montreux Jazz Festival 1978* (Atlantic 1979) ★★★, *3* (Atlantic 1980) ★★★, with Kaz Lux *Transparental* (Ariola 1980) ★★★, *Oil In The Family* (CNR 1981) ★★★, *Pleasure Point* (WEA 1982) ★★★, *It Could Happen To You* (Polydor 1982) ★★★, *Can't Stand Noise* (Columbia 1983) ★★★, *From The Basement* (Columbia 1984) ★★★★, *Heartware* (Skydancer 1987) ★★★, with Joachim Kühn *Live! Kiel/Stuttgart 1979* recording (Inak 1988) ★★★, *The Noise Of Art* (I.R.S. 1990) ★★★, *Puccini's Cafe* (EMI 1993) ★★★, *Blues Hearts* (EMI 1994) ★★★, *Focus In Time* (Patio 1996) ★★★, *10.000 Clowns On A Rainy Day: Live* (Patio 1997) ★★★★, *Live At The Priory* (Akkernet 1998) ★★★, with Curtis Knight *Blues Root* (Universe 1999) ★★★, *Passion* (Roadrunner 1999) ★★★★, *Live At Alexanders* (Akkernet 1999) ★★★.
● COMPILATIONS: *A Phenomenon* (Bovena Negram 1979) ★★★, *Best Of Jan Akkerman & Friends* (Atlantic 1980) ★★★, *A Talent's Profile* (EMI 1988) ★★★, *Guitar Special* (Sound Products 1991) ★★★.

## ALABAMA

Statistically the biggest US country rock act of the 80s and 90s, Alabama's origins can be traced back to Fort Payne in northern Alabama. They were originally formed in 1969 as Young Country by cousins Randy Owen (b. 14 December 1949, Fort Payne, Alabama, USA; vocals, guitar) and Teddy Gentry (b. 22 January 1952, Fort Payne, Alabama, USA; bass, vocals), with Jeff Cook (b. 27 August 1949, Fort Payne, Alabama, USA; vocals, guitar). Changing their name to Wild Country, they added Bennett Vartanian, the first of many drummers. After several misfires at the start of their career, their big breakthrough came with a residency at a club in Myrtle Beach, South Carolina, in 1973. Soon afterwards, they turned professional. They recorded for several small labels in the 70s before changing their name to Alabama in 1977.
The newly named band's career looked set to blossom following the Top 80 country success of 'I Wanna Be With You Tonight', a one-off single release on GRT Records. Following GRT's collapse, however, the band was forbidden from recording for two years. At this point, they sought out a full-time drummer to fill out their sound and recruited Mark Herndon (b. 11 May 1955, Springfield, Massachusetts, USA). After their third single, February 1980's 'My Home's In Alabama', on MDJ Records, reached the Country Top 20 they signed to RCA Records and found immediate success. A rich vein of country number 1 hits followed, including 'Tennessee River', 'Why Lady Why' and 'Feels So Right'. Singles such as 'Love In The First Degree' also acquired crossover pop success. Of their five platinum albums during the 80s, the most successful was *40 Hour Week*, which reached number 10 in the US chart. In 1986, they worked with Lionel Richie, but subsequent work has seen them return almost exclusively to the C&W charts. However, their environmental anthem, 'Pass

It On Down' in 1990, confirmed that they were still capable of surprising their audience.

In 1995 Alabama celebrated its 15th anniversary, in which time the band could lay claim to many outstanding achievements, including sales of over 50 million albums, and the Academy Of Country Music's Artist Of The Decade Award for their work in the 80s. Singer Randy Owen described their enduring appeal thus: 'What you see is what you get with Alabama. We're basically a blue-collar working band. We work really hard at what we do, and we work for our fans and listen to them.' 'Sad Lookin' Moon' in February 1997 took their total of country number 1s to a remarkable 41, as their worldwide record sales topped 58 million. *For The Record: 41 Number One Hits* debuted at lucky number 13 on the *Billboard* Top 200 in September 1998. Despite an increasingly formulaic sound, they remain a major live attraction.

● ALBUMS: *Wild Country* (LSI 1977) ★★★, *Deuces Wild* (LSI 1978) ★★★, *My Home's In Alabama* (RCA 1980) ★★★, *Feels So Right* (RCA 1981) ★★★, *Mountain Music* (RCA 1982) ★★★★, *The Closer You Get* (RCA 1983) ★★★, *Roll On* (RCA 1984) ★★★, *Alabama Christmas* (RCA 1985) ★★, *40 Hour Week* (RCA 1985) ★★★, *The Touch* (RCA 1986) ★★★, *Just Us* (RCA 1987) ★★★, *Alabama Live* (RCA 1988) ★★, *Southern Star* (RCA 1989) ★★★, *Pass It On Down* (RCA 1990) ★★★, *American Pride* (RCA 1992) ★★★, *Gonna Have A Party ... Live* (RCA 1993) ★★, *Cheap Seats* (RCA 1993) ★★★, *In Pictures* (RCA 1995) ★★★, *Alabama Christmas Volume II* (RCA 1996) ★★, *Dancin' On The Boulevard* (RCA 1997) ★★★, *Twentieth Century* (RCA 1999) ★★★, *When It All Goes South* (RCA 2001) ★★★.

● COMPILATIONS: *Wild Country* (LSI 1981) ★★★, *Greatest Hits* (RCA 1986) ★★★★, *Greatest Hits, Volume 2* (RCA 1991) ★★★, *Greatest Hits, Volume 3* (RCA 1994) ★★★, *Super Hits* (RCA 1996) ★★★, *Super Hits Volume 2* (RCA 1998) ★★★, *For The Record: 41 Number One Hits* (RCA 1998) ★★★★.

### ALARM

Formed in Rhyl, Wales, during 1981, this energetic pop outfit comprised Mike Peters (b. 25 February 1959; vocals, guitar), David Sharp (b. 28 January 1959; vocals, guitar), Eddie MacDonald (b. 1 November 1959; bass), and Nigel Twist (b. 18 July 1958; drums). Originally known as Seventeen, they changed their name after recording a self-penned song titled 'Alarm Alarm'. Peters was anxious to steer the band in the direction of U2, whose commitment and dedication appealed to his sense of rock as an expression of passion. However, by the time of the Alarm's first UK hit, 1983's '68 Guns', their style and imagery most closely recalled punk rockers the Clash. The declamatory verve continued on 'Where Were You Hiding When The Storm Broke' and the traditional rock influence was emphasized in their long spiked hair, skin-tight leather trousers and ostentatious belts. Behind the high energy, however, there was a lighter touch that was eloquently evinced on their reading of Pete Seeger's 'The Bells Of Rhymney', which they performed in aid of the coal miners' strike in 1984.

The original U2 comparisons began to make more sense on the fourth album, *Electric Folklore Live*, which displayed the power of their in-concert performance. *Change* (produced by Tony Visconti) saw them investigating their Celtic origins with the assistance of members from the Welsh Symphony Orchestra, and was released in a Welsh-language version (*Newid*). The much-maligned Mike Peters embarked on a solo career in the 90s following the dissolution of the band. He also recorded with Billy Duffy (ex-Cult) as Coloursound, before resurrecting the Alarm name for 20th anniversary tours during 2001.

● ALBUMS: *The Alarm* mini-album (I.R.S. 1983) ★★★, *Declaration* (I.R.S. 1984) ★★★, *Strength* (I.R.S. 1985) ★★★, *Eye Of The Hurricane* (I.R.S. 1987) ★★★, *Electric Folklore Live* mini-album (I.R.S. 1988) ★★★, *Change* (I.R.S. 1989) ★★, *Raw* (I.R.S. 1991) ★★, *Live On The King Biscuit Flower Hour* 1984 recording (King Biscuit Flower Hour 1999) ★★, *Acoustic Standards* (Conspiracy 2002) ★★★.

● COMPILATIONS: *Standards* (I.R.S. 1990) ★★★, *The Best Of The Alarm And Mike Peters* (EMI 1998) ★★★, *Collection* 8-CD box set (21st Century 2001) ★★★.

● VIDEOS: *Spirit Of '86* (Hendring Music Video 1986), *Change* (PMI 1990).

● FURTHER READING: *The Alarm*, Rick Taylor.

### ALIEN SEX FIEND

Essentially an alias for the eccentric Nick Wade, Alien Sex Fiend emerged as part of the early 80s gothic punk movement in the UK centred around London's Batcave venue. Wade previously served time with obscure acts such as the Earwigs and Mr. And Mrs. Demeanour, before releasing two singles as Demon Preacher. This was shortened to the Demons for a third single but, like its predecessors, it vanished without trace. After various short-lived projects, Wade eventually stumbled upon his long-term guise, Alien Sex Fiend, in 1982, aided by David James (guitar), partner Christine Wade (synthesizer) and Johnny 'Ha Ha' Freshwater (drums). On the strength of a nine-track demo tape, the band played the Batcave at the end of the year. Live tracks were added to the tape and released as the cassette-only release *The Lewd, The Mad, The Ugly And Old Nik*, before signing with Cherry Red Records subsidary, Anagram.

Wade, whose stage image of ghoulish, thick, white, pancake make-up revealed his strongest influence, Alice Cooper, further essayed that debt with 'Ignore The Machine' (1983). *Who's Been Sleeping In My Brain* was followed by 'Lips Can't Go' and in 1984 by 'R.I.P.'/'New Christian Music', 'Dead And Buried' and 'E.S.T. (Trip To The Moon)', to coincide with *Acid Bath*. Such was the album's reception in Japan that the band embarked on a tour there. *Liquid Head In Tokyo* celebrated the event, but was the last output for Johnny Ha Ha. As a three-piece, the band came up with 'I'm Doin' Time In A Maximum Security Twilight Home' (1985), accompanied by *Maximum Security*. *IT – The Album* arrived in time for a tour supporting Alice Cooper. A cover version of Red Crayola's late 60s classic, 'Hurricane Fighter Plane', surfaced in early 1987, followed by 'The Impossible Mission'. A retrospective, *All Our Yesterdays*, coincided with Yaxi Highriser's departure. Under the guise of the Dynamic Duo, Wade then issued 'Where Are Batman And Robin?' (on the Riddler label!). 'Bun Ho' was the next Alien Sex Fiend single, continuing a more open-minded musical policy. *Another Planet* confirmed this, while 'Haunted House' saw the adoption of out-and-out dance techniques. After a tour (with Rat Fink Junior and Doc Milton) was captured on the double album *Too Much Acid?*, the band returned with 'Now I'm Being Zombified' in September 1990. That same month, Alien Sex Fiend released the experimental *Curse*. They bounced back three years later with *The Altered States Of America*. The band then provided the music to the CD-ROM game *Inferno*, before establishing their own 13th Moon Records label and releasing the *Evolution* EP and *Nocturnal Emissions*.

● ALBUMS: *Who's Been Sleeping In My Brain* (Anagram 1983) ★★, *Acid Bath* (Anagram 1984) ★★★, *Liquid Head In Tokyo – Live* (Anagram 1985) ★★★, *Maximum Security* (Anagram 1985) ★★★, *IT – The Album* (Plague-Anagram 1986) ★★★, *Here Cum Germs* mini-album (Plague-Anagram 1987) ★★★, *Another Planet* (Plague-Anagram 1988) ★★★, *Too Much Acid?* (Plague-Anagram 1989) ★★, *Curse* (Plague-Anagram 1990) ★★★, *Open Head Surgery* (Plague-Anagram 1992) ★★★, *The Altered States Of America* (Anagram 1993) ★★★, *Inferno* (Anagram 1995) ★★★, *Nocturnal Emissions* (13th Moon 1997) ★★★, *Flashbacks: Live 1995–98* (Yeeah!/AlmaFame 2001) ★★.

● COMPILATIONS: *All Our Yesterdays* (Anagram 1988) ★★★, *The Legendary Batcave Tapes* (Plague-Anagram 1993) ★★, *The Singles 1983–1995* (Plague-Anagram 1995) ★★★, *Fiend At The Controls* (Anagram 1999) ★★★, *The Best Of Alien Sex Fiend* (Anagram 2001) ★★★.

● VIDEOS: *A Purple Glistener* (Jettisoundz 1984), *Edit* (Jettisoundz 1987), *Overdose* (Jettisoundz 1988), *Liquid Head In Tokyo* (ReVision 1991), *Re-Animated – The Promo Collection* (Visionary 1994).

## ALL ABOUT EVE

Originally called the Swarm, All About Eve emerged on the late 80s UK 'gothic' scene. The band's nucleus of erstwhile rock journalist and Gene Loves Jezebel bass player Julianne Regan (b. Coventry, England; vocals), along with Tim Bricheno (b. 6 July 1963, Huddersfield, Yorkshire, England; guitar, ex-Aemotti Crii), provided much of their song material. After various early personnel changes, the rhythm section was stabilized with Andy Cousin (bass; also ex-Aemotti Crii) and Mark Price (drums). Given encouragement by rising stars the Mission (for whom Regan had in the past sung backing vocals), All About Eve developed a solid following and with a backdrop of hippie mysticism and imagery, along with Regan's predilection for white-witchcraft and Tarot cards, provided a taste of the exotic with a mixture of goth rock and 70s folk.

Early singles 'Our Summer' and 'Flowers In Our Hair' achieved great success in the UK independent charts and after signing to Mercury Records, their modest showings in the national charts finally gave them a Top 10 hit in July 1988 with 'Martha's Harbour'. Both albums reached the UK Top 10, confirming their aspirations to be among the front-runners in UK rock in the late 80s. However, this ambition was dealt a blow in 1990 when a rift between the band and guitarist Bricheno resulted in his departure to join Sisters Of Mercy. The recruitment of Church guitarist Marty Willson-Piper on a part-time basis revitalized the band's drive, although the subsequent album, *Touched By Jesus*, only managed a brief visit to the UK Top 20, and indications that the band had undergone a born-again transformation were not vindicated. A stormy dispute with their distributor, Phonogram Records, over the company's alleged priority for chart single success saw All About Eve leave the label late in 1991 and shortly afterwards sign to MCA Records. After releasing the unfocused *Ultraviolet*, the band split, with Cousin going on to join the Mission. Regan formed Mice in 1995, recruiting Willson-Piper, Cousin and Price, among others. To the delight of their die-hard fans, Regan, Willson-Piper and Cousin embarked on an impromptu acoustic tour as All About Eve in early 2000. The highlights were captured on the two volumes of *Fairy Light Nights*.

● ALBUMS: *All About Eve* (Mercury 1987) ★★★, *Scarlet And Other Stories* (Mercury 1989) ★★★, *Touched By Jesus* (Vertigo 1991) ★★, *Ultraviolet* (MCA 1992) ★★, *Fairy Light Nights* (Yeaah/AlmaFame 2000) ★★★, *Fairy Light Nights Two: Live Acoustic* (Jamtart/AlmaFame 2001) ★★★, *Live & Electric At The Union Chapel* (Jamtart 2002) ★★★.

● COMPILATIONS: *Winter Words, Hits And Rarities* (MCA 1992) ★★★, *The Best Of All About Eve* (Spectrum 1999) ★★★.

● VIDEOS: *Martha's Harbour* (PolyGram Music Video 1988), *What Kind Of Fool* (PolyGram Music Video 1989), *Evergreen* (Channel 5 1989).

## ALLEN, DEBORAH

b. Deborah Lynn Thurgood, 30 September 1953, Memphis, Tennessee, USA. A singer-songwriter, whose songs have proved major successes for other artists, including 'Don't Worry 'Bout Me Baby' (Janie Fricke) and 'Can I See You Tonight?' (Tanya Tucker), Allen's own first US country chart success came in 1979 when she was working as a session singer. Thanks to the miracles of modern recording techniques and the thoughtfulness of RCA Records producer Bud Logan, she was chosen to superimpose her vocals over recordings made years earlier by Jim Reeves, a star then dead for almost 15 years. These so-called 'duets' produced three Top 10 US country hits, 'Don't Let Me Cross Over', 'Oh, How I Miss You Tonight' and 'Take Me In Your Arms And Hold Me'. Between 1980 and 1984, she had eight solo country singles including 'Baby I Lied' (a US country number 4 and US pop number 26) and 'I've Been Wrong Before' (a country number 2). She married songwriter Rafe Van Hoy, co-wrote songs with him and sang on the soundtrack of *The River Rat*.

After a long absence from the charts, which suggested that perhaps her solo singing career was over, she reappeared in December 1992. The reappearance, however, hardly matched the gentle vocals associated with the Reeves recordings. She joined the Giant label in 1992 and her debut album on the label contained 10 contemporary offerings either self-penned or written by Allen with others. She shared production with husband Van Hoy. 'Rock Me (In The Cradle Of Love)', the first single from the album, accompanied by a raunchy video, made the US country Top 30. A follow-up single, 'If You're Not Gonna Love Me', managed only a Top 50 placing and the year ended sadly for her when she and Rafe Van Hoy parted. The following year's *All That I Am* was another strong collection.

● ALBUMS: with Jim Reeves *Don't Let Me Cross Over* (RCA Victor 1979) ★★, *Trouble In Paradise* (Capitol 1980) ★★★, *Cheat The Night* mini-album (RCA 1983) ★★, *Let Me Be The First* (RCA 1984) ★★, *Delta Dreamland* (Giant 1993) ★★★, *All That I Am* (Giant 1994) ★★★.

● COMPILATIONS: *Anthology* (Renaissance 1998) ★★★, *The Best Of Deborah Allen* (Curb 2000) ★★★.

● VIDEOS: *Break These Chains* (Scene Three 1994).

### ALLEN, GERI

b. 12 June 1957, Pontiac, Michigan, USA. Pianist Allen grew up in Detroit, steeped in the city's strong bebop and black pop traditions (one early gig saw her playing with Mary Wilson and the Supremes), though Eric Dolphy, Herbie Nichols and Thelonious Monk were also major influences. She studied music at Washington's Howard University and at the University of Pittsburgh (with Nathan Davis) and later with Roscoe Mitchell. Moving to New York in the early 80s, she played with numerous contemporary jazz musicians, including James Newton and Lester Bowie, and recorded her debut *The Printmakers* in 1984 with a trio that featured Andrew Cyrille. She also became involved with the M-BASE and Black Rock Coalition organizations and the former's Steve Coleman and Robin Eubanks played on her *Open On All Sides In The Middle*. Later in the 80s she was a regular member of Oliver Lake's groups (*Plug It*, *Gallery*, *Impala*, *Otherside*) and toured and recorded with several leaders, including Dewey Redman (*Living On The Edge*), Frank Lowe (*Decision In Paradise*), Greg Osby (*Mindgames*) and Charlie Haden's Liberation Music Orchestra. With Haden and Paul Motian she formed an acoustic trio that has become celebrated for its intimate versions of modern mainstream jazz; and she also guested on Motian's own *Monk In Motian* and Betty Carter's *Droppin' Things*.

An acutely sensitive player with a lovely touch, in the early 90s Allen signed to Blue Note Records where she recorded several strong albums. Her most acclaimed recent work, however, was *The Gathering*, her 1998 debut for the Verve Records label. On this album, Allen was backed by Buster Williams (bass) and Lenny White (drums), with additional contributions from Vernon Reid on acoustic guitar.

● ALBUMS: *The Printmakers* (Minor Music 1984) ★★★, *Homegrown* (Minor Music 1985) ★★★★, *Open On All Sides In The Middle* (Minor Music 1987) ★★★, with Charlie Haden, Paul Motian *Etudes* (Soul Notes 1988) ★★★, with Haden, Motian *In The Year Of The*

*Dragon* (PolyGram 1989) ★★★, with Haden, Motian *Segments* (DIW 1989) ★★★, *Twylight* (Verve 1989) ★★★, with Haden, Motian *Live At The Village Vanguard* (DIW 1991) ★★★, *The Nurturer* (Blue Note 1991) ★★★, *Maroons* (Blue Note 1992) ★★★, *Eyes ... In The Back Of Your Head* (Blue Note 1997) ★★★, *The Gathering* (Verve 1998) ★★★★, *Some Aspects Of Water* 1996 recording (Storyville 1998) ★★★★.

### ALLISON, LUTHER

b. 17 August 1939, Mayflower, Arkansas, USA, d. 12 August 1997, Madison, Wisconsin, USA. Born into a family where he was the fourteenth child of 15, the young Allison worked with his siblings in the local cotton fields. In his youth, guitarist Allison sang with a family gospel group and moved to Chicago in 1951, where he attended school with one of Muddy Waters' children. Around 1957 he formed his own band with his brother Grant to work on the west side. They gigged occasionally under the name of the Rolling Stones and later the Four Jivers. After a year the group disbanded and Allison went on to work with Jimmy Dawkins, Magic Slim, Magic Sam, Muddy Waters, Little Richard, Freddie King and others until the mid-60s.

In March 1967, Allison recorded a session for Bill Lindemann, later issued by the collector label Delmark Records. He toured California, recording there as accompanist to Sunnyland Slim and Shakey Jake. He made his first album under his own name in 1969 and was one of the major successes of the Ann Arbor festivals of 1969 and 1970. In the early 70s, he recorded for Motown Records' subsidiary label Gordy and from the late 70s spent much of his time in France, living and working for a large and faithful following. He also recorded for many labels, usually live albums or studio sessions comprising funk or Jimi Hendrix- and Rolling Stones-influenced rock.

In the late 80s, following two well-received albums, *Serious* and *Soul Fixin' Man*, Allison found his career in ascendance. By the mid-90s, he was reaching a peak, winning W.C. Handy awards and experiencing financial success with a bestselling album, *Blue Streak*. This Indian summer of his career was cruelly cut short when in July 1997 he was diagnosed as having lung cancer; tragically, just over a month later, he died. It all happened so quickly that the interviews he had conducted for various magazines had not even gone to press. His son, Bernard Allison, released his debut album shortly before his father's death.

● ALBUMS: *Love Me Mama* (Delmark 1969) ★★★, *Bad News Is Coming* (Gordy 1973) ★★★, *Luther's Blues* (Gordy 1974) ★★★, *Night Life* (Gordy 1976) ★★★, *Love Me Papa* (Black & Blue 1977) ★★★, *Live In Paris* (Free Bird 1979) ★★★, *Live* (Blue Silver 1979) ★★★, *Gonna Be A Live One In Here Tonight* (Rumble 1979) ★★★, *Time* (Paris Album 1980) ★★★, *South Side Safari* (Red Lightnin' 1982) ★★★, *Lets Have A Natural Ball* (JSP 1984) ★★★, *Serious* (Blind Pig 1984) ★★★, *Here I Come* (Encore 1985) ★★★, *Powerwire Blues* (Charly 1986) ★★★, *Rich Man* (Entente 1987) ★★★, *Life Is A Bitch* (Encore 1988) ★★, *Love Me Mama* (Delmark 1988) ★★★, *Let's Try*

*It Again – Live '89* (Teldec 1989) ★★, *More From Berlin* (Melodie 1991) ★★, *Hand Me Down My Moonshine* (In-Akustik 1992) ★★, *Soul Fixin' Man* (Alligator 1994) ★★★, *Bad Love* (Ruf 1994) ★★★, *Blue Streak* (Ruf 1995) ★★★, *Reckless* (Ruf 1997) ★★★★, *Live In Paradise* (Ruf 1998) ★★★★, *Live In Chicago* (Alligator 1999) ★★★★, *South Side Safari* (Catfish 2000) ★★.
● COMPILATIONS: *Sweet Home Chicago* (Delmark 1993) ★★★, *The Motown Years 1972–1976* (Motown 1996) ★★★, *Where Have You Been? Live In Montreux 1976–1994* (Ruf 1997) ★★★★.
● VIDEOS: *Live In Paradise* (RUF 1998).

## ALMOND, MARC

b. Peter Marc Almond, 9 July 1956, Southport, Lancashire, England. Following the demise of the electro-pop duo Soft Cell and their adventurous offshoot Marc And The Mambas, Almond embarked on a solo career. With backing from the Willing Sinners, his first such venture was 1984's *Vermin In Ermine*, which barely consolidated his reputation and proved to be his last album for Phonogram Records. *Stories Of Johnny*, released on Some Bizzare Records through Virgin Records, was superior and displayed Almond's undoubted power as a torch singer. Prior to the album's release, he had reached the UK Top 5 in a camp disco-inspired duet with Bronski Beat titled 'I Feel Love (Medley)'. The single combined two Donna Summer hits ('Love To Love You Baby' and 'I Feel Love' ) with snatches of John Leyton's 'Johnny Remember Me', all sung in high register by fellow vocalist Jimmy Somerville. The controversial *Mother Fist And Her Five Daughters* did little to enhance his career, which seemed commercially in decline by the time of the *Singles* compilation. Another change of licensed label, this time to Parlophone Records, saw the release of 'Tears Run Rings' and Almond's old commercial sense was emphasized by 1989's opportune revival of 'Something's Gotten Hold Of My Heart' with Gene Pitney. This melodramatic single was sufficient to provide both artists with their first number 1 hit as soloists.
Almond returned in 1990 with a cover album of Jacques Brel songs and *Enchanted*, which featured the singer's usual flamboyant style complemented by flourishes of flamenco guitar and violin, and a solid production. In 1992, Almond revived the David McWilliams song 'The Days Of Pearly Spencer', reaching number 4 in the UK charts. The same year he staged an extravagant comeback concert at the Royal Albert Hall, documented on *12 Years Of Tears*. In contrast, *Absinthe: The French Album* was a strikingly uncommercial set that featured Almond performing Baudelaire and Rimbaud poems. He returned to the cold electronic sounds of the 80s with *Fantastic Star* in early 1996, the same year as he ended a 15-year contract with Stevo as his manager and signed an abortive deal with Echo Records. Almond returned in 1999 with *Open All Night*, released on his own Blue Star label. His profile was further raised by a Soft Cell reunion, and the release of the excellent *Stranger Things*. This collaboration with Icelandic producer Johann Johannson was

widely regarded to be the singer's strongest release since *Absinthe*.
● ALBUMS: *Vermin In Ermine* (Some Bizzare/ Phonogram 1984) ★★, *Stories Of Johnny* (Some Bizzare/Virgin 1985) ★★★, *A Woman's Story* mini-album (Some Bizzare/Virgin 1986) ★★★, *Violent Silence* mini-album (Virgin 1986) ★★★, *Mother Fist And Her Five Daughters* (Some Bizzare/Virgin 1987) ★★, *The Stars We Are* (Some Bizzare/Capitol 1988) ★★★, *Jacques* (Some Bizzare/Rough Trade 1989) ★★★, *Enchanted* (Some Bizzare/Capitol 1990) ★★★, *Tenement Symphony* (Some Bizzare/Sire 1991) ★★★, *12 Years Of Tears: Live At The Royal Albert Hall* (Some Bizzare/Sire 1993) ★★★, *Absinthe: The French Album* (Some Bizzare 1994) ★★★, *Fantastic Star* (Mercury 1996) ★★★, *Open All Night* (Blue Star 1999) ★★★, *Stranger Things* (XIII Bis 2001) ★★★.
● COMPILATIONS: *Singles 1984–1987* (Some Bizzare/Virgin 1987) ★★★, with Soft Cell *Memorabilia: The Singles* (Polydor 1991) ★★★, *A Virgin's Tale Vol. I* (Some Bizzare/Virgin 1992) ★★★, *A Virgin's Tale Vol. II* (Some Bizzare/Virgin 1992) ★★★, *Treasure Box* (Some Bizzare/EMI 1995) ★★.
● VIDEOS: *Marc Almond Videos: 1984–1987* (Virgin Vision 1987), *Marc Almond Live In Concert* (Windsong 1992), *12 Years Of Tears* (Sire 1993).
● FURTHER READING: *The Angel Of Death In The Adonis Lounge*, Marc Almond. *The Last Star: A Biography Of Marc Almond*, Jeremy Reed. *Gutterheart*, Paul Burston. *Beautiful Twisted Night*, Marc Almond. *Tainted Life: The Autobiography*, Marc Almond. *The End Of New York*, Marc Almond.

## ALTAN

This Irish traditional band, in the mould of De Dannan, has achieved popularity on its own merits. Their name was taken from Loch Altan (near Gweedore in north-western Donegal). The line-up of Frankie Kennedy (b. 30 September 1955, Belfast, Northern Ireland, d. 19 September 1994, Belfast, Northern Ireland; flute), Mairéad Ní Mhaonaigh (b. 26 July 1959, Donegal, Eire; vocals, fiddle), Ciaran Curran (b. 14 June 1955, Enniskillen, Co. Fermanagh, Northern Ireland; bouzouki), Dáithí Sproule (b. 23 May 1950, Co. Derry, Northern Ireland; guitar, vocals) and Ciaran Tourish (b. 27 May 1967, Buncrana, Co. Donegal, Eire; fiddle) built up a strong following both in Britain and the USA, where they first toured in 1988. The band was formed in 1987 following the release of *Altan*. At that point, the band was ostensibly Kennedy and Mhaonaigh, who were married in 1981, but with the others playing on the recording a more permanent arrangement was established. Their repertoire comes largely from Donegal, and due to the area's historical links with Scotland, the music has absorbed influences from both Irish and Scottish sources. Later recruits to the band included Mark Kelly (b. 15 March 1961, Dublin, Eire; guitar) and Dermot Byrne (b. Co. Donegal, Eire; accordion), although sadly Kennedy succumbed to cancer in 1994. Altan now regularly tour the USA and Europe, and have made frequent festival appearances. In 1996, the band signed a major label contract with Virgin Records, releasing the well-received albums

*Blackwater, Runaway Sunday* and *Another Sky*.

● ALBUMS: *Ceol Aduaidh* (Gael Linn 1983) ★★★, *Altan* (Green Linnet 1987) ★★★★, *Horse With A Heart* (Green Linnet 1989) ★★★, *The Red Crow* (Green Linnet 1990) ★★★, *Harvest Storm* (Green Linnet 1992) ★★★, *Island Angel* (Green Linnet 1993) ★★★, *Blackwater* (Virgin 1996) ★★★, *Runaway Sunday* (Virgin 1997) ★★★, *Another Sky* (Virgin 2000) ★★★, *The Blue Idol* (Narada 2002) ★★★★.

● COMPILATIONS: *The First Ten Years: 1986–1995* (Green Linnet 1995) ★★★, *The Best Of Altan* (Green Linnet 1997) ★★★★, *The Collection* (Eureka 1999) ★★★, *Altan's Finest* (Erin 2000) ★★★, *Once Again (1987–1993)* (Snapper 2000) ★★★.

## ALTERED IMAGES

Formed in 1979, this Scottish pop ensemble featured Clare Grogan (b. 17 March 1962, Glasgow, Scotland; vocals), Johnny McElhone (b. 21 April 1963; bass), Tony McDaid (guitar) and Michael 'Tich' Anderson (drums). Even before their recorded debut, Grogan found herself cast in a film, *Gregory's Girl*, by director Bill Forsyth. In 1980, Altered Images toured with Siouxsie And The Banshees and subsequently employed the services of their bass player, Steve Severin, as producer. Another champion of their work was the influential UK disc jockey John Peel. Their BBC radio sessions resulted in the offer of a major recording contract by Epic Records, and two unsuccessful singles followed – the early 80s indie classic 'Dead Pop Stars' and 'A Day's Wait'. With the addition of guitarist Jim McInven, the band completed their debut, *Happy Birthday*, in 1981. The infectious title track, produced by Martin Rushent, soared to number 2 in the UK charts, establishing the elfin Grogan as a punkish Shirley Temple. 'I Could Be Happy' and 'See Those Eyes' were also hits, but the band's second album, *Pinky Blue*, was not well received by the critics. With 1983's *Bite*, Grogan took on a more sophisticated, adult image, lost Anderson and McInven, gained Stephen Lironi (guitar, drums) and found new producers Tony Visconti and Mike Chapman. The experiment brought another Top 10 hit, 'Don't Talk To Me About Love'. Following a brief tour with the addition of David Wilde (drums) and Jim Prime (keyboards), Altered Images disbanded. Grogan pursued an acting career (notably in television sitcom *Red Dwarf*, and more recently on MTV and *EastEnders*), recorded an unreleased solo album, *Love Bomb*, and later reappeared fronting a new band, Universal Love School. Meanwhile, Altered Images guitarist Johnny McElhone moved on to Hipsway and Texas.

● ALBUMS: *Happy Birthday* (Epic 1981) ★★★, *Pinky Blue* (Epic 1982) ★★, *Bite* (Epic 1983) ★★.

● COMPILATIONS: *Collected Images* (Epic 1984) ★★★, *The Best Of Altered Images* (Receiver 1992) ★★★, *I Could Be Happy: The Best Of Altered Images* (Epic 1997) ★★★.

## AMAZULU

This predominantly female ska band earned themselves a string of UK hit singles in the mid-80s. The band comprised Annie Ruddock (b. Ann-Marie Teresa Antoinette Ruddock, 2 July 1961; lead vocals), Claire Kenny (bass), Lesley Beach (b. 30 September 1954; saxophone), Sharon Bailey (b. 22 November 1957; percussion) and Margo Sagov (guitar), plus the lone male of the group, Nardo Bailey (drums). They made their initial impact on the lower regions of the UK single charts with 'Cairo', but achieved greater success in July 1985 with 'Excitable', which reached the UK Top 20. This success was followed by other hits, including 'Don't You Just Know It', 'Too Good To Be Forgotten' (number 5) and 'Montego Bay'. Their album was released on Island Records in 1986. After an acrimonious break-up, Ruddock, Sharon Bailey and Beach briefly played on as Amazulu II. Claire Kenny later joined the initial line-up of Coming Up Roses and subsequently became a session player for Shakespears Sister and Sinéad O'Connor.

● ALBUMS: *Amazulu* (Island 1986) ★★★.

## AMERICAN MUSIC CLUB

One of their country's most undervalued bands, San Francisco, California, USA's American Music Club took a similar path to Australia's Go-Betweens in reaping rich harvests of critical acclaim that were not reflected in their sales figures. The band's mastermind and musical springboard was Mark Eitzel (b. 30 January 1959, Walnut Creek, San Francisco, California, USA; vocals, guitar), a lyricist of rare scope. The name of his publishing company, I Failed In Life Music, was a good indicator of Eitzel's world-view: 'I see humanity, including myself, as basically a bunch of sheep or ants. We're machines that occasionally do something better than machines.' The rest of American Music Club comprised Danny Pearson (b. 31 May 1959, Walnut Creek, San Francisco, California, USA; bass), Tim Mooney (b. 6 October 1958, Las Vegas, Nevada, USA; drums), Vudi (b. Mark Pankler, 22 September 1952, Chicago, Illinois, USA; guitar) and occasionally Bruce Kaphan (b. 7 January 1955, San Francisco, California, USA; steel guitar).

When he was seven, Eitzel's family moved to Okinawa, Taiwan, before settling in Southampton, England. He wrote his first songs aged 14, and was 17 when he saw the new punk bands. Two years later, he moved to Ohio with his family. There he put together Naked Skinnies, who moved to San Francisco in 1981. It was during their show at the San Francisco punk venue the Mabuhay Gardens that Vudi walked in and saw them. From his earliest appearances, Eitzel's onstage demeanour rivalled the extravagances of Iggy Pop. In the early days, he was also a fractious heavy drinker, until the day American Music Club signed to a major label after several acclaimed independent albums. Before this, he had left the band twice, once after the tour to support *Engine*, and once after *Everclear*. He also temporarily fronted Toiling Midgets. Following *Everclear*, in 1991, *Rolling Stone* magazine elected Eitzel their Songwriter Of The Year, but as he conceded: 'Yes, I'm songwriter of the year for 1991; a month later I'm still songwriter of the year, and still no one comes to see us play!'

*Mercury* was the band's debut for a major record label, although song titles such as 'What Godzilla Said To God When His Name Wasn't Found In The

Book Of Life' illustrated that Eitzel's peculiar lyrical scenarios were still intact. The album was primarily written while Eitzel was living in the decidedly down-at-heel Mission District of San Francisco. The critical acclaim customarily heaped on the band was repeated for 1994's *San Francisco*, and *Melody Maker* journalist Andrew Mueller grew exasperated when reviewing one of the singles drawn from it, 'Can You Help Me?' – 'We're obviously not explaining ourselves tremendously well . . . Every album they have ever made we have reviewed with prose in the most opulent hues of purple . . . We have, in short, shouted ourselves hoarse from the very rooftops in this band's name, and still nobody who doesn't work here owns any of their records'. Eitzel finally broke up the band for a solo career in 1995. The other members later recorded as Clodhopper.

● ALBUMS: *The Restless Stranger* (Grifter 1986) ★★★, *Engine* (Grifter/Frontier 1987) ★★★, *California* (Grifter/Frontier 1988) ★★★, *United Kingdom* (Demon 1990) ★★★, *Everclear* (Alias 1991) ★★★★, *Mercury* (Reprise 1993) ★★★★, *San Francisco* (Reprise 1994) ★★★.

● FURTHER READING: *Wish The World Away: Mark Eitzel And The American Music Club*, Sean Body.

## AND ALL BECAUSE THE LADY LOVES

Formed in 1987, this Newcastle, England-born female duo, Nicky Rushton (b. Nicola Rushton; guitar, vocals) and Rachel Collins (bass, vocals), achieved critical acclaim on the UK club circuit with their sets of bittersweet love songs, combined with a twist of political consciousness. Accompanied by simple, but effective, guitar and bass, their songs were offset with strong – almost a cappella – vocal harmonies and punchy melodies. They toured with Microdisney and Michelle Shocked while promoting their 1988 EP, *If You Risk Nothing*, and this led to an album on the small independent label Paint It Red, which won widespread critical acclaim. In 1989 they released their second album on the duo's own Newcastle-based label, Roundabout. Later work saw them employing backing musicians, both live and in the studio, remaining one of the north east's best-kept secrets. They enjoyed surprising popularity in German-speaking Europe, particularly Switzerland. And All Because The Lady Loves played their final concert in Switzerland in November 1994.

● ALBUMS: *Anything But A Soft Centre* (Paint It Red 1988) ★★★★, *Centred* (Roundabout 1989) ★★★, *Sugar Baby Love* (Roundabout 1991) ★★★, *Sister Bridget* (Roundabout 1993) ★★★.

## ANDERSON, JOHN

b. 12 December 1955, Apopka, Florida, USA. As an adolescent, Anderson was playing the songs of UK beat groups in his school band, but he then became enthused with country music. He joined his sister, Donna, in Nashville in 1972 and they played together in clubs and bars. In 1974, he began recording for the Ace Of Hearts label but none of his singles ('Swoop Down Sweet Jesus', 'Losing Again', 'A Heartbreak Ago') made any impression. He signed with Warner Brothers Records in 1977 and his first single was 'I Got A Feelin' (Somebody's Stealin')'.

Although Anderson had several country hits ('My Pledge Of Love', 'Low Dog Blues', 'Your Lying Blue Eyes' and a perfect country theme, 'She Just Started Liking Cheating Songs'), he was not allowed to make an album until he was established. Some regard Anderson as continuing the tradition of Lefty Frizzell and George Jones, and he was delighted when his song 'The Girl At The End Of The Bar' was covered by Jones. His revival of a poignant ballad, 'I Just Came Home To Count The Memories', originally a US country hit for Cal Smith, was given an identical arrangement to Elvis Costello's version of 'A Good Year For The Roses'. As well as honky tonk ballads, he recorded the cheerful Billy Joe Shaver song 'I'm Just An Old Chunk Of Coal (But I'm Gonna Be A Diamond Someday)' and his own up-tempo 'Chicken Truck'.

In 1982, Anderson had his first US country number 1 with a song recommended to him by his sister, 'Wild And Blue'. Anderson and his frequent co-writer, Lionel Delmore, the son of Alton Delmore, wrote 'Swingin'', which sold 1.4 million and became the biggest-selling country single in Warners' history. Anderson, who plays lead guitar in his road band, named his instrument after the character in 'Swingin'', Charlotte. Despite being one of country music's first video stars, the singer fell out with both his record label and his management. He fared relatively poorly on MCA, although there was a spirited duet with Waylon Jennings, 'Somewhere Between Ragged And Right'. Mark Knopfler wrote and played guitar on a 1991 release, 'When It Comes To You'. That song appeared on *Seminole Wind*, a triumphant comeback album that restored Anderson to the top rank of his profession, spawning a succession of hit singles (including the number 1 hit, 'Straight Tequila Night'). Its title track, a lament for the loss of traditional Indian lands, was reminiscent of Robbie Robertson's best work with the Band in its portrayal of history and American landscape. Since that time Anderson has become somewhat unfashionable as he has not embraced contemporary rock. From time to time, he enjoys country hits, including the number 1 'Money In The Bank', and continues to enjoy major label recognition as demonstrated by a new deal with Columbia Records at the turn of the century.

● ALBUMS: *John Anderson* (Warners 1980) ★★, *John Anderson 2* (Warners 1981) ★★★, *I Just Came Home To Count The Memories* (Warners 1981) ★★★, *Wild And Blue* (Warners 1982) ★★★, *All The People Are Talking* (Warners 1983) ★★★, *Eye Of The Hurricane* (Warners 1984) ★★★, *Tokyo, Oklahoma* (Warners 1985) ★★, *Countryfied* (Warners 1986) ★★★, *Blue Skies Again* (MCA 1987) ★★★, *10* (MCA 1988) ★★, *Too Tough To Tame* (MCA 1990) ★★, *Seminole Wind* (RCA 1992) ★★★★, *Solid Ground* (BNA 1993) ★★★★, *Country Till I Die* (BNA 1994) ★★★, *Christmas Time* (BNA 1994) ★★, *Paradise* (BNA 1996) ★★★, *Takin' The Country Back* (Mercury 1997) ★★★, *Nobody's Got It All* (Columbia 2001) ★★★.

● COMPILATIONS: *Greatest Hits* (Warners 1984) ★★★★, *Greatest Hits, Volume 2* (Warners 1990) ★★★, *Greatest Hits* (BNA 1996) ★★★★, *Super Hits* (BNA 1998) ★★★, *The Essential John Anderson* (BNA 1998)

★★★★, *Backtracks* aka *Somehow, Someway, Someday*
(Renaissance/Orpheus 1999) ★★★, *RCA Country
Legends* (RCA 2002) ★★★.
● VIDEOS: *Country 'Til I Die* (BNA 1994).

## ANDERSON, LAURIE

b. Laura Phillips Anderson, 5 June 1950, Chicago,
Illinois, USA. A product of New York's *avant garde* art
scene, Laurie Anderson eschewed her initial work as
a sculptor in favour of performing. *The Life And
Times Of Josef Stalin*, premiered at Brooklyn's
Academy of Music in 1973, was a 12-hour epic
containing many of the audio-visual elements the
artist brought to her subsequent canon. Anderson's
debut, *Big Science*, included the eight-minute
vocoder-laden 'O Superman', which had become a
cult hit in Europe in 1981 on the 1/10 label and
subsequently reached number 2 in the UK chart
after Warner Brothers Records picked up the record.
The song's looped, repeated pattern combined
with the singer's part-spoken intonation created
a hypnotic charm. *Mr. Heartbreak*, arguably
Anderson's most accessible release, featured
contributions from Peter Gabriel and writer William
Burroughs, while her next release, a sprawling five-
album set, *United States*, chronicled an ambitious,
seven-hour show.
*Home Of The Brave* resumed the less radical path of
her second album and was co-produced by former
Chic guitarist Nile Rodgers. *Strange Angels* was an
ambitious and largely successful attempt to combine
Anderson's *avant garde* leanings with simple pop
structures. The guests on her 1994 album, *Bright Red*,
meanwhile, included Lou Reed, Adrian Belew and
ex-Fixx guitarist Jamie West-Oram, with production
expertise lent by Gabriel. *The Ugly One With The
Jewels* captured a live performance of Anderson
reading from her book *Stories From The Nerve Bible*,
which examines her experience of travelling in the
Third World. Her next project was *Songs And Stories
From Moby Dick*, an ambitious show based on
Herman Melville's famous novel. *Life On A String*,
her first studio album in over six years, was released
in autumn 2001. Although operating at rock's outer,
experimental fringes, Laurie Anderson, like her
partner Lou Reed, remains an influential and
respected figure.
● ALBUMS: *Big Science* (Warners 1982) ★★★★, *Mr.
Heartbreak* (Warners 1984) ★★★, *United States* 5-LP
set (Warners 1985) ★★, *Home Of The Brave* (Warners
1986) ★★★, *Strange Angels* (Warners 1989) ★★★★,
*Bright Red* (Warners 1994) ★★★, *The Ugly One With
The Jewels And Other Stories* (Warners 1995) ★★★,
*Life On A String* (Nonesuch/Warners 2001) ★★★,
*Live At Town Hall New York City, September 19–20,
2001* (Nonesuch/Atlantic 2002) ★★★.
● COMPILATIONS: *Talk Normal: The Laurie
Anderson Anthology* (Rhino/WEA 2000) ★★★★.
● VIDEOS: *Home Of The Brave* (Warners 1986),
*Collected Videos* (Warner Reprise 1990).

## ANEKA

b. Mary Sandeman, Scotland. A respected traditional
vocalist, Aneka sang with the Scottish Fiddle
Orchestra, and taught herself to sing in Gaelic. In an
attempt to achieve a pop hit, she recorded 'Japanese
Boy', pretending she was Japanese. She promoted
the record by wearing a kimono and wig to further
the illusion, changing her name by looking through
the Edinburgh phone book. The record, combined
with the stage act, was more of a novelty number,
but it reached number 1 in the UK as well as topping
most of the European charts during 1981. However,
its follow-up, 'Little Lady', was little more than a
copy and only managed a brief spell in the charts.
Three subsequent singles and an album followed,
but none fared well. When the Aneka act had run its
course, Sandeman returned to performing her Gaelic
music and singing to Edinburgh Festival Fringe
audiences.
● ALBUMS: *Aneka* (Ariola Hansa 1982) ★★.

## ANGELIC UPSTARTS

This politically motivated, hardline punk quartet
formed in 1977, in South Shields, England. They
were the brainchild of Mensi (b. Thomas Mensforth;
vocals), and strongly influenced by the Clash, the
Damned and the Sex Pistols. With Mond (guitar),
Ronnie Wooden (bass) and Sticks (drums)
completing the line-up, they signed to the
independent Small Wonder label who re-released
their underground classic 'The Murder Of Liddle
Towers' in 1978. The song condemned police
brutality and identified strongly with the youth
culture of the day. It led to a contract with Warner
Brothers Records, which produced *Teenage Warning*
and *We Gotta Get Out Of This Place* in 1979 and 1980,
respectively. Both these albums were regarded by
some within the punk community as classics,
featuring provocative lyrics that ridiculed the
politics of the government under Margaret Thatcher.
Characterized by Mensi's nasal snarl, the Angelic
Upstarts suffered from regular outbreaks of violence
at their live shows from National Front fascist
supporters, who sought to counter the band's left-
wing politics after initially misinterpreting their
patriotic stance.
As the 80s progressed, the band gradually saw their
fanbase dwindle. They had become entrenched in a
musical style that was rapidly becoming outdated,
and continued to release material, but with declining
success. By 1983's *Reason Why?*, the line-up
comprised Mensi, Tony Feedback (bass), Bryan
Hayes (guitar) and Paul Thompson (drums; ex-Roxy
Music). The band ground to a halt in 1986, but re-
formed for a brief period in 1988 and then on a more
permanent basis in 1992, releasing *Bombed Out* on
the Roadrunner label. In the 90s, Mensi also became
a leading member of the Anti Fascist Action group.
The early 2002 version of Angelic Upstarts included
Mensi, Gaz Stoker (bass), Tony Van Frater (guitar),
and Lainey (drums).
● ALBUMS: *Teenage Warning* (Warners 1979) ★★★,
*We Gotta Get Out Of This Place* (WEA 1980) ★★★,
*2,000,000 Voices* (EMI 1981) ★★★, *Live* (EMI 1981)
★★, *Still From The Heart* (EMI 1982) ★★, *Reason
Why?* (Anagram 1983) ★★★, *Last Tango In Moscow*
(Picasso 1984) ★★, *Live In Yugoslavia* (Picasso 1985)
★★, *The Power Of The Press* (UK) *Brighton Bomb* (US)
(Gas/Chameleon 1986) ★★★, *Blood On The Terraces*

(Link 1987) ★★, *Live And Loud!!* (Link 1988) ★★, *Bombed Out* (Roadrunner 1992) ★★, *Anthems Against Scum* (Madbutcher/Insurgence 2001) ★★, *Live From The Justice League* (TKO 2002) ★★, *Sons Of Spartacus* (Captain Oi! 2002) ★★★.
● COMPILATIONS: *Angel Dust (The Collected Highs 1978–1983)* (Anagram 1983) ★★★, *Bootlegs And Rarities* (Dojo 1986) ★★, *Greatest Hits Live* (Streetlink 1992) ★★, *The Independent Punk Singles Collection* (Anagram 1995) ★★★, *Rarities* (Captain Oi! 1997) ★★, *Who Killed Liddle?* (Snapper 1999) ★★★, *Never 'Ad Nothing* (Harry May 1999) ★★, *The EMI Punk Years* (Captain Oi! 1999) ★★★, *The BBC Punk Sessions* (Captain Oi! 2000) ★★, *Bootlegs, Live And Rarities* (Rhythm Vicar 2002) ★★★.

## ANGRY SAMOANS
Formed in August 1978, in Van Nuys, California, USA, the Angry Samoans were one of the original Los Angeles punk bands, along with Fear, Black Flag, Circle Jerks and X. The fact that they never achieved quite as much as those other bands can be explained by a disappointingly curt discography. After numerous personnel changes, the most solid line-up consisted of core duo 'Metal' Mike Saunders (guitar, vocals) and Gregg Turner (guitar, vocals), plus Todd Homer (bass, vocals), Steve Drojensky (guitar) and Bill Vockeroth (drums). Leaning towards the humorous side of punk in the same way as the Ramones and Dickies, the Samoans' songs featured titles such as 'I'm A Pig', 'My Old Man's A Fatso', 'Attack Of The Mushroom People' and 'They Saved Hitler's Cock'. Following two EPs and one album for Bad Trip, they laid low for some time, before re-emerging in the late 80s via the auspices of Triple X Records. Saunders released a six-song solo EP as Metal Mike in 1991, before reuniting with Vockeroth to perform under the Angry Samoans banner.
● ALBUMS: *Inside My Brain* mini-album (Bad Trip 1980) ★★★, *Back From Samoa* (Bad Trip 1982) ★★★, *STP Not LSD* (PVC 1988) ★★, *Live At Rhino Records* (Triple X 1990) ★★,*The 90s Suck & So Do You* mini-album (Triple X 1999) ★★★.
● COMPILATIONS: *Gimme Samoa: 31 Garbage-Pit Hits* (PVC 1987) ★★★, *Return To Samoa* (Shakin' Street 1990) ★★, *The Unboxed Set* (XXX 1995) ★★★.
● VIDEOS: *True Documentary Video* (Triple X 1995).

## ANIMAL NIGHTLIFE
This early 80s UK pop/jazz group featured Andy Polaris (vocals), Steve 'Flid' Brown (guitar), Steve Shanley (bass), Billy Chapman (saxophone), Declan John Barclay (trumpet) and Mae (bongos). Their first single, 'Native Boy (Uptown)', reached the lower regions of the UK pop charts in 1983, but the following year's 'Mr. Solitaire' hit the Top 30, as did 1985's 'Love Is Just The Great Pretender'. The band's sparse output over a comparatively long period was probably exacerbated by their failure to capitalize on early media interest.
● ALBUMS: *Shangri-la* (Island 1985) ★★★, *Lush Life* (Ten 1988) ★★★.
● COMPILATIONS: *Unleashed: The Best Of Animal Nightlife* (Music Club 2000) ★★★.

## ANTHRAX
This New York, USA-based thrash metal outfit was formed in 1981 by Scott 'Not' Ian (b. Scott Rosenfeld, 31 December 1963; rhythm guitar) and Dan Lilker (bass). After a series of personnel changes, Ian and Lilker were joined by Neil Turbin (vocals), Dan Spitz (guitar) and Charlie Benante (drums). Managed by Johnny Zazula, head of the independent Megaforce Records, the quintet released *Fistful Of Metal* in 1984. Despite its tasteless sleeve, the album garnered fair reviews and was a small but steady seller. Lilker subsequently left Anthrax to pursue a hardcore direction with Nuclear Assault. Turbin also departed, with his initial replacement, Matt Fallon, being quickly succeeded by Joey Belladonna (b. 30 October 1960, Oswego, New York, USA). This line-up released the *Armed And Dangerous* EP in 1985, and their increasing popularity led to a contract with Island Records. *Spreading The Disease* was deservedly well received, and the band's European profile was raised considerably by their support slot on Metallica's Damage Inc tour.
In summer 1985, Ian and Benante formed S.O.D. (Stormtroopers Of Death, who were revived sporadically throughout the 90s), a hardcore band with a satirical outlook. They were joined in this venture by former bandmate Lilker and Billy Milano. *Among The Living*, co-produced by the band with Eddie Kramer, established Anthrax as a major force in the speed metal scene, producing UK hits in 'I Am The Law' and 'Indians', and their riotously entertaining live shows made them many friends among press and public alike. A humorous rap song, 'I'm The Man', became both a hit and a favourite encore. However, *State Of Euphoria* was a disappointing, patchy affair, with the band suffering an undeserved media backlash over their image. Sterling live work restored their reputation, with Anthrax's commitment to expanding their audiences' musical tastes demonstrated by their choice of UK support acts, Living Colour and King's X. *Persistence Of Time* showed a return to form, and was a dark and relentless work that produced another hit in the shape of a cover version of Joe Jackson's 'Got The Time'. Classed by the band as an EP, *Attack Of The Killer B's* was essentially a collection of b-sides for the curious fan, but became one of Anthrax's most popular albums, with the hit collaboration with Public Enemy, 'Bring The Noise', leading to the two bands touring together in a co-headlining package. Shortly after the band signed a new contract with Elektra Records, Belladonna was fired, with ex-Armored Saint frontman John Bush stepping in. *Sound Of White Noise* was hailed as the band's finest hour, a post-thrash *tour de force* of power metal with bursts of hardcore speed. Bush's creative input helped Ian and Benante to write some of their best work, while Dave Jerden's production updated and re-energized the Anthrax sound.
In 1994, Bush established his own R&B offshoot, Ho Cake, which included former Armored Saint personnel Joey Vera (bass) and Jeff Duncan (guitar), as well as Shawn Duncan (drums), Tony Silbert (keyboards) and Bruce Fernandez (ex-Dread Zeppelin). The following year Anthrax began work on

*Stomp 442*, an unremittingly brutal collection of hardcore and metal produced by the Butcher Brothers (best known for their work with Urge Overkill). However, Spitz was ejected from the band just before recording, and his guitar parts played instead by his former guitar technician, Paul Cook, Pantera's Dimebag Darrell and the band's drummer, Charlie Benante. In 1998, Ian guested on Tricky's *Angels With Dirty Faces*, shortly before Anthrax broke a three-year silence with *Volume 8 – The Threat Is Real*.

● ALBUMS: *Fistful Of Metal* (Megaforce 1984) ★★, *Spreading The Disease* (Island/Megaforce 1986) ★★★★, *Among The Living* (Island/Megaforce 1987) ★★★, *State Of Euphoria* (Island/Megaforce 1988) ★★, *Persistence Of Time* (Island/Megaforce 1990) ★★★★, *Attack Of The Killer B's* (Island/Megaforce 1991) ★★★, *Sound Of White Noise* (Elektra 1993) ★★★★, *Live – The Island Years* (Island 1994) ★★★, *Stomp 442* (Elektra 1995) ★★, *Volume 8 – The Threat Is Real* (Ignition 1998) ★★★, *We've Come For You All* (Beyond 2002) ★★★.

● COMPILATIONS: *Moshers 1986-1991* (Connoisseur Collection 1998) ★★★★, *Return Of The Killer A's* (Beyond/Spitfire 1999) ★★★, *Madhouse: The Very Best Of Anthrax* (Island 2001) ★★★★.

● VIDEOS: *Oidivnikufesin N.F.V.* (Island Visual Arts 1988), *Persistence Through Time* (Island Visual Arts 1990), *Through Time* (PolyGram Music Video 1991), *N.F.V.* (PolyGram Music Video 1991).

## ANTI-NOWHERE LEAGUE

Leading lights in the early 80s UK punk scene, along with contemporaries G.B.H. and the Exploited, this quartet from Tunbridge Wells, Kent, England, flaunted their talents in biker leather, chains and hardcore obscenity. Led by Animal (b. Nick Karmer; vocals) and Magoo (guitar), their catalogue of sexual outrage veered from the satirical to the genuinely offensive, with a string of four-letter words, rabid misogyny and the glorification of bestiality. Their most memorable moment was a thrashy rerun of Ralph McTell's 'Streets Of London', which replaced the song's folksy sentiments with the barbed, snarling rhetoric of the gutter. Thousands of copies of the single were seized and destroyed by the police as the b-side, 'So What', was deemed obscene. This action, however, could not prevent the band reaching number 1 in the UK Independent singles charts, a feat accomplished a further three times in 1982 with 'I Hate People', 'Woman' and 'For You'. As their punkish appeal receded, the Anti-Nowhere League abbreviated their name to the League and turned into a punk/metal hybrid in keeping with their biker image. Surprisingly, the results were not as appalling as might have been imagined, with *The Perfect Crime* boasting several fine songs, not least the almost subtle '(I Don't Believe) This Is My England'. The group disbanded in 1988 but there have been several revivals, including the one-off 1989 reunion recorded for release as *Live And Loud*. They bounced back with their 1997 album, *Scum*, which featured such treats as 'Fucked Up And Wasted' and a dubious cover version of Cher's 'Gypsies, Tramps And Thieves'.

● ALBUMS: *We Are ... The League* (WXYZ 1982) ★★,
*Live In Yugoslavia* (ID 1983) ★★, as The League *The Perfect Crime* (GWR 1987) ★★★, *Live And Loud* (Link 1990) ★★, *Scum* (SPV 1997) ★★, *Return To Yugoslavia* (Knock Out 1998) ★★, *So What?* (Harry May 2001) ★★★.

● COMPILATIONS: *Long Live The League* (Dojo 1986) ★★★, *Punk Singles & Rarities 1981-84* (Captain Oi! 2001) ★★★.

## ANY TROUBLE

In 1980, *Melody Maker* labelled Any Trouble: 'the most exciting new rock 'n' roll group since the Pretenders'. Formed in Stoke, England, by songwriter Clive Gregson (b. 4 January 1955, Ashton-Under-Lyne, Manchester, England) and Tom Jackson (vocals), they were part of a 'pub-rock' scene that also included Dr. Feelgood and Elvis Costello's Flip City. The line-up was completed with Chris Parks (lead guitar), Mel Harley (drums) and Phil Barnes (bass), although Jackson left before the band landed a recording contract. Stiff Records signed them and backed the single 'Yesterday's Love' with full-page adverts in the music press. *Where Are All The Nice Girls?* was an assured debut, but the promotional-only live album (just 500 were pressed) was a better example of their tough, bluesy music. They toured Europe and the USA as part of 'The Stiff Tour', but the label began concentrating on the US market because in the UK, Gregson, with his black-rimmed glasses and cynical lyrics, was frequently dismissed as an Elvis Costello imitator. *Wheels In Motion* lacked brightness, and Mike Howlett was an odd choice as producer, having just worked with OMD. Stiff lost faith and after releasing Any Trouble from their contract, drummer Martin Hughes (who had replaced Harley on the second album) and Chris Parks both quit. Any Trouble made a comeback in 1982, supporting John Martyn on a UK tour and signing to EMI America. Only Gregson and Barnes remained from the first line-up with new members Steve Gurl on keyboards and Andy Ebsworth on drums. *Any Trouble* was over-produced and Gregson himself later referred to it as 'dull'. *Wrong End Of The Race*, a double album, was their swansong but it was not backed by EMI America, and soon afterwards the band split. Their final performance was at London's Dingwalls venue at Christmas 1984. Gregson went on to work with Richard Thompson and record with the accomplished vocalist Christine Collister as Gregson And Collister.

● ALBUMS: *Where Are All The Nice Girls?* (Stiff 1980) ★★★, *Live At The Venue* (Stiff 1980) ★★★★, *Wheels In Motion* (Stiff 1981) ★★★, *Any Trouble* (EMI America 1983) ★★, *Wrong End Of The Race* (EMI America 1984) ★★★.

● COMPILATIONS: *Girls Are Always Right: The Stiff Years* (Cherry Red 2002) ★★★★.

## ARGENT, ROD

b. 14 June 1945, St. Albans, Hertfordshire, England. At this ancient town's fee-paying Abbey School, Argent studied clarinet, violin and, crucially, keyboards to scholarship level. Although his preferences lay in jazz and the classics, he was broad-minded enough to consider a career in pop. In

1962, he was a founder member of the Zombies, and became the quintet's principal composer – notably of the 1964 million-seller 'She's Not There'. After the Zombies broke up he formed Argent, who enjoyed several hit singles. Argent invested in a Worcester musical equipment shop and conducted session work for the Who, the Hollies, John Williams, Andrew Lloyd Webber and Cleo Laine and John Dankworth, before releasing *Moving Home* and its attendant single, 'Light Fantastic'. This was his first essay as a soloist (albeit with aid from famous friends). After collaborating with Lloyd Webber and Don Black on singer Marti Webb's *Tell Me On A Sunday* concept album in 1980, Argent penned *Masquerade*, an ambitious musical based on the Kit Williams book, which opened at the Young Vic in 1982. He continued as Lloyd Webber's principal pianist for a decade. That same year, he was also seen on the boards in person with John Hiscman and Barbara Thompson.

Argent's portfolio since then has embraced incidental music for films and new-age ventures, epitomized by 1988's *Red House* (named after his Bedfordshire studio) – which hedged its bets with vocal items. More lucrative, however, was his production (with drummer Peter Van Hooke) of Tanita Tikaram's first two albums, which sold millions. He co-composed two World Cup themes, and the use of the sturdy old 'She's Not There' (sung by former Zombie Colin Blunstone) in a 1990 British Telecom television advertisement was added to his vast amount of television work. Soundtracks to major series such as *Soldiers* and *Reach For The Sky* were co-composed by Argent.

In the 90s, Argent continued to work as a producer from his home studio. Successes included Joshua Kadison's *Painted Desert Serenade*, and a million-selling album by South American singer Soraya. Having maintained a friendship with his ex-Zombies (they performed together at a private party at the Jazz Cafe in 1997), it was no surprise when Argent started working with Blunstone. The result was *Out Of The Shadows*, a well-produced collection that was accompanied by a lengthy tour in 2001.

● ALBUMS: *Moving Home* (MCA 1979) ★★★, with Barbara Thompson *Ghosts* (MCA 1981) ★★★, *Siren Songs* (Miles Music 1983) ★★★, with Thompson *Shadow Show* (VeraBra 1985) ★★★, *Red House* (MMC 1988) ★★, with Colin Blunstone *Out Of The Shadows* (Red House 2001) ★★★.

## ARMORED SAINT

This Los Angeles, California, USA-based heavy metal quintet was formed in 1981. The band originally comprised John Bush (vocals), Dave Prichard (guitar), Phil E. Sandoval (guitar), Joey Vera (bass) and Gonzo Sandoval (drums). Their incessant gigging around the Los Angeles bar and club circuit led to them contributing a track to the *Metal Massacre II* compilation album. This, in turn, attracted the attention of Chrysalis Records, who signed them in 1984. *March Of The Saint* appeared the same year to widespread apathy. Poor production resulted in the band's dynamic energy being totally dissipated in a muddy wall of noise.

They moved away from the one-dimensional thrash approach on their next two albums, with Bush's powerful vocal style giving them a strong identity. With no commercial success after three albums, their contract with Chrysalis ended. The band returned with an excellent live album on Metal Blade Records. Sadly, Dave Prichard died of leukaemia on 27 February 1990. The remaining members, with the addition of touring guitarist Jeff Duncan, elected to complete *Symbol Of Salvation*, their most accomplished work to date.

In 1992, Bush left to replace Joey Belladonna in Anthrax and the rest of the band dispersed (though Vera and Duncan reunited with Bush in his side-project, Ho Cake). Vera released his solo debut, *A Thousand Faces*, for Metal Blade in 1994, and later recorded as Chroma Key for Massacre, and with Ray Alder (ex-Fates Warning) as Engine. The band reconvened in late 1998 to record the well-received *Revelation*.

● ALBUMS: *March Of The Saint* (Chrysalis 1984) ★★, *Delirious Nomad* (Chrysalis 1985) ★★★, *Raising Fear* (Chrysalis 1987) ★★★, *Saints Will Conquer – Live* (Metal Blade/Enigma 1989) ★★★, *Symbol Of Salvation* (Metal Blade/Enigma 1991) ★★★★, *Revelation* (Metal Blade 2000) ★★★.

● COMPILATIONS: *Nod To The Old School* (Metal Blade 2001) ★★★.

● VIDEOS: *A Trip Thru Red Times* (Video For Nations 1989).

## ARMOURY SHOW

Formed in 1984 by Richard Jobson (b. 6 October 1960, Dunfermline, Fife, Scotland; vocals, guitar) and Russell Webb (bass), both former members of the Skids, this band was initially completed by John McGeoch (b. 28 May 1955, Greenock, Strathclyde, Scotland; guitar), formerly of Magazine and Siouxsie And The Banshees, and John Doyle (drums). Although the quartet enjoyed two minor hit singles with 'Castles In Spain' (1984) and 'We Can Be Brave Again' (1985), the two latter musicians proved incompatible and left following the completion of the band's sole album. *Waiting For The Floods* was an uncomfortable mix of different styles, but a 1987 single, 'NY City', which featured Jobson, Webb and sundry session musicians, showed a greater sense of purpose. Although redolent of early Simple Minds, the release suggested a new-found confidence, but the band broke up in the wake of Jobson's burgeoning modelling and media-based career.

● ALBUMS: *Waiting For The Floods* (Parlophone 1985) ★★.

## ARROWS (CANADA)

A Canadian 80s pop rock outfit, the Arrows enjoyed some commercial success in their home country and mainland Europe during the duration of their two-album career. Making their debut with a four-track EP, *Misunderstood*, on Spontaneous Records, they went on to release two albums on A&M Records. Produced by Canadian songwriter David Tyson, who co-wrote most of the material with vocalist Dean McTaggart, they displayed a groundbreaking, sophisticated AOR sound and a flair for poppy choruses, setting standards at which the likes of A = 440 and Tim Feehan later aimed. *Stand Back* was released in 1984 and featured McTaggart, Rob Gusevs (keyboards), Earl Seymour (saxophone) and Doug Macaskill (guitars). With the addition of Bobby Economou (drums) and Glenn Olive (bass), the follow-up *The Lines Are Open* was released the following year. This included 'Talk Talk', which was their most successful single and was later covered by Gregg Rolie (ex-Santana; Journey) on his *Gringo* album; it was also taken as the name of the compilation released on Long Island Records in 1995.

● ALBUMS: *Stand Back* (A&M 1984) ★★★, *The Lines Are Open* (A&M 1985) ★★★.

● COMPILATIONS: *Talk Talk* (Long Island 1995) ★★★.

## ART OF NOISE

Formed in 1983, UK-based pop experimentalists Art Of Noise were the first artists to be signed to Trevor Horn's ZTT Records. The nucleus of the group was Horn, Anne Dudley (keyboard, arrangements), J.J. Jeczalik (keyboards, production) and Gary Langan (various instruments, production), with input from rock writer Paul Morley. Dudley had already achieved considerable experience arranging for a number of artists, including ABC, Frankie Goes To Hollywood and Paul McCartney. The band achieved early success as dancefloor favourites in America with the inventive *Into Battle With The Art Of Noise* EP. At the end of 1984, the ensemble registered a Top 10 UK hit with 'Close (To The Edit)', an inspired mix of hip-hop rhythms and vocal effects. The following year Dudley, Jeczalik and Langan fell out with ZTT over their marketing strategies and moved to the independent label China Records. Thereafter, their career consisted chiefly of work with other artists. A revival of 'Peter Gunn', with Duane Eddy, hit the UK Top 10 and this was followed by a collaboration with television's cartoon-animated character Max Headroom on 'Paranoimia'. Their finest and most bizarre backing role, however, was reserved for Tom Jones who made a Top 10 comeback courtesy of an amusing bump and grind version of Prince's 'Kiss'.

Having enjoyed several years of quirky chart success, Art Of Noise split in 1990, with Dudley going on to work with Phil Collins and Killing Joke's Jaz Coleman. Several remix collections have since been released, illustrating the band's (over-hyped) influence on dance music. Morley, Dudley and Horn re-formed the band in the late 90s, with the addition of the experienced Lol Creme, to work on the ambient concept album *The Seduction Of Claude Debussy*.

● ALBUMS: *Into Battle With The Art Of Noise* mini-album (ZTT 1983) ★★★, *(Who's Afraid Of?) The Art Of Noise!* (ZTT 1984) ★★★, *In Visible Silence* (Chrysalis 1986) ★★★, *Daft* (China 1987) ★★★, *In No Sense? Nonsense!* (China 1987) ★★, *Below The Waste* (China 1989) ★★, *The Ambient Collection* (China 1990) ★★★, *Drum And Bass Collection* (China 1996) ★★★, *State Of The Art* 3-CD remix box (China 1997) ★★★, *The Seduction Of Claude Debussy* (ZTT 1999) ★★★, *The Reduction* (ZTT 2000) ★★.

● COMPILATIONS: *The Best Of The Art Of Noise* (China 1988) ★★★★.
● VIDEOS: *In Visible Silence* (Channel 5 1988).
● FILMS: *Breakdance – The Movie* (1984).

## ASHMAN, HOWARD

b. 3 May 1950, Baltimore, Maryland, USA, d. 14 March 1991, Los Angeles, California, USA. A lyricist, librettist, playwright and director. After studying at Boston University and Indiana University, where he gained a master's degree in 1974, Ashman moved to New York and worked for publishers Grosset & Dunlap, while starting to write plays. One of his earliest works, *Dreamstuff*, a musical version of *The Tempest*, was staged at the WPA Theatre, New York, where Ashman served as artistic director from 1977 to 1982. In 1979, the WPA presented a musical version of Kurt Vonnegut's *God Bless You, Mr Rosewater*, written by Ashman in collaboration with composer Alan Menken (b. 22 July 1949, New Rochelle, New York, USA), which became a cult hit. In 1982, again at the WPA, they had even bigger success with *Little Shop Of Horrors*, an amusing musical about Audrey II, a man-eating plant. The show became the highest-grossing and third longest-running musical in off-Broadway history. It won the New York Drama Critics Award, Drama Desk Award and Outer Critics Circle Award The London production won *Evening Standard* awards for Best Musical and Best Score.

As well as writing the book and lyrics, Ashman also directed the show. One of the songs from the 1986 film version, 'Mean Green Mother From Outer Space', was nominated for an Academy Award. Disenchanted with Broadway following his flop show *Smile*, with music by Marvin Hamlisch, Ashman moved to Hollywood, and the animated features of Walt Disney. One of Ashman's own songs, with the ironic title 'Once Upon A Time In New York', was sung by Huey Lewis in *Oliver & Company* (1988), and the following year he was back with Menken for *The Little Mermaid*. Two of their songs for this film, 'Kiss The Girl' and 'Under The Sea', were nominated for Academy Awards. The latter won, and Menken received the Oscar for Best Score. Two years later, the duo did it again with their music and lyrics for *Beauty And The Beast* (1991) (one US theatre critic wrote: 'Disney's latest animated triumph boasts the most appealing musical comedy score in years, dammit'). Three songs from the film were nominated by the Academy, this time the title number emerged as the winner, along with the score. Menken received an unprecedented five BMI awards for this work on the film. In Ashman's case his Academy Award was posthumous – he died of AIDS on 14 March 1991.

Menken signed a long-term contract with Disney, the first result of which was *Newsies* (1992; retitled *The News Boys* in the UK), a turn-of-the-century live-action story, with lyrics by Jack Feldman. Before Ashman died he had been working with Menken on the songs for *Aladdin*, and one of them, 'Friend Like Me', was subsequently nominated for an Academy Award. Menken completed work on the film with UK lyricist Tim Rice, and their tender ballad, 'A

Whole New World', won an Oscar, as did Menken's score. 'A Whole New World' also won a Golden Globe award, and a version by Peabo Bryson and Regina Belle topped the US chart in 1993. Two years later, Menken worked with lyricist Stephen Schwartz on Disney's new movie, *Pocahontas*. The team won Oscars for Original Music Or Comedy Score and Original Song ('Colours Of The Wind'), and reunited for *The Hunchback Of Notre Dame* (1996). Menken's other film work has included *Rocky V* ('The Measure Of A Man', 1990), *Home Alone 2: Lost In New York* ('My Christmas Tree', with Jack Feldman, 1992), *Life With Mikey* (aka *Give Me A Break*, 1993), *Hercules* (1997) and *Little Mermaid II: The Return To The Sea* (2000). Early in the 90s, Menken returned to the stage, collaborating with David Spencer for the science-fiction musical *Weird Romance* (1992), at the WPA, and with Lynn Ahrens for a new $10 million musical version of the Charles Dickens classic *A Christmas Carol* (1994) at Madison Square Garden in New York. In April of that year, a spectacular stage production of *Beauty And The Beast* opened in New York, and three years later, Menken (with Tim Rice as librettist-lyricist) was back on Broadway with a limited, nine-performance run of the 'concert event' *King David*. Menken's other honours have included BMI, Golden Globe and Grammy awards.

## ASIA

A supergroup comprising well-known musicians from UK art-rock bands, Asia was formed in early 1981 by John Wetton (b. 12 June 1949, Derby, Derbyshire, England; vocals), Steve Howe (b. Stephen James Howe, 8 April 1947, Holloway, London, England; guitar), Geoff Downes (b. 25 August 1952, Stockport, Cheshire, England; keyboards) and Carl Palmer (b. Carl Frederick Kendall Palmer, 20 March 1950, Birmingham, West Midlands, England; drums, percussion). At the time, Wetton had recently left the English progressive band UK and released a solo album; Howe and Downes had just abandoned Yes; and Palmer had left Emerson, Lake And Palmer and released an album with PM. The band's self-titled debut album was released a year later and, although dismissed by critics as unadventurous and overly commercial, it topped the US album charts for nine weeks, becoming one of the year's bestsellers. A single, 'Heat Of The Moment', also reached the US Top 5. Neither fared as well in the band members' homeland. A follow-up single, 'Only Time Will Tell', was a moderate US success. The band released its second album, *Alpha*, in 1983 and, although it was a Top 10 hit in the USA, as was the single 'Don't Cry', its sales failed to match those of the debut. Wetton was subsequently replaced by Greg Lake (b. 10 November 1948, Bournemouth, Dorset, England), another Emerson, Lake And Palmer alumnus. As testament to the residual affection for the band, a live television concert from Japan drew over 20 million US viewers in late 1983. Lake's voice turned out to be unsuited to the band's material, and he was replaced by the returning Wetton. Ongoing personality clashes saw Howe leaving during recording sessions for a third album, with Mandy Meyer (b. Armand Meyer, 29

August 1960, Balcarres, Saskatchewan, Canada) brought in as his replacement. The comparatively low chart position of *Astra* precipitated the band's dissolution, with both Wetton and Downes going on to work on solo projects. The latter also produced Howe's new project, GTR, formed with Steve Hackett and Max Bacon.

Wetton recorded 'Gypsy Soul' under the name Asia for the soundtrack of the 1987 Sylvester Stallone movie *Over The Top*. During the same year, he teamed up with Downes and 21 Guns members Scott Gorham and Michael Sturgis for an abortive reunion, although some of the tracks would resurface on later albums. A more successful reunion took place in 1989, with Wetton and Palmer playing a series of European dates with various musicians. They were joined by Downes and Pat Thrall (ex-Hughes/Thrall) for a series of further dates to promote *Then & Now*, a compilation of new and old material that fulfilled their contractual agreement with Geffen Records. Wetton and Palmer subsequently moved on to other projects, leaving Downes as the sole remaining founder member. He inaugurated a new era for the band by forming a songwriting partnership with John Payne (bass, vocals). The duo recorded 1992's *Aqua* with Sturgis and Al Pitrelli (guitar), and occasional input from Palmer and Howe. The latter joined the subsequent tour as a 'special guest artist'. The Downes/Payne partnership has continued to release new albums, with the creative high point being 1996's *Arena*. They have been joined on these recordings by an ever-changing cast list of musicians, including Sturgis, Pitrelli, Thrall, Aziz Ibrahim (guitar), Elliott Randall (guitar), Ian Crichton (guitar) and Luis Jardim (percussion).

● ALBUMS: *Asia* (Geffen 1982) ★★★, *Alpha* (Geffen 1983) ★★, *Astra* (Geffen 1985) ★★, *Then & Now* (Geffen 1990) ★★★, *Live: 09-XI-90 Mockba* (Cromwell/Rhino 1991) ★★, *Aqua* (Musidisc/ Pyramid 1992) ★★, *Aria* (Intercord/I.R.S. 1994) ★★, *Arena* (Intercord/Bulletproof 1996) ★★★, *Now: Live Nottingham* 1990 recording (Blueprint 1997) ★★, *Live: Osaka – Japan – June 1992* (Blueprint 1997) ★★, *Live: Philadelphia – Chestnut Cabaret – 21st November 1992* (Blueprint 1997) ★★, *Live: Köln – Germany – 5th October 1994* (Blueprint 1997) ★★, *Live At The Town & Country Club* 1992 recording (Resurgence 1999) ★★, *Live Acoustic* 1997 recording (Resurgence 1999) ★★, *Aura* (Recognition 2001) ★★★, *Alive In Hallowed Halls* 1983 recording (Zoom Club 2001) ★★.

● COMPILATIONS: *Archiva 1* (Resurgence 1996) ★★, *Archiva 2* (Resurgence 1996) ★★, *Anthology* (Snapper 1997) ★★★, *Axioms* (Snapper 1998) ★★, *Rare* (Resurgence 2000) ★★, *The Very Best Of Asia: Heat Of The Moment (1982–1990)* (Geffen 2000) ★★★, *Anthologia* (Geffen 2002) ★★★.

● VIDEOS: *Asia In Asia* (Vestron Music Video 1984), *Asia (Live)* (Virgin Vision 1991).

● FURTHER READING: *The Heat Goes On*, David Gallant.

## ASSEMBLY

This one-off electronic project was inaugurated by Vince Clarke (b. 3 July 1960, South Woodford,

London, England), former synthesizers and keyboard player in Depeche Mode and Yazoo, and ex-Undertones singer Feargal Sharkey (b. Sean Feargal Sharkey, 13 August 1958, Londonderry, Northern Ireland). The resulting single, 'Never Never', reached the UK number 4 position in late 1983. No album was ever recorded by the duo. After many similar liaisons with Neil Arthur of Blancmange, The The's Matt Johnson and Paul Quinn of Orange Juice, Clarke found a stable rapport with Andy Bell in Erasure, while Sharkey departed for the USA and a solo career.

## ASSOCIATES

Vocalist Billy MacKenzie (b. 27 March 1957, Dundee, Scotland, d. 23 January 1997, Scotland) and Alan Rankine had performed in a variety of local bands before finally forming the Associates in 1979. They recorded a cover version of David Bowie's 'Boys Keep Swinging' for Double Hip Records, before being signed to Fiction Records where they released the critically acclaimed *The Affectionate Punch*. After a spell on the Beggars Banquet Records subsidiary Situation 2, they formed their own Associates label, distributed by WEA Records. The extra push provided a Top 10 chart breakthrough courtesy of 'Party Fears Two', which boasted an engaging and distinctive keyboard arrangement. Two further Top 30 hits followed with 'Club Country' and '18 Carat Love Affair'/'Love Hangover'. Meanwhile, MacKenzie became involved in other projects, most notably a cameo appearance on BEF's extravagant *Songs Of Quality And Distinction*, but split with Rankine in 1983. It was not until 1984 that MacKenzie reconvened the Associates, but this was followed by several very low chart entries and a relatively poor-selling album, *Perhaps*. The band's fifth album, *The Glamour Chase*, remained unreleased and MacKenzie was dropped from WEA in 1988. It was not until 1990 that he returned with a new album, *Wild And Lonely*, which was stylistically similar to the earlier work. The disappointing follow-up, *Outernational*, was released under MacKenzie's own name. An abortive reunion with Rankine took place in 1993, after which MacKenzie retired from the music business for several years to concentrate on breeding dogs. In 1996, he signed to the Nude label and demoed new material written in collaboration with Steve Aungle. Following a bout of depression after his mother's death, MacKenzie was found dead at his parents' home in January 1997. The posthumously released *Beyond The Sun* contained the new recordings on which he was working shortly before his death.
● ALBUMS: *The Affectionate Punch* (Fiction 1980) ★★★, *Sulk* (Associates/WEA 1982) ★★★★, *Perhaps* (WEA 1985) ★★, *Wild And Lonely* (Circa/Charisma 1990) ★★★.
Solo: Billy MacKenzie *Outernational* (Circa 1991) ★★, *Beyond The Sun* (Nude 1997) ★★★, with Paul Haig *Memory Palace* (Rhythm Of Life 1999) ★★, with Steve Aungle *Eurocentric* (Rhythm Of Life 2001) ★★★. Alan Rankine *The Day The World Became Her Age* (Les Disques Du Crepuscule 1986) ★★★, *She Loves Me Not* (Virgin 1987) ★★★, *The Big Picture*

*Sucks* (Les Disques Du Crepuscule 1989) ★★.
● COMPILATIONS: *Fourth Drawer Down* (Situation 2 1981) ★★★, *Popera: The Singles Collection* (East West 1991) ★★★, *The Radio 1 Sessions* (Nighttracks 1994) ★★★, *Double Hipness* (V2 2000) ★★, *The Glamour Chase/Perhaps* (Warners 2002) ★★★.
● FURTHER READING: *The Glamour Chase: The Maverick Life Of Billy MacKenzie*, Tom Doyle.

## ASTLEY, RICK

b. Richard Paul Astley, 6 February 1966, Newton-le-Willows, Lancashire, England. Astley was the drummer in a local band called Give Way, before joining soul outfit FBI in 1984 as lead vocalist. He was discovered by the successful producer/writer Pete Waterman in 1985 and worked at Waterman's PWL studios while waiting for a recording break. In 1987 he recorded a duet, 'Learning To Live', with Ochi Brown and was also part of Rick And Lisa, whose single 'When You Gonna' was released on RCA Records. He also sang on the UK number 1 hit 'Let It Be' by Ferry Aid, before achieving his first solo success with 'Never Gonna Give You Up'. This single topped the UK chart, became the biggest UK single of 1987 (winning a BRIT Award) and helped to make him the top singles act of the year. His debut album, *Whenever You Need Somebody*, also reached number 1 in the UK and sold over a million copies. When Astley was launched in the USA in 1988, he was an instant success. When 'Together Forever' followed 'Never Gonna Give You Up' to number 1, he became the first artist in the 80s to top the US charts with his first two singles. In 1988, Astley was the most played US club act and had the top-selling 12-inch record. Under the wing of Stock, Aitken And Waterman, Astley achieved seven UK and four US Top 10 singles. Despite the fact that he possessed one of the best voices in pop music, he became a target for the UK media who saw him as a puppet of his producers. Astley wanted to have more involvement in his recordings and he left the winning production and writing team. After a lengthy break, he resurfaced in 1991 with the successful album *Free*, which included guest appearances from Elton John and Mark King (of Level 42). This album also included the co-written single 'Cry For Help', which put him back into the Top 10 on both sides of the Atlantic. Astley left RCA in 1993, and very little was heard of him until he signed a new recording contract with Polydor Universal in May 2001. His first studio album in almost 10 years, *Keep It Turned On*, was released in Germany in December.
● ALBUMS: *Whenever You Need Somebody* (RCA 1987) ★★★, *Hold Me In Your Arms* (RCA 1988) ★★, *Free* (RCA 1991) ★★★, *Body & Soul* (RCA 1993) ★★★, *Keep It Turned On* (Polydor 2001) ★★★.
● COMPILATIONS: *Greatest Hits* (BMG Heritage/RCA 2002) ★★★★.
● VIDEOS: *Video Hits* (BMG Video 1989).

## ASTLEY, VIRGINIA

b. October 1960, Watford, Hertfordshire, England. Astley was a former member of the Ravishing Beauties along with Nicola Holland and Kate St. John. As classically trained musicians they attempted, with some degree of success, to cross over into the pop field, working with, among others, Echo And The Bunnymen, the Skids and the Teardrop Explodes. Astley broke away to pursue a solo career in 1982. Her single, 'Love's A Lonely Place To Be', was a melancholy paean to the feeling of isolation when a love affair breaks down, and the song's choral, almost boy soprano feel gave it an ephemeral quality. It reached number 7 in the UK Independent chart and conformed to the then current fashion for 'quiet pop'. Her debut album in 1983 confirmed her love of all things English and pastoral. Largely an instrumental album, this dreamy, atmospheric piece incorporated the sounds of the countryside on a summer's day. Complete with authentic bird songs and farm sounds, it gave the impression of a modern-day piece by Delius. It took three years for her second album to be released, and the Ryńichi Sakamoto-produced *Hope In Darkened Heart* concentrated on Astley's preoccupation with the loss of childhood innocence and uncertainty of adulthood. This accomplished musician has remained on the periphery of the music scene, but can occasionally be found guesting for other artists. In 1995 she collaborated with her old Ravishing Beauties partner Kate St. John on the latter's *Indescribably Night* album. She has also released two further solo albums in Japan where she retains a large fanbase.

● ALBUMS: *From Gardens Where We Feel Secure* (Rough Trade 1983) ★★★, *Hope In Darkened Heart* (Warners 1986) ★★★, *All Shall Be Well* (Columbia 1992) ★★★, *Had I The Heavens* (Columbia 1996) ★★.

● COMPILATIONS: *Promise Nothing* (Les Disques Du Crepuscule 1983) ★★★.

● FURTHER READING: *The World Of Virginia Astley*, Robert Brown and Deke Rivers.

## ATLANTIC STARR

Soul/dance act comprising Sharon Bryant (vocals), David Lewis (vocals, keyboards, guitar), Jonathan Lewis (keyboards, trombone), Wayne Lewis (vocals, keyboards), Koran Daniels (saxophone), William Suddeeth III (trumpet), Clifford Archer (bass), Joseph Phillips (percussion) and Porter Carroll Jnr. (drums). The Lewis component of the group comprises three brothers who had previously led their own bands – Newban, Exact Change and Unchained Youth – on the east coast of America. Atlantic Starr was formed in 1976 when they moved to Los Angeles. Later in the 70s, they enlisted the services of New York-born Bryant as lead singer, and signed to A&M Records. Under the auspices of Philadelphia producer Bobby Eli (whose other work includes Major Harris, Brenda And The Tabulations, Booker Newbury III and Ronnie Dyson), they recorded their first two albums. 'Gimme Your Lovin'', from the first of these, became a hit in the UK charts, before they switched to the production tutelage of James Anthony Carmichael (Commodores, Lionel Richie) for a series of three albums. Bryant departed after *Yours Forever* to marry Rick Brenna from Change. She then worked as a session singer before re-emerging in 1989 with

the solo *Here I Am* and the single 'Foolish Heart'. Her replacement in Atlantic Starr was Barbara Weathers, although Daniels, Suddeeth, Archer and Carroll also parted company around the same time. The nucleus of the Lewis brothers and Weathers continued, taking to producing themselves, starting with *As The Band Turns*, which spawned hits in 'Silver Shadow', 'One Love', 'Secret Lovers' and 'If Your Heart Isn't In It' during 1985 and 1986 – their first singles chart success since 1978. In 1987, they signed to Warner Brothers Records, an association that produced a US number 1 (UK number 3) in the ballad 'Always'. Weathers left in 1989 for a solo career (aided by Wayne Lewis and Maurice White from Earth, Wind And Fire), to be replaced by Porscha Martin, who was in turn replaced by Rachel Oliver in 1991. Aisha Tanner became the band's next vocalist, replacing Oliver in 1994. By the end of the decade, the line-up featured Wayne and Jonathan Lewis (David had left following the release of 1994's *Time*), the returning Oliver and male singer DeWayne Woods.

● ALBUMS: *Atlantic Starr* (A&M 1978) ★★★★, *Straight To The Point* (A&M 1979) ★★★, *Radiant* (A&M 1981) ★★★, *Brilliance* (A&M 1982) ★★★, *Yours Forever* (A&M 1983) ★★★, *As The Band Turns* (A&M 1986) ★★★, *All In The Name Of Love* (Warners 1987) ★★★, *We're Movin' Up* (Warners 1988) ★★★, *Love Crazy* (Reprise 1991) ★★★, *Time* (Arista 1994) ★★, *Legacy* (Street Solid 1999) ★★★.

● COMPILATIONS: *Secret Lovers: The Best Of Atlantic Starr* (A&M 1986) ★★★, *Ultimate Collection* (Hip-O 2000) ★★★★, *The Best Of Atlantic Starr: The Millennium Collection* (A&M 2001) ★★★★, *All-Time Greatest Hits* (K-Tel 2002) ★★★.

## ATTILA THE STOCKBROKER

b. John Baine, 21 October 1957, England. After graduating from the University of Kent with a degree in French, this performance poet really was a stockbroker, or on the way to becoming one, before he set out on the live music circuit. Accompanied on occasion by his own mandolin backing, he regaled his audience with good-humoured invective on the state of the world. Viewed as one of the new 'Ranting Poets', a term he disliked, his influences were poets Roger McCoughlan and Brian Patton, alongside the *Monty Python* team and the energy of punk.

After playing in forgotten punk bands English Disease and Brighton Riot Squad, Baine joined Brussels-based new wave band Contingent. His usual early environment, indeed, was supporting punk bands. Baine earned his unusual moniker during an unhappy but mercifully brief spell as a translator at the Stock Exchange. He made his first appearance as Attila The Stockbroker in September 1980, and played frequently enough to earn himself a session for BBC disc jockey John Peel, which in turn led to a contract with Cherry Red Records. The *Cocktails* EP, from October 1982, boasted some of his finest pieces, from the serious ('Contributory Negligence') to the absurd ('The Night I Slept With Seething Wells'), a reference to fellow 'ranting poet' and *New Musical Express* journalist Steven Wells.

The following year Attila released his full-length debut, *Ranting At The Nation*, a highly colourful selection of verse and spoken word, highlighting the absurdity of UK life. Nightmare visions of Soviets running the social security system and his affection for obscure European soccer clubs were among the targets: 'So go to your Job Centre – I'll bet you'll see, Albanian students get handouts for free, and drug-crazed punk rockers cavort and caress, in the interview booths of the D.H.S.S.' Critics were not convinced, however, one citing the contents as 'an inarticulate mish-mash of bad humour and popular clichés'.

*Sawdust And Empire* was released in 1984, and saw a greater emphasis on music. Increasingly Attila was seeing himself as a folk artist, and in between releases was becoming a near-permanent fixture at various festivals, working alongside John Otway and TV Smith. He was involved in the staging of *Cheryl – A Rock Opera*, alongside Otway and Blyth Power, for whom he occasionally plucks a fiddle, and has contributed to the pages of the *Guardian* with his essays on social change in eastern Europe while on tour in the region. In 1994, he emerged with a new venture, Barnstormer, which featured several members of the Fish Brothers. The band has released several albums that conceptualize Baine's long-standing interest in medieval/early music. The new millennium saw Baine marrying his long-time partner and becoming poet in residence at Brighton And Hove Albion Football Club.

● ALBUMS: *Ranting At The Nation* (Cherry Red 1983) ★★★, *Sawdust And Empire* (Cherry Red 1984) ★★★, *Libyan Students From Hell* (Cherry Red 1987) ★★★, *Scornflakes* (Probe 1988) ★★★, *Live At The Rivioli* (Festival 1990) ★★, *Donkey's Years* (Musidisc 1991) ★★★, with John Otway *Cheryl – A Rock Opera* (Strikeback 1991) ★★★, *This Is Free Europe* (Terz 1992) ★★, *668 – Neighbour Of The Beast* (Larrikin 1993) ★★★, *Live Auf St. Pauli* (Teerz 1993) ★★★.
● COMPILATIONS: *Attila The Stockbroker's Greatest Hits!* cassette only (Roundhead 1993) ★★★, *Poems Ancient & Modern: A Live Anthology 1981–1999* (Helmet 1999) ★★★, *The Pen & The Sword: Selected Songs 1981–1999* (Helmet 1999) ★★★.
● FURTHER READING: *Cautionary Tales For Dead Commuters*, Attila The Stockbroker. *Scornflakes*, Attila The Stockbroker. *The Rat-tailed Maggot And Other Poems*, Attila The Stockbroker.

## ATTRACTIONS
Formed in May 1977 to back Elvis Costello, the Attractions provided sympathetic support to the singer's contrasting, and often demanding, compositions. Steve Nieve (b. Steven Nason; keyboards), Bruce Thomas (b. Stockton-on-Tees, Cleveland, England; bass) and Pete Thomas (b. 9 August 1954, Sheffield, Yorkshire, England; drums) were already experienced musicians – Bruce Thomas with the Sutherland Brothers and Quiver, Pete Thomas with Chilli Willi And The Red Hot Peppers and John Stewart – while Nieve's dexterity on keyboards added colour to many of the unit's exemplary releases. In 1980, the Attractions completed a low-key album, *Mad About The Wrong*

*Boy*, but their position as Costello's natural backing group became increasingly unsure as their leader embarked on a plethora of guises. Nieve recorded a couple of solo collections and later led the house band, along with Pete Thomas as Steve Nieve And The Playboys, on UK television's *Jonathan Ross Show*, while Bruce Thomas began a literary career with *The Big Wheel* (1990), an impressionistic autobiography. The Attractions were reunited with Costello on the singer's 1994 release, *Brutal Youth*, and Pete Thomas and Nieve have continued to work with the singer into the new millennium.
● ALBUMS: *Mad About The Wrong Boy* (F-Beat 1980) ★★.

## AU PAIRS
Arguably the Midlands region's key contribution to the early 80s post-punk scene, Birmingham, England-based band the Au Pairs comprised Lesley Woods (lead vocals, guitar), Paul Foad (lead guitar), Jane Munro (bass) and Pete Hammond (drums). They began their career in 1980 with the *You* EP on their own Human label, which also housed their long-playing debut. Critically acclaimed for their social insight and thoughtful, agit-prop music, they continued with singles such as 'It's Obvious' and 'Inconvenience', which brought them closest to a hit. Covering a variety of subjects from the controversial ('Armagh') to the frankly personal ('Sex Without Stress'), they signed to Kamera Records and released a live album on a.k.a. Records in 1983, before vanishing when Woods failed to appear for a concert in Belgium. The latter artefact, recorded at the Berlin Women's Festival, is probably the best introduction to the band – omitting, as it does, some of the duff tracks that marred their previous studio efforts. Woods later blamed the split on 'lack of money, nervous breakdowns and drugs . . . the usual rock 'n' roll story'. She settled in Europe for a few years before returning to London to undertake a law degree and form all-female band the Darlings. Foad formed End Of Chat with Hammond and trumpeter Graham Hamilton (who deputized for Woods on that aborted Belgium date). Munro, who left six months before the band's eventual dissolution, spent the early 90s training as an aromatherapist.
● ALBUMS: *Playing With A Different Sex* (Human 1981) ★★★, *Sense & Sensuality* (Kamera 1982) ★★, *Live In Berlin* (a.k.a. 1983) ★★★.
● COMPILATIONS: *Equal But Different: BBC Sessions* (RPM 1994) ★★★, *Shocks To The System: The Very Best Of The Au-Pairs* (Cherry Red 1996) ★★★.

## AUSTIN, PATTI
b. 10 August 1948, New York City, New York, USA. Austin first sang on stage at the age of three at the famous Apollo Theatre in New York City during Dinah Washington's set. As a child performer, she appeared on television, including Sammy Davis Jnr.'s programme, and in the theatre. Her stage work included *Lost In The Stars* and *Finian's Rainbow*. At the age of nine, she travelled to Europe with the bandleader/arranger Quincy Jones. As a 16-year-old, she toured with Harry Belafonte and began

recording at the age of 17. Austin's first recordings were for Coral Records in 1965. 'Family Tree', recorded in 1969 for United Artists Records, was an R&B hit.

Austin's immaculate vocals brought her work on television jingles and during the 70s she was one of the busiest session singers in New York, with credits for Paul Simon, Billy Joel, Frankie Valli, Joe Cocker, George Benson and Roberta Flack. Her solo albums included material she had written herself, and revealed some jazz influences. Further session work during 1980 saw Austin working with Marshall Tucker, Steely Dan and the Blues Brothers. Her longstanding association with father figure Quincy Jones continued; his composition 'The Dude' featured her lead vocal, and won a Grammy in 1982. Austin had another hit with the title track of *Every Home Should Have One* on Jones' Qwest label. Although it only just made the US Top 100, 'Razzamatazz' (with Jones) was a UK number 11 hit in June 1981. Her duet with James Ingram, 'Baby Come To Me', became the theme music for the television soap opera *General Hospital* and was a US number 1 and a UK number 11 in 1983. Another Austin/Ingram duet, 'How Do You Keep The Music Playing?', from the movie *Best Friends*, was nominated for an Oscar. She also sang the theme tunes for *Two Of A Kind* (1984) and *Shirley Valentine* (1988), and had an R&B hit with 'Gimme, Gimme, Gimme' (a duet with Narada Michael Walden). *The Real Me* was a collection of standards ranging from Duke Ellington's 'Mood Indigo' to 'How Long' by the UK band Ace. Her 1990 set *Love's Gonna Getcha* was produced by Dave Grusin for GRP Records, while Austin was a guest vocalist on an album of George Gershwin songs released in 1992 by the Hollywood Bowl Orchestra. After two further studio albums for GRP in the early 90s, Austin subsequently recorded well-received sets for Concord Vista and Intersound. Already commercially successful, this smooth-toned vocalist has yet to receive the critical acclaim her achievements merit.

● ALBUMS: *End Of A Rainbow* (CTI 1976) ★★★, *Havana Candy* (CTI 1977) ★★★, *Live At The Bottom Line* (CTI 1979) ★★★, *Body Language* (CTI 1980) ★★★, *Every Home Should Have One* (Qwest 1981) ★★★★, *Patti Austin* (Qwest 1984) ★★★, *Gettin' Away With Murder* (Qwest 1985) ★★, *The Real Me* (Qwest 1988) ★★★, *Love's Gonna Getcha* (GRP 1990) ★★, *Carry On* (GRP 1991) ★★★, *Live* (GRP 1992) ★★★, *That Secret Place* (GRP 1994) ★★★, *In & Out Of Love* (Concord Vista 1998) ★★★, *Street Of Dreams* (Intersound 1999) ★★★, *On The Way To Love* (Intersound 2001) ★★★, *For Ella* (Playboy Jazz 2002) ★★★.

● COMPILATIONS: *The Best Of Patti Austin* (Columbia 1994) ★★★, *The Ultimate Collection* (GRP 1995) ★★★★, *Take Away The Pain Stain* (Body & Soul 1999) ★★★, *The CTI Collection* (Connoisseur 2000) ★★★★, *The Very Best Of Patti Austin* (Rhino 2001) ★★★★.

● FILMS: *It's Your Thing* (1970), *The Wiz* voice only (1978), *One Trick Pony* (1980), *Tucker: The Man And His Dream* (1988).

## AZTEC CAMERA

This acclaimed UK pop outfit was formed in 1980 by Roddy Frame (b. 29 January 1964, East Kilbride, Scotland) as a vehicle for his songwriting talents. The other members, Campbell Owens (bass) and Dave Mulholland (drums), soon passed through, and a regular turnover in band members ensued while Frame put together the songs that made up 1983's exceptionally strong debut *High Land, Hard Rain*. Two hits ('Just Like Gold' and 'Mattress Of Wire') in the UK independent charts on the influential Postcard Records label had already made the band a critics' favourite before they moved to London and signed to Rough Trade Records. The debut, recorded with Owens and drummer Dave Ruffy, was a sparkling and memorable album of light acoustic songs with a mature influence of jazz and Latin rhythms. 'Oblivious' reached number 18 in the UK singles chart the same year, while excellent songs such as the uplifting 'Walk Out To Winter' and the expertly crafted 'We Could Send Letters' indicated a major talent in the ascendant.

The Mark Knopfler-produced *Knife* broke no new ground but, now signed to the massive WEA Records, the band was pushed into a world tour to promote the album. Frame was happier writing songs on his acoustic guitar back home in Scotland and retreated there following the tour, until *Love* was released in 1987. This introverted yet over-produced album showed Frame's continuing development, with Elvis Costello-influenced song structures. The comparative failure of this collection was rectified the following year with two further UK hit singles, 'How Men Are' (number 25) and the catchy 'Somewhere In My Heart' (number 3). This stimulated interest in *Love* and the album became a substantial success, climbing to number 10 on the UK album chart. After a further fallow period, allowing Frame to create more gems, the band returned in 1990 with the highly acclaimed *Stray*, leaving no doubt that their brand of intelligent, gentle pop had a considerable following. 'Good Morning Britain', a bitter duet with Mick Jones, reached UK number 19 when released as a single. Frame then delivered the albums that fans and critics had waited for. *Dreamland*, recorded with composer Ryûichi Sakamoto, and *Frestonia* proved to be strong collections of emotionally direct, honest songs that rivalled Aztec Camera's sparkling debut from a decade earlier. The band disintegrated in 1996 as Frame worked on a solo project, *The North Star*, which was eventually released in late 1998 on Andy McDonald's Independiente Records label.

● ALBUMS: *High Land, Hard Rain* (Rough Trade/Sire 1983) ★★★★, *Knife* (WEA/Sire 1984) ★★★, *Love* (WEA/Sire 1987) ★★★, *Stray* (WEA/Sire 1990) ★★★, *Dreamland* (WEA 1993) ★★★, *Frestonia* (WEA/Sire 1995) ★★★★.

● COMPILATIONS: *The Best Of Aztec Camera* (WEA 1999) ★★★★.

● VIDEOS: *Aztec Camera* (WEA Music Video 1989).

## AZYMUTH

Azymuth were formed in Brazil in 1971 by José Roberto Bertrami (b. 21 February 1946, Tatui, Brazil;

piano, keyboards), Alex Malheiros (b. 19 August 1946, Niteroi, Brazil; bass) and Ivan Conti (b. 16 August 1946, Rio de Janeiro, Brazil; drums – sometimes joined in his percussion duties by Aleuda). Adopting the popular jazz-funk style, they enjoyed a worldwide hit in 1980 with 'Jazz Carnival', from their *Light As A Feather* set. As such, they were largely responsible for an upsurge of interest in Brazilian music, with a host of big-name American jazz acts journeying to South America to record. While commercial success for Azymuth was difficult to maintain, their subsequent releases were always of interest to the jazz-funk crowd. Both Bertrami (*Blue Wave*, 1983, and *Dreams Are Real*, 1986) and Malheiros (*Atlantic Forest*, 1985) also recorded solo outings for the Milestone label. Bertrami left Azymuth in the late 80s, and was replaced by keyboardist Jota Moraes. The latter featured on *Tudo Bem* and *Curumim* before making way for the returning Bertrami.

● ALBUMS: *Light As A Feather* (Black Sun 1979) ★★★★, *Outubro* (Milestone 1980) ★★★, *Telecommunication* (Milestone 1982) ★★, *Cascades* (Milestone 1982) ★★, *Rapid Transit* (Milestone 1983) ★★★, *Flame* (Milestone 1984) ★★★★, *Spectrum* (Milestone 1985) ★★, *Tightrope Walker* (Milestone 1986) ★★, *Crazy Rhythm* (Milestone 1987) ★★★★, *Carioca* (Milestone 1988) ★★★, *Tudo Ben* (Intima 1989) ★★★, *Carumim* (Intima 1990) ★★, *Carnival* (Far Out 1997) ★★★, *Woodland Warrior* (Far Out 1998) ★★★, *Live At The Copacabana Palace* (Iris 1999) ★★, *Pieces Of Ipanema* (Far Out 1999) ★★★, *Before We Forget* (Far Out 2000) ★★★.

● COMPILATIONS: *Early Years* (Crusader 1988) ★★★, *Jazz Carnival: Best Of Azymuth* (BGP 1988) ★★★★.

## B-52's

The quirky appearance, stage antics and lyrical content of the B-52's belie a formidable musical ability, as the band's rhythmically perfect pop songs show many influences, including 50s rock 'n' roll, punk and commercial dance music. However, it was the late 70s' new-wave music fans that took them to their hearts. The B-52's were formed in Athens, Georgia, USA, in 1976, and took their name from the bouffant hairstyles worn by Kate Pierson (b. 27 April 1948, Weehawken, New Jersey, USA; organ, vocals) and Cindy Wilson (b. 28 February 1957, Athens, Georgia, USA; guitar, vocals). The line-up was completed by Cindy's brother Ricky (b. 19 March 1953, Athens, Georgia, USA, d. 12 October 1985; guitar), Fred Schneider (b. 1 July 1951, Newark, Georgia, USA; keyboards, vocals) and Keith Strickland (b. 26 October 1953, Athens, Georgia, USA; drums). The lyrically bizarre but musically thunderous 'Rock Lobster' was originally a private pressing of 2,000 copies and came to the notice of the perceptive Chris Blackwell, who signed them to Island Records in the UK. Their debut, *B-52's*, became a strong seller and established the band as a highly regarded unit with a particularly strong following on the American campus circuit during the early 80s.

Their anthem, 'Rock Lobster', became a belated US hit in 1980 and they received John Lennon's seal of approval that year as his favourite band. Subsequent albums continued to defy categorization, their love of melodrama and pop culture running side by side with outright experimentalism (witness 50s sci-fi parody 'Planet Claire'). Ricky Wilson died of AIDS in 1985 (although it was initially claimed that cancer was the cause, to save his family from intrusion). Nevertheless, the band reached a commercial peak in 1989, winning a new generation of fans with the powerful hit single 'Love Shack', and its enticing accompanying video. *Cosmic Thing* showed that the band had not lost their touch and blended several musical styles with aplomb. In 1992 they parted company with Cindy Wilson and recorded *Good Stuff* under the eyes of previous producer Don Was and Nile Rodgers (Chic). During a Democratic party fund-raising concert in April 1992, actress Kim Basinger stood in for Wilson, as did Julee Cruise the following year. The B-52's achieved huge commercial success in 1994 with the theme song to *The Flintstones*, yet despite the 'cheese' factor, it remained hard not to warm to the full-blooded performances from Schneider and Pierson. Schneider recorded a solo album in 1996, while Wilson rejoined in 1998 as the band embarked on a tour to support that year's hits collection.

● ALBUMS: *B-52's* (Warners 1979) ★★★★, *Wild*

*Planet* (Warners 1980) ★★★, *Party Mix!* remix album (Warners 1981) ★★★, *Mesopotamia* mini-album (Warners 1982) ★★, *Whammy!* (Warners 1983) ★★, *Bouncing Off The Satellites* (Warners 1986) ★★, *Cosmic Thing* (Reprise 1989) ★★★, *Good Stuff* (Warners 1992) ★★★.

Solo: Fred Schneider *Fred Schneider And The Shake Society* (Warners 1984) ★★★, *Just Fred* (Reprise 1996) ★★★.

● COMPILATIONS: *Best Of The B-52's: Dance This Mess Around* (Island 1990) ★★★★, *Party Mix-Mesopotamia* (Warners 1991) ★★★, *Planet Claire* (Spectrum 1995) ★★★, *Time Capsule: Songs For A Future Generation* (Warners 1998) ★★★★, *Nude On The Moon: The B-52's Anthology* (Rhino 2002) ★★★★.

● VIDEOS: *Time Capsule: Videos For A Future Generation 1979–1998* (Warner Music Vision 1998).

## B-MOVIE

This post-punk keyboard and guitar combo originated from Mansfield, England. They were often falsely linked with the early 80s fad of New Romanticism. Graham Boffey (drums) and Paul Statham (guitar) were one-time members of punk band the Aborted, formed, like so many others, in the wake of the first Clash album. The duo invited Steve Hovington (vocals, bass) along to rehearsals, changing their name to Studio 10 before settling on B-Movie. Studio manager Andy Dransfield sent a demo tape of the band to Lincoln-based independent record label Dead Good. The result was two tracks on the compilation *East*. Soon afterwards, Rick Holliday joined as keyboard player. Their *Take Three* EP was warmly received by critics, ensuring several local radio sessions and a six-track 12-inch single, headed by 'Nowhere Girl'. Eccentric entrepreneur Stevo noticed the band and became their manager. Moving to Deram Records, 'Remembrance Day' became the second single to attract strong support in the press. Unfortunately, Stevo's connection saw the band categorized as part of the New Romantic movement, a perception that would act as a major constraint in their future. After 'Marilyn Dreams' only scraped the charts, the band set out on a major European tour, during which they acquired the services of Luciano Codemo on bass, allowing Hovington to concentrate on his vocals. In turn, he was replaced by Mike Pedan (ex-Everest The Hard Way), and soon Boffey also departed, joining Soft As Ghosts. Martin Smedley and Andy Johnson were the new recruits, but they arrived just in time to see the departure of a frustrated Holliday. He joined Six Sed Red then MCX while the reduced B-Movie line-up signed with Sire Records. A highly commercial but disappointing single, 'A Letter From Afar', was remixed by Jellybean. An album eventually followed, but by this time the band had effectively fallen apart (Al Cash and Martin Winter were among the latter-day cast). Statham went on to work with Pete Murphy and Then Jerico, Pedan formed the Chimes; Hovington formed One before returning to work with Holliday; and Boffey is currently a member of Slaughterhouse 5.

● ALBUMS: *Forever Running* (Sire 1985) ★★★, *The Dead Good Tapes* (Wax 1988) ★★★, *Remembrance*

*Days* (Dead Good 1991) ★★★, *Radio Days* (1991) ★★★.

## B., DEREK

b. Derek Bowland, 1966, Bow, East London, England. Derek grew up a fan of the Who as well as the more conventional black sounds of Aretha Franklin, Al Green and Bob Marley. He started out as a DJ when he was 15 as part of a mobile unit touring London clubs. He then moved into radio, working for pirate stations such as Kiss FM and LWR before beginning his own WBLS station. In 1987 he became bored with the disc jockey role and took a job at the Music Of Life label as an A&R man. Alongside Simon Harris (world yo-yo champion, it has been alleged) he signed several of the most notable early UK hip-hop groups, including Overlord X, MC Duke, Hijack, the She Rockers and Demon Boyz. He subsequently started to record his own material for the label. While in New York (visiting his family who had moved there), Derek met the DJ Mr Magic, who played his record to Profile Records, granting him a licensing contract in the USA. His debut single, 'Rock The Beat', and its follow-up, 'Get Down' (which featured the rapping of EZQ – Derek B under another pseudonym), both made an early impact. His hip-hop sounded a little ham-fisted in comparison to New York's more natural feel, which made the self-congratulatory raps sound increasingly hysterical: 'We kept on goin' for hours and hours/Straight after to the bathroom for a shower/Just before leaving she held me close and said/I think you're the greatest thing in bed' ('Get Down'). He hit the UK charts in 1988 with 'Goodgroove' and was the only rapper on the Free Mandela bill at Wembley Stadium. Further minor hits came with 'Bad Young Brother' and 'We've Got The Juice', after he set up his own Tuff Audio label through Phonogram. However, that relationship declined when he attempted to push for a harder sound. Further one-off contracts with a variety of labels failed to offer anything of significance, though while at SBK he did ghost-write tracks for Vanilla Ice. He then became a member of PoW.

● ALBUMS: *Bullet From A Gun* (Tuff Audio 1988) ★★★.

## B.A.L.L.

Formed in New York, USA, in 1987, B.A.L.L. comprised Mark Kramer (bass, vocals, production) and David Licht (drums) – both formerly of Shockabilly – and two ex-members of the Velvet Monkeys: Don Fleming (guitar, vocals) and Jay Spiegel (drums). The quartet's debut, *Period (Another American Lie)*, established their sound, wherein grunge-styled pop songs were driven by loud, distorted guitar work and the two drummers' solid, uncompromising beat. Humour was an equally integral part of the group's *raison d'être*, a facet that came to fruition on *Bird*. Its sleeve parodied the infamous Beatles 'butcher cover' and the second side was devoted to a pastiche of The Concert For Bangla Desh. Several sacred cows of rock were mercilessly savaged in a suite that married Ringo Starr's 'It Don't Come Easy', George Harrison's 'Wah Wah' and Marc

Bolan's 'Buick Mackane'. However, the concept was arguably stronger than the aural results and the group's own material lacked sparkle. Billed on the reverse as 'the disappointing third album', *Trouble Doll* was indeed inferior, consisting of one studio side and another recorded live at CBGB's, some of which was reprised from *Bird*. *Four (Hardball)* captures the quartet at their best, despite the fact that they fell apart during its recording. The first side is devoted to powerful pop songs, its counterpart comprised of ravaged instrumentals. Fleming left the group before completing vocals. The friction was latterly resolved – a similarly charged album, *Special Kiss*, appeared in 1991 under a new name, Gumball – but the four achieved a greater profile elsewhere. Spiegel and Fleming re-formed the Velvet Monkeys; the latter became a producer of note (Teenage Fanclub, Free Kitten), while Kramer continued to administer his Shimmy-Disc label (which issued B.A.L.L.'s albums) and to record with Bongwater and as a solo artist.

● ALBUMS: *Period (Another American Lie)* (Shimmy-Disc 1987) ★★★, *Bird* (Shimmy-Disc 1988) ★★, *Trouble Doll* (Shimmy-Disc 1989) ★★, *Four (Hardball)* (Shimmy-Disc 1990) ★★★.

## BAD BOY

The origins of this Milwaukee, USA rock band date back to the mid-70s, when Steve Grimm (guitar, vocals) teamed up with John Marcelli (bass). The first incarnation of Bad Boy had included Lars Hanson (drums) and Joe Luchessie (guitar, keyboards, vocals). The band chemistry was wrong, however, and their debut album was a disappointing, half-hearted affair. Their second release was a marked improvement, as the band moved in a heavier direction and made greater use of an up-front guitar sound, including Earl Slick (ex-David Bowie). Following a period of inactivity between 1978 and 1982, the band returned with a revamped line-up that saw Xeno (keyboards) and Billy Johnson (drums) alongside Grimm and Marcelli. Unfortunately, they reverted to a melodic pop-rock style. Both albums sold poorly and the band split as a result.

● ALBUMS: *The Band That Made Milwaukee Famous* (United Artists 1977) ★★, *Back To Back* (United Artists 1978) ★★★, *Private Party* (Indie 1982) ★★, *Electric Eyes* (Indie 1984) ★★.

## BAD BRAINS

This black American hardcore punk and dub reggae outfit originated in 1978, when the band were all playing together in an early fusion outfit. They moved from Washington, DC, to New York where they established a reputation as prime exponents, alongside the Dead Kennedys and Black Flag, of the new 'hardcore' hybrid of punk, based on a barely credible speed of musicianship. The line-up consisted of HR (b. Paul Hudson; vocals) and brother Earl Hudson (drums), Dr. Know (guitar) and Darryl Aaron Jenifer (bass). They broke up their sets with dub and reggae outings and attracted a mixed audience, which was certainly one of their objectives: 'We're a gospel group, preaching the word of unity.' It is frustrating that so little studio material

remains to document this early period, though the singles 'Pay To Cum' and 'Big Takeover' are regarded as punk classics, and later bands such as Living Colour sung their praises as one of the forerunners of articulate black rock music. Bad Brains were due to support the Damned in the UK in October 1979, having sold most of their equipment to buy aeroplane tickets. On arrival, however, they were denied work permits. They continued through the 80s, releasing only two full-length albums (*Rock For Light* and *I Against I*), although tension over the band's direction meant that HR left to pursue a solo career devoted to reggae music.

In May 1988 he was temporarily replaced by ex-Faith No More vocalist Chuck Mosley, while Mackie Jayson (ex-Cro-Mags) took over on drums. The move, which allowed the remaining founding members to gig, was singularly unsuccessful. A major label contract with Epic Records was a commercial disaster, but in 1994 Madonna offered them a place on her Maverick label, with HR returning to the fold. *God Of Love*, produced by ex-leader of the Cars, Ric Ocasek, concentrated more on dub and rasta messages than hardcore, but proved again there was still fire in the belly. In 1995 HR left the band after assaulting various Bad Brains members before a show on their promotional tour to support *God Of Love*. He was subsequently arrested at the Canadian border and charged with a drugs offence. The band was then dropped by Maverick, but have continued touring and recording under the new moniker Soul Brains.

● ALBUMS: *Bad Brains* cassette only (ROIR 1982) ★★, *Rock For Light* (PVC 1983) ★★★★, *I Against I* (SST 1986) ★★★★, *Live* (SST 1988) ★★, *Attitude: The ROIR Sessions* (In-Effect 1989) ★★★, *Quickness* (Caroline 1989) ★★★, *The Youth Are Getting Restless* (Caroline 1990) ★★★, *Rise* (Epic 1993) ★★★, *God Of Love* (Maverick 1995) ★★★, *Black Dots* (Caroline 1996) ★★★, *Omega Sessions* 1980 recordings (Victory 1997) ★★★.

## BAD ENGLISH

Towards the end of the 80s, a new generation of 'supergroups' emerged from the USA, including Mr. Big, Badlands, Damn Yankees, Alias and, arguably the most successful of them all, Bad English. The group was formed in 1988 by ex-Babys vocalist and successful solo artist John Waite (b. 4 July 1952, Lancaster, Lancashire, England), ex-Santana and Journey guitarist Neal Schon (b. 27 February 1954, San Mateo, California, USA), ex-Babys and Journey keyboard player Jonathan Cain (b. 26 February 1950, Chicago, Illinois, USA), ex-Babys bass player Ricky Phillips and ex-Wild Dogs drummer Deen Castronovo. Their 1989 self-titled debut album was an instant success in the USA, combining hard-edged, melodic rock with big ballads. It reached the US Top 10, helped on its way by the Dianne Warren-penned 'When I See You Smile', which was a US number 1 hit in 1990 (UK number 61). Success in the UK was not forthcoming and the album barely dented the Top 40, while a similar fate befell the single. The follow-up, *Backlash*, was promoted by the single 'Straight To Your Heart'. Internal disagreements plagued the band, causing them to split soon after its release, with Waite resuming his solo career; Phillips and Castronovo joined the Jimmy Page and David Coverdale project, while Schon and Cain re-formed Journey. Castronovo and Schon also formed Hardline. Despite their short history, Bad English left behind a legacy of high-quality melodic rock that achieved a considerable degree of commercial success.

● ALBUMS: *Bad English* (Epic 1989) ★★★, *Backlash* (Epic 1991) ★★★.

● VIDEOS: *Bad English* (CMV Enterprises 1990).

## BAD MANNERS

A formidable chart presence when the UK 2-Tone ska revival was at its peak, this north London-based outfit originally came together in 1976 as Stoop Solo And The Sheet Starchers. The unit came to be known as Buster Bloodvessel And His Bad Manners, and then simply Bad Manners, and comprised Buster Bloodvessel (b. Douglas Trendle, 6 September 1958; lead vocals), Gus 'Hot Lips' Herman (trumpet), Chris Kane (saxophone), Andrew 'Marcus Absent' Marson (saxophone), Winston Bazoomies (harmonica), Brian 'Chew-it' Tuitti (drums), David Farren (bass), Martin Stewart (keyboards) and Louis 'Alphonzo' Cook (guitar). Fronted by the exuberant Bloodvessel, whose shaven head, rotund build, protruding tongue and often outrageous costume provided a strong comic appeal, the band enjoyed a brief run of UK hits in the early 80s. Released on the Magnet label, their string of UK hits commenced with the catchy 'Ne-Ne Na-Na Na-Na Nu-Nu' followed by 11 UK chart entries, including four Top 10 hits, 'Special Brew', 'Can Can', 'Walking In The Sunshine' and a remake of Millie's hit retitled 'My Girl Lollipop'. Although this musically tight unit is still very popular on the live circuit, the band's mass novelty appeal had worn thin by the middle of 1983 when the hits ceased. In the late 80s Bloodvessel formed Buster's All-Stars to motivate the other members of Bad Manners into doing something. In recent years he has toured occasionally with the band, as well as trying his hand as an hotelier at the appropriately named Fatty Towers in Margate, Kent.

● ALBUMS: *Ska 'N' B* (Magnet 1980) ★★★, *Loonee Tunes* (Magnet 1981) ★★★, *Gosh It's ... Bad Manners* (Magnet 1981) ★★★★, *Forging Ahead* (Magnet 1982) ★★★, *Mental Notes* (Portrait 1985) ★★, *Live And Loud!!* (Link 1987) ★★★, *Eat The Beat* (Blue Beat/Squale 1988) ★★★, *Return Of The Ugly* (Blue Beat 1989) ★★, *Fat Sound* (Pork Pie 1992) ★★, *Don't Knock The Bald Head* (Receiver 1997) ★★.

● COMPILATIONS: *The Height Of Bad Manners* (Telstar 1983) ★★★, *The Collection* (Cleopatra 1998) ★★★★, *Rare & Fatty: Unreleased Recordings 1976-1997* (Moon Ska 1999) ★★, *Magnetism: The Very Best Of Bad Manners* (Magnet 2000) ★★★★.

● VIDEOS: *Bad Manners* (Videoform).

● FURTHER READING: *Bad Manners*, George Marshall.

## BAD NEWS

Originally written by Adrian Edmondson as part of UK television's *The Comic Strip Presents* series in 1982, *Bad News Tour* told the story of an ambitious (but inept) London heavy metal band, on tour and *en route* to Grantham with a television documentary crew. The members were played by Edmondson, as vocalist/guitarist Vim Fuego, Rik Mayall as bass player Colin Grigson, Nigel Planer as dim rhythm guitarist Den Dennis and Comic Strip co-writer/founder-member Peter Richardson as drummer Spider Webb. The music and lyrics for the show were put together by Edmondson and composer Simon Brint as a clever parody on the clichés of the UK heavy metal scene. After the success of Rob Reiner's film, *This Is Spinal Tap*, and its subsequent move into legend, Edmondson decided to revive Bad News for another Comic Strip episode, writing a basic storyline that required the band to play a genuine live gig. In 1986, armed with a recording contract with EMI Records, a producer in Queen's Brian May, clever management and photo sessions by Gerard Mankowitz, they set about recording an album of songs and sketches. The full promotional machinery of interviews, television appearances and a slot at the Donington Festival in August, all used in the film, was set in motion. Four months later, they organized a short tour that included several charity concerts with Iron Maiden. In 1987 *More Bad News* was shown in cinemas as support to another Comic Strip film, *Eat The Rich*, which, incidentally, starred Lemmy from Motörhead. This publicity was boosted by a cover version of Queen's 'Bohemian Rhapsody' on single, and a self-titled debut album. The music was badly received, but, in retrospect, revealed itself to be both well constructed and executed. Following the album, they embarked on a two-month tour and released a second single, 'Cashing In On Xmas'. However, by this time the joke had worn too thin for both press and public, and the actors returned to their day jobs. Their name briefly reappeared the following year, when EMI Records released a bootleg album that contained Edmondson-produced out-takes of music and comedy, and a Brian May remix of the 'Christmas' single.

● ALBUMS: *Bad News* (EMI 1987) ★★, *Bootleg* (EMI 1988) ★★.

● COMPILATIONS: *Collection* (Castle 1994) ★★.

● VIDEOS: *Bad News Tour And A Fistful Of Traveller's Cheques* (Virgin Vision 1986), *More Bad News* (Virgin Vision 1987), *Bohemian Rhapsody* (PMI 1987).

## BAD RELIGION

This US hardcore band was formed in 1980 in the suburbs of north Los Angeles, California. Their first incarnation comprised Greg Graffin (vocals), Brett Gurewitz (guitar), Jay Lishrout (drums) and Jay Bentley (bass), with the name originating from their mutual distaste for organized religion. Their debut release was the poorly produced EP *Bad Religion*, on Epitaph Records, formed by founder member Gurewitz. Following several appearances on local compilation albums, Pete Finestone took over as drummer in 1982. The milestone album *How Could Hell Be Any Worse?* was recorded in Hollywood, creating a fair degree of local and national interest. The subsequent *Into The Unknown* proved a minor disaster, disillusioning hardcore fans with the emphasis shifted to slick keyboard textures, though the record itself stands up well. In 1984 there were more changes and Graffin was soon the only surviving member from the previous year, with Greg Hetson and Tim Gallegos taking over guitar and bass, and Pete Finestone returning on drums, while Gurewitz took time out to conquer his drink and drug problems.

A comeback EP, *Back To The Known*, revealed a much more purposeful outfit. A long period of inactivity was ended in 1987 when Gurewitz rejoined for a show that Hetson (working with former band Circle Jerks once more) could not attend. New material was written, and *Suffer* was released in 1988 to wide critical acclaim. The band's subsequent releases featured intelligent lyrics set against their compelling punk sound. In 1993, they signed to Atlantic Records, making their major-label debut with the following year's *Stranger Than Fiction*. Despite this, Gurewitz retired in 1994 to spend more time looking after the Epitaph label, which was enjoying success with Offspring and others. *The Gray Race*, recorded by a line-up comprising Graffin, Hetson, Bentley, Brian Baker (guitar) and Bobby Schayer (drums), was an assured release that addressed famine, world disorder and politics. *Tested* collected powerful live performances from *The Gray Race* tour, but 1998's *No Substance* indicated a band struggling for new ideas. Former member Gurewitz made a guest appearance on the Todd Rundgren-produced follow-up, *The New America*, their final album for Atlantic. The band returned to Epitaph and welcomed back Gurewitz as a full-time member on 2002's *The Process Of Belief*.

● ALBUMS: *How Could Hell Be Any Worse?* (Epitaph 1982) ★★★★, *Into The Unknown* (Epitaph 1983) ★★★, *Suffer* (Epitaph 1988) ★★★★, *No Control* (Epitaph 1989) ★★★, *Against The Grain* (Epitaph 1990) ★★★, *Generator* (Epitaph 1992) ★★★, *Recipe For Hate* (Epitaph 1993) ★★★, *Stranger Than Fiction* (Atlantic 1994) ★★★, *The Gray Race* (Atlantic 1996) ★★★★, *Tested* (Epic 1997) ★★★, *No Substance* (Atlantic 1998) ★★, *The New America* (Atlantic 2000) ★★★, *The Process Of Belief* (Epitaph 2002) ★★★.

● COMPILATIONS: *80–85* (Epitaph 1991) ★★★, *All Ages* (Epitaph 1995) ★★★.

## BADOWSKI, HENRY

After serving his apprenticeship in UK bands Norman And The Baskervilles, Lick It Dry and the New Rockets, Badowski joined punk band Chelsea on bass, but in early 1978, after only a few months, he left to enlist as drummer for Stiff Records artist Wreckless Eric. During the summer of that year, he sang and played keyboards with the short-lived King, a punk/psychedelic group that included Dave Berk (drums; also Johnny Moped), Kym Bradshaw (bass) and Captain Sensible (guitar, ex-Damned). When King folded, Badowski took up the bass with the re-formed Damned offshoot, the Doomed. With the new year came the new position of drummer with the Good Missionaries, an experimental band created by Mark Perry from Alternative TV. This association led to the start of his solo career in the summer of 1979, with the release of 'Making Love

With My Wife' on Perry's Deptford Fun City label. Recorded at Pathway Studios, the track was performed completely by Badowski and displayed a strong 60s influence, with echoes of Syd Barrett and Kevin Ayers. The b-side, 'Baby Sign Here With Me', was originally part of the King live set and utilized the talents of James Stevenson (bass, guitar) from Chelsea, and Alex Kolkowski (violin) and Dave Berk (drums), both from the Johnny Moped Band. The single drew favourable reviews and within a month he had signed a contract with A&M Records, releasing a further two singles, 'My Face' and 'Henry's In Love', closely followed by the album *Life Is A Grand*, a classic slice of psychedelia that was to signal the end of Badowski's solo career.

● ALBUMS: *Life Is A Grand* (A&M 1981) ★★★.

## BAILEY, PHILIP

b. 8 May 1951, Denver, Colorado, USA. Bailey is a talented soul singer who originally joined Earth, Wind And Fire in 1972 as a co-vocalist and percussionist. By 1983 he had released his first solo effort, *Continuation*, produced by George Duke. However, more influential was Phil Collins' production of his second album. Collins provided percussion throughout, and also co-wrote the sparkling duet 'Easy Lover', which topped the UK charts in March 1985 and reached number 2 in the USA. Unfortunately, his only other UK hit to date has been the follow-up, 'Walking On The Chinese Wall', while his second album made number 11 in the USA. Bailey also released several pop-gospel albums during the 80s. He joined the re-formed Earth, Wind And Fire in the 90s, and has also released solo albums varying from pop to jazz.

● ALBUMS: *Continuation* (Columbia 1983) ★★, *The Chinese Wall* (Columbia 1984) ★★★, *The Wonders Of His Love* (Myrrh 1984) ★★★, *Inside Out* (Columbia 1986) ★★★★, *Triumph* (Myrrh 1986) ★★★, *Family Affair* (Myrrh 1989) ★★★, *Philip Bailey* (Zoo Entertainment 1995) ★★★, *Life & Love* (Eagle Rock 1998) ★★, *Dreams* (Heads Up 1998) ★★★, *Soul On Jazz* (Heads Up 2002) ★★★.

● COMPILATIONS: *The Best Of Philip Bailey: A Gospel Collection* (Word 1991) ★★★★.

## BAKER, ANITA

b. 26 January 1958, Toledo, Ohio, USA. The granddaughter of a minister, Baker had a religious upbringing that included church music and gospel singing. After vocal duties with local bands she joined the semi-professional Chapter 8 in 1979 and was the vocalist on their minor US chart hit, 'I Just Wanna Be Your Girl', the following year. Several years later she left the band and was working in an office when she persuaded the Beverly Glenn label to record and release her debut album in 1983. *The Songstress* brought her to wider notice and after disagreements with Beverly Glenn she chose to sign with Elektra Records. Her second album was partly funded by Baker herself, who also acted as executive producer, with former Chapter 8 colleague Michael Powell assisting with writing and production. *Rapture*, a wonderfully mature and emotional album, saw Baker hailed as 'a female Luther Vandross' and she began to win R&B awards with 'Sweet Love', 'Caught Up In The Rapture' and 'Giving You The Best That I Got'. In 1987 she appeared on the Winans' 'Ain't No Need To Worry' and in 1990 duetted with former Shalamar singer Howard Hewett. *Compositions* was self-penned bar two tracks and featured former Wonderlove musician Greg Phillinganes on keyboards, Steve Ferrone on drums, along with top Los Angeles session drummer Ricky Lawson, and Nathan East on bass. The album was recorded live in the studio with few overdubs. The birth of her first child delayed the release of her fourth Elektra album, the disappointing *Rhythm Of Love*. She subsequently signed a recording contract with Atlantic Records, and in 1998 made a guest appearance on jazz pianist Cyrus Chestnut's self-titled collection. Her own debut for the label has been much delayed.

● ALBUMS: *The Songstress* (Beverly Glenn 1983) ★★★, *Rapture* (Elektra 1986) ★★★★, *Giving You The Best That I've Got* (Elektra 1988) ★★★, *Compositions* (Elektra 1990) ★★★, *Rhythm Of Love* (Elektra 1994) ★★.

● COMPILATIONS: *Sweet Love: The Very Best Of Anita Baker* (Atlantic 2002) ★★★★.

● VIDEOS: *Sweet Love* (WEA Music Video 1989), *One Night Of Rapture* (WEA Music Video 1989).

### BAKER, ARTHUR

b. 22 April 1955, Boston, Massachusetts, USA. Arthur Baker began in music as a club DJ in Boston, Massachusetts, playing soul and R&B for the clubgoers. He moved into production for Emergency Records shortly thereafter, including work on Northend and Michelle Wallace's 'Happy Days' (his first record, only released in Canada, was Hearts Of Stone's 'Losing You'). This preceded a move to New York where he became intrigued by the rap scene of 1979. He entered the studios once more, this time in tandem with Joe Bataan, to record a pseudo rap record, 'Rap-O-Clap-O', but the projected record company, London, went under before its release. The proceeds of the session did emerge later, although Baker went uncredited, after he returned to Boston. His next project was 'Can You Guess What Groove This Is?' by Glory, a medley that hoped to find a novelty market. From there, back in New York, he joined Tom Silverman's Tommy Boy Records operation to record 'Jazzy Sensation' with Afrika Bambaataa and Shep Pettibone.

Afterwards, he partnered Bambaataa on his seminal 1982 'Planet Rock' single, before starting Streetwise Records. Though interwoven with the development of hip-hop, Baker's later releases were inspired by the club scene (Wally Jump Jnr.'s 'Tighten Up', Jack E Makossa's 'The Opera House' and Criminal Orchestra Element's 'Put The Needle On The Record'). He went on to become an internationally renowned producer, working with legends such as Bob Dylan and Bruce Springsteen, and performing important remixing work for artists including New Order. In 1989 he collaborated with the Force MD's, ABC and OMD, among others, on a showcase album that saw Baker working through various dance styles under his own auspices. A year was spent working on the biography of Quincy Jones' life before returning in 1991 with rapper and former MTV security guard Wendell Williams for club-orientated material such as 'Everybody', and a commercially unsuccessful follow-up to the *Merge* album.

● ALBUMS: with the Backbeat Disciples *Merge* (A&M 1989) ★★★, *Give In To The Rhythm* (Arista 1991) ★★★.

● COMPILATIONS: *Breakin'* (Perfecto 2001) ★★★★.

### BALAAM AND THE ANGEL

This UK rock band included both post-punk gothic and 60s elements in their output. The group originally consisted of the three Morris brothers, Jim (b. 25 November 1960, Motherwell, Scotland; guitar, occasional recorder, keyboards), Mark (b. 15 January 1963, Motherwell, Scotland; lead vocals, bass) and Des (b. 27 June 1964, Motherwell, Scotland; drums). They began their career playing working men's clubs as a children's cabaret act in their native Motherwell, encouraged by their father, who had insisted they all watch television's *Top Of The Pops* as children. They eventually moved to Cannock in Staffordshire. An early gig at the ICA in London in 1985 saw a completely different approach to that with which Balaam would later become identified. Playing in bare feet and pyjamas, they played numerous cover versions of 60s love paeans, and also included a recorder solo. Somewhat falsely categorized as a gothic group after supporting the Cult on three successive tours, they were, in fact, self-consciously colourful in both appearance and approach. Early in their career they founded Chapter 22 Records, along with manager Craig Jennings. Their debut on the label came when 'World Of Light' appeared in 1984, although 'Day And Night' was their most impressive release from this period. Their debut set, *The Greatest Story Ever Told*, was named after the headline under which their first interview in *Melody Maker* appeared, and saw them rehoused on Virgin Records. Apparently intended to be reminiscent of the Doors, although there were stylistic similarities, it fell some way short of the visionary qualities associated with the former band. In September 1988 Balaam's second album was released after they had returned from support slots with Kiss and Iggy Pop in the USA. A new guitarist, Ian McKean, was enlisted to perform additional guitar parts on *Live Free Or Die*. The band was dropped by Virgin, however, and their first tour for over four years took place in 1990. Press speculation that Mark would join the Cult as replacement bass player for Jamie Stewart collapsed when Ian Astbury decided he was too much of a 'frontman'. In 1991, they truncated their name to Balaam, marking the switch with the release of a mini-album, *No More Innocence*. By the advent of *Prime Time*, any residual press interest in their career had dried up completely.

● ALBUMS: *The Greatest Story Ever Told* (Virgin 1986) ★★★, *Live Free Or Die* (Virgin 1988) ★★, *No More Innocence* mini-album (Intense 1991) ★★, *Prime Time* (Bleeding Hearts 1993) ★★.

## BALL, DAVE

b. 3 May 1959, Blackpool, Lancashire, England. Ball came to notice as the keyboard player in the duo Soft Cell with Marc Almond. His early interest in electronics crystallized at Leeds Polytechnic where he joined a band that utilized three vacuum cleaners. This led to his composing music to accompany Almond's theatrical shows and the formation of Soft Cell in October 1979. Although contributing much to their sound, Ball maintained a low profile. In June 1983, he scored the music for a revival of Tennessee Williams' play *Suddenly Last Summer*. Later that year Ball released the solo instrumental *In Strict Tempo*, before the break-up of Soft Cell in December. The following year he wrote the score for the German film *Decoder* and produced the Virgin Prunes. The soundtrack to Derek Jarman's *Imagining Oktober* followed in 1985, and in 1987 he produced Jack The Tab. By the end of 1988 Ball had produced a single for train-robber Ronnie Biggs in Brazil and had started working with Jack The Tab's acid-house singer Richard Norris. This evolved into psychedelic dance outfit the Grid, which quickly found acceptance in ambient/new age/dance clubs by exploring the interface between Kraftwerk, Brian Eno and Pink Floyd. Other current activities include composing music for television commercials (Shell, TSB, etc.), film soundtracks, remix/production work for Art Of Noise, Bhundu Boys and Marc Almond, plus one-off collaborations with LSD guru Dr. Timothy Leary and Rolf Harris.

● ALBUMS: *In Strict Tempo* (Some Bizzare 1983) ★★★.

## BAMBI SLAM

An ambitious UK rock dance outfit, the Bambi Slam were formed in the mid-80s around would-be eccentric Roy Feldon (b. Lancashire, England). After a fairly inconsequential upbringing in the rosy suburbs of Pickering, Toronto, Canada, the expatriate Feldon moved to California for a spell. Coming to Britain to seek fame and fortune, he recruited Nick Maynard (drums) and Linda Mellor (cello) through an advert in the Royal Academy. Under the name Bambi Slam they toured the country, sending demos to dozens of record companies. The music contained on these cassettes resembled a rockier Public Image Limited. Product Inc., a subsidiary of Mute Records, picked up on them and released three singles, including 'Bamp Bamp' and the stirring 'Happy Birthday'. A tour supporting the Cult and a debut album were well under way and things were seemingly going to plan; however, Feldon suddenly underwent a period of artistic introspection, resulting in the band going way over budget. This led to a split with Product Inc. and an unfinished album on which they owed a considerable amount of money. However, Rough Trade Records supremo Geoff Travis thought they had promise and signed them to Blanco y Negro. There they released a flawed debut, after which Feldon jettisoned the rest of the band.

● ALBUMS: *The Bambi Slam* (Blanco y Negro 1987) ★★★.

## BANANARAMA

Formed in London in 1980, this all-female pop trio comprised Keren Woodward (b. 2 April 1961, Bristol, Avon, England), Sarah Dallin (b. 17 December 1961, Bristol, Avon, England) and Siobhan Fahey (b. Siobhan Marie Deidre Fahey, 10 September 1958, Dublin, Eire). After singing impromptu at various parties and pubs in London, the group were recorded by former Sex Pistols drummer Paul Cook on the Swahili Black Blood cover version, 'Ai A Mwana'. The single caught the attention of Fun Boy Three vocalist Terry Hall, who invited the girls to back his trio on their revival of 'It Ain't What You Do, It's The Way That You Do It'. In return, the Fun Boy Three backed Bananarama on their Velvelettes cover version, 'Really Saying Something', which reached the UK Top 5 in 1982. From the outset, Bananarama had a strong visual image and an unselfconsciously amateur approach to choreography that was refreshing and appealing. Although they initially played down their talents, they retained considerable control over their careers, eschewing the usual overt sexism associated with the marketing of female troupes in pop. A tie-up with producers Tony Swain and Steve Jolley brought them Top 10 hits with 'Shy Boy', the Steam cover version, 'Na Na Hey Hey Kiss Him Goodbye' and 'Cruel Summer'. Their high point during this phase was the clever and appealing 'Robert De Niro's Waiting', which justly reached the Top 3 in the UK. In an attempt to tackle more serious subject matter, they next released 'Rough Justice', a protest song on the political situation in Northern Ireland. The title prophetically summed up the disc's chart fate.

A lean period followed before the girls teamed up with the Stock, Aitken and Waterman production team for a remake of Shocking Blue's 'Venus', which brought them a US number 1 in 1986. 'I Heard A Rumour' maintained the quality of their recent output, with some excellent harmonies and a strong arrangement. Their biggest UK hit followed with the exceptional 'Love In The First Degree', which reached number 3 and proved to be their finest pop moment. In early 1988 Fahey left the group, married the Eurythmics' David A. Stewart and subsequently formed Shakespears Sister. Her replacement was Jacqui Sullivan (b. 7 August 1960, London, England), an old friend whose image fitted in reasonably well. During the early 90s, the hits continued making Bananarama the most consistent and successful British female group in pop history. This effective formula underwent yet another change in 1991 when Sullivan departed for a solo career, resulting in Dallin and Woodward continuing for the first time as a duo. The duo's last chart entry was 'More, More, More' in spring 1993, and they recorded one further album, *Ultra Violet*. The original line-up re-formed in 1998 to record a cover version of Abba's 'Waterloo' for Channel 4's *Eurotrash* Eurovision tribute. Dallin and Woodward went on to record a new album, *Exotica*, which was released in France in 2001.

● ALBUMS: *Deep Sea Skiving* (London 1983) ★★★, *Bananarama* (London 1984) ★★★, *True Confessions* (London 1986) ★★★, *Wow!* (London 1987) ★★★, *Pop*

*Life* (London 1991) ★★, *Please Yourself* (London 1993) ★★, *Ultra Violet* (Curb 1995) ★★, *Exotica* (Fr 2001) ★★★.
● COMPILATIONS: *The Greatest Hits Collection* (London 1988) ★★★★, *Bunch Of Hits* (London 1993) ★★★, *The Very Best Of Bananarama* (London 2001) ★★★.
● VIDEOS: *Bananarama* (PolyGram Music Video 1984), *Bananarama: Video Singles* (Channel 5 1987), *Love In The First Degree* (PolyGram Music Video 1988), *Greatest Hits: Bananarama* (Channel 5 1988), *And That's Not All* (Channel 5 1988), *Greatest Hits Collection* (PolyGram Music Video 1991).

## BAND AID/LIVE AID

Millions saw the 1984 BBC television news report narrated by Michael Buerk, showing the devastating famine in Ethiopia. Bob Geldof was so moved that he organized, promoted and produced a massive fund-raising enterprise. Geldof's likeable bullying and eloquently cheeky publicity endeared him to millions. The song 'Do They Know It's Christmas?', co-written with Midge Ure, assembled a cavalcade of rock and pop stars under the name Band Aid. It included members from Status Quo, Culture Club, Bananarama, Style Council, Duran Duran, Spandau Ballet, Heaven 17 and U2. Solo stars included Phil Collins, Sting, George Michael and Paul Young. Geldof bludgeoned artists, record companies, pressing plants, distributors and record shops to forgo their profit. The record scaled the UK charts and stayed on top for five weeks, eventually selling millions of copies. Geldof topped this masterstroke in July 1985 by organizing Live Aid. This spectacular rock and pop concert was televised worldwide, live from London and Philadelphia. Among the stellar cast were Sade, Queen, Bob Dylan, Neil Young, the Cars, Beach Boys, Pat Metheny, Santana, Madonna, Kenny Loggins, Bryan Adams, Crosby, Stills And Nash, Eric Clapton, Phil Collins (who via Concorde appeared at both venues), Judas Priest, REO Speedwagon, Jimmy Page, Robert Plant, Status Quo, Bryan Ferry, Sting, Paul Young, Simple Minds, U2, the Who, Paul McCartney, Mick Jagger, Adam Ant, Elvis Costello, Tina Turner, Elton John, Spandau Ballet and David Bowie. A huge television audience raised over £50 million through pledged donations. Geldof carried through his sincere wish to help starving children with integrity, passion and a sense of humour. The Live Aid concert remains one of the greatest musical events of all time. Geldof received an honorary knighthood in 1986 for his humanitarian activities.
● VIDEOS: *Do They Know It's Christmas?* (PolyGram Music Video 1986).
● FURTHER READING: *Live Aid: The Greatest Show On Earth*, Peter Hillmore.

## BAND OF SUSANS

The membership of this articulate, guitar-based US assembly was fluid but evolved around the songwriting partnership of Robert Poss (b. 20 November 1956, Buffalo, New York, USA; guitar, vocals) and Susan Stenger (b. 11 May 1955, Buffalo, New York, USA; bass, guitar, vocals). Poss had once

been offered the guitarist's role in Public Image Limited when Keith Levene left. Both he and Stenger formerly worked with guitar composers Rhys Chatham, and eventually formed their own group. Their title was drawn from the fact that the original line-up contained three Susans. Other members of the group have included Ron Spitzer (drums, replaced by Joey Kaye), Page Hamilton (b. 18 May 1960, Portland, Oregon, USA; guitar, vocals, who later formed Helmet in 1992) and Anne Husick, who took over from Karen Haglof as third guitarist. Bruce Gilbert from Wire also temporarily deputized for Haglof because of her aversion to touring. However, personnel changes have had little effect on the internal dynamics of the band because, when they audition new people, we're not looking for an influx of new ideas, we like the way the band is'. Two independent albums won them supporters on both sides of the Atlantic, after which they moved to Restless Records for 1991's *The Word And The Flesh*. The massed barrage of guitars onstage remains a unique visual and aural experience, which the *New Musical Express* described as 'nothing less than pure, demonic euphoria'. *Here Comes Success*, an ironic title given that the band was apparently on the verge of dissolution, opened with 'Elizabeth Stride (1843–1888)', the tale of a Jack The Ripper victim who had lived on the same street as Stenger.
● ALBUMS: *Hope Against Hope* (Further/Blast First 1988) ★★★, *Love Agenda* (Restless/Blast First 1989) ★★★, *The Word And The Flesh* (Restless/Blast First 1991) ★★★, *Veil* (Restless/Blast First 1993) ★★, *Here Comes Success* (Blast First 1995) ★★★.
● COMPILATIONS: *Wired For Sound: 1986–1993* (Blast First 1995) ★★★.

## BANGLES

Formerly known as the Colours, the Bangs and finally the Bangles, this all-female Los Angeles quartet mastered the art of melodic west coast guitar-based pop and, like the Go-Go's immediately before them, led the way for all-female outfits in the latter half of the 80s. The band was formed in 1981 and originally comprised Susanna Hoffs (b. 17 January 1962, Newport Beach, California, USA; guitar, vocals), Debbi Peterson (b. 22 August 1961, Los Angeles, California, USA; drums, vocals), Vicki Peterson (b. 11 January 1958, Los Angeles, California, USA; guitar, vocals) and Annette Zilinskas (bass, vocals). They emerged from the 'paisley underground' scene that spawned bands such as Rain Parade and Dream Syndicate. The Bangles' first recordings were made on their own Downkiddie label and then for Miles Copeland's Faulty Products set-up, which resulted in a flawed self-titled mini-album. On signing to the major CBS Records label in 1983, the line-up had undergone a crucial change. Zilinskas departed (later to join Blood On The Saddle) and was replaced by former Runaways member Michael Steele (b. 2 June 1954, USA; bass, vocals).
Their superb debut, 'Hero Takes A Fall', failed to chart, and an interpretation of Kimberley Rew's song 'Going Down To Liverpool' just scraped into the UK listing. The idea of four glamorous middle-class

American girls singing about trotting down to a labour exchange in Liverpool with their UB40 cards was both bizarre and quaint. The Bangles' energetic and harmonious style showed both a grasp and great affection for 60s pop with their Beatles and Byrds-like sound. Again they failed to chart, although their sparkling debut, *All Over The Place*, scraped into the US chart. Following regular live work they built up a strong following, although it was not until the US/UK number 2 hit single 'Manic Monday', written by Prince, and the huge success of *Different Light* that they won a wider audience. The media, meanwhile, were picking out the highly photogenic Hoffs as the leader of the band. This sowed the seeds of dissatisfaction within the line-up that would later come to a head. Both album and single narrowly missed the tops of the US and UK charts, and throughout 1986 the Bangles could do no wrong. Their interpretation of Jules Shear's 'If She Knew What She Wants' showed touches of mid-60s Mamas And The Papas, while 'Walk Like An Egyptian' (composed by former Rachel Sweet svengali Liam Sternberg) was pure 80s quirkiness and gave the band a US number 1/UK number 3 hit. The unusual choice as a cover version of the Simon And Garfunkel song 'Hazy Shade Of Winter', which was featured in the movie *Less Than Zero*, gave them a US number 2 hit in 1988.

The third album, *Everything*, offered another collection of classy pop that generated the hit singles 'In Your Room' (US number 5, 1988) and the controversial 'Eternal Flame' in the spring of 1989, which gave the band a transatlantic number 1. Both these songs featured lead vocals from Hoffs, but 'Eternal Flame' was viewed by the other band members as an unnecessary departure from the Bangles' *modus operandi*, with its use of string backing and barely any instrumental contribution from them. Rather than harking back to the 60s the song was reminiscent of the early to mid-70s pop ballads of Michael Jackson and Donny Osmond. It also once again compounded the illusion in the public's eye that the Bangles were Hoffs' band. The year that had started so well for the band was now disintegrating into internal conflict. 'Be With You' and 'I'll Set You Free' failed to emulate their predecessors' success, and by the end of the year the decision was made to dissolve the band. Susanna Hoffs embarked on a lukewarm solo career, while the remaining members failed to make any impact with their respective projects. They re-formed in 2000 for live dates and had further exposure in 2001 when Atomic Kitten took their cover version of 'Eternal Flame' to the top of the UK charts.

● ALBUMS: *All Over The Place* (Columbia 1985) ★★★, *Different Light* (Columbia 1986) ★★★★, *Everything* (Columbia 1988) ★★.
● COMPILATIONS: *The Bangles Greatest Hits* (Columbia 1991) ★★★★, *Twelve Inch Mixes* (Columbia 1993) ★★, *Eternal Flame: The Best Of* (Sony 2001) ★★★★.
● VIDEOS: *Bangles Greatest Hits* (SMV 1990).

## BANTON, BURO

b. *c*.1960, Western Kingston, Jamaica, West Indies. The nickname Buro has been with him from his schooldays and Banton was the title given to a lyrics champion. His early influences included Dillinger, Trinity, U. Brown and Ranking Trevor. He would frequent dances where his heroes performed and emulate their gestures and phrasings, which eventually evolved into his own presentation. In 1976, persuaded by his friends, he made his debut as a DJ at the renowned Skateland discotheque in Kingston when he entered a talent contest. Banton began his career in earnest on the Roots Unlimited sound system alongside Josey Wales. His success led to him becoming the resident DJ for the Gemini sound system, which resulted in his association with Henry 'Junjo' Lawes' Volcano sound. Performing alongside Peter Metro, Little John, Billy Boyo and Ranking Toyan, the sound clashed with People's Choice, where Banton battled with his old sparring partner, Josey Wales. Volcano won the contest and shortly after the event Wales joined the Volcano posse. In the early 80s, Banton's distinctive voice, which sounded similar to Prince Jazzbo, had only been heard on yard tapes. Throughout 1980–82 Henry 'Junjo' Lawes had proved to be a successful producer with Barrington Levy, Yellowman, Eek A Mouse and the aforementioned DJs. Having served his apprenticeship on the sound system, Banton went into the studio with Junjo for his vinyl debut, *Buro*. Notable inclusions were 'Better Than The Rest', 'Tell Me What You Want' and the sublime 'Tenement'. The album was overshadowed by the phenomenal success of Yellowman, which resulted in a vast number of distinguished DJs being disregarded by the media. He recorded 'Out A Hand' with references to the albino star, 'Seh, when I was a yout' dem a call me Buro – But now that I'm a man what I can't understand – Dey change fe mi name into the lyrics Banton – Me sing more church song than Yellowman', as part of a traditional dancehall confrontation. A similar encounter in 1983 with Peter Metro resulted in Banton winning the honours, although Metro maintained foul play. In 1984, Banton recorded 'Non Stop' with Junjo, toured Canada with DJ John Wayne and nurtured his protégé Little Buro. Banton continued to maintain his popularity in Jamaica where his perpetual chanting at the mike has become legendary. After leaving Volcano he was employed on the Stereo Mars system alongside Tenor Saw, Cocoa Tea, Major Worries, Supercat and Nicodemus. By the early 90s Banton was in New York and voiced the legality of his US residency on a remix of Shinehead's hit, 'Jamaican In New York'. In 1994, he was recording for the Brooklyn-based Massive B label, who specialized in both reggae and hip-hop. His initial output, including 'Boom Wha Dis' and 'Sensi Come From', was greeted with enthusiasm, leading to an album release in the summer of 1995.
● ALBUMS: *Buro* (CSA 1983) ★★★, *Original Banton* (Massive B 1995) ★★★★.

**BANTON, PATO**
b. Patrick Murray, Birmingham, England. Banton first came to the public's attention in 1982 on the Beat's *Special Beat Service* album, duelling with Ranking Roger on 'Pato And Roger A Go Talk', before releases on the Fashion Records and Don Christie labels. His debut single, 'Hello Tosh', was a novelty take on the Toshiba advertising campaign of 1985. His first long-playing effort saw him paired with the wizardry of the Mad Professor, a combination to which he would return four years later for the *Recaptured* set. On his solo debut Banton was backed by the Birmingham-based Studio 2 house band. Throughout, he coloured his Rasta toasting/dub with comic impersonations of the characters populating his songs. Since then, his records have leaned progressively towards pop and soul, blurring the dividing lines between Jamaican toasting and American rap. For *Wize Up!*, which contained an unlikely alternative radio hit in his cover version of the Police's 'Spirits In The Material World', Banton was joined by David Hinds of Steel Pulse. In the 90s Banton began to attract a large US following, where he was signed to I.R.S. Records. However, his tremendous live popularity was not translated into record sales, and in 1994 I.R.S. persuaded him to release a pop cover version. Backed by Robin and Ali Campbell of UB40 and written by Eddy Grant, 'Baby Come Back' became a worldwide success, selling one and a half million copies in Europe and Australasia. In its wake, Sting invited Banton to chat over his 'Cowboy Song' single, which became another major chart success.
● ALBUMS: with Mad Professor *Mad Professor Captures Pato Banton* (Ariwa 1985) ★★★, *Never Give In* (Greensleeves 1987) ★★★, *Visions Of The World* (I.R.S. 1989) ★★★, *Recaptured* (Ariwa 1989) ★★★, *Wize Up! (No Compromize)* (I.R.S. 1990) ★★★, *Collections* (I.R.S. 1995) ★★★, *Life Is A Miracle* (Surfdog 2000) ★★★.

**BARELY WORKS**
This eclectic folk group was assembled in 1988 by former Boothill Foot-Tappers singer and banjoist Chris Thompson (b. 19 March 1957, Ashford, Middlesex, England), together with Richard Avison (b. 9 July 1958, Rothbury, Northumberland, England; trombone, vocals, ex-Happy End; Dead Can Dance), Sarah Allen (b. 22 July 1964, Tiverton, Devon, England; accordion, tin whistle, flutes, ex-Happy End; Di's New Outfit), Alison Jones (b. 6 April 1965, Sketty, Swansea, West Glamorgan, Wales; violin, vocals, ex-Di's New Outfit), Keith Moore (tuba, also a member of poet John Hegley's Popticians), Mat Fox (b. 8 November 1956; hammer dulcimer, percussion, vocals) and former Redskins drummer Paul Hookham, later replaced in 1990 by Tim Walmsley (b. 29 March 1956, Paddington, London, England; ex-Happy End). This strange mixture of personalities signed to the radical world-music label Cooking Vinyl and emerged from the UK folk club circuit in the late 80s and early 90s. Their performances boasted a broad range of traditional ('Byker Hill') and original material, mostly from Thompson and Allen, as well as tackling the works of artists such as Captain Beefheart ('Tropical Hot Dog Nite'). The Barely Works managed to break away from the constrictive pigeonhole of an 'English folk group' and crossed over to the rock-club circuit where their virtuosity proved them more than capable of moving a rock audience. Mat Fox left the group in early 1992 and Keith Moore was replaced by Alice Kinloch. In 1993 the group disbanded.
● ALBUMS: *The Beat Beat* (Cooking Vinyl 1990) ★★★, *Don't Mind Walking* (Cooking Vinyl 1991) ★★★, *Shimmer* (Cooking Vinyl 1992) ★★★, *Glow* (Cooking Vinyl 1992) ★★★.
● COMPILATIONS: *Best Of The Barely Works* (Cooking Vinyl 1995) ★★★★.

**BARNES, JIMMY**
b. James Swan, 28 April 1956, Cowcaddens, Glasgow, Scotland. With the disintegration of the Australian band Cold Chisel in 1983, lead singer Jimmy Barnes embarked on a solo career with Mushroom Records. He teamed up with Jonathan Cain (ex-Babys) and produced two albums in quick succession. These were characterized by Barnes' rough and raunchy vocal delivery, and included erudite selections of blues, soul and R&B numbers. *Freight Train Heart* had a much bigger budget, as Geffen Records were hoping to break Barnes in America. With contributions from Journey's Neal Schon, Desmond Child, Mick Fleetwood and Jim Vallence, the result was a classic American rock album. Surprisingly, it did not take off and Geffen dropped Barnes in 1988. A credible double live album, appropriately titled *Barnestorming*, was recorded in Melbourne on his 1987–88 tour of Australia. This surfaced on import on the Mushroom label, and eventually led to a new international contract with Atlantic Records. *Two Fires* emerged in 1990, and represented yet another high-quality album of gritty rockers and gut-wrenching ballads. Once again, it made little impact outside Australia, a fate that befell all his subsequent albums. He returned to a re-formed Cold Chisel in the late 90s, before signing a new solo contract with Warner Music.
● ALBUMS: *Bodyswerve* (Mushroom 1984) ★★★, *For The Working Class Man* (Mushroom 1985) ★★★, *Freight Train Heart* (Mushroom/Geffen 1987) ★★★★, *Barnestorming* (Mushroom 1988) ★★★, *Two Fires* (Mushroom/Atlantic 1990) ★★★, *Soul Deep* (Mushroom 1991) ★★★, *Heat* (Mushroom/Atlantic 1993) ★★★, *Flesh And Wood* (Mushroom 1993) ★★★, *Psyclone* (Mushroom 1995) ★★★, *Love And Fear* (Mushroom 1999) ★★★, *Soul Deeper ... Songs From The Deep South* (Warner 2000) ★★★, *Double Jeopardy* (Warner 2001) ★★★, *Raw* (Warner 2001) ★★★.
● COMPILATIONS: *Barnes Hits* (Mushroom 1996) ★★★, *Double Jeopardy* (Rajon 2001) ★★★.
● VIDEOS: *Take One* (Mushroom 1989), *Take Two* (Mushroom 1991), *Soul Deep* (Mushroom 1992), *Flesh And Wood* (Mushroom 1994), *Barnes Hits* (Mushroom 1996).
● FURTHER READING: *Say It Loud*, Jimmy Barnes with Alan Whiticker.

## BARRACUDAS

Formed in London, England in 1978 as a neo-surfing band – their lone UK Top 40 entry in 1980 was the derivative 'Summer Fun' – Jeremy Gluck (b. Ottawa, Canada; vocals), Robin Wills (guitar, vocals), David Buckley (bass, vocals) and Nick Turner (b. 4 May 1959; drums, vocals) eschewed this direction during the recording of their debut album, *Drop Out With The Barracudas*. Newer tracks, including 'I Saw My Death In A Dream Last Night', bore a debt to US-styled psychedelia and garage bands (they had also taken their name from a Standells song), and the group became one of the genre's leading proponents during its revival in the early 80s. The original rhythm section then departed, with Nick Turner joining the Lords Of The New Church before taking a job at I.R.S. Records. Bass player Jim Dickson (b. Australia; ex-Survivors) and Graham Potter were the new recruits, although the latter was soon ousted by Terry Smith. However, the band only asserted an individual style with the arrival of Chris Wilson, formerly of the Flamin' Groovies. His influence was felt on the Barracudas' next two studio albums, *Meantime* and *Endeavour To Persevere*, the latter featuring new drummer Mark Sheppard, but these excellent releases were only issued in France.

Failure to generate a UK recording contract inevitably hampered the band's progress and they broke up in December 1984. Wilson and Wills were later reunited in a new venture, the Fortunate Sons, who recorded two albums for the Bam Caruso label. Gluck, a former columnist on the music paper *Sounds*, resumed his journalistic career, principally with Q magazine (as Jeremy Clarke) and also released two solo albums. Gluck and Wills re-formed the Barracudas in 1989 with Fortunate Sons bass player Steve Robinson and drummer Rick Sigmund, although the latter was quickly replaced by Jay Posner. They recorded the excellent *Wait For Everything* for the Canadian indie label Shake!, but the reunion was ultimately hampered by lack of money.

● ALBUMS: *Drop Out With The Barracudas* (Zonophone/EMI 1981) ★★★, *Meantime* (Closer 1983) ★★★, *Live 1983* (Coyote 1983) ★★★, *Endeavour To Persevere* (Closer 1984) ★★★, *The Big Gap* (Coyote 1984) ★★★, *Live In Madrid* (Impossible 1986) ★★, *Wait For Everything* (Shake! 1992) ★★★, *The Barracudas Again – Live In '93* (Impossible 1993) ★★.

● COMPILATIONS: *I Wish It Could Be 1965 Again* (GMG 1985) ★★★, *The Garbage Dump Tapes!* 1982 recordings (Shakin' Street 1989) ★★★, *The Complete EMI Recordings* (EMI 1991) ★★★, *Two Sides Of A Coin 1979–84* (Anagram 1993) ★★★, *Through The Mysts Of Time* (Snowdome 1998) ★★★, *This Ain't My Time* (Sanctuary 2001) ★★★.

## BARRY, JOHN

b. Jonathan Barry Prendergast, 3 November 1933, York, Yorkshire, England. Renowned as one of the leading composers of film soundtrack music, Barry began his career leading the John Barry Seven. This rousing instrumental unit enjoyed several notable UK hits between 1960 and 1962, the best-known of which were 'Hit And Miss' and a version of the Ventures' Walk Don't Run' (both 1960). The former, which reached number 11 in the UK charts, was the theme to *Juke Box Jury*, BBC Television's long-running record release show. Barry made regular appearances on several early pop programmes, including *Oh Boy* and *Drumbeat* and also enjoyed concurrent fame as a writer and arranger, scoring the distinctive pizzicato strings on numerous Adam Faith hits including the number 1 'What Do You Want' (1959) and 'Poor Me' (on which you can hear strong shades of the 'James Bond Theme' in the arrangement).

He also composed the soundtrack to *Beat Girl*, the singer's film debut, and later took up a senior A&R post with the independent Ember label. In 1962 Barry had a UK Top 20 hit with the 'James Bond Theme', which was part of Monty Norman's score for the film *Dr. No*, the first in a highly successful series. He produced music for several subsequent Bond films, including *From Russia With Love*, *Goldfinger* and *You Only Live Twice*, the title songs from which provided hit singles for Matt Monro (1963), Shirley Bassey (1964) and Nancy Sinatra (1967). Such success led to a series of stylish soundtracks that encompassed contrasting moods and music, including *The Ipcress File*, *The Knack ... And How To Get It* (both 1965), *Born Free* (which won two Oscars in 1966), *Midnight Cowboy* (1969) and *Mary, Queen Of Scots* (1971). Although his theme songs have enjoyed a high commercial profile, it is Barry's imaginative incidental music that has assured his peerless reputation. By contrast, he pursued another lucrative direction, composing television commercials for disparate household items.

Barry's consistency remained intact throughout the 70s and 80s, although several attendant movies, including the 1976 remake of *King Kong* and *Howard The Duck* (a second-rate DC comic character), were highly criticized. 'Down Deep Inside', the theme from *The Deep* (1977), was a UK Top 5 hit for Donna Summer, and this disco-influenced composition emphasized the writer's versatility. *A View To A Kill* (1985), *Peggy Sue Got Married* (1986), *The Living Daylights* and *Hearts Of Fire* (both 1987) demonstrated his accustomed flair, while his music for *Out Of Africa* (1985) and *Dances With Wolves* (1990) earned him further Oscars and Grammy Awards. In the early 90s his scores included Richard Attenborough's *Chaplin* (Oscar nomination), *Indecent Proposal*, *Ruby Cairo* aka *Deception* and *My Life* (all 1993), *The Specialist* (1994) and *Cry, The Beloved Country* (1995). His orchestrations combine elements of classical, jazz and popular themes and command the respect of enthusiastic aficionados. In April 1998 Barry conducted the 87-piece English Chamber Orchestra in a concert celebration of his own movie music at London's Royal Albert Hall, during which he previewed *The Beyondness Of Things*, a collection of 'string-driven musical poems'. Regarded as more subtle than his film scores, it was Barry's first non-soundtrack work for two decades. In the following year he returned to the Royal Albert Hall, and also released the soundtrack album *Playing By Heart*, which was inspired by the work of legendary trumpeter Chet Baker. In 2001 Barry composed the score for *Enigma*, in addition to recording a new album of non-soundtrack material, *Eternal Echoes*.

● ALBUMS: *Beat Girl* (Columbia 1959) ★★★, *Stringbeat* (Columbia 1961) ★★★, *Dr. No* (United Artists 1962) ★★★★, *It's All Happening* (Columbia 1963) ★★★, *A Handful Of Songs* (Ember 1963) ★★★, *Elizabeth Taylor In London* television soundtrack (Colpix 1963) ★★★, *From Russia With Love* (United Artists 1963) ★★★, *Zulu* (United Artists 1964) ★★★, *Man In The Middle* (20th Century Fox 1964) ★★★, *Goldfinger* (United Artists 1964) ★★★, *Sophia Loren In Rome* television soundtrack (Columbia 1964) ★★★, *The Ipcress File* (Decca 1965) ★★★, *King Rat* (Mainstream 1965) ★★★, *The Knack ... And How To Get It* (United Artists 1965) ★★★, *Four In The Morning* (Roulette 1965) ★★★, *Thunderball* (United Artists 1965) ★★★★, *Passion Flower Hotel* stage soundtrack (CBS 1965) ★★★, *The Wrong Box* (Mainstream 1966) ★★★, *The Chase* (Columbia 1966) ★★★, *Born Free* (MGM 1966) ★★★★, *The Quiller Memorandum* (Columbia 1966) ★★★, *You Only Live Twice* (United Artists 1967) ★★★★, *The Whisperers* (United Artists 1967) ★★★, *Deadfall* (20th Century Fox 1968) ★★★, *Petulia* (Warners 1968) ★★★, *Boom!* (MCA 1968) ★★★, *The Lion In Winter* (Columbia 1968) ★★★★, *On Her Majesty's Secret Service* (United Artists 1969) ★★★, *Midnight Cowboy* (United Artists 1969) ★★★★, *Monte Walsh* (FSM 1970) ★★★, *The Last Valley* (Dunhill 1970) ★★★, *Diamonds Are Forever* (United Artists 1971) ★★★★, *Lolita My Love* stage musical soundtrack (Blue Pearl 1971) ★★★, *The Persuaders* (Columbia 1971) ★★★, *Mary Queen Of Scots* (MGM 1971) ★★★, *Alice's Adventures In Wonderland* (Warners 1972) ★★★★, *Follow Me* (Victor 1972) ★★★★, *The Dove* (ABC 1974) ★★★★, *The Man With The Golden Gun* (United Artists 1974) ★★★, *Americans* non-soundtrack (Polydor 1976) ★★★, *The Day Of The Locust* (London 1975) ★★★, *Robin & Marian* (Probe 1976) ★★★, *King Kong* (Reprise 1976) ★★★, *The Deep* (Casablanca 1978) ★★★, *Game Of Death* (Tam 1979) ★★★, *The Black Hole* (Buena Vista 1979) ★★★★, *Moonraker* (United Artists 1979) ★★★, *Starcrash* (Durium 1979) ★★★, *Somewhere In Time* (MCA 1980) ★★★, *Body Heat* (Label X 1981) ★★★, *The Legend Of The Lone Ranger* (MCA 1981) ★★★, *Frances* (Southern Cross 1982) ★★★, *Hammett* (Prometheus 1982) ★★★, *Octopussy* (A&M 1983) ★★★, *Until September* (Varèse Sarabande 1984) ★★★, *Jagged Edge* (Varèse Sarabande 1985) ★★★, *Out Of Africa* (MCA 1985) ★★★★, *Peggy Sue Got Married* (Varèse Sarabande 1986) ★★★, *Howard The Duck* (MCA 1986) ★★★, *The Living Daylights* (Warners 1987) ★★★, *Dances With Wolves* (Epic 1990) ★★★★, *High Road To China* (A&R 1990) ★★★, *Chaplin* (Epic 1992) ★★★★, *Moviola* (Epic 1992) ★★★★, *Deception* (Sony 1993) ★★★, *My Life* (Epic 1993) ★★★, *The Specialist* (Epic 1994) ★★★, *Cry, The Beloved Country* (Epic 1995) ★★★, *The Scarlet Letter* (Epic 1995) ★★★, *Across The Sea Of Time* (Epic 1995) ★★★, *Moviola II – Action And Adventure* (Epic 1995) ★★★, *Swept From The Sea* (London 1997) ★★★, *Mercury Rising* (Varèse Sarabande 1998) ★★★, *The Beyondness Of Things* orchestral album (Decca 1998) ★★★, *Playing By Heart* (Decca 1999) ★★★★, *Eternal Echoes* (Decca 2001) ★★★.

● COMPILATIONS: *Six-Five Special* (Parlophone 1957) ★★★, *Oh Boy!* (Parlophone 1958) ★★★, *Drumbeat* (Parlophone 1959) ★★★, *Saturday Club* (Parlophone 1960) ★★★, *Blackpool Nights* (Columbia 1960) ★★★, *The Great Movie Sounds Of John Barry* (1966) ★★★, *John Barry Conducts His Great Movie Hits* (1967) ★★★, *Ready When You Are, John Barry* (1970) ★★★, *John Barry Revisited* (1971) ★★★, *Play It Again* (1974) ★★★, *The Music Of John Barry* (1976) ★★★, *The Very Best Of John Barry* (1977) ★★★, *The John Barry Seven And Orchestra* (EMI 1979) ★★★, *The Best Of John Barry* (Polydor 1981) ★★★, *The Big Screen Hits Of John Barry* (Columbia 1981) ★★★, *James Bond's Greatest Hits* (1982) ★★★, *Music From The Big Screen* (Pickwick 1986) ★★★, *Hit And Miss* (See For Miles 1988) ★★★, *The Film Music Of John Barry* (1989) ★★★, *John Barry Themes* (1989) ★★★, *The Ember Years Volume 1* (Play It Again 1992) ★★★, *The Ember Years Volume 2* (Play It Again 1992) ★★★, *The Best Of EMI Years Volume 2* (EMI 1993) ★★★, *The Ember Years Volume 3* (Play It Again 1996) ★★★, *The John Barry Experience* (Carlton 1997) ★★★, *Themeology: The Best Of John Barry* (Columbia 1997) ★★★★, *John Barry: The Hits And The Misses* (Play It Again 1998) ★★★, *The Music Of John Barry* (Columbia 1999) ★★★, *The Collection: 40 Years Of Film Music* 4-CD set (Silva Screen 2001) ★★★★.

● FURTHER READING: *John Barry: A Sixties Theme*, Eddi Fiegel. *John Barry: A Life In Music*, Geoff Leonard, Pete Walker, Gareth Bramley. *John Barry: A Sixties Theme*, Eddi Fiegel.

● FILMS: *It's All Happening* (1963).

## BASIL, TONI

b. Antonia Basilotta, 22 September 1943, Philadelphia, Pennsylvania, USA. American singer/dancer Basil was responsible for the choreography on the legendary US 60s pop shows, *Hullabaloo* and *Shindig*. She was also actively involved in the Monkees' 1968 cult movie *Head*, the following year's *Easy Rider* and the highly successful *American Graffiti* in 1974. David Bowie employed Basil's choreographical services for his elaborately staged *Diamond Dogs* tour and other rock artists followed his lead. By the early 80s, Basil had moved into the video field, co-directing Talking Heads among others. Backed by her own dance troupe, the Lockers, she recorded the hit album *Word Of Mouth* in 1981, which featured musical backing by two former members of Seatrain. The Chinn And Chapman composition 'Mickey' brought her a surprise UK number 2 in 1982 and several months later it reached number 1 in her homeland. With her related interests in different fields of the music business, Basil seemed unlikely to pursue an exclusively vocal career and failed to register any further major hits.

● ALBUMS: *Word Of Mouth* (Radialchoice 1981) ★★★, *Toni Basil* (Virgin 1983) ★★.

## BATORS, STIV

b. Stivin Bator, 22 October 1949, Cleveland, Ohio, USA, d. June 1990. Bators' first bands, Mother Goose and Frankenstein, were transmuted into seminal US 'no wave' band the Dead Boys. They moved to New

York in 1976, and although they officially split in 1978 there were frequent reunions. Bators moved to Los Angeles where he recorded demos with friend Jeff Jones (ex-Blue Ash). He also gigged with Akron band Rubber City Rebels. The first release from the demos was a version of the Choir's (later the Raspberries) 60s single, 'It's Cold Outside', which was released on Greg Shaw's Bomp label. A second guitarist and debut album (USA only) followed in 1980, on which the duo was augmented by guitarist Eddy Best and drummer David Quinton (formerly of Toronto's the Mods). After appearing in John Waters' cult movie *Polyester*, Bators formed a touring band, with Rick Bremner replacing Quinton. By 1981, Bators had become a permanent member of the Wanderers. The Stiv Bators Band played a final American tour in February 1981 with Brian James of the Damned guesting on guitar, after which Bators concentrated on the Wanderers until September 1981. After the impressive *Only Lovers Left Alive* (1981), Bators took Dave Treganna (ex-Sham 69) with him to join James and Nicky Turner (ex-Barracudas) in Lords Of The New Church. Following the Lords' demise, Bators resurfaced in London in 1989 for a 'Return Of The Living Boys' gig. This time his cohorts were drawn from a variety of local personnel, and it was not until he returned to Paris that he entered a recording studio once more. A new line-up included Dee Dee Ramone (Ramones), who had to be replaced by Neil X (Sigue Sigue Sputnik) before the sessions began, Kris Dollimore (ex-Godfathers) and guest appearances from Johnny Thunders. With six songs completed, Bators was hit by a car in June 1990, and died the following day. There are hopes that his sessions will receive a posthumous release.

● ALBUMS: *Where The Action Is* (Bomp! 1980) ★★★.
● COMPILATIONS: *The Church And The New Creatures* (Lolita 1983) ★★★.

## BAUHAUS

Originally known as Bauhaus 1919, this Northamptonshire, England-based quartet was formed by Peter Murphy (vocals), Daniel Ash (vocals/guitar), David Jay aka David J. (b. David Jay Haskins; vocals/bass) and Kevin Haskins (drums). Within months of their formation they made their recording debut in 1979 with the classic, brooding, nine-minute gothic anthem 'Bela Lugosi's Dead'. Their career saw them move to various independent labels (Small Wonder, Axix, 4AD Records and Beggars Banquet Records) and along the way they recorded some interesting singles, including 'Dark Entries', 'Terror Couple Kill Colonel' and a reworking of T. Rex's 'Telegram Sam'. Often insistent on spontaneity in the studio, they recorded four albums in as many years, of which 1981's *Mask* proved the most accessible. A cameo appearance in the movie *The Hunger*, starring David Bowie, showed them playing their memorable Bela Lugosi tribute. They later took advantage of the Bowie connection to record a carbon copy of 'Ziggy Stardust', which gave them their only UK Top 20 hit. Although there was further belated success with 'Lagartija Nick' and 'She's In Parties', the group disbanded in 1983. Vocalist Peter Murphy

briefly joined Japan's Mick Karn in Dali's Car and the remaining three members soldiered on under the name Love And Rockets. The original members reunited in the mid-90s for several live dates in Los Angeles, which led to a fully fledged reunion tour in 1998. *Gotham Live 1998* captured the band's performance at New York's Hammerstein Ballroom.

● ALBUMS: *In The Flat Field* (4AD 1980) ★★, *Mask* (Beggars Banquet 1981) ★★★, *The Sky's Gone Out* (Beggars Banquet/A&M 1982) ★★★, *Press The Eject And Give Me The Tape* (Beggars Banquet 1982) ★★, *Burning From The Inside* (Beggars Banquet/A&M 1983) ★★, *Rest In Piece: The Final Concert* (Nemo 1992) ★★, *Gotham Live 1998* (Cargo 2000) ★★.
● COMPILATIONS: *1979-1983* (Beggars Banquet 1985) ★★★, *Swing The Heartache: The BBC Sessions* (Beggars Banquet 1989) ★★, *Crackle: The Definitive Collection* (Beggars Banquet 1998) ★★★.
● VIDEOS: *Shadow Of Light* (Hendring 1984), *Archive* (Beggars Banquet 1984).
● FURTHER READING: *Dark Entries: Bauhaus And Beyond*, Ian Shirley.

## BEASTIE BOYS

Former hardcore trio who initially found international fame as the first crossover white rap act of the 80s, and later earned critical plaudits for their eclectic approach in a musical genre not known for its experimental nature. After forming at New York University, original guitarist John Berry departed after the release of the hardcore *Polly Wog Stew* EP, leaving Adam Yauch (b. 15 August 1967, Brooklyn, New York, USA), Mike Diamond (b. 20 November 1965, New York, USA), drummer Kate Schellenbach and guitarist Adam Horovitz (b. 31 October 1966, New York City, New York, USA), recently recruited from The Young And The Useless (one single, 'Real Men Don't Use Floss'), to hold the banner. Horovitz, it transpired, was the son of dramatist Israel Horovitz, indicating that far from being the spawn of inner-city dystopia, the Beasties all came from privileged middle-class backgrounds.

In 1983, the new line-up released the *Cooky Puss* EP, which offered the first evidence of them picking up on the underground rap phenomenon and the use of samples. 'Beastie Revolution' was later sampled for a British Airways commercial, earning them $40,000 in royalties. Schellenbach soon departed reducing the crew to the core trio of Yauch, Diamond and Horovitz, now going by the hip-hop monikers of MCA, Mike D and King Adrock respectively. Friend and sometime member Rick Rubin quickly signed them to his fledgling Def Jam Records. They did not prove hard to market. Their debut album revealed a collision of bad attitudes, spearheaded by the raucous single '(You Gotta) Fight For Your Right (To Party!)', and samples of everything from Led Zeppelin to the theme to *Mister Ed*. There was nothing self-conscious or sophisticated about the lyrics, Diamond and Yauch reeling off complaints about their parents confiscating their pornography or telling them to turn down the stereo. Somehow, however, it became an anthem for pseudo-rebellious youth everywhere, reaching US number 7 in December 1986, and UK number 11 in February 1987.

*Licensed To Ill* became the first rap album to top the US pop charts at the end of November 1986, and reached number 7 in the UK charts the following January. By the time follow-up singles 'No Sleep Till Brooklyn' (number 14, May 1987) and 'She's On It' (number 10, July 1987) charted in the UK, the Beastie Boys had become a media *cause célèbre*. Their stage shows regularly featured caged, half-naked females, while their Volkswagen pendants resulted in a crime wave, with fans stealing said items from vehicles throughout the UK. A reflective Horovitz recalled that this never happened in the USA, where they merely stole the car itself. More disturbing, it was alleged that the trio derided terminally ill children on a foreign jaunt. This false accusation was roundly denied, but other stories of excess leaked out of the Beastie Boys camp with grim regularity. There was also friction between the trio and Def Jam, the former accusing the latter of withholding royalties, the latter accusing the former of withholding a follow-up album.

The trio went their separate ways after finishing a fraught tour, with Yauch and Diamond working on solo projects and Horovitz appearing in Hugh Hudson's movie *Lost Angels*. By the time they reassembled on Capitol Records in 1989, the public, for the most part, had forgotten about them. Rap's ante had been significantly raised by the arrival of Public Enemy and NWA, yet *Paul's Boutique* remains one of the genre's most overlooked pieces, a complex reflection of pop culture that is infinitely more subtle than their debut. Leaving their adolescent fixations behind, the rhymes plundered cult fiction (Anthony Burgess' *A Clockwork Orange*) through to the Old Testament. It was co-produced by the Dust Brothers, who subsequently became a hot production item, but stalled at number 14 in the US album chart, and number 44 in the UK. Moving to California and setting up their own G-Son studio, *Check Your Head* saw them returning, partially, to their thrash roots, reverting to a guitar, bass and drums format, aided by the keyboard playing of Mark Nishita (Money Mark). The album proved popular, reaching US number 10 in May 1992. In the meantime, the Beasties had invested wisely, setting up their own magazine and label, Grand Royal, whose first release was the *In Search Of Manny* EP by Luscious Jackson (featuring the Beastie Boys' original drummer Schellenbach). Other signings included The Young And The Useless, DFL (Horovitz's hardcore punk project), DJ Hurricane (also of the Afros), Noise Addict and Moistboyz.

In 1993 Horovitz pleaded guilty to a charge of battery on a television cameraman during a memorial service for River Phoenix. He was put on two years' probation, ordered to undertake 200 hours' community service and pay restitution costs. His connections with the Phoenix family came through his actress wife Ione Sky. He himself had undertaken roles in underground movies *The Santa Anna Project* and *Roadside Prophets*, and also appeared in a television cameo for *The Equalizer*. By this time, both he and Diamond had become Californian citizens, while Yauch had become a Buddhist, speaking out in the press against US trade links with China because of the latter's annexation of Tibet. In 1994, Yauch set

up the Milarepa Fund to raise funds and public awareness of the situation in Tibet, and organized the hugely successful Tibetan Freedom Concerts from 1996 to 1998. *Ill Communication* was another successful voyage into inspired Beastie thuggism, featuring A Tribe Called Quest's Q-Tip, and a second appearance from rapper Biz Markie, following his debut on *Check Your Head*. An eclectic mix of hardcore, hip-hop and funk, the album debuted at number 1 on the US album chart. The trio then released the hardcore *Aglio E Olio EP*, which contained eight songs blasted out in only 11 minutes, followed by *The In Sound From Way Out!*, a space-filler of b-sides and instrumental cuts from their previous two albums. The long-awaited *Hello Nasty* (a title inspired by their agent's telephone greeting), their first full studio album in four years, was a return to a more sparse, hip-hop-dominated sound after the funky feel of *Ill Communication*. The album debuted at US number 1 in August 1998, staying at the top for three weeks. It also became their first UK chart-topper.

After eight years of sustained growth, the Grand Royal label was forced to close down in September 2001. Diamond cited 'mounting debts, decreasing assets, and increasingly harsh industry conditions' among the reasons for the closure.

● ALBUMS: *Licensed To Ill* (Def Jam/Columbia 1986) ★★★, *Paul's Boutique* (Capitol 1989) ★★★★, *Check Your Head* (Capitol 1992) ★★★★, *Ill Communication* (Grand Royal 1994) ★★★★, *Root Down EP* (Grand Royal 1995) ★★, *Aglio E Olio EP* (Grand Royal 1995) ★★★, *The In Sound From Way Out!* (Grand Royal 1996) ★★, *Hello Nasty* (Grand Royal 1998) ★★★★.
● COMPILATIONS: *Some Old Bullshit* (Capitol 1994) ★★★, *Beastie Boys Anthology: The Sounds Of Science* (Grand Royal 1999) ★★★★.
● VIDEOS: *Sabotage* (1994), *The Skills To Pay The Bills* (1994), *The Beastie Boys Video Anthology* (Criterion 2000).
● FURTHER READING: *Rhyming & Stealing: A History Of The Beastie Boys*, Angus Batey. *Beastie Boys 1991–1996*, Ari Marcopoulos.

## BEAT (UK)

Founded in Birmingham, England, in 1978, the original Beat comprised Dave Wakeling (b. 19 February 1956, Birmingham, England; vocals, guitar), Andy Cox (b. 25 January 1960, Birmingham, England; guitar), David Steele (b. 8 September 1960, Isle of Wight, England; bass) and Everett Morton (b. 5 April 1951, St. Kitts; drums). Local success on the pub circuit brought them to the attention of Jerry Dammers, who duly signed them to his Coventry-based 2-Tone label. In the meantime, the Beat had expanded their ranks to include black punk rapper Ranking Roger (b. Roger Charlery, 21 February 1961, Birmingham, England) and a saxophonist simply named Saxa (b. Jamaica, West Indies), who had the distinction of having played alongside that premier exponent of blue beat, Prince Buster.

The new line-up proved perfect for the ska/pop fusion that exemplified the Beat at their best. Their debut single, a cover version of Smokey Robinson's 'The Tears Of A Clown', was a surprise Top 10 hit, but the best was yet to come. After forming their own label, Go Feet, they registered several hits during 1980 that ably displayed their talents as sharp-witted lyricists with the necessary strong danceability quotient. The uplifting yet acerbic 'Mirror In The Bathroom' and 'Best Friend' worked particularly well, both as observations on personal relationships and more generalized put-downs of the 'Me' generation. This political awareness was more explicitly exposed on 'Stand Down Margaret', one of several anti-Thatcher songs that appeared during the British Prime Minister's reign. Donations to CND and benefit gigs for the unemployed linked the Beat with other radical 2-Tone outfits, such as the Specials. On record, the Beat sustained their verve, and their debut album, *I Just Can't Stop It*, proved a solid collection, boosted by the inclusion of several hit singles. Within a year, however, their essentially pop-based style was replaced by a stronger reggae influence. *Wha'ppen?* and *Special Beat Service* were generally well received, but the previously effortless run of chart hits had temporarily evaporated.

By April 1982, Saxa had retired to be replaced by Wesley Magoogan. Although the Beat continued to tour extensively, their dissolution was imminent. Ironically, they ended their career as it had begun, with an opportune cover version of a 60s song, this time Andy Williams' 'Can't Get Used To Losing You', which gave the group their biggest UK hit. After the split, Ranking Roger and Dave Wakeling formed General Public while Andy Cox and David Steele recruited Roland Gift to launch the Fine Young Cannibals.

● ALBUMS: *I Just Can't Stop It* (Go-Feet 1980) ★★★★, *Wha'ppen?* (Go-Feet 1981) ★★★, *Special Beat Service* (Go-Feet 1982) ★★★.

● COMPILATIONS: *What Is Beat* (Go-Feet 1983) ★★★, *BPM: The Very Best Of The Beat* (Arista 1995) ★★★, *The Best Of The Beat: Beat This!* (London 2000) ★★★.

● FURTHER READING: *The Beat: Twist And Crawl*, Malu Halasha.

## BEAT (USA)

Formed in San Francisco in 1979, the new wave/pop band the Beat was led by Paul Collins, who had previously played in power-pop band the Nerves, with Peter Case, who later joined the Plimsouls, and songwriter Jack Lee (whose 'Hanging On The Telephone' was a hit for Blondie). The Beat signed with Bill Graham's management company and secured a recording contract with Columbia Records. Their debut, *The Beat*, was popular on college radio but never broke nationally. Their second album and a 1983 EP for Passport Records, recorded with a new line-up, failed to garner much interest and the group broke up.

● ALBUMS: *The Beat* (Columbia 1979) ★★★, *The Kids Are The Same* (Passport 1982) ★★★, as Paul Collins' Beat *To Beat Or Not To Beat* mini-album (Passport 1983) ★★.

## BEAT FARMERS

The Beat Farmers were formed in 1983 in San Diego, California, USA, by drummer/vocalist 'Country'

Dick Montana (b. Dan McLain 1955, USA, d. 8 November 1995, Whistler, British Columbia, Canada). A veteran of previous San Diego bands the Crawdaddys and Penetrators, he was deeply immersed in the local underground music scene, having established the city's first alternative music record shop and formed the local Kinks Preservation Society. The Beat Farmers' intelligent hybrid of punk, pop and country always benefited from Montana's endearing sense of comedy, which often focused on agricultural issues – as did his annual fanzine, the *Beat Farmer's Almanac* (a parody of the Farmer's Almanac). The group's debut album came in 1985 with *Tales Of The New West*, a record that included appearances from Peter Case, Chip and Tony Kinman (Rank And File) and Sid Griffin (Long Ryders). Prior to *The Pursuit Of Happiness* Montana's primary partner was guitarist Buddy Blue (later a member of the Jacks), who was now replaced by Joey Harris. Their most eloquent album to date, alongside cover versions of Johnny Cash and Tom Waits, the material included typically rustic concerns such as 'Texas' and the sceptical 'God Is Here Tonight'. Harris emerged as a songwriter on the subsequent *Poor & Famous*, alongside vocalist/guitarist Jerry Raney, with Montana taking a back seat for the first time in the group's career (leading to claims that *Poor & Famous* fits unevenly with the rest of the Beat Farmers' discography). Although *Loud And Plowed* (a typically punning title) includes cover versions of the Kinks and George Jones, the highlight of the live album was its documentation of Montana's idiosyncratic, effervescent stage presence. In the 90s Montana suffered from thyroid cancer, which limited the Beat Farmers' activities until they signed to Dallas independent label Sector 2, for whom they completed two albums. Montana was also a member of the Pleasure Barons, an *ad hoc* roots band that also included Dave Alvin (Blasters), John Doe (X), Mojo Nixon and Harris (who also worked with his own band the Speedsters, releasing a self-titled album in 1983). Montana died while on stage with the Beat Farmers at the Longhorn Saloon in British Columbia, promoting the release of *Manifold*. A posthumous solo collection was released in 1996.

● ALBUMS: *Tales Of The New West* (Rhino 1985) ★★★, *Van Go* (Curb 1986) ★★★, *The Pursuit Of Happiness* (Curb 1987) ★★★, *Poor & Famous* (Curb 1989) ★★, *Loud And Plowed And ... LIVE!!* (Curb 1990) ★★, *Viking Lullabies* (Sector 2 1994) ★★, *Manifold* (Sector 2 1995) ★★.

Solo: Country Dick Montana *The Devil Lied To Me* (Sector 2 1996) ★★★.

## BEAT HAPPENING

Formed in Olympia, Washington, USA, the guitar band Beat Happening are led by Calvin Johnson. Two five-song tapes, *Beat Happening* and *Three Tea Breakfast*, introduced their primitive art, which echoed the jejune style of Jonathan Richman. The group's charming amateurism flourished on their debut album, *Beat Happening*, issued on their own K label and produced by Wipers guitarist Greg Sage. Their work drew parallels with Scottish act the

Pastels, and a 12-inch EP, *Crashing Through*, was released in Britain on 53rd & 3rd, a label co-founded by Stephen Pastel. Scottish acts Teenage Fanclub and Melody Dog reciprocally recorded for K. *Jamboree* revealed a more electric sound although the group's overall innocence remained intact. A collaborative EP with the Screaming Trees ensued, notable for the Cream-inspired 'Tales Of Brave Aphrodite', before the disappointing *Black Candy* appeared in 1989. Its inconsistent shortcomings were ironed out for *Dreamy* and *You Turn Me On*, which showed the band maturing without sacrificing their charm, but proved to be their final recording of the decade.

● ALBUMS: *Beat Happening* (K 1985) ★★★, *Jamboree* (K 1988) ★★★, *Black Candy* (K 1989) ★★, *Dreamy* (K 1991) ★★★, *You Turn Me On* (K 1992) ★★★.
● COMPILATIONS: *1983–85* (K 1990) ★★★.

## BEATMASTERS

This UK writing and production team consisted of Richard Walmsley (b. 28 September 1962), Amanda Glanfield and Paul Carter, and were initially most famous for their work with Betty Boo on tracks such as 'Hey DJ, I Can't Dance To The Music You're Playing'. Among their other UK chart coups were the Cookie Crew's breakthrough hit, 'Rok Da House' (number 5), Yazz's 'Stand Up For Your Love Rights' (number 2), and MC Merlin's 'Who's In The House' (number 8). They also worked on the P.P. Arnold comeback hit, 'Burn It Down'. This production line of pop hits won them few critical admirers, but their methodology had been honed when Glanfield and Carter spent time working on television commercial jingles for a production house (Brook Street's 'Get A Job', among them). Although they fell short of the commercial knack of Stock, Aitken and Waterman, they did manage notable hits under their own steam, such as 1988's 'Burn It Up'. A second album for Rhythm King Records saw guest appearances from JC001 and MC Precious. The group enjoyed something of a creative renaissance with 'Boulevard Of Broken Dreams' in 1991, built on Young-Holt Unlimited's 'Light My Fire', after lacklustre efforts including 'I Dunno What It Is'.

● ALBUMS: *Anywayawanna* (Rhythm King 1989) ★★, *Life And Soul* (Rhythm King 1991) ★★.

## BEAUSOLEIL

Widely considered to be the pre-eminent Cajun band of the 80s and 90s, BeauSoleil (the capitalized 'S' having been added in the 90s) have amassed a substantial discography that features some of the most exciting music extant within the traditional music realm. Rather than contemplate retirement, if anything, their output seems to have increased and intensified during recent years. They were almost entirely responsible for the Cajun music boom of the late 80s when their music was featured extensively in the movie *The Big Easy*.

Formed in 1975 by fiddler, vocalist and songwriter Michael Doucet (who had formerly piloted a Cajun group entitled Coteau which he revived in the mid-90s), the regular group additionally comprises brother David Doucet (guitar, vocals), Tommy Alesi (drums), Al Tharp (bass), Billy Ware (percussion)

and Jimmy Breaux (accordion). Other prominent members over the years include guitarist Bessyl Duhon (of Riff Raffs fame), while guest collaborators have included artists of the calibre of Richard Thompson, Keith Richards, the Grateful Dead and Augie Meyers. Despite their already vast recorded legacy, BeauSoleil remain predominantly a live attraction, the group having rarely left the road for any extended period during their 25 years together. *Bayou Cadillac* and *Cajun Conja*, a collaboration with Thompson that was nominated for a Grammy, are but two stand-out albums in a distinguished recording career. Despite their genre popularity, they have too often had to rely on the recommendations or lip service of others to gain media prominence. For example, they received a major boost in 1991 when Mary-Chapin Carpenter mentioned the group in the lyrics to her hit 'Down At The Twist And Shout'. The video for the award-winning song prominently featured BeauSoleil themselves. In 1997, the group joined Carpenter for a reprise of the song at the Super Bowl, in New Orleans. *Cajunization* in 1999 ventured into blues and rock territories.

● ALBUMS: *The Spirit Of Cajun Music* (Swallow 1977) ★★★, *Zydeco Gris Gris* (Rounder 1980) ★★★, *Parlez-Nous À Boire* (Arhoolie 1981) ★★★, *Bayou Boogie* (Rounder 1986) ★★★, *Allons À Lafayette* (Arhoolie 1986) ★★★, *Belizaire The Cajun* film soundtrack (Arhoolie 1986) ★★★, *Hot Chili Mama* (Arhoolie 1988) ★★★★, *Live! From The Left Coast* (Rounder 1989) ★★★, *Bayou Cadillac* (Rounder 1989) ★★★★, *Déja Vu* (Swallow 1990) ★★★, *Cajun Conja* (Rhino 1991) ★★★★, *L'Echo* (Rhino 1995) ★★★, *L'Amour Ou La Folie* (Rhino 1997) ★★★, *Cajunization* (Rhino 1999) ★★★★, *Looking Back Tomorrow: Beausoleil Live* (Rhino 2001) ★★★★.
● COMPILATIONS: *Their Swallow Recordings* (Ace 1992) ★★★★, *Vintage BeauSoleil* (Music Of The World 1995) ★★★★, *The Very Best Of BeauSoleil* (Nascente 1998) ★★★, *The Best Of The Crawfish Years* (Rounder 2001) ★★★★.

## BEF

The BEF (or British Electric Foundation) was a UK duo formed by ex-Human League members Martyn Ware (b. 19 May 1956, Sheffield, England) and Ian Craig Marsh (b. 11 November 1956, Sheffield, England). The first in the *Music Of Quality And Distinction* series arrived in 1982, featuring a series of guest artists covering songs of their own selection. Among them were Gary Glitter, Tina Turner, Billy MacKenzie (ex-Associates) and Sandie Shaw. The concept was innovative and achieved minor commercial success, but the project was abandoned when Ware and Marsh reunited with vocalist Glenn Gregory in their other incarnation, Heaven 17. When that group ended, a lucrative career in production ensued, notably with Terence Trent D'Arby and Tina Turner. It was only in 1991 that they managed to burrow through the legal contracts binding the second volume's artists, and repeated the formula. This time the album was more cohesive, consisting entirely of soul cover versions. It saw the return of Tina Turner, alongside Terence Trent D'Arby (his version of Bob Dylan's 'Its Alright Ma, I'm Only Bleeding' was approached as Otis Redding might have sung it), Chaka Khan, Billy Preston and Mavis Staples, among others. Most surprising of all was the appearance of Billy MacKenzie's version of Deniece Williams' 'Free'. Another unexpected facet of the recordings was the duo's use of traditional instruments and a backing band.

● ALBUMS: *Music Of Quality And Distinction Volume 1* (10 1982) ★★★, *Music Of Quality And Distinction Volume 2* (10 1991) ★★★.

## BELEW, ADRIAN

b. 23 December 1949, Kentucky, USA. Guitarist Adrian Belew has enjoyed a rich and varied career, with a number of left-field stars having used his skills. His chameleon-like style, which ranges from overwrought progressive rock to impish and self-deprecating pop, has helped make his contributions more anonymous than otherwise might have been the case. Having cut his teeth with Frank Zappa, Belew contributed admirably to Talking Heads' tensely orchestrated early 80s output (*Remain In Light*, *The Name Of This Band Is ...*, *Stop Making Sense*, etc.). His other clients included the Talking Heads spin-off group the Tom Tom Club. He also joined the re-formed King Crimson before Robert Fripp decided to resurrect his solo career, and spurred Belew to do the same. The funk-influenced style with which he had spiced *Remain In Light* resurfaced on his debut. Ill-focused and without a prevailing musical ethos to guide it (the album lurches from funk to rock), it failed to illustrate his proven skills to their best advantage. *Twang Bar King* concentrated on technique and, although occasionally draining, would have appealed to committed King Crimson fans. *Desire Caught By The Tail*, its title taken from Picasso's play, was a one-man home studio exercise, which prefaced his sojourn with the Bears. Recruiting with former friends the Raisins, Belew embarked on creating a set of originals that could accommodate his musical effects and guitar improvizations within an offbeat pop framework. The Bears' debut invoked comparisons with Squeeze and XTC, and for good reason. Far more accessible than previous offerings, Belew clearly had a knack for pop composition and performance that had previously been buried under layers of musicianship. Even the lyrics, though not yet quite in the stately Difford/Tilbrook or Moulding/Partridge sphere, were coming along well. The same was true of the second and final Bears album, which repeated this successful formula. However, despite their obvious qualities and rave reviews in the more discerning musical papers, sales were not great and the three remaining Bears formed the Psychodots. Belew carried over some of his new-found accessibility and pop instinct to his second attempt at a solo career, this time on Atlantic Records. It became clear that Belew was now composing songs on the piano, which altered the feel of subsequent recordings, even if they retained the occasional outbreak of fretboard abandon. *Young Lions* featured two songs written and sung by David Bowie, with whom Belew was about to tour as

guitarist and musical director. Bowie's 'Pretty Pink Rose' was certainly a highlight but so were some of Belew's own songs. 'Men In Helicopters' was a particularly affecting one, depicting rogue hunters gunning down rhinos. The cover versions of Buddy Holly's 'Heartbeat' and the Traveling Wilburys' 'Not Alone Anymore' filled out the set. *Inner Revolution*, meanwhile, saw a full-scale Beatles pastiche, with superbly observed singing and playing, before Belew regrouped with Fripp for a new King Crimson album, *Thrak*, in 1995. Belew's 90s releases have varied from two acoustic collections to the *Experimental Guitar Series* album.

● ALBUMS: *Lone Rhino* (Island 1982) ★★, *Twang Bar King* (Island 1983) ★★★, *Desire Caught By The Tail* (Island 1986) ★★★, with the Bears *The Bears* (Primitive Man 1987) ★★★, with the Bears *Rise And Shine* (Primitive Man 1988) ★★★, *Mr. Music Head* (Atlantic 1989) ★★★, *Young Lions* (Atlantic 1990) ★★, *Inner Revolution* (Atlantic 1992) ★★★★, *Here* (Caroline 1994) ★★★, *The Acoustic Adrian Belew* (Discipline 1995) ★★★, *The Experimental Guitar Series Volume 1: The Guitar As Orchestra* (Adrian Belew Presents 1996) ★★★, *Op Zop Too Wah* (Passenger 1996) ★★★, *Belewprints* (Discipline 1998) ★★★.

## BELLE STARS

This UK all-female group were formed in 1981, when Jennie McKeown (vocals) and Lesley Shone (b. 23 September 1958, London, England; bass, vocals) lined up with Stella Barker (guitar, vocals), Sarah-Jane Owen (guitar, vocals), Miranda Joyce (saxophone, vocals) Judy Parsons (drums) and Penny Leyton (keyboards, vocals). The band quickly generated a strong live following, playing select club dates in London at such established venues as Dingwalls, Hope & Anchor and the Marquee, and were signed to the legendary UK indie label Stiff Records, who released their debut single 'Hiawatha'/'Slick Trick', a UK indie chart hit. Constant touring consolidated the band's status, both in the UK and abroad. By this time, Claire Hirst (saxophone) had replaced Leyton in the band's line-up. Their UK chart breakthrough came in June 1982, with a raucous version of the Dixie Cups classic, 'Iko Iko'. Further chart hits with versions of Shirley Ellis' 'The Clapping Song' and 'Mockingbird' followed, and in January 1983 they scored their most successful singles hit with the memorable 'Sign Of The Times', a catchy song with a spoken word section reminiscent of the great girl group sound of the 60s. It made the UK Top 3 and charted heavily on the international scene.

A regime of further touring followed, opening for the likes of the Clash, the Beat and the Police, as well as headlining tours in their own right. Numerous UK television appearances helped score more chart success with singles such as 'Sweet Memory' and 'Indian Summer'. By late 1985, however, the original seven-piece line-up fragmented, leaving Shone, Joyce and Owen to carry on as the Belle Stars. The trio recorded an album for the ZTT label, but despite the US club chart success of the single 'World Domination' the album was never released.

The out of the blue US chart success of 'Iko Iko' in 1989 (the song formed part of the *Rain Man* soundtrack) saw McKeown and Shone flying the Belle Stars flag by promoting the hit in clubs and on television. The Belle Stars were an innovative combo for their time, an all-female band that played their own instruments.

● ALBUMS: *The Belle Stars* (Stiff 1983) ★★★.
● COMPILATIONS: *The Best Of The Belle Stars* (Stiff 1993) ★★★, *The Very Best Of The Belle Stars* (Repertoire 1994) ★★★.
● VIDEOS: *Live Signs, Live Times* (PolyGram Music Video 1989).

## BELOVED

Initially known in 1983 as the Journey Through and comprising Jon Marsh, Guy Gousden and Tim Havard, this UK outfit fell into place a year later when Cambridge University student and ex postman Steve Waddington joined on guitar. It was no straightforward initiation ceremony. Marsh had placed an advert in the music press that ran thus: 'I am Jon Marsh, founder member of the Beloved. Should you too wish to do something gorgeous, meet me in exactly three years' time at exactly 11 am in Diana's Diner, or site thereof, Covent Garden, London, WC2'. Tentative stabs at heavy psychedelia evolved into a more pop-orientated formula by the mid-80s, with the Beloved's dark, danceable sounds often being compared to New Order and garnering attention throughout Europe. Marsh became a contestant on television quiz show *Countdown* in 1987, featuring on nine programmes before being knocked out in the semi-finals. It was not until 1988, however, that the Beloved started living up to their name; Waddington and Marsh, heavily influenced by the nascent rave scene in London at that time, split from Gousden and Harvard and started forging their own path.

Unshackled from the confines of a four-cornered set-up, the revitalized duo dived into the deep end of the exploding dance music movement, subsequently breaking into commercial waters with the ambient textures of 'Sun Rising' (a future chill-out classic). The *Happiness* album, backed by Marsh and Waddington's enthusiastic chatter concerning the virtues of flotation tanks and hallucinogenic substances, perfectly embodied the tripped-out vibe of the times and sealed the Beloved's fashionable success in worldwide territories. By 1993's *Conscience*, Marsh had left his former partner Waddington (who joined Steve Hillage's System 7), using his wife Helena as his new creative foil. The resultant album was more whimsical and understated than previous affairs, with a pop rather than a club feel. Their third album relied too heavily on electronic gimmickry, detracting attention from individual songs. Returning in 1996 with *X*, the duo's sound showed no signs of progression. They left East West Records shortly afterwards, concentrating on remixing and DJing duties.

● ALBUMS: *Happiness* (Atlantic 1990) ★★★, *Blissed Out* remix of *Happiness* (East West 1990) ★★★, *Conscience* (East West 1993) ★★★, *X* (East West 1996) ★★.

## BENATAR, PAT

b. Patricia Andrzejewski, 10 January 1953, Brooklyn, New York City, New York, USA. After training as an opera singer, Pat Benatar became a major hitmaker in the early 80s, adept at both mainstream rock and powerful ballads, often focusing on personal relationships and sexual politics. She married Dennis Benatar after graduating from high school and relocated to Virginia. By the 70s she had returned to New York, where she was discovered by Rick Newman in 1979 at the latter's Catch A Rising Star club. With Newman as manager, she signed to Chrysalis Records that year and released her debut album, *In The Heat Of The Night*, produced by Mike Chapman, which became a substantial hit and spawned three US chart singles. Benatar (who retained the name after divorcing) released her second album, *Crimes Of Passion*, in 1980. This collection, which later won a Grammy for Best Female Rock Vocal Performance, rose to number 2 in the US charts, while the hard-rocking 'Hit Me With Your Best Shot' became her first *Billboard* Top 10 single. *Precious Time* was released in 1981 and this time reached number 1 in the USA. Although no Top 10 singles resulted, Benatar won another Grammy for 'Fire And Ice'.

In 1982 Benatar married producer Neil Giraldo, who played guitar in her band and wrote most of her material, and released *Get Nervous*, which reached US number 4. The following year, a live album, also featuring two new studio tracks, was released. One of these tracks, 'Love Is A Battlefield', reached number 5 in the USA, the same position attained in 1984 by 'We Belong', from the next album, *Tropico*. The former single eventually became a UK Top 20 hit in 1985, reissued in the wake of the British success of 'We Belong', after initially stalling a year earlier at number 49. Also in 1985, 'Invincible', from the movie *Legend Of Billie Jean*, was Benatar's last US Top 10 single of the decade. An album, *Seven The Hard Way*, followed later that year but signalled a decline in Benatar's popularity. Musical inactivity marked the next couple of years as Benatar devoted her attentions to motherhood. A compilation album, *Best Shots*, was released in 1987. Although moderately successful in her homeland, it became a major hit in Europe, putting her into the UK Top 10 album chart for the first time. The blues-influenced *True Love* was a commercial and critical disaster, and subsequent albums have seen Benatar struggling to regain lost sales.

● ALBUMS: *In The Heat Of The Night* (Chrysalis 1979) ★★★, *Crimes Of Passion* (Chrysalis 1980) ★★★, *Precious Time* (Chrysalis 1981) ★★, *Get Nervous* (Chrysalis 1982) ★★, *Live From Earth* (Chrysalis 1983) ★★, *Tropico* (Chrysalis 1984) ★★, *Seven The Hard Way* (Chrysalis 1985) ★★★, *Wide Awake In Dreamland* (Chrysalis 1988) ★★, *True Love* (Chrysalis 1991) ★★, *Gravity's Rainbow* (Chrysalis 1993) ★★, *Innamorata* (CMC 1997) ★★★, *8-15-80* (CMC 1998) ★★★, with Neil Giraldo *Live* (Gold Circle 2002) ★★★.
● COMPILATIONS: *Best Shots* (Chrysalis 1987) ★★★, *The Very Best Of Pat Benatar: All Fired Up* (Chrysalis 1994) ★★★, *16 Classic Performances* (EMI

1996) ★★★, *Synchronistic Wanderings: Recorded Anthology 1979 To 1999* 3-CD set (Chrysalis 1999) ★★★, *The Very Best Of Pat Benatar* (Chrysalis 2000) ★★★.
● VIDEOS: *Hit Videos* (RCA/Columbia 1988), *Best Shots* (Chrysalis Music Video 1988), *Benatar* (RCA/Columbia 1988).
● FURTHER READING: *Benatar*, Doug Magee.
● FILMS: *Union City* (1980).

## BENITEZ, JELLYBEAN
(see Jellybean)

## BENOIT, DAVID
b. Bakersfield, California, USA. Benoit gained an early appreciation of music from his parents, who played guitar and piano. He began piano lessons at the age of 14, by which time he was steeped in the influences of both Ramsey Lewis and Henry Mancini. Following his musical studies at El Camino College, he met with composer Richard Baskin and played piano on the movie soundtrack to *Nashville* in 1975. He gained valuable experience playing in clubs and bars and became Gloria Lynne's pianist. He toured with the Duke Ellington Orchestra in 1976 as Lainie Kazan's arranger and accompanist.
Benoit's debut recording was with drummer Alphonse Mouzon and it was during these sessions he met with Dave Grusin, who became an important figure in his future career. He recorded a number of albums on the small AVI label that demonstrated his fluid and skilful playing, although these recordings suffered from an overall blandness that resulted in disappointing sales.
*This Side Up* in 1985 changed everything. It contained the stunning 'Beach Trails', put Benoit in the US jazz bestseller lists and led to a call from Larry Rosen, Dave Grusin's partner at GRP Records. Benoit has now become one of their leading artists, with a series of bestselling albums of easy, yet beautifully constructed, music, forging a similar path to that of Grusin and bridging the gap between jazz and pop. Each album contains a balanced mixture but it is Benoit's delicate rippling style on some of the quieter numbers that best demonstrates his dexterity. 'Kei's Song' from *Freedom At Midnight* and 'The Key To You' from *Every Step Of The Way* are fine compositions. His pure acoustic style was highlighted on *Waiting For Spring*, a concept album featuring Emily Remler and Peter Erskine. Imaginative readings of 'Cast Your Fate To the Wind', 'Secret Love' and 'My Romance' were mixed with Benoit originals. He maintained this high standard with *Inner Motion* in 1990, which opened with the Grusin-styled 'M.W.A.' and peaked with the sublime tribute to the late Remler, '6-String Poet'. Benoit's *Letter To Evan* was another acoustic excursion, enlisting the talent of Larry Carlton. The collaboration with guitarist Russ Freeman in 1993 was a whole-hearted success and stayed in the *Billboard* jazz chart for many weeks. That same year, Benoit attempted another theme album, this time echoing his remembrances of the 60s, as good as *Shaken Not Stirred* was, it sounded just like another David Benoit album, clean, accessible and easy.

Benoit is now an established artist, having refined his brand of music to perfection. In his own words, 'I didn't want instant stardom like those artists whose fall is as quick as their rise.' Jazz purists may throw their arms up in horror but until another genre is invented, jazz remains the closest category for his music.
● ALBUMS: *Heavier Than Yesterday* (AVI 1977) ★★★, *Can You Imagine* (AVI 1980) ★★★, *Stages* (AVI 1983) ★★, *Digits* (AVI 1984) ★★, *This Side Up* (AVI 1985) ★★★★, *Christmastime* (AVI 1985) ★★, *Freedom At Midnight* (GRP 1987) ★★★, *Every Step Of The Way* (GRP 1988) ★★★★, *Urban Daydreams* (GRP 1989) ★★★, *Waiting For Spring* (GRP 1989) ★★★★, *Inner Motion* (GRP 1990) ★★★, *Shadows* (GRP 1991) ★★★, *Letter To Evan* (GRP 1992) ★★★, with Russ Freeman *The Benoit/Freeman Project* (GRP 1993) ★★★, *Shaken Not Stirred* (GRP 1994) ★★★, *Remembering Christmas* (GRP 1996) ★★, *American Landscape* (GRP 1997) ★★★, *Professional Dreamer* (GRP 1999) ★★★, *Here's To You Charlie Brown: 50 Great Years* (GRP 2000) ★★★★, *Fuzzy Logic* (GRP 2002) ★★★.
● COMPILATIONS: *The Best Of David Benoit 1987-1995* (GRP 1995) ★★★★.

## BENSON, GEORGE
b. 22 March 1943, Pittsburgh, Pennsylvania, USA. This guitarist and singer successfully planted his feet in both the modern jazz and easy-listening pop camps in the mid-70s when jazz-pop as well as jazz-rock became a most lucrative proposition. Before a move to New York in 1963, he had played in various R&B outfits local to Pittsburgh, including the Altairs and the Four Counts, and recorded a single, 'It Should Have Been Me', in 1954. By 1965, Benson was an established jazz guitarist, having worked with Brother Jack McDuff, Herbie Hancock – and, crucially, Wes Montgomery, whose repertoire was drawn largely from pop, light classical and other non-jazz sources. When Montgomery died in 1969, critics predicted that Benson – contracted to Columbia Records in 1966 – would be his stylistic successor. Further testament to Benson's prestige was the presence of Hancock, Earl Klugh, Miles Davis, Joe Farrell and other jazz musicians on his early albums. Four of these were produced by Creed Taylor, who signed Benson to his own CTI label in 1971. Benson was impressing audiences in concert with extrapolations of songs such as 'California Dreamin'', 'Come Together' and, digging deeper into mainstream pop, 'Cry Me A River' and 'Unchained Melody'. From *Beyond The Blue Horizon*, an arrangement of Jefferson Airplane's 'White Rabbit' was a turntable hit, and chart success seemed inevitable – especially as he was now recording a majority of vocal items. After *Bad Benson* reached the US album lists and, via disco floors, the title song of *Supership* cracked European charts, he was well placed to negotiate a favourable contract with Warner Brothers Records, who immediately reaped a Grammy-winning harvest with 1976's *Breezin'* (and its memorable 'This Masquerade'). As a result, companies with rights to the prolific Benson's earlier product cashed in, with reissues such as *The Other*

*Side Of Abbey Road*, a track-for-track interpretation of the entire Beatles album.

Profit from film themes such as 'The Greatest Love Of All' (from the Muhammed Ali biopic *The Greatest*), the million-selling *Give Me The Night* and the television-advertised *The Love Songs* have allowed him to indulge artistic whims, including a nod to his jazz roots via 1987's excellent *Collaboration* with Earl Klugh, and a more commercial merger with Aretha Franklin on 'Love All The Hurt Away'. Moreover, a fondness for pop standards has also proved marketable, epitomized by revivals of 'On Broadway' – a US Top 10 single from 1978's *Weekend In LA* – and Bobby Darin's 'Beyond The Sea' ('La Mer'). Like Darin, Benson also found success with Nat 'King' Cole's 'Nature Boy' (a single from *In Flight*) – and a lesser hit with Cole's 'Tenderly' in 1989, another balance of sophistication, hard-bought professionalism and intelligent response to chart climate. In 1990, he staged a full-length collaboration with the Count Basie Orchestra, accompanied by a sell-out UK tour. In the mid-90s Benson moved to the GRP Records label, debuting with the excellent *That's Right*. The follow-up *Standing Together* was a disappointing contemporary R&B collection, and Benson wisely returned to instrumentals on *Absolute Benson*. Benson is one of a handful of artists who have achieved major critical and commercial success in different genres, and this pedigree makes him one of the most respected performers of the past 30 years.

● ALBUMS: with the Brother Jack McDuff Quartet *The New Boss Guitar Of George Benson* (Prestige 1964) ★★★★, *It's Uptown* (Columbia 1965) ★★★★, *Most Exciting* (Columbia 1966) ★★★, *Benson Burner* (Columbia 1966) ★★★★, *The George Benson Cook Book* (Columbia 1967) ★★★, *Giblet Gravy* (Verve 1968) ★★★, *Goodies* (Verve 1969) ★★★, *Shape Of Things To Come* (A&M 1969) ★★, *Tell It Like It Is* (A&M 1969) ★★, *The Other Side Of Abbey Road* (A&M 1970) ★★★, *Beyond The Blue Horizon* (CTI 1971) ★★★, *White Rabbit* (CTI 1972) ★★, *Body Talk* (CTI 1973) ★★★, *Bad Benson* (CTI 1974) ★★, *Supership* (CTI 1975) ★★★, *Breezin'* (Warners 1976) ★★★★, *Good King Bad* (CTI 1976) ★★★, with Joe Farrell *Benson And Farrell* (CTI 1976) ★★★, *George Benson In Concert: Carnegie Hall* (CTI 1977) ★★, *In Flight* (Warners 1977) ★★★★, *George Benson And Jack McDuff* (Prestige 1977) ★★★, *Weekend In LA* (Warners 1978) ★★, *Living Inside Your Love* (Warners 1979) ★★, *Give Me The Night* (Warners 1980) ★★★★, *Blue Benson* (Polydor 1983) ★★★, *In Your Eyes* (Warners 1983) ★★★, *Stormy Weather* (Columbia 1984) ★★, *20/20* (Warners 1985) ★★, *The Electrifying George Benson* (Affinity 1985) ★★★, *In Concert* (Premier 1985) ★★, *Love Walked In* (Platinum 1985) ★★, *While The City Sleeps* (Warners 1986) ★★, with Earl Klugh *Collaboration* (Warners 1987) ★★★★, *Love For Sale* (Masters 1988) ★★★, *Twice The Love* (Warners 1988) ★★, *Detroit's George Benson* (Parkwood 1988) ★★★, *Tenderly* (Warners 1989) ★★, with the Count Basie Orchestra *Big Boss Band* (Warners 1990) ★★★, *Lil' Darlin'* (Thunderbolt 1990) ★★★, *Live At The Casa Caribe Volumes 1–3* (Jazz View 1992) ★★★, *Love Remembers* (Warners 1993) ★★, *That's Right* (GRP 1996) ★★★, *Standing Together* (GRP 1998) ★★, *Absolute Benson* (GRP 2000) ★★★.

● COMPILATIONS: *The George Benson Collection* (Warners 1981) ★★★★, *Early Years* (CTI 1982) ★★★, *Best Of George Benson* (A&M 1982) ★★★, *The Wonderful Years* (Proton 1984) ★★★, *The Love Songs* (K-Tel 1985) ★★★★, *The Silver Collection* (Verve 1985) ★★★, *Compact Jazz* (Verve 1988) ★★★, *Best Of* (Epic 1992) ★★, *Guitar Giants* (Pickwick 1992) ★★★, *The Best Of George Benson* (Warners 1995) ★★★, *Essentials: The Very Best Of George Benson* (Jive 1998) ★★★, *George Benson Anthology* 2-CD box set (Rhino/Warner Archives 2000) ★★★★.

## BERLIN

This US band from Los Angeles was formed in 1977 as a new wave/electro pop group. The original band included main songwriter John Crawford (b. 17 January 1960; bass, synthesizer, ex-Videos), Terri Nunn (b. 26 June 1961; vocals), Jo Julian (b. 22 January 1948; synthesizer), Chris Velasco (b. Germany; guitar, vocals) and Dan Van Patten (drums, ex-Barbies). This line-up released a single for Renegade Records before Nunn left to pursue her acting career. She was briefly replaced by Toni Childs before Virginia Macolino took over the lead vocalist slot. This line-up released an album on their own Zone H Records label before signing to I.R.S. Records in the USA. They only managed one single for I.R.S. before breaking up in 1981.

They re-formed a few months later, but a series of personnel changes saw only Crawford and Nunn, who had returned to the band, remaining from the original line-up. David Diamond (guitar, synthesizer, vocals), Ric Olsen (b. 20 August 1956; guitar), Matt Reid (b. 15 April 1958; keyboards) and Rod Learned (drums) joined the duo in the new look Berlin. They completed recording 1982's mini-album *Pleasure Victim* (not released in the UK), followed by the full long-player *Love Life*. They gained a US Top 30 hit in April 1984 with 'No More Words', before dropping down to a three-piece of Crawford, Nunn and Rob Brill (b. 21 January 1956; drums) the following year. In 1986 they had a number 1 hit on both sides of the Atlantic with a song with which they became almost exclusively associated, 'Take My Breath Away'. It was the theme song to the highly lucrative movie *Top Gun*, and had been produced and co-written by veteran producer Giorgio Moroder. Follow-up singles fared less well, and the band broke up for a second time in the late 80s.

'Take My Breath Away' has proved to be a perennial favourite, re-entering the charts in 1988 and going into the UK Top 3 on reissue in 1990 as a result of its use in television car commercials. Nunn released a solo album, *Moment Of Truth*, in 1991, and has continued to lead Berlin on numerous nostalgia tours. She assembled a new line-up to record Berlin's first new studio album in over 15 years, *Voyeur*.

● ALBUMS: *Information* (Zone H 1980) ★★, *Pleasure Victim* mini-album (Geffen 1982) ★★, *Love Life* (Geffen 1984) ★★★, *Count Three And Pray* (Geffen 1986) ★★, *Live: Sacred And Profane* (Time Bomb 2000) ★★, *Voyeur* (Beyond 2002) ★★.

● COMPILATIONS: *Best Of Berlin 1979–1988* (Geffen 1988) ★★★, *Greatest Hits Remixed* (Cleopatra 2000) ★★.

## BERLINE, BYRON
b. 6 July 1944, Caldwell, Kansas, USA. This masterful newgrass fiddle player has been a much sought-after session man in addition to his spells with a number of prestigious country rock groups, notably the Dillards, Dillard And Clark Expedition, the Flying Burrito Brothers and his own highly respected Country Gazette and Sundance. His father Luke was also a bluegrass fiddler and Byron started playing at the age of five. Later on he studied music at the University Of Oklahoma and it was there that he formed his first band. He joined the Dillards after a spell with Bill Monroe and followed Doug Dillard when he teamed up with Gene Clark in 1968. Over the years he has appeared on albums by the Rolling Stones ('Honky Tonk Woman', and 'Country Honk' from *Let It Bleed*), Dan Baird and Vince Gill, in addition to his ongoing work with Dan Crary and John Hickman as BCH, and with Crary, Hickman and John Moore (mandolin, vocals) as California. Berline owns and operates the Double Stop Fiddle Shop and Concert Hall in Guthrie, Oklahoma. The latter hosts the annual International Bluegrass Festival.
● ALBUMS: *Dad's Favorites* (Rounder 1977) ★★★, *Live At McCabes* (Takoma 1978) ★★★, *Byron Berline & The L.A. Fiddle Band* (Sugar Hill 1980) ★★★, *Outrageous* (Flying Fish 1980) ★★★, with Dan Crary, John Hickman *Berline-Crary-Hickman* (Sugar Hill 1981) ★★★, *Night Run* (Sugar Hill 1984) ★★★, with Crary, Hickman *B-C-H* (Sugar Hill 1986) ★★★★, with Hickman *Double Trouble* (Sugar Hill 1986) ★★★, with Crary, Hickman, Steve Spurgin *Now They Are Four ...* (Sugar Hill 1989) ★★★, with California *Traveler* (Sugar Hill 1992) ★★★, *Fiddle & A Song* (Sugar Hill 1995) ★★★★, *Jumpin' The Strings* (Sugar Hill 1996) ★★★, *Live At The Music Hall* (Double Stop 1997) ★★★, *One-Eyed Jack* (Double Stop 1999) ★★★.
● COMPILATIONS: with Dan Crary, John Hickman *Chambergrass: A Decade Of Tunes From The Edges Of Bluegrass* (Sugar Hill 2002) ★★★★.

## BERRY, HEIDI
An American singer and songwriter, and former painter, who has lived in London since childhood, Berry saw the first of her compositions released on Creation Records in 1987 on the mini-album *Firefly*. Numerous members of the Creation fold were used as backing musicians, notably Martin Duffy (Felt) on keyboards. Two years later the line-up also included her brother Christopher on acoustic guitar and Rocky Holman on piano and synthesizer. However, after appearing on This Mortal Coil's *Blood*, singing a version of Rodney Crowell's 'Til I Gain Control Again', she switched to 4AD Records. The nucleus of Christopher Berry and Holman was retained for her second full-length album *Love*, which proved to be her most accomplished and satisfying set to date. The album contained contributions from, among others, Terry Bickers and Laurence O'Keefe of

Levitation and veteran saxophonist Lol Coxhill. The original compositions were augmented by a cover version of Bob Mould's 'Up In The Air'. *Heidi Berry* included the artist's first ever single, 'The Moon And The Sun', and saw Bickers return to provide guitar assistance. After one final album for 4AD, Berry left the label to collaborate with Patrick Fitzgerald (ex-Kitchens Of Distinction) as Lost Girls.
● ALBUMS: *Firefly* mini-album (Creation 1987) ★★, *Below The Waves* (Creation/Rockville 1989) ★★★, *Love* (4AD 1991) ★★★, *Heidi Berry* (4AD 1993) ★★★, *Miracle* (4AD 1996) ★★★.
● COMPILATIONS: *Pomegranate: An Anthology* (4AD 2001) ★★★.

## BERRY, NICK
b. 1961, Woodford, Essex, England. Berry attended the Sylvia Young Theatre School in north London. Minor appearances in movies, television and West End plays led to a leading role in the BBC 1 soap opera *EastEnders* as 'Wicksy', a youth with aspirations to become a musical entertainer. Fiction became truth when 'Every Loser Wins', a song Simon Wicks sang in one episode, was issued as a single. Co-written by Simon May and produced by Mike Batt, it reached the top of the UK charts in 1986, necessitating a hastily recorded Berry album and a round of personal appearances in discos and nightclubs. Nevertheless, his duty as a pop star done, he returned to full-time acting. His voice was heard on the Buddy Holly title theme of the 1992 television series, *Heartbeat*, in which he played a police constable, and once again Berry returned to the UK charts.
● ALBUMS: *Nick Berry* i (BBC 1986) ★★, *Nick Berry* ii (Columbia 1992) ★★.

## BEVIS FROND
Often mistakenly believed to be a group, the Bevis Frond is actually just one person: Nick Saloman. Influenced by Jimi Hendrix and Cream, Saloman formed the Bevis Frond Museum while still at school. The group disbanded and after a period playing acoustic sets in the Walthamstow area of London he formed the Von Trap Family, later known as Room 13. In 1982 Saloman was seriously hurt in a motorcycle accident. He used the money he received in compensation to record *Miasma* in his bedroom and it quickly became a collector's item. *Pulsebeat* magazine described the tracks as being 'like fireworks for inside your head'. Saloman then released *Inner Marshland* and *Triptych* on his own Woronzow Records, and his long psychedelic guitar workouts mapped out a style that was shamelessly archaic but nevertheless appealing. London's Reckless Records re-released his first three albums and in 1988 provided *Bevis Through The Looking Glass* and, a year later, *The Auntie Winnie Album*. Saloman's brand of raw, imaginative blues guitar drew many converts and *Any Gas Faster*, recorded in better-equipped studios, was widely lauded. *Rolling Stone* magazine said of it: 'With so much modern psychedelia cheapened by cliché or nostalgia, the Bevis Frond is the actual out-there item.' *Magic Eye* was an inconsistent collaboration with ex-Pink

Fairies drummer Twink. In 1991 Saloman released a double set, *New River Head*, on his own Woronzow Records, distributed in the USA by Reckless. He followed it up with 1992's *It Just Is*, again a double, and *Beatroots*, recorded under the pseudonym Fred Bison Five. As a tireless believer in the need for communication, he set up an underground magazine, *Ptolemaic Terrascope*, in the late 80s and, like Saloman's music, it is a loyal correspondent of the UK psychedelic scene. Still a prolific songwriter, Saloman's recent albums have included *Superseeder*, an appealing blend of electric and acoustic styles, the 26-track *North Circular*, and *Valedictory Songs*, the final Bevis Frond album for the immediate future.

● ALBUMS: *Miasma* (Woronzow 1987) ★★★, *Inner Marshland* (Woronzow 1987) ★★★, *Triptych* (Woronzow 1987) ★★★, *Bevis Through The Looking Glass* (Reckless 1988) ★★★, *Acid Jam* (Woronzow 1988) ★★★, *The Auntie Winnie Album* (Reckless 1989) ★★★, *Any Gas Faster* (Woronzow 1990) ★★★★, as Bevis and Twink *Magic Eye* (Woronzow 1990) ★★★, *New River Head* (Woronzow 1991) ★★★★, *London Stone* (Woronzow 1992) ★★★, *It Just Is* (Woronzow 1993) ★★★, *Sprawl* (Woronzow 1994) ★★★, *Superseeder* (Woronzow 1995) ★★★, *North Circular* (Woronzow 1997) ★★★, *Live* (Woronzow 2000) ★★★, *Valedictory Songs* (Woronzow 2000) ★★★.

● COMPILATIONS: *A Gathering Of Fronds* (Woronzow 1992) ★★★.

## BHUNDU BOYS

The Bhundu Boys were formed in Harare, Zimbabwe, in 1980 by Biggie Tembo (b. Rodwell Marasha, 30 September 1958, Chinhoye, Mashonaland, d. 30 July 1995, London, England; guitar, vocals, leader), Rise Kagona (guitar), David Mankaba (d. 1991; bass guitar), Shakie Kangwena (b. 16 August 1956, Salisbury, Rhodesia, d. 5 December 1993, Harare, Zimbabwe; keyboards) and Kenny Chitsvatsa (drums), most of whom had previously played together in another Harare outfit, the Wild Dragons. Although the Bhundu Boys achieved prominence both at home in Zimbabwe and overseas in Britain with their own idiosyncratic jit style of dance music, their rise in both territories owed much to the work of bandleader and vocalist Thomas Mapfumo. He was the first modern Zimbabwean performer to make traditionally rooted music acceptable and stylish in a social climate where previously all things European had been deemed preferable to anything African (the result of a national cultural inferiority complex engendered by decades of white colonial rule). The band itself was a product of Zimbabwe's late 70s war of liberation, the name Bhundu ('bush') being chosen to commemorate the freedom fighters who fought against the white settlers in rural areas.

As the Wild Dragons, a back-up group for vocalist Son Takura, the quintet had already forged a reputation as respectful modernizers of traditional Zimbabwean folk music, and after 1980 – in the cultural renaissance that followed independence – they replaced any lingering vestiges of rock and soul for a wholly Zimbabwean approach. However,

while Mapfumo's style was based on traditional, rural Shona mbira ('thumb piano') music, the Bhundu Boys approach, which did from time to time embrace the mbira, was altogehue more eclectic and urban, drawing on the traditions of all the tribal peoples in Zimbabwe. Their early style also drew freely on the mbaqanga township music of neighbouring South Africa. Jit found almost immediate acceptance amongst the youth of post-independence Zimbabwe and between 1981 and 1984 the band had four number 1 hits – 'Baba Munini Francis', 'Wenhamo Haaneti', 'Hatisitose' and 'Ndimboze'. Three albums, *The Bhundu Boys*, *Hupenyu Hwenasi* and *Shabini*, proved equally popular.

In 1986, the band decided to make a sustained onslaught on the British music scene and moved to the country in readiness for a long stay. Basing themselves first in Scotland and then in London, they spent most of the following two years on a near-permanent tour, establishing a reputation as one of the most exciting bands in the country (BBC Radio 1 disc jockey John Peel described them as playing 'the most perfect music I've ever heard'). The incessant touring boosted British sales of *Shabini* (released in the UK in 1986 on the independent label Discafrique), which sold some 10,000 copies in the first six months of its release and reached number 1 in the *Melody Maker* independent charts. Early in 1987, the band signed to major label WEA Records, released a second Discafrique album, *Tsvimbodzemoto*, and supported Madonna at London's Wembley Stadium. However, while the sales of *Shabini* had made the Bhundus stars of the independent scene, sales of 10,000 copies were insignificant to a major international label and, as WEA were unable to lift them beyond this plateau, they, as a consequence, lost interest in the band, dropping them from the roster early in 1990. A few months later, Biggie Tembo was asked to leave, before several members succumbed to AIDS. The Bhundu Boys re-emerged with the excellent live set, *Absolute Jit!*, recorded in Zimbabwe, which saw them return to the Discafrique label. Nevertheless, their crushing late 80s run-in with the record industry had shrunk the band's fanbase and, when Tembo was discovered hanged in 1995, it served as a chilling epitaph to the original line-up of this once pioneering group. By 2001 the name resurfaced together with a compilation album and news of new recordings in the pipeline.

● ALBUMS: *The Bhundu Boys* (1981) ★★★, *Hupenyu Hwenasi* (1984) ★★★, *Shabini* (Discafrique 1985) ★★★★, *Tsvimbodzemoto* (Discafrique 1987) ★★★★, *True Jit* (WEA 1987) ★★★★, *Pamberi* (WEA 1989) ★★★, *Absolute Jit! Live At King Tut's Wah Wah Hut* (Discafrique 1990) ★★★, *Friends On The Road* (Cooking Vinyl 1993) ★★★, *Muchiyedza (Out Of The Dark)* (Cooking Vinyl 1997) ★★★.

● COMPILATIONS: *The Shed Sessions* (Sadza 2001) ★★★.

## BIBLE

This acclaimed band was formed in Cambridge, England. Their 1986 debut single, 'Gracelands', was a classy pop song, as was its follow-up, 'Mahalia' (a tribute to the gospel singer Mahalia Jackson). The band comprised Boo Hewerdine (vocals, guitar), Tony Shepherd (keyboards, percussion), Dave Larcombe (drums) and Leroy Lendor (bass), and by the time Chrysalis Records had signed them, they already had an album's worth of well-crafted songs in *Walking The Ghost Back Home*. Chrysalis duly reissued 'Gracelands' in early 1987, but it eluded the charts, and the band spent the year recording a second album. Released in January 1988, *Eureka* shared the melodic quality of the Bible's debut, but neither of the singles, 'Crystal Palace' in April and 'Honey Be Good' in September, made much impression. Desperate for success, they tried revamping 'Gracelands' and, when that failed, reissued 'Honey Be Good'. A compilation release in late 1989, *The Best Of The Bible*, signalled the end of the band's association with their label. Hewerdine, who had previously played in short-lived bands such as the Great Divide, subsequently embarked on a solo career. The band re-formed in 1993, and were signed to Warner Brothers Records subsidiary Blanco y Negro. An EP of new songs was released, but with Hewerdine contributing songs to Eddi Reader's debut album, and Tony Shepherd and Dave Larcombe working with Oasis, the band split again in December 1994. Tracks on which they had been working eventually surfaced on Hewerdine's second solo set, *Baptism Hospital*, and *Dodo*.

● ALBUMS: *Walking The Ghost Back Home* (Backs 1986) ★★★★, *Eureka* (Ensign/Chrysalis 1988) ★★★, *Dodo* 1993 recording (Haven 2000) ★★★.

● COMPILATIONS: *The Best Of The Bible* (Ensign/Chrysalis 1989) ★★★★, *Random Acts Of Kindness* (Haven 1995) ★★★★.

## BIFF BANG POW!

Biff Bang Pow! – a name derived from a song by 60s cult group the Creation – is an outlet for the musical aspirations of Glaswegian Alan McGee, the motivating force behind Creation Records, one of the UK's most inventive independent outlets. The group also featured business partner Dick Green (guitar) and, despite its part-time nature, completed several excellent releases, including the neo-psychedelic singles '50 Years Of Fun' (1984) and 'Love's Going Out Of Fashion' (1986). *Pass The Paintbrush Honey* and *The Girl Who Runs The Beat Hotel* offered idiosyncratic, and often contrasting, views of pop, while *Love Is Forever* showed the influence of Neil Young, notably on 'Ice Cream Machine'. In the 90s, however, with his record label achieving major success with the likes of Oasis and the Boo Radleys, McGee has found less time for his own band.

● ALBUMS: *Pass The Paintbrush Honey* (Creation 1985) ★★★, *The Girl Who Runs The Beat Hotel* (Creation 1987) ★★★, *Oblivion* (Creation 1987) ★★★, *Love Is Forever* (Creation 1988) ★★★, *Songs For The Sad Eyed Girl* (Creation 1990) ★★★, *Me* (Creation 1991) ★★★.

● COMPILATIONS: *The Acid House Album* (Creation 1989) ★★★, *L'amour, Demure, Stenhousemuir: A Compilation 1984–1991* (Creation 1991) ★★★★.

## BIG AUDIO DYNAMITE

After Clash guitarist Mick Jones (b. 26 June 1955, Brixton, London, England) was fired from that band in 1984, he formed an ill-fated outfit with former Clash drummer Topper Headon, before linking up with DJ and film-maker Don Letts to form Big Audio Dynamite (or B.A.D., as they were commonly known). With Jones on guitar and Letts on keyboards and effects, they completed the line-up with Dan Donovan (keyboards), son of famed photographer Terence Donovan, Leo Williams (bass) and Greg Roberts (drums). *This Is Big Audio Dynamite* was a natural progression from tracks such as 'Inoculated City' on *Combat Rock*, the last Clash album to feature Jones, with cut-up funk spiced with sampled sounds (the first time this technique had been used). The follow-up album included writing contributions from the former Clash vocalist Joe Strummer, who happened across the band while they were recording in Soho, London. They continued to record but faced their first crisis in 1988 when Jones came close to death from pneumonia, which caused a delay in the release of *Megatop Phoenix*. This in turn led to the break-up of the band and by 1990 and *Kool-Aid*, Jones had assembled a completely new line-up (B.A.D. II) featuring Nick Hawkins (guitar), Gary Stonadge (bass) and Chris Kavanagh (drums, ex-Sigue Sigue Sputnik). DJ Zonka was drafted in to provide live 'scratching' and mixing. Jones also contributed to the *Flashback* soundtrack and 'Good Morning Britain' single from Aztec Camera.

Meanwhile, he attracted disdain, not least from former colleagues, by insisting on putting a B.A.D. track on the b-side to the posthumous Clash number 1, 'Should I Stay Or Should I Go'. Donovan proved to be no stranger to controversy either, having married and separated from the actress and Eighth Wonder vocalist Patsy Kensit. He went on to join the re-formed Sigue Sigue Sputnik, while his former employers were being hailed as a great influence on the new wave of 90s British dance-pop (EMF, Jesus Jones). Jones regrouped in 1995 for the accomplished *F-Punk*, which mixed imported west coast hip-hop beats with jungle textures and rock 'n' roll. Although the commercial fortunes of Big Audio Dynamite (as they were now, again, named) were in free-fall following Columbia Records' decision to drop his band, *F-Punk* reaffirmed Jones' status as an intelligent artist working on the periphery of the rock scene. Radioactive Records elected not to release the follow-up *Entering The New Ride*, although tracks have been made available by the band on their official website.

● ALBUMS: *This Is Big Audio Dynamite* (CBS 1985) ★★★★, *No. 10 Upping Street* (CBS 1986) ★★★★, *Tighten Up, Vol. 88* (CBS 1988) ★★★, *Megatop Phoenix* (CBS 1989) ★★★, as B.A.D. II *Kool-Aid* (CBS 1990) ★★, as B.A.D. II *The Globe* (Columbia 1991) ★★, as Big Audio *Higher Power* (Columbia 1994) ★★, as Big Audio *Looking For A Song* (Columbia 1994) ★★, as Big Audio Dynamite *F-Punk* (Radioactive 1995) ★★★.

● COMPILATIONS: *Planet B.A.D.: Greatest Hits* (Columbia 1995) ★★★, *Super Hits* (Columbia 1999) ★★★★.

## BIG BLACK

Initially based in Evanstown, Illinois, USA, Big Black made its recording debut in 1983 with the six-track EP *Lungs*. Fronted by guitarist/vocalist Steve Albini, the band underwent several changes before completing *Bulldozer* the following year. A more settled line-up was formed around Albini, Santiago Durango (guitar) and Dave Riley aka David Lovering (bass) as Big Black began fusing an arresting, distinctive sound, and *Atomizer* (1986) established the trio as one of America's leading independent acts. This powerful, compulsive set included 'Kerosene', a lyrically nihilistic piece equating pyromania with teenage sex as a means of escaping small-town boredom. The combined guitar assault of Albini and Durango was underpinned by Riley's emphatic bass playing, which propelled this metallic composition to its violent conclusion. Melvin Belli (guitar) replaced Durango, who left to study law, for *Songs About Fucking*, Big Black's best-known and most popular album. Once again their blend of post-hardcore and post-industrial styles proved exciting, but Albini had now tired of his creation: 'Big Black are dumb, ugly and persistent, just like a wart' – and announced the break-up of the group prior to the record's release. He later became a respected but idiosyncratic producer, working with the Pixies (*Surfer Rosa*), the Breeders (*Pod*) and Tad (*Salt Lick*), before forming a new venture, the controversially named and short-lived Rapeman. When that band shuddered under the weight of criticism at its name (though Albini insisted this was merely a UK phenomenon), he returned to production duties. Undoubtedly the highest profile of these would be PJ Harvey's *Rid Of Me* and Nirvana's *In Utero*. Afterwards he returned to a group format with Shellac. Durango recorded two EPs as Arsenal.

● ALBUMS: *Atomizer* (Homestead/Blast First 1986) ★★★, *Sound Of Impact* live album (Walls Have Ears 1987) ★★, *Songs About Fucking* (Touch And Go/Blast First 1987) ★★★, *Pigpile* (Blast First 1992) ★★★.

● COMPILATIONS: *The Hammer Party* (Homestead/Blast First 1986) ★★★, *The Rich Man's Eight-Track Tape* (Homestead/Blast First 1987) ★★★.

## BIG COUNTRY

Stuart Adamson (b. William Stuart Adamson, 11 April 1958, Manchester, England, d. 16 December 2001, Honolulu, Hawaii, USA; guitar/vocals) formed Big Country in June 1981 upon his departure from Scottish new wave outfit the Skids. His first recruit was childhood friend Bruce Watson (b. 11 March 1961, Timmins, Ontario, Canada; guitar), but early plans to work solely as a studio ensemble were quickly abandoned. An initial line-up completed by Clive Parker and brothers Peter and Alan Wishart proved incompatible, so in April 1982 Adamson and Watson brought in Mark Brzezicki (b. 21 June 1957, Slough, Buckinghamshire, England; drums) and Tony Butler (b. 13 February 1957, London, England; bass), two former members of On The Air, a band that had supported the Skids on an earlier tour. A month later the new line-up signed a recording contract with Mercury Records. Despite several overtures, Adamson preferred to remain close to his adopted home town of Dunfermline, emphasizing a prevalent Scottish influence in his music. Both guitarists wove a ringing, 'bagpipe' sound from their instruments and the band's debut album, which included the UK Top 20 hit singles 'Fields Of Fire (400 Miles)' and 'In A Big Country', established their rousing, anthemic approach. Both the latter single and the album broached the US Top 20. Two further single releases, 'Chance' and the non-album track 'Wonderland', both reached the UK Top 10, while a second collection, *Steeltown*, like their debut produced by Steve Lillywhite and Will Gosling, was also a commercial success climbing to the top of the UK album charts. However, the band seemed unable to tackle fresh directions and despite achieving their highest-charting UK single in 1986 with 'Look Away' (number 7), the attendant *The Seer* was disappointing.

Despite a two-year hiatus, their fourth album offered little that was new, although its leading single, 'King Of Emotion', broached the UK Top 20. The band struggled into the early 90s, only reaching the lower end of the singles charts and beset by inter-band tension and record company problems. Brzezicki had left the band in July 1989 and was replaced by Pat Ahern and then Chris Bell, the latter completing sessions for 1991's *No Place Like Home*. Simon Phillips was recruited as drummer for *The Buffalo Skinners*, the band's debut for the new Compulsion label. This album rocked out to good effect, but *Without The Aid Of A Safety Net*, featuring a returning Brzezicki, failed to capture the band's exciting in-concert sound. Quite different, however, was the energetic single 'I'm Not Ashamed', which preceded their 1995 album. Despite changing labels yet again the band sounded fresh, embellishing their sound with more contemporary influences. *Eclectic*, featuring guest artists Steve Harley, Kym Mazelle and violin maestro Bobby Valentino, was the band's attempt at an unplugged album, and although not wholly satisfying on CD, the accompanying tour was a revelation, showing a much-revitalized outfit. It also allowed, possibly for the first time, the essence of the band's folk roots to show through, without the chiming guitars masking the quality of some of their songs. Additionally, an acoustic Adamson belting out songs by Bruce Springsteen, Bob Dylan and Neil Young (notably 'Rockin' In The Free World') was a rare treat.

Adamson relocated to Nashville in 1997, with the rest of the band joining him to record *Driving To Damascus*. Their debut for the legendary Track Records label, the album featured two songs co-written by Ray Davies. While recording the album, the band featured as special guests on the Rolling Stones' tour of Europe. In November 1999, Adamson briefly went 'missing' causing much furore in the media. The following year the band embarked on what they claimed was their farewell tour. Various releases in 2001 included a cover versions album, a second rarities compilation, and a collection of 12-inch mixes. Adamson, meanwhile, began working with Marcus Hummon in the Raphaels but was increasingly troubled by personal problems. He went missing again and was found hanged in a Hawaii hotel room in December.

● ALBUMS: *The Crossing* (Mercury 1983) ★★★★, *Steeltown* (Mercury 1984) ★★★, *The Seer* (Mercury 1986) ★★, *Peace In Our Time* (Mercury/Reprise 1988) ★★★, *No Place Like Home* (Vertigo 1991) ★★, *The Buffalo Skinners* (Compulsion 1993) ★★★, *Without The Aid Of A Safety Net* (Compulsion 1994) ★★, *BBC Live In Concert* (Windsong 1995) ★★, *Why The Long Face* (Transatlantic 1995) ★★★, *Eclectic* (Transatlantic 1996) ★★★, *Big Country* (King Biscuit Flower Hour 1997) ★★★, *Brighton Rock* (Snapper 1997) ★★, *Driving To Damascus* (Track 1999) ★★★, *Come Up Screaming* (Track 2000) ★★, *Under Cover* (Track 2001) ★★★, *Live In Cologne* (Eastworld 2002) ★★★.

● COMPILATIONS: *Through A Big Country: Greatest Hits* (Mercury 1990) ★★★, *The Collection* (Castle 1993) ★★★, *Radio 1 Sessions* 1982/1983 recordings (Strange Fruit 1994) ★★, *Restless Natives & Rarities* (Mercury 1998) ★★★, *Kings Of Emotion* (Recall 1998) ★★★, *Rarities II* (Track 2001) ★★, *The Greatest Hits Of Big Country And The Skids: The Best Of Stuart Adamson* (Universal 2002) ★★★★.

● VIDEOS: *Big Country Live* (Channel 5 1986), *King Of Emotion* (PolyGram Music Video 1988), *In A Big Country* (PolyGram Music Video 1988), *Peace In Our Time: Moscow 1988* (Channel 5 1989), *Greatest Hits: Big Country* (Channel 5 1990), *Through A Big Country* (PolyGram Music Video 1991), *The Seer: Live* (Virgin Vision 1991), *Without The Aid Of A Safety Net – Live* (PMI/EMI 1994).

● FURTHER READING: *Big Country: A Certain Chemistry*, John May.

**BIG DISH**

Formed in Airdrie, Lanarkshire, Scotland in 1983, the Big Dish, comprising Steven Lindsay (vocals, guitar, keyboards), Brian McFie (guitar), Raymond Docherty (bass) and Ian Ritchie (saxophone, programming), rose to prominence in 1986 with the release of their debut album, *Swimmer*, which garnered a succession of positive reviews. Commentators compared their crafted pop with Prefab Sprout, Aztec Camera and Danny Wilson, but a series of excellent singles, including 'Prospect Street' and 'Big New Beginning', failed to chart. The trio of Lindsay, McFie and Docherty then completed *Creeping Up On Jesus*. This second effort betrayed a greater debt to American music, yet despite a more commercial sound, it also proved unsuccessful, and the group was dropped from its record label when Lindsay refused to countenance recording a 'cover' version. In 1991 the Big Dish re-emerged with a new contract, an official line-up of Lindsay and McFie, and a minor hit single in 'Miss America'. The attendant release, *Satellites*, maintained the unit's quest for excellence, yet lacked the depth and purpose of their initial work.

● ALBUMS: *Swimmer* (Virgin 1986) ★★★, *Creeping Up On Jesus* (Virgin 1988) ★★★, *Satellites* (East West 1991) ★★.

● COMPILATIONS: *Rich Man's Wardrobe – A Concise History Of ...* (Virgin 1993) ★★★.

**BIG FUN**

This UK group comprised Philip Creswick (b. 12 October 1965, Charlwood, Surrey, England; vocals), Mark Gillespie (b. 28 November 1966, Elgin, Scotland; vocals) and Jason John (b. 18 March 1967, Coventry, Warwickshire, England; vocals). Encouraged by their friends, they started singing and dancing together, and then recorded with the house specialist, Marshall Jefferson. These sessions were enough to interest Stock, Aitken and Waterman, whose production work contributed significantly to their UK number 4 hit in 1989, with a revival of the Jacksons' 'Blame It On The Boogie'. The fresh-faced youths' next single also went into the UK Top 10. Stock, Aitken and Waterman then teamed them with Sonia and achieved success on 'You've Got A Friend'. Their biggest claim to fame was having three simultaneous Top 15 hits in Spain.

● ALBUMS: *Pocketful Of Dreams* (Jive 1990) ★★.

● VIDEOS: *Pocketful Of Dreams* (BMG Video 1990).

**BIG IN JAPAN**

For a band that issued very few recordings, Big In Japan received strong critical acclaim. The main reason for this interest was their line-up: Jayne Casey (vocals, later formed Pink Military/Industry), Bill Drummond (guitar, later formed Lori And The Chameleons, ran the Zoo Records label, released a solo album and comprised half of the KLF), Dave Balfe (bass, worked with Drummond in Lori And The Chameleons, was later enrolled as keyboard player in the Teardrop Explodes and then founded the Food Records label), Budgie (drums, later briefly with the Slits then, more permanently, Siouxsie And The Banshees), Ian Broudie (guitar, who subsequently joined the Original Mirrors before carving out a successful career as a producer, and later enjoyed great success under the guise of the Lightning Seeds) and finally Holly on bass. After two country-styled singles, Holly joined Frankie Goes To Hollywood and later embarked on a solo career as Holly Johnson. On the b-side of their 1977 self-titled debut single was a track from the Chuddy Nuddies, who turned out to be the Yachts. After Big In Japan split, Drummond used four of their tracks for the first Zoo single, *From Y To Z And Never Again*, which stands as a delightfully quirky period piece. The remaining members of Big In Japan (vocalist Ken Ward and drummer Phil Allen) failed to emulate the success of their fellow travellers.

**BIG SOUND AUTHORITY**

This promising UK band was formed in 1983 by two vocalists Tony Burke (who handled the rock material) and Julie Hadwin (who sang the blues parts), and the band were complemented by a fine brass section. On the small Source label they released the 60s-influenced 'This House (Is Where Your Love Stands)', which was a minor UK hit early in 1985. The follow-up, 'A Bad Town', did less well and, despite moving to Source's distributing label and being produced by Tony Visconti, subsequent singles 'Moving Heaven And Earth' and 'Don't Let Our Love Start A War' also failed.

● ALBUMS: *An Inward Revolution* (Source 1985) ★★★.

## BILLY AND THE BEATERS

Formed in 1979 around songwriter Billy Vera (b. William McCord, 28 May 1944, Riverside, California, USA; vocalist, guitarist), Billy And The Beaters was an aggregation comprised of Los Angeles studio musicians. A 10-piece group, whose best-known member other than Vera was Steely Dan/Doobie Brothers guitarist Jeff 'Skunk' Baxter, the other members at various times included Barry Beckett (keyboards), Gene Chrisman (drums), Tommy Cogbill (bass), Ron Viola (saxophones), Pete Carr (guitar), Jim Ehinger (piano), Jimmy Johnson (guitar), Lon Price (saxophone), Beau Segal (drums) and Jerry Peterson (saxophone). The band initially came together to work a club date at LA's Troubadour nightclub. They banded together officially following that engagement and solidified their act during a six-week residency there. 'Here Comes The Dawn Again' was their live show-stopper, featuring a biting saxophone solo. In 1981 they signed with the small Alfa Records and recorded a live album at LA's Roxy club. Two singles, 'I Can Take Care Of Myself' and 'At This Moment', became moderate chart successes, but the latter made a comeback in 1986 after being used in the US television programme *Family Ties*, and ultimately became a million-selling number 1 in the US. Vera has since become a highly respected songwriter and record producer, in addition to working as a vintage soul and R&B album compiler.
● ALBUMS: *Billy Vera And The Beaters* (Alfa 1981) ★★, *Retro Nuevo* (Capitol 1988) ★★, *Out Of The Darkness* 1977 recordings (Unidisc 1993) ★★.
● COMPILATIONS: *By Request (The Best Of Billy Vera & The Beaters* (Rhino 1986) ★★★.

## BINGI BUNNY

b. Eric Lamont, 23 September 1955, Kingston, Jamaica, West Indies, d. 31 December 1993. Lamont began his career working with Bongo Herman as Bunny, recording 'Know For I' with producer Derrick Harriott. In 1973, he joined forces with Maurice Wellington in the Morwells, who in 1974 released 'Mafia Boss' and 'You Got To Be Happy'. While remaining a member of the band, he was also employed as a session musician playing rhythm guitar with other artists, including Errol Holt who joined the Morwells. As members of the group they continued to enjoy hits with 'Crab Race' and 'Proverbs'. In the late 70s they recorded 'Kingston 12 Tuffy' which was a big sound system hit and still enjoys cult status. They were associated with the Sir Jesus Sound Of Shepherds Bush and a number of their recordings would debut on the sound exclusives. The duo of Eric and Maurice also worked as the Morwell production team; notable releases came from the Jah Lloyd The Black Lion (*The Humble One*) and Prince Hammer (*Bible*). In 1981 when the Morwells disbanded, Lamont and Holt joined forces with Lincoln Valentine 'Style' Scott and Noel 'Sowell' Bailey to form the Roots Radics. The band became the island's most in-demand session group, providing backing for Michael 'Dread' Campbell, Gregory Isaacs and Bunny Wailer, as well as a number of sessions for producers Henry 'Junjo' Lawes and Linval Thompson. With Gregory Isaacs

they were the featured musicians on *More Gregory, Night Nurse* and *Out Deh*. With Bunny Wailer they provided backing on *Rock And Groove*, which found the singer in a change of style, winning over new supporters. With Lawes they featured on Barrington Levy's debut, *Bounty Hunter*, heralding the arrival of a new sound that remained popular through to the mid-80s, by which time they faced competition from the Sagittarius Band. As well as playing guitar, Lamont had provided vocals with the Morwells, and in the spring of 1982 he returned to singing as a soloist. He released 'Young Lover', which had been included on the compilation *The Best Of The Morwells*. The b-side featured 'Him A Natty Dread' with DJ Nicodemus. Other singles followed, including 'Me And Jane' and 'Street Lover'. Lamont died of prostate cancer in December 1993. The posthumous 1995 release of *Live At Channel One* included the track 'Tribute To Bingi Bunny'.
● ALBUMS: *Me And Jane* (Cha Cha 1982) ★★★, *Live At Channel One* (Live And Love 1995) ★★★.

## BIRTHDAY PARTY

One of the most creative and inspiring 'alternative' acts of the 80s, this Australian outfit had its roots in the new wave band Boys Next Door. After one album, the band relocated to London and switched names. In addition to featuring the embryonic genius of Nick Cave (b. 22 September 1957, Warracknabeal, Australia; vocals), their ranks were swelled by Roland S. Howard (guitar, ex-Obsessions; Young Charlatans), Mick Harvey (b. 29 September 1958, Rochester, Australia; guitar, drums, organ, piano), Tracy Pew (d. 5 July 1986; bass) and Phil Calvert (drums). They chose the newly launched 4AD Records offshoot of Beggars Banquet Records as their new home, and made their debut with the impressive 'Fiend Catcher'. Music critics and BBC disc jockey John Peel became early and long-serving converts to the band's intense post-punk surges. Back in Australia, they recorded their first album, a transitional piece that nevertheless captured some enduring aggressive rock statements. Their finest recording, however, was the single 'Release The Bats'. It was John Peel's favourite record of 1981, though its subject matter unwittingly connected the band with the emerging 'gothic' subculture populated by Bauhaus and Sex Gang Children.
As Pew was imprisoned for three months for drink-driving offences, Barry Adamson (ex-Magazine), Roland Howard's brother Harry and Chris Walsh helped out on the recording of the follow-up and the band's increasingly torrid live shows. After collaborating with the Go-Betweens on the one-off single 'After The Fireworks', as the Tuf Monks, they shifted to Berlin to escape the constant exposure and expectations of them in the UK. Calvert was dropped (moving on to Psychedelic Furs), while the four remaining members moved on to collaborative projects with Lydia Lunch and Einstürzende Neubauten, among others. They had already recorded a joint 12-inch, 'Drunk On The Pope's Blood', with Lunch, and Howard featured on much of her subsequent output. When Harvey left in the summer of 1983, the band seemed set to fulfil their

solo careers, even though he was temporarily replaced on drums by Des Heffner. However, after a final gig in Melbourne, Australia, in June the band called it a day. Howard went on to join Crime And The City Solution alongside his brother and Harvey, who also continued in Cave's solo band, the Bad Seeds.

● ALBUMS: *The Birthday Party* (Missing Link 1980) ★★★, *Prayers On Fire* (Thermidor 1981) ★★★, *Drunk On The Pope's Blood* mini-album (4AD 1982) ★★★, *Junk Yard* (4AD 1982) ★★★, *It's Still Living* live recording (Missing Link 1985) ★★★.

● COMPILATIONS: *A Collection* (Missing Link 1985) ★★★, *Hee Haw* (4AD 1989) ★★★, *The Peel Sessions Album* (Strange Fruit 1991) ★★★, *Hits* (4AD 1992) ★★★★, *Definitive Missing Link Recordings 1979-1982* (Missing Link 1994) ★★★★, *Live 1981-82* (4AD 1999) ★★★★.

● VIDEOS: *Pleasure Heads Must Burn* (IKON 1988).

## BLACK

Originally a three-piece pop outfit from Roby, near Liverpool, England, the group featured Colin Vearncombe (vocals), Dave Dickie (keyboards) and Jimmy Sangster (bass). Vearncombe was previously in the Epileptic Tits at the age of 16, playing punk cover versions. He then moved on to producing his own tapes until Dickie (ex-Last Chant) and Sangster formed a unit together. Vearncombe and Dickie had previously released 'Human Features' on the local Rox label in 1981. Black's next base was the Liverpool independent record label Eternal, sponsored by Pete Wylie and Wah!. However, Vearncombe's distinctive voice soon attracted the attention of WEA Records. Unfortunately, after the failure of two singles, 'Hey Presto' (written about existential novel *The Dice Man*) and 'More Than The Sun', they dropped the band. Despite this setback, the solo Vearncombe soon found himself with an unexpected hit on his hands. He was approached after a gig by two brothers who wanted to release one of the band's singles on their Ugly Man label. That single was the seductive, bittersweet ballad 'Wonderful Life' and, after using a record plugger, it was played regularly on the radio and took off in the independent charts. Its success attracted the attention of A&M Records, and the second single for the label, 'Sweetest Smile', climbed to number 8 in June 1987, a position matched by a reissue of 'Wonderful Life' two months later. Their debut album followed, though 1988's *Comedy* was the more impressive long-player, highlighting Vearncombe's natural romanticism. A hiatus followed that allowed Vearncombe time for marriage and new material, before a third album, titled simply *Black*. Produced by Robin Millar, guest vocalists included Robert Palmer and Sam Brown. A single featuring the latter, 'Fly To The Moon', also boasted an ironic cover version of Janet Jackson's 'Control'. *Are We Having Fun Yet?* continued in a similar vein but received little commercial reward, and was originally issued as a mail-order-only release on Black's Nero Schwarz label. Following this album, Vearncombe bowed out of the music scene for several years. He returned in 1999 with the critically fêted *The Accused*, which was released

under his own name.

● ALBUMS: *Wonderful Life* (A&M 1987) ★★★, *Comedy* (A&M 1988) ★★★★, *Black* (A&M 1991) ★★★, *Are We Having Fun Yet?* (A&M 1993) ★★★, as Colin Vearncombe *The Accused* (Nero Schwarz 1999) ★★★.

## BLACK FLAG

Formed in 1977 in Los Angeles, California, Black Flag rose to become one of America's leading hardcore outfits. The initial line-up – Keith Morris (vocals), Greg Ginn (guitar), Chuck Dukowski (bass) and Brian Migdol (drums) – completed the *Nervous Breakdown* EP in 1978, but the following year Morris left to form the Circle Jerks. Several members joined and left before Henry Rollins (b. Henry Garfield, 13 February 1961, Washington, DC, USA; vocals), Dez Cadenza (guitar) and Robo (drums) joined Ginn and Dukowski for *Damaged*, the group's first full-length album. Originally scheduled for release by MCA Records, the company withdrew support, citing outrageous content, and the set appeared on the quintet's own label, SST Records. This prolific outlet has not only issued every subsequent Black Flag recording, but also has a catalogue that includes Hüsker Dü, Sonic Youth, the Minutemen, the Meat Puppets and Dinosaur Jr. Administered by Ginn and Dukowski, the latter of whom left the band to concentrate his efforts on the label, the company has become one of America's leading, and most influential, independents. Ginn continued to lead Black Flag in tandem with Rollins, and although its rhythm section was subject to change, the music's power remained undiminished. Pivotal albums included *My War* and *In My Head*, while their diversity was showcased on *Family Man*, which contrasted one side of Rollins' spoken-word performances with four excellent instrumentals. However, the band split up in 1986 following the release of a compulsive live set, *Who's Got The 10 1/2?*, after which Ginn switched his attentions to labelmates Gone. Rollins went on to a successful solo career. The glory days of Black Flag are warmly recalled in one of Rollins' numerous books for his 2.13.61. publishing empire, *Get In The Van*.

● ALBUMS: *Damaged* (SST 1981) ★★★★, *My War* (SST 1984) ★★★, *Family Man* (SST 1984) ★★, *Slip It In* (SST 1984) ★★★, *Live '84* (SST 1984) ★★, *Loose Nut* (SST 1985) ★★, *In My Head* (SST 1985) ★★★, *Who's Got The 10 1/2?* (SST 1986) ★★★.

● COMPILATIONS: *Everything Went Black* (SST 1982) ★★★, *The First Four Years* (SST 1983) ★★★★, *Wasted ... Again* (SST 1988) ★★★★.

● VIDEOS: *Black Flag Live* (Jettisoundz 1984).

## BLACK LACE

This duo, consisting of Colin Routh (b. 8 December 1953, England) and Alan Barton (b. 16 September 1953, Barnsley, Yorkshire, England, d. 23 March 1995, Germany), was responsible for a string of hits in the mid-80s that enjoyed enormous popularity in discos and parties across the UK. However, those in pursuit of music with a marginally more cerebral nature made Black Lace a target for their relentless scorn. After failing to represent Great Britain in the

1979 Eurovision Song Contest with 'Mary Ann', Black Lace carried on regardless, unleashing upon the nation (via Spanish holiday discos) a series of party songs initiated by 'Superman (Gioca Jouer)', which reached the UK Top 10 and was succeeded in 1984 by 'Agadoo', which reached the UK number 2 slot and remained in the charts for 30 weeks. This was followed by 'Do The Conga' (UK number 10), 'El Vino Collapso', 'I Speaka Da Lingo' and 'Hokey Cokey'. The duo's last UK chart entry came in the summer of 1989 with 'I Am The Music Man', which reached number 52. Barton joined a re-formed Smokie who proved popular on the German touring circuit. Tragedy struck on 19 March 1995 when the band's car crashed at Gummersbach on the way to Dusseldorf airport. Barton died after spending five days in a coma.

● ALBUMS: *Party Party: 16 Great Party Icebreakers* (Telstar 1984) ★★, *Party Party 2* (Telstar 1985) ★, *Party Crazy* (Telstar 1986) ★.
● VIDEOS: *The Ultimate Party Video* (Prism 1995).

## BLACK ROOTS

Black Roots, not to be confused with Sugar Minott's project of the same name, formed in Bristol, England in the early 80s. The line-up comprised Errol Brown (vocals), Delroy Ogilvie (vocals), Kondwani Ngozi (congas, vocals), Jabulani Ngozi (rhythm guitar), Cordell Francis (lead guitar), Carlton Roots (keyboard, vocals), Trevor Seivwright (drums) and Derrick King (bass). The group soon established an ardent clique of local supporters following a series of live appearances where they demonstrated their awesome talent. They gained wider exposure when they appeared on the first televised edition of *Rockers Roadshow*, a showcase of British black music screened in the early days of Channel 4. The group, introduced by Mikey Dread, performed the popular hits 'Move On', 'Survival Time', 'Africa' and opened the show with a tribute to one of the UK's first immigrant slaves, Scipio Africanus, buried in Whiteladies Road on Blackboy Hill in the St. Pauls district of Bristol. They established themselves as a powerful and potent force in reggae and initiated an exhaustive touring programme promoting *Black Roots*. The collection appeared on their own Nubian label and was met with much acclaim from the reggae media, and even crossed into the mainstream when reviewed in *The Guardian*. The growing interest in the band inspired the BBC to commission the group to provide the theme tune to *The Front Line*, a situation comedy featuring two black brothers, one a streetwise dreadlocked rasta and the other a policeman. The opening sequence of the show featured the band performing the song and led to an album of the same name. In the same year the group released 'Juvenile Delinquent', which bubbled under the national chart when licensed to the Kick label. The group accompanied Linton Kwesi Johnson and Eek A Mouse on European tours, attracting favourable reviews. In 1985 the group maintained their profile, performing at the WOMAD festival in Essex alongside Toots And The Maytals and Thomas Mapfumo. Deemed as a conscientious roots outfit, the group enrolled the production skills

of the Mad Professor to produce their third album, which also featured accompaniment from Vin Gordon and Michael 'Bammi' Rose. The compilation included a remarkable lovers rock track, 'Seeing Your Face', with Carlton Roots on lead vocals, which was sadly overlooked for a single release, as was a cover version of the Fat Larry's Band hit, 'Zoom'. In 1988 the group released 'Start Afresh', which was moderately successful, and demonstrated their versatility with the appropriately titled *In A Different Style*. Further sessions with the Mad Professor followed in the late 80s when the depleted band enrolled the multi-talented Black Steel to amplify the sound, resulting in the enchanting 'Guide Us', 'Voice Of The People' and 'Natural Reaction'.

● ALBUMS: *Black Roots* (Nubian 1982) ★★★, *The Front Line* (BBC 1984) ★★, *All Day All Night* (Nubian 1985) ★★★, *In A Different Style* (Nubian 1988) ★★★, *Live Power* (Nubian 1989) ★★★, *Natural Reaction* (Nubian 1990) ★★.
● VIDEOS: *Celebration* (Nubian 1989).

## BLACK SLATE

A large roots reggae ensemble consisting of members drawn from both Jamaica and the UK, Black Slate originally comprised Anthony Brightly, Desmond Mahoney (b. 1955, St. Thomas, Jamaica, West Indies; drums), Keith Drummond (b. 1955, Mandeville, Jamaica, West Indies; lead vocals), Chris Hanson (b. 1956, Kingston, Jamaica, West Indies; lead guitar), Cledwyn Rogers (b. 1955, Anguilla; rhythm guitar) and Ras Elroy (b. Elroy Bailey, 1958, London, England; bass and vocals). Subsequent members included Henschell Holder, Rudy Holmes, Ray Carness and Nicky Ridguard. Formed in 1974, they found their first employment as backing band to Dennis Brown, Delroy Wilson, Ken Boothe and many other visiting Jamaican musicians. After gigging heavily on the London reggae circuit, their first hit under their own steam came with the anti-mugging 'Sticks Man' in 1976. They embarked on their first nationwide tour in 1978, launching their own TCD label and going on to their debut chart appearance with 'Mind Your Motion'. The band's watershed year was 1980: a simple Rastafarian rallying call, 'Amigo', was picked up by Ensign and, with the extra corporate muscle, the single rose to number 7 in the UK charts. It became their signature tune, and although follow-ups brushed the charts, notably 'Boom Boom', the band's initial impact was never repeated.

● ALBUMS: *Black Slate* (TCD 1979) ★★★, *Sirens In The City* (Ensign 1981) ★★, *Six Plus One* (Top Ranking 1982) ★★, *Black Slate* (Sierra 1985) ★★★.

## BLACK UHURU

Formed in Jamaica by Rudolph 'Garth' Dennis, Derrick 'Duckie' Simpson and Euvin 'Don Carlos' Spencer in 1974, Black Uhuru first recorded a version of Curtis Mayfield's 'Romancing To The Folk Song' for Dynamic's Top Cat label as Uhuru (the Swahili word for 'freedom'), which met with limited success. Dennis then joined the Wailing Souls and McCarlos (as Don Carlos) went on to a solo career. Simpson then enlisted Michael Rose as lead singer, who himself had previously recorded as a solo artist for Yabby You (on the excellent 'Born Free') and for Winston 'Niney' Holness, including the first recording of 'Guess Who's Coming To Dinner', inspired by the Sidney Poitier movie. Errol Nelson, from the Jayes, was used for harmonies. This line-up sang on an album for Prince Jammy in 1977 entitled *Love Crisis*, later reissued and retitled *Black Sounds Of Freedom*, after the band had found success. Nelson returned to the Jayes soon afterwards and Puma Jones (b. Sandra Jones, 5 October 1953, Columbia, South Carolina, USA, d. 28 January 1990, New York, USA) took over. Formerly a social worker, she had worked with Ras Michael And The Sons Of Negus as a dancer in a bid to retrace her African ancestry via Jamaica.

This combination began work for Sly And Robbie's Taxi label in 1980, and Black Uhuru mania gripped the Jamaican reggae audience. The solid bedrock of Sly And Robbie's rhythms with Jones' and Simpson's eerie harmonies provided a perfect counterpoint to Rose's tortured vocals, as his songs wove tales of the hardships of Jamaican life that managed to convey a far wider relevance. Their first album for Taxi, *Showcase*, later reissued as *Vital Selection*, gave equal prominence to the vocal and instrumental versions of songs such as 'General Penitentiary', 'Shine Eye Gal' and 'Abortion', and was a massive reggae seller. Island Records signed the band and they became a hot property throughout the musical world over the next few years. Their albums for Mango/Island continued in the same militant vein, and *Anthem* was remixed for the American market and earned a Grammy for the band. They toured the globe with the powerhouse rhythm section of Sly And Robbie, in addition to a full complement of top Jamaican session musicians. For a time they were widely touted as the only reggae band with the potential to achieve international superstar status, but although their popularity never waned after their initial breakthrough, it sadly never seemed to grow either.

Michael Rose left the band in the mid-80s for a solo career that always promised more than it has actually delivered, although his 1990 album *Proud* was very strong. Junior Reid took over on lead vocals, but in retrospect, his approach was too deeply rooted in the Jamaican dancehalls at the time for Black Uhuru's international approach, and after a couple of moderately well-received albums, he also left for a solo career, which to date has been remarkably successful. Puma Jones, who had left the band after *Brutal* and was replaced by soundalike Olafunke, died of cancer in 1990. During this period the original members reunited to tour and record. Subsequent albums proved less successful, and by the end of the decade only Simpson remained from the original line-up. Black Uhuru will always remain one of *the* great reggae acts, despite the fact that the international status that they deserved proved elusive.

● ALBUMS: *Love Crisis* (Prince Jammys/Third World 1977) ★★★, *Showcase* (Taxi/Heartbeat 1979) ★★★, *Sinsemilla* (Mango/Island 1980) ★★★, *Red* (Mango/Island 1981) ★★★★, *Black Uhuru* (Virgin 1981) ★★★, *Chill Out* (Mango/Island 1982) ★★★,

*Tear It Up – Live* (Mango/Island 1982) ★★★, *Guess Who's Coming To Dinner* (Heartbeat 1983) ★★★, *The Dub Factor* (Mango/Island 1983) ★★★, *Anthem* (Mango/ Island 1984) ★★★, *Uhuru In Dub* (CSA 1985) ★★★, *Brutal* (RAS 1986) ★★★★, *Brutal Dub* (RAS 1986) ★★★, *Positive* (RAS 1987) ★★★, *Positive Dub* (RAS 1987) ★★★, *Live In New York City* (Rohit 1988) ★★★, *Now* (Mesa 1990) ★★★, *Now Dub* (Mesa 1990) ★★★★, *Iron Storm* (Mesa 1991) ★★, *Mystical Touch* (Mesa 1993) ★★★, *Unification* (Five Star General 1999) ★★★, *Dynasty* (RAS 2001) ★★★.

● COMPILATIONS: *Reggae Greats* (Mango/Island 1985) ★★★★, *Liberation: The Island Anthology* 2-CD box set (Mango/Island 1993) ★★★★, *What Is Life? An Introduction To Black Uhuru* (Island 1999) ★★★, *Ultimate Collection* (Hip-O 2000) ★★★★, *The Best Of Black Uhuru: The Millennium Collection* (Island 2002) ★★★★.

● VIDEOS: *Tear It Up* (Channel 5 1988), *Black Uhuru Live* (PolyGram Music Video 1991).

## BLACK, MARY

b. 22 May 1955, Eire. Mary is a member of the Black Family, who all have musical backgrounds, and with whom she has recorded and performed. Her father was a fiddle player and her mother a singer. Her early days were spent singing in the folk clubs of Dublin, but with *Mary Black* reaching number 4 in the Irish charts in 1983, it was obvious that she was destined for bigger things. In addition, she was awarded the Irish Independent Arts Award for Music for the album. Shortly after this, Black joined De Dannan, recording two albums with them, *Song For Ireland* and *Anthem*, before leaving the group in 1986. Although not credited, she provided some backing vocals and production work for *The Black's Family Favourites* in 1984. Black maintained her solo career while with De Dannan, and teamed up with producer Declan Sinnott for *Without The Fanfare*, featuring mostly contemporary songs, which subsequently went gold. In 1987 and 1988, Black was voted Best Female Artist in the Irish Rock Music Awards Poll. *No Frontiers*, apart from being one of Ireland's bestselling albums in 1989, also reached the Top 20 of the New Adult Contemporary charts in the USA, in 1990. The album also had a great deal of success in Japan, resulting in Black's first Japanese tour in December 1990.

Although, in the eyes of some critics, more recent works have seen Black tagged as 'middle of the road', she defies straight categorization, still retaining an honest feel for her traditional background. Nevertheless, she also remains a fine interpreter of more contemporary works. With the Black Family, she has only made two albums, owing to many of them living in different parts of the world. Apart from backing Nanci Griffith in concert, Black also sang with Emmylou Harris and Dolores Keane, in Nashville, in the television series *Bringing It All Back Home*. In April 1991, Black returned from an American tour in order to finish *Babes In The Wood*, released in July the same year. The album went straight to number 1 in the Irish charts, staying there for five weeks. 1991 saw a concerted effort to capitalize on her success and reach a wider audience, with tours of England and another of Japan. Until *Babes In The Wood*, her albums, all on Dara, had not previously had a full distribution in Britain. Further albums built on her success, culminating in *Shine* and *Speaking With The Angel*, her most commercial outings to date.

● ALBUMS: *Mary Black* (Dara 1983) ★★★, *Collected* (Dara 1984) ★★★, *Without The Fanfare* (Dara 1985) ★★★, with the Black Family *The Black Family* (Dara 1986) ★★★, *By The Time It Gets Dark* (Dara 1987) ★★★, with the Black Family *Time For Touching Home* (Dara 1989) ★★★, *No Frontiers* (Dara 1989) ★★★, *Babes In The Wood* (Grapevine 1991) ★★★★, *The Holy Ground* (Gifthorse 1993) ★★★, *Circus* (Grapevine 1995) ★★★, *Shine* (Grapevine 1997) ★★★, *Speaking With The Angel* (Grapevine 1999) ★★★.

● COMPILATIONS: *The Best Of Mary Black* (Dara 1991) ★★★★, *The Collection* (Dara 1992) ★★★★, *Looking Back: The Best Of Mary Black* (Curb 1995) ★★★★, *The Best Of Mary Black 1991–2001* (Grapevine 2001) ★★★★.

## BLACKFOOT

Southern US rock practitioners Blackfoot initially comprised Rick Medlocke (guitar, vocals), Charlie Hargrett (guitar), Greg Walker (bass) and Jakson Spires (drums, vocals). The quartet shared common origins with Lynyrd Skynyrd (Medlocke co-writing four songs and singing lead on two tracks on the latter's platinum *First And Last*) and in turn offered a similar blues/rock-based sound, centred on their leader's confident playing. Medlocke himself was the grandson of Shorty Medlocke, a popular Jacksonville, Florida bluegrass musician of the 50s, whose 'Train, Train' was successfully covered by Blackfoot and, in the 90s, Warrant. Rick Medlocke took the name Blackfoot from his own native Indian tradition. Session pianist Jimmy Johnson produced Blackfoot's early work at the revered Muscle Shoals studio but, despite this impressive pedigree, the group was unable to translate an in-concert popularity, especially in the UK, into record sales. *Blackfoot Strikes*, the unit's first release for Atlantic/Atco Records, offered a heavier perspective, while the cream of their early work was captured live on *Highway Song*. After these releases, the group bowed to record company pressure and pursued a more commercial approach that was not always convincing. Ken Hensley (b. 24 August 1945, London, England), formerly of Uriah Heep, joined the line-up for *Siogo* and *Vertical Smiles*, and was eventually replaced by Bobby Barth of Axe, but Blackfoot was disbanded following the latter's release. The name was revived at the end of the decade with a revised line-up, with Medlocke backed by Neal Casal (b. 2 November 1968, Denville, New Jersey, USA; guitar), Rikki Mayer (bass, ex-Lizzy Borden) and Gunner Ross (drums). However, none of these members remained for Blackfoot's 1994 album with new label Bullet Proof/Music For Nations, with Mark Woerpel (guitar, vocals, ex-Wardrive), Benny Rappa (drums, vocals) and Tim Stunson (bass) stepping in to support the venerable Medlocke. Rappa was replaced by ex-W.A.S.P.

drummer Stet Howland for touring.

● ALBUMS: *No Reservations* (Island 1976) ★★★, *Flyin' High* (Epic 1977) ★★★, *Blackfoot Strikes* (Atco 1978) ★★★, *Tomcattin'* (Atco 1980) ★★★, *Maurauder* (Atco 1981) ★★★, *Highway Song* (Atco 1982) ★★★, *Siogo* (Atco 1983) ★★★, *Vertical Smiles* (Atco 1984) ★★★, *Medicine Man* (Loop 1990) ★★, *After The Reign* (Bullet Proof 1994) ★★, *Blackfoot Live On The King Biscuit Flower Hour* 1983 recording (King Biscuit 1998) ★★.

● COMPILATIONS: *Rattlesnake Rock 'N' Roll: The Best Of Blackfoot* (Rhino 1995) ★★★.

## BLADE RUNNER

Of the few rock bands of any note to emerge from the Humberside region in England (in the two decades that the area was not designated as part of Lincolnshire or Yorkshire), most seemed to draw their principal influence from Status Quo. Blade Runner were no exception, despite the fact that they took their name from a futuristic science fiction film. Comprising Steve Mackay (vocals), Gary Jones (guitar), Mark Wilde (guitar), Mick Cooper (bass) and Gregg Ellis (drums), they made their debut in 1984 with *Hunted* for Ebony Records. It was followed two years later by *Warriors Of Rock*, but with neither record selling substantially, the members of Blade Runner settled back into semi-retirement, with some members remaining active on the local club rock scene.

● ALBUMS: *Hunted* (Ebony 1984) ★★, *Warriors Of Rock* (Ebony 1986) ★★.

## BLADES

Formed in Dublin, Eire, in 1977 by Paul Cleary (b. 9 September 1959, Dublin, Eire; guitar, vocals), the original line-up of the Blades featured his brother Lar Cleary (b. 2 June 1957, Dublin, Eire; bass/vocals) and Pat Larkin (b. 25 November 1956, Dublin, Eire; drums). Unlike other swaggering contenders at the time of punk rock in Ireland and the UK, there was substance to the claims for the Blades' greatness. Inspired by a mixture of punk rock, soul and pop, the pyrrhic victory of national critical acclaim did not lead to a major label record deal until 1983. When they did sign (to Elektra America), what at first seemed like the capture of the Holy Grail quickly deteriorated into the time-honoured music industry nightmare, resulting in being dropped before they had a chance to release a record. By this stage, the Blades line-up had lost Lar Cleary and Pat Larkin, their places taken by Brian Foley (b. 23 July 1957, Dublin, Eire; bass, vocals) and Jake Reilly (b. 2 May 1958, Dublin, Eire; drums) as well as being augmented by the inclusion of Frank Duff (b. 16 July 1964, Dublin, Eire; trombone), Paul Grimes (b. 3 December 1963, Dublin, Eire; trumpet) and Conor Brady (b. 16 February 1961, Cork, Eire; guitar). Between the two line-ups, the Blades were, effortlessly, one of the best bands in Ireland. They had the pop songs ('Hot For You', 'The Bride Wore White', 'Downmarket', 'Animation', 'Revelations Of Heartbreak', 'Ghost Of A Chance' – the latter regarded as one of the best Irish singles of all time), the working-class street credibility which resonated throughout the lyrics, an eloquent frontman and ambition. When they split up in 1986, Paul Cleary formed the Partisans. This band split up in the late 80s, with Cleary effectively disappearing until the re-release of the Blades material (for the first time on CD) in late 2000.

● ALBUMS: *The Last Man In Europe* (Reekus 1985) ★★★, *Raytown Revisited* (Reekus 1986) ★★★★.
● COMPILATIONS: *Those Were The Days* (Reekus 2000) ★★★★.

## BLADES, RUBÉN

b. 16 July 1948, Panama City, Panama. Blades was brought up in a musical family, with his mother Anoland an accomplished pianist and singer, and his father Rubén Snr. a bongo player. In 1966, while still at school, he became a vocalist with the band Conjunto Latino. He then switched to Los Salvajes Del Ritmo, staying with this band until 1969. In 1970, he travelled to New York to record *De Panama A Nuevo York* with the band of ex-boogaloo star Pete 'El Conde' Rodríguez. After graduating from the University of Panama, he worked as a lawyer with the National Bank of Panama. In 1974, while visiting his family in Miami (they had relocated there in 1973), Blades made a side trip to New York and secured a job in the mailroom of Fania Records. When Tito Allen left Ray Barretto's band in 1974, Blades was recommended to the bandleader. Barretto auditioned him in the mailroom, and in July of that year Blades appeared at Madison Square Garden with Barretto's band, and performed on the following year's *Barretto*.

When Barretto left to form a fusion concert band, Blades stayed with his former musicians (renamed Guarare) for a short while, as well as appearing on the *Barretto Live: Tomorrow*, the debut set by Barretto's new band. He composed and sang lead vocals on Willie Colón's hit track 'El Cazangero', featured on his 1975 set *The Good, The Bad, The Ugly*. The song won him the Composer Of The Year award in the 1976 *Latin NY* magazine poll. Blades supplied songs for a number of bands and artists during the 70s, including Ricardo Ray and Bobby Cruz, Ismael Miranda, Bobby Rodríguez Y La Compañia, Cheo Feliciano, Conjunto Candela, Tito Rodríguez II, Tito Puente, Roberto Roena, Tito Gómez, Héctor Lavoe and Pete 'El Conde' Rodríguez. Twelve original recordings of his compositions by other artists were collected on 1981's *Interpretan A Rubén Blades*. In 1976 he joined the Fania All Stars, making his debut with them on that year's *Tribute To Tito Rodríguez*. He continued as a member until 1980. Three years earlier, he sang lead and chorus on Larry Harlow's acclaimed salsa suite *La Raza Latina*.

Blades' partnership with Willie Colón began in earnest with 1977's *Metiendo Mano!* (released in the UK on the Caliente label in 1988). They collaborated on four more albums. *Siembra* (1978) went gold and was regarded as 'the Renaissance of Salsa'. The controversial double album *Maestra Vida* (1980), incorporated theatrical elements and also received a gold record. *Canciones Del Solar De Los Aburridos* (Songs From The Place Of Bored People) was nominated for a Grammy Award. *The Last Fight* was released in tandem with the 1982 movie of the same name, in which Blades and Colón both starred. The movie was Fania Records' boss Jerry Masucci's attempt to break into the film industry, but it fared badly. At the same time, Blades was playing a leading role over the issue of alleged non-payment of royalties by the label and there was speculation that he tried to form a union of Fania's artists in 1979. Masucci eventually sold Fania for a million dollars to an Argentinian business group called Valsyn and retained a constancy affiliation with the label. Blades switched to Elektra Records in 1984. His debut for the label, *Buscando America*, was recorded with a sextet, Seis Del Solar. The album also introduced modern rock and pop elements into the mix, substituting synthesizers for salsa's traditional horns. Blades starred in 1985's low-budget *Crossover Dreams*, and also contributed songs to the soundtrack album.

He made his UK concert debut with Seis Del Solar in 1986, but his plunge into crossover territory with 1988's rock-orientated, English-language *Nothing But The Truth* flopped. He returned to a more traditional style for the same year's Spanish-language, Grammy award-winning *Antecedente*, on which his backing band (renamed Son Del Solar) was augmented by a trombone section. The arrangements (by keyboard player Oscar Hernández and bass player Mike Viñas) were reminiscent of his work with Colón. Blades has subsequently developed a productive and successful acting career, starring in movies including *Critical Condition* (with Richard Pryor), *The Milagro Beanfield War* (with Robert Redford), *The Lemon Sisters* (with Diane Keaton) and *The Two Jakes* (with Jack Nicholson). He was the first Latino to win an ACE (American Cable Excellence) award for his portrayal of a death-row prisoner in 1989's *Dead Man Out*. He also composed the music for Sidney Lumet's *Q And A*. Blades provoked controversy in Panama, and his mother's wrath, when he criticized the 1990 US invasion of Panama. In 1994 he finished a credible second in the Panamanian presidential elections. Musically Blades was relatively quiet until the release of 1996's *La Rosa De Los Vientos*. Blades' most significant contribution to salsa has been the quality of his lyrical content, which introduced a modern political edge and a wider perspective to the genre's traditional forms. He has described his own work as 'musical journalism' and an 'urban chronicle'. He is a giant figure of Latin music.

● ALBUMS: with Willie Colón *Metiendo Mano!* (Fania 1977) ★★★, with Colón *Siembra* (Fania 1978) ★★★★, *Bohemio Y Poeta* (Fania 1979) ★★★, with Colón *Canciones Del Solar De Los Aburridos* (Fania 1981) ★★★★, with Colón *The Last Fight* (Fania 1982) ★★★, *el que la hace la paga* (Fania 1983) ★★★, *Buscando America* (Warners 1984) ★★★★, *Mucho Mejor* (Fania 1984) ★★★, *Crossover Dreams* film soundtrack (Elektra 1985) ★★★★, *Escenas* (Elektra 1985) ★★★★, *Agua De Luna* (Elektra 1987) ★★★★, *Doble Filo* (Fania 1987) ★★★, *With Strings* (Fania 1988) ★★, *Nothing But The Truth* (Elektra 1988) ★★★, *Antecedente* (Warners 1988) ★★★★, *Rubén Blades Y Son Del Solar ... Live!* (Elektra 1990) ★★★★, *Caminando* (Sony Discos 1991) ★★★, *Amor Y Control*

(Sony Discos 1992) ★★★, with Colón *Tras La Tormenta* (Sony Discos 1995) ★★★, *La Rosa De Los Vientos* (Sony Discos 1996) ★★★, *Tiempos* (Sony Discos 1999) ★★★, *Mundo* (Columbia 2002) ★★★.
● COMPILATIONS: *Best Of Rubén Blades* (Sony Discos 1992) ★★★★, *Poeta Latino* (Charly 1993) ★★★, *Greatest Hits* (WEA 1996) ★★★★, *Best Of: Prohibido Olvidar* (World Up! 2000) ★★★★, *Salsa Caliente De Nu York!* (Nascente 2002) ★★★★.
● VIDEOS: *The Return Of Rubén Blades* (Rhapsody 1995).
● FILMS: *The Last Fight* (1982), *Crossover Dreams* (1985), *Critical Condition* (1987), *The Milagro Beanfield War* (1988), *Dead Man Out* (1989).

## BLAKE BABIES
This trio from Boston, Massachusetts, USA was formed by Juliana Hatfield (b. 2 July 1967, Duxbury, Massachusetts, USA), John Strohm (guitar, vocals) and Freda Love (drums). As part of a succession of bands that emerged from a healthy rock scene in the Boston area in the late 80s/early 90s, Blake Babies were able to mature slowly, showing signs of a major breakthrough in early 1992. Their debut, *Nicely Nicely*, was released on the band's own Chewbud label, and the follow-up, the mini-album *Slow Learners*, on Billy Bragg's reactivated Utility label. Signed to the North Carolina Mammoth Records label, *Earwig* and *Sunburn* consolidated the praise garnered from the music press, often drawing comparisons with fellow Bostonians the Lemonheads. Hatfield would enjoy a celebrated romance with Evan Dando of the Lemonheads, while Strohm had also briefly been a member during their *Creator* sessions. The release of the EP *Rosy Jack World*, coupled with sell-out dates on a UK visit early in 1992, promised a bright future for the trio. However, Hatfield turned solo just as *Sunburn* began to attract rave reviews. On her departure Hatfield concluded: 'When Blake Babies was happening it was really romantic to sleep on floors and not have any money. But when I look back on it, I can't believe some of the stuff we did.' Strohm and Love, meanwhile, went on to form Antenna. The trio reunited in 2000 to record a new album, *God Bless The Blake Babies*.
● ALBUMS: *Nicely, Nicely* (Chew-bud 1987) ★★★, *Slow Learners* mini-album (Utility 1989) ★★★, *Earwig* (Mammoth 1989) ★★★, *Sunburn* (Mammoth 1990) ★★★, *God Bless The Blake Babies* (Rounder 2001) ★★★.
● COMPILATIONS: *Innocence And Experience* (Mammoth 1993) ★★★.

## BLANCMANGE
This UK electro-pop duo featured Neil Arthur (b. 15 June 1958, Lancashire, England; vocals, guitar) and Steven Luscombe (b. 29 October 1954; keyboards). After debuting with an EP, *Irene And Mavis*, they were invited by disc jockey/entrepreneur Stevo to appear on his influential 1981 Some Bizzare compilation. This led to a contract with London Records and a synthesizer-based album, *Happy Families*, which spawned two Top 10 singles, 'Living On The Ceiling' and 'Blind Vision'. Ambitiously

eclectic at times, Blancmange employed orchestration and raga influences on their second album, *Mange Tout*, and enjoyed an unlikely hit with a cover version of Abba's 'The Day Before You Came'. By 1985, the Blancmange experiment had effectively run its course and after a final album, *Believe You Me*, Luscombe and Arthur went their separate ways.
● ALBUMS: *Happy Families* (London 1982) ★★★, *Mange Tout* (London 1984) ★★★, *Believe You Me* (London 1985) ★★.
● COMPILATIONS: *Second Helping: The Best Of Blancmange* (London 1990) ★★★, *Heaven Knows* (Elite 1992) ★★, *The Third Course* (Karussel 1994) ★★, *Best Of Blancmange* (Connoisseur Collection 1997) ★★★.
● VIDEOS: *Live At The Haçienda* (London 1994).

## BLASTERS
Formed in Los Angeles, California, USA, in 1979, the Blasters were one of the leading proponents of the so-called US 'roots-rock' revival of the 80s. Originally comprising Phil Alvin (vocals), his songwriter brother Dave (guitar), John Bazz (bass) and Bill Bateman (drums), the group's first album in 1980 was *American Music* on the small Rollin' Rock label. Incorporating rockabilly, R&B, country and blues, the album was critically applauded for both Dave Alvin's songwriting and the band's ability to update the age-old styles without slavishly recreating them. With a switch to the higher-profile Slash label in 1981, the group released a self-titled album that was also well received. Pianist Gene Taylor was added to the line-up and 50s saxophonist Lee Allen guested (and later toured with the group). With Slash picking up distribution from Warner Brothers Records, the album reached the Top 40, due largely to good reviews (three later albums would chart at lower positions). A live EP recorded in London followed in 1982 but it was the following year's *Non Fiction*, a thematic study of the working class likened by critics to Bruce Springsteen and Tom T. Hall, that earned the band its greatest acclaim so far. By this time saxophonist Steve Berlin had also joined the fold, playing on 1985's *Hard Line*. The album included a song by John Mellencamp and guest backing vocals by the Jordanaires. Dave Alvin departed from the group upon its completion to join X, and was replaced by Hollywood Fats, who died of a heart attack at the age of 32 while a member of the band. Phil Alvin and Steve Berlin kept a version of the group together until 1987, at which point it folded. Both Alvin brothers have recorded solo albums and worked on other projects.
● ALBUMS: *American Music* (Rollin' Rock 1980) ★★★, *The Blasters* (Slash 1981) ★★★★, *Non Fiction* (Slash 1983) ★★★, *Hard Line* (Slash 1985) ★★★.
● COMPILATIONS: *The Blasters Collection* (Slash 1991) ★★★★, *Testament: The Complete Slash Recordings* (Rhino 2002) ★★★★.
● FURTHER READING: *Any Rough Times Are Now Behind You*, Dave Alvin.

## BLEGVAD, PETER

b. 1951, New York City, New York, USA. Blegvad is a playful and witty songwriter and singer who has built up a cult following in the UK and the USA. Moving to England in the early 70s, he formed Slapp Happy with singer Dagmar Krause and keyboard player Anthony Moore. Described by one critic as a 'mutant cabaret group', they made two albums for Virgin Records and two more with *avant garde* band Henry Cow. When that group split in 1977, Blegvad worked briefly with the Art Bears before returning to New York. There he performed with John Zorn, the Ambitious Lovers and, from 1985–87, Anton Fier's 'supergroup', the Golden Palaminos. Blegvad's solo recording career began in the mid-80s, when he made two albums for Virgin, with Andy Partridge of XTC producing *The Naked Shakespeare*. Previously he had recorded for the same label in 1977 in tandem with John Greaves. After making *Downtime* for *avant garde* label Recommended, Blegvad signed to Silvertone Records where Palaminos colleague Chris Blamey co-produced *King Strut*. Guest artists on the album included Syd Straw (vocals) and Danny Thompson (bass). Blegvad also began to contribute a weekly cartoon strip to the London newspaper *The Independent On Sunday*, entitled *Leviathan*, which displayed the same world-weary wit as his songwriting. *Unearthed* was a spoken-word piece featuring John Greaves, while *Just Woke Up* showed Blegvad back in word-playing singer-songwriter mode. In 1997 Blegvad joined up with Krause and Moore again to record a new Slapp Happy album, *Ça Va*.

● ALBUMS: with John Greaves *Kew. Rhone* (Virgin 1977) ★★★, *The Naked Shakespeare* (Virgin 1983) ★★, *Knights Like This* (Virgin 1985) ★★, *Downtime* (Recommended 1988) ★★★, *King Strut & Other Stories* (Silvertone 1991) ★★★, with John Greaves *Unearthed* (Sub Rosa 1995) ★★★, *Just Woke Up* (East Side Digital/RER 1996) ★★★, *Hangman's Hill* (RER 1998) ★★★★.

● COMPILATIONS: *Choices Under Pressure: An Acoustic Retrospective* (Resurgence 2001) ★★★★.

● FURTHER READING: *The Book Of Leviathan*, Peter Blegvad.

## BLOCK, RORY

b. 6 November 1949, Greenwich Village, New York, USA. American blues singer and guitarist, raised in New York. Her father played classical violin, but at the age of 10, Block started learning to play folk music on the guitar. She later became involved in the burgeoning Greenwich Village folk scene. It was as a teenager that she first heard the blues, and went on to play with such names as Rev. Gary Davis and Mississippi John Hurt; meeting up with Stefan Grossman when she was 13 further encouraged her interest in the music. However, she took a 10-year break to raise her family, and only returned to music in 1975 with a self-titled debut for RCA-Victor Records. A studio release for the small Blue Goose label was followed by two disappointing albums for Chrysalis Records.

Block's first release for Rounder Records, 1982's *High Heeled Blues*, was co-produced with John Sebastian. She continued in the same vein of recording and performing traditional blues and country blues material alongside her own compositions. The recording of *I've Got A Rock In My Sock* featured such luminaries as Taj Mahal and David Bromberg. In 1986, her 19-year-old son, Thiele, was killed in a car accident. The subsequent tribute album, *House Of Hearts*, contained 10 tracks, with all but one Block originals. *Turning Point*, despite having a bigger production sound overall, did not detract from her earlier blues influences. *Tornado* in 1996 was her most commercial offering to date and was bolstered by some guest 'heavy friends', including Mary-Chapin Carpenter and guitarist David Lindley. Her track record speaks for itself, with her one-time apprehension that a white girl from New York might not sound authentic singing the blues, proving quite unfounded. Receiving the W.C. Handy Award for Traditional Blues Female Artist of the Year in 1997 and 1998 was ample justification. In 1997 she was elected to the CAMA Hall Of Fame.

● ALBUMS: *Rory Block* (RCA Victor 1975) ★★★, *Rory Block (I'm In Love)* (Blue Goose 1976) ★★★, *Intoxication, So Bitter Sweet* (Chrysalis 1977) ★★, *How To Play The Blues Guitar* (Kicking Mule 1978) ★★★, *You're The One* (Chrysalis 1979) ★★, *High Heeled Blues* (Rounder 1982) ★★★, *Blue Horizon* (Rounder 1983) ★★★, *Rhinestones & Steel Strings* (Rounder 1983) ★★★, *I've Got A Rock In My Sock* (Rounder 1986) ★★★, *House Of Hearts* (Rounder 1987) ★★★, *Color Me Wild* (Alcazar 1990) ★★★, *Mama's Blues* (Rounder 1991) ★★★, *Ain't I A Woman* (Rounder 1992) ★★★★, *Angel Of Mercy* (Rounder 1994) ★★★, *When A Woman Gets The Blues* (Rounder 1995) ★★★, *Tornado* (Rounder 1996) ★★★, *Confessions Of A Blues Singer* (Rounder 1998) ★★★, *I'm Every Woman* (Rounder 2002) ★★★.

● COMPILATIONS: *Best Blues And Originals* (Rounder 1987) ★★★★, *Turning Point* (Munich 1989) ★★★, *The Early Tapes 1975/1976* (Alcazar 1990) ★★★, *Best Blues & Originals Volume 2* (Munich 1994) ★★★★, *Gone Woman Blues (The Country Blues Collection)* (Rounder 1997) ★★★★.

● VIDEOS: *Classics Of Country Blues Guitar* (Homespun Video 1984).

## BLONDY, ALPHA

b. Seydou Kone, 1 January 1953, Dimbokoro, Ivory Coast. During the mid-80s, reggae vocalist Blondy, whose name translates as First Bandit, became one of West Africa's most successful bandleaders, his songs widely covered by other local reggae artists. Adopting not only the rhythms and instrumental arrangements of Jamaican reggae, Blondy also followed its tradition of militant protest lyrics. His embracing of reggae and rasta was not without its problems; after he returned in 1981 from two years' study at Columbia University in the USA, his parents committed him to a psychiatric hospital for 18 months because of his Rasta beliefs. Although he dressed as a Rasta, Blondy took to travelling everywhere with the Star of David, a copy of the Bible and one of the Koran.

After releasing 1985's searing *Apartheid Is Nazism* album, Blondy took the logical next step of flying to Jamaica to record the follow-up, *Jerusalem*, with the

Wailers. By the early 90s he had established himself as an international star with such releases as *Revolution* and *Masada*. Blondy continues to release a steady stream of studio albums, and is particularly popular and commercially successful in France.

● ALBUMS: *Jah Glory* (Celluloid 1983) ★★★, *Cocody Rock!!!* (Shanachie 1984) ★★★, *Apartheid Is Nazism* (Shanachie 1985) ★★★★, *Jerusalem* (Tuff Gong/ Shanachie 1986) ★★, *Revolution* (Shanachie 1987) ★★, *The Prophets* (Capitol 1989) ★★★, *Masada* (World Pacific 1992) ★★★, *Live Au Zenith (Paris)* (World Pacific 1992) ★★★, *Dieu* (World Pacific 1994) ★★★, *Yitzhak Rabin* (Tuff Gong/Lightyear 1998) ★★★, *Paris Percy* (Shanachie 2001) ★★★.

● COMPILATIONS: *Best Of Alpha Blondy* (Shanachie 1990) ★★★, *Merci* (Shanachie 2002) ★★★.

## BLOOD BROTHERS

After transferring from the Liverpool Playhouse, this distinctly contemporary stage musical opened at the Lyric Theatre in London on 11 April 1983. Its tough and realistic setting – Liverpool in the depths of that city's despairing inner-urban collapse – mirrored the harshly unsentimental tale of twin brothers Eddie (Andrew C. Wadsworth) and Mickey (George Costigan), separated as children, who grow up in radically different situations. Despite being worlds apart in their social lives, they are drawn together, but the reunion ends tragically. With book, music and lyrics by Willy Russell, one of a handful of brilliant chroniclers of Liverpool's contemporary traumas and dramas, the show starred Barbara Dickson as Mrs. Johnstone (the twins' mother), accompanied by what author and critic Sheridan Morley referred to as 'a hit-squad cast capable of slamming Russell's score out across the footlights'. Prominent amongst the performers were Peter Christian (Sammy), Amanda York (Linda), Wendy Murray (Mrs. Lyons), Alan Leith (Mr. Lyons) and Andrew Scholfield (Narrator). *Blood Brothers* was generally well received by the critics (although there was talk of 'a sordid melodrama'), and earned an Ivor Novello Award for Best British Musical, and Laurence Olivier Awards for Best Musical and Actress (Dickson). However, by the time it began to become popular with the public, aided by radio play of Dickson's 'Tell Me It's Not True', closing notices had been posted, and the show ran for only six months. In the years that followed, many productions were mounted in the UK and abroad. West End impresario Bill Kenwright acquired the national touring rights, and it was his production, headed by Kiki Dee, that opened at London's Albery Theatre on 28 July 1988. With audiences now more familiar with the material, this new *Blood Brothers* was acclaimed from the start. Highlights of the score, which included 'My Child', 'Kids Game', 'Bright New Day', 'That Guy', 'Miss Jones' and 'Light Romance', were the mother's catchy opening 'Marilyn Monroe', the melancholy 'Easy Terms' and the affecting 'Tell Me It's Not True'; Eddie's tender 'I'm Not Saying A Word', Eddie and Mickey's bluesy 'Long Sunday Afternoon' and the Narrator's 'Shoes Upon The Table' were also noteworthy.

Con O'Neill (Mickey) won the Olivier Award for Best Actor In A Musical Entertainment, and he and Stephanie Lawrence, with Mark Michael Hutchinson (Eddie) and Warwick Evans (Narrator), led *Blood Brothers* into New York's Music Box Theatre on 25 April 1993. Co-directed by Kenwright and Bob Tomson, it was damned by leading critic Frank Rich ('Not much dancing, and not much to dance about') and, in spite of enjoying regular standing ovations, was about to be withdrawn when leading cast members were succeeded by more mature artists from the world of popular music, such as Petula Clark, David Cassidy and his step-brother Shaun Cassidy. Business then picked up considerably, and the show completed 839 performances before recouping its losses during a US tour headed by Clark and David Cassidy. Meanwhile, the London production had transferred to the larger Phoenix Theatre in December 1991, and continued a remarkable run, celebrating its 10th anniversary in July 1998, having taken nearly £50 million at the box office. Lyn Paul, former member of the New Seekers, was Mrs. Johnstone on that occasion, and others to fill the role in London and/or New York or Australia, have included Angela Richards, Siobhán McCarthy, Helen Reddy, Carole King and Delia Hannah. Several more stars from the worlds of pop and television have also been in various *Blood Brothers* ensembles, such as Carl Wayne (of 60s pop group the Move), David Soul (*Starsky And Hutch*) and Stefan Dennis (*Neighbours*). Chief albums issued feature the 1988 and 1995 London casts, and *The International Recording*, with Clark and the Cassidy brothers accompanied by the Royal Philharmonic Orchestra.

## BLOW MONKEYS

Led by the politically opinionated Dr Robert (b. Bruce Robert Howard, 2 May 1961, Norfolk, England; guitar), the Blow Monkeys took their name from Australian slang for Aboriginal didgeridoo players, something Robert picked up while living in Australia as a teenager. The nickname Doctor was pinned on him at boarding school because he was seen as a sympathetic listener. Before the Blow Monkeys began in the early 80s, he also had a spell at Norwich City Football Club and dabbled in pop journalism. The other constituent elements of the band were Tony Kiley (b. 16 February 1962; drums), Neville Henry (saxophone) and Mick Anker (b. 2 July 1957; bass). They started recording for RCA Records in 1984 but singles such as 'Man From Russia', 'Atomic Lullaby' and 'Forbidden Fruit' made no headway in the charts. The band finally broke through in 1986 with the jazz-tinged 'Digging Your Scene', one of the earliest songs about AIDS. The following January they had their biggest hit with 'It Doesn't Have To Be This Way'. Come May, this strongly socialist and vehemently anti-Thatcher band found their latest single, '(Celebrate) The Day After You', banned from the airwaves by the BBC until the General Election was over. The record also featured the voice of Curtis Mayfield.

Although reasonably successful, the band were sent a financial lifeline by contributing the track 'You Don't Own Me' to the hugely successful *Dirty Dancing* soundtrack. A series of minor hits followed, and 1989 opened with Dr Robert recording a duet (under his own name) with soul singer Kym Mazelle. 'Wait' went into the UK Top 10, and the year ended with 'Slaves No More' back with the Blow Monkeys, also featuring the vocal prowess of Sylvia Tella. Their last minor hit was 1990's 'Springtime For The World'. Following the break-up of the band, Dr Robert worked with Paul Weller and started a solo career.

● ALBUMS: *Limping For A Generation* (RCA 1984) ★★★, *Animal Magic* (RCA 1986) ★★★★, *She Was Only A Grocer's Daughter* (RCA 1987) ★★★, *Whoops! There Goes The Neighbourhood* (RCA 1989) ★★★, *Springtime For The World* (RCA 1990) ★★★.

● COMPILATIONS: *Choices: The Singles Collection* (RCA 1989) ★★★★, *The Best Of* (RCA 1993) ★★★, *For The Record* (BMG 1996) ★★★, *Atomic Lullabies: Very Best Of The Blow Monkeys* (Camden 1999) ★★★★.

● VIDEOS: *Video Magic* (Hendring Music Video 1988), *Digging Your Scene* (RCA/Columbia 1988), *Choices* (BMG Video 1989).

## BLOW, KURTIS

b. Kurt Walker, 9 August 1959, Harlem, New York, USA. A producer and rap pioneer who had one of the genre's earliest hits with 'Christmas Rappin' in 1979, written for him by J.B. Ford and *Billboard* journalist Robert Ford Jnr. Blow had previously studied vocal performance at the High School Of Music and Art at the City College of New York. Afterwards, he began working as a DJ in Harlem where he added his first tentative raps to liven up proceedings. By this time he had made the acquaintance of fellow City College student Russell Simmons, who convinced him to change his name from Kool DJ Kurt to Kurtis Blow. Playing in small clubs alongside other early innovators such as Grandmaster Flash, he signed to Mercury Records just as the Sugarhill Gang achieved the first rap chart success with 'Rapper's Delight'. Blow in turn became the first rap artist to cut albums for a major label. His 1979 hit, 'The Breaks', for which his partner Davy D (b. David Reeves Jnr.; originally titled Davey DMX, and best known for recording 'One For The Table (Fresh)') provided the first of his backing tracks, was a massive influence on the whole hip-hop movement.

The early 80s were quiet in terms of chart success, before he re-emerged in 1983 with the *Party Time EP* and an appearance in the movie *Krush Groove*. *Ego Trip* was an impressive selection, bolstered by the presence of Run-DMC on the minor hit '8 Million Stories'. He rapped on Rene And Angela's hit 'Save Your Love (For Number One)', doubtless an experience of which he would not wish to be reminded. He also produced for the Fearless Four and Dr. Jeckyll And Mr Hyde, among others. His yearly album cycle continued with the patriotic *America*, whose earnest, sensitive moments (particularly, 'If I Ruled The World', which appeared on the soundtrack to *Krush Groove* and as a single) were rather undermined by the presence of 'Super Sperm'. The following year he organized the all-star King Dream Chorus and Holiday Crew who recorded the Martin Luther King tribute, 'King Holiday', which campaigned for King's birthday to be enshrined as a national holiday. *Kingdom Blow*

featured guest appearances from the likes of Bob Dylan and George Clinton on an amazing interpretation of 'Zip-A-Dee-Doo-Dah'. However, Blow was largely overtaken by the young guns of the genre (notably Run-DMC, ironically) that he helped to create, a fact underlined by the miserable reception offered the misnomered *Back By Popular Demand*, and he has not enjoyed a chart hit since 'I'm Chillin'' in 1986.

● ALBUMS: *Kurtis Blow* (Mercury 1980) ★★★, *Deuce* (Mercury 1981) ★★, *Tough* (Mercury 1982) ★★, *Ego Trip* (Mercury 1984) ★★★, *America* (Mercury 1985) ★★★, *Kingdom Blow* (Mercury 1986) ★★, *Back By Popular Demand* (Mercury 1988) ★★.

● COMPILATIONS: *The Best Of Kurtis Blow* (Mercury 1994) ★★★.

## BLOWZABELLA

Essentially a UK folk dance band, formed in 1978, which achieved a deal of success both on the live music circuit and on record. The band were almost as well known for the frequent changes of personnel as their music. In 1987, sole remaining founder-member John Swayne (b. Jonathan Rock Phipps Swayne, 26 June 1940, Hereford, England; alto and soprano saxophones, bagpipes) left, and Jo Fraser (b. Jo-Anne Rachel Newmarch Fraser, 4 December 1960, St. Albans, Hertfordshire, England; saxophone, vocals, whistles, ex-Old Swan Band) joined. In 1989, Fraser changed her name to Freya, as there was an Equity member with the same name. The rest of the group were Paul James (b. 4 April 1957, Southampton, Hampshire, England; bagpipes, soprano saxophone, percussion, ex-Dr. Cosgill), Nigel Eaton (b. 3 January 1966, Lyndhurst, Hampshire, England; hurdy-gurdy), Ian Luff (b. 4 January 1956, Brighton, Sussex, England; cittern, bass guitar), Dave Roberts (d. 23 February 1996; melodeon, darabuka) and Dave Shepherd (fiddle). Shepherd had joined the group in 1982, having previously played with folk rock band Dr. Cosgill's Delight, alongside James. Luff joined in 1985. Blowzabella toured Brazil for the British Council in 1987, playing a large number of concerts, and *Pingha Frenzy* emerged from over 50 hours of taped sessions. *A Richer Dust* came from the music the band had written for the 500th Anniversary of the Battle of Stoke Field. A concert featuring the piece was performed on 18 June 1987. James and Eaton formed Ancient Beatbox as a part-time project. Freya, by 1989, was also pursuing a career outside Blowzabella, notably touring with Kathryn Locke (b. 30 May 1961, Upminster, Essex, England; 'cello). Shepherd left to get married and moved to live in Germany, and Andy Cutting (b. 18 March 1969, West Harrow, Middlesex, England; melodeon) joined in 1989. Cutting had previously filled in on occasional dates when Shepherd was unavailable. Later that same year, Swayne rejoined the band. The band's repertoire included a wealth of dance material from northern Europe and France. Although considered a dance band, Blowzabella gave many concerts in such places as Ghana, Nigeria, Sierra Leone, Europe and Brazil. They played a 'farewell tour' in 1990 as it had become uneconomical to stay together and tour. The various members have become involved in their own projects and continue to perform.

● ALBUMS: *Blowzabella* (Plant Life 1982) ★★★, *Blowzabella In Colour* (Plant Life 1983) ★★, *Bobbityshooty* (Plant Life 1984) ★★★, with Frankie Armstrong, Brian Pearson *Tam Lin* (Plant Life 1985) ★★★, *The Blowzabella Wall Of Sound* (Plant Life 1986) ★★★, *The B To A Of Blowzabella* (1987) ★★★, *Pingha Frenzy* (Some Bizzare 1988) ★★★, *Vanilla* (Topic 1990) ★★.

● COMPILATIONS: \*\*\* (Osmosys 1995) ★★★.

## BLUE AEROPLANES

Since forming in Bristol, England, in the early 80s, the Blue Aeroplanes have had endless line-up changes, but maintained their original aim, a desire to mix rock and beat poetry and to involve a large number of musicians in an almost communal manner. The nucleus of the band originally revolved around deadpan vocalist Gerard Langley, his brother John (drums, percussion), Nick Jacobs (guitar), Dave Chapman (multi-instrumentalist) and dancer Wojtek Dmochowski. Along the way, individuals such as Angelo Bruschini (guitar, bass, organ), John Stapleton (tapes), Ruth Coltrane (bass, mandolin), Ian Kearey (guitar, banjimer, harmonium), Rodney Allen (guitar), Simon Heathfield (bass) and Caroline Halcrow (guitar – who later left to pursue a solo career as Caroline Trettine) have all contributed to the Aeroplanes' melting pot. After a debut album for the Abstract label, *Bop Art*, in April 1984, the band signed with the fledgling Fire Records. Several well-received EPs followed – *Action Painting And Other Original Works* (1985), *Lover And Confidante And Other Stories Of Travel* and *Religion And Heartbreak* (March 1986) – succeeded by their second album, *Tolerance* (October 1986).

The Blue Aeroplanes' third set, *Spitting Out Miracles*, surfaced in 1987. All were characterized by Langley's monotone verse and a deluge of instruments and sounds hinged around the guitar. 'Veils Of Colour' (1988) coincided with the release of *Night Tracks*, their February 1987 session for BBC Radio disc jockey Janice Long. A double album, *Friendloverplane*, neatly concluded their time with Fire, compiling the Aeroplanes' progress to date. It was not until the start of the new decade that, following a stint supporting R.E.M. in the UK, the band re-emerged on the Ensign label with 'Jacket Hangs' in January 1990 and a new album, *Swagger*, the following month. Both suggested a more direct, straightforward approach, and this was confirmed on the EP *And Stones*. In 1991, an eight-strong line-up now comprising Langley, Bruschini, Dmochowski, Allen, Paul Mulreany (drums – a former member of the Jazz Butcher), Andy McCreeth, Hazel Winter and Robin Key released the roundly acclaimed *Beatsongs*, co-produced by Elvis Costello and Larry Hirsch. Further activity in 1994 indicated a major push forward with that year's album for new home Beggars Banquet Records. *Life Model* sounded as fresh as the band ever has and engendered further press acclaim, and featured new recruits Marcus Williams (bass, ex-Mighty Lemon Drops), Susie Hugg (vocals, ex-Katydids). Following a ten-year

anniversary tour, *Rough Music* proved to be their best album since *Beatsongs*, but commercial success was still elusive. After a long hiatus, the band re-emerged in 2000 with the excellent *Cavaliers*.

● ALBUMS: *Bop Art* (Abstract 1984) ★★★, *Tolerance* (Fire 1986) ★★★, *Spitting Out Miracles* (Fire 1987) ★★★, *Swagger* (Ensign 1990) ★★★, *Beatsongs* (Ensign 1991) ★★★★, *Life Model* (Beggars Banquet 1994) ★★★, *Rough Music* (Beggars Banquet 1995) ★★★, *Cavaliers* (Swarf Finger 2000) ★★★.

Solo: Gerard Langley/Ian Kearey *Siamese Boyfriends* mini-album (Fire 1986) ★★.

● COMPILATIONS: *Friendloverplane* (Fire 1988) ★★★★, *Friendloverplane 2* (Ensign 1992) ★★★, *Fruit* (Fire 1996) ★★★, *Huh! The Best Of The Blue Aeroplanes 1987–1992* (Chrysalis 1997) ★★★, *Weird Shit* (Swarf Finger 2001) ★★★.

## BLUE NILE

The Blue Nile formed in Glasgow, Scotland, in 1981 and consist of Paul Buchanan (b. Glasgow, Scotland; vocals, guitar, synthesizers), Robert Bell (b. Glasgow, Scotland; synthesizers) and Paul Joseph Moore (b. Glasgow, Scotland; piano, synthesizers). Their debut single, 'I Love This Life', was recorded independently and subsequently picked up by RSO Records, which promptly folded. Eventually, their demo tapes found their way to hi-fi specialists Linn Products, so that the company could test various types of music at their new cutting plant. In spite of their lack of experience in the record retail market, Linn immediately signed the band to make *A Walk Across The Rooftops*, which was released in 1984 to considerable praise. Suddenly, thanks to some gently emotive synthetics and an overall mood which seemed to revel in nocturnal atmospherics, the unsuspecting trio were thrust into the limelight. Blue Nile pondered over the reasons for their success and, as a consequence, found themselves incapable of repeating the feats of the first album.

Indeed, it was to be five years before the follow-up, *Hats*, finally continued the shimmering legacy of its predecessor, whereupon the studio-bound collective took their first tentative steps into the live arena with enthusiastically received shows in the USA and Britain before returning to the studio for another anticipated lengthy recording period. Another hold-up was caused by contractual difficulties with Linn and Virgin Records ('It's amazing how you can be generating fantastically small amounts of money and still have fantastically complicated scenarios'). In the 90s the band journeyed to California to record backing vocals for Julian Lennon, eventually working with Robbie Robertson and several others. They also signed a new contract with Warner Brothers Records in 1993, and by 1995 stated they had a large stockpile of songs written in the interim on which to draw. The greatly anticipated *Peace At Last* was highly praised (the UK's *Q* magazine bestowed five stars); however, once the dust had settled its modest success was soon forgotten and fans returned to the first two albums, both minor-masterpieces.

● ALBUMS: *A Walk Across The Rooftops* (Linn/Virgin 1984) ★★★★, *Hats* (Linn/Virgin 1989) ★★★★, *Peace At Last* (Warners 1996) ★★★.

## BLUE ORCHIDS

This experimental pop group was a spin-off from the Manchester band the Fall. Una Baines (keyboards, vocals) and Martin Bramah (guitar, vocals) both found themselves outcasts from that band as the 80s dawned. They put together the Blue Orchids with Rick Goldstar (guitar), Steve Toyne (bass) and Joe Kin (drums) producing a sound that echoed the less esoteric moments of their former employer. Lyrics were usually spoken or half-sung, leaving a sinister and enticing set of songs that deserved a wider audience. These included their debut single, 'The Flood', after which Ian Rogers became the first in a succession of drumming replacements. After the follow-up, 'Work', the band embarked on a debut album. Toyne had left, leaving Bramah to fill in on bass, as their third drummer, 'Toby' (ex-Ed Banger And The Nosebleeds), came into the line-up. *The Greatest Hit (Money Mountain)* was ambitious and slightly flawed. Mark Hellyer filled the vacant bass position, while Goldstraw departed, leaving Bramah to handle guitar duties on his own. 'Agents Of Chance' was the final Blue Orchids release for some time, before they returned with one 12-inch single, 'Sleepy Town', in 1985. Nick Marshall (drums) was the back-up to Baines and Bramah this time, on an effort produced by another ex-Fall man, Tony Friel. Bramah moved on to Thirst, working, inevitably, with another Fall alumnus, Karl Burns. He would finally return to the Fall fold in 1989 to complete the cycle. However, the Blue Orchids re-formed once more in 1991 with a single, 'Diamond Age', and the retrospective *A View From The City*. Contained among other forgotten period classics is 'Bad Education', better known for the cover treatment given to it by Aztec Camera. The new line-up featured Bramah, Craig Gannon (guitar, ex-Bluebells; Smiths), Martin Hennin (bass) and Dick Harrison (drums). Baines, now Bramah's ex-wife, had departed. His new girlfriend was the Fall keyboard player Marcia Schofield who made a guest appearance on 'Diamond Age'.

The Blue Orchids' influence continued to be felt in the revival of the Hammond organ sound, especially on the records of bands such as the Inspiral Carpets (who once asked Bramah to join as singer).
● ALBUMS: *The Greatest Hit (Money Mountain)* (Rough Trade 1982) ★★★, *A View From The City* (Rough Trade 1991) ★★★.
● COMPILATIONS: *A Darker Bloom: The Blue Orchids Collection* (Cherry Red 2002) ★★★.

## BLUE RONDO A LA TURK

Named after a Dave Brubeck tune, this UK-based group comprised Moses Mount Bassie (saxophone), Mick 'Lloyd' Bynoe (drums, percussion), Art Collins (saxophone), Geraldo d'Arbilly (b. Brazil; percussion), Kito Poncioni (b. Rio de Janeiro, Brazil; bass), Mark Reilly (b. 20 February 1960, High Wycombe, Buckinghamshire, England; guitar), Chris Sullivan (vocals), Christos Tolera (vocals), Tholo Peter Tsegona (trumpet) and Daniel White (b. 26 August 1959, Letchwood, Hertfordshire, England; keyboards). Founder-member and chief lyricist Sullivan formed the core of the band in early 1981.

The group were heavily promoted in the fashion and style magazines of the period, but were received less enthusiastically by the music press. Their debut, *Chewing The Fat*, produced by Clive Langer and Alan Winstanley, nevertheless showed promise. 'Me And Mr Sanchez' peaked at number 40 and 'Klactoveesedstein' just made the Top 50, and a parting of the ways had occurred even before the second album. Reilly and White went on to form Matt Bianco.
● ALBUMS: *Chewing The Fat* (Diable Noir 1982) ★★, *Bees Knees And Chicken Elbows* (Virgin 1984) ★★.

## BLUEBELLS

This Scottish quintet was formed in 1982, and originally comprised brothers David McCluskey (b. 13 January 1964; drums) and Ken McCluskey (b. 8 February 1962; vocals, harmonica), plus Robert 'Bobby Bluebell' Hodgens (b. 6 June 1959; vocals, guitar), Russell Irvine (guitar) and Lawrence Donegan (bass). The latter two were later replaced, respectively, by Craig Gannon (b. 30 July 1966) and Neal Baldwin. The group were fine exponents of the 'jangly pop' common to Scottish bands such as Orange Juice and Aztec Camera. Despite strong airplay on UK radio, the inexplicable failure of 'Cath' to rise any further than number 62 in the UK chart in 1983 perplexed critics and fans, as did the similar fate that befell 'Sugar Bridge' in the same year. The Bluebells did at last gain their deserved success in 1984 with the number 11 hit 'I'm Falling', and 'Young At Heart' (co-written by Siobhan Fahey of Bananarama/Shakespears Sister), which reached the UK Top 10, while their solitary album for London Records achieved Top 30 status. Riding on the wave of this success, a reissued 'Cath'/'She Will Always Be Waiting' belatedly hit the Top 40. After splitting, siblings Ken and David formed the McCluskey Brothers, releasing an album, *Aware Of All*, while Hodgens formed Up and later worked with Paul Quinn (ex-Bourgie Bourgie). Craig Gannon stood in, briefly, for the Smiths bass player Andy Rourke, who was having drug problems, then, on Rourke's return, Gannon continued with the Smiths as second guitarist, subsequently joining the Adult Net and working with Terry Hall. In 1993 Volkswagen used 'Young At Heart' in one of their television advertisements. The song re-entered the UK charts in April, reaching number 1 and staying there for a month. However, the group promised 'not to outstay their welcome', with the McCluskey brothers returning to folk-singing (releasing a new album, *Favourite Colours*). Bobby Bluebell was to be found in Bob's, his Glasgow house/hip-hop club, while Russell Irvine had become a chef, but returned for their appearances on *Top Of The Pops*, replacing Donegan. The Bluebells' former bass player had been ejected after a previous appearance on the programme, when he used the opportunity to write an exposé of the show for the *Guardian* newspaper.
● ALBUMS: *Sisters* (London 1984) ★★★, *Bloomin' Live* (London 1993) ★★.
● COMPILATIONS: *Second* (London 1992) ★★★, *The Singles Collection* (London 1993) ★★★.
● VIDEOS: *The Bluebells* (Dubious Video 1989).

## BLUES BAND

This vastly experienced British blues-rock outfit was put together – initially 'just for fun' – in 1979 by former Manfred Mann band colleagues Paul Jones (b. Paul Pond, 24 February 1942, Portsmouth, England; vocals, harmonica) and Tom McGuinness (b. 2 December 1941, London, England; guitar). They brought in slide guitarist and singer Dave Kelly (b. 1948, London, England; ex-John Dummer Blues Band and Rocksalt), who suggested the bass player from his then-current band Wildcats, Gary Fletcher (b. London, England). On drums was McGuinness' hit-making partner from the early 70s, Hughie Flint (b. 15 March 1942, Manchester, England). Such a confluence of 'name' players brought immediate success on the pub/club/college circuit and, despite the group's humble intentions, recordings followed. *The Official Blues Band Bootleg Album* was literally just that: inability to pay studio bills had forced them to press copies privately from a second copy tape. It sold extremely well, however, and Arista Records soon stepped in, releasing the master recording and issuing four further albums by 1983. The band split in 1982, but re-formed three years later after a one-off charity performance. Recent releases have placed far more emphasis on original material and augur well for the future. Ex-Family drummer Rob Townsend (b. 7 July 1947, Leicester, England) replaced Flint in 1981. The band regularly performed during the 90s, even though Jones and Kelly had substantial careers of their own. Jones has become one of the UK's leading blues/R&B broadcasters and Kelly has released a number of solo albums. The latest Blues Band venture is their version of the 'Unplugged' phenomenon, recorded not for MTV, but at the famous Snape Maltings in Aldeburgh, Suffolk. The Blues Band has such a pedigree that even the most stubborn pro-American purist accepts them. Jones alone has made an immense contribution to promoting the blues and authentic R&B over four decades.

● ALBUMS: *The Official Blues Band Bootleg Album* (Blues Band 1980) ★★★★, *Ready* (Arista 1980) ★★★, *Itchy Feet* (Arista 1981) ★★★, *Brand Loyalty* (Arista 1982) ★★★, *Live: Bye-Bye Blues* (Arista 1983) ★★★, *These Kind Of Blues* (Date 1986) ★★★, *Back For More* (Arista 1989) ★★★, *Fat City* (RCA 1991) ★★★, *Live* (RCA 1993) ★★★, *Homage* (Essential 1993) ★★★, *Wire Less* (Cobalt 1995) ★★★, *Juke Joint Blues* (Ichiban 1995) ★★, *18 Years Old And Alive* (Cobalt 1996) ★★★★, *Brassed Up* (Cobalt 1999) ★★★★, *Scratchin' On My Screen* (Cobalt 2001) ★★★, *Steppin Out* (Hypertension 2002) ★★★, *Greenstuff* 1982 live recording (Hux 2002) ★★★.

● FURTHER READING: *Talk To Me Baby: The Story Of The Blues Band*, Roy Bainton.

## BLUES BROTHERS, THE

John Landis, director of *An American Werewolf In London* and Michael Jackson's promotional video for *Thriller*, was responsible for this 1980 feature film. John Belushi (b. 24 January 1949, Chicago, Illinois, USA, d. 5 March 1982, Los Angeles, California, USA), star of a previous Landis project, *National Lampoon's Animal House*, shared top billing with Dan Aykroyd (b. 1 July 1952, Ottawa, Ontario, Canada) as Jake and Elwood Blues, who re-form their R&B band following the former's release from jail. 'We're on a mission from God,' the pair proclaim when, after a vision, they attempt to raise funds for the orphanage in which they were raised. A highly popular slapstick comedy, *The Blues Brothers* contains some priceless scenes, notably when the band attempt to play soul at a redneck venue. However, it is equally prone to cliché, in particular, the car chase and wrecking sequences, and it is reported that the shot in which one vehicle is dropped from a crane cost more than the rest of the film put together. Despite the presence of former Booker T. And The MGs members Steve Cropper and Duck Dunn, many critics sensed a patronizing, almost pantomime, view of R&B in its content. Cameo roles for James Brown, Ray Charles, Aretha Franklin and John Lee Hooker, however memorable, seemed to marginalize performers actually at the forefront of the genre. However, there is little doubt many of the musicians and singers featured found their careers galvanized by their appearances therein. A successful soundtrack album ensued, while Belushi and Aykroyd, aided by Cropper and Dunn, recorded further albums under the Blues Brothers banner. Belushi's sudden death brought that pastime to a premature end. The film, nevertheless, has retained its appeal and remains one of the most popular musical features of its era. Long planned by Aykroyd, a sequel, *Blues Brothers 2000*, was released in 1998 to general critical disapproval. Reprising his role as Elwood, Aykroyd was this time paired with ex-*Roseanne* star John Goodman; the film retrod the original virtually step for step and featured more lazy cover versions of R&B classics.

● FILMS: *The Blues Brothers* (1980).

## BLYTH POWER

The driving force behind this collection of post-punk train-spotters (their name derives from the name of a steam engine) is drummer, lead singer and songwriter Josef Porta (b. Joseph Porter, 21 February 1962, Templecombe, Somerset, England). He had previously worked with a variety of bands, Valley Forge, while in Somerset in 1978, and on moving to London in 1979, Attitudes and the Entire Cosmos – which primarily comprised the road-crew of Here And Now. After brief stints joining and recording with Zounds, Null And Void and the Mob, Porta formed Blyth Power in 1983 with Curtis Youé. Porta's eloquent lyrics, coupled with a punk-influenced mixture of folk and rock, drew analogies from England's history, such as Watt Tyler and Oliver Cromwell's army, with the state of present-day politics, in particular, resistance against the Conservative government. His attacks on the ruination of the common man's right to English heritage have endeared him to an audience of kindred spirits, though this has been no exercise in austerity – Porta being just as likely to document the rise and fall of a cricket match as a government's fortunes. Though many of Blyth Power's albums have been blighted by inadequate production, each has achieved a consistent quality, with the highlight

Porta's mocking social analysis. The group's debut cassette, for example, included songs such as their debut single, 'Chevy Chase' – 'And from Yorkshire to Somerset I was king of the field/With my barn-door defence of my lofty ideals/They tell me that anarchy and peace became real/And it lives in a field outside Reading'. Vivid characters, historical, rural and cricketing, have continued to populate Porta's songs ever since. They certainly have their supporters, among them *Folk Roots*' editor Ian A. Anderson: '(They) are among the rare outfits who have sufficient roots in our culture to bring that unmistakable feeling of swelling, thrilling pride; whose lyrical literacy and grasp of a great, powerful melody line lift them way above just about any multi-millionaire household-name pop icons you can name.' Their sixth studio album was released in 1995, this time without the services of long-serving member 'Wob', who had departed for a solo career. Nevertheless, *Paradise Razed*, completed in 10 days with Whisky Priests collaborator Fred Purser, was as accessible an introduction to the band as any, with Porta (now calling himself Porter) offering further entertaining insights into British history in songs such as 'Ghilbert De Haace' and 'Rowan's Riding'.

● ALBUMS: *A Little Touch Of Harry In The Middle Of The Night* cassette only (96 Tapes 1984) ★★★, *Wicked Women, Wicked Men And Wicket Keepers* (Midnight 1986) ★★★, *The Barman And Other Stories* (Midnight 1988) ★★★, *Alnwick And Tyne* (Midnight 1990) ★★★, *The Guns Of Castle Cary* (Downward Spiral 1991) ★★★, *Pastor Skull* (Downward Spiral 1993) ★★★, *Paradise Razed* (Downward Spiral 1995) ★★★, *Out From Under The King* (Downward Spiral 1996) ★★★, *The Bricklayer's Arms* (Downward Spiral 2000) ★★★. Solo: Joseph Porter *When Death Went To Bed With A Lady* (Downward Spiral 1998) ★★★. Wob *I Can't Stay Long* (Cycle 1996) ★★★.

● COMPILATIONS: *Pont Au-Dessus De La Brue* (Midnight 1988) ★★★.

## BODINES

This UK rock/pop combo achieved a degree of critical success in the mid- to late 80s, principally, and unjustly, through their connections with the fashionable Creation Records label. The band's line-up featured lyricist Mike Ryan (vocals), Paul Brotherton (guitar), Tim Burtonwood (bass) and John Rowland (drums). Ryan and Rowland were school friends from Glossop, Lancashire, while Brotherton grew up in Salford. The band was put together while its members were unemployed. Their first demo tape included raw versions of songs that would surface later, and Alan McGee at Creation decided he was interested. They became the youngest band to play the Factory Funhouse (at the Haçienda, Manchester), and two singles on Creation, 'God Bless' and 'Therese', produced by Ian Broudie (Lightning Seeds), were impressive. However, they soon moved on when record sales failed to follow their good press. Subsequent singles 'Skankin' Queen' and 'Slip Slide' were undeservedly ignored, though their debut album was critically revered: 'Mick Ryan . . . is not going suddenly to sing songs

about being happy; he's still stuck with betrayal, guilt and worry, but these feelings aren't smothered in some wet blanket, they're distilled into a crystal glass.' By this time they employed a brass section (Graham Lambyekski and Nelson Pandela), but when new label Magnet disappeared, so did the Bodines.

● ALBUMS: *Played* (Magnet 1987) ★★★.

## BOLLOCK BROTHERS

The Bollock Brothers started off as an 'in joke' that rapidly became very unfunny indeed. Formed in the UK in 1982 and led by the 'legendary' Jock McDonald, they attempted to satirize the philosophy of punk by blatantly using songs, images and ideas that were the property of the Sex Pistols. However, their music was less than exciting and more akin to inept cabaret. They included funk, blues, soul, rock and even folk styles, but struggled to produce anything that was even vaguely memorable or original. The full-scale Pistols pastiche, *Never Mind The Bollocks*, is worthy of note, however, for including Michael Fagin on guest vocals. Fagin had been widely celebrated in the media for having broken into the Queen's bedroom in the middle of the night for a chat. Arguably stranger still, McDonald managed to enlist songwriters Vangelis and Alex Harvey for *Four Horsemen Of The Apocalypse*, but this set was still marred by his abominable vocals. Several albums/bootlegs credited to the Ex-Pistols also had McDonald's dubious fingerprints all over them.

● ALBUMS: *Last Supper* (Charly 1983) ★★, *Never Mind The Bollocks 1983* (Charly 1983) ★★, *Live Performances* (Charly 1983) ★, *77, 78, 79* (Konnexion 1985) ★★, *Four Horsemen Of The Apocalypse* (Charly 1985) ★, *Rock 'N' Roll Suicide* (Konnexion 1986) ★★, *Live – In Public In Private* (Charly 1985) ★, *The Prophecies Of Nostradamus* (Blue Turtle 1987) ★★.

## BOLTON, MICHAEL

b. Michael Bolotin, 26 February 1954, New Haven, Connecticut, USA. Bolton became one of the most successful rock balladeers of the late 80s and early 90s. He grew up listening to soul artists such as Stevie Wonder, Ray Charles and Marvin Gaye before recording his first single (under his real name) for Epic Records in 1968. Among the backing musicians on Bolotin's first solo album for RCA Records were Bernard Purdie, David Sanborn and Muscle Shoals session musician Wayne Perkins. Critics made frequent comparisons between Bolotin and Joe Cocker. In the late 70s, Bolotin became lead singer with hard rock band Blackjack. However, despite the presence of top producers Tom Dowd (Allman Brothers Band and Eric Clapton) and Eddy Offord (Yes), their two albums for Polydor Records sold poorly. After the band split, guitarist Bruck Kulick played with Billy Squier, while drummer Sandy Gennaro joined the Pat Travers Band and bass player Jimmy Haslip became a session musician. Bolotin himself turned to songwriting and to a new solo recording contract with Columbia Records. Initially, he had greater success as a composer, providing Laura Branigan with the 1983 hit 'How Am I

Supposed To Live Without You', co-written with Doug James.

He started using the more accessible name Bolton in 1983. As a solo performer, he persevered with a heavy rock approach and it was not until he shifted to a soul-ballad style on *The Hunger* that he had his own first Top 20 single, 'That's What Love Is All About', in 1987. From that point Bolton had a series of blue-eyed soul hits that included a new US chart-topping version of 'How Am I Supposed To Live Without You' in 1990, as well as 'How Can We Be Lovers' (US number 3) and the 1991 successes 'Love Is A Wonderful Thing' (US number 4), 'Time, Love And Tenderness' (US number 7) and his second US chart-topper, a cover version of 'When A Man Loves A Woman'. He also enjoyed a brief, and unexpected, songwriting collaboration with Bob Dylan, but by the middle of the 90s his career had peaked. In 1995, he resurfaced with a hit single, 'Can I Touch You ... There?', and a greatest hits package.

After the commercial failure of *All That Matters*, Bolton reappeared in the late 90s performing quasi-operatic material. Years of litigation with the Isley Brothers ended in January 2001 when Bolton was ordered to pay them over $5 million in a plagiarism lawsuit. His first recording for Jive Records was released the following year.

● ALBUMS: as Michael Bolotin *Michael Bolotin* (RCA 1975) ★★, as Michael Bolotin *Every Day Of My Life* (RCA 1976) ★★, with Blackjack *Blackjack* (Polydor 1979) ★★, with Blackjack *Worlds Apart* (Polydor 1980) ★★, *Michael Bolton* (Columbia 1983) ★★, *Everybody's Crazy* (Columbia 1985) ★★, *The Hunger* (Columbia 1987) ★★★, *Soul Provider* (Columbia 1989) ★★★, *Time, Love And Tenderness* (Columbia 1991) ★★, *The One Thing* (Columbia 1993) ★★, *This Is The Time - The Christmas Album* (Columbia 1996) ★, *All That Matters* (Columbia 1997) ★★★, *My Secret Passion: The Arias* (Sony Classical 1998) ★★, *Only A Woman Like You* (Jive 2002) ★★★.

● COMPILATIONS: *Timeless - The Classics* (Columbia 1992) ★★★, *Greatest Hits 1985-1995* (Sony 1995) ★★★, *The Early Years* (RCA 1997) ★★, *Timeless - The Classics, Vol. 2* (Columbia 1999) ★★, *Love Songs* (Columbia 2002) ★★★.

● VIDEOS: *Soul Provider: The Videos* (CMV Enterprises 1990), *This Is Michael Bolton* (SMV 1992), *Decade: Greatest Hits 1985-1995 The Videos* (SMV 1995).

## BON JOVI

This commercial hard rock band, formed in New Jersey, USA, is fronted by Jon Bon Jovi (b. John Francis Bongiovi Jnr., 2 March 1962, Perth Amboy, New Jersey, USA; vocals). His four co-members were Richie Sambora (b. Richard Stephen Sambora, 11 July 1959, Perth Amboy, New Jersey, USA; guitar, ex-Message), David Bryan (b. David Rashbaum, 7 February 1962, Edison, New Jersey, USA; keyboards), Tico Torres (b. 7 October 1953; drums, ex-Franke And The Knockouts) and Alec John Such (b. 14 November 1956; bass, ex-Message). Bongiovi, of Italian descent, met Bryan (ex-Phantom's Opera) at Sayreville High School, where they shared a mutual interest in rock music. They soon joined eight other musicians in the R&B cover band Atlantic City Expressway. When Bryan moved to New York to study at the Juilliard School of Music, Bongiovi followed. After charming his way into the Power Station recording studios, which was owned by his cousin Tony, he performed menial tasks for two years before Billy Squier agreed to produce his demo tape. One track, 'Runaway', was played on local radio and appeared on a local artist compilation album (his work would also grace oddities such as the novelty track, 'R2D2 I Wish You A Merry Christmas'). Reunited with Bryan, he acquired the services of Sambora, an established session musician, Such (ex-Phantom's Opera) and Torres (ex-Knockouts).

By July 1983, they had a recording contract with PolyGram Records and support slots with Eddie Money and ZZ Top, the latter at Madison Square Garden. Jon Bon Jovi's looks attracted immediate attention for the band, and he turned down the lucrative lead role in the dance movie *Footloose* in order to concentrate on his music. Their debut album preceded a headline tour and support slots with the Scorpions, Whitesnake and Kiss. Their second album, *7800 Degrees Fahrenheit*, was greeted with cynicism by the music press, which was already hostile towards the band's manicured image and formularized heavy rock - this mediocre album only fuelled their scorn. The band responded in style: *Slippery When Wet* was the biggest-selling rock album of 1987, although it originally appeared in August 1986. Collaborating with songwriter Desmond Child, three of its tracks - 'Wanted Dead Or Alive', 'You Give Love A Bad Name' and 'Livin' On A Prayer' - were US and European hits. Headlining the Monsters Of Rock shows in Europe, they were joined on stage by Gene Simmons and Paul Stanley (Kiss), Dee Snider (Twisted Sister) and Bruce Dickinson (Iron Maiden) for an encore of 'We're An American Band'. It merely served to emphasize the velocity with which Bon Jovi had reached the top of the rock league. The tour finally finished in Australia after 18 months, while the album sold millions of copies. When *New Jersey* followed, it included 'Living In Sin', a Jon Bon Jovi composition that pointed to his solo future, although the song owed a great debt to his hero Bruce Springsteen.

The rest of 1989 was spent on more extensive touring, before the band temporarily retired. As Jon Bon Jovi commented, it was time to 'Ride my bike into the hills, learn how to garden, *anything* except do another Bon Jovi record.' He subsequently concentrated on his solo career, married karate champion Dorothea Hurley and appeared in his first movie, *Young Guns II*, and released a quasi-soundtrack of songs inspired by the film as his debut solo album in 1990. However, the commercial incentive to return to Bon Jovi was inevitably hard to resist. *Keep The Faith*, with a more stripped-down sound, was an impressive album, satisfying critics and anxious fans alike who had patiently waited almost four years for new material. To those who had considered the band a spent commercial force, the success of the slick ballad, 'Always', a chart fixture in 1994, announced no such decline. On the back of its success, Bon Jovi occupied the UK number 1 spot with the compilation set *Crossroad*, amid rumours that bass player Alec John Such was about to be replaced by Huey McDonald. Meanwhile, Bryan released his first solo album, through Phonogram in Japan, and Sambora married Hollywood actress Heather Locklear (ex-*Dynasty*).

*These Days* was a typically slick collection of ballads and party rock, and included the hit single 'This Ain't A Love Song'. With their position already secure as one of the world's most popular rock bands, the album lacked ambition, and the band seemed content to provide fans with more of the same old formula. Their profile had never been greater than in 1995, when, in the annual readers poll of the leading UK metal magazine *Kerrang!*, the band won seven categories, including best band and best album (for *These Days*) and, astonishingly, worst band and worst album (for *These Days*)! *These Days Tour Edition* was a live mini-album released only in Australia.

Jon Bon Jovi began to nurture an acting career in the 90s with starring roles in *Moonlight And Valentino* and *The Leading Man*, and enjoyed further solo success with 1997's *Destination Anywhere*. The band regrouped two years later to record their new album, *Crush*. They continue to bridge the gap between heavy metal and AOR with both style and ease, and somehow manage to remain in fashion.

● ALBUMS: *Bon Jovi* (Mercury 1984) ★★, *7800 Degrees Fahrenheit* (Mercury 1985) ★★, *Slippery When Wet* (Mercury 1986) ★★★★, *New Jersey* (Mercury 1988) ★★★, *Keep The Faith* (Jambco/Mercury 1992) ★★★★, *These Days* (Mercury 1995) ★★★, *These Days Tour Edition* mini-album (Mercury 1996) ★★, *Crush* (Island/Mercury 2000) ★★★, *One Wild Night: Live 1985–2001* (Island/Mercury 2001) ★★★, *Bounce* (Mercury 2002) ★★.

● COMPILATIONS: *Crossroad – The Best Of* (Mercury 1994) ★★★★.

● VIDEOS: *Breakout* (PolyGram Music Video 1986), *Slippery When Wet* (Channel 5 1988), *New Jersey* (Channel 5 1989), *Dead Or Alive* (PolyGram Music Video 1989), *Access All Areas* (PolyGram Music Video 1990), *Keep The Faith: An Evening With Bon Jovi* (PolyGram Music Video 1993), *Crossroad: The Best Of* (PolyGram Music Video 1994), *Live From London* (PolyGram Music Video 1995), *The Crush Tour* (Mercury 2000).

● FURTHER READING: *Bon Jovi: An Illustrated Biography*, Eddy McSquare. *Faith And Glory*, Malcolm Dome. *Bon Jovi: Runaway*, Dave Bowler and Bryan Dray. *The Illustrated Biography*, Mick Wall. *The Complete Guide To The Music Of Bon Jovi*, Mick Wall and Malcolm Dome. *Bon Jovi*, Neil Jeffries.

## BONGO MAN, KANDA

b. Kanda Bongo, Inongo, Belgian Congo. Soukous vocalist and bandleader Bongo Man is the nephew of the celebrated Zairean singer-songwriter Jean Bokelo, who was instrumental in encouraging his musical talent as a child and later helped him to gain his first foothold in the local music scene. In 1973, with the brothers Soki and Dianzenza Vangu, Bongo Man formed his first band, Orchestre Bella Mambo

(later known as Orchestre Bella Bella). Stylistically, Bella Mambo struck a balance between the older big bands and younger dance groups such as Zaiko Langa Langa. The outfit toured widely in Zaire, Tanzania, Uganda and Kenya before Bongo Man left in 1979, to settle in Paris, then a powerful European magnet for Francophone African musicians. He spent his first two years in the city working as a labourer, before signing to the Afro Rythmes label in 1981 and releasing two superb albums, *Iyole* and *Djessy*, which mixed soukous with internationally appealing pop melodies. With *Djessy*, he further broadened soukous' established style by adding Latin-American-derived beguine rhythms. In 1983, he visited the UK to play an acclaimed set at the high-profile WOMAD (World Music And Dance) Festival. Setting up his own Paris-based label, Bongo Man Records, in 1984, he released his third album, *Amour Fou*. In 1985 British-based specialist label Globestyle released the compilation *Non Stop Non Stop*. *Malinga* followed in 1986, then the zouk-influenced *Lela Lela* in 1987. His flirtation with that year continued when he played on Kassav's classic album *Zouk Time*. As the decade closed Kanda immersed himself in dance trends such as the Kwassa Kwassa and Mayebo, though his style was still located primarily in the high-speed soukous tradition that he had pioneered.

● ALBUMS: *Iyole* (Afro Rythmes 1981) ★★★★, *Djessy* (Afro Rythmes 1982) ★★★★, *Amour Fou* (Bongo Man 1984) ★★, *Malinga* (Bongo Man 1986) ★★★, *Lela Lela* (Bongo Man 1987) ★★, *Sai Liza* (Bongo Man/Melodié 1988) ★★★, *Kwassa Kwassa* (Hannibal 1989) ★★★, *Isambe Monie* (Bongo Man/Melodié 1990) ★★★, *Zing Zong* (Hannibal 1991) ★★★, *Sango* (Celluloid 1992) ★★★, *Soukous In Central Park* (Hannibal 1993) ★★★★, *Sweet* (Air B 1995) ★★★, *Welcome To South Africa* (Melodié 1995) ★★★.

● COMPILATIONS: *Non Stop Non Stop* (Globestyle 1985) ★★★, *The Very Best Of Kanda Bongo Man* (Nascente 2001) ★★★★.

## BONGWATER

Bongwater evolved in New York, USA, in 1987 when (Mark) Kramer (guitar), formerly of Shockabilly and the Butthole Surfers, joined forces with vocalist/performance artist Ann Magnuson. The pair were already acquainted from the latter's previous group, Pulsallama, and the new act was one of the first to record for Kramer's Shimmy-Disc label. The duo completed their debut EP, *Breaking No New Ground*, with the help of guitarist Fred Frith, and its content ranged from original material to a reconstructed interpretation of the Moody Blues' 'Ride My See-Saw'. The expansive *Double Bummer* introduced Dave Rick (guitar) and David Licht (drums) to a unit that would remain largely informal, although both contributed to subsequent releases. The new set included 'Dazed And Chinese', a version of Led Zeppelin's 'Dazed And Confused' sung in Chinese, as well as songs drawn from the Soft Machine, Monkees and Gary Glitter. Self-penned compositions embraced psychedelia, taped documentaries, pop culture and the *avant garde*, and, if derided as self-indulgent by some, the album confirmed the group's sense of adventure. *Too Much Sleep* was more conventional and while 'Splash 1' (the 13th Floor Elevators) and 'The Drum' (Slapp Happy) continued the duo's dalliance with the obscure, their original material, notably the title song and 'He Loved The Weather', showed an unerring grasp of melody. Magnuson's semi-narrative intonation flourished freely on *The Power Of Pussy*, which encompassed sexuality in many contrasting forms. Layers of guitar lines and samples enhanced a genuinely highly crafted collection, which confirmed the promise of earlier recordings. Bongwater also undertook several entertaining live appearances, proving them to be one of the most imaginative acts on the independent circuit of the early 90s. Rick was replaced by Randolph A. Hudson III in 1991, but following the release of *The Big Sell Out* the group split due to personal clashes between Kramer and Magnuson. The ensuing legal squabbles led to the closure of Shimmy-Disc.

● ALBUMS: *Breaking No New Ground* mini-album (Shimmy-Disc 1987) ★★★, *Double Bummer* (Shimmy-Disc 1988) ★★★, *Too Much Sleep* (Shimmy-Disc 1989) ★★★, *The Power Of Pussy* (Shimmy-Disc 1991) ★★★★, *The Peel Sessions* (Strange Fruit 1991) ★★★, *The Big Sell Out* (Shimmy-Disc 1992) ★★★★.
● COMPILATIONS: *The Complete Bongwater Collection* 4-CD box set (Shimmy-Disc 1999) ★★★.

## BONNET, GRAHAM

b. 12 December 1947, Skegness, Lincolnshire, England. Bonnet first garnered attention in 1968 as one half of the Marbles, who enjoyed a UK Top 5 hit with the emotional 'Only One Woman'. Subsequent singles, both with the group and as a solo act, proved unsuccessful and he later turned to acting, starring in the film *Three For All*. Bonnet resumed recording in 1977 on Ringo Starr's Ring O Records, but although *Graham Bonnet* was not a major seller in Britain, the album achieved gold status in Australia. In 1979 Bonnet replaced Ronnie James Dio in Ritchie Blackmore's Rainbow. With his almost James Dean-like image, the choice of Bonnet as Dio's replacement was the subject of some consternation amongst the group's more traditional heavy metal fans. The singer was featured on *Down To Earth*, one of the group's most popular albums, and also graced the hit singles 'Since You've Been Gone' and 'All Night Long'. However, Rainbow's legendary instability led to Bonnet's departure the following year. He resumed his solo career with *Line Up* in 1981 and earned himself a UK Top 10 single with 'Night Games'. Later, he returned to collectivism by joining MSG for one album, *Assault Attack*, before relocating to the west coast of the USA to become vocalist for Alcatrazz. In 1987 he joined Chris Impellitteri's group, recording the hard rock classic *Stand In Line*. In 1993 he assembled metal 'supergroup' Blackthorne, whose repertoire included an update of 'All Night Long'.

● ALBUMS: *Graham Bonnet* (Ring O 1977) ★★★, *Line Up* (Vertigo 1981) ★★★, *The Day I Went Mad* (Escape 2001) ★★.

## BOOGIE DOWN PRODUCTIONS

This Bronx, New York-based rap duo comprised DJ Scott LaRock (b. Scott Sterling, d. 27 August 1987, South Bronx, New York City, New York, USA) and rapper KRS-One (b. Lawrence Krisna Parker, 20 August 1965, New York, USA). KRS-One (aka KRS-1) is an acronym for Knowledge Reigns Supreme Over Nearly Everyone, and 'edutainment' remained a central theme in the work of Boogie Down Productions. Similar to most New York rap crews, their lyrics highlighted the problems faced by the black community in a modern urban environment, compounded by the increasing drug problems, gang wars and use of weaponry on the streets. Indeed, LaRock and KRS-One, who had formerly worked with 'joke' rap act 12:41 ('Success Is The Word'), met at a homeless people's shelter in the Bronx, where LaRock was a counsellor and KRS-One a client. Following their first release, 'Crack Attack', their debut album, *Criminal Minded*, was produced in conjunction with fellow Bronx crew, the Ultramagnetic MC's. It was a set that actively suggested that young blacks were entitled to use 'any means necessary' in order to overcome years of prejudice and discrimination. It sold over 500,000 copies and was instrumental in kick-starting the gangsta rap movement.

After Scott LaRock became the victim of an unknown assassin while sitting in a parked car in the South Bronx, KRS-One's lyrics enforced an even stronger need for a change in attitude, demanding an end to violence and the need for blacks to educate themselves. *Criminal Minded* had, of course, depicted the duo wielding guns on its sleeve. The follow-up sets, *By All Means Necessary* and *Ghetto Music: The Blueprint Of Hip-Hop*, were arguably just as convincing. Tracks such as 'The Style You Haven't Done Yet' took pot shots at KRS-One's would-be successors. There was certainly much to admire in KRS-One's style, his method becoming the most frequently copied in aspiring new rappers. He was also setting out on lecture tours of American universities, even writing columns for the *New York Times*. Like contemporaries Public Enemy, Boogie Down Productions retained the hardcore edge necessary to put over their message and, in doing so, brought a more politically aware and mature conscience to the rap scene. However, 1990's *Edutainment* possibly took the message angle too far, featuring only lacklustre musical accompaniment to buoy KRS-One's momentous tracts. The live set that followed it was not the first such hip-hop album (2 Live Crew beating KRS-One to the punch), but it was certainly the best so far, with a virulent, tangible energy. After the release of *Sex And Violence*, KRS-One elected to release new material under his own name and abandoned the Boogie Down Productions moniker.

● ALBUMS: *Criminal Minded* (B-Boy 1987) ★★★★, *By All Means Necessary* (Jive/RCA 1988) ★★★★, *Ghetto Music: The Blueprint Of Hip Hop* (Jive/RCA 1989) ★★★★, *Edutainment* (Jive/RCA 1990) ★★★, *Live Hardcore Worldwide: Paris, London & NYC* (Jive/RCA 1991) ★★★★, *Sex And Violence* (Jive 1992) ★★★.

● COMPILATIONS: *Man And His Music* (B-Boy 1987) ★★.

## BOOTHILL FOOT-TAPPERS

Formed in 1982 by Chris Thompson (b. 19 March 1957, Ashford, Middlesex, England; banjo/vocals) and Kevin Walsh (guitar, vocals), the Boothills' full line-up was completed by Wendy May (b. Wendy May Billingsley; vocals), Slim (b. Clive Pain; accordion/piano), Marnie Stephenson (washboard/vocals), Merrill Heatley (vocals) and her brother Danny (drums). As part of an emerging 'country cow-punk' movement in the UK during the mid-80s (along with such acts as Helen And The Horns and Yip Yip Coyote), the Boothill Foot-Tappers proved to be the most adept at the genre and certainly one of the best live performers. They enjoyed a minor UK hit on the Go! Discs/Chrysalis label with 'Get Your Feet Out Of My Shoes' in July 1984. Slim, who had been enjoying a parallel career as part of the Blubbery Hellbellies, left the group in 1983 before the recording of the Boothills' debut album and was replaced by Simon Edwards (melodeon) – although he occasionally rejoined the group for live performances. The group folded at the end of 1985 after touring to promote the album, which failed to set the charts alight. After briefly working with B.J. Cole and Bob Loveday in the Rivals and later with the Devils In Disguise, Chris Thompson went on to form the Barely Works. Wendy May decided to concentrate on the running of the successful disco club Locomotion at the Town And Country Club in Kentish Town, London.

● ALBUMS: *Ain't That Far From Boothill* (Mercury 1985) ★★.

## Bow Wow

The name translates literally as 'Barking Dog', a fitting title for Japan's finest exponents of melodic heavy metal. Formed in 1976, the band comprised Kyoji Yamamoto (vocals/guitar), Mitsuhiro Saito (vocals/guitar), Kenji Sano (bass) and Toshiri Niimi (drums). Intriguingly, they incorporated classical Japanese musical structures within a framework of westernized hard rock. Influenced by Kiss, Led Zeppelin and Aerosmith, they released a sequence of impressive albums during the late 70s. Characterized by explosive guitar work and breathtaking arrangements, the only disappointment to western ears was the Japanese vocals, which doubtless restricted their international appeal. On *Asian Volcano*, their eleventh album, released in 1982, the vocals were sung in English for the first time, but the band sounded uncomfortable with the transition. They played the Reading Festival the same year and were afforded an encouraging reception. Two subsequent shows at London's Marquee Club were recorded for the live album *Holy Expedition*, which followed in 1983. At the end of that year the band changed their name to Vow Wow, adding an extra vocalist and keyboard player to pursue a more melodic direction. Lead guitarist Yamamoto has released two solo albums representing an instrumental fusion of classical, rock and jazz styles, *Horizons* and *Electric Cinema* in 1980 and 1982,

respectively. Beyond the Far East, success has continued to elude this first-class rock outfit, despite Whitesnake's Neil Murray joining for a short time in 1987.

● ALBUMS: *Bow Wow* (Invitation 1976) ★★★, *Signal Fire* (Invitation 1977) ★★★, *Charge* (Invitation 1977) ★★★, *Super Live* (Invitation 1978) ★★★, *Guarantee* (Invitation 1978) ★★★, *The Bow Wow* (Invitation 1979) ★★★, *Glorious Road* (SMS 1979) ★★★, *Telephone* (SMS 1980) ★★★, *X Bomber* (SMS 1980) ★★★, *Hard Dog* (SMS 1981) ★★★, *Asian Volcano* (VAP 1982) ★★, *Warning From Stardust* (VAP 1982) ★★, *Holy Expedition* (Heavy Metal 1983) ★★. As Vow Wow: *Beat Of Metal Motion* (VAP 1984) ★★★, *Cyclone* (Eastworld 1985) ★★★, *III* (Eastworld 1986) ★★★, *Live* (Passport 1987) ★★, *V* (Arista 1987) ★★★, *VIB* (EMI 1989) ★★★, *Helter Skelter* (Arista 1989) ★★★.

## Bow Wow Wow

Formed in London, England, in 1980 by former Sex Pistols manager Malcolm McLaren, Bow Wow Wow comprised three former members of Adam And The Ants: Dave Barbe (b. David Barbarossa, Mauritius; drums), Matthew Ashman (b. London, England, d. 21 November 1995) and Leigh Gorman (bass). This trio was called upon to back McLaren's latest protégée, a 14-year-old Burmese girl whom he had discovered singing in a dry cleaners in Kilburn, north London. Annabella Lwin (b. Myant Myant Aye, Rangoon, Burma) was McLaren's female equivalent of Frankie Lymon, a teenager with no previous musical experience who could be moulded to perfection. Bow Wow Wow debuted with 'C30, C60, C90, Go', a driving, Burundi Black-influenced paean to home taping composed by McLaren. Its follow-up, the cassette-only *Your Cassette Pet*, featured eight tracks in an EP format (including the bizarre 'Sexy Eiffel Towers'). In addition to the African Burundi influence, the band combined a 50s-sounding Gretsch guitar, complete with echo and tremolo. Although innovative and exciting, the band enjoyed only limited chart rewards during their stay with EMI Records, and, like the Sex Pistols before them, soon sought a new record company.

After signing with RCA Records, McLaren enlivened his promotion of the band with a series of publicity stunts, amid outrageous talk of paedophiliac pop. Annabella had her head shaven into a Mohican style and began appearing in tribal clothes; further controversy ensued when she was photographed semi-nude on an album-sleeve pastiche of Manet's *Déjeuner sur l'Herbe*. A deserved UK Top 10 hit followed with 'Go Wild In The Country', a frenzied, almost animalistic display of sensuous exuberance. An average cover version of the Strangeloves/Brian Poole And The Tremeloes' hit 'I Want Candy' also clipped the Top 10, but by then McLaren was losing control of his concept. A second lead singer was briefly recruited in the form of Lieutenant Lush, who threatened to steal the limelight from McLaren's ingénue and was subsequently ousted, only to reappear in Culture Club as Boy George. By 1983, amid uncertainty and disillusionment, Bow Wow Wow folded. The backing musicians briefly soldiered on as the Chiefs Of Relief, while Annabella took a sabbatical, reappearing in 1985 for an unsuccessful solo career. Matthew Ashman died in 1995 following complications after suffering from diabetes. At the time of his death he was working with Agent Provocateur. Lwin and Gorman reunited in 1997, touring America with new members Dave Calhoun (guitar) and Eshan K (drums).

● ALBUMS: *Your Cassette Pet* cassette only (EMI 1980) ★★★★, *See Jungle! See Jungle! Go Join Your Gang, Yeah, City All Over! Go Ape Crazy!* (RCA 1981) ★★★, *I Want Candy* (RCA 1982) ★★, *When The Going Gets Tough, The Tough Get Going* (RCA 1983) ★★, *Wild In The U.S.A.* (Cleopatra 1999) ★★★. Solo: Annabella *Fever* (RCA 1986) ★★.

● COMPILATIONS: *The Best Of Bow Wow Wow* i (Receiver 1989) ★★★, *Girl Bites Dog: Your Compact Disc Pet* (EMI 1993) ★★★, *The Best Of Bow Wow Wow* ii (RCA 1996) ★★★.

## BOX OF FROGS

Box Of Frogs were welcomed with widespread excitement in the UK press on their arrival in the early 80s by dint of their collective heritage. Jim McCarty (b. 25 July 1943, Liverpool, Lancashire, England; drums), Paul Samwell-Smith (b. 8 May 1943, Richmond, Surrey, England; bass) and Chris Dreja (b. 11 November 1945, Surbiton, Surrey, England; guitar) had all previously been founding members of the Yardbirds. The fourth member, vocalist John Fiddler, had been recruited from Medicine Head. Box Of Frogs released its debut album for Epic Records in 1984. *Box Of Frogs* saw them reprise the spirit of energized R&B for which the Yardbirds had been renowned, though the quality of the songwriting barely hinted at a 'For Your Love' or 'Heart Full Of Soul'. Although it was not a commercial success, pockets of nostalgic fans throughout the world and particularly in the USA purchased it. It included a cameo appearance from Jeff Beck, while both Rory Gallagher and Jimmy Page contributed to the follow-up collection, *Strange Land*. However, deterred by the lack of commercial activity their reunion had created, Box Of Frogs dispersed shortly after its release. McCarty subsequently played with the British Invasion All-Stars and the Yardbirds Experience, and re-formed his original band with Dreja and new personnel.

● ALBUMS: *Box Of Frogs* (Epic 1984) ★★★, *Strange Land* (Epic 1986) ★★★.

## BOY GEORGE

b. George O'Dowd, 14 June 1961, Eltham, Kent, England. During the early 80s O'Dowd became a regular on the London 'New Romantic' club scene. His appearances at clubs such as Billy's, Blitz, Heaven and Hell were regularly featured in the pages of magazines such as *Blitz* and *The Face*. Flaunting a series of flamboyant cross-dressing styles he caught the attention of pop svengali Malcolm McLaren who enrolled him to appear alongside Bow Wow Wow's Annabella Lwin, as Lieutenant Lush, at a concert at London's Rainbow Theatre. This partnership proved short-lived but useful as George's name was pushed further into the spotlight. A meeting with former disc jockey Mikey

Craig (b. 15 February 1960, Hammersmith, London, England; bass) resulted in the forming of a band, In Praise Of Lemmings. After the addition of former Adam And The Ants drummer Jon Moss (b. 11 September 1957, Wandsworth, London, England; drums) plus Roy Hay (b. 12 August 1961, Southend-on-Sea, Essex, England; guitar, keyboards), the group was renamed Culture Club. To the public, however, Culture Club was, to all intents and purposes, Boy George, and his appetite for publicity and clever manipulation of the media seemed effortless. His barely concealed homosexuality, though no problem to his many fans, caused considerable comment in the tabloid press. Ultimately, however, it was not his sexuality but his involvement with drugs that brought his downfall. A week after he teased journalists with the proclamation that he was 'your favourite junkie' at an anti-apartheid concert in London, the British national press revealed that he was indeed addicted to heroin.

No sooner had this episode hit the headlines than another scandal broke. A visiting New York keyboard player, Michael Rudetski, died of a heroin overdose while staying at George's London home. Soon afterwards, George was arrested on a charge of possession of cannabis, resulting in successful treatment for his drug dependence. His public renouncement of drugs coincided with the dissolution of Culture Club and the launch of a solo career. His debut effort, a cover version of the Bread/Ken Boothe hit, 'Everything I Own', in the spring of 1987, gave him his first UK number 1 since 'Karma Chameleon' in 1983. George's outspoken opposition to the Conservative government's anti-homosexual bill, Clause 28, triggered a series of releases damning the bill. He formed his own record label, More Protein, in 1989, and fronted a band, Jesus Loves You, which reflected his new-found spiritual awareness and continuing love of white reggae and soul. Releases with the E-Zee Possee, meanwhile, demonstrated his increasing involvement in the UK's club scene. His pop career was revived in 1992 by a cover version of 'The Crying Game', which was featured in the hit movie of the same name. *Cheapness And Beauty* was a blend of punky glam pop, at odds with his perceived 90s image of fading superstar. The songs, co-written with guitarist John Themis, were the result of a more confident Boy George, altogether more comfortable with his publicly gay persona and completely free of heroin addiction. The album was preceded by an unlikely cover version of Iggy Pop's 'Funtime', while its release date in 1995 coincided with the publication of the artist's self-deprecating autobiography. Now recognized as a leading club DJ, George contributed vocals to a drum 'n' bass version of 'Police And Thieves', released by London dance collective Dubversive in 1998. He has also produced, often in collaboration with Pete Tong, several mix compilations for the Ministry Of Sound label.

The singer returned to his New Romantic days in a new musical, *Taboo*, which opened at The Venue in London on 29 January 2002. The cast, featuring Euan Morton as George, Mark McGee as Marilyn and Matt Lucas as performance artist Leigh Bowery, performed new songs written by George specifically for the show. The producer was Christopher Renshaw.

● ALBUMS: *Sold* (Virgin 1987) ★★★, *Tense Nervous Headache* (Virgin 1988) ★★, *Boyfriend* (Virgin 1989) ★★, *High Hat* (US) (Virgin 1989) ★★, *Cheapness And Beauty* (Virgin 1995) ★★★, *The Unrecoupable One Man Bandit* (Back Door/Nu Gruv 1999) ★★★, *U Can Never B2 Straight* (Virgin 2002) ★★★.

● COMPILATIONS: with Jesus Loves You *The Martyr Mantras* (More Protein/Virgin 1991) ★★★, *At Worst ... The Best Of Boy George And Culture Club* (Virgin 1993) ★★★★, as Jesus Loves You *The Devil In Sister George* (More Protein/Virgin 1994) ★★, *The Annual – Pete Tong & Boy George* (MOS 1995) ★★★, *Dance Nation 2 – Pete Tong & Boy George* (MOS 1996) ★★★, *The Annual II – Pete Tong & Boy George* (MOS 1996) ★★★★, *Dance Nation 4 – Pete Tong & Boy George* (MOS 1997) ★★★★, *Dance Nation 5 – Pete Tong & Boy George* (MOS 1998) ★★★, *The Annual IV – Pete Tong & Boy George* (MOS 1998) ★★★★, *Essential Mix* (London/Sire 2001) ★★★★, *BoyGeorgeDj.com* (Trust The DJ 2001) ★★★★, *Lucky For Some* (J-Bird 2001) ★★★, *Classic Masters* (EMD 2002) ★★★, *Night Out* (Moonshine 2002) ★★★.

● FURTHER READING: *Take It Like A Man*, Boy George.

## BOYS DON'T CRY

The members of Boys Don't Cry had all variously played with Sad Café, Andy Brown, Jackson Heights, Byzantium and Mike Oldfield. Nick Richards, Brian Chatton, Nico Ramsden, Mark Smith and Jeff Seopardi had first played together in an earlier incarnation of the group known as the Jazz Sluts. With unlimited studio time owing to Richards' ownership of the Maison Rouge studio, their recording career began in 1983 with 'Heart's Bin Broken'. They signed to US label Profile Records in the mid-80s and secured an immediate hit single with 'I Wanna Be A Cowboy'. With a video featuring Motörhead's Lemmy, it reached number 12 in the US charts in 1986. Its follow-up, 'The Cities On Time', failed to repeat its success. Following one charting album the group then switched labels to Atlantic Records. Subsequent efforts such as 'Who The Am Dam Do You Think I Am?' failed to revive their career. The members eventually returned to session work.

● ALBUMS: *Boy's Don't Cry* (Legacy/Profile 1986) ★★.

## BRADY, PAUL

b. 19 May 1947, Strabane, Co. Tyrone, Northern Ireland. A member of an R&B group, the Kult, while a student in Dublin, Brady later embraced folk music with the Johnstons. Renowned as a commercial attraction, the group enjoyed a minor success with a version of Joni Mitchell's 'Both Sides Now'. Brady subsequently joined Planxty, a much-respected traditional unit, where the multi-instrumentalist forged an empathy with fellow member Andy Irvine. *Andy Irvine/Paul Brady* prefaced Brady's solo career which began with the much-lauded *Welcome Here Kind Stranger* in 1978. The singer abandoned folk in 1981 with *Hard Station*, which included the Irish chart-topping single 'Crazy Dreams'. The song was then covered by Roger Chapman and Dave Edmunds while a further inclusion, 'Night Hunting Time', was later recorded by Santana. *True For You* followed a prolific period where Brady toured supporting Dire Straits and Eric Clapton, winning the approbation of their audiences. Bob Dylan and U2's Bono also professed admiration for the artist's talents while Tina Turner's versions of 'Steel Claw' and 'Paradise Is Here' cemented Brady's reputation as a songwriter. He collaborated with Mark Knopfler on the soundtrack to *Cal*, before completing a strong live album, *Full Moon*. Subsequent releases show the flowering of a mature talent, reminiscent of Van Morrison. *Trick Or Treat* was recorded under the aegis of former Steely Dan producer Gary Katz. Bonnie Raitt, an admirer of Brady's work, gave his career a significant boost by including two of his songs on her outstanding 1991 album, including the title track, 'Luck Of The Draw'. It is hoped that Brady's work will receive major recognition in the future as he is clearly an important songwriter, although the signs are that, as with talented artists such as Richard Thompson and John Martyn, his work will not get the exposure it certainly deserves. He enlisted outside help in the shape of Ronan Keating, Connor Reeves, Carole King and Will Jennings on May 2000's *Oh What A World*, his first album in over five years.

● ALBUMS: with Andy Irvine *Andy Irvine/Paul Brady* (Mulligan 1976) ★★★★, with Tommy Peoples *The High Part Of The Road* (Shanachie 1976) ★★★, *Welcome Here Kind Stranger* (Mulligan 1978) ★★★, *Hard Station* (Polydor 1981) ★★★, *True For You* (Polydor 1983) ★★★, *Full Moon* (Demon 1984) ★★★★, *Back To The Centre* (Mercury 1985) ★★★, with Peoples, Matt Molloy *Molloy, Brady, Peoples* (Mulligan 1986) ★★★, *Primitive Dance* (Mercury 1987) ★★★★, *Trick Or Treat* (Fontana 1990) ★★★, *Songs And Crazy Dreams* (Fontana 1992) ★★★, *Spirits Colliding* (Fontana 1995) ★★★★, *Oh What A World* (Rykodisc 2000) ★★★.

● COMPILATIONS: *Nobody Knows: The Best Of Paul Brady* (Rykodisc 1999) ★★★★, *The Liberty Tapes* (Compass 2002) ★★★.

● VIDEOS: *Echoes And Extracts* (Fontana 1991).

## BRAGG, BILLY

b. Steven William Bragg, 20 December 1957, Barking, Essex, England. Popularly known as 'The Bard Of Barking' (or variations of), Bragg is generally regarded as one of the most committed left-wing political performers working in popular music. After forming the ill-fated punk group Riff Raff, Bragg briefly joined the British Army (Tank Corp), before buying his way out with what he later described as the most wisely spent £175 of his life. Between time working in a record store and absorbing his new-found love of the blues and protest genre, he launched himself on a solo musical career. Armed with guitar, amplifier and voice, Bragg undertook a maverick tour of the concert halls of Britain, ready at a moment's notice to fill in as support for almost any act. He confounded the local youth with what would usually be a stark contrast to the music billed for that evening. Seeing himself as a 'one-man Clash', his lyrics, full of passion, anger and wit, made him a truly original character on the UK music scene.

During this time, managed by ex-Pink Floyd manager Peter Jenner, his album *Life's A Riot With Spy Vs Spy*, formerly on Charisma Records, but now with the emergent independent label Go! Discs/Utility, had begun to take a very firm hold on the UK independent charts, eventually peaking in the UK national charts at number 30. His follow-up, *Brewing Up With Billy Bragg*, reached number 16 in the UK charts. As always, at Bragg's insistence, and helped by the low production costs, the albums were kept at a below-average selling price. His credentials as a songwriter were given a boost in 1985 when Kirsty MacColl reached number 7 in the UK charts with his song 'A New England'. Bragg became a fixture at political rallies and benefits, particularly during the 1984 Miners' Strike with his powerful pro-Union songs 'Which Side Are You On', 'There Is Power In The Union' and the EP title track 'Between The Wars'. He was instrumental in creating the socialist musicians' collective 'Red Wedge', which included such pop luminaries as Paul Weller, Junior Giscombe and Jimmy Somerville. Despite the politicizing, Bragg was still able to pen classic love songs such as the much acclaimed 'Levi Stubbs' Tears', which appeared on the UK Top 10 album *Talking With The Taxman About Poetry*. Bragg's political attentions soon spread to Russia and Central/South America. He often returned the host musicians' hospitality by offering them places as support acts on his forthcoming UK tours.

In 1988 Bragg reached the UK number 1 slot with a cover version of the Beatles song 'She's Leaving Home', on which he was accompanied by Cara Tivey on piano – this was part of a children's charity project of contemporary artists performing various John Lennon and Paul McCartney songs. Bragg shared this double a-side single release with Wet Wet Wet's version of 'With A Little Help From My Friends', which received the majority of radio play, effectively relegating Bragg's contribution to that of a b-side. The following year Bragg reactivated the label Utility, for the purposes of encouraging young talent who had found difficulty in persuading the increasingly reticent major companies to take a gamble. These artists included Coming Up Roses, Weddings Parties Anything, Clea And McLeod, Caroline Trettine, Blake Babies, Jungr And Parker and Dead Famous People. In 1991, Bragg issued the critically acclaimed *Don't Try This At Home*, arguably his most commercial work to date. The album featured a shift towards personal politics, most noticeably on the liberating hit single 'Sexuality'. It also featured contributions from R.E.M.'s Michael Stipe and Peter Buck, following several live appearances with the band.

Following a five-year hiatus Bragg returned in 1996 with his new studio recording, *William Bloke*. Less angry and more ironic than he had ever sounded, the material also displayed an almost graceful confidence and maturity. On this album Bragg ceased to be the 'bard from Barking' or the 'quirky left-wing troubadour', and established himself as a major 'English' songwriter. The following year he collaborated with Woody Guthrie's daughter on a musical project to interpret several of the hundreds of completed lyrics bequeathed by the great American folk singer. Working with American country rockers Wilco and Natalie Merchant (on the achingly beautiful 'Birds & Ships'), Bragg fashioned a respectful testament to Guthrie that avoided nostalgia and easy sentiment. In 1999, in addition to performing, he was heard regularly on national BBC Radio 2 as a presenter. A second Guthrie collection was released the following year. Bragg resumed his solo career in 2002 with *England, Half-English*, recorded with his regular backing band the Blokes.

● ALBUMS: *Life's A Riot With Spy Vs Spy* (Utility 1983) ★★★, *Brewing Up With Billy Bragg* (Go! Discs 1984) ★★★★, *Talking With The Taxman About Poetry* (Go! Discs 1986) ★★★★, *Workers Playtime* (Go! Discs 1988) ★★★, *Help Save The Youth Of America – Live And Dubious* US/Canada release (Go! Discs 1988) ★★★, *The Internationale* (Utility 1990) ★★★, *Don't Try This At Home* (Go! Discs 1991) ★★★★, *William Bloke* (Cooking Vinyl 1996) ★★★★, with Wilco *Mermaid Avenue* (East West 1998) ★★★★, with Wilco *Mermaid Avenue Vol II* (East West 2000) ★★★, *England, Half English* (Cooking Vinyl/Elektra 2002) ★★★.

● COMPILATIONS: *Back To Basics* a repackage of the first two albums (Go! Discs 1987) ★★★, *The Peel Sessions Album* 1983–88 recordings (Strange Fruit 1992) ★★★, *Reaching To The Converted (Minding The Gaps)* (Cooking Vinyl 1999) ★★★.

● VIDEOS: *Billy Bragg Goes To Moscow And Norton, Virginia Too* (ReVision 1990), with Wilco *Man In The Sand* (Union Productions 1999).

● FURTHER READING: *Midnight In Moscow*, Chris Salewicz. *Still Suitable For Miners: Billy Bragg – The Official Biography*, Andrew Collins.

## BRANIGAN, LAURA

b. 3 July 1957, Brewster, New York, USA. A former backing vocalist with Leonard Cohen, Branigan's breakthrough came in 1982, when her energetic voice was demonstrated to its full effect on a belting rendition of Umberto Tozzi's 1979 Italian hit 'Gloria'. It reached number 2 on the *Billboard* Hot 100, and stayed in the charts for eight months. The song was a transatlantic bestseller, reaching number 6 in the UK. Her debut album *Branigan*, achieved a million sales and broke into the US Top 40. The follow-up, *Branigan 2*, was another million-seller, and included 'Solitaire', another US Top 10 smash in 1983. She was first choice to sing 'All Time High', the title tune to the James Bond movie *Octopussy*, but lost out to Rita Coolidge. Branigan's US chart success continued with 1983's emotional 'How Am I Supposed To Live Without You' (a US number 1 for Michael Bolton in 1989), which reached number 12, and 'Self Control', a US and UK Top 5 hit the following year. After several minor hits she returned to the US Top 30 in late 1987 with her rousing interpretation of Jennifer Rush's 1985 UK chart-topper, 'The Power Of Love'. Her recording career has subsequently taken a back seat to acting work.

● ALBUMS: *Branigan* (Atlantic 1982) ★★★, *Branigan 2* (Atlantic 1983) ★★, *Self Control* (Atlantic 1984) ★★★, *Hold Me* (Atlantic 1985) ★★, *Touch* (Atlantic 1987) ★★, *Laura Branigan* (Atlantic 1990) ★★, *Over My Heart* (Atlantic 1993) ★★.
● COMPILATIONS: *The Best Of Laura Branigan* (Atlantic 1988) ★★★, *The Best Of Branigan* (Atlantic 1995) ★★★, *Back In Control* (Gallo 1999) ★★.
● VIDEOS: *Laura Branigan* (Pioneer Artists 1984).
● FILMS: *Delta Pi* aka *Mugsy's Girls* (1985), *Backstage* (1988).

## BRASS MONKEY

This folk group, formed in 1981, originally comprised John Kirkpatrick (b. 8 August 1947, Chiswick, London, England; anglo-concertina, melodeon, accordion, vocals), Roger Williams (b. 30 July 1954, Cottingham, Yorkshire, England; trombone), Howard Evans (b. 29 February 1944, Chard, Somerset, England; trumpet, flügelhorn), Martin Brinsford (b. 17 August 1944, Gloucester, England; saxophone, mouth organ, percussion) and Martin Carthy (b. 21 May 1940, Hatfield, Hertfordshire, England; guitar, mandolin, vocals). Brinsford had earlier been a member of the Old Swan Band. Meanwhile, another band, Home Service, still included Evans and Williams as members. Williams was replaced in 1984 by Richard Cheetham (b. 29 January 1957, Ashton-under-Lyne, Manchester, England; trombone). The group proved something of an eyebrow-raiser when their combination of traditional folk instruments were played alongside brass instruments. The combination of folk stalwarts Carthy and Kirkpatrick and classically trained brass musicians produced the highly acclaimed *Brass Monkey*. The group appeared on the Loudon Wainwright III release *More Love Songs* in 1986, but with the various members of the band having so many other commitments, they went their separate ways the following year. To great delight the group reunited in the late 90s, releasing the wondrous *Sound & Rumour*. They are not to be confused with the Brass Monkey who record for Prestige Elite Records.
● ALBUMS: *Brass Monkey* (Topic 1983) ★★★, *See How It Runs* (Topic 1986) ★★★, *Sound & Rumour* (Topic 1998) ★★★★, *Going & Staying* (Topic 2001) ★★★.
● COMPILATIONS: *The Complete Brass Monkey* (Topic 1993) ★★★.

## BRAVE COMBO

Formed in Denton, Texas, USA, during 1979, the Brave Combo ensemble has pioneered a wholly refreshing sound that matches musical discipline with learned eclecticism and good humour. The seeds of the band were sewn in 1974 when Carl Finch (b. 29 November 1951, Texarkana, Arkensas, USA) became bored with contemporary music and began to delve more deeply into the obscurities of folk and ethnic sounds. As a result he fell in love with polka records. By 1979 he had decided to put a band together in an attempt to revitalize the tradition. Having previously played in rock bands as a guitarist and keyboard player, he now switched to the accordion. However, this early formation of the Brave Combo was greeted with confusion by onlookers, who imagined them to be a satirical group. Nothing could be further from the truth, and Finch eventually found a more sympathetic audience at punk and new wave gigs, where viewers proved more open-minded. Their most successful early performance came at a Czech polka festival in the town of West (near Waco). By this time they had already begun releasing material on their own Four Dots record label. They made their debut in 1980 with the *Polkamania* double EP. Numerous line-up changes (including the addition of wind player Jeffrey Barnes in 1983) followed before the release of their debut album, *World Dance Music*. By now the band had established its sound. Although polkas remained the central component, there were flashes of Latin, Middle Eastern and Cajun music. They were also becoming renowned for their sense of humour (for example, segueing a version of 'Tubular Bells' into 'Little Brown Jug'). Following the release of a cassette album, *Polkatharsis*, released to sell at live performances, the band was picked up by Rounder Records, who re-released the album with four extra songs. Subsequent albums for Rounder, particularly *Humansville* and *A Night On Earth*, have seen the band develop a strong bond with both roots music and purist polka fans. Tours of Japan have also extended their international audience, particularly through the band's efforts to record material such as 'Eejhanaika' in the Japanese language. The Brave Combo have recorded with Japanese ondo star Kikusuimaru as well as US singer-songwriter Lauren Agnelli (ex-Washington Squares), Tish Hinjosha and Tiny Tim. The band's 1995 set, *Polkas For A Gloomy World*, was nominated for a Grammy as Best Polka Album. Other activities included the issue of a 1991 Christmas album (*It's Christmas, Man!*), which included a samba recording of 'O, Christmas Tree' and a ska version of 'The Christmas Song', and the establishment of a new label, Dentone Records.
● ALBUMS: *World Dance Music* (Four Dots 1984) ★★★, *No Sad Faces* (Four Dots 1985) ★★, *Polkatharsis* cassette only (Four Dots 1986) ★★, *Polkatharsis* re-recorded version with new tracks (Rounder 1986) ★★, *Humansville* (Rounder 1989) ★★★, *It's Christmas, Man!* (Rounder 1991) ★★, *A Night On Earth* (Rounder 1992) ★★★, *Polkas For A Gloomy World* (Rounder 1995) ★★★, *Polka Party* (Rounder 1998) ★★★, *Polkasonic* (Cleveland International 1999) ★★★, *The Process* (Rounder 2000) ★★★★, *Kick Ass Polkas* (Cleveland International 2001) ★★★.
● COMPILATIONS: *Musical Varieties* (Rounder 1987) ★★★, *Early Brave Combo* (Japan 1994) ★★.

## BREAKING GLASS

This 1980 film covers the time-honoured plot of a singer's rise to stardom and the subsequent pressures that cause her to crack. New wave music and clashes between the National Front and the Anti-Nazi League provide the only deviation in this clichéd 'sex and drugs and rock 'n' roll' pot-boiler. Hazel O'Connor took the role of the 'tortured' artist in question, while *Quadrophenia* star Phil Daniels also appeared in a cast that included Zoot Money and former Heavy Metal Kids vocalist Gary Holton. Producer Tony Visconti was the film's musical director while O'Connor sang and composed each of the soundtrack songs, bar one that featured Victy Silva. The *Breaking Glass* album reached number 5 in the UK chart, while 'Eighth Day' reached the same position in the singles chart. For all its punk bravura, *Breaking Glass* owed more to *A Star Is Born* than *Jubilee*.

## BRECKER BROTHERS

Randy Brecker (b. 27 November 1945, Philadelphia, Pennsylvania, USA) and Michael Brecker (b. 29 March 1949, Philadelphia, Pennsylvania, USA) are two of the most in-demand studio musicians around, having supplied the horn licks to untold major records over the last 30 years. Randy originally attended Indiana University to study under David Baker, and undertook a lengthy State Department tour with the university's band, directed by Jerry Coker. He relocated to New York in 1966 and joined Blood, Sweat And Tears, staying for a year before joining up with Horace Silver's quintet. Michael, another Indiana University student, turned professional at the age of 19 with Edwin Birdsong's band, before teaming up with his older brother, Billy Cobham, Chuck Rainey and Will Lee in the pop-jazz co-operative Dreams. Both became in demand for session work (notably on Cobham's three Atlantic Records albums of the mid-70s), but by 1974, the brothers were ready to branch out on their own. They signed with Arista Records early the following year, releasing their debut, 'Sneakin' Up Behind You', in a style reminiscent of the Average White Band. It received heavy club rotation, although it was 'East River' from their second album that broke onto the singles charts in 1978. The group split in 1982, with both brothers recording solo albums in addition to session work (Michael with Ashford And Simpson and Spyro Gyra, Randy with Breakwater, among others). The commercial success of 1992's *Collection* compilations reunited the brothers as a touring and recording unit.

● ALBUMS: *The Brecker Brothers* (One Way/Arista 1975) ★★★★, *Back To Back* (One Way/Arista 1976) ★★★, *Don't Stop The Music* (One Way/Arista 1977) ★★★, *Heavy Metal Be-Bop* (One Way/Arista 1978) ★★★, *Detente* (One Way/Arista 1980) ★★, *Straphangin'* (One Way/Arista 1981) ★★★, *Return Of The Brecker Brothers* (GRP 1992) ★★★, *Out Of The Loop* (GRP 1994) ★★.

● COMPILATIONS: *The Brecker Brothers Collection Volume One* (RCA 1989) ★★★, *The Brecker Brothers Collection Volume Two* (RCA 1992) ★★.

● VIDEOS: *Return Of The Brecker Brothers: Live In Barcelona* (GRP 1993).

## BRECKER, RANDY

b. 27 November 1945, Philadelphia, Pennsylvania, USA. Brecker studied classical trumpet at school, at the same time playing in local R&B bands. He turned to jazz when at Indiana University and was a member of a student band that visited Europe. He quit the band and the university, remaining in

Europe for a while before returning to the USA to take up a career in music. In 1967 he was with Blood, Sweat And Tears and thereafter played with various jazz groups including those led by Horace Silver, Art Blakey and Clark Terry. He also accompanied performers from the worlds of rock and pop, including Janis Joplin, Stevie Wonder and James Brown. In 1969 he became co-leader with his brother, Michael Brecker, of the band Dreams. In the early 70s he worked in the studios, playing jazz gigs with Larry Coryell, Billy Cobham, Hal Galper and others. He also formed another band with his brother, this time simply named the Brecker Brothers, which made some enormously successful albums and became one of the most popular and musically skilled and influential jazz-rock bands. In the late 70s he played with Charles Mingus and in the early 80s Brecker led his own groups and also worked with his wife, Eliane Elias, and with various jazzmen including Lew Tabackin. An exceptionally talented musician with great technical facility and flair, Brecker has become one of the major figures in jazz-rock and has evolved into a fine all-rounder.

● ALBUMS: *Amanda* (Sonet 1986) ★★★, *In The Idiom* (Denon 1987) ★★, *Live At Sweet Basil* (Sonet 1988) ★★★, *Toe To Toe* (MCA 1989) ★★, *Mr Max!* (Nable 1990) ★★, *Score* (Blue Note 1993) ★★★, *Into The Sun* (Concord Vista 1997) ★★★, *Thank You Gerry: Our Tribute To Gerry Mulligan* (Arkadia 1999) ★★★, with the JazzTimes Superband *Bob Berg, Randy Brecker, Joey DeFrancesco, Dennis Chambers* (Stretch 2000) ★★★, *Hangin' In The City* (Escapade 2001) ★★★, with Frank Catalano *Live At The Green Mill* (Delmark 2001) ★★★.

## BRICKELL, EDIE, AND THE NEW BOHEMIANS

The Dallas, Texas, USA-based band the New Bohemians – Kenny Withrow (guitar), John Bush (percussion), Brad Houser (bass), and Brandon Aly (drums) already existed as a unit in their own right before Edie Brickell (b. 10 March 1966, Oak Cliff, Texas, USA; guitar, vocals) jumped up on stage to sing with them. Following their contribution to the Island Records compilation *Deep Ellum*, Aly left and was replaced by Matt Chamberlain, with Wes Martin joining as additional guitarist. The new line-up signed to Geffen Records and recorded their 1988 debut, *Shooting Rubberbands At The Stars*, which featured the US number 7 hit single 'What I Am'. The album reached US number 4 and immediately established Brickell as one of the most interesting new songwriters of her era, and introduced her distinctive vocal style to a wider public. The band subsequently toured with Bob Dylan. Their follow-up single 'Circle' scraped into the US Top 50 in April 1989. The attendant *Ghost Of A Dog* included guest vocals by John Lydon on 'Strings Of Love' and displayed Brickell's characteristically oblique lyrics. In May 1992, she married Paul Simon with whom she worked on a poorly received solo album. She continues to work with the New Bohemian and in 1999 the original line-up got together in Long Island to record the independent release, *The Live Montauk Sessions*.

● ALBUMS: *Shooting Rubberbands At The Stars*

(Geffen 1988) ★★★, *Ghost Of A Dog* (Geffen 1991) ★★★, *The Live Montauk Sessions* (New Bohemians 2000) ★★★.
Solo: Edie Brickell *Picture Perfect Morning* (Geffen 1994) ★★.

## BRIGADIER JERRY

b. Robert Russell, 28 September 1957, Kingston, Jamaica, West Indies. Now considered one of the most influential Jamaican DJs of the 80s, it is surprising to learn that Brigadier Jerry made such an impact mainly through sound tapes (live recordings of sound system dances). He is without equal as a lyrical improvizer, despite the relative rarity of his recordings. Born in the Papine area of eastern Kingston, his early interest in music led him to U-Roy's King Sturgav Hi-Fi, and he acknowledges U-Roy's huge influence. In 1978, he was spreading the word of the Twelve Tribes of Israel organization on the Jah Love sound system, and sometimes recorded with other members such as Fred Locks. Freddie McGregor and Judah Eskender Tafari encouraged him to record three tracks for Studio One in 1982, before Delroy Stansbury released 'Pain' and 'Gwan A School' on the Jwyanza label. Aside from Jah Love he worked with several other sound systems, such as Supreme Love, Wha Dat and Black Star. While in the USA, he worked with Downbeat International and acquired a growing following of DJ admirers who often recorded his lyrics. *Jamaica Jamaica*, was released on Jah Love Musik in 1985 and is still considered one of his best albums. It contained a classic version of 'Amagideon' by Bunny Wailer. He also recorded several tracks for the Supreme, Techniques and George Phang labels, but there was not much recorded output until *On The Road* in early 1991. He recorded *Hail Him* for Tapper Zukie in 1992.
● ALBUMS: *Live At The Controls* (Vista Sounds 1983) ★★★, *Jamaica Jamaica* (RAS 1985) ★★★★, *On The Road* (RAS 1989) ★★, *Hail Him* (Tappa 1992) ★★★.

## BRIGHTMAN, SARAH

b. 14 August 1961, London, England. An actress and singer who first came to notice in 1978 when, with the dance group Hot Gossip, she made the UK Top 10 with the disco-pop single 'I Lost My Heart To A Starship Trooper'. It was all a far cry from her childhood ambition to become a ballet dancer. Three years after her chart success, she won a part in Andrew Lloyd Webber's musical *Cats*, and was noticed again – this time by the composer himself – and they were married in 1984. The marriage lasted for six years, and, during that time, Brightman became established as one of the premier leading ladies of the musical theatre. After *Cats*, she appeared for a season at the Old Vic in Frank Dunlop's 1982 adaptation of *Masquerade*, and later in the year she was in Charles Strouse's short-lived musical *Nightingale*. All this time she was taking singing lessons, training her superb soprano voice so that she could undertake more demanding roles than those in conventional musical comedy. In 1984 she appeared in the television version of Lloyd Webber's *Song And Dance*, and also sang on the Top

30 album. A year later, she made her operatic debut in the role of Valencienne in *The Merry Widow* at Sadlers Wells, and gave several concerts of Lloyd Webber's *Requiem* in England and America, which resulted in another bestselling album. It also produced a Top 5 single, 'Pie Jesu', on which Brightman duetted with the 12-year-old Paul Miles-Kingston. In 1986 Brightman enjoyed a great personal triumph when she co-starred with Michael Crawford in *The Phantom Of The Opera*, and recreated her role two years later on Broadway. She had UK Top 10 hits with three songs from the show, 'The Phantom Of The Opera' (with Steve Harley), 'All I Ask Of You' (with Cliff Richard) and 'Wishing You Were Somehow Here Again'.
In the late 80s and early 90s, Brightman toured many parts of the world, including Japan and the UK, in a concert production of *The Music Of Andrew Lloyd Webber*. In December 1991, at the end of the American leg of the tour, she took over the leading role of Rose in *Aspects Of Love* for the last few weeks of the Broadway run. She also joined the West End production for a time, but, while her presence was welcomed and her performance critically acclaimed, she was unable to prevent its closure in June 1992. In the same year Brightman was high in the UK chart again, this time duetting with opera singer José Carreras on the Olympic Anthem, 'Amigos Para Siempre (Friends For Life)', which was written, inevitably, by Andrew Lloyd Webber, with lyric by Don Black. In 1993 she made her debut in the straight theatre with appearances in *Trelawny Of The Wells* and *Relative Values*. For some years it had been forecast that Lloyd Webber would write a stage musical or film for her based on the life of Jessie Matthews, the graceful star of many 20s and 30s musicals, and to whom she bears an uncanny facial resemblance. However, in 1994 the composer dropped his option on Michael Thornton's biography of Matthews, and announced that there 'no further plans to develop the project'. Based mostly in Germany in the 90s, Brightman continued to perform in Australia, Canada, America and elsewhere. In 1997 her duet with the blind Tuscan tenor Andrea Bocelli, 'Time To Say Goodbye', topped the charts throughout Europe. In the same year, her tour of the UK, in company with the English National Orchestra, included a concert at London's Royal Albert Hall. She had another surprise UK hit single in 1997 when 'Timeless' went near the top of the charts. She also established herself as a bestselling diva in the USA with albums such as *Time To Say Goodbye*, *Eden* and *La Luna*.
● ALBUMS: *Britten Folk Songs* (Angel 1988) ★★★, *The Songs That Got Away* (Really Useful 1989) ★★, *As I Came Of Age* (Polydor 1990) ★★★, with José Carreras *Amigos Para Siempre* (East West 1992) ★★★, *Dive* (A&M 1993) ★★★, *Sings The Music Of Andrew Lloyd Webber* (Really Useful 1994) ★★★, *Surrender: The Unexpected Songs* (Really Useful 1995) ★★★, *Fly* (Coalition 1995) ★★★, *Just Show Me How To Love You* (Coalition 1996) ★★★, *Timeless* (Coalition 1997) ★★★, with the London Symphony Orchestra *Time To Say Goodbye* (Nemo 1998) ★★★, *Eden* (Coalition/East West 1998) ★★★★, *La Luna*

(Angel/Nemo 2000) ★★★, *Classics* (Angel 2001) ★★★, and Original Cast recordings.
● COMPILATIONS: *The Andrew Lloyd Webber Collection* (Decca 1998) ★★★, *The Very Best Of 1990–2000* (East West 2001) ★★★.
● VIDEOS: *One Night In Eden: Sarah Brightman Live In Concert* (Capitol Video 1999).

## BRILLIANT CORNERS

Purveyors of intelligent and undervalued pop music, the Brilliant Corners originated from Bristol, England, and took their name from a Thelonious Monk jazz passage. Davey Woodward (b. Avonmouth, Bristol, England; vocals, guitar), Chris Galvin (b. 1959, d. 22 December 1998; bass), Winston (percussion, backing vocals), Bob (drums) and Dan (occasional keyboards) comprised the line-up. Early material was absorbed into the *New Musical Express'* C86 phenomenon, and comparisons to other 'shambling' bands became a near-permanent albatross around the their necks. Their own SS20 label was home to their first three singles and mini-album *Growing Up Absurd*. However, their latter-day career was characterized by an absence of press coverage, bearing no relation to the quality of the band's output. Thus far they had sustained only a single line-up change, losing a trumpeter, though a substitute guitarist was drafted in when Woodward broke his arm. In March 1988 the band set up their own label McQueen, and released the definitive *Somebody Up There Likes Me*. Woodward and Galvin formed the Experimental Pop Band in 1995. Galvin died from cancer in 1998.
● ALBUMS: *Growing Up Absurd* mini-album (SS20 1985) ★★★, *What's In A Word* (SS20 1986) ★★★, *Somebody Up There Likes Me* (McQueen 1988) ★★★★, *Joyride* (McQueen 1989) ★★★, *Hooked* (McQueen 1990) ★★★, *A History Of White Trash* (1993) ★★★.
● COMPILATIONS: *Everything I Ever Wanted* collection of first two EPs (McQueen 1988) ★★★.
● VIDEOS: *Creamy Stuff* (Jettisoundz 1991).

## BRONSKI BEAT

This Anglo-Scottish band was formed in 1983 by Jimmy Somerville (b. 22 June 1961, Glasgow, Scotland; vocals), Steve Bronski (keyboards) and Larry Steinbachek (keyboards). After establishing themselves in London's gay community, the trio was awarded a support slot for a Tina Turner show, and subsequently signed to London Records. Their memorable debut single, 'Smalltown Boy' immediately drew attention to Somerville's arresting falsetto vocal, which became the hallmark of their sound. The single climbed to number 3 in the UK charts and also fared well in Europe and in the US dance charts. The follow-up, 'Why?', another Top 10 single, emphasized their debt to producer Giorgio Moroder, whose Euro disco sound they so admired. The song was inspired by a paedophile friend of theirs, whose illegal sexual activities had forced him to flee the country. By the end of 1984, Somerville was already well known as a tireless homosexual rights campaigner. The band's debut album, *The Age Of Consent*, emphasized their homosexual politics

and met with a mixed reaction in the music press. The summer of 1984 saw them supporting Elton John at Wembley, London, and a major UK tour followed that winter. Meanwhile, a third single, a sprightly cover version of George Gershwin's 'It Ain't Necessarily So', scaled the charts. Early the following year, the Bronskis teamed up with Marc Almond for an extraordinary version of Donna Summer's 'I Feel Love', interwoven with the refrains of 'Love To Love You Baby' and 'Johnny Remember Me'. The single climbed into the UK Top 3 during April 1985, but at the end of that same month, Somerville left, citing disillusionment as a major factor. He later resurfaced in the Communards, before relocating to San Francisco. Bronski Beat found a replacement in John Jon (b. John Foster) and initially enjoyed some success. The catchy 'Hit That Perfect Beat' returned them to the Top 3 and two further albums followed. The impetus was gradually lost, however, although Bronski Beat carried on into the 90s with new vocalist Jonathan Hellyer.
● ALBUMS: *The Age Of Consent* (Forbidden Fruit/London 1984) ★★★, *Hundreds And Thousands* remix album (Forbidden Fruit/London 1985) ★★★, *TruthDareDoubleDare* (Forbidden Fruit/London 1986) ★★, *Rainbow Nation* (ZYX 1995) ★★★.
● COMPILATIONS: *The Very Best Of Jimmy Somerville, Bronski Beat And The Communards* (Warners 2001) ★★★.
● VIDEOS: *The First Chapter* (Channel 5 1986).

## BROS

Twins Matthew and Luke Goss (b. 29 September 1968, London, England), along with school friend Craig Logan (b. 22 April 1969, Fife, Scotland), formed a group called Cavier before changing the name to Bros. After securing the services of Pet Shop Boys manager Tom Watkins and producer Nicky Graham, they scraped into the lower regions of the UK charts with 'I Owe You Nothing'. Well groomed and ambitious, the group were well marketed and soon attracted a fanatical teenage fan following. Their second single, the catchy, dance-orientated 'When Will I Be Famous' was promoted aggressively and climbed to number 2. 'Drop The Boy' soon followed, again just missing the number 1 spot. By now established as the teen-idols of 1988, the trio's first single, 'I Owe You Nothing', was repromoted and reached the chart summit in June 1988. A string of Top 10 singles followed, including 'I Quit', 'Cat Among The Pigeons', 'Too Much', 'Chocolate Box' and 'Sister'. Their fortunes gradually took a downward turn, however. In January 1989, bass player Craig Logan was ousted and Bros subsequently became embroiled in an acrimonious legal battle with their manager (well documented in Luke Goss' autobiography). Written off as mere teenybop fodder, they actively pursued a more serious direction and returned to the UK Top 20 with 'Are You Mine?' and the album *Changing Faces* in 1991. By 1993 the phenomenon had passed, with the twins now going their separate ways. Matt pursued a solo career while Luke Goss turned to acting, enjoying success as a stage actor and appearing as Nomak in *Blade II*.

● ALBUMS: *Push* (CBS 1988) ★★★, *The Time* (CBS 1989) ★★, *Changing Faces* (Columbia 1991) ★★.
● VIDEOS: *Live: The Big Push Tour* (CMV Enterprises 1988), *Push Over* (CMV Enterprises 1989).
● FURTHER READING: *I Owe You Nothing: My Story*, Luke Goss.

## BROWN, SAM
b. Samantha Brown, 7 October 1964, Stratford, London, England. The daughter of Joe Brown, Sam made her recording debut aged 12, on the Small Faces' *78 In The Shade*. Three years later she toured singing with the National Youth Jazz Orchestra, and that year started writing songs. She continued to gain experience providing backing vocals on records for Adam And The Ants and Dexys Midnight Runners, and toured with Spandau Ballet when she was 19. After demoing her songs with some help from her brother, Brown signed to A&M Records in 1986. The debut single and album had a distinctive white soul sound, and both went into the UK Top 5 in 1988. Her powerful version of 'Can I Get A Witness' charted the following year. The band she formed to promote the first album also recorded the second. In August 1990 she produced an album for her mother Vikki Brown, shortly before the latter's death. In 1991 she released a single with Jools Holland, 'Together Again', the proceeds of which went to AIDS research. During the 90s Brown was often a featured singer in Holland's Rhythm And Blues Orchestra, but her own work struggled to find an audience beyond her loyal fanbase. *Box* suffered from weak material, especially with some clumsy lyrical links, although Brown's magnificent voice was a redeeming factor. *Reboot*, released in autumn 2000, was a more cohesive and jazz-orientated album.
● ALBUMS: *Stop* (A&M 1988) ★★★★, *April Moon* (A&M 1990) ★★, *43 Minutes* (A&M 1993) ★★, *Box* (Demon 1997) ★★, *Reboot* (Mud Hut 2000) ★★★.
● VIDEOS: *The Videos* (A&M Sound Pictures 1990).

## BROWN, T. GRAHAM
b. Anthony Graham Brown, 30 October 1954, Arabi, Georgia, USA. As much a southern R&B singer as a country singer-songwriter, Brown was at school in Athens, Georgia, with members of the B-52's. He earned extra money singing cover versions in lounge bars, until he saw a television documentary on David Allen Coe, after which he formed Rio Diamond, an 'outlaw' band, in 1976. By 1979, he was fronting T. Graham Brown's Rack Of Spam, a white soul band, singing Otis Redding material. In 1982, he moved to Nashville, where he worked as a demo singer, recording songs for publishers who wanted famous artists to record their copyrighted material. A song he demoed as '1962' was later recorded by Randy Travis as '1982', but more lucrative was the use of his voice on jingles for products such as Budweiser beer and McDonald's hamburgers. Signed to a major label in 1985, he was known as T. Graham Brown to avoid confusion with the noted Nashville producer Tony Brown. His first album *I Tell It Like It Used To Be*, included two US country number 1 singles, 'Hell Or High Water' and 'Don't Go To Strangers', and he returned to the top again in 1988

with 'Darlene'. His albums were never huge hits, however, and an attempt to penetrate the European market in the late 80s was unsuccessful. After leaving Capitol Records in the early 90s, Brown spent a fruitless period moving between different labels before signing with the independent Intersound and releasing a strong comeback album, *Wine Into Water*. The title-track dealt frankly with Brown's fight against alcoholism.
● ALBUMS: *I Tell It Like It Used To Be* (Capitol 1986) ★★★, *Brilliant Conversationalist* (Capitol 1987) ★★★, *Come As You Were* (Capitol 1988) ★★★, *Bumper To Bumper* (Capitol 1990) ★★★, *You Can't Take It With You* (Capitol 1991) ★★★, *Wine Into Water* (Intersound 1998) ★★★★, *Lives!* (Madacy 2001) ★★.
● COMPILATIONS: *The Best Of T. Graham Brown* (Liberty 1992) ★★★★.

## BRUFORD, BILL
b. William Scott Bruford, 17 May 1949, Sevenoaks, Kent, England. A founder-member of progressive rock outfit Yes in 1968, Bruford left four years later at the height of the band's popularity. An accomplished drummer, he opted to join King Crimson, where his skills were put to even greater test, and remained there until leader Robert Fripp dissolved the line-up in 1974. Bruford subsequently worked with Pavlov's Dog, before forming the jazz-rock ensemble UK. The initial line-up also featured guitarist Allan Holdsworth, who joined the drummer for his solo debut, *Feels Good To Me*. The two musicians then broke away to found Bruford, which was completed by Dave Stewart (keyboards) and Jeff Berlin (bass). However, the artist's independent career was sidelined in 1981 when Fripp invited him to join the reconstituted King Crimson. Following the second collapse of King Crimson, Bruford toured with Al Di Meola and David Torn. Bruford subsequently returned to his jazz roots with Earthworks, which included keyboard player Django Bates, saxophonist Iain Ballamy and bass player Mick Hutton. The latter was replaced by Tim Harries on subsequent albums. Bruford became involved with the reunion of Yes in the late 80s, touring and recording under the banner of Anderson, Bruford, Wakeman, Howe until such legal matters as to the ownership of the Yes name had been resolved. He rejoined King Crimson for their mid-90s set, *Thrak*, and the attendant world tour. Following the release of an Earthworks compilation, Bruford collaborated with Ralph Towner and Eddie Gomez on the 'chamber trio' outing *If Summer Had Its Ghosts*. In 1998, he inaugurated a second line-up of Earthworks featuring Steve Hamilton (keyboards), Patrick Clahar (tenor saxophone), and Mark Hodgson (bass). One of the finest drummers in British music, Bruford refuses to rest on his laurels.
● ALBUMS: with Bruford *Feels Good To Me* (EG 1977) ★★★, with Bruford *One Of A Kind* (EG 1978) ★★, with Bruford *The Bruford Tapes* (EG 1979) ★★★★, with Bruford *Gradually Going Tornado* (EG 1980) ★★★, with Patrick Moraz *Music For Piano And Drums* (Editions EG 1983) ★★★, with Patrick Moraz *Flag* (EG 1985) ★★★, with Earthworks *Earthworks* (EG 1987) ★★★★, with Earthworks *Dig?* (Editions

EG 1989) ★★★, with Earthworks *All Heaven Broke Loose* (Editions EG 1991) ★★★, with Earthworks *Stamping Ground* (Virgin 1994) ★★, with Ralph Towner, Eddie Gomez *If Summer Had Its Ghosts* (Discipline 1997) ★★, with Tony Levin *Upper Extremities* (Papa Bear 1998) ★★★, with Earthworks *A Part, And Yet Apart* (Discipline 1999) ★★★, with Levin *Blue Nights* (Papa Bear 2000) ★★★, with Earthworks *The Sound Of Surprise* (Discipline 2001) ★★★★, with Earthworks *Footloose And Fancy Free* (Discipline 2002) ★★★.

● COMPILATIONS: *Master Strokes 1978-1985* (EG 1986) ★★★, with Earthworks *Heavenly Bodies* (Virgin 1997) ★★★.

● VIDEOS: *Bruford & The Beat* (1982).

● FURTHER READING: *When In Doubt, Roll!*, Bill Bruford.

## BRYSON, PEABO

b. Robert Peabo Bryson, 13 April 1951, Greenville, South Carolina, USA. This talented soul singer and producer is a former member of Moses Dillard and the Tex-Town Display and Michael Zager's Moon Band. Between 1976 and 1978, Bryson had hits with this latter group, with 'Reaching For The Sky' and 'I'm So Into You'. His numerous appearances in *Billboard*'s R&B chart include 'Underground Music', 'Feel The Fire', 'Crosswinds', 'She's A Woman' and 'Minute By Minute'. 'Gimme Some Time', a 1979 duet with Natalie Cole, was the first of several successful partnerships. However, despite hits with Melissa Manchester and Regina Belle, the singer is best known for his work with Roberta Flack, and in particular the dewy-eyed ballad 'Tonight, I Celebrate My Love', which reached number 5 on the US R&B chart and number 2 in the UK pop chart in 1983. Such releases have obscured Bryson's own career, which included, notably, the US Top 10 hit 'If Ever You're In My Arms Again' from 1984, but he remains an able and confident performer blessed with an effortless voice. Soundtrack duets with Celine Dion ('Beauty And The Beast') and Regina Belle ('A Whole New World (Aladdin's Theme)') in 1992 provided Bryson with further chart success.

● ALBUMS: *Reaching For The Sky* (Capitol 1978) ★★★, *Crosswinds* (Capitol 1978) ★★★, with Natalie Cole *We're The Best Of Friends* (Capitol 1979) ★★★, *Paradise* (Capitol 1980) ★★★, with Roberta Flack *Live And More* (Atlantic 1980) ★★★, *Turn The Hands Of Time* (Capitol 1981) ★★★, *I Am Love* (Capitol 1981) ★★★, *Don't Play With Fire* (Capitol 1982) ★★★, with Roberta Flack *Born To Love* (Capitol 1983) ★★★, *Straight From The Heart* (Elektra 1984) ★★★, *Take No Prisoners* (Elektra 1985) ★★★, *Quiet Storm* (Elektra 1986) ★★★, *Positive* (Elektra 1988) ★★★, *Can You Stop The Rain* (Columbia 1991) ★★★, *Unconditional Love* (Private Music 1999) ★★★.

● COMPILATIONS: *The Peabo Bryson Collection* (Capitol 1984) ★★★★, *I'm So Into You: The Passion Of Peabo Bryson* (EMI 1997) ★★★★, *Anthology* (The Right Stuff 2001) ★★★★.

## BUCKINGHAM, LINDSEY

b. 3 October 1949, Palo Alto, California, USA. The pop mastermind behind Fleetwood Mac's golden era,

Buckingham began his career as a folk-singer before joining Fritz, an aspiring Bay Area rock band that also featured vocalist Stevie Nicks. When Fritz folded in 1971, the couple, now linked professionally and romantically, formed a new unit, Buckingham Nicks. The group's 1973 self-titled album offered glimpses of the harmonized style the duo later forged, but it made little commercial impression and Buckingham undertook session work. However, the album was later used to demonstrate technical facilities when Mick Fleetwood was researching likely studio locations for Fleetwood Mac's next album. By chance, both Buckingham and Nicks were in an adjacent room and the seeds of a fruitful partnership were sown. When Bob Welch left Fleetwood Mac in December 1974, Fleetwood invited the pair to join as replacements. Their arrival signalled a renaissance in the group's fortunes when *Fleetwood Mac* and the multi-million-selling *Rumours* established them as one of the world's top-selling acts. Buckingham's skills as a singer, composer, guitarist and producer were crucial to this success, but, following the release of the ambitious *Tusk*, both he and Nicks, who had, by now, severed their romantic attachment, embarked on solo careers. Buckingham's debut album, *Law And Order*, continued the craftsmanship displayed on earlier work, but although one of the tracks, 'Trouble', reached the US Top 10, it failed to match the profile Nicks had achieved with her first release. Both artists resumed their roles with Fleetwood Mac for the 1982 album *Mirage*, but subsequently pursued individual paths. The title song from a second collection, *Go Insane*, provided another hit single, and although he returned to the parent group's fold for the excellent *Tango In The Night* (1987), Buckingham officially parted from the unit the following year rather than embark on a promotional tour. A decade later, having found little in the way of solo success, he returned to work with the 1973 *Rumours* line-up of Fleetwood Mac.

● ALBUMS: *Law And Order* (Asylum 1981) ★★★, *Go Insane* (Elektra 1984) ★★, *Out Of The Cradle* (Reprise 1992) ★★.

## BUCKS FIZZ

'Britain's answer to Abba', Bucks Fizz was originally conceived as a vehicle for singer, producer and manager Nichola Martin to appear in the Eurovision Song Contest. With her partner, and later husband, Andy Hill producing and composing material, Martin auditioned hundreds of applicants before deciding on Mike Nolan (b. 7 December 1954), Bobby Gee (b. Robert Gubby, 23 August 1957, Epsom, Surrey, England), Jay Aston (b. 4 May 1961, London, England) and Cheryl Baker (b. Rita Crudgington, 8 March 1954, Bethnal Green, London, England). Of the four, Baker had the most experience, having previously appeared as a Eurovision entrant with Coco. So impressed was Martin with her discoveries that she suppressed her singing ambitions and reverted to a wholly managerial role. Having signed the group for publishing, she soon abandoned the management reins, which were passed over to Jill Shirley of the

Razzmatazz agency. Armed with the catchy 'Making Your Mind Up', the manufactured Bucks Fizz duly won the 1981 Eurovision Song Contest and enjoyed a UK number 1 in the process. During the next 12 months they had two further UK number 1 hits, 'The Land Of Make Believe' and 'My Camera Never Lies'. For the next two years all was well, but after 'When We Were Young', their chart performance declined significantly. In 1984 the group was involved in a much publicized coach crash and Nolan was incapacitated for a considerable period. Matters worsened when Aston became involved in an affair with Hill, thereby straining the relationship with Martin. Feeling ostracized, guilty and emotionally confused, Aston attempted suicide, sold her dramatic story to the press and sought legal redress against Martin's Big Note Music after departing from the group. Martin and Shirley subsequently conducted another mass audition to find a replacement before choosing the totally unknown 21-year-old Shelley Preston (b. 16 May 1964, Salisbury, Wiltshire, England).

Although the new line-up did not recapture the success of its predecessor, the aptly titled 'New Beginning (Mamba Seyra)' returned them to the UK Top 10. They had further minor entries in the late 80s, with 'Love The One You're With', 'Keep Each Other Warm' and 'Heart Of Stone'. Nolan left the group in 1996, to be replaced by former Dollar frontman David Van Day. Amid a certain amount of acrimony, Nolan subsequently returned to launch his own version of Bucks Fizz with Day, Lianna Lee and Sally Jacks. In 1998 they released a revamped 'Making Your Mind Up', faster in tempo and with 'lots of pingy electronic bits'. Meanwhile, Bobby Gee's rival outfit, which is accepted by many to be the official Bucks Fizz since he kept the group alive when the others had left, comprises himself Graham Crisp, Heidi Manton and Louise Hart. Since the original group disbanded, founder-member Cheryl Baker has become a popular UK television personality, hosting shows such as *Eggs 'N' Baker*, *The Survival Guide To Food* and *Record Breakers*. In the wake of the coach crash, she also founded the charity Headfirst.

● ALBUMS: *Bucks Fizz* (RCA 1981) ★★, *Are You Ready?* (RCA 1982) ★★, *Hand Cut* (RCA 1983) ★★, *I Hear Talk* (RCA 1984) ★★, *The Writing On The Wall* (Polydor 1986) ★★.

● COMPILATIONS: *Greatest Hits* (RCA 1983) ★★★, *The Story So Far* (Stylus 1988) ★★, *Golden Days* (RCA 1992) ★★★, *The Best And The Rest* (RCA 1993) ★★, *Greatest Hits Of Bucks Fizz* (RCA/Camden 1996) ★★★, *Making Your Mind Up: The Very Best Of Bucks Fizz* (Hallmark 1998) ★★★.

● VIDEOS: *Greatest Hits: Bucks Fizz* (RCA/Columbia 1986).

## BUCKWHEAT ZYDECO

Founded by Stanley Dural (b. Lafayette, Louisiana, USA). Dural started his musical career playing piano and organ in local bands around south-east Louisiana. In the late 80s and early 90s, Buckwheat Zydeco emerged as one of the leaders of zydeco music, the accordion-led dance music of southern

Louisiana's French-speaking Creoles. Dural, taking the nickname 'Buckwheat', worked with R&B singers Joe Tex, Barbara Lynn and Clarence 'Gatemouth' Brown during the 60s. Following a period playing keyboards in Clifton Chenier's band, he took up accordion and moved to the indigenous sound of zydeco. He formed his own funk band, the Hitchhikers, in the 70s, followed by the Ils Sont Partis Band in 1979. That outfit recorded eight albums for Blues Unlimited, Black Top and Rounder Records before Dural formed Buckwheat Zydeco. Signed to Island Records in 1987, the group recorded three albums for the label, with *Where There's Smoke There's Fire* produced by David Hidalgo of Los Lobos. Newcomers to this music should start with the excellent compilation *Menagerie* or the more recent *A 20 Year Party*, which was released on Dural's own label after he had obtained the rights to his own masters. A remarkable artist.

● ALBUMS: *One For The Road* (Blues Unlimited 1979) ★★, *Take It Easy Baby* (Blues Unlimited 1980) ★★★, *100% Fortified Zydeco* (Rounder 1983) ★★★, *Turning Point* (Rounder 1984) ★★★, *Waitin' For My Ya Ya* (Rounder 1985) ★★★, *Buckwheat Zydeco* (Rounder 1986) ★★★, *Zydeco Party* (Rounder 1987) ★★★, *On A Night Like This* (Island 1987) ★★★★, *Taking It Home* (Island 1988) ★★★, *Buckwheat Zydeco And The Ils Sont Partis Band* (Island 1988) ★★★, *Where There's Smoke There's Fire* (Island 1990) ★★★★, *On Track* (Charisma 1992) ★★★, *Five Card Stud* (Mercury 1994) ★★★, *Trouble* 1987 recording (Tomorrow 1997) ★★★, *Down Home Live!* (Tomorrow 2001) ★★★★.

● COMPILATIONS: *Menagerie: The Essential Zydeco Collection* (Mango 1994) ★★★★, *The Buckwheat Zydeco Story: A 20 Year Party* (Tomorrow 1999) ★★★★, *Ultimate Collection* (Hip-O 2000) ★★★★, *Buckwheat's Zydeco Party* (Rounder 2002) ★★★★.

● VIDEOS: *Taking It Home* (Island Visual Arts 1989), *Buckwheat Zydeco Live* (PolyGram Music Video 1991).

## BURNEL, JEAN JACQUES

b. 1952, London, England. Of the four original members of the Stranglers, bass player Burnel was probably the most forthright. Born of French parents, he was staunchly pro-European. A keen biker and former skinhead, with a black belt in karate and an economics degree from Bradford University, he was employed as a van driver in Guildford, Surrey, when he first met Hugh Cornwell through the American lead singer of the band Bobbysox, with whom Cornwell was playing guitar in the early 70s. Original plans to become a karate instructor were shelved (although he later returned to this profession part-time), so that he could play bass and sing in a band with Cornwell. As the Stranglers soared to success Burnel waged a personal battle with the press who dismissed the band as either being of higher intellect than their punk cohorts or, alternatively, abject and brutal chauvinists. Several well-documented episodes led to violent resolutions at Burnel's hands. Burnel was the first Strangler to work on a solo project, *Euroman Cometh*. As the title implied, this was a plea for the cause of European federalism. It was released early in 1979 with guests Brian James (guitar, ex-Damned), Lew Lewis (harmonica, ex-Eddie And The Hot Rods), with Carey Fortune (ex-Chelsea) and Pete Howells (ex-Drones) both playing the drums. A short tour to promote the album was something of a disaster. The Euroband assembled for the tour featured John Ellis (ex-Vibrators – who was also playing for the support band Rapid Eye Movement), Lewis, Howells and Penny Tobin on keyboards. In 1980 'Girl From The Snow Country' was scheduled as a solo release but was withdrawn. Despite a later bootleg, the copies that slipped out are among the most collectable of new wave releases. The next musical project outside of the Stranglers was a collaboration with Dave Greenfield on a soundtrack for the Vincent Coudanne film *Ecoutez Vos Murs*. Ensuing years saw Burnel becoming involved with a number of bands as either producer, guest musician or both. Typically the groups were largely non-English, including Taxi Girl (France), Ping Pong (Norway), the Revenge (Belgium) and ARB (Japan). The next major project was the formation in 1986 of a 60s covers band called the Purple Helmets. Consisting of Burnel, Ellis, Alex Gifford and Laurent Sinclair, the group was put together for a one-off gig at the Trans Musicale Avant Festival in France. So successful was the concert that the Helmets became an ongoing concern, with Greenfield replacing Sinclair and Tears For Fears drummer Manny Elias joining. Burnel's second solo album, *C'est Un Jour Parfait*, was recorded almost entirely in French and released just about everywhere in Europe except Britain.

● ALBUMS: *Euroman Cometh* (United Artists 1979) ★★★, with Dave Greenfield *Fire And Water* (Epic 1983) ★★, *C'est Un Jour Parfait* (Columbia 1989) ★★.

## BURNETT, T-BONE

b. John Henry Burnett, 18 January 1945, St. Louis, Missouri, USA. Burnett, a member of Bob Dylan's Rolling Thunder Revue in the mid-70s, is a highly regarded producer and songwriter. He grew up in Texas playing guitar in local bands before travelling to Los Angeles to produce Delbert And Glen and recorded a solo album for Uni. After touring with Delaney And Bonnie and the B-52's, he joined Dylan's touring troupe. When the Rolling Thunder concerts were over, Burnett founded the Alpha Band with ex-Dylan accompanist Steven Soles (guitar) and David Mansfield (guitar, mandolin). The group made three albums between 1976 and 1979. After the demise of the Alpha Band, Burnett made a solo album for Takoma which introduced his rootsy style and overtly moralistic lyrical approach. His growing reputation was evidenced by the presence of guitarists Ry Cooder and Richard Thompson on 1983's excellent *Proof Through The Night*. He later toured with Thompson and Elvis Costello, releasing a 1985 single with the latter as the Coward Brothers and producing his *King Of America*. Increasingly active as a producer, among the artists Burnett has worked with are Leo Kottke, Los Lobos, Roy Orbison, Counting Crows, Bruce Cockburn, the Wallflowers, Gillian Welch and Sam Phillips, the former Christian singer who he later married. In the new millennium Burnett helped spearhead a bluegrass revival after

being commissioned by the Coen Brothers to organise the bestselling soundtrack to their *O Brother, Where Art Thou?*

● ALBUMS: as J. Henry Burnett *The B-52 Band & The Fabulous Skylarks* (Uni 1972) ★★★, *Truth Decay* (Takoma 1980) ★★★, *Trap Door* mini-album (Warners 1982) ★★★, *Proof Through The Night* (Warners 1983) ★★★★, *Behind The Trap Door* mini-album (Demon 1984) ★★★, *T-Bone Burnett* (Dot 1986) ★★★, *The Talking Animals* (Columbia 1987) ★★★, *The Criminal Under My Own Hat* (Columbia 1992) ★★★★.

● FILMS: *Renaldo And Clara* (1978), *Heaven's Gate* (1980), *Bob* (2001).

## BUSH, KATE

b. Catherine Bush, 30 July 1958, Bexleyheath, Kent, England. While still at school, the precocious Bush was discovered by Pink Floyd's David Gilmour, who was so impressed by the imaginative quality of her songwriting that he financed some demo recordings. EMI Records were equally taken with the product and in an unusual act of faith decided not to record her immediately. Instead, she was encouraged to develop her writing, dancing and singing in preparation for a long-term career. The apprenticeship ended in 1978 with the release of the extraordinary 'Wuthering Heights'. Inspired by Emily Bronte's novel, Bush had created a hauntingly original piece, complete with an ethereal, almost demented, vocal that brilliantly captured the obsessive love of the novel's heroine, and her namesake, Cathy. It was no surprise when the single rapidly reached number 1 in the UK and established Bush in Europe. An attendant album, *The Kick Inside*, recorded over the previous three years, was a further example of her diversity and charm as a songwriter. A follow-up single, 'The Man With The Child In His Eyes', was typical of her romantic, sensual style of writing, and provided her with another Top 10 success. Bush consolidated her position with a new album, *Lionheart*, and during 1979 undertook her first major tour. The live shows were most notable for her characteristically extravagant mime work and elaborate stage sets, but it was to be the last time the singer would tour. An EP from the show, *Kate Bush On Stage*, gave her another Top 10 hit. After guesting on Peter Gabriel's 'Games Without Frontiers', Bush was back in the charts with 'Breathing' and 'Babooshka'. The latter was her most accomplished work since 'Wuthering Heights' with a clever storyline and strong vocal. Her next album, *Never For Ever*, entered the UK album charts at number 1 and further hits followed with 'Army Dreamers' and the seasonal 'December Will Be Magic Again'.

At this point, Bush was still regarded as a mainstream pop artist whose charm and popularity was likely to prove ephemeral. Her self-produced 1982 album *The Dreaming* suggested a new direction, with its experimental song structures, even though its less melodic approach alienated some critics. A comparative commercial failure, the album nevertheless proved to be highly influential on other 80s pop musicians, and in particular on Gabriel's increasingly studio-bound work.

A two-year hiatus followed, during which Bush perfected a work that would elevate her to new heights in the pop pantheon. The pilot single, 'Running Up That Hill (A Deal With God)', was arguably her greatest work to date, a dense and intriguing composition with a sound uniquely her own. The album *Hounds Of Love* soon followed and was greeted with an acclaim that dwarfed all her previous accolades and efforts. By any standards, it was an exceptional work and revealed Bush at the zenith of her powers. Songs such as the eerily moving 'Mother Stands For Comfort' and the dramatic 'Cloudbusting' underlined her strengths not only as a writer and singer, but most crucially as a producer. The outstanding video accompanying the latter featured Donald Sutherland. An entire side of the album, titled 'The Ninth Wave', fused Arthurian legend and Jungian psychology in a musical framework, part orchestral and part folk. After this, Bush could never again be regarded as a quaint pop artist.

Following another brief tie-up with Peter Gabriel on the hit 'Don't Give Up', Bush took an extended sabbatical to plot a follow-up album. In 1989 she returned with *The Sensual World*, a startling musical cornucopia in which she experimented with various musical forms, even using a Bulgarian folk troupe. The arrangements were as evocative and unusual as her choice of instrumentation, which included uillean pipes, whips, valiha, Celtic harp, tupan and viola. There was even a literary adaptation *à la* 'Wuthering Heights', with Bush adapting Molly Bloom's soliloquy from James Joyce's *Ulysses* for the enticing title track. The album attracted the keen attention of the highbrow rock press and Bush found herself celebrated as one of the most adventurous and distinctively original artists of her era.

Sadly, the music world has heard less and less of Bush in subsequent years as she has devoted her time to her own family, guitarist/partner Danny McIntosh and son Bertie. A variety of artists contributed to her sole release of the 90s, *The Red Shoes*, including Eric Clapton, Prince, Jeff Beck, Trio Bulgarka and Gary Brooker. Though it rarely reached the creative heights of her 80s recordings, the album was a notable success for the singer in the American market.

● ALBUMS: *The Kick Inside* (EMI 1978) ★★★★, *Lionheart* (EMI 1978) ★★, *Never For Ever* (EMI 1980) ★★★, *The Dreaming* (EMI 1982) ★★★★, *Hounds Of Love* (EMI 1985) ★★★★, *The Sensual World* (EMI 1989) ★★★★, *The Red Shoes* (EMI 1993) ★★★★.
● COMPILATIONS: *The Whole Story* (EMI 1986) ★★★, *This Woman's Work* (EMI 1990) ★★★★.
● VIDEOS: *Live At Hammersmith Odeon* (PMI 1984), *The Whole Story* (PMI 1986), *Hair Of The Hound* (PMI 1986), *Sensual World* (PMI 1990), *The Single File* (Music Club Video 1992), *The Line, The Cross & The Curve* (PMI 1994).
● FURTHER READING: *Kate Bush: An Illustrated Biography*, Paul Kerton. *Leaving My Tracks*, Kate Bush. *The Secret History Of Kate Bush (& The Strange Art Of Pop)*, Fred Vermorel. *Kate Bush: The Whole Story*, Kerry Juby. *Kate Bush: A Visual Documentary*, Kevin Cann and Sean Mayes.

## BUTLER, JONATHAN

b. 1961, Capetown, South Africa. Butler began his professional career as a guitarist, leaning strongly towards jazz. Later, resident in England, he added engaging vocals to his instrumental skills and broadened his repertoire to incorporate urban, reggae, gospel and Brazilian music. Underscoring all of his work, however, are Butler's African musical roots. He began performing at an early age in his native South Africa, where he was discovered by British record producer Clive Calder. His debut single was one of the first by a black artist to be played on white radio stations. Butler relocated to England in 1984, having signed a recording contract with Calder's Jive Records label. He enjoyed success two years later duetting with Ruby Turner on the Top 30 hit, 'If You're Ready (Come Go With Me)'. A track, 'Lies', from the following year's self-titled set broke into the US Top 30 and earned Butler a Grammy nomination. Much of this smoothly swinging guitarist's work is presented in a thoroughly accessible form, and as such is matched by his persuasive tenor voice. Nevertheless, the gentle flow of his work and the often poetic imagery of his lyrics, sometimes displays a harder edge that owes its origins to his early years under the repression of apartheid.
● ALBUMS: *Jonathan Butler* (Jive/Novus 1987) ★★★★, *More Than Friends* (Jive 1988) ★★★★, *7th Avenue* (Pro Jazz 1988) ★★★, *Gospel Days* (Pro-Arte 1989) ★★★, *Heal Our Land* (Jive 1990) ★★★, *Deliverance* (Jive 1990) ★★★, *Head To Head* (Mercury 1994) ★★★, *Do You Love Me?* (N-Coded 1997) ★★★, *Story Of Life* (N-Coded 1999) ★★★, *The Source* (N-Coded 2000) ★★★, *Surrender* (Warners 2002) ★★★.
● COMPILATIONS: *The Best Of Jonathan Butler* (Jive 1993) ★★★★.
● VIDEOS: *Heal Our Land* (Jive/RCA 1991).

## BUTTHOLE SURFERS

Formerly known as the Ashtray Baby Heads, this maverick quartet from Austin, Texas, USA, made its recording debut in 1983 with a self-titled mini-album (the name Butthole Surfers comes from an early song about beach transvestites). Gibson 'Gibby' Haynes (vocals) Paul Leary Walthall aka Paul Sneef (guitar) and King Coffey (drums) were initially indebted to the punk/hardcore scene, as shown by the startling 'The Shah Sleeps In Lee Harvey's Grave', but other selections were inspired by a variety of sources. Loping melodies, screaming guitar and heavy-metal riffs abound in a catalogue as zany as it is unclassifiable. Lyrically explicit, the group has polarized opinion between those who appreciate their boisterous humour and those deeming them prurient. Having endured a succession of bass players, including Kramer from Shockabilly and Bongwater, the Buttholes secured the permanent services of Jeff Pinker, alias Tooter, alias Pinkus, in 1985. The Surfers' strongest work appears on *Locust Abortion Technician* and *Hairway To Steven*, the former memorably including 'Sweet Loaf', a thinly disguised version of Black Sabbath's 'Sweet Leaf'. On the latter set, tracks are denoted by various simple drawings, including a defecating deer, rather than song titles. In 1991 the release of *Digital Dump*, a house project undertaken by Haynes and Pinkus under the Jack Officers epithet, was followed closely by the Buttholes' ninth album, *piouhgd*, which showed that their ability to enrage, bewilder and excite remained as sure as ever. It was marked by a curiously reverential version of Donovan's 'Hurdy Gurdy Man'.

In 1991, Pinkus also recorded the frenetic *Cheatos* as Daddy Longhead. This set was closely followed by Paul Leary's excellent solo debut, *The History Of Dogs*, and the band's shock signing to Capitol Records. The delay of *Electriclarryland* was as a result of objections received from the estate of Richard Rodgers/Oscar Hammerstein II when the band wanted to call the album *Oklahoma!*. It is difficult to be indifferent about this band, it's a simple love or loathe. Tagged as the sickest band in the world, they thrive on their own antics which include simulated sex, urinating and masturbation on stage. This tends to mask their musical ability and commercial potential which *Electriclarryland* clearly demonstrated. Haines also appeared alongside actor Johnny Depp in *P*, while Coffey recorded 1992's *Pick Up Heaven* as Drain on his own Trance Syndicate Records label. Following the release of 1998's *After The Astronaut*, the band signed a contract with Surfdog. Their first album for the label, *Weird Revolution*, was released in August 2001.

● ALBUMS: *Butthole Surfers* (Alternative Tentacles 1983) ★★★, *Live PCPPEP* (Alternative Tentacles 1984) ★★★, *Psychic ... Powerless ... Another Man's Sac* (Touch And Go 1985) ★★★, *Rembrandt Pussyhorse* (Touch And Go 1986) ★★★, *Locust Abortion Technician* (Touch And Go 1987) ★★★, *Hairway To Steven* (Touch And Go 1988) ★★★, *piouhgd* (Rough Trade 1991) ★★★, *Independent Worm Saloon* (Capitol 1994) ★★, *Electriclarryland* (Capitol 1996) ★★★★, *After The Astronaut* (Capitol 1998) ★★★, *Weird Revolution* (Surfdog 2001) ★★★.
Solo: Paul Leary *The History Of Dogs* (Rough Trade 1991) ★★★.
● COMPILATIONS: *Double Live* (Latino Buggerveil 1989) ★★★, *The Hole Truth ... And Nothing Butt!* (Trance Syndicate 1995) ★★★, *Classic Masters* (EMD 2002) ★★★, *Humpty Dumpty LSD* (Latino Bugger Veil 2002) ★★.
● VIDEOS: *Blind Eye Sees All* (Touch And Go).

## BYRNE, DAVID

b. 14 May 1952, Dumbarton, Scotland, but raised in Baltimore, Maryland, USA. Briefly a student of the Rhode Island School of Design, Byrne abandoned his training in visual and conceptual arts in favour of rock. He teamed up fellow design student, Chris Frantz, in the Artistics. After relocating to New York's Lower East Side, Byrne, Frantz and Tina Weymouth formed Talking Heads in 1974. This highly respected unit, completed with the addition of seasoned multi-instrumentalist Jerry Harrison, evolved from its origins in the New York punk milieu into one of America's leading new post-punk attractions. Much of its appeal was derived from

Byrne's quirky, almost paranoid, diction and imaginative compositions, but the band rapidly proved too limiting for his widening artistic palette. *My Life In The Bush Of Ghosts*, a 1981 collaboration with Brian Eno, was widely praised by critics for its adventurous blend of sound collages, ethnic influences and vibrant percussion, which contrasted with Byrne's ensuing solo debut, *The Catherine Wheel*. The soundtrack to Twyla Tharp's modern ballet, this fascinating set was the prelude to an intensive period in the parent act's career, following which the artist began composing and scripting a feature film. Released in 1986, *True Stories*, which Byrne also directed and starred in, was the subject of an attendant Talking Heads album. *Music For The Knee Plays*, on which Byrne worked with playwright Robert Wilson, confirmed interests emphasized in 1987 by his collaboration with Ryûichi Sakamoto and Cong Su on the soundtrack for Bernardo Bertolucci's *The Last Emperor*.

This highly acclaimed movie won several Oscars, including one for Best Original Score. Byrne, meanwhile, continued recording commitments to Talking Heads, but by the end of the 80s intimated a reluctance to appear live with them. He instead assembled a 14-strong Latin-American ensemble that toured the USA, Canada, Europe and Japan to promote *Rei Momo*, while a 1991 statement established that Talking Heads were on 'indefinite furlough'. *The Forest*, another collaboration with Wilson, confirmed the artist's prodigious talent by invoking European orchestral music. His Luaka Bop label, founded in 1988, established itself as a leading outlet for world music albums with a pop edge, including several devoted to Brazilian recordings. After two lacklustre rock-orientated releases, 1997's *Feelings* gained Byrne some of his best reviews for years. The album employed several guest producers, including UK trip-hop outfit Morcheeba. The follow-up *Look Into The Eyeball* was even better, a perfect fusion of exotic world rhythms and pop melody. Byrne's profile was further raised by his collaboration with UK dance act X-Press 2 on 'Lazy'. Featuring Byrne's witty lyrics and distinctive vocal delivery, the track stirred a great deal of excitement in the UK music media and was released amid much press and radio hype in March 2002. It eventually reached number 2 in the UK singles chart.

● ALBUMS: with Brian Eno *My Life In The Bush Of Ghosts* (Sire/Polydor 1981) ★★★★, *The Complete Score From The Broadway Production Of 'The Catherine Wheel'* soundtrack (Sire 1981) ★★★★, *Music For The Knee Plays* (ECM 1985) ★★★, *Sounds From True Stories* film soundtrack (Sire 1986) ★★★, with Ryûichi Sakamoto, Cong Su *The Last Emperor* film soundtrack (Virgin 1988) ★★★★, *Rei Momo* (Luaka Bop/Sire 1989) ★★★, *The Forest* (Luaka Bop/ Warners 1991) ★★★, *Uh-Oh* (Luaka Bop/Warners 1992) ★★★, *David Byrne* (Luaka Bop/Warners 1994) ★★, *Feelings* (Luaka Bop/Warners 1997) ★★★★, *The Visible Man* remix album (Luaka Bop 1998) ★★★, *In Spite Of Wishing And Wanting* dance soundtrack (Luaka Bop 1999) ★★★, *Look Into The Eyeball* (Luaka Bop/Virgin 2001) ★★★★.

● VIDEOS: *Catherine Wheel* (Elektra Entertainment 1982), *David Byrne: Between The Teeth* (Warner Reprise Video 1994).
● FURTHER READING: *American Originals: David Byrne*, John Howell. *Strange Ritual*, David Byrne. *Your Action World: Winners Are Losers With A New Attitude*, David Byrne.
● FILMS: *Stop Making Sense* (1984), *True Stories* (1986), *Heavy Petting* (1988), *Checking Out* (1989), *Between The Teeth* (1994), *Lulu On The Bridge* (1998).

## CABARET VOLTAIRE

Formed in Sheffield, Yorkshire, England, in 1972, and named after a 1930s Dadaist collective based in Zurich, this experimental, innovative electronic outfit proved to be a huge influence on later, more commercially successful bands such as the Human League, Depeche Mode and New Order. By the late 80s they were also recognised as a pioneering force on the UK's dance music scene.

Cabaret Voltaire was formed by Stephen Mallinder (bass, vocals), Richard H. Kirk (guitar, wind instruments) and Chris Watson (electronics and tapes). Influenced by Can and Brian Eno, the trio strived to avoid the confines of traditional pop music and their early appearances veered towards performance art. Their brutal, rhythmic sound was christened 'industrial' by a bemused music press. The trio's sound and attitude initially attracted the attention of Factory Records and they contributed two tracks to the Manchester label's 1978 double EP, *A Factory Sample*. They eventually signed to Rough Trade Records that same year, producing the *Extended Play EP*, which confirmed their experimental stance, although 'Nag, Nag, Nag' (1979) was a head-on rush of distorted guitar with a driving beat. The trio continued to break new ground, using sampled 'noise', cut-up techniques (inspired by author William Burroughs) and tape loops. Often viewed as inaccessible, in the ensuing years Cabaret Voltaire released the UK Independent Top 10 singles 'Silent Command' (1979), 'Three Mantras' and 'Seconds Too Late' (both 1980). Their 1979 debut *Mix-Up*, was followed by the more conventional *The Voice Of America*. After *Live At The YMCA 27.10.79*, the trio widened their horizons with video and collaborative work, including outings on the Belgian label Les Disques du Crépescule and two Industrial label cassettes, *1974-1976* (their early recordings) and Kirk's solo *Disposable Half Truths*.

In 1981, their prolific output was increased by the morbid but successful *Red Mecca* and by another cassette, *Live At The Lyceum*. They also set up their own Western Works studio in Sheffield. Watson left in October 1981 to work in television and later resurfaced in the Hafler Trio. In 1982, Eric Random was recruited on guitar for a Solidarity benefit concert, performing under the name Pressure Company. The resulting album, *Live In Sheffield 19 January 1982*, was released on Paradox Product. The year also saw the release of *2 x 45* (the last recording to feature Watson), 'Temperature Drop', plus the Japanese live album *Hai!* and a solo set from Mallinder, *Pow Wow*. Departing from Rough Trade in 1983, while also releasing 'Fools Game' on Les Disques du Crépuscule and 'Yashar' on Factory, they signed a joint contract with Some Bizzare/Virgin

Records. The first fruits of this move, 'Just Fascination' and 'Crackdown', confirmed Cabaret Voltaire's new approach and signalled a drastic shift towards rhythmic dancefloor sounds (assisted by keyboard player Dave Ball's presence). Yet another label entered the frame when Doublevision released the soundtrack *Johnny YesNo*. Kirk's double set, *Time High Fiction*, came at the end of this productive year. Aside from a compilation video, *TV Wipeout*, 1984 was a quiet year, until 'Sensoria' (on Some Bizzare) ripped the dance charts apart, setting the tone for much of Cabaret Voltaire's subsequent work, including 'James Brown', both featuring on *Micro-Phonies*, and 'I Want You' (1985). In between, the pair concentrated on the video *Gasoline In Your Eye*, paralleled by the similarly titled, double 12-inch 'Drinking Gasoline'. The critically acclaimed *The Arm Of The Lord* echoed their earlier phase.

Kirk's solo work continued apace in 1986 with *Black Jesus Voice*, and a mini-album, *Ugly Spirit*, plus a project with the Box's Peter Hope resulting in *Hoodoo Talk* on Native Records in 1987. By July of the same year, the duo had transferred to Parlophone Records, debuting with 'Don't Argue'. As with the follow-up releases, 'Here To Go' and *Code*, its sound introduced a more commercial club-orientated slant, lacking the pair's earlier, experimental approach. In 1988, Mallinder collaborated with Dave Ball and Mark Brydon, collectively known as Love Street, releasing 'Galaxy'. A new Cabaret Voltaire single, 'Hypnotised' (1989), reflected their visit to the house music capital, Chicago, while Kirk's highly influential single 'Testone' (1990), issued under the guise of Sweet Exorcist (with DJ Parrot, later of the All Seeing I), was pure techno. Cabaret Voltaire continued in this style with 'Keep On' and *Groovy, Laidback And Nasty*, working with some of the leading lights of the US house and techno scene. In the meantime, Mute Records methodically reissued their early back catalogue on CD. Leaving EMI, who were bemused by their new direction, Cabaret Voltaire signed to Les Disques Du Crepuscule for 'What Is Real' (1991). The well-received *Body And Soul* consolidated Cabaret Voltaire's pivotal position on the UK's dance scene, which they had, without fanfare, helped develop over a decade and a half. *International Language* and *The Conversation* were more minimalist pieces that appeared on their own Plastex label. Mallinder emigrated to Australia in late 1993, which effectively spelt the end for Cabaret Voltaire as a recording unit. Kirk has continued to release challenging dance-orientated material under a variety of guises, including Electronic Eye, Sandoz, Xon, Citrus, and Richard H. Kirk.

● ALBUMS: *Mix-Up* (Rough Trade/Go 1979) ★★★, *Three Mantras* mini-album (Rough Trade 1980) ★★, *The Voice Of America* (Rough Trade 1980) ★★, *Live At The YMCA 27.10.79.* (Rough Trade 1981) ★★, *Red Mecca* (Rough Trade 1981) ★★★, *Live At The Lyceum* cassette only (Rough Trade 1982) ★★★, *2 x 45* (Rough Trade 1982) ★★★, *Hai! Live In Japan* (Nichion/Rough Trade 1982) ★★★, *Johnny YesNo* film soundtrack (Doublevision 1983) ★★★, *The Crackdown* (Some Bizzare/Virgin 1983) ★★★, *Micro-Phonies* (Some Bizzare/Virgin 1984) ★★★, *The Arm Of The Lord* aka *The Covenant, The Sword And The Arm Of The Lord* (Some Bizzare/Virgin 1985) ★★★, *Drinking Gasoline* (Some Bizzare/Virgin 1985) ★★★, *Code* (Parlophone/EMI Manhattan 1987) ★★★★, *Groovy, Laidback And Nasty* (Parlophone 1990) ★★★, *Body And Soul* (Les Disques du Crépuscule 1991) ★★★, *Percussion Force* mini-album (Les Disques du Crépuscule 1991) ★★★, *Colours* mini-album (Plastex/Mute 1991) ★★★, *Plasticity* (Plastex 1992) ★★★, *International Language* (Plastex 1993) ★★★, *The Conversation* (Instinct/Apollo 1994) ★★★.

● COMPILATIONS: *74–76* cassette only (Industrial 1978) ★★, *The Golden Moments Of Cabaret Voltaire* (Rough Trade 1987) ★★★★, *Eight Crépuscule Tracks* (Giant 1988) ★★★, *Listen Up With Cabaret Voltaire* (Mute 1990) ★★★, *The Living Legends* (Mute 1990) ★★, *Technology: Western Re-Works 1992* (Virgin 1992) ★★★, *Radiation* (New Millennium 1998) ★★★, *Remixed* (EMI 2001) ★★★, *Conform To Deform: '82/'90. Archive;* 3-CD box set (Virgin 2001) ★★★, *The Original Sound Of Sheffield: '83/'87. Best Of;* (Virgin 2001) ★★★★.

● VIDEOS: *Doublevision Presents Cabaret Voltaire* (Doublevision 1983), *TV Wipeout* (Doublevision 1984), *Gasoline In Your Eye* (Doublevision/Virgin Vision 1985).

● FURTHER READING: *Cabaret Voltaire: The Art Of The Sixth Sense*, M. Fish and D. Hallbery. *Industrial Evolution: Through The Eighties With Cabaret Voltaire And Local Government*, Mick Fish.

## CALL

The Call's stadium-friendly rock songs prompted comparisons with U2 from the very outset of their career. A California, USA-based quartet, the songs written by vocalist Michael Been (ex-Aorta) recalled the passion and melodrama of *Boy*-era U2, an impression compounded by the band's spiritual inclinations. The band, originally known as Motion Pictures, was formed in 1980 in Santa Cruz, California, by Been, Tom Ferrier (guitar), Greg Freeman (bass) and Scott Musick (drums). Their 1982 debut was recorded in England with Hugh Padgham producing and Garth Hudson of the Band guesting on keyboards. The following year's *Modern Romans* included the minor US hit single 'The Walls Came Down'. Following the release of *Scene Beyond Dreams*, keyboard player Jim Goodwin was brought into the line-up and Been replaced the departing Freeman on bass. The band subsequently signed a new contract with Elektra Records. Their debut for the label, *Reconciled*, was given over to rather self-satisfied Christian mysticism, but occasionally they struck the right note with more classy and less pretentious numbers such as 'Everywhere I Go'. The album also included guest appearances from Robbie Robertson, Peter Gabriel and Jim Kerr. *Let The Day Begin* produced another memorable single in the title track, as the Call switched to MCA Records. *Red Moon* emerged as pressure mounted on Been to produce another hit. Despite this, it was a rewarding set, finding a more natural studio context to complement vocals that were always in danger of ill-advised grandeur. Again, the title cut was a stand-out track, though this was ably backed up by a rash of bold songwriting ventures including 'What's Happened To You' and the evocative 'This Is Your Life'. A subsequent compilation covering the band's Mercury Records years was compiled by Been and titled after the band's first breakthrough hit. However, the Call's long-term fate was, as one reviewer suggested, to be 'too politically tuff to be the Police, too strident to be the Cars, and too late to be the Clash'. Been, who made his acting debut as John The Apostle in Martin Scorsese's *The Last Temptation Of Christ*, recorded a strong solo album in 1994. The Call re-formed three years later, releasing the overtly Christian *To Heaven And Back* on their own Fingerprint label.

● ALBUMS: *The Call* (Mercury 1982) ★★★, *Modern Romans* (Mercury 1983) ★★★, *Scene Beyond Dreams* (Mercury 1984) ★★★, *Reconciled* (Elektra 1986) ★★, *Into The Woods* (Elektra 1987) ★★★, *Let The Day Begin* (MCA 1989) ★★★, *Red Moon* (MCA 1990) ★★★, *To Heaven And Back* (Fingerprint 1997) ★★★, *Live Under The Red Moon* 1990 recording (Conspiracy 2000) ★★★.
Solo: Michael Been *On The Verge Of A Nervous Breakthrough* (WEA 1994) ★★★.

● COMPILATIONS: *The Walls Came Down – The Mercury Years* (PolyGram 1991) ★★★★, *The Best Of The Call* (Warners 1997) ★★★★, *The Best Of The Call: The Millennium Collection* (Universal 2000) ★★★★.

## CAMEO

This US soul/funk act, originally called the New York City Players, was formed in 1974 by Larry 'Mr. B' Blackmon (b. New York City, New York, USA; drums, vocals) and vocalists Tomi Jenkins and Nathan Leftenant. Building up a strong following by undergoing rigorous touring schedules, with their backing group at times numbering almost a dozen members, they signed with the Casablanca subsidiary label Chocolate City, where they recorded their 1977 debut, *Cardiac Arrest*, produced by Blackmon. Touring alongside Parliament and Funkadelic enhanced their reputation and subsequent album releases gained modest positions in the US pop chart. In Britain, they enjoyed a loyal cult following, but it was not until their seventh album release, *Knights Of The Sound Table*, that they were afforded an UK release. However, in 1984, the single 'She's Strange' crossed over into the pop market and Cameo found themselves with their first UK Top 40 single. After the success of the following year's 'Single Life' (UK Top 20), 'She's Strange' was remixed and peaked at number 22. Three sell-out shows at London's Hammersmith Odeon followed. Having won over the UK pop market, it was not until 1986 that they finally broke into the US Top 40 chart; 'Word Up' had reached number 3 in the UK, and subsequently reached number 1 in the US R&B chart and number 6 in the *Billboard* pop chart. Having trimmed down the group to the core trio of Blackmon, Jenkins and Leftenant, and only using additional session players when necessary, Blackmon attracted most of the media attention. His image was helped in no small degree by the expansive, bright red codpiece he wore on stage. Blackmon's own studio, Atlanta Artists, allowed him almost total control over Cameo's sound and helped him to promote and nurture local musical talent. By the 90s, their commercial success had dramatically waned, but they continue to tour and release the occasional new album.

● ALBUMS: *Cardiac Arrest* (Chocolate City 1977) ★★, *We All Know Who We Are* (Chocolate City 1977) ★★★, *Ugly Ego* (Chocolate City 1978) ★★, *Secret Omen* (Chocolate City 1979) ★★, *Cameosis* (Chocolate City 1980) ★★★, *Feel Me* (Chocolate City 1980) ★★★, *Knights Of The Sound Table* (Chocolate City 1981) ★★★, *Alligator Woman* (Chocolate City 1982) ★★, *Style* (Atlanta Artists 1983) ★★★, *She's Strange* (Atlanta Artists 1984) ★★★, *Single Life* (Atlanta Artists/Club 1985) ★★★★, *Word Up!* (Atlanta Artists/Club 1986) ★★★★, *Machismo* (Atlanta Artists/Club 1988) ★★★, *Real Men ... Wear Black* (Atlanta Artists 1990) ★★★, *Emotional Violence* (Reprise 1992) ★★★, *In The Face Of Funk* (Way 2 Funky 1994) ★★, *Nasty* (Intersound 1996) ★★, *Sexy Sweet Thing* (Private I 2000) ★★★.

● COMPILATIONS: *The Best Of Cameo* (Phonogram 1993) ★★★★, *The Best Of Cameo, Volume 2* (Phonogram 1996) ★★★, *Live: Word Up* (CEMA 1998) ★★★, *The Ballads Collection* (PolyGram 1998) ★★★, *Cameo: The Hits Collection* (Spectrum 1998) ★★★★, *Greatest Hits* (PolyGram 1998) ★★★★, *The Best Of Cameo: The Millennium Collection* (PolyGram 2001) ★★★★, *Anthology* (Mercury 2002) ★★★.

● VIDEOS: *Cameo: The Video Singles* (Channel 5 1987), *Back And Forth* (Club 1987).

## CAMPBELL, JOHN

b. 20 January 1952, Shreveport, Louisiana, USA, d. 13 June 1993, New York, USA. Campbell, a white man, became an authentic-sounding blues singer/guitarist after a serious drag racing accident in 1967, which left him without one of his eyes and a mass of stitches in his face, which became permanently scarred. Prior to this crash, he had been curious about music – his grandmother played lap steel guitar – but he was more interested in being a tearaway. During his lengthy period of recuperation, much of it spent in solitude, he taught himself to play guitar and became devoted to the work of the black bluesmen who had recorded for the local Jewel label in Shreveport – in particular, John Lee Hooker and Lightnin' Hopkins, the latter of whom became his major influence. Leaving school in the late 60s, he became a travelling troubadour, working as the opening act for Clarence 'Gatemouth' Brown and Hubert Smith, ultimately relocating to New York where he played local clubs for many years. His recording debut came in 1988, when guitarist Ronnie Earl sent a tape of Campbell to the specialist Crosscut label in Germany. Earl produced his first album, *A Man And His Blues*, but it had little distribution in the USA, and he remained an obscure cult figure until he began working with guitarist Alexander Kennedy. He and Kennedy were opening for Albert King in New York when he was signed by Elektra Records, and in 1991 he released *One Believer*, produced by Dennis Walker (also Robert

Gray's producer), and backed by members of both Gray's band and Joe Ely's group. Campbell played solely amplified acoustic guitar, and his songwriting partnership with Walker and Kennedy produced several modern blues classics such as 'Devil In My Closet', 'Tiny Coffin' and 'Take Me Down'. *Howlin' Mercy* consolidated Campbell's standing as an important (although cult) figure in the new blues boom, but he died of heart failure in 1993 prior to undertaking a European tour.

● ALBUMS: *A Man And His Blues* (Crosscut 1988) ★★★, *One Believer* (Elektra 1991) ★★★★, *Howlin' Mercy* (Elektra 1993) ★★★, *Tyler, Texas Session* (Sphere 2000) ★★.

## CAMPER VAN BEETHOVEN

A band for whom the term 'alternative' might first have been coined; in fact, principal songwriter David Lowery suggests that is exactly the case: '(We) were arguably the prototypical alternative band. I remember first seeing that word applied to us. The nearest I could figure is that we seemed like a punk band, but we were playing pop music, so they made up the word "alternative" for those of us who do that'. Camper Van Beethoven were a witty, often sarcastic garage rock band formed in Redlands, California, USA, in 1983 by school friends, transferring to Santa Cruz when members attended college there. They were given their name by early member David McDaniels, though initial line-ups were frequently unstable. Lowery (b. 10 October 1960, San Antonio, USA; vocals, guitar) was originally joined by Greg Lisher (guitar), Chris Pedersen (drums), Chris Molla, Jonathan Segel (violin) and Victor Krummenacher (bass). Krummenacher was formerly a member of jazz ensemble Wrestling Worms. Their debut, *Telephone Free Landslide Victory*, contained the classic single cut 'Take The Skinheads Bowling', as well as the surreal ethnic instrumentation of 'Balalaika Gap' and 'Border Ska', and a strange Black Flag cover version ('Wasted'). It was typical of an armoury of songs that included titles such as 'The Day Lassie Went To The Moon', 'Joe Stalin's Cadillac' and 'ZZ Top Goes To Egypt'. They played their UK debut in March 1987, where 'Take The Skinheads Bowling' had become something of a cult hit, but neither there nor in the USA did their critical popularity transfer into sales.

*Vampire Can Mating Oven* wrapped up the last of their Rough Trade Records-distributed fare before a move to Virgin Records. *Our Beloved Revolutionary Sweetheart* found them in fine form with a bigger budget and a sympathetic producer, Dennis Herring. However, the tone of *Key Lime Pie* proved infinitely more sombre than previous outings and prophesied their split. In retrospect it is hard to listen to a track like 'When I Win The Lottery' without reading it as allegory for the band's unsuccessful transition from independent to major label chart prospect. A bizarre cover version of Status Quo's 'Pictures Of Matchstick Men', released as a single, serves as a reminder of their former discordant eclecticism.

Four members of Camper Van Beethoven, Lisher, Krummenacher, Pederson and former Ophelias guitarist David Immerglück (who joined the band over their final recordings), put together Monks Of Doom. Segel, who had been replaced by Morgan Fichter before *Key Lime Pie* was released, worked on released solo projects, and main songwriter David Lowery, after waiting fruitlessly for his former colleagues to return from their 'stupidity', finally made the deserved transition to a major band with Cracker. He reunited with Krummenacher and Segel in late 1999 to promote the rarities set, *Camper Van Beethoven Is Dead, Long Live Camper Van Beethoven*, and to undertake a handful of live dates.

● ALBUMS: *Telephone Free Landslide Victory* (Independent Project 1985) ★★★, *Take The Skinheads Bowling* mini-album (Pitch-A-Tent 1986) ★★★, *II/III* (Pitch-A-Tent 1986) ★★★★, *Camper Van Beethoven* (Pitch-A-Tent 1986) ★★★, *Vampire Can Mating Oven* mini-album (Pitch-A-Tent 1987) ★★★, *Our Beloved Revolutionary Sweetheart* (Virgin 1988) ★★★★, *Key Lime Pie* (Virgin 1989) ★★★.

● COMPILATIONS: *Camper Vantiquies* (I.R.S. 1994) ★★★, *Camper Van Beethoven Is Dead, Long Live Camper Van Beethoven* (Pitch-A-Tent 2000) ★★★.

## CAPERCAILLIE

The line-up of this traditional Scottish outfit includes Karen Matheson (b. 11 February 1963, Oban, Argyll, Scotland; vocals), Marc Duff (b. 8 September 1963, Ontario, Canada; bodhran, whistles), Manus Lunny (b. 8 February 1962, Dublin, Eire; bouzouki, vocals), Charlie McKerron (b. 14 June 1960, London, England; fiddle), John Saich (b. 22 May 1960, Irvine, Scotland; bass, vocals, guitar) and Donald Shaw (b. 6 May 1967, Ketton, Leicestershire, England; keyboards, accordion, vocals). Formed in 1984 at Oban High School in Scotland, initially to play for local dances, the band have now built a strong reputation for their treatment of traditional and Gaelic music from the West Highlands of Scotland. The strong musicianship of Manus Lunny, who is equally well known for his work with Andy M. Stewart, and the haunting vocals of Karen Matheson have established the band wherever they have performed. Having toured the Middle East, South America and the USA between 1984 and 1990, the band's appeal has widened beyond the restrictions of the folk music market. In 1988, Capercaillie were commissioned to compose and record the music for *The Blood Is Strong*, a television series about the history of the Gaelic Scots. The resultant success of both the series and music led to the soundtrack being released, and within six months it had been awarded a platinum disc for sales in Scotland.

In 1990, the band signed to Survival Records and, as evidence of their broadening appeal, the single from *Delirium*, 'Coisich A Ruin' (Walk My Beloved), a traditional Gaelic work song, achieved daytime airplay on BBC's Radio 1. Touring and promoting *Delirium*, Capercaillie were on the bill at Loch Lomond, Scotland, in the summer of 1991, the venue for a 40,000-strong concert by Runrig. *To The Moon* moved the band further from traditional folk into a stronger rock-based sound using African rhythm; it also introduced the band to a much wider audience, which they had deserved for some time. The same year the BBC commissioned the band to provide a soundtrack to a documentary marking the 250th anniversary of the last Jacobite Rebellion. Matheson sang the French entry, 'Diwanit Bugale', in the 1996 Eurovision Song Contest, and released her solo debut the same year. Saich and McKerron also collaborated with vocalist Laura McKerron, Charlie's cousin, on the Big Sky project.

● ALBUMS: *Cascade* (SRT 1984) ★★★, *Crosswinds* (Green Linnet 1987) ★★★, *The Blood Is Strong* (Celtic Music 1988) ★★★, *Sidewaulk* (Green Linnet 1989) ★★★, *Delirium* (RCA 1991) ★★★, *Secret People* (Survival 1993) ★★★, *Capercaillie* (Survival 1994) ★★★, *To The Moon* (Survival 1995) ★★★, *Beautiful Wasteland* (Survival 1997) ★★★★, *Glenfinnan (Songs Of The '45)* mini-album (Survival 1999) ★★★, *Nàdurra* (Survival 2000) ★★★.
Solo: Karen Matheson *The Dreaming Sea* (Survival 1996) ★★★.
● COMPILATIONS: *Get Out* (Survival 1992) ★★★, *Dusk Till Dawn: The Best Of Capercaillie* (Survival 1998) ★★★★, *Waulk Roots* (Eureka 1999) ★★★, *An Introduction To Capercaillie* (BMG 2002) ★★★★.
● VIDEOS: *The Capercaillie Collection 1990-1996* (Survival 2000).

## CAPTAIN SENSIBLE

b. Raymond Burns, 24 April 1954, Balham, London, England. Having drifted from job to job after leaving school, Burns fell in with fellow reprobate Chris Miller while working at the Croydon Fairfield Halls. Sharing common interests in drink, chaos and music, they eventually found themselves part of the burgeoning punk scene in west London in 1976. Together with Dave Vanian and Brian James, Miller (Rat Scabies) and Burns (Captain Sensible) formed what was to be one of the major punk bands of the period: the Damned. Initially enrolled as their bass player, he moved on to guitar following James' departure. A riotous character with an unnerving sense of charm, Sensible frequently performed at gigs dressed in various guises, often in a tu-tu, a nurse's uniform or even nothing at all. Behind the comic-strip façade lurked a keen fan of 60s and 70s psychedelia; he was often quoted in later interviews as being influenced by Jimi Hendrix, Syd Barrett-era Pink Floyd and the Soft Machine. This went against the punk ethos of the time.
Sensible was able to indulge his esoteric taste in music by carving out a solo career by accident rather than design, owing to the frequent bouts of forced inactivity by the Damned. With ex-Chelsea bass player Henry Badowski, Sensible formed King, an outfit that lasted barely three months. That same year, he recorded 'Jet Boy, Jet Girl', a lyrically improbable translation of Plastic Bertrand's 'Ca Plane Pour Moi' with the Softies, and also performed on Johnny Moped's *Cycledelic*. A fervent campaigner for animal rights, and a CND supporter, he confirmed his anti-establishment credentials by recording an EP on the Crass label, *This Is Your Captain Speaking* in 1981. With fellow Damned member Paul Gray, he produced the Dolly Mixture singles 'Been Teen' and 'Everything And More'. Signed by A&M Records as a solo act, he recorded a cover version of Richard Rodgers and Oscar

Hammerstein II's 'Happy Talk', which included Dolly Mixture on backing vocals. The single shot to the UK number 1 position in the summer of 1982. With his distinctive red beret and round shades, he become an instant media and family favourite, revealing an endearing fondness for rabbits, cricket and trains. He subsequently released two albums in close collaboration with lyricist Robyn Hitchcock, and had further hit singles with 'Wot!' and the glorious anti-Falklands war song 'Glad It's All Over'. Although he was keen not to let his solo success interfere with the Damned's activities, Sensible found himself gradually becoming isolated from the other members due to internal politics and managerial disputes, resulting in his leaving the band in 1984, although he occasionally dropped in to guest on live performances. One single in 1985 in partnership with girlfriend Rachel Bor of Dolly Mixture, billed as Captain Sensible And The Missus, 'Wot! No Meat?', emphasized his commitment to vegetarianism. He undertook a national tour in 1985, as well as studio work, which culminated in the formation of his own Deltic label. His 1991 set *Revolution Now* received less favourable reviews. The double set did, however, show that his talent for catchy pop had not deserted him. He reunited with Paul Gray for some live performances in 1991, and set up another record company, Humbug Records. In 1994, he released *Live At The Milky Way*, an album which managed to capture both his humour and considerable songwriting talent. The band performs as if it is their last day on the planet on rewarding versions of 'Neat Neat Neat', 'New Rose' and 'Happy Talk'. At the same time Sensible was playing bass in the psychedelically inclined the Space Toad Experience, who released *Time Machine* in 1996. In 1995 Sensible put together Captain Sensible's Punk Floyd with Dreadful and Monty The Moron (keyboards), and, following live work with Dave Vanian, re-formed the Damned in 1996.
● ALBUMS: *Women And Captains First* (A&M 1982) ★★★, *The Power Of Love* (A&M 1983) ★★, *Revolution Now* (Deltic 1989) ★★, *The Universe Of Geoffrey Brown* (Deltic 1993) ★★, *Live At The Milky Way* (Humbug 1994) ★★★★, *Mad Cows & Englishmen* (Scratch 1996) ★★★.
● COMPILATIONS: *Sensible Singles* (A&M 1984) ★★★, *A Day In The Life Of Captain Sensible* (A&M 1984) ★★★, *Meathead* (Humbug 1995) ★★★, *A Slice Of ... Captain Sensible* (Humbug 1996) ★★★, *Sensible Lifestyles: The Best Of Captain Sensible* (Cleopatra 1997) ★★★, *The Masters* (Eagle 1999) ★★★.

## CARA, IRENE

b. Irene T. Escalera, 18 March 1959, New York City, New York, USA. Having spent most of her childhood as a successful actor, singer and dancer, Cara's role as Coco Hernandez in the 1980 Alan Parker movie *Fame* was tailor-made. Based around the lives, loves and ambitions of students at the New York School of Performing Arts, Cara's rendition of the jubilant title song was an Oscar-winning international hit, reaching the number 1 spot, belatedly, in the UK. This sparked off an entire 'Fame' industry and a worldwide boost for sales of leg warmers. Another movie song, 'Flashdance ... What A Feeling', from *Flashdance*, earned Cara a US number 1, a UK number 2 and yet another Oscar for Best Song. Signing to Geffen Records, Cara enjoyed further US hits with 'Why Me' (1983), a further movie hit with 'The Dream (Hold On To Your Dream)' from *DC Cab*, and the Top 10 hit 'Breakdance' (both 1984). Contractual disputes delayed her recording career in the mid-80s, before she re-emerged with a new album in 1987 on Elektra Records.

● ALBUMS: *Anyone Can See* (Network 1982) ★★, *What A Feelin'* (Geffen 1983) ★★, *Carasmatic* (Elektra 1987) ★★.

● FILMS: *Sparkle* (1976), *Apple Pie* (1976), *Fame* (1980), *Killing 'Em Softly* (1982), *D.C. Cab* (1983), *City Heat* (1984), *Certain Fury* (1985), *Busted Up* (1986), *Happily Ever After* voice only (1990), *Caged In Paradise* (1990), *Die Abenteuer Von Pico Und Columbus* voice only (1992).

## CARDIACS

Formed in 1978 by Tim Smith (b. 3 July 1961, Carshalton, Surrey, England; guitar, vocals), brother Jim (b. 14 April 1958, Carshalton, Surrey, England; bass, vocals), Peter Tagg (b. London, England; drums) and Mick Pugh (b. 21 September 1958, Kingston, Surrey, England; vocals), this UK indie band started life known as Philip Pilf And The Filth, which, although bizarre, was to be no less strange than the rest of a career riddled with personnel changes and eccentric activities. The name was soon switched to Cardiac Arrest, whereupon Colvin Myers (b. London, England; keyboards) joined for the first single, 'A Bus For A Bus On The Bus', in 1979. In the same year, Mark Cawthra replaced Tagg, who went on to form the Trudy. His departure was followed by that of Pugh and Myers, who joined the Sound.

The Cardiacs resolutely strived to avoid the traditional machinations of the record business by releasing a series of cassette-only albums. Saxophonist Sarah Smith (b. 30 November 1960, Coleford, Gloucestershire, England) and drummer Dominic Luckman (b. 29 November 1961, Brighton, East Sussex, England) both merged with the ranks, as had William D. Drake (b. 7 February 1962, Essex, England; keyboards) and Tim Quy (b. 14 August 1961, Brixton, London, England; percussion) towards the end of 1983. Fortunately, this line-up was to remain stable for the next six years, allowing the Cardiacs to build a devoted live following with oddball performances involving flour, ill-fitting suits and several other crazy theatrical elements. Long-overdue vinyl album releases followed, revealing how the band were perfecting a thoroughly unique musical sound that flummoxed the critics, although one offered the opinion that 'Genesis on a frantic amphetamine overdose' fitted the bill adequately.

By 1988, the Cardiacs started to infringe upon the hitherto alien mainstream, reaching number 80 in the UK singles chart with the epic 'This Is The Life', but changes were on the way again as Sarah Smith, Quy and Drake all left and guitarist Christian Hayes (b. 10 June 1964, London, England) joined briefly before departing for the equally indefinable Levitation in 1991, paving the way for more chapters

in the Cardiacs' fairy story. In 1995 the entire Cardiacs back catalogue was reissued, together with a specially priced sampler CD. This featured one track from each of their previous albums and one each from projected new releases from Tim Smith, Drake and Sara Smith (*The Sea Nymphs*), Tim Smith's solo album (*Oceanland World*) and the forthcoming group album. They then joined with Sidi Bou Said for a widespread UK tour and supported long-standing fans Blur at the Mile End Stadium concert in London. *Sing To God* proved to be an excellent comeback release.

● ALBUMS: *The Obvious Identity* cassette only (Own Label 1980) ★★★, *Toy World* cassette only (Own Label 1981) ★★★, *Archive Cardiacs* cassette only (Alphabet 1983) ★★★, *The Seaside* cassette only (Alphabet 1983) ★★★, *Mr & Mrs Smith & Mr Drake* cassette only (Alphabet 1984) ★★★, *Rude Bootleg* (Alphabet 1986) ★★★, *A Little Man And A House And The Whole World Window* (Alphabet 1988) ★★★★, *Cardiacs Live: Recorded Live At The 'Paradiso' Amsterdam, Holland* (Alphabet 1988) ★★★, *On Land And In The Sea* (Alphabet 1989) ★★★, *Songs For Ships And Irons* (Alphabet 1990) ★★★★, *Heaven Born And Ever Bright* (Alphabet 1992) ★★★, *All That Glitters Is A Mares Nest* (Alphabet 1993) ★★★, *Sing To God Parts I & II* (Alphabet 1996) ★★★, *Guns* (Alphabet 1999) ★★★.

● COMPILATIONS: *Cardiacs Sampler* (Alphabet 1995) ★★★, *A Remorseless And Insouciant Compendium Of Songs By Cardiacs And Affectionate Friends* (Org 2001) ★★★.

● VIDEOS: *All That Glitters Is A Mares Nest* (FotoDisk Video 1993).

## CARLISLE, BELINDA

b. 17 August 1958, Hollywood, California, USA. When the Go-Go's broke up in 1985, Carlisle remained with the I.R.S. Records label and pursued a solo career. After the excesses of her former band, Carlisle underwent a period of physical recuperation and image remodelling – emerging as the quintessential modern young Californian female. With artistic assistance from former band mate Charlotte Caffey, Carlisle hit the US Top 3 with her debut single 'Mad About You' in 1986 and her first album peaked at number 13 in the *Billboard* chart. It was not until a move to the MCA label in the USA and on signing to Virgin Records in the UK that she achieved international acclaim with the release of 'Heaven Is A Place On Earth'. This infectious piece of perfect pop reached number 1 in the USA and UK and gave her a whole new generation of fans who had previously never heard of the Go-Go's. This winning formula was subsequently used for a string of albums and other chart singles such as 'I Get Weak' (US number 2/UK Top 10, 1988), 'Circle In The Sand' (US number 7/UK number 4, 1988), 'Leave A Light On' (UK number 4, 1989) and 'We Want The Same Thing' (UK number 6). Using her new found position as a respected pop star, Carlisle and Jane Wiedlin put their names to various environmental and humanitarian/animal rights causes. *A Woman And A Man* featured an eclectic mix of bedfellows, notably ex-Kajagoogoo bass player

Nick Beggs, Susannah Hoffs and Brian Wilson. In the late 90s, Carlisle reunited with her former colleagues to record a new Go-Go's album.
● ALBUMS: *Belinda* (I.R.S. 1986) ★★★, *Heaven On Earth* (Virgin 1987) ★★★, *Runaway Horses* (Virgin 1989) ★★, *Live Your Life Be Free* (Virgin 1991) ★★, *Real* (Virgin 1993) ★★, *A Woman And A Man* (Chrysalis 1996) ★★.
● COMPILATIONS: *Her Greatest Hits* (MCA 1992) ★★★, *A Place On Earth: The Greatest Hits* (Virgin 1999) ★★★.
● VIDEOS: *Belinda Live* (Virgin Vision 1988), *Runaway – Live* (Castle Music Pictures 1990), *Runaway Videos* (Virgin Vision 1991), *The Best Of ... Volume 1* (Virgin 1992).

## CARLTON, LARRY
b. 2 March 1948, Torrance, California, USA. Often cited as the guitarist's guitarist, Carlton has courted rock, jazz and acoustic new age with considerable success. The former member of the Crusaders carved a career during the 70s as a sought-after session musician. His profile improved following some outstanding, fluid playing over a number of years with Steely Dan (in particular, his solo on 'Kid Charlemagne' from 1976's *The Royal Scam*). His distinctive 'creamy' Gibson 335 guitar sound was heard on countless records and his work on numerous Joni Mitchell albums arguably contributed to their success, with notable examples including *Court And Spark* and *Hejira*. His major label debut appeared in 1978. It was not until *Sleepwalk*, including its title track (formerly a hit for Santo And Johnny), that Carlton was fully accepted as a solo artist in his own right. *Alone But Never Alone* found Carlton playing acoustic guitar and the record proved a critical and commercial success. Both that album and *Discovery* broadened Carlton's following. The live *Last Nite*, however, saw a return to his jazz roots, and contained flashes of breathtaking virtuosity, in particular on his stand-out version of Miles Davis' 'So What'.
Carlton demonstrated a stronger rock influence with *On Solid Ground*, producing a credible cover version of Eric Clapton's 'Layla' and Steely Dan's 'Josie'. He was awarded a Grammy in 1981 and again in 1987 for his version of 'Minute By Minute'. The following year Carlton was shot in the neck by an intruder at his studio. After an emergency operation and many months of physiotherapy he made a full recovery. Carlton joined the GRP Records stable in 1991 and found a home that perfectly suited his music. His duet with labelmate Lee Ritenour in 1995 was wholly satisfying, and boded well for future collaborations. His 2001 live album with Steve Lukather was also noteworthy. Carlton remains a master musician with a catalogue of accessible and uplifting music that occasionally catches fire.
● ALBUMS: *With A Little Help From My Friends* (Uni 1968) ★★, *Singing/Playing* (Blue Thumb 1973) ★★★, *Larry Carlton* (Warners 1978) ★★, *Live In Japan* (Flyover 1979) ★★★, *Strikes Twice* (MCA 1980) ★★★, *Sleepwalk* (MCA 1981) ★★★, *Eight Times Up* (Warners 1983) ★★★, *Friends* (MCA 1983) ★★★, *Alone But Never Alone* (MCA 1986) ★★★★, *Discovery* (MCA 1986) ★★★★, *Last Nite* (MCA 1986) ★★★★, *On Solid Ground* (MCA 1989) ★★★, *Renegade Gentleman* (GRP 1991) ★★★, *Kid Gloves* (GRP 1992) ★★★, with Lee Ritenour *Larry And Lee* (GRP 1995) ★★★★, *The Gift* (GRP 1996) ★★★, *Fingerprints* (Warners 2000) ★★★, with Steve Lukather *No Substitutions: Live In Osaka* (Favored Nations 2001) ★★★★, *Deep Into It* (Warners 2001) ★★★.
● COMPILATIONS: *The Collection* (GRP 1990) ★★★★.

## CARMEL
This UK act was formed in Manchester in 1981 by Carmel McCourt (b. 24 November 1958, Scunthorpe, Lincolnshire, England; vocals) and former members of Bee Vamp, Jim Parris (b. 13 January 1957, Finchley, London, England; double bass) and Gerry Darby (b. 13 October 1959, Finchley, London, England; drums, percussion). On the release of the single 'Storm' and a mini-album in 1982 on the independent Red Flame label, Carmel drew praise for the fiery passion of all three members. Parris and Darby remarkably conjured the effect of a full ensemble backing to McCourt's powerful vocals, and were able to alternate between soulful ballads, gospel, blues and stomping jazz. The stand-out 'Tracks Of My Tears' was performed with confidence, as though the song had been a group original rather than a new arrangement of the Smokey Robinson classic. An appearance at the 1983 ICA Rock Week led to Carmel signing to London Records, while a sell-out date at the prestigious Ronnie Scott's jazz club confirmed their status within the British 'new jazz/pop' scene. In accentuating the 'jazz' motif, the music and 'style' press unfortunately saddled the singer with an unwanted Billie Holiday image, which was eventually passed on to future 'rival' Sade. Carmel tasted success for the first time that August when the glorious, gospel-tinged 'Bad Day', featuring the Attractions' Steve Nieve and the swooping backing vocals of Helen Watson and Rush Winters, reached number 15 in the UK singles chart. Carmel's '50s jazz club' image was evocatively captured on the single's cover by Serge Clerc, who supplied the artwork to the subsequent 'Willow Weep For Me', February 1984's number 23 hit 'More, More, More' and the album, *The Drum Is Everything*. Despite reaching number 19 in the charts, the album failed to capture the vitality of the singles or of the earlier Red Flame issues.
While the jazz fashion faded in the UK, Carmel found a much more attentive and appreciative audience in Europe, particularly France. A more satisfying release, *The Falling* saw the trio achieve their most successful studio performance up to that time, aided by several producers including Brian Eno and Hugh Johns. Subsequent albums displayed an increasing maturity that manifested itself in original compositions such as 'Easy For You', 'Nothing Good', 'Napoli' and 'I'm Over You'. Their earlier talent for producing imaginative cover versions saw them tackling Randy Newman's 'Mama Told Me Not To Come', Charles Dawes and Carl Sigman's hit for Tommy Edwards, 'It's All In The Game', and Duke Ellington's 'Azure'. Despite the disappointing lack of

mass appeal in the home market, Carmel continue to command respect from critics and fans alike and are able to work equally well within the confines of an intimate jazz club or in the larger auditoriums. After a long association with London Records, Carmel left the label in 1991, signing with East West in 1992. The trio recorded two indifferent major label releases in the mid-90s, but they remain a compelling live attraction as documented on the live sets for Musidisc and Indigo.

● ALBUMS: *Carmel* (Red Flame 1982) ★★★, *The Drum Is Everything* (London 1984) ★★, *The Falling* (London 1986) ★★★, *Everybody's Got A Little ... Soul* (London 1987) ★★★, *Set Me Free* (London 1989) ★★★, *Good News* (East West 1992) ★★★, *World's Gone Crazy* (East West 1995) ★★★, *Live In Paris* (Musidisc 1997) ★★★★, *Live At Ronnie Scott's* (Indigo 1998) ★★★.

● COMPILATIONS: *Collected* (London 1990) ★★★★.

● VIDEOS: *Collected: A Collection Of Work 1983–1990* (London 1990).

## CARNES, KIM

b. 20 July 1945, Pasadena, California, USA. The gravelly voiced Carnes is best known for her 1981 pop classic 'Bette Davis Eyes', which won a Grammy award. Her career started as a member of the influential New Christy Minstrels in 1966, and she also appeared alongside future songwriting partner Jackie DeShannon in the low budget 1967 movie *C'mon, Let's Live A Little*. Her second solo album, 1975's *Kim Carnes*, brought her critical favour, although she was reaping greater success as a songwriter with her husband Dave Ellingson, whom she had met in the New Christy Minstrels. Renowned artists such as Frank Sinatra and Barbra Streisand recorded her songs, as did another old New Christy Minstrels sparring partner Kenny Rogers who duetted with her on their US Top 5 hit 'Don't Fall In Love With A Dreamer' in 1980. The previous year Carnes/Ellingson had written all the material for Rogers' bestselling *Gideon*.

In 1981, the Jackie DeShannon/Donna Weiss composition 'Bette Davis Eyes' topped the US charts for an impressive nine weeks. This lyrically strong number featured Carnes' husky vocal over a chiming guitar, utilizing one of the best examples of 'flanging guitar effect' ever recorded. The follow-up, 'Draw Of The Cards', gave prominence to a contagious, swirling, organ-dominated sound, and stalled inside the US Top 30. *Mistaken Identity* contained both these tracks and topped the US chart for a month during its year long stay. Subsequent albums made a respectable showing in the bestsellers with Carnes enjoying regular visits to the US singles chart. During 1984 she had two major duetted hits, the first, 'What About Me?', with Kenny Rogers and James Ingram; three months later she had success duetting with Barbra Streisand on 'Make No Mistake, He's Mine'. Carnes was one of the stars to appear on the 1985 USA For Africa charity single 'We Are The World', and enjoyed a solo Top 20 hit later in the year with 'Crazy In The Night (Barking At Airplanes)'. She returned to her country roots for 1988's *View From The House*, which featured the

country chart hit 'Speed Of The Sound Of Loneliness', with Lyle Lovett on backing vocals. During the 90s she established herself in Nashville as a reliable hit songwriter for artists such as Reba McEntire, Tim McGraw, Mindy McCready and Trisha Yearwood, although her own recording career was limited to a 1991 Japanese album and three new tracks on a 1993 compilation. Carnes has now completed a full circle, proving herself as a successful songwriter in rock, pop and country and entering the record books for one of the longest stays at the coveted number 1 position.

● ALBUMS: *Rest On Me* (Amos 1971) ★★, *Kim Carnes* (A&M 1975) ★★★, *Sailin'* (A&M 1976) ★★★, *St Vincent's Court* (EMI America 1979) ★★, *Romance Dance* (EMI America 1980) ★★★, *Mistaken Identity* (EMI America 1981) ★★★★, *Voyeur* (EMI America 1982) ★★★, *Cafe Racers* (EMI America 1983) ★★, *Barking At Airplanes* (EMI America 1985) ★★, *Light House* (EMI America 1986) ★★★, *View From The House* (MCA 1988) ★★★★, *Checking Out The Ghosts* (Teichiku 1991) ★★★.

● COMPILATIONS: *The Best Of You* (A&M 1988) ★★★, *Crazy In The Night* (CEMA 1990) ★★★, *Gypsy Honeymoon: The Best Of Kim Carnes* (EMI America 1993) ★★★, *The Mistaken Identity Collection* (Razor & Tie 1999) ★★★.

● FILMS: *C'mon, Let's Live A Little* (1967).

## CARRACK, PAUL

b. 22 April 1951, Sheffield, Yorkshire, England. Justified success finally arrived for keyboard/vocalist Paul Carrack during the late 80s. As an unassuming personality, it seemed that he would only be remembered as the man who sang 'How Long'. This memorable pop song from pub-rock band Ace took Carrack's voice into the UK Top 20 in 1974, and to number 3 in the US charts in 1975. When investigated, Carrack's career reveals first-class credentials. Following the demise of Ace in 1977 he joined Frankie Miller's band and the following year moved on to Roxy Music, appearing on *Manifesto* and *Flesh And Blood*. After recording a solo album, *Nightbird*, Carrack was invited to join Squeeze as Jools Holland's replacement. He sang lead vocal on the sublime 'Tempted' (1981), and made a considerable contribution to their *East Side Story*. Carrack then teamed up with Nick Lowe under various guises, during which time he released his second solo album, *Suburban Voodoo*, and achieved a US Top 40 hit with 'I Need You'. He was seen as a regular member of Eric Clapton's band in the mid-80s, before being enlisted as lead singer of Mike And The Mechanics in 1985. His distinctive voice was heard on two major hits, 'Silent Running (On Dangerous Ground)' (1986) and 'The Living Years' (1989).

During 1987, again as a solo artist, he had a minor UK hit with 'When You Walk In The Room', but still suffered from anonymity with the mass British record-buying public. His standing in the USA, however, was much more respected, endorsed that same year with the Top 10 hit, 'Don't Shed A Tear'. In 1989 *Groove Approved* was highly successful in America and did much to place his name in the foreground of male vocalists. As a session musician, his pedigree has always secured him positions alongside many of the top acts of the day and his smooth and effortless delivery gives him one of the most distinctive voices in pop music, albeit one to which it is difficult to put a face.

In the 90s, Carrack's career was mostly taken up with his participation with Mike And The Mechanics. He stepped outside in the mid-90s with an excellent solo album that spawned two hit singles, notably a beautiful reworking of 'How Long' and the equally fine 'Eyes Of Blue'. *Blue Views* at last gave him the critical recognition he has long deserved. *Satisfy My Soul* further established the songwriting partnership he has developed with former Squeeze colleague Chris Difford.

● ALBUMS: *Nightbird* (Vertigo 1980) ★★, *Suburban Voodoo* (Epic 1982) ★★, *One Good Reason* (Chrysalis 1987) ★★★, *Groove Approved* (Chrysalis 1989) ★★★, *Blue Views* (I.R.S. 1996) ★★★★, *Beautiful World* (Ark 21 1997) ★★★, *Satisfy My Soul* (Compass 2000) ★★★, *Groovin'* (Carrack 2001) ★★★.

● COMPILATIONS: *Ace Mechanic* (Demon 1987) ★★★, *Carrackter Reference* (Demon 1991) ★★★.

## CARROLL, CATH

b. 25 August 1960, Chipping Sodbury, Avon, England. Carroll had previously made a name for herself on the Manchester club and music scene, founding with friend Liz Naylor the magazine *City Fun*, forming the short-lived Gay Animals and developing a penchant for cross-dressing. On moving south to London, she pursued a parallel career as a journalist and gossip columnist for the rock weekly *New Musical Express* and listings magazine *City Limits*. An often-used pseudonym, Myrna Minkoff (inspired by the character in John Kennedy Toole's novel *A Confederacy Of Dunces*) was a direct contradiction of Carroll's true quiet nature. Leading the mid-80s 'indie' band Miaow, which also comprised Chris Fenner (drums), Ron Caine (bass, guitar) and Steve MacGuire (guitar), she found herself linked with the *NME*'s seminal C86 project, contributing 'Sport Most Royal' for the album and appearing at London's ICA rock week celebration. Her smooth vocals, coupled with the jangling rhythm section, won critical acclaim, particularly with the anti-Thatcher song 'Grocer's Devil Daughter' on the Venus label, and the triumphant 'yodelling' high point, 'When It All Comes Down', on Factory Records, which reached the UK Independent Top 20. Their final single, 'Break The Code', gave some clue as to the musical direction Carroll was later to pursue.

She subsequently became involved in low-key collaborations with Julian Henry in the Hit Parade, then married Big Black's guitarist Santiago Durango (who had left the group to study law), and continued her own solo career, spending recording time in São Paulo, Brazil, as well as London and Sheffield, England. Remaining with Factory as a solo artist (and becoming the label's first artist actually to sign a contract), Carroll recorded her debut album, assisted by Mark Brydon (guitar), Sim Lister (saxophone, drums, keyboards), Oswaldinho da

Cuica (congas), Antenor Soares Gandra Neto (guitar), Dirceu Simoes de Medeiros (drums), Vincente da Paula Silva (piano), Valerie A. James (backing vocals), Steve Albini (guitar) and Santiago Durango (guitar). The result was the critically acclaimed *England Made Me*, released in the summer of 1991. The set confirmed the complete departure from Carroll's past English 'indie' workings, revealing a set of smooth, steamy Latin-samba, mixed with electro-dance rhythms. She relocated to Chicago, USA, and released the lyrically strong *True Crime Motel* in 1995.

● ALBUMS: *England Made Me* (Factory 1991) ★★★, *True Crime Motel* (Matador 1995) ★★★.

## CARROLL, JIM

b. 1951, New York City, USA. Jim Carroll was a poet and author who became a rock singer in the late 70s. He had a difficult childhood on New York's rough streets, but became a proficient basketball player before his teens. He then became exposed to the seedy aspects of city life. He began writing down his experiences at the age of 12, describing his initiation to heroin at 13 as well as his encounters with sex and crime. (Those notes were later published as a critically acclaimed book, *The Basketball Diaries*, in 1980.) Carroll became interested in poetry through reading the works of modern poets such as Jack Kerouac and Allen Ginsberg and had his own first book of poetry, *Living At The Movies*, published when he was 16. He spent three months in jail for heroin possession in 1966, and continued his obsessions with drugs, literature and basketball upon his release. Having already befriended writer William Burroughs and the rock group the Velvet Underground, Carroll was introduced to poet Patti Smith in the early 70s. Smith was in the process of setting her poetry to music and after Carroll moved to Marin County, north of San Francisco, in 1974 to rid himself of his heroin habit, he maintained contact with Smith. When Smith and her group went to California in the late 70s, Carroll, having also taken an interest in setting his poetry to music, and having been inspired by the punk movement, performed as her opening act. He produced a demo tape of his music in 1979 and was signed to Atco Records. Carroll recorded his debut album, *Catholic Boy*, that year and formed the Jim Carroll Band, with Brian Linsley (guitar), Steve Linsley (bass), Terrell Winn (guitar) and Wayne Woods (drums). The album reached only number 73 but was a critical success, particularly the song 'People Who Died', a graphic description of individuals known to the singer who met with horrible deaths. Carroll made two further albums, *Dry Dreams* and *I Write Your Name*, with several personnel changes in the band for each album. He performed music infrequently after the mid-80s, concentrating instead on giving poetry readings. Carroll published his second book, *Forced Entries* in 1987. In 1991, Carroll signed with Giant Records and released a spoken-word album, *Praying Mantis*, recorded live at St. Mark's Church in New York City.

● ALBUMS: *Catholic Boy* (Atco 1980) ★★★★, *Dry Dreams* (Atco 1982) ★★★, *I Write Your Name* (Atco

1984) ★★★, *Praying Mantis* spoken word (Giant 1991) ★★★, *Pools Of Mercury* (Mercury 1998) ★★★.
● COMPILATIONS: *A World Without Gravity: The Best Of The Jim Carroll Band* (Rhino 1993) ★★★★ .

## CARS

In a recording career that started in 1977 the Cars' output was a meagre six albums. Each one, however, sold over a million copies and reached high chart positions in the USA. Formerly known as Cap'n Swing, the stable line-up comprised Ric Ocasek (b. Richard Otcasek, 23 March 1949, Baltimore, Maryland, USA; guitar, vocals), Benjamin Orr (b. Benjamin Orzechowski, 9 August 1947, Cleveland, Ohio, USA, d. 3 October 2000, USA; bass, vocals), Greg Hawkes (keyboards), Elliot Easton (b. Elliot Shapiro, 18 December 1953, Brooklyn, New York, USA; guitar) and David Robinson (drums). Their catchy pop/rock songs were hard to categorize and when they arrived with 'Just What I Needed', they were embraced by the new wave art-rock fraternity in the USA. They were an instant success in Britain, notching up a number of hits, and debuting with a Top 3 single, the irresistible 'My Best Friend's Girl'. The Cars never deviated from writing catchy, well-crafted songs, each containing at least one memorable and instantly hummable riff, which enabled them to gain acceptance on the lucrative AOR market.
In 1984 they enjoyed worldwide success with 'Drive', and a year later the same song was opportunistically but tastefully used to pull at people's consciences during the Live Aid concert. A film accompanying the song, showing the appalling famine in Ethiopia, will forever remain in people's minds; as the lyric 'Who's gonna plug their ears when you scream' was played, it was replaced by a heart-rending scream from a small child. This memorable yet tragic segment left few dry eyes in the world, and predictably the song became a hit once more. The band broke up at the end of the 80s in favour of solo work, and Ocasek became busy as a record producer, notably with Weezer in 1994. Elliot Easton produced *Middlescence* for Amy Rigby in 1998, and toured with Creedence Clearwater Revisited. Orr formed Big People, but in October 2000 succumbed to cancer of the pancreas.
● ALBUMS: *The Cars* (Elektra 1978) ★★★★, *Candy-O* (Elektra 1979) ★★★, *Panorama* (Elektra 1980) ★★, *Shake It Up* (Elektra 1981) ★★★, *Heartbeat City* (Elektra 1984) ★★★★, *Door To Door* (Elektra 1987) ★.
Solo: Elliot Easton *Change No Change* (Elektra 1985) ★★. Greg Hawkes *Niagara Falls* (Passport 1983) ★★. Benjamin Orr *The Lace* (Elektra 1986) ★★.
● COMPILATIONS: *The Cars Greatest Hits* (Elektra 1985) ★★★, *Just What I Needed: The Cars Anthology* (Elektra/Rhino 1995) ★★★★, *Complete Greatest Hits* (Rhino 2002) ★★★★.
● VIDEOS: *Heartbeat City* (Warner Music Video 1984), *Cars Live* (Vestron Music Video 1988).
● FURTHER READING: *The Cars*, Philip Kamin.

## CARTER, CARLENE

b. Rebecca Carlene Smith, 26 September 1955, Nashville, Tennessee, USA. Carter is the daughter of country singers Carl Smith and June Carter and the granddaughter of Maybelle Carter of the Carter Family. She learned piano at six years of age and guitar at 10, having lessons from Carl Perkins. Her parents divorced and, when she was 12, her mother married Johnny Cash. Carlene Carter herself first married when 16, and had a daughter Tiffany, but she and Joe Simpkins were divorced within two years. After college she joined her mother and stepfather on the road and was featured on Johnny Cash's family album *The Junkie And The Juicehead Minus Me* in 1974. Carlene then met Jack Routh, a writer for Cash's publishing company, and within three months they were married. They had a son, John Jackson Routh, but they separated in 1977. Carter brought her new boyfriend, Rodney Crowell, to the UK where she made an appealing, upbeat rock album with Graham Parker And The Rumour. Crowell's song 'Never Together But Close Sometimes' was almost a UK hit, and her song 'Easy From Now On' was recorded by Emmylou Harris.
Carter had an assertive personality but she struggled with the dance tracks on her second album, *Two Sides To Every Woman*, which was made in New York. *Musical Shapes* was produced by her new husband Nick Lowe; the songs included her 'Appalachian Eyes' and a duet with Dave Edmunds, 'Baby Ride Easy'. Her 1981 album *Blue Nun* was also produced by Lowe and featured members of Rockpile and Squeeze. The album, with such titles as 'Do Me Lover' and 'Think Dirty', was an explicit celebration of sex but, just as she seemed to be rejecting her country roots, she joined her family onstage at the Wembley Country Music Festival for 'Will The Circle Be Unbroken?'. Carter, whose marriage to Lowe broke up, was prevented from calling her next album *Gold Miner's Daughter*, and settled for *C'est Bon*. She was featured in *Too Drunk To Remember*, a short film shown at the London Film Festival, based on one of her songs. In 1985 she won acclaim for her role as one of the waitresses in the London cast of the country musical *Pump Boys And Dinettes*, which starred Paul Jones and Kiki Dee. In 1990 Carter, by making an album, *I Fell In Love*, aimed to please rather than alienate country fans. Produced by Howie Epstein, the musicians included Dave Edmunds, Kiki Dee, Albert Lee, Jim Keltner, and such songs as 'Me And Wildwood Rose' celebrated her country music heritage. Carter has the potential of a fine country songwriter, and the song 'Guardian Angel' shows she has enough experiences on which to draw. Unfortunately, Carter may have discarded much of her personality in order to become a mainstream country artist. *Little Acts Of Treason* was comparatively bland, a word not previously associated with her.
● ALBUMS: *Carlene Carter* (Warners 1978) ★★★, *Two Sides To Every Woman* (Warners 1979) ★★, *Musical Shapes* (F-Beat 1980) ★★★, *Blue Nun* (F-Beat 1981) ★★, *C'est Bon* (Epic 1983) ★★★, with Anita, Helen and June Carter *Wildwood Flower* (Mercury 1988) ★★★, *I Fell In Love* (Reprise 1990) ★★, *Little*

*Love Letters* (Giant 1993) ★★★, *Little Acts Of Treason* (Giant 1995) ★★★.
● COMPILATIONS: *Hindsight 20/20* (Giant 1996) ★★★★.
● VIDEOS: *Open Fire* (Hendring Video 1990).

## CASE, PETER

b. 5 April 1954, USA. This Los Angeles, California-based folk-rock singer-songwriter first worked as part of pop-rock bands the Nerves (whose compositions included 'Hanging On The Telephone') and the Plimsouls. His solo career kicked off with an album of stylistic diversity. Intelligent and considered, there was little in the songs to excite but plenty to provoke thought. With co-production from T-Bone Burnett (who also wrote some of the songs) and Mitchell Froom, this was a fine collection combining Case's plaintive delivery with intelligent lyrics. The best examples included 'Steel Strings', later covered by Marshall Crenshaw, and a cover of the Pogues' 'A Pair Of Brown Eyes', on which Roger McGuinn played guitar. The second album mined a narrower seam. This time the assembled personnel included David Lindley, Jim Keltner and David Hidalgo (Los Lobos), although Case's remained the dominant voice. Spiritual matter was covered in 'Hidden Love' while his remarkable observational streak offered further excellent character and place studies in songs such as 'Poor Old Tom' and 'This Town's A Riot'. Despite its many attractive features, critics judged Case to have lost the light-fingered touch his earlier pop incarnations and first album had demonstrated. This was redressed by the issue of a third collection, three years later, in 1992. *Six Pack Of Love* threw in elevated Beatles harmonies alongside jangling guitars and soul influences. His second album without a binding musical ethos, it nevertheless marked a return to the uplifting, optimistic Case of old. Having been released by Geffen Records, Case recorded the compellingly low-key *Peter Case Sings Like Hell*, which subsequently led to a new recording contract. Vanguard Records have since released two strong albums, *Torn Again* and *Full Service No Waiting*, which showcased Case as the folk troubadour. Case joined the Plimsouls recording reunion in 1997 while still working as a solo artist, although *Flying Saucer Blues* did not appear until April 2000.
● ALBUMS: *Peter Case* (Geffen 1986) ★★★★, *The Man With The Blue Postmodern Fragmented Neo-Traditionalist Guitar* (Geffen 1989) ★★★, *Six Pack Of Love* (Geffen 1992) ★★, *Peter Case Sings Like Hell* (Vanguard 1993) ★★★★, *Torn Again* (Vanguard 1995) ★★★, *Full Service No Waiting* (Vanguard 1997) ★★★, *Flying Saucer Blues* (Vanguard 2000) ★★★, *Thank You St. Jude* (Travelin' Light 2001) ★★★.

## CASH, ROSANNE

b. 24 May 1955, Memphis, Tennessee, USA. The daughter of Johnny Cash from his first marriage to Vivian Liberto, Cash lived with her mother in California after her parents divorced in 1966. Perhaps inevitably, she returned to Nashville, where she studied drama at Vanderbilt University, before relocating to Los Angeles to study 'method' acting at

Lee Strasberg's Institute, after which she worked for three years on her father's roadshow. In the late 70s, she spent a year in London working for CBS Records, the same label as her father, and signed a recording contract in Germany with Ariola, resulting in her debut album, which has become a collector's item. Mainly recorded and produced in Germany with German-based musicians, it also included three tracks recorded in Nashville and was produced by Rodney Crowell. At the time, Cash was influenced by punk which she had experienced in Britain, but on her return to Nashville, she worked on demos with Crowell which gained her a contract with CBS as a neo-country act. She married Crowell in 1979, the same year her first CBS album, *Right Or Wrong*, was released. While not a huge success, the album, again produced by Crowell, included three US country hits: 'No Memories Hangin' Round' (a duet with Bobby Bare), 'Couldn't Do Nothin' Right and 'Take Me, Take Me', while many of the backing musicians were also members of Emmylou Harris' Hot Band.
*Seven Year Ache* followed in 1981, again produced by Crowell, and went gold, reaching the Top 30 of the US pop chart. It included three US country chart number 1 singles: the title track, her own composition, which reached the Top 30 of the US pop chart, 'My Baby Thinks He's A Train' (written by Leroy Preston, then of Asleep At The Wheel) and another of her own songs, 'Blue Moon With Heartache'. *Somewhere In The Stars* also reached the Top 100 of the US pop album charts, and included three US country chart singles, 'Ain't No Money', 'I Wonder' and 'It Hasn't Happened Yet', but overall the album was considerably less successful than its predecessor. Her next album, *Rhythm And Romance*, included four US country hit singles, two of which were overseen by Crowell; 'Never Be You', another number 1, was written by Tom Petty and Benmont Tench. David Malloy produced most of the album, including another country number 1 single, 'I Don't Know Why You Don't Want Me' (which Cash co-wrote with Crowell) and 'Second To No-One'. After another two years' hiatus came *King's Record Shop*, named after and featuring a sleeve picture of the store of that name in Louisville, Kentucky. This album included four US country number 1 singles: John Hiatt's 'The Way We Make A Broken Heart', her revival of her father's 1962 country hit, 'Tennessee Flat-Top Box', 'If You Change Your Mind', which she co-wrote with pedal steel ace Hank DeVito, and 'Rainway Train', written by John Stewart. This album was again produced by Crowell, with whom she duetted on her fifth US country number 1 within 13 months, 'It's A Small World'. This song was included on Crowell's *Diamonds And Dirt*. Cash won a Grammy award in 1985 for Best Country Vocal Performance Female, and in 1988 won *Billboard*'s Top Single Artist Award.
A wife and mother, Cash has rarely had time to work live, but this has clearly had little effect on her recording career. In 1989 came a compilation album, *Hits 1979-1989* (retitled *Retrospective 1979-1989* for UK release), and in late 1990, *Interiors*, a hauntingly introspective album which was criticized for its apparently pessimistic outlook. The video for

*Interiors* shows her berating Crowell in song after song, only then to have him come on for a guest appearance. Its release was later followed by the news that the couple's marriage had broken down. The emotional fall-out was subsequently explored by Cash on 1993's bleak and compelling *The Wheel*. Three years later she demoed new material for Capitol Records who persuaded her to release the songs in their unadorned state, feeling the sparse arrangements complemented the introspective nature of the material. Cash, meanwhile, seemed more interested in promoting her collection of short stories, *Bodies Of Water*.

One of the pioneers of the 'new country' movement of the late 80s, Cash's relative unavailability – she places her family firmly before her career – may ultimately result in others taking the glory. Nevertheless, her achievements to date have ensured that the Cash family heritage in country music is far from disgraced.

● ALBUMS: *Rosanne Cash* (Ariola 1978) ★★, *Right Or Wrong* (Columbia 1979) ★★★, *Seven Year Ache* (Columbia 1981) ★★★, *Somewhere In The Stars* (Columbia 1982) ★★★, *Rhythm And Romance* (Columbia 1985) ★★★, *King's Record Shop* (Columbia 1988) ★★★, *Interiors* (Columbia 1990) ★★★★, *The Wheel* (Columbia 1993) ★★★, *10 Song Demo* (Capitol 1996) ★★★★.

● COMPILATIONS: *Hits 1979-1989* (Columbia 1989) ★★★★, *Retrospective* (Columbia 1995) ★★★★.

● VIDEOS: *Live – The Interiors Tour* (1994).

● FURTHER READING: *Bodies Of Water*, Rosanne Cash.

## CATS

Following the termination of his partnership with Tim Rice which had resulted in 70s hits such as *Jesus Christ Superstar*, *Joseph And The Amazing Technicolor Dreamcoat* and *Evita*, in 1980 the composer Andrew Lloyd Webber turned for the source of his next musical to a favourite collection of poems from his childhood, T.S. Eliot's *Old Possum's Book Of Practical Cats*, that was first published in 1939. After hearing some of his songs, the author's widow, Valerie Eliot, gave Lloyd Webber access to her late husband's letters and an unpublished poem about Grizabella the Glamour Cat, who became one of the show's leading characters, and introduced the hit song 'Memory'. Together with producer Cameron Mackintosh, Lloyd Webber assembled a highly impressive creative team that included Trevor Nunn (director), Gillian Lynne (associate director and choreographer), John Napier (designer), and John Hersey (lighting designer). Finance was not easy to come by – not many of the regular 'angels' (theatrical investors) fancied putting money into an English show about cats, but Lloyd Webber toured the television chat-show circuit and provided personal monetary guarantees so that *Cats* could open at London's New London Theatre on 11 May 1981.

The show's action is played out on Napier's spectacular (permanent) set representing a gigantic rubbish dump, which, after dark, becomes alive with cats of all types, shapes and sizes. Soon, there are cats all over the place – in the aisles – everywhere, gathering for the Jellicle Ball during which one cat will be selected by the Jellicle leader and allotted an extra precious life. The main contenders in this 'match of the moggies' are Grizabella (Elaine Paige), Rum Tum Tugger (Paul Nicholas), Asparagus (Stephen Tate), Mr. Mistoffolees (Wayne Sleep), Deuteronomy and Bustopher Jones (Brian Blessed), Skimbleshanks (Kenn Wells), Griddlebone (Susan Jane Tanner), Rumpleteazer (Bonnie Langford), Mungojerrie (John Thornton) and Munkustrap (Jeff Shankley). Sarah Brightman, who, with the dance group Hot Gossip, had climbed high in the UK chart with 'I Lost My Heart To A Starship Trooper' in 1978, was in the chorus, and subsequently became Lloyd Webber's second wife. The opening night had to be postponed when the celebrated actress Judi Dench suffered a torn Achilles tendon, and Elaine Paige, who had made such an impact in *Evita*, took over the role of Grizabella. She is the one, the former Glamour Cat-turned-dishevelled outcast, who, at the end of the evening, is chosen by Deuteronomy to receive the prized additional life. Paige delivered her big number, 'Memory', a highly dramatic reading, and her recorded version entered the UK Top 5. The song, with a tune from Lloyd Webber's trunk of unused items, had a lyric by Trevor Nunn that was based on Eliot's poem *Rhapsody On A Windy Night*. Because all the text in the show was taken from Eliot's writings, with a few minor revisions, the only other 'extra lyrics' credit was given to Richard Stilgoe. The remainder of the score included 'Prologue: Jellicle Songs For Jellicle Cats', 'The Naming Of The Cats', 'The Invitation To The Jellicle Ball', 'Moments Of Happiness', 'The Journey To The Heavyside Layer', 'The Ad-Dressing Of Cats' and several numbers in the names of the various characters, such as 'Old Gumbie Cat', 'Gus, Theatre Cat' and 'Growltiger's Last Stand'.

Initial reviews were mixed, but word-of-mouth about Napier's environmental set and slinky black cat costumes, as well as Lynne's exciting and innovative choreography and the show's special effects, ensured full houses for a 'performance extravaganza that was then a radical departure from anything seen on the musical stage'. Napier and Lynne were both involved again in the Broadway production of *Cats* which opened at the Winter Garden Theatre on 7 October 1982, with Betty Buckley in the role of Grizabella. Since those days *Cats* has undertaken several US tours, and played in the major cities of Europe, Canada, Australia, Britain, and many other countries. Its awards have included: 1981 *Evening Standard*, Ivor Novello, and Laurence Olivier Awards for Best Musical; 1983 Tony Awards for Best Musical, Book, Score, Director (Nunn), Supporting Actress (Buckley), Costumes (Napier), Lighting (Hersey), and Drama Desk Awards for Music, Costumes, Lighting; and 1989 Moliere Award for Best Musical.

In 1992 Lloyd Webber's Really Useful Company announced that it was aware of 150 different recorded versions of 'Memory' (it even listed them). In January 1996 the West End production of his most enduring show, *Cats*, went one step further in justifying its billing of 'Now And Forever' by overtaking *A Chorus Line* as the longest-running musical of all time, having resided at the New London Theatre for 6,138 performances. On 19 June 1997, the New York production also reached that magic figure, thereby replacing *A Chorus Line* as the longest-running show (musical or play) in Broadway history. It was then estimated that in the past 16 years, *Cats* had grossed $2.2 billion worldwide and played to more than 50 million people in 42 productions. *Cats* finally closed on Broadway on 10 September 2000, after a run of almost 18 years – a total of 7,485 performances. The West End production closed on its 21st anniversary on 11 May 2002.

In 1998, a video version was released. Directed by David Mallet, the cast included Elaine Paige (Grizabella), James Barron (Bustopher), John Mills (Gus), Rosemarie Ford (Bombalurina), Geoffrey Garratt (Skimbleshanks), Jo Gibb (Rumpleteazer), John Partridge (Rum Tum Tugger), Michael Gruber (Munkustrap), Aeva May (Demeter), Ken Page (Old Deuteronomy), Susie McKenna (Jennyanydots), Jacob Brent (Magical Mr. Mistoffolees), and Susan Jane Turner (Jellyorum).

● VIDEOS: *Andrew Lloyd Webber's Cats* (PolyGram 1998).

## CAVE, NICK

b. Nicholas Edward Cave, 22 September 1957, Warracknabeal, Australia. After the Birthday Party disbanded, the enigmatic vocalist Nick Cave retained his association with Berlin by teaming up with ex-Einstürzende Neubauten member Blixa Bargeld (b. 12 January 1959, Berlin, Germany; guitar), together with ex-Magazine personnel Barry Adamson (b. 1 June 1958, Moss Side, Manchester, England; bass) and multi-instrumentalist Mick Harvey (b. 29 September 1958, Rochester, Australia), who became the Bad Seeds. The debut album, *From Her To Eternity*, was accompanied by a startling rendition of the Elvis Presley classic 'In The Ghetto', and showed that Cave had lost none of his passion or ability to inject dramatic tension into his music. *The Firstborn Is Dead* followed a year later, promoted by the excellent 'Tupelo', but the Bad Seeds made their mark with *Kicking Against The Pricks* in the summer of 1986, bolstered by the UK Independent number 1, 'The Singer'. Cave had always drawn from a variety of sources, from Captain Beefheart to delta blues, and the Bad Seeds' material betrayed a claustrophobic, swamp-like aura. Although purely cover versions, *Kicking Against The Pricks* (which featured drummer Thomas Wylder) fully displayed his abilities as an original interpreter of other artists' material. The subsequent *Your Funeral, My Trial* emphasized the power of his self-penned compositions, with improved production giving his vocals added clarity.

After a brief hiatus from recording, it was two years before Cave returned, but it was worth the wait. 'The Mercy Seat' was a taut, brooding example of Cave's ability to build a story, followed by the milder 'Oh Deanna', which still contained considerable menace in its lyric. Both elements were present on October 1988's *Tender Prey*, as well as a more melodious

approach to both his song constructions and singing voice. 'The Ship Song', released in February 1990, continued Cave's exploration of the more traditional ballad, and was followed by another strong album, *The Good Son*, in April. This accentuated several themes previously explored, notably spirituality and mortality, aided by the introduction of strings.

Cave's literary aspirations had already been given an outlet by Black Spring Press in 1989, who published his first novel, *And The Ass Saw The Angel*. He also appeared in the Wim Wenders' movie *Wings Of Desire*, following it with a powerful performance as a prison inmate in the Australian production *Ghosts ... Of The Civil Dead*. Still prolific on the music side, Cave released the comparatively pedestrian *Henry's Dream* in 1992. It was followed by a live collection and contributions to the soundtrack of Wenders' *Faraway, So Close!* The brooding, self-obsessed *Let Love In* was recorded during an increasingly turbulent period in Cave's personal life, but was one of his finest releases. In 1995 Cave (with the Dirty Three) provided a live soundtrack to Carl Dreyer's 1928 silent classic *La Passion De Jeanne d'Arc*, while an unlikely musical coupling with Kylie Minogue on 'Where The Wild Roses Grow' proved to be a commercial success. This in turn spawned *Murder Ballads*, a dark concept album. In 1997 Cave released another excellent album, *The Boatman's Call*, arguably one of his best. Sounding deeply introspective yet never mundane, he came over like a cross between Tom Waits and a depressed Leonard Cohen. The dark and dangerous *No More Shall We Part* was equally impressive.

● ALBUMS: *From Her To Eternity* (Mute 1984) ★★★, *The Firstborn Is Dead* (Mute 1985) ★★★, *Kicking Against The Pricks* (Mute 1986) ★★★, *Your Funeral, My Trial* (Mute 1986) ★★★, *Tender Prey* (Mute 1988) ★★★, with Mick Harvey, Blixa Bargeld *Ghosts Of The Civil Dead* film soundtrack (Mute 1989) ★★★, *The Good Son* (Mute 1990) ★★★★, *Henry's Dream* (Mute 1992) ★★★, *Live Seeds* (Mute 1993) ★★★, *Let Love In* (Mute 1994) ★★★★, *Murder Ballads* (Mute/Reprise 1996) ★★★★, with Harvey, Bargeld *To Have And To Hold* film soundtrack (Mute 1996) ★★★, *The Boatman's Call* (Mute 1997) ★★★★, *The Secret Life Of The Love Song/The Flesh Made Word* spoken word (King Mob 2000) ★★★, *No More Shall We Part* (Mute 2001) ★★★★.

● COMPILATIONS: *The Best Of Nick Cave & The Bad Seeds* (Mute 1998) ★★★★.

● VIDEOS: *Kings Of Independence* (Studio 1989), *The Road To God Knows Where* (BMG Video 1990), *Live At The Paradiso* (Mute 1992), *Ritual Habitual* (PolyGram Music Video 1996), *The Videos* (Mute 1998).

● FURTHER READING: *King Ink*, Nick Cave. *And The Ass Saw The Angel*, Nick Cave. *Fish In A Barrel: Nick Cave & The Bad Seeds On Tour*, Peter Milne. *Hellfire: Life According To Nick Cave*, Jeremy Dean. *Bad Seed: The Biography Of Nick Cave*, Ian Johnston. *Nick Cave: The Birthday Party And Other Epic Adventures*, Robert Brokenmouth. *King Ink II*, Nick Cave. *The Complete Lyrics: 1978–2001*, Nick Cave.

● FILMS: *Der Himmel Über Berlin* aka *Wings Of Desire* (1987), *Dandy* (1987), *Ghosts ... Of The Civil Dead* (1988), *The Road To God Knows Where* (1990),

*Johnny Suede* (1991), *Jonas In The Desert* (1994), *Rhinoceros Hunting In Budapest* (1996).

## CETERA, PETER

b. 13 September 1944, Chicago, Illinois, USA. Peter Cetera was the last musician to join the original line-up of Chicago, and he remained with that highly successful outfit through its first 17 albums as lead singer and bass player. In 1981, Cetera recorded a self-titled solo album on Full Moon Records, which only reached number 143 on the US album chart. He left the group in 1985 to pursue a solo career and achieved immediate success with the single 'Glory Of Love', the theme from the movie *The Karate Kid Part II*, which reached US number 1 and UK number 3 in the summer of 1986. The second solo album, *Solitude/Solitaire*, reached number 23. In September of that year, Cetera recorded a duet with pop-gospel singer Amy Grant, 'The Next Time I Fall', which also reached US number 1. In 1987, he worked with former Abba member Agnetha Fältskog on her WEA Records debut, duetting on the minor US hit single 'I Wasn't The One (Who Said Goodbye)'. Cetera's third solo album, *One More Story*, was released in 1988 and included the US Top 5 single, 'One Good Woman'. In 1989, 'After All', a duet with Cher from the Cybil Shepherd/Robert Downey Jnr. movie *Chances Are*, returned Cetera to the US Top 10. *World Falling Down* was released in 1992, following which Cetera moved to the independent River North label. *You're The Inspiration: A Collection* featured re-recordings of old songs alongside some new material.

● ALBUMS: *Peter Cetera* (Full Moon 1981) ★★, *Solitude/Solitaire* (Full Moon 1986) ★★★★, *One More Story* (Full Moon 1988) ★★★, *World Falling Down* (Warners 1992) ★★, *One Clear Voice* (River North 1995) ★★, *You're The Inspiration: A Collection* (River North 1997) ★★, *Another Perfect World* (DDE 2001) ★★★.

● COMPILATIONS: *Greatest Hits* (Edel 2002) ★★★.

## CHAMELEONS

Formed in 1981 in Middleton, Manchester, England this highly promising but ill-fated band was formed by Mark Burgess (vocals, bass), Reg Smithies (guitar), Dave Fielding (guitar) and Brian Schofield (drums), although the latter was soon replaced by John Lever. After some successful BBC radio sessions, the band signed to the CBS Records subsidiary Epic and released 'In Shreds' in March 1982. Its lack of success saw the band switch to the independent label Statik, where they issued 'As High As You Can Go' and 'A Person Isn't Safe Anywhere These Days'. Their *Script Of The Bridge* and *What Does Anything Mean? Basically* revealed them as a promising guitar-based outfit with a strong melodic sense. Regular touring won them a contract with Geffen Records and their third album, *Strange Times*, was very well received by the critics. Just as a breakthrough beckoned, however, their manager Tony Fletcher died, and amid the ensuing chaos the band folded.

Various spin-off bands, the Sun And The Moon (who released a solid album in 1988), Music For Aborigines, Weaveworld and the Reegs lacked the charm of the powerful but unrealized mother group.

Burgess also released a solo album, *Zima Junction*, with backing band the Sons Of God. The Chameleons re-formed in 2000 to play some live dates. They commemorated the success of this reunion with the release of *Strip*, a collection of acoustic versions of previous recordings along with two new tracks. The quartet subsequently began work on their brand new studio album. *Why Call It Anything* proved to be a stunning reaffirmation of the brilliance of this unsung band.

● ALBUMS: *Script Of The Bridge* (Statik/MCA 1983) ★★★, *What Does Anything Mean? Basically* (Statik 1985) ★★★★, *Strange Times* (Geffen 1986) ★★★★, *Tripping Dogs* 1985 recordings (Glass Pyramid 1990) ★★, *Live In Toronto* 1987 recording (Imaginary 1992) ★★★, *Free Trade Hall Rehearsal* 1985 recordings (Imaginary 1993) ★★, *Dali's Picture* (Imaginary 1993) ★★, *Aufführung In Berlin* (Imaginary 1993) ★★★, *Live At The Gallery Club Manchester 18 December 1982* (Visionary 1996) ★★★, *Strip* (Paradiso 2000) ★★★, *Why Call It Anything* (Artful/Cleopatra 2001) ★★★★, *Live At The Academy* (Paradiso 2002) ★★★.

● COMPILATIONS: *The Fan And The Bellows* (Hybrid 1986) ★★★, *John Peel Sessions* (Strange Fruit 1990) ★★, *Here Today ... Gone Tomorrow* (Imaginary 1992) ★★, *The Radio 1 Evening Show Sessions* (Nighttracks 1993) ★★★, *Northern Songs* (Bone Idol 1994) ★★★, *Live Shreds* (Cleopatra 1996) ★★, *Return Of The Roughnecks: The Best Of The Chameleons* (Dead Dead Good 1997) ★★★★.

● VIDEOS: *Live At The Camden Palace* (Jettisoundz 1985), *Live At The Hacienda* (Jettisoundz 1994), *Arsenal* (Jettisoundz 1995), *Live At The Gallery Club 1982* (Jettisoundz 1996).

## CHANDRA, SHEILA

b. 14 March 1965, Waterloo, London, England. Born of Indian parentage, Chandra was enrolled at the Italia Conti stage school at the age of 11, where she was taught song and dance as well as acting skills. However, the school's preoccupation with show tunes argued against her personal instincts for jazz, soul and gospel. This inclination saw her instigate her own rehearsal and practice schedules in opposition to the prescribed timetable. The school did allow her to record an audition tape for Hansa Records, however, and this was eventually passed to songwriter and producer Steve Coe. He was in the process of forming a new group, Monsoon, to fuse pop music with Indian classical structures such as fixed note scales. Chandra's heritage made her the perfect choice of singer, and three months before she left the Conti school she had enrolled as Monsoon's full-time vocalist. After an independent EP the group was signed to Phonogram Records, for whom their debut single, 'Ever So Lonely', provided a UK Top 20 success in 1982 (Chandra would also feature on Jakatta's dance update of the song 20 years later).

Chandra had suddenly become Britain's first mainstream Asian pop star at the age of 17. However, following disagreements between artist and record company Monsoon disbanded at the end of the year. Chandra spent the next two years furthering her studies into Indian and Asian music, which eventually resulted in her debut solo album in

1984. Both this and a follow-up collection, also released in that year, demonstrated her growing technique and fascination with vocal experimentation. *Quiet* was the first record to include her own compositions, and her blossoming talent was given further vent in 1985 with two more studio collections. *The Struggle* was firmly song based, leaning towards the pop dance culture she had known as a child, while *Nada Brahma* offered a more experimental song cycle, absorbing influences from not only the East but also Afro-Caribbean music (notably the ragga-tinged title-track). However, after four albums in two years some rest and recuperation were required. A gap of five years preceded the release of her fifth album, *Roots & Wings*. This accentuated the Indian tradition of 'drone' music at one level, while continuing her fascination with cross-matching cultures. As she stated: 'I am often unaware of the precise joining point between two styles of vocal from different traditions, it seems so natural to slip from one to the other.' In 1991, she signed to Real World Records, through her own production company Moonsong, and provided them with *Weaving My Ancestors' Voices*. A year later she made her live debut singing at the Spanish WOMAD Festival. The *Zen Kiss* was inspired jointly by the spirituality implicit in its title and her new found passion for live performance. The densely layered *ABoneCroneDrone* was the final part of the Real World cycle, completing a powerful vocal odyssey.
● ALBUMS: *Out On My Own* (IndiPop 1984) ★★, *Quiet* (IndiPop 1984) ★★★, *The Struggle* (IndiPop 1985) ★★★, *Nada Brahma* (IndiPop 1985) ★★★★, *Roots & Wings* (Moonsung 1990) ★★★, *Weaving My Ancestors' Voices* (Real World 1991) ★★, *The Zen Kiss* (Real World 1994) ★★★, *ABoneCroneDrone* (Real World 1996) ★★★, *This Sentence Is True (The Previous Sentence Is False)* (Shakti 2001) ★★★.
● COMPILATIONS: *Silk* (Shanachie 1991) ★★★★, *Moonsung: A Real World Retrospective* (Real World 1999) ★★★★.

## CHAPMAN, TRACY
b. 30 March 1964, Cleveland, Ohio, USA. During Nelson Mandela's satellite-linked 70th birthday concert at Wembley Stadium, London in 1988, this guitar-playing singer-songwriter got her big break when, owing to headliner Stevie Wonder's enforced walk out, her spot was extended. She won the hearts of enough viewers worldwide for her debut album, *Tracy Chapman* to climb to number 1 on the UK album chart within days, and become an international success. Following the Mandela show sales shot past the 3 million mark, and the album topped the US album chart. 'Fast Car' became a UK Top 5/US Top 10 hit and the track 'Talkin' Bout A Revolution' became a concert favourite.
Chapman was neither a second Joan Armatrading nor the overnight sensation many thought her to be. The daughter of estranged but well-heeled parents, she had attended a Connecticut school before attending the University of Massachusetts to study anthropology, where she became the toast of the campus folk club. Contracted by SBK Publishing, her

first album had the advantage of the sympathetic production of David Kershenbaum who had worked previously with Joan Baez and Richie Havens. Next, she acquired a most suitable manager in Elliot Roberts – who also had Neil Young on his books – and a deal with the similarly apposite Elektra Records. She appeared with Peter Gabriel, Sting and other artists for a world-wide tour in aid of Amnesty International. Afterwards, she lost momentum. Although the impact of her second album, *Crossroads* was not insubstantial (UK number 1/US number 9), its title track single was only a minor hit. The pedestrian folk-rock material on *Matters Of The Heart* suffered as a result of Chapman's lengthy spell away from the spotlight, and failed to make the US Top 50. Another three-year hiatus ensued before the release of *New Beginning*, which found a much wider audience in the USA thanks to the left-field hit 'Give Me One Reason'. *Telling Stories* was arguably her best collection of songs since her debut, leavening her trademark self-absorption on affecting material such as the title track and 'It's OK'.
● ALBUMS: *Tracy Chapman* (Elektra 1988) ★★★★, *Crossroads* (Elektra 1989) ★★★, *Matters Of The Heart* (Elektra 1992) ★★, *New Beginning* (Elektra 1995) ★★★, *Telling Stories* (Elektra 2000) ★★★★.
● COMPILATIONS: *Tracy Chapman Collection* (East West 2001) ★★★★.

## CHEFS
The Chefs, from Brighton, East Sussex, England, only survived three singles before splitting, and one of those was a reissue. Along with other aspiring local talent in the late 70s, the Chefs – Helen McCookerybook (b. Helen McCallum; vocals, bass), James McCallum (guitar), Russell Greenwood (drums) and Carl Evans (guitar) – were signed to the town's resident label, Attrix Records. The EP *Sweetie*, issued in September 1980, was far from being sweet, dealing frankly with sex, personal hygiene and other matters. However, '24 Hours' (1981) was nothing short of a great pop song and was strong enough to warrant a reissue on the Midlands label Graduate Records. The band changed their name to Skat for a guitar-based cover version of the Velvet Underground's 'Femme Fatale'. Helen McCookerybook then left to form Helen And The Horns, a bold brass-dominated group with influences taken from the American west. 'Pioneer Town' and a remake of Doris Day's 'Secret Love' were both interesting excursions, although the band eventually floundered due to McCallum's increasing stage fright.

## CHER
b. Cherilyn Sarkisian La Pierre, 20 May 1946, El Centro, California, USA. Cher began working as a session singer in an attempt to finance an acting career. She recorded with producer Phil Spector as a backing vocalist, having become romantically attached to his studio assistant and PR man Sonny Bono. After releasing two singles under the name Caesar And Cleo, the duo then achieved international acclaim as Sonny And Cher. Throughout this period Cher also sustained a solo

career, initially singing a paean to Ringo Starr ('Ringo I Love You') under the pseudonym Bonnie Jo Mason. Thereafter, she secured several hits, including an opportunistic cover version of the Byrds' 'All I Really Want To Do' (US number 15, July 1965; UK number 9, August 1965). The sultry 'Bang Bang (My Baby Shot Me Down)', with its gypsy beat and maudlin violins was a worldwide smash in March 1966 (US number 2; UK number 3), leading Cher to tackle more controversial themes in 'I Feel Something In The Air' and 'You Better Sit Down Kids' (US number 9, October 1967). Although her acting aspirations seemed long forgotten, she did appear in two minor 60s movies, *Good Times* (1967) and *Chastity* (1969). In September 1971, the zestful, US chart-topping 'Gypsies, Tramps And Thieves' and its attendant album saw her back in the ascendant. Two further US number 1 hits ('Half Breed' in August 1973, 'Dark Lady' in January 1974) preceded her divorce from Sonny, though for a time the duo continued to appear together on stage and television. In 1975, she switched to Warner Brothers Records for the Jimmy Webb-produced *Stars*, while her on-off relationship with Gregg Allman (whom she divorced in 1979) resulted in one album, the punningly titled *Allman And Woman: Two The Hard Way*.

By the late 70s, she became a regular fixture in gossip columns and fashion magazines, which lauded over her sartorial outrageousness and much publicized musical and personal relationships with Allman, Gene Simmons (of Kiss) and Les Dudek. In 1981, Cher appeared on Meat Loaf's 'Dead Ringer For Love' but recording interests increasingly took a back seat to her first love: acting. A leading role in *Come Back To The Five And Dime, Jimmy Dean, Jimmy Dean* (1982) was followed by a lucrative part in *Silkwood* (1983), and an Oscar nomination. Appearances in *Mask* (1985), *The Witches Of Eastwick* (1987) and *Suspect* (1987) emphasized that her thespian aspirations were no mere sideline. For *Moonstruck* (1987), she won an Oscar for Best Actress and celebrated that honour with another musical comeback courtesy of *Cher* and 'I Found Someone' (US number 10, November 1987; UK number 5, December 1987). In 1989, she enjoyed three US Top 10 singles courtesy of 'After All', a duet with Peter Cetera that reached number 6 in March, 'If I Could Turn Back Time' (number 3 in July; UK number 6 in September) and 'Just Like Jesse James' (number 8 in October). Her April 1991 UK number 1 'The Shoop Shoop Song (It's In His Kiss)', a cover of the Betty Everett song, was the theme song to another screen appearance in *Mermaids*.

In March 1995, in the company of Chrissie Hynde, Neneh Cherry and Eric Clapton, she topped the UK charts with the charity single 'Love Can Build A Bridge'. The same year she did a credible cover of Marc Cohn's 'Walking In Memphis' which preceded *It's A Man's World*. In addition to the James Brown title track her voice admirably suited a reworking of the Walker Brothers classic, 'The Sun Ain't Gonna Shine Anymore'. Her astonishing popularity was confirmed by the worldwide hit single 'Believe', which topped the UK charts for seven weeks in late 1998. The attendant album featured notable contributions from dance gurus Junior Vasquez and Todd Terry. The next single to be lifted from the album, 'Strong Enough', entered the UK charts at number 5 in March 1999, and in the same month 'Believe' completed its long climb up the US *Billboard* Hot 100 to the top. Oddly enough, Cher's next album, *Not.com.mercial*, was only made available through her own website.

With her professional life as a singer and actress now scrutinized by the mass media, as well as the added intrigue of her love life and public fascination for her penchant for cosmetic surgery, Cher has become one of the great American icons of the modern age. Her powerful voice is often overlooked amidst the AOR glitz and perfect skin.

● ALBUMS: *All I Really Want To Do* (Imperial 1966) ★★, *The Sonny Side Of Cher* (Imperial 1966) ★★, *Cher* i (Imperial 1966) ★★★, *Backstage* (Imperial 1967) ★★, *Sings The Hits* (Springboard 1967) ★★, *With Love* (Imperial 1967) ★★, *3614 Jackson Highway* (Atco 1969) ★★, *Gypsys, Tramps & Thieves* (Kapp 1971) ★★★, *Foxy Lady* (Kapp 1972) ★★, *Half Breed* (MCA 1973) ★★, *Dark Lady* (MCA 1974) ★★, *Bittersweet White Light* (MCA 1974) ★★, *Stars* (Warners 1975) ★★, *I'd Rather Believe In You* (Warners 1976) ★★, with Gregg Allman as Allman And Woman *Two The Hard Way* (Warners 1977) ★, *Take Me Home* (Casablanca 1979) ★★, *Prisoner* (Casablanca 1980) ★★, *Black Rose* (Casablanca 1980) ★★, *I Paralyze* (Columbia 1982) ★★, *Cher ii* (Geffen 1987) ★★, *Heart Of Stone* (Geffen 1989) ★★, *Love Hurts* (Geffen 1991) ★★★★, *It's A Man's World* (Warners 1995) ★★★, *Believe* (Warners 1998) ★★★, *Not.com.mercial* (CherDirect.Com 2000) ★★★, *Living Proof* (Warners 2001) ★★.

● COMPILATIONS: *Cher's Golden Greats* (Imperial 1968) ★★, *The Best Of Cher* 60s recordings (EMI America 1991) ★★★, *Greatest Hits* (Geffen 1992) ★★★, *The Casablanca Years* (PolyGram 1996) ★★★, *Bang, Bang: The Early Years* (EMI 1999) ★★★, *Behind The Door: 1964-1974* (Raven 2000) ★★★, *The Way Of Love* (MCA 2000) ★★★.

● VIDEOS: *Extravaganza: Live At The Mirage* (1992), *Cher: Live In Concert* (Warner Music Vision 1999).

● FURTHER READING: *Cher: Simply Cher*, Linda Jacobs. *Sonny And Cher*, Thomas Braun. *Cher*, J. Randy Taraborrelli. *Totally Uninhibited: The Life & Times Of Cher*, Lawrence J. Quirk. *Cher: In Her Own Words*, Nigel Goodall. *Cher: The Visual Documentary*, Mick St. Michael. *The First Time*, Cher. *Cher: If You Believe*, Mark Bego.

● FILMS: *Wild On The Beach* aka *Beach House Party* (1965), *Good Times* (1967), *Chastity* (1969), *Come Back To The Five And Dime, Jimmy Dean, Jimmy Dean* (1982), *Silkwood* (1983), *Mask* (1985), *The Witches Of Eastwick* (1987), *Suspect* (1987), *Moonstruck* (1987), *Mermaids* (1990), *The Player* (1992), *Prêt-à-Porter* aka *Ready To Wear* (1994), *Faithful* (1996), *Tea With Mussolini* (1999).

## CHERRELLE

b. Cheryl Norton, Los Angeles, California, USA. This cousin of soul singer Pebbles is an accomplished drummer as well as a vocalist. She was discovered by her neighbour Michael Henderson, with whom she

toured widely and appeared on his *In The Night Time* (1978). Five years later she made her solo debut with *Fragile* for Tabu, featuring the production team of Jimmy Jam And Terry Lewis. The album included two lynchpin cuts, 'I Didn't Mean To Turn You On' (later a hit for Robert Palmer) and 'When I Look In Your Eyes'. In 1985 she achieved her first hit, with 'Saturday Love', a duet with labelmate Alexander O'Neal, hitting the UK Top 10, eventually provoking interest in her homeland the following year. However, she has continued to enjoy considerably greater success in the UK, with another O'Neal duet, 'Never Knew Love Like This', reaching the Top 30. The 90s saw her move to a new contract with A&M Records.
● ALBUMS: *Fragile* (Tabu 1984) ★★★, *High Priority* (Tabu 1985) ★★★, *Affair* (Tabu 1988) ★★★, *The Woman I Am* (A&M 1991) ★★★.
● COMPILATIONS: *The Best Of Cherrelle* (Tabu 1995) ★★★.

## CHERRY RED RECORDS

Founded in London during 1978 by Iain McNay, Cherry Red enjoyed almost immediate commercial success during the immediate punk era through releases by US hardcore act the Dead Kennedys. This led to the founding of subsidiary labels specializing in thrash punk/Oi. The acquisition of early recordings by Marc Bolan, issued as *You Scare Me To Death* was another early commercial coup. Meanwhile, at the instigation of A&R director Mike Alway, Cherry Red forged a distinctive style of introspective, willowy pop, heard in Headtime, Felt, the Marine Girls, Monochrome Set, Ben Watt and Tracey Thorn. The latter pair subsequently united as Everything But The Girl. A brief reissue imprint saw Cherry Red pressings for the Misunderstood and Merrell Fankhauser And HMS Bounty, but this was discontinued when Alway left in 1983 to launch Blanco y Negro but rejoined in 1985 to form the critically acclaimed El records, under the Cherry Red banner. Meanwhile McNay started Anagram Records, another subsidiary with harder-edged acts such as the Meteors, Alien Sex Fiend, Angelic Upstarts and the Vibrators. Cherry Red also focused on building Complete Music, its publishing arm, and presently has over 27,000 copyrights ranging from the Stranglers, Buzzcocks, Primal Scream and Roddy Frame to Sir Malcolm Arnold. Recent acquisitions and initiatives has seen the launch of a number of labels; British Steel (heavy metal), Zebra (rock), the Football Collectors Series, Goth Collectors, Psychobilly Collectors, Punk Collectors 7T's (70s reissues), Thunderbird (80s reissues) and the RPM label.
● COMPILATIONS: *Ambition: The History Of Cherry Red Records Volumes 1 & 2* (Cherry Red 1997) ★★★★.

## CHESS

As with two of his big hit shows of the 70s, *Jesus Christ Superstar* and *Evita* (both written with Andrew Lloyd Webber), Tim Rice opted to introduce this show by way of a studio concept album, which made the UK Top 10 in 1984. For *Chess*, Rice wrote the book and lyrics, and the composers were Björn

Ulvaeus and Benny Andersson, two ex-members of the record-breaking Swedish pop group Abba. The album spawned two hit singles: Murray Head's 'disco-rap-style' 'One Night In Bangkok', which reputedly sold several million copies worldwide and did particularly well in the UK and the USA; and the atmospheric ballad 'I Know Him So Well', a UK number 1 for Elaine Paige with Barbara Dickson. The show itself opened at London's Prince Edward Theatre (replacing *Evita*) on 14 May 1986. Rice's book was generally considered at the time to be the weakest element in the show. It dealt with the familiar conflict between East and West – the Reds and the rest – but this time the different sides were personified by two chess grandmasters, the US world champion Frederick Trumper (Murray Head) and Anatoly Sergeievsky (Tommy Korgerg) from the USSR. After the prologue ('The Story Of Chess'), Frederick dumps the Russian challenger under the table in the middle of the World Championships which are being held in a Tyrolean township, and eventually loses not only his crown, but his devoted 'second', Florence Vassy (Elaine Paige), to Anatoly, who defects in the best Nureyev tradition. During the dark intrigues that follow, Anatoly defends his title (with the help of a reformed Frederick) against another Russian challenger and, reversing his original career move, bids a heartfelt farewell to Florence at the airport before flying off into the (red) sunset. The 'part opera – part chorale' score was generally well received for its 'witty, stylish lyrics and consistently listenable music' (although some called it sheer Euro-pop), not only for 'One Night In Bangkok' and 'I Know Him So Well', which were important elements within the context of the show, but for the touching ballad, 'Heaven Help My Heart', and other numbers such as 'Pity The Child' and 'Where I Want To Be', As befitted a musical of the 80s, *Chess* was full of 'technological glitz' and much of its £4 million budget was visible onstage in the form of an elaborate rolling and revolving hydraulic set, a vast bank of television monitors and various other high-tech gear. Despite the sniping of the critics, *Chess* ran in London until April 1989, a total of 1102 performances. The show's director, Trevor Nunn, who had taken over from the renowned American director-choreographer, Michael Bennett, when he became ill (he died from AIDS in 1987), also staged the 1988 Broadway version which was savaged by the critics and flopped, despite having been 'Americanized' and fitted with a new cast and book. *Chess* returned to the USA in 1990 for a 40-week tour, and then, two years later, the musical 'with more past lives than Shirley MacLaine' was reworked yet again for a limited run off-Broadway.

## CHILDISH, BILLY

b. Stephen Hamper, 1959, Chatham, Kent, England. This cult songwriter, guitarist, producer, poet and painter's career is a testament to his passionate commitment to the DIY spirit of the post-punk scene. Since the late 70s, Childish has recorded a prodigious number of independently released albums, published over 30 collections of his poetry, and produced over 1,000 paintings. Remarkably, he has achieved this despite suffering from serious dyslexia.

A gifted teenage artist, Childish left school at 16 to work as an apprentice stonemason at the Naval Dockyard in his native Chatham. He managed to escape this employment by gaining a place at St. Martin's School of Art, but was later expelled for failing to adhere to the institution's strict guidelines. After spending years without gainful employment, Childish emerged on to the UK music scene in 1979 with his first band, the Pop Rivets, who released three ramshackle studio albums before changing their name to Mickey And The Milkshakes. Later known as simply the Milkshakes and occasionally Thee Milkshakes, the band's unpretentious garage rock style earned them two independent Top 20 hits ('Brand New Cadillac' and 'Ambassadors Of Love').

By 1985, Childish had formed a new band, Thee Mighty Caesars, taking with him the Milkshakes' rhythm section. He maintained the prolific output of his previous band, much of which was released on Childish's own outlet, Hangman Records. Hangman also became the outlet for his various spin-off projects, including numerous solo albums, one-off recordings and collaborations with Medway poet Sexton Ming, while the publishing imprint issued several volumes of his poetry. Childish's solo recordings offered the usual primal rock 'n' roll alongside his idiosyncratic readings of blues material.

Thee Mighty Caesars' members Bruce Brand and John Agnew were present in Childish's next project, Thee Headcoats. Formed in 1989, this combo continued to churn out garage rock-inspired recordings of variable quality until the mid-90s, when, in a typically uncompromising move, Childish announced he was retiring from the music business. Unsurprisingly, he reunited with Thee Headcoats three years later to record a new album, The Messerschmitt Pilot's Severed Hand. He then moved on to another new band, the Buff Medways, with whom he recorded his 100th album, Steady The Buffs. The album was released on Blur guitarist Graham Coxon's Transcopic label.

● ALBUMS: with Sexton Ming Which Dead Donkey Daddy? (Hangman 1987) ★★, with Sexton Ming Plump Prizes And Little Gems ... (Hangman 1987) ★★, with Sexton Ming Ypres 1917 Overture (Verdun Ossuary) (Hangman 1987) ★★, with Russ Wilkins Laughing Gravy (Empire 1987) ★★★, I've Got Everything Indeed (Hangman 1987) ★★★, The 1982 Cassettes (Hangman 1988) ★★★, I Remember ... (Hangman 1988) ★★★, with the Blackhands Play: Capt'n Calypso's Hoodoo Party (Hangman 1988) ★★★★, Poems Of Laughter And Violence (Hangman 1988) ★★, with the Natural Born Lovers Long Legged Baby (Hangman 1989) ★★★, 50 Albums Great (Hangman 1991) ★★★★, The Sudden Fart Of Laughter (Dog Meat 1992) ★★, Der Henkermann (Tom 1992) ★★★, with the Blackhands The Original Chatham Jack (Sub Pop 1992) ★★★, with the Blackhands Live In The Netherlands (Hangman 1993) ★★★, with the Singing Loins At The Bridge (Damaged Goods 1993) ★★★, Hunger At The Moon spoken word (Sympathy For The Record Industry 1994) ★★★, with Dan Melchior Devil In The Flesh

(Sympathy For The Record Industry 1998) ★★★, with Sexton Ming The Cheeky Cheese (Damaged Goods 1999) ★★★, with Holly Golightly In Blood (Wabana 1999) ★★★★, with the Buff Medways Steady The Buffs (Transcopic 2002) ★★★★.

● COMPILATIONS: I Am The Billy Childish: 50 Songs From 50 Albums (Sub Pop 1991) ★★★★, Native American Sampler: A History 1983–1993 (Sub Pop 1993) ★★★, Made With A Passion: Kitchen Demo's (Sympathy For The Record Industry 1996) ★★★, Crimes Against Music: Blues Recordings 1986–99 (Sympathy For The Record Industry 1999) ★★★★.

## CHINA CRISIS

This Liverpool, England-based band was formed in 1979 around the core of Gary Daly (b. 5 May 1962, Kirkby, Merseyside, England; vocals) and Eddie Lundon (b. 9 June 1962, Kirkby, Merseyside, England; guitar). In 1982, their first single, 'African And White', initially on the independent Inevitable label, was picked up for distribution by Virgin Records and made a critical impact, despite only just breaking into the UK Top 50. The single's b-side was 'Red Sails', a perfect early example of China Crisis' pastoral electro-pop. Having now signed to the Virgin label, the duo formed a more permanent line-up with the recruitment of Gazza Johnson (bass) and Kevin Wilkinson (drums). The following single, 'Christian', taken from the debut album Difficult Shapes And Passive Rhythms, was a UK number 12 hit. With the follow-up to their second album, they had two further Top 50 hits with 'Tragedy And Mystery' and 'Working With Fire And Steel', the former featuring the trademark on the forthcoming album – the ethereal oboe accompaniment. 'Wishful Thinking' in 1984 gave the group a Top 10 hit, while the following year gave them two further Top 20 hits with 'Black Man Ray' and 'King In A Catholic Style (Wake Up)'. While Flaunt The Imperfection, produced by Walter Becker, reached the UK Top 10, the uneven follow-up What Price Paradise? (produced by Clive Langer and Alan Winstanley), saw a drop in China Crisis' fortunes, when the album peaked at number 63. A two-year hiatus saw a reunion with Becker, which resulted in the critically acclaimed Diary Of A Hollow Horse, although this success was not reflected in sales. After their split with Virgin and the release of a deserved reappraisal of their career with a compilation in 1990, activities within the China Crisis camp were restricted to low-key releases on independent labels, none of which helped restore the band's commercial standing.

● ALBUMS: Difficult Shapes And Passive Rhythms (Virgin 1983) ★★★, Working With Fire And Steel – Possible Pop Songs Volume Two (Virgin 1983) ★★★, Flaunt The Imperfection (Virgin 1985) ★★★, What Price Paradise? (Virgin 1986) ★★, Diary Of A Hollow Horse (Virgin 1989) ★★★, Warped By Success (Stardumb 1994) ★★★, Acoustically Yours (Telegraph 1995) ★★★.

● COMPILATIONS: The China Crisis Collection (Virgin 1990) ★★★, China Crisis Diary (Virgin 1992) ★★★, Wishful Thinking (Recall 1998) ★★★.

● VIDEOS: Showbiz Absurd (Virgin Vision 1992).

## CHRIS AND COSEY

Chris Carter and Cosey Fanni Tutti (b. Christine Newby) became partners while with late 70s 'industrial' sound pioneers Throbbing Gristle. When the latter split in 1981, the couple decided to operate both as Chris And Cosey and as CTI (Creative Technology Institute). Their debut album, *Heartbeat*, credited to CTI, drew from Throbbing Gristle's rhythmic undercurrents, but the pair's next collection, *Trance*, was soured by a disagreement with Rough Trade Records over its selling price. 1983 yielded two singles, the Japanese-only 'Nikki' (a collaboration with John Duncan) and the relatively mainstream 'October (Love Song)'. These were followed in 1984 by *Songs Of Love And Lust*. That year the duo also issued *Elemental 7* in collaboration with John Lacey on Cabaret Voltaire's Doublevision label and further projects, as CTI, with Lustmord's Brian Williams and Glenn Wallis of Konstructivitis. These projects were also accompanied by *European Rendezvous*. *Mondo Beat*, released in 1985, was originally conceived by Carter as a 12-inch single, but expanded beyond that format. By this time, the pair's relationship with Rough Trade had become strained and they left after *Techno Primitiv* and 'Sweet Surprise', a project with the Eurythmics. They then joined Vancouver label Nettwerk Productions, while in Europe they were handled by renowned Brussels label Play It Again Sam (who have also reissued much of their product). After that, Chris And Cosey gradually steered towards the 'new beat' dance sound, with singles such as 'Obsession', 'Exotica' (both 1987) and 'Rise' (1989). The early 90s albums *Reflection* and *Pagan Tango* confirmed their adoption of hi-tech dance music.

● ALBUMS: *Heartbeat* (Rough Trade 1981) ★★, *Trance* (Rough Trade 1982) ★★, *Songs Of Love And Lust* (Rough Trade 1984) ★★★, as CTI *Elemental 7 – The Original Soundtrack* (Rough Trade 1984) ★★★, *European Rendezvous* (Doublevision 1984) ★★★, *Techno Primitiv* (Rough Trade 1985) ★★, *Action* (Licensed 1987) ★★★, *Exotica* (Nettwerk 1987) ★★★, *Trust* (Play It Again Sam 1989) ★★★, *Reflection* (Play It Again Sam 1990) ★★★, *Pagan Tango* (Play It Again Sam 1991) ★★★, *Muzik Fantastique* (Play It Again Sam 1992) ★★★.
Solo: Chris Carter *Mondo Beat* (Conspiracy International 1986) ★★.
● COMPILATIONS: *Best Of Chris And Cosey* (Play It Again Sam 1989) ★★★, *Collectiv 1, 2, 3, & 4* (Play It Again Sam 1990) ★★★, *The Essential Chris & Cosey Collection* (CTI 2002) ★★★.

## CHRISTIAN DEATH

This incredibly prolific art-rock band was formed in Los Angeles, California, USA, in 1979 by singer Rozz Williams (b. Roger Alan Painter, 1964, d. 1 April 1998, West Hollywood, California, USA). The original line-up additionally comprised Rikk Agnew (guitar, ex-Adolescents), James McGearly (bass) and George Belanger (drums), but afterwards the group's composition would fluctuate rapidly. Finding success in their homeland elusive, the group relocated to Europe in 1983, where they fitted in perfectly with the gothic rock fashion. Shunning the easy route to success, the band have since remained on the periphery of rock, and Christian Death's independence from prevailing trends has secured themselves a strong cult following, if little commercial or critical recognition. In 1986 the group fell under the control of songwriter and singer Valor Kand (b. Australia), who made radical changes to the line-up. Principal members now included Gitane Demone (vocals, keyboards) and David Glass (drums). Their often provocative material made as its principal target grand passion and organized religion, particularly that of Catholicism, citing corruption in the church and links with politicians. Album cover artwork, such as that which bedecked *Sex, Drugs And Jesus Christ*, depicting a Christ-like figure injecting heroin, caused a suitable furore of publicity and controversy, as did *All The Hate*'s 'poignant' use of swastika imagery. Despite the attention-seeking nature of some of their product, their vast discography has rarely risen above such crude devices. It is complicated, too, by the fact that during the 90s there were at least two bands operating under the same banner, resulting in all manner of litigation and dubious album issues. Williams hanged himself in April 1998 following a troubled period of heroin addiction.

● ALBUMS: *Only Theatre Of Pain* (Frontier 1982) ★★★, *Catastrophe Ballet* (L'Invitation Au Suicide 1984) ★★, *Ashes* (Nostradamus 1985) ★★★, *The Decomposition Of Violets* cassette only (ROIR 1986) ★★, *An Official Anthology Of Live Bootlegs* (Nostradamus 1986) ★★, *Atrocities* (Normal 1986) ★★, *Scriptures* (Jungle 1987) ★★★, *Sex, Drugs And Jesus Christ* (Jungle 1988) ★★★, *The Heretics Alive* (Jungle 1989) ★★, *All The Love* (Jungle 1989) ★★★, *All The Hate* (Jungle 1989) ★★★, *Insanus, Ultio, Proditio Misericordiaque* (Supporti Fonografici 1990) ★★, *Love And Hate* (Jungle 1992) ★★, *Iconolgia: Apparitions, Dreams And Nightmares* live recording (Triple X 1993) ★★, *Sleepless Nights* live recording (Cleopatra 1993) ★★, *Invocations: 1981-1989* live recording (Cleopatra 1993) ★, *The Doll's Theatre* live recording (Cleopatra 1994) ★★★, *Sexy Death God* (Bullet Proof 1994) ★★★, *The Rage Of Angels* (Cleopatra 1994) ★★★, *Death In Detroit* (Cleopatra 1995) ★★, *Pornographic Messiah* (Trinity 1998) ★★, *Born Again Anti Christian* (Candlelight 2000) ★★.
● COMPILATIONS: *The Wind Kissed Pictures (Past And Present)* (Supporti Fonografici 1988) ★★, *The Wind Kissed Pictures (Past, Present And Future)* (Supporti Fonografici 1990) ★★, *Jesus Points The Bone At You* singles collection from 1986–90 (Jungle 1992) ★★★, *Tales Of Innocence: A Continued Anthology* (Cleopatra 1994) ★★★, *Best Of* (Cleopatra 1999) ★★★.

## CHRISTIANS

This UK band was formed in Liverpool in 1984 by Henry Priestman (b. 21 June 1955, Hull, Humberside, England; keyboards, ex-Yachts; It's Immaterial) and brothers Roger (b. 13 February 1950, Merseyside, England), Russell (b. 8 July 1956, Merseyside, England) and Garry Christian (b. 27 February 1955, Merseyside, England; vocals). Up until then, the brothers, who came from a family of

11, with a Jamaican immigrant father and Liverpudlian mother, had performed as a soul a cappella trio and had previously worked under a variety of names, most notably as Natural High when they made an appearance on UK television's *Opportunity Knocks* talent show in 1974. The Christian brothers met Priestman, who became the band's main songwriter, at Pete Wylie's Liverpool studios, where Priestman convinced the trio to try recording his compositions. The resulting demo session tapes eventually led to the Christians signing to Island Records.

The band's combination of pop and soul earned them a string of UK hits including, in 1987, 'Forgotten Town', 'Hooverville (And They Promised Us The World)', 'When The Fingers Point' and 'Ideal World'. The media usually focused their attention on the striking appearance of the tall, shaven-headed Garry. This, and a reluctance to tour, led to Roger quitting the band in 1987. The Christians' self-titled album, meanwhile, would become Island's bestselling debut. With the exception of the Top 30 hit 'Born Again' in the spring, 1988 was much quieter, with the band touring and recording. The year was brought to a climax, however, with the Top 10 cover version of the Isley Brothers hit, 'Harvest For The World'.

The Hillsborough football crowd disaster in April 1989 prompted a charity record, 'Ferry Across The Mersey', on which they were given joint credit alongside Paul McCartney, Gerry Marsden, Holly Johnson and Stock, Aitken and Waterman. In 1989, Roger Christian released a solo single, 'Take It From Me', achieving a minor UK hit (number 63), plus a well-received album that did not chart. The Christians' only hit that year came with the Top 20 'Words'. The labours over recording *Colour* paid off when it reached UK number 1 on its first week in the chart. Subsequent singles failed to break into the top reaches of the chart, and 1992's *Happy In Hell* proved to be a commercial failure. Island recouped their losses with a compilation album the following year (including new material).

The band subsequently pursued solo projects, officially splitting up in 1997. Garry Christian released the acclaimed *Your Cool Mystery* the same year, while Priestman and Russell Christian teamed up with singer Desi Campbell in Blu-Dog. Priestman and Russell Christian reunited with Garry Christian in 1999 to play live dates and record a new Christians album. *Prodigal Sons* was released in 2002 and was backed by a UK tour.

● ALBUMS: *The Christians* (Island 1987) ★★★★, *Colour* (Island 1990) ★★★, *Happy In Hell* (Island 1992) ★★★.
● COMPILATIONS: *The Best Of The Christians* (Island 1993) ★★★★.
● VIDEOS: *The Best Of The Christians* (Island 1993).

## CHRON GEN

The name an abbreviation of 'chronic generation', this early 80s, third-generation UK punk band, ranked only below the Exploited, Vice Squad and Discharge in popularity. More melodic than the vast majority of their peers, Chron Gen earned early comparisons to the Buzzcocks, though they never really justified such heady praise. The band was originally formed as the Condemned in 1977 in Hitchin, Hertfordshire, England. At this time Glynn Baxter (guitar/vocals) and John Johnson (drums) were still at school, and they were joined by bass player Adam in the formative line-up. The early repertoire consisted of ramshackle versions of old Sex Pistols and Ramones standards, and Adam was soon replaced by Pete Dimmock, before Jon Thurlow was drafted in on rhythm guitar to complete the band's enduring line-up. While frontman Baxter's lyrics were fuelled by a life on the dole, his fellow guitarist Thurlow actually admitted to a job as a civil servant. The band made their debut with the *Puppets Of War* EP, a spirited four-tracker where the production partially deprived the band of their live punch. Released initially on the group's own Gargoyle label, the record sold out of its 1,000 pressing and was picked up for wider distribution by Fresh Records. Following national exposure on the infamous Apocalypse Now tour (with the Exploited, Anti-Pasti, etc.), it rose into the Top 5 of *Sounds* music paper's Alternative Chart. *Sounds*, with its coverage of both the Oi! and new punk movements, remained the band's only real advocates within the mainstream. Chron Gen then lost many of their new found supporters with a debut album that was an unfocused, patchy affair. The promise of songs such as 'Hound Of The Night' was tempered by the lack of power and studio skill employed elsewhere, and Chron Gen never really recovered from the blow. They soldiered on for a couple of years, but to diminishing rewards.

● ALBUMS: *Chronic Generation* (Secret 1982) ★★, *Nowhere To Run* (Picasso 1985) ★★.
● COMPILATIONS: *The Best Of ...* (Captain Oi! 1994) ★★★.

## CHURCH

Formed in Canberra, Australia, in 1980, the Church, led by Steve Kilbey (b. 13 September 1954, England; bass/vocals), who emigrated with his family at an early age, originally comprised Peter Koppes (b. 21 November 1955, Australia; guitar/vocals), Marty Willson-Piper (b. 7 May 1958, Liverpool, England; guitar/vocals) and Nick Ward (drums). Richard Ploog (b. 22 March 1962, Australia; drums) would replace the latter after the completion of the band's debut album. That release came in 1981, when *Of Skins And Heart* gained some radio and television exposure. The European release *The Church*, which included stand-out cut 'The Unguarded Moment' (with its accompanying early pixilated image effect video), gave indications of great promise. The Church's 60s/Byrds revivalist stance, coupled with a distinctive 12-stringed 'jangly' guitar approach, was exemplified on *The Blurred Crusade* by such songs as 'Almost With You', 'When You Were Mine' and 'Fields Of Mars'.

*Starfish* saw the band gain college radio airplay in the USA, earning them a US Top 30 hit with 'Under The Milky Way', and strengthened their audiences in parts of Europe – although generally they found themselves restricted to a loyal cult following. The band's activities have been interrupted periodically due to internal problems and extensive solo projects and collaborations. Ploog's departure in 1990 saw the addition of former Patti Smith and Television drummer Jay Dee Daugherty, who appeared on 1992's *Priest = Aura*. Willson-Piper released several solo albums and took on a part time role as guitarist for All About Eve in 1991, appearing on their final two releases *Touched By Jesus* and *Ultraviolet*. Kilbey also recorded several solo albums, as well as publishing a book of poems. In 1991, he teamed up with Go-Betweens guitarist/vocalist Grant McLennan under the name of Jack Frost, recording a self-titled album for Arista Records in 1991. Peter Koppes completed an EP, *When Reason Forbids*, in 1987, and embarked on his own sequence of album releases, briefly leaving the group in the mid-90s (*Sometime Anywhere* was recorded by Kilbey, Willson-Piper and new drummer Tim Powles). Kilbey and McLennan made a second Jack Frost album, *Snow Job*, released by Beggars Banquet Records in 1996. The Church signed a new recording contract with Cooking Vinyl Records in the late 90s, releasing the covers collection *A Box Of Birds* and *After Everything Now This*.

● ALBUMS: *Of Skins And Heart* (Parlophone/Arista 1981) ★★★, *The Church* US version of debut (Carrere/Capitol 1982) ★★★, *The Blurred Crusade* (Parlophone/Carrere 1982) ★★★, *Séance* (Parlophone/Carrere 1983) ★★★, *Remote Luxury* (Parlophone/Warners 1984) ★★★★, *Heyday* (EMI/Warners 1985) ★★★, *Starfish* (Mushroom/Arista 1988) ★★★, *Gold Afternoon Fix* (Mushroom/Arista 1990) ★★★★, *Priest = Aura* (Mushroom/Arista 1992) ★★★, *Sometime Anywhere* (Mushroom/Arista 1994) ★★★, *Magician Among The Spirits* (Deep Karma/Mushroom 1996) ★★★, *Hologram Of Baal* (Cooking Vinyl/Thirsty Ear/Festival 1998) ★★★, *A Box Of Birds* (Cooking Vinyl/Thirsty Ear 1999) ★★★, *After Everything Now This* (Cooking Vinyl 2002) ★★★.

● COMPILATIONS: *Hindsight 1980–1987* (EMI 1987) ★★★, *Conception* (Carrere 1988) ★★★, *A Quick Smoke At Spot's (Archives 1980–1990)* (Arista 1991) ★★★, *Almost Yesterday 1981–1990* (Raven 1994) ★★★★, *Under The Milky Way: The Best Of The Church* (Buddah 1999) ★★★★.

● VIDEOS: *The Church* (EMI Australia 1986), *Goldfish (Jokes, Magic & Souvenirs)* (Arista/BMG Video 1990).

## CIRCLE JERKS

Formed in Los Angeles, California, USA, in 1980, this powerful hardcore band featured vocalist Keith Morris (ex-Black Flag) and guitarist Greg Hetson (ex-Redd Kross, later Bad Religion). Roger (Dowding) Rogerson (bass) and Lucky Lehrer (drums) completed the line-up featured on the quartet's forceful debut album. Their second, *Wild In The Streets*, was initially issued on Police manager Miles Copeland's Step Forward/Faulty label. It featured the services of hardcore's number one drummer, Chuck Biscuits (ex-D.O.A.), but he would leave in 1984 for a career in Danzig. Appearances on several influential 'new music' compilations, including *The Decline Of*

*Western Civilisation* (they also had a starring role in the film of the same name) and *Let Them Eat Jelly Beans* confirmed the Circle Jerks' position at the vanguard of California's virulent hardcore movement. Long-standing members Morris and Hetson remained at the helm of this compulsive group which, by 1985, was fleshed out with the addition of Zander 'Snake' Schloss (bass; later Weirdos and Joe Strummer) and Keith 'Adolph' Clark (drums). *Wönderful*, from the same year, was something of a disappointment, but the Circle Jerks rescued their reputation with the staunch, Dictators-influenced *VI*. After releasing a live anthology, the group went their own ways, before unexpectedly returning in the mid-90s to sign with PolyGram Records. The ensuing *Oddities Abnormalities And Curiosities* featured one truly bizarre track, with former teen star Debbie Gibson providing lead vocals for a thrashy cover version of the Soft Boys' 'I Wanna Destroy You'.

● ALBUMS: *Group Sex* (Frontier 1980) ★★★, *Wild In The Streets* (Faulty 1982) ★★★, *Golden Shower Of Hits* (LAX 1983) ★★, *Wönderful* (Combat Core 1985) ★★, *VI* (Relativity 1987) ★★★, *Oddities Abnormalities And Curiosities* (Mercury 1995) ★★★.

● COMPILATIONS: *Gig* (Relativity 1992) ★★★.

## CLANNAD

This family band, from Gweedore in Co. Donegal, Eire, enjoyed transatlantic commercial success by skilfully crossing the bridge between folk and rock. Clannad was formed in 1968 by brothers Pól Brennan (b. Pol Ó Braonáin, Eire; guitar, vocals, percussion, flute) and Ciarán Brennan (b. Ciaran Braonáin, Eire; guitar, bass, vocals, keyboards), and their twin uncles Pádraig Duggan (b. Pádraig Ó Dúgáin, February 1949, Eire; guitar, vocals, mandolin) and Noel Duggan (b. Noel Ó Dúgáin, February 1949, Eire; guitar, vocals). They were originally known as An Clann As Dobhar (Gaelic for a family from the townland of Dore), and although the name was soon abbreviated to Clannad the band continued to sing mainly in their native tongue. They played at local folk festivals and Leo's Tavern, run by Leo Brennan, a former showband musician and father of the Brennan group members of Clannad. Máire Brennan (b. Marie Ní Bhraonáin, 4 August 1952, Eire; harp/vocals) subsequently joined the band, who earned a recording contract with Philips Records by winning first prize at the Letterkenny Folk Festival. Their somewhat derivative 1973 debut was followed by two stronger efforts on the Gael-Linn label. The band's breakthrough success came in Germany, where they toured in 1975. The following year the band decided to commit themselves to music full-time. Máire's sister, Enya (b. Eithne Ní Bhraonáin, 17 May 1961, Dore, Gweedore, Co. Donegal, Eire) joined the line-up in 1980 and appeared on the transitional *Fuaim*, before leaving in 1982 to pursue a highly successful solo career. Clannad initially caught the attention of the wider public in the UK when they recorded the theme tune for the ITV drama *Harry's Game* in 1982. The single, which later appeared as the opening track on *Magical Ring*, reached number 5 in the UK charts, and received an Ivor Novello Award. In 1984, they recorded the soundtrack to UK television's *Robin Of Sherwood* and reached the Top 50. The following year the band received a British Academy Award for Best Soundtrack. Further chart success followed with the 1986 UK Top 20 hit 'In A Lifetime', on which Máire Brennan duetted with Bono from U2.

Pól Brennan left at the end of the decade to concentrate on solo work, but in his absence Clannad continued to release enchanting and distinctive albums that stayed true to their Celtic roots. They have been particularly successful in America, where 'Theme From Harry's Game' gained belated exposure on the movie soundtrack *Patriot Games* and a Volkswagen television commercial. Their work on the soundtrack to *The Last Of The Mohicans* also gained widespread stateside exposure. Máire Brennan, meanwhile, has established a successful solo career as a contemporary Christian artist.

● ALBUMS: *Clannad* (Philips 1973) ★★★, *Clannad 2* (Gael-Linn/Shanachie 1974) ★★★, *Dúlamán* (Gael-Linn/Shanachie 1976) ★★★, *Clannad In Concert* (Ogham/Shanachie 1978) ★★★, *Crann Ull* (Ogham/Tara 1980) ★★★, *Fuaim* (Tara 1982) ★★★★, *Magical Ring* (RCA 1983) ★★★, *Legend* (RCA 1984) ★★★, *Macalla* (RCA 1985) ★★★, *Sirius* (RCA 1987) ★★, *Atlantic Realm* television soundtrack (BBC 1989) ★★★, with narration by Tom Conti *The Angel And The Soldier Boy* (RCA 1989) ★★★, *Anam* (RCA/Atlantic 1990) ★★★, *Banba* (RCA/Atlantic 1993) ★★★, *Lore* (RCA 1996) ★★★, *Lore/Themes* (RCA 1996) ★★★, *Landmarks* (RCA 1998) ★★★.

● COMPILATIONS: *Clannad: The Collection* (K-Tel 1986) ★★★, *Past Present* (RCA 1989) ★★★, *Themes* (K-Tel/Celtic Heartbeat 1992) ★★★, *Rogha: The Best Of Clannad* (RCA 1997) ★★★, *The Ultimate Collection* (RCA 1997) ★★★, *Magic Elements: The Best Of Clannad* (BMG 1998) ★★★, *An Díolaim: The Folk Roots Of One Of Ireland's Finest Groups* (Music Club 1998) ★★★★, *Celtic Collection* (BMG 1999) ★★★, *Greatest Hits* (RCA 2000) ★★★, *The Celtic Voice* (Erin 2000) ★★★, *A Magical Gathering: The Clannad Anthology* (Rhino 2002) ★★★★.

● VIDEOS: *Past Present* (BMG Video 1989).

● FURTHER READING: *The Other Side Of The Rainbow*, Máire Brennan.

## CLAPTON, ERIC

b. Eric Patrick Clapp, 30 March 1945, Ripley, Surrey, England. The world's premier living rock guitarist will be forever grateful to his grandparents, for they gave him his first guitar. The young Eric was raised by his grandparents Rose and Jack Clapp when his natural mother could not face bringing up an illegitimate child at the age of 16. He received a £14 acoustic guitar for his fourteenth birthday, then proceeded to copy the great blues guitarists note for note. His first band was the Roosters, a local R&B group that included Tom McGuinness, a future member of Manfred Mann, and latterly part of the Blues Band. Clapton stayed for eight months until he and McGuinness left to join Casey Jones And The Engineers. This brief sojourn ended in 1963 when

Clapton was sought out by the Yardbirds, an aspiring R&B band, who needed a replacement for their guitarist Tony Topham. The reputation swiftly established by the Yardbirds was largely centred on Clapton, who had already been nicknamed 'Slowhand' by the partisan crowd at Richmond's Crawdaddy club. Clapton stayed for 18 months until musical differences interfered. The Yardbirds were taking a more pop-orientated direction and he just wanted to play the blues. He departed shortly after the recording of 'For Your Love'.

The perfect vehicle for his musical frustrations was John Mayall's Bluesbreakers, one of Britain's top blues bands. It was with Mayall that Clapton would earn his second nickname: 'God'! Rarely had there been a similar meteoric rise to such an exalted position. Clapton only made one album with Mayall but the record is now a classic; on its famous cover Clapton is sitting reading a copy of *The Beano* comic. Between Mayall and his next band, Clapton made numerous session appearances and recorded an interesting session with a conglomeration called the Powerhouse. They recorded three tracks – 'Crossroads', 'I Want To Know' and 'Steppin' Out' – the line-up comprising Paul Jones, Steve Winwood, Jack Bruce, Pete York and Clapton.

Clapton was elevated to superstar status with the formation of Cream in 1966, and together with ex-Graham Bond Organisation members Jack Bruce and Ginger Baker, he created one of the most influential rock bands of our time. Additionally, due to his close friendship with George Harrison, he was asked to play the beautiful lead solo on Harrison's 'While My Guitar Gently Weeps' on *The Beatles* ('The White Album'). Cream lasted just over two years, and shortly after their demise he was back with Baker, this time in Blind Faith. The line-up was completed by Steve Winwood and Ric Grech. This 'supergroup' was unable to stay together for more than one self-titled album, although their financially lucrative American tour made the impending break-up easier to bear. During the tour Clapton befriended Delaney And Bonnie, decided that he wanted to be their guitarist, and then joined them before the sweat had dried following his last Blind Faith gig in January 1970. He played on one album, *Delaney And Bonnie On Tour*, and three months later he had again absconded and finished up recording the disappointing *Eric Clapton*. Most of the previous band sessioned on that recording and three members (Jim Gordon, Bobby Whitlock and Carl Radle) ended up flying over to the UK to join Clapton again.

The band then metamorphosed into Derek And The Dominos. This memorable unit, together with Duane Allman, recorded one of his most famous compositions, the perennial 'Layla'. This clandestine love song was directed at George Harrison's wife Pattie, with whom Clapton had become besotted. Harrison, unaware of this, invited him to play at his historic The Concert For Bangla Desh in August 1971. Clapton then struggled to overcome a heroin habit that had grown out of control, since being introduced to the drug during the recording of *Layla And Other Assorted Love Songs*. During the worst moments of his addiction he began to pawn some of his precious guitars and spent up to £1,500 a week to feed his habit. Pete Townshend of the Who was appalled to discover that Clapton was selling his guitars and proceeded to try to rescue him and his girlfriend Alice Ormsby-Gore. Townshend organized the famous Eric Clapton At The Rainbow concert as part of his rehabilitation crusade, along with Steve Winwood, Ric Grech, Ron Wood and Jim Capaldi. His appearance broke two years of silence, and wearing the same suit he had worn at the Bangla Desh concert, he played a majestic and emotional set. Although still addicted, this represented a turning point in his life, and following pleas from his girlfriend's father, Lord Harlech, he entered the Harley Street clinic of Dr Meg Patterson for treatment.

A rejuvenated Clapton began to record again and released the buoyant 461 Ocean Boulevard in August 1974. The future pattern was set on this album; gone were the long guitar solos, replaced instead by relaxed vocals over shorter, more compact songs. The record was an incredible success, a number 1 hit in the USA and number 3 in the UK. The singles drawn from it were also hits, notably his number 1 US hit with Bob Marley's 'I Shot The Sheriff'. Also included was the autobiographical message to himself, 'Give Me Strength', and the beautifully mantric 'Let It Flow'. Clapton ended 1974 on a high note; not only had he returned from the grave, but he had finally succeeded in winning the heart of Pattie Harrison. During 1975 he maintained his drug-free existence, although he became dependent on alcohol. That same year he had further hits with There's One In Every Crowd and the live E.C. Was Here. Both maintained his reputation, and since then Clapton has continued to grow in stature. During 1977 and 1978 he released two more major albums, Slowhand and Backless. Further singles success came with the gentle 'Lay Down Sally' (co-written with Marcella Detroit, later of Shakespears Sister) and 'Promises', while other notable tracks were 'Wonderful Tonight', J.J. Cale's 'Cocaine' and John Martyn's 'May You Never'. Clapton had completely shrugged off his guitar hero persona and had now become an assured vocalist and songwriter, who, by chance, played guitar. A whole new audience, many of whom had never heard of the Yardbirds or Cream, saw Clapton as a wholesome, healthy individual with few vices, and no cobwebs in his attic. Clapton found additional time to play at the Band's historic The Last Waltz concert.

The 80s were kinder to Clapton, with every album selling in vast quantities and being critically well received. Another Ticket and Money And Cigarettes, which featured Ry Cooder, were particularly successful at the beginning of the decade. Behind The Sun benefited from the firm production hand of Clapton's close friend Phil Collins. Collins played drums on his next album, August, which showed no sign of tiredness or lack of ideas. This particularly strong album contained the excellent hit 'Behind The Mask', and an exciting duet with Tina Turner on 'Tearing Us Apart'. Throughout the record Clapton's voice was in particularly fine form. Journeyman in

1989 went one better; not only were his voice and songs creditable but 'Slowhand' had rediscovered the guitar. The album contains some of his finest playing and, not surprisingly, it was a major success.

Clapton has enjoyed a high profile in recent years with his touring, television documentaries, numerous biographies, and the now annual season of concerts at London's Royal Albert Hall. His 24 nights there in 1991 represented a record – such is his popularity that he could fill the Albert Hall every night for a year. As a final bonus for his many fans he played three kinds of concerts, dividing the season with a series of blues nights, orchestral nights and regular nights. In the 90s Clapton's career went from strength to strength, although the tragic death of his son Connor in 1991 halted his career for some months. In December of the same year he toured Japan with George Harrison, giving Harrison the moral support that he had received more than a decade earlier. Unplugged in 1992 became one of his most successful albums (US sales alone were 10 million copies by 1996). On this he demonstrated his blues roots, playing acoustically in relaxed circumstances with his band (including Andy Fairweather-Low), and oozing supreme confidence. The poignant 'Tears In Heaven', about the death of his son, was a major hit worldwide. From The Cradle was a worthy release, bringing him full circle in producing an electric blues album. Those guitar buffs who mourned his departure from Mayall and despaired when Cream called it a day could rejoice once again: 'God' had returned. The follow-up, Pilgrim, was a long time coming, giving rise to doubts about what he would do next and in which direction, blues or AOR. He fooled everyone by releasing a great soul-influenced album, sounding more like Curtis Mayfield than anybody else. Clapton has already earned the title as the greatest white blues guitarist of our time, but at the present time he seems to be working on his voice and his songwriting.

Clapton has contributed to numerous artists' albums over many years, including John Martyn, Phil Collins, Duane Allman, Marc Benno, Gary Brooker, Joe Cocker, Roger Daltrey, Jesse Davis, Dr. John, Bob Dylan, Aretha Franklin, Rick Danko, Champion Jack Dupree, Howlin' Wolf, Sonny Boy Williamson, Freddie King, Alexis Korner, Ronnie Laine, Jackie Lomax, Christine McVie, the Mothers Of Invention, the Plastic Ono Band, Otis Spann, Vivian Stanshall, Stephen Stills, Ringo Starr, Leon Russell, Doris Troy, Roger Waters and many, many more. He also appeared as the Preacher in Ken Russell's film of Pete Townshend's rock opera Tommy.

In 1998, he parted company with his long-time manager Roger Forrester and aimed to spend more time working with Crossroads, the drug rehabilitation centre he founded in Antigua. The auction sale of over 100 of his personal guitars raised money for this establishment. He changes his styles of rock music as often as he changes his hairstyle and spectacles. Ultimately he returns time and time again to his first love affair, the blues. His wonderful collaboration with B.B. King, Riding With The King, was an artistic and commercial success. Reptile built upon the soulful direction taken on *Pilgrim*. While guitar aficionados might be disappointed, those monitoring his 'new improved voice' will be impressed, notably with the slick cover version of James Taylor's 'Don't Let Me Be Lonely Tonight'.

● ALBUMS: three tracks as the Powerhouse with Steve Winwood, Jack Bruce, Pete York, Paul Jones *What's Shakin'?* (Elektra 1966) ★★★, *Eric Clapton* (Polydor 1970) ★★★, *Eric Clapton's Rainbow Concert* (RSO 1973) ★★★, *461 Ocean Boulevard* (RSO 1974) ★★★★, *There's One In Every Crowd* (RSO 1975) ★★★, *E.C. Was Here* (RSO 1975) ★★, *No Reason To Cry* (RSO 1976) ★★★, *Slowhand* (RSO 1977) ★★★★, *Backless* (RSO 1978) ★★★, *Just One Night* (RSO 1980) ★★★, *Another Ticket* (RSO 1981) ★★★, *Money And Cigarettes* (Duck 1983) ★★★, *Behind The Sun* (Duck 1985) ★★★, *August* (Duck 1986) ★★★, with Michael Kamen *Homeboy* television soundtrack (Virgin 1989) ★★, *Journeyman* (Duck 1989) ★★★★, *24 Nights* (Duck 1991) ★★, *Rush* film soundtrack (Reprise 1992) ★★, *MTV Unplugged* (Sony 1992) ★★★★, *From The Cradle* (Duck 1994) ★★★, *Pilgrim* (Warners 1998) ★★★★, with B.B. King *Riding With The King* (Reprise 2000) ★★★, *Reptile* (Reprise 2001) ★★★.

● COMPILATIONS: *Time Pieces – The Best Of Eric Clapton* (RSO 1982) ★★★, *Time Pieces Volume II: Live In The Seventies* (RSO 1983) ★★★, *Backtrackin'* (Starblend 1984) ★★★★, *Crossroads* 4-CD box set (Polydor 1988) ★★★★★, *The Cream Of Eric Clapton* (Polydor 1989) ★★★★, *Stages* (Spectrum 1993) ★★★, *Crossroads 2: Live In The 70s* (Polydor 1996) ★★★★, *Blues* (Polydor 1999) ★★★★, *Clapton Chronicles: The Best Of Eric Clapton* (Reprise 1999) ★★★★.

● VIDEOS: *Eric Clapton On Whistle Test* (BBC Video 1984), *Live '85* (PolyGram Music Video 1986), *Live At The NEC Birmingham* (MSD 1987), *The Cream Of Eric Clapton* (Channel 5 1989), *Man And His Music* (Video Collection 1990), *Eric Clapton In Concert* (Abbey Music Video 1991), *24 Nights* (Warner Music Video 1991), *Unplugged* (1992), *Clapton Chronicles: The Best Of Eric Clapton* (Warner Music Vision 1999), *Eric Clapton & Friends In Concert* (Warner Music 2000).

● FURTHER READING: *Conversations With Eric Clapton*, Steve Turner. *Eric Clapton: A Biography*, John Pidgeon. *Survivor: The Authorized Biography Of Eric Clapton*, Ray Coleman. *Clapton: The Complete Chronicle*, Marc Roberty. *Eric Clapton: The New Visual Documentary*, Marc Roberty. *Eric Clapton: Lost In The Blues*, Harry Shapiro. *Eric Clapton: The Complete Recording Sessions*, Marc Roberty. *The Man, The Music, The Memorabilia*, Marc Roberty. *Edge Of Darkness*, Christopher Sandford. *The Complete Guide To The Music Of*, Marc Roberty. *Crossroads: The Life And Music Of Eric Clapton*, Michael Schumacher.

● FILMS: *Tommy* (1975), *Water* (1985), *Blues Brothers 2000* (1998).

## CLASSIX NOUVEAUX

This 80s UK experimental quartet was fronted by the shaven-headed Sal Solo (b. 5 September 1954, Hatfield, Hertfordshire, England), whose uncompromising vocal style gelled uneasily with his musicians' synthesizer dance beat. Originally appearing on Stevo's Some Bizzare Records sample album, the group signed to Liberty Records in 1981 and recorded a series of albums, ranging from the gargantuan to the quirky unmelodic. Four of their singles reached the UK Top 75 during 1981 and the following year they scored their biggest success with 'Is It A Dream', which climbed to number 11. Perpetually on the periphery, the group's limited chart success and affiliation with a major label did little to offset their determinedly *avant garde* approach. By the mid-80s, the unit folded with Sal going solo and releasing *Heart And Soul* in 1985.

● ALBUMS: *Night People* (Liberty 1981) ★★★, *La Verité* (Liberty 1982) ★★★, *Secret* (Liberty 1983) ★★★.

● COMPILATIONS: *The Very Best Of Classix Nouveaux* (EMI 1997) ★★★.

## CLAYDERMAN, RICHARD

b. Philippe Pages, 28 December 1953, Paris, France. This highly popular pianist, specializes in light classical compositions, with a romantic, yet low profile image. His father was a piano teacher, and at the age of 12, Pages enrolled at the Conservatoire in Paris, and won the first prize four years later. He was encouraged to study classical piano, but his ambition was to be in a rock band. The dream was never realized, although in the 70s he did play with French pop stars such as Johnny Halliday and Michel Sardou. After working as a bank clerk, the newly renamed Clayderman (his great-grandmother's last name) was signed to the Delphine label, and had a hit in several European countries with 'Ballade Pour Adeline', which sold several million copies. He followed up with albums that contained show tunes, film themes and familiar classical pieces, with his relaxed, low-key piano playing cushioned by a large string orchestra. In the early 80s, he was reputed to be the top album seller in France, and in other countries such as South Africa and Japan. In 1982, he broke into the UK market with the number 2 hit album *Richard Clayderman* and, the following year, with the television-promoted *The Music Of Richard Clayderman*. In the same year, he played his first sell-out UK concerts and appeared several times on television. Clayderman is widely considered the most successful pianist in the world, having sold in excess of 66 million copies of his albums. At the peak of his popularity Clayderman was dubbed 'the Prince of Romance' by Nancy Reagan.

● ALBUMS: many albums contain a mixture of new recordings and previously released tracks *Ballade Pour Adeline (The Love Song)* (Decca 1981) ★★★, *Dreaming (Traumereien)* (IMS 1981) ★★★, *Dreaming (Traumereien) 2* (Teldec 1981) ★★★, *Dreaming (Traumereien) 3* (Teldec 1981) ★★★, *Richard Clayderman* (Decca 1982) ★★★, *A Comme Amour* (Teldec 1982) ★★★, *Lettre A Ma Mere* (Teldec 1982) ★★★, *Musiques De L'Amour* (Decca 1982) ★★★, *The Music Of Richard Clayderman* (Decca 1983) ★★★, *A Pleyel* (Delphine 1983) ★★★, *Marriage Of Love* (Delphine 1984) ★★★, *The Music Of Love* (Delphine 1984) ★★★, *Christmas* (Decca 1984) ★★, with the Royal Philharmonic Orchestra *The Classic Touch* (Decca 1985) ★★, *Hollywood And Broadway* (Delphine 1986) ★★★, *Songs Of Love* (Decca 1987)

★★★, *A Little Night Music* (Delphine 1988) ★★★, *Eleana* (Delphine 1988) ★★★, *The Love Songs Of Andrew Lloyd Webber* (Delphine 1989) ★★, *My Classic Collection* (Delphine 1990) ★★★, *Together At Last* (Delphine/Polydor 1991) ★★★, *The Carpenters Collection* (PolyGram 1995) ★★★, *Mexico Con Amor* (PolyGram 1996) ★★.

● COMPILATIONS: *The Very Best Of Richard Clayderman* (Delphine 1992) ★★★, *Candle In The Wind: A Collection Of His Finest Recordings* (Music Club 1998) ★★★, *With Love* (Music Collection 1999) ★★.

● VIDEOS: *Richard Clayderman In Concert* (Channel 5 1988), *Richard Clayderman* (Spectrum 1989), *Richard Clayderman: Live In Concert* (Pickwick Video 1990).

## CLIMIE FISHER

This UK songwriting duo featured Simon Climie (b. 7 April 1960, Fulham, London, England; vocals/keyboards) and Rob Fisher (b. 5 November 1959, Cheltenham, Gloucestershire, England, d. 25 August 1999, England; keyboards). Climie was a songwriter and Fisher had been one half of the duo Naked Eyes with Pete Byrne who had had a US Top 10 hit with a cover of 'Always Something There To Remind Me' in 1983. They met in London in 1986 and signed to EMI Records as Climie Fisher. After a few flops, the ballad, 'Rise To The Occasion' – featuring a beefier mix on the 12-inch single – rose to number 10 in the UK in early 1988. A remix of one of their previous misses, the white soul ballad, 'Love Changes (Everything)', with Climie sounding like Rod Stewart, made UK number 2 and the US Top 30. Subsequent singles failed to make any noticeable impact. Climie later embarked on a solo career, before concentrating on songwriting. He has penned hit singles for and produced various acts including George Michael, Pat Benatar, Louise, Eternal and Eric Clapton (notably his co-songwriting credits on *Pilgrim*). Fisher also worked as a songwriter for other artists, including Rick Astley, but died of severe pancreatitis in August 1999.

● ALBUMS: *Everything* (EMI 1988) ★★★, *Coming In For The Kill* (EMI 1989) ★★.

● COMPILATIONS: *The Best Of Climie Fisher* (Disky 1996) ★★★.

● VIDEOS: *The Best Of Everything* (EMI 1988).

## CLINT EASTWOOD AND GENERAL SAINT

Clint Eastwood (b. Robert Brammer, Jamaica, West Indies), the younger brother of Trinity, came to prominence with UK reggae fans in the late 70s with a series of big-selling singles recorded in his home country, and albums such as *African Youth*, *Death In The Arena* and *Sex Education*. In the early 80s he teamed up with General Saint (b. Winston Hislop), who had already established a devoted following working in London's Front Line International sound system, and the pair formed a talented pop-reggae duo. Their first release, a tribute to the late General Echo, topped the reggae charts, and the follow-up, 'Another One Bites The Dust', repeated the feat in 1981, reaching as far as the lower rungs of the national chart. Their subsequent records and live

appearances enhanced their reputation further and they were instrumental in the Jamaican DJ style crossing over to the early 80s pop audience.

● ALBUMS: Clint Eastwood *African Youth* (Third World 1978) ★★★, *Death In The Arena* (Cha Cha 1978) ★★★, *Love & Happiness* (Burning Sounds 1979) ★★★, *Sex Education* (Greensleeves 1980) ★★★; Clint Eastwood And General Saint *Jah Lights Shining* (Vista Sounds 1984) ★★★.

● COMPILATIONS: *Two Bad DJ* (Greensleeves 1981) ★★★, *Stop That Train* (Greensleeves 1983) ★★★, *Best Of Clint Eastwood* (Culture Press 1984) ★★★★.

## CLINTON, GEORGE

b. 22 July 1940, Kannapolis, North Carolina, USA. The mastermind behind the highly successful Parliament and Funkadelic, George 'Dr Funkenstein' Clinton's seemingly impregnable empire crumbled at the beginning of the 80s. Restrained from recording by a damaging breach-of-contract lawsuit and unable to meet the running expenses of his considerable organization, he found himself personally and professionally destitute. Clinton, nonetheless, tackled his problems. He settled most of his outstanding debts, overcame an addiction to freebase cocaine and resumed recording. An *ad hoc* group, the P-Funk All Stars, secured two minor hits with 'Hydrolic Pump' and 'One Of Those Summers' (both 1982), before the singer introduced a solo career with the magnificent 'Loopzilla', a rhythmic *tour de force* abounding with references to black music past (the Supremes and the Four Tops) and present (Afrika Bambaataa's 'Planet Rock'). The ensuing album, *Computer Games*, featured several ex-Funkadelic/Parliament cohorts, including Bernie Worrell and Bootsy Collins, while a further track, 'Atomic Dog', was a US R&B number 1 single in 1983. Clinton then continued to work both as a soloist and with the P-Funk All Stars, pursuing his eclectic, eccentric vision on such innovatory albums as *Some Of My Best Jokes Are Friends* and *The Cinderella Theory*. The latter was the first of a succession of recordings released on Prince's Paisley Park label. His *Hey Man ... Smell My Finger* set featured a cameo by ex-N.W.A. artist Dr. Dre, who in turn invited Clinton to guest rap on 'You Don't Wanna See Me' from Dre's collaboration with Ice Cube, *Helter Skelter*. As Dre and many other recent American rappers confess, they owe a great debt to Clinton, not least for their liberal use of his music. Clinton was not one to complain, however, as the young guns' heavy use of Parliament and Funkadelic samples had helped him overcome a crippling tax debt in the early 80s. Ironically enough, Clinton too makes use of samples in his recent recordings, returning to his past ventures for beats, breaks and riffs as so many of his legion of admirers have done before him. Clinton's 1996 album *The Awesome Power Of A Fully Operational Mothership* was a superb blend of the Funkadelic and Parliament sounds.

● ALBUMS: *Computer Games* (Capitol 1982) ★★★, *You Shouldn't-Nuf Bit Fish* (Capitol 1984) ★★★★, with the P-Funk All Stars *Urban Dance Floor Guerillas* (Sony 1984) ★★★, *Some Of My Best Jokes Are Friends* (Capitol 1985) ★★★★, *R&B Skeletons In The Closet*

(Capitol 1986) ★★★, *The Cinderella Theory* (Paisley Park 1989) ★★★, *Sample A Bit Of Disc And A Bit Of Dat* (AEM 1993) ★★★, *Hey Man ... Smell My Finger* (Paisley Park 1993) ★★★, *A Fifth Of Funk* (Castle Communications 1995) ★★★, *The Music Of Red Shoe Diaries* (Wienerworld 1995) ★★★, *Mortal Kombat* (London 1996) ★★★, with the P-Funk All Stars *The Awesome Power Of A Fully Operational Mothership* (Epic 1996) ★★★, *P-Funk All Stars Live At The Beverly Theatre* (Westbound 1996) ★★★, with the P-Funk All Stars *Live And Kickin'* (Intersound 1997) ★★★, with the P-Funk All Stars *Dope Dogs* (Dogone 1999) ★★★.
● COMPILATIONS: *The Best Of George Clinton* (Capitol 1986) ★★★★, *Family Series: Testing Positive 4 The Funk* (Essential 1994) ★★★, *Greatest Funkin' Hits* (Capitol 1996) ★★★★, *Extended Pleasure* (EMI 2000) ★★★, *Greatest Hits* (Right Stuff 2000) ★★★★.
● VIDEOS: *Mothership Connection* (Virgin Vision 1987).

## CLOCK DVA

One of a batch of groups forming the so-called 'industrial' scene of Sheffield in the early 80s, Clock DVA's first release was, appropriately, on Throbbing Gristle's Industrial label. The cassette-only (until its re-release in 1990) *White Souls In Black Suits* featured Adi Newton (vocals, ex-the Studs; the Future; Veer), Stephen James 'Judd' Turner (bass, vocals, guitar, ex-Block Opposite), David J. Hammond (guitar), Roger Quail (drums) and Charlie Collins (saxophone). However, there had already been three previous line-ups, including synthesizer players Joseph Hurst and Simon Mark Elliot-Kemp. In 1981, the band (with new guitarist Paul Widger) offered *Thirst*, available through independent label Fetish. With the ground for such 'difficult music' having been prepared by Throbbing Gristle, the press reaction was remarkably favourable. Nevertheless, the band disintegrated at the end of the year, and tragedy struck with the death of co-founder Turner.

Newton kept the name while the three other surviving members joined the Box. By 1983, replacements had been found in John Valentine Carruthers (guitar), Paul Browse (saxophone), Dean Dennis (bass) and Nick Sanderson (drums). A brace of singles prefaced *Advantage*, their first album for Polydor Records. The following year Carruthers and Sanderson departed, and Clock DVA continued as a trio. Though it would be five years before a follow-up, Newton was kept busy with his visual project the Anti Group (TAGC) and several singles. *Buried Dreams* finally arrived in 1989. By the time of 1991's *Transitional Voices*, Browse had been replaced by Robert E. Baker, a veteran of TAGC. The departure of Dennis left the remaining duo of Newton and Baker to record a selection of material for the Contempo label in the middle of the decade. Newton has long since described the process of making music as his research: 'We feel music is something that should change and not remain too rigid, evolve with ourselves as we grow, change our perception'. Although their recorded history is sparse, it represents a more thoughtful and reflective body of work than that which dominates their peer group. In particular, Newton's grasp of the philosophical connotations of technology placed him apart from the majority of its practitioners.
● ALBUMS: *White Souls In Black Suits* cassette (Industrial 1980) ★★, *Thirst* (Fetish 1981) ★★★, *Advantage* (Polydor 1983) ★★★, *Buried Dreams* (Interfisch 1989) ★★★, *Transitional Voices* (Interfisch 1990) ★★★, *Man-Amplified* (Contempo 1992) ★★★, *Sign* (Contempo 1992) ★★★, *Digital Soundtrack* (Contempo 1993) ★★★, *Anterior* (Contempo 1995) ★★★.
● COMPILATIONS: *Collective: The Best Of Clock DVA* (Cleopatra 1994) ★★★★.
● VIDEOS: *Kinetic Engineering* (Contempo 1994).

## CLOSE LOBSTERS

This atypical example of the 'indie shambling band' was formed in 1985 by Andrew Burnett (b. 11 February 1965, Johnstone, Scotland; vocals), brother Robert Burnett (b. 11 September 1962, Johnstone, Scotland; bass), Stewart McFadyen (b. 26 September 1965, Paisley, Scotland; drums), Graeme Wilmington (b. 22 August 1965, Johnstone, Scotland; guitar) and Thomas Donnelly (b. 29 August 1962, Johnstone, Scotland; guitar). The Close Lobsters first crept into the limelight by featuring 'Firestation Towers' on the *C86* cassette organized by the *New Musical Express*, designed to bring together the best of the new independent bands appearing in 1986. Thanks to an intense mixture of agitated guitars and Andrew Burnett's peculiar – and frequently unfathomable – lyrics, Close Lobsters manufactured a partisan following in Britain and garnered an enthusiastic response from US college radio stations. An invitation to the prestigious New York Music Seminar in 1989 led to an extensive Stateside tour as the band virtually emigrated to America in a bid to crack that market. In spite of respectable sales, the pressure was too much for Donnelly, who departed at the close of the year. His ex-colleagues followed this example by taking a two-year break from the public eye before returning to the live circuit at the start of 1991. Sadly, when a Close Lobsters song did crack the UK Top 20 the following year ('Let's Make Some Plans'), it was as the b-side cover version to the Wedding Present's 'California'.
● ALBUMS: *Foxheads Stalk This Land* (Fire 1987) ★★★, *Headache Rhetoric* (Fire 1989) ★★★.

## CLUB NOUVEAU

This disco act from Sacramento, California, USA, was formed by producer Jay King and comprised Valerie Watson, Denzil Foster, Thomas McElroy and Samuelle Prater. All bar Prater had previously been members of the Timex Social Club, a local vocal group. With Watson singing lead, a 1987 revival of Bill Withers' 'Lean On Me' – issued on King's own King Jay Records – climbed to number 1 in the USA and reached the Top 10 in most European countries. However, the follow-up, 'Why You Treat Me So Bad', was only a modest domestic hit. Some later singles made ripples regionally, but the replacement in 1988 of McElroy and Prater with David Agent and Kevin Irving failed to rekindle chartbusting enthusiasm for the group. Foster and McElroy went on to form a production duo and record as FMob.

● ALBUMS: *Life, Love & Pain* (Warners 1986) ★★★, *Listen To The Message* (Warners 1988) ★★, *Under A Nouveau Groove* (Warners 1989) ★★.
● COMPILATIONS: *The Collection Volume 1* (WEA 1998) ★★★, *Greatest Hits* (Thump 2001) ★★★.

## COCKNEY REJECTS

Discovered by Jimmy Pursey of Sham 69, this skinhead band came to the fore in London, England, in 1980 with an irreverent brand of proletarian-focused punk. The band comprised Jefferson Turner (vocals), Vince Riordan (bass, vocals), Micky Geggus (guitar, vocals) and Keith Warrington (drums). Daring and anti-everything, they were virtually a parody of the 'kick over the traces' punk attitude, while also betraying a stubborn parochialism in keeping with their band title. The 'anarchic' contents of their albums were reflected in their garishly tasteless record sleeves. Nevertheless, they had a certain subversive humour, titling their first two albums *Greatest Hits* when the sum of their UK Top 40 achievements rested with 'The Greatest Cockney Ripoff' at number 21 and the West Ham United football anthem, 'I'm Forever Blowing Bubbles', at number 35. On their second album they included the 'Oi! Oi! Oi!' song/chant, thereby giving birth to a musical genre that came to define the brash inarticulacy of skinhead politics. Their gigs during this time also became an interface for working-class culture and the extreme right and, like Sham 69, the Rejects were judged guilty by default. By the time of 1982's *The Wild Ones* the band were veering away from their original punk influences towards heavy metal. Significantly, their new producer was UFO bass player Pete Way. Equally significantly, their career was well on the decline by this point. They disbanded in 1985 but re-formed to public apathy at the turn of the decade, *Lethal* hardly living up to its title.
● ALBUMS: *Greatest Hits Vol. 1* (Zonophone 1980) ★★★, *Greatest Hits Vol. 2* (Zonophone 1980) ★★★, *Greatest Hits Vol. 3 (Live And Loud)* (Zonophone 1981) ★★, *The Power & The Glory* (Zonophone 1981) ★★, *The Wild Ones* (AKA 1982) ★★★, *Rock The Wild Side* (Heavy Metal 1984) ★★, *Live And Loud!! Bridgehouse Tapes* 1981 recording (Link 1987) ★★, *Lethal* (Neat 1990) ★★, *Greatest Hits Vol. 4* (Rhythm Vicar 2000) ★★.
● COMPILATIONS: *Unheard Rejects* early unreleased recordings (Wonderful World 1985) ★, *We Are The Firm* (Dojo 1986) ★★, *The Best Of Cockney Rejects* (Castle 1994) ★★★, *The Great Cockney Rip Off* (Harry May 1999) ★★.
● VIDEOS: *Destroying Statues: An Interview With The Cockney Rejects* (Visionary 1996).

## COCOA TEA

b. Calvin Scott, 3 September 1959, Rocky Point, Clarendon, Jamaica, West Indies. Cocoa Tea began his career while still a child in Kingston in 1974, singing on a couple of obscure records for an equally obscure producer, Willie Francis; 'Searching In The Hills' was issued under the name of Calvin Scott. He vanished again until 1983, when, sporting dreadlocks and his new nickname, he began to carve a niche in dancehall reggae with producer Henry 'Junjo' Lawes, hitting with 'Rockin' Dolly', and 'I Lost My Sonia'. Unlike other dancehall singers, he did not find it necessary to attempt to dominate a song with energy, instead preferring a subtler, more melodic approach. His 1985 album debut, *Wha Them A Go Do, Can't Stop Cocoa Tea*, suggested a great future, which proved to be correct as *The Marshall*, *Sweet Sweet Cocoa Tea*, *Come Again* and *Cocoa Tea* established him further. A collaboration with producer Gussie Clarke led to the formation of a group alongside the trio Home T and DJ Shabba Ranks. Their *Holding On* and the single 'Pirate's Anthem' were huge Jamaican hits in 1989. As a solo artist, *Riker's Island* established that he had more to say than most. The 'No Blood For Oil' single was a lucid comment on the Gulf war, and was also to be found on *Another One For The Road* (1991), recorded with Home T after Cutty Ranks had replaced Shabba in the group. In 1997 he successfully revived the King Sporty hit, 'I'm Not A King'. The only thing currently preventing Cocoa Tea from becoming a major musical star is his apparent reluctance to travel.
● ALBUMS: *Wha Them A Go Do, Can't Stop Cocoa Tea* (Volcano 1985) ★★★★, *Sweet Sweet Cocoa Tea* (Blue Mountain 1986) ★★★, *The Marshall* (Jammys 1986) ★★★, *Cocoa Tea* (Firehouse 1986) ★★★★, with Tenor Saw *Clash* (Witty 1987) ★★★, *Come Again* (Super Power 1987) ★★★, with Shabba Ranks, Home T *Holding On* (Greensleeves 1989) ★★★, *Rikers Island* (Greensleeves 1991) ★★★, with Cutty Ranks, Home T *Another One For The Road* (Greensleeves 1991) ★★★, *Authorized* (Greensleeves 1992) ★★★, *I Am The Toughest* (King Jammys 1992) ★★★, *Kingston Hot* (Greensleeves 1992) ★★★, *One Up* (Exterminator/Greensleeves 1993) ★★★, *Tune In* (Greensleeves 1994) ★★★, with Freddie McGregor, Mykal Roze, Bunny Rugs *Grafton 4 By 4* (Mesa 1997) ★★★★, *One Way* (Xterminator 1998) ★★★, *Feel The Power* (VP 2001) ★★★.

## COCTEAU TWINS

Formed in 1982 in Grangemouth, Scotland, the Cocteau Twins originally comprised Elizabeth Fraser (b. 29 August 1963, Scotland), Robin Guthrie (b. 4 January 1962, Scotland) and bass player Will Heggie. Able to convey an astonishing variety of moods and emotions, using words more for their sound than their meaning, Fraser's voice has become one of the most recognizable and imitated of the last two decades. The accompanying musical backdrop assembled by Guthrie used guitar, tape loops, echo boxes and drum machines.
Guthrie formed the band with Heggie after seeing Fraser dancing at a disco. Demo tapes were passed to Ivo Watts-Russell, the owner of 4AD Records and his enthusiasm for the Cocteau Twins' music prompted the band's move to London to record for the label. The first album generated enormous interest and airplay from BBC Radio 1 disc jockey John Peel. *Garlands* was initially rather lazily compared to Siouxsie And The Banshees, but the Cocteau Twins soon began to carve out their own niche. By spring 1983, Heggie had departed (later to join Lowlife).

*Head Over Heels* smoothed over the rougher edges of its predecessor with Guthrie adding layers of echo and phased drum effects that allowed Fraser's voice full rein. During this period the band were also involved in the 4AD label project This Mortal Coil, for which Fraser and Guthrie's version of the Tim Buckley song 'Song To the Siren', has since been acknowledged as one of the finest independent label recordings of the 80s. Simon Raymonde (b. 3 April 1962, Tottenham, London, England) had by now been enrolled as bass player, eventually becoming a valuable asset in composing, arranging and production. The release of two superb EP collections, *Sunburst And Snowblind* and *Pearly-Dewdrops' Drops*, dominated the independent charts, with the latter broaching the UK Top 30.

The Cocteau Twins' reluctance to reveal anything of their private lives or play the music business game won them respect from many quarters and annoyance from others. This did leave them, however, less able to counter the image imposed upon them by fans as fey, mystical creatures – in the interviews to which the band did acquiesce, the principals appeared to be earthy, occasionally cantankerous and most definitely of this world. One benefit of their refusal to have their photographs taken for record sleeves was the superb cover art produced by the 23 Envelope studio, a presentational aspect utterly synonymous with their early career. The arrival of *Treasure* in 1984 saw the band scaling new heights, and over the next couple of years they released several EPs, *Aikea-Guinea*, *Tiny Dynamine* and *Echoes In A Shallow Bay*, each displaying rich, complex textures without ever repeating themselves. *Victorialand*, recorded without Raymonde, had a lighter, acoustic sound and featured Richard Thomas (saxophone, tablas) of 4AD stablemates Dif Juz. Raymonde returned for the *Love's Easy Tears* EP and the collaboration with Harold Budd in late 1986. *Blue Bell Knoll* seemed to confirm that the Cocteau Twins had lost their touch, but the emotional impact of the birth of Fraser and Guthrie's child revived their career on the stunning *Heaven Or Las Vegas*. The single 'Iceblink Luck' reached the UK Top 40 and the band started to tour again.

In 1991, Guthrie continued with studio production work, notably with 4AD labelmates Lush. The Cocteau Twins signed a new contract with Fontana Records in March 1992 and following work with a speech therapist, Fraser returned to recording and completed *Four-Calendar Café*. There were some surprises in store for the band's long-term fans – for the first time Fraser's lyrics were audible, and the band then released a Christmas single, 'Frosty The Snowman'. *Milk & Kisses* was recorded in Brittany and the band's own September Sound Studios in Twickenham, and was preceded by two EP releases, the 'ambient' *Otherness* (with Mark Clifford of Seefeel) and the 'acoustic' *Twinlights*. The latter was accompanied by the band's first film short. The Cocteau Twins announced they were splitting up in June 1998.

● ALBUMS: *Garlands* (4AD 1982) ★★★, *Head Over Heels* (4AD 1983) ★★★, *Treasure* (4AD 1984) ★★★, *Victorialand* (4AD 1986) ★★★, as Harold Budd, Elizabeth Fraser, Robin Guthrie, Simon Raymonde *The Moon And The Melodies* (4AD/Relativity 1986) ★★★, *Blue Bell Knoll* (4AD/Capitol 1988) ★★, *Heaven Or Las Vegas* (4AD/Capitol 1990) ★★★★, *Four-Calendar Café* (Fontana/Capitol 1993) ★★★, *Milk & Kisses* (Fontana/Capitol 1996) ★★★.

● COMPILATIONS: *The Pink Opaque* (4AD/Relativity 1986) ★★★, *Cocteau Twins* box set (Capitol 1991) ★★★, *BBC Sessions* (Bella Union 1999) ★★★★, *Stars And Topsoil: A Collection (1982–1990)* (4AD 2000) ★★★★.

## COLE, LLOYD

b. 31 January 1961, Buxton, Derbyshire, England. Despite his birthplace, this literate singer-songwriter emerged from Glasgow's post-punk renaissance. The Commotions, Neil Clark (b. 3 July 1955; guitar), Blair Cowan (keyboards), Lawrence Donegan (b. 13 July 1961; bass) and Stephen Irvine (b. 16 December 1959; drums) completed the line-up responsible for *Rattlesnakes*, a critically lauded set that merged Byrds-like guitar figures to Cole's languid, Lou Reed-inspired intonation. A representative selection from the album, 'Perfect Skin', reached the UK Top 30 when issued as a single, while a follow-up album, *Easy Pieces*, spawned two Top 20 entries in 'Brand New Friend' and 'Lost Weekend'. However, the style that came so easily on these early outings seemed laboured on *Mainstream*, after which Cole disbanded his group. Retaining Cowan, he switched bases to New York, and emphasized the infatuation with Lou Reed's music by recruiting sidemen Robert Quine (guitar) and Fred Maher (drums), the latter of whom also acted as producer. *Lloyd Cole* showed signs of an artistic rejuvenation, but Cole was yet to stamp a wholly original persona and capitalize on his undoubted talent. Both *Don't Get Weird On Me, Babe* and *Bad Vibes* failed to lift the atmosphere of bookish lyrics rendered without the requisite soul, but neither were these collections without merit. Instead, the listener was once again left to reminisce about the power of writing and performance that coalesced on tracks such as 'Down On Mission Street' and 'Forest Fire' from the artist's debut. His recent band the Negatives, features the occasional services of talented singer-songwriter Jill Sobule.

● ALBUMS: with the Commotions *Rattlesnakes* (Polydor 1984) ★★★★, with the Commotions *Easy Pieces* (Polydor 1985) ★★★, with the Commotions *Mainstream* (Polydor 1987) ★★★, *Lloyd Cole* (Polydor 1989) ★★★, *Don't Get Weird On Me, Babe* (Polydor 1991) ★★★, *Bad Vibes* (Fontana 1993) ★★, *Love Story* (Fontana 1995) ★★★, with the Negatives *The Negatives* (What Are/XIII Bis 2000) ★★★.

● COMPILATIONS: *1984–1989* (Polydor 1989) ★★★★, *The Collection* (Mercury 1998) ★★★★, *An Introduction To Lloyd Cole & The Commotions* (Polydor 2001) ★★★★, *2001: The Collected Recordings By Lloyd Cole* 4-CD box set (XIII Bis 2001) ★★★.

● VIDEOS: *Lloyd Cole & The Commotions* (Channel 5 Video 1986), *From The Hip* (PolyGram Music Video 1988), *1984–1989 (Lloyd Cole & The Commotions)* (Channel 5 Video 1989).

## COLE, NATALIE

b. 6 February 1950, Los Angeles, California, USA. The daughter of celebrated singer/pianist Nat 'King' Cole, Natalie survived early pressures to emulate her father's laid-back singing style. Signed to Capitol Records in 1975, her debut release, 'This Will Be', was a US Top 10 hit and the first of three consecutive number 1 soul singles. This early success was continued with 'I've Got Love On My Mind' and 'Our Love' (both 1977), which continued the astute, sculpted R&B style forged by producers Chuck Jackson and Marvin Yancey, who, like herself, attended Jerry Butler's Writers Workshop. Yancey and Cole later married. Cole's work continued to enjoy plaudits, and although it lacked the intensity of several contemporaries, there was no denying its quality and craft.

She maintained her popularity into the 80s but an increasing drug dependency took a professional and personal toll. Her marriage ended in divorce, but in May 1984, the singer emerged from a rehabilitation centre. Now cured, Cole picked up the pieces of her career, and a 1987 album, *Everlasting*, provided three hit singles, 'Jump Start', 'I Live For Your Love' and 'Pink Cadillac', the latter reaching number 5 in the UK and US pop charts. This Bruce Springsteen song was uncovered from the b-side of 'Dancing In The Dark'. Further pop hits followed with 'Miss You Like Crazy' and 'Wild Women Do', the latter taken from the soundtrack of the movie *Pretty Woman*.

In 1991, she recorded a unique tribute to her late father – a 'duet' with him on his original recording of the song 'Unforgettable'. The song took on a moving significance, with the daughter perfectly accompanying her deceased father's voice. The single's promotional video featured vintage black-and-white footage of Nat 'King' Cole at his peak on his US television show, interspersed with colour clips of Natalie. The accompanying album on Elektra Records later won seven Grammy Awards, including best album and song the following year. *Unforgettable ... With Love* marked a stylistic turning point in Cole's career, with the singer moving away from the urban contemporary market and embracing the smooth jazz-pop sound of her father on subsequent albums. *Take A Look* included a superb cover version of the standard 'Cry Me A River', while her Christmas albums *Holly & Ivy* and *The Magic Of Christmas* brought new life to some old chestnuts. Her revealing autobiography was published in November 2000.

● ALBUMS: *Inseparable* (Capitol 1975) ★★★★, *Natalie* (Capitol 1976) ★★★, *Unpredictable* (Capitol 1977) ★★★, *Thankful* (Capitol 1977) ★★★, *Natalie ... Live!* (Capitol 1978) ★★★★, *I Love You So* (Capitol 1979) ★★★, with Peabo Bryson *We're The Best Of Friends* (Capitol 1979) ★★★, *Don't Look Back* (Capitol 1980) ★★, *Happy Love* (Capitol 1981) ★★, with Johnny Mathis *Unforgettable: A Musical Tribute To Nat 'King' Cole* (Columbia 1983) ★★★, *I'm Ready* (Epic 1983) ★★, *Dangerous* (Modern 1985) ★★, *Everlasting* (Manhattan 1987) ★★, *Good To Be Back* (EMI 1989) ★★, *Unforgettable ... With Love* (Elektra 1991) ★★★★, *Take A Look* (Elektra 1993) ★★★★, *Holly & Ivy* (Elektra 1994) ★★★, *Stardust* (Elektra 1996) ★★★, with José Carreras, Placido Domingo *Celebration Of Christmas* (Elektra 1996) ★★★, *Snowfall On The Sahara* (Elektra 1999) ★★★, with the London Symphony Orchestra *The Magic Of Christmas* (Elektra 1999) ★★★, *Ask A Woman Who Knows* (Verve 2002) ★★★.

● COMPILATIONS: *The Natalie Cole Collection* (Capitol 1988) ★★★, *The Soul Of Natalie Cole (1974–80)* (Capitol 1991) ★★★★, *Greatest Hits: Volume 1* (Elektra 2000) ★★★★.

● VIDEOS: *Video Hits* (PMI 1989), *Holly & Ivy* (Warner Music Vision 1995).

● FURTHER READING: *Angel On My Shoulder: The Autobiography Of Natalie Cole*, Natalie Cole with Digby Diehl.

## COLLINS, PHIL

b. 30 January 1951, Chiswick, London, England. This former child actor has, in a comparatively short time, established himself as the world's premier singing drummer. His broad public appeal was not unlike that bestowed upon the Beatles in their heyday, and Collins also earned the respect of his fellow musicians as a technically brilliant drummer. The appearance of the self-confessional *Face Value* in 1981, immediately confirmed Collins as a songwriter of note, outside of his existence as vocalist/drummer with the highly successful rock band Genesis. The record focused on Collins' distinctive voice, something that had previously been underrated and under-used. Collins, who had spent a number of years as their drummer had also recorded with Brand X. He came out from behind the drum-stool in 1975 and took over the vocals previously handled by the departed Peter Gabriel. Collins' vocal delivery owed much to Gabriel. *Face Value* was recorded during the collapse of his first marriage and he conveyed all the intense emotional feelings of that crumbled relationship into most of the compositions. *Face Value* contained such stand-outs as the melancholic 'If Leaving Me Is Easy', the stark, yet beautiful piano-accompanied 'You Know What I Mean' and the soulful 'It Must Be Love'. The album's main axis was the hauntingly powerful 'In The Air Tonight'. A song that slowly builds until it reaches a climax that explodes with such a clamour of drums that the listener cannot fail to be moved. The single narrowly failed to make the top spot in the UK singles chart, while the album became a worldwide success. In the UK it became a number 1, and spent over five years in the charts.

Following *Face Value*'s extraordinary success and media interest, Collins went to great lengths to insist that he would not be leaving Genesis, and went on to make a further five albums with them. Collins' next solo work, *Hello, I Must Be Going*, was similarly successful although the angst had disappeared now that Collins was happily ensconced in a relationship with his future wife. The excellent cover version of the Supremes 'You Can't Hurry Love' was another worldwide hit in 1982, reaching the top spot in the UK. Collins continued with a gruelling schedule of work, which he managed to complete with enthusiasm and King Midas-like success. He became a highly successful record producer and session drummer, working with such artists as John Martyn, Robert Plant, Adam And The Ants, Frida, Eric Clapton, Brand X and Howard Jones. Additionally, his specially commissioned film soundtrack song for *Against All Odds* reached the top of the US charts and narrowly missed the top spot in the UK. A few weeks later he appeared on television giving a confident performance as an actor in one episode of *Miami Vice*, resulting in a glut of film scripts being sent to him. He played drums on the famous Band Aid single, 'Do They Know It's Christmas?', which spent the early weeks of 1985 at the top of the charts. A few weeks later he was again near the top of the US charts duetting with Philip Bailey on the infectious 'Easy Lover', and, barely pausing for breath, released *No Jacket Required* which topped the charts in most countries in the world, for many weeks.

Collins made history on 13 July 1985 by appearing at the Live Aid concert twice, both at Wembley, and, following a dash to catch Concorde, in Philadelphia. Incredibly, he found further energy a few hours later to play drums with Jimmy Page and Robert Plant and Eric Clapton. A second duet and film soundtrack, this time with Marilyn Martin for the film *White Nights* made 'Separate Lives' his fourth chart-topper in the US at the end of a phenomenal year. Collins had a comparatively quiet time during 1986, spending part of it touring the world as drummer with Eric Clapton's band. The following year was spent filming for his starring role as a great train robber, Buster Edwards in *Buster*, which was released the following year to mainly good reviews. His fourth solo album was released in 1989 and immediately topped the charts, spawning further hit singles.

In the 90s in addition to continuing with Genesis he contributed to David Crosby's album *Thousand Roads*, co-writing the hit 'Hero' and starred in the movie *Frauds*. *Both Sides* in 1993 was a return to the stark emotion of *Face Value*. Collins, although he stated in interviews that he was a happily married man, opened old relationship wounds with powerful lyrics. He was rewarded by the album debuting at number 1 in the UK chart and finding similar success in the USA and most countries in the world. There seemed little else left to achieve for the teenager who played the Artful Dodger in *Oliver!* onstage in 1964. However, his untarnished image suffered a major setback when it was revealed that his highly publicised second marriage was over, following his defection with a much younger woman. Collins relocated to Switzerland leaving his wife alone together with the almost unanimous support of the UK public and press, and allowing the lyrical intensity of *Both Sides* to be viewed in a different light.

Collins left Genesis in March 1996, and when the underwhelming *Dance Into The Light* was released later in the year, the singer went to great lengths during interviews to regain credibility with his public. The *Hits* compilation restored Collins to the top of the UK charts in October 1998, and broke into the US Top 20. The following year Collins composed the songs for the Disney movie *Tarzan*, enjoying particular success with the ballad 'You'll Be In My

Heart', which later won the Oscar for Best Original Song. He recorded a big band live album, which was ignored by the rock press, but given a fair hearing from the quality media.

● ALBUMS: *Face Value* (Virgin 1981) ★★★★, *Hello, I Must Be Going* (Virgin 1982) ★★★★, *No Jacket Required* (Virgin 1985) ★★★, *... But Seriously* (Virgin 1989) ★★★, *Serious Hits ... Live!* (Virgin 1990) ★★, *Both Sides* (Virgin 1993) ★★★, *Dance Into The Light* (Face Value 1996) ★, *Tarzan* film soundtrack (Disney 1999) ★★, *A Hot Night In Paris* (Warners 1999) ★★.
● COMPILATIONS: *Hits* (Virgin 1998) ★★★.
● VIDEOS: *Live: Phil Collins* (Thorn-EMI 1984), *Video EP: Phil Collins* (PMI/EMI 1986), *No Ticket Required* (WEA Music Video 1986), *Live At Perkin's Palace* (PMI/EMI 1986), *You Can't Hurry Love* (Gold Rushes 1987), *No Jacket Required* (Virgin Vision 1988), *The Singles Collection* (Virgin Vision 1989), *Seriously Live* (Virgin Vision 1990), *But Seriously, The Videos* (Virgin Vision 1992), *Live And Loose In Paris* (Warner Vision 1998).
● FURTHER READING: *Phil Collins* Johnny Waller.

## COLORBLIND JAMES EXPERIENCE
From Rochester, New York, USA, this eccentric outfit was led by the evidently talented but somewhat unhinged Colorblind James (b. Chuck Cuminale, 1952, Oswego, New York, USA, d. 10 July 2001, USA; vocals, vibraphone, guitar), with Phillip Marshall (lead guitar, vocals), Bernie Heveron (bass, vocals) and Jim McAvaney (drums). Together they utilized the myriad forms of North American musical expression open to them, from country, cocktail-lounge jazz, folk, rockabilly and blues to goodtime rock 'n' roll, in order to express James' oddball view of the world. It was BBC disc jockey John Peel who first gave them the exposure necessary to make them realize they were producing something that an audience might also appreciate. Their 1987 debut album was an eclectic work, notable for its engaging black humour. The high point of the collection, the sprawling 'I'm Considering A Move To Memphis', was reminiscent of David Byrne's less self-conscious efforts. By the time of the release of their second album, *Why Should I Stand Up?*, the line-up had increased to a sextet with the addition of John Ebert (trombone, tuba, vocals), Ken Frank (bass, violin, vocals – replacing Heveron) and Dave McIntire (saxophone, clarinet, vocals). In 1990, the group put aside their electric instruments, thereby standing revealed as Colorblind James And The Death Valley Boys, and indulging in more basic country blues, gospel and jug band music. The result of these sessions was *Strange Sounds From The Basement*, which continued Colorblind's infatuation with the underside of contemporary American life. He really did move to Memphis in the 90s, although his attempts to break into the local songwriting community were unsuccessful. He returned to New York state and continued to release records with the Colorblind James Experience, before succumbing to a heart attack in his swimming pool in July 2001.
● ALBUMS: *The Colorblind James Experience* (Earring 1987) ★★★, *Why Should I Stand Up?* (Death Valley/Cooking Vinyl 1989) ★★★★, as Colorblind

James And The Death Valley Boys *Strange Sounds From The Basement* (Death Valley/Cooking Vinyl 1990) ★★★, *Solid! Behind The Times* (Red House 1992) ★★★★, *I Could Be Your Guide* (Scout 1996) ★★★, *Call Of The Wild* (Death Valley 1999) ★★★.
● COMPILATIONS: *Greatest Hits!* (Stub Daddy 2000) ★★★★.

## COLOUR FIELD

After appearing with the Specials and the Fun Boy Three, Terry Hall (b. 19 March 1959, Coventry, West Midlands, England; guitar, vocals) formed the Colour Field with Karl Sharle (bass) and Toby Lyons (guitar, keyboards) in 1983. Having been involved in a band that was responsible for the ska/mod revival, and then a vocal-based trio, Hall's third band of the 80s was a basic group of three musicians. He was aided by friends, and produced strong pop songs featuring his rather flat vocals. After the instant success of his two previous bands, Colour Field found the going hard. Although they had positive reviews from the music press, it took nearly 18 months for the band to break into the UK Top 20 with 'Thinking Of You' in 1985. Their debut album reached number 12 in the UK, but the failure of subsequent singles soon reduced them to a duo of Hall and Lyons. They reappeared in 1987 with a weak cover version of Sly And The Family Stone's 'Running Away' and a second album that gave a poor showing on the UK chart; this was soon followed by the dissolution of the group. In 1989, Hall released an album with assistance from Blair Booth (keyboards, vocals) and Anouchka Grooe (guitar), before going on a critically acclaimed but commercially unrewarding solo career.
● ALBUMS: *Virgins And Philistines* (Chrysalis 1985) ★★★, *Deception* (Chrysalis 1987) ★★★.

## COLOURBOX

This mid-80s UK indie act recorded several singles and two albums for 4AD Records that attracted a cult following, but never rivalled the mainstream breakthrough of stablemates such as the Cocteau Twins. Colourbox were formed in London, England, in 1982, by brothers Martyn (guitar) and Steve Young (drums), together with Debian Curry (vocals) and Steve Biggs (bass). Their 4AD debut followed in November with 'Breakdown', after which the group personnel shuffled with the replacement of Curry with Lorita Grahame. Guests Steve Wright (guitar), Michael Smith (drums) and Bunny McKenzine (harmonica) then appeared on the group's adventurous 1983 mini-album, *Untitled*. By July 1985 and 'The Moon Is Blue', Biggs had been replaced by Ian Robbins on bass, as the group embarked on sessions for their debut album proper. *Colourbox* was a kaleidoscopic marriage of dance music, including dub reggae, funk and R&B, with effortless pop/soul songwriting, which bore little resemblance to other music on the 4AD roster. This approach eventually resulted in success when the Young brothers joined with members of AR Kane to produce M.A.R.R.S.' hugely influential 'Pump Up The Volume'. There was only one further Colourbox single, 'The Colourbox Unofficial World Cup Theme', released in May 1986.

The Young brothers also collaborated with This Mortal Coil while Grahame joined Love Child Orchestra.
● ALBUMS: *Untitled* mini-album (4AD 1983) ★★, *Colourbox* (4AD 1985) ★★★.
● COMPILATIONS: *Best Of 82/87* (4AD/Beggars Banquet 2001) ★★★.

## COMING UP ROSES

This unit was formed in 1986 by the songwriting partnership of ex-Dolly Mixture members Deborah Wykes (b. 21 December 1960, Hammersmith, London, England; guitar, vocals) and Hester Smith (b. 28 October 1960, West Africa; drums), along with Nicky Brodie (vocals, percussion), Patricia O'Flynn (saxophone, ex-Shillelagh Sisters), Leigh Luscious (guitar) and Claire Kenny (bass, ex-Amazulu), later replaced by bass player Sophie Cherry. Their melodic pop/dance style, described by the band as 'ballroom soul', mixed witty and caustic lyrics – in 'I Could Have Been Your Girlfriend (If You'd Asked Me To)' Wykes sang: 'She's so dumb, she's so sweet/I didn't think she'd last a week . . . She's so pretty she's so fine, she is such a waste of time/Well so she's cute, well I don't care, she's got stinking underwear!'. They signed to Billy Bragg's Utility Records label releasing one album in 1989. The band had already toured the UK as part of the pop-socialist collective Red Wedge troupe in 1987. After various personnel changes, but retaining the nucleus of Wykes and Smith along with Brodie, the band settled on a more stable line-up in 1990 with Tony Watts (lead guitar), Midus (bass) and Jane Keay (saxophone). However, disillusion with the music business' preoccupation with current trends prompted the band's demise in March 1991, leaving behind a legacy of timeless pop songs. Wykes later worked with Saint Etienne and formed Birdie with their guitarist Paul Kelly.
● ALBUMS: *I Said Ballroom* (Utility 1989) ★★★.

## COMMUNARDS

After leaving Bronski Beat in the spring of 1985, vocalist Jimmy Somerville (b. 22 June 1961, Glasgow, Scotland) teamed up with the classically trained pianist Richard Coles (b. 23 June 1962, Northampton, England) to form the Committee. When a rival group laid claim to that name, they became the Communards, a title borrowed from a nineteenth-century group of French Republicans. Their debut single, the disco-styled 'You Are My World' reached the UK Top 30. The follow-up, 'Disenchanted', was another minor hit, after which the duo decided to augment the line-up with various backing musicians. Meanwhile, their self-titled debut album climbed to number 2 in the UK. In September 1986, the group unexpectedly reached number 1 with a revival of Harold Melvin's 'Don't Leave Me This Way'. The song was most memorable for the vocal interplay between the falsetto of Somerville and the husky tones of guest singer Sarah Jane Morris. Her statuesque presence added much to the group's live appeal, especially when dancing alongside the diminutive Somerville. A further UK Top 10 hit followed with 'So Cold The Night'.
After touring extensively, the group issued a second

album, *Red.*, produced by Stephen Hague. A series of singles were culled from the album, including 'Tomorrow', their comment on wife beating, which reached number 23. The group returned to the Top 5 with a stirring revival of Gloria Gaynor's 'Never Can Say Goodbye'. During 1988, they registered two more minor UK hits with 'For A Friend' and 'There's More To Love'. With their fusion of disco-revival and falsetto pop, the Communards proved one of the more accomplished new acts of the mid-late 80s and seemed likely to enjoy further success in the new decade. As with Bronski Beat, however, Somerville showed a restlessness with the British music scene and wound down the group's activities, after which he went solo and scored hits with a cover of Sylvester's 'You Make Me Feel (Mighty Real)' and 'Read My Lips' before relocating to San Francisco.

● ALBUMS: *Communards* (London 1986) ★★★, *Red* (London 1987) ★★★.
Solo: Jimmy Somerville *Read My Lips* (London 1989) ★★★, *Dare To Love* (London 1995) ★★, *Manage The Damage* (Gut 1999) ★★.
● COMPILATIONS: *The Singles Collection, 1984–1990* includes recordings from Bronski Beat, Communards, Jimmy Somerville (London 1990) ★★★★, *The Very Best Of Jimmy Somerville, Bronski Beat And The Communards* (Warners 2001) ★★★.
● VIDEOS: *Communards: The Video Singles* (Channel 5 1987).

## COMSAT ANGELS

Three major recording contracts, no hit singles, legal complications – and yet the Comsat Angels survived to make thoughtful, expressive guitar music for more than 15 years. Formed in Sheffield, England, at the end of the 70s as Radio Earth, they initially merged the zest of punk with a mature songwriting approach, using a strong keyboard element on their promising debut, *Waiting For A Miracle*. The line-up of Stephen Fellows (guitar, vocals), Mik Glaisher (drums), Kevin Bacon (bass) and Andy Peake (keyboards) was to remain constant throughout their early career. In the USA they were forced to shorten their name to CS Angels after the communications giant Comsat threatened legal action. *Sleep No More* was their highest UK chart placing at number 51 but after *Fiction* only skimmed the lower reaches of the Top 100, Polydor Records lost patience and the band moved to the CBS Records subsidiary Jive. *Land* spawned a near-hit single with the catchy 'Independence Day', which had previously appeared on their first album. It was released in various formats, including a double-single set, but did not provide the success the band or their label envisioned. Other acts with a similar driving guitar sound fared better and they were surpassed commercially by the likes of Simple Minds and U2. The Comsat Angels invested heavily in their recording studio in Sheffield, which subsequently became a focus for the city's musical creativity. Another attempt to regenerate their career was made by Island Records in the late 80s but early in 1990, the Comsat Angels announced they were changing their name to Dream Command in the hope that it would bring about a change of fortune, and released the album *Fire On The Moon*. Bacon quit the band only to join up again when they reverted to their original name, signing to RPM Records for the release of a new album, *My Minds Eye*, in addition to two compilations of radio sessions. *The Glamour*, with new members Terry Todd (bass) and Simon Anderson (guitar), saw the Comsat Angels story end in familiar fashion – their superbly crafted, wry rock pop heard only by their existing clutch of die-hard European and American fans. Bacon now plays with Jonathan Quarmby as trip-hop duo Manna.

● ALBUMS: *Waiting For A Miracle* (Polydor 1980) ★★, *Sleep No More* (Polydor 1981) ★★★, *Fiction* (Polydor 1982) ★★★, *Land* (Jive 1983) ★★★, *Seven Day Weekend* (Jive 1985) ★★★, *Chasing Shadows* (Island 1987) ★★★, as Dream Command *Fire On The Moon* (Island 1990) ★★, *My Minds Eye* (RPM 1992) ★★★, *The Glamour* (Thunderbird 1995) ★★★.
● COMPILATIONS: *Enz* Dutch release (Polydor 1984) ★★, *Time Considered As A Helix Of Semi-Precious Stones* (RPM 1992) ★★★★, *Unravelled* (RPM 1994) ★★★, *From Beyond 2: 1987–1995* (Cherry Red 2002) ★★★★.

## CONFLICT

This anarchist punk band was formed in south-east London, England, in 1979, previously existing under a variety of names such as Splattered Rock Stars. Having followed Crass around the country they were essentially motivated by similar concerns: pacifism, animal welfare and anarchism. 'We call ourselves anarchists. That doesn't mean we believe in chaos – our ideal society would be one of small self-governing communities, with people being able to run their own lives. But above all we're trying to say that we don't want to be used by the political left or right.' Conflict played their first gig in their native Eltham in April 1981. The band's line-up remains very fluid, but revolves around singer Colin Jerwood (b. 6 May 1962, London, England; vocals), with Paul Fryday the technician, visuals supervisor and general motivator. Their debut EP *The House That Man Built* was released on Crass Records in June 1982. 'To A Nation Of Animal Lovers', on which Crass' Steve Ignorant guested, saw the band faced with incitement charges over the cover. Their policy of direct action in protest for many causes, in particular the Orkney seal hunters, led to many live appearances being broken up by police action. Other controversial releases included 'The Serenade Is Dead' and 'Better Dead Than Wed', the latter a joint venture with Class War released to celebrate the royal wedding of Prince Andrew and Sarah Ferguson in 1986. Of the band's numerous line-up changes, the most significant was the two-year tenure of Ignorant as joint vocalist between 1987 and 1989. Jerwood, meanwhile, was assaulted at a pub in Eltham, nearly losing the use of his eye in the process. Conflict set up their own Mortarhate label, going on to release albums throughout subsequent decades for a loyal audience of social miscreants. The best of these efforts were the studio side of *Increase The Pressure* and *The Ungovernable Force*, in 1984 and 1985, respectively. The wide-scale rioting that occurred after the band's 1987 Brixton Academy gig was documented by *Turning Rebellion Into Money*. In 1993, the band recorded their first 7-inch single ('These Colours Don't Run') since 1984, followed in December by an album, *Conclusion*. After several years inactivity in the mid-90s, the band has resumed touring and recording.

● ALBUMS: *It's Time To See Who's Who* (Corpus Christi 1983) ★★★, *Increase The Pressure* (Mortarhate 1984) ★★★, *The Ungovernable Force* (Mortarhate 1985) ★★★, *Only Stupid Bastards Help EMI* (Mortarhate 1986) ★★, *Turning Rebellion Into Money* (Mortarhate 1987) ★★, *The Final Conflict* (Mortarhate 1988) ★★★, *Against All Odds* (Mortarhate 1989) ★★, *Conclusion* (Mortarhate 1993) ★★, *It's Time To See Who's Who Now* expanded reissue (Mortarhate 1994) ★★★, *In The Venue* (Mortarhate 1994) ★★.

● COMPILATIONS: *From Protest To Resistance* (Mortarhate 1986) ★★★, *Standard Issue 82–87* (UK) *Employing All Means Necessary* (US) (Mortarhate 1988) ★★★, *Standard Issue 2* (Mortarhate 1994) ★★★, *Deploying All Means Necessary* (Mortarhate 1996) ★★★, *There Must Be Another Way: The Singles* (Mortarhate 2001) ★★★.

## CONNICK, HARRY, JNR.

b. Joseph Harry Fowler Connick, 11 September 1967, New Orleans, Louisiana, USA. As a pianist and singer, Connick is a young man with a sound that has been around for some time, often being favourably compared to Frank Sinatra. Connick's studied influences take in many from the late 40s and 50s, encompassing bebop, 'cocktail' jazz and swing. Despite the critical acclaim afforded to his first two albums, it was not until he sung a group of standard songs on the soundtrack of the 1989 movie *When Harry Met Sally*, that Connick came to national prominence. His work on the film earned him the Grammy Award for Male Jazz Vocal, and his clean cut, chisel-jawed good looks, plus a penchant for sharp suits, made him a favourite with the ladies. He won another Grammy in 1990 for *We Are In Love*. Supported by Shannon Powell (drums) and Ben Wolfe (bass), Connick's Trio has earned sufficient plaudits from their jazz peers, endorsed by *Blue Light, Red Light* elevation to number 1 on the *Billboard* jazz chart. In 1990, he extended himself further when he played the role of a crewmember of a US B17 bomber aircraft in the World War II movie, *Memphis Belle*, and a year later co-starred with Jodie Foster in *Little Man Tate*.

In 1992, Connick was arrested, and charged with having a 9mm pistol in his possession while passing through Kennedy Airport, New York. He spent a night in jail before agreeing to make a public service television commercial warning against breaking gun laws, in exchange for a promise to drop the charges if he stayed out of trouble for six months. After giving a splendid, 'old-fashioned' rendering of the Oscar-nominated 'A Wink And A Smile' in the 1993 movie *Sleepless In Seattle*, Connick's 1994 album *She*, and his *Funk Tour* of the UK in the same year, came as somewhat of a surprise. It signalled a departure from the 'smooth crooning' and a move to down-home New Orleans funk – or as one of the many disillusioned fans who left before the end of each performance put it: 'We expected Frank Sinatra but we got Motörhead instead.' Connick continues to balance his music and acting careers, and in 1998 made a credible leading man alongside Sandra Bullock in *Hope Floats*. In autumn 2001, he released a solo piano album and a disc of Hollywood show tunes recorded with his big band and orchestra, in addition to providing the music to the Broadway musical *Thou Shalt Not*.

● ALBUMS: *Harry Connick Jr.* (Columbia 1987) ★★★, *20* (Columbia 1988) ★★★, *When Harry Met Sally* film soundtrack (Columbia 1989) ★★★★, *We Are In Love* (Columbia 1990) ★★★, as the Harry Connick Jnr. Trio *Lofty's Roach Souffle* (Columbia 1990) ★★, *Blue Light, Red Light* (Columbia 1991) ★★★, *Eleven* (Columbia 1992) ★★★, *25* (Columbia 1992) ★★★, *When My Heart Finds Christmas* (Columbia 1993) ★★, *She* (Columbia 1994) ★★, *Star Turtle* (Columbia 1996) ★★★, *To See You* (Columbia 1997) ★★★, *Come By Me* (Columbia 1999) ★★★, *Songs I Heard* (Columbia 2001) ★★, *30* (Columbia 2001) ★★★.

● VIDEOS: *Singin' And Swingin'* (Sony Music Video 1990), *Swinging Out Live* (Sony Music Video 1992), *The New York Big Band Concert* (Sony Music Video 1993).

● FURTHER READING: *Wild About Harry: The Illustrated Biography*, Antonia Felix.

● FILMS: *Memphis Belle* (1990), *Little Man Tate* (1991), *Copycat* (1995), *Independence Day* (1996), *Excess Baggage* (1997), *Action League Now!!* voice (1997), *Hope Floats* (1998), *The Iron Giant* voice only (1999), *Wayward Son* (1999), *My Dog Skip* voice only (2000), *The Simian Line* (2000), *Life Without Dick* (2001), *Mickey* (2002).

## COPE, JULIAN

b. 21 October 1957, Deri, Glamorgan, Wales. Cope first attracted attention as an integral part of Liverpool's post-punk renaissance, most notably as a member of the short-lived but seminal group the Crucial Three, which also included Ian McCulloch and Pete Wylie. In 1978 Cope began writing songs with Ian McCulloch in A Shallow Madness, but the pair quickly fell out over the direction of the group. While McCulloch formed Echo And The Bunnymen, Cope founded the Teardrop Explodes whose early releases enjoyed critical acclaim. The band had several hit singles but an introspective second album, *Wilder*, was heavily criticized before dissent within the ranks led to their demise. In 1984 Cope embarked on a solo career with *World Shut Your Mouth*, but misfortune dogged his progress. The singer intentionally gashed his stomach with a broken microphone stand during an appearance at London's Hammersmith Palais and his pronouncements on the benefits of mind-expanding substances exacerbated an already wayward, unconventional image.

The sleeve of his second album, *Fried*, featured a naked Cope cowering under a turtle shell and commentators drew parallels with rock casualties Roky Erickson and Syd Barrett, both of whom Cope admired. Another of his heroes, Scott Walker, enjoyed an upsurge in interest in his recordings when Cope constantly gave the reclusive 60s singer name-checks in interviews. A third album, *Skellington*, was rejected by his label, which resulted in Cope switching to Island Records. Paradoxically he then enjoyed a UK Top 20 single with 'World Shut Your Mouth'. *Saint Julian* became the artist's bestselling album to date, but a tour to promote Cope's next collection, *My Nation Underground*, was abandoned when he became too ill to continue. Over subsequent months Cope maintained a low profile, but re-emerged in 1990 at London's anti-Poll Tax demonstration dressed in the costume of a space alien, Mr Sqwubbsy. However, this unconventional behaviour was tempered by a new realism and in 1991 he enjoyed another major hit with 'Beautiful Love'. Commentators also noted a new-found maturity on the attendant double album, *Peggy Suicide*, which garnered considerable praise.

Two albums for his mail-order record companies followed. However, none of this was enough to discourage Island from dropping the artist following the release of *Jehovakill*, though the move caused considerable surprise within critical circles (in retrospect it may have had more to do with Cope's legendary contrariness and recessionary times than any comment on his ability). *Autogeddon* provided no clear-cut evidence as to whether or not his powers were on the wane, but kept the faithful happy for another year. *Julian Cope Presents 20 Mothers* was conceived as a double album of 'devotional songs ranging from pagan rock 'n' roll through sci-fi pop to bubblegum trance-music'. In a review of 1996's *Interpreter*, *Q* magazine succinctly labelled Cope 'the Andrew Lloyd Webber of garage rock', but the singer has been relatively quiet on the recording front since then. He teamed up with Kevlar and Dogman to form the 'psycho metal supergroup' Brain Donor, who released *Love Peace And Fuck* in 2001.

Cope is also a respected writer, publishing two witty autobiographical volumes, the passionate *Krautrocksampler*, a study of the German 'Krautrock' bands who had such a great musical influence on him, and *The Modern Antiquarian*, a weighty guide to Great Britain's megalithic sites which Cope spent most of the 90s researching.

● ALBUMS: *World Shut Your Mouth* (Mercury 1984) ★★★, *Fried* (Mercury 1984) ★★★, *Saint Julian* (Island 1987) ★★★★, *My Nation Underground* (Island 1988) ★★★, *Skellington* (Capeco-Zippo 1990) ★★★, *Droolian* (Mofoco-Zippo 1990) ★★, *Peggy Suicide* (Island 1991) ★★★★, *Jehovakill* (Island 1993) ★★, *Autogeddon* (Echo 1994) ★★, *Rite* (Echo 1994) ★★, *Queen Elizabeth* (Echo 1994) ★★, *Julian Cope Presents 20 Mothers* (Echo 1995) ★★★, *Interpreter* (Echo 1996) ★★★★, *Rite 2* (Head Heritage 1997) ★★, *Discover Odin: Julian Cope At The British Museum* (Head Heritage 2001) ★★.

● COMPILATIONS: *Floored Genius – The Best Of Julian Cope And The Teardrop Explodes 1981–91* (Island 1992) ★★★★, *Floored Genius 2 – Best Of The BBC Sessions 1983–91* (Nighttracks 1993) ★★★, *The Followers Of Saint Julian* (Island 1997) ★★★, *Leper Grin: An Introduction To Julian Cope* (Island 1999)

★★★★, *Floored Genius 3: Julian Cope's Oddicon Of Lost Rarities & Versions (1978–98)* (Head Heritage 2000) ★★★, *The Collection* (Spectrum 2002) ★★★.

● VIDEOS: *Copeulation* (Island Visual Arts 1989).

● FURTHER READING: *Head-On: Memories Of The Liverpool Punk Scene And The Story Of The Teardrop Explodes (1976–82)*, Julian Cope. *Krautrocksampler: One Head's Guide To Great Kosmische Music*, Julian Cope. *The Modern Antiquarian: A Pre-Millennial Odyssey Through Megalithic Britain*, Julian Cope. *Repossessed: Shamanic Depressions In Tamworth & London (1983–89)*, Julian Cope.

## COPELAND, STEWART

b. 16 July 1952, Alexandria, Egypt. Following the dissolution of the hugely successful Police in 1986, Copeland has kept his career going without ever overworking chart compilers. He began his career in the progressive group Curved Air (his long-time girlfriend and later wife Sonja Kristina was the singer), and then took up the mantle of 'Welsh' artist Klark Kent, under whose guise he issued a 10-inch album, shaped as a 'K', and pressed on green vinyl. He was also widely rumoured to have been involved as the drummer in the UK's notorious Moors Murderers.

After the Police disbanded, Copeland immersed himself in television and film recording projects. He wrote, produced, and played most of the music for Francis Ford Coppola's movie *Rumble Fish*. Without an obvious reliance on percussion, Copeland's score was hugely effective, though like so many soundtracks it failed to transfer to vinyl successfully. However, 'Don't Box Me In', co-written and sung by ex-Wall Of Voodoo vocalist Stan Ridgway, is perfectly listenable. A second album, *The Rhythmatist*, offered a Paul Simon-like cultural survey of the sounds of Africa within a rock idiom. Fusing rhythms from Zaire, Burundi, Kenya, Tanzania and the Congo, Copeland found a rich seam of ethnic music to mine. The album also introduced solo artist Ray Lema to the west, and it is his vocals that are the record's high point. Copeland's next soundtrack work was to become his most famous as he penned the theme tune to morally asinine and gratuitously violent US television serial *The Equalizer*. Despite the subject matter, Copeland's compositions were never less than interesting and, in the case of the synthesizer-driven title track, they could be genuinely tuneful. After this and other oddments from the series were cobbled together for a patchy album released in 1988, Copeland moved on to work with Stanley Clarke and Deborah Holland in Animal Logic. During the following decade, he worked on the soundtracks for *Rapa Nui*, *The Leopard Son*, *Four Days In September* and *Simpatico*.

● ALBUMS: *Rumble Fish* film soundtrack (A&M 1983) ★★, *The Rhythmatist* (A&M 1985) ★★★, *The Equalizer & Other Cliff Hangers* soundtrack (I.R.S. 1988) ★★, *Rapa Nui* film soundtrack (Milan 1994) ★★★, *Silent Fall* film soundtrack (Morgan Creek 1994) ★★★, *The Leopard Son* film soundtrack (Ark 21 1996) ★★★.

● VIDEOS: *The Rhythmatist* (A&M Sound Pictures 1988).

## CORNWELL, HUGH

b. 28 August 1949, London, England. Cornwell had long since launched his solo career before his defection in August 1990 from the Stranglers, with whom he was lead vocalist and guitarist. His extracurricular activities began in 1979, when he recorded an album, *Nosferatu*, with Captain Beefheart drummer Robert Williams, which also featured contributions from members of Devo. It is of considerable interest to Stranglers fans as it prefigures some of the lyrical and musical concerns of the band in the next decade. Cornwell returned to the Stranglers for much of the 80s, enduring several adventures, not least a jail term for heroin possession which he would later recall in a privately published indictment of the justice system – *Who Guards The Guards?*. He also appeared alongside Bob Hoskins in a London stage play. Cornwell's next album, *Wolf*, was a hugely disappointing affair, a limp attempt to carve a pop niche. Rightly considered a potent songwriter for his work with the Stranglers, this attempt to convert himself into a gruff Ray Davies fell flat, despite the presence of old pals Jools Holland and Mani Elias (Tears For Fears). The album had been prefaced by one notable single, 1987's 'Facts + Figures', which featured on the soundtrack of the animated film *When The Wind Blows*.

Following his departure from the Stranglers after 16 years, Cornwell started to develop songs he had already half-written while still with the band. Before unveiling these, he collaborated with Roger Cook and Andy West for the largely ignored *CCW* album. Afterwards he recruited former collaborator Williams (drums), Alex Gifford (bass), Ted Mason and Chris Goulstone (guitars) and Art Of Noise producer Gary Langan to shape *Wired*. Far superior to its predecessor, this collection of songs revealed a grasp of vibrant pop. *Guilty*, released in 1997, continued this move towards the mainstream. The album was given an American release, under the title *Black Hair Black Eyes Black Suit*, two years later (*Wired* was also issued in the US under a different title, *First Bus To Babylon*). At the end of the decade Cornwell released three Internet-only albums on his own His Records imprint, and recorded tracks for his new studio album, *Hi Fi*.

● ALBUMS: with Robert Williams *Nosferatu* (United Artists 1979) ★★★, *Wolf* (Virgin 1988) ★★, with CCW *CCW* (UFO 1992) ★★, *Wired* (UK) *First Bus To Babylon* (US) (Transmission/Velvel 1993) ★★★, *Guilty* (UK) *Black Hair Black Eyes Black Suit* (US) (Madfish/Velvel 1997) ★★★, *Mayday* (His 1999) ★★★, *Solo* (His 1999) ★★★, *Sons Of Shiva* (His 1999) ★★, *Hi Fi* (Koch 2000) ★★★, *Footprints In The Desert* (Track 2002) ★★★.

## CORROSION OF CONFORMITY

This mid-80s American hardcore crossover band, originally known as No Labels, was formed in Raleigh, North Carolina, USA, in 1982 by Reed Mullin (drums), Woody Weatherman (guitar) and Mike Dean (bass/vocals), and rose to become one of the biggest draws on the US underground scene with their stunning live shows. *Eye For An Eye*, with

vocals supplied by Eric Eyke, separated them from the pack by mixing hardcore speed with Black Sabbath and Deep Purple-influenced power riffing. A more metallic crossover style became evident with *Animosity*, although the band lost neither their aggression nor their hardcore ideals. Following the blistering *Technocracy*, with Simon Bob (ex-Ugly Americans) on vocals, the size of the band's audience expanded with the rise of thrash, but record company problems and the loss of Simon Bob and Dean led to Corrosion Of Conformity's collapse. However, just when it seemed that *Six Songs With Mike Singing* would be their epitaph, Corrosion Of Conformity returned, with Mullin and Weatherman joined by Karl Agell (vocals, ex-School Of Violence), Pepper Keenan (guitar/vocals) and Phil Swisher (bass).

Impressive tours with D.R.I. and Danzig helped to gain a new recording contract, and the acclaimed *Blind* saw the band adopt a slower, more melodic, but still fiercely heavy style. It also continued the hardcore lyrical stance of an increasingly politically active band, challenging social, political, and ecological issues. Success with 'Vote With A Bullet' and electrifying live shows, including a UK tour supporting Soundgarden, re-established Corrosion Of Conformity as a force, but the departure of Agell and Swisher slowed the momentum once more. *Deliverance*, with Keenan taking lead vocals and Dean back in place, saw the band incorporate ever more diverse influences into their weighty sound, adding southern rock grooves and, perhaps most surprisingly, Thin Lizzy-style guitar harmonies for a varied album that was a considerable departure from their hardcore musical roots. The hardcore image continued to fade as *Wiseblood* demonstrated an excellent grasp of 70s heavy rock. After a four-year recording gap they returned in 2000 with *America's Volume Dealer*, once again demonstrating a continuing influence from the Allman Brothers Band and the Marshall Tucker Band.

● ALBUMS: *Eye For An Eye* (No Core 1984) ★★★, *Animosity* (Combat 1985) ★★★, *Technocracy* mini-album (Combat 1987) ★★★, *Six Songs With Mike Singing* mini-album, 1985 recording (Caroline 1988) ★★, *Blind* (Combat 1991) ★★★, *Deliverance* (Sony 1994) ★★★, *Wiseblood* (Sony 1996) ★★★, *America's Volume Dealer* (Sanctuary 2000) ★★★, *Live Volume* (Sanctuary 2001) ★★.

## COSTELLO, ELVIS

b. Declan McManus, 25 August 1954, Paddington, London, England, but brought up in Liverpool. The son of singer and bandleader Ross McManus first came to prominence during the UK punk era of 1977. The former computer programmer toured A&R offices giving impromptu performances. While appealing to the new wave market, the sensitive issues he wrote about, combined with the structures in which he composed them, indicated a major talent that would survive and outgrow this musical generation. Following a brief tenure in the country rock act Flip City he was signed as a solo act to Dave Robinson's pioneering Stiff Records. Costello failed to chart with his early releases, which included the anti-fascist 'Less Than Zero' and the sublime ballad 'Alison'. His Nick Lowe-produced debut, *My Aim Is True*, featured members of the cult west coast band Clover, who in turn had Huey Lewis as their vocalist. The album introduced a new pinnacle in late 70s songwriting. Costello spat, shouted and crooned through a cornucopia of radical issues, producing a set that was instantly hailed by the critics.

Costello's first hit single, 'Watching The Detectives', contained scathing verses about wife-beating over a beautifully simple reggae beat. His new band, the Attractions, gave Costello a solid base: the combination of Bruce Thomas (b. Stockton-on-Tees, Cleveland, England; bass), ex-Chilli Willi And The Red Hot Peppers' Pete Thomas (b. 9 August 1954, Sheffield, Yorkshire, England; drums) and Steve Nieve (b. Steven Nason; keyboards), became an integral part of the Costello sound. The Attractions provided the backing on the strong follow-up, *This Year's Model*, and further magnificent singles ensued prior to the release of another landmark album, *Armed Forces*. This vitriolic collection narrowly missed the coveted number 1 position in the UK and reached the Top 10 in the USA. Costello's standing across the Atlantic was seriously dented by his regrettably flippant dismissal of Ray Charles as 'an ignorant, blind nigger', an opinion he later recanted. 'Oliver's Army', a major hit taken from the album, was a bitter attack on the mercenary soldier, sung over a contrastingly upbeat tune.

By the end of the, 70s Costello was firmly established as both performer and songwriter, with Linda Ronstadt and Dave Edmunds having success with his compositions. In 1980 he released the soul-influenced *Get Happy!!*, another fine album which failed to repeat the sales success of *Armed Forces*. The increasingly fraught nature of the Attractions' recording sessions informed the follow-up, *Trust*, and during the same year Costello elected to relocate to Nashville to record a country covers album, *Almost Blue*, with the Attractions and legendary producer Billy Sherrill. A version of George Jones' 'Good Year For The Roses' became the album's major hit, although a superb reading of Patsy Cline's 'Sweet Dreams' was a comparative failure. The following year, with seven albums already behind him, the prolific Costello returned to his own material and released the outstanding collection, *Imperial Bedroom*. Many of the songs herein were romantic excursions into mistrust and deceit, including 'Man Out Of Time' and 'Tears Before Bedtime'. The fast paced 'Beyond Belief' was a perfect example of vintage Costello lyricism: 'History repeats the old conceits/the glib replies the same defeats/keep your finger on important issues with crocodile tears and a pocketful of tissues'. That year Robert Wyatt recorded arguably the best-ever interpretation of a Costello song. The superlative 'Shipbuilding' offered an imposingly subtle indictment of the Falklands War, with Wyatt's strained voice giving extra depth to Costello's seamless lyric. The next year Costello as the Imposter released 'Pills And Soap', a similar theme cleverly masking a bellicose attack on Thatcherism.

Both *Punch The Clock* and *Goodbye Cruel World*

favoured a rich production sound, courtesy of Clive Langer and Alan Winstanley. The prolific Costello also found the time to produce albums by the Specials, Squeeze, the Bluebells and the Pogues (where he met future wife, Cait O'Riordan), and during 1984 played a retarded brother on BBC television in Alan Bleasdale's *Scully*, which would not be the last time he would attempt a low-key acting career. The following year Costello took to a different stage at Live Aid, and in front of millions sang John Lennon's 'All You Need Is Love'. His cover version of the Animals' 'Don't Let Me Be Misunderstood' was a minor hit in 1986 and during another punishing year, Costello released two albums. First was the rock 'n' roll-influenced *King Of America*, with notable production from T-Bone Burnett and guitar contributions from the legendary James Burton. Then, reunited with the Attractions and producer Nick Lowe, Costello stalled with the less successful *Blood & Chocolate*.

Towards the end of the 80s he collaborated with Paul McCartney, co-writing a number of songs for *Flowers In The Dirt*. A new recording contract with Warner Brothers Records was now in place, and Costello returned after a brief hiatus (by his standards) with the eclectic *Spike* in 1989. During 1990, he wrote and sang with Roger McGuinn for his 1991 comeback album *Back To Rio*. During that year, a hirsute Costello co-wrote the soundtrack to the controversial television series *G.B.H.* (written by Alan Bleasdale) and delivered another artistic success, *Mighty Like A Rose*. With lyrics as sharp as any of his previous work, this introspective and reflective album had Costello denying he was ever cynical – merely realistic. His perplexing collaboration with the Brodsky Quartet in 1993 was a brave yet commercially ignored outing. *Brutal Youth* brought him back to critical approbation and reunited him with the Attractions. *Kojak Variety* was a second album of cover versions recorded in 1991 but released four years later, with selections from major artists such as 'Screamin'' Jay' Hawkins, the Supremes, Bob Dylan, Willie Dixon, Ray Davies and Bert Bacharach and Hal David. The new studio set, *All This Useless Beauty* (again with the Attractions), although containing songs offered to or recorded by other artists, was as lyrically sharp as ever. The *Extreme Honey* compilation marked the end of Costello's contract with Warners. Collecting a varied selection of material, the album included a new track, 'The Bridge I Burned', which demonstrated that Costello's creative abilities were as sharp as ever.

Costello signed a worldwide deal with PolyGram Records in February 1998. Following their collaboration on the track 'God Give Me Strength', featured in the 1996 movie *Grace Of My Heart*, Costello and songwriting legend Burt Bacharach joined forces on 1998's *Painted From Memory*, a finely crafted collection of ballads. 'I Still Have That Other Girl' won a 1999 Grammy for Best Pop Collaboration With Vocals. The two worked together again on a cover version of Bacharach and David's 'I'll Never Fall In Love Again' for the soundtrack to Mike Myers' *Austin Powers: The Spy Who Shagged Me*. Costello's cover version of Charles Aznavour's 'She' also figured prominently in the Hugh Grant/Julia Roberts film, *Notting Hill*, and returned the singer to the UK Top 20 in July. The following year he composed the orchestral score for Italian ballet troupe Aterballetto's adaptation of *A Midsummer Night's Dream*. A stirring collaboration with opera singer Anne Sofie Van Otter in 2001 preceded a new 'pop' album, *When I Was Cruel*.

Although Costello no longer tops the charts he remains a critics' favourite, and is without doubt one of the finest songwriter/lyricists England has ever produced. His contribution was acknowledged in 1996 when he collected Q magazine's songwriter award. His left-of-centre political views have not clouded his horizon and he is now able to assimilate all his musical influences and to some degree, rightly indulge himself.

● ALBUMS: *My Aim Is True* (Stiff/Columbia 1977) ★★★★, with the Attractions *This Year's Model* (Radar/Columbia 1978) ★★★★★, with the Attractions *Armed Forces* (Radar/Columbia 1979) ★★★, with the Attractions *Get Happy!!* (F-Beat/Columbia 1980) ★★★★, with the Attractions *Trust* (F-Beat/Columbia 1981) ★★★★, with the Attractions *Almost Blue* (F-Beat/Columbia 1981) ★★★, with the Attractions *Imperial Bedroom* (F-Beat/Columbia 1982) ★★★★★, with the Attractions *Punch The Clock* (F-Beat/Columbia 1983) ★★★, with the Attractions *Goodbye Cruel World* (F-Beat/Columbia 1984) ★★★, *King Of America* (Demon/Columbia 1986) ★★★★, with the Attractions *Blood & Chocolate* (Demon/Columbia 1986) ★★★, *Spike* (Warners 1989) ★★★, *Mighty Like A Rose* (Warners 1991) ★★★, with Richard Harvey *G.B.H.: Original Music From The Channel Four Series* (Demon Soundtracks 1991) ★★★, with the Brodsky Quartet *The Juliet Letters* (Warners 1993) ★★★★, with the Attractions *Brutal Youth* (Warners 1994) ★★★, *Kojak Variety* (Warners 1995) ★★, with Bill Frisell *Deep Dead Blue: Live 25 June 95* (Nonesuch 1995) ★★★, with Harvey *Original Music From Jake's Progress* (Demon Soundtracks 1996) ★★, with the Attractions *All This Useless Beauty* (Warners 1996) ★★★, with Steve Nieve *Costello & Nieve* (Warners 1996) ★★★, with Burt Bacharach *Painted From Memory: The New Songs Of Bacharach & Costello* (Mercury 1998) ★★★, with Anne Sofie Von Otter *For The Stars* (Deutsche Grammophon 2001) ★★★★, *When I Was Cruel* (Mercury 2002) ★★★.

● COMPILATIONS: *Taking Liberties* (Columbia 1980) ★★★★, *Ten Bloody Marys And Ten Hows Your Fathers* (Demon 1980) ★★★★, *The Best Of Elvis Costello – The Man* (Telstar 1985) ★★★★, *Out Of Our Idiot* (Demon 1987) ★★★, *Girls Girls Girls* (Demon 1989) ★★★★★, *The Very Best Of ... 1977–1986* (Demon 1994) ★★★★, *Extreme Honey: The Very Best Of The Warner Bros. Years* (Warners 1997) ★★★★, various artists *Bespoke Songs, Lost Dogs, Detours & Rendezvous: Songs Of Elvis Costello* (Rhino 1998) ★★★★, *The Very Best Of Elvis Costello* (Universal 1999) ★★★★.

● VIDEOS: *Best Of Elvis Costello* (Palace Video 1986), with Brodsky Quartet *The Juliet Letters* (Warner Vision 1993), *The Very Best Of* (1994), *Live: A Case*

*For Song* (Warner Vision 1996), with Burt Bacharach *Painted From Memory: The New Songs Of Bacharach & Costello* (Mercury 1998).

● FURTHER READING: *Elvis Costello: Completely False Biography Based On Rumour, Innuendo And Lies*, Krista Reese. *Elvis Costello*, Mick St. Michael. *Elvis Costello. A Man Out Of Time*, David Gouldstone. *The Big Wheel*, Bruce Thomas. *Going Through The Motions (Elvis Costello 1982–1985)*, Richard Groothuizen and Kees Den Heyer. *Elvis Costello: A Biography*, Tony Clayton-Lea. *Elvis Costello: A Bio-Bibliography*, David E. Perone. *Let Them All Talk: The Music Of Elvis Costello*, Brian Hinton. *Elvis Costello*, David Sheppard.

● FILMS: *Americathon* (1979), *No Surrender* (1985), *Straight To Hell* (1987), *Spice World* (1997), *200 Cigarettes* (1999), *Austin Powers: The Spy Who Shagged Me* (1999), *Sans Plomb* aka *Unleaded* (2000), *Prison Song* (2000).

## COUGHLAN, MARY

b. 5 May 1956, Co. Galway, Eire. This acclaimed Irish singer's troubled upbringing manifested itself in an erratic career path, including stints as a model and a street-sweeper. After moving to London in the mid-70s, she married and began raising a family, before terminating the union and returning to Galway with her children. She began her singing career in 1984, working with Dutch musician Erik Visser (who became her long-term collaborator). The following year she made an acclaimed appearance on the *Late Late Show* and recorded her first album, which showcased her powerful and bluesy jazz stylings and became an unexpected bestseller in her native Ireland. Despite her ongoing personal problems, Coughlan continued to reap praise for her recorded output on WEA Records. On *Under The Influence* she revived the 1948 Peggy Lee hit 'Don't Smoke In Bed' and the Billie Holiday ballad 'Good Morning Heartache', as well as Christy Moore's 'Ride On'.

In 1988, Coughlan made her acting debut in Neil Jordan's *High Spirits*, and released *Ancient Rain*. Her fourth album, *Uncertain Pleasures*, was recorded in England with producer Peter Glenister, former musical director for Terence Trent D'Arby. It included new compositions by Mark Nevin (Fairground Attraction) and Bob Geldof as well as cover versions of the Rolling Stones' 'Mother's Little Helper' and the Elvis Presley hit 'Heartbreak Hotel'. Coughlan began straightening her personal life out in the mid-90s, and signed a new recording contract with Big Cat Records. The label issued an excellent live set and her US debut, *After The Fall*. In June 2000, Coughlan presented a series of multimedia shows in Dublin celebrating Billie Holiday, a singer whose life story has close parallels to Coughlan's own. The best of these shows was collected on the wonderful *Sings Billie Holiday*. A new studio album was released the following April.

● ALBUMS: *Tired And Emotional* (WEA 1985) ★★★, *Under The Influence* (WEA 1987) ★★★★, *Ancient Rain* (WEA 1988) ★★★, *Uncertain Pleasures* (East West 1990) ★★★★, *Sentimental Killer* (East West 1992) ★★★, *Love For Sale* (Demon 1993) ★★★, *Live In Galway* (Big Cat 1996) ★★★★, *After The Fall* (Big

Cat/V2 1997) ★★★, *Sings Billie Holiday* (Evangeline 2000) ★★★★, *Long Honeymoon* (Evangeline 2001) ★★★, *Red Blues* (Tradition & Moderne 2002) ★★★.
● COMPILATIONS: *Love Me Or Leave Me: The Best Of Mary Coughlan* (WEA 1994) ★★★★.
● FILMS: *High Spirits* (1988), *The Miracle* (1991).

## COUNTY, JAYNE/WAYNE

b. Wayne Rogers, 13 July 1947, Dallas, Georgia, USA. One of the most intriguing artists thrown up by the 'no rules' exchanges of late 70s punk was transsexual vocalist and songwriter Wayne County. The artist had grown up on stages in seedy New York clubs playing alongside the New York Dolls, revelling in an act that approximated the Dolls' sleaze rock combined with various acts of vulgarity. Adopting the name Wayne County, he soon found kindred spirits in Andy Warhol's enclave and the Max's Kansas City crowd, and formed the bands Queen Elizabeth and Wayne And The Backstreet Boys. County then migrated to London, England, just as the punk scene in that metropolis was taking hold. Consequently none of County's albums were ever released in his/her own country. Together with a rudimentary but competent backing band, titled the Electric Chairs, the group made its debut with a self-titled album for Safari Records in 1978. The Electric Chairs' most popular live numbers at this stage were the enduring low-rent punk favourites 'Fuck Off' and 'Cream In My Jeans'. 'Eddie And Sheena', meanwhile, became a minor hit in the genre, with its depiction of a crushed love affair between a Ted (rock 'n' roll revivalist) and a punk – two warring factions during the late 70s. However, two subsequent albums, with a new line-up of the Electric Chairs, proved less inspiring, with the shock value of County's performances provoking a diminishing reaction. *Rock 'N' Roll Resurrection*, a live show in Toronto, Canada, was the first to be credited to Jayne County, and it was subsequently reported that the artist had undergone a sex change (this was not true – the assumption was largely based on speculation caused by the change of name). After a career lull (and, allegedly, a nervous breakdown) the artist returned in 1986 with the self-produced *Private Oyster*, though there had been little other artistic development. A second return came in 1994, at which time she unveiled her new band, Queen Elizabeth. The ensuing *Deviation* was as warped as ever, while 1996's no holds-barred-biography proved as entertaining as expected.
● ALBUMS: *The Electric Chairs* (Safari 1978) ★★★, as Wayne County And The Electric Chairs *Storm The Gates Of Heaven* (Safari 1978) ★★★, as Wayne County And The Electric Chairs *Things Your Mother Never Told You* (Safari 1979) ★★, as Jayne County And The Electric Chairs *Rock 'N' Roll Resurrection* (Safari 1980) ★★★, as Jayne County *Private Oyster* (Revolver 1986) ★★, as Jayne County *Betty Grable's Legs* mini-album (Freud 1989) ★★, as Jayne County And The Electric Chairs *Deviation* (CSA/Royalty 1995) ★★.
● COMPILATIONS: *The Best Of Jayne/Wayne County And The Electric Chairs* (Safari 1981) ★★★, as Jayne County *Goddess Of Wet Dreams* (ESP 1993) ★★, as

Wayne County And The Electric Chairs *Rock 'N' Roll Cleopatra* (RPM/Royalty 1993) ★★★, as Jayne County And The Electric Chairs *Let Your Backbone Slip* (RPM 1995) ★★.
● FURTHER READING: *Man Enough To Be A Woman*, Jayne County with Rupert Smith.
● FILMS: *Jubilee* (1977).

## COWBOY JUNKIES

Toronto-based musicians Michael Timmins (b. 21 April 1959, Montreal, Canada; guitar) and Alan Anton (b. Alan Alizojvodic, 22 June 1959, Montreal, Canada; bass) formed a group called Hunger Project in 1979. It was not successful and, now basing themselves in the UK, they formed the experimental instrumental outfit, Germinal. Returning to Toronto, they joined forces with Timmins' sister Margo (b. 27 January 1961, Montreal, Canada; vocal) and brother Peter (b. 29 October 1965, Montreal, Canada; drums). As the Cowboy Junkies (which was simply an attention-grabbing name), they recorded their first album, *Whites Off Earth Now!!*, in a private house. Their second album, *The Trinity Session*, was made with one microphone in the Church of Holy Trinity, Toronto, for $250. The band's spartan, less-is-more sound captivated listeners and, with little publicity, the second album sold 250,000 copies in North America. The tracks included a curious reinterpretation of 'Blue Moon' called 'Blue Moon Revisited (Song For Elvis)' and the country standards, 'I'm So Lonesome I Could Cry' and 'Walkin' After Midnight'. Lou Reed praised their version of his song 'Sweet Jane', and in 1991, they contributed 'To Lay Me Down' to a tribute to the Grateful Dead, *Deadicated*. Their previous year's album *The Caution Horses* included several vintage country songs, which, true to form, were performed in their whispered, five miles-per-hour style.

The extent of the Cowboy Junkies' fast-growing reputation was sufficient for them to promote the 1992 album *Black Eyed Man* at London's Royal Albert Hall. By the release of 1995's *Lay It Down*, their debut for Geffen Records, the band had firmly settled into such a distinctive style that it was hard to see how they could expand their appeal to reach a wider audience. Critically acclaimed and cultishly adored, the album was recorded to the highest standards. Michael Timmins' understated guitar was very much the lead instrument, with barely a hint of a solo, perfectly complementing Margo Timmins' eerie vocals. *Miles From Our Home* was too well recorded for some, although there was no denying the quality that permeates everything the band releases. The live *Waltz Across America* documents highlights from the 1999/2000 North American tour.
● ALBUMS: *Whites Off Earth Now!!* (Latent/RCA 1986) ★★★, *The Trinity Session* (Latent/RCA 1988) ★★★★, *The Caution Horses* (RCA 1990) ★★★, *Black Eyed Man* (RCA 1992) ★★★, *Pale Sun, Crescent Moon* (RCA 1993) ★★★, *Lay It Down* (Geffen 1996) ★★★★, *Miles From Our Home* (Geffen 1998) ★★★, *Waltz Across America* (Latent 2000) ★★★, *Open* (Zöe/Cooking Vinyl 2001) ★★★.
● COMPILATIONS: *200 More Miles: Live Performances 1985–1994* (RCA 1995) ★★★★, *Selected*

*Studio Recordings 1986–1995* (RCA 1996) ★★★★, *Rarities, B-Sides And Slow, Sad Waltzes* (Latent 1999) ★★★.
● VIDEOS: *Open Road* (Zöe 2002).

## CRAIG, CARL

A prolific techno third columnist from Detroit, Michigan, Craig rose to prominence on Derrick May's Transmat Records imprint, releasing material under names like Psyche (famed for the pre-trance 'Crackdown' epic) and BFC (notably 'Static Friendly'). Originally he had been inspired by Kraftwerk and early Human League, but after supporting May as a component of Rhythm Is Rhythm his tastes broadened, taking a more ethno-centric view of his surroundings. Following recording sessions for 'Stringz Of Life '89' with May he set up his own label, Planet E, before a six-month sabbatical to England in 1990 (during which time Fragile released 'Galaxy').

Increasingly welcomed across two continents as a prime mover in the Detroit techno sound, Craig issued a plethora of subsequent material. Most notable among these were his collaboration with Maurizio ('Mind') and his work as Paperclip People ('Remake Uno'), which were licensed from Planet E to the Ministry Of Sound's Open label in the UK. He signed his 69 moniker to R&S Records in 1994. That name had first been employed for the epic 1991 12-inch track 'Ladies And Gentleman', which latterly found favour as a Sound On Sound reissue with DJs like DJ Pierre, Andrew Weatherall and Amsterdam's Dimitri. In the meantime the duo remixed 'Le Funk Mob' for Planet E, while Craig offered a new version of 'Throw' for Open. Craig has also performed remix work for prominent artists including the Orb, Yello and Tori Amos. He released his debut long-player (on Blanco y Negro) in 1995, but the follow-up *More Songs About Food And Revolutionary Art* offered more compelling evidence of Craig's superb melodic talent. Craig has subsequently recorded as Innerzone Orchestra.
● ALBUMS: *Landcruising* (Blanco y Negro 1995) ★★★, *More Songs About Food And Revolutionary Art* (SSR/Planet 1997) ★★★★, as Innerzone Orchestra *Programmed* (Talkin' Loud 1999) ★★★, *More Songs About Food* (Planet E 1999) ★★★.
● COMPILATIONS: *DJ-Kicks* (!K7 1996) ★★★, *Designer Music: The Remixes, Volume 1* (Planet E 2000) ★★★★, *Onsumothasheeat* (Shadow 2001) ★★★, *Abstract Funk Theory* (Obsessive 2001) ★★★★.

## CRAMPS

Formed in Ohio, USA, in 1976, the original Cramps, Lux Interior (b. Erick Lee Purkhiser; vocals), 'Poison' Ivy Rorschach (b. Kirsty Marlana Wallace; guitar), Bryan Gregory (d. 10 January 2001, Anaheim, California, USA; guitar) and his sister, Pam Balam (drums), later moved to New York, where they were embroiled in the emergent punk scene centred on the CBGB's rock venue. Miriam Linna briefly replaced Balam, before Nick Knox (b. Nick Stephanoff) became the band's permanent drummer. The Cramps' early work was recorded at the famed

Sun Records studio under the aegis of producer Alex Chilton. Their early singles and debut album blended the frantic rush of rockabilly with a dose of 60s garage-band panache and an obvious love of ghoulish b-movies. Bryan Gregory's sudden departure followed the release of the compulsive 'Drug Train' single. Former Gun Club acolyte Kid Congo (Powers) (b. Brian Tristan), appeared on *Psychedelic Jungle*, but he later rejoined his erstwhile colleagues and the Cramps subsequently employed several, often female, replacements, including Fur and Candy Del Mar.

Despite the band's momentum being rudely interrupted by a protracted legal wrangle with the I.R.S. Records label during the early 80s, the Cramps' horror-cum-trash style, supplemented with a healthy dose of humour and sex, has nonetheless remained intact throughout their career. However, the best examples of their work can still be found on their early albums (and compilations), with songs such as 'You've Got Good Taste', 'Human Fly' and 'I'm Cramped' perfectly capturing a moment in time in the evolution of alternative rock music. Next best is probably 1986's *A Date With Elvis*, which appealed because the formula was still relatively fresh.

Wary of outside manipulation, the Cramps continue to steer their own course by touring and recording, proving themselves the masters of their particular (limited) genre. Their live shows, especially, are rarely found wanting in terms of entertainment value. In 1991, Interior and Rorschach re-emerged fronting a rejuvenated line-up with Slim Chance (bass) and Jim Sclavunos (drums). *Flamejob*, released in 1994, showed that the band had become virtually a pantomime act, a fact that their most recent albums have sadly confirmed.
● ALBUMS: *Songs The Lord Taught Us* (Illegal/I.R.S. 1980) ★★★, *Psychedelic Jungle* (I.R.S. 1981) ★★★, *Smell Of Female* (Enigma 1983) ★★★, *A Date With Elvis* (Big Beat 1986) ★★★, *Rockinnreelininauucklandnewzelandxxx* (Vengeance 1987) ★★★, *Stay Sick* (Enigma 1990) ★★★, *Look Mom No Head!* (Big Beat 1991) ★★, *Flamejob* (Medicine 1994) ★★★, *Big Beat From Badsville* (Epitaph 1997) ★★.
● COMPILATIONS: *Off The Bone* (I.R.S. 1983) ★★★, *Bad Music For Bad People* (I.R.S. 1984) ★★★, *Greatest Hits* (BMG 1998) ★★★.
● FURTHER READING: *The Wild Wild World Of The Cramps*, Ian Johnston.

## CRASS

Formed in the UK in 1978 by Steve Ignorant and Penny Rimbaud, Crass' music was a confrontational hybrid of buzzsaw, offbeat guitars, military drumming and shouted vocals, but this was always secondary to their message. They believed in anarchy (which they defined as 'respect for yourself and others as human beings') and took their performances to hundreds of unlikely venues. Formed by the members of a commune based in North Weald, Essex, England, Crass had a fluid line-up. Its members wore black and adopted pseudonyms to 'save their message becoming diluted by personalities'. *Feeding Of The 5000* was raw and frantic, peppered with swear words but clearly authentic and heartfelt. *Stations Of The Crass*, a double album, offered more of the same and challenged contemporary issues such as the dissolution of the punk ethos ('White Punks On Hope') and British class divisions ('Time Out').

The band's most notorious offering was the post-Falklands war single, directed at the Prime Minister, Margaret Thatcher, 'How Does It Feel (To Be The Mother Of A 1,000 Dead)', which topped the UK Independent chart. The line-up at the time was listed as: Ignorant (vocals), Rimbaud (drums), Eve Libertine (vocals), Joy De Vivre (vocals), Phil Free (guitar), N.A. Palmer (guitar), Pete Wright (bass) and Mick 'G' Duffield (backing vocals). Crass maintained a high degree of autonomy through their own Crass Records label and supported other like-minded groups, notably Flux Of Pink Indians and Conflict. They issued three compilation albums of other people's music, *Bullshit Detectors 1, 2* and *3* (a title borrowed from the Clash song, a group that Crass often accused of 'selling out'), and released records by the Poison Girls, Captain Sensible, Rudimentary Peni, the Mob (which included Josef Porta, later of Blyth Power), the aforementioned Conflict and Flux, and many others. On *Penis Envy* the female members took on lead vocals and the record was a sustained and tuneful attack on sexism in modern society. It marked the band's creative apex; by *Christ The Album* and *Yes Sir, I Will* – where poetry and experimental music were combined – the initial energy and inspiration were missing. They split in 1984, as they often said they would, and to this day remain one of the few bands to loyally adhere to their original ideals. Steve Ignorant joined Conflict in the latter part of the 80s.

● ALBUMS: *Feeding Of The 5000* (Small Wonder 1978) ★★★, *Stations Of The Crass* (Crass 1980) ★★★, *Penis Envy* (Crass 1981) ★★★, *Yes Sir, I Will* (Crass 1982) ★★, *Christ The Album* (Crass 1983) ★★, *10 Notes On A Summer's Day* (Crass 1986) ★★★, *You'll Ruin It For Everyone* 1981 live recording (Pomona/Crass 1993) ★★★.
Solo: Penny Rimbaud And Eve Libertine *Acts Of Love* (Crass 1985) ★★.

● COMPILATIONS: *Best Before 1984* (Crass 1987) ★★★.

● VIDEOS: *Christ The Movie* (Exit Films).

● FURTHER READING: *Shibboleth: My Revolting Life*, Penny Rimbaud.

## CRAWFORD, RANDY

b. Veronica Crawford, 18 February 1952, Macon, Georgia, USA. Raised in Cincinnati, from the age of 15 Crawford was a regular performer at the city's nightclubs. She later moved to New York and began singing with several jazz musicians including George Benson and Cannonball Adderley. Crawford was subsequently signed to Warner Brothers Records as a solo act, but achieved fame as the (uncredited) voice on 'Street Life', a major hit single for the Crusaders in 1979. Crawford toured extensively with the group, whose pianist, Joe Sample, provided her with 'Now We May Begin', a beautiful ballad that established the singer's independent career. Crawford enjoyed

further successes with 'One Day I'll Fly Away' (UK number 2), 'You Might Need Somebody', 'Rainy Night In Georgia' (both UK Top 20 hits) and her 1981 album *Secret Combination*, considered by many to be her finest, reached number 2 in the UK. After a five-year respite, she made a return to the top flight of the chart in 1986 with 'Almaz', which reached the Top 5. Curiously, this soulful, passionate singer has found greater success in the UK than in her homeland, and the 1989 album *Rich And Poor* was recorded in London. By the new millennium, Crawford was fronting the gospel group the Kingsmen.

● ALBUMS: *Miss Randy Crawford* (Warners 1977) ★★★, *Raw Silk* (Warners 1979) ★★★★, *Now We May Begin* (Warners 1980) ★★★, *Everything Must Change* (Warners 1980) ★★, *Secret Combination* (Warners 1981) ★★★★, *Windsong* (Warners 1982) ★★, *Nightline* (Warners 1983) ★★★, *Abstract Emotions* (Warners 1986) ★★★, *Rich And Poor* (Warners 1989) ★★★, *Naked And True* (Bluemoon 1995) ★★★★, *Every Kind Of Mood: Randy, Randi, Randee* (Atlantic 1998) ★★★, *Permanent* (Warners 2001) ★★★★.

● COMPILATIONS: *Miss Randy Crawford – Greatest Hits* (K-Tel 1984) ★★★, *Love Songs* (Telstar 1987) ★★★, *The Very Best Of* (Dino 1992) ★★★, *The Best Of* (Warners 1996) ★★★★.

## CRAY, ROBERT

b. 1 August 1953, Columbus, Georgia, USA. The popularity of guitar-based blues during the 80s had much to do with the unassuming brilliance of Cray. Although he formed his first band in 1974, it was not until *Bad Influence* in 1983 that his name became widely known. His debut, *Who's Been Talkin'*, failed because the record label folded (it has since been reissued on Charly Records). Cray's music is a mixture of pure blues, soul and rock and his fluid, clean style owes much to Albert Collins and Peter Green, while on faster numbers a distinct Jimi Hendrix influence is heard. The Robert Cray Band features long-time bass player Richard Cousins, Dave Olson (drums) and Peter Boe (keyboards). *Strong Persuader* in 1987 became the most successful blues album for over two decades and Cray has taken this popularity with calm modesty. He is highly regarded by experienced stars like Eric Clapton, who in addition to recording Cray's 'Bad Influence', invited him to record with him and play at his 1989 marathon series of concerts at London's Royal Albert Hall.

In 1988 Cray consolidated his reputation with the superb *Don't Be Afraid Of The Dark*, which featured some raucous saxophone playing from David Sanborn. *Midnight Stroll* featured a new line-up that gave Cray a tougher-sounding unit and moved him out of mainstream blues towards R&B and soul. *Some Rainy Morning* was Cray's vocal album: there were no blinding solos to be found, but rather, a mature and sweet voice that prompted Cray to be viewed as a soul singer rather than a blues guitarist. Cray's quartet in the mid-90s featured Kevin Hayes (drums), Karl Sevareid (bass) and Jim Pugh (keyboards). *Sweet Potato Pie* featured the Memphis Horns on a cover version of Isaac Hayes and David

Porter's 'Trick Or Treat'. Cray moved to Rykodisc Records for 1999's *Take Your Shoes Off*, a loose-limbed and funky affair that was, to all intents and purposes, a soul record. *Shoulda Been Home* moved even further away from the blues and was a pure southern soul recording, with Cray putting his guitar aside and concentrating on his singing.

● ALBUMS: *Who's Been Talkin'* (Tomato 1980) ★★★, *Bad Influence* (HighTone 1983) ★★★★, *False Accusations* (HighTone 1985) ★★★, with Albert Collins, Johnny Copeland *Showdown!* (Alligator 1985) ★★★★, *Strong Persuader* (Mercury 1986) ★★★, *Don't Be Afraid Of The Dark* (Mercury 1988) ★★★★, *Midnight Stroll* (Mercury 1990) ★★★★, *Too Many Cooks* (Tomato 1991) ★★★, *I Was Warned* (Mercury 1992) ★★★, *The Score* reissue of *Who's Been Talkin'* (Charly 1992) ★★★, *Shame And A Sin* (Mercury 1993) ★★★, *Some Rainy Morning* (Mercury 1995) ★★★, *Sweet Potato Pie* (Mercury 1997) ★★★★, *Take Your Shoes Off* (Rykodisc 1999) ★★★, *Robert Cray With Albert Collins In Concert* 1977 recording (Indigo 1999) ★★★, *Shoulda Been Home* (Rykodisc 2001) ★★★★.

● COMPILATIONS: *Heavy Picks: The Robert Cray Band Collection* (Mercury 1999) ★★★★.

● VIDEOS: *Smoking Gun* (PolyGram Music Video 1989), *Collection: Robert Cray* (PolyGram Music Video 1991).

## CREATURES
This on-off collaboration between Siouxsie And The Banshees members Siouxsie Sioux (b. Susan Dallion, 27 May 1957, London, England) and drummer/percussionist Budgie (b. Peter Clark, 21 August 1957) won them a string of UK hits starting with 'Mad Eyed Screamer' (number 24, October 1981) and 'Miss The Girl' (number 21, April 1983) – both achieving Top 30 status. Their greatest success came with Herbie Mann and Carl Sigman's swing composition, 'Right Now' which reached number 14 in the UK chart in July 1983. Away from the more rock-orientated constraints of the parent group, the Creatures allowed Budgie to experiment with exotic percussive instruments and give the sound a freer, more expressive feel. Conceived primarily as a studio-only set-up, the Creatures did not make their live debut until 1990. Following the Banshees' initial dissolution in 1996, Siouxsie and Budgie continued to record as the Creatures, releasing *Anima Animus* on their own Sioux label in 1999.

● ALBUMS: *Feast* (Wonderland 1983) ★★, *Boomerang* (Wonderland 1989) ★★★, *Anima Animus* (Sioux 1999) ★★★, *Hybrids* remixes (Hydrogen Dukebox 1999) ★★★.

● COMPILATIONS: *A Bestiary Of* (PY 1997) ★★★.

## CRENSHAW, MARSHALL
b. 11 November 1953, Detroit, Michigan, USA. After portraying John Lennon in the stage show *Beatlemania*, Crenshaw forged a solo career as a solid and dependable performer of the classic urban American pop song. His rock 'n' roll songs were sprinkled with lyrics discoursing on the perennial problems of the lovelorn and the trials of being in love. With an echo-laden guitar sound that harked back to the 60s (with a little Buddy Holly and Eddie Cochran thrown in for effect), Crenshaw's future looked bright with the release of his first album for Warner Brothers Records in 1982. Performing alongside his brother Robert (drums, vocals) and Chris Donato (bass, vocals), this debut album contained Crenshaw's only US hit single to date, 'Someday, Someway'. His album of modern pop also contained such classics as 'Cynical Girl' and 'Mary Ann', but only reached number 50 on the US chart. His follow-up was dealt a similar fate. Although the album was packed with what seemed to be 'radio-friendly' hits, songs such as 'Whenever You're On My Mind', 'What Time Is It?' and 'For Her Love' found only cult-status appreciation.

The lean period of commercial success was relieved by the success of Owen Paul's cover of his 'My Favourite Waste Of Time', which reached the UK Top 3 in 1986. Crenshaw made film appearances in *Peggy Sue Got Married* and portrayed Buddy Holly in *La Bamba*. Further acclaimed album releases have seen the guitarist cover other artists' songs, including sterling performances of Richard Thompson's 'Valerie' and John Haitt's 'Someplace Where Love Can't Find Me' on *Good Evening*. A split with Warners in 1990 saw Crenshaw sign to MCA Records and the release of *Life's Too Short*. In the mid-90s, Crenshaw guested on various tribute albums for Nilsson, Arthur Alexander and Merle Haggard in addition to finding a new audience with his contribution on the Gin Blossoms' 'Til I Hear It From You'. He broke a five-year silence with a new album in 1996, although his enduring cult status is unlikely to break new ground for this underrated talent.

● ALBUMS: *Marshall Crenshaw* (Warners 1982) ★★★★, *Field Day* (Warners 1983) ★★★, *Downtown* (Warners 1985) ★★★, *Sings Mary Jean & Nine Others* (Warners 1987) ★★★, *Good Evening* (Warners 1989) ★★★, *Life's Too Short* (MCA 1991) ★★★, *My Truck Is My Home* (Razor & Tie 1994) ★★★, *Miracle Of Science* (Razor & Tie 1996) ★★★, *The 9 Volt Years: Battery Powered Home Demos And Curios* (Razor & Tie 1998) ★★, *#447* (Razor & Tie 1999) ★★★, *I've Suffered For My Art ... Now It's Your Turn* (King Biscuit Flower Hour 2001) ★★★.

● COMPILATIONS: *This Is Easy: The Best Of Marshall Crenshaw* (Rhino 2000) ★★★★.

● FILMS: *Peggy Sue Got Married* (1986), *La Bamba* (1987).

## CRISWELL, KIM
b. Hampton, Virginia, USA. An actress and singer who came to prominence in stage musicals during the 80s, with a style and voice reminiscent of the much-missed Ethel Merman. Criswell grew up in Chattanooga, Tennessee, where, so she says, the 'live' theatre used to arrive in a bus and stay for just two nights. Her early influences were Julie Andrews, Barbra Streisand and Judy Garland, and, like them, she started performing from an early age. After graduating from high school, she studied musical theatre at the University of Cincinnatti's College Conservatory of Music before moving to New York where she gained a featured part in a revival of *Annie Get Your Gun*. She made her

Broadway musical debut in *The First* (1981), and then appeared in *Nine*, which was staged by Tommy Tune and had a cast of 21 women and only one male adult. Her other Broadway credits during the 80s included revivals of the *Three Musketeers* and *The Threepenny Opera* (retitled as *3 Penny Opera*). In the latter show, Criswell played Lucy, one of the leading roles in a production that was headed by the popular rock singer Sting. She has appeared as the featured soloist with several of America's leading symphony orchestras, and took part in concert stagings of Jerome Kern's *Sitting Pretty* at Carnegie Hall, and George and Ira Gershwin's *Girl Crazy* at the Lincoln Centre. She won the Helen Hayes award for her performance in *Side By Side By Sondheim*, and played the role of Grizabella (the feline who sings 'Memory') for six months in the Los Angeles production of Andrew Lloyd Webber's *Cats*. Between 1989 and 1991 Criswell starred in three London studio recordings of famous Broadway shows, *Anything Goes*, *Kiss Me, Kate*, and *Annie Get Your Gun*, accompanied by a large orchestra directed by John McGlinn. He also conducted the London Sinfonietta when Criswell joined Brent Barrett in *Cole Porter And The American Musical* at the Royal Festival Hall. In September 1991, she presented her one-woman show, *Doin' What Comes Naturally*, at the Shaw Theatre in London, and, just over a year later, co-starred with John Diedrich in a West End revival of *Annie Get Your Gun*. The show was acclaimed by the critics ('Criswell is the best Annie we have seen since Dolores Gray') but it folded after less than two months. In 1993 she appeared in two very different kind of shows in the UK. The first, *Elegies For Angels, Punks And Raging Queens*, was a musical play that purported to tell the real-life stories of 33 individuals who have met their death through AIDS; while the other, a touring nostalgia show, *Hollywood And Broadway II*, with Bonnie Langford and Wayne Sleep, found her on more familiar ground. Her 1993 record releases were dissimilar, too: *The Lorelei* contained a mixture of well-known and neglected show tunes, while *Human Cry* turned out to be a pop album in a contemporary, and sometimes funky style, and the single, 'Moment Of Weakness', demonstrated her ability to cross over to the pop scene.

During the remainder of the 90s Criswell starred in musicals such as *Dames At Sea* (1996, Covent Garden Festival), *The Slow Drag* (1997, Freedom and Whitehall theatres), *Of Thee I Sing* (1998, Opera North), and featured prominently in *Side By Side ... By Cole Porter* (1998), a tribute to the famous composer at London's Palace Theatre, with the BBC Concert Orchestra conducted by John McGlinn. She also continued to appear regularly on the concert platform, in cabaret with pianist and musical director Wayne Marshall, as well as recording a number of studio cast albums, including Simon Rattle's setting of *Wonderful Town*.

● ALBUMS: with the Cincinnati University Singers *I Wants To Be An Actor Lady* (New World 1978) ★★★, *Human Cry* (Angel 1993) ★★, *The Lorelei* (Angel 1994) ★★★, *Back To Before* (TER 1999) ★★★, and Original Cast recordings.
● FILMS: *True Colors* (1991).

## CROKER, BRENDAN

b. 15 August 1953, Bradford, Yorkshire, England. Croker studied sculpture at art school before becoming a British Rail guard, a refuse collector and a theatre set designer. It was while toiling away at the last job that he met fellow guitarist Steve Phillips, with whom he formed the duo Nev And Norris. During the early 80s, when Phillips temporarily retired from music to concentrate on his own art career, Croker set about assembling his own band, the 5 O'Clock Shadows, comprising Croker, Marcus Cliffe (bass) and Mark Cresswell (guitar). Cresswell also played alongside Tanita Tikaram. The 5 O'Clock Shadow's debut, *A Close Shave*, emerged on the Leeds independent label Unamerican Activities, and was promoted with the single 'That's The Way All My Money Goes' in 1986. They moved to Red Rhino but released an album and single before that company ceased trading. Croker gained a high profile for his work with Mark Knopfler, Guy Fletcher and Steve Phillips as the Notting Hillbillies and was signed to Andrew Lauder's Silvertone label. In 1989, the Notting Hillbillies released a self-titled album, with guest appearances by Tikaram, Eric Clapton, Steve Goulding and Katie Kissoon (of Mac And Katie Kissoon) amongst others. Croker and Cresswell also guested on Tikaram's *Ancient Heart*. Croker enjoyed some success in Nashville as a songwriter during the 90s, writing 'What It Takes' for Wynonna's debut album. His solo career, meanwhile, has continued to follow an eccentric path.
● ALBUMS: *A Close Shave* (Unamerican Activities 1986) ★★★, *Boat Trips In The Bay* (Red Rhino 1987) ★★★★, *Brendan Croker And The 5 O'Clock Shadows* (Silvertone 1989) ★★★, *The Great Indoors* (Silvertone 1991) ★★★, *The Acoustic Sessions* (Windsong 1995) ★★★, *The Kershaw Sessions* (Strange Fruit 1996) ★★★.
● COMPILATIONS: *Not Just A Hillbilly: More Like A Best Of* (Essential 2000) ★★★★.

## CROSS, CHRISTOPHER

b. Christopher Geppert, 3 May 1951, San Antonio, Texas, USA. Formerly a member of Texas heavy rock band Flash, Cross was signed to Warner Brothers Records on the strength of his songwriting talents. His 1980 debut, full of smooth AOR songs ideal for radio-play, spawned hits in 'Ride Like The Wind' (US number 2 – featuring Michael McDonald), 'Sailing (US number 1)', 'Never Be The Same' and 'Say You'll Be Mine'. Cross won five Grammy Awards in 1981, including Best Album of the Year. Cross also sang and co-wrote, along with Carole Bayer Sager, Burt Bacharach and Peter Allen, the theme song, 'Arthur's Theme (Best That You Can Do)' for the top-grossing Dudley Moore movie *Arthur* in 1981. The song gave Cross another US number 1 hit and his only UK Top 10 single. Despite having a UK Top 20 album, Cross' singles sales propelled him no further than number 48 ('Sailing'). His sophomore album, *Another Page*, supplied him with a further US Top 10 hit with 'Think Of Laura' in 1983, which was featured on US ABC television's *General Hospital* series.

Later years saw a decline in Cross' sales, indicating either a loss of touch in songwriting or in popularity, or both. He was dropped by Warners following the release of 1988's *Back Of My Mind*. A revamped dance version of 'Ride Like The Wind' was used by East Side Beat in late 1991 and reached the UK Top 10. Cross' subsequent releases include 1998's *Walking In Avalon*, a double album containing a new studio work and a live set which was later re-released in the US as two single albums, *Red Room* (studio) and *Greatest Hits Live* (live).

● ALBUMS: *Christopher Cross* (Warners 1980) ★★★, *Another Page* (Warners 1983) ★★★, *Every Turn Of The World* (Warners 1985) ★★, *Back Of My Mind* (Warners 1988) ★★, *Rendezvous* (BMG 1992) ★★★, *Window* (BMG 1995) ★★★, *Walking In Avalon* (CMC 1998) ★★★, *Red Room* (CMC 1999) ★★★, *Greatest Hits – Live* (CMC 1999) ★★★.

● COMPILATIONS: *The Definitive Christopher Cross* (Rhino 2001) ★★★★.

● VIDEOS: *An Evening With Christopher Cross* (BMG 1998).

## CROWD

The Crowd was a brief component of the 'beach punk' scene of Huntington Beach, California, USA, in the early 80s. Featuring Jim 'Trash' Decker (vocals), Jay Decker (bass), Jim Kaa (guitar, vocals), Tracy Porterfield (vocals) and Barry 'Cuda' Miranda (drums), they were almost completely divorced from the prevailing hardcore punk ethos. Dressed in dayglo beachwear, and with their own version of communal dancing (it is often suggested that Decker invented the 'slam dance'), the Crowd specialized in trashy surf punk, akin to a less skilled Agent Orange. Their debut album, *A World Apart*, failed to build on their early impact, however, and the Crowd were quickly overtaken by many of the bands they had helped influence. When Cuda departed, Dennis Walsh (aka Dennis Racket) joined from the Flyboys. The Crowd broke up shortly afterwards, leaving Decker and Porterfield's ambition to be 'the Frankie and Annette of the 80s' unrealized. Various ex-members went on to join Sextet, before the Deckers, Kaa and Walsh reunited in 1987 to record a second Crowd album, *Big Fish Stories*. They have continued to balance Crowd work with other projects, although Jay Decker announced he was leaving for good in 1997.

● ALBUMS: *A World Apart* (Posh Boy 1980) ★★★, *Big Fish Stories* (Flipside 1989) ★★, *Letter Bomb* (Flipside 1996) ★★, *Punk Off* (Unity Squad 2001) ★★.

## CROWELL, RODNEY

b. 7 August 1950, Houston, Texas, USA. Combining careers as a country songwriter, producer and artist, Crowell has become an influential figure in Nashville's new breed, along with Emmylou Harris, in whose Hot Band he worked for three years, Rosanne Cash, and fellow songwriters such as Guy Clark. His songs have been covered by Bob Seger, Waylon Jennings, George Jones and others, while he has also produced albums for Sissy Spacek, Guy Clark and Bobby Bare.

Crowell's introduction to playing music came before he was a teenager, when he played drums in his Kentucky-born father's bar band in Houston. He dropped out of college in the early 70s to move to Nashville, where he was briefly signed as a songwriter at Jerry Reed's publishing company, and in 1973 was appearing on local 'writers' night' with contemporaries such as Clark, John Hiatt and Richard Dobson. In 1974, a demo tape of his songs was heard by Brian Ahern, who was about to produce *Pieces Of The Sky* for Emmylou Harris, and that album eventually began with Crowell's 'Bluebird Wine'. Harris' 1975 album *Elite Hotel* included Crowell's 'Till I Gain Control Again', and her 1979 release, *Quarter Moon In A Ten Cent Town*, featured his 'I Ain't Living Long Like This' and 'Leaving Louisiana In The Broad Daylight'. During this period, Crowell also worked as a permanent member of Harris' Hot Band, playing rhythm guitar and singing harmony and duet vocals.

In 1978, Crowell recorded his own debut album for Warner Brothers Records, *Ain't Living Long Like This*, using Ahern as producer and an all-star line-up of musicians including the entire Hot Band plus Ry Cooder, Jim Keltner and Willie Nelson. Although it included two minor US country hit singles, the album was not a commercial success.

In 1979, Crowell married Rosanne Cash, and subsequently produced most of her albums. In 1980, he tried again on his own account with *But What Will The Neighbors Think*, which he co-produced with Craig Leon. It remained in the US album charts for 10 weeks, and included a US Top 40 single, 'Ashes By Now'; in 1981, he released the self-produced *Rodney Crowell*, which just failed to reach the Top 100 of the US album chart. These albums were later the basis for *The Rodney Crowell Collection*, a 1989 compilation that was virtually a 'Best Of' of his early career. In 1984, he delivered *Street Language* to Warner Brothers, who rejected it, whereupon Crowell changed four tracks and leased it to Columbia Records. The album, released in 1986, included three US country chart singles, and established him as a country artist. *Diamonds And Dirt*, co-produced by Crowell and his erstwhile Hot Band colleague Tony Brown, was much more successful, spawning five US country number 1 singles, 'It's Such A Small World' (a duet with Rosanne Cash), 'I Couldn't Leave You If I Tried' and 'She's Crazy For Leavin''. In 1989, Crowell and Brown co-produced *Keys To The Highway*, which was largely recorded with his fine band, the Dixie Pearls, whose personnel included Stewart Smith (lead guitar), Jim Hanson (bass), Vince Santoro (drums) and another erstwhile Hot Band colleague, Hank DeVito (pedal steel).

His 1992 album, *Life Is Messy*, followed shortly after the revelation that his marriage to Rosanne Cash had broken down. Taken by most observers as a reply to Cash's stunning *Interiors*, the album attempted – with some success – to marry melancholy themes to up-tempo songs. Subsequent albums such as *Let The Picture Paint Itself* and *Jewel Of The South* also chronicled his personal problems. As long as life is messy, it appears Crowell will be able to write great songs, although his marriage to Claudia Church in September 1998 indicated he had found personal happiness once more. The self-financed *The Houston Kid* was regarded as one of the finest albums of

Crowell's career.

● ALBUMS: *Ain't Living Long Like This* (Warners 1978) ★★★★, *But What Will The Neighbors Think* (Warners 1980) ★★★, *Rodney Crowell* (Warners 1981) ★★★, *Street Language* (Columbia 1986) ★★★★, *Diamonds And Dirt* (Columbia 1988) ★★★★, *Keys To The Highway* (Columbia 1989) ★★★★, *Life Is Messy* (Columbia 1992) ★★★, *Let The Picture Paint Itself* (MCA 1994) ★★★, *Soul Searchin'* (Excelsior 1994) ★★★, *Jewel Of The South* (MCA 1995) ★★★, *The Cicadas* (Warners 1997) ★★★, *The Houston Kid* (Sugar Hill 2001) ★★★★.
● COMPILATIONS: *The Rodney Crowell Collection* (Warners 1989) ★★★★, *Greatest Hits* (Columbia 1993) ★★★★, *Super Hits* (Columbia 1995) ★★★.

## CUBAN HEELS
This UK band was headed by John Malarky (vocals), previously a member of Johnny And The Self Abusers, the Scottish punk band that metamorphosed into Simple Minds. Cuban Heels' formation in Glasgow 1978 was completed with the addition of Laurie Cuffe (guitar), Paul Armour (bass) and Davie Duncan (drums). Initially an R&B band with the occasional punk track, they soon found growing popularity with the mod revival crowd. Consequently, their live set was balanced between originals such as 'Modern Girl', 'Too Much, Too Loud', 'Samantha's World' and 'Young Pretender', plus cover versions such as Cat Stevens' 'Matthew And Son' and Cliff Richard's 'On The Beach'. The debut single, released on the Housewives Choice label in March 1978, was a pop-punk reworking of Petula Clark's hit 'Downtown'. With the new year came a change in line-up, with Nick Clarke (bass) and Ali McKenzie (drums), replacing Armour and Duncan. Throughout 1979–80 they continued an exhausting live schedule and released two more independent singles, 'Little Girl' and 'Walk On Water'. Their lack of commercial success prompted the band to settle on a more comfortable pop sound, with an image to match. A contract with Virgin Records saw *Walk Our Way To Heaven* and a string of singles, 'Sweet Charity', 'My Colours Fly' and a remake of 'Walk On Water', suffer the same fate as previous offerings. The band split during 1982.
● ALBUMS: *Walk Our Way To Heaven* (Virgin 1981) ★★.

## CUDDLY TOYS
Emerging from the ashes of glam-punk outfit Raped, the Ireland-based Cuddly Toys consisted of Sean Purcell (vocals), Tony Baggett (bass), Faebhean Kwest (guitar), Billy Surgeoner (guitar) and Paddy Phield (drums). Both their 1980 offerings, *Guillotine Theatre* and a cover of Marc Bolan and David Bowie's 'Madmen', were co-releases for Raped's old label Parole and Fresh Records. 'Astral Joe' came later that year, followed by 'Someone's Crying' in 1981, but the band seemed derivative in comparison to more exciting members of their peer group and soon endured line-up changes. Terry Noakes joined on guitar and Robert Parker on drums. After 'It's A Shame' and a second album, *Trials And Crosses*, in 1982, the band disappeared from view.

● ALBUMS: *Guillotine Theatre* (Fresh 1981) ★★★, *Trials And Crosses* (Fresh 1982) ★★★.
● COMPILATIONS: *Young And Dangerous: The Best Of Cuddly Toys* (Cherry Red 2001) ★★★.

## CULT
Originally known as first Southern Death Cult, then Death Cult, the band was formed by lead singer Ian Astbury (b. 14 May 1962, Heswall, Cheshire, England) in 1981. After a youth spent in Merseyside, Scotland and Canada (where he gained early exposure to the culture of native Indians on the Six Nations Reservation, informing the early stages of the band's career), Astbury moved into a house in Bradford, Yorkshire, and discovered a band rehearsing in the basement. The personnel included Haq Qureshi (drums), David 'Buzz' Burrows (guitar) and Barry Jepson (bass) As their vocalist, Astbury oversaw a rapid rise in fortunes, their fifth gig and London debut at the Heaven club attracting a near 2,000-strong audience. Southern Death Cult made their recording debut in December 1982 with the double a-side 'Moya'/'Fatman', and released a self-titled album on Beggars Banquet Records. They supported Bauhaus on tour in early 1983. However, by March the band had folded, Astbury reeling from his perceived image of 'positive punk' spokesman, and the fact that his native Indian concept was being diluted by the band's format.
His new outfit, operating under the truncated name Death Cult, would, he vowed, not become a victim of hype in the same way again (Qureshi, Jepson and Burrows would go on to join Getting The Fear, subsequently becoming Into A Circle before Qureshi re-emerged as the centrepiece of Fun-Da-Mental's 'world dance' ethos under the name Propa-Ghandi). A combination of the single, demo and live tracks was posthumously issued as the sole SDC album. Death Cult comprised the rhythm section of recently deceased gothic band Ritual, namely Ray 'The Reverend' Mondo (b. Ray Taylor-Smith; drums) and Jamie Stewart (bass), plus guitarist Billy Duffy (b. William Henry Duffy, 12 May 1961, Hulme, Manchester, England; ex-Ed Banger And The Nosebleeds and Theatre Of Hate). They made their debut in July 1983 with an eponymous four-track 12-inch, at which time Astbury also changed his own name (he had previously been using Ian Lindsay, which, it later transpired, was his mother's maiden name).
After an appearance at the Futurama festival Mondo swapped drumming positions with Sex Gang Children's Nigel Preston (d. 7 May 1992), a former colleague of Duffy's in Theatre Of Hate. However, 1984 brought about a second and final name change – with the band feeling that the Death prefix typecast them as a 'gothic' act, they became simply the Cult. They recorded their first album together, *Dreamtime*, for release in September 1984, its sales boosted by a number 1 single in the independent charts with the typically anthemic 'Spiritwalker'. Another strong effort followed early the next year, 'She Sells Sanctuary', but this was to prove Preston's swansong. Mark Brzezicki of Big Country helped out on sessions for the forthcoming album until the

permanent arrival of Les Warner (b. 13 February 1961), who had previously worked with Johnny Thunders, Julian Lennon and Randy California. The band's major commercial breakthrough came with *Love* in 1985, which comprised fully fledged hard rock song structures and pushed Duffy's guitar lines to the fore. It reached number 4 in the UK, and spawned two UK Top 20 hit singles in the aforementioned 'She Sells Sanctuary' and 'Rain'. *Electric* saw the band's transition to heavy rock completed. There was no disguising their source of inspiration, with Led Zeppelin being mentioned in nearly every review. Part-produced by Rick Rubin, *Electric* was a bold and brash statement of intent, if not quite the finished item. It became a success on both sides of the Atlantic, peaking at number 4 and 38 in the UK and US charts, respectively. The gigs to promote it saw the band add bass player Kid 'Haggis' Chaos (ex-Zodiac Mindwarp And The Love Reaction), with Stewart switching to rhythm guitar.

Both Haggis and Warner were dispensed with in March 1988, the former joining Four Horsemen. Reduced to a three-piece of Astbury, Stewart and Duffy, the sessions for *Sonic Temple* saw them temporarily recruit the services of drummer Mickey Curry. It was an album which combined the atmospheric passion of *Love* with the unbridled energy of *Electric*, and reached number 3 in the UK and number 10 on the US *Billboard* chart. A 1989 world tour saw the band augmented by Matt Sorum (b. 19 November 1960, Mission Viejo, California, USA; drums) and Mark Taylor (keyboards). Stewart quit in 1990, while Sorum would go on to a tenure with Guns N'Roses. *Ceremony* was released in 1991, with the help of Charlie Drayton (bass), Benmont Tench (keyboards) and the returning Mickey Curry. This was a retrogressive collection of songs, which had more in common with *Love* than their previous two albums. Nevertheless, having already established an enormous fanbase, success was virtually guaranteed. The *Pure Cult* compilation duly topped the UK charts in February 1993. Introducing new drummer Scott Garrett, *The Cult* saw them reunited with producer Bob Rock on a set that included the rather clumsy Kurt Cobain tribute 'Sacred Life'. By this time, however, Astbury had departed and later resurfaced with a new band, the Holy Barbarians.

In 1999, Astbury, Duffy, Sorum and Martyn LeNoble (b. 14 April 1969, Vlaardingen, Netherlands; bass, ex-Porno For Pyros) re-formed the Cult, although the latter was soon replaced by Chris Wyse. Astbury released the solo *Spirit/Light/Speed* the following year, while the band worked on their debut album for Lava Records, *Beyond Good And Evil*.

● ALBUMS: as Southern Death Cult *The Southern Death Cult* (Beggars Banquet 1983) ★★, *Dreamtime* (Beggars Banquet 1984) ★★, *Dreamtime Live At The Lyceum* (Beggars Banquet 1984) ★★, *Love* (Beggars Banquet/Sire 1985) ★★, *Electric* (Beggars Banquet/Sire 1987) ★★★, *Sonic Temple* (Beggars Banquet/Sire 1989) ★★★, *Ceremony* (Beggars Banquet/Sire 1991) ★★, *The Cult* (Beggars Banquet/Sire 1994) ★★, *Live Cult: Marquee London MCMXCI* (Beggars Banquet 1999) ★★, *Beyond Good And Evil* (Lava 2001) ★★★.

● COMPILATIONS: as Southern Death Cult *Complete Recordings* (Situation Two 1991) ★★★, *Pure Cult* (Beggars Banquet 1993) ★★★, as Death Cult *Ghost Dance* (Beggars Banquet 1996) ★★★, *High Octane Cult* (Beggars Banquet 1996) ★★★, *Rare Cult* 6-CD box set (Beggars Banquet 2000) ★★, *Best Of Rare Cult* (Beggars Banquet 2000) ★★★.

● VIDEOS: *Dreamtime At The Lyceum* (Beggars Banquet 1984), *Electric Love* (Beggars Banquet 1987), *Cult: Video Single* (One Plus One 1987), *Sonic Ceremony* (Beggars Banquet 1992), *Pure Cult* (Beggars Banquet 1993), *Dreamtime Live At The Lyceum* (Beggars Banquet 1996).

## CULTURE CLUB

Harbingers of the so-called 'new pop' that swept through the UK charts in the early 80s, Culture Club comprised Boy George (b. George O'Dowd, 14 June 1961, Eltham, Kent, England; vocals), Roy Hay (b. 12 August 1961, Southend-on-Sea, Essex, England; guitar, keyboards), Mikey Craig (b. 15 February 1960, Hammersmith, London, England; bass) and Jon Moss (b. 11 September 1957, Wandsworth, London, England; drums). The band came together in 1981 after George, a nightclub *habitué*, had briefly appeared with Bow Wow Wow (under the name Lieutenant Lush) and played alongside Craig in the Sex Gang Children. The elder drummer Moss had the most band experience having already appeared with London, the Damned and Adam Ant. After failing an audition with EMI Records, Culture Club were signed to Virgin Records in the spring of 1982, and released a couple of non-chart singles, 'White Boy' and 'I'm Afraid Of Me'. By autumn of that year, however, the band was firmly established as one of the most popular new acts in the country. The melodic and subtly arranged 'Do You Really Want To Hurt Me?' took them to number 1 in the UK and they deserved another chart-topper with the Top 3 follow-up, 'Time (Clock Of The Heart)'.

Although their first album *Kissing To Be Clever* lacked the consistent excellence of their singles, it was still a fine pop record. By this time, George was already one of pop's major talking points with his dreadlocks, make-up and androgynous persona. Never short of a quote for the press, he would later stress such virtues as celibacy with the anti-sex quip, 'I'd rather have a cup of tea'. The launching of MTV in the USA ensured that many UK acts were infiltrating the American charts and the colourful persona of George, coupled with the irresistible charm of Culture Club's melodies, effectively broke them Stateside early in 1983. *Kissing To Be Clever* climbed into the Top 20 of the US album charts, while their two UK singles hits both reached number 2. Suddenly, Culture Club was one of the most popular bands in the world. Back at home, the passionate 'Church Of The Poison Mind', with Helen Terry on counter vocals with George, gave them another number 2 hit. The band reached their commercial peak later that year with the release of the infectious 'Karma Chameleon', which topped the charts on both sides of the Atlantic and sold in excess of a million copies. The second album, *Colour By Numbers* was another UK number 1 and was only kept off the top in the US by Michael Jackson's mega-selling *Thriller*.

The momentum was maintained through 1983–84 with strong singles such as 'Victims', 'It's A Miracle' and 'Miss You Blind', which charted in either the US or UK Top 10. Ironically, it was one their biggest UK hits which presaged Culture Club's fall from critical grace. In October 1984, 'The War Song' hit number 2 but was widely criticized for its simplistic politicizing. Thereafter, chart performances took an increasing backseat to the tabloid newspaper adventures of George. Indeed, 1986's 'Move Away' was to be their only other Top 10 hit during the 80s. The media-conscious singer had signed a Faustian pact with Fleet Street, which led to his downfall in 1986. Having confessed that he was a heroin addict, he was persecuted by the press and was eventually arrested for possession of cannabis. Early in 1987, he appeared on the high-rating UK television chat show *Wogan* and declared that he was cured. The announcement coincided with the news that Culture Club no longer existed.

George would continue to enjoy chart-topping success as a soloist and later as an in-demand DJ. A resurgence of all things eighties led to Culture Club re-forming in 1998, with the sweet reggae ballad 'I Just Wanna Be Loved' debuting at number 4 in the UK singles chart in October. Another excellent song, 'Your Kisses Are Charity', stalled outside the Top 20 the following August. Their first studio album since 1986, *Don't Mind If I Do*, was released shortly afterwards.

● ALBUMS: *Kissing To Be Clever* (Virgin 1982) ★★★, *Colour By Numbers* (Virgin 1983) ★★★★, *Waking Up With The House On Fire* (Virgin 1984) ★★, *From Luxury To Heartache* (Virgin 1986) ★★★, *Don't Mind If I Do* (Virgin 1999) ★★★.

● COMPILATIONS: *This Time: The First Four Years* (Virgin 1987) ★★★, *The Best Of Culture Club* (Virgin 1989) ★★★, *At Worst ... The Best Of Boy George & Culture Club* (Virgin 1993) ★★★★, *Greatest Moments* (Virgin 1998) ★★★★.

● VIDEOS: *Kiss Across The Ocean* (Virgin Vision 1984), *This Time: The First Four Years* (Virgin Vision 1987).

● FURTHER READING: *Culture Club: When Cameras Go Crazy*, Kasper de Graaf and Malcolm Garrett. *Mad About The Boy: The Life And Times Of Boy George & Culture Club*, Anton Gill. *Boy George And Culture Club*, Jo Dietrich. *Like Punk Never Happened: Culture Club And The New Pop*, Dave Rimmer.

## CURE

Formed in 1976 as the Easy Cure, this UK band originally comprised Robert Smith (b. 21 April 1959, Crawley, Sussex, England; guitar, vocals), Michael Dempsey (bass) and Laurence 'Lol' Tolhurst (b. 3 February 1959; drums). After struggling to find a niche during the first flashes of punk, the band issued the Albert Camus-inspired 'Killing An Arab' on the independent Small Wonder Records in mid-1978. It proved sufficient to draw them to the attention of producer and Fiction Records label manager Chris Parry, who reissued the single the following year. By May 1979, the band were

attracting glowing reviews, particularly in the wake of 'Boys Don't Cry', whose style recalled mid-60s British beat, with the added attraction of Smith's deadpan vocal. The attendant album, *Three Imaginary Boys*, was also well received, and was followed by a support spot with Siouxsie And The Banshees, on which Smith joined the headliners onstage. Another strong single, 'Jumping Someone Else's Train', performed predictably well in the independent charts but, in common with previous releases, narrowly missed the national chart. A pseudonymous single, 'I'm A Cult Hero', under the name the Cult Heroes, passed unnoticed and, soon after its release, Dempsey was replaced on bass by Simon Gallup. Amid the shake-up, keyboards player Mathieu Hartley was added to the line-up.

By the spring of 1980, the Cure was developing less as a pop outfit than a guitar-laden rock band. The atmospheric 12-inch single 'A Forest' gave them their first UK Top 40 hit, while a stronger second album, *17 Seconds*, reached the Top 20. Thereafter, the Cure's cult following ensured that their work regularly appeared in the lower regions of the charts. After consolidating their position during 1981 with 'Primary', 'Charlotte Sometimes' and 'Faith', the band looked to the new year for a new direction. A major breakthrough with *Pornography* threatened to place them in the major league of new UK acts, but there were internal problems to overcome. The keyboard player, Hartley, had lasted only a few months and, early in 1982, the other 'new boy', Gallup, was fired and replaced by Phil Thornalley and Steve Goulding. Meanwhile, Smith briefly joined Siouxsie And The Banshees as a temporary replacement for John McGeogh. As well as contributing the excellent psychedelic-tinged guitar work to their hit 'Dear Prudence', Smith subsequently teamed up with Banshee Steve Severin and Jeanette Landray in the Glove.

The Cure, meanwhile, continued to record and during the summer enjoyed their first UK Top 20 single appearance with the electronics-based 'The Walk'. Four months later, they were in the Top 10 with the radically contrasting pop single 'The Love Cats' (Smith subsequently attempted to distance himself from this song, which was initially intended more as a parody). Further success followed with 'The Caterpillar', another unusual single, highlighted by Smith's eccentric violin playing. This chart success confirmed the Cure as not only one of the most eclectic and eccentric ensembles working in British pop, but one of the very few to make such innovations accessible to a wider audience. Smith's heavy eye make-up, smudged crimson lipstick and shock-spiked hair was equally as striking, while the band's videos, directed by Tim Pope, became increasingly wondrous. In 1985, the band released their most commercially successful album yet, *The Head On The Door*. The following year, they re-recorded their second single, 'Boys Don't Cry', which this time became a minor UK hit.

By now, the band was effectively Smith and Tolhurst, with members such as Gallup and others flitting through the line-up from year to year. With the retrospective *Standing On A Beach* singles collection the Cure underlined their longevity during an otherwise quiet year. During 1987, they undertook a tour of South America and enjoyed several more minor UK hits with 'Why Can't I Be You?', 'Catch' and 'Just Like Heaven'. The latter also reached the US Top 40, as did their double album, *Kiss Me, Kiss Me, Kiss Me*. A two-year hiatus followed before the release of the follow-up, *Disintegration*. A fiendishly downbeat affair, with some of Smith's most moribund lyrics, it nevertheless climbed into the UK Top 3. During the same period, the band continued to register regular hits with such singles as 'Lullaby', 'Lovesong', 'Pictures Of You' and the fiery 'Never Enough'. Along the way, they continued their run of line-up changes, which culminated in the departure of Tolhurst (to form Presence), leaving Smith as the sole original member.

Although it was assumed that the Cure would attempt to consolidate their promising sales in the USA, Smith announced that he would not be undertaking any further tours of America. *Mixed Up*, a double album compiling re-recordings and remixes of their singles, was released at the end of 1990. By 1992, the Cure line-up comprised Smith, a reinstated Gallup, Perry Bamonte (keyboards, guitar), Porl Thompson (guitar) and Boris Williams (drums), and with the critically acclaimed *Wish*, the Cure consolidated their position as one of the world's most consistently successful bands. Thompson left the unit in June 1993, at which time former member Tolhurst sued Smith, the band and its record label for alleged unpaid royalties. The ensuing court transcripts made for colourful reading, and confirmed the Cure's reputation for drinking excess (Tolhurst was summarily defeated in the action and left with a huge legal debt). Following a successful bill-topping gig at the 1995 Glastonbury Festival the band started work on what was to become *Wild Mood Swings*, issued in May 1996. The line-up on this album was Smith, Bamonte, Gallup, Jason Cooper (drums) and Roger O'Donnell (keyboards). The revealing lyrics hinted at Smith's personal insecurities. *Galore*, a useful follow-up to the earlier compilations, preceded the excellent *Bloodflowers* which Smith claimed was to be the final Cure album.

● ALBUMS: *Three Imaginary Boys* (Fiction 1979) ★★★, *Boys Don't Cry* (Fiction 1979) ★★, *Seventeen Seconds* (Fiction 1980) ★★★, *Faith* (Fiction 1981) ★★★★, *Pornography* (Fiction 1982) ★★★★, *The Top* (Fiction 1984) ★★★, *Concert - The Cure Live* (Fiction 1984) ★★, *Concert And Curiosity - Cure Anomalies 1977-1984* (Fiction 1984) ★★, *Head On The Door* (Fiction 1985) ★★★, *Kiss Me, Kiss Me, Kiss Me* (Fiction 1987) ★★★★, *Disintegration* (Fiction 1990) ★★★★, *Entreat* (Fiction 1991) ★★★, *Wish* (Fiction 1992) ★★★★, *Show* (Fiction 1993) ★★★, *Paris* (Fiction 1993) ★★★, *Wild Mood Swings* (Fiction 1996) ★★★, *Bloodflowers* (Fiction 2000) ★★★★.
● COMPILATIONS: *Japanese Whispers - The Cure Singles Nov 1982-Nov 1983* (Fiction 1983) ★★★, *Standing On The Beach - The Singles* titled *Staring At The Sea* on CD (Fiction 1986) ★★★★, *Mixed Up* (Fiction 1990) ★★★, *Galore - The Singles 1987-1997* (Fiction 1997) ★★★, *Greatest Hits* (Fiction 2001) ★★★.

● VIDEOS: *Staring At the Sea: The Images* (Palace Video 1986), *The Cure In Orange* (PolyGram Music Video 1987), *In Between Days* (PolyGram Music Video 1988), *Close To Me* (PolyGram Music Video 1989), *Cure Picture Show* (PolyGram Music Video 1991), *The Cure Play Out* (Windsong 1991), *The Cure Show* (PolyGram Music Video 1993), *Galore - The Videos* (PolyGram Music Video 1997), *Greatest Hits* (Warner Music Vision 2001).
● FURTHER READING: *The Cure: A Visual Documentary*, Dave Thompson and Jo-Anne Greene. *Ten Imaginary Years*, Lydia Barbarian, Steve Sutherland and Robert Smith. *The Cure Songwords 1978-1989*, Robert Smith (ed.). *The Cure: Success Corruption & Lies*, Ross Clarke. *The Cure On Record*, Daren Butler. *The Cure: Faith*, Dave Bowler and Bryan Dray. *The Making Of: The Cure's Disintegration*, Mary Elizabeth Hargrove. *Catch: Robert Smith And The Cure*, Daniel Patton.

## CURIOSITY KILLED THE CAT

This late-80s UK pop act graced the covers of all the teen-pop magazines. The various group members all had showbusiness/theatrical backgrounds. The line-up comprised: Ben Volpeliere-Pierrot, (b. Martin Benedict Volpeliere-Pierrot, 19 May 1965, Earls Court, London, England; vocals), Julian Godfrey Brookhouse, (b. 15 May 1963, Putney, London, England; guitar), Nicholas Bernard Thorpe (b. 25 October 1964, Sunbury-On-Thames, London, England; bass) and Migi (b. Miguel John Drummond, 27 January 1964, Strawberry Hill, London, England; drums). Volpeliere-Pierrot's father was a celebrity photographer and his mother a model - Ben's surname was a double-barrelled convolution of their surnames. His childhood was dotted with visits from various Beatles, Rolling Stones and other faces of the 60s who held court at his parents' home. A pretty child, he was in a Kodak commercial in 1970 and by his teens was a regular model in teenage girls' magazines. He also appeared in videos for XTC and the Thompson Twins in the early 80s. Volpeliere-Pierrot first played alongside the other members in the punk-influenced Twilight Children. Drummond was the son of a film and video maker and brushed with the stars when his father's company made videos for bands such as the Police. After discovering punk, he took up drumming, and met Throp at art school before an invitation to join the Twilight Children. In mid-1984 Volpeliere-Pierrot was dating Drummond's sister and the boys invited him to sing in their band, kicking out the old vocalist in the process. Later that same year Toby Anderson also joined the band as keyboard player and songwriter. A demo of a song called 'Curiosity Killed the Cat' was heard by businessman Peter Rosengard who became their manager and they changed their name to that of the song. A debut gig was held at the Embassy Club in December 1984 at which point there were still numerous extra musicians and singers on stage. They shed the excess baggage although Anderson remained the 'fifth' Cat until late 1986. Signed to Phonogram in 1985, they started recording towards the end of the year. Their album was held up for almost a year after original producers Sly Dunbar and Robbie Shakespeare were dropped in favour of Stewart Levine. 'Misfit' followed in July but flopped. Another face from the 60s, Andy Warhol, met the band at a London art exhibition and he championed them, even appearing in a video for 'Misfit'. His involvement, though useful, was cut short when he died in 1987. Several television appearances helped to push the second single 'Down To Earth', which entered the charts in December 1986 reaching the Top 5 in the New Year. A series of further hits followed, including 'Ordinary' and a re-issued 'Misfit', and *Keep Your Distance* rose to the top of the UK album charts. However, after the flop single 'Free' in September 1987 they underwent a quiet period but returned in 1989 (minus Thorpe and now simply known as Curiosity) with the Top 20 hit 'Name And Number'. The band's fortunes were restored in 1992, when a cover version of Johnny Bristol's 'Hang On In There Baby' rose to number 3 in the UK charts. Further single releases failed to dent the upper regions of the chart and the band quietly faded away. They re-formed in the new millennium, making an appearance on the UK's National Lottery television show singing 'Down To Earth'.

● ALBUMS: *Keep Your Distance* (Mercury 1987) ★★★, *Getahead* (Mercury 1989) ★★★, *Back To Front* (Japan 1994) ★★.

● COMPILATIONS: *The Very Best Of Curiosity Killed The Cat* (PolyGram 1996) ★★★.

● VIDEOS: *Running The Distance* (Channel 5 1988).

## CURRY, TIM

b. Timothy James Curry, 19 April 1946, Grappenhall, Cheshire, England. A versatile actor and singer, with much flair and a dashing style, Curry studied drama and English at Birmingham University. In the 60s, he was a member of the Royal Shakespeare Company, and joined the cast of *Hair* early on in its run. After appearing in a supporting role in the 1970 flop musical, *Lie Down, I Think I Love You*, three years later he created the role of the outrageous Frank 'N' Furter in Richard O'Brien's phenomenally successful *The Rocky Horror Show*. In 1975, he reprised the part in the short-lived New York production, and starred in the film adaptation which was entitled *The Rocky Horror Picture Show*. In 1981 Curry was nominated for a Tony Award for his performance in the title role of the Broadway production of *Amadeus*, and in the following year received a Variety Club Award when he played the role of the Pirate King, with George Cole and Bonnie Langford, in a West End revival of *The Pirates Of Penzance*. In 1986 he was 'bold, muscular and in fine ample baritone voice' as Macheath in the UK National Theatre's *The Threepenny Opera*, and two years later played Bill Sibson in the US tour of *Me And My Girl*. In 1993, Curry received another Tony nomination for his performance as the ageing and alcoholic swashbuckler Alan Swann in *My Favorite Year*. The musical, which had a book by Joseph Dougherty and a score by Lynn Ahrens And Stephen Flaherty, was based on the 1982 Peter O'Toole movie of the same name. Negative revues forced its closure after 37 performances, but Curry's own film career

has flourished since the mid-70s. As well as his on-screen performances, on numerous occasions he has provided the voice for feature and television productions. These have included the voice of the evil spirit Hexxus who sang Thomas Dolby's 'Toxic Love' in *FernGully: The Last Rainforest* (1992). Three years later he was the voice of the 'macho, strutting Drake' in MGM's animated *The Pebble And The Penguin*. Curry has appeared extensively on television, especially in the USA, in films or television series such as *Oliver Twist* (1982, as Bill Sikes), *The Worst Witch* (1986), *Wiseguy* (1989), *The Three Musketeers* (1993), *Daisy-Head Mayzie* (1995), *Mighty Ducks* (1996), and *Charlie's Angels* (2000).

● ALBUMS: *Read My Lips* (A&M 1978) ★★★, *Fearless* (A&M 1979) ★★, *Simplicity* (A&M 1981) ★★★.

● COMPILATIONS: *The Best Of Tim Curry* (A&M 1989) ★★★.

● FILMS: *The Rocky Horror Picture Show* (1975), *The Shout* (1978), *Times Square* (1980), *Annie* (1982), *The Ploughman's Lunch* (1983), *Legend* (1985), *Clue* (1985), *Pass The Ammo* (1988), *The Little Mermaid* voice only (1989), *The Hunt For Red October* (1990), *Oscar* (1991), *FernGully: The Last Rainforest* voice only (1992), *Passed Away* (1992), *Home Alone 2: Lost In New York* (1992), *Loaded Weapon 1* (1993), *The Three Musketeers* (1993), *The Shadow* (1994), *The Pebble And The Penguin* voice only (1995), *Congo* (1995), *Muppet Treasure Island* (1996), *Lover's Knot* (1996), *McHale's Navy* (1997), *A Christmas Carol* voice only (1997), *The Rugrats Movie* voice only (1998), *Pirates Of The Plain* (1999), *The Titanic Chronicles* (1999), *Robots Of Mars* voice only (1999), *Four Dogs Playing Poker* (1999), *Sorted* (2000), *Charlie's Angels* (2000), *Rugrats In Paris: The Movie* voice only (2000), *Lion Of Oz* voice only (2000), *Scary Movie 2* (2001), *Ritual* (2001), *The Scoundrel's Wife* (2002).

## CUTTING CREW

Fronted by vocalist/guitarist Nick Van Eede (b. Nicholas Van Eede, 14 June 1958, East Grinstead, West Sussex, England), Cutting Crew was formed when he began working with Canadian guitarist Kevin Scott MacMichael (b. 7 November 1951, Halifax, Nova Scotia, Canada). The duo came together when MacMichael's group Fast Forward were supporting Eede's unit the Drivers on a Canadian tour. The two subsequently recorded some demos in Toronto and during 1986 added Colin Farley (b. 24 February 1959, England; bass) and Martin Beedle (b. 18 September 1961, Hull, North Humberside, England; drums) to form Cutting Crew. The title of their debut single '(I Just) Died In Your Arms' was a phrase Van Eede coined after making love to his girlfriend. This memorable song reached number 4 in the UK but surpassed expectations by climbing to number 1 in the USA in the spring of 1987. A further US Top 40 hit followed with the frantic 'One For The Mockingbird', backed with the anti-cocaine 'Mirror And A Blade'. The plaintive 'I've Been In Love Before' returned them to the US Top 10 later that year, yet the single struggled to reach the UK Top 30 the following year after its third chart entry. Cutting Crew never regained their commercial impetus, and disbanded following the release of a third album, 1992's *Compus Mentus*, which was recorded by the core duo of Van Eede and MacMichael.

● ALBUMS: *Broadcast* (Siren/Virgin 1986) ★★★, *The Scattering* (Siren/Virgin 1989) ★★, *Compus Mentus* (Virgin 1992) ★★.

● COMPILATIONS: *The Best Of Cutting Crew* (Virgin 1993) ★★★, *Best Of The 80's* (Simply The Best 2000) ★★★.

## CZUKAY, HOLGER

b. 24 March 1938, Danzig, Germany. Czukay was a founder member of influential German band Can. His own solo work has adopted a more experimental approach, using tape loops and *musique concrete* methods. After being expelled from Berlin's Music Academy for his disregard for musical conventions, he studied with *avant garde* composer Karlheinz Stockhausen from 1963 to 1966, before joining Can as bass player in 1968. They pioneered the use of electronics in a rock context and made numerous albums and composed several film soundtracks before Czukay left in the late 70s. As Cluster, he worked with Brian Eno, recording two albums for RCA Records before creating the highly praised *Movies*. Its backing musicians included African percussionist Reebop Kwaku Baah and his former Can colleagues. Among Czukay's later collaborators were Jah Wobble (for 1981's pioneering, sample-heavy *On The Way To The Peak Of Normal*) and David Sylvian (1988–89). Czukay caused an outcry in 1986 when 'Blessed Easter' included a 'cut-up' extract of a Papal speech. In 1989, Czukay rejoined Can to record *Rite Time*. Although he released two albums in the early 90s, Czukay concentrated on production work and the remastering of the Can back-catalogue. In 1997, he toured the US with Dr. Walker from Air Liquide, and returned to the studio to work on *Good Morning Story*.

● ALBUMS: with Rolf Dammers *Canaxis* (Music Factory 1969) ★★★, *Movies* (EMI 1979) ★★★★, with Jah Wobble *On The Way To The Peak Of Normal* (EMI 1982) ★★★★, with The Edge, Jah Wobble *Snake Charmer* (Island 1983) ★★★★, with Jaki Liebezeit, Jah Wobble *Full Circle* (Virgin 1983) ★★★, *Der Osten 1st Rot* (Virgin 1984) ★★★, *Rome Remains Rome* (Virgin 1986) ★★, with David Sylvian *Plight & Premonition* (Virgin 1988) ★★★, with Sylvian *Flux + Mutability* (Virgin 1989) ★★★★, *Radio Wave Surfer* (Virgin 1991) ★★★, *Moving Pictures* (Mute 1993) ★★★, with Dr. Walker *Clash* (Tone Casualties 1998) ★★★, *Good Morning Story* (Tone Casualties 1999) ★★★★, *La Luna* (Tone Casualties 2000) ★★★.

## D-MOB

D-Mob is essentially the creative vehicle of 'Dancin'' Danny D (b. Daniel Kojo Poku, England), an ex-McDonald's employee. He found solace by DJing for three or four years in the evenings, at one point working with journalist James Hamilton at Gullivers in Park Lane, London. He subsequently started club promotions for Loose Ends (for whom he contributed his first remix), Total Contrast and Full Force, before taking up an A&R post at Chrysalis Records. This brought a number of further remixing opportunities, including Nitro Deluxe, Kid 'N Play, Adeva and Eric B And Rakim's 'I Know You Got Soul' in tandem with Norman Cook. By the time he had started using the name D-Mob he had already released two records, as the Taurus Boys, which were minor hits in the US. Then came 'Warrior Groove', about the tribe (the Ashantis) his Ghanaian parents came from. The first D-Mob release was 1989's UK Top 5 hit 'We Call It Acieed' which featured Gary Haisman on vocals. It was a stirring acid house tune, bringing the underground scene a good deal of notoriety when politicians and papers determined its subject matter was drugs-related. The BBC, in its wisdom, banned it from *Top Of The Pops*. However, as Poku confirmed to the press: 'I don't take any form of drugs. I don't even go to the doctor to get something for my cold.' Follow-up hits included 'It Is Time To Get Funky' (with London Rhyme Syndicate), 'C'mon And Get My Love' and 'That's The Way Of The World' (with Cathy Dennis) and 'Put Your Hands Together' (with Nuff Juice). He also produced/remixed records for Adeva, Juliet Roberts ('Another Place, Another Day, Another Time'), Monie Love, Diana Ross ('Working Overtime'), Chaka Khan ('I'm Every Woman') and the Cookie Crew ('Love Will Bring Us Together'), plus dozens more. In 1993, he brought back Dennis (who had enjoyed huge subsequent solo success) for vocals on 'Why', his 'comeback' single as D-Mob. As an in-demand producer and remixer he had never been away.

● ALBUMS: *A Little Bit Of This, A Little Bit Of That* (ffrr 1989) ★★★.

## D-TRAIN

This US soul group was formed in a Brooklyn, New York, USA high school in the early 80s by Hubert Eaves III (keyboards) and James Williams (lead vocals). Having signed to the Epic/Prelude label, they found greater success in the UK than in their home country. They enjoyed three UK Top 30 hits with 'You're The One For Me' (1982), 'Music, Part 1' (1983) and 'You're The One For Me (Remix)' (1985). D-Train's biggest US hit was the *Billboard* R&B Top 5 single, 'Something's On Your Mind' (1983). However, the anticipated breakthrough in the USA never materialized and the group split in 1985 with Williams pursuing a solo career. Again, restricted to R&B chart success, Williams' three notable hits were 'Misunderstanding' (number 10, 1986), 'Oh, How I Love You (Girl)' (number 22, 1987), and 'In Your Eyes' (number 11, 1988).

● ALBUMS: *D-Train* (Prelude 1982) ★★★, *Music* (Prelude 1983) ★★★, *Something's On Your Mind* (Prelude 1984) ★★, *You're The One For Me* (Prelude 1985) ★★.

● COMPILATIONS: *The Best Of D-Train* (Unidisc 1990) ★★★, *The Best Of The 12" Mixes* (Unidisc 1992) ★★★, *Essential Dancfloor Artists Volume 2* (Sequel 1994) ★★★.

### D.A.F.

This German band, based in Dusseldorf, specialized in minimalist electro-dance music, epitomized by their big dancefloor hit 'Der Mussolini'. The initials stood for Deutsch Amerikanische Freundschaft, a term first invoked on local posters to symbolize postwar American-German friendship, and the line-up comprised Robert Görl (drums, synthesizer), Michael Kehmer (bass), Chrislo Hass (saxophone, synthesizer, bass), and Gabi Delgado-Lopez (vocals). *Die Kleinen Und Die Bösen* was their first album available in the UK because *Produkt* had only been available in Germany. *Die Kleinen* (the title translates as The Small And The Evil) was released on the Mute Records label in 1980. Recorded in London, the album was uneven and is generally considered as unrepresentative, dominated by 'songs' whose heritage combined *Pink Flag*-era Wire and Can influences. Afterwards Görl and Delgado-Lopez continued as a duo (Haas would later join Crime And The City Solution), recording three acclaimed albums for Virgin Records in an 18-month period. These comprised a mixture of Teutonic fantasy, love songs, and social statements. Delgado-Lopez's refusal to sing in English condemned them to a minority international market. Contrary to their dour image, there was much to admire in the exemplary pop of singles such as 'Verlieb Dich In Mich'. Indeed, in 1981 they guested on the Eurythmics first album, *In The Garden*. Later Annie Lennox would return the compliment by adding vocals to Gorl's solo 'Darling Don't Leave Me' single and several tracks on the accompanying album. Görl and Delgado-Lopez reformed in 1986 to record an out-and-out dance album, before returning to solo projects.

● ALBUMS: *Ein Produkt Der D.A.F.* (Warning/Atatack 1979) ★★★, *Die Kleinen Und Die Bösen* (Mute 1980) ★★, *Alles Ist Gut* (Virgin 1981) ★★★, *Gold Und Liebe* (Virgin 1981) ★★★, *Für Immer* (Virgin 1982) ★★★, *Live In London* (Music For Midgets 1984) ★★, *1st Step To Heaven* (Ariola 1986) ★★.

Solo: Gabi Delgado *Mistress* (Virgin 1983) ★★★. Robert Görl *Night Full Of Tension* (Elektra 1984) ★★.

● COMPILATIONS: *Deutsche Amerikanische Freundschaft* (Virgin 1988) ★★★.

### D.O.A.

This explosive band was based in Vancouver, Canada, and formed in 1978, before emerging as their country's most popular and influential hardcore act. The line-up featured Joey 'Shithead' Keithley (lead vocals, guitar), Randy Rampage (bass, vocals), Chuck Biscuits (drums), and Brad Kent (guitar, ex-Avengers). Early releases included the *Disco Sucks* EP on their own Sudden Death Records, an incredibly rare artefact. Dave Gregg was added as second guitarist in 1980 to expand the band's sound (Kent was only a temporary member). In the early 80s, they toured incessantly, and not only defined their own sound but much of the subsequent 'hardcore' genre. The *Positively D.O.A.* EP and *Hardcore 81* proved hugely important to the development of North American punk. The latter album even gave the movement an identity, not only in name, but as a political agenda.

The band's most successful line-up collapsed in 1982. Biscuits left to join the Circle Jerks (and subsequently Black Flag and Danzig), while Randy Rampage went on to a solo career. Greg 'Dimwit' James (drums, ex-Subhumans, Pointed Sticks, and actually Chuck Biscuits' elder brother) and Brian 'Wimpy Boy' Goble (bass, vocals, ex-Subhumans) then joined. D.O.A.'s product in this incarnation was almost as invigorating. However, the third album realized fully the potential of its two predecessors: *Let's Wreck The Party* was a definitive, hard-rocking, intelligent punk record. After its release, James departed and was replaced on drums by Jon Card (ex-Personality Crisis and SNFU). Chris Prohourn aka 'Humper The Dumper' (guitar, vocals, ex-Red Tide) also joined when Dave Gregg started his own band, Groovaholics. Keithley formed Joey Keithley's Instinct when D.O.A. briefly disbanded, but reformed the group in 1990 with Goble and new drummer Ken Jensen (d. January 1995). Keithley also appeared as a biker cop alongside old friend Jello Biafra in the movie *Terminal City Ricochet*. D.O.A. would subsequently record a ferocious minialbum in tandem with the former Dead Kennedys vocalist. Asked in 1994 if he saw himself as a punk Tom Jones (D.O.A. having covered one of the Welshman's songs), Keithley offered this career summation: 'Well, D.O.A. can't keep going on forever, though some people say it already has, but I gotta think of my career later on in life, y'know, down in Vegas and Reno.' Morbidly compelling, *The Black Spot* commemorated Jensen, who died in a house fire in January 1995, and several other former members and friends of the band who had recently died.

● ALBUMS: *Something Better Change* (Friend's 1980) ★★★, *Hardcore '81* (Friend's 1981) ★★★, *Let's Wreck The Party* (Alternative Tentacles 1985) ★★★★, *True (North) Strong And Free* (Rock Hotel/Profile 1987) ★★★, *Murder* (Restless 1990) ★★, with Jello Biafra *Last Scream Of The Missing Neighbors* mini-album (Alternative Tentacles 1990) ★★★, *Talk Minus Action Equals Zero* (Roadrunner 1990) ★★★, *13 Flavours Of Doom* (Alternative Tentacles 1992) ★★, *Loggerheads* (Alternative Tentacles 1993) ★★★, *The Black Spot* (Essential Noise/Virgin 1995) ★★★, *Festival Of Atheists* (Sudden Death 1998) ★★★.

● COMPILATIONS: *Bloodied But Unbowed* (CD Presents 1984) ★★★★, *The Dawning Of A New Error*

(Alternative Tentacles 1991) ★★★, *The Lost Tapes* (Orchard 2000) ★★★.
● VIDEOS: *Assassination Club* (JettiSoundz 1984).

## DALEK I LOVE YOU

From the ashes of Liverpool, England-based punk band Radio Blank, Alan Gill (guitar, vocals) and David Balfe (bass, vocals, synthesizer), formed Dalek I Love You in November 1977. Disagreement over the band's name – Balfe wanted the Daleks, whereas Gill preferred Darling I Love You – resulted in the compromised title, and with the addition of Dave Hughes (keyboards), Chris 'Teepee' Shaw (synthesizer), plus a drum machine, the first of many loose line-ups was complete. In July 1978, Balfe left to join Big In Japan. After a string of critically acclaimed synthesizer-pop singles, *Compass Kum'pass* was released in 1980, arriving in the wake of acts such as OMD and Tubeway Army who had brought electronics into the mainstream charts. A worldwide contract with Korova Records produced the singles 'Holiday In Disneyland' and 'Ambition', and the album *Dalek I Love You*, which meshed layered synth and psychedelic fragments with starry-eyed vocals, augmented by excellent harmonies. Again, none achieved any real commercial success and Phil Jones decided to put the band 'on ice'. During this period he was busy writing and recording the soundtrack for the movie *Letter To Brezhnev* (1985), and formed the Bopadub label in Birkenhead, which issued a series of cassettes culminating in 1985 with *Naive*, recorded by the re-formed Dalek I. In 1986, after eight years of tentative existence, there was still optimism about future releases and, subsequently, *Compass Kum'pass* was re-released by Fontana Records in 1989, acknowledging the importance of this seminal electronic band.
● ALBUMS: *Compass Kum'pass* (Backdoor 1980) ★★★, *Dalek I Love You* (Korova 1983) ★★★, as Dalek I *Naive* (Bopadub 1985) ★★.

## DALTON, LACY J.

b. Jill Byrem, 13 October 1948, Bloomsburg, Pennsylvania, USA. Dalton's father played guitar and mandolin, but she was originally determined to be an artist. At the age of 18, she moved to Los Angeles and then settled in Santa Cruz, where she played the clubs for 12 years. She worked as a protest singer and then became the lead singer with a psychedelic band, Office, under the name of Jill Croston. A demo tape brought her to the attention of record producer Billy Sherrill, who signed her to Columbia Records in Nashville in 1979. Her gravelly, bluesy voice was unusual for country singers and thus made her work distinctive. Her 1980 debut *Lacy J. Dalton* is regarded by many as a classic, and she is often described by the title of one of its songs, 'Hillbilly Girl With The Blues'. Her US country hits include 'Crazy Blue Eyes', 'Tennessee Waltz', 'Hard Times' and '16th Avenue'. *Highway Diner* (1986) moved her into Bruce Springsteen territory, and she had a pop hit with 'Working Class Man'. By way of contrast, she was featured alongside Bobby Bare, George Jones and Earl Scruggs on her album *Blue Eyed Blues*. Dalton

recorded for Capitol Records and Liberty Records in the late 80s and early 90s. Her most recent release, *Wild Horse Crossing*, appeared on the independent Let 'Em Run label.
● ALBUMS: *Lacy J. Dalton* (Columbia 1980) ★★★★, *Hard Times* (Columbia 1980) ★★★, *Takin' It Easy* (Columbia 1981) ★★★, *16th Avenue* (Columbia 1982) ★★★, *Dream Baby* (Columbia 1983) ★★★, *Can't Run Away From Your Heart* (Columbia 1985) ★★, *Highway Diner* (Columbia 1986) ★★, *Blue Eyed Blues* (Columbia 1987) ★★, *Survivor* (Universal 1989) ★★★, *Lacy J.* (Capitol Nashville 1990) ★★★, *Crazy Love* (Capitol Nashville 1991) ★★★, *Chains On The Wind* (Liberty 1992) ★★, *Wild Horse Crossing* (Let 'Em Run 1999) ★★★.
● COMPILATIONS: *Greatest Hits* (Columbia 1983) ★★★★, *The Best Of Lacy J. Dalton* (Liberty 1994) ★★★, *Pure Country* (Sony 1998) ★★★, *Anthology* (Renaissance 2000) ★★★★.

## DANIELS, PHIL, AND THE CROSS

Daniels (b. 25 October 1958, London, England), a graduate of London's Anna Scher Theatre School and a member of the Royal Shakespeare Company, had flirted with pop as part of Renoir. Following his involvement in the Mod blockbuster *Quadrophenia*, the persona of Jimmy the Mod was launched into the rock world with the aid of Peter Hugo-Daly (keyboards), Barry Neil (bass) and John McWilliams (drums), Daniels himself handling both vocal and guitar duties. A solitary album on RCA Records was released, but sales were minimal, despite full-page advertisements in the music press, a charitable reaction from some critics and a concert itinerary centred on the metropolis. Daniels returned to stage, television and film work, notably satirizing the music industry in Hazel O'Connor's *Breaking Glass*. In 1994 he was to be found singing in a new West End production of *Carousel*, while also being celebrated as a cult icon of the 70s and 80s (being featured on the cover of the hip dance compilation *The Junior Boy's Own Collection*). His vocals on the title track to Blur's *Parklife* (1994) gave him further exposure.
● ALBUMS: *Phil Daniels And The Cross* (RCA 1980) ★★.

## DANNY WILSON

This quality pop act from Dundee, Scotland featured Kit Clark (guitar/vocals), Gary Clark (guitar/vocals), and Ged Grimes (keyboards/vocals). Named after Frank Sinatra's character in the movie *Meet Danny Wilson*, their clean-cut image was enshrined by their reputation for tidying up hotel rooms after 'trashing' them. The trio emerged in 1985, blending Steely Dan and soul harmonics on their promising debut album. *Meet Danny Wilson* boasted the hit singles 'Mary's Prayer', an extended Catholic metaphor, and 'Davy'. The subsequent album was too derivative in its focus on 60s beat, although it did provide another hit in 'Second Summer Of Love'. *Sweet Danny Wilson* is a retrospective compiling the best of the two aforementioned albums.
After Danny Wilson split up, vocalist Gary Clark released his debut, *Ten Short Songs About Love*,

before embarking on a fruitful career as a songwriter. Kit Clark went on to record as part of the Swiss Family Orbison, while Grimes now pursues a career writing music for computer games and advertisements.

● ALBUMS: *Meet Danny Wilson* (Virgin 1987) ★★★, *Be Bop Mop Top* (Virgin 1989) ★★★.

● COMPILATIONS: *Sweet Danny Wilson* (Virgin 1991) ★★★.

## DANSE SOCIETY

These UK gothic rock innovators evolved from Sheffield bands Y? and Lips-X. The two acts merged as Danse Crazy, establishing the line-up as Steve Rawlings (vocals) Paul Gilmartin (drums) Lyndon Scarfe (keyboards) and Paul Nash (guitar), as additional guitar and keyboard players were jettisoned. These included Paul Hampshire (aka Bee and Paul Hertz). They came to prominence first at the Futurama Festival 2 in Leeds, which was filmed by the BBC. After a slight change of name to Danse Society, and the filling of the bass position with Tim Wright, they performed their first gig at the Marples venue in Sheffield. The self-produced 'Clock' single provided the band with some acclaim, despite its short run of 1,000 copies. Management duties were taken over by Marcus Featherby, who released their EP, *No Shame In Death*, on his own Pax Records label. However, they soon returned to their own Society Records. The 1982 mini-album *Seduction* garnered strong support in the media and the band embarked on a series of interviews and live dates. Following one more independent single they signed to Arista Records: 'We'd done the Society Records thing and taken it as far as we could independently, we were totally out of money.' The dramatic 'Wake Up' was their debut, its sense of mystery and dark charm pre-dating the 'gothic' scene by at least a year. *Heaven Is Waiting* provided their first full album's worth of material, and further airplay from BBC disc jockeys John Peel and Janice Long kept them in the ascendant. However, internal rifts saw the replacement of Scarfe with former Music For Pleasure member David Whitaker. Relations with their record company also deteriorated when Arista failed to back a US tour. Litigation delayed further activities until a compromise was reached in March 1985. When they returned with 'Say It Again' (produced by Stock, Aitken and Waterman), it was to a bemused audience who had not anticipated such a sudden shift in style. The more commercial nature of their subsequent work failed to impress, and Arista rejected their proposed second album, *Heaven Again*. When they split in April 1986, Rawlings attempted to persevere with the funk-orientated Society, while the rest of the band continued briefly as Johnny In The Clouds. Since then Rawlings has only dabbled with music, while Wright and Scarfe both work in the computer industry.

● ALBUMS: *Seduction* mini-album (Society 1982) ★★, *Heaven Is Waiting* (Arista 1984) ★★★, *Looking Through* (Society 1986) ★★.

● COMPILATIONS: *Seduction: The Society Collection* (Anagram 2001) ★★★.

## DARLING BUDS

Formed in Wales in 1987 by Andrea Lewis (b. 25 March 1967, Newport, Wales; vocals), Harley Farr (b. 4 July 1964, Singapore; guitar), Bloss (drums) and Chris McDonagh (b. 6 March 1962, Newport, Wales; bass), the early part of the Darling Buds' career was as much a pure adrenalin rush as was their poppy/punk music. Following in the tradition of classic pop records by Blondie and the Waitresses, the Buds produced a series of sparkling sub-three-minute singles on the independent Native Records label ('Shame On You', etc.), becoming embroiled in the superfluous 'Blond' scene of that time alongside the Primitives. With the added incentive of increasingly celebrational live performances, Epic Records swiftly signed the band in 1988 and earned moderate chart success for the subsequent singles 'Burst' and 'Hit The Ground'. Unfortunately, in the true spirit of bubblegum pop, the Darling Buds' balloon soon began to deflate. Drummer Bloss was replaced by Jimmy Hughes (b. Liverpool, England) and the band's second album, *Crawdaddy*, witnessed a new sophisticated approach to recording that was at odds with their early material, creating few ripples in the musical pond. *Erotica* then emerged just one month before Madonna's opus of the same title, though doubtless it would have been ignored by a now disinterested music media regardless of its title. Following one further American tour the Darling Buds disbanded, with Lewis moving into acting.

● ALBUMS: *Pop Said ...* (Epic 1989) ★★★, *Crawdaddy* (Epic 1990) ★★★, *Erotica* (Epic 1992) ★★★.

## DAX, DANIELLE

b. Southend, Essex, England. Dax first came to prominence in 1980 with Karl Blake in the engaging Lemon Kittens. After *We Buy A Hammer For Daddy* and *The Big Dentist*, the group broke up in 1982. Dax next pursued a more straightforward pop route, mixed with forays into ethnic music and the *avant garde*. Her first solo album, *Pop-Eyes*, featured her playing 15 instruments, as well as composing and producing. She also displayed talents as a sleeve designer, contributing to Robert Fripp's *League Of Gentlemen*, among others. After a brief detour into acting, during which she appeared in the movie *The Company Of Wolves*, she returned with 1984's *Jesus Egg That Wept* and an extensive UK tour, during which she was backed by Dave Knight, Steve Reeves, Ian Sturgess and Martin Watts. Former artistic partner Blake also made a comeback on that album's 'Ostrich'. Her 1985 single, 'Yummer Yummer Man', was well received and revealed her love of 60s psychedelia. *Inky Bloaters* was an exceptionally eclectic work that maintained this reputation, and saw reviewers recall a myriad of influences in an attempt to gain some grasp of its contents. After appearing at the new music seminar in Boston, she was signed more permanently by Seymour Stein to Sire Records. He launched her on the US market with *Dark Adapted Eye*, which added five new picks to selections from *Inky Bloaters*. Her fourth album, *Blast The Human Flower*, produced by Stephen Street, included a revival of the Beatles' 'Tomorrow

Never Knows', but was an unhappy mainstream compromise that sacrificed Dax's earlier esotericism for accessibility. Her back-catalogue later became available again through her own Biter Of Thorpe label. Curiously, Dax was most recently seen as the winner of the 1997 Amateur Decorator Of The Year award on BBC Television's *Home Front*.

● ALBUMS: *Pop-Eyes* (Awesome 1983) ★★★, *Jesus Egg That Wept* mini-album (Awesome 1984) ★★★, *Inky Bloaters* (Awesome 1987) ★★★, *Dark Adapted Eye* (Sire 1988) ★★★, *Blast The Human Flower* (Sire 1990) ★★.
● COMPILATIONS: *Comatose-Non-Reaction: The Thwarted Pop Career Of Danielle Dax* (Biter Of Thorpe 1995) ★★★.
● VIDEOS: *Live From London* (Dubious Video 1987).
● FILMS: *The Company Of Wolves* (1984), *The Chimera*.

## DAZZ BAND

Bobby Harris masterminded the formation of the Dazz Band in the late 70s when he combined two Cleveland funk outfits, Bell Telefunk and the Kinsman Grill house band. The result was an eight-piece line-up, with Harris, Pierre DeMudd and Skip Martin III handling horns and vocals, and Eric Fearman (guitar), Kevin Frederick (keyboards), Kenny Pettus (percussion), Michael Wiley (bass) and Isaac Wiley (drums) providing the instrumental support. Coining the word 'Dazz' as a contraction of 'danceable jazz', Harris initially named the band Kinsman Dazz, under which moniker they registered two minor US hits in 1978 and 1979. The following year, they signed to Motown Records, where their irresistible blend of dance rhythms and commercial melodies established them as one of the label's hottest acts of the 80s. Their early albums were firmly in the jazz-funk style pioneered by Earth, Wind And Fire and George Benson. They graduated towards a harder, less melodic funk sound, enjoying a US Top 10 hit with 'Let It Whip' in 1982, which won them a Grammy award for the best performance by an R&B Vocal Duo or Group. Notable British success followed with the tougher, sparse rhythm of 'Let It All Blow'. *Jukebox* marked a transition towards a more rock-orientated sound which brought them continued success in the specialist black music charts, though crossover recognition among pop fans proved more elusive. The band suffered two personnel changes in 1985, when Marlon McClain and Keith Harrison replaced Eric Fearman and Kevin Frederick. A switch to Geffen Records in 1986 proved unfulfilling, and the group quickly moved on to RCA Records, but failed to re-establish their hit-making form.

● ALBUMS: *Invitation To Love* (Motown 1980) ★★★, *Let The Music Play* (Motown 1981) ★★★, *Keep It Live* (Motown 1982) ★★★, *On The One* (Motown 1983) ★★★, *Joystick* (Motown 1983) ★★★, *Jukebox* (Motown 1984) ★★★, *Hot Spot* (Motown 1985) ★★, *Wild And Free* (Geffen 1986) ★★, *Rock The Room* (RCA 1988) ★★, *Under The Streetlights* (Lucky 1995) ★★★, *Double Exposure* (Intersound 1997) ★★, *Here We Go Again* (Intersound 1998) ★★, *Time Traveler* (Eagle 2001) ★★★.

● COMPILATIONS: *Greatest Hits* (Motown 1987) ★★★★, *Funkology: The Definitive Dazz Band* (Motown 1994) ★★★★, *The Best Of The Dazz Band: The Millennium Collection* (Motown 200) ★★★★.

## dB's

Founder members of the US pop unit the dB's, Chris Stamey (b. Chapel Hill, North Carolina, USA; guitars, vocals), Gene Holder (bass) and Will Rigby (drums) had made their name around North Carolina, USA, with the Sneakers, alongside Mitch Easter (guitar, vocals). After two EPs (in 1976 and 1978) on Alan Betrock's Car label, Easter departed (later surfacing with Let's Active), the remaining three teamed up with keyboard player Peter Holsapple (ex-H-Bombs), to create the dB's. Stamey and Holsapple had previously worked together in Rittenhouse Square as early as 1972, while Stamey had indulged in a solo effort, 'Summer Sun' on Ork, in 1977. The dB's' debut single, 'I Thought (You Wanted To Know)', on the Car label, was issued towards the end of 1978, by which time the band had relocated to New York City. Signing with Shake, they then came up with 'Black And White', attracting attention in the UK and sealing a contract with Albion. The dB's delivered two albums in as many years for Albion, both capturing an evocative blend of melodic, occasionally Beatles-styled songs and new wave sensibilities. 'Dynamite', 'Big Brown Eyes' and 'Judy' were drawn from *Stands For Decibels* (1981), while the following year's *Repercussion* spawned 'Amplifier', 'Neverland' and 'Living A Lie'. However, the dB's failed to make any significant commercial impact, and Stamey left to resume his solo career. In the meantime, the dB's replaced him with Jeff Beninato and reunited for *The Sound Of Music* on I.R.S., joined by guests Van Dyke Parks and Syd Straw. In the 90s, Stamey and Holsapple reconvened as a duo to record an album, *Mavericks* (1991), before resurrecting the dB's name for *Paris Avenue*. Holsapple has been intermittently working in the wings with R.E.M. since the beginning of the 90s.

● ALBUMS: *Stands For Decibels* (Albion 1981) ★★★★, *Repercussion* (Albion 1982) ★★★★, *Like This* (Bearsville 1985) ★★★★, *The Sound Of Music* (I.R.S. 1987) ★★★, *Paris Avenue* (Monkey Hill 1994) ★★★. Solo: Will Rigby *Sidekick Phenomenon* (Egon 1985) ★★★.
● COMPILATIONS: *Amplifier* (Dojo 1986) ★★★, *Ride The Wild Tom Tom* (Rhino 1993) ★★★★, *Neverland* (Line 1999) ★★★★.

## DE BURGH, CHRIS

b. Christopher John Davidson, 15 October 1948, Argentina. The son of a UK diplomat, De Burgh began writing pop songs while studying at Trinity College in Dublin. After being signed to A&M Records, he was pushed out as support act for Supertramp, when they were enjoying massive success in 1975. His debut *Far Beyond These Castle Walls* was inspired by his family home in Ireland, a medieval castle which his father had turned into a hotel. The album had strong shades of the cosmic progressive rock period Moody Blues, although De Burgh's tales of historical fantasy were deemed a little fey by the critics. A single, 'Flying', taken from the album, failed to sell in the UK, but became a number 1 hit in Brazil. His follow-up *Spanish Train & Other Stories* also failed to sell, but one track, the hauntingly catchy 'A Spaceman Came Travelling', was picked up by British disc jockeys and became a perennial Christmas radio hit.

Whilst De Burgh could not break through in Britain and the USA, he was highly successful in Canada, South Africa, Europe and South America. His fifth album *Eastern Wind* outsold the Beatles' *Let It Be* in Norway, as it topped their charts. After an interminable wait, he finally had a UK success in 1982 with the Rupert Hine-produced *The Getaway*, containing the infectious minor hit 'Don't Pay The Ferryman'. The superior *Man On The Line*, released in 1984, featured another minor hit, 'High On Emotion', but it was the same year's compilation on the Telstar label that made De Burgh a big name in the UK.

After 11 years of touring and two dozen singles, De Burgh finally made it to the top of the UK charts in 1986 with the irresistibly romantic 'The Lady In Red'. The record became a worldwide hit and established him as a major artist. His back catalogue began to sell to a new generation of fans and the re-released 'A Spaceman Came Travelling' finally made the UK charts in 1987. De Burgh maintained his ability to write a perfect pop song with the infectious 'Missing You' in 1988, which narrowly missed the top spot in the UK, while *Into The Light* was another bestseller. *Flying Colours* became his biggest-selling album to date when it topped the UK album lists in 1988. In 1991, following the Gulf War, De Burgh donated all proceeds from his song 'The Simple Truth' to the Kurdish refugees. His 1992 release, *Power Of Ten*, maintained his standards, with De Burgh sticking to his guns by not changing his musical direction for the sake of commercial gain. In the words of a letter De Burgh sent to the A&M Records chairman: 'There is life after the Sex Pistols'.

Much controversy surrounded the singer in 1995 when he had a brief affair with his children's nanny. A few months later De Burgh was again hitting the headlines when he confessed that 'The Lady In Red' was not about his wife after all. At the end of a turbulent year, he released *Beautiful Dreams*, a live album on which the singer was backed by an orchestra. On this collection, De Burgh revisited his past by covering tracks by Elvis Presley, the Beatles and Roy Orbison. One of the singer's most notable recent songs is 'A New Star In Heaven Tonight', a tribute to the late Diana, Princess Of Wales available on the US-only compilation *The Lady In Red*.

● ALBUMS: *Far Beyond These Castle Walls* (A&M 1975) ★★, *Spanish Train & Other Stories* (A&M 1975) ★★, *At The End Of A Perfect Day* (A&M 1977) ★★★, *Crusader* (A&M 1979) ★★★, *Live In S.A.* (A&M 1979) ★★, *Eastern Wind* (A&M 1980) ★★, *The Getaway* (A&M 1982) ★★★, *Man On The Line* (A&M 1984) ★★★, *Into The Light* (A&M 1986) ★★★, *Flying Colours* (A&M 1988) ★★★, *High On Emotion: Live From Dublin* (A&M 1990) ★★★, *Power Of Ten* (A&M 1992) ★★★, *This Way Up* (A&M 1994) ★★, *Beautiful Dreams* (A&M 1995) ★★, *Love Songs* (A&M 1997)

★★, *Quiet Revolution* (Mercury 1999) ★★, *Timing Is Everything* (Mercury 2002) ★★.
● COMPILATIONS: *Best Moves* (A&M 1981) ★★★, *The Very Best Of Chris De Burgh* (Telstar 1984) ★★★, *From A Spark To A Flame: The Very Best Of Chris De Burgh* (A&M 1989) ★★★, *The Lady In Red: The Very Best Of Chris De Burgh* (Ark 21 2000) ★★★, *Notes From Planet Earth: The Ultimate Collection* (Mercury 2001) ★★★.

## DE GRASSI, ALEX

b. 13 February 1952, Yokosuka, Japan. The acoustic guitar sound of de Grassi had much to do with the growth and success of the Windham Hill Records label during the 80s. His clean, open-tuned new-age music was similar, although more complex, to that of founder William Ackerman. Together with another Windham Hill artist Michael Hedges, they pioneered much of the solo acoustic guitar terrain to which the new-age market was receptive.

Although he started his musical education on trumpet, De Grassi took up the guitar at 13. Like Ackerman he was drawn to the music of John Fahey and Leo Kottke but also cites John Renbourn as a major influence. De Grassi's music is both sombre and uplifting, good examples are the title track from 'Western' from 1980's *Clockwork* and 1984's *Southern Exposure*. The arrangements include minimal accompaniment from a small ensemble. De Grassi moved away from the label in the mid-80s, wanting to expand his musical horizon and feeling constricted by the stigma attached to Windham Hill. On *Altiplano* he used piano and guitar synthesizer and, with an expanded line-up including bass player Mark Egan, demonstrated a strong South American and Middle-Eastern influence. Recent releases appeared on the Earthbeat label, although he founded his own Tropo label in 1998.

● ALBUMS: *Turning: Turning Back* (Windham Hill 1978) ★★★, *Slow Circle* (Windham Hill 1979) ★★, *Clockwork* (Windham Hill 1981) ★★★, *Southern Exposure* (Windham Hill 1984) ★★★★, *Altiplano* (RCA/Novus 1987) ★★★, *Deep At Night* (Windham Hill 1991) ★★, *The World's Getting Loud* (Windham Hill 1993) ★★★, *Beyond The Night Sky: Lullabies For Guitar* (Earthbeat! 1996) ★★★, *The Water Garden* (Tropo 1998) ★★★★, *Alex de Grassi's Interpretations Of James Taylor* (Auditorium 1999) ★★★, *Bolivian Blues Bar* (Narada 1999) ★★★, with Quique Cruz *TataMonk* (Tropo 2000) ★★★, with G.E. Stinson *Shortwave Postcard* (Auditorium 2002) ★★★.
● COMPILATIONS: *A Windham Hill Retrospective* (Windham Hill 1992) ★★★★.
● VIDEOS: *The Artist's Profile* (Ecliptic Productions 1998), *Adventures In Fingerstyle Guitar: The Techniques And Arrangements Of Alex de Grassi* (Homespun Video).
● FURTHER READING: *Guitar Collection*, Alex de Grassi.

## DEAD CAN DANCE

Based in London, England, but tracing their origins to Australia, Dead Can Dance's long campaign in the music industry rarely attracted attention outside of a devoted following. Whether this was a result of wilful obscurism or a disciplined artistic vision is a moot point, but the band left behind more than a decade's worth of, by turns, infuriating and blissful, *avant garde* pop.

The band's name had the unfortunate effect of nailing their colours to the gothic masthead, though in truth they were light years away from this genre. Their 1984 debut collection was not as focused as later efforts, mingling their trademark male/female vocals with an uncoordinated mesh of chants and drawling guitar. However, from packaging to production it fitted the 4AD Records aesthetic perfectly, and there were enough hints of the less prosaic gems to come to distinguish the band. Reduced to the core duo of Brendan Perry and Lisa Gerrard, *Spleen And Ideal* was an altogether more thrilling and cohesive record, with the discordant guitar barrage abandoned in favour of a considered array of instruments, including cello, trombones and timpani. The clean production also lent the improved material greater clarity, though what the songs actually concerned was, typically, something for listeners to decide for themselves. *Within The Realm Of A Dying Sun* gave further indication of their talent, though some critics balked at the idea of giving the two singers one side each of the record, making its tone uneven. It also revealed a debt to music from the Middle East, a process that was further explored by the less satisfying *The Serpent's Egg*. *Aion* took as its premise medieval or 'early music', using Gregorian chants, similar in many ways to the work of Bel Canto, and baroque stylistics, played with genuine folk instruments (including hurdy gurdy and bagpipes). *Into The Labyrinth* confirmed Perry's greater awareness of electronics and samplers, and while *Towards The Within* is a basic live album, it primarily contains a phenomenal live repertoire never before committed to vinyl.

By 1995, Perry had begun work on his own album, while Gerrard's stunning vocal presence was heard to great effect on her solo debut, *The Mirror Pool*. The mother band's seventh studio album, *Spiritchaser*, arrived at a time when Dead Can Dance was being acknowledged as influences on the UK dance music community (Black Grape and Future Sound Of London have both sampled their work). This time the band moved away from the Celtic influences that exerted themselves on *Into The Labyrinth*, towards sounds reminiscent of African and South American music. However, as Gerrard succinctly informed the press: 'It's gone past the point of being "this" and "that". Music has come to a new age, where we're exposed to music from all over the world, from a much larger palate of colours.' For similar reasons, *Spiritchaser* served to validate the reason for Dead Can Dance's continuation into the 90s, the band having proved themselves among the most accurate cultural conductors in popular music, shifting emphasis effortlessly in keeping with the zeitgeist. Dead Can Dance was put on indefinite hold following the release of *Spiritchaser*. Gerrard collaborated with Australian keyboard player Pieter Bourke on 1998's haunting *Duality*, and Perry released his solo debut (*Eye Of The Hunter*) a year later.

● ALBUMS: *Dead Can Dance* (4AD 1984) ★★★★, *Spleen And Ideal* (4AD 1985) ★★★, *Within The Realm Of A Dying Sun* (4AD 1987) ★★★, *The Serpent's Egg* (4AD 1988) ★★★, *Aion* (4AD 1990) ★★★, *Into The Labyrinth* (4AD 1993) ★★★, *Towards The Within* (4AD 1994) ★★★★, *Spiritchaser* (4AD 1995) ★★★★.
● COMPILATIONS· *A Passage In Time* (Rykodisc 1991) ★★★★, *1981–1998* box set (Rhino 2001) ★★★★.
● VIDEOS: *Toward The Within* (Warners 1994).

## DEAD KENNEDYS

The undoubted kings of US punk, the Dead Kennedys, formed in San Francisco, California, USA, arrived on the 80s music scene with the most vitriolic and ultimately persuasive music ever to marshal the US underground (at least until the arrival of Nirvana). Even today, the sight of their name can send the uninitiated into a fit of apoplexy. Originally a quintet with a second guitarist called 6025, the latter left before recordings for the debut album took place, leaving a core group of Jello Biafra (b. Eric Boucher, 17 June 1958, Denver, Colorado, USA; vocals), Klaus Flouride (b. Geoffrey Lyall; bass), East Bay Ray Glasser (b. Ray Pepperell; guitar) and Ted (b. Bruce Slesinger; drums). As soon as they hit a studio, the results were extraordinary. Biafra, weaned partially on 70s Brit Punk as well as local San Francisco bands such as Crime and the Nuns, was the consummate frontman, his performances never far away from personal endangerment, including stage-diving and verbally lambasting his audience. He was certainly never destined to be an industry conformist – some of his more celebrated stunts included getting married in a graveyard, running for Mayor of San Francisco (he finished fourth) and allowing the crowd to disrobe him on stage. Lyrically, the Dead Kennedys always went for the jugular but twisted expectations; writing an anti-neutron bomb song called 'Kill The Poor' is a good example of their satire.

The band's debut single, 'California Uber Alles', attacked the 'new age' fascism of Californian governor Jerry Brown, a theme developed over a full-blown musical rollercoaster ride. Just as enduring is its follow-up, 'Holiday In Cambodia', which mercilessly parodied college student chic and the indifference to the suffering caused to others by America's foreign policy: 'Playing ethnicky jazz to parade your snazz on your five grand stereo/Bragging that you know how the niggers feel cold and the slum's got so much soul'. 'Too Drunk To Fuck', despite (naturally) a complete absence of airplay, made the UK Top 40 (there were a number of prosecutions linked to those wearing the accompanying T-shirt). Biafra established his own Alternative Tentacles Records after a brief flirtation with Miles Copeland's I.R.S. Records label (Cherry Red Records in the UK), and this has gone on to be a staple of the US alternative record scene, releasing music by both peers and progeny: Hüsker Dü, TSOL, D.O.A., NoMeansNo, Beatnigs and Alice Donut. Slesinger broke away to form the Wolverines at this point, having never been quite in tune with the Dead Kennedys' musical dynamic. His eventual replacement was Darren H. Peligro (b. Darren Henley; ex-Nubs, Speedboys, Hellations, SSI, who had also played guitar with the Jungle Studs and was the drummer for an early incarnation of Red Hot Chili Peppers).

If the band's debut album, *Fresh Fruit For Rotting Vegetables*, had followed a broadly traditional musical format, *In God We Trust, Inc.* indulged in ful-blown thrash. Undoubtedly the long-term inspiration behind literally hundreds of US noise merchants, it certainly took many by surprise with its minimalist adrenaline ('Dog Bite/On My Leg/S'Not Right, S'posed to Beg' practically encompassed the entire lyrics to one song). *Plastic Surgery Disasters* saw the band branch out again. Though it did not share *Fresh Fruit*'s immediacy, there were several stunning songs on offer once more ('Trust Your Mechanic', with Biafra's typically apocalyptic delivery, attacked the values of the service industry, and 'Well Paid Scientist' mocked the career ladder). *Frankenchrist* was more considered, allowing songs such as 'Soup Is Good Food' to bite hard. The cornerstone of the recording was 'Stars And Stripes Of Corruption', which predicted some of Biafra's later solo excursions by relentlessly pursuing a single theme. *Bedtime For Democracy* was the band's final studio recording, and a return to the aggressive speed of the previous mini-album, though without the shock value. Meanwhile, Biafra was on trial for the artwork given away with *Frankenchrist*, a pastiche of American consumerism by H.R. Giger (*Landscape #20* – often referred to as 'Penis Landscape'), which made its point with a depiction of row upon row of male genitalia entering anuses (i.e. everybody fucking everybody else).

Long an irritant to the US moral 'guardians', the PMRC now had Biafra in their sights. In truth the band had elected to call it a day anyhow, but there was a long hibernation while Biafra weathered the storm (he was eventually cleared on all counts and the case thrown out of court) before embarking on his next creative phase – an episodic solo career marked by collaborations with D.O.A. and NoMeansNo. Flouride released three albums for Alternative Tentacles, while East Bay Ray formed Scrapyard. Flouride, East Bay Ray and D.H. Peligro went to court in 2000 to successfully gain control of the Dead Kennedys' catalogue from Jello Biafra. Two years later, they embarked on a tour with Brandon Cruz as frontman.

Despite the ill-natured bickering of later years, the Dead Kennedys' contribution to music is best measured not by the number of copy bands who sprung up around the world, but by the enduring quality of their best records and Biafra's admirable and unyielding stance on artistic censorship.
● ALBUMS: *Fresh Fruit For Rotting Vegetables* (I.R.S./Cherry Red 1980) ★★★★, *In God We Trust, Inc.* mini-album (Alternative Tentacles/Faulty Products 1981) ★★★, *Plastic Surgery Disasters* (Alternative Tentacles 1982) ★★★, *Frankenchrist* (Alternative Tentacles 1985) ★★★, *Bedtime For Democracy* (Alternative Tentacles 1986) ★★★, *Mutiny On The Bay: Live From The San Francisco Bay Area* 1982, 1986 recordings (DKD 2001) ★★★.

Solo: Klaus Flouride *Cha Cha Cha With Mr. Flouride* (Alternative Tentacles 1985) ★★, *Because I Say So* (Alternative Tentacles 1988) ★★, *The Light Is Flickering* (Alternative Tentacles 1991) ★★.
● COMPILATIONS: *Give Me Convenience Or Give Me Death* (Alternative Tentacles 1987) ★★★★.
● VIDEOS: *Live In San Francisco* (Hendring Music Video 1987), *Dead Kennedys Live At DMPO's* (Visionary 1998).

## DEAD MILKMEN

This US crypto-punk band came from the active Philadelphian underground scene of the mid-80s and drew members who rejoiced in the unlikely names Joe Jack Talcum (guitar, vocals), Rodney Anonymous Melloncamp (vocals), Dave Blood (bass), and Dean Clean (drums). With each of their album titles punning a more famous rock release and songs such as 'Takin' Retards To The Zoo', 'Beach Party Vietnam', and 'The Thing That Only Eats Hippies', the Dead Milkmen were always destined for college favouritism. Utilizing an uncomplicated adolescent punk rock foundation, the band's 1985 debut album set out its stall by loading up on youthful satire and demanding to know the answer to the eternal questions – like why anybody likes the Doors. As basic but slightly more astute was *Eat Your Paisley!*, its b-movie song titles suggesting there was no immediate end in sight for the Milkmen's hyperactive juvenilia. *Bucky Fellini* saw a more fully fledged musical format, aided by guest musicians and improved songwriting – although with lyrical targets including '(Theme From) Blood Orgy Of The Atomic Fern' and 'Nitro Burning Funny Cars', it was obvious that the band had not yet turned into a 'proper' rock group. *Beelzebubba* boasted the minor hit single 'Punk Rock Girl', but was undistinguished elsewhere. The best song title yet arrived in 'If You Love Somebody, Set Them On Fire', drawn from the improved *Metaphysical Graffiti*. Guests included Butthole Surfers' Gilby Clarke, on the near-hysterical prog-rock bluff 'Anderson, Walkman, Buttholes and How!'. The band then moved to the Hollywood label and released two albums worthy of their name, the musical backing matching the lyrics at last. *Chaos Rules* was a haphazard live trawl through the band's greatest hits, and was followed by their final release, *Stoney's Extra Stout (Pig)*, a disappointingly lacklustre end to their recording career. Anonymous later resurfaced as the lead singer of Burn Witch Burn.
● ALBUMS: *Big Lizard In My Back Yard* (Fever/Enigma 1985) ★★★, *Eat Your Paisley!* (Fever/Restless 1986) ★★, *Bucky Fellini* (Fever/Enigma 1987) ★★★, *Instant Club Hit (You'll Dance To Anything)* mini-album (Fever/Enigma 1987) ★★, *Beelzebubba* (Fever/Enigma 1988) ★★★, *Metaphysical Graffiti* (Enigma 1990) ★★, *Soul Rotation* (Hollywood 1992) ★★★, *Not Richard, But Dick* (Hollywood 1993) ★★★, *Chaos Rules: Live At The Trocadero* (Restless 1994) ★★, *Stoney's Extra Stout (Pig)* (Restless 1996) ★★.
● COMPILATIONS: *Death Rides A Pale Cow: The Ultimate Collection* (Restless 1997) ★★★★, *Cream Of The Crop: The Best Of The Dead Milkmen* (BMG 1998) ★★★.

## DEAD OR ALIVE

One of this band's principal assets is the androgynous persona of Pete Burns (b. 5 August 1959, Port Sunlight, England; vocals) who had fronted Liverpool's Mystery Girls in 1977, then Nightmares In Wax, in which he was accompanied by Mick Reid (guitar), Martin Healey (keyboards), Walter Ogden (bass), and ex-Mystery Girl Phil Hurst (drums). This line-up recorded an EP for a local label and a track for a 1980 compilation *Hicks From The Sticks*, before Burns and Healey formed Dead Or Alive with Sue James (bass), Joe Musker (drums) and a flux of guitarists including Wayne Hussey, who later found fame with the Mission. The line-up stabilized when the act was signed to Inevitable for some flop singles before soliciting the attentions of Epic, who saw their singer as an 'answer' to Boy George. With Burns now joined by Mike Percy (bass), Steve Coy (drums), and Tim Lever (keyboards), the band's television plugs sent a revival of KC And The Sunshine Band's 'That's The Way (I Like It)' into the UK Top 30 in 1984. Slowly but surely, 'You Spin Me Round (Like A Record)', from *Youthquake*, arrived at number 1 in the New Year and was the first UK chart-topper for Stock, Aitken and Waterman. Soundalike follow-ups fared less well but, after the UK chart-topper entered the US Top 20, the band enjoyed further major record success in the late 80s with *Youthquake* featuring in *Billboard*'s album list, and its title track returning them to the UK Top 10. Lever and Percy left following the release of 1989's *Nude*. In the 90s, after a brief period known as International Chrysis, Burns and Coy found greater success abroad, especially in Japan where *Nukleopatra* was a major hit. The duo has worked hard to maintain their overseas following.

● ALBUMS: *Sophisticated Boom Boom* (Epic 1984) ★★, *Youthquake* (Epic 1985) ★★★, *Mad, Bad, And Dangerous To Know* (Epic 1987) ★★, *Rip It Up* (Epic 1987) ★★★, *Nude* (Epic 1989) ★★, *Nukleopatra* (Sony/Cleopatra 1995) ★★, *Fragile* (Avex 2000) ★★.
● VIDEOS: *Youthquake* (CBS-Fox 1988).

## DEBARGE

One sister, Bunny DeBarge, and four brothers, Mark, James, Randy and El DeBarge, combined to form this family group in Grand Rapids, Michigan, USA, in 1978. Signed to Motown Records in 1979, they were viewed and marketed as successors to the young Jackson Five, a ploy helped by the physical similarity between El DeBarge and Michael Jackson. After several years of grooming from Motown's A&R department, the group (then known as the DeBarges) were launched with the album *The DeBarges* in March 1981, and gained their initial soul hit 18 months later. 'I Like It' repeated this success and crossed over into the pop charts, while two 1983 hits, 'All This Love' and 'Time Will Reveal', established DeBarge as one of America's most popular acts in the teenage market. A support slot on Luther Vandross' 1984 US tour brought them to a wider audience, and in 1985 they scored their biggest hit with the seductive 'Rhythm Of The Night', taken from the soundtrack to Motown's movie *The Last Dragon*, in which the group also appeared. This single reached number 3 in the US charts, a success that the follow-up release, 'Who's Holding Donna Now?' came close to repeating. Lead vocalist El DeBarge had become synonymous with the group's name, and his decision to go solo in February 1986 effectively sabotaged the group's career. In 1987, Bunny also departed when the rest of the group signed to Striped Horse Records. In the event, only Mark and James (who had briefly been married to Janet Jackson in the mid-80s) appeared on the resulting *Bad Boys*, by which time their commercial impetus had been lost. The group's wholesome image was seriously damaged by the arrest and conviction of their other brothers Bobby and Chico DeBarge in 1988 on cocaine trafficking charges.

● ALBUMS: *The DeBarges* (Gordy 1981) ★★★, *All This Love* (Gordy 1982) ★★★, *In A Special Way* (Gordy 1983) ★★★, *Rhythm Of The Night* (Gordy 1985) ★★, *Bad Boys* (Striped Horse 1988) ★★.
● COMPILATIONS: *Greatest Hits* (Motown 1986) ★★★, *Ultimate Collection* (Motown 1997) ★★★, *The Best Of DeBarge: The Millennium Collection* (Motown 2000) ★★★.

## DEBARGE, BUNNY

b. 15 March 1955, Grand Rapids, Michigan, USA. Bunny DeBarge was a vocalist in the family group DeBarge from their inception in 1978 until 1987. She was the first member of the group to be married, and missed several national tours during her three pregnancies, although she appeared regularly on their Motown Records releases. In 1987, she chose to remain as a solo artist with the label rather than follow the rest of the group to Striped Horse Records. Her loyalty was rewarded when *In Love*, a light pop/soul concoction, was a minor US hit album, and 'Save The Best For Me' became a US Top 20 black music hit.

● ALBUMS: *In Love* (Motown 1987) ★★.

## DEBARGE, CHICO

b. Jonathan Arthur DeBarge, 1966, Grand Rapids, Michigan, USA. Chico DeBarge was too young to join the family group DeBarge in 1978, but he was signed to a solo contract with Motown Records in 1986, issuing a self-titled album in a harder, funk-rooted style than his brothers and sisters. His debut single, 'Talk To Me', was a major US hit, and he had four more black music chart entries up to 1988. His promising career was effectively ended when he and his brother Bobby DeBarge (a former member of the Motown group Switch) were arrested and then convicted on charges of trafficking cocaine in October 1988. Released after six years' imprisonment, DeBarge returned to music in the late 90s with *Long Time No See*.

● ALBUMS: *Chico DeBarge* (Motown 1986) ★★★, *Kiss Serious* (Motown 1988) ★★★, *Long Time No See* (Universal 1997) ★★★, *The Game* (Motown 1999) ★★★.

## DEBARGE, EL

b. Eldra DeBarge, 4 June 1961, Grand Rapids, Michigan, USA. El DeBarge became the lead singer of the family vocal group DeBarge from their formation in 1978. He was featured on all the group's hits between 1982 and 1985, when he elected to pursue a solo career, leaving DeBarge the following year. His eponymous debut album was an attractive mixture of pop and soul, fashioned in the style of Michael Jackson, on whom DeBarge modelled his career. He achieved a US number 1 black music hit in 1986 with 'Who's Johnny?', the theme song of the movie *Short Circuit*, and re-emerged after a two-year pause in his career with the single 'Real Love' in 1989, which was soon followed by *Gemini*. In 1990, he co-wrote and sang lead on Quincy Jones' 'The Secret Garden', before moving to Warner Brothers Records.

● ALBUMS: *El DeBarge* (Gordy 1986) ★★★, *Gemini* (Motown 1989) ★★★, *Heart, Mind & Soul* (Warners/Reprise 1994) ★★★.

## DEEP FREEZE MICE

Deep Freeze Mice was effectively a front operation for Alan Jenkins (b. 16 March 1959, Dudley, West Midlands, England; guitar, clarinet, vocals). Jenkins' one-man battle against the heads (and underlings) of the corporate music industry has seen him lead various bands since the late 70s. Along with the Chrysanthemums, Jody And The Creams and Ruth's Refrigerator, the majority of his 80s output was released under the Deep Freeze Mice moniker. Formed in 1979, the band's line-up included Sherree Lawrence (b. 24 May 1959, Rushden, Northamptonshire, England; keyboards), Michael Bunnage (b. 21 December 1958, Romford, Essex, England; bass) and Graham Summers (b. 30 July 1958, Wellingborough, Northamptonshire, England; drums). Peter Gregory replaced Summers in 1983. Deep Freeze Mice's brand of English psychedelia, which drew upon such influences as Syd Barrett, Captain Beefheart, the Mothers Of Invention, Soft Machine, plus a soupçon of the Velvet Underground, often made for uncomfortable listening, but conversely also displayed a talent for commercial pop songs.

Following the break–up of Deep Fried Mice, Jenkins privately published a booklet entitled *How To Be In A Pop Group* (1990), an accurate and highly amusing account of the pitfalls to be endured along the road to possible fame and failure, naming names in the process. He continues to record with the Creams and Thurston Lava Tube, remaining on the periphery of the music business, which he studiously despises for its lack of adventure.

● ALBUMS: *My Geraniums Are Bulletproof* (Mole Embalming 1979) ★★★, *Teenage Head In My Refrigerator* (Mole Embalming 1981) ★★★, *The Gates Of Lunch* (Mole Embalming 1982) ★★★, *Saw A Ranch House Burning Last Night* (Mole Enbalming 1983) ★★★, *I Love You Little BoBo With Your Delicate Golden Lions* (Cordelia 1984) ★★★, *Hang On Constance Let Me Hear The News* (Cordelia 1985) ★★★, *Rain Is When The Earth Is Television* (Cordelia 1986) ★★★, *Live In Switzerland* (In Der Tat/Logical Fish 1986) ★★★, *War, Famine, Death, Pestilence And Miss Timberlake* (Cordelia 1987) ★★★, *The Tender Yellow Ponies Of Insomnia* (Cordelia 1989) ★★★.

## DEF JAM RECORDS

Russell Simmons (b. Hollis, Queens, New York, USA) and Rick Rubin's (b. Frederick Rubin, Long Island, New York, USA) New York, USA street rap label, Def Jam Records brought the world, amongst other things, the skewed genius of the Beastie Boys and the militancy of Public Enemy. The label made its debut with T. La Rock and Jazzy Jay's 'It's Yours', a record released in conjunction with Partytime/Streetwise Records. Managing director Simmons (brother of Run-DMC's Joe Simmons) was described as 'The mogul of rap' by *The Wall Street Journal* as early as 1984, following his early managerial coups. A year later Def Jam had netted a landmark distribution deal with Columbia Records, the first results of which were the LL Cool J smash, 'I Can't Live Without My Radio'. Simmons also concurrently managed the affairs of Whodini, Kurtis Blow, Dr Jeckyll And Mr Hyde and Run DMC, co-producing the latter's first two albums alongside Larry Smith. Rubin's credits included the label debut by T. La Rock and Jazzy Jay. Together they produced Run-DMC's platinum set *Tougher Than Leather*, before Rubin's productions of LL Cool J and the Beastie Boys' enormously successful debut sets. The biggest signing, however, would be Public Enemy, though Simmons was at first unconvinced of their potential.

The Rubin/Simmons partnership dissolved in acrimony in 1987. As Rubin recalled: 'Russell's and my visions were going in different directions. My taste was growing more extreme, toward more aggressive and loud music, and Russell would say, like, "You made a hit record with the Bangles, why are you wasting your time with this stuff like Public Enemy?"' Simmons would go on to head several other business ventures, including Rush Management, the Phat Farm clothing line and HBO's Def Comedy Jam, continuing to manage the careers of R&B artists including Alyson Williams, Oran' Juice Jones, Tashan and the Black Flames. However, he lost the Beastie Boys in litigation over unpaid royalties on their debut album.

Rubin, meanwhile, set up Def American Records in 1988. There he continued to enjoy success with a variety of artists, including several thrash metal outfits such as Slayer, then the Black Crowes. He earned himself a series of rebukes in hip-hop circles when he released a record by the latter with lyrics that gloried in allusions to an Aryan race war. He maintained his links with rap, however, via similarly outrageous concerns such as the Geto Boys. On 27 August 1993 Rubin officially dropped the 'Def' from the Def American imprint, reasoning that now the word Def had been incorporated into the latest edition of a major US dictionary, it no longer had the street value it once enjoyed. He 'buried' it via an elaborate New Orleans style funeral, complete with a dixieland jazz band. Def Jam continued in its own right, though it left its original deal with Columbia and teamed up with PolyGram Records. In 1992, Simmons opened a west coast subsidiary, DJ West, to follow the action there, signing Boss and MC Sugs. However, despite its continued presence, Def Jam never regained its standing of the 80s, when it became the most significant rap label ever and one of the decade's most vital musical outlets. Kevin Liles was appointed as the company's first president in 1998.

● COMPILATIONS: *Def Jam, The First Ten Years Volumes 1–4* (Def Jam 1995) ★★★★, *The Box Set 1985–1995* 4-CD box set (Def Jam 1995) ★★★★, *The History Of Hip Hop, Volume 1: 1985–2001* (Def Jam 2001) ★★★★.

● FURTHER READING: *Life And Def: Sex, Drugs, Money, + God*, Russell Simmons with Nelson George. *The Men Behind Def Jam: The Radical Rise Of Russell Simmons And Rick Rubin*, Alex Ogg.

## DEF LEPPARD

This perennially popular UK hard rock band was formed in 1977 in Sheffield, Yorkshire by Pete Willis (b. 16 February 1960, Sheffield, Yorkshire, England; guitar), Rick Savage (b. 2 December 1960, Sheffield, Yorkshire, England; bass) and Tony Kenning (drums), as Atomic Mass. They assumed their current name when Joe Elliott (b. 1 August 1959, Sheffield, Yorkshire, England; vocals) joined the band. The quartet initially hired a tiny room in a spoon factory, which served as a rehearsal area, for £5 per week. Early in 1978, Willis met another young guitarist, Steve Clark (b. 23 April 1960, Sheffield, Yorkshire, England, d. 8 January 1991, London, England), and invited him to join. Clark agreed only on condition that they would play some 'proper' shows, and in July that year, Def Leppard debuted at Westfield School before an audience of 150 children. After several gigs, the band voted to dismiss their drummer, replacing him with Frank Noon, who was working with another Sheffield group, the Next Band.

In 1979, Def Leppard recorded a debut EP for Bludgeon Riffola Records, which included 'Ride Into The Sun', 'Getcha Rocks Off' and 'The Overture'. Shortly after its release, Noon returned to the Next Band, and Rick Allen (b. 1 November 1963, Sheffield, Yorkshire, England) became Def Leppard's permanent drummer. Later that year, the band supported Sammy Hagar and AC/DC on short UK tours. This generated considerable interest and the band was offered a contract by Vertigo Records. Their Tom Allom-produced debut, *On Through The Night*, was issued in 1980, climbing to number 15 in the UK album charts. The band subsequently staged their first headlining tour of Britain and also visited America for the first time – a move that prompted fans to accuse them of 'selling out', making their displeasure known by throwing cans at the band during their appearance at the Reading Festival that summer. The following year's *High 'N' Dry* was recorded with producer Robert 'Mutt' Lange, and reached number 26 in the UK and number 38 in the USA. *Pyromania* in 1983 saw the first change in the band's line-up since 1979. After missing many pre-production meetings and arriving drunk for a recording session, Pete Willis was sacked and replaced by ex-Girl guitarist Phil Collen (b. 8 December 1957, Hackney, London, England). *Pyromania* was Def Leppard's most successful to date, climbing to number 2 in the US album charts,

but they were unable to build on that momentum. On New Year's Eve 1984, tragedy struck when drummer Rick Allen was involved in a car crash in which he lost his left arm. The band maintained faith in their percussionist, and did not resume work until Allen had perfected a specially designed kit that made it possible for him to play most of the drums with his feet. His recovery severely delayed the recording of *Hysteria*, which was finally released in 1987 and eventually sold a staggering 15 million copies worldwide. It topped both the British and American charts, and produced two Top 5 US singles, 'Armageddon It' and the anthemic 'Pour Some Sugar On Me', and the October 1988 number 1 'Love Bites'. To promote the album, the band embarked on a 14-month world tour, which ended at the Memorial Arena, Seattle, in October 1988. This was destined to be Steve Clark's last show with the band. As they began work on their belated follow-up to *Hysteria*, Clark was found dead in his London flat after consuming a lethal mixture of drugs and alcohol. The rest of the band subsequently revealed that they had spent years trying to divert Clark from his self-abusive lifestyle.

Faced once again by tragedy, Def Leppard soldiered manfully through the recording sessions for their fifth album, *Adrenalize*, which was released in March 1992 and immediately scaled the charts, topping the UK and US lists on release (unlike *Hysteria*, which had taken 49 weeks to crawl to the top in the USA). Greeted with the usual mixture of critical disdain and public delight (the band's fans had chosen the title), Def Leppard celebrated by performing at the Freddie Mercury tribute concert at Wembley Stadium. This event also introduced replacement guitarist Vivian Campbell (b. 25 August 1962, Belfast, Northern Ireland; ex-Dio; Trinity; Whitesnake; and Shadow King), who had made his debut at a low-key Dublin gig. In 1995, Rick Allen faced the possibility of two years in jail after he was arrested for assaulting his wife in America. In the meantime, a greatest hits package and a new studio collection, *Slang*, were released. The following year Joe Elliott appeared in the soccer-inspired film *When Saturday Comes*. Championed as a return to the classic Def Leppard sound, 1999's *Euphoria* sounded a little tired and cliché-ridden although it leaped into the bestselling charts in the UK and USA. 'Demolition Man' featured UK racing driver Damon Hill on guitar.

● ALBUMS: *On Through The Night* (Mercury 1980) ★★★, *High 'N' Dry* (Mercury 1981) ★★★★, *Pyromania* (Mercury 1983) ★★★★, *Hysteria* (Mercury 1987) ★★★★, *Adrenalize* (Mercury 1992) ★★★, *Slang* (Mercury 1996) ★★★, *Euphoria* (Bludgeon Riffola 1999) ★★, *X* (Mercury/Island 2002) ★★★.

● COMPILATIONS: *Retro Active* (Mercury 1993) ★★★, *Vault: Def Leppard Greatest Hits 1980–1995* (Mercury 1995) ★★★★.

● VIDEOS: *Love Bites* (PolyGram Music Video 1988), *Historia* (PolyGram Music Video 1988), *Rocket* (PolyGram Music Video 1989), *Rock Of Ages* (PolyGram Music Video 1989), *In The Round – In Your Face* (PolyGram Music Video 1989), *Animal*

(PolyGram Music Video 1989), *Visualise* (PolyGram Music Video 1993), *Unlock The Rock: Video Archive 1993–1995* (PolyGram Music Video 1995).
● FURTHER READING: *Def Leppard: Animal Instinct*, David Fricke. *Def Leppard*, Jason Rich. *Biographize: The Def Leppard Story*, Dave Dickson.

## DEFUNKT

This hard-funk act from the USA centers around trombonist Joseph Bowie (b. St. Louis, Missouri, USA) who rose to prominence as a member of the Black Artists Group, an *avant garde* collective, based in St. Louis, and patterned after the Art Ensemble Of Chicago. Defunkt drew on this 'new wave' tradition but fused such radical jazz with the dancefloor punch of Parliament and Funkadelic to create a thrilling, invigorating style. Bowie, the brother of trumpeter Lester Bowie and Broadway arranger Byron K. Bowie, was an inspired frontman and several propulsive albums, notably 1982's *Thermonuclear Sweat*, captured their exciting style.

Defunkt undertook an enforced four-year sabbatical while its leader battled heroin addiction but emerged anew with 1988's *In America*. Bill Bickford, Ronnie Drayton (guitars), John Mulkerik (trumpet), Kim Annette Clarke (bass) and Kenny Martin (drums) joined Bowie for this compulsive set which, if shorn of melody, compensated with sheer excitement. Since then, Bowie and Defunkt have steered between dance music and *avant garde* jazz with a verve that makes nonsense of the usual pigeonholes.
● ALBUMS: *Defunkt* (Hannibal 1980) ★★★, *Razor's Edge* (Hannibal 1981) ★★★, *Thermonuclear Sweat* (Hannibal 1982) ★★★★, *In America* (Antilles/New Direction 1988) ★★★★, *Heroes* (DIW 1990) ★★★, *Live At The Knitting Factory* (Enemy 1991) ★★★, *Crisis* (Enemy 1992) ★★★, *Cum Funky* (Enemy 1993) ★★★, *Live & Reunified* (Enemy 1994) ★★★, *A Blues Tribute: Muddy Waters & Jimi Hendrix Tribute* (Enemy 1994) ★★★, *One World* (Blue Funk 1995) ★★★.
● COMPILATIONS: *Avoid The Funk: A Defunkt Anthology* (Hannibal 1988) ★★★★, *The Legend Continues* (Music Avenue 2001) ★★★.

## DEL AMITRI

This Glaswegian semi-acoustic rock band emerged in the wake of the Postcard Records scene, when they were formed by 16-year-old singer, pianist and bass player Justin Currie (b. 11 December 1964, Scotland) and his guitarist friend Iain Harvie (b. 19 May 1962, Scotland). They were joined for 'Sense Sickness', their 1983 debut on the No Strings independent label, by Bryan Tolland (guitar) and Paul Tyagi (drums). Numerous sessions for disc jockey John Peel and tours with everyone from the Fall to the Smiths ensured a cult following and a growing reputation for Currie's wry lyrics. They came to the attention of Chrysalis Records who signed them to their own 'indie' label, Big Star. Del Amitri, meaning 'from the womb' in Greek, released their debut album in 1985 but fell foul of the label shortly afterwards.

The band's career entered a restorative period during which they toured via a network of fans who organized and promoted events in individual regions. A tour of the USA led to Del Amitri being signed to A&M Records in 1987 and resuming their recording career, with Andy Alston (keyboards) and Mick Slaven joining Currie, Harvie and Tyagi in the line-up. They hit the UK singles chart with 'Kiss This Thing Goodbye', 'Nothing Ever Happens' (from 1989's *Waking Hours*) and 'Spit In The Rain'. The reissue of 'Kiss This Thing Goodbye' helped to break them in the USA, while domestically the plaintive protest ballad 'Nothing Ever Happens' won many supporters: 'And computer terminals report some gains, On the values of copper and tin, While American businessmen snap up Van Goghs, For the price of a hospital wing'. Though their singles success abated somewhat, this was tempered by the platinum success of 1992's *Change Everything*, which featured new members Brian McDermott (drums) and David Cummings (guitar). Touring continued throughout that year while most of 1993 was spent at Haremere House in East Sussex, working on their fourth album. *Twisted* was produced by Al Clay (Frank Black, Pere Ubu) and featured new drummer Chris Sharrock. The album further refined the band's familiar AOR formula, with the lyrics almost exclusively dealing in loneliness and the establishment and breakdown of relationships. Of their transition from indie wordsmiths to stadium rockers, Currie philosophically preferred to think that 'Del Amitri fans only hold ironic lighters aloft'.

There were enough ironic electric 12-string soundalikes on the energetic and excellent 1997 album *Some Other Sucker's Parade* (if you love the Byrds and Crazy Horse you will appreciate Del Amitri). The album saw the mainstays Currie, Harvie and Alston joined by Ashley Soan (drums) and Jon McLoughlin (guitar). The following year the band provided the Scottish soccer team with the typically wry 'Don't Come Home Too Soon' for their official World Cup song. It struggled to reach number 15 in June 1998. The downbeat *Can You Do Me Good?* featured the sublime single 'Just Before You Leave' and a number of other soul-influenced tracks. Kris Dollimore (guitar) and Mark Price (drums) joined Currie, Harvie and Alston for the sessions. The album was Del Amitri's final recording for A&M/Mercury.
● ALBUMS: *Del Amitri* (Chrysalis 1985) ★★★, *Waking Hours* (A&M 1989) ★★★, *Change Everything* (A&M 1992) ★★★★, *Twisted* (A&M 1995) ★★★, *Some Other Sucker's Parade* (A&M 1997) ★★★★, *Can You Do Me Good?* (A&M/Mercury 2002) ★★★.
● COMPILATIONS: *The Best Of Del Amitri: Hatful Of Rain* (A&M/Mercury 1998) ★★★★, *Lousy With Love: The B-Sides* (A&M/Mercury 1998) ★★★.
● VIDEOS: *Let's Go Home* (VVL 1996), *The Best Of Del Amitri: Hatful Of Rain* (VVL 1998).

## DEL FUEGOS

Roots rock 'n' roll revivalists from Boston, Massachusetts, USA, whose early 80s recordings stand as a fine testament to their influences, even if some of their later output was dulled by commercial considerations. The band, led by vocalist Dan Zanes and guitarist brother Warren, with Tom Lloyd (bass) and Brent 'Woody' Giessmann (drums), was formally introduced to its public on a 1984 debut album for Slash Records. A winning collection of rounded songs drawing principally from the 60s beat boom, it explored a full complement of moods with energy and belief. The follow-up, 1985's *Boston, Mass.*, a eulogy to their working-class origins, was a more commercially orientated affair, though it lacked something of the sparkle of their debut. If this set had mapped out the possibility of future indulgence, that fear was confirmed with the arrival of *Stand Up*. With numerous guest appearances (including Tom Petty and James Burton), neither the songwriting nor performances possessed the same spirit or character of old. It was universally panned by reviewers. Presumably as a result, drummer Giessmann (who had formerly worked with the underrated Embarrassment) and Warren Zanes departed. The new line-up's *Smoking In The Fields* marked a partial return to form. With the addition of harp player Magic Dick (ex-J. Geils Band), the band's sound had now soothed to a classy R&B/soul timbre. Producer David Thoener gave the new dynamic a sympathetic treatment and restored the Del Fuegos to critical favour. The band fizzled out in 1990, however, with Dan Zanes going on to record as a solo artist.

● ALBUMS: *The Longest Day* (Slash 1984) ★★★, *Boston, Mass.* (Slash/Warners 1985) ★★★, *Stand Up* (Slash/Warners 1987) ★★, *Smoking In The Fields* (RCA 1989) ★★★.

● COMPILATIONS: *The Best Of The Del Fuegos: The Slash Years* (Slash/Warners 2001) ★★★.

## DEL LORDS

This Bronx, New York, USA rock band was founded by ex-Dictators guitarist/vocalist Scott Kempner (then known as 'Top Ten'), whose straightforward enthusiasm for uncomplicated rock brought a new lustre to a tried and tested formula. Backed by the equally strident guitar (and occasional lead vocals) of Eric 'Roscoe' Ambel, the band's 1984 debut featured basic but impressive rock 'n' roll in 'Burning In The Flame Of Love', 'Feel Like Going Home' and 'How Can A Poor Man Stand Such Times And Live' (a cover version of Alfred Reed's classic, revitalized by the unlikely urban blues of the Del Lords). Drafting in Pat Benatar's producer husband Neil Geraldo, *Johnny Comes Marching Home*, from its title onwards, was a set that utilized folk tradition, but squeezed it through a taut electric guitar mesh, producing peerless rock songs that defied both its roots and its participants' ages. A third album pushed the strident choruses and strong melody lines to the forefront, in an obvious effort on Geraldo's part to convert critical reverence into commercial accessibility. Though *Based On A True Story* was consequently weakened, the natural strengths of songs such as 'Judas Kiss' and 'The Cool And The Crazy', an anthemic party rocker, won through. Guests included Mojo Nixon ('Rivers Of Justice') and Syd Straw. *Howlin' At The Halloween Moon* was a disappointingly mediocre live set, but this proved an uncharacteristic qualitative hitch. *Lovers Who Wander* saw Kempner and Ambel produce the best

work of their respective careers. Abandoning the commercial ambition of their previous studio set, this collection focused instead on the innate strengths of previous Del Lords releases – spirited, emotive rock songs delivered with unreconstructed passion. Of no small consequence was the band's most sympathetic production yet – courtesy of Thom Panunzio and bass player Manny Caiati. Shortly after release, Ambel would depart for a solo career (having already recorded one album, *Roscoe's Gang*, in 1988) and the band fizzled out shortly afterwards.

● ALBUMS: *Frontier Days* (Enigma/EMI 1984) ★★★, *Johnny Comes Marching Home* (Enigma/EMI 1986) ★★★, *Based On A True Story* (Enigma 1988) ★★★, *Howlin' At The Halloween Moon* (Restless 1989) ★★, *Lovers Who Wander* (Enigma 1990) ★★★.

● COMPILATIONS: *Get Tough: The Best Of The DelLords* (Restless 1999) ★★★.

## DELTA 5

Leeds, England-originated post-punk band who had much in common with the Au Pairs – though the inspired amateurism that fuelled their early releases proved more reminiscent of the Slits. They released several singles on Rough Trade Records that highlighted insipid but endearing hooklines, the John Peel favourite 'Mind Your Own Business' being a good example (they also recorded two 1980 radio sessions for the programme). The line-up featured Julz Sale (vocals), Alan Riggs (guitar), Ros Allen (bass, ex-Mekons), Bethan Peters (bass, vocals) and Kelvin Knight (drums). Sale and Peters were the only two remaining following a major transformation in personnel as they moved to Pre Records. They split up shortly afterwards, though history would prove them a great influence on mid-80s indie pop bands such as the Shop Assistants and Tallulah Gosh.

● ALBUMS: *See The Whirl* (Pre 1981) ★★★.

## DEMON RECORDS

Demon Records was founded in 1980 by Andrew Lauder, fresh from his employment as A&R executive for United Artists Records, and Jake Riviera, manager of Elvis Costello, Nick Lowe and the Damned. Previously, both had worked together in establishing Radar Records in 1978, which they formed to provide an outlet for Costello and Lowe after both had broken from Stiff Records in 1977. After Radar they established F-Beat Records, for whom Elvis Costello And The Attractions recorded 'I Can't Stand Up For Falling Down'. Initially, the Demon label geared itself for one-off single releases. Among the featured artists were the Subterraneans (who featured *New Musical Express* journalist Nick Kent), the Spectres (formed by former Sex Pistols' bass player Glen Matlock), TV21 and Department S. The latter band gave Demon its first chart success with 'Is Vic There?' in 1981. Further chart success followed when Bananarama's debut single, 'Aie-A-Mwana', was released (though it was later picked up for distribution by Phonogram Records). Soon the singles-only policy was abandoned with the hope of launching long-term artists. Lauder left the label to join Island Records in 1981. At the same time, Demon launched its own subsidiary label, Edsel Records, as a reissue/archive imprint. Edsel's early releases included a single by mod pioneers the Action (with a sleeve note by Paul Weller), the Escorts and 'Screamin' Jay' Hawkins. It boldly reissued Moby Grape, the Byrds and Gene Clark when they were out of fashion (they continued this policy in the 90s with Spooky Tooth and Ronnie Lane). The parent label, Demon, also moved into reissues as the market for deleted records boomed in the mid-80s. By 1982, Lauder had rejoined the label, which had now expanded to incorporate further labels such as the soul specialist label Hi (Ann Peebles, Willie Mitchell, Al Green) and the psychedelic rock-orientated Drop Out imprint. Through the 80s Demon became closely identified with imported American roots rock, and in particular what became known as the Paisley Underground scene (Green On Red, Long Ryders, Giant Sand, Beat Farmers and Replacements). Among the UK album acts featured on the roster at this time were The Men They Couldn't Hang, Shamen, Paul Brady, That Petrol Emotion and Christy Moore. All these acts used Demon as a stepping-stone to a major recording contract. Lauder left the label for a final time in 1988 (to establish Silvertone and then the This Way Up labels), with Demon concentrating increasingly on the reissue market. Newer artists included Lowe, Martin Stephenson, Clive Gregson and Kate Campbell. Much of the respect the company enjoyed was due to the genuine and tireless enthusiasm of their long-term director of press Alan Robinson, who ensured Demon remained a 'dream indie', loving and nurturing their product. In March 1997 Jake Riviera and Elvis Costello sold their shares as F-Beat Records was taken over by Kingfisher Plc. Robinson was without a job a few weeks later.

## DEPECHE MODE

During the UK post-punk backlash at the turn of the 80s, when bands dispensed with guitars and drums in favour of synthesizers and drum machines, Depeche Mode were formed, taking their name from the title of a French style magazine. More than 20 years later, they are recognized as the most successful 'electro-synth' band ever. Ironically enough, given their reputation as the kings of synth-pop, they had made their debut as a trio playing only guitars at Scamps club in Southend-on-Sea, Essex, England. The band originally came together in the neighbouring borough of Basildon in 1980, and comprised Vince Clarke (b. 3 July 1960, South Woodford, London, England; synthesizer, ex-No Romance In China), Andy Fletcher (b. 8 July 1960, Basildon, Essex, England; synthesizer) and Martin Gore (b. 23 July 1961, Basildon, Essex, England; synthesizer, ex-The French Look; Norman And The Worms).

Following a series of concerts that attracted packed houses at the Bridge House Tavern in London's Canning Town, they were spotted by Daniel Miller. Shortly afterwards they were signed to his independent Mute Records, which became their long-term record label. They had already tasted vinyl exposure by issuing one track on Stevo's *Some Bizzare* compilation in 1981. This had been recorded by the original trio, with Clarke on vocals, before they elected to recruit Dave Gahan (b. 9 May 1962, Epping, Essex, England) as their permanent lead vocalist. 'Dreaming Of Me' in 1981 started a remarkable run of hit singles. Principal songwriter Vince Clarke left shortly after *Speak & Spell* to form Yazoo with Alison Moyet, and the writing reins were taken over by Martin Gore, as Alan Wilder (b. 1 June 1959, England; synthesizer, vocals, ex-Dragons; Hitmen) settled into Clarke's place. The gentle, hypnotic ambience of 'See You' was an early demonstration of Gore's sense of melody. Only briefly in their early years did Depeche Mode find their craft compatible with the tastes of the music press, yet their success remained a testament to the power of their music. Lyrically, Gore tended to tackle subjects a shade darker than the musical content might suggest, including sado-masochism ('Master And Servant'), capitalism ('Everything Counts') and religious fetishism ('Personal Jesus'). As the 90s dawned their albums continued to reach the UK Top 10, and they had made important inroads on the US market. The *Violator* tour made them huge concert stars in America, where they became stars on the burgeoning alternative scene. *Violator* presented a harder sound, informed by Gahan's patronage of the American rock scene, which was continued on *Songs Of Faith And Devotion*. As their standing throughout the world continued to be enhanced by ambitious stage shows, the latter album debuted in both the US and UK charts at number 1 on its week of release – this despite the fact that thinly veiled acrimony seemed to surround the Depeche Mode camp as it entered the 90s. Wilder departed in 1996 (resurfacing in 1997 as the cinematic Recoil).

The change in Gahan during this period saw him relocate from Essex to Los Angeles, divorce his wife, remarry to his tattooed American girlfriend, divorce her and then attempt suicide. Gahan's serious drug dependency reached a peak when he came close to death in 1996. In a revealing interview with the *New Musical Express*, he spoke about his drug problems to such an extent that the reader was convinced of his determination to stay clean and pursue a future with his longest love affair, his band. The following year's *Ultra* was a surprisingly good album, considering the fragmentation that had been occurring within the ranks. The renaissance continued with the excellent *Exciter* in 2001, which ranks as one of their strongest albums.

● ALBUMS: *Speak & Spell* (Mute/Sire 1981) ★★★, *A Broken Frame* (Mute/Sire 1982) ★★, *Construction Time Again* (Mute/Sire 1983) ★★★, *Some Great Reward* (Mute/Sire 1984) ★★★, *Black Celebration* (Mute/Sire 1986) ★★★, *Music For The Masses* (Mute/Sire 1987) ★★★, *101* (Mute/Sire 1989) ★★, *Violator* (Mute/Sire 1990) ★★★★, *Songs Of Faith And Devotion* (Mute/Sire 1993) ★★★★, *Songs Of Faith And Devotion Live* (Mute/Sire 1993) ★★★, *Ultra* (Mute/Reprise 1997) ★★★, *Exciter* (Mute/Reprise 2001) ★★★★.

● COMPILATIONS: *People Are People* US only (Sire 1984) ★★★, *Catching Up With Depeche Mode* US only (Sire 1985) ★★★★, *The Singles 81 > 85* (Mute/Reprise 1985) ★★★★, *The Singles 86 > 98* (Mute/Reprise 1998) ★★★★, *The Singles 81 > 98* 3-CD box set (Mute 2001) ★★★★.

● VIDEOS: *Some Great Videos* (Virgin Vision 1986), *Strange* (Virgin Vision 1988), *101* (Virgin Vision 1989), *Strange Too – Another Violation* (BMG Video 1990), *Devotional* (Virgin Vision 1993), *Live In Hamburg* (Virgin Vision 1993), *The Videos 86 > 98* (Mute 1998), *One Night In Paris: Exciter Tour 2001* (Mute 2002).

● FURTHER READING: *Depeche Mode*, Dave Thomas. *Depeche Mode: Strangers – The Photographs*, Anton Corbijn. *Depeche Mode: Some Great Reward*, Dave Thompson. *Depeche Mode: A Biography*, Steve Malins.

## DESCENDENTS

Los Angeles, California, USA punk band, formed in 1978, whose first stage of development was as a three-piece. Frank Navetta (vocals, guitar), Tony Lombardo (vocals, bass) and Bill Stevenson (drums) played power pop along the lines of the Buzzcocks. It was this line-up that recorded the debut 'Ride The Wild' single, and they collaborated with singer Cecilia for some six months before the near-legendary Milo Aukerman became the first regular vocalist. The resulting period was characterized by songs about fishing and food; titles such as 'Weinerschnitzel' and the self-parodying 'Fat' hail from these merry times. The band also had a predilection for loading up on caffeine and measuring the results in song velocity on tour. Shortly afterwards, things became more serious, as the quartet recorded their debut album, 1981's *Milo Goes To College*, for posterity; again the title was self-explanatory, with Aukerman indeed being college-bound. He remembers his choice of career as being a question of priorities: 'I went to El Camino College for my first year, then I went to UC San Diego. I have a problem. I like to immerse myself in things. I'm obsessed with music and I'm obsessed with biology – so what can I do?'

There was something of a hiatus in the band's fortunes following this traumatic experience, with Stevenson joining up with Black Flag. The band re-formed in 1985, with Ray Cooper replacing Navetta on guitar (he originally tried out as vocalist). *I Don't Want To Grow Up* followed swiftly on the heels of the reunion. This time the production values were more polished, with Aukerman commenting: 'On *I Don't Want To Grow Up* I was more melancholy. We're singing about the same things, just approaching it in a different way. To bring out the feeling behind it rather than just punking it out'. Doug Carrion (bass, ex-Anti) replaced Lombardo in 1986 and featured on the pop-orientated *Enjoy!*. Aukerman and Stevenson were then joined by Karl Alvarez (bass) and Stephen Egerton (guitar) on the Descendents' disappointing swansong, *All*.

Aukerman returned to college to pursue his academic career, eventually gaining a doctorate in biochemistry. After the Descendents disbanded the members, with Aukerman replaced by Dave Smalley, formed All, who have continued in much the same vein. Stevenson, Alvarez and Egerton unexpectedly reunited with Aukerman in 1996, embarking on a national tour and recording a new studio album. Further collaborations have followed, as both the Descendents and All.

The Descendents were hugely popular in the USA because they addressed the burning issues facing their audience: relationships and the hassles of being young. Their influence on UK pop punk outfits such as Mega City Four, and particularly the Senseless Things (who covered 'Marriage'), should not be underestimated.

● ALBUMS: *Milo Goes To College* (New Alliance 1982) ★★★, *I Don't Want To Grow Up* (New Alliance 1985) ★★★, *Enjoy!* (New Alliance 1986) ★★★, *All* (SST 1987) ★★, *Liveage!* (SST 1987) ★★, *Hallraker Live!* (SST 1989) ★★, *Everything Sucks* (Epitaph 1996) ★★★.

● COMPILATIONS: *Two Things At Once* (SST 1988) ★★★, *Somery* (SST 1990) ★★★.

## DESERT ROSE BAND

Formed in the mid-80s, the Desert Rose Band were akin to a mini-supergroup of country rock musicians. Lead vocalist and guitarist Chris Hillman was formerly a member of the Byrds, the Flying Burrito Brothers, Manassas, the Souther, Hillman, Furay Band and McGuinn, Clark And Hillman; Herb Pedersen (vocals/guitar) was one of the most famous session players on the country scene and a former member of the Dillards and Country Gazette; Bill Bryson (vocals/bass) was another Country Gazette alumnus and had also played in the Bluegrass Cardinals, as well as working on various movie soundtracks; Jay Dee Maness (b. 14 January 1945, Loma Linda, California, USA) was one of the world's most famous pedal-steel guitarists, and among his past credentials were appearances with Gram Parsons' International Submarine Band, the Byrds and Buck Owens' Buckaroos; John Jorgenson, who played guitar, mandolin and six-string bass was the 'wunderkind' of the outfit; while Steve Duncan had drummed behind several new country artists, including Dwight Yoakam.

The band was signed to the independent Curb Records label by Dick Whitehouse, and their highly accomplished self-titled first album appeared in 1987. Among its delights was a highly effective reworking of 'Time Between', previously recorded by Hillman on the Byrds' *Younger Than Yesterday*. The follow-up *Running* was another strong work, particularly the title track, which dealt with the suicide of Hillman's father, a matter never previously mentioned in any interview. By the end of the 80s, the band were touring extensively and registering regular hits in the country charts. A third album, *Pages Of Life*, consolidated their position, and featured the memorable anti-drugs song, 'Darkness On The Playground'. In 1991, Jay Dee Maness left the group to be replaced by Tom Brumley, formerly of Rick Nelson's Stone Canyon Band. The departure of Maness made little difference to the Desert Rose Band's sound, but John Jorgenson's decision the following year to pursue a solo career threatened the group's momentum. He was replaced by Jeff Ross (formerly with Los Angeles cow-punk band Rank And File), who for a time brought a harsher, rock-flavoured edge to their show. It was not to last and the Desert Rose Band have now broken up.

● ALBUMS: *The Desert Rose Band* (MCA 1987) ★★★, *Running* (MCA 1988) ★★★★, *Pages Of Life* (MCA 1989) ★★★★, *True Love* (Curb 1991) ★★, *Traditional* (Curb 1993) ★★, *Life Goes On* (Curb 1993) ★★.

● COMPILATIONS: *A Dozen Roses: Greatest Hits* (MCA 1991) ★★★★, *Greatest Hits* (Curb 1994) ★★★★.

## DeVille, Willy

b. William Borsey, 27 August 1950, Stamford, Connecticut, USA. DeVille put the lid on his previous outfit, Mink DeVille, following the release of *Sportin' Life* in 1985. Having embarked on a solo career, he was unexpectedly chosen to sing and write the theme tune to *The Princess Bride*, which brought his name back into the media after several years away from the mainstream. 'Storybook Love' was subsequently awarded an Academy Award Nomination, and was the closing track on *Miracle* – a soft rock/pop soul collection produced by Mark Knopfler (Dire Straits), who also played guitar throughout. Although unmistakably the voice of Willy DeVille, there was little else in slushy songs such as 'Angel Eyes' and the Van Morrison cover version, 'Could You Would You?', to appease long-standing fans. After moving to New Orleans, DeVille signed to the local Orleans label. The 1990 release *Victory Mixture* proved far more interesting, partnering the rejuvenated rocking DeVille with blues and soul legends such as Dr. John and Alan Toussaint. Two years later, DeVille shone on a tribute to the late Doc Pomus. His studio albums during this period were predominantly aimed at the European market. DeVille's louche fusion of rock 'n' roll, Tex-Mex and country styles has matured with age, and his most recent work is among the finest of his recording career.

● ALBUMS: *Miracle* (Atlantic/A&M 1987) ★★, *Victory Mixture* (Orleans 1990) ★★★, *Backstreets Of Desire* (Fnac/East West 1992) ★★★, *Live* (Fnac/East West 1993) ★★★, *Loup Garou* (East West/Discovery 1995) ★★★★, *Horse Of A Different Color* (East West 1999) ★★★★.

● COMPILATIONS: *Love & Emotion: The Atlantic Years* (East West 1996) ★★★, *His Greatest Hits* (Arcade 1997) ★★★, *Les Inoubliables* (Wagram 1999) ★★★.

● VIDEOS: *DeVille: 25 Years Of Heart & Soul* (2002).

## Devoto, Howard

b. Howard Trafford, 1955, Manchester, England. One writer perceptively dubbed the bespectacled new wave intellectual as 'the Orson Welles of punk'. After leaving the Buzzcocks just as they seemed destined for greatness (which they actually managed to achieve without him), Manchester student Howard Devoto formed the altogether more sober Magazine. After widespread critical acclaim, the band split in the early 80s, and Devoto briefly embarked on a

straightforward solo career with 1983's *Jerky Visions Of The Dream*. Despite two singles ('Rainy Season' and 'Cold Imagination'), the album failed to achieve the impact that Magazine had attained. Devoto approached later work using various disguises, such as Luxuria. Highly influential during the punk era, Devoto's role as a much-quoted spokesperson and innovator declined in the 80s. He now works as a photograph archivist in London, but in October 2000 reunited with Shelley under the Buzzkunst moniker. The duo recorded a well-received album, which owed little to their respective musical pasts.

● ALBUMS: *Jerky Visions Of The Dream* (Virgin 1983) ★★★, with Pete Shelley *Buzzkunst* (Cooking Vinyl/spinART 2002) ★★★.

● FURTHER READING: *It Only Looks As If It Hurts: The Complete Lyrics Of Howard Devoto 1976–90*, Howard Devoto.

## Dexys Midnight Runners

Conceived by the uncompromising Kevin Rowland (b. 17 August 1953, Wolverhampton, West Midlands, England), Dexys Midnight Runners proved one of the most original, eclectic and fascinating UK bands to achieve success in the 80s. Their career was marked by a series of broken contracts, band upheavals, total changes of image, diverse musical forays and an often bitter association with the music press. Vocalist Rowland and rhythm guitarist Al Archer were previously members of punk outfit the Killjoys, before rehearsing the soul-inspired Dexys Midnight Runners in July 1978. A further six members were added to the first line-up: Pete Williams (bass), Bobby Junior (drums), Pete Saunders (piano/organ), Jeff 'JB' Blythe (tenor saxophone), Steve 'Baby Face' Spooner (alto saxophone) and Big Jim Paterson (trombone).

The unit took their name from the amphetamine Dexedrine, a stimulant favoured by northern soul dancers. Their name notwithstanding, the band gained an almost puritanical reputation for their aversion to drink and drugs. Rowland cleverly fashioned their image, using Robert De Niro's movie *Mean Streets* as an inspiration for their New York Italian docker chic. The band's debut, 'Dance Stance', was an extraordinary single, its simple title belying what was a lyrically devastating attack on racism directed at the Irish community, with a superb background litany extolling the virtues of Ireland's finest literary figures. The single crept into the UK Top 40, but the follow-up 'Geno' (a tribute to 60s soul singer Geno Washington featuring new keyboard player Mick Talbot) climbed confidently to number 1 in May 1980. Two months later, *Searching For The Young Soul Rebels* was released to critical acclaim and commercial success. Many polls perhaps rightly suggested that it one of the finest debut albums ever issued; it showed Rowland's mastery of the pop-soul genre to spectacular effect. The epistolary 'There, There My Dear', taken from the album, brought the band another UK Top 10 hit. The flip was a revival of Cliff Noble's instrumental 'The Horse', in keeping with the band's soul revivalism.

The first signs of Rowland's artistic waywardness

occurred with the release of the blatantly uncommercial 'Keep It Part Two (Inferiority Part One)', much against the band's wishes. Unquestionably his most intensely passionate work from the band's first phase, the song's almost unbearably agonized vocal line was double-tracked to create a bizarre but riveting effect. The song precipitated the fragmentation of the original line-up. With Blythe, Spooner, Talbot and Williams defecting to the Bureau, Rowland and Paterson found a fresh line-up: former Secret Affair drummer Seb Shelton, Micky Billingham (keyboards), Paul Speare (tenor saxophone), Brian Maurice (alto saxophone), Steve Wynne (bass) and Billy Adams (guitar). After another single for EMI Records, the excellent 'Plan B', the band switched to Phonogram. By 1981, they had abandoned soul revivalism in order to investigate different music and a new look. Out went the balaclavas to be replaced by a new uniform of red anoraks, boxing boots, tracksuit bottoms, hoods and pony tails. Their 'ascetic athlete' phase saw the release of the more commercial 'Show Me' produced by Tony Visconti. This was followed by the idiosyncratic 'Liars A To E'. A highly acclaimed live show 'The Projected Passion Review' followed, including a performance at London's Old Vic. Early 1982 saw the band augmented by a fiddle section, the Emerald Express, featuring Helen O'Hara, Steve Brennan and Roger McDuff. Rowland's latest experiment was to fuse Northern soul with Irish traditional music. As before, the shift in musical style was reflected in the image as Rowland created his own brand of hoedown gypsy chic – neckerchiefs, earrings, stubble and leather jerkins. The first release from the new line-up, 'The Celtic Soul Brothers', was a vital work that failed to chart. Shortly afterwards Paterson, Maurice and Speare departed, having become disillusioned by their role in the band. 'Come On Eileen' restored Dexys Midnight Runners to number 1 in the summer of 1982. The second album, Too-Rye-Ay, was another startling work and a bestseller, reaching number 2 in the UK album charts. The band subsequently undertook an extensive tour, which revealed Rowland's love of theatre in its self-conscious grandeur.

Further line-up changes followed, with the departure of Rowland's right-hand man Jim Paterson and two other brass players. Continuing under the autocratic title 'Kevin Rowland And Dexys Midnight Runners', the band went on to reap considerable success in the USA where 'Come On Eileen' reached number 1 in 1983. Further hits followed with a snappy cover version of Van Morrison's 'Jackie Wilson Said' and 'Let's Get This Straight (From The Start)' before the band underwent a long hibernation. They returned as a quartet comprising Rowland, Adams, O'Hara and Nicky Gatfield, and boasting a radically new image 'College Preppie' – chic shirts and ties and neatly cut hair. Don't Stand Me Down received favourable reviews but sold poorly in spite of its qualities. Featuring some of Rowland's most impassioned material, the album also featured a rambling conversation between the singer and Adams running on and off through the first four

tracks. An edited version of 'This Is What She's Like' was belatedly issued as a single, but received little airplay. A director's cut version was issued in 2002. Adams subsequently left and, although Rowland and O'Hara charted again in 1986 with 'Because Of You' (the theme for BBC Television's comedy series Brush Strokes), the commercial failure of the latest experiment forced Rowland to think again, and he finally dissolved the band in 1987. He returned the following year as a soloist with the light pop album The Wanderer, which failed to produce a hit single. In 1990, Rowland, amid not unusual record company trouble, announced that he was resurrecting Dexys Midnight Runners and bringing back his old colleague Jim Paterson. A similar announcement came in 1993, but in 1996 Creation Records signed Rowland for a one-album deal. My Beauty was an idiosyncratic cover versions album, which received a wide-ranging batch of reviews and sold poorly. Some enlightened sources quoted 300 copies. For all this, Rowland remains a fascinating renegade; original, temperamental and brutally uncompromising at times, yet still capable of producing a surprise hit out of the hat.

● ALBUMS: Searching For The Young Soul Rebels (Parlophone/EMI America 1980) ★★★★, as Kevin Rowland And Dexys Midnight Runners Too-Rye-Ay (Mercury 1982) ★★★★, Don't Stand Me Down (Mercury 1985) ★★★★, BBC Radio One Live In Concert 1982 recording (Windsong 1994) ★★★, Don't Stand Me Down: The Director's Cut (EMI 2002) ★★★★.
Solo: Kevin Rowland The Wanderer (Mercury 1988) ★★, My Beauty (Creation 1999) ★.
● COMPILATIONS: Geno (EMI 1983) ★★★, The Very Best Of Dexys Midnight Runners (Mercury 1991) ★★★★, 1980–1982: The Radio One Sessions (Nighttracks 1995) ★★★, It Was Like This (EMI 1996) ★★★★.

## DIAMOND HEAD

Formed in Stourbridge, England, in 1979, the original line-up of Diamond Head comprised Sean Harris (vocals), Brian Tatler (guitar), Colin Kimberley (bass) and Duncan Scott (drums). The band was one of the pioneers of the New Wave Of British Heavy Metal and their debut single, 'Sweet And Innocent', showcased the band's blues influences and Harris' impressive vocal talents. After gigging extensively, the band recorded a session for the Friday night rock show on BBC Radio 1. 'Play It Loud' and 'Shoot Out The Lights' were both released in 1981 to minor critical acclaim. The press even went as far as to hail the band as the new Led Zeppelin. With interest growing, they decided to self-finance their debut, which they sold through the pages of Sounds magazine under the title Lightning To The Nations. This was quickly snapped up by the German-based Woolfe Records in the same year, and released on import. The album was full of hard rock, soaring vocals and tasteful guitar work, and attracted the attention of several major record companies.
As a stopgap, the band released a 12-inch EP, Diamond Lights, again on DHM Records, in 1981, before signing to MCA Records. Their first release for

the label was an EP, *Four Cuts*, which was quickly followed by their most popular album, *Borrowed Time*. Again, the material was Led Zeppelin-style hard rock, and the band included a couple of re-recorded tracks that had originally appeared on their first album. During sessions for the follow-up, *Canterbury*, both Kimberley and Scott left the band. They were quickly replaced by ex-Streetfighter bass player Mervyn Goldsworthy (later a member of FM) and drummer Robbie France, with keyboardist Josh Phillips-Gorse also added to the line-up. The album represented a brave change of direction, still melodic but much more inventive and unconventional. Unfortunately, this change in style was not well received and despite a very successful appearance at the Donington Festival, it flopped, and the band split up in 1985.

Tatler then remixed their debut album, dropped two of the original tracks and added four previously released single tracks. The result was later released under the new title of *Behold The Beginning*. Tatler went on to form Radio Moscow while Sean Harris teamed up with guitarist Robin George in the ill-fated Notorious album project. Even though Diamond Head were no longer in existence, they retained a healthy press profile owing to the acclaim accorded them by Metallica drummer Lars Ulrich, who made no secret of the fact that the band were one of his main influences and inspired him to begin his musical career. Metallica subsequently recorded a cover version of Diamond Head's old stage favourite, 'Am I Evil'.

Early in 1991 Harris and Tatler re-formed Diamond Head with newcomers Karl Wilcox (drums) and Eddie 'Chaos' Moohan (bass). The band undertook a short, low-key UK club tour using the name Dead Reckoning, and declared officially that they had re-formed. The first release from this new incarnation was a limited edition 12-inch single, 'Wild On The Streets'. Housed on the newly relaunched Bronze label in 1991 it showed the band had returned in fine form and rediscovered their previous spirit. By the time they had pieced together a new collection (after shelving a projected mini-album the previous year), many of the rock world's biggest names were only too pleased to help out (including Tony Iommi of Black Sabbath, Dave Mustaine of Megadeth, and still-fervent supporter Lars Ulrich). The album featured new bass player Pete Vukovic. The band broke up after the tour to support the release of *Death & Progress* in 1993. Tatler went on to play with Jean Genie, Dizzy Lizzy and the folk rock band Quill, while Vukovic re-emerged in the late 90s with 3 Colours Red. Tatler and Harris returned to their enduring creation in the new millennium, playing electric and acoustic Diamond Head shows.

● ALBUMS: *Lightning To The Nations* (Happy Face/Woolfe 1981) ★★★, *Borrowed Time* (MCA 1982) ★★★★, *Canterbury* (MCA 1983) ★★★, *The Friday Rock Show Sessions/Live At Reading* (Raw Fruit 1992) ★★, *Death & Progress* (Bronze 1993) ★★★, *Evil Live* (Bronze 1994) ★★, *Live In The Heat Of The Night* (Zoom Club 2000) ★★.

● COMPILATIONS: *Am I Evil* (FM 1987) ★★★, *Behold The Beginning* (Heavy Metal 1991) ★★★,

*Singles* (MCA 1992) ★★★, *The Best Of* (Half Moon 1999) ★★★.

## DIAMOND, JIM

b. 28 September 1951, Glasgow, Scotland. Diamond is a veteran of several Glasgow-based groups. He sang with the Jade, which featured bass player Chris Glen, later of the Sensational Alex Harvey Band, but did not achieve prominence until the mid-70s when he joined Bandit. This traditionally styled rock band struggled in the face of punk, but Diamond's persistence paid dividends in 1982 when, as a member of PhD, he was the featured voice on their UK number 3 hit, 'I Won't Let You Down'. The singer then embarked on a solo career, and in 1984 he enjoyed an unexpected UK chart-topper with the emotional ballad, 'I Should Have Known Better'. Diamond next scored two minor hits, before achieving another major success with 'Hi Ho Silver', the theme song to the popular British television series *Boon*. A UK television advertised compilation album released in 1993 put Diamond back in the UK Top 20.

● ALBUMS: *Double Crossed* (A&M 1985) ★★, *Desire For Freedom* (A&M 1986) ★★.

● COMPILATIONS: *Jim Diamond* (PolyGram 1993) ★★★.

## DIANNO

This British band was formed in 1982 by ex-Iron Maiden vocalist Paul Di'Anno (17 May 1959, Chingford, London, England; vocals), John Wiggins (guitar), Peter J. Ward (guitar, vocals), Mark Venables (keyboards, vocals), Kevin Browne (bass, vocals) and Mark Stuart (drums). Originally known as Lonewolf, they spent their first year touring Europe playing American-style melodic AOR rock. In 1983 John Wiggins was replaced on guitar by Lee Slater and Lonewolf signed to FM Revolver. Soon after the contract was in place, Lonewolf were forced to change their name following complaints from a group of the same title. On their debut album *Dianno*, they came across as an English band trying to sound American, although their version of Cliff Richard's 'Heart User' was a surprise inclusion. The album did not sell well and at the end of the year, Dianno fell apart, with Paul Di'Anno going on to form Paul Di'Anno's Battlezone, then Killers.

● ALBUMS: *Dianno* (FM Revolver 1984) ★★.

## DIE KRUPPS

German unit Die Krupps has been a pioneering force in experimental music ever since being formed in 1980 by Jürgen Engler (b. 12 October 1960, Germany; vocals, keyboards, guitars) and band spokesman Bernward Malaka (bass, vocals; ex-Male), together with keyboard/vocalist Ralf Dörper (b. 11 January 1960, Dusseldorf, Germany; ex-S.Y.P.H and later of Propaganda). Together with Front 242, they formulated the Body Music subgenre of Euro rock, a sound lush in electronics but harsh in execution. Several albums of synthesized material emerged, venerated by a loyal fanbase. However, Engler spent the mid-80s, which were largely quiet for the band, absorbing the new sounds pioneered by Metallica, pushing back the frontiers of metal. When Die Krupps eventually returned in 1992, Engler and Dörper added layers of metal guitar. The most famous of two excellent sets in that year included a tribute to the band who had revolutionized Engler's thinking: 'Metallica were coming to Germany for some dates and I wanted to present something to them because I really admired what they did. So we put together this tape, and that's all it was intended for, but our label heard of it and wanted to put it out . . .' On *II: The Final Option* Lee Altus (guitar, ex-Heathen), Rüdiger Esch (bass) and Darren Minter (drums) were brought in, and Die Krupps adhered to their bleak lyrical themes, notably on 'Crossfire', a reaction to the Yugoslavian conflict. A remix album, with contributions from Gunshot, Jim Martin (ex-Faith No More), Andrew Eldritch (Sisters Of Mercy) and Julian Beeston (Nitzer Ebb, who in 1989 had remodelled the band's classic 'Wahre Arbeit, Wahrer Lohn'), was also unveiled. On *III: Odyssey Of The Mind* embraced still further the metallic guitar sound, which now subsumed their distinctive hard dance electronics. Engler said of it, 'The guitars are definitely louder on this one. We still get put into different sections in record stores all over the world. In Germany we're in the independent section. In France the techno, and in England in the metal. It's all right, but it's all wrong too. We should be in every section!'. Following one further Die Krupps release, 1997's *Paradise Now*, Engler set up his Dkay.Com project.

● ALBUMS: *Stahlwerksinfonie* (Zick Zack 1981) ★★★, *Volle Kraft Voraus* (WEA 1982) ★★, *Entering The Arena* (Static 1984) ★★, *I* (Rough Trade 1992) ★★★, *II: The Final Option* (Rough Trade 1993) ★★★, *The Final Remixes* (Rough Trade 1994) ★★★, *III: Odyssey Of The Mind* (Rough Trade/Cleopatra 1995) ★★★, *Paradise Now* (Rough Trade 1997) ★★★.

● COMPILATIONS: *Metall Maschinen Musik: 91–81 Past Forward* (Mute 1991) ★★★, *Die Krupps Box* 3-CD box set (Rough Trade 1993) ★★★, *Rings Of Steel* (Cleopatra 1995) ★★, *Metalmorphosis Of Die Krupps '81–'92* (Cleopatra 1996) ★★★, *Foundation* (Captain Trip 1997) ★★★.

## DIESEL PARK WEST

Purveyors of epic guitar rock, Diesel Park West – John Butler (b. 17 April 1954; guitar/lead vocals), Rick Willson (b. 1 December 1959; guitar/vocals), Richie Barton (b. June 1957; guitar/vocals), Geoff Beavan (b. 24 January 1953; bass/vocals) and Dave Anderson (b. 27 April 1967; drums) – made its recording debut in August 1987 with 'When The Hoodoo Comes'. Twelve months of solid groundwork followed, during which time the quintet toured and composed new material. This resulted in a series of singles, 'Jackie's Still Sad', 'All The Myths On Sunday', 'Like Princes Do', each of which was featured on the critically acclaimed *Shakespeare Alabama*. However, despite contributing a version of Jesus Jones' 'Info Freako' to their label's *Food Christmas E.P.*, Diesel Park West withdrew from both live and studio work in order to write new material and *Flipped*, a collection of b-sides, cover versions and out-takes, was released to fill the gap. The band

resurfaced in 1991 with a new single, 'Boy On Top Of The News', and the favourably reviewed *Decency*, although by the mid-90s their star appeared to have waned. An acrimonious fall-out with Food saw the band resurfacing on Demon Records with the bitter *Diesel Park West Versus The Corporate Waltz*. Ian Mitchie then replaced Beavan as the band changed label again, releasing the excellent *FreakGene* on Permanent. Butler took a break in 1997 to record his excellent solo debut, *The Loyal Serpent*, since when the original line-up of the band has reunited and now maintain a steady recording and touring schedule.

● ALBUMS: *Shakespeare Alabama* (Food/EMI 1989) ★★★★, *Decency* (Food/EMI 1991) ★★★, *Diesel Park West Versus The Corporate Waltz* (Fiend 1993) ★★★, *FreakGene* (Permanent 1995) ★★★★, *HIP Replacement* (Thunderbird 1998) ★★★, *Thought For Food* (Hypertension 2000) ★★★.

● COMPILATIONS: *Flipped* (Food 1990) ★★, *Left Hand Band: The Very Best Of Diesel Park West* (EMI 1997) ★★★.

● VIDEOS: *The Complete And Continuing Diesel Park West* (Food 1993).

## DIFFORD AND TILBROOK

The two principal songwriters of Squeeze met after Chris Difford (b. 4 November 1954, London, England) had placed an advert in a Blackheath, south London shop window in search of a guitarist to join a (non-existent) band with a (non-existent) record contract. In answering the advert, Glenn Tilbrook (b. 31 August 1957, London, England) found a compatible songwriting partner and together they led one of the most popular British groups of the late 70s/early 80s. After suffering from the strain of holding Squeeze together, the duo decided to reassess their situation in 1982. Prior to recording an album, the duo had worked on the fringe theatre production of *Labelled With Love* at the Albany Theatre in their home area of Deptford. The album received a mixed reception and the only single to make any impact upon the UK charts was 'Love's Crashing Waves', narrowly missing out on the Top 50. Assisted by Andy Duncan (drums), Keith Wilkinson (bass), Guy Fletcher (keyboards), with a production credit by Tony Visconti, the album was an improvement on the last Squeeze offering, *Sweets From A Stranger*. Tracks like 'You Can't Hurt The Girl', 'Hope Fell Down' and 'On My Mind Tonight' particularly stood out. Having given themselves a sufficient rest from the group set-up, the duo resurrected Squeeze in 1985 after a successful charity reunion pub-date which led to the recording the excellent *Cosi Fan Tutti Frutti* that same year.

● ALBUMS: *Difford And Tilbrook* (A&M 1984) ★★★.

## DINOSAUR JR

This uncompromising alternative rock band from the university town of Amherst, Massachusetts, USA, was originally called simply Dinosaur. Their musical onslaught eventually dragged them, alongside the Pixies, into the rock mainstream of the late 80s. Both J. Mascis (b. 10 December 1965, Amherst, Massachusetts, USA; vocals, guitar) and Lou Barlow (bass) were formerly in the hardcore band Deep Wound, along with a singer called Charlie. The latter recruited his best friend Murph (b. Patrick Murphy; ex-All White Jury) from Connecticut, and was rewarded by the first line-up of Dinosaur ejecting him and thus becoming a trio. Mascis had by this time switched from drums to guitar to accommodate the new arrival. Mascis, apparently a huge fan of Sham 69 and the UK Oi! movement, had actually known Murphy at high school but they had never been friends. He formed Deep Wound as a response to seeing 999 play live when he was 14 years old.

During Dinosaur Jr's career internal rifts never seemed far from the surface, while their leader's monosyllabic press interviews and general disinterest in rock 'n' roll machinations gave the impression of 'genius anchored by lethargy'. SST Records saw them establish their name as a credible underground rock act – You're Living All Over Me featured backing vocals from Sonic Youth's Lee Ranaldo. However, their debut album for Homestead had brought them to the attention of ageing hippie group Dinosaur, who insisted the band change their name. Mascis elected to add the suffix Junior. Real recognition came with the release of the huge underground anthem 'Freak Scene', which more than one journalist called the perfect pop single. Its sound was constructed on swathes of guitar and Mascis' laconic vocals, which were reminiscent of Neil Young. However, the parent album (Bug) and tour saw Barlow depart (to Sebadoh) and Donna became a temporary replacement. This line-up recorded a version of the Cure's 'Just Like Heaven', which so impressed Robert Smith that it led to joint touring engagements. Soon afterwards they signed to Warner Brothers Records subsidiary Blanco y Negro, remixing their Sub Pop Records track 'The Wagon' as their debut major label release. Subsequent members included Don Fleming (Gumball, etc.), Jay Spiegel and Van Conner (Screaming Trees), while Mascis himself flirted with other bands such as Gobblehoof, Velvet Monkeys and satanic metal band Upside Down Cross, principally as a drummer.

By the advent of Green Mind, Dinosaur Jr had effectively become the J. Mascis show, with him playing almost all the instruments. Although critically acclaimed, Where You Been did not manage to build on the commercial inroads originally made by Green Mind. Without A Sound included several strong compositions such as 'Feel The Pain' and 'On The Brink', with the bass now played by Mike Johnson (b. 27 August 1965, Grant's Pass, Oregon, USA). Mascis also produced other artists including the Breeders and Buffalo Tom, and wrote the soundtrack for and appeared in Allison Anders' movie Gas Food Lodging. A new album, Hand It Over, was released in March 1997, and proved a full-bodied Dinosaur Jr recording that sounded like Mascis was once more committed to his music. While the lyrics were often muddied, Mascis' melodic grunge was very much intact. However, Mascis formally announced the end of Dinosaur Jr in December 1997. He subsequently collaborated with Kevin Shields (My Bloody Valentine) and Bob Pollard (Guided By Voices) on his next project, J Mascis And

The Fog, releasing the excellent More Light in September 2000.

● ALBUMS: as Dinosaur Dinosaur (Homestead 1985) ★★★, You're Living All Over Me (SST 1987) ★★★, Bug (SST 1988) ★★★★, Green Mind (Blanco y Negro/Sire 1991) ★★★, Whatever's Cool With Me mini-album (Blanco y Negro/Sire 1993) ★★, Where You Been (Blanco y Negro 1993) ★★★★, Without A Sound (Blanco y Negro 1994) ★★★, Hand It Over (Blanco y Negro 1997) ★★★, In Session 1988 recording (Strange Fruit 1999) ★★★.
Solo: J Mascis Martin + Me (Baked Goods/Reprise 1996) ★★★, as J Mascis + The Fog More Light (Ultimatum/City Slang 2000) ★★★★.

● COMPILATIONS: Ear Bleeding Country: The Best Of Dinosaur Jr. (Rhino 2001) ★★★★.

## DINOSAURS

Formed in 1982 in San Francisco, California, USA, the Dinosaurs consisted of former members of the popular San Francisco rock bands of the 60s. The initial line-up comprised, guitarist Barry Melton (ex-Country Joe And The Fish), guitarist John Cipollina (ex-Quicksilver Messenger Service), bass player Peter Albin (formerly of Big Brother And The Holding Company), drummer Spencer Dryden (Jefferson Airplane) and songwriter/vocalist Robert Hunter (Grateful Dead). The band came together with the intent of recreating the sound and ambience of the era from which the members sprang. Long, winding improvisations were the norm whether the group performed new, original material or songs associated with the 60s. They played locally in the San Francisco area. In 1985, Hunter left and was replaced by keyboard player Merl Saunders, who worked with the Grateful Dead's Jerry Garcia in a number of extra-curricular bands during the 70s. They recorded their only album in 1988. After Cipollina's death in 1989, the group went on a hiatus, but by the mid-90s had replaced him with violinist Papa John Creach, formerly of Jefferson Airplane/Starship and Hot Tuna. Creach died in February 1994.

● ALBUMS: Dinosaurs (Big Beat 1988) ★★★.

## DIRE STRAITS

Few groups can claim to be synonymous with a lifestyle, but Dire Straits are an exception, whether they like it or not. Brothers In Arms, released in 1985, established them as the first real darlings of the compact disc 20-something generation that grew out of the boom years of the 80s. Their accessible, traditional blues-based music made them perfect for the massive, mature, relatively wealthy strata of the public that likes its music tightly performed and readily digestible. The album was number 1 in the US charts for nine weeks and spent three years in the UK chart.

Surprisingly, Dire Straits first surfaced during a period that was the antipathy of what they were to become – the London punk scene of 1976/7. Mark Knopfler (b. 12 August 1949, Glasgow, Scotland) and his brother David Knopfler (b. 27 December 1952, Glasgow, Scotland) were the sons of an architect who moved to Newcastle-upon-Tyne, England, when the boys were young. Mark Knopfler studied English literature at Leeds University, and for a short while worked as a junior reporter with the *Yorkshire Evening Post* and with an Essex local newspaper. After university he played in a part-time pub band called Brewer's Droop but his main income was drawn from teaching. The Knopflers moved to London during the early 70s and Mark met bass player John Illsley (b. 24 June 1949, Leicester, England) and drummer Pick Withers. Illsley, a sociology graduate, was working in a record shop and Withers had been a session drummer for many years. The climate was not right for the group as punk took a grip on music and almost every UK record label passed on the offer to press up Dire Straits' polished music. One song began to stand out from their repertoire, a basic blues progression with dry, affectionate lyrics, called 'Sultans Of Swing'. It was picked up by Radio London DJ and Oval Records proprietor, Charlie Gillett, and by the end of 1977 the group were recording their debut, Dire Straits, for Vertigo Records with producer Muff Winwood. 'Sultans Of Swing' was a hit first in Holland and later made the UK Top 10. The powerful Warner Brothers Records took over distribution in the USA and aggressively backed the album until in March 1979 it had reached number 2 in the *Billboard* chart. Their second single, 'Lady Writer', was a relative failure but it did not impair their attraction as an 'albums band'. *Communique*, produced by Jerry Wexler and Barry Beckett, sold three million copies worldwide. It missed the commercial edge of the debut but developed Knopfler's trademark incisive, cynical lyricism.

Before the recording of *Making Movies*, David Knopfler opted out to begin a solo career and has since released several records with various small independent labels. He was replaced by Hal Lindes, formerly a member of Darling, with Alan Clark joining on keyboards at the same time. Knopfler was heavily criticized for not varying his songwriting formula but the album still spawned a UK Top 10 single with the poignant love ballad, 'Romeo And Juliet'. *Love Over Gold* fared better than its predecessor in the USA and the single from it, 'Private Investigations', reached number 2 in the UK during September 1982.

Following the *Love Over Gold* album, Knopfler took time off to produce Bob Dylan's *Infidels* (1983), and wrote Tina Turner's comeback hit, 'Private Dancer'. Now respected as both a songwriter and an exceptionally gifted guitarist, it looked for a while as if Dire Straits might not record again because of Knopfler's other production commitments with artists as diverse as Aztec Camera, Randy Newman and Willy DeVille. They reassembled, however, in 1983 with ex-Man drummer Terry Williams replacing Withers, and completed an arduous world tour. A live double album, *Alchemy Live*, filled the gap before the band's next studio album release, *Brothers In Arms*. Like many others, Dire Straits' appearance at the Live Aid concert boosted sales and their own 200-date tour helped it become one of the decade's biggest-selling albums. Knopfler used it to make several wry observations on his own position as a rock star, laughing at the folly of videos and MTV on 'Money For Nothing' – a number 1 in the USA. Three other songs from the record, 'Walk Of Life', 'So Far Away' and the title track, also charted on both sides of the Atlantic, with 'Walk Of Life' reaching number 2 in the UK. With *Brothers In Arms* still riding high in the charts, Knopfler turned once again to other projects. Having already written three film scores in 1983 and 1984 (for *Local Hero*, *Cal*, and *Comfort And Joy*), he wrote the music for the fantasy comedy film, *The Princess Bride* in 1987. With Dire Straits on extended sabbatical, bass player John Illsley also took the chance to release two solo albums, *Never Told A Soul* in 1984 and *Glass* in 1988, neither of which sold in significant quantities. In 1990, Knopfler formed an *ad hoc* and low-key pub band with Brendan Croker and Steve Phillips, called the Notting Hillbillies. Their self-titled debut album was a disappointing, soporific release and the group disbanded after one UK tour.

During the summer of 1991 Dire Straits announced a massive 'comeback' tour and the release of a new album, *On Every Street*. While Knopfler strove to find new challenges in various other music-related spheres, his group was able to leave a six-year gap between album releases and still maintain their incredible popularity. This was owing, in no small measure, to masterful global marketing and the unflinching mainstream appeal of their music. Their world tour, taking two years to complete, marked their first concerts since their 1988 appearance as part of the Nelson Mandela birthday concert at London's Wembley Stadium, and was captured on their second live album, *On The Night*. With Dire Straits on indefinite hold, Knopfler released his first solo album in 1996.

● ALBUMS: *Dire Straits* (Vertigo 1978) ★★★★, *Communique* (Vertigo 1979) ★★, *Making Movies* (Vertigo 1980) ★★★★, *Love Over Gold* (Vertigo 1982) ★★★, *Alchemy – Live* (Vertigo 1984) ★★, *Brothers In Arms* (Vertigo 1985) ★★★, *On Every Street* (Vertigo 1991) ★★★, *On The Night* (Vertigo 1993) ★★, *Live At The BBC* (Windsong 1995) ★★★.

● COMPILATIONS: *Money For Nothing* (Vertigo 1988) ★★★★, *Sultans Of Swing: The Very Best Of Dire Straits* (Mercury 1998) ★★★★.

● VIDEOS: *Brothers In Arms* (PolyGram Music Video 1988), *Alchemy Live* (Channel 5 1988), *The Videos* (PolyGram Music Video 1992).

● FURTHER READING: *Dire Straits*, Michael Oldfield. *Mark Knopfler: The Unauthorised Biography*, Myles Palmer.

## DIRTY DANCING

If films that adhered to a conventional musical formula could be counted on the fingers of one hand in the 80s, the excitement of dance never ceased to attract enthusiastic audiences. Following in the dance steps of the success of *Footloose* and *Flashdance*, *Dirty Dancing*, released in 1987, caught the imagination of many with its combination of raunchy dancing, romance and upbeat soundtrack. Directed by Emile Ardolino, with a screenplay by Eleanor Bergstein, it tells the story of Baby (Jennifer Grey), her father's favourite daughter, who suffers the ups-and-downs of growing up while on a family holiday at a Catskills resort in the summer of 1963. Baby is an idealistic girl, soon to begin at college, who thinks she can right any problem, and help anyone, whatever the situation. These are all characteristics which one of the resort's leading dancers, Johnny (Patrick Swayze), finds refreshing and attractive. When someone is desperately needed to fill the shoes of Johnny's dancing partner, Penny (Cynthia Rhodes), it's hardly surprising that Baby is chosen to substitute, learning all the steps from scratch – almost a mild modern variation of the chorus girl becomes star routine. It's at this point that Baby and Johnny begin to fall in love, and despite the protestations of most of the adults around them – particularly Baby's father (Jerry Orbach) – the young lovers are isolated for a time before the inevitable happy ending. The uplifting finale features the film's biggest song hit, '(I've Had) The Time Of My Life' sung by Bill Medley and Jennifer Warnes, which won an Oscar and a Grammy, and topped the US chart. Many of the other tracks reflect the film's theme of 60s nostalgia with contributions from Frankie Valli, the Four Seasons, Otis Redding, the Shirelles and Mickey And Sylvia. There is even one song on the soundtrack, 'She's Like The Wind', performed and written by Swayze (with Stacy Widelitz). *Dirty Dancing* was the first feature release for the home video company Vestron Pictures. While its plot is simplistic, it is a sensitive and original portrayal of a young girl's coming of age, helped along by fine performances and some great frenetic and exciting dancing.

## DIVINYLS

Led by the provocative Chrissie Amphlett, whose songwriting with guitarist Mark McEntee is the basis of the band, the Divinyls have recorded some excellent work. Amphlett's sexy image complemented the mesmerizing urgency of the music, and the band was guaranteed the audience's undivided attention. They formed in Sydney, Australia, in 1981, and their first mini-album was written for the 1982 film *Monkey Grip*; it produced the Australian Top 10 single 'Boys In Town' as well as the excellent ballad 'Only The Lonely'. Signing with the UK label Chrysalis Records, their first album *Desperate* was a hit in Australia. Several hit singles and extensive touring bridged the gap to *What A Life!* (1985), which was greeted enthusiastically; however, the sales did not match the reviews. Later material, with the exception of the next single 'Pleasure And Pain', did not compare well with their earliest work. The band became a duo when bass player Rick Grossman left in 1988 to join Hoodoo Gurus, with musicians added whenever a tour was undertaken. The Divinyls underwent a mini-revival with the controversial single 'I Touch Myself', a deliberately blatant reference to masturbation, which reached the UK Top 10 in 1991. In recent years, Amphlett has established herself as a stage actor, appearing in Australian productions of *Blood Brothers* and *The Boy From Oz*.
● ALBUMS: *Desperate* (Chrysalis 1983) ★★★, *What A Life!* (Chrysalis 1985) ★★★, *Temperamental* (Chrysalis 1988) ★★★, *Divinyls* (Virgin America 1991) ★★★, *Underworld* (RCA 1996) ★★★.
● COMPILATIONS: *Essential* (Chrysalis 1987) ★★★, *Make You Happy (1981–1993)* (Raven 1997) ★★★.

## DJ JAZZY JEFF AND THE FRESH PRINCE

The Fresh Prince, aka Will Smith (b. 25 September 1968, Philadelphia, Pennsylvania, USA) is now just as famous for his acting career, which started when he played the streetwise tough suffering culture shock when transplanted into the affluent Beverly Hills household of television series *The Fresh Prince of Bel Air*. However, this was initially very much a second career for Smith. Together with DJ Jazzy Jeff (b. Jeffrey Townes, 22 January 1965, Philadelphia, Pennsylvania, USA), this young duo had already cut a highly successful debut album in 1987, and charted with the hit single 'Girls Ain't Nothing But Trouble'. Musically the duo operated in familiar territory, working a variety of inoffensive, borrowed styles to good effect and in marked contrast to the threatening 'street style' of other rap artists.
Jazzy Jeff started DJing in the mid-70s when he was a mere 10 years old (though he is not to be confused with the similarly titled Jazzy Jeff who cut an album, also for Jive, in 1985). He was frequently referred to in those early days as the 'bathroom' DJ, because, hanging out with better-known elders, he would only be allowed to spin the decks when they took a toilet break. He met the Fresh Prince at a party, the two securing a recording deal after entering the 1986 New Music Seminar, where Jeff won the coveted Battle Of The Deejays. Embarking on a recording career, the obligatory James Brown lifts were placed next to steals from cartoon characters like Bugs Bunny, which gave some indication of their debut album's scope. In the late 80s, they cemented their reputation with million-selling teen anthems like 'Girls Ain't Nothing But Trouble', which sampled the *I Dream Of Jeannie* theme, and was released three weeks before Smith graduated from high school. They became the first rap act to receive a Grammy Award for their second album's 'Parents Just Don't Understand', even though the ceremony was boycotted by most of the prominent hip-hop crews because it was not slated to be 'screened' as part of the television transmission. In its wake, the duo launched the world's first pop star 900 number (the pay-phone equivalent of the UK's 0898 system). By January 1989, 3 million calls had been logged.
*He's The DJ, I'm The Rapper* contained more accessible pop fare, the sample of *Nightmare On Elm Street* being the closest they came to street-level hip-hop. The raps were made interesting, however, by the Prince's appropriation of a variety of personas. This is doubtless what encouraged the television bosses to make him an offer he could not refuse, and *The Fresh Prince Of Bel Air*'s enormous success certainly augmented his profile. He has since moved on to dramatic film roles, beginning with *Where The Day Takes You* and *Six Degrees Of Separation* (1993), and reaching a peak with *Independence Day* (1996) and *Men In Black* (1997), two of the highest-grossing movies of all time. Townes, meanwhile, formed A Touch Of Jazz Inc., a stable of producers working on

rap/R&B projects. The duo picked up a second Grammy for 'Summertime' in 1991, before scoring a surprise UK number 1 in 1993 with 'Boom! Shake The Room', the first rap record (Vanilla Ice and MC Hammer aside) to top the British singles chart. The same year's *Code Red* was the duo's final album, with Smith concentrating on his acting career and releasing his solo debut in 1997. Townes concentrated on production duties, with his most notable work coming on Jill Scott's debut, *Who Is Jill Scott?*. He released his own solo debut, *The Magnificent*, in August 2002.

● ALBUMS: *Rock The House* (Word Up 1987) ★★, *He's The DJ, I'm The Rapper* (Jive 1988) ★★★, *And In This Corner* (Jive 1990) ★★★, *Homebase* (Jive 1991) ★★★, *Code Red* (Jive 1993) ★★★.

● COMPILATIONS: *Greatest Hits* (Jive 1998) ★★★★, *Before The Willennium* (BMG 2000) ★★★.

## DJ PIERRE

Beginning his DJing career in 1983, Pierre was his second choice of name after hosting a disastrous set under his original title. He would play at several early Lil' Louis parties, before he was credited with developing acid house, alongside his collaborator Spanky, in a Chicago basement in 1986. The duo had just purchased a bass machine, the Roland TB 303. Through a process of experimentation the 'acid squelch' sound came forth, which was recorded and passed on to DJ Ron Hardy to play at his Warehouse club. These quickly became known as Hardy's 'Acid Tracks' and the term stuck. Pierre went on to form Phuture Records, started in 1987, which consolidated on his invention with the hugely influential *Acid Trax* series. From there, his name first became synonymous with the Acid House movement, before tiring of Chicago and moving to New York to help establish the Strictly Rhythm empire. His work there in the capacity of A&R head, producer and artist was pivotal. Pierre's discography is a varied and prolific one, beginning with singles like 'Annihilating Rhythm' (as Darkman), 'Masterblaster', 'Rise From Your Grave', 'Musik' and 'Generate Power'. In New York he perfected the 'Wyld Pitch' musical style, and in later years operated more as a free agent (releasing material like 'More Than Just A Chance' on the UK's Vinyl Solution, and 'I Might Be Leaving U' for Moving, which featured a vocal from LaVette), though he maintained links with Strictly Rhythm. He also remixed widely, his clients including Yo You Honey, Midi Rain and DIY. Not to be confused with the similarly titled DJ Pierre (Pierre Fieroldi) from Italy, who, along with Gianfranco Bortolotti has been responsible for Euro hits by the 49ers, Cappella and others, plus his own cuts like 'We Gonna Funk'. Various heated letters were exchanged between the two as confusion increased.

## DMC

The hugely influential and important Dance Music Club was established by the former DJ and head of programming at Radio Luxembourg, Tony Prince. In 1982, Prince was impressed by one of the many 'demo' tapes he was sent by aspiring radio DJs. It featured no speech between the tracks which were

also segued into each other. Inspired, he set about establishing DMC and in 1983 released the organisation's first 'megamix' cassette, featuring a sequence of hits by Shalamar. The notion of the megamix of one artist's material was in itself revolutionary. DMC pioneered the idea of mixing and the notion of the DJ as the star, releasing a succession of megamixes and remixes. In 1985, DMC established its now world-famous annual World DJ Mixing Championship, sponsored by electronics company, Technics. The competition attracts DJing talent from all over the world and has helped to launch the career of many famous DJs, including Chad Jackson, Cash Money, Carl Cox and Cutmaster Swift. UK DJs Dave Seaman and Guy Ornadel were both employed by DMC in the early 90s, Seaman as an A&R man and Ornadel as manager of their US office in New York City. Sasha was also managed by DMC for some time. It was DMC's newsletters that, in 1989, evolved into the clubber's bible, *MixMag*. In 1990, DMC established two subsidiary imprints, Stress Records and FBI to release the work of recording artists rather than mixes by DJs, including John Digweed (Bedrock). In June 1999, DMC launched the world's first dance music weekly, *7* magazine.

## DNA

This US band was a short-lived collaboration between guitarist Rick Derringer (b. Richard Zehringer, 5 August 1947, Fort Recovery, Ohio, USA) and drummer Carmine Appice (b. 15 December 1946, Staten Island, New York, USA). With the assistance of Duane Hitchings (keyboards) and Jimmy Johnson (bass), they released *Party Tested* in 1983. This featured a wide range of styles that included jazz, rock, funk, blues and pop. The playing was beyond criticism, but the songs were devoid of soul, and the album as a whole lacked unity and cohesion. Failing to win support in the media, DNA disintegrated when Carmine Appice accepted an offer to join Ozzy Osbourne's band. He subsequently formed King Kobra.

● ALBUMS: *Party Tested* (Polydor 1983) ★★.

## DOCTOR AND THE MEDICS

This psychedelic UK pop-rock outfit led by Clive Jackson (b. 7 July 1961, Liverpool, England) came to prominence in 1986 with a cover version of Norman Greenbaum's 'Spirit In The Sky'. The single hit number 1 in the UK, but they found it difficult to consolidate their success, with the subsequent 'Burn' and 'Waterloo' only achieving UK chart placings of 29 and 46, respectively. *Laughing At The Pieces* peaked at number 25 in the charts, primarily on the back of major single success. Following this every release sunk without trace, and the band was dropped by their label, although they are still sighted, playing irregular live dates. They also run their own Madman Records label.

● ALBUMS: *Laughing At The Pieces* (I.R.S. 1986) ★★★, *I Keep Thinking It's Tuesday* (I.R.S. 1987) ★★, *The Adventures Of Boadicea And The Beetle* (Castle 1993) ★★.

## DOGS D'AMOUR

This rock outfit was originally formed in Birmingham, England, during 1983, with a line-up comprising Tyla (guitar), Ned Christie (vocals), Nick Halls (guitar), Carl (bass) and Bam Bam (drums). After making their London debut in April 1983 and recording a track for the Flicknife compilation *Trash On Delivery*, they underwent a rapid series of personnel changes. Halls, Bam Bam and Christie departed, prompting Tyla to assume lead vocal responsibilities. He and Carl recruited replacements Dave Kusworth (guitar) and Paul Hornby (drums). They relocated to Finland, where their hard rock style won them an underground following. After returning to the UK in 1985, further changes in the line-up were underway, with Bam Bam replacing Hornby, while Kusworth departed in favour of the elegantly named Jo-Dog (b. Jo Almeida). Later that year, the procession of changes continued with the departure of Carl in favour of Doll By Doll bass player Mark Duncan, and then Mark Drax who lasted until 1987 when Steve James arrived. The group finally broke through with the minor hit 'How Come It Never Rains', and the mini-album *A Graveyard Of Empty Bottles*. The follow-up, 'Satellite Kid', also reached the UK Top 30 in August 1989, as did their album, *Errol Flynn*. The latter met with some resistance in the USA where it was forcibly retitled *The King Of The Thieves*. Having at last stabilized their line-up, Dogs D'Amour failed to establish themselves in the top league of hard rock acts, but continued to tour extensively

During a lull in the early 90s James formed the Last Bandits, while Bam Bam joined the Wildhearts. Dogs D'Amour re-formed in 1993 with Darrell Barth (ex-Crybabys) replacing Almeida. However, by 1994 the group had ground to a halt, with Tyla embarking on a solo career and Steve James and Bam Bam forming Mary Jane. Tyla, Almeida and Bam Bam reunited to record *Happy Ever After*, which featured the latter's wife Share Pedersen on bass.

● ALBUMS: *The State We're In* (Kumibeat 1984) ★★, *The (Un)Authorised Bootleg* (China 1988) ★★, *In The Dynamite Jet Saloon* (China 1988) ★★★, *A Graveyard Of Empty Bottles* mini-album (China 1989) ★★★, *Errol Flynn* (UK) *The King Of The Thieves* (US) (China 1989) ★★★, *Straight??!!* (China 1990) ★★★, *More Uncharted Heights Of Disgrace* (China 1993) ★★, *Happy Ever After* (Artful 2001) ★★.

● COMPILATIONS: *Dog's Hits And The Bootleg Album* (China 1991) ★★★, *Skeletons – The Best Of The Dogs D'Amour* (Nectar 1997) ★★★.

## DOKKEN

This Los Angeles, USA heavy metal band was put together by vocalist Don Dokken. His first break came when producer Dieter Dierks recruited him to supply (eventually unused) back-up vocals on the Scorpions' *Blackout* in 1982. Dierks then allowed Dokken the remaining studio time to produce demos. These rough recordings impressed Carrere Records enough to secure him a contract, and he enlisted the services of guitarist George Lynch, drummer Mick Brown and bass player Juan Croucier (who later left to form Ratt and was replaced by Jeff Pilson) to form Dokken. The band's intimate fusion of hard rock, melody and atmospherics led to a major label deal with Elektra Records. They remixed and re-released their Carrere debut, *Breaking The Chains*, which made the lower end of the US *Billboard* album chart. Thereafter, Elektra allowed the band a substantial recording budget, with producers Michael Wagener, Geoff Workman, Tom Werman and Roy Thomas Baker being used at different times. The band recorded three excellent studio albums for Elektra (*Back For The Attack* reaching US number 13 in December 1987) before internal disputes between Lynch and Don Dokken led the band to split in 1988. A farewell live album, *Beast From The East*, followed, and provided a fitting epitaph.

Lynch went on to form Lynch Mob, while Don Dokken negotiated a solo contract with Geffen Records and released *Up From The Ashes* in 1990. Pilson fronted War And Peace, but soon began writing with Dokken once more. Having been begged by Dokken fans over the preceding years for some form of reunion, they eventually elected to make it permanent. With Brown already on board, Lynch finally settled his differences with Don Dokken and rejoined in May 1994. The original line-up released the acoustic live set *One Live Night* (from a December 1994 concert), and recorded the lacklustre studio albums *Dysfunctional* and *Shadow Life*. Lynch left in November 1997, and was replaced by Reb Beach (ex-Winger). The latter appeared on 1999's *Erase The Slate* before in turn being replaced by John Norum on 2002's surprisingly sound *Long Way Home*. This album also featured new bass player Barry Sparks.

● ALBUMS: *Breaking The Chains* (Carrere/Elektra 1982) ★★★, *Tooth And Nail* (Elektra 1984) ★★★, *Under Lock And Key* (Elektra 1985) ★★★, *Back For The Attack* (Elektra 1987) ★★★★, *Beast From The East* (Elektra 1988) ★★★, *Dysfunctional* (Columbia 1995) ★★, *One Live Night* (CMC 1995) ★★★, *Shadow Life* (CMC 1997) ★★, *Erase The Slate* (CMC 1999) ★★, *Live From The Sun* (CMC 2000) ★★, *Long Way Home* (CMC 2002) ★★★.
Solo: Don Dokken *Up From The Ashes* (Geffen 1990) ★★.

● COMPILATIONS: *The Very Best Of Dokken* (Elektra 1999) ★★★.

● VIDEOS: *One Live Night: The Concert Video* (CMC International 1996).

## DOLBY, THOMAS

b. Thomas Morgan Robertson, 14 October 1958, Cairo, Egypt. Dolby is a self-taught musician/vocalist/songwriter and computer programmer. After studying meteorology and projectionism at college, he started building his own synthesizers at the age of 18. With his own hand-built PA system he acted as sound engineer on tours by the Members, Fall and the Passions. Afterwards, he co-founded Camera Club with Bruce Wooley in January 1979, before joining the Lene Lovich backing group in September 1980, for whom he wrote 'New Toy'. His first solo output was the single 'Urges' on the Armageddon label in 1981, before he scored hits the following year with 'Europa' and 'The Pirate Twins'. For a series of 1982 concerts at the Marquee he recruited ex-Soft Boys Matthew Seligman and Kevin Armstrong of the Thompson Twins, while finding time to contribute to albums by M, Joan Armatrading and Foreigner. Other collaborations included Stevie Wonder, Herbie Hancock, Dusty Springfield, Howard Jones and Grace Jones. The most visual of such appearances came when he backed David Bowie at Live Aid. A strong 'mad scientist' image proliferated in his videos, which also featured famous British eccentric Magnus Pike. These earned him a strong media profile, but, surprisingly, his best-known singles, 'She Blinded Me With Science' and 'Hyperactive', only peaked at numbers 31 and 17, respectively. The latter did, however, reach the Top 5 in the USA, and charted in the UK again when re-released in 1996. As well as production for Prefab Sprout and Joni Mitchell, Dolby scored music for several movies including *Howard: A New Breed Of Hero*. He married actress Kathleen Beller (Kirby Colby from *Dynasty*). In 1993, he founded the computer software company Headspace, an enterprise which began to take precedence over his musical activities. Dolby commands high respect in the music business, as his back-room contributions have already been considerable.

● ALBUMS: *The Golden Age Of Wireless* (Venice In Peril 1982) ★★★★, *The Flat Earth* (Parlophone 1984) ★★★, *Aliens Ate My Buick* (Manhattan 1988) ★★, *Astronauts & Heretics* (Virgin 1992) ★★★, *The Gate To The Mind's Eye* (Giant 1994) ★★★.

● COMPILATIONS: *The Best Of Thomas Dolby: Retrospectacle* (Capitol 1995) ★★★★, *Hyperactive* (EMI 1999) ★★★.

● VIDEOS: *The Gate To The Mind's Eye* (Miramar Images 1994).

## DOLCE, JOE

b. Painesville, Ohio, USA. Of Italian/American extraction, Dolce was supposedly a member of Sugar Creek, an obscure country/rock act which released an album *Please Tell A Friend*, on Metromedia Records in 1968. By 1974, he was touring the USA east coast, fronting a 'poetry/rock' group, but he emigrated to Australia in the second half of the 70s, where he formed the Joe Dolce Music Theatre, a comedy act, with Dolce himself playing a character known as Giuseppe. In this guise, he recorded a novelty single, 'Shaddap You Face', which became a major hit in Australia, and was licensed to Epic in the UK and MCA in the USA. No doubt it appealed to Italian immigrants on both sides of the Atlantic, and while it stalled just outside the US Top 50 in mid-1981, it had already topped the UK singles chart for three weeks in February 1981, supplanting 'Woman' by John Lennon, whose records were dominating the UK chart in the wake of his recent murder. As with many novelty acts, Dolce was unable to follow up this success, although (remarkably) an album titled after the hit spent a month in the US Top 200 album chart also in 1981.

● ALBUMS: *Shaddap You Face* (Epic/MCA 1981) ★★.

## DOLLY MIXTURE

This female UK pop trio comprised Deborah Wykes (b. 21 December 1960, Hammersmith, London, England; bass, piano, vocals), Rachel Bor (b. 16 May 1963, Wales; guitar, cello, vocals) and Hester Smith (b. 28 October 1960, West Africa; drums). The band was formed by the three school friends in Cambridge, with a musical style that echoed the Shangri-Las and the 70s Undertones. Championed by influential UK disc jockey John Peel, the band released a cover version of the Shirelles hit 'Baby It's You' on Chrysalis Records in 1980 – which at the time of issue they disowned, protesting at the label's attempted manipulation of their image. They were one of the first bands to record for Paul Weller's Respond label, releasing 'Been Teen' (1981) and 'Everything And More' (1982), both of which were produced by Captain Sensible and Paul Gray of the Damned. The UK record-buying public found difficulty coming to terms with the trio's idiosyncratic mode of dress and independent attitude, something with which a portion of the music press also had problems. They proved their worth, however, with exhilarating live performances. In 1982, they released a double album on their own Dead Good Dolly Platters label, featuring demo tapes collected over the previous four years. The album has since achieved cult status among later 80s independent groups. Dolly Mixture eventually found national fame by acting as Sensible's backing vocalists on his UK number 1 single 'Happy Talk', in 1982. They also guested on his subsequent singles and albums, while Rachel and the Captain formed a romantic partnership. Meanwhile, their own career floundered, despite the critical plaudits. The trio dissolved as a working band in 1984, leaving as their swan-song *The Fireside* EP, released on Cordelia Records, a set consisting mainly of 'pop/chamber' music, featuring their often ignored talents on piano and cello. In 1986, Wykes and Hester resurfaced with Coming Up Roses.

● ALBUMS: *The Demonstration Tapes* (Dead Good Dolly 1982) ★★★.

## DOMINGO, PLACIDO

b. 21 March 1941, Madrid, Spain. One of the world's leading tenors who, along with Luciano Pavarotti, has attempted to give opera in recent years a widespread, classless appeal. Domingo's family emigrated to Mexico in 1950, where he studied piano, conducting and singing. He debuted as a baritone in 1957, and his first major tenor role came in 1960 performing in Giuseppe Verdi's *La Traviata*. Domingo became a member of the Israel National Opera from 1962 to 65 and latter made acclaimed performances at the New York City Opera and Metropolitan, and at La Scala (Milan) and Covent Garden (London) – singing alongside sopranos such as Katria Ricciarelli, Rosalind Plowright and Montserrat Caballe. His first flirtation with the pop world came in 1981, when he recorded as duet with John Denver, 'Perhaps Love'. This Denver-penned song reached the UK Top 50 and US Top 20, consequently opening up a parallel career for Domingo in light entertainment and simultaneously introducing to the mass-market the delights of the operatic aria as well as Spanish love-songs. In 1985 he joined forces with Sarah Brightman and Lorin Maazel for Andrew Lloyd Webber's *Requiem*, which became a UK Top 10 album. 'Till I Loved You', a duet with Jennifer Rush, reached the UK Top 30 in 1989. Domingo's efforts, plus those of similar promotions from Luciano Pavarotti, Nigel Kennedy and José Carreras, signalled the beginnings of the early 90s boom in sales of populist classical and operatic music. In particular, the 'Three Tenors' concert with Carreras and Pavarotti, promoting the 1990 soccer World Cup in Italy, gained the three men widespread media coverage and huge record sales. They repeated the concert for the 1998 World Cup in France. The same year Domingo released *Por Amor*, an album dedicated to the work of Mexican composer Agustín Lara.

● ALBUMS: with John Denver *Perhaps Love* (Columbia 1981) ★★, *Domingo-Con Amore* (RCA 1982) ★★★, *My Life For A Song* (Columbia 1983) ★★★, *Be My Love* (DGS 1984) ★★★, *Christmas With Placido Domingo* (Columbia 1984) ★★, *Placido Domingo Sings Zarzuelas* (HMV 1988) ★★★, *Goya ... A Life In A Song* (Columbia 1989) ★★★, with José Carreras, Luciano Pavarotti *In Concert* (Decca 1990) ★★★, *Be My Love ... An Album Of Love* (EMI 1990) ★★★, with the London Symphony Orchestra *The Broadway I Love* (East West 1991) ★★★, *Domingo: Arias And Spanish Songs* (Deutsche Grammophon 1992) ★★★, with Montserrat Caballe, Carreras, Domingo *From The Official Barcelona Games Ceremony* (RCA 1992) ★★★, with Carreras, Diana Ross *Christmas In Vienna* (Sony Classical 1993) ★★★, with José Carreras, Natalie Cole *Celebration Of Christmas* (Elektra 1996) ★★★, *Por Amor* (WEA 1998) ★★★, with Carreras, Pavarotti *The 3 Tenors Live In Paris* (Decca 1998) ★★★, with Carreras, Pavarotti *A Tenors Christmas* (Sony Classical 1998) ★★★, with Carreras, Pavarotti *A Tenors Valentine* (Sony Classical 1999) ★★★, *100 Años De Mariachi* (EMI Latin 1999) ★★★, *The Three Tenors Christmas* (Sony Classical 1999) ★★★.

● COMPILATIONS: *Placido Domingo Collection* (Stylus 1986) ★★★, *Greatest Love Songs* (Columbia 1988) ★★★, *The Essential Domingo* (Deutsche Grammophon 1989) ★★★★.

● VIDEOS: *The 3 Tenors – Paris 1998* (PolyGram Music Video 1998), *The Three Tenors Christmas* (Sony 2000).

## DONINGTON FESTIVAL

Held annually during August at the Castle Donington racetrack in north Leicestershire, England, the Donington Festival has come to represent the highlight of the UK heavy metal calendar. First staged in 1980, Donington was conceived as an alternative to the Reading Festival when the latter moved away from its hard-rock roots to encompass new wave and indie acts. Donington's one-day event, billed 'Monsters Of Rock', generally features at least six top-flight rock bands, with the opening slot reserved for 'talented newcomers'. This has resulted in commercially successful acts such as Mötley Crüe (1984), Cinderella (1987), Thunder

(1990) and the Black Crowes (1991) all using the spot as a platform to launch their international careers. Among the headliners, AC/DC have returned three times (1982, 1984, 1991), and Iron Maiden (1988, 1992) and Whitesnake (1983, 1990) twice. Although the festival has encountered fewer public disorder problems than most, in 1988 two attendees were killed during Guns N'Roses' performance when a video screen and supporting scaffolding collapsed at the side of the stage. Two years previously, heavy metal satirists Bad News were 'bottled off' as their caricatures of the heavy metal lifestyle wore thin. In 1992, BBC Radio 1 presented its first live broadcast of the festival in its entirety – with the provision of a 15-second delay before 9pm so engineers could delete any expletives. Though that year's audience fell 10,000 below the 72,500 maximum capacity imposed by safety regulators, Donington continues to be the one annual festival for heavy metal and hard rock fans that remains uncontaminated by the presence of other forms of music.

## DONOVAN, JASON

b. Jason Sean Donovan, 1 June 1968, Malvern, Melbourne, Australia. Donovan appeared in the Australian television soap-opera *Neighbours*, which, when shown on British television, commanded a considerable viewing audience of pre-pubescent/teenage girls who instantly took his character, Scott Robinson, to their hearts. His co-star Kylie Minogue had already begun to forge a career in pop music when he also signed to the Stock, Aitken and Waterman label, PWL. In 1988 his first single, 'Nothing Can Divide Us Now', reached the UK Top 5. The follow-up was a collaboration with Minogue, 'Especially For You', which topped the UK charts in January the following year. Donovan consolidated his position as Britain's top teen pin-up by scoring four more Top 10 hits, including 'Too Many Broken Hearts' (a number 1 hit), 'Sealed With A Kiss', 'Every Day (I Love You More)' and 'When You Come Back To Me'. His album, *Ten Good Reasons*, reached number 1 and became one of 1989's bestsellers. His success the following year was endorsed by Top 10 hits in 'Hang On To Your Love' and a remake of the 1963 Cascades hit, 'Rhythm Of The Rain'. By this time Donovan had left the cast of *Neighbours*. His performances in the stage show of the Andrew Lloyd Webber/Tim Rice musical, *Joseph And The Amazing Technicolor Dreamcoat*, at the London Palladium, drew sell-out crowds and mostly good reviews, taking many of his regular critics by surprise. A single from the show, 'Any Dream Will Do', reached number 1 in the UK chart, scotching any notion that Donovan was wavering as a hit-maker. He was perceived by many as simply being a teen-idol, yet his obvious talent in acting and singing, and the extent of his loyal following, echoed previous teen-idols made good as all-round entertainers (Tommy Steele for example).

In the spring of 1992, Donovan won a libel action he brought against *The Face* magazine. Later in the same year, his high-profile concert tour was greeted with a good deal of apathy and critical derision ('Jason's big rock dream turns sour'), and it was considered by many to be a retrograde career move when he returned to *Joseph And The Amazing Technicolor Dreamcoat* the following year. For some time he alternated with other leading performers, before taking over for the last few weeks before the show closed in February 1994. After he had collapsed several times in public during 1995, there was inevitably speculation in the press regarding drugs and alcohol abuse. However, the following year he was in London playing Mordred in the Covent Garden Festival production of Camelot, and had his first non-singing role as a psychopath who keeps his first victim's head in a hat box, in Emlyn Williams' classic 1935 thriller, *Night Must Fall*, at the Theatre Royal Haymarket. Having also dressed in a black bin liner and Dr. Marten boots in order to host *Mr. Gay UK*, a beauty contest for men, he went one step further and donned the obligatory stockings and suspenders for the role of Frank 'N' Furter in an Australian production of *The Rocky Horror Show*. In 1998, he headed the 25th Anniversary tour of that cult show in Britain.

● ALBUMS: *Ten Good Reasons* (PWL 1989) ★★, *Between The Lines* (PWL 1990) ★★, *Joseph And The Amazing Technicolor Dreamcoat* stage show soundtrack (PolyGram 1991) ★★★, *All Around The World* (Polydor 1993) ★★.

● COMPILATIONS: *Greatest Hits* (PWL 1991) ★★★, *The Very Best Of Jason Donovan* (Music Club 1999) ★★★.

● VIDEOS: *Jason, The Videos* (PWL 1989), *The Videos 2* (PWL 1990), *Into The Nineties: Live* (Castle Music Pictures 1991), *Greatest Video Hits* (PWL 1991), *The Joseph Mega-Remix* (PolyGram Music Video 1992), *Live* (1993).

## DORE, CHARLIE

b. Pinner, Middlesex, England. Dore is a respected UK songwriter who originally trained as an actress, and is best known for her 1979 hit 'Pilot Of The Airwaves', which reached number 11 on the US charts. Her 1977 country influenced band Prairie Oyster included Pick Withers on drums, who was also playing with the early Dire Straits, at that time playing the same UK pub circuit. The band evolved through various personnel changes into Charlie Dore's Back Pocket (guitarist Julian Littman having since become a long-time songwriting collaborator). When the band broke up, Dore started a solo career. *Where To Now* was recorded partly in Nashville, and produced by the Shadows' Bruce Welch and songwriter Alan Tarney, with session musicians such as Sonny Curtis. The first single 'Fear Of Flying' failed to make a commercial impact, although it was a major 'turntable hit', but 'Pilot' charted on both sides of the Atlantic and received extensive airplay. She signed to Chrysalis Records in 1981 and released *Listen*, but unable to capitalize on her early success, focused her varied talents on songwriting and acting. As well as repertory work with Michael Bogdanov, she co-starred with Jonathan Pryce in Richard Eyre's award-winning film *The Ploughman's Lunch*, and appeared in several television series, including *Hard Cases* (playing in a band with former Cockney Rebel drummer Stuart Elliot) and *South Of The Border*. She

was also a founder-member of the London-based comedy improvisation team Dogs On Holiday, who have been resident at their own Hurricane Club since 1990. Her songwriting credits include many album tracks and a number of highly successful singles. 'Strut' was a worldwide hit for Sheena Easton, reaching number 4 in the US, where it also won an ASCAP award. She wrote a range of material for Barbara Dickson, and in 1992 scored a UK number 1 with Jimmy Nail's 'Ain't No Doubt', which she co-wrote. 'Refuse To Dance', taken from Celine Dion's hugely successful *The Colour Of My Love*, was released as a single in 1995. Following a return to the recording studio, working with Julian Littman, Danny Schogger (co-writer of 'Ain't No Doubt' and 'Refuse To Dance'), Ricky Fataar and Paul Carrack on a collection of new material, Dore released *Things Change* in 1995, an album co-produced by Littman. Dore's ability, enthusiasm and commitment have helped many others to commercial success while she remains something of a hidden talent.

● ALBUMS: *Where To Now* (Island 1979) ★★★, *Listen* (Chrysalis 1981) ★★★, *Things Change* (Grapevine 1995) ★★★.

## DOUG E. FRESH

b. Douglas E. Davis, 17 September 1966, St. Thomas, Virgin Islands, though he grew up in the Bronx and Harlem districts of New York, USA. Self-proclaimed as The Original Human Beatbox, i.e. being able to imitate the sound of a rhythm machine, Fresh broke through in 1985 with the release of one of rap's classic cuts, 'The Show'. Joined by partner MC Ricky D (aka Slick Rick), the single matched rhymes with a bizarre array of human sound effects, courtesy of Fresh. It marked a notable departure in rap's development, and was so distinctive it began a small flurry of similarly inclined rappers, as well as Salt-N-Pepa's answer record, 'Showstopper'. Despite its impact, it was a song that was hardly representative of Fresh fare: far too much of his recorded material was workmanlike and soundalike. A debut album included live contributions from Bernard Wright (synthesiser) and veteran jazz man Jimmy Owens (trumpet), as well as a dubious anti-abortion cut. The follow-up saw him allied to Public Enemy's Bomb Squad production team.

To give him his due Fresh was very nearly rap's first superstar, but rather than capitalise on 'The Show', he would end up in court trying to sue Reality Records for non-payment of royalties on the song. He was also the first genuine rapper to appear at Jamaica's Reggae Sunsplash festival, stopping in the West Indies long enough to record alongside Papa San and Cocoa Tea. He made something of a comeback at the end of 1993 with the release of party record 'I-Right (Alright)', after he was reunited with Slick Rick (recently returned from a period of incarceration), and signed with Gee Street Records. Fresh has also enjoyed the distinction of seeing a 'Doug E. Fresh' switch added to the Oberheim Emulator, in order to provide samples of his human beat box talents. On *Play* Fresh employed Luther Campbell of 2 Live Crew to add a gangsta edge.

● ALBUMS: *Oh, My God!* (Reality 1985) ★★★, *The*

*World's Greatest Entertainer* (Reality 1988) ★★★, *Doin' What I Gotta Do* (Bust It 1992) ★★, *Play* (Gee Street 1995) ★★, *Alright* (Gee 1996) ★★★.
● COMPILATIONS: *Greatest Hits, Volume 1* (Bust It 1996) ★★★.

## DOWNING, WILL

b. New York, USA. Downing was an in-demand session singer during the late 70s, appearing on recordings by artists including Rose Royce, Billy Ocean, Jennifer Holliday and Nona Hendryx. The soul singer's career was really launched when he met producer/performer Arthur Baker in the mid-80s. This led to him joining Baker's group Wally Jump Jnr. And The Criminal Element, whose other members included Brooklyn-bred Wally Jump, Craig Derry (ex-Moments; Sugarhill Gang), Donny Calvin and Dwight Hawkes (both ex-Rockers Revenge), Rick Sher (ex-Warp 9), Jeff Smith, and the toasting pair Michigan And Smiley. After a spell with Wally Jump Jnr. recording for Baker's Criminal Records label, Downing secured a solo contract with Island Records and recorded his debut album in 1988 with Baker producing. The first release under Downing's own name was 'A Love Supreme', which set lyrics to one of John Coltrane's most famous compositions. The single reached number 1 in the UK, while his first album, produced by Baker, was a Top 20 hit. He had further hits with 'In My Dreams' and a remake of the Roberta Flack and Donny Hathaway duet 'Where Is The Love', on which he partnered Mica Paris. Downing himself produced the second album, co-writing tracks with Brian Jackson, Gil Scott-Heron's collaborator. Neither this nor *A Dream Fulfilled*, on which Barry J. Eastmond and Wayne Braithwaite co-produced, was able to approach the popularity of his debut. *Moods* and *Invitation Only* put Downing firmly in the smooth late-night music category, and although his exquisite vocals were suitably melancholic on both albums, they came uncomfortably close to sounding merely lethargic.
● ALBUMS: *Will Downing* (4th & Broadway 1988) ★★★★, *Come Together As One* (4th & Broadway 1989) ★★★, *A Dream Fulfilled* (4th & Broadway 1991) ★★, *Love's The Place To Be* (4th & Broadway 1993) ★★, *Moods* (4th & Broadway 1995) ★★★, *Invitation Only* (Mercury 1997) ★★★, with Gerald Albright *Pleasures Of The Night* (Verve 1998) ★★★, *All The Man You Need* (Motown 2000) ★★★, *Sensual Journey* (GRP 2002) ★★★.

## DRAMARAMA

The 80s were littered with US alt-rock bands that paved the way for the genre's big commercial breakthrough in the early 90s, but never seem to receive proper credit. Top in this category would be the Replacements, the Pixies, and Hüsker Dü, as well as several lesser-known outfits, such as the pop art-inspired Dramarama. Comprising John Easdale (vocals), Mark Englert (guitar), Chris Carter (bass), Peter Wood (guitar), plus a revolving door of drummers, Dramarama originally formed during 1983 in Wayne, New Jersey. They released an obscure single and EP, while their debut album, *Cinéma Vérité*, compiled their previous output

alongside six new songs, including what would become their best known track, 'Anything, Anything (I'll Give You)'. The album helped the band build a sizeable following among college rock devotees and became a major regional hit in Los Angeles. The excellent *Box Office Bomb* and *Stuck In Wonderamaland* failed to make any headway in a music scene still in thrall to corporate rock. Further releases continued throughout the early 90s, but despite alternative rock's emergence into the mainstream (via bands like Nirvana), Dramarama failed to latch on to a wider mainstream audience. They split up in 1994, with Easdale eventually launching a solo career during the latter part of the decade.
● ALBUMS: *Cinéma Vérité* (New Rose 1985) ★★★★, *Box Office Bomb* (Questionmark 1987) ★★★★, *Stuck In Wonderamaland* (Chameleon 1990) ★★★★, *Live At The China Club* mini-album (Chameleon 1990) ★★★, *Vinyl* (Chameleon/Elektra 1991) ★★★★, *Hi-Fi Sci-Fi* (Chameleon/Elektra 1993) ★★★.
● COMPILATIONS: *The Days Of Wayne And Roses* (No Label 1992) ★★★, *The Best Of Dramarama: 18 Big Ones* (Rhino 1996) ★★★★.

## DREAM ACADEMY

This 80s UK band comprised Nick Laird-Clowes (guitar/vocals, ex-the Act), Gilbert Gabriel (keyboards) and Kate St. John (vocals/oboe/saxophone, ex-Ravishing Beauties). Laird-Clowes, who as a child experienced the last days of the London underground movement at first hand, revived memories of that earlier era with the polished folky-pop 'Life In A Northern Town', dedicated to the memory of singer songwriter Nick Drake. The single, released on the Blanco y Negro label, reached UK number 15 in 1985 (and US number 7 the following year). Hailed, or conversely, derided as one the leading lights of the new breed of English psychedelic revivalists, the band's momentum was halted by the relative failure of 'The Love Parade'. They periodically released albums which stuck gamely to their formula, with Pink Floyd member David Gilmour contributing guitar and production work to their third album. St. John, meanwhile, found plentiful work composing incidental music for British television programmes, while Laird-Clowes later resurfaced on Creation Records as Trashmonk.
● ALBUMS: *The Dream Academy* (Blanco y Negro 1985) ★★★, *Remembrance Days* (Blanco y Negro 1987) ★★, *A Different Kind Of Weather* (Blanco y Negro 1990) ★★.

## DREAM SYNDICATE

The early 80s were exciting times for those with a taste for American west coast rock. Several aspiring new acts appeared in the space of a few months who were obviously indebted to the late 60s, but managed to offer something refreshingly vital in the process. The Dream Syndicate's self-titled debut EP and the follow-up *The Days Of Wine And Roses* (recorded in September 1982), more than justified the attention that the 'Paisley Underground' bands were attracting. Consisting of songwriter Steve Wynn (b.

21 February 1960, Los Angeles, California, USA; guitar, vocals), Karl Precoda (guitar), Kendra Smith (bass) and Dennis Duck (drums), the band chose their finest song, 'Tell Me When It's Over', for their first UK single, issued on Rough Trade Records in late 1983. A contract with A&M Records followed, and *Medicine Show* appeared in 1984. Like their debut, there was a definite acknowledgement of the influence of both Lou Reed and Neil Young. By this time, however, Kendra Smith had joined partner David Roback in Opal (she would also release a sumptuous solo album in 1995), and was replaced by Dave Provost (ex-Droogs).

*This Is Not The New Dream Syndicate Album ... Live!*, featured new bass player Mark Walton, but it was to be their last engagement with A&M. Another move, this time to Chrysalis Records offshoot Big Time, resulted in 1987's *Out Of The Grey*. Recorded by Wynn, Walton, Duck and new guitarist Paul B. Cutler, the band's approach was now gradually shifting to the mainstream. After a 12-inch single, '50 In A 25 Zone', the Dream Syndicate moved to the Enigma Records label, distributed in the UK by Virgin Records. *Ghost Stories* was followed by the live swan-song offering, *Live At Raji's*, in 1989. However, the band never surpassed the dizzy heights of their first album, leaving Wynn to go on to a similarly acclaimed but commercially unsuccessful solo career. Pat Thomas' Normal Records label unearthed some excellent unreleased Dream Syndicate recordings during the 90s.

● ALBUMS: *The Dream Syndicate* mini-album (Down There 1982) ★★★★, *The Days Of Wine And Roses* (Ruby/Rough Trade 1983) ★★★★, *Medicine Show* (A&M 1984) ★★★, *This Is Not The New Dream Syndicate Album ... Live!* mini-album (A&M 1984) ★★, *Out Of The Grey* (Big Time 1986) ★★★, *Ghost Stories* (Enigma 1988) ★★★, *Live At Raji's* (Enigma 1989) ★★★, *The Days Before Wine And Roses* 1982 live recording (Normal 1994) ★★★.
● COMPILATIONS: *It's Too Late To Stop Now* (Another Cowboy 1989) ★★★, *The Lost Tapes: 1985–1988* (Normal 1993) ★★★, *The Days Of Wine And Roses* expanded version (Rino 2001) ★★★★.
● VIDEOS: *Weathered & Torn* (Enigma 1988).

## DROOGS

Formed in 1972, this long-serving Los Angeles, California, USA-based band initially included Rich Albin (vocals), Roger Clay (guitar, vocals), Paul Motter (bass) and Kyle Raven (drums). Unashamedly inspired by 60s garage bands, the quartet founded their own label, Plug-n-Socket, on which they recorded cover versions of favourite songs and originals inspired by their heroes. Having completed a mere six singles in the space of 10 years, during which time the group's rhythm section underwent several changes, the Droogs found themselves avatars of the then in-vogue 'Paisley Underground' scene. *Stone Cold World*, which saw Albin and Clay joined by David Provost (bass) and Jon Gerlach (drums), was sadly obscured in the flurry to praise Green On Red, the Long Ryders and Bangles, but Albin and Clay doggedly pursued their chosen direction when the fashion faded. The unit's

later work was issued on the German Music Maniac label. *Want Something* compiled material from previously released European albums.
● ALBUMS: *Stone Cold World* (Making Waves/Plug-n-Socket 1984) ★★★, *Kingdom Day* (PVC 1987) ★★★, *Mad Dog Dreams* (Music Maniac 1989) ★★★, *Live In Europe* (Music Maniac 1990) ★★, *Guerrilla Love-In* (Music Maniac 1991) ★★★, *Atomic Garage* (Lakota 1997) ★★★.
● COMPILATIONS: *Anthology* (Music Maniac 1987) ★★★★, *Want Something* (Skyclad 1990) ★★★.

## DRUMMOND, BILL

b. 29 April 1953, Butterworth, South Africa. After relocating to Scotland as a child, Drummond rose to fame in the music business during the late 70s rock renaissance in Liverpool. Drummond formed the Merseyside trio Big In Japan, which lasted from 1977 to 78. Drummond subsequently founded the influential Zoo Record label and backed Lori Larty in Lori And The Chameleons. He then enjoyed considerable success as a manager, overseeing the affairs of Echo And The Bunnymen and the Teardrop Explodes. When the Liverpool group scene saw artists moving south, Drummond left the city, and during the next decade was involved in a number of bizarre projects, which testified to his imagination and love of novelty. The controversial JAMS (Justified Ancients Of Mu Mu), whose irreverent sampling was extremely innovative for the period, was a typical example of Drummond's pseudonymous mischief. The chart-topping Timelords was another spoof and, by the 90s, Drummond found himself at the heart of the creative sampling technology with the critically acclaimed and bestselling KLF. Along the way, the eccentric entrepreneur even managed to record a minor solo album, most notable for the track 'Julian Cope Is Dead', an answer song to the former Teardrop Explodes singer's witty 'Bill Drummond Said'.
● ALBUMS: *The Man* (Creation 1987) ★★★.
● FURTHER READING: *Bad Wisdom*, Bill Drummond and Mark Manning. *45*, Bill Drummond.

## DUB SYNDICATE

An On U Sound offshoot which Roots Radics drummer Lincoln Valentine 'Style' Scott and Adrian Sherwood have used as a flag of convenience for various collaborations, working with reggae greats such as U-Roy, Lee Perry and Aswad. Scott and Sherwood's exploration of dancehall, dub and reggae is an enduring project which was inaugurated in 1982 by the *Pounding System* release. Personnel are recruited as the need arises, with Errol Holt, Skip McDonald and Carlton 'Bubblers' Ogilvie the most regularly featured players. The *Classic Selection* series was given focus by the voice of poet Andy Fairley, who also appeared on 'Lack Of Education'. Dub Syndicate's later material included ethnic chants and mantras in a nod to the global ambient school of dance music.
● ALBUMS: *Pounding System* (On U Sound/ROIR 1982) ★★★★, *One Way System* (On U Sound/ROIR 1983) ★★★, with Dr. Pablo *North Of The River Thames* (On U Sound 1984) ★★★, *Tunes From The*

*Missing Channel* (On U Sound/EMI 1985) ★★★, *Strike The Balance* (On U Sound/Mango 1990) ★★★, *Stoned Immaculate* (On U Sound 1991) ★★★, *Echomania* (On U Sound 1993) ★★★★, *Ital Breakfast* (On U Sound 1996) ★★★, *Fear Of A Green Planet* (Shanachie 1998) ★★★, *Mellow & Colly* (On U Sound/EFA 1998) ★★★, *Live At The T+C 1991* (On U Sound 1999) ★★★★, *Live At The Maritime Hall* (On U Sound/Artists Only 2000) ★★★, *Acres Of Space* (Lion & Roots/EFA 2001) ★★★.
● COMPILATIONS: *Classic Selection Vol. 1* (On U Sound 1989) ★★★★, *Classic Selection Vol. 2* (On U Sound 1991) ★★★, *Research & Development* (On U Sound 1996) ★★★.

## DUFFY

b. 30 May 1960, Birmingham, Worcestershire, England. Having appeared in an early line-up of Duran Duran, Stephen Duffy first came to prominence in the UK under the moniker of Stephen 'Tin Tin' Duffy, with the release of his second single, 'Kiss Me', in early 1985. The track, which reached UK number 4, confirmed Duffy's power as a weaver of engaging pop melodies. His debut *The Ups And Downs* divided the critics, but his formula pop was most suitable for daytime radio play. 'Icing On The Cake' restored him to the UK Top 20, but his subsequent solo work proved less enticing. He later formed the folk-rock outfit, the Lilac Time. Following their demise in their early 90s, Duffy recorded an album with classical violinist Nigel Kennedy, and signed with Indolent Records, relaunching himself as Duffy. Having been around for more than a decade his self-depreciating quote 'it's an accident of birth, that had me a born loser' seemed to cover him against any lack of future success. His debut album as Duffy, however, was a sparkling collection of guitar pop with some occasionally glorious harmonies. He had matured into a witty perceptive songwriter and even though there was more than a glance over his shoulder to the Kinks, Beatles and quality 60s pop, the songs (many dealing with the death of his father) stood up well. Produced by Mitch Easter and featuring wistful harmony vocals from Velvet Crush, for once the press release description of a bejewelled guitar album was accurate. *I Love My Friends*, featuring backing from Aimee Mann and Blur's Alex James, confirmed Duffy's mastery of sweet pop music. The following year Duffy revived the Lilac Time as a recording unit.
● ALBUMS: as Stephen 'Tin Tin' Duffy *The Ups And Downs* (10 1985) ★★★, *Because We Love You* (10 1986) ★★, *Music In Colors* (Parlophone 1993) ★★, *Duffy* (Indolent 1995) ★★★, *I Love My Friends* (Cooking Vinyl 1998) ★★★.
● COMPILATIONS: *They Called Him Tin Tin* (Virgin 1998) ★★★.

## DUKES OF STRATOSPHEAR

An alter ego of XTC, this group was a vehicle for Andy Partridge's psychedelic frustrations of being born a decade or two out of time. Both albums the group released contained brilliant pastiches of virtually every pop band of the mid to late 60s period. In many cases the Dukes' tongue-in-cheek

parables were far superior to the songs to which they gently alluded. It was suggested that their albums actually outsold the XTC product available at the same time.
● ALBUMS: *25 O'Clock* mini-album (Virgin 1985) ★★★, *Psonic Psunspot* (Virgin 1987) ★★★★.
● COMPILATIONS: *Chips From The Chocolate Fireball* (Virgin 1987) ★★★★.

## DUNN, HOLLY

b. Holly Suzette Dunn, 22 August 1957, San Antonio, Texas, USA. Dunn's father was a preacher and her mother a professional artist, but they encouraged their children to sing and entertain. Dunn learned guitar and became a lead vocalist with the Freedom Folk Singers, representing Texas in the White House bicentennial celebrations. After university, she joined her brother, Chris Waters (Chris Waters Dunn), who had moved to Nashville as a songwriter (he wrote 'Sexy Eyes' for Dr. Hook). Together they wrote 'Out Of Sight, Not Out Of Mind' for Cristy Lane. Among her other songs are 'An Old Friend' (Terri Gibbs), 'Love Someone Like Me' (New Grass Revival), 'Mixed Emotions' (Bruce Murray, brother of Anne Murray) and 'That Old Devil Moon' (Marie Osmond). Dunn sang on numerous demos in Nashville. Her self-named album for the MTM label in 1986, and her own composition 'Daddy's Hands', drew considerable attention. *Across The Rio Grande*, was a traditional yet contemporary country album featuring Vince Gill and Sam Bush and it won much acclaim. However, MTM went into liquidation and Dunn moved to Warner Brothers Records. Her up-tempo 'You Really Had Me Going' was a country number 1 and other country hits include 'Only When I Love', 'Strangers Again' and 'That's What Your Love Does To Me'. Her 'greatest hits' set, *Milestones*, aroused some controversy when she issued one of its tracks, the newly recorded 'Maybe I Mean Yes' as a single. The song was accused of downplaying the trauma of date rape, and Dunn was sufficiently upset to ask radio stations not to play the record. Her career was restored to equilibrium with the low-key, but impressive, *Getting It Dunn* in 1992. *Getting It Dunn* was her last album for Warner, and she subsequently signed to the independent label River North. Her debut for that label, *Life And Love And All The Stages*, was undistinguished, and she may find it difficult returning to the mainstream.
● ALBUMS: *Holly Dunn* (MTM 1986) ★★★, *Cornerstone* (MTM 1987) ★★★, *Across The Rio Grande* (MTM 1988) ★★★, *The Blue Rose Of Texas* (Warners 1989) ★★★, *Heart Full Of Love* (Warners 1990) ★★★, *Getting It Dunn* (Warners 1992) ★★★, *Life And Love And All The Stages* (River North 1995) ★★, *Leave One Bridge Standing* (A&M 1997) ★★.
● COMPILATIONS: *Milestones: Greatest Hits* (Warners 1991) ★★★.
● VIDEOS: *Cowboys Are My Weakness* (River North 1995).

## DURAN DURAN

Borrowing their name from a character in the cult 60s science fiction movie *Barbarella*, this UK pop band achieved global fame in the early 80s thanks to a series of catchy synth-pop tunes, a strong visual image, and expensively produced promotional videos which enjoyed endless rotation on the nascent MTV music channel. The band's classic line-up featured vocalist Simon Le Bon (b. 27 October 1958, Bushey, Hertfordshire, England), keyboard player Nick Rhodes (b. Nicholas James Bates, 8 June 1962, Moseley, Birmingham, West Midlands, England), guitarist Andy Taylor (b. 16 February 1961, Wolverhampton, England), bass player John Taylor (b. Nigel John Taylor, 20 June 1960, Birmingham, West Midlands, England) and drummer Roger Taylor (b. 26 April 1960, Castle Bromwich, Birmingham, West Midlands, England). Formed by Rhodes and John Taylor in 1978, the early line-ups of the band included Simon Colley (bass/clarinet), Stephen 'Tin Tin' Duffy (b. 30 May 1960, Birmingham, Worcestershire, England; vocals), Andy Wickett (vocals), Alan Curtis (guitar), and Jeff Thompson.

They established a residency at the Rum Runner in Birmingham, and the club's owners Michael and Paul Berrow became the band's first managers. Duran Duran came to prominence in late 1980 when they toured with Hazel O'Connor and won a contract with EMI Records. Firmly in the 'new romantic' bracket, they enjoyed early publicity and reached the UK Top 20 the following year with their debut single, 'Planet Earth'. The follow-up 'Careless Memories' barely scraped into the UK Top 40, but this proved merely a minor setback. 'Girls On Film', which was accompanied by a risqué Godley And Creme video that featured nude models, brought them their first UK Top 5 hit. Two albums quickly followed and hits like 'Hungry Like The Wolf', 'Save A Prayer', and 'Rio' revealed that there was considerable songwriting substance behind the hype. By 1983, they were in the ascendant, having broken into the US Top 10 three times. 'Is There Something I Should Know?', a gloriously catchy pop song, entered the UK charts at number 1, thereby underlining the strength of their fanbase. They were now, unquestionably, the most popular teen idols in the country. An impressive run of transatlantic Top 10 hits followed over the next two years, including 'Union Of The Snake', 'New Moon On Monday', 'The Reflex' (a UK/US number 1), 'The Wild Boys', and 'A View To A Kill', the latter a James Bond movie theme which gave the band their second US chart-topper.

At the peak of their success, they decided to wind down and venture into other projects, such as the Power Station and Arcadia, while Le Bon caused many a teenage heart to flutter when he was almost killed in a yachting accident in 1986. The same year the band regrouped, minus Roger and Andy Taylor, to record Notorious with producer Nile Rodgers. Although the title track was a big hit the band had by now lost many of their original fans, and excellent follow-up singles such as 'Skin Trade' and 'Meet El Presidente' failed to break into the Top 20 either side of the Atlantic. The trio of Le Bon, Rhodes and John Taylor continued recording, however, knowing that they had already secured a place in pop history. Pointlessly tinkering with their name (to DuranDuran) failed to restore the band's commercial

fortunes, and the release of a singles compilation raised question marks about their future. Guitarist Warren Cuccurullo (b. 8 December 1956, Brooklyn, New York City, USA; ex-Missing Persons), who first featured on Notorious, and Sterling Campbell became permanent members in June 1989, although the latter left two years later, going on to play with Cyndi Lauper and David Bowie among others.

Renewed interest in Duran Duran came about in 1993 when 'Ordinary World' became a major transatlantic hit (USA number 3/UK number 6). It was followed by 'Come Undone', which reached number 7 in America. Both tracks were taken from Duran Duran, which caused critics who had written them off to amend their opinions. In 1995 they released Thank You, a covers album that paid tribute to the band's influences, although they attracted hostile criticism for versions of rap classics 'White Lines (Don't Do It)' and '911 Is A Joke'. Two years later John Taylor left the band, leaving Le Bon and Rhodes to carry on with the long-serving Cuccurullo. Their contract with EMI ended following the record company's refusal to release Medazzaland in the UK, although Greatest sold well on the back of an 80s revival. Pop Trash, released on the Hollywood label, was a deliberate attempt to escape the pop tag with which Rhodes and Le Bon will forever be associated. The following May, the five original members announced they were to play together for the first time in over 15 years.

● ALBUMS: Duran Duran (EMI/Harvest 1981) ★★★, Rio (EMI/Harvest 1982) ★★★★, Seven And The Ragged Tiger (EMI/Capitol 1983) ★★, Arena (Parlophone/Capitol 1984) ★★, Notorious (EMI/Capitol 1986) ★★★, as DuranDuran Big Thing (EMI/Capitol 1988) ★★, Liberty (Parlophone/Capitol 1990) ★, Duran Duran aka The Wedding Album (Parlophone/Capitol 1993) ★★★, Thank You (Parlophone/Capitol 1995) ★★, Medazzaland (Capitol 1997) ★★★, Pop Trash (Hollywood 2000) ★★★★.

● COMPILATIONS: Decade (EMI/Capitol 1989) ★★★★, Essential Duran Duran (Night Versions) (EMI 1998) ★★★, Greatest (EMI/Capitol 1998) ★★★★, Strange Behaviour (EMI 1999) ★★, Girls On Film: 'The Collection' (EMI 2000) ★★★, Classic Masters (EMD 2002) ★★★.

● VIDEOS: Duran Duran (The First 11 Videos) (PMI 1983), Dancing On The Valentine (PMI 1984), Sing Blue Silver (PMI 1984), Arena: An Absurd Notion (PMI 1984), The Making Of Arena (PMI 1985), Working For The Skin Trade (PMI 1987), Three To Get Ready (BMG/Aurora 1987), 6ix By 3hree (PMI 1988), Decade (PMI 1989), Extraordinary World (PMI 1993), Greatest: The Videos (EMI 1998).

● FURTHER READING: Duran Duran: Their Story, Kasper deGraff and Malcolm Garrett. Duran Duran: An Independent Story In Words And Pictures, John Carver. Duran Duran, Maria David. Duran Duran: A Behind-The-Scenes Biography Of The Supergroup Of The Eighties, Cynthia C. Kent. Everything You Want To Know About Duran Duran, Toby Goldstein. Duran Duran, Susan Martin. Duran Duran Live, Peter Goddard and Philip Kamin. Inside Duran Duran, Robyn Flans. Duran Duran, Annette Weidner.

## DURUTTI COLUMN

One of the more eclectic bands to emerge from Manchester, England's punk scene, Vini Reilly (b. Vincent Gerard Reilly, August 1953, Manchester, England) and his Durutti Column combined elements of jazz, electronic and even folk in their multitude of releases. However, Reilly's musical beginnings were as guitarist in more standard 1977 hopefuls Ed Banger And The Nosebleeds. Two other groups from 1977 – Fastbreeder and Flashback – had since merged into a new group, who were being managed by Manchester television presenter and Factory Records founder Tony Wilson. Wilson invited Reilly to join guitarist Dave Rowbotham and drummer Chris Joyce in January 1978, and together they became the Durutti Column (after a political cartoon strip used by the SI in Strasbourg during the 60s). They were joined by vocalist Phil Rainford and bass player Tony Bowers and recorded for the famous 'A Factory Sampler EP' with the late Martin Hannett producing. These were the only recordings made by this line-up and the band broke up. Reilly carried on with the Durutti Column alone, while the others (except Rainford) formed the Moth Men. The debut, *The Return Of The Durutti Column*, appeared on Factory in 1980 and was largely recorded by Reilly, although Hannett, Pete Crooks (bass), and Toby (drums) also contributed.

Durutti Column soon established a solid cult following, particularly abroad, where Reilly's moving instrumental work was widely appreciated. Live appearances had been sporadic, however, as Reilly suffered from an eating disorder and was frequently too ill to play. The album was notable for its sandpaper sleeve, inspired by the anarchist movement Situationist Internatiside. Reilly and producer Hannett helped out on Pauline Murray's first solo album later in 1980. The Durutti Column's own recordings over the next few years were a mixed batch recorded by Reilly with assistance from drummers Donald Johnson, then Bruce Mitchell (ex-Alberto Y Lost Trios Paranoias), Maunagh Flemin and Simon Topping on horns, and much later, further brass players Richard Henry, Tim Kellett, and Mervyn Fletcher, plus violinist Blaine Reininger and cellist Caroline Lavelle.

Dozens of other musicians have joined the nucleus of Reilly and Mitchell over the years and the band are still active today. A striking example of mid-period Durutti Column was captured on *Vini Reilly*, released in 1989. The guitarist cleverly incorporated the sampled voices of Joan Sutherland, Tracy Chapman, Otis Redding and Annie Lennox into a moving world of acoustic/electric ballads. Reilly has also lent some mesmerizing guitar to a host of recordings by artists such as Anne Clarke and Richard Jobson, and fellow Mancunian and friend Morrissey. On 8 November 1991, former Durutti guitarist Dave Rowbotham was discovered axed to death at his Manchester home, leading to a murder hunt. Following Factory's bankruptcy in 1992, Reilly released the excellent *Sex And Death* on their new label Factory Too. Although *Fidelity* saw him on yet another label, the Durutti sound was still the same.

● ALBUMS: *The Return Of The Durutti Column* (Factory 1980) ★★★, *LC* (Factory 1981) ★★★, *Another Setting* (Factory 1983) ★★★, *Live At The Venue, London* (VU 1983) ★★★, *Amigos En Portugal* (Fundacio Atlantica 1984) ★★, *Without Mercy* (Factory 1984) ★★★, *Domo Arigato* (Factory 1985) ★★★, *Circuses And Bread* (Factory 1985) ★★★, *Live At The Bottom Line New York* cassette only (ROIR 1987) ★★★, *The Guitar And Other Machines* (Factory 1987) ★★★, *Vini Reilly* (Factory 1989) ★★★★, *Obey The Time* (Factory 1990) ★★★, *Lips That Would Kiss Form Prayers To Broken Stone* (Factory 1991) ★★★, *Dry* (Materiali Sonori 1991) ★★★, *Sex & Death* (Factory Too 1994) ★★★, *Fidelity* (Les Disques Du Crepuscule 1996) ★★★, *Time Was GIGANTIC ... When We Were Kids* (Factory Too 1998) ★★★, *A Night In New York* (Shellshock 1999) ★★★, *Rebellion* (Artful 2001) ★★★.
Solo: Vini Reilly *The Sporadic Recordings* (Sporadic 1989) ★★★.

● COMPILATIONS: *Valuable Passages* (Factory 1986) ★★★, *The Durutti Column: The First Four Albums* (Factory 1988) ★★★.

## E., SHEILA

b. Sheila Escovedo, 12 December 1959, Oakland, California, USA, Sheila E. came to prominence as a solo artist in 1984 but had been playing conga drums since the age of three. Her father, Pete Escovedo, worked briefly with Santana and led the Latin-jazz fusion band Azteca, with which Sheila sat in while in high school. She briefly gave up the idea of a musical career but eventually left school to join her father's band, appearing on two of his albums for Fantasy Records. She was discovered by Prince in 1984 and appeared as a vocalist on his 'Erotic City', the b-side of the US number 1 'Let's Go Crazy'. With that exposure she was able to sign a solo record contract with Warner Brothers Records; her debut was *Sheila E. In The Glamorous Life*. The album yielded the US Top 10 single of the same name and the UK Top 20 hit, 'The Belle Of St. Mark'. Her follow-up, *Sheila E. In Romance 1600*, appeared on Prince's Paisley Park label in 1985 and featured the US hit single, 'A Love Bizarre', with Prince himself on backing vocals. Her third solo album, self-titled, was released in 1987 but failed to garner the attention or sales of the first two. That same year she joined Prince's touring group as drummer, also appearing in the movie *Sign O' The Times*.

After a four-year lapse in recording, she returned in 1991 with the dance-orientated *Sex Cymbal*, which was self-written and produced with assistance from her brother, Peter Michael, and David Gamson. Escovedo subsequently retreated behind the scenes, writing and recording with other artists and working as music director on Magic Johnson's television show *The Magic Hour*. She also worked extensively with charitable organisations. In 2000, she produced and co-composed the music for the first Latin Grammy Awards and returned to recording with the stylish Latin jazz album, *Writes Of Passage*.

● ALBUMS: *Sheila E. In The Glamorous Life* (Warners 1984) ★★★, *Sheila E. In Romance 1600* (Paisley Park 1985) ★★★, *Sheila E.* (Paisley Park 1987) ★★★, *Sex Cymbal* (Warners 1991) ★★★, with Pete Escovedo *Solo Two/Happy Together* 80s recordings (Fantasy 1997) ★★★, with the E. Train *Writes Of Passage* (Concord Vista 2000) ★★★, with the E. Train *Heaven* (Concord Vista 2001) ★★★.

● FILMS: *Krush Groove* (1985), *Sign O' The Times* (1987), *The Adventures Of Ford Fairlane* (1990).

## EARLE, STEVE

b. 17 January 1955, Fort Monroe, Virginia, USA. Earle's father was an air-traffic controller and the family was raised in Schertz, near San Antonio, Texas. Earle played an acoustic guitar from the age of 11, but he also terrorized his school friends with a sawn-off shotgun. He left home many times and

sang 'Help Me Make It Through The Night' and 'all that shit' in bars and coffee houses. He befriended Townes Van Zandt, whom he describes as a 'a real bad role model'. Earle married at the age of 19 but when his wife went with her parents to Mexico, he moved to Nashville, playing for tips and deciding to stay. He took several jobs to pay his way but they often ended in arguments and violence. He appeared as a backing vocalist on Guy Clark's 1975 classic *Old No. 1*, before signing a publishing deal with Sunbury Dunbar. Elvis Presley almost recorded 'Mustang Wine', and Johnny Lee had a Top 10 hit in 1982 with 'When You Fall In Love'. His second marriage was based, he says, 'on a mutual interest in drug abuse'. Earle formed a back-up band in Texas, the Dukes, and was signed to Epic Records, who subsequently released the rockabilly influenced *Early Tracks*.

Recognition came when he and the Dukes signed to MCA and made a famed 'New Country' album, *Guitar Town*, the term being the CB handle for Nashville. The title track, with its Duane Eddy-styled guitar riff, was a potent blend of country and rock 'n' roll. 'Good Ol' Boy (Gettin' Tough)' was Earle's response to President Reagan's firing of the striking air-traffic controllers, including Earle's brother. Like Bruce Springsteen, his songs often told of the restlessness of blue-collar workers. 'Someday' is a cheerless example – 'There ain't a lot you can do in this town/You drive down to the lake and then you turn back around.' Earle wrote 'The Rain Came Down' for the Farm Aid II benefit, and 'Nothing But A Child' was for an organization to provide for homeless children. Waylon Jennings recorded 'The Devil's Right Hand' and Janie Fricke, 'My Old Friend The Blues'. Earle saw in the 1988 New Year in a Dallas jail for punching a policeman and during that year, he married his fifth wife and released an album with a hard rock feel, *Copperhead Road*, which included the Vietnam saga 'Johnny Come Lately', which he recorded with the Pogues. *The Hard Way* and a live album followed, before Earle's contract expired with MCA. His drug problems escalated and he was imprisoned for narcotics possession.

Following a successful detox program, Earle returned in 1995 with a fine album. *Train A Comin'* was mellow, acoustic and emotional, and featured some exceptional playing from Peter Rowan and harmony vocals from Emmylou Harris. Some of Earle's compositions are regarded as redneck anthems, but the views are not necessarily his own: he writes from the perspective of his creation, Bubba, the archetypal redneck. Another is The Beast: 'It's that unexplainable force that causes you to be depressed. As long as The Beast is there, I know I'll always write.'

In the mid-90s, fired by the acclaim for *Train A Comin'*, a cleaned-up Earle started his own label, E Squared, and contributed to the soundtrack of *Dead Man Walking*. Earle is determined never to return to drugs. He stated in January 1996, 'I am real, real active and that is how I stay clean. It's a matter of survival to me. My life's pretty together right now. I got my family back.' Earle continued his renaissance with *I Feel Alright* and *El Corazón*, and recorded a superb bluegrass album with the Del McCoury Band. He also published the short stories collection, *Doghouse Roses*. *Sidetracks* was a collection of his cover versions featuring a particularly powerful version of Dylan's 'My Back Pages'.

● ALBUMS: *Guitar Town* (MCA 1986) ★★★★, *Exit O* (MCA 1987) ★★★, *Copperhead Road* (MCA 1988) ★★★★, *The Hard Way* (MCA 1990) ★★★, *Shut Up And Die Like An Aviator* (MCA 1991) ★★★★, *BBC Radio 1 Live In Concert* (Windsong 1992) ★★★, *Train A Comin'* (Winter Harvest/Transatlantic 1995) ★★★★, *I Feel Alright* (E-Squared/Transatlantic 1996) ★★★, *El Corazón* (E-Squared/Warners 1997) ★★★★, with the Del McCoury Band *The Mountain* (E-Squared/Grapevine 1999) ★★★★, *Transcendental Blues* (E Squared 2000) ★★★, with Townes Van Zandt, Guy Clark *Together At The Bluebird* (Catfish 2001) ★★★★, *Jerusalem* (Artemis 2002) ★★★.

● COMPILATIONS: *Early Tracks* (Epic 1987) ★★★, *We Ain't Ever Satisfied: Essential Steve Earle* (MCA 1992) ★★★★, *Essential Steve Earle* (MCA 1993) ★★★★, *This Highway's Mine* (Pickwick 1993) ★★★, *Fearless Heart* (MCA 1995) ★★★, *The Very Best Of Steve Earle: Angry Young Man* (Nectar 1996) ★★★, *Ain't Ever Satisfied: The Steve Earle Collection* (Hip-O 1996) ★★★★, *The Devil's Right Hand: An Introduction To Steve Earle* (MCA 2000) ★★★★, *Sidetracks* (E-Squared/Artemis 2002) ★★★.

● FURTHER READING: *Doghouse Roses*, Steve Earle.

## EASTERHOUSE

Formed in Manchester, England, by the Perry brothers, singer Andy and guitarist Ivor, during the mid-80s, Easterhouse first came to prominence after being championed by Morrissey of the Smiths. Taking their name from a working-class area of Glasgow, they signed to Rough Trade Records and were widely praised for early singles 'Inspiration' and 'Whistling In The Dark', which merged Andy's left-wing political rhetoric with Ivor's echo-laden guitar patterns. *Contenders*, a confident debut, also featured Peter Vanden (bass), Gary Rostock (drums) and Mike Murray (rhythm guitar). Contained within were entirely convincing accommodations between music and politics – the hard line of Andy Perry's lyrics exemplified by the compelling 'Nineteen Sixty Nine', a bitter assault on the betrayal of the working classes by Britain's Labour Party. Arguments broke out soon after its release and Ivor Perry went on to form the short-lived Cradle. Andy Perry kept the name Easterhouse, but by the time of 1989's *Waiting For The Red Bird* he was the only remaining original band member. He was joined on this disappointing, over ambitious record by David Verner (drums), Neil Taylor (lead guitar), Lance Sabin (rhythm guitar) and Steve Lovell (lead guitar). 'Come Out Fighting', with its anthemic rock pretensions, failed to make the singles chart and the new Easterhouse, with all songs written solely by Perry, was heavily criticized: the political content was still high with tracks such as 'Stay With Me (Death On The Dole)', but the soul and subtle melodies were no longer present. Easterhouse's impact was, aside from one great album, probably minimal, but along with other Manchester guitar groups like the Chameleons, they

laid the foundations for the explosion of interest in the city in the late 80s.

● ALBUMS: *Contenders* (Rough Trade 1986) ★★★, *Waiting For The Red Bird* (Rough Trade 1989) ★★.

## EASTON, SHEENA

b. Sheena Shirley Orr, 27 April 1959, Bellshill, Scotland. Orr began performing while studying speech and drama at the Royal Scottish Academy of Music And Drama, studying by day and singing with the band Something Else in the evenings. Her short-lived marriage to actor Sandi Easton gave Orr her new name, and as Sheena Easton she was signed to EMI Records in 1979 following an audition for a planned documentary following a budding pop star. The resulting television film, *The Big Time*, about the creation of her chic image helped her debut single 'Modern Girl' into the UK charts. This was followed by the chirpy '9 To 5', which reached number 3 and propelled a reissued 'Modern Girl' into the Top 10. The former sold over a million copies in the USA (there known as 'Morning Train (Nine To Five)') and topped the singles chart for two weeks.

Extraordinary success followed in America where she spent most of her time. Now established as an easy-listening rock singer, Easton was offered the theme to the 1981 James Bond movie, *For Your Eyes Only*, which became a US Top 5 hit. Further hits followed from her second album, including 'When He Shines' and the title track, 'You Could Have Been With Me'. In 1983, Easton, who by now had emigrated to California, joined the trend towards celebrity duets, recording the country chart-topper 'We've Got Tonight' with Kenny Rogers. The Top 10 hit 'Telefone (Long Distance Love Affair)' was in a funkier dance mode and her career took a controversial turn in 1984 with attacks by moralists on the sexual implications of 'Sugar Walls', a Prince song that became one of her biggest hits. Easton also sang on Prince's 1987 single, 'U Got The Look', and appeared in *Sign 'O' The Times*. The same year she starred as Sonny Crockett's wife in several episodes of *Miami Vice*.

Easton's later albums for EMI included *Do You*, produced by Nile Rodgers, and the Japan-only release *No Sound But A Heart*. In 1988, she switched labels to MCA, releasing *The Lover In Me*. When the title track was issued as a single, it soared to number 2 on the US charts. The album's list of producers read like the Who's Who of contemporary soul music, with L.A. And Babyface, Prince, Jellybean and Angela Winbush among the credits. *What Comes Naturally*, released in 1991, was a hard and fast dance record produced to the highest technical standards but lacking the charm of her earlier work. The same year she starred in the revival of *Man Of La Mancha*, which reached Broadway a year later. The same year Easton finally became a US citizen, but during the 90s she enjoyed most success in Japan, with several of her new albums only released in that territory. By now her focus had switched towards her acting career, and in 1996 she appeared as Rizzo in the Broadway production of *Grease*. She signed a new recording contract with Universal International in 2000, and appeared opposite David Cassidy in the

Las Vegas production, *At The Copa*.

● ALBUMS: *Take My Time* aka *Sheena Easton* (EMI 1981) ★★, *You Could Have Been With Me* (EMI 1981) ★★, *Madness, Money And Music* (EMI 1982) ★★, *Best Kept Secret* (EMI 1983) ★★, *Todo Me Recuerda A Ti* (EMI 1984) ★★★, *A Private Heaven* (EMI 1984) ★★★★, *Do You* (EMI 1985) ★★, *No Sound But A Heart* (EMI 1987) ★★, *The Lover In Me* (MCA 1988) ★★★, *What Comes Naturally* (MCA 1991) ★★★, *No Strings* (MCA 1993) ★★★, *My Cherie* (MCA 1995) ★★★, *Freedom* (SkyJay Trax/MCA 1997) ★★★, *Home* (Universal Japan 1999) ★★★, *Fabulous* (Universal International 2000) ★★★.

● COMPILATIONS: *The Best Of Sheena Easton* (EMI America 1989) ★★★, *For Your Eyes Only: The Best Of Sheena Easton* (EMI 1989) ★★★, *The World Of Sheena Easton: The Singles Collection* (EMI America 1993) ★★★★, *Greatest Hits* (CEMA 1995) ★★★, *The Best Of Sheena Easton* (Disky 1996) ★★★, *The Gold Collection* (EMI 1996) ★★★, *Body & Soul* (Universal 1997) ★★★, *20 Great Love Songs* (Disky 1998) ★★★, *Classic Masters* (Capitol 2002) ★★★.

● VIDEOS: *Live At The Palace, Hollywood* (Sony 1982), *Sheena Easton* (Sony 1983), *A Private Heaven* (Sony 1984), *Sheena Easton Act 1* (Prism 1986), *Star Portraits* (Gemini Vision 1992).

● FILMS: *Sign 'O' The Times* (1987), *Indecent Proposal* (1993), *All Dogs Go To Heaven 2* voice only (1996), *An All Dogs Christmas Carol* (1998).

## ECHO AND THE BUNNYMEN

The origins of this renowned Liverpool, England-based band can be traced back to the spring of 1977 when vocalist Ian McCulloch (b. 5 May 1959, Liverpool, England) was a member of the short-lived Crucial Three with Julian Cope and Pete Wylie. While the latter two later emerged in the Teardrop Explodes and Wah!, respectively, McCulloch put together his major band at the end of 1978. Initially the trio of McCulloch, Will Sergeant (b. 12 April 1958, Liverpool, England; guitar), and Les Pattinson (b. 18 April 1958, Ormskirk, Merseyside, England; bass) was joined by a drum machine that they named 'Echo'. After making their first appearance at the famous Liverpool club Eric's, they made their vinyl debut in March 1979 with 'Pictures On My Wall'/'Read It In Books', produced by whiz kid entrepreneurs Bill Drummond and Dave Balfe. The production was sparse but intriguing and helped the band to establish a sizeable cult following. McCulloch's brooding live performance and vocal inflections were already drawing comparisons with the Doors' Jim Morrison.

After signing to Korova Records (distributed by Warner Brothers Records), they replaced 'Echo' with a human being – Pete De Freitas (b. 2 August 1961, Port Of Spain, Trinidad, West Indies, d. 14 June 1989). The second single, 'Rescue', was a considerable improvement on its predecessor, with a confident driving sound that augured well for their forthcoming album. *Crocodiles* proved impressive with a wealth of strong arrangements and compulsive guitar work. After the less melodic single 'The Puppet', the band toured extensively and issued an EP, *Shine So Hard*, which crept into the UK Top 40. The next album, *Heaven Up Here*, saw them regaled by the music press. Although a less accessible and melodic work than its predecessor, it sold well and topped numerous polls. *Porcupine* reinforced the band's appeal, while 'The Cutter' gave them their biggest UK hit so far, reaching number 8 in January 1983. The same year Sergeant released a solo set, *Themes For Grind*. In January 1984 they reached UK number 9 with 'The Killing Moon', an excellent example of McCulloch's ability to summon lazy melodrama out of primary lyrical colours. The epic quality of his writing remained perfectly in keeping with the band's grandiloquent musical character. The accompanying 1984 album, *Ocean Rain*, broadened their appeal further and brought them into the US Top 100 album charts.

In February 1986 De Freitas left to be replaced by former Haircut 100 drummer Mark Fox, but he returned the following September. However, it now seemed the band's best days were behind them. The uninspired title *Echo And The Bunnymen* drew matching lacklustre performances, while a cover version of the Doors' 'People Are Strange' left both fans and critics perplexed. This new recording was produced by Ray Manzarek, who also played on the track, and it was used as the haunting theme for the cult movie *The Lost Boys*. Yet, as many noted, there were simply dozens of better Echo And The Bunnymen compositions that could have benefited from that type of exposure.

In 1988, McCulloch made the announcement that he was henceforth pursuing a solo career. While he completed the well-received *Candleland*, his bandmates made the unexpected decision to carry on. Large numbers of audition tapes were listened to before they chose McCulloch's successor, Noel Burke, a Belfast boy who had previously recorded with St Vitus Dance. Just as they were beginning rehearsals, De Freitas was killed in a road accident. The band struggled on, recruiting new drummer Damon Reece and adding road manager Jake Brockman on guitar/synthesizer. In 1992, they entered the next phase of Bunnymen history with *Reverberation*, but public expectations were not high and the critics unkind. The Bunnymen Mark II broke up in the summer of the same year, with Pattinson going on to work with Terry Hall, while Sergeant conducted work on his ambient side project, B*O*M, and formed Glide. McCulloch, whose solo career had stalled after a bright start, and Sergeant eventually reunited in 1993 as Electrafixion, also pulling in Reece from the second Bunnymen incarnation.

In 1996, an announcement was made that the three remaining original members would go out as Echo And The Bunnymen once again. McCulloch, Pattinson and Sergeant completed a remarkable comeback when 'Nothing Lasts Forever' reached number 8 in the UK charts, and their new album, *Evergreen*, was released to widespread acclaim. Pattinson left before the recording of their second new album, a remarkably mellow set from a band not normally associated with such a concept. McCulloch and Sergeant parted company with London Records later in the year, and the following year's mini-album *Avalanche* was an Internet-only release. The full-length *Flowers*, picked up for release by Cooking Vinyl Records, marked a return to the trademark Echo And The Bunnymen sound, with Sergeant's guitar work to the fore.

● ALBUMS: *Crocodiles* (Korova 1980) ★★★★, *Heaven Up Here* (Korova 1981) ★★★, *Porcupine* (Korova 1983) ★★★★, *Ocean Rain* (Korova 1984) ★★★, *Echo And The Bunnymen* (Warners 1987) ★★, *Reverberation* (Korova 1990) ★★, *Evergreen* (London 1997) ★★★, *What Are You Going To Do With Your Life?* (London 1999) ★★★, *Avalanche* mini-album (Gimmemusic 2000) ★★★, *Flowers* (Cooking Vinyl 2001) ★★★, *Live In Liverpool* (Cooking Vinyl/spinART 2002) ★★★.

● COMPILATIONS: *Songs To Learn And Sing* (Korova 1985) ★★★★, *Live In Concert* (Windsong 1991) ★★★, *The Cutter* (Warners 1993) ★★★, *The Peel Sessions* (Strange Fruit 1995) ★★★, *Ballyhoo: The Best Of Echo And The Bunnymen* (Warners 1997) ★★★★, *Crystal Days (1979-1999)* 4-CD box set (Rhino 2001) ★★★★.

● VIDEOS: Porcupine (Virgin Video 1983), *Live In Liverpool* (Cooking Vinyl 2002).

● FURTHER READING: *Liverpool Explodes: The Teardrop Explodes, Echo And The Bunnymen*, Mark Cooper. *Never Stop: The Echo & The Bunnymen Story*, Tony Fletcher. *Ian McCulloch: King Of Cool*, Mick Middles.

## EEK A MOUSE

b. Ripton Joseph Hilton, 19 November 1957, Kingston, Jamaica, West Indies. It is not only Eek A Mouse's 6 feet 6 inches height that make him one of Jamaica's most individual talents. Hilton's unusual name was originally that of a racehorse upon which he frequently lost money; when the horse finally won a race, he had, of course, refused to back it. 'My Father's Land' and 'Creation', his first two releases, came out under his real name in the mid-70s. In 1980, he started recording with Joe Gibbs after working briefly with the Papa Roots, Black Ark, Gemini, Jah Life, Black Scorpio and Virgo sound systems. By 1981, he had teamed up with producer and Volcano sound owner Henry 'Junjo' Lawes and had achieved significant hits with 'Once A Virgin', 'Modelling Queen' and 'Virgin Girl'. Between 1980 and 1984, Lawes and Linval Thompson used the Roots Radics at Channel One with Scientist mixing, to help record a number of hit albums and singles by the DJ. In 1981, after his debut *Wa Do Dem* , Eek A Mouse was the surprise star of Reggae Sunsplash. 'Ganja Smuggling', 'For Hire And Removal' and 'Do You Remember' and the album *Skidip* sustained his high profile. High profile singles 'Terrorists In The City', 'Anarexol' and 'Operation Eradication' (a response to his friend Errol Scorcher's death) followed, along with *The Mouse And The Man* and *Assassinator* and several appearances on live dancehall albums. Nevertheless, it was not long before his characteristic 'biddy biddy bengs' started to wear thin and his popularity diminished somewhat after *Mouseketeer*, the last of his albums with Lawes. He made something of a comeback with 1991's major label release *U-Neek*, which included tracks produced by Gussie Clarke, Daddy-O and Matt Robinson. He also made a cameo appearance in the movie, *New Jack City* and recorded for Wild Apache and former Channel One engineer, Soljie.

● ALBUMS: *Wa Do Dem* (Greensleeves 1981) ★★★, *Skidip* (Greensleeves 1982) ★★★, with Michigan And Smiley *Live At Reggae Sunsplash* (Sunsplash 1982) ★, *The Mouse And The Man* (Greensleeves 1983) ★★★, *Assassinator* (RAS 1983) ★★★, *Mouseketeer* (Greensleeves 1984) ★★★, *King And I* (RAS 1987) ★★, *U-Neek* (Mango/Island 1991) ★★★, *Black Cowboy* (Explicit 1996) ★★★, *Eeksperience* (Coach House 2001) ★★★.

● COMPILATIONS: *The Very Best Of Eek A Mouse* (Greensleeves 1987) ★★★, *RAS Portraits* (RAS 1997) ★★★.

## EIGHTH WONDER

A vehicle for 'sex-kitten' singer Patsy Kensit (b. Patricia Jude Francis Kensit, 4 March 1968, Waterloo, London, England), a former child actress at one time known for her role in a UK television advertisement. She pursued a parallel career as an actress, including a role in the Royal Shakespeare Company production of *Silas Marner* in 1984, and as a pop singer in Eighth Wonder, which was comprised of Geoff Beauchamp (guitar), Alex Godson (keyboards) and Jamie Kensit (guitar). The band gained a minor UK hit with 'Stay With Me' in 1985. Kensit later landed the role of Crêpe Suzette in Julien Temple's 1986 film of Colin McInnes' novel, *Absolute Beginners*. Surrounded by an intense media hype, the film, which also featured David Bowie, Sade and Ray Davies of the Kinks, was a critical and commercial flop. Kensit and Eighth Wonder found greater success in 1988 with the UK Top 10 single 'I'm Not Scared'. Two more chart singles followed that same year, including the Top 20 hit 'Cross My Heart' and a Top 50 album, *Fearless*. Kensit later restored her credibility as an actress in the 1991 Don Boyd film, *Twenty-One*, although the subsequent *Blame It On The Bellboy* drew less favourable reviews.

Her first marriage in 1988 to Dan Donovan (of Bad Audio Dynamite) ended in 1991. She then married Simple Minds singer Jim Kerr in January 1992, which caused considerable interest in the UK tabloid press. They divorced in 1996. Since then she has been a favourite of the paparazzi lens, which reached a peak during 1996/7 when she started a relationship with Liam Gallagher of Oasis. Their three-year marriage ended in 2000.

● ALBUMS: *Fearless* (Columbia 1988) ★★.

## EINSTÜRZENDE NEUBAUTEN

Formed out of the Berlin arts conglomerate Die Geniale Dilletanten, Einstürzende Neubauten (inspired by the collapse of the Kongresshalle) made their live debut on April 1 1980 at the Moon. The line-up comprised Blixa Bargeld (b. Christian Emmerich, 12 January 1959, Berlin, Germany), N.U. Unruh (b. Andrew Chudy, 9 June 1957, New York, USA), Beate Bartel and Gudrun Gut, the latter two from the punk band Mania D. Alexander Van Borsig (b. Alexander Hacke, 11 October 1965, Berlin, Germany), an occasional contributor, joined in time for the band's first single, 'Für Den Untergang'. When

Bartel and Gut departed to form Malaria and Matador they were replaced by F.M. Einheit (b. Frank Strauss, 18 December 1958, Dortmund, Germany; ex-Abwärts). Einheit and Unruh formed the band's rhythmic backbone, experimenting with a variety of percussive effects, while Bargeld provided discordant vocals and guitar.

The band's first official album (there were previously many tapes available) was Kollaps, a collage of sounds created by unusual rhythmic instruments ranging from breaking glass and steel girders to pipes and canisters. Their 1982 12-inch single, 'Durstiges Tier', involved contributions from the Birthday Party's Rowland S. Howard and Lydia Lunch, at which point Hacke had joined the band permanently as guitarist alongside new bass player Marc Chung (b. 3 June 1957, Leeds, England; ex-Abwärts). A UK tour with the Birthday Party introduced them to Some Bizzare Records, which released 1983's Die Zeichnungen Des Patienten O.T. The following year's Strategien Gegen Architekturen 80=83 was compiled with the help of Jim Thirlwell of Foetus, while the band performed live at the ICA in London. Joined by Genesis P. Orridge (Psychic TV), Frank Tovey (Fad Gadget) and Stevo (Some Bizzare), the gig ended violently and attracted heated debate in the press. Bargeld spent the rest of the year touring as bass player for Nick Cave, going on to record several studio albums as a member of Cave's backing band, the Bad Seeds. He returned to the Einstürzende Neubauten set-up for the more structured Halber Mensch. Following the release of this enthralling album the band temporarily broke-up, but reunited in 1987 to perform the soundtrack for Andi, a play at the Hamburg Schauspielhaus, and record Fünf Auf Der Nach Oben Offenen Richterskala. This was intended as a farewell album, but they, nevertheless, continued after its release.

Bargeld's part-time career with the Bad Seeds continued, and in 1987 he featured alongside them in Wim Wenders' movie Der Himmel Über Berlin. Hacke, ironically, was now contributing to the work of Crime And The City Solution, featuring Cave's old Birthday Party colleagues. Einheit restarted the Abwärts and inaugurated his solo project, Stein, while Chung formed Freibank, the band's own publishing company. The various members reunited, however, in time for 1989's Haus Der Lüge, which included the sounds of riots around the Berlin Wall as a backdrop. They also signed a deal with Mute Records and set up their own Ego subsidiary to house their soundtrack work, which has included the music for the radio play Die Hamletmaschine and Faustmusik. Their 1993 album Tabula Rasa was another politically inclined collection exploring the reunification of Germany. It also demonstrated the band's growing commitment to conventional musical structure, with their trademark industrial sound effects now used to accentuate the atmosphere of a piece rather than just being a case of art for art's sake. Ende Neu, with the departed Chung replaced by Andrew Chudy, completed Einstürzende Neubauten's gradual transition to atmospheric rock band. Jochen Arbeit and Rudi Moser were added to the line-up for the sparse,

melodic Silence Is Sexy, a title that would have been untenable at the start of the band's career.

● ALBUMS: Kollaps (Zick Zack 1981) ★★★, Die Zeichnungen Des Patienten O.T. (Some Bizzare/Rough Trade 1983) ★★★★, 2x4 cassette-only (ROIR 1984) ★★, Halber Mensch (Some Bizzare 1985) ★★★, Fünf Auf Der Nach Oben Offenen Richterskala (Some Bizzare/Relativity 1987) ★★★, Haus Der Lüge (Some Bizzare/Rough Trade 1989) ★★★, Die Hamletmaschine film soundtrack (Ego 1991) ★★, Tabula Rasa (Mute 1993) ★★★, Faustmusik film soundtrack (Ego 1996) ★★, Ende Neu (Mute 1996) ★★★, Ende Neu Remixes (Mute 1997) ★★, Silence Is Sexy (Mute 2000) ★★★.

● COMPILATIONS: Strategien Gegen Architekturen 80=83 (Mute 1984) ★★★, Strategies Against Architecture II (Ego/Mute 1991) ★★★, Strategies Against Architecture III (Mute 2001) ★★★.

● VIDEOS: Halber Mensch (Doublevision/Mute 1986), Liebenslieder (Mute 1993).

## ELECTRIBE 101

This electro-dance band featured the voice of vocalist Billie Ray Martin (b. Hamburg, Germany). She moved to Berlin in the hope of setting up a R&B band with 60s Motown Records influences. However, following several unsuccessful attempts she moved to London in 1985. Two years later, she met Joe Stevens, Les Fleming, Rob Cimarosti and Brian Nordhoff and formed Electribe 101. Their first two singles, 'Tell Me When The Fever Ended' and 'Talking With Myself', were instant hits with the acid house generation and Martin's voice drew comparisons to Marlene Dietrich and Aretha Franklin. Despite the acclaim, Electribe 101 broke up shortly afterwards, with Martin pursuing a solo career, while the others formed Groove Corporation. Martin's 'Your Loving Arms', taken from Deadline For My Memories, was a major club hit and went on to reach number 6 in the UK charts in May 1995.

● ALBUMS: Electribal Memories (Mercury 1990) ★★★.

## ELECTRO HIPPIES

This eccentric 'grindcore' outfit formed in Liverpool, England, in 1985. Specializing in low-technology studio techniques, they went on to issue a sequence of albums for Peaceville, and, later, Necrosis. In each case, a distorted, bass-laden barrage was overridden by stomach-churning vocals that consciously lacked both finesse and cohesion. The band's initial line-up featured Simon (drums), Bruno (bass), Andy (guitar) and Jeff Walker (vocals) After recording a split-single with Generic, Jeff and Bruno left the band, with the former joining Carcass. Bruno was replaced by Dom, with all three members assuming vocal duties. Chaotic and extreme, Electro Hippies used their platform to chastise the whole recording industry. Their mantle was upheld in the first case by Radio 1 disc jockey John Peel, for whom the band recorded a July 1987 session consisting of nine tracks. Titles such as 'Starve The City (To Feed The Poor)' and 'Mega-Armageddon Death Part 3' summed up both their appeal and limitations. The Electro Hippies split-up in 1989.

● ALBUMS: *Peel Sessions* (Strange Fruit 1987) ★★★, *The Only Good Punk ... Is A Dead One* (Peaceville 1988) ★★★, *Live* (Peaceville 1989) ★★, *Play Fast Or Die* (Necrosis 1989) ★★.
● COMPILATIONS: *The Peaceville Recordings* (Peaceville 1989) ★★★, *The Only Good Punk ... Is A Dead One* (Peaceville 2002) ★★★.

## ELY, JOE

b. 9 February 1947, Amarillo, Texas, USA. Singer, songwriter and guitarist Ely, latterly regarded as the link between country rock and so-called new country, moved with his parents in 1958 to Lubbock, the major city of the flatlands of Texas, from which such luminaries as Buddy Holly, Roy Orbison and Waylon Jennings had previously emerged. Ely formed his first band at the age of 13, playing a fusion of country and R&B, before dropping out of high school and following in the footsteps of Woody Guthrie and the writer Jack Kerouac, hopping freight trains and working at a variety of non-musical jobs (including a spell with a circus) before finding himself stranded in New York with nothing but his guitar. He joined a theatrical company from Austin, Texas, and travelled to Europe with his theatrical employers in the early 70s before returning to Lubbock, where he teamed up with fellow singer-songwriters Jimmie Dale Gilmore and George 'Butch' Hancock and a couple of other local musicians (including a musical saw player!) in an informal combo known as the Flatlanders. Although they were never immensely successful, the group did some recording in Nashville for Shelby Singleton's Plantation label, but only a couple of singles were released at the time. Later, when Ely was signed to MCA Records in the late 70s, the recordings by the Flatlanders, which had achieved legendary status, were anthologized on *One Road More*, an album that was first released by European label Charly Records in 1980, but did not appear in the USA until the mid-80s (the album is also available with the title *More A Legend Than A Band*).

In 1976 Ely formed his own band, whose members included Jesse Taylor (guitar), Lloyd Maines (steel drum), Gregg Wright (bass) and Steve Keeton (drums), plus auxiliary picker Ponty Bone (accordion). This basic line-up recorded three albums, *Joe Ely*, *Honky Tonk Masquerade*, and *Down On The Drag*, before Keeton was replaced by Robert Marquam and Wright by Michael Robertson for *Musta Notta Gotta Lotta*, which also featured Reese Wyhans (keyboards), among others. Although these albums were artistic successes, featuring great songs mainly written by Ely, Hancock (especially) and Gilmore, the musical tide of the times was inclined far more towards punk and new wave music than towards Texan singer-songwriters. In 1980, the Ely Band had toured extensively as opening act for the Clash, with whom Ely became very friendly, and *Live Shots* was released that year. The album featured Taylor, Marquam, Wright, Bone and Maines and was recorded on dates with the Clash, but was no more successful than the three studio albums that preceded it. In 1984 he recorded *Hi-Res*, which featured a completely new band of little-known

musicians, but was no more successful than the previous albums in commercial terms.

By 1987, Ely had assembled a new band that has largely remained with him to date: David Grissom (lead guitar), Jimmy Pettit (bass) and Davis McLarty (drums). This line-up recorded two artistically stunning albums for the US independent label HighTone, *Lord Of The Highway* and *Dig All Night*, the latter featuring for the first time a repertoire totally composed of Ely's own songs. Both albums were licensed in the UK to Demon Records; in the wake of this renewed interest, Sunstorm Records, a tiny London label launched by Pete O'Brien, the editor of *Omaha Rainbow* fanzine, licensed two albums worth of Ely's early material. *Milkshakes And Malts*, a compilation of Ely's recordings of songs by Butch Hancock, appeared in 1988, and *Whatever Happened To Maria?*, which similarly compiled Ely's own self-penned songs, was released in 1989. At this point, the band had been together for three years and had achieved an incredible onstage empathy, especially between Ely and Grissom, whose R&B guitar work had moved the band's music away from country. In 1990, they recorded a powerhouse live album in Austin, *Live At Liberty Lunch*, which was sufficiently impressive for Ely's old label, MCA, to re-sign him.

Ely's extra-curricular activities include contributions to the soundtrack of *Roadie*, a movie starring Meat Loaf, in which he can be heard playing 'Brainlock' and 'I Had My Hopes Up High', and his participation as a member of the *ad hoc* group Buzzin Cousins, in which his colleagues are John Mellencamp, John Prine, Dwight Yoakam and James McMurtry, on the soundtrack to the Mellencamp movie *Falling From Grace*. Ely, Terry Allen and Butch Hancock have together written a stage musical about a prostitute, *Chippy*. His 1995 album *Letter To Laredo* was a return to the sound of his first MCA albums and included an update of Butch Hancock's 'She Never Spoke Spanish To Me' as 'She Finally Spoke Spanish To Me'. The key track is a fine version of Tom Russell's song about cockfighting, 'Gallao Del Cielo'. Joe Ely is one of the most completely realized artists in contemporary country music, especially in the live situation where he excels.

● ALBUMS: *Joe Ely* (MCA 1977) ★★★★, *Honky Tonk Masquerade* (MCA 1978) ★★★★, *Down On The Drag* (MCA 1979) ★★★★, *Live Shots* (MCA 1980) ★★★, *One Road More* (Charly 1980) ★★★, *Musta Notta Gotta Lotta* (SouthCoast 1981) ★★★, *Hi-Res* (MCA 1984) ★★★, *Lord Of The Highway* (HighTone 1987) ★★★★, *Dig All Night* (HighTone 1988) ★★★★, *Milkshakes And Malts* (Sunstorm 1988) ★★★, *Whatever Happened To Maria* (Sunstorm 1989) ★★★, *Live At Liberty Lunch* (MCA 1990) ★★★★, *Love And Danger* (MCA 1992) ★★★, *Letter To Laredo* (Transatlantic 1995) ★★★★, *Twistin' In The Wind* (MCA 1998) ★★★★, *Live At The Cambridge Folk Festival* 1990 recording (Strange Fruit 1998) ★★★, *Live @ Antone's* (Rounder 2000) ★★★★.
● COMPILATIONS: *No Bad Talk Or Loud Talk '77-'81* (Edsel 1995) ★★★★, *The Time For Travellin': The Best Of ... Volume 2* (Edsel 1996) ★★★★, *The Best Of Joe Ely* (MCA 2000) ★★★★, *From Lubbock To Laredo: The Best Of Joe Ely* (MCA 2002) ★★★.

## ENYA

b. Eithne Ní Bhraonáin, 17 May 1961, Dore, Gweedore, Co. Donegal, Eire. Enya, a classically trained pianist, was formerly a member of Clannad before embarking on a solo career that blossomed unexpectedly with her 1988 UK chart-topper, 'Orinoco Flow'. Daughter of noted Irish Showband leader Leo Brennan (Brennan is the non-Gaelic form of Bhraonáin) who led the Slieve Foy Band, Enya was born into a highly musical family. Her mother was also a musician, and in 1968 two of her brothers and two of her uncles formed the band An Clann As Dobhar (Gaelic for a family from the townland of Dore). The name was soon shortened to Clannad and another family member, harpist/vocalist Máire Brennan, added to the line-up. Enya joined the band on keyboards in 1980 and shared in some of their success as they recorded haunting themes for a variety of television programmes, giving them their first chart success. However, Enya, who has professed she has little time for conventional pop music, never quite fitted into the band and left amicably in 1982. Her first recordings appeared on the score to David Puttnam's 1985 feature, *The Frog Prince*. The following year Enya recorded the music for the BBC Television series *The Celts*, which was subsequently released as her debut album in 1987. An endearing blend of ethereal singing (in Gaelic and English) and lush synthesisers, the album was largely ignored, as was the accompanying single, 'I Want Tomorrow'. However, the following year, Enya signed to WEA Records and released *Watermark*. Climbing to number 5 in the UK charts, the album also generated a surprise number 1 with the hypnotic single 'Orinoco Flow (Sail Away)'. Working with her long-time collaborators, Roma Ryan (her lyric writer) and Nicky Ryan (her producer), Enya followed the chart-topper with two smaller hits – 'Evening Falls' and 'Storms In Africa Part II'. The album also enjoyed a long chart run in America, eventually attaining multi-platinum status and establishing Enya as a fixture on the New Age album chart.

Enya adopted a lower profile for the next couple of years except for an appearance with Sinéad O'Connor. She returned in 1991 with the UK chart-topper *Shepherd Moons*, which by the mid-90s had attained world sales of 10 million copies. The album was hugely successful in America, and in 1993 won the Grammy for Best New Age Album. Her third collection, *The Memory Of Trees*, didn't alter the winning formula, but at some stage her warm, ambient music will begin to pale as listeners realize it is the same delicious cake with a different topping. The artist spent the remainder of the decade contributing soundtrack material to various projects, before returning to the studio to record *A Day Without Rain*. The album shot up the US and several European charts almost a year after its release, thanks to the use of the track 'Only Time' in news coverage of the terrorist attacks on the World Trade Center in New York.

● ALBUMS: *Enya* aka *The Celts* (BBC 1987) ★★, *Watermark* (WEA/Geffen 1988) ★★★★, *Shepherd Moons* (WEA/Reprise 1991) ★★★, *The Memory Of Trees* (WEA/Reprise 1995) ★★★, *A Day Without Rain* (WEA/Reprise 2000) ★★★.
● COMPILATIONS: *Paint The Sky With Stars: The Best Of Enya* (WEA/Reprise 1997) ★★★★, *A Box Of Dreams* 3-CD box-set (WEA 1997) ★★★.
● VIDEOS: *Moonshadows* (Warner Music Vision 1991), *The Video Collection* (Warner Music Vision 2001).
● FURTHER READING: *Enya: A Beginning Discography*, Matt Hargreaves.

## EPMD

Erick Sermon (b. 25 November 1968, Bayshore, Long Island, New York City, New York, USA) and Parrish Smith (b. 13 May 1968, Brentwood, Long Island, New York, USA) are two rappers who did much to revitalize a flagging rap scene with an early outburst of controlled creative energy, *Unfinished Business*. Taking samples from rock sources such as Steve Miller, as well as underground dance music, EPMD worked up a healthy, funk-fuelled groove. Particularly effective among their early recordings was the rap manifesto on 'So Whatcha Sayin''. Their early struggles to attract record company interest are best observed in the 1989 single, 'Please Listen To My Demo', which documents their malaise. By then, however, they had recorded their first two albums. *Strictly Business* was distinguished by an idea for a new dance entitled 'The Steve Martin', while the fun continued on *Unfinished Business*, which in many ways sounded just like its title. Unrestrained anarchy in the studio appeared to be the order of the day, with improvised lines, interruptions and jokey singing forming the basis of proceedings. It included contributions from K-Solo, who had previously worked in a pre-EPMD band with Smith, and would go on to record a solo album under his tutelage.

They moved to Def Jam Records in time for their third album, a much more accomplished affair (at least musically) with tighter production and harder beats. Despite the prevailing ethos, they never felt the need to provide a direct political agenda like many rap groups, seeing music as a source of personal self-advancement. This is openly demonstrated by the titles of their LPs, and the fact that their initials stand for Erick And Parrish Making Dollars. However, the manner in which EPMD tried to accommodate new lyrical concerns was less than satisfactory. Their raps continued to chastise their peers as 'sucker MC's', which was by now little more than cliché. Ironically, one of the better cuts on *Business As Usual* was 'Rampage', a collaboration with LL Cool J, whose artistic fortunes had witnessed a similar decline in recent years. *Business Never Personal* simply continued in remorseless EPMD style. The duo split in 1993, Sermon being the first to embark on a solo career with 'Stay Real' and *No Pressure*. The latter's title reflected, wryly, on the fact that most considered Smith to be the talent of the band. Yet, *No Pressure* was an excellent collection that did much to lay that myth to rest. Smith released his own solo debut a year later, billing himself as PMD. Sermon and Smith reunited in the late 90s to release *Back In Business* and *Out Of Business*, before returning to their solo projects.

● ALBUMS: *Strictly Business* (Fresh 1988) ★★★★, *Unfinished Business* (Fresh 1989) ★★★★, *Business As Usual* (Def Jam 1991) ★★★, *Business Never Personal* (Def Jam 1992) ★★, *Back In Business* (Def Jam 1997) ★★, *Out Of Business* (Def Jam 1999) ★★★.

## ERASURE

Keyboard player and arranger Vince Clarke (b. 3 July 1960, South Woodford, London, England) had already enjoyed success as a member of Depeche Mode, Yazoo, and the Assembly when he decided to undertake a new project in 1985. The plan was to record an album with 10 different singers, but after auditioning vocalist Andy Bell (b. 25 April 1964, Peterborough, Cambridgeshire, England), the duo Erasure was formed. Erasure broke into the UK chart in 1986 with 'Sometimes', which reached number 2 and was followed by 'It Doesn't Have To Be Me' in 1987. The following month their second album, *The Circus*, reached the UK Top 10 and their popularity rapidly grew. Memorable and infectious hits such as 'Victim Of Love', 'The Circus', 'Ship Of Fools', 'A Little Respect', *Crackers International* EP, 'Drama!', 'Blue Savannah', 'Chorus', 'Love To Hate You' and 'Breath Of Life' established the band as serious rivals to the Pet Shop Boys as the world's leading vocal/synthesizer duo. Their appeal lay in the unlikely pairing of the flamboyant Bell and the low-profile keyboards wizard and songwriter Clarke. Their stage-shows were spectacular events, whilst the overtly gay Bell's taste in clothes was campily outrageous. During the 90s, their singles and album sales continued to increase, with *The Innocents*, *Wild!*, *Chorus* and *I Say, I Say, I Say* all reaching number 1 on the UK album chart. Their excellent pastiche of Abba, 1992's *Abba-Esque* EP, topped the UK singles chart. Subsequent releases saw a dip in the duo's popularity, however, and they took a sabbatical following 1997's *Cowboy* before recording the follow-up, *Loveboat*. It is worth stressing that Clarke and Bell achieved their extraordinary success working through an independent label, Mute Records.

● ALBUMS: *Wonderland* (Mute 1986) ★★★, *The Circus* (Mute/Sire 1987) ★★★, *The Two Ring Circus* remix album (Mute/Sire 1988) ★★★, *The Innocents* (Mute/Sire 1988) ★★★, *Wild!* (Mute/Sire 1989) ★★★, *Chorus* (Mute/Sire 1991) ★★★, *I Say, I Say, I Say* (Mute 1994) ★★, *Erasure* (Mute 1995) ★★★, *Cowboy* (Mute/Maverick 1997) ★★★, *Loveboat* (Mute 2000) ★★★.

● COMPILATIONS: *Pop! – The First 20 Hits* (Mute/Sire 1992) ★★★★.

● VIDEOS: *Pop – 20 Hits* (Mute 1993).

## ERIC B AND RAKIM

This Queens, New York, USA-based rap duo comprised Eric Barrier (b. Elmhurst, New York, USA) and William 'Rakim' Griffin (b. William Griffin Jnr., Long Island, New York, USA), using additional musicians such as Sefton the Terminator and Chad Jackson as required. Rakim was the lyricist, Eric B the DJ, or, as Rakim himself put it in 'I Ain't No Joke': 'I hold the microphone like a grudge, Eric B hold the record so the needle don't budge'. They met in 1985 when Eric was working for the New York radio station WBLS and was looking for the city's top MC. They started working together before emerging with the demo 'Eric B. Is President'. Released as a single on an obscure Harlem independent, Zakia Records, in the summer of 1986, it eventually led to a deal with 4th & Broadway. Their long-playing debut was preceded by a stand-out single of the same name, 'Paid In Full', which inspired over 30 remixes. When the album arrived it caused immediate waves. Representatives of James Brown and Bobby Byrd took legal action over the sampling of those artists' works. Conversely, they helped to galvanize Brown's career as a legion of rap imitators drew on his back catalogue in search of samples. They also originated the similarly coveted 'Pump Up The Volume' sample. As well as Eric B putting the funk back into rap music, Rakim was responsible for introducing a more relaxed, intuitive delivery that was distinctly separate from the machismo of Run-DMC and LL Cool J, and was probably the biggest single influence on 90s hip-hop artists such as Wu-Tang Clan, Nas and Dr. Dre. The duo hit the UK charts in 1987 with 'Paid In Full (The Coldcut Remix)', though they themselves hated the version. Later hits included 'Move The Crowd', 'I Know You Got Soul', 'Follow The Leader', 'The Microphone' and 1989's US Top 10 collaboration with Jody Watley, 'Friends'. Label moves may have diminished their probable impact, though the duo themselves never went out of their way to cross over into the mainstream. Instead, each of their albums offered a significant musical development on the last, Rakim's raps growing in maturity without sacrificing impact. The split came in the early 90s, with Rakim staying with MCA to deliver solo material like 'Heat It Up', produced by new co-conspirator Madness 4 Real, and included on the soundtrack to the Mario van Peebles movie, *Gunmen*.

● ALBUMS: *Paid In Full* (4th & Broadway 1987) ★★★★, *Follow The Leader* (Uni 1988) ★★★, *Let The Rhythm Hit 'Em* (MCA 1990) ★★★★, *Don't Sweat The Technique* (MCA 1992) ★★★, *Paid In Full: The Platinum Edition* (Island 1998) ★★★★.

## ESCAPE CLUB

A quartet of Trevor Steel (vocals), John Holliday (guitar), Johnnie Christo (bass) and Milan Zekavica (drums), the Escape Club took their central influence from the glam rock era of T. Rex and David Bowie. Formed in Essex, England, in 1983, they signed to EMI Records after the release of their first single, 'Breathing', for Bright Records. Afterwards they played regularly at the Marquee Club and supported China Crisis and the Alarm on tour. However, several singles and a debut album for EMI failed to provide a breakthrough. The band alleged 'under-promotion' by EMI and ended their association. That decision was rewarded when they found huge if fleeting success in the USA for Atlantic Records. Their single, 'Wild Wild West', became a surprise *Billboard* number 1 hit in 1988, accompanying an album of the same title, which also achieved gold sales. However, that was the end of their commercial good fortune and further efforts failed to penetrate the American charts.

● ALBUMS: *White Fields* (EMI 1985) ★★★, *Wild Wild West* (Atlantic 1988) ★★★, *Dollars And Sex* (Atlantic 1991) ★★.

## ESTEFAN, GLORIA, AND MIAMI SOUND MACHINE

Formed in Miami, Florida, USA in 1973, this Latin/funk/pop group was originally a trio called the Miami Latin Boys, comprising Emilio Estefan (b. 4 March 1953, Cuba; keyboards), Juan Avila (bass) and Enrique 'Kiki' Garcia (drums), each of whom was born in Cuba and raised in Miami. The following year the group played at a friend's wedding where they were joined onstage by singer Gloria Fajardo (b. 1 September 1957, Havana, Cuba). The latter at first refused to join the group, then agreed to sing with them part-time as she pursued her studies. In 1975, the quartet changed its name to Miami Sound Machine. They recorded their first single, 'Renecer', for a local Hispanic company that year. Emilio and Gloria married in 1978. In 1979, the group recorded its first album, sung entirely in Spanish; it was picked up for distribution by CBS Records International. They recorded seven Spanish-language records during the next six years, becoming successful in predominantly US Hispanic areas, Central and South America, as well as in Europe. Meanwhile, the group's membership grew to nine musicians. Their first English-language single, 'Dr. Beat', was released in 1984 and became a club/Top 10 hit in the UK, where the group then flew to appear on the BBC Television programme *Top Of The Pops*. The following year the group toured Japan successfully, and was honoured by their hometown Miami, which renamed a local street Miami Sound Machine Boulevard. Signed to Epic Records, their first US chart single was 'Conga' in 1985, reaching number 10 by early 1986. That same year saw two other US Top 10 singles, 'Bad Boy' and the ballad 'Words Get In The Way', and *Billboard* named them the year's top singles act. Their first English-language album, *Primitive Love*, reached number 23 that same year.

The group officially changed its name to Gloria Estefan And Miami Sound Machine in 1987, a year that brought one Top 10 single, 'Rhythm Is Gonna Get You', and *Let it Loose*, which reached number 6 by the spring of 1988. Another Top 10 single, 'Can't Stay Away From You', and the number 1 ballad, 'Anything For You', were highlights of early 1988. The year closed with another US/UK Top 10 single, '1-2-3'. Gloria Estefan released a solo album, *Cuts Both Ways*, which also made the Top 10, in the summer of 1989, after which she went on to enjoy a hugely successful pop career under her own name.

● ALBUMS: *Miami Sound Machine* (Columbia 1976) ★★★, *Rio* (Columbia 1978) ★★★, *Eyes Of Innocence* (Columbia 1984) ★★★, *Primitive Love* (Epic 1986) ★★★, as Gloria Estefan And Miami Sound Machine *Let it Loose* (US) *Anything For You* (UK) (Epic 1987) ★★★★.

● COMPILATIONS: *Greatest Hits* (Epic 1992) ★★★★.

● FURTHER READING: *Gloria Estefan*, Grace Catalano.

## EUROPE

This Swedish heavy rock outfit enjoyed brief international success in the late 80s. The origins of the band can be traced back to 1978, when Joey Tempest (b. 19 August 1963, Stockholm, Sweden; vocals), John Norum (guitar), and Tony Reno (b. Tony Niemstö; drums) joined Peter Olsson in Force. Olsson quit the band in 1981 and was replaced by John Léven (bass). After winning a national talent contest, the newly renamed Europe recorded two Rush-influenced albums for the Swedish market before signing to Epic Records in 1986. By this time, Norum had left the band and the new line-up featured his replacement Ian Haughland (drums) and Michael Michaeli (b. Gunnar Michaeli; keyboards). The first Epic album was produced by Kevin Elson and included three hits, 'The Final Countdown' (UK number 1/US number 8), 'Rock The Night' (UK number 12/US number 30), and 'Carrie' (UK number 22/US number 3). *The Final Countdown* went on to multi-platinum status, but also set the band a standard they subsequently failed to maintain. Norum was replaced shortly after the release of *The Final Countdown* by Kee Marcello (b. Kjell Lövbom). The new line-up's continued success in Japan and the USA was assisted by their lengthy world tours, and later hits included 1988's 'Superstitious' (UK number 34/US number 31) from the Ron Nevison-produced second album. *Prisoners In Paradise*, with Beau Hill as producer, sold poorly, despite containing the UK number 28 hit single 'I'll Cry For You'. Joey Tempest signed a solo contract with PolyGram Records in 1994 and released his debut, *A Place To Call Home*, in 1995.

● ALBUMS: *Europe* (Hot 1983) ★★, *Wings Of Tomorrow* (Hot 1984) ★★★, *The Final Countdown* (Epic 1986) ★★★, *Out Of This World* (Epic 1988) ★★, *Prisoners In Paradise* (Epic 1991) ★★★.

● COMPILATIONS: *Europe 1982-1992* (Epic 1993) ★★★, *Super Hits* (Columbia 1998) ★★★.

## EURYTHMICS

David A. Stewart (b. 9 September 1952, Sunderland, Tyne and Wear, England) and Annie Lennox (b. 25 December 1954, Aberdeen, Scotland). The worldwide popularity and critical acclaim of one of pop music's leading duos came about by fastidious determination and Stewart's remarkably good ear in being able to write the perfect song for his musical partner Lennox. Both artists relied heavily on each other's considerable talent and, as former lovers, they knew better than most their strengths and weaknesses.

Stewart met Lennox in London while he was still a member of the folk/rock band Longdancer. She was supplementing her income by waitressing while a student at the Royal College of Music. Together they formed the Tourists, a fondly remembered band that was able to fuse new wave energy with well-crafted pop songs. Following the Tourists' split, with Lennox and Stewart now embroiled in their much publicized doomed love affair, they formed the Eurythmics in 1980. The debut *In The Garden* was a rigidly electronic sounding album, very Germanic, haunting and cold. The record failed to sell. During one of the low points in their lives, having ended their four-year relationship, the duo persevered professionally and glanced the charts in November 1982 with the synthesizer-based 'Love Is A Stranger'. This gave them the confidence they needed, and the material on the subsequent *Sweet Dreams* (which climbed to number 3 in the albums chart) was superb, bringing deserved success. The album spawned a number of hits, all accompanied by an imaginative series of self-produced videos with the stunning Lennox in countless guises, showing incredible natural confidence in front of a camera. The spooky 'Sweet Dreams (Are Made Of This)' narrowly missed the top of the UK chart in February 1983, but made the top spot in the US in May. It was followed in quick succession by a reissued 'Love Is A Stranger' (UK number 6, April 1983) and 'Who's That Girl?' (UK number 3, July 1983). Released in November 1983, the UK chart-topping *Touch* became a huge success, containing a varied mixture of brilliantly accessible pop music, including the celebratory 'Right By Your Side' (UK number 10, November 1983) and 'Here Comes The Rain Again' (UK number 8/US number 4, January 1984). A remixed mini-LP of four tracks from *Touch* followed before they embarked upon scoring the music for the movie *1984*, starring John Hurt, which generated a UK number 4 hit in November 1984 with 'Sexcrime (Nineteen Eighty Four)'. Their lacklustre work on the soundtrack was immediately remedied by the excellent *Be Yourself Tonight*, which featured another huge transatlantic single 'Would I Lie To You?' (UK number 17, US number 5, April 1985). The album contained less synthesized pop and more rock music, with Stewart using guitar-based songs including a glorious soul duet with Aretha Franklin on 'Sisters Are Doin' It For Themselves' and the earthy 'Ball And Chain'.

During 1985, Lennox experienced serious throat problems, which forced the band to cancel their appearance at July's Live Aid charity concert. That same month, however, the duo enjoyed their sole UK chart-topper, the exuberant 'There Must Be An Angel (Playing With My Heart)'. Lennox made her big-screen debut in *Revolution* with Donald Sutherland and Al Pacino. Stewart, meanwhile, became one of the most sought-after record producers, working with Bob Dylan, Tom Petty, Feargal Sharkey, Daryl Hall (of Hall And Oates), Bob Geldof and Mick Jagger. The following year another gem, *Revenge*, was released, which included the group's last UK Top 10 single 'Thorn In My Side' (number 5, September 1986), 'Missionary Man' and the comparatively lightweight 'The Miracle Of Love'. *Savage* in 1987 maintained the standard and featured one of Lennox's finest vocal performances with the R&B rocker 'I Need A Man'. In 1988, their performance at the televised Nelson Mandela Concert from Wembley was one of its highlights, and the acoustic 'You Have Placed A Chill In My Heart' was a triumph. Later that year Lennox duetted with Al Green for a rousing and soulful version of Jackie DeShannon's 'Put A Little Love In Your Heart'. *We Too Are One* at the end of 1989 became their most successful album, staying at number 1 into 1990, but

proved to be their last.

The Eurythmics gained a mass following during the 80s by the sheer quality of their songs and managed to stay favourites with the media. It helped that Lennox was one of the most visually striking female performers of her era, with a voice of rare quality. Following their split, Stewart stayed in the background, using his talent as a producer and songwriter, and releasing his own solo albums. In 1992, Lennox issued her successful solo debut, *Diva*, and consolidated her reputation with *Medusa* in 1995. She reunited with Stewart in June 1998 at a tribute concert for journalist Ruth Picardie, and again at the following year's BRIT awards where the duo were honoured for their 'outstanding contribution' to British music. Buoyed by the successful reunion, Stewart and Lennox returned to the studio to record *Peace*. The ability to still write well together after such a break was the most striking aspect of the album, especially in view of the duo's past romantic relationship. The most revealing lyrics are in '17 Again', where Lennox sings: 'You in all your jewellery, and my bleeding heart, who couldn't be together, and who could not be apart'.

● ALBUMS: *In The Garden* (RCA 1981) ★★, *Sweet Dreams (Are Made Of This)* (RCA 1983) ★★★★, *Touch* (RCA 1983) ★★★★, *Touch Dance* (RCA 1984) ★★, *1984 (For The Love Of Big Brother)* film soundtrack (Virgin 1984) ★★, *Be Yourself Tonight* (RCA 1985) ★★★★, *Revenge* (RCA 1986) ★★★★, *Savage* (RCA 1987) ★★★, *We Too Are One* (RCA 1989) ★★★, *Peace* (RCA 1999) ★★★.

● COMPILATIONS: *Greatest Hits* (RCA 1991) ★★★★, *Eurythmics Live 1983–1989* (RCA 1993) ★★★.

● VIDEOS: *Sweet Dreams* (Eagle Rock 2000).

● FURTHER READING: *Eurythmics: Sweet Dreams: The Definitive Biography*, Johnny Waller. *Annie Lennox: The Biography*, Bryony Sutherland and Lucy Ellis.

## EVERYTHING BUT THE GIRL

Tracey Thorn (b. 26 September 1962, Hertfordshire, England) and Ben Watt (b. 6 December 1962, Barnes, London, England) first began performing together when they were students at Hull University, taking their name coming from a local furniture shop. Thorn was a member of the Marine Girls, and released the acoustic mini-album *A Distant Shore*, which was a strong seller in the UK independent charts during 1982. Watt released the critically acclaimed *North Marine Drive* the following year, by which time the duo had made their recording debut with a gentle and simply produced version of Cole Porter's 'Night And Day'.

They subsequently left Cherry Red Records and signed to the major-distributed Blanco y Negro label. In 1984, they made the national Top 30 with 'Each And Everyone', which preceded the superb *Eden*. This jazz-flavoured pop collection hallmarked the duo's understated compositional skills, displaying a great leap from the comparative naïveté of their previous offerings. Subsequent albums revealed a much more gradual growth in songwriting, though many of their older fans contend they have never surpassed that debut. Their biggest single breakthrough, meanwhile, came when a cover version of Danny Whitten's 'I Don't Want To Talk About It' reached UK number 3 in 1988. The attendant *Idlewild* enjoyed critical and commercial success. *The Language Of Life*, a collection more firmly fixated with jazz stylings, found further critical acclaim; one track, 'The Road', featured Stan Getz on saxophone. However, a more pop-orientated follow-up, *World-wide*, was released to mediocre reviews in 1991.

Watt's increasingly busy DJing schedule and Thorn's vocal contributions to trip-hop pioneers Massive Attack's 1994 opus, *Protection*, demonstrated their increasing interest in the UK's dance music scene. This was reflected in the textures of *Amplified Heart*, which featured contributions from Danny Thompson, Dave Mattacks, Richard Thompson and arranger Harry Robinson. The album was recorded following Watt's recovery from a life-threatening illness (chronicled in the quirky *Patient: The History Of A Rare Illness*). Todd Terry's remix of the track 'Missing' provided their big breakthrough, becoming a huge club hit and reaching the UK and US Top 5. The duo's new approach was confirmed on *Walking Wounded*, their Virgin Records debut, which embellished their acoustic songs with drum 'n' bass and trip-hop rhythms to stunning effect. The title track and 'Wrong' both reached the UK Top 10. Watt's involvement in the club scene meant that the follow-up did not appear until 1999. *Temperamental* retained some of the low-key charm of *Walking Wounded*, although three years on the duo's work sounded less groundbreaking.

● ALBUMS: *Eden* (Blanco y Negro 1984) ★★★★, *Love Not Money* (Blanco y Negro 1985) ★★, *Baby The Stars Shine Bright* (Blanco y Negro 1986) ★★, *Idlewild* (Blanco y Negro 1988) ★★★★, *The Language Of Life* (Blanco y Negro 1990) ★★★, *World-wide* (Blanco y Negro 1991) ★★, *Amplified Heart* (Blanco y Negro 1994) ★★★★, *Walking Wounded* (Virgin 1996) ★★★★, *Temperamental* (Virgin 1999) ★★★.
Solo: Tracey Thorn *A Distant Shore* mini-album (Cherry Red 1982) ★★★. Ben Watt *North Marine Drive* (Cherry Red 1983) ★★★.
● COMPILATIONS: *Home Movies: The Best Of Everything But The Girl* (Blanco y Negro 1993) ★★★★, *The Best Of Everything But The Girl* (Blanco y Negro 1997) ★★★★, *Back To Mine* (DMC/Ultra 2001) ★★★★.
● FURTHER READING: *Patient: The History Of A Rare Illness*, Ben Watt.

## EXILE

Formed in Berea, Kentucky, USA, in 1963 as the Exiles, Exile first reached the pop charts in the late 70s before changing musical direction and becoming one of the most successful country bands of the 80s. They toured with the Dick Clark Caravan of Stars in 1965 as back-up band for artists including Brian Hyland and Tommy Roe. In the late 60s, they recorded for Date Records and Columbia Records, and in the early 70s for SSS International, Date, Curb and Wooden Nickel. In 1973, they changed their name to Exile and in 1977, recording for Atco

Records, they had their first chart single. Following a switch to Warner Brothers Records, Exile had a number 1 pop hit with 'Kiss You All Over', in 1978. After two more pop chart singles they switched to country. The group's membership in 1978, when they had their first hit, was guitarist and vocalist J.P. Pennington, keyboard player Buzz Cornelison, vocalist and guitarist Les Taylor, keyboard player and vocalist Marlon Hargis, bass player and vocalist Sonny LeMaire and drummer Steve Goetzman.

Exile's second, and more lucrative, career as a country group began in 1983 (by which time Cornelison had left). The first country chart single, 'High Cost Of Leaving', reached number 27, but was followed by four successive number 1 country singles in 1984: 'Woke Up In Love', 'I Don't Want To Be A Memory', 'Give Me One More Chance' and 'Crazy For Your Love'. There were six further number 1 country singles by 1987: 'She's A Miracle', 'Hang On To Your Heart', 'I Could Get Used To You', 'It'll Be Me', 'She's Too Good To Be True' and 'I Can't Get Close Enough'. Hargis was replaced by Lee Carroll in 1985 and Pennington left in 1989, replaced by Paul Martin. The group signed to Arista Records in 1989 with a noticeable decline in commercial success. They were dropped by the label in 1993 and broke up soon afterwards, but a new version with Pennington and Taylor was on the road in 1996.

● ALBUMS: *Exile* (Wooden Nickel 1973) ★★★★, *Mixed Emotions* (Epic 1978) ★★★, *All There Is* (Epic 1979) ★★★, *Don't Leave Me This Way* (Epic 1980) ★★★, *Heart And Soul* (Epic 1981) ★★★, *Exile* (Epic 1983) ★★★, *Kentucky Hearts* (Epic 1984) ★★, *Hang On To Your Heart* (Epic 1985) ★★, *Shelter From The Night* (Epic 1987) ★★★, *Still Standing* (Arista 1990) ★★★★, *Justice* (Arista 1991) ★★★.
● COMPILATIONS: *The Best Of Exile* (Curb 1985) ★★★★, *Exile's Greatest Hits* (Epic 1986) ★★★, *The Complete Collection* (Curb 1991) ★★★★, *Super Hits* (Epic 1993) ★★★.

## EXPLOITED

This abrasive and unruly Scottish punk quartet was formed in East Kilbride in 1980 by vocalist Wattie Buchan and guitarist 'Big John' Duncan. Recruiting drummer Dru Stix (b. Drew Campbell) and bass player Gary McCormick, they signed to the Secret Records label the following year. Specializing in two-minute blasts of high-speed blue vitriol, they released their first album, *Punk's Not Dead*, in 1981. Lyrically they sketched out themes such as war, corruption, unemployment and police brutality, amid a chaotic blur of crashing drums and flailing guitar chords. The band quickly become entrenched in their own limited musical and philosophical ideology, and earned themselves a certain low-life notoriety. Songs such as 'Fuck A Mod', for example, set youth tribe against youth tribe without any true rationale. 'Sid Vicious Was Innocent', meanwhile, deserves no comment whatsoever. Nevertheless, they were the only member of the third-generation punk set to make it on to BBC Television's *Top Of The Pops*, with 1981's 'Dead Cities'. Continuing to release material on a regular basis, they have retained a small, but ever-declining, cult following. The line-ups have fluctuated wildly, with Duncan going on to join Goodbye Mr. Mackenzie and, very nearly, Nirvana, while Buchan remained in place. The diminutive but thoroughly obnoxious lead singer, with a multi-coloured mohican haircut, strikes an oddly anachronistic figure today as he presides over his dubious musical curio.

● ALBUMS: *Punk's Not Dead* (Secret 1981) ★★★, *On Stage* (Superville 1981) ★★★, *Troops Of Tomorrow* (Secret 1982) ★★★, *Let's Start A War (Said Maggie One Day)* (Combat/Pax 1983) ★★★, *Horror Epics* (Combat/Konnexion 1985) ★★★, *Live At The Whitehouse* (Combat Core 1985) ★★, *Death Before Dishonour* (Rough Justice 1989) ★★, *The Massacre* (Rough Justice 1991) ★★, *Beat The Bastards* (Rough Justice 1996) ★★.

● COMPILATIONS: *Totally Exploited* (Dojo 1984) ★★, *Live On The Apocalypse Now Tour '81* (Chaos 1985) ★★★, *Live And Loud!!* (Link 1987) ★★, *Inner City Decay* (Snow 1987) ★★★, *On Stage 91/Live At The Whitehouse 1985* (Dojo 1991) ★★, *The Singles Collection* (Cleopatra 1993) ★★★, *Dead Cities* (Harry May 2000) ★★★, *Punk Singles And Rarities* (Captain Oi! 2001) ★★★.

● VIDEOS: *Live At The Palm Cove* (Jettisoundz 1983), *1983–87* (Jettisoundz 1987), *Sexual Favours* (Jettisoundz 1987), *Live In Japan* (Jettisoundz 1991), *Live In Buenos Aires* (Jettisoundz 1993), *Rock & Roll Outlaws* (Jettisoundz 1995).

## EXTREME NOISE TERROR

A band whose name truly encapsulates their sound, Extreme Noise Terror formed in January 1985 and were signed by Manic Ears Records after their first ever gig. Their debut release was a split album with Chaos U.K., and although there were musical similarities, ENT, along with Napalm Death, were already in the process of twisting traditional punk influences into altogether different shapes. Along with the latter, they became the subject of disc jockey John Peel's interest in 1987, recording a session (one of three) that would eventually see release on Strange Fruit Records. Afterwards, drummer Mick Harris, who had left Napalm Death to replace the band's original drummer Pig Killer, in turn departed, joining Scorn. His replacement was Stick (b. Tony Dickens), who joined existing members Dean Jones (vocals), Phil Vane (vocals) and Pete Hurley (guitar). Mark Bailey had by now replaced Mark Gardiner, who himself had replaced Jerry Clay, on bass. Touring in Japan preceded the release of *Phonophobia*, while continued Peel sessions brought the band to the attention of the KLF's Bill Drummond. He asked them to record a version of the KLF's '3 A.M. Eternal', with the intention of the band appearing on *Top Of The Pops* live at Christmas to perform the tune (BBC Television, however, decided this was not in the best interests of their audience). Eventually released as a limited edition single, the two bands paths crossed again in 1992 when the KLF were invited to perform live at the 1992 BRIT Awards. This crazed event, which included the firing of blanks into the audience, has already passed into music industry legend.

Back on their own, 1993 saw Extreme Noise Terror touring widely, and the band signed to Earache Records the following year. By this time, the line-up had expanded to include Lee Barrett (bass; also Disgust) replacing Bailey, Ali Firouzbakht (lead guitar) and original member Pig Killer on drums. Together they released *Retro-bution*, ostensibly a compilation, but nevertheless featuring the new line-up on re-recorded versions of familiar material. Pig Killer was replaced by Was (ex-Cradle Of Filth) shortly afterwards, but a greater shock was the departure of Vane to join Napalm Death. That band's departed vocalist Mark 'Barney' Greenway was brought in to help record *Damage 381*. Bizarrely, Vane and Greenway then swapped places once more.

● ALBUMS: split with Chaos UK *Radioactive* (Manic Ears 1985) ★★, *A Holocaust In Your Head* (Hurt 1987) ★★, *The Peel Sessions* (Strange Fruit 1990) ★★★, *Phonophobia* (Vinyl Japan 1992) ★★, *Retro-bution* (Earache 1995) ★★★, *Damage 381* (Earache 1997) ★★★, *Being And Nothing* (Candlelight 2001) ★★★.

● VIDEOS: *From One Extreme To The Other* (Jettisoundz 1989).

## EYELESS IN GAZA

Taking their name from Aldous Huxley's famous novel, this UK outfit is the brainchild of vocalists/musicians Martyn Bates and Peter Becker. Known for their tortured vocals and impressive arranging skills, the band established a reasonable following on the independent circuit with their 1981 debut, *Photographs As Memories*. Several more albums for Cherry Red Records saw them alternate between a melodramatic and meandering style that increasingly veered towards improvisation.

Bates subsequently teamed up with former Primitives bass player Steve Gullaghan in Hungry I, also working solo. Eyeless In Gaza re-formed in 1992, releasing an album titled *Fabulous Library* the following year as a trio comprising Bates, Becker and chanteuse Elizabeth S. Reverting to the original two-piece line-up later in 1993, the two recorded and toured Europe and the USA extensively with self-styled 'performance poet' Anne Clark, also collaborating with Derek Jarman film soundtrack composer Simon Fisher Turner. In 1995, they relaunched the Ambivalent Scale imprint in co-operation with World Serpent Distribution. Their own releases on the label included *Bitter Apples* and *All Under Leaves, The Leaves Of Life*. The first Eyeless In Gaza album in almost five years, *Song Of The Beautiful Wanton*, was released by the US label Soleilmoon in 2000.

● ALBUMS: *Photographs As Memories* (Cherry Red 1981) ★★★, *Caught In Flux* (Cherry Red 1981) ★★★, *Pale Hands I Loved So Well* (Uniton 1982) ★★★, *Drumming The Beating Heart* (Cherry Red 1982) ★★★, *Rust Red September* (Cherry Red 1983) ★★★, *Back From The Rains* (Cherry Red 1986) ★★★, *Fabulous Library* (Orchid 1993) ★★★, *Saw You In Reminding Pictures* (Hive-Arc 1994) ★★★, *Bitter Apples* (A-Scale 1995) ★★★, *All Under Leaves, The Leaves Of Life* (A-Scale 1996) ★★★, *Song Of The Beautiful Wanton* (Soleilmoon 2000) ★★★.

● COMPILATIONS: *Kodak Ghosts Run Amok* (Cherry Red 1987) ★★★, *Transience Blues* (Integrity 1990) ★★★, *Orange Ice & Wax Crayons* (Cherry Red 1992) ★★★, *Voice: The Best Of Eyeless In Gaza (Recollections 1980–1986)* (Cherry Red 1993) ★★★★, *Sixth Sense: The Singles Collection* (Cherry Red 2002) ★★★★.
● VIDEOS: *Street Lamps N'Snow* (Visionary 1994).

## FABULOUS THUNDERBIRDS

Formed in Texas, USA, in 1977, the Thunderbirds originally comprised Jimmy Vaughan (b. 20 March 1951, Dallas, Texas, USA; guitar), Kim Wilson (b. 6 January 1951, Detroit, Michigan, USA; vocals, harmonica), Keith Ferguson (b. 23 July 1946, Houston, Texas, USA, d. 29 April 1997; bass) and Mike Buck (b. 17 June 1952; drums). They emerged from the post-punk vacuum with a solid, unpretentious brand of R&B. Their debut album, *The Fabulous Thunderbirds* aka *Girls Go Wild*, offered a series of powerful original songs as well as sympathetic cover versions, including a vibrant reading of Slim Harpo's 'Baby Scratch My Back'. This mixture has sustained the group throughout its career, although it took a move from Chrysalis Records to the Epic label to provide the success that their exciting music deserved. The Thunderbirds line-up has undergone some changes, with former Roomful Of Blues drummer Fran Christina (b. 1 February 1951, Westerly, Rhode Island, USA) replacing Mike Buck in 1980, and Preston Hubbard (b. 15 March 1953, Providence, Rhode Island, USA) joining after Ferguson departed.

Throughout these changes, Wilson and Vaughan, the brother of the late blues guitarist Stevie Ray Vaughan, remained at the helm until Vaughan jumped ship in 1995. Drummer Buck formed the LeRoi Brothers in 1980, while Ferguson went on to forge a new career with the Tail Gators. Although both of these groups offer similar bar band fare, the Thunderbirds remain, unquestionably, the masters. The Danny Kortchmar-produced *Roll Of the Dice* was the first album with Kim Wilson leading the band in the wake of Vaughan's departure and showed the new lead guitarist, Kid Ramos (b. David Ramos, 13 January 1959, Fullerton, California, USA), having a difficult job to fill. The recent line-up in addition to Wilson and Ramos comprises Gene Taylor (piano), Jim Bott (drums) and Ronnie James Weber (bass).

● ALBUMS: *The Fabulous Thunderbirds* aka *Girls Go Wild* (Chrysalis 1979) ★★★★, *What's The Word* (Chrysalis 1980) ★★★, *Butt Rockin'* (Chrysalis 1981) ★★★, *T-Bird Rhythm* (Chrysalis 1982) ★★★, *Tuff Enuff* (Columbia 1986) ★★★, *Hot Number* (Columbia 1987) ★★★, *Powerful Stuff* (Columbia 1989) ★★★, *Walk That Walk, Talk That Talk* (Columbia 1991) ★★★, *Roll Of The Dice* (Private Music 1995) ★★, *High Water* (High Street 1997) ★★★★, with Al Copley *Good Understanding* 1992 recording (Bullseye Blues 1998) ★★★, *Live* (Sanctuary 2001) ★★★.
● COMPILATIONS: *Portfolio* (Chrysalis 1987) ★★★★, *Hot Stuff: The Greatest Hits* (Columbia 1992) ★★★★, *Different Tacos* (Country Town Music 1998) ★★★★.
● VIDEOS: *Tuff Enuff* (Hendring Music Video 1990).

## FACTORY RECORDS

Cambridge graduate Anthony H. Wilson (b. 1950, Salford, Lancashire, England) was a regional television reporter working in Manchester when he started the Factory label in 1978. He was also responsible for the *So It Goes* and *What's On* television programmes, which in themselves had acted as an invaluable platform for the emerging new wave scene. Previously he had edited his university's *Shilling Paper*. From there, he joined television news company ITN as a trainee reporter, writing bulletins for current events programmes. It was on regional news programmes based in Manchester that he first encountered his future collaborators in the Factory operation; Alan Erasmus, Peter Saville, Rob Gretton (manager of Joy Division) and producer Martin Hannett. Erasmus and Wilson began their operation by jointly managing the fledgling Durutti Column, opening the Factory Club venue soon after. The label's first catalogue number, FAC 1, was allocated to the poster promoting its opening event. This typified Wilson's approach to the whole Factory operation, the most famous assignation of which was FAC 51, the Haçienda nightclub. However, it was their records, and the impersonal, nondescriptive packaging accompanying them, that saw the label make its mark. Among the first releases were OMD's 'Electricity' (later a hit on Dindisc) and A Certain Ratio's 'All Night Party'. However, it was Joy Division, harnessing the anxieties of Manchester youth to a discordant, sombre musical landscape, that established the label in terms of public perception and financial security. With Curtis gone, New Order continued as the backbone of the Factory operation throughout the 80s, establishing themselves in the mainstream with the biggest-selling 12-inch up to that time, 'Blue Monday'. Other mainstays included Section 25 and Stockholm Monsters, who steered a path too close to that of New Order, and the resourceful Durutti Column. It took the brief arrival of James to restore a pop sensibility (their subsequent departure would be a huge body blow), while New Order, somewhat astonishingly, took the England Football Squad to number 1 in the UK Charts with 'World In Motion'. The latter-day success of Electronic, the most successful of various New Order offshoots, and the Happy Mondays, a shambolic post-punk dance conglomerate, diffused accusations of Factory being too reliant on a single band.

Reported cash flow problems in 1991 were vehemently denied by Wilson, but the label went bankrupt the following year. London Records bought Factory Communications and its associated trademarks, and Wilson set up the Factory Too imprint. The four-album compilation *Palatine* showcased the label's achievements, of which Wilson has never been reticent: 'In my opinion (popular art) is as valid as any other art form . . . a lot of the tracks on *Palatine* are phenomenal art. We're 35 years into pop now, and great records do not lose their power. The deference with which we treat this stuff is deserved.' Ten years later, Wilson and Factory's story was made into an entertaining

film, *24 Hour Party People*.

● COMPILATIONS: *Palatine* 4-LP box set (Factory 1991) ★★★.

● FURTHER READING: *From Joy Division To New Order*, Mick Middles. *24 Hour Party People: What The Sleeve Notes Never Tell You*, Tony Wilson. *The True Story Of Anthony H. Wilson And Factory Records*, Mick Middles.

## FAD GADGET

Effectively a moniker for UK-born vocalist and synthesizer player Frank Tovey (b. 1956, London, England, d. 3 April 2002, London, England), Fad Gadget enjoyed cult success with a series of bizarre releases on the Mute Records label during the early 80s. Tovey's background lay in his study of performance art at Leeds Art College. After moving to London, he transferred this interest into an unpredictable, often self-mutilating stage show. The first artist to sign with Daniel Miller's Mute label, Fad Gadget's 'Back To Nature' was released in 1979. 'Ricky's Hand' further combined Tovey's lyrical skill (observing the darker aspects of life) with an innovative use of electronics. Both these traits were evident on 'Fireside Favourites', a single and also the title of Fad Gadget's debut album. For the latter, Tovey was joined by Eric Radcliffe (guitar, bass), Nick Cash (drums), John Fryer (percussion, noises), Daniel Miller (drum machine, synthesizer) and Phil Wauquaire (bass synthesizer, guitar). After 'Make Room' in 1981 came *Incontinent*, which was more violent, unnerving and disturbing than before. Tovey had also recruited new staff, working with Peter Balmer (bass, rhythm guitar), David Simmons (piano, synthesizer), singers B.J. Frost and Anne Clift, plus drummer Robert Gotobed of Wire. In 1982, 'Saturday Night Special' and 'King Of The Flies' preceded a third album, *Under The Flag*. Dealing with the twin themes of the Falklands conflict and Tovey's new born child, the album featured Alison Moyet on saxophone and backing vocals. The following year saw new extremes as Tovey returned from a European tour with his legs in plaster, having broken them during a show. On the recording front, the year was fairly quiet, apart from 'For Whom The Bell Tolls' and 'I Discover Love', and in October the band supported Siouxsie And The Banshees at London's Royal Albert Hall. 'Collapsing New People' continued an impressive run of singles at the start of 1984, and was followed by Fad Gadget's final album, *Gag*. However, Tovey opted to use his real identity from this point on. In November, he teamed up with American conceptualist Boyd Rice for *Easy Listening For The Hard Of Hearing*, and went on to release several solo works, each of them as highly distinct and uncompromising as Fad Gadget's material.

Despite Tovey's relative inactivity during the 90s, Fad Gadget's reputation as a pioneering electronic act continued to grow. Fad Gadget's return to live performance, headlining Elektrofest 2001 at The Mean Fiddler in London with Austrian band Temple X, demonstrated that the years had not diminished Tovey's remarkable stage energy. His artistic renaissance was cruelly curtailed by his death from heart failure the following April.

● ALBUMS: *Fireside Favourites* (Mute 1980) ★★★, *Incontinent* (Mute 1981) ★★★, *Under The Flag* (Mute 1982) ★★★★, *Gag* (Mute 1984) ★★★.
● COMPILATIONS: *The Fad Gadget Singles* (Mute 1985) ★★★★, *The Best Of Fad Gadget* (Mute 2001) ★★★★.

## FAIR, JAD

b. Ann Arbor, Michigan, USA. This US singer-songwriter has pursued his wildly eccentric muse for over three decades, as a solo performer or with Half Japanese, the band he formed in the mid-70s with his brother David Fair. Drawing equal inspiration from Jonathan Richman's primitive rock and classic 60s pop, Fair's recorded output has been dismissed as tuneless drivel by some, and as the work of a childlike savant by others. Whatever the verdict (and his music generates such extreme responses), Fair has stuck with his rudimentary style over the years and resolutely refuses to learn how to play guitar or sing properly.

Fair began recording as a solo artist in 1980, shortly after Half Japanese released their long-playing debut, a three-record box set! His own full-length debut, *Everyone Knew ... But Me*, chronicled Fair's problems with girls over an interminable 27 tracks (plus two James Brown covers). The follow-up, *Best Wishes*, comprised 42 brief instrumentals titled either 'O.K.' or 'A.O.K.'. The majority of his work since the late 80s has been 'collaborations' with other artists, including Kramer, Daniel Johnston, the Pastels, Yo La Tengo and Teenage Fanclub, although with Fair unwilling or unable to alter his DIY approach, the results have often been disjointed and sometimes unlistenable. Confirming his status as a cult underground hero, in 1993 Fair and his band were recruited by Kurt Cobain as the opening act on Nirvana's In Utero tour. Fair has also recorded several albums with Half Japanese guitarist Tim Foljahn and Sonic Youth drummer Steve Shelley as Mosquito.

● ALBUMS: *The Zombies Of Mora-Tau* mini-album (Armageddon 1980) ★★, *Everyone Knew ... But Me* (Press 1982) ★★, as Between Meals *Oh No I Just Knocked Over A Cup Of Coffee* (Iridescence 1983) ★★, *Monarchs* (Iridescence 1984) ★★, *Best Wishes* (Iridescence 1987) ★★, with Kramer *Roll Out The Barrel* (Shimmy-Disc 1988) ★★, *Great Expectations* (Bad Alchemy 1989) ★★★, *Jad Fair And Daniel Johnston* aka *It's Spooky* (50 Skidillion Watts/ Paperhouse 1989) ★★★, *Greater Expectations* (Psycho-Acoustic Sounds/T.E.C. Tones 1991) ★★★, *I Like It When You Smile* (T.E.C. Tones/Paperhouse 1992) ★★★, *Jad Fair/Jason Willett/Gilles Rieder* (Megaphone 1992) ★★★, with Nao *Half Robot* (Paperhouse 1993) ★★, with Phono-Comb *Monsters, Lullabies ... And The Occasional Flying Saucer* (Shake 1996) ★★★, with the Shapir-O'Rama *We Are The Rage* (Avant 1996) ★★★, with David Fair *Best Friends* (Vesuvius 1996) ★★★, with Jason Willett *Honey Bee* (Dr. Jim 1997) ★★★, with Willett *Wild* (Megaphone 1997) ★★, with Yo La Tengo *Strange But True* (Matador 1998) ★★★, with David Fair *26 Monster Songs For Children* (Kill Rock Stars 1998) ★★, with Willett *Enjoyable Songs* (Alternative Tentacles 1999)

★★★, with the Shapir-O'Rama *I Like Your Face* (Wire Monkey 1999) ★★★, as the Lucky Sperms *Somewhat Humorous* (Jagjaguwar 2001) ★★★, with Teenage Fanclub *Words Of Wisdom And Hope* (Geographic/ Alternative Tentacles 2002) ★★★, *DQE And Jad Fair* (Dark Beloved Cloud 2002) ★★★, with R. Stevie Moore *FairMoore* (Old Gold 2002) ★★.

## FAIRGROUND ATTRACTION

This jazz/folk-tinged Anglo/Scottish pop band comprised Eddi Reader (b. Sadenia Reader, 28 August 1959, Glasgow, Scotland; vocals), Mark Nevin (guitar), Simon Edwards (guitaron, a Mexican acoustic guitar-shaped bass) and Roy Dodds (drums). After art school Reader made her first musical forays as backing singer for the Gang Of Four. She moved to London in 1983 where session and live work with the Eurythmics and Alison Moyet kept her gainfully employed. She first linked with Nevin for the Compact Organisation sampler album *The Compact Composers*, singing on two of his songs. Nevin and Reader began their first collaborations in 1985, after Nevin had graduated by playing in one of the numerous line-ups of Jane Aire And The Belvederes. He was also closely involved with Sandie Shaw's mid-80s comeback. Around his songs they built Fairground Attraction, adding Edwards and Dodds, a jazz drummer of over 20 years' standing who had spent time with Working Week and Terence Trent D'Arby. They signed to RCA Records and quickly set about recording a debut album, as the gentle skiffle of 'Perfect' topped the UK singles charts in May 1988. They subsequently won both Best Single and Best Album categories at the BRIT awards.

A slight hiatus in their career followed when Reader became pregnant. They followed their natural inclinations by filming the video for their 1989 single 'Clare' in Nashville, and were supplemented on tour by Graham Henderson (accordion) and Roger Beaujolais (vibraphone). Their promise was cut short when the band split, and Reader went on to acting (appearing in a BBC drama *Your Cheatin' Heart*, about the Scottish country and western scene) and a solo career, releasing her debut, *Mirmama*, in 1992. Nevin established a productive career as a songwriter, and later worked with Brian Kennedy in Sweetmouth.

● ALBUMS: *The First Of A Million Kisses* (RCA 1988) ★★★.
● COMPILATIONS: *Ay Fond Kiss* (RCA 1990) ★★★.

## FAITH BROTHERS

A passionate brand of rock, spiced with an old soul feel, allowed the Faith Brothers to address important political and moral issues without needing to preach. Their debut single, 'Country Of The Blind', in 1985, set the tone, an attack on a nation in the clutches of consumer fever and a decaying welfare state. 'Stranger On Home Ground' (1985) was closer to their hearts, dealing with the band's attitude towards the loss of community, not least where they grew up around west London's Fulham area. The year ended with the more optimistic 'Eventide (A Hymn For Change)', a title shared by the Faith Brothers' debut album released on the Virgin Records subsidiary 10.

Alongside the main songwriter Billy Franks (guitar, vocals) were Lee Hirons (bass), his brother Mark (guitar), Henry Trezise (keyboards), Mark Waterman (saxophone), Will Tipper (trumpet) and Steve Howlett (drums). The immediacy of the singles seemed to be lost on *Eventide*, which sounded strained and tame in comparison. 'Whistling In The Dark' was taken as a further single in 1986, but failed to chart. The Faith Brothers returned in 1987 with *A Human Sound*, but like its two singles, 'That's Just The Way It Is To Me' and 'Consider Me', it made little impression and they disbanded shortly thereafter.
● ALBUMS: *Eventide* (10 1985) ★★, *A Human Sound* (Siren 1987) ★★★.

## FALCO

b. Johann Hölzel, 19 February 1957, Vienna, Austria, d. 6 February 1998, Puerto Plata, Dominican Republic. Using a droll mixture of German and English lyrics, Falco had several international hits in the 80s. After completing his studies at the Vienna Conservatoire, he played bass guitar in the punk band Drahdiwaberl, composing 'Ganz Wien' which appeared on their *Psycho Terror* in 1979, and was banned because it contained the line 'all Vienna is on heroin today'. His solo career began in 1982 with the rap-style European hit 'Der Kommissar' and the controversial tale of prostitution 'Jeanny', which topped the German charts despite a complete radio ban. Falco's first impact on the English-speaking world came with 1985's 'Rock Me Amadeus'. Co-written with Dutch producers Rob and Ferdi Bolland, the song's zany mixture of speech and singing made it a US/UK chart-topper the following year at the same time as *Falco 3* broke into the US Top 10. After releasing the rock ballad 'Vienna Calling', Falco returned to the 'Amadeus' mode on 'The Sound Of Musik', which was an attack on Austrian president Kurt Waldheim. Despite his collaboration with model and film star Brigitte Nielsen on 'Body Next To Body', Falco's later records, such as 'Titanic' in 1992 were not successful outside German-speaking territories. Moving to the Dominican Republic for tax purposes, he was building his own recording studio when he was killed in a car accident in February 1998.
● ALBUMS: *Einzelhaft* (A&M 1982) ★★★, *Jung Roemer* (A&M 1984) ★★★, *Falco 3* (A&M 1986) ★★★★, *Emotional* (Sire 1986) ★★★, *Data De Groove* (ARD 1987) ★★★, *Wiener Blut* (Warners 1988) ★★.
● COMPILATIONS: *The Final Curtain: The Ultimate Best Of Falco* (EMI 1999) ★★★★, *Greatest Hits* (Buddha 1999) ★★★★.

## FALL

Formed in Manchester, England, in 1977, the Fall is the brainchild of the mercurial Mark E. Smith (b. Mark Edward Smith, 5 March 1957, Salford, Manchester, England). Over the years, Smith has ruthlessly utilized a battalion of musicians while taking the band on a personal odyssey defined by his wayward musical and lyrical excursions. His truculent press proclamations, by turns hysterically funny or sinister, also illuminated their career. Just as importantly, BBC disc jockey John Peel became their most consistent and fervent advocate, with the band recording a record number of sessions for his Radio 1 show.

The first Fall line-up, featuring Una Baines (electric piano), Martin Bramah (guitar), Karl Burns (drums) and Tony Friel (bass), made their debut on 'Bingo Master's Breakout', a good example of Smith's surreal vision, coloured by his relentlessly northern working-class vigil. Initially signed to the small independent label Step Forward the band recorded three singles, including the savage 'Fiery Jack', plus *Live At The Witch Trials*. In 1980 the unit signed to Rough Trade Records and went on to release the critically acclaimed but still wilful singles 'How I Wrote Elastic Man' and 'Totally Wired'. Meanwhile, a whole series of line-up changes saw the arrival and subsequent departures of Mike Leigh, Martin Bramah and Yvonne Pawlett. The band's most stable line-up featured Marc Riley, Steve Hanley, Paul Hanley and Craig Scanlon backing Smith. The Fall's convoluted career continued to produce a series of discordant, yet frequently fascinating albums, from the early menace of *Dragnet* to the chaotic *Hex Enduction Hour*. At every turn Smith worked hard to stand aloof from any prevailing trend, his suspicious mind refusing to make concessions to the mainstream. An apparent change in the band's image and philosophy occurred during 1983 with the arrival of future wife Brix (Laura Elise Smith), and the departure of Riley to form the Creepers. As well as appearing with the Fall as singer and guitarist, Brix later recorded with her own outfit, the pop-orientated Adult Net. She first appeared on the Fall's *Perverted By Language*, and her presence was felt more keenly when the Fall unexpectedly emerged as a potential chart act, successfully covering R. Dean Taylor's 'There's A Ghost In My House' and later the Kinks' 'Victoria'. Despite this, Mark E. Smith's deadpan voice and distinctive, accentuated vocals still dominated the band's sound, along with his backing band's ceaseless exploration of the basic rock riff.

On later albums such as the almost flawless *This Nation's Saving Grace* and *The Frenz Experiment*, they lost none of their baffling wordplay or nagging, insistent rhythms, but the work seemed more focused and accessible. The line-up changes had slowed, although more changes were afoot with the arrival of drummer Simon Woolstenscroft and Marcia Schofield. Proof of Smith's growing stature among the popular art cognoscenti was the staging of his papal play *Hey! Luciani* and the involvement of dancer Michael Clarke in the production of *I Am Kurious Oranj*. Any suggestions that the Fall might be slowly heading for a degree of commercial acceptance underestimated Smith's restless spirit.

By the turn of the decade Brix had left the singer and the band (he maintains he 'kicked her out'), and Schofield followed soon afterwards. A succession of labels did little to impair the band's 90s output, with the Fall's leader unable to do wrong in the eyes of their hugely committed following, which now had outposts throughout America. Brix returned in time to guest on *Cerebral Caustic*, although Smith had persevered in her absence, recording four strong albums, with 1993's *The Infotainment Scam* even reaching number 9 in the UK album charts. *In The City* featured a live set recorded in 1996, and was followed by Smith's thirtieth album, *Levitate*, which experimented with dance rhythms. *Oxymoron* and *The More You Look The Less You Find* are among the glut of compilations of unreleased or alternative material to have flooded the market. Long-term bass player Steve Hanley walked out, along with two other musicians, following an onstage fight at a show in New York in April 1998. True to form, Smith assembled a new band and returned with two excellent, thoroughly contemporary albums, *The Marshall Suite* and *The Unutterable*. Unpredictable and unique, the Fall under Smith's guidance remains one of the UK's most uncompromising bands.

● ALBUMS: *Live At The Witch Trials* (Step Forward 1979) ★★★★, *Dragnet* (Step Forward 1979) ★★★★, *Totale's Turns (It's Now Or Never) (Live)* (Rough Trade 1980) ★★, *Grotesque (After The Gramme)* (Rough Trade 1980) ★★★, *Slates* mini-album (Rough Trade 1981) ★★★, *Hex Enduction Hour* (Kamera 1982) ★★★★, *Room To Live* (Kamera 1982) ★★★, *Perverted By Language* (Rough Trade 1983) ★★★, *The Wonderful And Frightening World Of ...* (Beggars Banquet 1984) ★★★★, *This Nation's Saving Grace* (Beggars Banquet 1985) ★★★★, *Bend Sinister* (Beggars Banquet 1986) ★★★★, *The Frenz Experiment* (Beggars Banquet 1988) ★★★★, *I Am Kurious Oranj* (Beggars Banquet 1988) ★★★, *Seminal Live* (Beggars Banquet 1989) ★★★, *Extricate* (Cog Sinister/Fontana 1990) ★★★, *Shiftwork* (Cog Sinister/Fontana 1991) ★★★★, *Code: Selfish* (Cog Sinister/Fontana 1992) ★★★, *The Infotainment Scan* (Cog Sinister/Permanent 1993) ★★★, *BBC Live In Concert* 1987 recording (Windsong 1993) ★★★, *Middle Class Revolt* (Permanent 1994) ★★★★, *Cerebral Caustic* (Permanent 1995) ★★★★, *The Twenty-Seven Points* (Permanent 1996) ★★★, *The Light User Syndrome* (Jet 1996) ★★★, *In The City* (Artful 1997) ★★★, *Levitate* (Artful 1997) ★★★, *Live To Air In Melbourne '82* (Cog Sinister 1998) ★★★★, *The Marshall Suite* (Artful 1999) ★★★★, *The Unutterable* (Eagle 2000) ★★★★, *Liverpool 78* (Cog Sinister 2001) ★, *Are You Are Missing Winner* (Cog Sinister 2001) ★★★, *2G + 2* (Action 2002) ★★.
Solo: Mark E. Smith *The Post Nearly Man* (Artful 1998) ★★.

● COMPILATIONS: *77 – Early Years – 79* (Step Forward 1981) ★★★, *Live At Acklam Hall, London, 1980* cassette only (Chaos 1982) ★★★, *Hip Priests And Kamerads* (Situation 2 1985) ★★★, *In Palace Of Swords Reversed (80–83)* (Cog Sinister 1987) ★★★★, *458489 A Sides* (Beggars Banquet 1990) ★★★★, *458489-B Sides* (Beggars Banquet 1990) ★★★, *The Collection* (Castle 1993) ★★★, *Sinister Waltz* archive recordings (Receiver 1996) ★★, *Fiend With A Violin* archive recordings (Receiver 1996) ★★★, *Oswald Defence Lawyer* archive recordings (Receiver 1996) ★★, *Oxymoron* (Receiver 1997) ★★, *The More You Look The Less You Find* (Trojan 1998) ★★, *Slates/A Part Of America Therein, 1981* (Castle 1998) ★★★, *Smile ... It's The Best Of The Fall* (Castle 1998) ★★★, *Northern Attitude: An Alternative Selection* (Music Club 1998) ★★, *The Peel Sessions* (Strange Fruit 1999) ★★★, *A Past Gone Mad: The Best Of The Fall 1990–2000* (Artful 2000) ★★★★, *Psykick Dance Hall: Classic Archive Recordings From The Fall 1977–1982* 3-CD set (Eagle 2000) ★★★, *A World Bewitched: Best Of 1990–2000* (Artful 2001) ★★★★, *Totally Wired: The Rough Trade Anthology* (Castle 2002) ★★★★, *The Rough Trade Singles Box* (Essential 2002) ★★★.

● VIDEOS: *VHS0489* (Beggars Banquet 1991), *Perverted By Language Bis* (IKON 1992).

● FURTHER READING: *Paintwork: A Portrait Of The Fall*, Brian Edge.

## FÄLTSKOG, AGNETHA

b. 5 April 1950, Jönköping, Sweden. Fältskog started her musical career in 1965 at the age of 15, when she sang for a Swedish dance band. In 1968 she released her debut single – 'Jag Var Så Kär' ('I Was So In Love'). It was a smash in Sweden and the rest of Scandinavia, and she successfully followed it up with further hits. In 1969 she appeared on a television show where she met Björn Ulvaeus, a former member of the Hootenanny Singers, and a songwriting partner of Hep Star Benny Andersson. Agnetha (who was normally known as Anna) and Björn married on 7 July 1971. By this time Ulvaeus and Anderson were recording together, and Anna and Andersson's girlfriend Anni Fred Lyngstad were singing backing vocals for the boys. Eventually a permanent group was formed and in 1974, they became Abba who first conquered Sweden then took the UK by storm when they won the Eurovision Song Contest. Fältskog's relationship with Ulvaeus ended with divorce in 1979 and by 1982 the group had worked together for the last time. Neither Lyngstad nor Fältskog wasted anytime in launching their solo careers. Fältskog opened with an album – *Wrap Your Arms Around Me* – produced by famed pop producer Mike Chapman and hit the singles chart three times in 1983 with 'The Heat Is On', 'Wrap Your Arms Around Me' and 'Can't Shake Loose'; the latter written by Russ Ballard. In 1988, Fältskog moved to WEA Records with ex-Chicago vocalist Peter Cetera as producer. However, the album and the single 'The Last Time' made little impact and latterly Fältskog seems to have retired from the music business. She published her autobiography in 1997.

● ALBUMS: *Agnetha* (Embassy 1974) ★★, *Wrap Your Arms Around Me* (Epic 1983) ★★★, *Eyes Of A Woman* (Epic 1987) ★★, *I Stand Alone* (Warners 1988) ★★.

● COMPILATIONS: *My Love My Life* (Columbia 1996) ★★, *That's Me – Greatest Hits* (Polydor 1998) ★★.

● FURTHER READING: *As I Am: Abba Before And Beyond*, Agnetha Fältskog with Brita Åhman. *Abbamania Volume 2: The Solo Years*, Peter Bingham and Bernadette Dolan.

## *FAME*

Exiled British director Alan Parker (*Bugsy Malone*, *The Commitments*) took the reins for this 1980 film, which followed the lives of young showbusiness aspirants in time-honoured fashion. Set in Manhattan's High School for the Performing Arts, *Fame* charts the lives of a group of teenagers over a period of four years. Parker cast disparate characters – homosexuals, Puerto Ricans, individuals drawn from New York's uptown and downtown environments – in what turned out to be a box-office blockbuster. Star Irene Cara's recording of Michael Gore and Dean Pitchford's title song, which won an Academy Award, went to number 1 in the UK, and there was another Oscar for Gore's exciting score. The rest of the songs included 'Red Light', 'I Sing The Body Electric', 'Dogs In The Yard', 'Hot Lunch Jam', 'Out Here On My Own' and 'Is It OK If I Call You Mine?'. Prominent among the cast were Paul McCrane, Gene Anthony Ray, Lee Carreri and Barry Miller as a slick and hip Puerto Rican. Produced by David De Silva and Alan Marshall, with a screenplay by Christopher Gore, *Fame* proved popular enough to inspire a spin-off television series, which in turn spawned more chart successes for *The Kids From Fame*. This played in more than 60 countries, and prompted De Silva to conceive and develop a version for the stage. He formed a new creative team that included composer Steven Margoshes, lyricist Jacques Levy, and librettist Jose Fernandez.

*Fame: The Musical* made its debut at the Coconut Grove Playhouse, Miami, on 21 October 1988. Despite positive audience reaction in Miami, and later, Philadelphia, a Broadway transfer fell through, but *Fame* subsequently proved a hit in Stockholm, Sweden and other European countries. West End audiences were introduced to the show at the Cambridge Theatre on 27 June 1995. Gore and Pitchford's title song was still in there, along with numbers such as 'Hard Work', 'I Want To Make Magic', 'Dance Class' (after Beethoven's 'Spring Sonata'), 'Can't Keep It Down', 'Tyrone's Rap', 'There She Goes', 'Let's Play A Love Scene', 'Bring On Tomorrow', 'The Teachers' Argument', 'Mabel's Prayer', 'Dancin' On The Sidewalk', 'These Are My Children' and 'In L.A.'. Loraine Velez played Carmen with dash and authority, and Sonia Swaby (Mabel) tore into the amusing 'Think Of Meryl Streep'. Also cast were Marcus D'Cruze (Joe), Scott Sherrin (Tyrone), Jonatha Aris (Schlomo), Richard Dempsey (Nick) and Gemma Wardle (Serena). Directed by Runa Borge and choreographed by Lars Bethke, *Fame* ran until 28 September 1996. The UK touring version called in on London's West End for Christmas seasons in 1997 and 1998, while elsewhere productions during 1998/9 were being forecast for Toronto, Paris, Sydney, Berlin, Chicago, Warsaw, Tokyo, Vienna, Oslo, Munich, Caracas, Milan, Budapest, Montreal and Los Angeles.

## FARLEY JACKMASTER FUNK

The resident DJ at Chicago's Playground between 1981 and 1987 (often combining live drum machine with his selection of Philly soul and R&B), Farley was also one of the earliest house producers, with 'Yellow House' being the first record on Dance Mania Records. He was also a key component of the Hot Mix 5, the DJ group which provided Chicago's WBMX radio station with its groundbreaking mix shows. As Chicago backroom boy Mike 'Hitman' Wilson once stated: 'To me Farley started house. Because while Frankie [Knuckles] had an audience of 600, Farley reached 150,000 listeners.' He had a hit in 1986 with a cover version of 'Love Can't Turn Around', with a vocal from Greater Tabernacle Baptist Choir's Daryl Pandy (although this actually hijacked a Steve 'Silk' Hurley song). Other notable releases include 'Aw Shucks', 'As Always' (with Ricky Dillard) and 'Free At Last' (with the Hip House Syndicate). When WBMX went off air his career ground to a halt, an intermission he occupied by exploring rap and R&B. He returned to DJing in England in the 90s, where his reputation had not diminished, and started a new Chill-London label.

## FARMERS BOYS

Along with the Higsons, the Farmers Boys emerged from Norwich, Norfolk, England, in the early 80s with an amusing brand of wacky guitar pop. Baz, Frog, Mark and Stan (they never used surnames) issued the excellent 'Whatever Is He Like?' (on the Backs label) in the summer. On the follow-up 'More Than A Dream' (also on Backs), the band veered towards country and western, a formula successful enough to warrant its reissue as the Farmers Boys' first single for EMI Records. 'Muck It Out', issued in early 1983, played on the band's rural name in the search for a novelty hit, but chart success was something that would always elude them. The band's debut album appeared in the autumn, but despite charm and melodic strength (exemplified by the catchy single 'For You') *Get Out & Walk* could not sustain the impact of their singles over two sides. 'Apparently', issued in the late spring of 1984, benefited from the band's horn section of Andrew Hamilton (saxophone), Noel Harris (trumpet) and John Beecham (trombone), while a cover version of Cliff Richard's 'In The Country' became the closest thing to a Farmers Boys hit in August. However, after the release of the excellent 'I Built The World' early in 1985, the writing was on the wall and the band split up soon afterwards. After a long hiatus, Baz, Mark and Stan reconvened as the Great Outdoors in the late 90s to record two singles for the Fierce Panda label. A new album followed on the revived Backs label in 2001.
● ALBUMS: *Get Out & Walk* (EMI 1983) ★★★, *With These Hands* (EMI 1985) ★★★.

## FAT BOYS

From the Bronx, New York City, New York, USA, the Fat Boys were originally known as the Disco 3, before deciding to trade in the appellation in exchange for something more gimmicky. The bulk of their material dealt with just that, emphasizing their size, and did little to avert the widely held perception of them as a novelty act. The trio consisted of Darren 'The Human Beatbox/Buff Love' Robinson (b. 1968, New York, USA, d. 10 December 1995), Mark 'Prince Markie Dee' Morales, and Damon 'Kool Rockski' Wimbley. They were discovered by Charlie Stetler (later manager of MTV's Dr. Dre and Ed Lover), whose interest was aroused by Robinson's amazing talent for rhythmic improvization, effectively using his face as an instrument. It was Stetler who suggested they take the name-change, after winning a nationwide talent contest at Radio City Music Hall in 1983. Legend has it that this was prompted during an early European tour when Stetler was presented with a bill of $350 for 'extra breakfasts'.

The initial run of records were produced by Kurtis Blow, and largely discussed the size of the group's appetites. All their LPs for Sutra offered a consistent diet (a phrase not otherwise within the Fat Boy lexicon) of rock, reggae and hip-hop textures, with able if uninspiring raps. Their fortunes improved significantly once they signed up with Polydor Records, however. *Crushin'* is probably their best album, crammed with party anecdotes that stand up to repeated listening better than most of their material. It yielded a major hit with the Beach Boys on 'Wipe Out' in 1987. One year and one album later they scored with another collaboration, this time with Chubby Checker on 'The Twist (Yo' Twist)'. It peaked at number 2 in the UK chart, the highest position at the time for a rap record. In truth the Fat Boys had become more pop than hip-hop, though the process of revamping rock 'n' roll chestnuts had begun as far back as 1984 with 'Jailhouse Rock'. Also contained on *Coming Back Hard Again* was a strange version of 'Louie Louie' and 'Are You Ready For Freddy', used as the theme song for one of the *Nightmare On Elm Street* films. They also starred in another movie, *Disorderlies*, after appearing with Checker as part of Nelson Mandela's 70th Birthday Party at Wembley Stadium in June 1988 (they had previously been the only rap participants at Live Aid).

The decade closed with the release of *On And On*. It proved a hugely disappointing set, overshadowed by its 'concept' of being a 'rappera', and offering a lukewarm adaptation of gangsta concerns. News broke in the 90s of a $6 million lawsuit filed against their former record company, while Robinson was put on trial in Pennsylvania for 'sexual abuse of a minor'. Prince Markie Dee went on to a solo career, recording an album as Prince Markie Dee And The Soul Convention. He also produced and wrote for Mary J. Blige, Christopher Williams, Father, El DeBarge, Trey Lorenz and others. Their career never recovered from the bad press after Robinson was found guilty and the Fat Boys' true legacy remains firmly in the era of rap party records, Swatch television ads and cameo appearances on television's *Miami Vice*. Robinson died in 1995 after a cardiac arrest following a bout of respiratory flu.

● ALBUMS: *Fat Boys* (Sutra 1984) ★★★, *The Fat Boys Are Back!* (Sutra 1985) ★★★, *Big & Beautiful* (Sutra 1986) ★★★, *Cruisin'* (Tin Pan Apple/Polydor 1987) ★★★★, *Coming Back Hard Again* (Tin Pan Apple/Polydor 1988) ★★★, *On And On* (Tin Pan Apple/Mercury 1989) ★★.
Solo: Prince Markie Dee *Free* (Columbia 1992) ★★.
● COMPILATIONS: *The Best Part Of The Fat Boys* (Sutra 1987) ★★★, *Krush On You* (Blatant 1988) ★★, *All Meat No Filler!* (Rhino 1997) ★★★.

## FAT LARRY'S BAND

'Fat' Larry James (b. 2 August 1949, Philadelphia, Pennsylvania, USA, d. 5 December 1987; drums) formed this funk/disco outfit in Philadelphia following his spell as a back-up musician for the Delfonics and Blue Magic. The group comprised Art Capehart (trumpet, flute), Jimmy Lee (trombone, saxophone), Doug Jones (saxophone), Erskine Williams (keyboards), Ted Cohen (guitar), Larry LaBes (bass), Darryl Grant (percussion). James found success easier in the UK than in his homeland, having a Top 40 hit with 'Center City' in 1977, and in 1979 achieving a Top 50 with 'Boogie Town' under the title of FLB. That same year, one of James' other projects, the studio group Slick, had two UK hit singles with 'Space Bass' and 'Sexy Cream'. These two releases established them with the disco market. However, it was not until 1982 that the group secured a major national hit, with a recording of the Commodores' song 'Zoom' taking them to number 2 in the UK charts, although it only managed to scrape into the US soul chart at 89. It proved, however, to be their last success of any note, and hope of a regeneration was cut short on their founder's death in 1987.

● ALBUMS: *Feel It* (WMOT 1977) ★★★, *Off The Wall* (Stax 1978) ★★★, *Lookin' For Love* (Fantasy 1979) ★★, *Stand Up* (Fantasy 1980) ★★, *Breakin' Out* (WMOT 1982) ★★★, *Straight From The Heart* (WMOT 1983) ★★, *Nice* (Omni 1986) ★★.
● COMPILATIONS: *Bright City Lights* (Fantasy 1980) ★★, *The Best Of Fat Larry's Band* (WMOT 1994) ★★★, *Close Encounters Of A Funky Kind* (Southbound/Ace 1995) ★★★.

## FEELIES

Formed in New Jersey, USA in 1976, the Feelies originally comprised Glenn Mercer (b. Haledon, New Jersey, USA; lead guitar, vocals), Bill Million (b. William Clayton, Haledon, New Jersey, USA; rhythm guitar, vocals), Keith DeNunzio aka Keith Clayton (b. 27 April 1958, Reading, Pennsylvania, USA; bass) and Dave Weckerman (drums). Weckerman departed from the line-up and was replaced by Vinny DeNuzio (b. 15 August 1956), and this new line-up began making a name for themselves on New York's club circuit. DeNuzio was replaced by Anton Fier prior to the band's 1980 debut, *Crazy Rhythms*. This exceptional release brought to mind the jerky paranoia of an early Talking Heads and the compulsion of the Velvet Underground, while at the same time it established the Feelies' polyrhythmic pulsebeats and Mercer's scratchy but effective guitar work.

Despite critical acclaim, *Crazy Rhythms* was a commercial failure and the band fizzled out. Fier subsequently formed the Golden Palaminos, an *ad hoc* unit featuring contributions from various musicians. Mercer and Million then embarked on several diverse projects (as well as contributing the soundtrack to *Smithereens*), which included work with three different groups: the Trypes, the Willies and Yung Wu. Mercer and Million reactivated the Feelies name in 1983, and were joined by a returning Weckerman and two of their Willies associates, Stanley Demeski (drums) and Brenda Sauter (bass). With Weckerman switching to percussion, the re-formation was complete. The Feelies' second album, *The Good Earth*, was produced by R.E.M. guitarist Peter Buck, a long-time fan of *Crazy Rhythms*. Despite the gap between the releases, the new quintet showed much of the same fire and purpose, a factor confirmed by the albums *Only Life* and *Time For A Witness* (distributed by A&M Records). The Feelies split up again in 1991, with Mercer and Weckerman forming Wake Ooloo and then Sunburst, and Demeski going on to play with Dean Wareham's Luna. They remain one of America's most inventive post-punk ensembles.

● ALBUMS: *Crazy Rhythms* (Stiff 1980) ★★★★, *The Good Earth* (Coyote/Twin/Tone 1986) ★★★★, *Only Life* (Coyote/A&M 1988) ★★★, *Time For A Witness* (Coyote/A&M 1991) ★★★.

### FELT

Cultivated, experimental English pop outfit formed in 1980 whose guru was the enigmatic Lawrence Hayward (b. Birmingham, West Midlands, England; vocals, guitar). Early collaborators included Maurice Deebank (guitar) and Nick Gilbert (bass), who practised together in a small village called Water Orton just outside Birmingham. By the time of their first album, released on Cherry Red Records, drummer Tony Race was replaced by Gary Ainge, and Gilbert departed to be replaced on bass by Mick Lloyd. Martin Duffy joined on organ for *Ignite The Seven Cannons*. Cult status had already arrived with the archetypal Felt cut 'Penelope Tree'. The critical respect they were afforded continued, although they enjoyed little in the way of commercial recognition. The nearest they came was the 1985 single 'Primitive Painters', where they were joined by Elizabeth Fraser of the Cocteau Twins in a stirring, pristine pop song produced by fellow Cocteau Robin Guthrie.

They signed to Creation Records in 1985. However, as Felt's contract with Cherry Red expired, so did the tenure of Hayward's fellow guitarist and co-writer, Deebank. The latter, classically trained, had been an important component of the Felt sound, and was chiefly responsible for the delicate but intoxicating drama of early releases. Their stay at Creation saw high points in *Forever Breathes The Lonely Word* (1986) and *Poem Of The River* (1987). On the latter they were joined by Marco Thomas, Tony Willé and Neil Scott to add to the melodic guitar broadside. Felt bowed out with *Me And A Monkey On The Moon*, after a final move to Él Records, at which time guitar duties had switched to John Mohan.

By the end of the 80s the band were no more, having achieved their stated task of surviving 10 years, 10 singles and 10 albums (*Bubblegum Perfume* is an archive release of their Creation material, *The Felt Box Set* compiles their Cherry Red recordings). Hayward chose to concentrate on his new project, 70s revivalists Denim. Duffy joined Primal Scream, while Ainge and Thomas formed Italian Paper and then Fly.

● ALBUMS: *Crumbling The Antiseptic Beauty* mini-album (Cherry Red 1982) ★★★, *The Splendour Of Fear* mini-album (Cherry Red 1983) ★★★, *The Strange Idols Pattern And Other Short Stories* (Cherry Red 1984) ★★★, *Ignite The Seven Cannons* (Cherry Red 1985) ★★★, *Let The Snakes Crinkle Their Heads To Death* (Creation 1986) ★★★, *Forever Breathes The Lonely Word* (Creation 1986) ★★★★, *Poem Of The River* (Creation 1987) ★★★, *The Pictorial Jackson Review* (Creation 1988) ★★★, *Train Above The City* (Creation 1988) ★★★, *Me And A Monkey On The Moon* (Él 1989) ★★.

● COMPILATIONS: *Gold Mine Trash* (Cherry Red 1987) ★★★, *Bubblegum Perfume* (Creation 1990) ★★★★, *Absolute Classic Masterpieces Volume 2* (Creation 1993) ★★★, *The Felt Box Set* 4-CD box set (Cherry Red 1993) ★★★★.

### FIELDS OF THE NEPHILIM

This UK rock band was formed in Stevenage, Hertfordshire, in 1983. The line-up comprised Carl McCoy (vocals), Tony Pettitt (bass), Peter Yates (keyboards) and the Wright brothers, Nod (b. Alexander; drums) and Paul (guitar). Their image, that of neo-western desperados, was borrowed from movies such as *Once Upon A Time In the West* and *The Long Ryders*. They also had a bizarre habit of smothering their predominantly black clothes in flour and/or talcum powder for some of the most hysterically inept videos ever recorded. Their version of goth-rock, tempered with transatlantic overtones, found favour with those already immersed in the sounds of the Sisters Of Mercy and the Mission. Signed to the Situation Two label, Fields Of The Nephilim had two major UK independent hit singles with 'Preacher Man' and 'Blue Water', while their first album, *Dawnrazor*, made a modest showing on the UK album chart. The second set, *The Nephilim*, reached number 14, announcing the band's arrival as one of the principal rock acts of the day. Their devoted following also ensured a showing on the national singles chart, giving them minor hits with 'Moonchild' (also an independent chart number 1), 'Psychonaut' and 'Summerland (Dreamed)'. In October 1991, McCoy left the group, taking the 'Fields Of The Nephilim' name with him. The remaining members vowed to carry on. With the recruitment of a new vocalist, Alan Delaney, they began gigging under the name Rubicon in the summer of 1992, leaving McCoy to unveil his version of the Nephilim (renamed Nefilim). Rubicon released two albums on Beggars Banquet Records (1993's *What Starts, Ends* and 1995's *Room 101*) before disbanding. They joined in the goth-rock revival by re-forming in the late 90s.

● ALBUMS: *Dawnrazor* (Situation 2 1987) ★★, *The Nephilim* (Situation 2 1988) ★★★, *Elizium* (Beggars Banquet 1990) ★★, *Earth Inferno* (Beggars Banquet 1991) ★★, *BBC Radio 1 In Concert* (Windsong 1992) ★★, *Revelations* (Beggars Banquet 1993) ★★.

● COMPILATIONS: *From Gehenna To Here* (Jungle 2001) ★★.

● VIDEOS: *Forever Remain* (Situation 2 1988), *Morphic Fields* (Situation 2 1989), *Earth Inferno* (Beggars Banquet 1991), *Visionary Heads* (Beggars Banquet 1992), *Revelations* (Beggars Banquet 1993).

### FINE YOUNG CANNIBALS

This sophisticated English pop trio from the Midlands appeared after the demise of the Beat in 1983. Former members Andy Cox (b. 25 January 1960, Birmingham, England; guitar) and David Steele (b. 8 September 1960, Isle of Wight, England; bass/keyboards) invited Roland Gift (b. 28 April

1961, Birmingham, England; vocals, ex-Acrylic Victims and actor for the Hull Community Theatre) to relinquish his tenure in a London blues combo to join them. Taking their name from the Robert Wagner movie of similar name (relinquishing the 'All The' prefix), the trio was quickly picked up by London Records after a video screening on the UK music television show *The Tube*. 'Johnny Come Home' was soon released on single, with the band joined on percussion by Martin Parry and on trumpet by Graeme Hamilton. Dominated by Gift's sparse and yearning vocal, it reached the UK Top 10 in June 1985 and defined the band's sound for years to come. The follow-up 'Blue' set out an early political agenda for the band, attacking Conservative Government policy and its effects.

After the band's debut album rose to UK number 11, the first of a series of distinctive cover versions emerged with the UK Top 10 single 'Suspicious Minds'. Backing vocals were handled by Jimmy Somerville. It was followed by a surprise, and radical, rendition of 'Ever Fallen In Love', which the Buzzcocks' Steve Diggle claimed he preferred to his band's original. Meanwhile Gift's parallel acting career got under way with the parochial *Sammy And Rosie Get Laid*, after all three members of the band had appeared in the previous year's *Tin Men*. While Gift's commitments continued Cox and Steele became involved in the release of an opportunistic house cut, 'I'm Tired Of Being Pushed Around', under the title Two Men, A Drum Machine And A Trumpet. On the back of regular club airings it became a surprise Top 20 hit in February 1988. More importantly, it attracted the interest of several dance music acts who would seek out the duo for remixes, including Wee Papa Girl Rappers and Pop Will Eat Itself.

Before the unveiling of Gift's latest film, *Scandal*, the band scored their biggest hit to date with 'She Drives Me Crazy', a US number 1 single. The second album duly followed, featuring cultivated soul ballads to complement further material of a politically direct nature. It would top the charts on both sides of the Atlantic. Of the five singles taken from the album 'Good Thing' was the most successful, claiming a second US number 1. In 1990 they won both Best British Group and Best Album categories at the BRIT Awards, but felt compelled to return them because: '. . . it is wrong and inappropriate for us to be associated with what amounts to a photo opportunity for Margaret Thatcher and the Conservative Party'. It led to a predictable backlash in the right-wing tabloid press.

In 1990 Gift appeared in Hull Truck's *Romeo And Juliet* stage performance, and left Cox and Steele to work on a remixed version of *The Raw And The Cooked*. Still with the ability to bounce back after long pauses, the band's 1996 compilation included new track 'The Flame'. Gift began performing solo in the late 90s and issued a solo album in 2002.

● ALBUMS: *Fine Young Cannibals* (London 1985) ★★★, *The Raw And The Cooked* (London 1989) ★★★★, *The Raw And The Remix* (London 1990) ★★★.
● COMPILATIONS: *The Finest* (London 1996) ★★★★.
● VIDEOS: *The Finest* (London 1996).
● FURTHER READING: *The Sweet And The Sour: The Fine Young Cannibals' Story*, Brian Edge.

## FINITRIBE

Scottish dance music unit, who shared the same One Little Indian label as their fellow countrymen the Shamen, but failed to replicate their success. It was not through want of effort, or, for that matter, talent. The band took their name from 'Finny Tribe', a name given to the entire fish species by Irish religious sect the Rosicrucians, as well as by the common people of that country. Originally a six-piece formed in Edinburgh in 1984, they founded their own label, striking out with a debut EP, *Curling And Stretching*, in October. One month later they played their first gig together supporting Danielle Dax at London ULU. By 1986, they had acquired their first sampler, and released 'DeTestimony', an influential cut in both the Balearic and, later, house movements. The following year they began an ill-fated liaison with Chicago's Wax Trax! Records, releasing a version of Can's 'I Want More'. Following problems with the label, vocalist Chris Connelly eventually elected to remain, ostensibly as part of Ministry and Revolting Cocks, but also recording solo.

Finitribe re-emerged in 1989 with the curtailed line-up of Mr Samples (b. John William Vick, 6 November 1965, Edinburgh, Scotland), Philip Pinsky (b. Philip David Pinsky, 23 March 1965, Appleton, Wisconsin, USA) and David Miller (b. David Francis Ashbride Miller, 20 July 1962, Moffat, Dunfrewshire, Scotland). Vick and Pinsky had previously been colleagues in Rigor Mortis and Miller had served in Explode Your Heart. Their influences remained both traditional rock and indie giants (Dog Faced Hermans, Magazine) and a myriad of new and old dance innovators (Jah Wobble, Tackhead, Sparks, Sub Sub, Orbital). A succession of well-regarded releases on One Little Indian failed to deliver them much in the way of commercial reward. The first and most notable of these was the acidic 'Animal Farm', which sampled the 'Old McDonald' nursery rhyme and laid torrents of abuse at the door of the McDonald's hamburger chain. The ensuing fuss, hardly deflated by a 'Fuck Off McDonald's' poster campaign, brought the band significant media exposure for the first time.

Entering the 90s, they looked as though they might expand beyond cult tastes with a new, kitsch image (white boiler suits peppered with stars) and more pop-dance-orientated material. As critics pointed out, they resembled an underground version of the Pet Shop Boys. By 1992, they had resurrected the Finiflex label and opened their own studio complex in Leith. Reduced to a nucleus of Miller and new vocalist Katy Morrison, Finitribe released a new studio album (*Sleazy Listening*) in 1998.

● ALBUMS: *Noise Lust And Fun* (Finiflex 1988) ★★★, *Grossing 10K* (One Little Indian 1990) ★★★, *An Unexpected Groovy Treat* (One Little Indian 1992) ★★★, *Sheigra* (London 1995) ★★, *Sleazy Listening* (Infectious 1998) ★★★.

## FINN, TIM

b. 25 June 1952, Te Awamutu, New Zealand. As lead singer of the New Zealand band Split Enz, Finn was soon recognized as a major songwriter and vocalist with a very distinctive singing voice. Even before the dissolution of the band in 1985, he had recorded his first solo album, *Escapade,* on A&M Records, which became the Top Album of 1983 in Australia. It featured the singles, 'Fraction Too Much Friction', 'Made My Day' and 'Staring At The Embers', all excellent melodic pop tunes. The set also made a minor impact on the US charts. However, despite a high budget and more emphasis on production, his follow-up albums were not internationally successful. Moving from A&M to Virgin Records in 1985, he released *Big Canoe,* but the concentration on production buried his songs under layers of sound and the melodies were lost. A move to Capitol Records resulted in a critically acclaimed, self-titled third album, but commercial success continued to elude him. However, the switch to Capitol made it possible for Finn to join stablemates Crowded House in 1991 – the band formed by his brother Neil after the break-up of Split Enz six years earlier.

After achieving international success with Crowded House following the release of *Woodface,* which had originally been mooted as a one-off project helmed by the brothers, Tim elected to return to a solo career in 1992. *Before & After,* inspired by his two-week sojourn in the Blue Mountains of Australia, utilized two tracks the Finn brothers were working on during the sessions for *Woodface,* and also boasted the services of guest contributors Andy White and Liam O Maonlai (Hothouse Flowers). Tim briefly reunited with his brother on the Finn project in 1995 and worked with White and O Maonlai in Alt. After appearing with Split Enz in December 1999 for two reunion concerts in Auckland, Finn self-released his fifth album, *Say It Is So,* which was recorded in Nashville and Sydney. His brother was featured as one of the core musicians.

● ALBUMS: *Escapade* (A&M 1983) ★★★★, *Big Canoe* (Virgin 1986) ★★, *Tim Finn* (Capitol 1989) ★★★, *Before & After* (Capitol 1993) ★★★, *Say It Is So* (What Are?/Hypertension 2000) ★★★, *Feeding The Gods* (What Are? 2001) ★★★.

## FIRE ENGINES

Alongside fellow Postcard Records bands such as Orange Juice and Josef K, the Fire Engines were part of a burgeoning Scottish music scene in the early 80s. Formed in 1979 by Davey Henderson (vocals, guitar), Murray Slade (guitar), Russell Burn (drums, percussion) and Graham Main (bass), the band's debut surfaced on independent label Codex Communications, in late 1980. 'Get Up And Use Me' was a manic burst of estranged, frenetically delivered guitar broken by sharp vocal outbursts. It also cut through the surrounding tendency for dense, synthesized sounds or second-rate punk. The band received considerable promotion in the music press and was strongly tipped for success by the *New Musical Express. Lubricate Your Living Room (Background Music For Action People!),* a mini-album's

worth of near-instrumentals on the Accessory label, contained a similar barrage of awkward, angular funk guitar riffs. By spring 1981, the band had signed with aspiring Scottish label Pop: Aural, releasing the excellent 'Candy Skin'. More overtly pop (Henderson's nasal tones were to the forefront for the first time), the single was backed by 'Meat Whiplash', a superb slab of nasty, breakneck guitar work conflicting with an aggressive drum rhythm. By comparison, 'Big Gold Dream' (1981) was relatively melodic, perhaps in an attempt to reach a wider audience. It failed, although all the Fire Engines' product fared well in independent terms, and it was to be the band's last release. Ideologically, the Fire Engines tapped a similar aesthetic to Josef K, fuelled by a vehement hatred of 'rock' in the general sense and the realization that punk's spirit of innovation had to be continued. Both bands remained true to that ethic, imploding rather than growing stale. Henderson went on to form Win, managed by Postcard founder Alan Horne, then Nectarine No.9.

● ALBUMS: *Lubricate Your Living Room (Background Music For Action People!)* (Pop: Aural 1981) ★★★.
● COMPILATIONS: *Fond* (Creation 1992) ★★★.

## FIREHOSE

This propulsive US hardcore trio (usually titled fIREHOSE) was formed by two ex-members of the Minutemen, Mike Watt (vocals, bass) and George Hurley (drums), following the death of the latter band's founding guitarist, David Boon, in 1985. Ed Crawford aka eD fROMOHIO, completed the new venture's line-up, which made its debut in 1986 with the impressive *Ragin', Full-On.* Although undeniably powerful, the material Firehose offered was less explicit than that of its predecessor, and showed a greater emphasis on melody rather than bluster. Successive releases, *If'n* and *fROMOHIO,* revealed a band that, although bedevilled by inconsistency, was nonetheless capable of inventive, exciting music. At their best, these songs merged knowing sarcasm (see 'For The Singer Of R.E.M.') with an unreconstructed approach to music making (as on drum solo 'Let The Drummer Have Some'). In 1989, Watt and Hurley also collaborated with Elliott Sharp on the *avant garde Bootstrappers* project. The band's variety argued against commercial fortune, but they were still picked up by a major, Columbia Records, in 1991, who released the slightly more disciplined *Flyin' The Flannel* that year. Following the disappointing critical and commercial response to *Mr. Machinery Operator,* the band decided to call it a day in 1995, with Watt having already begun a solo career.

● ALBUMS: *Ragin', Full-On* (SST 1986) ★★★, *If'n* (SST 1987) ★★, *fROMOHIO* (SST 1989) ★★★, *Flyin' The Flannel* (Columbia 1991) ★★★, *Live Totem Pole* mini-album (Columbia 1992) ★★, *Mr. Machinery Operator* (Columbia 1993) ★★.

## FIRM

It seemed to be a marriage made in heaven when ex-Led Zeppelin guitarist Jimmy Page (b. James Patrick Page, 9 January 1944, Heston, Middlesex,

England) and former Free/Bad Company vocalist Paul Rodgers (b. 17 December 1949, Middlesbrough, Cleveland, England) began working together as the Firm in 1984. Enlisting ex-Uriah Heep/Manfred Mann drummer Chris Slade (b. 30 October 1946) and virtual unknown Tony Franklin on bass (an acquaintance of Page's from work with Roy Harper), the partnership never quite gelled in a manner that matched either protagonist's earlier achievements. However, the band was not without musical merit, with Slade's precise backbeat providing a solid base for Page and the stylish Franklin. On *The Firm*, Rodgers was in fine voice on varied material, from the lengthy and Zeppelinesque 'Midnight Moonlight' to the more commercial strains of 'Radioactive', which was a minor hit, plus a cover version of 'You've Lost That Loving Feeling'. Live dates proved successful, with Page producing his customary show-stopping solo spot, replete with laser effects, although neither Page nor Rodgers were willing to reprise their previous work. *Mean Business* continued in the warm, understated and bluesy style of the debut, but failed to raise the band to new heights, and the Firm split after the subsequent world tour. Page and Rodgers returned to their respective solo careers, while Slade joined AC/DC and Franklin teamed up with John Sykes in Blue Murder.
● ALBUMS: *The Firm* (Atlantic 1985) ★★★, *Mean Business* (Atlantic 1986) ★★★.

## FISHER, MORGAN
Beginning his apprenticeship with the Love Affair and then Mott The Hoople as a pianist in 1973, initially only for live appearances, Fisher went on to form the abbreviated Mott in May 1975 with Dale Griffin and Overend Watts. They were completed by new members Ray Major and Nigel Benjamin, becoming the British Lions in May 1977 with John Fidler (ex-Medicine Head) replacing Benjamin. After two albums they split in the late 70s, and Fisher produced two albums for Cherry Red Records as Hybrid Kids (*A Collection Of Classic Mutants* and *Claws*). The first of these was supposedly filled by unknown new wave acts doing cover versions, but was actually Fisher and a few cronies. The tracks included Jah Wurzel's (Jah Wobble meets the Wurzels) 'Wuthering Heights', British Standard Unit's 'Do Ya Think I'm Sexy', the Burton's 'MacArthur Park', and a new version of 'All The Young Dudes'. Another 'concept' album, *Miniatures*, came out on Fisher's own Pipe label, and featured various artists doing songs less than a minute long. Included among the 51 tracks are Dave Vanian (Damned), John Otway, Andy Partridge (XTC), Robert Wyatt, George Melly, the Residents and David Cunningham. The album was later reissued on micro-cassette, presumably suitable solely for playing on dictaphones. Fisher continued to record for Cherry Red throughout the 80s, later relocating to Japan where he changed his name to Veetdharm.
● ALBUMS: with Lol Coxhill *Slow Music* (Voiceprint 1980) ★★★, *A Collection Of Classic Mutants* (Cherry Red 1980) ★★★, *Miniatures* (Pipe 1980) ★★★, *Claws* (Cherry Red 1982) ★★★, *Seasons* (Cherry Red 1983)

★★★, *Look At Life* (Cherry Red 1984) ★★★, *Ivories* (Cherry Red 1987) ★★★.

## FIVE STAR
This commercial pop act was formed by the five siblings of the Pearson family, all of whom shared vocal duties and were born in Romford, Essex, England; Deniece (b. 13 June 1968), Doris (b. 8 June 1966), Lorraine (b. 10 August 1967), Stedman (b. 29 June 1964) and Delroy (b. 11 April 1970). Their father, Buster, had been a professional guitarist with a variety of acts including Wilson Pickett, Desmond Dekker and Jimmy Cliff. After his retirement from the live circuit he formed reggae label K&B, then the more commercially disposed Tent Records. His daughters persuaded him to let them record a version of his recently written composition, 'Problematic'. It showed promise and he decided to throw his weight behind their career as manager, while the brothers elected to expand the group to a five-piece. Although 'Problematic' failed to chart, Buster secured a licensing agreement for Tent with RCA Records, but follow-ups 'Hide And Seek' and 'Crazy' also missed out. However, when Nick Martinelli took over production duties, 1985's 'All Fall Down' reached the charts. Heavy promotion, and the group's choreographed dance routines, ensured that next single, 'Let Me Be The One', followed it into the Top 20. By the time the band's debut album was released, they had worked through six different producers and countless studios. Despite the relative disappointment of chart placings for subsequent singles 'Love Take Over' and 'R.S.V.P.', the band departed for a major US promotional tour. The Walt Disney organization immediately stepped in to offer the band their show, but Buster declined. Back in the UK, 'System Addict', the seventh single milked from *Luxury Of Life*, became the first to break the Top 10. Both 'Can't Wait Another Minute' and 'Find The Time' repeated the feat, before the band acquired the sponsorship of Crunchie Chocolate Bars for their UK tour. Their next outings would attract the sponsorship of Ultrabite toothpaste, much to the derision of critics who were less than enamoured by their 'squeaky clean' image.
Meanwhile, *Silk And Steel*, the second album, climbed slowly to the top of the UK charts. It would eventually earn triple platinum status, unleashing another steady stream of singles. The most successful of these, 'Rain And Shine', achieved their best placing in the singles chart, at number 2. Continued success allowed the family to move from Romford, Essex, to a mansion in Sunningdale, Berkshire, where they installed a massive studio complex. Ever a favourite for media attacks, Buster was variously accused of keeping his offspring in a 'palatial prison' and of spending wanton sums of money on trivia. However, as their records proved increasingly unsuccessful, the family was the subject of several media stories concerning their financial instability. These hit a peak when the band was forced to move from their home in 1990. Attempts to resurrect their career in America on Epic failed, with their fortunes hitting an all-time low in October 1991

when Stedman Pearson was fined for public indecency. Although their chart days appear to be over, they are still performing and are now based in California, reduced to a trio (Stedman, Deniece and Lorraine) and still managed by their father.

● ALBUMS: *Luxury Of Life* (Tent 1985) ★★, *Silk And Steel* (Tent 1986) ★★★, *Between The Lines* (Tent 1987) ★★, *Rock The World* (Tent 1988) ★★, *Five Star* (Tent 1990) ★★.

● COMPILATIONS: *Greatest Hits* (Tent 1989) ★★★.

## FIXX

This durable UK new wave band originally comprised Cy Curnin (13 December 1957; vocals/guitar), Adam Woods (b. 8 April 1953; drums), Rupert Greenall (keyboards), Jamie West-Oram (guitar) and Charlie Barret (bass). They formed at the turn of the 80s when college friends Curnin and Woods made the decision to pursue music as a full-time vocation. After advertising in the music press for new members, the band released a 'one off' single for Ariola Records 'Hazards In The Home' credited as 'The Portraits'. A year later with a more complete line-up, they changed their name to the Fixx, and recorded the quirky 'Lost Planes' which led to the band's signing with MCA Records. Their debut album *Shuttered Room* remained on the US album chart for over a year, but UK reaction was less than enthusiastic and the album and subsequent releases suffered the same fate in their home country. *Reach The Beach* was released in 1983 and earned platinum status in the US, and marked the recording debut of Dan K. Brown, who had replaced Barret.

In 1984, the Fixx's contribution to the soundtrack of the movie *Streets Of Fire* was arguably the most interesting. Further success followed with a string of single and album hits in America and Europe, with the band proving themselves to be musicians able to maintain credibility and longevity through a willingness to change with the times without compromising their creative vision. Their commercial fortunes had declined by the late 80s. Following the critical backlash that greeted 1991's dance-orientated *Ink* the band remained quiet for several years. They returned to the studio in the late 90s.

● ALBUMS: *Shuttered Room* (MCA 1982) ★★★, *Reach The Beach* (MCA 1983) ★★★, *Phantoms* (MCA 1984) ★★★, *Walkabout* (MCA 1986) ★★★, *React* (MCA 1987) ★★, *Calm Animals* (RCA 1988) ★★, *Ink* (MCA 1991) ★★, *Elemental* (CMC International 1998) ★★★, *1011 Woodland* (CMC International 1999) ★★.

● COMPILATIONS: *One Thing Leads To Another: Greatest Hits* (MCA 1989) ★★★★, *The Ultimate Collection* (Hip-O 1999) ★★★, *The Best Of Fixx: The Millennium Collection* (MCA 2000) ★★★★, *Happy Landings & Lost Tracks* (Beyond 2001) ★★★.

## FLAMING LIPS

Formed in Oklahoma City, Oklahoma, USA, the Flaming Lips won a deserved reputation in the 80s and 90s for their discordant, psychedelia-tinged garage rock, and have recorded a fine body of off-kilter and unpredictable work. They are led by lyricist, vocalist and guitarist Wayne Coyne (b. Wayne Ruby Coyne, 17 March 1965, Pittsburgh, Pennsylvania, USA), who started playing music during his high school days. Coyne was joined in the band by his brother, Mark Coyne, who is best remembered for his vocals on the debut album's 'My Own Planet'. Taking up the microphone following his brother's departure, Wayne Coyne fronted a line-up completed by Steven Drozd (b. Steven Gregory Drozd, 6 December 1969, Houston, Texas, USA; drums/vocals, replacing Richard English and Nathan Roberts), Ron Jones (b. Ronald Lee Jones, 26 November 1970, Angeles, Philippines; guitars/vocals) and Michael Ivins (b. Michael Lee Ivins, 17 March 1965, Omaha, Nebraska, USA; bass/vocals). John 'Dingus' Donahue, of Mercury Rev fame, was also a member during the sessions for *In A Priest Driven Ambulance*.

In 1993, they played at the Reading Festival in the UK and toured with Porno For Pyros, Butthole Surfers and Stone Temple Pilots. They returned to Reading in 1994 to support the release of 'She Don't Use Jelly', which finally took off on MTV over the following year. This, combined with a storming appearance on the second stage at Lollapalooza, at last helped to build a substantial popular as well as critical following. A two-year break preceded the release of *Clouds Taste Metallic*, their seventh album, a typically confusing but arresting exercise in wide-eyed, skewed pop rock, akin to a restrained Pavement. Song titles such as 'Guy Who Got A Headache And Accidentally Saved The World' and 'Psychiatric Explorations Of The Fetus With Needles' continued the penchant for adolescent shock value. Guitarist Jones departed shortly after the album was released. Reduced to a trio, the band returned with *Zaireeka*, a defiantly uncommercial 'experiment in listener participation, using multiple sound sources', whereby four separate CDs needed to be played simultaneously to hear the final mix. *The Soft Bulletin* and *Yoshimi Battles The Pink Robots* were far more satisfying records, representing the perfect fusion of the band's experimental urges and pop instincts.

● ALBUMS: *The Flaming Lips* (Lovely Sorts Of Death 1985) ★★★, *Hear It Is* (Pink Dust 1986) ★★★, *Oh My Gawd!!! ...The Flaming Lips* (Restless 1987) ★★★, *Telepathic Surgery* (Restless 1988) ★★, *Live* cassette only (Lovely Sorts Of Death 1989) ★★, *In A Priest Driven Ambulance* (Restless 1990) ★★★, *Hit To Death In The Future Head* (Warners 1992) ★★★, *Transmissions From The Satellite Heart* (Warners 1993) ★★★, *Providing Needles For Your Balloons* (Warners 1995) ★★, *Clouds Taste Metallic* (Warners 1995) ★★★★, *Zaireeka* 4-CD set (Warners 1998) ★★, *The Soft Bulletin* (Warners 1999) ★★★★, *Yoshimi Battles The Pink Robots* (Warners 2002) ★★★★.

● COMPILATIONS: *A Collection Of Songs Representing An Enthusiasm For Recording ... By Amateurs ... Or The Accidental Career* (Restless 1998) ★★★, *Finally, The Punk Rockers Are Taking Acid* (Restless 2002) ★★★, *The Day They Shot A Hole In The Jesus Egg* (Restless 2002) ★★★.

## FLASHDANCE

Alex Owens (Jennifer Beals) yearns to be a ballet star, and is encouraged and coached by former classical dancer, Hanna Long (Lilia Skala). However, until the real thing comes along, there is always the erotic disco dancing in the evening, and a day job working as a female welder in a Pittsburg factory. Nick (Michael Nouri), the foreman, is her boyfriend, and Alex puts a brick through his window just to remind him, after he has been seen with another girl (it was his sister). Life can be tough, but Hanna's death inspires Alex to pass the audition and finally achieve her dream. With a screenplay (Tom Hedley and Joe Eszterhas) like that, no wonder the critics saw this film as a series of rock videos, especially as it is full of slick, gaudy images (choreography: Jeffrey Hornaday) and a super-high energy score, composed mainly by Giorgio Moroder, one of the most successful and inventive dance music producers of the 80s. The numbers include 'Imagination' and 'Gloria' (performed by Laura Branigan), 'Flashdance ... What A Feeling' (Irene Cara), 'I'll Be Here Where The Heart Is' (Kim Carnes), 'Seduce Me Tonight' (Cycle V), 'Lady, Lady, Lady' (Joe Esposito), 'Manhunt' (Karen Kamon), 'Love Theme From Flashdance' (Helen St. John), 'Maniac' (Michael Sembello), 'He's A Dream' (Shandi), 'Romeo' (Donna Summer), 'It's Just Begun' (Jimmy Castor and the Jimmy Castor Bunch), 'I Love Rock 'N' Roll' (Joan Jett And The Blackhearts) and, somewhat incongruously, Hoagy Carmichael and Ned Washington's oldie 'The Nearness Of You'. Directed by Adrian Lyne and produced by PolyGram Records for Paramount in 1983, *Flashdance* was immensely successful worldwide, grossing over $36 million at the North American box office alone. The soundtrack album won a Grammy Award and spent 10 weeks at the top of the US chart, and there was another Grammy for Moroder's 'Love Theme From Flashdance'. Two number one singles, Irene Cara's 'Flashdance ... What A Feeling' and 'Maniac' sung by Michael Sembello, also came from the score, with the former song (lyric by Keith Forsey) winning an Oscar and other honours. Not surprisingly, there was a Worst Screenplay Razzie nomination for Hedley and Eszterhas.

## FLESH FOR LULU

This UK rock band was the creation of singer/guitarist Nick Marsh and drummer James Mitchell and took their name from an American cult movie. They were joined by Rocco Barker (ex-Wasted Youth) on guitar and Glen Bishop, replaced by Kevin Mills (ex-Specimen) on bass after the single 'Restless'. Derek Greening (keyboards, guitar) became the fifth member shortly afterwards, although he continued to play with his other band, Peter And The Test Tube Babies. Previously their debut single had been 'Roman Candle', prefacing a first album that they would 'rather forget about'. *Blue Sisters Swing*, on the tiny Hybrid label, followed as a stop-gap. The sleeve illustration of two nuns kissing resulted in bans in the USA and Europe. The release of *Big Fun City* was the first to do the band justice, even though it was hampered by artwork problems

at Polydor Records, and featured everything from country ballads to basic rock 'n' roll. Their succession of labels grew longer as they moved on to Beggars Banquet Records in 1986. *Long Live The New Flesh* followed a year later, recorded at Abbey Road Studios and produced by Mike Hedges. Their approach to the sophistication of their new surroundings was typical: 'Forget the cerebral approach – just turn up them guitars!' Their most pop-orientated album, *Plastic Fantastic*, was recorded in Australia by Mark Opitz, several titles from which were later employed for film soundtracks (*Uncle Buck* and *Flashback*). By this time, original members Marsh, Barking and Greening had been joined by Hans Perrson (drums) and Mike Steed (bass). Despite stronger songwriting than on previous recordings, the album failed and Beggars Banquet did not renew their option.
● ALBUMS: *Flesh For Lulu* (Polydor 1984) ★★, *Blue Sisters Swing* mini-album (Hybrid 1985) ★★, *Big Fun City* (Caroline 1985) ★★★, *Long Live The New Flesh* (Beggars Banquet 1987) ★★★, *Plastic Fantastic* (Beggars Banquet 1989) ★★★.

## FLESHEATERS

Innovative rock outfit built around cult hero Chris 'D' Desjardins (vocals), who had been active on the Los Angeles, California scene from the 70s, making movies and acting as well as co-ordinating the Flesheaters. Their first established line-up added Robyn Jameson (bass), Don Kirk (guitar), and Chris Wahl (drums). However, something of the nature of the band can be surmised by the frequency of its personnel shifts. Those passing through the ranks include: Bill Bateman (drums), Steve Berlin (saxophone), Gene Taylor (keyboards), John Bazz (bass), Dave Alvin (guitar), all ex-Blasters; Pat Garrett (guitar, bass), Joe Ramirez (bass), Joe Nanini (drums), all ex-Black Randy; John Doe (bass), D.J. Bonebrake (drums), Excene Cervenka (vocals), all ex-X. Stan Ridgway (Wall Of Voodoo; guitar) and Tito Larriva (Plugz; guitar) were also present in an early incarnation. These represent only a fraction of former members in a band that effectively operated in a 'pick up and play' mode. This did not diminish their appeal, however: 'The one thing that we do that mystifies our audience is we don't play in one category. The music that we play is real loud. Its real metallic. It could be described as heavy metal, or what was in 1977 punk.' Chris D split the band at the end of the 80s after the years of cut-and-paste line-ups finally took their toll. By the 90s, however, they were back on the circuit once more. *Dragstrip Riot*, with which Desjardins reinstated the band after years of inactivity, was a sprawling double album set that saw the band crashing out riotous swamp rock of a virulent, Cramps-type character. The intervening years had seen him operate with his own band, the Divine Horsemen, while Jameson also played with Alex Gibson and Passionel.
● ALBUMS: *No Questions Asked* (Upsetter 1979) ★★★, *A Minute To Pray, A Second To Die* (Ruby 1981) ★★★, *Forever Came Today* (Ruby 1982) ★★★, *A Hard Road To Follow* (Upsetter 1983) ★★★, *Dragstrip Riot* (SST 1991) ★★, *The Sex Diary Of Mr Vampire* (SST

1991) ★★★, *Ashes Of Time* (Upsetter 2001) ★★.
● COMPILATIONS: *Greatest Hits: Destroyed By Fire* (SST 1986) ★★★, *Prehistoric Fits* (SST 1990) ★★★.

## FLESHTONES
Formed in 1976 in the Queens district of New York City, the Fleshtones were first heard on British shores as part of a 'package' tour in 1980 with the dB's, the Raybeats and the Bush Tetras. Each band was different, drawing energy from punk but ideas from a myriad of other musical forms. In the Fleshtones' case, Keith Streng (guitar), Peter Zaremba (vocals, keyboards), Jan Marek Pukulski (bass) and Bill Milhizer (drums, ex-Harry Toledo Band and Action Combo), this involved the fusion of the new wave with R&B and rockabilly. The group caught the attention of Miles Copeland's I.R.S. Records label via 'American Beat', their debut single from 1979 on the Red Star label. The 12-inch EP *Up-Front* duly surfaced in 1980 in America, although it was not until 1981 that its strongest track, 'The Girl From Baltimore', secured a British release. It was followed by 'The World Has Changed' (though only in the USA), and 'Shadow-Line' in early 1982. This coincided not only with the band's first official long-player, *Roman Gods*, but also *Blast Off!*, a cassette of their unreleased 1978 studio album on Reach Out International (ROIR) Records.
All was comparatively quiet for over a year until the Fleshtones unleashed their best record, *Hexbreaker!*, promoted by two singles, 'Right Side Of A Good Thing' and the evocative 'Screaming Skull' (both 1983). The material shared the hard rock 'n' roll sound of *Roman Gods*, but the band soon curtailed their activities, apart from the strange *Fleshtones Vs Reality* set in 1987 and three live albums. Meanwhile, Streng collaborated with R.E.M.'s Peter Buck and most of the Fleshtones as the Full Time Men, and Zaremba released an album as the Love Delegation. However, the parent group was back on the case come 1996 with *Laboratory Of Sound* and further examples of how three chords can be milked to great effect. *More Than Skin Deep* and *Hitsburg Revisited* repeated the formula.
● ALBUMS: *Roman Gods* (I.R.S. 1981) ★★★, *Blast Off!* cassette only (ROIR 1982) ★★, *Hexbreaker!* (I.R.S. 1983) ★★★★, *Speed Connection* (I.R.S. 1985) ★★, *Speed Connection II* (I.R.S. 1985) ★★★, *Fleshtones Vs Reality* (Emergo 1987) ★★★, *Soul Madrid* (Impossible 1989) ★★★, *Beautiful Light* (Naked Language 1994) ★★★, *Laboratory Of Sound* (Musidisc 1996) ★★★, *More Than Skin Deep* (Epitaph 1998) ★★★, *Hitsburg Revisited* (Epitaph 1999) ★★★.
● COMPILATIONS: *Time Bomb! The Big Bang Theory* (Skyclad 1988) ★★★, *Living Legends Series* (I.R.S. 1989) ★★★, *Angry Years 84–86* (Amsterdamned 1997) ★★★.

## FLIPPER
San Francisco hardcore band Flipper formed in 1979 with original members Will Shatter (d. 1987; bass, vocals), Steve DePace (drums), both former members of Negative Trend, Bruce Lose (bass, vocals) and Ted Falconi (guitar), also of Negative

Trend, on drums. Following the single 'Love Canal'/'Ha Ha', on Subterranean Records, the group released its debut and best-known album, *Generic*, in 1982. Sporting topical lyrics and both hardcore punk and noise dirges, the collection was instantly recognized as a classic of west coast punk. However, these were no stereotypical three-chord thrashes, the band experimenting instead with the wildly overblown 'Sex Bomb Baby' and the super-minimalist 'Life'. Other albums followed on Subterranean in 1984 and 1986 but failed to match their debut's impact, and the following year Shatter died of an accidental heroin overdose. The three surviving members of Flipper reunited in 1990, resulting in the eventual release of *American Grafishy*. This was the first official release on the new label founded by Henry Rollins and Rick Rubin. Flipper are now cited as being highly influential in the development of Nirvana's sound.
● ALBUMS: *Generic* (Subterranean 1982) ★★★★, *Blow 'n Chunks* (ROIR 1984) ★★, *Gone Fishin'* (Subterranean 1984) ★★★, *American Grafishy* (Def American 1992) ★★★, *Live At CBGB's* 1983 recording (Overground 1997) ★★★★.
● COMPILATIONS: *Public Flipper Limited Live 1980–1985* (Subterranean 1986) ★★★, *Sex Bomb Baby!* (Subterranean 1988) ★★★★.

## FLOOD
b. Mark Ellis, 16 August 1960, England. Although Ellis is now a world-renowned producer, he began his career as a 'runner' for a London recording studio before becoming its in-house engineer and then working as a freelance. His unusual nickname is said to have originated from his willingness to make tea – another studio technician was christened 'Drought'. Flood is now known for his tough, techno-tinged production work for high-profile artists including U2, Depeche Mode, Smashing Pumpkins and PJ Harvey. His first career break came when he engineered New Order's 1981 debut, *Movement*. This auspicious start was followed by work with new wave bands such as Soft Cell, Psychic TV, Cabaret Voltaire and the Associates. Flood quickly graduated to production, beginning with the Nick Cave And The Bad Seeds' albums *The Firstborn Is Dead, Kicking Against The Pricks, Your Funeral, My Trial* and Erasure's first two albums. Flood's long association with U2 began when he worked as the engineer on 1987's bestselling *The Joshua Tree*. He developed his trademark electronic edge on productions such as Nine Inch Nails' *Pretty Hate Machine*, Pop Will Eat Itself's *This Is The Day, This Is The Hour, This Is This!*, and 1990's acclaimed *Violator* by Depeche Mode. The latter recording was engineered by François Kevorkian, himself a highly acclaimed producer and remixer. This metallic, edgy sound was also strongly evident on the following year's U2 release, *Achtung Baby*. Although Flood engineered that album, he progressed to co-production with Brian Eno for 1993's *Zooropa*. In the intervening time, however, he had produced Nitzer Ebb's *Ebbhead*, the Charlatans' *Between 10th And 11th*, and Curve's *Doppelgänger*. In 1993, Flood collaborated with Depeche Mode again on *Songs Of*

*Faith & Devotion* before working on PJ Harvey's *To Bring You My Love* and Smashing Pumpkins' *Mellon Collie And The Infinite Sadness*. More production work with U2 followed with 1997's post-modern extravaganza *Pop*. In late 1998, Flood began to produce Smashing Pumpkins' new album, work that did not finish until November 1999. Despite the praise for his productions and the international fame of the artists with whom he has worked, Flood prefers to remain out of the limelight and in the studio where he can get on with a craft at which he clearly excels.

## FLUX OF PINK INDIANS

This UK punk band was formed from the ashes of the Epileptics (who later changed their name to Epi-X due to letters of complaint from The British Epilepsy Association). Two surviving members were Colin Latter (vocals) and Derek Birkett (b. 18 February 1961, London, England; bass), who would go on to form Flux Of Pink Indians, with guitarist Andy and drummer Sid. Their debut EP *Neu Smell* emerged on Crass Records. Alongside standard rejections of society, war, and the eating of flesh lay the joyful 'Tube Disasters', the sort of humour that was in short order in the grim world of anarcho punk. Sid (later Rubella Ballet) was soon replaced by Bambi, formerly of Discharge, while Andy was replaced by Simon. However, both departed quickly for their original band, the Insane, and were replaced by old Epileptics guitarist Kevin Hunter and drummer Martin Wilson. Their debut album, 1982's *Strive To Survive Causing Least Suffering Possible*, confirmed the promise of the single, and premiered the band's own Spiderleg label. Alongside standard thrash numbers were highly perceptive attacks on consumer society. The anti-religious 'Is Anybody There' was a particularly effective example, using simple but jarring lyrics to emphasize its point. The follow-up, *The Fucking Cunts Treat Us Like Pricks*, was unsurprisingly banned by retailers HMV, and copies were seized by Greater Manchester police from Eastern Bloc record shop, which was charged with displaying 'Obscene Articles For Publication For Gain'. The album, ironically, concerned violence between men and women, based on the experiences of a band member who had been sexually assaulted. The music contained within was little short of a directionless cacophony, however. *Uncarved Block* was the most unexpected of the band's three studio albums, delivering more polemic allied to dance and funk rhythms that left their previous audience totally nonplussed. It was a brave effort, and one that, alongside their debut, stands up to repeated listening. Birkett, making use of his experiences with Spiderleg, has gone on to set up the highly successful One Little Indian Records, and still uses the Flux title for occasional projects.
● ALBUMS: *Strive To Survive Causing Least Suffering Possible* (Spiderleg 1982) ★★★, *The Fucking Cunts Treat Us Like Pricks* (Spiderleg 1984) ★★, as Flux *Uncarved Block* (One Little Indian 1986) ★★★.
● COMPILATIONS: *Not So Brave* (Overground 1997) ★★★.

## FLYING PICKETS

This a cappella UK sextet were formed in 1980 with a line-up comprising actors Rick Lloyd (tenor), Brian Hibbard (tenor), Gareth Williams (bass), David Brett (tenor), Ken Gregson (baritone) and Red Stripe (baritone). Originally, they came together informally and were warmly received at the 1982 Edinburgh Festival. In keeping with their unusual group title and their background with the politically motivated 7:84 theatre company, they played at benefit concerts for the National Union of Mineworkers and subsequently performed in pubs and clubs. Their novel cover of Yazoo's hit 'Only You' proved spectacularly successful, bringing them the coveted UK Christmas number 1 spot in 1983. Although their appeal seemed ephemeral, they enjoyed a second Top 10 hit with the Marvelettes' '(When You're) Young And In Love' and their albums included spirited reworkings of familiar vocal classics from different eras, ranging from the Teddy Bears' 'To Know Him Is To Love Him' through Bob Dylan's 'Masters Of War' and even Talking Heads' 'Psycho Killer'. Their last appearance on the UK charts was a lowly 71 with a rendition of the Eurythmics' 'Who's That Girl' in 1984. Two years later Gary Howard and Hereward Kaye were the first new members to join, and the group lost its last original member in 1990 with the departure of Brett. Howard and Kaye carried on with various personnel, although the original group re-formed briefly in 1994 to record a new album.
● ALBUMS: *Live At The Albany Empire* (VAM 1983) ★★, *Lost Boys* (10/Moving Target 1984) ★★★, *Live* (10 1985) ★★, *Waiting For Trains* (10 1988) ★★★, *Blue Money* (Forlane 1991) ★★, *The Warning* (Hey U 1992) ★★★, *The Original Flying Pickets Volume One* (Warners 1994) ★★, *Politics Of Need* (Alora 1996) ★★★, *Vox Pop* (Alora 1998) ★★.
● COMPILATIONS: *The Best Of The Flying Pickets* (Virgin 1991) ★★★.

## FOETUS

You've Got Foetus On Your Breath, Scraping Foetus Off The Wheel, Foetus Interruptus, Foetus Uber Alles, Foetus Inc – all these titles are actually the pseudonym of one person: Australian émigré Jim Thirlwell, alias Jim Foetus and Clint Ruin. After founding his own record company, Self Immolation, in 1980, he set about 'recording works of aggression, insight and inspiration'. Backed with evocatively descriptive musical slogans such as 'positive negativism' and 'bleed now pay later', Foetus released a series of albums, several of which appeared through Stevo's Some Bizzare Records. With stark one-word titles such as *Deaf*, *Ache*, *Hole* and *Nail*, Thirlwell presented a harrowing aural netherworld of death, lust, disease and spiritual decay. In November 1983, Foetus undertook a rare tour, performing with Marc Almond, Nick Cave and Lydia Lunch in the short-lived Immaculate Consumptive. Apart from these soul mates, Foetus has also played live with the Swans' Roli Mossiman as Wiseblood (who released *Dirtdish* in 1986), Lydia Lunch in Stinkfist, and appeared on albums by several artists including The The, Einstürzende

Neubauten, Nurse With Wound and Anne Hogan. Thirlwell also records instrumental work as Steroid Maximus, releasing *Quilombo* (1991) and *Gonwanaland* (1992) on the Big Cat label. In 1995, Thirlwell announced plans to release his first studio album in seven years. The result was the major-label release *Gash*, an album that led to a reappraisal of his work as one of the key figures in the development of the industrial music movement. Thirlwell subsequently returned to independent label status with his reputation and legendary status still intact.

● ALBUMS: as You've Got Foetus On Your Breath *Deaf* (Self Immolation 1981) ★★★, as You've Got Foetus On Your Breath *Ache* (Self Immolation 1982) ★★★, as Scraping Foetus Off The Wheel *Hole* (Self Immolation 1984) ★★★, as Scraping Foetus Off The Wheel *Nail* (Self Immolation/Some Bizzare 1985) ★★★, as Foetus Interruptus *Thaw* (Self Immolation/Some Bizzare 1988) ★★★, as Foetus Corruptus *Rife* (No Label 1989) ★★★, as Foetus In Excelsis Corruptus DeLuxe *Male* recorded 1990 (Big Cat 1993) ★★★, *Gash* (Columbia 1995) ★★★, *Boil* (Cleopatra 1996) ★★★, as The Foetus Symphony Orchestra *York* mini-album (Thirsty Ear 1997) ★★★, *Flow* (Thirsty Ear 2001) ★★★, *Blow* Flow remixed (Noise-O-Lution 2002) ★★.

● COMPILATIONS: as Foetus Inc *Sink* (Self Immolation/Wax Trax! 1989) ★★★.

● VIDEOS: *!Male!* (Visionary 1994).

### FORBERT, STEVE

b. 15 December 1954, Meridian, Mississippi, USA. Forbert played guitar and harmonica in local rock bands before moving to New York in 1976. There he busked at Grand Central Station before making his first recordings in 1977 for Nemperor and was briefly heralded as 'the new [Bob] Dylan' because of the tough poetry of his lyrics. Forbert's biggest commercial success came when he had a Top 20 hit with 'Romeo's Tune' (1979). After four albums, his contract was terminated. For most of the 80s and 90s, Forbert was based in Nashville, songwriting and playing concerts around the South with a touring group including Danny Counts (bass), Paul Errico (keyboards) and Bobby Lloyd Hicks (drums). His 1988 album for Geffen Records had Garry Tallent from Bruce Springsteen's E Street Band as producer. Nils Lofgren was a guest musician. After a four-year gap, Forbert returned with the highly praised *The American In Me*, produced by Pete Anderson. He switched labels once again to record *Mission Of The Crossroad Palms* and *Rocking Horse Head*, two well-crafted collections of mature, roots rock material that confirmed Forbert as one of America's most celebrated singer-songwriters. He also began to attract the attention of the burgeoning alt-country movement, and responded to the challenge with 2000's excellent studio album *Evergreen Boy* and the following year's *Live At The Bottom Line*.

● ALBUMS: *Alive On Arrival* (Nemperor/Epic 1978) ★★★, *Jackrabbit Slim* (Nemperor/Epic 1979) ★★★, *Little Stevie Orbit* (Nemperor/Epic 1980) ★★★, *Steve Forbert* (Nemperor/Epic 1982) ★★, *Streets Of This Town* (Geffen 1988) ★★★, *The American In Me* (Geffen 1992) ★★★★, *Be Here Now: Solo Live* (Rolling Tide 1994) ★★★, *Mission Of The Crossroad Palms* (Giant 1995) ★★★, *In Concert* 1982 recording (King Biscuit Flower Hour 1995) ★★★, *Rocking Horse Head* (Giant 1996) ★★★, with the Rough Squirrels *Here's Your Pizza* 1987 recording (Paladin 1998) ★★★, *Be Here Again Live Solo 1998* (Rolling Tide 1998) ★★★, *Evergreen Boy* (Koch 2000) ★★★★, *Acoustic Live: The WFUV Concert* (Rolling Tide 2000) ★★★, with the Rough Squirrels *Live At The Bottom Line* (Koch 2001) ★★★.

● COMPILATIONS: *The Best Of Steve Forbert: What Kinda Guy?* (Columbia/Legacy 1993) ★★★★, *Young, Guitar Days* (Madacy/Relentless 2001) ★★★, *More Young, Guitar Days* (Rolling Tide 2002) ★★★.

### FORCE M.D.'s

Often neglected next to the adventures of Afrika Bambaataa or Grandmaster Flash, Force M.D.'s (from Staten Island, New York City) were nevertheless a vital component in the early 80s in rap's development. They were originally titled the LDs, working as a street-corner act in the manner of the Jackson Five, with Antoine 'TCD' Lundy, Stevie D, Trisco Pearson and Charles 'Mercury' Nelson holding the reigns. Alongside Planet Patrol, they were the first to instigate doo wop hip-hop, before changing tack to largely soul-based harmonies which were an early influence on the swingbeat outfits of the late 80s and early 90s. They employed formation steps alongside breakdance routines as visual inducement, adding impersonations of television theme tunes and popular stars of the day, often performing on the Staten Island ferry. They became Dr. Rock And The MCs when they were joined by a DJ of that title, introducing scratching into their nascent act (in his absence a DJ Shock would deputize). When they signed to Tommy Boy Records in 1984 they were billed simply as the Force M.D.'s (the M.D. component of the name is short for Musical Diversity). They enjoyed several R&B hits during the latter part of the decade, including the chart-topping 'Love Is A House'. Their pop career peaked with 1986's 'Tender Love', a US Top 10 ballad written by Jimmy Jam and Terry Lewis. Nelson and Pearson were replaced by Rodney 'Khalil' Lundy and Shaun Waters in 1990, but the premature death of Antoine Lundy was a sad loss.

● ALBUMS: *Love Letters* (Tommy Boy 1984) ★★★, *Chillin'* (Tommy Boy 1986) ★★★★, *Touch And Go* (Tommy Boy 1987) ★★★★, *Step To Me* (Tommy Boy 1990) ★★★.

● COMPILATIONS: *For Lovers And Others: Force M.D.'s Greatest Hits* (Tommy Boy 1992) ★★★, *Let Me Love You: The Greatest Hits* (Tommy Boy 2001) ★★★.

### FORD, LITA

b. 23 September 1959, London, England. Ford was one of the original members of the Kim Fowley-conceived Runaways, first joining the band at age 15. In 1980 a disagreement within the ranks over musical direction led to the Runaways' break-up, leaving Ford to explore a solo career on the US glam metal circuit (initially subsidized by her day job as a beautician). Her debut album was recorded for

Mercury Records with the assistance of Neil Merryweather on bass, though it was Ford's guitar playing that took centre stage. *Dancin' On The Edge* made a minor impact on the US album charts, reaching number 66, although it was a less slick collection. Almost four years later in 1988 came *Lita*. Housed on RCA Records (a third album for MCA, *The Bride Wore Black*, had been abandoned), it reached the Top 30 and spawned the US number 12 hit, 'Kiss Me Deadly' (April 1988), plus a Top 10 hit with a duet with Ozzy Osbourne, 'Close My Eyes Forever' (March 1989). She later married W.A.S.P. guitarist Chris Holmes, although the marriage did not last. *Stiletto* continued to display Ford's commitment to the formula rock format prevalent in the USA, but she left RCA following disappointing sales for 1991's *Dangerous Curves*.
● ALBUMS: *Out For Blood* (Mercury 1983) ★★★, *Dancin' On The Edge* (Mercury 1984) ★★, *Lita* (RCA 1988) ★★★, *Stiletto* (RCA 1990) ★★★, *Dangerous Curves* (RCA 1991) ★★, *Black* (ZYX 1995) ★★.
● COMPILATIONS: *The Best Of Lita Ford* (BMG 1992) ★★★, *Greatest Hits* (RCA 1993) ★★★.
● VIDEOS: *Lita Live* (BMG Video 1988), *A Midnight Snack* (BMG Video 1990).

### FORD, ROBBEN
b. Robben Lee Ford, 16 December 1951, Woodlake, California, USA. A jazz, blues and rock guitarist, Robben is the most celebrated member of the musical Ford family. His father Charles was a country musician, and his brothers Patrick and Mark are bluesmen, playing drums and harmonica, respectively. Inspired initially by Mike Bloomfield and Eric Clapton, Ford's first professional engagement was with Charlie Musslewhite in 1970. He formed the Charles Ford Band with his brothers in 1971, then backed Jimmy Witherspoon from 1972-74. He toured and recorded with Joni Mitchell (as part of L.A. Express) and George Harrison in 1974, the resulting exposure bringing him a considerable amount of session work. In 1978, he formed the Yellowjackets with keyboards player Russell Ferrante and found time to record a patchy solo debut, *The Inside Story*. The early 80s saw him performing with Michael McDonald and saxophonist Sadao Watanabe; in 1986 he joined the Miles Davis band on its tour of the USA and Europe. The solo *Talk To Your Daughter* was a triumphant return to his blues roots, and picked up a Grammy nomination in the 'Contemporary Blues' category. In 1992, he formed a new unit, the Blue Line, featuring Roscoe Beck (bass) and Tom Brechtlein (drums), augmented by Bill Boublitz (keyboards). The unit recorded three acclaimed albums before disbanding in 1997. *Tiger Walk* was recorded with Keith Richard's rhythm section, but lacked the urgency of the Blue Line set-up captured on the following year's *The Authorized Bootleg*. Ford plays cleanly in an uncluttered style (like Mike Bloomfield), but occasionally with the frantic energy of Larry Carlton.
● ALBUMS: with the Charles Ford Band *The Charles Ford Band* (Arhoolie 1972) ★★★, *The Inside Story* (Elektra 1978) ★★★, with the Charles Ford Band *A Reunion Live* (Blue Rockit 1982) ★★★, *Talk To Your Daughter* (Warners 1988) ★★★★, with Joe Diorio *Minor Elegance* (MGI 1990) ★★★, *Robben Ford & The Blue Line* (Stretch/Blue Thumb 1992) ★★★★, with Jimmy Witherspoon *Live At The Notodden Blues Festival* (Blue Rockit 1993) ★★★★, with the Blue Line *Mystic Mile* (Stretch/Blue Thumb 1993) ★★★, with the Blue Line *Handful Of Blues* (Blue Thumb 1995) ★★★★, with Witherspoon *Live At The Mint* (On The Spot 1996) ★★★, *Blues Connotation* 1992 recording (Pacific 1996) ★★★, *Tiger Walk* (Blue Thumb 1997) ★★, with the Blue Line *The Authorized Bootleg* (Blue Thumb 1998) ★★★, *Sunrise* 1972 recording (Rhino 1999) ★★★, *Supernatural* (Blue Thumb 1999) ★★★, with the Ford Blues Band *A Tribute To Paul Butterfield* (Blue Rockit 2001) ★★★, *Blue Moon* (Concord Jazz 2002) ★★★, with Vinnie Colaiuta, Jimmy Haslip *Jing Chi* (Tone Center 2002) ★★★★.
● COMPILATIONS: *The Blues Collection* (Blue Rockit/Crosscut 1997) ★★★★, *Anthology: The Early Years* (Rhino 2001) ★★★.
● VIDEOS: *Highlights* (Warner Music Video 1995).

### FORDHAM, JULIA
b. 10 August 1962, Portsmouth, Hampshire, England. Formerly one of Mari Wilson's backing vocalists, the Wilsations, Fordham embarked on a solo career in 1986 as the archetypal angst-woman of the 80s. She achieved an initial UK chart hit with the Top 30 'Happy Ever After' (which also reached number 1 in Japan) in 1988, and a self-titled debut album and the follow-up both reached the UK Top 20. However, her biggest success came with the non-original '(Love Moves In) Mysterious Ways', which reached number 19 in February 1992. These releases, and the subsequent *Swept*, all on the Circa label, established the singer with a 'thirtysomething' audience, enabling her to perform headlining dates at venues such as London's Royal Albert Hall. Her fifth album, 1997's *East West*, saw Fordham teaming up with producer Michael Brook. Following a label change to Atlantic Records, the subsequent *Concrete Love* teamed her with producer Larry Klein and keyboard player Billy Preston.
● ALBUMS: *Julia Fordham* (Circa 1988) ★★★, *Porcelain* (Circa 1989) ★★★, *Swept* (Circa 1991) ★★★, *Falling Forward* (Circa 1994) ★★★, *East West* (Virgin 1997) ★★★, *Concrete Love* (Atlantic 2002) ★★★.
● COMPILATIONS: *The Julia Fordham Collection* (Circa 1998) ★★★.
● VIDEOS: *Porcelain* (Virgin Video 1990).

### FOREIGNER
This AOR band derives its name from the fact that the original members were drawn from both sides of the Atlantic, and this mixture of influences is much in evidence in their recorded legacy. Mick Jones (b. 27 December 1944, London, England; guitar, vocals) formed the band in 1976, having spent time in Nero And The Gladiators (two minor hits, 'Entry Of The Gladiators' and 'In The Hall Of The Mountain King', in 1961). The rest of the 60s were taken up working as a songwriter and musical director for French singer Johnny Halliday, alongside ex-Gladiator

Tommy Brown, with whom Jones also recorded several singles and EPs. During the early 70s, he worked with ex-Spooky Tooth keyboard player Gary Wright in Wonderwheel, which led to Jones playing on three albums with the reformed Spooky Tooth. Jones then worked with Leslie West and Ian Lloyd before taking a job as an A&R man, although he never actually signed anyone.

Prepared to make one final attempt on the music scene, Jones auditioned musicians, eventually forging a line-up that consisted of Ian McDonald (b. 25 June 1946, London, England; guitar, keyboards, horns, vocals, ex-King Crimson), Lou Gramm (b. Lou Grammatico, 2 May 1950, Rochester, New York, USA; vocals), who had played with Black Sheep in the early 70s, Dennis Elliott (b. 18 August 1950, Peckham, London, England; drums, ex-If), Al Greenwood (b. New York, USA; keyboards), and Edward Gagliardi (b. 13 February 1952, New York, USA; bass). In 1977 the band released *Foreigner*, and in a poll conducted by *Rolling Stone* magazine, emerged as top new artists. The album was an immediate success in America, climbing to number 4 in the *Billboard* chart. Jones and Gramm wrote most of the band's material, including classic tracks such as 'Feels Like The First Time' (US number 4, March 1977) and 'Cold As Ice' (US number 6, July 1977). Despite playing at the Reading Rock Festival in England twice in the 70s, Foreigner had more consistent success in the USA, where 'Hot Blooded' (number 3, July 1978) and 'Double Vision' (number 2, September 1978) were both million-sellers. In 1979 Rick Wills (b. England; bass) replaced Gagliardi, having served a musical apprenticeship with King Crimson and Peter Frampton; Gagliardi reportedly 'fell on the floor and passed out' on being told the news. *Head Games*, meanwhile, proved most notable for its 'exploitative' sleeve design, which contrasted with the subtle brand of rock it contained.

In 1980 McDonald and Greenwood departed to form Spys, leading to the guest appearances of Thomas Dolby and Junior Walker on the following year's US chart-topping *4*, produced by Mutt Lange. The album also broke the band in the UK, reaching number 5 in July of that year. 'Waiting For A Girl Like You' was the hit single lifted from the album, spending 10 weeks at number 2 in the US charts, and providing the group with their first UK Top 10 single. Although it was representative of the band's highly musical approach, taking the form of a wistful yet melodious ballad, it pigeonholed the group as purveyors of the epic AOR song. This reputation was only endorsed in December 1984 by the release of 'I Want To Know What Love Is', which proved to be Foreigner's greatest commercial success. It topped the charts on both sides of the Atlantic and featured the New Jersey Mass Choir backing Gramm's plaintive vocal. *Agent Provocateur*, meanwhile, topped the UK album charts and reached number 4 in America.

In the mid-80s the members of Foreigner were engaged in solo projects, and the success of Gramm's *Ready Or Not* in 1987 led to widespread speculation that Foreigner were about to disband. This was not the case, as *Inside Information* proved, though in other respects it was a poor record and a portent of things to come, despite containing the US Top 10 hit singles 'Say You Will' and 'I Don't Want To Live Without You'. In 1989, Gramm enjoyed success with another solo project, *Long Hard Look*, before officially leaving the band in May 1990 to form Shadow King. Jones refused to face the inevitable, and, amid much press sniping, recruited Johnny Edwards (ex-King Kobra) to provide vocals for *Unusual Heat*.

In 1992, both Jones and Gramm grasped the nettle and reunited, launching a re-formed Foreigner, though both Wills and Elliott were deemed surplus to requirements. The 1994 model boasted a line-up of Bruce Turgon (bass; a former colleague of Gramm in Black Sheep and Shadow King), Jeff Jacobs (keyboards, ex-Billy Joel circa *Storm Front*) and Mark Schulman (drums), in addition to Jones and Gramm. The band was back on the road during the early part of 1995 to promote *Mr Moonlight*. The album was only a moderate success, even though it was a typical Foreigner record. At their well-attended gigs, however, it was still 'Cold As Ice', 'Urgent' and 'I Want To Know What Love Is' that received the biggest cheers. Gramm was successfully treated for a brain tumour before the band reconvened in 1999. Whether or not their legacy grows further, Foreigner will continue to epitomize better than most the classic sound of 'adult-orientated rock'.

● ALBUMS: *Foreigner* (Atlantic 1977) ★★★, *Double Vision* (Atlantic 1978) ★★★, *Head Games* (Atlantic 1979) ★★★, *4* (Atlantic 1981) ★★★★, *Agent Provocateur* (Atlantic 1985) ★★★, *Inside Information* (Atlantic 1987) ★★★, *Unusual Heat* (Atlantic 1991) ★★★, *Mr Moonlight* (BMG 1994) ★★★.
● COMPILATIONS: *Records* (Atlantic 1982) ★★★★, *The Very Best Of Foreigner* (Atlantic 1992) ★★★★, *The Very Best ... And Beyond* (Atlantic 1992) ★★★★, *Classic Hits Live* (Atlantic 1993) ★★★, *Anthology: Jukebox Heroes* (Rhino/Atlantic 2000) ★★★★, *Complete Greatest Hits* (Rhino 2002) ★★★★.
● FILMS: *Footloose* (1984).

## 4AD RECORDS

Few independent record labels can boast as distinctive a roster as 4AD, both aesthetically and musically. The label was formed in early 1980 by Ivo Watts-Russell and Peter Kent (who were both then working at Beggars Banquet Records) reputedly after hearing a demo from new act Modern English. At first, the label was called Axis for the initial clutch of singles by the Fast Set, the Bearz, Shox and most importantly, Bauhaus, but this was changed to avoid confusion with a similarly named company, and 4AD was born. A loan of £2,000 from Beggars Banquet ensured that 4AD got off the ground, signing Modern English, In Camera, Mass, Dance Chapter and Rema Rema, among others. Kent soon left to set up Situation 2, working heavily with Bauhaus who shortly graduated to Beggars Banquet. 4AD, however, steered away from their parent company, witnessing a one-off single for the then-unknown The The (and later, Matt Johnson's solo album), plus several uncompromising recordings from Australian outfit the Birthday Party, and providing a home for ex-Wire personnel Bruce

Gilbert, Graham Lewis/Cupol and Colin Newman. From 1981–82 new acts as eclectic as Sort Col, the Past Seven Days, My Captains, Dif Juz and the Happy Family, appeared alongside solo works from ex-Bauhaus individuals David Jay and Daniel Ash/Tones On Tail and a collaboration between Lydia Lunch and the Birthday Party's Rowland S. Howard. More significantly, Watts-Russell stumbled upon the Cocteau Twins, who were to prove the act that, aside from emerging as the label's major artists, crystallized the ethereal nature often associated with 4AD product, aided later by the oblique yet attractive sleeve designs from Vaughn Oliver's 23 Envelope art studio. There was also Colourbox, another 4AD mainstay who embodied the label's experimental approach to recording and the studio, as well as the more sinister Xmal Deutschland.

Watts-Russell teamed with the Cocteau Twins among others, for his own project in 1983, This Mortal Coil, which enjoyed both critical and commercial support. Apart from Dead Can Dance, Xymox, Richenel and the Wolfgang Press, the mid-80s saw few signings as 4AD concentrated on their existing roster. The late 80s, on the other hand, signalled a slight reappraisal, with the departure of Colourbox and the signing of new American acts Throwing Muses, Boston exports the Pixies and New York's Ultra Vivid Scene. The influential but often-ignored AR Kane also arrived for a brief time, which spawned a one-off project with members of Colourbox, M.A.R.R.S' 'Pump Up The Volume'. A UK number 1 hit, this pivotal single was perhaps the first successful mesh of white rock and rhythm, paving the way for a commercial and artistic revolution in both British dance and independent music.

Then came the two-pronged attack of guitar bands Lush and the Pale Saints to see in the new decade, as the Pixies made serious commercial headway. When the Pixies dissolved it was to much wringing of hands in the music press, but 4AD soon picked up Frank Black as a solo artist (though he would eventually be dropped after two albums). Greater consolation came with the commercial approbation of Throwing Muses spin-off, Belly, which was just as well, as the quintessential 4AD group, the Cocteau Twins, had now moved on to a major. 4AD moved its operational base to California when Watts-Russell relocated to Los Angeles in the mid-90s, and continued to discover exciting new talent including Gus Gus, Kristin Hersh and Mojave 3. Treading a tightrope between financial well-being and artistic purity, 4AD has spotlighted an impressive yet diverse roster since its inception, and continues to excel in bringing idiosyncratic music into the commercial mainstream.

● COMPILATIONS: *Lonely Is An Eyesore* (4AD 1987) ★★★★, *Anakin* (4AD 1998) ★★★.

## 4 SKINS

As their name suggests, this London, England band comprised four skinheads, who specialized in vitriolic three-chord 'yob-rock'. Their membership was fluid, including no less than four lead singers, with only Hoxton Tom (bass) still resident between their first and second albums. Taking their musical brief from outfits such as Sham 69, the Angelic Upstarts and the Cockney Rejects, they were a third generation punk band heavily associated with the Oi! Movement, alongside fellow travellers the Business. With a blatantly patriotic image, the band attracted National Front supporters to their live shows, which occasionally erupted into full-scale riots. Lyrically they expounded on racism, police brutality and corrupt governments. However, musically they were not so adventurous, being rigidly formularized and unable to develop from their simplistic origins (basic punk spiced by the odd foray into skinhead's 'other' music, ska). From a creative standpoint, the band had ground to a halt by 1983. Their fanbase continued to contract and they soon faded into oblivion, although re-releases and compilations have reminded many of their enduring street popularity.

● ALBUMS: *The Good, The Bad And The 4 Skins* (Secret 1982) ★★, *A Fistful Of 4 Skins* (Syndicate 1983) ★★, *From Chaos To 1984* (Syndicate 1984) ★★.
● COMPILATIONS: *The Wonderful World Of The 4 Skins* (Link 1987) ★★★, *A Few 4 Skins More Vol. 1* (Link 1987) ★★, *A Few 4 Skins More Vol. 2* (Link 1987) ★★, *Live And Loud!* (Link 1989) ★★, *Clockwork Skinhead* (Harry May 1999) ★★★, *Singles & Rarities* (Captain Oi 1999) ★★★, *The Secret Life Of The 4 Skins* (Captain Oi! 2002) ★★★.

## FOX, SAMANTHA

b. 15 April 1966, London, England. While studying for her O-level examinations, 16-year-old Fox was 'discovered' by the *Sun* newspaper and promoted as a topless model. Before long she became something of a British institution and a recording career beckoned. Her debut single in 1986, 'Touch Me' elicited almost universally favourable reviews with critics registering surprise at her strong vocal performance. After the disc charted at number 3, she followed up with the sultry 'Do Ya, Do Ya (Wanna Please Me)', which also hit the UK Top 10. Further major British hits followed with 'Hold On Tight', 'Nothing's Gonna Stop Me Now' and 'I Surrender'. Having proven that former newspaper models can be hit artists, Fox defied all expectations by exporting her talents to the USA, where she enjoyed even greater chart success with three Top 10 hits including 'Naughty Girls', recorded with Full Force. Her albums were uneven but displayed her range to some effect, most notably on the acid house-inspired 'Love House', which was also an UK hit.

Over-exposure and increasing media prejudice finally persuaded her to relocate to America, but despite her strong visual appeal, particularly to the MTV audience, further hits were not forthcoming and Fox attempted to launch an acting and television career. In January 1996, she was banned from singing at a charity concert in Calcutta, India, owing to police fears she might cause a riot.

● ALBUMS: *Touch Me* (Jive 1986) ★★★, *Samantha Fox* (Jive 1987) ★★, *I Wanna Have Some Fun* (Jive 1989) ★★, *Just One Night* (Jive 1991) ★★, *21st Century Fox* (Ichiban 1998) ★★.
● COMPILATIONS: *Greatest Hits* (Jive 1992) ★★★, *Hot Tracks: The Best Of Samantha Fox* (BMG 2000)

★★★.
● FILMS: *Rock Dancer* (1994), *The Beautiful Game* aka *The Match* (1999).

## FOXTON, BRUCE
b. 1 September 1955, Woking, Surrey, England. Following the break-up of the Jam, guitarist Foxton set out on a predictably difficult solo career. During the summer of 1983, he enjoyed UK Top 30 success with 'Freak'. His strong, straightforward pop, with often distinct Jam overtones, was generally well produced, with 'This Is The Way' proving particularly effective. In 1984, Foxton released *Touch Sensitive*, which featured all-original compositions and another solid production. While deserving of chart success, Foxton's work was, not surprisingly, compared unfavourably with that of the Jam and consequently, his solo career failed to ignite.
● ALBUMS: *Touch Sensitive* (Arista 1984) ★★★.
● FURTHER READING: *Our Story*, Bruce Foxton and Rick Buckler with Alex Ogg.

## FOXX, JOHN
b. Dennis Leigh, Chorley, Lancashire, England. Foxx moved to London in 1974 where he became a key instigator in the rise of the UK electro-pop scene. He was a founder member of Ultravox, with whom he wrote, sang and dabbled in synthetic noises. Gary Numan cited Foxx as his main influence, which was some consolation for the fact that Numan was having hits when Ultravox were dropped by Island Records in 1978. They subsequently regrouped, without Foxx but with new singer Midge Ure, and enjoyed great success during the 80s with a string of synth-pop singles. Foxx went solo in 1979 and formed his own label Metal Beat, distributed by Virgin Records. The infectious 'Underpass' began a short string of minor Top 40 UK hits that included further electronic pop classics 'No-One Driving', 'Burning Car' and 'Europe After The Rain'. The stark, minimalist *Metamatic* has since been hailed as a pioneering influence on the UK's dance music scene.

Foxx's appearances on the singles and album charts ended in the mid-80s, since which time he has balanced work as a graphic designer with his ongoing musical explorations, which included a foray into the dance scene with Nation XII. He resurfaced in the late 90s, releasing several albums on his own Metamatic label. The lush, atmospheric *Cathedral Oceans* had originally been recorded in the mid-80s, too early to reap the benefits of the ambient house explosion of the early 90s. *Shifting City*, a collaboration with Louis Gordon, was a largely successful fusion of Foxx's early 80s sound with modern electronica.
● ALBUMS: *Metamatic* (Metal Beat 1980) ★★★★, *The Garden* (Virgin 1981) ★★★, *The Golden Section* (Virgin 1983) ★★★, *In Mysterious Ways* (Virgin 1985) ★★★, *Cathedral Oceans* (Metamatic 1997) ★★★, with Louis Gordon *Shifting City* (Metamatic 1997) ★★★, *Exotour 97* mini-album (Metamatic 1997) ★★★, *Subterranean Omnidelic Exotour* (Metamatic 1998) ★★★, with Louis Gordon *The Pleasures Of Electricity* (Metamatic 2002) ★★★.

● COMPILATIONS: *Assembly* (Virgin 1992) ★★★★, *Modern Art: The Best Of John Foxx* (Music Club 2001) ★★★★.

## FRANKIE GOES TO HOLLYWOOD
Formed in the summer of 1980, this Liverpool, England-based outfit comprised former Big In Japan vocalist Holly Johnson (b. William Johnson, 19 February 1960, Khartoum, Sudan) backed by Paul Rutherford (b. 8 December 1959, Liverpool, England; vocals), Nasher Nash (b. Brian Nash, 20 May 1963; guitar), Mark O'Toole (b. 6 January 1964, Liverpool, England; bass) and Peter Gill (b. 8 March 1964, Liverpool, England; drums). It was a further two years before they started to make any real headway with television appearances and a record deal with Trevor Horn's ZTT Records. Their debut single, 'Relax', produced by Horn, was a pyrotechnic production and superb dance track with a suitably suggestive lyric that led to a BBC radio and television ban in Britain. Paradoxically, the censorship produced even greater public interest in the single, which topped the UK charts for five weeks, selling close to two million copies in the process. The promotion behind Frankie Goes To Hollywood, engineered by former music journalist Paul Morley, was both clever and inventive, utilizing marketing techniques such as single word slogans and the production of best selling T-shirts that offered the enigmatic message 'Frankie Says ...' The band's peculiar image of Liverpool laddishness coupled with the unabashed homosexuality of vocalists Johnson and Rutherford merely added to their curiosity value and sensationalism, while also providing them with a distinctive identity that their detractors seriously underestimated.

The follow up to 'Relax' was the even more astonishing 'Two Tribes'. An awesome production built round a throbbing, infectiously original riff, it showed off Johnson's distinctive vocal style to striking effect. Like all the band's singles, the record was available in various 7-inch and 12-inch remixed formats with superb packaging and artwork. The power of the single lay not merely in its appropriately epic production but the topicality of its lyric, which dealt with the escalation of nuclear arms and the prospect of global annihilation. In order to reinforce the harrowing theme, the band included a chilling voice over from actor Patrick Allen taken from government papers on the dissemination of information to the public in the event of nuclear war. Allen's Orwellian instructions on how to avoid fall out while disposing of dogs, grandparents and other loved ones gave the disc a frightening authenticity that perfectly captured the mood of the time. Johnson's closing lines of the song, borrowed from an unnamed literary source, provided a neat rhetorical conclusion: 'Are we living in a land where sex and horror are the new gods?' The six-minute plus version of 'Two Tribes' was played in its entirety on UK lunch time radio shows and duly entered the chart at number 1, remaining in the premier position for an incredible nine weeks while the revitalized 'Relax' nestled alongside its successor at number 2. A Godley And Creme promotional film of 'Two Tribes' which featured caricatures of US President Reagan and Soviet leader Mr. Chernenko wrestling was rightly acclaimed as one of the best videos of the period and contributed strongly to the Frankie Goes To Hollywood package. Having dominated the upper echelons of the chart like no other artist since the Beatles, the pressure to produce an album for the Christmas market was immense. *Welcome To The Pleasure Dome* finally emerged as a double with a number of cover versions including interesting readings of Bruce Springsteen's 'Born To Run', Dionne Warwick's 'Do You Know The Way To San Jose?' and Gerry And The Pacemakers' 'Ferry Across The Mersey'. Like all the band's recordings, the sound was epic and glorious and the reviews proclaimed the album an undoubted hit, though some commentators felt its irresistible charm might prove ephemeral. 1984 ended with a necessary change of style as the band enjoyed their third number 1 hit with the moving festive ballad 'The Power Of Love'. Thus they joined Gerry And The Pacemakers as only the second act in UK pop history to see their first three singles reach the top. History repeated itself the following year when, like Gerry And The Pacemakers, Frankie Goes To Hollywood saw their fourth single ('Welcome To The Pleasure Dome') stall at number 2.

Thereafter, they were never again to attain the ascendancy that they had enjoyed during the golden year of 1984. A sabbatical spent in Eire for tax purposes meant that their comeback in 1986 had to be emphatic. Having failed to conquer America during the same period, merely increased the pressure. Critics had long been claiming that the band were little more than puppets in the hands of a talented producer despite the fact that they sang, played and even wrote their own material. The grand return with 'Rage Hard' (the title borrowed from Dylan Thomas) won them a number 4 UK hit, but that seemed decidedly anti-climactic. The second album, *Liverpool*, cost a small fortune but lacked the charm and vibrancy of its predecessor. Within a year Johnson and Rutherford had quit, effectively spelling the end of the band, although the remaining three attempted to continue with new vocalist Grant Boult. Johnson prevented them using the Frankie Goes To Hollywood name, and attempts to record as the Lads came to nothing.

It brought an end to the band's remarkable rise and fall, when they had managed to cram a decade of sales, creativity and controversy into less than 24 months. In many ways, their fate was the perfect pop parable of the 80s. For a band that was so symptomatic of their age, it was appropriate that the Frankie Goes To Hollywood saga should end not in the recording studio, but in the High Court. In a battle royal between Johnson and his former record company ZTT in early 1988, the artist not only won his artistic freedom but substantial damages which were to have vast implications for the UK music business as a whole.

● ALBUMS: *Welcome To The Pleasure Dome* (ZTT 1984) ★★★★, *Liverpool* (ZTT 1986) ★★.
● COMPILATIONS: *Bang! The Greatest Hits Of Frankie Goes To Hollywood* (ZTT 1993) ★★★★,

*Maximum Joy* (ZTT 2000) ★★★, *Twelve Inches* (ZTT 2001) ★★★.
● VIDEOS: *Shoot!: The Greatest Hits* (ZTT 1993), *Hard On* (ZTT 2000).
● FURTHER READING: *Give It Loads: The Story Of Frankie Goes To Hollywood*, Bruno Hizer. *Frankie Say: The Rise Of Frankie Goes To Hollywood*, Danny Jackson. *A Bone In My Flute*, Holly Johnson.

## FRANTIC ELEVATORS

This Manchester, England-based punk/pop unit is notable for starting the musical career of Mick Hucknall (b. 8 June 1960, Denton, Greater Manchester, England). Together with his school chum Neil Moss (guitar), Kevin Williams (drums) and Brian Turner (bass), they released a number of interesting but undistinguished singles during 1979 and the early 80s. Their debut single, comprising the tracks 'Voice In The Dark', 'Passion' and 'Every Day I Die', was an independent production of 2,000 copies. A planned second release failed to materialize and the white label pressings are now much sought after. Three further singles were eventually released, including a version of Hucknall's modern classic, 'Holding Back The Years'. Hucknall folded the Frantic Elevators in 1983 to pursue his plans for a white soul band, which became Simply Red. Various members gigged as the Elevators for a brief while. When listening to the Frantic Elevators material, it is hard to place Hucknall the vocalist, in punk staccato, against the smooth pop stylist he became in Simply Red. Interesting, but primitive.
● COMPILATIONS: *Singles* mini-album (Essential 2000) ★★.

## FRAZIER CHORUS

Originally a four-piece band from Brighton, Sussex, England, this mid-80s pop outfit, originally under the name Plop!, set out with the grand ambition of being the antithesis of Wham!. Singer and keyboard player Tim Freeman's songs were circulated on a demo tape and he and the rest of the band, Michele Allardyce (percussion), Kate Holmes (flute) and Chris Taplin (clarinet), were signed to 4AD Records under the name Frazier Chorus, a name taken from the back of a 50s US baseball jacket. With their unusual instrumental line-up, which lent an almost synth-pop/pastoral feel, their 4AD debut, 'Sloppy Heart' (1987), did not fit easily with the harder edge towards which the label was moving. As a consequence, the band soon switched to Virgin Records. In 1989, they released their debut album, *Sue*, which featured orchestral arrangements from David Bedford and contributions from Tim Sanders (tenor saxophone), Roddy Lorimer (trumpet, flügelhorn) and Simon Clarke (piccolo, saxophones). Minor UK hits with 'Dream Kitchen' and 'Typical' promised much, but none reached the Top 50. A reissue of 'Sloppy Heart' featured a laconic version of the Sex Pistols' 'Anarchy In The UK' on its b-side. Allardyce left acrimoniously during the recording of the second album (with the Lightning Seeds' Ian Broudie on production), leaving the band as a trio. Allardyce, whose orientation was geared towards dance music, would continue to work as a journalist for disc jockey magazine *Jocks*. Freeman had previously collaborated on the 4AD house project This Mortal Coil. Further minor Frazier Chorus hits included the Paul Oakenfold remixes of 'Cloud 8' and 'Nothing'. The disappointing performance of 1991's 'Walking On Air' confirmed that Frazier Chorus' cult appeal had apparently peaked, but the band pressed on regardless. Freeman's muse had not deserted him, and their final album, 1995's *Wide Awake*, included further strong songwriting in songs such as 'If The Weather Was Up To Me'. Holmes later recorded for Creation Records before forming the electronic duo Technique with Xan Tyler. She is now married to Alan McGee.

● ALBUMS: *Sue* (Virgin 1989) ★★★, *Ray* (Virgin 1991) ★★, *Wide Awake* (Pinkerton 1995) ★★★.

## FREEEZ

This British funk group was led by John Rocca (b. 23 September 1960, London, England), and included Peter Maas (bass), Andy Stennet (keyboards) and Paul Morgan (drums). Rocca, a former van salesman for the dance music specialist shop Disc Empire, formed the group in 1978. They released their first single, 'Keep In Touch', on their own Pink Rythm (sic) label (one of the first British acts to form their own label), and it narrowly missed the UK Top 40 in 1980 when picked up by Calibre. After moving to Beggars Banquet Records in 1981, they hit the UK Top 10 with 'Southern Freeze', which included vocals by Ingrid Mansfield-Allman (b. London, England). The album of the same name reached the Top 20. The group expanded to a seven piece with the addition of Gordon Sullivan, George Whitmore, and new vocalist Alison Gordon. Later reduced to the basic duo of Rocca and Maas, they had their biggest success in 1983 with 'I.O.U.', written and produced in the USA by Arthur Baker with mixing assistance from Jellybean. In 1985, Rocca and Stennet recorded as Pink Rhythm while Freeez continued with Maas, Morgan, Billy Crichton and Louis Smith and recorded on Siren in 1986. As a solo artist Rocca had a US dance number 1 with 'I Want To Be Real' in 1987; the same year a remix of Freeez's 'I.O.U.' on Citybeat made the UK Top 30. Rocca later recorded on Who'd She Coo and Cobra (where he re-recorded 'Southern Freeze') and reappeared in 1991 as Midi Rain on the Vinyl Solution label.

● ALBUMS: *Southern Freeze* (Beggars Banquet 1981) ★★★, *Gonna Get You* (Beggars Banquet 1983) ★★★.

## FREY, GLENN

b. 6 November 1948, Detroit, Michigan, USA. Frey's early career was forged as singer, guitarist in a number of local attractions, including the Mushrooms and Subterraneans. He appeared on several sessions by the Bob Seger System, singing back-up on 'Ramblin' Gamblin' Man', a 1968 hit, before moving to Los Angeles. Here Frey formed Longbranch Pennywhistle with J.D. Souther, but this harmony duo floundered on record label intransigence and in 1972, the now-disengaged musician opted for singer Linda Ronstadt's backing group. Frey then joined fellow band members Bernie

Leadon, Don Henley and Randy Meisner in the Eagles which grew from humble country-rock origins into one of America's most successful attractions. Frey co-wrote many of the unit's best-known songs, including 'Take It Easy', 'Lyin' Eyes', 'Take It To The Limit' and 'Hotel California', while his distinctive vocal formed the ideal counterpoint to that of Henley.

The Eagles broke up in 1980 amid rancorous professional and personal circumstances. A new found partnership with songwriter Jack Tempchin formed the basis of Frey's solo debut, *No Fun Aloud*, which achieved gold status and spawned US hits in 'I Found Somebody' and 'The One You Love'. In 1984, he wrote and performed 'The Heat Is On', the hit theme to the highly successful movie, *Beverly Hills Cop*, before resuming his association with Tempchin for *The Allnighter*. The following year Frey reached number 2 in the US charts with 'You Belong To The City', a song culled from the soundtrack of *Miami Vice*. He subsequently took an acting role in this popular television crime series and in 1988 completed *Soul Searchin'*, the third in a series of slick, professional AOR-styled albums. Frey was a key member of the highly successful Eagles reunion in 1994 During their financially lucrative *Hell Freezes Over* tour in 1995 he was taken seriously ill and received surgery for a stomach complaint. The following year he made a guest appearance in the Don Johnson television series, *Nash Bridges*, and acted in the Tom Cruise movie *Jerry Maguire*.

● ALBUMS: *No Fun Aloud* (Asylum 1982) ★★, *The Allnighter* (MCA 1984) ★★★, *Soul Searchin'* (MCA 1988) ★★, *Strange Weather* (MCA 1992) ★★, *Live* (MCA 1993) ★★.

● COMPILATIONS: *Solo Collection* (MCA 1995) ★★★, *The Best Of Glenn Frey: The Millennium Collection* (MCA 2000) ★★★.

● FILMS: *Let's Get Harry* aka *The Rescue* (1986), *Jerry Maguire* (1996).

## FRICKE, JANIE

b. Jane Frickie, 19 December 1947, on the family farm near South Whitney, Indiana, USA. Fricke, who adopted the spelling in 1986 to avoid mispronunciation, has sung in public since the age of 10. Her father was a guitarist and her mother a piano teacher and organist. Fricke sang jingles to pay her university fees and then moved to Los Angeles to find work as a session singer. As this was not productive, she moved to Nashville and joined the Lea Jane Singers, often recording three sessions a day, five days a week. Fricke has added background vocals to thousands of records, mostly country, including ones by Crystal Gayle ('I'll Get Over You'), Ronnie Milsap ('(I'm A) Stand By My Woman Man'), Elvis Presley ('My Way'), Tanya Tucker ('Here's Some Love') and Conway Twitty ('I'd Love To Lay You Down'). Fricke's uncredited contribution on Johnny Duncan's 'Jo And The Cowboy' led to several other records with Duncan. The disc jockeys and public alike were curious about the mystery voice on his country hits 'Stranger', 'Thinkin'' Of A Rendezvous' and 'It Couldn't Have Been Any Better', and she was finally given equal billing on 'Come A

Little Bit Closer'. This led to considerable interest in her first solo recordings and she had US country hits with 'What're You Doing Tonight?' and a revival of 'Please Help Me, I'm Falling'. At first, she was reluctant to tour because she found herself in continuing demand as a session singer. She joined Vern Gosdin for 'Till The End' and 'Mother Country Music' and Charlie Rich for a US country number 1, 'On My Knees'.

In 1982, Fricke had her first solo US country number 1 with 'Don't Worry 'Bout Me, Baby', co-written by 60s hitmaker Bruce Channel and featuring Ricky Skaggs' harmony vocals. Johnny Rodriguez's road manager, Randy Jackson, proposed to Fricke on a radio phone-in show and later married her and became her manager. Fricke, who toured with Alabama, had a US country number 1 with a similarly styled, high-energy performance, 'He's A Heartache (Looking For A Place To Happen)' (1983). It was taken from It Ain't Easy, which she made with her own Heart City Band and which was produced by Bob Montgomery. 'It Ain't Easy Bein' Easy' (1982) and 'Tell Me A Lie' (1983) were other US country number 1s from the same album. She joined Merle Haggard for another number 1, 'A Place To Fall Apart' (1985), which was based on a letter he had written about his ex-wife, Leona Williams, and Fricke's other duet partners include George Jones ('All I Want To Do In Life'), Ray Charles ('Who Cares?'), Tommy Cash ('The Cowboy And The Lady') and Larry Gatlin ('From Time To Time'). Her Black And White album was more blues based, while Labor Of Love was produced by Chris Waters and included an ingenious song he had written with his sister, Holly Dunn, 'Love Is One Of Those Words', as well as Steve Earle's 'My Old Friend The Blues'. She recorded albums for Intersound and Branson Entertainment in the 90s, reverting to the original spelling of her surname.

● ALBUMS: Singer Of Songs (Columbia 1978) ★★★, Love Notes (Columbia 1979) ★★★, with Johnny Duncan Nice 'N' Easy (Columbia 1979) ★★, From The Heart (Columbia 1980) ★★★, I'll Need Someone To Hold Me When I Cry (Columbia 1981) ★★★, Sleeping With Your Memory (Columbia 1981) ★★★, It Ain't Easy (Columbia 1982) ★★★, Love Lies (Columbia 1983) ★★★, The First Word In Memory Is Me (Columbia 1984) ★★★, Somebody Else's Fire (Columbia 1985) ★★, Black And White (Columbia 1986) ★★★★, After Midnight (Columbia 1987) ★★★, Saddle The Wind (Columbia 1988) ★★★, Labor Of Love (Columbia 1989) ★★★, Janie Fricke (Intersound 1990) ★★★, Crossroads (Branson 1992) ★★★, Now & Then (Branson 1993) ★★★, Bouncin' Back (JMF 1999) ★★★★.

● COMPILATIONS: Greatest Hits (Columbia 1982) ★★★, The Very Best Of Janie Fricke (Columbia 1986) ★★★★, 17 Greatest Hits (Columbia 1986) ★★★, Country Store: Janie Fricke (Country Store 1988) ★★★.

### FRIDA

b. Anni-Frid Synni-Lyngstad, 15 November 1945, Narvik, Norway. Frida attempted a career as a solo singer after the break-up of Abba in 1981. She was the first of the group to make a solo album, which was produced by Phil Collins. Somewhat downbeat in tone (many thought it reflected the recent breakdown of the separate marriages of both Frida and Collins) it included songs by Per Gessle, later of Roxette. The most successful track, 'I Know There's Something Going On' reached the US Top 20 and was written by Russ Ballard who also composed the first solo hit for another ex-Abba soloist Agnetha Fältskog. 'To Turn To Stone' was also successful in Europe. The following year, Frida's duet with B.A. Robertson, 'Time' was a minor British hit but her second solo album made little impact on either side of the Atlantic, although the title track was a hit across Europe.

● ALBUMS: Frida (Columbia 1970) ★★, Something's Going On (Epic 1982) ★★★, Shine (Epic 1984) ★★, Djupa Andetag (Anderson 1996) ★★.

● COMPILATIONS: Frida 1967–1972 (EMI 1997) ★★.

● FURTHER READING: Abbamania Volume 2: The Solo Years, Peter Bingham and Bernadette Dolan.

### FRITH, FRED

b. 17 February 1949, Heathfield, East Sussex, England. One of the leading avant garde guitarists in contemporary music, Frith played violin and piano as a child before falling in love with the guitar. In 1968, he co-founded the left-field rock group Henry Cow and in 1974 recorded an innovative album of electric guitar improvisations, Guitar Solos. After Henry Cow's demise in the late 70s, he worked with several ex-members in the Art Bears (releasing Hopes And Fears, Winter Songs and The World As It Is Today). During the 80s Frith was based mostly in New York City, where he guested with Material (Memory Serves) and played in the groups Skeleton Crew (Learn To Talk and The Country Of Blinds), Massacre (Killing Time) and Naked City. He also recorded two superb albums (Live, Love, Larf & Loaf and Invisible Means) with fellow guitarists Henry Kaiser, Jim French and Richard Thompson.

At the end of the decade, Frith began to branch out, writing music for films, theatre and dance projects, while continuing to play with his own groups, Keep The Dog and the Fred Frith Guitar Quartet. His own prolific solo output, meanwhile, continued to showcase a quirky blend of guitar experimentation, free jazz, hard rock, fold music and improvization. Long-time collaborators John Zorn, Larry Ochs, Miya Masaoka, Chris Cutler, Tom Cora, Bob Ostertag, Ikue Mori and Zeena Parkins frequently join him. Frith has worked as a session guitarist on records by innumerable artists (including Brian Eno, Robert Wyatt, the Golden Palominos, Gavin Bryars and the Residents); has played total improvisation with Lol Coxhill, Phil Minton, Hans Reichel and many others; and has had several of his compositions recorded by the ROVA Saxophone Quartet (Long On Logic). He continues to hold improvising workshops throughout the world, and in 1995 moved to Germany before becoming Composer-in-Residence at l'Ecole Nationale de Musique in Villeurbanne, France. In 1997 he relocated to America to become Composer-in-Residence at Mills College, Oakland, California. Two years later he became Professor of

Composition at the college.

● ALBUMS: *Guitar Solos* (Caroline 1974) ★★★, with Henry Kaiser *With Friends Like These* (Metalanguage 1979) ★★★, *Gravity* (Ralph 1980) ★★★, *Speechless* (Ralph 1981) ★★★, *Live In Japan* (Recommended 1982) ★★★, with Phil Minton, Bob Ostertag *Voice Of America* (Rift 1982) ★★★, with Totsuzen Danball *Live At Loft Shinjuku Tokyo Japan 23 July '81* (Floor 1983) ★★★, *Cheap At Half The Price* (Ralph 1983) ★★★, with Chris Cutler *Live In Prague And Washington* (Re 1983) ★★★, with Lol Coxhill *French Gigs* (AAA 1983) ★★★, with Kaiser *Who Needs Enemies?* (Metalanguage 1983) ★★★, with Rene Lussier *Nous Autres* (Victo 1987) ★★★, with Kaiser, John French, Richard Thompson *Live, Love, Larf & Loaf* (Rhino/Demon 1987) ★★★★, *The Technology Of Tears* (RecRec/SST 1988) ★★★★, *The Top Of His Head* film soundtrack (Crammed Discs 1989) ★★★, with French, Kaiser, Thompson *Invisible Means* (Windham Hill/Demon 1990) ★★★, *Step Across The Border* film soundtrack (RecRec/East Side Digital 1990) ★★★, with Ferdinand Richard *Dropera* (RecRec 1991) ★★★, with Tim Hodgkinson *Live Improvisations* (Woof/Megaphone 1992) ★★★, with Francois-Michel Pesenti *Helter Skelter* (RecRec 1993) ★★★, *Quartets* 1992 recordings (RecRec 1994) ★★★, with Marc Ribot *Subsonic 1: Sound Of A Distant Episode* (Sub Rosa/Subsonic 1994) ★★★★, with Cutler *Live In Trondheim, Berlin, Limoges* (ReR 1994) ★★★, with John Zorn *Art Of Memory* (Incus 1995) ★★★, *Middle Of The Moment* (RecRec 1995) ★★★, with Kato Hidcki, Ikue Mori *Death Ambient* (Tzadik 1995) ★★★★, with Karin Scholl, Daniel Erismann, Lucas N. Niggli, Hans Koch, Peter Kowald *Nil* (Unit 1995) ★★★, *Allies* (RecRec 1996) ★★★, *Eye To Ear* (Tzadik 1997) ★★★, *Ayaya Moses* (Ambiances Magnetiques 1997) ★★★, with Jean-Pierre Drouet *Improvisations* (Transes Europeennes 1997) ★★★, with Noel Akchote *Reel* (Rectangle 1997) ★★★, *The Previous Evening* (ReR Megacorp 1997) ★★★, with Tom Cora *Etymology* 1995 recordings (Rarefaction 1997) ★★★, with Percy Howard, Charles Hayward, Bill Laswell *Meridiem* (Materiali Sonori 1998) ★★★, *Upbeat* (Ambiances Magnetiques 1999) ★★★, *Traffic Continues* (Winter & Winter 2000) ★★★, with Cutler *2 Gentlemen In Verona* (ReR Megacorp 2000) ★★★★.

● COMPILATIONS: with Henry Kaiser *With Enemies Like These, Who Needs Friends?* (SST 1987) ★★★★, *Live In Moscow, Prague And Washington* 1979, 1989 live recordings (ReR 1990) ★★★, *Guitar Solos* (RecRec/East Side Digital 1991) ★★★★★, with Kaiser *Friends & Enemies* (Cuneiform 1999) ★★★★, *Stone, Brick, Glass, Wood, Wire (Graphic Scores 1986–1996)* (I Dischi Di Angelica 1999) ★★★.

## FRONT 242

A duo of Patrick Codenys (b. 16 November 1958, Brussels, Belgium; composition, computers, synthesizers, guitars, vocals) and Daniel Bressanutti (b. 27 August 1954, Brussels, Belgium; programming, samples), Front 242 earned their long-standing reputation within the industrial/*avant garde* community via a largely compelling series of experimental exercises in sound. Originally, Front 242 comprised Codenys alone, for the 1982 single

'Principles', then became a trio with Jean-Luc De Meyer and Bressanutti. These early releases were more in tune with the elementary synth-pop of artists such as Depeche Mode, and it was not until after the release of *Geography* that they appeared live. A fourth member, Geoff Bellingham, was added for this purpose, although he was later replaced by ex-roadie and concurrent Revolting Cocks member Richard 23. Front 242's journey through the 80s gradually saw them becoming a more distinctive unit, however, with politically motivated samples filtering through the repetition. On the back of an awesome reputation for live events and visuals, they were launched out of cult status by the success of *Official Version*. This introduced the intemperate, militaristic rhythms that would become a signature, as well as a diversity enshrined by nods to disco and pop in other tracks. It was not until the advent of *Tyranny For You* that the ingredients were significantly rearranged once more, this time to instil a darker overtone to proceedings (the album emerged at the same time as the Gulf War and proclamations of a New World Order). Influenced by the German anti-rock movement (Can, Neu!, Faust), cinema and architecture, the duo (following De Meyer's departure in 1995) continue to run the Art & Strategy design company and record label.

● ALBUMS: *Geography* (RRE 1982) ★★, *No Comment* mini-album (Wax Trax! 1985) ★★★, *Official Version* (Wax Trax! 1987) ★★★★, *Front By Front* (Wax Trax! 1988) ★★★, *Tyranny (for You)* (RRE/Epic 1991) ★★★, *Live Target* (Guzzi 1993) ★★★, *06:21:03:11 Up Evil* (RRE/Epic 1993) ★★★, *05:22:09:12 Off* (RRE/Epic 1993) ★★★, *Mut@ge Mix@ge* (RPE 1995) ★★★, *Re-Boot: Live '98* (Metropolis 1998) ★★★, *Headhunter 2000* remixes (Metropolis 1998) ★★★.

● COMPILATIONS: *Backcatalogue* (Wax Trax! 1987) ★★★, *Geography 1981–1983* (RRECD 1992) ★★★, *No Comment 1984–1985* (RRECD 1992) ★★★, *Back Catalogue 1981–1985* (RRECD 1992) ★★★, *Official Version 1986–1987* (RRECD 1992) ★★★, *Front By Front 1988–1989* (RRECD 1992) ★★★.

## FUN BOY THREE

When the Specials topped the UK charts in June 1981 with the spellbinding 'Ghost Town' few would have guessed that three of their members would depart immediately to form an offshoot group. By October, Terry Hall (b. 19 March 1959, Coventry, England; vocals), Neville Staples (vocals, drums) and Lynval Golding (b. 24 July 1951, Coventry, England; guitar) had launched the Fun Boy Three. Their UK Top 20 debut single was the extraordinary 'The Lunatics (Have Taken Over The Asylum)', a haunting protest against political conservatism, made all the more effective by Hall's deadpan, languid vocal. The single effectively established the trio as both original and innovative commentators, whose work compared favourably with that of their mother group, the Specials. For their follow-up, the Fun Boy Three teamed up with the then unknown Bananarama for a hit revival of bandleader Jimmie Lunceford's 'It Ain't What You Do, It's The Way That You Do It'. The Bananarama connection continued when the Fun Boy Three appeared on their hit

'Really Saying Something (He Was Really Sayin' Somethin')'. The girl trio also sang on several tracks of their mentors' self-titled debut album.

By 1982, the Fun Boy Three were proving themselves adept at writing political songs and reviving classic songs, which they moulded into their own distinctive style. Hall's lazy vocal on George Gershwin's 'Summertime' was a typical example of this and provided another Top 20 hit. The wonderfully cynical comment on teenage love and pregnancy, 'Tunnel Of Love', and the Top 10 hit 'Our Lips Are Sealed' proved the trio's last major statements. Following a second album, they split during 1983, with Hall going on to form the Colour Field and work as a solo artist.

● ALBUMS: *Fun Boy Three* (Chrysalis 1982) ★★★, *Waiting* (Chrysalis 1983) ★★★.
● COMPILATIONS: *Really Saying Something: The Best Of Fun Boy Three* (Chrysalis 1997) ★★★★.

## FUREYS

This musical family group from Ballyfermont, Dublin, Eire, originally featured George Furey (b. 11 June 1951, Dublin, Eire; vocals, guitar, accordion, mandola, autoharp, whistles), Finbar Furey (b. 28 September 1946, Dublin, Eire; vocals, uillean pipes, banjo, whistles, flute), Eddie Furey (b. 23 December 1944, Dublin, Eire; guitar, mandola, mandolin, harmonica, fiddle, bodhrán, vocals) and Paul Furey (b. 6 May 1948, Dublin, Eire; accordion, melodeon, concertina, whistles, bones, spoons, vocals). During the 60s Finbar and Eddie Furey had performed as a duo, playing clubs and doing radio work. Despite the offer of a recording contract, they turned it down, and went to Scotland to play. Having established a reputation for themselves, they later signed to Transatlantic Records, and joined the Clancy Brothers on the latter group's American tour in 1969. In 1972, the duo toured most of Europe, but while they were away, Paul and George had formed a group called the Buskers, with Davy Arthur (b. 24 September 1954, Edinburgh, Scotland; multi-instrumentalist, vocals). This group was involved in a road crash, bringing Finbar and Eddie back home, where they formed Tam Linn with Davey and Paul, and played the Cambridge Folk Festival. George later joined the line-up, and they became the Fureys And Davey Arthur. The following year, 1981, the group, credited as the Fureys And Davy Arthur, reached the UK Top 20 with 'When You Were Sweet Sixteen'. By contrast, the album, having the same title, only just made the Top 100 in the UK during 1982. A follow-up single, 'I Will Love You (Every Time When We Are Gone)' failed to make the Top 50. *Golden Days*, released on K-Tel, made the UK Top 20 in 1984, selling in excess of 250,000 copies, while *At The End Of A Perfect Day*, also on K-Tel, made the UK Top 40 in 1985.

Numerous compilations abound, but *The Sound Of The Fureys And Davey Arthur*, on PolyGram Records, was released only in Ireland. *Golden Days* and *At The End Of A Perfect Day* were re-packaged, in 1991, as *The Very Best Of The Fureys And Davy Arthur*. The group has successfully followed the middle-of-the-road folk musical path, by producing melodic and

popular music. Folk purists argue that this detracts from 'real' folk music, whilst their supporters say that the group has encouraged people to listen to folk music. Either way, their concerts are popular worldwide, and while not a hugely successful chart act domestically, their records still sell extremely well. Towards the end of 1993, Davy Arthur left the group and formed Davy Arthur And Co.

● ALBUMS: *When You Were Sweet Sixteen* (Castle Classics 1982) ★★★, *Steal Away* (Ritz 1983) ★★★, *In Concert* (Ritz 1984) ★★★, *Golden Days* (K-Tel 1984) ★★★★, *At The End Of A Perfect Day* (K-Tel 1985) ★★★, *The First Leaves Of Autumn* (Ritz 1986) ★★★, *The Scattering* (BMG/Ariola 1989) ★★★.
● COMPILATIONS: *The Sound Of The Fureys And Davey Arthur* (PolyGram Ireland 1981) ★★★, *The Fureys Finest* (Telstar 1987) ★★★★, *The Fureys Collection* (Castle Communications 1989) ★★★★, *The Very Best Of The Fureys And Davy Arthur* (Music Club 1991) ★★★★, *Winds Of Change* (Ritz 1992) ★★★, *The Essential Fureys* (Erin 2001) ★★★★.

## FURNITURE

Led by James Irvin (b. 20 July 1959, Chiswick, London, England; vocals), UK guitar band Furniture originally formed in 1981 with the intention of marrying the influences of 'the Undertones and Chic'. With their line-up completed by Tim Whelan (b. 15 September 1958, London, England; guitar) and Hamilton Lee (b. 7 September 1958, London, England; drums), they released their debut single, 'Shaking Story', on their own The Guy From Paraguay label. Afterwards they were joined by Sally Still (b. 5 February 1964, London, England; bass) and Maya Gilder (b. 25 April 1964, Poonak, India; keyboards), and recorded a debut mini-album for independent label Survival Records in September 1983. Reaction was almost non-existent, and the group considered an early exit before Stiff Records heard one of the new songs they had written, 'Brilliant Mind', and signed them. Released as a single, this evocative, understated song reached number 21 in the UK charts in May 1986. Stiff, however, collapsed after the release of only one further single, 'Love Your Shoes' (itself a new version of a 1985 Premonition single). ZTT Records acquired the Stiff catalogue, and Furniture spent the next two years attempting to free themselves from their contract. They finally achieved this in 1989 via a new contract with Arista Records, but their chart stature had long since declined. Arista released an album, *Food Sex And Paranoia*, but sacked almost half of its A&R department (including the team that had signed Furniture) immediately afterwards. Underexposed and overlooked, the album that should have resurrected their career managed only 5,000 sales.

Irvin broke up the group after a farewell performance at the 1990 Reading Festival, before recording his debut solo album (attributed to Because) in 1991. He became Reviews Editor at *Melody Maker* magazine, then Features Editor at *Mojo* magazine. His former colleagues, Lee and Whelan, enjoyed notable success as members of Transglobal Underground. Gilder joined the BBC.

● ALBUMS: *When The Boom Was On* mini-album (Premonition 1983) ★★★, *The Wrong People* (Stiff 1986) ★★★, *Food Sex And Paranoia* (Arista 1990) ★★★.
Solo: Jim Irvin as Because *Mad, Scared, Dumb And Gorgeous* (Haven 1991) ★★★.
● COMPILATIONS: *The Lovemongers* (Survival 1986) ★★★, *She Gets Out The Scrapbook – The Best Of Furniture* (Survival 1991) ★★★.

## GABRIEL, PETER

b. 13 February 1950, London, England. After seven years fronting Genesis, Gabriel tired of the extensive touring and band format and went solo in 1975. Until the release of 1983's *Peter Gabriel Plays Live*, his solo albums for Charisma Records were all called *Peter Gabriel*. His 1977 debut included the track 'Solsbury Hill', a metaphorical account of his split from Genesis, which made the Top 20 in the UK. The album charted in the UK Top 10 and the *Billboard* Top 40 and Gabriel began his solo touring career in the USA, expressing a nervousness of facing his home country audiences. Unlike his earlier extravagant, theatrical presentations, he favoured minimalism and often played shows in a plain boiler suit. Robert Fripp was brought in as producer for the second album, which made the UK Top 10. The album contained chiefly introspective, experimental music, but healthy sales figures were encouraging. However, Atlantic Records refused to distribute his third album in the USA, claiming its maudlin nature would mean 'commercial suicide'. Mercury Records stepped in and with Steve Lillywhite's disciplined production the striking collection was far from the flop Atlantic feared, narrowly failing to break into the Top 20 (the album topped the UK chart). 'Games Without Frontiers' was a UK Top 5 hit and the track 'Biko', about the murdered South African activist Stephen Biko, became an anti-racist anthem.

Continuing his deliberated approach, his fourth album, given the full title of *Peter Gabriel (Security)*, was not released until 1982 and appeared to be hinting at a more accessible approach, tempering the third album's dense electronic production values with African and Latin rhythms. The album was distributed by Geffen Records in the USA, and a German-language edition was also released. In 1985, Gabriel composed the haunting soundtrack to the Alan Parker movie, *Birdy*. The journey to complete commercial acceptance was finished in 1986 with his Virgin Records debut *So*. The album contained the hit single 'Sledgehammer' (US number 1/UK number 4), which was supported by a pioneering, award-winning video featuring puppetry and animation. He was celebrated as an artist whose work was popular without being compromised. A duet with Kate Bush, 'Don't Give Up', also lifted from *So*, became a UK Top 10 hit in November 1986.

Throughout the 80s, Gabriel dedicated much of his time to absorbing world music and in 1982 inaugurated the WOMAD (World Of Music And Dance) Festival. He also became heavily involved in Amnesty International and recorded with Senegalese star Youssou N'Dour. The pair toured the USA under the banner of 'Conspiracy Of Hope' and raised money for Amnesty. He invited musicians from all over the world to record at his luxurious self-built Real World studios in Bath and incorporated many non-Western ideas into his own music. In 1989, Gabriel was commissioned to write the score for Martin Scorsese's *The Last Temptation Of Christ*. Virgin Records, now the owners of the Charisma back-catalogue, released a greatest hits collection in 1990, *Shaking The Tree: Sixteen Golden Greats*. The title track was written by Gabriel with N'Dour and was included originally on N'Dour's album, *The Lion*. Although 1992's *Us* fell short of the high standard set by *So*, it put Gabriel back in the public eye with a series of outstandingly creative videos for singles such as 'Steam' (a UK number 10 hit), 'Digging In The Dirt' and 'Kiss That Frog'.

In 1999, Gabriel was commissioned to contribute music and act as musical director for the Millennium Dome show in London. The soundtrack was released the following year on the *Ovo* album. Gabriel's next project was the soundtrack to Australian film *The Rabbit-Proof Fence*, released in June 2002. His brand new studio album followed three months later.

● ALBUMS: *Peter Gabriel* (Charisma/Atco 1977) ★★★, *Peter Gabriel* (Charisma/Atlantic 1978) ★★★, *Peter Gabriel* (Charisma/Mercury 1980) ★★★★, *Peter Gabriel (Security)* (Charisma/Geffen 1982) ★★★★, *Peter Gabriel Plays Live* (Charisma/Geffen 1983) ★★, *Birdy* film soundtrack (Charisma/Geffen 1985) ★★, *So* (Virgin/Geffen 1986) ★★★★, *Passion: Music For The Last Temptation Of Christ* (Virgin/Geffen 1989) ★★, *Us* (Real World/Geffen 1992) ★★★, *Secret World – Live* (Real World 1994) ★★★, *Ovo* (Real World 2000) ★★★, *Long Walk Home: Music From The Rabbit-Proof Fence* (Real World 2002) ★★★, *Up* (Charisma/Geffen 2002) ★★★.

● COMPILATIONS: *Shaking The Tree: Sixteen Golden Greats* (Virgin/Geffen 1990) ★★★★.

● VIDEOS: *Point Of View (Live In Athens)* (Virgin Vision 1989), *The Desert And Her Daughters* (Hendring Music Video 1990), *CV* (Virgin Vision 1991), *All About Us* (Real World 1993), *Secret World Live* (Real World 1994), *Computer Animation: Vol. 2.* (Real World 1994).

● FURTHER READING: *Peter Gabriel: An Authorized Biography*, Spenser Bright. *In His Own Words*, Mick St. Michael.

## GALAXIE 500

Ex-Harvard College alumni Dean Wareham (b. New Zealand; guitar, vocals), Naomi Yang (bass, vocals) and Damon Krukowski (drums) formed this group (named after an American car) in Boston, Massachusetts, USA. Having released one track, 'Obvious', on a flexi-disc given away with the magazine *Chemical Imbalance*, they moved to New York. Maverick producer Kramer allowed the trio's brittle amateurism to flourish on *Today*, wherein Wareham's plaintive voice and scratchy guitar work inspired comparisons with the Velvet Underground and Jonathan Richman. A version of the latter's 'Don't Let Our Youth Go To Waste' was featured on this engaging set which inspired Rough Trade Records to sign the band. *On Fire* continued their established métier, and a growing self-confidence imbued the songs with resonance and atmosphere.

*This Is Our Music* provided a greater emphasis on light and shade, sacrificing some of Yang's silky bass lines for traditional dynamism. A cover version of Yoko Ono's 'Listen, The Snow Is Falling' proved captivating, but the set lacked the warmth of its predecessors.

Rumours of internal disaffection proved true when Wareham left in 1991. He subsequently formed the enthralling Luna 2, later known simply as Luna. His former Galaxie 500 partners continued as Pierre Etoile, issuing a self-titled EP in August, then simply Damon And Naomi. After releasing a 1992 album (*More Sad Hits*), Yang and Krukowski collaborated with Kate Biggar of Crystallised Movements as Magic Hour. The duo released another album with Kramer, 1995's *The Wondrous World Of ...*, before concentrating on their publishing company Exact Change. In 1996, they issued a box set containing the entire recorded output of Galaxie 500, and returned to the studio two years later with the self-produced *Playback Singers*.

● ALBUMS: *Today* (Aurora 1989) ★★, *On Fire* (Rough Trade 1989) ★★★, *This Is Our Music* (Rough Trade 1990) ★★★, *Copenhagen* 1990 live recording (Rykodisc 1997) ★★★.

● COMPILATIONS: *1987–1991* 4-CD box set (Rykodisc 1996) ★★★, *The Portable Galaxie 500* (Rykodisc 1998) ★★★.

## GANG OF FOUR

Formed in Leeds, Yorkshire, England in 1977, Gang Of Four – Jon King (vocals, melodica), Andy Gill (guitar, vocals), Dave Allen (bass) and Hugo Burnham (drums) – made their debut on Fast Records the following year with *Damaged Goods*. This uncompromising three-track EP introduced the band's strident approach, wherein Burnham's pounding, compulsive drumming and Gill's staccato, stuttering guitar work, reminiscent of Wilko Johnson from Dr. Feelgood, framed their overtly political lyrics. The quartet maintained this direction on *Entertainment!*, while introducing the interest in dance music that marked future recordings. Its most impressive track, 'At Home He's A Tourist', was issued as a single, but encountered censorship problems over its pre-AIDS reference to prophylactics ('rubbers').

Following the release of *Solid Gold*, internal strife resulted in Allen's departure, later to join Shriekback, in July 1981. He was replaced by Sara Lee, formerly of Jane Aire And The Belvederes, as the band pursued a fuller, more expansive sound. *Songs Of The Free* featured the tongue-in-cheek single 'I Love A Man In Uniform', which seemed destined for chart success until disappearing from radio playlists in the wake of the Falklands conflict. Burnham was fired in 1983 and a three-piece line-up completed *Hard* with sundry session musicians. This disappointing release made little difference to a band unable to satisfy now divergent audiences and they split up the following year. However, following several rather inconclusive projects, King and Gill exhumed the Gang Of Four name in 1990. The reunion was marked by *Mall* for Polydor Records, which justified the decision to resume their career with a set of typically bracing, still politically motivated songs. However, it did little to revive their commercial fortunes, and was never released in the UK.

Gill and King subsequently worked on movie soundtracks, one of which, *Delinquent*, formed the basis of the energetic and full-sounding *Shrinkwrapped*, on which the duo was joined by Curve members Dean Garcia and Steve Monti. The furious rhythms and dark musical scenarios of earlier years made a welcome return, while the lyrics continued to paint the agents of capitalism as the enemy (notably on 'Lord Of The Anthill'). Gill and King played some rare live dates to a rapturous reception, but shortly afterwards the latter retired from the music business. Gill teamed up with Burnham and Allen in 1998 to compile the excellent *100 Flowers Bloom* compilation.

● ALBUMS: *Entertainment!* (EMI/Warners 1979) ★★★★, *Solid Gold* (EMI/Warners 1981) ★★★, *Songs Of The Free* (EMI/Warners 1982) ★★★, *Hard* (EMI/Warners 1983) ★★, *At The Palace* (Mercury/Phonogram 1984) ★★, *Mall* (Polydor 1991) ★★★, *Shrinkwrapped* (When! 1995) ★★★★.

● COMPILATIONS: *The Peel Sessions* (Strange Fruit 1990) ★★★, *A Brief History Of The Twentieth Century* (EMI/Warners 1990) ★★★★, *100 Flowers Bloom* (Rhino 1998) ★★★★.

## GAUGHAN, DICK

b. Leith, Scotland. A veteran of Scotland's thriving folk circuit, Gaughan rose to national prominence in the 70s as a member of the Boys Of The Lough. From there, he became a founder member of Five Hand Reel, an electric folk group that enjoyed considerable critical acclaim. Gaughan left them in 1978 following the release of their third album, *Earl O' Moray*, having already embarked on a concurrent solo career. His early releases, *No More Forever* and *Kist O' Gold*, concentrated on traditional material, while *Coppers And Brass* showcased guitar interpretations of Scottish and Irish dance music. However, it was the release of *Handful Of Earth* that established Gaughan as a major force in contemporary folk. This politically charged album included the beautifully vitriolic 'Worker's Song' and 'The World Turned Upside Down' while at the same time scotched notions of nationalism with the reconciliatory 'Both Sides The Tweed'. This exceptional set is rightly regarded as a landmark in British traditional music, but its ever-restless creator surprised many commentators with *A Different Kind Of Love Song*, which included a version of Joe South's 60s protest song, 'Games People Play'.

Gaughan has since enjoyed a fervent popularity both at home and abroad while continuing to pursue his uncompromising, idiosyncratic musical path. Gaughan calls himself a 'hard-nosed Communist' and is a passionate lover and supporter of Scotland, while not tolerating any anti-English feeling. Both his playing and singing come from the heart and by the 90s he was being lauded as arguably Scotland's greatest living troubadour.

Gaughan was part of the folk 'supergroup' Clan Alba in the mid-90s, alongside veteran artists Mary

MacMaster, Brian McNeill, Fred Morrison, Patsy Seddon, Davy Steele, Mike Travis and Dave Tulloch. He made a return to solo work with 1996's *Sail On*, a typically inspired album featuring a superb cover version of the Rolling Stones' 'Ruby Tuesday'.

● ALBUMS: *No More Forever* (Trailer 1972) ★★, *Coppers And Brass* (Topic 1977) ★★, *Kist O' Gold* (Trailer 1977) ★★★, with Dave Burland, Tony Capstick *Songs Of Ewan MacColl* (Rubber 1978) ★★★, *Gaughan* (Topic 1978) ★★★, *Handful Of Earth* (Topic 1981) ★★★★, with Andy Irvine *Parallel Lines* (Folk Freak 1982) ★★★, *A Different Kind Of Love Song* (Celtic 1983) ★★★, with Ken Hyder *Fanfare For Tomorrow* (Impetus 1985) ★★★, *Live In Edinburgh* (Celtic 1985) ★★★, *True And Bold* (Stuc 1986) ★★★, *Call It Freedom* (Celtic 1988) ★★★, *Sail On* (Greentrax 1996) ★★★, *Redwood Cathedral* (Greentrax 1998) ★★★, *Outlaws & Dreamers* (Greentrax 2001) ★★★.

## GAYE BYKERS ON ACID

This UK rock band employed an image that combined traditional biker attire with elements of psychedelia and hippie camp. They were led by the colourful figure of Mary Millington, aka Mary Mary (b. Ian Garfield Hoxley; vocals), alongside Kevin Hyde (drums), Robber (b. Ian Michael Reynolds; bass) and Tony Horsfall (b. Richard Anthony Horsfall; guitar). They were later complemented by disc jockey William Samuel Ronald Monroe ('Rocket Ronnie'). Mary Mary, who had once come second in Leicester's Alternative Miss Universe competition, was often to be seen in platform shoes and dresses, which fuelled the critics' confusion with regard to the band's name and gender orientation. Their debut album, *Drill Your Own Hole*, required purchasers to do just that, as the record was initially issued without a hole in its centre. After leaving Virgin Records, they set up their own label, Naked Brain, quite conceivably because nobody else would have them. Subsequent to the band's demise, Hyde instigated a new band, GROWTH, with Jeff (ex-Janitors), Horsfall teamed up with Brad Bradbury in Camp Collision, Reynolds worked as a DJ, and Rocket Ronnie went on to collaborate with the Grid's Richard Norris and run the drum 'n' bass label Warm Interface. Mary Mary joined ex-members of Killing Joke, Ministry and Public Image Limited in the multi-member outfit Pigface. The 90s brought a more permanent home for his talents with Hyperhead, a band he formed with Karl Leiker (ex-Luxuria; Bugblot), and breakbeat dance outfit Apollo 440.

● ALBUMS: *Drill Your Own Hole* (Virgin 1987) ★★★, *Stewed To The Gills* (Virgin 1989) ★★★, *GrooveDiveSoapDish* (Bleed 1989) ★★★, *Cancer Planet Mission* (Naked Brain 1990) ★★, as PFX *Pernicious Nonsense* (Naked Brain 1991) ★★, *From The Tomb Of The Near Legendary* (Receiver 1993) ★★.

● VIDEOS: *Drill Your Own Hole* (Virgin Vision 1987).

## GEFFEN, DAVID

b. David Lawrence Geffen, 21 February 1943, Brooklyn, New York City, New York, USA. Geffen became one of the richest individuals in rock through his activities as manager, label owner and film producer. After failing to complete his studies at the University Of Texas, Geffen got his start in showbusiness in 1963 with a job at CBS Television in Los Angeles, before moving to the mailroom of the William Morris Agency. In 1968, after establishing himself as one of the company leading agents, he become the manager of Laura Nyro, helping her sign to Columbia Records after he had befriended Clive Davis. Next Geffen formed a company with Elliott Roberts, to manage Crosby, Stills And Nash, Joni Mitchell (her song 'Free Man In Paris' was about Geffen), Jackson Browne, Linda Ronstadt and others. In 1970, he founded his first label, Asylum Records, signing Mitchell and the Eagles. Two years later it was sold to WEA Records for $7,000,000 although Geffen stayed on as chairperson. During this time he had a lengthy relationship with Cher, at one stage they were close to being married. He was promoted to chief of Elektra/Asylum in 1973, signing Bob Dylan for a brief stay at the label. He became vice-chairman of Warner Brothers Pictures two years later, but was fired by chairman Ted Ashley a year later.

Cancer of the bladder forced Geffen to leave the music business for several years but he returned in 1980 with another new label, Geffen Records, whose initial roster included John Lennon and Elton John. The following year he also started Geffen Films, with distribution by Warner Brothers. Among his movies productions were *Risky Business* and *Little Shop Of Horrors* while on Broadway he backed *Cats* and *Dreamgirls*. In 1986, Geffen Records enjoyed huge international success with Peter Gabriel's *So*, and signed Guns N'Roses and Nirvana. In 1990, Geffen sold his label to MCA for $540 million in stock and when MCA itself was bought by Japanese company Matsushita he made over $700 million. At MCA, he remained chairman of Geffen Records and introduced a new label, DGC. In 1994, he founded the multi-media company DreamWorks with Steven Spielberg and Jeffrey Katzenberg. Geffen has been shown to be a ruthless businessman, sometimes forsaking friendships over business. Much of this is revealed in Tom King's compelling biography. What is not in dispute is that he is probably the most successful person the music business has ever known, both commercially, and certainly financially.

● FURTHER READING: *The Hit Men*, Frederick Dannen. *The Operator: David Geffen Builds, Buys, And Sells The New Hollywood*, Tom King.

## GELDOF, BOB

b. Robert Frederick Zenon Geldof, 5 October 1951, Dún Laoghaire, Co. Dublin, Eire. Geldof initially entered the music scene as a journalist on Canada's premier underground rock journal *Georgia Straight*. Further experience with the *New Musical Express* and *Melody Maker* sharpened his prose and upon returning to Dublin, he formed the band Nightlife Thugs, which subsequently evolved into the Boomtown Rats, one of the first acts to emerge during the punk/new wave explosion of 1976/77.

After a series of hits, including two UK number 1 singles, the band fell from favour, but Geldof was about to emerge unexpectedly as one of the most well known pop personalities of his era. He had always had an acerbic wit and provided excellent interviews with an energy and enthusiasm that matched any of his articulate rivals. After starring in the film of Pink Floyd's *The Wall*, he turned his attention to the dreadful famine that was plaguing Ethiopia in 1984. Shocked by the horrific pictures that he saw on television, Geldof organized the celebrated Band Aid aggregation for the charity record which he co-wrote with Midge Ure, 'Do They Know It's Christmas?' The single sold in excess of three million copies and thanks to Geldof's foresight in gaining financial control of every aspect of the record's production, manufacture and distribution, famine relief received over 96 pence of the £1.35 retail price. The record inspired 1985's mammoth Live Aid extravaganza in which Geldof herded together rock's elite to play before a worldwide television audience of over 1,000,000,000.

Geldof continued to help with the administration of Band Aid, which effectively put his singing career on hold for a couple of years. After receiving a knighthood in June 1986 and publishing his autobiography, he recorded the solo album, *Deep In The Heart Of Nowhere*, which spawned the minor hit 'This Is The World Calling'. Unfortunately, Geldof's celebrity status seemed to have worked against him in the fashion-conscious pop world, a fact that he freely admitted. His second album, 1990's *The Vegetarians Of Love*, was recorded in a mere five days and proved a hit with critics and fans alike. Complete with folk and Cajun flavourings and an irreverent stab at apathy in the hit single 'The Great Song Of Indifference', the album brought some hope that Geldof might be able to continue his recording career, despite the perennial publicity that associates his name almost exclusively with Live Aid.

A further album was poorly received, and the singer's attention began to be diverted by other interests. By now he had established himself as a highly astute businessman with his co-ownership of the television production house Planet 24, which began life as Planet Pictures back in the mid-80s. The company broke into the big time by launching the pioneering early morning television series *The Big Breakfast* in 1992. Geldof was once again in the headlines in late 1994, although this time not by his choosing. His marriage to television presenter/writer Paula Yates had seemingly broken up following her affair with Michael Hutchence of INXS. Throughout the whole tawdry media exposure Geldof remained calm and kept his dignity.

In the late 90s, Geldof moved into new media, founding the online travel agency site deckchair.com and the mobile portal WapWorld. He also held a major share in the online music retailer clickmusic.com, prior to its financial problems. Geldof returned to the music scene in September 2001 with his first new recording in over eight years. A raw and brutally frank album dealing in unflinching detail with the recent emotional upheavals of Geldof's personal life, *Sex, Age & Death* was in marked contrast to his previous studio set, the relatively upbeat *The Happy Club*.

● ALBUMS: *Deep In The Heart Of Nowhere* (Mercury/Atlantic 1986) ★★★, *The Vegetarians Of Love* (Mercury/Atlantic 1990) ★★★, *The Happy Club* (Vertigo 1992) ★★, *Sex, Age & Death* (Eagle 2001) ★★★.

● COMPILATIONS: *Loudmouth: The Best Of The Boomtown Rats And Bob Geldof* (Vertigo 1994) ★★★, *Great Songs Of Indifference: The Best Of Bob Geldof & The Boomtown Rats* (Columbia 1997) ★★★.

● FURTHER READING: *Is That It?*, Bob Geldof. *Bob Geldof*, Charlotte Gray.

● FILMS: *The Wall* (1982), *Diana & Me* (1997), *Spice World* (1997).

## GENE LOVES JEZEBEL

Identical twins Jay (John) and Mike Aston, ostensibly Gene Loves Jezebel, enjoyed cult appeal, largely within the UK gothic rock community, but achieved greater success in America. The pair grew up in the South Wales town of Porthcawl, together with guitarist Ian Hudson. After moving to London, they made their debut in late 1981 supporting the Higsons. A recording contract with Situation 2 resulted in 'Shavin' My Neck' (a collection of demos) the following May. The dense, experimental sound was matched by live performances, featuring bass player Julianne Regan and drummer Dick Hawkins, where they mixed almost tribal rhythms with furious guitar work. Hawkins was replaced by a succession of drummers, including John Murphy (ex-Associates; SPK) and Steve Goulding, while Regan left to front All About Eve. Her space was filled by Hudson, allowing Albio De Luca (later of Furyo) to operate as guitarist in time for 'Screaming (For Emmalene)' in 1983.
Following Luca and Goulding's departure, Hudson reverted to guitar and Hawkins/Murphy offered a two-pronged drum attack. Murphy then left before a third single, the strong commercial sound of 'Bruises' (1983). Hot on its heels came their powerful debut album, *Promise*, promoted by a John Peel BBC radio session. A trip to the USA in 1984 to work with John Cale ensued, before returning for two quick-fire singles, 'Influenza (Relapse)' and 'Shame (Whole Heart Howl)'. Marshall then left, Mike Aston briefly switching from rhythm guitar to play bass, before Peter Rizzo was recruited. Ex-Spear Of Destiny drummer Chris Bell arrived in place of Hawkins, but it was a year before 'The Cow' hit the UK independent charts, preceding *Immigrant* in June 1985. After 'Desire' in November, the band left for a further north American tour, a traumatic time that led to Hudson's departure, ex-Generation X guitarist James Stevenson taking his place. The band skirted the Top 75 with 'Sweetest Thing' and *Discover* (which included a free live album), while 'Heartache' hinted at a passing interest in dance music. They subsequently concentrated their efforts on the US market. However, all was not well in their camp, and Mike Aston left the band in mid-1989.
In 1993 Gene Loves Jezebel, now comprising Jay Aston, Rizzo, Stevenson and Robert Adam, released the ill-fated *Heavenly Bodies*. The band subsequently

ground to a halt, with the various members moving on to different projects. The Astons reunited with Stevenson, Bell and Rizzo to record new material for a 1995 compilation set, before re-forming Gene Loves Jezebel on a more permanent basis in the late 90s.

● ALBUMS: *Promise* (Situation 2 1983) ★★★, *Immigrant* (Beggars Banquet 1985) ★★★, *Discover* (Beggars Banquet 1986) ★★★, *The House Of Dolls* (Beggars Banquet 1987) ★★, *Kiss Of Life* (Beggars Banquet 1990) ★★, *Heavenly Bodies* (Savage/Arista 1993) ★★★, *VII* (Robison 1999) ★★★, *Love Lies Bleeding* (Robison 1999) ★★★, *Live In The Voodoo City* (Triple X 1999) ★★, *Giving Up The Ghost* (Triple X 2001) ★★, *Live At Nottingham* (Perris 2002) ★★.

● COMPILATIONS: *Some Of The Best Of Gene Loves Jezebel: From The Mouths Of Babes* (Avalanche 1995) ★★★, *Voodoo Dollies: The Best Of Gene Loves Jezebel* (Beggars Banquet 1999) ★★★.

## GENERAL KANE

US group fronted by Mitch McDowell (b. 1954, San Bernadino, California, USA, d. January 1992). McDowell took the professional name General Kane (formerly General Caine) in tribute to an officer who had supported his artistic ambitions when he was at military school. After leaving that institution, he formed the group Booty People with several future members of War, before assembling an eight-piece rap group and signing with Groove Time Records in 1978. Two albums for the label preceded a move to Tabu Records. A slimmed-down version of the group signed a recording contract with Motown Records in the mid-80s. Their debut single for the label, 'Crack Killed Applejack', was an uncompromising reflection of drug addiction on the inner city streets, and reached number 12 in the black music charts despite being barred from airplay. Subsequent releases mellowed General Kane's approach, without losing their commitment to the basic rap sound of the late 80s – though the group's album, *Wide Open*, did include a romantic ballad, 'Close Your Eyes', which featured vocals from two of the group's less prominent members, Cheryl McDowell and Danny Macon. Mitch McDowell was murdered in January 1992. General Kane's catalogue remained in print through the efforts of their former producer, Grover Wimberly III, who runs his own label, King Bee Records.

● ALBUMS: *General Caine* (Groove Time 1978) ★★★, *Get Down Attack* (Groove Time 1981) ★★★★, *Girls* (Tabu 1982) ★★, *Dangerous* (Tabu 1984) ★★★, *In Full Chill* (Motown 1986) ★★★, *Wide Open* (Motown 1987) ★★★.

## GENERAL PUBLIC

When the Birmingham, England-based Beat disbanded, the band's two vocalists, Dave Wakeling and Ranking Roger, formed General Public with ex-Specials bass player Horace Panter (bass), Stoker (drums), Micky Billingham (keyboards) and Kevin White (guitar), plus veteran saxophonist Saxa. A self-titled debut single on Virgin Records combined a strong pop sound with an underlying dance feel and brushed the UK charts. 'Tenderness', in October, fared better in the USA (on I.R.S. Records), coinciding with a fine debut album, ... *All The Rage*. Without a British hit, the band's blend of musical influences, characterized by Roger's all-round skills, was largely ignored. General Public tried again in 1986 with *Hand To Mouth*, but despite aiming at the singles market with 'Faults And All', the world seemed oblivious and the band disappeared. Ranking Roger surfaced in a revitalized International Beat, before a new album finally appeared in 1995, with the line-up consisting of Wakeling, Ranking Roger, Michael Railton (vocals, keyboards), Norman Jones (vocals, percussion), Wayne Lothian (bass), and Dan Chase (drums). Produced by Jerry Harrison, the album sounded fresh and energetic. In addition to invigorating originals such as 'It Must Be Tough' and 'Rainy Days', there was an interesting ska/reggae version of Van Morrison's 'Warm Love'.

● ALBUMS: ... *All The Rage* (Virgin/I.R.S. 1984) ★★★, *Hand To Mouth* (Virgin/I.R.S. 1986) ★★★, *Rub It Better* (Epic 1995) ★★★.

● COMPILATIONS: *Classic Masters* (Capitol 2002) ★★★.

## GENESIS

This leading UK rock band first came together at the public school Charterhouse. Peter Gabriel (b. 13 May 1950, London, England; vocals), Tony Banks (b. 27 March 1951, East Heathly, Sussex, England; keyboards) and Chris Stewart (drums) were in an ensemble named the Garden Wall, and joined forces with Anthony Philips (guitar/vocals) and Mike Rutherford (b. 2 October 1950; bass/guitar/vocals), who were in a rival group, the Anon. In January 1967, the student musicians sent a demonstration tape to another Charterhouse alumnus, Jonathan King, then at Decca Records. King financed further recordings and christened the band Genesis. They recorded one single, 'The Silent Sun' in 1968, but it was not until the following year that their debut album *From Genesis To Revelation* was issued. Its lack of success left them without a label until the enterprising Tony Stratton-Smith signed them to his recently formed Charisma Records in 1970. The band had already lost three drummers from their line-up before finding the perfect candidate that August. Phil Collins (b. 31 January 1951, London, England) had already worked with a professional group, Flaming Youth, and his involvement would later prove crucial in helping Genesis achieve international success.

The already recorded *Trespass* was issued in October 1970, but sold poorly. Further line-up changes ensued with the arrival of new guitarist Steve Hackett (b. 12 February 1950, London, England). The band was known for their highly theatrical stage act and costumes, but this did not help record sales. When the 1971 album *Nursery Cryme* also failed commercially, the band was again in danger of being dropped from their label. Success on the continent brought renewed faith, which was vindicated with the release of *Foxtrot*. The album reached the UK Top 20 and included the epic live favourite 'Supper's Ready'. Over the next two-and-a-half years, Genesis increased their profile with the bestselling albums *Selling England By The Pound* and *The Lamb Lies Down On Broadway*.

Having reached a new peak, however, their prospects were completely undermined by the shock departure of singer Gabriel in May 1975. Many commentators understandably wrote Genesis off at this point, particularly when it was announced that the new singer was to be their drummer Collins. The streamlined quartet proved remarkably resilient, however, and the succeeding albums *A Trick Of The Tail* and *Wind And Wuthering* were well received. In the summer of 1977, Hackett left to pursue a solo career, after which Genesis carried on as a trio, backed by various short-term employees. Amazingly, the band appeared to grow in popularity with the successive departure of each key member. During 1978, they received their first gold disc for the appropriately titled *And Then There Were Three* and two years later enjoyed a chart-topping album with *Duke*. With various solo excursions underway, Genesis still managed to sustain its identity as a working group and reached new levels of popularity with hits in the USA. By late 1981, they were in the US Top 10 with *Abacab* and could rightly claim to be one of the most popular rock acts in the world. Helped by Collins' high profile as a soloist, they enjoyed their biggest UK singles hit with 'Mama' and followed with 'Thats All' and 'Illegal Alien'. In America, they scored a number 1 single in 1986 with 'Invisible Touch', while the following four singles all made the US Top 5. Both *Genesis* and *Invisible Touch* topped the UK charts, while the latter also reached number 1 in the USA.

By the mid-80s, the group format was not sufficient to contain all their various projects and Collins pursued a parallel solo career, while Rutherford formed the hit act Mike And The Mechanics. In 1991, the trio reconvened to record and issue *We Can't Dance*. Although this was their first album in over five years, it immediately topped the charts throughout the world confirming their status as one of the world's leading dinosaur bands. Collins decided that his solo career and relocation to Switzerland had put too much pressure on trying to maintain his role in the band and he officially resigned. Although either of Mike's Mechanics, Paul Carrack or Paul Young would have fitted the bill perfectly, his replacement was Ray Wilson, the former lead singer of Stiltskin. He was heard on *Calling All Stations* released in August 1997, which proved to be the final Genesis recording as Rutherford and Banks also elected to call it a day.

● ALBUMS: *From Genesis To Revelation* (Decca 1969) ★, *Trespass* (Charisma 1970) ★★, *Nursery Cryme* (Charisma 1971) ★★★, *Foxtrot* (Charisma 1972) ★★★, *Genesis Live* (Charisma 1973) ★★, *Selling England By The Pound* (Charisma 1973) ★★★, *The Lamb Lies Down On Broadway* (Charisma 1974) ★★★★, *A Trick Of The Tail* (Charisma 1976) ★★★, *Wind And Wuthering* (Charisma 1977) ★★★, *Seconds Out* (Charisma 1977) ★★, *And Then There Were Three* (Charisma 1978) ★★★, *Duke* (Charisma 1980) ★★★★, *Abacab* (Charisma 1981) ★★★, *3 Sides Live* (Charisma 1982) ★★, *Genesis* (Charisma 1983) ★★★, *Invisible Touch* (Charisma 1986) ★★★, *We Can't*

*Dance* (Virgin 1991) ★★★, *The Way We Walk – Volume 1: The Shorts* (Virgin 1992) ★★, *Live The Way We Walk – Volume 2: The Longs* (Virgin 1993) ★★, *Calling All Stations* (Virgin 1997) ★★.
● COMPILATIONS: *Archive 1967–75* 4-CD box set (Virgin 1998) ★★★★, *Turn It On Again ... The Hits* (Virgin 1999) ★★★★, *Archive #2 1976–1992* 3-CD box set (Virgin 2000) ★★★★.
● VIDEOS: *Three Sides Live* (Virgin 1986), *Live: The Mama Tour* (Virgin 1986), *Visible Touch* (Virgin 1987), *Genesis 2* (Virgin 1988), *Genesis 1* (Virgin 1988), *Invisible Touch Tour* (Virgin 1989), *Genesis: A History 1967–1991* (Virgin 1991), *Live: The Way We Walk* (Virgin 1993), *Songbook* (Eagle Vision 2001).
● FURTHER READING: *Genesis: The Evolution Of A Rock Band*, Armando Gallo. *Genesis Lyrics*, Kim Poor. *Genesis: Turn It On Again*, Steve Clarke. *Genesis: A Biography*, Dave Bowler and Brian Dray. *Opening The Musical Box*, Alan Hewitt. *Genesis: Inside & Out*, Robin Platts.

## GEORGIA SATELLITES

This rock quartet was formed as the Hellhounds in 1980 in Atlanta, USA, when Dan Baird (b. Daniel John Baird, 12 December 1953, San Diego, California, USA; vocals) and Rick Richards (guitar) started jamming together inspired by the Rolling Stones, the Kinks and the Pretty Things. Rick Price (bass) and Mauro Magellan (drums) completed the band. Magellan was the only one of the four not to originate from the Deep South, hailing from Miami. After a small-budget independent EP, they signed to Elektra Records. Their debut album rose to number 5 in the US charts in 1987, thanks to the Top 5 success of the inspired single 'Keep Your Hands To Yourself'. They followed up with two cover versions; the Woods' 'Battleship Chains' and Chan Romero's 'Hippy Hippy Shake' (featured on the soundtrack of the Tom Cruise movie *Cocktail*). One of their heroes, Ian McLagan of the Small Faces, later joined them for *In The Land Of Salvation And Sin*, following which Baird left to start a solo career. The rest of the band went their separate ways shortly afterwards, although Richards and Price re-formed the Georgia Satellites in 1996, recruiting Billy Pitts (drums) and Joey Huffman (keyboards) to help record *Shaken Not Stirred*. Richards and Price continue to play together as the Hellhounds in addition to their commitments to the Georgia Satellites.
● ALBUMS: *Keep The Faith* mini-album (Making Waves 1985) ★★★, *Georgia Satellites* (Elektra 1986) ★★★★, *Open All Night* (Elektra 1988) ★★★, *In The Land Of Salvation And Sin* (Elektra 1989) ★★★, *Shaken Not Stirred* (CMC/3NM 1997) ★★.
● COMPILATIONS: *Let It Rock* (Elektra 1993) ★★★★, *Greatest & Latest* (Disky 2001) ★★★, *The Essentials* (Rhino 2002) ★★★★.

## GIBBONS, WALTER

b. 1954, USA, d. 1994. Gibbons is often cited as the first 'remixer'. It was he who transformed Double Exposure's 'Ten Percent' from a three-minute album track into a nine-minute dancefloor epic and subsequently the first commercially available 12-inch single in 1975. Gibbons moved away from disco's emphasis on orchestration towards percussion, and developed contemporary mixing techniques with his DJing at clubs such as New York's Galaxy 21, Fantasia, Buttermilk Bottom, Philadelphia's Second Storey and the Monastery in Seattle. It was his DJing skills that influenced the respected producer François Kevorkian – whose live drumming accompanied Gibbons' sets. Gibbons not only advanced the skills of the DJ but also developed the art of 'remixing', adding dub-inspired effects to early disco records, often transforming them from mediocre dance music tracks into epic-sounding disco anthems for labels such as Salsoul, West End and Gold Mind. He also worked with artists such as Loleatta Holloway (remixing her 'Hit And Run' and 'Catch Me On The Rebound') and the Salsoul Orchestra ('Nice 'N' Nasty'). At the peak of his popularity, Gibbons rejected the decadence of disco to become a born-again Christian, even refusing to play records with a sexual content. However, in 1984, he released a 12-inch single, 'Set It Off' by Strafe, on his own independent Jus' Born label that had a massive impact on the emergent Chicago house scene. The record was a sensation at Levan's Garage in New York City and spawned covers by C. Sharpe and Masquerade and a 'response' single in the form of number 1'Set It Off (Party Rock)'. The track determined the tone for much of the house music that followed, with its seductive vocal refrain repeated over sparse and atmospheric beats. 'Set It Off' did just that, becoming massively popular in Chicago's nascent house clubs, where it was played by Frankie Knuckles and Farley Jackmaster Funk, and by the city's influential radio DJs. Gibbons also completed remix work on two tracks by Arthur Russell in 1986: Indian Ocean's 'Tree House'/'School Bell' on Sleeping Bag Records before leaving the music business.

## GIBSON, DEBBIE

b. Deborah Ann Gibson, 31 August 1970, Brooklyn, New York, USA. This pop singer/songwriter generated massive sales in the late 80s, particularly in her homeland. Following training in piano and early songwriting ventures, Gibson was signed to the management of Doug Breithart by the time she was 13 years old. The following three years saw her apprenticeship in recording studios as she produced and wrote over 100 original compositions, mostly in her own multi-track home studio. Before leaving school, she had signed to Atlantic Records and was only turned down for the lead role in a US production of *Les Misérables* when the producers discovered her age. By the end of 1987, she emerged alongside a rash of female teenage singers in the US charts, hitting number 4 twice with 'Only In My Dreams' and 'Shake Your Love'. Her songwriting status and production involvement on *Out Of The Blue* was duly noted by critics. When 'Foolish Beat' topped the charts in 1988, she became the youngest artist to have written, produced and performed a US number 1 single. 'Lost In Your Eyes', a sentimental ballad replaced the high-energy pop of previous singles, and topped the US charts once more after the disappointing 'Staying Together'. The equivalent accolade in the album chart would be hers for five weeks with *Electric Youth*, co-produced, as was her debut, by Fred Zarr. However, a batch of subsequent singles, including the album's title track, 'No More Rhyme' and 'We Could Be Together' fared progressively worse in the US charts. The sales of the third album *Anything Is Possible* proved similarly disappointing, despite the appearance of Freddie Jackson and Lamont Dozier in the studio.

In 1991, Gibson finally got to appear in *Les Misérables*, playing the part of Eponine in the Broadway production. She continued in the theatre after releasing 1993's *Body Mind Soul*, appearing as Sandy in the London, England production of *Grease*. She switched to the character of Betty Rizzo in the National Touring Company Of Grease, which performed throughout the USA from October 1995 to March 1996. Further acting roles have included stints in productions of *Funny Girl*, *Beauty And The Beast*, *Gypsy* and *Cinderella*. Her recording career has largely taken a back seat to her theatre work, and has moved away from the dance-pop of her teen years to a more considered AOR style.

● ALBUMS: *Out Of The Blue* (Atlantic 1987) ★★★★, *Electric Youth* (Atlantic 1989) ★★★, *Anything Is Possible* (Atlantic 1990) ★★, *Body Mind Soul* (Atlantic 1993) ★★, *Think With Your Heart* (EMI 1995) ★★★, *Deborah* (Espiritu 1997) ★★★, *M.Y.O.B.* (Golden Egg 2001) ★★★.

● COMPILATIONS: *Greatest Hits* (Atlantic 1996) ★★★.

● VIDEOS: *Live: Out Of The Blue* (Atlantic Video 1989), *Smart Pack* (Atlantic Video 1990), *Live Around The World* (Atlantic Video 1990).

## GILL, JOHNNY

b. Washington, DC, USA. Gill's expertly delivered soul vocal chords have been working since an early age. At the age of seven, he was singing with his three brothers in the gospel quartet the Wings Of Faith. His debut album was recorded when he was only 16. Following his meeting and subsequent recording with Stacey Lattishaw (*Perfect Combination*), she proffered his rough demo to Ahmet Ertegun at Atlantic Records, resulting in 1985's *Chemistry*. Although Gill failed to dent the charts he had built a considerable reputation with his voice, and replaced Bobby Brown in New Edition towards the end of their heyday, singing on their comeback hit 'If It Isn't Love' in 1988. He reinvented himself once again, following a similar pattern: working with Lattishaw, followed by another self titled solo album, this time on Motown Records. The mix was favourable, having been produced by Jimmy Jam and Terry Lewis and LA Reid and Babyface. The album was a major success and established him as a potential modern R&B giant, spawning a number of US hits including 'Rub You The Right Way', 'My My My' and 'Fairweather Friend'. Further success came as a featured vocalist with Shanice ('Silent Prayer') and Shabba Ranks ('Slow And Sexy'). 'This Floor' kept Gill's profile alive in 1993, together with *Provocative*, but it was not until 1996 that a new solo album was released. In 1997 Gill joined with Gerald LeVert and Keith Sweat

for the 'soul supergroup' LSG.

● ALBUMS: *Johnny Gill* (Cotillion 1983) ★★, with Stacey Lattishaw *Perfect Combination* (Cotillion 1984) ★★, *Chemistry* (Atlantic 1985) ★★★, *Johnny Gill* (Motown 1990) ★★★★, *Provocative* (Motown 1993) ★★★, *Let's Get The Mood Right* (Motown 1996) ★★★.

● COMPILATIONS: *Favorites* (Motown 1997) ★★★★, *Ultimate Collection* (Hip-O 2002) ★★★★.

## GIPSY KINGS

These popular flamenco artists initially formed as an offshoot of the family group Los Reyes (the Kings), who in the 70s and 80s were led by father José Reyes. Together with sons Nicolas and Andre Reyes, they enjoyed significant domestic success in Spain, though contrary to popular belief their origins lay on the other side of the French border. In 1982, Nicolas and Andre Reyes teamed up with Chico Bouchikhi when he married into the family. The Gipsy Kings were formed when they joined with three cousins from the Baliardo family (Diego, Tonino and Paci), each member singing and playing guitar with Nicolas Reyes as their lead vocalist. As the Gipsy Kings they attempted to reach a worldwide market for the first time, initially earning their reputation by playing to film stars and royalty at France's St. Tropez holiday resort. They made their worldwide debut with a self-titled album for Elektra Records in 1988, by which time several collections had already been released in Spain and mainland Europe. As before, the music blended elements of the Nueva Andalucia flamenco style, with the inclusion of percussive foot stamps, handclaps and vocals drawn from Arabic music. In addition to their trademark multi-guitar sound, they also added other components, including drums, bass, percussion and synthesizers. This effort to broaden their appeal resulted in a massive international breakthrough, including number 1 status in the Canadian and Australian charts, with *Gipsy Kings* peaking at number 16 in the UK. The ensuing *Mosaique*, though marginally less successful, saw the group incorporate elements of jazz (collaborating with Rubén Blades) and 50s/60s pop. In the early 90s, the personnel shuffled, and the Gipsy Kings began to lose much of the momentum they had built up in the previous decade, despite the release of a live album in 1993. *Cantos De Amor* reversed the trend, becoming a major success for them in 1998.

● ALBUMS: *Luna De Fuego* (Philips 1983) ★★★, *Allegria* (Elektra 1986) ★★★, *Gipsy Kings* (Elektra 1988) ★★★, *Mosaique* (Elektra 1989) ★★★, *Love & Liberty* (Elektra 1993) ★★, *Tierra Gitana* (Atlantic 1996) ★★, *Compas* (Atlantic 1997) ★★★★, *Cantos De Amor* (Nonesuch 1998) ★★★★, *Somos Gitanos* (Nonesuch 2001) ★★★.

● COMPILATIONS: *The Best Of The Gipsy Kings* (Elektra 1995) ★★★, *Volare! The Very Best Of The Gipsy Kings* (Columbia 1999) ★★★★.

## GIRLSCHOOL

The all-female heavy metal band had its origins in Painted Lady, founded by teenagers Enid Williams (bass, vocals) and Kim McAuliffe (b. 13 April 1959; guitar, vocals). The remaining members of Painted

Lady went on to form Tour De Force. After Kelly Johnson (guitar, vocals) and Denise Dufort (drums) had joined in 1978 the name became Girlschool and the independently produced single 'Take It All Away' for City Records, led to a tour with Motörhead. As a direct result of Lemmy's sponsorship of the band they signed to the Bronze label in 1980, for whom Vic Maile produced the first two albums. There was a minor hit with a revival of Adrian Gurvitz's 'Race With The Devil', a 1968 success for Gun, before the band combined with Motörhead to reach the UK Top 10 as Headgirl with an EP entitled *St Valentine's Day Massacre*. The lead track was a frenetic version of Johnny Kidd's 'Please Don't Touch'.

Girlschool had smaller hits later in 1981 with 'Hit And Run' and 'C'mon Let's Go', but soon afterwards a bored Williams was replaced by former Killjoys bass player Gill Weston-Jones (introduced to the band by Lemmy). Williams went on to form melodic rockers Framed, record two singles with Sham 69's Dave Parsons, and work on sessions with disco producer Biddu, before joining Moho Pack. Later she also sang, variously, country and opera (appearing in Fay Weldon's *The Small Green Space* and her own opera, *The Waterfall*) and taught performance and vocal skills. Girlschool, meanwhile, persevered, with Slade's Noddy Holder and Jim Lea producing the glam-influenced *Play Dirty*, which found the band opting for a more mainstream rock sound. In 1984 Johnson left for an unsuccessful solo career (later abandoning music and taking up sign language to work with the deaf) and Girlschool added guitarist Cris Bonacci, and keyboard player and singer Jackie aka Jacqui Bodimead from Canis Major. The new line-up recorded an album for Mercury Records before Bodimead became the next member to leave. The band switched visual style towards a more glam rock look as they recorded 'I'm The Leader Of The Gang (I Am)' with Gary Glitter. After the departure of Weston in 1987, ex-Rock Goddess bass player Tracey Lamb was enlisted to help record *Take A Bite*. Girlschool split following a Russian tour supporting Black Sabbath.

McAuliffe left to work with punk singer Beki Bondage and present the cable show *Raw Power*, and later formed Strangegirls with Toyah, Dufort and Williams. In 1992, Girlschool reunited with the addition of ex-Flatmates bass player Jackie Carrera. The new line-up recorded a self-titled album for Progressive Records. Three years later Kelly Johnson returned for a series of European dates before being replaced by another original member, Enid Williams. Several live albums were released during the 90s, featuring additional guitarist Jackie Chambers and various original members. McAuliffe, Dufort, Chambers and Williams recorded 2002's new studio album, with additional input from Johnson and Lamb.

● ALBUMS: *Demolition* (Bronze 1980) ★★, *Hit 'N' Run* (Bronze 1981) ★★★, *Screaming Blue Murder* (Bronze 1982) ★★★, *Play Dirty* (Bronze 1983) ★★★, *Running Wild* (Mercury 1985) ★★, *Nightmare At Maple Cross* (GWR 1986) ★★★, *Take A Bite* (GWR 1988) ★★, *Girlschool* (Progressive 1992) ★★, *Live On*

*The King Biscuit Flower Hour* 1984 recording (Strange Fruit 1997) ★★, *Race With The Devil: Live 1982* (Receiver 1998) ★★, *Live* (Communiqué 1998) ★★, *21st Anniversary: Not That Innocent* (Communiqué 2002) ★★.

● COMPILATIONS: *Race With The Devil* (Raw Power 1986) ★★★, *Cheers You Lot* (Razor 1989) ★★, *Collection* (Castle 1991) ★★★, *From The Vaults* (Sequel 1994) ★★.

● VIDEOS: *Play Dirty Live* (Bronze 1984), *Bronze Rocks* (Bronze 1985).

## GISCOMBE, JUNIOR

b. Norman Giscombe, 10 November 1961, England. Known simply as Junior, this young performer promised much in his early years when he achieved a UK Top 10 hit with 'Mama Used To Say' (picking up a Grammy award). The follow-up, 'Too Late', was his last Top 20 hit in the UK. The tag he was given as 'the future of UK soul' hung heavily around him, and his career ended up being handled by a variety of labels from Mercury Records and London Records to MCA. Each one found difficulty, despite good reviews, in breaking Giscombe. He did make a brief return to the UK Top 10 in April 1987 when he duetted with Kim Wilde on 'Another Step Closer To You'. He became involved with the formation of Red Wedge in 1986 with Billy Bragg, Jimmy Somerville and Paul Weller. During the 90s, he recorded as Junior Giscombe.

● ALBUMS: *JI* (Mercury 1982) ★★★, *Inside Lookin' Out* (Mercury 1983) ★★★, *Acquired Taste* (London 1986) ★★★, *Sophisticated Street* (MCA 1988) ★★, *Stand Strong* (MCA 1990) ★★★, *Renewal* (MCA 1992) ★★.

● COMPILATIONS: *The Best Of Junior* (Mercury 1995) ★★★.

## GO WEST

Peter Cox (b. 17 November 1955, London, England; vocals) and Richard Drummie (b. 20 March 1959, England; guitar/keyboard/vocals) were a songwriting partnership before forming Go West in 1982. The publishers, ATV Music, had teamed them up to write with artists such as Peter Frampton and David Grant. Chrysalis Records signed the duo and the result was a string of quality pop rock hits in 1985 with, 'We Close Our Eyes', 'Call Me', 'Don't Look Down' and a successful debut album. Sylvester Stallone heard the latter and liked it, and they wrote 'One Way Street' for the *Rocky IV* soundtrack. The songs were well crafted, well arranged and produced and they used a regular session crew of talented and innovative players. Cox's voice was strong and distinctive and the Godley And Creme video for 'We Close Our Eyes' was extremely inventive. *Indian Summer* came after a lengthy gap and they demonstrated that they had developed and matured since they were first viewed as pop pin-ups. It contained the transatlantic hit 'King Of Wishful Thinking'. Following the album's release, Cox and Drummie elected to disband Go West and concentrate on solo projects.

● ALBUMS: *Go West* (Chrysalis 1985) ★★★, *Bangs And Crashes* (Chrysalis 1985) ★★, *Dancing On The*

*Couch* (Chrysalis 1987) ★★, *Indian Summer* (Chrysalis 1992) ★★★.
● COMPILATIONS: *Aces And Kings: The Best Of Go West* (Chrysalis 1993) ★★★, *Greatest Hits* (EMI 1999) ★★★.
● VIDEOS: *Aces And Kings: The Best Of The Videos* (Chrysalis 1993).

## GO-BETWEENS

Critics' favourites the Go-Betweens were formed in Brisbane, Australia, by Robert Forster (b. 29 June 1957, Brisbane, Queensland, Australia; guitar, vocals) and Grant McLennan (b. 12 February 1958, Rockhampton, Queensland, Australia; bass, guitar, vocals). These two songwriters were influenced by Bob Dylan, the Velvet Underground, the Monkees and the then-burgeoning New York no wave scene involving Television, Talking Heads and Patti Smith. Although sharing the same subject matter in trouble-torn love songs, melancholy and desolation, Forster and McLennan's very different compositional styles fully complemented each other.

The Go-Betweens first recorded as a trio on the Able label with drummer Dennis Cantwell. McLennan took on bass playing duties for 'Lee Remick'/'Karen' (1978) and 'People Say'/'Don't Let Him Come Back' (1979). By the time of the latter release, the line-up had expanded to include Tim Mustafa (drums), Malcolm Kelly (organ) and Candice and Jacqueline on tambourine and vocals. The duo soon reverted to the trio format on recruiting ex-Zero drummer Lindy Morrison (b. 2 November 1951, Australia). At the invitation of Postcard Records boss Alan Horne, the band came to Britain to record a single, 'I Need Two Heads'. After this brief visit, they returned to Australia and recorded *Send Me A Lullaby* for the independent label Missing Link. This roughly hewn but still charming set was heard by Geoff Travis at Rough Trade Records in London, who picked it up for distribution in the UK. Travis proposed that the Go-Betweens return to the UK, sign a recording contract and settle in London, which the band accepted. *Before Hollywood* garnered favourable reviews, prompting many to predict a rosy future for the Go-Betweens. The highlight of this set was McLennan's evocative 'Cattle And Cane', one of the Go-Betweens' most enduring tracks (later covered by the Wedding Present).

The problem of finding a permanent bass player was solved with the enrolment of Brisbane associate Robert Vickers (b. 25 November 1959, Australia) in the post, thus enabling McLennan to concentrate on guitar and giving the band a fuller sound. The move to a major label, Sire Records, brought expectations of a 'big breakthrough' in terms of sales, but for all the critical acclaim heaped upon *Spring Hill Fair*, success still eluded them. The break with Sire left the band almost on the brink of returning to Australia. The intervention of Beggars Banquet Records led them to a relationship that allowed the band to develop at their own pace. *Liberty Belle And The Black Diamond Express* presented what was by far their best album to date. The successful use of violins and oboes led to the introduction of a fifth member, Amanda Brown (b. 17 November 1965,

Australia; violin, oboe, guitar, keyboards), adding an extra dimension and smoother texture to the band's sound. With *Tallulah* in 1987, the Go-Betweens made their best showing so far in the UK album chart, peaking at number 91. That same year, Robert Vickers left to reside in New York and was replaced by John Willsteed (b. 13 February 1957, Australia). Prior to the release of *16 Lovers Lane* in 1988, the single 'Streets Of Your Town', an upbeat pop song with a dark lyric tackling the subject of wife-battering, was given generous airplay. However, once again, the single failed to make any impact on the charts despite being lavished with praise from the UK music press. The album only managed to peak at number 81, a hugely disappointing setback for the band.

After touring with the set, Forster and McLennan dissolved the Go-Betweens in December 1989. Remaining with Beggars Banquet they both released solo albums, while McLennan released an album with fellow antipodean Steve Kilbey, from the Church, under the title Jack Frost. He then credited himself as G.W. McLennan for his full solo set, *Watershed*, which proved that neither artist was lost without the other. Lindy Morrison and Amanda Brown, meanwhile, had formed Cleopatra Wong. When McLennan joined Forster onstage in 1991, subsequent rumours of a Go-Betweens reunion were strengthened by a Forster/McLennan support slot with Lloyd Cole in Toronto that same year. However, both artists continued to release solo records at regular intervals throughout the 90s, although critical acclaim was not matched by commercial success. In 1997, McLennan and Forster re-formed for special live dates. They subsequently teamed up with Sleater-Kinney to record the excellent new Go-Betweens set, *The Friends Of Rachel Worth*.
● ALBUMS: *Send Me A Lullaby* (Missing Link/Rough Trade 1981) ★★, *Before Hollywood* (Rough Trade 1983) ★★★, *Spring Hill Fair* (Sire 1984) ★★★★, *Liberty Belle And The Black Diamond Express* (Beggars Banquet 1986) ★★★★, *Tallulah* (Beggars Banquet 1987) ★★★, *16 Lovers Lane* (Beggars Banquet 1988) ★★★★, *78 Til 79: The Lost Album* (Tag Five 1999) ★★, *The Friends Of Rachel Worth* (Circus/Jet Set 2000) ★★★★.
● COMPILATIONS: *Very Quick On The Eye* (Man Made 1982) ★★★, *Metals And Shells* (PVC 1985) ★★★, *Go-Betweens 1978-1990* (Beggars Banquet 1990) ★★★★, *Bellavista Terrace: Best Of The Go-Betweens* (Beggars Banquet 1999) ★★★★.
● VIDEOS: *That Way* (Visionary 1993).
● FURTHER READING: *The Go-Betweens*, David Nichols.

## Go-Go's

This all-female band, originally called the Misfits, was formed in California, USA, in 1978 by Belinda Carlisle (b. 17 August 1958, Hollywood, California, USA; lead vocals) and Jane Wiedlin (b. 20 May 1958, Oconomowoc, Wisconsin, USA; rhythm guitar, vocals). They were joined by Charlotte Caffey (b. 21 October 1953, Santa Monica, California, USA; lead guitar, keyboards), Elissa Bello (drums) and Margot Olaverra (bass). Inspired by the new wave scene, the

Go-Go's performed bright, infectious harmony pop songs and were initially signed to the UK independent label Stiff Records and to Miles Copeland's I.R.S. Records in the USA, where they would enjoy practically all their success. By the time of the release of debut album *Beauty And The Beat*, Olaverra was replaced by ex-Textone Kathy Valentine and Bello by Gina Schock. Produced by Rob Freeman and Richard Gottehrer, who had earlier worked with a long line of female singers in the 60s, the sprightly pop qualities of *Beauty And The Beat* drew comparisons with Blondie, with whom Gottehrer and Freeman had also worked. The album, which stayed at the US number 1 spot for 6 weeks in 1981, included 'Our Lips Are Sealed' (US Top 20), which was co-written by Wiedlin with Terry Hall of the Fun Boy Three, and 'We Got The Beat', which gave the band a US number 2 hit the following year. The second album provided a further US Top 10 hit with the title track, but the band was by now showing signs of burnout. Despite their 'safe' image, it later transpired that the Go-Go's were more than able to give the average all-male outfit a run for their money when it came to on-the-road excesses, which eventually took their toll. *Talk Show* reached the US Top 20, as did the most successful single culled from the set, 'Head Over Heels' (1984).

With the break-up of the band in 1985, Belinda Carlisle subsequently pursued a successful solo career with assistance from Charlotte Caffey, who, for a time, appeared in her backing group. Caffey later formed the Graces with Meredith Brooks and Gia Campbell and recorded for A&M Records, releasing *Perfect View* in 1989, before moving into soundtrack work (*Clueless*). Schock formed the short-lived House Of Shock, releasing a self-titled album for Capitol Records in 1988. As well as recording as a solo artist, Wiedlin attempted to break into acting with a few minor movie roles. Galvanized by her, the Go-Go's re-formed briefly in 1990 for a benefit for the anti-fur trade organization PETA (People for the Ethical Treatment of Animals).

A fuller reunion took place in 1994 for well-paid shows in Las Vegas, prompted by which I.R.S. issued *Return To The Valley Of The Go-Go's*, a compilation of the band's best-known moments with the addition of two new tracks. Carlisle and Wiedlin then resumed their solo careers, whilst Valentine and Schock formed the Delphines. Another reunion took place in summer 2000 for a US tour alongside the B-52's, with a new album released in May 2001.

● ALBUMS: *Beauty And The Beat* (I.R.S. 1981) ★★★, *Vacation* (I.R.S. 1982) ★★★, *Talk Show* (I.R.S. 1984) ★★, *God Bless The Go-Go's* (Go-Go's/Beyond 2001) ★★★.

● COMPILATIONS: *Go-Go's Greatest* (I.R.S. 1990) ★★★, *Return To The Valley Of The Go-Go's* (I.R.S. 1995) ★★★, *Go-Go's Collection* (A&M 2000) ★★★.

## GODARD, VIC, AND THE SUBWAY SECT

Godard, of Mortlake, London, England, put his band together during 1976, centring it on the friends with whom he used to attend Sex Pistols gigs. Subway Sect made their live debut on 20 September 1976 at the 100 Club, featuring Godard (vocals), Paul Myers (bass), Robert Miller (guitar), and Paul Smith (drums). Their name came from brief flirtations with busking upon their inauguration. Rehearsing in the Clash's studio, a series of short sets followed around the capital, featuring embryonic songwriting prowess to add to the abrasiveness they learnt at the hands of the Pistols. They opened for the Clash at Harlesdon and subsequently joined them for their White Riot tour. Mark Laff had replaced Smith, but he too was lured away (to Generation X) before they set out on their first European trek. Bob Ward was their new drummer when they released their April 1978 debut 'Nobody's Scared'. However, a major split followed, leaving Ward and Godard to recruit John Britain (guitar), Colin Scott (bass) and Steve Atkinson (keyboards) in the summer of 1978.

'Ambition' was a trailblazing single, but afterwards the band fell into inactivity before reviving in 1980 with another new line-up with definite New Romantic leanings. This time the band featured Rob Marche§ (b. 13 October 1962, Bristol, England; guitar), Dave Collard (b. 17 January 1961, Bristol, England; keyboards), Chris Bostock (b. 23 November 1962, Bristol, England; bass) and Sean McLusky (b. 5 May 1961, Bristol, England; drums). *Songs For Sale* presented a collection of slick, swing-style songs with Godard adopting a cocktail lounge, crooner image. Supports with the Clash and Buzzcocks had transformed into guest spots on the Altered Images tour, and Godard's new backing band departed to find commercial success with JoBoxers. *T.R.O.U.B.L.E.*, a collection of jazz songs, was recorded with Working Week, but a bad mix sunk the album. Disillusioned, Godard retired from the music scene until, in 1992, the death of Johnny Thunders inspired him to show some interest in music again, and he began experimenting in his home recording studio. With support from Edwyn Collins and ex-Sex Pistols drummer Paul Cook, Godard subsequently released two solo albums.

● ALBUMS: *What's The Matter Boy?* (Oddball 1980) ★★, *Songs For Sale* (London 1982) ★★★, as Vic Godard *T.R.O.U.B.L.E.* (Upside 1986) ★★, as Vic Godard *The End Of The Surrey People* (Overground 1993) ★★★, as Vic Godard *Long Term Side Effect* (Tugboat 1998) ★★★.

● COMPILATIONS: *A Retrospective (1977–81)* (Rough Trade 1984) ★★★, *Twenty Odd Years: The Story Of* (Motion 1999) ★★★.

## GODLEY AND CREME

This highly talented duo began recording together in 1976, having already enjoyed an illustrious career in British pop. Kevin Godley (b. 7 October 1945, Manchester, England; vocals/drums) and Lol Creme (b. 19 September 1947, Manchester, England; vocals/guitar) had previously been involved with such groups as the Mockingbirds, Hotlegs and, most crucially, 10cc. After leaving the latter, they intended to abandon mainstream pop in favour of a more elaborate project. The result was a staggeringly overblown triple album *Consequences*, whose concept was nothing less than 'The Story Of Man's Last Defence Against An Irate Nature'. The work was lampooned in the music press, as was the duo's invention of a new musical instrument the 'Gizmo' gadget, which had been used on the album. As their frustrated manager Harvey Lisberg sagely noted: 'They turned their back on huge success. They were brilliant, innovative – and what did they do? A triple album that goes on forever and became a disaster'. An edited version of the work was later issued but also failed to sell.

The duo reverted to a more accessible approach for 1981's UK Top 10 hit 'Under My Thumb', a ghost story in song. Although they enjoyed two more singles hits with 'Wedding Bells' and 'Cry', it was as video makers that they found their greatest success. Their video of 'Cry' won many awards and is a classic of the genre. This monochrome film superimposes a series of faces which gradually change. Visage, Duran Duran, Toyah, the Police and Herbie Hancock were some of the artists that used their services. Then, in 1984, they took the rock video form to new heights with their work with Frankie Goes To Hollywood. Godley And Creme are regarded as arguably the best in their field having pushed rock videos into a highly creative and competitive new market. Creme joined the Art Of Noise in the late 90s.

● ALBUMS: *Consequences* (Mercury 1977) ★★, *L* (Mercury 1978) ★★, *Freeze Frame* (Polydor 1979) ★★, *Ismism* (Polydor 1981) ★★★, *Birds Of Prey* (Polydor 1983) ★★, *The History Mix Volume 1* (Polydor 1985) ★★★★, *Goodbye Blue Sky* (Polydor 1988) ★★.
● COMPILATIONS: *The Changing Face Of 10cc And Godley And Creme* (Polydor 1987) ★★★, *Images* (Polydor 1993) ★★★.
● VIDEOS: *Changing Faces – The Very Best Of 10cc And Godley And Creme* (PolyGram Music Video 1988), *Cry* (PolyGram Music Video 1988), *Mondo Video* (Virgin 1989).

## GOLDEN PALOMINOS

This unorthodox rock act's profile has been much enhanced by the glittering array of celebrities who have contributed to their work. They are led by drummer Anton Fier (b. 20 June 1956, Cleveland, Ohio, USA), who gave birth to the Golden Palominos in 1981. Prior to this he had spent time in the ranks of experimental bands Lounge Lizards, the Feelies and Pere Ubu. The band's albums have seen guest appearances by John Lydon (the Sex Pistols, PiL), Michael Stipe (R.E.M.), Arto Lindsay, Bill Laswell, John Zorn, Daniel Ponce, Richard Thompson, T-Bone Burnett, Jack Bruce and Syd Straw, among others. The other core members of the band have included Nicky Skopelitis (guitar), Robert Kidney (guitar, vocals), and Amanda Kramer (vocals).

Both Thompson and Stipe made their bow with the Golden Palominos on 1985's *Visions Of Excess*, along with Henry Kaiser and Lydon. The maverick talents employed on the follow-up *Blast Of Silence* included Peter Blegvad and Don Dixon, though it failed to match the impact of the first two albums – an obvious example of the sum not being as great as the parts. *Drunk With Passion* featured Stipe on 'Alive And Living Now', while Bob Mould provided vocals on the excellent 'Dying From The Inside Out'. For *This Is How It Feels* in 1993, Fier avoided the super-session framework, recruiting instead singer Lori Carson who added both warmth and sexuality to that and the subsequent *Pure*. Mainstays Skopelitis and Laswell were additionally joined by the guitar of Bootsy Collins.

The Golden Palominos more recent work has also seen Fier adopted by the techno cognoscenti of Britain, where he believes the most innovative modern music is being made. This has led to remixes of the band's work from Bandulu and Psychick Warriors Of Gaia appearing in UK clubs. *Dead Inside* was largely the work of Fier, Knox Chandler (guitar) and Nicole Blackman (vocals).

● ALBUMS: *The Golden Palominos* (OAO/Celluloid 1983) ★★★★, *Visions Of Excess* (Celluloid 1985) ★★★★, *Blast Of Silence* (Celluloid 1986) ★★★, *A Dead Horse* (Celluloid 1989) ★★★, *Drunk With Passion* (Nation/Charisma 1991) ★★★★, *This Is How It Feels* (Restless 1993) ★★★, *Pure* (Restless 1994) ★★★, *Dead Inside* (Restless 1996) ★★★.
● COMPILATIONS: *A History (1982-1985)* (Metrotone/Restless 1992) ★★★★, *A History (1986-1989)* (Metrotone/Restless 1992) ★★★, *The Best Of The Golden Palominos 1983–1989* (Music Club 1997) ★★★, *Surrealistic Surfer* (Dressed To Kill 2001) ★★★, *Run Pony Run: An Essential Collection* (Varèse Sarabande 2002) ★★★★.

## GOOMBAY DANCE BAND

This Germany-based theatrical band was in a similar vein to the more successful Boney M. They were led by Olivier Bendt, and included his wife Alicia, children Danny and Yasmin, plus Dorothy Hellings, Wendy Doorsen, and Mario Slijngaard. Olivier is by profession a fire-eater who learned his trade in St. Lucia, West Indies. By 1980, the Goombay Dance Band were one of the most successful acts in Germany, and entered the UK charts with '7 Tears'. Originally recorded in 1980, it was only released in the UK in 1982 and, after many previous flops, its success was something of a surprise. It eventually went all the way to number 1, only the second UK chart-topper by a German act following Kraftwerk's 'The Model'. The follow up 'Sun Of Jamaica' fared less well and the band returned to Germany to continue their domestic success. However, occasional singles still received a UK release, such as 1986's 'A Typical Jamaican Mess'.
● ALBUMS: *Seven Tears* (Epic 1982) ★★.

## GORKA, JOHN

b. New Jersey, USA. Singer-songwriter Gorka, who possesses a rich and emotive baritone, honed his craft in America's north-eastern folk scene of the early 80s before recording a succession of acclaimed albums. Influenced by Tom Paxton, Richard Thompson and Tom Waits, amongst others, his musical career began in 1986 when he was attending Moravian College in Bethlehem, with the intention of studying history and philosophy. A small coffee-house folk scene had sprung up at a nearby venue called Godfrey Daniels, and Gorka graduated from open-mic spots to leading a group, the Razzy Dazzy Spasm Band. However, he packed his guitar and took his songs out to the wider world, playing throughout north-east America, then travelling to Texas where he won the Kerrville Folk Festival's New Folk Award in 1984. His debut album, *I Know*, was released on Red House Records in 1987, and featured the best of his early songwriting, including 'Blues Palace', 'Downtown Tonight', and 'Down In The Milltown'. Afterwards, he would enjoy a more stable relationship with High Street/Windham Hill Records. The ensuing albums explored a multi-faceted talent, with earnest vocals bedecking Gorka's dry wit and sharp observations and character sketches.

By the advent of *Temporary Road* in 1993, the artist found increased exposure, touring with Mary-Chapin Carpenter and Nanci Griffith. Meanwhile, a single drawn from the album, 'When She Kisses Me', was voted the CMT Best Independent Video Of The Year. For *Out Of The Valley* Gorka relocated from Bethlehem to Nashville, teaming up with producer/guitarist John Jennings. Together they recruited an all-star cast to accompany the singer, including Mary-Chapin Carpenter, Kathy Mattea, Leo Kottke and Dave Mattacks. Gorka also drew on the rich musical environment that surrounded him in the studio, using a guitar once owned by Buddy Holly, the piano with which Carole King had recorded *Tapestry* and a mixing board that had been used for sessions with Elvis Presley and Roy Orbison. This time the songs were less personally defined, using a third person mechanism to allow the artist to explore his characters, giving them individual motivation and colour.

Following a final album for High Street, Gorka relocated to Minnesota, married and become a parent. He returned to the Red House label in 1998 to release the acclaimed *After Yesterday*. Gorka's creative roll showed no sign of coming to an end on the follow-up *The Company You Keep*, which included the wry baby boomer sketch 'People My Age' and the Republican-baiting 'Oh Abraham'.

● ALBUMS: *I Know* (Red House 1987) ★★★★, *Land Of The Bottom Line* (Windham Hill 1990) ★★★★, *Jack's Crows* (High Street 1992) ★★★, *Temporary Road* (High Street 1993) ★★★, *Out Of The Valley* (High Street 1994) ★★★★, *Between Five And Seven* (High Street 1996) ★★★, *After Yesterday* (Red House 1998) ★★★★, *The Company You Keep* (Red House 2001) ★★★★.

● VIDEOS: *Good Noise* (High Street 1994).

## GRAHAM, JAKI

b. Birmingham, England. Graham is a soul artist who sang at school before taking a secretarial position. In the evenings she continued her singing in a band called Ferrari with David 'Dee' Harris (later of Fashion), before moving on to the Medium Wave band. She was spotted there by Rian Freshwater, who managed David Grant (ex-Linx) and singer/producer Derek Bramble, formerly of Heatwave, who became her producer and songwriter. She signed to EMI Records, who released her debut 45 'What's The Name Of Your Game' (1984). Her first chart appearance came via a duet with production stablemate David Grant on 'Could It Be I'm Falling In

Love' in 1985. She followed that success with the solo hits 'Round And Round' and 'Heaven Knows', before another Grant duet, 'Mated' (written by Todd Rundgren). The second album provided a trio of hits; 'Set Me Free', 'Breaking Away' and 'Step Right Up'. Her only notable UK chart entry since then has been 1994's Top 50 hit 'Ain't Nobody'. She remains hugely popular on the Japanese market, although her studio albums are now only available in her native England on import.

● ALBUMS: *Heaven Knows* (EMI 1985) ★★★, *Breaking Away* (EMI 1986) ★★★, *From Now On* (EMI 1989) ★★, *Real Life* (BMG 1995) ★★★, *Don't Keep Me Waiting* (WEA 1997) ★★★, *My Life* (Phantom 1998) ★★★.

● VIDEOS: *Set Free* (PMI 1986).

## GRAHAM, LARRY

b. 14 August 1946, Beaumont, Texas, USA. Graham moved to Oakland, California while still a child and by his late teens had established a proficiency on several instruments. A member of Sly And The Family Stone between 1967 and 1972, he left to form Graham Central Station, one of the era's most popular funk bands. In 1980, he embarked on a solo career which opened successfully with 'One In A Million You', a US Top 10 hit. The singer enjoyed R&B hits with 'When We Get Married' (1980) and 'Just Be My Lady' (1981), while his last chart entry was 'If You Need My Love Tonight', a 1987 duet with Aretha Franklin. At the end of the 90s, Graham revived the Graham Central Station moniker for a new studio album.

● ALBUMS: *One In A Million You* (Warners 1980) ★★★, *Just Be My Lady* (Warners 1981) ★★★, *Sooner Or Later* (Warners 1982) ★★, *Victory* (Warners 1983) ★★, *Fired Up* (Warners 1985) ★★★.

● COMPILATIONS: *The Jam: The Larry Graham & Graham Central Station Anthology* (Rhino 2001) ★★★★.

## GRANDMASTER FLASH

b. Joseph Saddler, 1 January 1958, Barbados, West Indies, but raised in the Bronx, New York City, New York, USA. This pivotal force in early rap music grew up in the South Bronx, studying at Samuel Gompers Vocational Technical High School, spending his leisure time attending DJ parties thrown by early movers such as Grandmaster/DJ Flowers, MaBoya and DJ Pete Jones. The latter took him under his wing, and Flash intended to combine Jones' timing on the decks with the sort of records that Kool Herc was spinning. Hence in the early 70s Saddler set about discovering the way to segue records smoothly together, highlighting the 'break' – the point in a record where the drum rhythm is isolated or accentuated – and repeating it. With admirable fortitude, Saddler spent upwards of a year in his apartment on 167th Street experimenting. The basis of his technique was to adapt Herc's approach, using two turntables each spinning the same record. He would then interrupt the flow of the disc offering the basic rhythm by overlaying the 'break', repeating the process by switching channels on the mixer, as necessary. The complexity and speed of the operation (the second desk would have to be rotated backwards to the beginning of the 'break' section) earned him the nickname Flash when he brought the style to his public, owing to the rapid hand movements. However, attention grabbing though this was, the style had not yet quite gelled into what Flash required. He decided, instead, to invite a vocalist to share the stage with him. He worked in this respect with first Lovebug Starski, then Keith Wiggins. Wiggins would eventually come to be known as Cowboy within Grandmaster Flash's Furious Five, in the process becoming one of the first 'MCs', delivering rhymes to accompany Flash's turntable wizardry. Flash continued in the block/park party vein for a considerable time, often illegally by hooking up his sound system to an intercepted mains cable until the police arrived. One person, at least, saw some commercial potential in his abilities, however. Ray Chandler stepped up and invited Flash to allow him to promote him, and charge an entrance fee (previous hip-hop events had always been free). Initially incredulous at the thought that anyone would actually pay to see them, Flash nevertheless accepted.

Flash put together a strong line-up of local talent to support him: Grandmaster Melle Mel (b. Melvin Glover, New York City, New York, USA) and his brother Kid Creole (b. Nathaniel Glover) joining Cowboy, this line-up initially titled Grandmaster Flash And The 3MCs. Two further rappers, Duke Bootee (b. Ed Fletcher) and Kurtis Blow subsequently joined, but were eventually replaced by Rahiem (b. Guy Todd Williams; ex-Funky Four) and Scorpio (b. Eddie Morris, aka Mr Ness). The Zulu Tribe was also inaugurated, with the express purpose of acting as security at live events: with Flash popularising the rap format, rival MCs sprang up to take their mentor and each other on. These head to heads often had the result of garnering the participants equipment as prize money. A crew who were not popular could expect to see their turntables and sound system rehabilitated for their troubles. Just as Jamaican sound system owners like Duke Reid and Coxsone Dodd had done in the 60s, Flash, Kool Herc and Afrika Bambaataa would hide their records from prying eyes to stop their 'sound' being pirated. Similarly, record labels were removed to avoid identifying marks.

The Furious Five, meanwhile, made their debut proper on 2 September 1976. Shortly afterwards they released their first record, 'Super Rappin'', for Enjoy Records. Although hugely popular within the hip-hop fraternity, it failed to make commercial inroads, and Flash tried again with 'We Rap Mellow' (as the Younger Generation on Brass). However, it would be Joe Robinson Jnr. of Sugarhill Records who finally bought out their Enjoy contract. He had seen the Grandmaster in action at Disco Fever, 'hip-hop's first home', which had opened in the Bronx in 1978. His wife, Sylvia, wrote and produced their subsequent record, a relationship which kicked off with 'Freedom'. On the back of a major tour, certainly the first in rap's embryonic history, the single sold well, going on to earn a gold disc. The follow-up 'Birthday Party' was totally eclipsed by 'The Adventures Of Grandmaster Flash On The Wheels Of Steel', the first rap record to use samples, and a musical *tour de force*, dramatically showcasing the Flash quickmixing and scratching skills. Memorable enough, it too was overshadowed when Sugarhill brought the band in to record one of Robinson's most memorable compositions (written in tandem with Bootee): 'The Message'. The single, with its daunting, apocalyptic rumblings, significantly expanded not just rap but black music's boundaries, though the Furious Five had been less convinced of its worth when it was first offered to them in demo form. In just over a month the record achieved platinum sales. In the wake of the record's success Flash enquired of his Sugarhill bosses why no money was forthcoming. When he did not receive satisfactory explanation, he elected to split, taking Kid Creole and Rahiem with him, signing to Elektra Records. The others, headed by Melle Mel, would continue as Melle Mel And The Furious 5, scoring nearly instantly with another classic, 'White Lines (Don't Do It)'. Bearing in mind the subject matter of Mel's flush of success, it was deeply ironic that Flash had now become a freebase cocaine addict.

In the 80s Flash's name largely retreated into the mists of rap folklore until he was reunited with his Furious Five in 1987 for a Paul Simon hosted charity concert in New York, and talk of a reunion in 1994 eventually led to the real thing. Back with the Furious Five he hosted New York's WQHT Hot 97 show, 'Mic Checka', spinning discs while prospective rappers rang up to try to pitch their freestyle rhymes down the telephone. Unfortunately, the reunion would not include Cowboy, who died on 8 September 1989 after a slow descent into crack addiction. Flash also helped out on Terminator X's *Super Bad* set, which brought together many of the old school legends. In January 2002, he released an acclaimed mix album recreating the sounds of his legendary mid-70s block parties.

● ALBUMS: as Grandmaster Flash And The Furious Five *The Message* (Sugarhill 1982) ★★★★, as Grandmaster Flash And The Furious Five *Greatest Messages* (Sugarhill 1983) ★★★, as Grandmaster Flash And The Furious Five *On The Strength* (Elektra 1988) ★★, *They Said It Couldn't Be Done* (Elektra 1985) ★★, *The Source* (Elektra 1986) ★★, *Ba-Dop-Boom-Bang* (Elektra 1987) ★★★.

● COMPILATIONS: as Grandmaster Flash And The Furious Five/Grandmaster Melle Mel *Greatest Hits* (Sugarhill 1989) ★★★★, *The Best Of ...* (Rhino 1994) ★★★★, *The Greatest Mixes* (Deepbeats 1998) ★★★, *Adventures On The Wheels Of Steel* 3-CD set (Sequel 1999) ★★★, *The Official Adventures Of Grandmaster Flash* (Strut 2002) ★★★★.

## GRANDMIXER DST

b. Derek Howells, 23 August 1960, New York City, New York, USA. Born and raised in the south Bronx area – the tough spawning ground of many of the finest first-generation hip-hop artists – scratch DJ DST was a member of Afrika Bambaataa's street gang/sound system crew the Zulu Nation, before quitting to carve out a solo career in 1982 with the single 'Grandmixer Cuts It Up' on French label

Celluloid, backed by the Infinity Rappers (KC Roc and Shahiem). With a formidable underground reputation behind him, he achieved international breakthrough in 1983 as the scratcher on Herbie Hancock's 'Rockit', and was prominently featured on other tracks from Hancock's album *Future Shock* the same year. It was the first collaboration between jazz and hip-hop, until then seen as mutually exclusive forms. In 1984, he enjoyed an international dancefloor hit with his own single, 'Crazy Cuts'. He raised his profile further with a series of collaborations with avant-funk/jazz producer Bill Laswell, producer of *Future Shock* and 'Rockit', appearing on a wide range of Laswell-produced tracks by Deadline, Manu Dibango, Foday Musa Suso and Material. A supremely talented, musical scratcher, DST's star faded in the late 80s as new generations of DJs replaced him in hip-hop's notoriously short-shelf-life marketplace. (DST derived his tag from the New York garment district's Delancey Street, where the young DJ was often to be found in the late 70s adding to his collection of fashion wear.)
● ALBUMS: *Crazy Cuts* (Celluloid 1984) ★★★.

## GRANT, AMY

b. 25 November 1960, Augusta, Georgia, USA. A huge influence on the development of modern gospel music, Grant's perennially youthful but always convincing vocal has imbued her many recordings with a purity of spirit and performance that can be awe-inspiring. Songs such as 'Angels', 'Raining On The Inside' and 'Find A Way', scattered through a consistently high-quality recording career, have endeared her to her massive contemporary and gospel audience as well as critics. Though originally a primarily religious performer, her material also blends in rhythms derived from modern R&B and soul, while her lyrics contemplate subjects outside of the average gospel singer's repertoire. However, when secular subjects are tackled, there is an abiding spirituality to Grant's treatment of them that ensures her position as a gospel singer despite her 90s R&B success: 'The point of my songs is never singer-focused. It's experience focused. When I go in the studio, I'm taking my experience as a wife and a mother with me.'
Though earlier albums had flirted with pop, rock, soul and country, and she enjoyed a US number 1 single as far back as 1986, duetting with Peter Cetera on 'The Next Time I Fall', Grant's first truly secular release arrived in 1991 with *Heart In Motion*. Featuring the US number 1/UK number 2 single 'Baby Baby', this move into the contemporary pop world was rewarded with platinum sales, the album spending 52 consecutive weeks on the US *Billboard* chart. Subsequent singles carried on Grant's commercial renaissance, with 'Every Heartbeat' (number 2), 'That's What Love Is For' (number 7) and 'Good For Me' (number 8) all breaking into the US Top 10 in 1991–92. Long-term collaborators Keith Thomas and Michael Omartian were again in place for the follow-up, *House Of Love*. Boosted by a strong duet with Vince Gill on the title track and the presence of another hit single, 'Lucky One', this

collection also included a cover version of the Joni Mitchell standard 'Big Yellow Taxi'. Grant took a giant leap in credibility with *Behind The Eyes* in 1997. This was an album of much greater depth that dispelled the perception of her as merely a vacuous pop diva. In March 2000, Grant married Vince Gill.
● ALBUMS: *My Father's Eyes* (Myrrh/Reunion 1979) ★★★, *Never Alone* (Myrrh/Reunion 1980) ★★★, *In Concert* (Myrrh/Reunion 1981) ★★★★, *In Concert Volume Two* (Myrrh/Reunion 1981) ★★★, *Age To Age* (Myrrh/Reunion 1982) ★★★★, *Straight Ahead* (A&M 1984) ★★★★, *Unguarded* (A&M 1985) ★★★, *A Christmas Album* (Myrrh/Reunion 1988) ★★★, *Lead Me On* (A&M 1988) ★★★, *Heart In Motion* (A&M 1991) ★★★, *Home For Christmas* (A&M 1992) ★★★, *House Of Love* (A&M 1994) ★★★, *Behind The Eyes* (A&M 1997) ★★★★, *A Christmas To Remember* (A&M 1999) ★★★.
● COMPILATIONS: *The Collection* (Myrrh/Reunion 1986) ★★★★, *Her Great Inspirational Songs* (BMG Heritage/RCA 2002) ★★★, *Legacy: Hymns & Faith* (A&M 2002) ★★★★.
● VIDEOS: *Building The House Of Love* (A&M 1994).

## GRANT, DAVID

b. 8 August 1956, Kingston, Jamaica, West Indies. By the time everyone realized that Linx was not the spearhead of a new UK soul movement, singer David Grant had swapped his glasses and moustache for a sweatband and aerobics gear and gone solo. Suddenly he was Britain's answer to Michael Jackson. He could dance; he was pretty and his voice was high; and 'Stop And Go', 'Watching You Watching Me' and 'Love Will Find A Way' all made the UK Top 30 in 1983. His songwriting partnership with Derek Bramble developed, resulting in the Steve Levine-produced self-titled album. More memorable, however, were his duets with Jaki Graham in 1985, on the Spinners' 'Could It Be I'm Falling In Love' and Todd Rundgren's 'Mated'. 'Hopes And Dreams' was an altogether weightier offering, with contributions from Aswad and Go West, but it just made the Top 100. Grant penned further hits for Gavin Christopher, Cheryl Lynn and Hot Chocolate. He maintained a loyal club following for a time, where his energetic 'soul' music was highly popular. In the 90s he was active in session work, acting and television.
● ALBUMS: *David Grant* (Chrysalis 1983) ★★★, *Hopes And Dreams* (Chrysalis 1985) ★★, *Change* (Polydor 1987) ★★, *Anxious Edge* (4th & Broadway 1990) ★★.
● COMPILATIONS: *The Best Of David Grant And Linx* (Chrysalis 1993) ★★★.

## GRANT, EDDY

b. Edmond Montague Grant, 5 March 1948, Plaisance, Guyana, West Indies. Grant moved to England in 1960. Over the next few years, he wrote a number of ska songs, some of which have become classics, including the suggestive hit for Prince Buster 'Rough Rider'. During the late 60s he enjoyed pop success as part of the Equals, with 'Baby Come Back' topping the UK singles chart. Grant was 24 years old, with several further Equals hits to his credit, when he left the band to form his own production company. After producing other acts, he made his own debut in 1977 with *Message Man*. It was certainly a solo effort: not only did he sing and play every note, but it was recorded in his own studio, the Coach House, and released on his own label, Ice Records. Grant had developed his own sound – part reggae, part funk, with strong musical motifs and strong melodies – producing pop with credibility. More than 10 years after the Equals' first hit, 'Living On The Front Line' (1979) was a UK number 11 hit, and the now dreadlocked Grant had found himself a whole new audience. 'Do You Feel My Love' and 'Can't Get Enough Of You' kept him in the UK Top 20.

In 1982, Grant moved his home and studio to Barbados, signed Ice Records to RCA Records, and achieved a memorable UK number 1 hit with 'I Don't Wanna Dance'. The following year 'Electric Avenue' reached number 2 on both sides of the Atlantic, and the parent album *Killer On The Rampage* proved his biggest seller. The huge hits eluded him for four years until he stormed back in January 1988 with 'Gimme Hope Jo'anna', as if he had never been away. The dressing of the anti-apartheid message in the apparent simplicity of a pop song was typically inspired. In recent years, Grant has continued recording and writing quality material, but has concentrated his efforts on building a successful music publishing company and record label in Barbados. A dance remix of 'Electric Avenue' was a huge club hit in 2001.

● ALBUMS: *Message Man* (Ice 1977) ★★★, *Walking On Sunshine* (Ice 1979) ★★★, *Love In Exile* (Ice 1980) ★★★, *Can't Get Enough* (Ice 1981) ★★★, *Live At Notting Hill* (Ice 1981) ★★, *Paintings Of The Soul* (Ice 1982) ★★★, *Killer On The Rampage* (Ice/RCA 1982) ★★★, *Can't Get Enough* (Ice/RCA 1983) ★★★, *Going For Broke* (Ice/RCA 1984) ★★, *Born Tuff* (Ice 1987) ★★, *File Under Rock* (Parlophone 1988) ★★★, *Paintings Of The Soul* (Ice 1992) ★★★, *Hearts And Diamonds* (Ice 1999) ★★★.
● COMPILATIONS: *All the Hits: The Killer At His Best* (K-Tel 1984) ★★, *Hits* (Starr 1988) ★★, *Walking On Sunshine (The Best Of Eddy Grant)* (Parlophone 1989) ★★★, *Greatest Hits Collection* (Ice/Castle 1999) ★★★★, *Hits From The Frontline* (Music Club 1999) ★★★, *The Greatest Hits* (Ice/East West 2001) ★★★★.
● VIDEOS: *Live In London* (PMI 1986), *Walking On Sunshine* (PMI 1989).

## GREEN ON RED

Formed as the Serfers in Tucson, Arizona, USA, in 1981, this influential band featured Dan Stuart (guitar, vocals), Jack Waterson (bass) and Van Christian (drums). Christian was replaced by Alex MacNicol, and Chris Cacavas added on keyboards for the first EP, *Two Bibles*, released under their new name. The band attracted attention as part of the 60s-influenced 'paisley underground' alongside the Rain Parade and the Dream Syndicate. However, Green On Red's sound owed more to Neil Young and country/blues traditions, an influence that became more apparent when Chuck Prophet IV joined on lead guitar in 1984. Sophisticated arrangements on

1987's *The Killer Inside Me* saw the band pushing for mainstream recognition, but shortly afterwards Waterson and Cacavas left to pursue solo careers. The remaining duo, Prophet and Stuart, forged ahead, using session musicians for the excellent *Here Come The Snakes*. Both members also operated outside the confines of Green On Red, most notably Stuart's involvement on *Danny And Dusty*, featuring Steve Wynn and members of the Long Ryders.

In 1991, Prophet and Stuart re-emerged with a new Green On Red collection, *Scapegoats*, recorded in Nashville with the help of Al Kooper on keyboards. Following one further Green On Red release, they elected to concentrate on solo work, with Prophet's career taking off in 1993 with the well-received *Balinese Dancer*. Stuart relocated to Spain where he settled for a quiet life away from the music business.
● ALBUMS: *Green On Red* (Down There 1982) ★★★, *Gravity Talks* (Slash 1983) ★★★, *Gas Food Lodging* (Demon 1985) ★★★★, *No Free Lunch* (Mercury 1985) ★★★, *The Killer Inside Me* (Mercury 1987) ★★★★, *Here Come The Snakes* (Red Rhino 1989) ★★★★, *Live At The Town And Country Club* mini-album (China/Polydor 1989) ★★, *This Time Around* (China 1989) ★★★, *Scapegoats* (China 1991) ★★★, *Too Much Fun* (Off Beat 1992) ★★★.
● COMPILATIONS: *Little Things In Life* (Music Club 1991) ★★★★, *The Best Of Green On Red: Rock 'n' Roll Disease* (China 1994) ★★★, *What Were You Thinking?* (Normal 1998) ★★★.

## GREENWOOD, LEE

b. Melvin Lee Greenwood, 27 October 1942, Southgate, California, USA. Because of his parents' divorce, Greenwood was brought up by his grandparents in Sacramento, California, but he inherited their musical talent (his mother played piano and his father woodwind). In his teens, he played in various bands in Sacramento and Los Angeles and was even part of a dixieland jazz band at Disneyland. He played saxophone for country star Del Reeves and then formed his own band, Apollo, which found work in Las Vegas in 1962. He turned down an opportunity to join the Young Rascals and for many years he was arranging and playing music for bands in casinos (and working as a blackjack dealer by day). The environment narrowed his vocal range and he developed a husky-voiced approach to ballads similar to Kenny Rogers.

In 1979, his career took a major step forward when he was heard by Larry McFaden of Mel Tillis' band, who became his manager. His first MCA single, 'It Turns Me Inside Out', was a US Top 20 country hit in 1981. This was followed by several other hits including two number 1s, 'Somebody's Gonna Love You' and 'Going, Going, Gone'. His songs were also recorded by several other performers including Kenny Rogers who found success with 'A Love Song'. In 1984 he recorded an album with Barbara Mandrell and they made the US country charts with 'To Me' and he recorded his own patriotic song, 'God Bless The USA', which won the Country Music Association's Song Of The Year. His other number 1 country singles are 'Dixie Road', 'I Don't Mind The Thorns (If You're The Rose)', 'Don't Underestimate

My Love For You', 'Hearts Aren't Made To Break (They're Made To Love)', and the sensual 'Mornin' Ride'. He has won numerous country awards and a Grammy for Best Vocal Performance, and is known as the original performer of 'The Wind Beneath My Wings'.

Greenwood switched labels to Capitol Records, but this was not enough to stop the decline of his career during the 90s. He subsequently concentrated on performing at his own theatre in Sevierville, Tennessee, while continuing to release the occasional album of new material. 'God Bless The USA' enjoyed a chart revival in the wake of the terrorist attacks in America on 11 September 2002.

● ALBUMS: *Inside Out* (MCA 1982) ★★★, *Somebody's Gonna Love You* (MCA 1983) ★★, *You've Got A Good Love Coming* (MCA 1984) ★★★, with Barbara Mandrell *Meant For Each Other* (MCA 1984) ★★★, *Streamline* (MCA 1985) ★★★, *Christmas To Christmas* (MCA 1985) ★★, *Love Will Find It's Way To You* (MCA 1986) ★★★★, *If There's Any Justice* (MCA 1987) ★★★, *This Is My Country* (MCA 1988) ★★★, *If Only For One Night* (MCA 1989) ★★★, *Holdin' A Good Hand* (Capitol 1990) ★★★, *A Perfect 10* (Capitol 1991) ★★, *American Patriot* (Liberty 1992) ★★★, *Totally Devoted To You* (Arrival 1995) ★★, *Super Hits* (Epic 1996) ★★, *Wounded Heart* (Kardina 1998) ★★, *Same River, Different Bridge* (FreeFalls 2000) ★★★, *Have Yourself A Merry Little Christmas* (FreeFalls 2001) ★★.

● COMPILATIONS: *Greatest Hits* (MCA 1985) ★★★★, *Greatest Hits Volume Two* (MCA 1988) ★★★, *Best Of Lee Greenwood* (Curb 1992) ★★★, *The Best Of Lee Greenwood* (Liberty 1993) ★★★, *God Bless The USA: Best Of Lee Greenwood* (Curb 1996) ★★★, *The Best Of Lee Greenwood: The Wind Beneath My Wings* (Half Moon 1998) ★★★, *The Best Of Lee Greenwood: The Millennium Collection* (MCA 2002) ★★★★, *Inspirational Songs Featuring 'God Bless The USA'* (Curb 2002) ★★★.

## GREGSON AND COLLISTER

Comprising Clive Gregson (b. 4 January 1955, Ashton-under-Lyne, Manchester, England; guitar, keyboards, vocals), and Christine Collister (b. 28 December 1961, Douglas, Isle of Man; guitar, percussion, vocals), this UK act was one of the most notable duos working in folk music. Gregson was already known as the writer and prominent front man of the band Any Trouble, with whom he recorded five albums before turning solo. He released *Strange Persuasions* in 1985, and then became a member of the Richard Thompson Band. In addition, he acquired the role of producer on albums by such artists as the Oyster Band, Stephen Fearing and Keith Hancock. Another solo album was released in 1990, *Welcome To The Workhouse*, comprising material that had hitherto been unreleased. Collister had made a living singing and playing guitar in Italian bars, and as a session singer for Piccadilly Radio in Manchester. She was discovered performing in a local club by Gregson and this led to her place in the Richard Thompson Band, and subsequent position in the duo with Gregson himself. Collister also provided backing vocals for Loudon Wainwright III and Mark Germino. Her warm sensuous vocals were instantly recognizable as the soundtrack to the BBC television series *The Life And Loves Of A She Devil*.

Gregson's lyrical ability and harmonies, together with Collister's unmistakable vocal style produced a number of critically acclaimed albums of note. The duo toured extensively throughout the UK, USA and Canada, and also played in Japan and Europe. In 1990, the duo completed their first tour of Australia. In March 1992, they announced the start of a farewell tour. Later that year following the tour, Collister worked with Barb Jungr (of Jungr And Parker) and Heather Joyce in a part-time unit, the Jailbirds. Both Gregson and Collister continue to work and perform but no longer together. Collister toured with Richard Thompson in the mid-90s, and Gregson worked with Boo Hewerdine in addition to releasing his own solo records.

● ALBUMS: *Home And Away* (Eleventh Hour 1986) ★★★, *Mischief* (Special Delivery 1987) ★★★, *A Change In The Weather* (Special Delivery 1989) ★★★★, *Love Is A Strange Hotel* (Special Delivery 1990) ★★★, *The Last Word* (Special Delivery 1992) ★★★★.

## GRIFFIN

US rock band Griffin was originally formed in 1981 around a trio of William Rodrick McCay (vocals), Rick Cooper (guitar), and Rick Wagner (drums). However, it was only with the expanded line-up of Yaz (guitar) and Thomas Sprayberry (bass) that they began to make progress. Signed to Shrapnel/SPV Records in 1985, they made their debut with *Flight Of The Griffin*, a solid hard rock collection with the material consistently accentuating McCay's vocal delivery. Yaz and Sprayberry then left the group, leaving Cooper to double up on bass for Griffin's second album, 1987's *Protectors Of The Lair*. Once again, this failed to expand their audience and the original trio parted soon after its release.

● ALBUMS: *Flight Of The Griffin* (Shrapnel/SPV 1985) ★★★, *Protectors Of The Lair* (SPV 1987) ★★★.

## GRIFFITH, NANCI

b. 6 July 1953, Seguin, Texas, USA. This singer-songwriter brilliantly straddles the boundary between folk and country music, with occasional nods to the mainstream rock audience. Her mother was an amateur actress and her father a member of a barbershop quartet. They passed on their interest in performance to Nanci, and although she majored in education at the University of Texas, she eventually chose a career in music in 1977, by which time she had been performing in public for 10 years. In 1978 her first album, *There's A Light Beyond These Woods*, was released by a local company, BF Deal Records. Recorded live in a studio in Austin, it featured mainly her own compositions, along with 'Dollar Matinee', written by her erstwhile husband Eric Taylor. The most notable song on the album was the title track, and as a souvenir of her folk act of the time, the album was adequate. In 1982, *Poet In My Window* was released by another local label, Featherbed Records; like its predecessor, this album was re-released in 1986 by nationally distributed Philo/Rounder Records. It displayed a pleasing maturity in composition, the only song not written by Griffith herself being 'Tonight I Think I'm Gonna Go Downtown', penned by Jimmie Gilmore and John Reed (once again, Eric Taylor was involved as associate producer/bass player), while the barbershop quartet in which her father, Marlin Griffith, sang provided harmony vocals on 'Wheels'. By 1984, Griffith had met Jim Rooney, who produced her third album, Once In A Very Blue Moon, released in 1985 by Philo/Rounder. This album featured such notable backing musicians as lead guitarist Phillip Donnelly, banjo wizard Bela Fleck, Lloyd Green and Mark O'Connor. It was recorded at Jack Clement's Nashville studio. As well as more of her own songs, the album included her version of Lyle Lovett's 'If I Was The Woman You Wanted', Richard Dobson's 'Ballad Of Robin Wintersmith' and the superb title track written by Pat Alger – Griffith named the backing band she formed in 1986 the Blue Moon Orchestra. Following on the heels of this artistic triumph came 1986's Last Of The True Believers. Released by Philo/Rounder, the album had a similar feel to its predecessor, and one that set it apart from run-of-the-mill albums by singer-songwriters. It included two songs that would later achieve US country chart celebrity as covered by Kathy Mattea, Griffith's own 'Love At The Five And Dime' and Alger's 'Goin' Gone', as well as several other tracks that would become Griffith classics, including the title track, 'The Wing And The Wheel' (which inspired Griffith's music publishing company), 'More Than A Whisper' and 'Lookin' For The Time (Working Girl)', plus the fine Tom Russell song 'St. Olav's Gate'. The album became Griffith's first to be released in the UK when it was licensed by Demon Records.

Signed by MCA Records, her debut album for the label, Lone Star State Of Mind, was released in 1987, and was produced by MCA's golden-fingered Tony Brown, the influential A&R representative in Nashville who had signed Steve Earle and Lyle Lovett as well as Griffith herself (she also co-produced the album). The stunning title track again involved Alger as writer, while other notable tracks included the remake of 'There's A Light Beyond These Woods' from the first album, Robert Earl Keen's 'Sing One For Sister' and Griffith's own 'Ford Econoline' (about the independence of 60s folk singer Rosalie Sorrels). However, attracting most attention was Julie Gold's 'From A Distance', a song that became a standard by the 90s as covered by Bette Midler, Cliff Richard and many others, but which received its first major exposure with Griffith's own version. Little Love Affairs, released in 1988, was supposedly a concept album, but major songs included 'Outbound Plane', which she co-wrote with Tom Russell, veteran hit writer Harlan Howard's '(My Best Pal's In Nashville) Never Mind' and John Stewart's 'Sweet Dreams Will Come', as well as a couple of collaborations with James Hooker (ex-Amazing Rhythm Aces), and keyboard player of the Blue Moon Orchestra. Later that year Griffith recorded and released a live album, One Fair Summer

Evening, recorded at Houston's Anderson Fair Retail Restaurant. Although it only included a handful of songs that she had not previously recorded, it was at least as good as Little Love Affairs, and was accompanied by a live video. However, it seemed that Griffith's appeal was falling between the rock and country audiences, the latter apparently finding her voice insufficiently radio-friendly, while Kathy Mattea, who recorded many of the same songs some time after Griffith, became a major star. In 1989 came Storms, produced by the legendary Glyn Johns, who had worked with the Beatles, the Rolling Stones, the Eagles, Steve Miller, the Who, Joan Armatrading and many others. Johns deliberately geared the album's sound towards American radio, and it became Griffith's biggest seller. The album featured Hooker, Irish drummer Fran Breen, Bernie Leadon (ex-Eagles), guitarist Albert Lee and Phil Everly of the Everly Brothers providing harmony vocals on 'You Made This Love A Teardrop'.

Although Storms was a sales breakthrough for Griffith, it failed to attract country audiences, although it reached the album chart in the UK, where she had regularly toured since 1987. However, her major European market was Ireland, where she was accorded near-superstar status. Late Night Grande Hotel was produced by the British team of Rod Argent and Peter Van Hooke, and again included a duet with Phil Everly on 'It's Just Another Morning Here', while English singer Tanita Tikaram provided a guest vocal on 'It's Too Late'. In 1991, singing 'The Wexford Carol', she was one of a number of artists who contributed tracks to the Chieftains' The Bells Of Dublin. Other Voices, Other Rooms was a wholehearted success artistically and commercially. Griffith interpreted some outstanding songs by artists such as Bob Dylan ('Boots Of Spanish Leather'), John Prine ('Speed Of The Sound Of Loneliness') and Ralph McTell ('From Clare To Here'). Flyer, another exquisite record, maintained her popularity with some excellent new material that indicated a strengthening and hardening of her vocals, with greater power and a hint of treble.

Griffith continues to fail to put a foot wrong. Other Voices, Too (A Trip Back To Bountiful) saw Griffith returning to the cover versions format once again, with superb readings of Richard Thompson's 'Wall Of Death', Sandy Denny's 'Who Knows Where The Time Goes?' and Woody Guthrie's 'Deportee'. On 1999's The Dust Bowl Symphony, Griffith reinterpreted songs from her back catalogue with the help of the London Symphony Orchestra. Clock Without Hands, her first album to comprise largely original material since 1997, was released in July 2001.

● ALBUMS: There's A Light Beyond These Woods (BF Deal 1978) ★★, Poet In My Window (Featherbed 1982) ★★, Once In A Very Blue Moon (Philo 1985) ★★★, Last Of The True Believers (Philo 1986) ★★★★, Lone Star State Of Mind (MCA 1987) ★★★★, Little Love Affairs (MCA 1988) ★★★★, One Fair Summer Evening (MCA 1988) ★★★★, Storms (MCA 1989) ★★★★, Late Night Grande Hotel (MCA 1991) ★★★★, Other Voices, Other Rooms (Elektra 1993) ★★★★, Flyer (Elektra 1994) ★★★★, Blue Roses From The

*Moon* (East West 1997) ★★★★, *Other Voices, Too (A Trip Back To Bountiful)* (Elektra 1998) ★★★★, *The Dust Bowl Symphony* (Elektra 1999) ★★★, *Clock Without Hands* (Elektra 2001) ★★★★.
● COMPILATIONS: *The Best Of Nanci Griffith* (MCA 1993) ★★★★, *Wings To Fly And A Place To Be: An Introduction To Nanci Griffith* (MCA 2000) ★★★, *From A Distance: The Very Best Of Nanci Griffith* (MCA 2002) ★★★★.
● FURTHER READING: *Nanci Griffith's Other Voices: A Personal History Of Folk Music*, Nanci Griffith and Joe Jackson.

## GROOVERIDER

b. Raymond Bingham, 16 April 1967, Dulwich, London, England. Best-known for his DJ partnership with Fabio, Grooverider's work has seen him proclaimed by at least one UK magazine as 'the Godfather' of contemporary dance music. A major contributor to both the hardcore and jungle phenomenons (frequent collaborator Goldie rates him as a pivotal influence), Grooverider has been active as a DJ at house parties since the mid-80s. He was particularly associated (alongside Fabio) with the outdoor rave movement of the late 80s when he was one of the few recognisable champions of a music which matched huge popularity with barely concealed hostility from the mainstream press. The base element of his music has always been exclusive dub plates, from whose breakbeats he fashioned what subsequently became known as drum 'n' bass music. His partnership with Fabio started in the early 80s when both were invited to DJ on a pirate radio station called Phase One. The show's creator was sufficiently impressed to invite the duo to host a new club he was opening in Brixton, south London. His recording career began much later, with tracks such as 'Sinister' and 'Dreams Of Heaven'. However, rather than ride his current boom in popularity, Grooverider has remained almost exclusively a performance DJ, earning his reputation by playing sets at venues throughout the country, and also appearing regularly on the Kiss FM radio station and at Goldie's Metalheadz Sunday Sessions at the Blue Note club in London. He also launched his own label, Prototype Records, in the early 90s, working with a new wave of breakbeat artists such as Photek, Ed Rush, Origin Unknown, Boymerang, Dillinja and Lemon D, and recording the hugely influential tracks 'Dreams Of Heaven' and 'Deep Inside' under his alter ego Codename John. His debut album, the two-hour drum 'n' bass marathon *Mysteries Of Funk*, finally appeared in 1998.
● ALBUMS: *Mysteries Of Funk* (Higher Ground 1998) ★★★.
● COMPILATIONS: *Grooverider Presents: The Prototype Years* (Prototype/Higher Ground 1997) ★★★★.

## GUN CLUB

Briefly known as Creeping Ritual, the Gun Club was formed in Los Angeles, California, USA, in 1980. Led by vocalist Jeffrey Lee Pierce (b. 27 June 1958, El Monte, California, USA, d. 31 March 1996, Salt Lake City, Utah, USA), the band was initially completed

by Kid Congo Powers (b. Brian Tristan; guitar), Rob Ritter (bass; ex-Bags) and Terry Graham (drums; ex-Bags). *Fire Of Love* established the unit's uncompromising style, which drew from delta blues and the psychobilly tradition of the Cramps. The set included anarchic versions of Robert Johnson's 'Preachin' The Blues' and Tommy Johnson's 'Cool Drink Of Water'. Pierce's own compositions followed a similar pattern. There would be some clumsy 'deep southisms' in his early lyrics: 'Searching for niggers down in the dark', being one example, but generally most of Pierce's lyrics were non-specific in their hate-mongering (example: 'I'm gonna buy me a gun just as long as my arm, And kill everyone who ever done me harm'). However, the Gun Club's progress was undermined by Congo's defection to the Cramps.
*Miami* was the first Gun Club recording for Animal Records, owned by ex-Blondie guitarist Chris Stein (Pierce had previously been president of the Blondie fan club). Although lacking the passion of its predecessor, it established the band as one of America's leading 'alternative' acts, but further changes in personnel, including the return of the prodigal Congo, ultimately blunted Pierce's confidence (which itself was hardly aided by a self-destructive alcohol problem). He disbanded Gun Club for a solo career in 1985; *Two Sides Of The Beast* was then issued in commemoration, but the band re-formed in 1987 to record *Mother Juno* (produced by Robin Guthrie of the Cocteau Twins). Subsequent albums were disappointing and the singer, frequently based in London, continued to battle with his personal demons while the Gun Club's ranks fluctuated. Former members of the Gun Club, including Patricia Morrison who joined Sisters Of Mercy, looked elsewhere for employment.
In the 90s, Pierce reconstituted the Gun Club with a returning Kid Congo, Nick Sanderson (drums) and his Japanese wife Romi Mori on bass. The occasional inspired live performance was all that remained, however, in continuation of the benchmark for impulsive, powerful music he had established in the early 80s. By the mid-90s, Pierce's self-destructive lifestyle had begun to catch up with him, and he died in March 1996 from a brain haemorrhage, although years of alcoholism and drug problems had probably been a contributing factor.
● ALBUMS: *Fire Of Love* (Ruby 1981) ★★★, *Miami* (Animal 1982) ★★, *Sex Beat 81* (Lolita 1984) ★★, *The Las Vegas Story* (Animal 1984) ★★★, *Danse Kalinda Boom: Live In Pandora's Box* (Dojo 1985) ★★, *Mother Juno* (Fundamental 1987) ★★★, *Pastoral Hide And Seek* (Fire 1990) ★★★, *Divinity* (New Rose 1991) ★★★, *The Gun Club Live In Europe* (Triple X 1992) ★★, *Lucky Jim* (New Rose 1993) ★★★.
● COMPILATIONS: *The Birth, The Death, The Ghost* (ABC 1984) ★★, *Two Sides Of The Beast* (Dojo 1985) ★★★, *In Exile* (Triple X 1992) ★★★, *Early Warning* (Sympathy 1998) ★★★.
● VIDEOS: *Preaching The Blues* (Visionary 1995).

## GUNS N'ROSES

The founder members of the most controversial heavy rock band of the late 80s included Axl Rose (an anagram of Oral Sex) (b. William Bailey, 6 February 1962, Lafayette, Indiana, USA) and Izzy Stradlin (b. Jeffrey Isbell, 8 April 1962, Lafayette, Indiana, USA). Vocalist Rose, who had first sung at the age of five in a church choir, met guitarist Stradlin in Los Angeles in 1984 He changed his name to Rose at the age of 17 when he discovered who his real father was, the Axl prefix coming from a band with whom he had rehearsed in Indiana. With Tracii Guns (guitar) and Rob Gardner (drums), they formed a rock band called, in turn, Rose, Hollywood Rose and L.A. Guns. Soon afterwards, Guns and Gardner left, to be replaced by two members of local band Road Crew, drummer Steven Adler (b. 22 January 1965, Cleveland, Ohio, USA) and guitarist Slash (b. Saul Hudson, 23 July 1965, Stoke-on-Trent, Staffordshire, England), the son of a clothes designer and an album cover artist. With bass player Duff McKagan (b. Michael McKagan, 5 February 1964, Seattle, Washington, USA; ex-Fartz; Fastbacks; Ten Minute Warning; and approximately 30 other north-west bands), the band was renamed Guns N'Roses.

Following the disastrous US Hell Tour '85, Guns N'Roses released an EP, *Live?!*@ Like A Suicide*, on the independent Uzi/Suicide label. This brought intense interest from critics and record companies and in 1986, the band signed to Geffen Records, who reissued the EP the following year. During 1987, they toured extensively, though the band's appetite for self-destruction became readily apparent when Fred Coury of Cinderella was recruited to replace Adler temporarily, after the latter had broken his hand in a brawl. February 1988 also saw the first internal rift when Rose was kicked out, then reinstated, within three days. Their debut, *Appetite For Destruction*, produced by Mike Clink, went on to sell 20 million copies worldwide and reached number 1 in the USA a year after its release date. 'Welcome To The Jungle' was used on the soundtrack of the Clint Eastwood movie *Dead Pool*, and reached the Top 30 in the UK. The band's regular live shows in the USA and Europe brought frequent controversy, notably when two fans died during crowd disturbances at the Monsters Of Rock show at the Donington Festival in 1988. In 1989, the eight-track album *G N' R Lies* was issued, becoming a big hit on both sides of the Atlantic, as were the singles 'Sweet Child O' Mine' (written about Rose's girlfriend and later wife Erin Everly, daughter of Don Everly), 'Paradise City' and 'Patience'. However, Rose's lyrics for 'One In A Million' were widely criticized for their homophobic sentiments. Although Guns N'Roses appeared at the Farm Aid IV charity concert, their career was littered with incidents involving drugs, drunkenness and public disturbance offences in 1989/90. At times their excesses made the band seem like a caricature of a 60s supergroup, with headlines screaming of Stradlin urinating in public on an aeroplane, Slash and McKagan swearing live on television while collecting trophies at the American Music Awards, and Rose's on-off relationship with Everly. In September 1990, Adler was replaced by Matt Sorum (b. 19 November 1960, Mission Viejo, California, USA) from the Cult. Apparently more restrained in their private life, Guns N'Roses added Dizzy Reed (b. Darren Reed;

keyboards) for a 1991 world tour, where their exciting and unpredictable performances brought favourable comparisons with the heyday of the Rolling Stones. In September the band released the highly publicized pair of albums, *Use Your Illusion I* and *Use Your Illusion II*, preceded by a version of Bob Dylan's 'Knockin' On Heaven's Door' from the soundtrack of *Days Of Thunder*. Further hit singles, 'You Could Be Mine' (featured in the movie *Terminator II*) and 'Don't Cry', followed. The *Illusion* brace immediately sat astride the top two album positions in the *Billboard* chart, the first occasion on which they had been thus dominated since Jim Croce in 1974.

Izzy Stradlin found the pressure too much and left late in 1991, going on to form the Ju Ju Hounds. He was replaced by Gilby Clarke (ex-Kill For Thrills). Meanwhile, Slash's growing reputation brought guest appearances on recordings by Dylan and Michael Jackson. He also contributed to tribute albums to Muddy Waters and Les Paul, and subsequently established his own spin-off band, Slash's Snakepit. Guns N'Roses' appearance at the 1992 Freddie Mercury AIDS Benefit concert prompted the reissue of 'Knockin' On Heaven's Door', and while Dylan fans groaned with disbelief, the band's vast following was happy to see its heroes scale the charts shortly after the single's release.

While both of their previous albums remained on the US chart, having sold more than four million copies each, it was not until the end of 1993 that any new material emerged. When it arrived, it came in the form of *The Spaghetti Incident*, a much-vaunted collection of cover versions with a punk foundation. A perfunctory affair, it was mainly notable for lining the pockets of several long-forgotten musicians (UK Subs, Nazareth, Misfits, Fear, etc.), and for including a song written by mass murderer Charles Manson. The main inspiration behind the project, Duff McKagan, had his debut solo album released at the same time. However, reports of an unhappy camp continued to filter through in 1994, leading to the dismissal of Gilby Clarke towards the end of the year, following his own, highly public, outbursts about Rose. His replacement was Paul Huge, a former flatmate of Rose from his Indiana days. Huge's first recording with the band was a cover version of the Rolling Stones' 'Sympathy For The Devil' for the soundtrack to *Interview With The Vampire*. However, Huge stayed only briefly with the band, as did his replacement, Zakk Wylde, who failed to record a single note with the band before falling out irreconcilably with Rose.

In May 1995, Izzy Stradlin was reinstated as second guitarist, but by the end of the year Rose and Slash were again at loggerheads and no new album was imminent. Sorum and McKagan, meanwhile, teamed up with guitarist Steve Jones for the spin-off band the Neurotic Outsiders. Slash confirmed Rose's departure in November 1996, although this situation was reversed in February 1997 when Rose allegedly purchased the rights to the Guns N'Roses name. Later in the year, this was seemingly confirmed by the recruitment of Robin Finck, formerly of Nine Inch Nails, to replace Slash. In November 1999, Rose surprised everyone by contributing the industrial metal track 'Oh My God' to the soundtrack of *End Of Days*. Backed by new personnel, he embarked on *The Chinese Democracy* tour and claimed to have finally finished the band's long-awaited new album.

● ALBUMS: *Appetite For Destruction* (Geffen 1987) ★★★★, *G N'R Lies* (Geffen 1989) ★★★, *Use Your Illusion I* (Geffen 1991) ★★★, *Use Your Illusion II* (Geffen 1991) ★★★, *The Spaghetti Incident* (Geffen 1993) ★★.

● COMPILATIONS: *Live Era '87–'93* (Geffen 1999) ★★.

● VIDEOS: *Use Your Illusion I* (Geffen Video 1992), *Making Fuckin' Videos Vol. 1* (Geffen Video 1993), *Making Fuckin' Videos Vol. 2* (Geffen Video 1993), *The Making Of Estranged – Part IV Of The Trilogy* (Geffen Video 1994), *Guns N'Roses: Welcome To The Videos* (Geffen Video 1998).

● FURTHER READING: *Guns N'Roses: The World's Most Outrageous Hard Rock Band*, Paul Elliot. *Appetite For Destruction: The Days Of Guns N'Roses*, Danny Sugerman. *The Most Dangerous Band In The World*, Mick Wall. *Over The Top: The True Story Of ...* , Mark Putterford. *In Their Own Words*, Mark Putterford. *The Pictures*, George Chin (ed.). *Lowlife In The Fast Lane*, Eddy McSquare. *Live!*, Mick St. Michael.

## GURVITZ, ADRIAN

b. 26 June 1949, London, England. Also known to have worked under the name of Adrian Curtis, this accomplished guitarist began his career backing 60s pop singer Crispian St. Peters for whom his father Sam Curtis was road manager. Spells with Billie Davis and Screaming Lord Sutch followed before Gurvitz joined Rupert's People, a group enjoying a sizeable hit in Europe with 'Reflections Of Charles Brown' (1967). He formed Gun with brother Paul the following year, which in turn evolved into Three Man Army. The siblings also made numerous session appearances before teaming with drummer Ginger Baker in the Baker Gurvitz Army, following which Adrian embarked on a solo career. *Sweet Vendetta* included contributions by US studio musicians Jeff, Joe and Steve Porcaro and David Paich, all later of Toto, but neither it nor *Il Assassino* made a commercial impression. However, in 1982 Gurvitz scored a surprise UK Top 10 hit with 'Classic'. This soft-rock masterpiece contained the immortal line; 'Gonna write a classic, gonna write it in my attic'. Sadly, subsequent appearances by this artist have now greatly lessened. By the 90s, he had turned his hand to a more jazz-influenced direction.

● ALBUMS: *Sweet Vendetta* (Jet 1979) ★★★, *Il Assassino* (Jet 1980) ★★, *Classic* (RAK 1982) ★★★, *No Compromise* (RAK 1983) ★★, *Acoustic Heart* (Playfull 1996) ★★★.

● COMPILATIONS: *Classic Songs* (Cool Sound 2000) ★★★.

## HAGAR, SAMMY

b. 13 October 1947, Monterey, California, USA. Hagar is a singer, guitarist, and songwriter whose father was a professional boxer. Legend has it that Elvis Presley persuaded him not to follow in his father's footsteps, and instead he started out in 60s San Bernardino bands the Fabulous Castillas, Skinny, Justice Brothers and rock band Dust Cloud. He joined Montrose in 1973 (formed by ex-Edgar Winter guitarist Ronnie Montrose) and became a minor rock hero in the Bay Area of San Francisco, in particular acquiring a reputation as a potent live performer. After two albums with Montrose, he left to go solo, achieving a string of semi-successful albums and singles. He took with him Bill Church (bass) and added Alan Fitzgerald (keyboards), and later Denny Carmassi (drums, also ex-Montrose). The band attracted good press on support tours with Kiss, Boston and Kansas, but by 1979 Hagar had fashioned a radically altered line-up, with Gary Pihl (guitar), Chuck Ruff (drums) and Geoff Workman (keyboards) joining Hagar and Church. 1983's *Three Lock Box* became their first Top 20 entry, and included 'Your Love Is Driving Me Crazy', which reached number 13 in the singles chart. Hagar then took time out to tour with Journey guitarist Neal Schon, Kenny Aaronson (bass) and Michael Shrieve (drums, ex-Santana), recording a live album under the band's initials HSAS. Under this title they also cut a studio version of Procol Harum's 'Whiter Shade Of Pale'. Returning to solo work, Hagar enjoyed his biggest hit to date with the *Voice Of America* out-take, 'I Can't Drive 55'. In 1985, he surprised many by joining Van Halen, from whom Dave Lee Roth had recently departed. However, he continued to pursue a parallel, if intermittent, solo career which continues to be characterized by a refreshing lack of bombast in a genre not noted for its subtlety. Hagar left Van Halen in 1996.

● ALBUMS: *Nine On A Ten Scale* (Capitol 1976) ★★, *Red* (Capitol 1977) ★★, *Musical Chairs* (Capitol 1978) ★★★, *All Night Long – Live* (Capitol 1978) ★★, *Street Machine* (Capitol 1979) ★★★, *Danger Zone* (Capitol 1979) ★★★, *Live, Loud And Clear* (Capitol 1980) ★★, *Standing Hampton* (Geffen 1982) ★★★, *Three Lock Box* (Geffen 1983) ★★, *Live From London To Long Beach* (Capitol 1983) ★★★, *VOA* (Geffen 1983) ★★★, as Hagar, Schon, Aaronson And Shrieve *Through The Fire* (Geffen 1984) ★★, *Sammy Hagar* (Geffen 1987) ★★, *Red* (Geffen 1993) ★★★, *Unboxed* (Geffen 1994) ★★, *Marching To Mars* (MCA 1997) ★★★, *Red Voodoo* (MCA 1999) ★★★, *Ten 13* (Cabo Wabo 2000) ★★★.

● COMPILATIONS: *Rematch* (Capitol 1983) ★★★, *The Best Of Sammy Hagar* (Geffen 1992) ★★★.

● VIDEOS: *Sammy Hagar & The Waboritas: Cabo*

*Wabo Birthday Bash Tour* (Aviva International 2001).
● FILMS: *Footloose* (1984).

## HAGEN, NINA

b. 11 March 1955, Berlin, Germany. After her parents divorced in 1957, Hagen was raised in a suburb in the eastern bloc by her actress mother and her stepfather, dissident poet and songwriter Wold Biermann. In 1964, she joined the Thalmann-Pioneers, a Communist youth organization and, four years later, the Freie Deutsche Jugend – from which she was excluded for her hand in a demonstration (instigated by Biermann) against the participation of East German militia in the Soviet invasion of Czechoslovakia. On failing a 1972 entrance test for a Berlin-Schönweide drama college, she sang a mixture of blues and soul with a Polish outfit for several months prior to enrolment at the Studio Für Unterhaltungsmusik (Studio For Popular Music) where she was an outstanding student. For a few years, she toured East Germany as featured vocalist with the Alfons Wonneberg Orchestra before fronting Automobil and then Fritzens Dampferband (Fred's Steamboat Band) but when Biermann was expelled from Soviet territory in 1976, she followed him to West Germany where her worth as an entertainer was sufficiently known for a recording contract to be offered. Her imagination captured by punk, she flew to London where she and Ari Up of the Slits collaborated on a number of songs. On returning to Germany, she formed the Nina Hagen Band with former members of Lok Kreuzberg – Bernhard Potschka (guitar) and Manfred Praeker (bass) – plus Herwig Mitteregger (drums). Released in 1979, 'African Reggae' was enough of a 'turntable hit' to bring Hagen a cult following – particularly in Australia – that grew steadily during the 80s. Nevertheless, the saga of her rise to qualified fame remains more intriguing than her subsequent career, which faltered outside her native Germany. One oddity was the *Punk Wedding EP*, a four song 'celebration' of Hagen's 1987 marriage.
● ALBUMS: as Nina Hagen Band *The Nina Hagen Band* (Columbia 1978) ★★★, as Nina Hagen Band *Unbehagen* (Columbia 1979) ★★, *Nunsexmockrock* (Columbia 1982) ★★, *Angstios* (Columbia 1983) ★★, *Fearless* (Columbia 1983) ★★★, *In Ekstasy* (Columbia 1985) ★, *Nina Hagen* (Mercury 1989) ★, *Love* (PolyGram 1990) ★★, *Revolution Ballroom* (Activ 1995) ★★.
● COMPILATIONS: *14 Friendly Abductions: The Best Of Nina Hagen* (Columbia/Legacy 1996) ★★★.

## HAIN, KIT

b. 15 December 1956, Cobham, Surrey, England. Formerly a member of the Marshall Hain band with former partner Julian Marshall. Following the huge success of their 1979 single 'Dancing In The City', Marshall found the pressure too much and left the team. Hain's first release after the band was predictably dropped by their record company was 'The Joke's On You', for Harvest Records. She then signed to Decca Records and subsequently Mercury Records for several singles and albums. Hain moved to the USA in 1985 and forged a successful career as

a songwriter. Her portfolio includes 'Fires Of Eden' (Cher), 'Back To Avalon' (Heart), 'Rip In Heaven' and 'Crash And Burn' ('Til Tuesday), 'Further From Fantasy' (Annie Haslam), 'Remind My Heart' and 'Every Time We Fall' (*Miss Saigon*'s Lea Salonga). Her songs have also been recorded by Roger Daltrey, Kiki Dee, Barbara Dickson, Nicki Gregoroff, Cheryl Beattie and Kim Criswell.
● ALBUMS: *Spirits Walking Out* (Deram 1981) ★★★, *School For Spies* (Mercury 1983) ★★★.

## HAIRCUT 100

Formed in Beckenham, Kent, England in 1980, Haircut 100 began on a part-time basis with a line-up comprising Nick Heyward (b. 20 May 1961, Beckenham, Kent, England; vocals), Les Nemes (b. 5 December 1960, Croydon, Surrey, England; bass) and Graham Jones (b. 8 July 1961, Bridlington, North Yorkshire, England; guitar). Early the following year they were augmented by Memphis Blair Cunningham (b. 11 October 1957, Harlem, New York, USA; drums), Phil Smith (b. 1 May 1959, Redbridge, Ilford, Essex, England; saxophone) and Mark Fox (b. 13 February 1958; percussion). Engineer/manager Karl Adams secured them a deal with Arista Records where they were placed in the hands of producer Bob Sargeant. Their teen appeal and smooth punk-pop sound was perfect for the time and it came as no surprise when their debut single 'Favourite Shirts (Boy Meets Girl)' climbed to number 4 in the UK charts. The follow-up, 'Love Plus One', did even better, firmly establishing the band as premier pop idols in 1982. Their career received a serious setback, however, when the engaging frontman Nick Heyward split for a solo career. In January 1983, Haircut 100 was relaunched with Mark Fox on vocals. Although the band hoped to succeed with a new audience, their singles sold poorly, and following the release of their 1984 album *Paint On Paint*, they disbanded. Drummer Cunningham later reappeared in one of the many line-ups of the Pretenders.
● ALBUMS: *Pelican West* (Arista 1982) ★★★★, *Paint On Paint* (Arista 1984) ★★.
● COMPILATIONS: *Best Of Nick Heyward And Haircut 100* (Ariola 1989) ★★★★, *The Greatest Hits Of Nick Heyward & Haircut 100* (RCA Camden 1996) ★★★★.
● FURTHER READING: *The Haircut 100 Catalogue*, Sally Payne. *Haircut 100: Not A Trace Of Brylcreem*, no editor listed.

## *HAIRSPRAY*

A 1988 film set in America in 1962, *Hairspray* featured rock and pop luminaries Deborah Harry (as Velma Von Tussle), Sonny Bono (as Franklin Von Tussle) and Divine (as Edna Turnblad). It is among writer/director John Waters most famous 'schlock classics'. The plot introduced later mainstream chat show host Ricki Lake's character, Tracy Turnblad. By entering the Baltimore *Corny Colins* television show and winning their talent contest, she proves that 'fat girls can dance'. However, jealous school friends and anxious teachers make her life a misery after Tracy becomes the regular star of the show. She and friend

Penny travel to Baltimore's black quarter and find boyfriends – Tracy's an Elvis impersonator/look-a-like. However, when their new boyfriends are brought back to the studio their colour causes problems. Eventually it is decided that a live *Corny Colins* show is to be broadcast from Mr and Mrs Von Tussle's amusement arcade. A riot follows and Tracy is arrested. This means she is unable to compete at the car show pageant and Amber Von Tussle (Colleen Anne Fitzpatrick aka Vitamin C) usurps her place. Predictably, Tracy is returned to her rightful position as queen of the pageant after the students protest. As a nostalgia spoof the film included some nice touches – not least cameos by Ric Ocasek of the Cars as 'the beatnik cat' and an excellent period soundtrack – but failed to convince cinema reviewers. Divine died just two weeks after the film's premiere.

## HALF JAPANESE

Formed by brothers David Fair (drums) and Jad Fair (b. Ann Arbor, Michigan, USA; vocals, guitar) in Chicago, Illinois, USA in the mid-70s, this eccentric band has undergone numerous personnel changes since its inception. Despite an erratic history, the unit remains an important outlet for the considerable but anachronistic talents of Jad Fair, who has also pursued a musically indistinguishable solo career. Half Japanese performances were events in the truest sense, often featuring two sets of drums, brass bands, magicians and up to four guitars. The most regular outside contributor was David Stansky, though all sorts of guest appearances punctuate the band's extensive recording career, Kramer (Shockabilly, Bongwater), Don Fleming (B.A.L.L., Gumball), Fred Frith (ex-Henry Cow) and John Zorn among them.

All releases are hallmarked by Jad Fair's idiosyncratic talent, which combines the naïvety of Jonathan Richman with a love of classic 60s pop. Half Japanese's body of work taken as a whole represents an almost inconceivable playground of diversity and experimentation. Early songs such as 'I Want Something New' could easily be classified as unlistenable. Later titles such as 'Thing With A Hook', 'Rosemary's Baby', and 'Vampire' (all from the *Horrible* EP) illustrate Fair's ability to take any genre (in this case gothic punk-pop) and sound absolutely convincing. Their best-known releases, including the more mainstream-sounding *The Band That Would Be King*, were issued on the 50 Skidillion Watts label, for which Maureen 'Mo' Tucker also recorded. In 1991, Tucker produced 'Everybody Knows' for Half Japanese in gratitude for having accompanied her as backing band on three tours. However, it should not be a rollcall of distinguished colleagues that provides Jad Fair and Half Japanese with their notoriety, but the stature of their music and lyrics, which have played a large part in shaping the development of the American underground rock scene (influencing artists as diverse as Beck and Sebadoh). As critics are esteemed as Robert Christagau ('Practically redefines rock 'n' roll') and Lester Bangs ('Half Japanese: an entirely new genre of music') have

noted, Fair's compelling sincerity and absolute conviction are unique. In 1993, a film, *Half Japanese: The Band That Would Be King*, toured small cinemas.
● ALBUMS: *1/2 Gentlemen, Not Beasts* (Armageddon 1979) ★★, *Loud* (Armageddon 1981) ★★, *Our Solar System* (Iridescence 1984) ★★★, *Sing No Evil* (Iridescence 1984) ★★★, *Music To Strip By* (50 Skidillion Watts 1987) ★★★, *Charmed Life* (50 Skidillion Watts 1988) ★★★, with Velvet Monkeys *Big Big Sun* cassette (K 1988) ★★, *The Band That Would Be King* (50 Skidillion Watts 1989) ★★★, *We Are They Who Ache With Amorous Love* (T.E.C. Tones 1990) ★★★, *Fire In The Sky* (Paperhouse/Safe House 1993) ★★★, *Boo! Live In Europe* (T.E.C. Tones 1994) ★★★, *Hot* (Safe House 1995) ★★★, *Bone Head* (Alternative Tentacles 1997) ★★★, *Heaven Sent* (Emperor Jones 1997) ★★, *Hello* (Alternative Tentacles 2001) ★★★.
● COMPILATIONS: *Best Of Half Japanese* (Timebomb 1993) ★★★, *Best Of Half Japanese Vol. 2* (Timebomb 1995) ★★★, *Greatest Hits* (Safe House 1995) ★★★★.
● FILMS: *Half Japanese: The Band That Would Be King* (1993).

## HALF MAN HALF BISCUIT

Five-piece 'scally' outfit whose penchant for seeing the funny side of British society's underbelly won them many friends in the mid-80s. From Birkenhead, Merseyside, England, they were formed by songwriter Nigel Blackwell (vocals, guitar), Si Blackwell (guitar), Neil Crossley (vocals, bass) and Paul Wright (drums), with David Lloyd (keyboards) joining shortly after the band began recording their debut, *Back In The DHSS*. Their original demo tape for Skeleton Records had been heard by Probe Plus boss Geoff Davies, who signed the band to his label in 1985. Test pressings of their first release were dispatched to disc jockey John Peel who immediately arranged a session. *The Trumpton Riots* 12-inch EP, released in February 1986, became a resident in the indie charts for weeks, propelled by Blackwell's endearing view of the idiosyncrasies of British life. Their songwriting vernacular included cult television programmes and celebrities (snooker referee Len Ganley; sports presenter Dickie Davies) in unforgettable song titles: '99% Of Gargoyles Look Like Bob Todd', 'I Love You Because (You Like Jim Reeves)', 'Rod Hull Is Alive – Why?'. Throughout their work they displayed an admirable lack of careerism, turning down key television appearances due to favoured football club Tranmere Rovers playing at home that night. They also decided to split up at the peak of their success, though they did re-form in mid-1990 to release a remarkable version of 'No Regrets', featuring another cult television personality, Margi Clarke, on vocals. The subsequent *McIntyre, Treadmore And Davitt* and *This Leaden Pall* continued to mine the band's parochial good humour and downbeat view of life, including songs of the calibre of 'Outbreak Of Vitas Geralitis', 'Everything's AOR' and '13 Eurogoths Floating In The Dead Sea'. The band has subsequently become something of a British institution, although the

quality of Blackwell's songwriting has never dipped.
● ALBUMS: *Back In The DHSS* (Probe Plus 1985) ★★★★, *McIntyre, Treadmore And Davitt* (Probe Plus 1991) ★★★, *This Leaden Pall* (Probe Plus 1993) ★★★, *Some Call It Godcore* (Probe Plus 1995) ★★★, *Voyage To The Bottom Of The Road* (Probe Plus 1997) ★★★, *Four Lads Who Shook The Wirral* (Probe Plus 1998) ★★★, *Trouble Over Bridgwater* (Probe Plus 2000) ★★★.
● COMPILATIONS: *Back Again In The DHSS* (Probe Plus 1987) ★★★, *ACD* (Probe Plus 1988) ★★★.
● VIDEOS: *Live* (Alternative Image 1993).

## HALL AND OATES

Like 60s predecessors the Righteous Brothers (and their 90s successor Michael Bolton), Hall And Oates' decade-spanning string of hit singles was proof of the perennial appeal of white soul singing. The duo achieved their success through the slick combination of Hall's falsetto and Oates' warm baritone. A student at Temple University, Daryl Hall (b. Daryl Franklin Hohl, 11 October 1949, Pottstown, Pennsylvania, USA) sang lead with the Temptones and recorded a single produced by Kenny Gamble in 1966. He first met Oates (b. 7 April 1949, New York City, New York, USA), a former member of Philadelphia soul band the Masters, in 1967. After briefly performing together, the duo went their separate ways. Hall subsequently made solo records and formed soft-rock band Gulliver with Tim Moore, recording one album in 1969. Hall and Oates were reunited the same year, and the two men began to perform around Philadelphia and write acoustic-leaning songs together. They were discovered by Tommy Mottola, then a local representative of Chappell Music. He became their manager and negotiated a recording contract with Atlantic Records. Their three albums for the label had star producers (Arif Mardin on *Whole Oats* and Todd Rundgren for *War Babies*) but sold few copies. However, *Abandoned Luncheonette* included the first version of one of Hall And Oates' many classic soul ballads, 'She's Gone'.
The duo came to national prominence with the million-selling 'Sara Smile', their first single for RCA Records. It was followed into the US Top 10 by a re-released 'She's Gone' and the tough 'Rich Girl', which reached US number 1 in 1977. However, they failed to capitalize on this success, dabbling unimpressively in the then fashionable disco style on *X-Static*. The turning point came with the Hall And Oates-produced *Voices*. The album spawned four hit singles, notably a remake of the Righteous Brothers' 'You've Lost That Lovin' Feelin'', 'You Make My Dreams', and the US chart-topper 'Kiss On My List'. It also included the haunting 'Every Time You Go Away', a big hit for English singer Paul Young in 1985. For the next five years the pair could do no wrong, as hit followed hit. These included four US chart-toppers, the pounding 'Private Eyes', 'I Can't Go For That (No Can Do)', 'Maneater' (their biggest UK hit at number 6) and 'Out Of Touch' (co-produced by Arthur Baker), in addition to the Top 10 hits 'Did It In A Minute', 'One On One', 'Family Man' (a Mike Oldfield composition), 'Say It Isn't So',

'Adult Education' and 'Method Of Modern Love'.
On *Live At The Apollo* they were joined by Temptations members Eddie Kendricks and David Ruffin. This was the prelude to a three-year hiatus in the partnership, during which time Hall recorded his second solo album with production by Dave Stewart and enjoyed a US Top 5 hit with 'Dreamtime'. Reunited in 1988, Hall And Oates had another US Top 5 hit with 'Everything Your Heart Desires', released on their new label Arista Records. On the 1990 Top 20 hit 'So Close', producers Jon Bon Jovi and Danny Kortchmar added a strong rock flavour to their sound. The duo did not record together again until 1997's *Marigold Sky*, by which time their brand of white soul was out of fashion in a world of 'urban R&B'. However, Hall and Oates' passion for soul music remains undiminished. Their contribution to the cause is a significant one.
● ALBUMS: *Whole Oats* (Atlantic 1972) ★★★, *Abandoned Luncheonette* (Atlantic 1973) ★★★★, *War Babies* (Atlantic 1974) ★★, *Daryl Hall & John Oates* (RCA 1975) ★★, *Bigger Than Both Of Us* (RCA 1976) ★★★, *Beauty On A Back Street* (RCA 1977) ★★★, *Livetime* (RCA 1978) ★★, *Along The Red Ledge* (RCA 1978) ★★★, *X-Static* (RCA 1979) ★★, *Voices* (RCA 1980) ★★★, *Private Eyes* (RCA 1981) ★★★★, *H2O* (RCA 1982) ★★★★, *Big Bam Boom* (RCA 1984) ★★★, with David Ruffin, Eddie Kendrick *Live At The Apollo* (RCA 1985) ★★★★, *Ooh Yeah!* (Arista 1988) ★★, *Change Of Season* (Arista 1990) ★★, *Marigold Sky* (Push 1997) ★★★, *Ecstasy On The Edge* 1979 recording (Burning Airlines 2001) ★★, *Greatest Hits Live* (RCA 2002) ★★★.
Solo: Daryl Hall *Sacred Songs* (RCA 1980) ★★, *Three Hearts In The Happy Ending Machine* (RCA 1986) ★★, *Soul Alone* (Epic 1993) ★★★, *Can't Stop Dreaming* (Untied/RSI 1996) ★★★, John Oates *Phunk Shui* (Rhythm & Groove 2002) ★★★.
● COMPILATIONS: *No Goodbyes* (Atlantic 1977) ★★★, *Greatest Hits: Rock 'N Soul Part 1* (RCA 1983) ★★★★, *2Gether* (Delta 1987) ★★, *The Best Of Daryl Hall + John Oates: Looking Back* (Arista 1991) ★★★, *Really Smokin'* (Thunderbolt 1993) ★★, *The Early Years* (Javelin 1994) ★★, *The Best Of Times: Greatest Hits* (Arista 1995) ★★★, *The Atlantic Collection* (Rhino 1996) ★★★, *Greatest Hits* (Razor & Tie 1997) ★★★, *With Love From ... Hall & Oates: The Best Of The Ballads* (BMG 1998) ★★★, *Past Times Behind* (Legacy 1998) ★★, *Rich Girl* (Camden 1999) ★★, *Backtracks* (Renaissance 1999) ★★, *Master Hits* (Arista 1999) ★★★, *The Very Best Of Daryl Hall And John Oates* (RCA 2001) ★★★★, *The Essential Collection* (BMG 2001) ★★★★, *Behind The Music: The Daryl Hall And John Oates Collection* (BMG 2002) ★★★★.
● VIDEOS: *Rock 'N Soul Live* (RCA 1984), *The Daryl Hall & John Oates Video Collection: 7 Big Ones* (RCA 1984), *The Liberty Concert* (RCA 1986), *Live At The Apollo* (RCA 1987), *Sara Smile* (Master Tone 1995), *The Best Of MusikLaden Live* (Encore Music Entertainment 1999).
● FURTHER READING: *Dangerous Dances*, Nick Tosches.

## HANNETT, MARTIN

b. May 1948, Northside, Manchester, England, d. 9 April 1991, England. In his role as producer Hannett worked with practically all the bands from the Manchester area that came to prominence in the late 70s. He also intermittently produced the bands of the 80s that established Manchester's international reputation as a hotbed of young musical talent. After completing further education, where he had spent all his time playing bass guitar in bands and promoting local concerts, he toured with Paul Young (ex-Sad Café, later Mike And The Mechanics). He also managed a musicians' co-operative and worked as a soundman before being approached by the Buzzcocks to produce their *Spiral Scratch* EP in 1977. Following this, he helped Joy Division fashion their sound in the studio, producing them, and encouraging their use of synthesizers. This resulted in the brutal and isolating feel of *Unknown Pleasures* on the one hand, and the mesmerizing beauty of *Closer* on the other, both now considered classic albums. The band worked with Hannett on 1981's *Movement*, their debut as New Order, but were disappointed with the results; this was to be their last collaboration. An integral part of the band's subsequent success, Hannett was made co-director of their label, Factory Records. This, however, did not interfere with his production schedule, working with U2, the Only Ones, OMD, Psychedelic Furs, Magazine and numerous other bands in the early 80s.

As Manchester flourished for a second time in the late 80s, again it was Hannett who helped shape the sound that had a profound influence on the UK music scene. He produced the Stone Roses' debut single, 'So Young', and Happy Mondays' *Bummed* album, which provided the blueprint for a host of young hopefuls as the 90s began. He was held in high regard throughout the UK music business, described by those who worked with him as a genius whose instincts behind the mixing desk almost always paid off. However, away from the studio he had a reputation for irresponsible behaviour and his drink-and-drugs lifestyle accelerated his declining health. He died from a heart attack in 1991.

● COMPILATIONS: *Martin* (Factory 1991) ★★★, *And Here Is The Young Man: Martin Hannett Productions 1978–91* (Debutante 1998) ★★★.

## HANOI ROCKS

This Finnish heavy rock band was distinguished by their leanings towards 70s glam rock, which they carried off with more style and conviction than any of their peers. Initially the brainchild of Andy McCoy (b. Antti Hulkko, 11 November 1962, Finland) and Michael Monroe (b. Matti Fagerholm, 17 June 1960, Helsinki, Finland) in 1975, the band was not formed until 1980 when singer Monroe enlisted Nasty Suicide (b. Jan Stenfors, 4 September 1963, Finland; guitar), Stefan Piesmack (guitar), Pasi Sti (bass) and Peki Senola (drums). By September, when they recorded their debut album, *Bangkok Shocks, Saigon Shakes, Hanoi Rocks* (initially only released in Scandinavia), the line-up was Monroe, Suicide, McCoy (guitar), Sam Yaffa (b. Sami Takamaki, 4 August 1963; bass) and Gyp Casino (b. Jesper Sporre;

drums). McCoy had previously played with two Finnish punk bands, Briard and Pelle Miljoona Oy. In addition, Suicide had played in Briard, while Yaffa had also been a member of Pelle Miljoona Oy at various times.

Hanoi Rocks' debut single – 'I Want You', was released on the Finnish Johanna label in 1980 and preceded the album. The band then travelled to London where they began recording *Oriental Beat*. Soon after it was finished, Casino was sacked (and joined the Road Rats) and replaced by Razzle (b. Nicholas Dingley, 2 December 1960, Leamington Spa, England, d. 9 December 1984, Redondo Beach, California, USA), who had previously played with Demon Preacher and the Dark. In 1983, they were signed to CBS Records and started to attract attention in the British music press. They hit the UK charts for the first and only time in 1984 with a cover version of Creedence Clearwater Revival's 'Up Around The Bend', but the year ended in tragedy. The band was in the USA when Razzle was killed following a car crash on 8 December. The car driver – Vince Neil of Mötley Crüe – was later found guilty of Vehicular Manslaughter. Former Clash drummer Terry Chimes was brought in as a replacement and when Yaffa left (to form Chain Gang, and then join Jetboy), Rene Berg (ex-Idle Flowers) also joined the band. However, Monroe never accepted the loss of Razzle and in early 1985 he informed the other members that he intended to quit. Hanoi Rocks played their final gig in May 1985.

Monroe has since embarked on a solo career, Piesmack joined Pelle Miljoona Oy, then abandoned music, and Sti and Senola also left the music scene. McCoy, who had already formed a side-project in 1983 – the Urban Dogs with Charlie Harper, Alvin Gibbs (UK Subs) and Knox (Vibrators), went on to form the Cherry Bombz with Suicide, Chimes and ex-Toto Coelo vocalist Anita Chellemah. The Cherry Bombz barely lasted a year and the members went on to play in various short-lived outfits, most notably Suicide (with Gibbs once more) in Cheap 'N' Nasty. A near-reunion of Hanoi Rocks, featuring Monroe with Suicide and Sam Yaffa, emerged as Demolition 23 in 1993.

● ALBUMS: *Bangkok Shocks, Saigon Shakes, Hanoi Rocks* (Johanna 1981) ★★★, *Oriental Beat* (Johanna 1981) ★★★, *Back To Mystery City* (Johanna 1983) ★★★, *All Those Wasted Years!* (Johanna 1984) ★★, *Two Steps From The Move* (Johanna/CBS 1984) ★★★, *Rock 'N' Roll Divorce* (Lick 1985) ★★, *Lean On Me* (Lick 1992) ★★.
● COMPILATIONS: *Self Destruction Blues* (Johanna 1982) ★★★, *The Best Of Hanoi Rocks* (Johanna 1985) ★★★, *Dead By Christmas* (Raw Power 1985) ★★, *Tracks From A Broken Dream* (Lick 1990) ★★★, *Decadent Dangerous Delicious* (Essential 2000) ★★★★.
● VIDEOS: *All Those Wasted Years: Live At The Marquee* (Mercury 1984), *Up Around The Bend* aka *The Nottingham Tapes* (Mercury 1990).

## HAPPY MONDAYS

Few debut records could lay claim to have had the impact (or length of title) of the Happy Mondays'

*Squirrel And G-Man Twenty Four Hour Party People Plastic Face Carnt Smile (White Out).* The sextet's raw brand of urban folk, with Shaun Ryder's accented, drawled vocals, was almost universally acclaimed. John Cale, formerly of the Velvet Underground, produced and gave the record a fresh, live feel. The original line-up remained unchanged (apart from the addition of backing singer Rowetta) from the band's formation in Manchester, England, early in the 80s. Joining singer Ryder (b. 23 August 1962) was his brother, Paul Ryder (b. 24 April 1964; bass), Mark Day (b. 29 December 1961; guitar), Gary Whelan (b. 12 February 1966; drums), Paul Davis (b. 7 March 1966; keyboards) and Mark Berry aka Bez (percussion), the latter widely noted for his manic onstage antics.

Martin Hannett, famous for his work with a number of Manchester bands including Joy Division, produced the follow-up *Bummed*, which layered their music with diverse but strong dance music rhythms. The following year's Paul Oakenfold remix of 'Wrote For Luck' (retitled 'WFL') crystallized the band's emergent sound. The subsequent *Madchester Rave On* EP, which featured the club favourite 'Hallelujah', broke into the UK Top 20 and gave a name to the new Manchester scene led by the Happy Mondays and the Stone Roses. In 1990, the band covered John Kongos' 'He's Gonna Step On You Again' (retitled 'Step On') and reached the UK Top 10. Their manic third album *Pills 'N' Thrills And Bellyaches* went to number 1 in the UK and established the band as a major pop force. The album also coincided with support and re-promotion of 60s singer Donovan, who appeared alongside them on the front covers of the music press. They even recorded a tribute song, 'Donovan', which paraphrased the lyrics of the singer's 60s hit, 'Sunshine Superman'.

Strong support from Factory Records and an unusually consistent output meant Happy Mondays quickly rose to the status of favourite sons of the readership of the *New Musical Express* and *Melody Maker*, and they were achieving sales to match. However, the band's successes were tempered with a fair share of unpleasant publicity which came to a head when Shaun Ryder announced he was a heroin addict and was undergoing detoxification treatment. A highly publicized strife-torn recording session in the Caribbean, with producers Tina Weymouth and Chris Frantz (of Talking Heads), resulted in ... *Yes Please!*. However, its impact was dulled by a decline in press interest, at least outside of Ryder's drug habits. Fittingly, the Happy Mondays' eventual collapse could not be tied to a specific date, with various members breaking off at various points throughout 1993. The band's focal points, Shaun Ryder and Bez, eventually re-emerged in 1995 as part of a new coalition, Black Grape, after Ryder had contributed vocals to 'Can You Fly Like You Mean It' by fellow Mancunians Intastella. Following the break-up of Black Grape, Ryder re-formed the Happy Mondays for several live dates and a new recording of the Thin Lizzy classic, 'The Boys Are Back In Town'. The 1999 line-up comprised both Ryder, Bez, Gary Whelan and new member Nuts.

● ALBUMS: *Squirrel And G-Man Twenty Four Hour Party People Plastic Face Carnt Smile (White Out)* (Factory 1987) ★★★, *Bummed* (Factory 1988) ★★★★, *Pills 'N' Thrills And Bellyaches* (Factory 1990) ★★★★, *Live* (Factory 1991) ★★, *Yes Please!* (Factory 1992) ★★, *The Peel Sessions* (Strange Fruit 1996) ★★. ● COMPILATIONS: *Loads – The Best Of* (London 1995) ★★★, *Loads More* limited edition (London 1995) ★★, *Greatest Hits* (London 1999) ★★★.
● FURTHER READING: *Shaun Ryder: Happy Mondays, Black Grape And Other Traumas*, Mick Middles. *High Life 'N' Low Down Dirty: The Thrills And Spills Of Shaun Ryder*, Lisa Verrico. *Freaky Dancin'*, Bez. *Hallelujah! The Extraordinary Return Of Shaun Ryder And Happy Mondays*, John Warburton with Shaun Ryder.

## HARDCASTLE, PAUL

b. 10 December 1957, London, England. This producer, mixer, composer and keyboard wizard was one of the UK dance music scene's first crossover successes. He first worked in a hi-fi shop and developed an interest in electronics in his teens. Hardcastle made his recording debut in 1981 on 'Don't Depend On Me', a single by UK soul act Direct Drive. He subsequently formed First Light with vocalist Derek Green, with whom he had worked on the Direct Drive sessions. First Light's output included a deplorable cover version of America's 'A Horse With No Name'. Hardcastle then formed his own Total Contral Records label and enjoyed two number 1 dance hits in 1984 with 'You're The One For Me'/'Daybreak'/'A.M.' and 'Rainforest'. The latter was released on the Bluebird label in the UK, and became a big club hit in America on the Profile Records label.

Hardcastle's big breakthrough came with the following year's '19', a record about the Vietnam conflict utilising samples of spoken news reports. The single went to number 1 in 13 countries, including his native England, and received the Ivor Novello award for The Bestselling Single Of 1985. The follow-up, 'Just For The Money', was based on the Great Train Robbery and boasted the voices of Bob Hoskins and Sir Laurence Olivier. Further singles were progressively less successful before he scored with 'Papa's Got A Brand New Pigbag' under the pseudonym Silent Underdog. He also wrote the *Top Of The Pops* theme, 'The Wizard', in 1986, before switching to production for young funk band LW5, providing remixes for anyone from Third World to Ian Dury. Another production credit was the last ever Phil Lynott single, coincidentally called 'Nineteen'. Other engagements came with Carol Kenyon (previously vocalist on Heaven 17's 'Temptation') most notably on the 1986 Top 10 hit 'Don't Waste My Time'.

Hardcastle subsequently 'retired' to his Essex home studio, where he continues to release records under pseudonyms such as the Deff Boyz, Beeps International, Kiss The Sky (with vocalist Jaki Graham) and the bestselling Jazzmasters (with vocalist Helen Rogers). The latter showcases his preference for smooth jazz grooves, and is particularly popular in the USA and Japan. He is also founder of the labels Fast Forward and Hardcastle

Records, and has written the theme music to two BBC nature series, *Supersense* and its sequel, *Lifesense*, and contributed to the soundtrack of *Spiceworld – The Movie* and the S Club 7 television series.

● ALBUMS: *Paul Hardcastle* (Chrysalis 1985) ★★★, *Rain Forest* US only (Profile 1985) ★★★, *No Winners* (Chrysalis 1988) ★★, as The Jazzmasters *The Jazzmasters* (Push 1991) ★★★★, *Hardcastle* (Push 1994) ★★★, as The Jazzmasters *The Jazzmasters II* (Push 1995) ★★★, *Hardcastle 2* (Push 1996) ★★, as The Jazzmasters *The Jazzmasters III* (Push 1999) ★★★.

● COMPILATIONS: *The Definitive Collection* (K-Tel 1993) ★★★, *Cover To Cover: A Musical Autobiography* (Push 1997) ★★★, as The Jazzmasters *The Greatest Hits* (New Note 2000) ★★★.

## HARDY, RON

b. *c*.1956, USA, d. 1991. Hardy's name is often mentioned alongside his fellow Chicago DJ, Frankie Knuckles. It is sometimes claimed that Hardy was the true originator of the essence of house music, while Knuckles simply refined the idea. Hardy began his DJing career at the club Den One in 1974 and had already developed continuous mixes of music using edited reel-to-reel tapes and dual turntables. He later played at seminal club the Warehouse with Knuckles, before relocating to Los Angeles for several years. When he returned to Chicago in the early 80s to establish the Music Box, it was Knuckles' name that was associated with the new sound of house. In the meantime, Knuckles had also set up the Powerplant. Hardy's club was a raw, wild and hedonistic gay night, playing a mixture of disco, European electronic music and early house tracks. In the southern part of the city, the sound of Knuckles' Powerplant was firmly rooted in disco and was beginning to draw a heterosexual audience. The Music Box became famous for Hardy's 72-hour parties, during which he would DJ throughout, often sleeping in the DJ booth and practising his mixing skills when the club closed. Several key DJ-producers on the Chicago scene were regular attendees at the Music Box, including Marshall Jefferson, Larry Heard, Chip E, DJ Pierre and Adonis. They were undoubtedly influenced by the sound that Hardy was developing and all of them tried out their early productions by giving Hardy tapes or acetates to play at the Music Box. Hardy left the Music Box in 1986 but continued to DJ around Chicago. Hardy lived the decadent party lifestyle to the full and was unable to kick a heroin habit that had plagued him for many years. He died of an AIDS-related illness in 1991.

● COMPILATIONS: *Sensation* (Trax 1998) ★★★.

## HARLEQUIN

An underachieving melodic rock act formed in Winnipeg, Canada, in 1975, Harlequin attracted a modicum of interest over a multi-album career without ever threatening to break into the mainstream. Originally comprising George Belanger (vocals), Glen Willows (guitar), Gary Golden (keyboards), Ralph James (bass) and David Budzak

(drums), they made their debut for Epic Records in 1978 with *Victim Of A Song*. The follow-up, 1980's *Love Crimes*, is widely considered to be the band's strongest set, with Willows' guitar and Golden's keyboards moulding a distinctive AOR sound. Subsequent albums failed to produce any showing in the US charts, however, and a number of personnel changes hindered the band's progress. Despite splitting up at the end of the decade, they have occasionally reunited to play on the popular Canadian revival circuit.

● ALBUMS: *Victim Of A Song* (IGM 1979) ★★, *Love Crimes* (Epic 1980) ★★★, *One False Move* (Epic 1982) ★★, *Radio Romances* (Epic 1983) ★★, *Harlequin* (Epic 1985) ★★.

● COMPILATIONS: *Greatest Hits* (Epic 1986) ★★★.

## HARRISON, JERRY

b. Jeremiah Griffin Harrison, 21 February 1949, Milwaukee, Wisconsin, USA. Harrison, a graduate of Harvard University, built his reputation as guitarist and keyboard player for Talking Heads. Previously he had played in a similar capacity for Jonathan Richman And The Modern Lovers, between 1970 and 1974. He returned to Boston to teach at Harvard, but was recruited by Talking Heads in 1976. Like the other core members of Talking Heads, he enjoyed several fruitful extra-curricular pursuits. These began with a debut solo album in 1981, titled *The Red And The Black*. Recorded while the parent band was enjoying a sabbatical, many of those who had contributed to recent Talking Heads fare such as *Remain In Light* – including Adrian Belew, Bernie Worrell and Nona Hendryx – were on hand to aid Harrison. However, apart from scant critical interest there was little public support for this excellent exploration of international rhythms and ethnic music. Harrison then returned to his role in Talking Heads before 1984 brought a solitary 12-inch release for rap label Sleeping Bag Records. Titled '5 Minutes' and credited to Bonzo Goes To Washington, this combined a Bootsy Collins bass riff with a sample of President Reagan declaring 'We begin bombing . . .'. Although a footnote to Harrison's own career, this document pre-empted much of the politically motivated sampling that spread through the remainder of the 80s.

The artist retained a political agenda for his second album, released in 1987. Joined by a core of accomplished musicians (the 13-piece Casual Gods), the music was once again primarily a rhythmic experience, moving from funk to hip-hop. Three years later, and with the Talking Heads' career seemingly on permanent hold, Harrison returned to the Casual Gods. The resultant album, *Walk On Water*, credited to Jerry Harrison's Casual Gods, revealed a more pop/rock-orientated sound. The additional personnel this time included former Modern Lovers colleague Ernie Brooks, Dan Hartman, Bernie Worrell and the Thompson Twins. Although the musicianship remained exemplary, critics were still dissuaded from the overall merits of the project by Harrison's somewhat untutored vocal delivery. Perhaps this has given impetus to his position in later decades as overseer of a steady influx of production work (notably Live, Kenny Wayne Shepherd, Crash Test Dummies, Foo Fighters). He reunited with Chris Frantz and Tina Weymouth as the Heads, to record 1996's *No Talking Just Head*.

● ALBUMS: *The Red And The Black* (Sire 1981) ★★★, *Casual Gods* (Sire 1987) ★★★, as Jerry Harrison's Casual Gods *Walk On Water* (Sire/Fontana 1990) ★★★.

## HARRY, DEBORAH

b. 1 July 1945, Miami, Florida, USA. Raised in New Jersey, Harry was drawn to the alternative music emanating from New York's Greenwich Village in the mid-60s. Spells in a succession of *avant garde* groups, including the First National Unaphrenic Church And Bank, preceded her tenure in the Wind In The Willows, a baroque folk/rock act which completed an album for Capitol Records in 1968. For five years Harry abandoned music altogether, but resumed singing in 1973 as a member of the Stilettos, an exaggerated version of girl-group the Shangri-Las. The following year she formed Blondie with Fred Smith (bass), Billy O'Connor (drums) and long-time boyfriend Chris Stein (guitar). Having made its debut at the New York punk haven CBGB's, the band rose to become one of the leading pop attractions of the late 70s, scoring a succession of hits in the US and UK. Meanwhile, Harry established herself as the leading female rock sex symbol of the time. However, as the dividing line between the band and its photogenic lead singer became blurred, so inner tensions proved irreconcilable.

In 1981, Harry released her solo debut *Koo Koo*, produced by Chic mainstays Nile Rodgers and Bernard Edwards. Despite the presence of Stein, the set failed to capture Blondie's sense of simple pop and the singer resumed her commitment to the parent act. Stein's recurrent ill health brought the band to an end and a further period of retirement ensued. Harry did pursue an acting career, including roles in *Union City Blue*, *Videodrome* and a memorable comic role in John Water's movie, *Hairspray*. In 1986, she released *Rockbird* which featured the UK Top 10 hit 'French Kissing In The USA'. It was not until three years later that Harry made a return to the UK Top 20, this time with the Tom Bailey and Alannah Currie (aka the Thompson Twins) composition 'I Want That Man'. The accompanying album, *Def, Dumb And Blonde*, credited to Deborah Harry, achieved a similar chart position, since when the singer has completed several tours, performing material drawn from Blondie and her subsequent work. Subsequent compilations were credited to and included, tracks from Harry's solo career and with Blondie. In the late 90s, she appeared as a featured vocalist with the experimental Jazz Passengers, before appearing alongside Stein, Burke and Destri in a re-formed Blondie.

● ALBUMS: *Koo Koo* (Chrysalis 1981) ★★, *Rockbird* (Chrysalis 1986) ★★, *Def, Dumb And Blonde* (Chrysalis 1989) ★★★, *Debravation* (Chrysalis 1993) ★★, with The Jazz Passengers *Individually Twisted*

(32 Records 1997) ★★★.

● COMPILATIONS: *Once More Into The Bleach* (Chrysalis 1988) ★★★, *The Complete Picture: The Very Best Of Deborah Harry And Blondie* (Chrysalis 1990) ★★★★, *Most Of All: The Best Of Deborah Harry* (Chrysalis 1999) ★★★.

● FURTHER READING: *Deborah Harry: Platinum Blonde*, Cathay Che.

## HART, COREY

b. 31 May 1962, Montreal, Canada. Corey Hart was one of the biggest-selling Canadian acts of the 80s before his career entered what seemed to be terminal decline at the end of that decade. He had always intended to become a singer from childhood, an ambition hardly qualified by exposure to other musical traditions when his father moved the family to Malaga, Spain, when he was four, then Mexico City when he was nine. While living in Key Biscayne, Florida, his sister introduced him to Tom Jones, who recommended his abilities to Canadian superstar Paul Anka. Anka personally financed the recording of two Hart songs in Las Vegas when the young artist was just 13 years old. Hart eventually made his recording debut with a version of Anka's 'Ooh Baby' for United Artists Records in 1974, but it failed to chart and his contract was not renewed. After an abortive attempt to launch a songwriting career in Los Angeles, he returned to Montreal. There he struck a deal with the EMI Records-distributed Aquarius label, making his long-playing debut in 1983 with *First Offense*. This became a major success both in Canada and the USA when the singles, 'Sunglasses At Night' and 'It Ain't Enough', both reached the Top 20 of the *Billboard* charts. After only six warm-up performances, he made his professional performing debut supporting Culture Club in Toronto in 1984. His second album, *Boy In The Box*, also featured another major hit single, 'Never Surrender', a number 1 hit in Canada which peaked at number 3 in the US charts. The single won a Juno Award and Hart was also nominated for a Grammy. However, his commercial bubble burst in 1987 when *Fields Of Fire* stalled at US number 55. Hart was also exhausted from excessive touring, leading to the cancellation of dates in Canada. His commercial decline continued over the course of two further albums until, in 1991, he made the move to Sire Records. However, *Attitude And Virtue* failed to resurrect his career, and Hart retired from the music industry. He finally returned in 1996 with a suite of songs written about, among other things, the break-up of his marriage to graphic designer Erika Gagnon, and his relationship with Quebec singer Julie Masse and the birth of their child, India.

● ALBUMS: *First Offense* (Aquarius 1983) ★★★, *Boy In The Box* (Aquarius 1985) ★★, *Fields Of Fire* (Aquarius 1986) ★★★, *Young Man Running* (Aquarius 1988) ★★★, *Bang!* (Aquarius 1990) ★★, *Attitude And Virtue* (Sire 1991) ★★★, *Corey Hart* (Columbia 1996) ★★★, *Jade* (Columbia 1998) ★★★.

● COMPILATIONS: *The Singles* (EMI 1992) ★★★★, *Best Of Corey Hart* (CEMA 1998) ★★★, *Classic Masters* (EMI 2002) ★★★★.

## HARVEY, RICHARD

b. 25 September 1953, Enfield, Middlesex, England. Harvey originally took up the recorder at the age of four, and by the time he was sixteen was playing the instrument with the Music Reservata. He also studied clarinet, piano and viol at the Royal College of Music, where he co-founded Gryphon with fellow student Brian Gulland. Gryphon created a distinctive and visionary blend of medieval music and progressive rock, but Harvey continued to pursue his interest in classical recorder music while still in the band, recording *Divisions On A Ground* in 1975. Following the break up of Gryphon in the late 70s, Harvey moved into the advertising world to compose jingles and television scores. His credits include the soundtrack to Channel 4's award-winning television play *G.B.H.*, written with Elvis Costello, with whom he also collaborated on the score to *Jake's Progress*. The rare release *A New Way Of Seeing*, meanwhile, was the result of a commission from ICL. Despite working in a new area, it proved to be a logical extension of his work with Gryphon.

● ALBUMS: *Divisions On A Ground: An Introduction To The Recorder And Its Music* (Transatlantic 1975) ★★★, *Italian Recorder Concertos* (ASV 1982) ★★, *Brass At La Sauve-Majeure* aka *Fanfare For The Common Man* (ASV 1983) ★★★, *The Genteel Companion* (ASV 1986) ★★★, *Evening Falls* (Telstar 1989) ★★★, with Elvis Costello *G.B.H.: Original Music From The Channel Four Series* (Demon Soundtracks 1991) ★★★, with Costello *Original Music From Jake's Progress* (Demon Soundtracks 1995) ★★.

● COMPILATIONS: *Shroud For A Nightingale: The Screen Music Of Richard Harvey* (Silva Screen 1996) ★★★★.

## HAWKINS, TED

b. Theodore Hawkins Jnr., 28 October 1936, Biloxi, Mississippi, USA, d. 1 January 1995, Los Angeles, California, USA. Hawkins was more of a modern-day 'songster' than a bluesman, his repertoire encompassing pop hits, country and folk standards, soul numbers and originals. He grew up with gospel music, and learned to play guitar at the age of 12, taught in the bluesy 'Vestapol' (or open C) style by local musicians. He played with such force that he protected his left hand with a glove. As a boy, he was sent to a reformatory, and spent several terms in prison. He left home in the 50s, hoboing first to Chicago, Illinois, then to New York, Pennsylvania and New Jersey, eventually settling in California. He recorded 'Baby'/'Whole Lot Of Women' for the Hollywood-based Money label in 1966; in 1971 he was spotted busking by producer Bruce Bromberg with whom he made an album. Apart from a single 'Sweet Baby', the recordings remained unreleased until Rounder Records issued *Watch Your Step* in 1982. Hawkins continued to perform on street corners and California's Ocean Front Walk; this aspect of Hawkins' career was documented on the *Venice Beach Tapes*, recorded, ironically, in Nashville, Tennessee in 1985 by H. Thorp Minister, III. *Happy Hour* consolidated his reputation, particularly in Britain where he had a sizeable following. An upturn in his career when he signed to Geffen Records in the early 90s was sadly curtailed by his death following a stroke. Despite retaining an undoubtedly 'rural' feel in performance, Hawkins owed much vocally to his hero Sam Cooke and to the great soul stylists of the 60s. Above all, he was one of the finest contemporary interpreters of melancholic material.

● ALBUMS: *Watch Your Step* (Rounder 1982) ★★★★, *Happy Hour* (Rounder 1986) ★★★, *On The Boardwalk: The Venice Beach Tapes* (American Activities 1986) ★★★★, *On The Boardwalk: At Venice Beach, California, Vol. II* (American Activities 1987) ★★★, *I Love You Too* aka *Nowhere To Run* (PT/Catfish 1989) ★★, *The Next Hundred Years* (DGC 1994) ★★★, *The Final Tour* 1994 live recording (Evidence 1998) ★★, *Love You Most Of All: More Songs From Venice Beach* 1985 recordings (Evidence 1998) ★★★, *The Unstoppable Ted Hawkins* 1988 recording (Catfish 2001) ★★★.

● COMPILATIONS: *The Best Of Venice Beach Tapes* (Munich 1989) ★★★★, *Songs From Venice Beach* (Evidence 1995) ★★★★, *The Kershaw Sessions* 1986–1989 recordings (Strange Roots 1995) ★★★★, *The Ted Hawkins Story: Suffer No More* (Rhino 1998) ★★★★.

● VIDEOS: *Ted Hawkins: Amazing Grace* (Geffen Home Video 1995).

## HAYSI FANTAYZEE

This colourful London-based disco trio comprised Jeremy Healy (b. Jeremiah Healy, 18 January 1962, Woolwich, London, England), Kate Garner (b. 9 July 1953, Wigan, Lancashire, England) and the less conspicuous Paul Caplin. Garner was formerly a fashion photographer; Healy was a disc jockey and Caplin a keyboard player with Animal Magnet. Heavily touted in the clubs, their debut 'John Wayne Is Big Leggy' brought instant success by reaching number 11 in the UK charts in 1982. Three further minor hits followed; 'Holy Joe', 'Shiny Shiny' and 'Sister Friction'. After they split in 1983, Healy went on to become one of the UK's most in-demand DJs, and also enjoyed chart success with the E-Zee Possee and Bleachin'.

● ALBUMS: *Battle Hymns For Children Singing* (RCA 1983) ★★.

## HAZA, OFRA

b. 19 November 1957, Tel Aviv, Israel, d. 23 February 2000, Tel Aviv, Israel. Haza was the daughter of Yemenite parents who had fled from the Muslim regime in Yemen. At the age of 12 she joined the theatre group Hatikva, run by Bezalel Aloni. In her seven years with the group, Haza recorded with them and won a Grammy award for an outstanding performance. After serving two years national service in the Israeli army she recorded her first solo album and quickly rose to become one of Israel's top singers. She was voted second in the 1983 Eurovision Song Contest with 'Ani Od Hai' (translated: 'I'm still alive'). In February 1987, Haza survived a horrific aeroplane crash on the Israeli/Jordanian border. Later in the year her singing was sampled on Eric B And Rakim hit remix of 'Paid In Full'. Her unlikely success, in her own right, in the US dance charts in 1988 with 'Im Nin'alu' spread to Europe where it topped the German charts and broke into the UK Top 20. The attendant *Shaday* went on to sell over a million copies worldwide.

Haza's visual image with her colourful national dress and the exotic mixture of middle-eastern ballads and rhythms blended with western styles, helped to make her Israel's best-known female solo singer. This success saw Haza fêted by artists in various fields of music; from world music and traditional folk, to disco and dance music. In an unlikely alliance in 1992, Haza linked with the Sisters Of Mercy for the remix of their single, 'Temple Of Love'. That same year also saw the release of *Kirya*, which involved both Don Was and Iggy Pop and was nominated for a Grammy Award. Two years later, she performed at the Nobel Peace Prize ceremony in Oslo, Norway. Following the release of a self-titled album for BMG-Ariola in 1997, Haza collaborated with composer Edward Shearmur on the soundtrack for *The Governess*. The following year she sang the role of Moses' mother in DreamWorks' star-studded animation *The Prince Of Egypt*, and featured on Jonathan Elias' Sony Classical release, *The Prayer Cycle*. She also worked with techno act Black Dog Productions on their *Babylon* project. Haza died suddenly of massive organ failure in February 2000, with many believing that her death was AIDS-related.

● ALBUMS: *Songs For Children* (1982) ★★★, *Temptations* (1982) ★★★, *Earth* (1982) ★★★, *Shirei Moledet* (Hed Arzi 1983) ★★★, *Shirei Teiman* aka *Fifty Gates Of Wisdom* (Shanachie 1984) ★★★, *Shirei Moledet 2* (Hed Arzi 1985) ★★★, *Yamim Nishbarim* aka *Broken Days* (Hed Arzi 1986) ★★★, *Shaday* (Sire 1988) ★★★★, *Desert Wind* (Sire 1989) ★★★, *Kirya* (Shanachie 1992) ★★★, *Ofra Haza* (BMG 1997) ★★★, *Live @ Montreux Jazz Festival* 1990 recording (1998) ★★★, with Black Dog Productions *Babylon* (Warners 1999) ★★★.

● COMPILATIONS: *The Golden Album* (Hed Arzi 1987) ★★★★.

● FILMS: *Shlager* (1979), *Na'arat Haparvarim* aka *West Side Girl* (1979), *Tzedek Muchlat* aka *Primal Justice* (1998), *The Prince Of Egypt* voice only (1998).

## HEARD, LARRY

b. 31 May 1960, Chicago, Illinois, USA. Heard is often credited as the single biggest influence on contemporary dance music, a claim that gains credence when his groundbreaking run of mid-80s house singles is taken into consideration. Heard was given the nickname 'Mr. Fingers' because of his dexterity when spinning records. He started off playing percussion in several bands before becoming fascinated by electronics and its musical possibilities. He made his recording debut in 1985 as the It with street poet Harry Dennis, releasing the singles 'Donnie' and 'Gallimaufry Gallery', the latter named after a Chicago club. As well as his solo work under the Mr. Fingers moniker, Heard formed Fingers Inc. with vocalists Robert Owens and Ron Wilson. Seminal house tracks such as 'Mystery Of Love' and 'Can You Feel It?' (as Mr. Fingers), and 'Distant Planet', 'You're Mine' and 'Bring Down The Walls' (as Fingers Inc.) followed on DJ International and Trax Records.

Some say that Heard (as Mr. Fingers) invented acid house music in 1986 on the track 'Washing Machine', although others say that DJ Pierre and Marshall Jefferson got there first. There can be no dispute, however, about the strength of Heard's mid-80s releases such as 'Slam Dance', or his production of Owens' 'I'm Strong'. Fingers then established Alleviated Records, and in 1988 under the name of the House Factors released 'Play It Loud', and his first album, this time under the name Fingers Inc. In 1989, he produced records by Kym Mazelle ('Treat Me Right'), Lil' Louis ('Touch Me'), Blakk Society ('Just Another Lonely Day') and Trio Zero ('Twilight'), and as Mr. Fingers released 'What About This Love?' on ffrr Records. The 1984 demos of his later club classics were also released on the *Amnesia* album. Heard also undertook remixing and production work for artists including Adamski, Electribe 101 and Massive Attack.

After signing a major label contract with MCA Records, Heard released the Mr. Fingers album *Introduction*, which included the club favourite 'Closer' and the fusion experiment, 'On A Corner Called Jazz'. He subsequently moved away from the dancefloor with a series of experimental albums released under his own name. The Mr. Fingers album *Back To Love* had originally been refused a release by MCA, and finally saw the light of day on Ren Galston's Black Market label. It was a restrained and mature collection of mellow house tracks that broke few musical barriers but cemented Heard's reputation as one of house music's pivotal forces. Although constantly threatening to retire from the music scene Heard has continued to produce a steady flow of well-received albums.

● ALBUMS: as Fingers Inc. *Another Side* (Jack Trax 1988) ★★★★, as Mr. Fingers *Amnesia* 1984 recordings (Jack Trax 1989) ★★★★, as Mr. Fingers *Introduction* (MCA 1992) ★★★★, as Mr. Fingers *Back To Love* (Black Market 1994) ★★★, *Sceneries Not Songs, Vol. 1* (Black Market 1995) ★★★, *Sceneries Not Songs, Vol. Tu* (Black Market 1996) ★★★, *Alien* (Black Market 1996) ★★★, *Dance 2000* (Distance 1997) ★★★, *Dance 2000, Part 2* (Distance 1998) ★★★, *Ice Castles* (Mecca 1998) ★★★, *Genesis* (Mecca 1999) ★★★, *Love's Arrival* (Track Mode 2001) ★★★★.

● COMPILATIONS: *Classic Fingers* (Black Market 1995) ★★★★, *Les Parrains De La House* (Mirakkle 1998) ★★★★, *Can You Feel It: Trax Classics* (Crown Japan 2001) ★★★.

## HEAVEN 17

An offshoot project from the UK production company BEF, this featured the synthesizer duo Ian Craig Marsh (b. 11 November 1956, Sheffield, England) and Martyn Ware (b. 19 May 1956, Sheffield, England) and vocalist Glenn Gregory (b.16 May 1958, Sheffield, England). Heaven 17's first UK hit was the dance-orientated '(We Don't

Need This) Fascist Groove Thang', which reached number 45. In late 1981, they released the bestselling album *Penthouse And Pavement*, which reflected the hedonistic themes of the period. Alternating with BEF projects and various guest appearances, Heaven 17 recorded intermittently. In May 1983, they achieved their finest moment with the electrifying UK Top 10 hit 'Temptation', which featured guest vocalist Carol Kenyon. A series of albums followed, but Heaven 17 always appeared to be a predominantly studio-based concern, whose name was used irregularly as an outlet to experiment with various new ideas. Meanwhile, the group's services as producers were still in demand and Ware co-produced Terence Trent D'Arby's best selling *The Hardline According To Terence Trent D'Arby*. In 1991, Marsh and Ware completed another ambitious BEF album of star cover versions. In 1996, they surprised the market by re-forming and recording a new studio album.

● ALBUMS: *Penthouse And Pavement* (Virgin 1981) ★★★, *Heaven 17* (Virgin 1983) ★★★, *The Luxury Gap* (Virgin 1983) ★★★, *How Men Are* (BEF 1984) ★★, *Endless* (Virgin 1986) ★★, *Pleasure One* (Virgin 1987) ★★★, *Teddy Bear, Duke & Psycho* (Virgin 1988) ★★★, *Bigger Than America* (Warners 1996) ★★, *How Live Is* (Almafame 1999) ★★.

● COMPILATIONS: *Higher & Higher (The Very Best Of Heaven 17)* (Virgin 1993) ★★★, *Retox/Detox* (Eagle 1998) ★★.

## HEDGES, MICHAEL

b. 31 December 1958, California, USA, d. 30 November 1997, Mendocino County, USA. This American guitarist, singer and composer moved from a highly individual instrumental style to a growing acclaim as a singer and composer, cut short by his death in a car accident. Hedges grew up in Enid, Oklahoma, and began playing the piano at the age of four. At high school he played cello and clarinet, then flute and guitar. He underwent a formal musical education, studying flute and composition at Philips University in Oklahoma then classical guitar and electronic music at the Peabody Conservatory in Baltimore. Hedges cited as his early influences, the Beatles, guitarist Leo Kottke and the twentieth century composers Morton Feldman, Bela Bartok and Anton Webern. In 1980, he moved to California to study computer music at Stanford University and was signed by Windham Hill Records.

The company's image, as purveyors of ethereal 'new age' music was, in part, forged by Hedges' early recordings with them, in particular *Breakfast In The Field* and *The Shape Of The Land*. While mysticism was a force behind his songwriting and he admitted being deeply influenced by the ideas of the anthropologist Joseph Campell, Hedges built a solid and grittier reputation as a musical innovator. Freewheeling experiments with tuning, two handed-fretwork tapping and harmonics pre-figured in later work in both recordings and concerts, which also saw the use of the harp guitar (an obscure instrument augmenting the standard six-strings with a tangential set of five bass strings) and synthesizers. The experiments are not merely embellishments to the music, but structural – Hedges' route to a distinctive musical voice. He was not, he said, an instrumentalist, but a composer. That was clearly disputed by his standing with the specialist music press who saw him as one of the great guitarists of the past two decades.

● ALBUMS: *Breakfast In The Field* (Windham Hill 1981) ★★★, *Aerial Boundaries* (Windham Hill 1984) ★★★★, with Kelly McGillis *Santabear's First Christmas* (Windham Hill 1986) ★★★, *Watching My Life Go By* (Windham Hill 1987) ★★★, *Live On The Double Planet* (Windham Hill 1987) ★★★, *Taproot* (Windham Hill 1990) ★★★, with Geena Davis *Princess Scargo & The Birthday Pumpkin* (Rabbit Ears 1993) ★★★, *The Road To Return* (Windham Hill 1994) ★★★, *Oracle* (Windham Hill 1996) ★★★★, *Torched* (Windham Hill 1999) ★★★.

● COMPILATIONS: *Strings Of Steel* (Windham Hill 1993) ★★★, *Best Of Michael Hedges* (Windham Hill 2000) ★★★★, *Beyond Boundaries: Guitar Solos* (Windham Hill 2001) ★★★.

● VIDEOS: *The Artist's Profile: Michael Hedges* (Artist's Profile 1996).

## HELLANBACH

Formed in Newcastle-upon-Tyne, England, in 1980, Hellanbach were one of the many groups to emerge from the New Wave Of British Heavy Metal. The band consisted of Jimmy Brash (vocals), Dave Patton (guitar), Kev Charlton (bass) and Steve Walker (drums). Instead of taking the usual route of making demos to secure a recording contract, the band went straight ahead with recording and releasing a four-track EP at their own expense – like many other NWOBHM groups, adopting the 'do it yourself' punk creed. *Out To Get You* was a heavy yet melodic debut. Hellanbach then kept a low profile until re-emerging on the Neat Records label and releasing their debut album, *Now Hear This*, in 1983. It was afforded a mixed reaction by the press, however, and the comparisons to Van Halen dogged them for the rest of their career. By the time *The Big H* was released in 1984, the band had clearly taken note of the criticisms levelled against them. Again, this was a worthy release from a dedicated band (now featuring Barry Hopper on drums), deftly executed and full of melodic choruses. Owing to a continued lack of media interest, the band quickly folded.

● ALBUMS: *Now Hear This* (Neat 1983) ★★★, *The Big H* (Neat 1984) ★★★.

● COMPILATIONS: *The Big H: The Hellanbach Anthology* (Sanctuary 2002) ★★★.

## HELLOWEEN

Formed in 1984 in Hamburg, Germany, from the ashes of local bands Second Hell and Iron Fist, the original line-up of this durable heavy metal band comprised Kai Hansen (b. 17 January 1963, Hamburg, Germany; guitar, vocals), Michael Weikath (b. 7 August 1962, Hamburg, Germany; guitar), Markus Grosskopf (b. 21 September 1965, Hamburg, Germany; bass) and Ingo Schwichtenberg (b. 18 May 1965, Hamburg, Germany, d. 8 March

1995; drums). After having two tracks included on the *Death Metal* compilation album released by Noise Records in 1984, the label issued their self-titled debut mini-album in 1985. This was soon followed by *Walls Of Jericho* and an EP, *Judas*. The band gained a strong following with their unique brand of high-speed power metal. Soon after its release, Helloween decided to add a vocalist/frontman, namely Michael Kiske (b. 24 January 1968, Hamburg, Germany), a charismatic 18-year-old. *Keeper Of The Seven Keys*, released in 1987, showed the band to be pursuing a much more melodic approach and Kiske proved himself a worthy addition.

Helloween then toured Europe relentlessly, building a sizeable following in the process. *Keeper Of The Seven Keys Part II* was released in 1988, together with a successful appearance at the Donington Festival that year. After this came an EP, *Dr. Stein*, but behind the scenes, all was not well. The band had become increasingly unhappy with their record company and started to negotiate with several major labels who had previously shown an interest. As a stopgap the band released *Live In The UK*, recorded at the Hammersmith Odeon in 1989. Kai Hansen then left to form his own outfit, Gamma Ray. His replacement was Roland Grapow (b. 30 August 1959, Hamburg, Germany). A protracted legal battle with their record company ensured that it was not until 1990 that the band was back in action. They finally signed to EMI Records and gained major management in the form of the Smallwood/Taylor organization. The band's debut for their new label, *Pink Bubbles Go Ape*, released in 1991, depicted Helloween as a shadow of their former selves, sadly missing Kai Hansen and his songwriting skills. Shortly after the dismissal of Kiske, Schwichtenberg was also given his marching orders due to personal health problems and a clash with Weikath, who was now the main force behind the band. Their former drummer took his own life by jumping in front of a train in March 1995. The new band members were Andi Deris (b. 18 August 1964, Karlsruhe, Germany; vocals, ex-Pink Cream 69) and Uli Kusch (b. 11 March 1967, Aachen, Germany; drums), who were in place in time for their Castle/Raw Power debut, *Master Of The Rings*. This became Helloween's most successful album for several years, topping the Japanese charts. *The Time Of The Oath* featured writing contributions from Weikath, Deris and Kusch, while the group composition 'Mission Motherland' saw the band tackle one of the social problems affecting Germany since the fall of the Berlin wall – refugees. Grapow and Kusch left the band in 2001, with English drummer Mark Cross (b. 2 August 1965, London, England) being brought in to replace the latter.

● ALBUMS: *Helloween* mini-album (Noise 1985) ★★, *Walls Of Jericho* (Noise 1986) ★★, *Keeper Of The Seven Keys* (Noise 1987) ★★★, *Keeper Of The Seven Keys Part II* (Noise 1988) ★★★, *Live In The U.K.* (Noise 1989) ★★, *Pink Bubbles Go Ape* (EMI 1991) ★★, *Chameleon* (EMI 1993) ★★, *Master Of The Rings* (Raw Power 1994) ★★★, *The Time Of The Oath* (Raw Power 1996) ★★★, *High Live* (Raw Power 1996) ★★,

*Better Than Raw* (Raw Power 1998) ★★★, *Metal Jukebox* (Raw Power 1999) ★★, *The Dark Ride* (Nuclear Blast 2000) ★★★.
● COMPILATIONS: *Pumpkin Tracks* (Noise 1989) ★★★, *The Best The Rest The Rare* (Noise 1991) ★★★, *Pumpkin Box* 4-CD box set (Label 1998) ★★★, *Treasure Chest* (Sanctuary 2002) ★★★.

## HENDRYX, NONA

b. Wynona Hendryx, 18 August 1945, Trenton, New Jersey, USA. A former member of both the Blue-Belles and LaBelle, the singer's departure from the latter group in 1977 precipitated their demise. Hendryx began a solo career in which strong visual elements were combined with a black rock direction. During the 80s, she enjoyed a consistent run of R&B hits, notably with 'Keep It Confidential' (number 22, March 1983), 'I Sweat (Going Through The Motions)' (number 28, March 1984) and 'Why Should I Cry?' (number 5, April 1987), the latter also reaching number 58 on the *Billboard* Hot 100 singles chart. In addition to soul material, though, Hendryx also produced a series of hard-rock albums and collaborated with acts as diverse as Material, Talking Heads, Peter Gabriel, Laurie Anderson and Afrika Bambaataa. *Skindiver* was a very personal creation defying easy musical categorization. In 1992, she returned to her soul roots with a fine album, *You Have To Cry Sometime*, which she shared with blue-eyed soulman Billy Vera. The album included a duet of 'Storybook Children', a demo of which Vera and Hendryx had cut together in 1967 before Vera recorded a hit version with Judy Clay.
● ALBUMS: *Nona Hendryx* (Epic 1977) ★★★, *Nona* (RCA 1983) ★★★★, *The Art Of Defence* (RCA 1984) ★★★, *The Heat* (RCA 1985) ★★★, *Female Trouble* (EMI 1987) ★★★, *Skindiver* (Private 1989) ★★★, with Billy Vera *You Have To Cry Sometime* (Shanachie 1992) ★★★.
● COMPILATIONS: *Transformation: The Best Of* (Razor & Tie 1999) ★★★.

## HEYWARD, NICK

b. 20 May 1961, Beckenham, Kent, England. The original lead vocalist in UK chart act Haircut 100, Heyward left for a solo career in late 1982. Early the following year he returned with a couple of chart hits, 'Whistle Down The Wind' and 'Take That Situation', both close to the 'boy next door blue-eyed soul' style developed by his former group. His debut solo album, *North Of A Miracle*, which included the up-tempo 'Blue Hat For A Blue Day', was a solid effort that won critical approval and sold well. It featured Beatles engineer Geoff Emerick as co-producer. An uneasy move away from his teenage audience was completed with the funk-influenced 'Warning Sign' but like many former teenage pin-ups the transition brought only limited commercial success. In 1988, he moved to Warner Brothers Records, but both the single, 'You're My World', and accompanying album, *I Love You Avenue*, failed to re-establish him in the mainstream.
For the next four years, Heyward concentrated on his second career as a graphic artist, until returning in 1992 with a new album for Epic Records and tour

dates alongside Squeeze. Over the next two years, he toured regularly, particularly in the USA, where he supported such alternative luminaries as Belly, Lemonheads, Mazzy Star and Therapy? (arguably the most unlikely coupling, given Heyward's reputation for gentle, pastoral songs). Much effort was put into *Tangled*; resulting in an outstanding album full of great melodies and fascinating lyrics. Released at the height of renewed interest in the Beatles, Heyward's album identifies him with the fab four and much of the late-60s quality pop song era. Neither the album nor the singles taken from it found much commercial favour, and it was difficult to imagine what he would have to do in the future, as on this showing Heyward had reached a creative peak. He worked on Edward Ball's 1996 solo album, and signed to Creation Records in 1997. The album that followed was perplexing; all the regular Heyward trademarks were present, catchy hooks and vocals were up to standard yet the overall impression was strangely disappointing. It would appear that Heyward had been listening to the Beatles' *Revolver* prior to entering the recording studio. Stand out tracks were 'My Heavy Head', 'The Man You Used To Be' and 'Stars In Her Eyes', but the next classic Heyward pop song was not on this album. Creation released him from his contract in 1998. Heyward's next release was a collection of his poetry, read by actor Greg Ellis.

● ALBUMS: *North Of A Miracle* (Arista 1983) ★★★, *Postcards From Home* (Arista 1986) ★★, *I Love You Avenue* (Warners 1988) ★★, *From Monday To Sunday* (Epic 1992) ★★, *Tangled* (Epic 1995) ★★★★, *The Apple Bed* (Creation 1998) ★★★, with Greg Ellis *Open Sesame Seed* spoken word (Greg Ellis 2001) ★★★.

● COMPILATIONS: *Best Of Nick Heyward And Haircut 100* (Ariola 1989) ★★★★, *The Greatest Hits Of Nick Heyward & Haircut 100* (RCA Camden 1996) ★★★★.

● FURTHER READING: *The Haircut 100 Catalogue*, Sally Payne. *Haircut 100: Not A Trace Of Brylcreem*, no editor listed.

## HIATT, JOHN

b. 1952, Indianapolis, Indiana, USA. The archetypal musicians' musician, John Hiatt is a powerful singer, guitarist and talented songwriter whose material has been recorded by various acts, including Dr. Feelgood, Searchers, Iggy Pop, Three Dog Night, Desert Rose Band, Bonnie Raitt, Bob Dylan, Nick Lowe, Rick Nelson and the Neville Brothers. Hiatt started out in local R&B bands in the late 60s, most notably the White Ducks. Moving to Nashville in 1970, he signed to Epic and recorded two highly acclaimed albums. After the second album, he left the label and toured for a spell as a solo performer before being offered a new contract by MCA at the end of the decade. This resulted in two further albums.

In 1980, guitarist Ry Cooder was looking for some new songs and was recommended Hiatt's material. Cooder received a tape of demos from Hiatt's publisher, and although he was not convinced the material was suitable for him, he decided he could use the talented guitarist in his own band. Hiatt duly accepted Cooder's offer and played with him on *Borderline* and on several subsequent albums and tours. His first solo album after his engagements with Cooder was 1982's *All Of A Sudden* and it was followed by almost one new album every year produced by Tony Visconti and Nick Lowe. Lowe regularly formed part of Hiatt's band both in the studio and on tour. The duo later became half of a new 'supergroup' when they teamed up with Cooder and Jim Keltner (veteran journeyman drummer) to form Little Village, who released their first disappointing self-titled album in 1992.

Since then Hiatt's reputation as a songwriter has grown and his own output has included some of his best work; the title tracks to *Perfectly Good Guitar* and *Walk On* are two of his most infectious songs. Equally arresting was *Crossing Muddy Waters* on which Hiatt was supported by some excellent musicians, most notably David Immerglück. Hiatt's music walks a fine line between country and folk, but he comfortably fits in the middle to create a genre of music which is entirely his own.

● ALBUMS: *Hanging Around The Observatory* (Epic 1974) ★★★, *Overcoats* (Epic 1975) ★★★, *Slug Line* (Epic 1979) ★★★, *Two Bit Monsters* (MCA 1980) ★★★, *All Of A Sudden* (MCA 1982) ★★, *Riding With The King* (Geffen 1983) ★★★★, *Warming Up To The Ice Age* (Geffen 1985) ★★★, *Bring The Family* (A&M 1987) ★★★★, *Slow Turning* (A&M 1988) ★★★, *Stolen Moments* (A&M 1990) ★★★, *Perfectly Good Guitar* (A&M 1993) ★★★★, with The Guilty Dogs *Hiatt Comes Alive At Budokan?* (A&M 1994) ★★★, *Walk On* (Capitol 1995) ★★★★, *Little Head* (Capitol 1997) ★★★, *Crossing Muddy Waters* (Vanguard/Sanctuary 2000) ★★★★, *The Tiki Bar Is Open* (Vanguard/Sanctuary 2001) ★★★.

● COMPILATIONS: *Y'All Caught?: The Ones That Got Away 1979-1985* (Geffen 1991) ★★★, *The Best Of John Hiatt* (Parlophone 1998) ★★★, *Greatest Hits: The A&M Years '87-'94* (A&M 1998) ★★★★, *Anthology* (Hip-O 2001) ★★★★.

## HIGHWAY 101

Like the Monkees, Highway 101 is a manufactured US band. Chuck Morris, the manager of the Nitty Gritty Dirt Band and Lyle Lovett, wanted to form an outfit that would play 'traditional country with a rock 'n' roll backbeat'. He recruited session man Scott 'Cactus' Moser to help him. He worked with bass player Curtis Stone, the son of Cliffie Stone, in the movie *Back To School*, and then added session guitarist Jack Daniels. Morris then heard some demos by Paulette Carlson. She had previously had songs recorded by Gail Davies and Tammy Wynette and made a cameo role as a nightclub singer in the movie *Twins*. Their first single, 'Some Find Love', was not successful, but in 1987, they had their first US country hits with 'The Bed You Made For Me' (number 4), which Carlson wrote, and 'Whiskey, If You Were A Woman' (number 2). They topped the US country charts with 'Somewhere Tonight' with its songwriting credit of 'old' and 'new' country, Harlan Howard and Rodney Crowell. In 1988, they had further chart-toppers with 'Cry, Cry, Cry' (which was a new song and not a revival of the Johnny Cash hit), 'If You Love Me, Just Say Yes' (being based on the slogan of Nancy Reagan's anti-drugs campaign, 'Just say no') and 'Who's Lonely Now' in 1989. Paulette Carlson took a turn off the Highway in 1990, and Nikki Nelson was recruited for *Bing Bang Boom*. The title track was an infectious and successful single, but the album failed to sell in the same quantities as before.

Daniels quit in 1992 and the group made a final album, *The New Frontier*, before disbanding. In 1995, Carlson initiated a reunion, missing only Moser from the line-up, and the band released a new album the following year. Carlson and Daniels were absent from the line-up that recorded 2000's *Big Sky*, which features new singer Chrislynn Lee and songs by the returning Moser and the stalwart Stone.

● ALBUMS: *Highway 101* (Warners 1987) ★★★, *101 2* (Warners 1988) ★★★, *Paint The Town* (Warners 1989) ★★★, *Bing Bang Boom* (Warners 1991) ★★★, *The New Frontier* (Liberty 1993) ★★★, *Reunited* (Willow Tree 1996) ★★★, *Big Sky* (Navarre/ FreeFalls 2000) ★★★.

● COMPILATIONS: *Greatest Hits* (Warners 1990) ★★★★, *Latest & Greatest* (Intersound 1997) ★★★.

## HIGSONS

Formed at Norwich University, England, in 1980 by Charlie 'Switch' Higson (lead vocals), Terry Edwards (guitar, saxophone, trumpet), Stuart McGeachin (guitar), Simon Charterton (drums), Colin Williams (bass) and Dave Cummings (guitar), who left the line-up early on, the band originally appeared under a plethora of guises such as the Higson 5, the Higson Brothers and the Higson Experience. They had settled for the Higsons by the time their first single, 'I Don't Want To Live With Monkeys' (1981), on the independent label Romans In Britain, was released. The song typified the Higsons' brand of quirky, tongue-in-cheek funk/pop and was treated to extensive airplay by the influential BBC radio disc jockey John Peel, achieving a number 2 position in the UK independent chart. A new label, Waap, brought with it a second single, 'The Lost And The Lonely' (1981), followed by 'Conspiracy' (1982). A contract with Chrysalis Records ensued for two singles, 'Tear The Whole Thing Down' (1982) and 'Run Me Down' (1983). They returned to Waap for 'Push Out The Boat' in 1983 and yet another change of label (Uptight) for a cover version of Andy Williams' 'Music To Watch Girls By'. The single failed to provide that elusive hit and was followed by the album *The Curse Of The Higsons*, combining several single sides with new material. Another move, to EMI Records' R4 label, yielded 'Take It' in 1985, but although Cummings had rejoined for the single, the Higsons played their final gig in March 1986.

A posthumous release by Waap, *Attack Of The Cannibal Zombie Businessmen*, married both sides of the first three 45s with six unreleased cuts, including a cover version of the Buddy Miles track 'Them Changes'. By that time, Charlie Higson had turned his hand to writing comedy, notably with comedians Harry Enfield and Vic Reeves; he later became the co-writer and star of BBC Television's *The Fast Show*, and published a number of serious novels. Charterton formed the short-lived Eat My Bed, and then Brazilian Nightmare with ex-Serious Drinking pair Pete Saunders and Jem Moore. Terry Edwards later performed with, and produced, Yeah Jazz, released a single as New York, New York ('Roger Wilson Said'), teamed up with Madness' Mark 'Bedders' Bedford as the Butterfield 8, and worked with Tindersticks and Gallon Drunk. Dave Cummings, meanwhile, joined Lloyd Cole's Commotions in 1986 and later joined Del Amitri.

● ALBUMS: *Live At The Jacquard Club, Norwich* (Own Label 1982) ★★★, *The Curse Of The Higsons* (Waap 1984) ★★★, *Attack Of The Cannibal Zombie Businessmen* (Waap 1987) ★★★.

● COMPILATIONS: *It's A Wonderful Life* (Hux 1998) ★★★.

## HIPSWAY

Hipsway emerged in the mid-80s on to a Scottish pop scene that had enjoyed a high profile, both commercially and critically, with acts such as Orange Juice, the Associates, Simple Minds and Altered Images. It was ex-Altered Images bass player Johnny McElhone (b. 21 April 1963) who teamed up with guitarist Pim Jones, drummer Harry Travers and vocalist Graham Skinner (previously in the White Savages) around 1984. As Hipsway, the band secured a contract with Mercury Records who were impressed enough to promote strongly both 'The Broken Years' in June and the catchy 'Ask The Lord' later in 1985, although neither made much impact. However, the momentum led to a UK number 17 chart hit with their third single, 'The Honeythief', in February 1986, and in its wake came both Hipsway's self-titled album and a reissue of 'Ask The Lord' in April. Unfortunately, Graham Skinner's dramatic vocal style was the only distinctive feature aside from the previous promising singles. 'Long White Car' was released in August, but fell quickly by the wayside after a modest chart run. McElhone went on to form the more successful Texas with Sharleen Spiteri and Ally McErlaine. It was three years before Hipsway returned but unfortunately they failed even to manage what their second album, *Scratch The Surface*, suggested. 'Your Love' disappeared without trace, the album followed suit, and Hipsway broke up soon afterwards. Skinner and Jones moved on to Witness.

● ALBUMS: *Hipsway* (Mercury 1986) ★★★, *Scratch The Surface* (Mercury 1989) ★★.

## HITCHCOCK, ROBYN

b. 3 March 1953, London, England. The possessor of a lyrical vision of a latter-day Syd Barrett, Hitchcock made his early reputation with the post-punk psychedelic band the Soft Boys, having previously appeared in various acts including the Beetles and Maureen And The Meat Packers. After the Soft Boys split in 1981, he spent some time writing for Captain Sensible, then formed his own band, the Egyptians, around erstwhile colleagues Andy Metcalfe (bass), Morris Windsor (drums) and Roger Jackson (keyboards). Hitchcock's live performances were punctuated by epic, surreal monologues of comic invention capable of baffling the uninitiated and delighting the converted. His sharp mind and predilection for the bizarre has revealed itself in many titles, such as 'Man With The Light Bulb Head' ('. . . I turn myself on in the dark'), 'My Wife And My Dead Wife', a tragi-comedy of a man coming to accept the intrusion into his life of a deceased spouse, 'Trash', a well-aimed diatribe against hopeless rock star hangers-on, 'Trams Of Old London', a love and remembrance saga of an era long gone, and a guide to bringing up children in the a cappella 'Uncorrected Personality Traits'.

A move to A&M Records saw the release of Globe Of Frogs, which included the 'Ballroom Man', a favourite on US college radio that went some way to breaking new ground and earning Hitchcock a fresh audience. As a result, and despite his devoted cult following in the UK, the artist had by the early 90s concentrated more on recording and performing in the USA (occasionally guesting with R.E.M.). He also played from time to time with the Soft Boys and saw his back-catalogue repackaged with loving commitment by Sequel Records. It remains to be seen whether the oddball workings of this endearing eccentric's mind will find a way into anything other than the US collegiate consciousness. Warner Brothers Records were prepared to take the risk in 1996 when a revitalized Hitchcock released Moss Elixir and its vinyl-only companion piece, Mossy Liquor. In 1998, cult director Jonathan Demme filmed Hitchcock playing live in a New York department store window, later released as Storefront Hitchcock. The singer's second and final Warners album was followed by a typically eccentric collection of outtakes from the sessions. A more permanent Soft Boys reunion saw the original line-up undertaking an extensive transatlantic tour in 2001, and recording a new studio album (Nextdoorland) the following year.

● ALBUMS: Black Snake Diamond Role (Armageddon 1981) ★★★★, Groovy Decay (Albion 1982) ★★, I Often Dream Of Trains (Midnight Music 1984) ★★★, with The Egyptians Fegmania! (Midnight Music/Slash 1985) ★★★★, with The Egyptians Gotta Let This Hen Out! (Midnight Music/Relativity 1985) ★★★★, Groovy Decoy original demos of Groovy Decay (Midnight Music 1985) ★★★, with The Egyptians Element Of Light (Glass Fish/Relativity 1986) ★★★★, with The Egyptians Globe Of Frogs (A&M 1988) ★★★, with The Egyptians Queen Elvis (A&M 1989) ★★, Eye (Glass Fish/Twin/Tone 1990) ★★★, with The Egyptians Perspex Island (Go! Discs/A&M 1991) ★★★, with The Egyptians Respect (A&M 1993) ★★★, Mossy Liquor (Outtakes And Prototypes) (Warners 1996) ★★★, Moss Elixir (Warners 1996) ★★★, with The Egyptians Live At The Cambridge Folk Festival (Strange Fruit 1998) ★★★, Storefront Hitchcock (Warners 1998) ★★★, Jewels For Sophia (Warners 1999) ★★★, A Star For Bram (Editions PAF! 2000) ★★★, Robyn Sings (Editions PAF! 2002) ★★★.

● COMPILATIONS: Invisible Hitchcock (Glass Fish/Relativity 1986) ★★★, Robyn Hitchcock And The Egyptians: The Kershaw Sessions (Strange Roots 1994) ★★★, You & Oblivion (Rhino/Sequel 1995) ★★★, Robyn Hitchcock (Sequel 1995) ★★★, Gravy Deco (Rhino 1995) ★★★, with The Egyptians Greatest Hits (A&M 1996) ★★★, Uncorrected Personality Traits (Rhino/Sequel 1997) ★★★★.

● VIDEOS: Gotta Let This Hen Out! (Jettisoundz 1985), Brenda Of The Lightbulb Eyes (A&M 1990).

● FILMS: Storefront Hitchcock (1998).

## HOLLIDAY, JENNIFER

b. 19 October 1960, Houston, Texas, USA. This powerful vocalist first attracted attention as lead in the Broadway show Your Arms Too Short To Box With God. She is, however, better known for her Tony Award-winning role in the musical Dreamgirls, a thinly disguised adaptation of the Supremes' story, which former member Mary Wilson took as the title of her autobiography. The show's undoubted highlight was Holliday's heart-stopping rendition of 'And I Am Telling You I'm Not Going', one of soul's most emotional, passionate performances. The single's success in 1982 prompted Holliday's solo career, but subsequent work was overshadowed by that first hit. She returned to the stage in 1985 in Sing, Mahalia Sing and acted in the television series The Love Boat. Holliday was also part of the backing choir on Foreigner's 1984 UK number 1 hit single, 'I Wanna Know What Love Is'. Say You Love Me won her a second Grammy award in 1985. She appeared in the musical Grease in the 90s and has recorded only sporadically. Holliday possesses an outstandingly powerful and emotional voice, the range of which has seen her compared to Aretha Franklin.

● ALBUMS: with Loretta Devine, Cleavant Derricks Dreamgirls (Geffen 1982) ★★★, Feel My Soul (Geffen 1983) ★★★, Say You Love Me (Geffen 1985) ★★★, Get Close To My Love (Geffen 1987) ★★★, I'm On Your Side (Arista 1991) ★★★, On And On (Inter Sound 1994) ★★★.

● COMPILATIONS: The Best Of Jennifer Holliday (Geffen 1996) ★★★★, The Best Of Jennifer Holliday: The Millennium Collection (Interscope 2000) ★★★.

## HOME SERVICE

Formed in 1980 as the First Eleven, this UK band evolved from the ever-changing Albion Band, which at the time included John Kirkpatrick in the line-up. Led by John Tams (vocals), the group featured Bill Caddick (b. 27 June 1944, Hurst Hill, Wolverhampton, England; vocals/guitar/dobro), Graeme Taylor (b. 2 February 1954, Stockwell, London, England; vocals/guitar), Michael Gregory (b. 16 November 1949, Gower, South Wales; drums/percussion), Roger Williams (b. 30 July 1954, Cottingham, Yorkshire, England; trombone), Howard Evans (b. 29 February 1944, Chard, Somerset, England; trumpet), and Jonathan Davie (b. 6 September 1954, Twickenham, Middlesex, England; bass). Both Evans and Williams were concurrently members of Brass Monkey, and Caddick had already released a number of solo albums. The group was involved with work for the National Theatre, for which they provided the music for the York Mystery Plays. The resultant album appeared in 1985. This release included guest vocals from Linda Thompson, and covered both traditional and contemporary material. By 1985, Caddick had left the group, unhappy with the lack of live concert work. This situation was caused by the many commitments the group had to theatre, television, and film work. The following year, 1986, Andy Findon (saxophone) and Steve King (keyboards) were added to the line-up. It was 1991 before the line-up played together again, on the Hokey Pokey charity compilation *All Through The Year*.

● ALBUMS: *The Home Service* (Jigsaw 1984) ★★★, *The Mysteries* (Coda 1985) ★★★, *Alright Jack* (Celtic Music 1986) ★★★★, *Wild Life* 1992 live recording (Fledg'ling 1995) ★★★.

## HONEYMAN-SCOTT, JAMES

b. 4 November 1956, Hereford, England, d. 16 June 1982, London, England. This flaxen-headed guitarist who doubled on keyboards was a founder member of the Pretenders in 1978. If less prominent onstage than Chrissie Hynde, he was solidly at the music's heart: loud enough for vocal harmonies, but quietly ministering to overall effect instrumentally. Remembered principally as a guitarist, his riffs and solos were constructed to integrate with melodic and lyrical intent, rather than a flashier reaction to underlying chord sequences. This style was commensurate with a personality that permitted Hynde to take increasing control of the band's destiny after *Pretenders II* in 1981 – the year he married Peggy Sue Fender. Weakened by a detoxification course for drug addiction, his death in June 1982 occurred shortly after snorting cocaine at a London party. The Pretenders found a replacement in Robbie McIntosh, a Honeyman-Scott soundalike.

## HOODOO GURUS

An Australian rock band whose belief in the power of the bar chord never diminished, Sydney's Hoodoo Gurus shared links with that city's other major alternative rock attraction of the 80s, the Scientists (after both relocated from Perth). That connection was instigated by singer-songwriter Dave Faulkner, who had previously played in a band called the Gurus, before joining Scientists guitarist Rod Radalj (guitar) in an untitled band. Bolstered by the arrival of another ex-Scientist member, drummer Jim Baker, the trio named their new band Le Hoodoo Gurus. That outfit would eventually evolve into the tight, hypnotic garage rock machine that, under a slightly abbreviated title, became widely venerated in underground circles through their releases for a variety of American labels. Indeed, much of their popularity stemmed from the USA, where tours of the west coast made them as popular as the musically aligned Fleshtones.

Led by the power-pop playing of Faulkner, Brad Sheperd (guitar, harmonica), with the rhythm section of Baker (drums) and Clyde Bramley (bass), the Hoodoo Gurus ceaseless exploration of the riff saw them compared to everyone from the Cramps to the Fall, beginning with their influential *Stoneage Romeos* debut of 1983. Dedicated to US television

sitcom legends Arnold Ziffel and Larry Storch, it included the stage favourite '(Let's All) Turn On' and the nonsensical 'I Was A Kamikaze Pilot'. *Mars Needs Guitars!*, with Mark Kingsmill taking over on drums, was slightly hampered by inferior production, but the tunes were still memorable and even adventurous given their limited musical range, which veered from country punk to booming, bass-driven sleaze rock. A rarer outbreak of melodicism was introduced on *Blow Your Cool!*, with the band joined by the Bangles on several selections, although elsewhere they retreated to pounding rhythms and tough rock 'n' roll. The gap between albums in 1988 saw Bramley replaced by Rick Grossman on bass. More feedback and heightened songwriting tension, together with improved production, produced the band's finest album in 1989's *Magnum Cum Louder*. *Kinky* mined a similar furrow, drawing lyrical targets from US and Australian pop culture, though there was little stylistic variation to the band's themes. *Crank* brought in Ramones producer Ed Stasium, but, like follow-up *Blue Cave*, was a weaker effort. The band elected to call it a day in late 1997, although they played one final show in January 1998. Faulkner, Shepherd, Grossman and Kingsmill later formed the Persian Rugs, although Grossman was replaced by Kendall James following a Hoodoo Gurus reunion show in December 2001.

● ALBUMS: *Stoneage Romeos* (Big Time/A&M 1983) ★★★, *Mars Need Guitars!* (Big Time/Elektra 1985) ★★★, *Blow Your Cool!* (Big Time/Elektra 1987) ★★★, *Magnum Cum Louder* (RCA 1989) ★★★★, *Kinky* (RCA 1991) ★★★, *Crank* (RCA 1994) ★★, *Blue Cave* (Zoo 1996) ★★.

● COMPILATIONS: *Electric Soup: The Singles Collection* (RCA 1992) ★★★★, *Gorilla Bisquit: B-Sides And Rarities* (RCA 1992) ★★★, *Bite The Bullet* (Mushroom 1998) ★★★, *Ampology* (Acadia 2000) ★★★★.

## HOOTERS

This long-running Philadelphia, USA-based band became well versed in the fickle nature of fame since their formation in 1978. Originally a quintet fusing folk, rock and ska, they spent the early 80s building a formidable live reputation throughout surrounding states. Led by Rob Hyman and Eric Bazilian, the Hooters took their name from the distinctive keyboard and harmonica sound that dominated their early recordings. They had several US hits in the mid-80s as MTV exposure took 'All You Zombies' (number 58), 'And We Danced' (number 21) 'Day By Day' (number 18), and 'Where Do The Children Go' (number 38) into the *Billboard* charts. All four were included on their 1985 debut album, which received universally strong reviews. Two more singles, 'Johnny B' and 'Satellite', failed to break the Top 50, although the latter did become a strong international seller, topping several European lists. On *Zig Zag* they pursued a more sober direction, with songs such as 'Give The Music Back' and 'Don't Knock It 'Til You Try It' adding darker shades to their repertoire. However, when the sales of the album were only moderate, a dramatic self-appraisal was undertaken. 'We did talk about ending the band, but we came to the conclusion that we still have too much energy.' *Out Of Body* revealed plenty of the Hooters' customary catchy rock verve, but with a new focus on folk-rock (including the use of a mandolin, violin and accordion). They had also moved to a new label, following Columbia Records' purchase by Sony (which had upset the promotion of their previous album). They also changed producers (Richard Chertoff departing in favour of Steve Earle collaborator Joe Hardy). Multi-instrumentalist Mindy Jostyn (formerly part of Donald Fagen's New Rock 'N' Soul Revue) was also added as a sixth member. Despite a revitalized sound, the Hooters failed to regain the commercial ground lost in the early 90s, and the band returned to session playing. Most in-demand was Hyman who worked with Sophie B. Hawkins, Willie Nelson, Johnny Clegg, and Cyndi Lauper. He worked with Bazilian on Joan Osborne's debut *Relish*, including the transatlantic hit single 'One Of Us'.

● ALBUMS: *Nervous Night* (Columbia 1985) ★★★★, *One Way Home* (Columbia 1987) ★★★, *Zig Zag* (Columbia 1989) ★★★, *Out Of Body* (MCA 1993) ★★★, *Live* (MCA 1998) ★★.

● COMPILATIONS: *We Came To Play* (Sony 1995) ★★★, *Hooterization: A Retrospective* (Columbia 1996) ★★★★, *Super Hits* (Sony 2001) ★★★.

## HORNETS ATTACK VICTOR MATURE

Until the mid-80s, this American band was one of the most influential groups that never existed. During the late 70s, against the backdrop of new wave, legions of young rockers with thin ties and excessive safety-pins were congregating under increasingly strange names that eschewed the rakishness and romance of earlier eras (for example, the Searchers, the Telstars, the Temptations, the Kinks), using everything from body parts (the Brains) to *realpolitik* (Gang Of Four) to establish mystique. One afternoon two rock journalists, both neighbours and columnists for competing music weeklies, saw a perfect new name for a band in a headline in the *Los Angeles Times*: 'Hornets Attack Victor Mature'. The actor had been whisked off to the Encino burn centre. It is unknown whether he was still under observation several days later when both scribes faced Wednesday deadlines for their rather similar columns, both devoted to reporting the latest news in Hollywood music circles. What is known is that both reporters encountered a not uncommon problem, a surfeit of committed editorial space against a shortfall of compelling fact, and that both reporters arrived at the same solution. As many journalistic professionals know, a misstatement of fact is a gross miscarriage of the truth; a misstatement followed by a question mark is entirely legal. Thus, these resourceful members of the Fourth Estate wondered aloud: 'Will Hornets Attack Victor Mature be the next L.A. power pop band to snare big bucks in a record deal?' The following week, two respected industry journals both queried a heretofore disinterested collective readership about the fate of this group. A week thereafter, a rock radio newsletter not known for its exhaustive fact-checking protocols reprinted the information, *sans* question mark. Thus was the long and largely fruitless career of Hornets Attack Victor Mature launched, accumulating momentum and new copy lines without benefit of a single, album, video, tour or lawsuit. In 1980, *Musician* magazine named the band winner in both the Best Name For A New Band and Worst Name For A New Band categories. At the beginning of the 80s, a buxom centrefold in *Oui* magazine was quoted as loving new wave and punk, naming Hornets Attack Victor Mature alongside the Clash as among her favourites (possibly the bio was ghosted by one of our former columnists). This virtual career might have gone on indefinitely, but in the mid-80s the members of R.E.M. actually booked themselves into an Athens club under this very name.

● ALBUMS: *The Underground Car Park Tapes* (Redmond West 1997) ★★, *The Barnes Sutherland Expedition* (Redmond West 1998) ★★★.

## HORNSBY, BRUCE

b. 23 November 1954, Williamsburg, Virginia, USA. After many years working in the music business as pianist and contract songwriter for 20th Century Fox, Hornsby burst on to the market in 1986 with a superb debut. The single 'The Way It Is', with its captivating piano introduction and infectious melody, was a transatlantic hit. Hornsby has a technique of hitting the piano keys hard, which still results in a clean melodic sound, reminiscent of Floyd Cramer. The first album, part produced by Huey Lewis, contained a plethora of piano based southern American rock songs, with Hornsby's strong voice, reminiscent of Bruce Springsteen, making it one of the year's best rock albums. Many of the 'American heritage' songs on the album were co-written with his brother John. The line-up of the Range comprised David Mansfield (violin, mandolin, guitar), Joe Puerta (bass), John Molo (drums), and George Marinelli (guitar). Hornsby and the Range followed the first album with *Scenes From The South Side*, an even stronger collection including the powerful 'The Valley Road' and 'Defenders Of The Flag'. The former song won him a composers' Grammy for the best bluegrass recording, as performed by the Nitty Gritty Dirt Band. The third collection *Night On The Town* in 1990 was a move away from the piano-dominated sound and featured Jerry Garcia on guitar. Following the death of the Grateful Dead's Brent Mydland in July 1990, Hornsby joined as a temporary replacement. In addition to many session/guest appearances during the early 90s, Hornsby (by now recording without the Range and writing on his own) found time to record *Harbor Lights*, a satisfying and acoustic sounding record. In forsaking an overtly commercial direction, Hornsby sounded both confident and happy with his recent 'sound'. *Hot House* and its follow up *Spirit Trail* were both credible records, demonstrating Hornsby's penchant for jazzy improvization, yet commercially they were disappointing. Hornsby continues to perform regularly with his own band and with the excellent The Other Ones, Bob Weir and Phil Lesh's post-Grateful Dead unit. Hornsby, however, is sliding dangerously towards the 'criminally underrated' pages of rock history.

● ALBUMS: as Bruce Hornsby & The Range *The Way It Is* (RCA 1986) ★★★, as Bruce Hornsby & The Range *Scenes From The South Side* (RCA 1988) ★★★★, as Bruce Hornsby & The Range *Night On The Town* (RCA 1990) ★★★, *Harbor Lights* (RCA 1993) ★★★★, *Hot House* (RCA 1995) ★★★, *Spirit Trail* (RCA 1998) ★★★, *Here Come The Noise Makers* (RCA 2000) ★★★, *Big Swing Face* (RCA 2002) ★★★.

## HOTHOUSE FLOWERS
This folk-inspired Irish rock band, who took their name from the title of a Wynton Marsalis album, are based around the nucleus of vocalist and keyboard player Liam O Maonlai and guitarist Fiachna O Braonain. The pair played in a punk band called Congress, before performing as the Incomparable Benzini Brothers. The duo busked in their native Dublin, and in 1985 won the Street Entertainers Of The Year Award. Recruiting bass player Peter O'Toole, saxophonist Leo Barnes, drummer Jerry Fehily and backing vocalist Maria Doyle, they became the Hothouse Flowers and landed a regular gig at the Magic Carpet Club just outside Dublin. Their notoriety spreading, they were highly praised in *Rolling Stone* magazine before they had even secured a recording contract. An appearance on RTE's Saturday night chat programme *The Late Show* led to the issue of a single on U2's Mother label. 'Love Don't Work That Way' came out in 1987 and though it was not a great success, it brought them to the attention of PolyGram Records subsidiary, London Records, who signed them up. Their debut single for the major, 'Don't Go', was a number 11 UK hit. Further hits followed, including a cover version of Johnny Nash's 'I Can See Clearly Now' (number 23), 'Give It Up' (number 30) and 'Movies'. Their bestselling debut, *People*, reached number 2 in the UK charts. The band existed as part of a larger, looser 'Raggle Taggle' musical community, and members could be heard on material by the Indigo Girls, Adventures, Michelle Shocked, and Maria McKee. In the early 90s, they made their 'acting' debut in an episode of the UK television series *Lovejoy*. Further albums continued to chart in the UK Top 10, but showed little musical progression from their debut. In 1995, O Maonlai formed a side project, Alt, with Andy White and Tim Finn. Hothouse Flowers returned in 1998 with the uninspiring *Born*.

● ALBUMS: *People* (London 1988) ★★★, *Home* (London 1990) ★★, *Songs From The Rain* (London 1993) ★★★, *Born* (London 1998) ★★.

● COMPILATIONS: *The Best Of* (London 2000) ★★★.

## HOUSE
House music takes its name from a Chicago, USA nightclub, the Warehouse, where a pulsating, mesmerizing, predominantly electronic form of disco music became hugely popular in the early and mid-80s. House can be characterized by its relentless 4/4 tempo, its emphasized percussion (notably the bass or kick drum and hissing high-hat

cymbals) combined with looped vocal codas, dramatic piano vamps, drum rolls and repetitive synthesizer riffs. Although he cannot be credited with its invention, DJ Frankie Knuckles from the South Bronx, New York, was certainly instrumental in refining the form. Knuckles was a protégé of David Mancuso's pivotal Manhattan 'house parties' whose heyday was in the early to mid-70s. Knuckles had also worked with another groundbreaking DJ/sound engineer, Larry Levan and Nicky Siano – DJ at the famous New York club, the Gallery. In 1977, aged 22, Knuckles re-located from New York to Chicago to help establish a new club. The club became known as the Warehouse and an abbreviated form of the name eventually became synonymous with the extended, turbo-charged disco records that were invented specifically for its dancefloor. Between 1977 and 1981, the club's crowd was mainly black and gay, and Knuckles played disco anthems from labels such as Philadelphia International Records and Salsoul. To add extra zest to his sets, Knuckles began to manipulate the records themselves by transferring them on to reel-to-reel tape. He would then remix them to extend certain parts, such as the breakdown to bass and drums, and to emphasise and repeat others such as vocal codas or brass and orchestral 'stabs'. These effects have since become the hallmarks of early house music. Although Levan and others had tried similar techniques in New York, in Chicago they were still striking and the impact of Knuckles' sets soon made the Warehouse the hottest Saturday night in town. An important innovation was Knuckles' introduction of pre-set percussion patterns from an early drum machine that he played in synchronicity with the records, to boost their kick and high-hat drum sounds.

In 1984, Knuckles left the Warehouse to set up a new club, the Powerplant. Around this time, he bought a Roland TR-909 drum instrument from the then unknown techno pioneer from Detroit, Derrick May. Again, Knuckles was able to supercharge the percussion sections of his records by adding the forceful and distinctive sound of the 909 to crash in dramatically, bridge between discs or 'pump up the bass' – a technique he practised endlessly during the week in readiness for Saturday night. In parallel with these improvizations, radio DJs on Chicago's WBMX station – Farley Jackmaster Funk, Ralph Rosario, Kenny 'Jammin'' Jason, Mickey 'Mixin'' Oliver and Scott Seals (known as the Hot Mix 5) were perfecting the art of mixing – creating dynamic turntable collages by switching between record decks using a mixing unit. It was not long before they too incorporated drum machines and eventually synthesizers. It was here that the division between artist and DJ began to blur, as the manipulation of pre-recorded sound became more pronounced. Another Chicago club, the Music Box, was home to DJ, Ron Hardy, who was also creating powerful new sound with stripped down and extended synthetic drum sections. Like many clubs and raves before and since, the Music Box did not serve alcohol, tacitly embracing the use of drugs (PCP, large quantities of LSD and MDMA).

This only served to intensify the atmosphere of abandon and ecstasy. This 'symbiosis' between narcotics – including alcohol – and the music has remained at the heart of club culture ever since.

The new accessibility of technology, such as that made by Roland of Japan, served to empower those hedonists, dancers and DJs wishing to create their own soundscapes for the dancefloor. Many machines (the Roland 808, 909 and 727 for example) had been discontinued and were available cheaply on the second-hand market. Their futuristic fizzles, squelches and cracks sounded astonishing through the powerful sound systems of the clubs. Cheap and portable, the user could assemble a miniature studio in a small space and create space-age dance music. Later, of course, sampling took these homemade possibilities to new dimensions. The sounds of the disco diva, the orchestra, the drummer and the piano could all be conjured up and manipulated to sound like they never had – all from within the space of a bedsit. The early 80s' boom in cheap studio equipment had a huge impact on all forms of popular music but hip-hop, techno and house positively celebrated the flexibility and the new sound that this technology had brought.

Necessity being the mother of invention, the improvizations that Knuckles and others had made for their DJ sets soon became records, often transferred from homemade tapes on to acetates for the club before being crudely pressed 12-inches on Chicago's two largest independent labels, Trax Records and DJ International. Early house recordings included 'On And On Trax' by Vince Lawrence and 'Waiting On My Angel' by Jamie Principle. As with rock 'n' roll 30 years previously, it was radio that brought house music to the mainstream and in this case it was Chicago radio DJs such as Julian Peruse, Frankie Rodríguez, Mike 'Hitman' Wilson, Bad Boy Bill, Tim Shomer, Brian Middleton and the aforementioned Hot Mix 5, that took house to new audiences. Further ground-breaking releases included Colonel Abrams' 'Music Is The Answer', J.M. Silk's answer record 'Music Is The Key' and Farley Jackmaster Funk's 'Aw Shucks'. It was Steve Hurley's 'Jack Your Body' that emphatically announced house's arrival on the world stage when it reached the UK's number 1 in January 1987. It is somewhat easy to forget the impact these new sounds had on the uninitiated ear – their harsh, mechanically precise percussion and bass lines and repetitive vocal samples sounding alien to a generation of dancers used to the strings and smooth vocals of traditional disco records.

Of course, garage and techno developed in parallel with house in the USA but particularly because of the acid house explosion the UK and Ibiza, house would transmogrify into sub-genres during the next 10 years. (For a more detailed account of the UK's scene, see the entry on dance music.) Italy and Germany was also instrumental in forming new styles. These included deep house, epic house, 'handbag', ambient, tribal, tech-house and trance, the latter itself a mutation of house music.

'Deep' house remained slightly down-tempo from its sibling forms and used funkier bass sections and subtle, repetitive melodies, building slowly to a dancefloor climax. Moby's early recordings, including the 1991 hit 'Go' are perhaps a good example of this form. 'Epic' house, an early form of trance, was notable for its sweeping, panoramic use of strings, its long breakdowns and pauses before rising to bombastic snare rolls, melodic synthesizer riffs and choral samples – all orchestrated to maximize the effects of the Ecstasy high. This form was initially popularized by UK DJs such as Sasha and John Digweed – BT's 'Embracing The Sunshine' and Robert Miles' 'Children' are good examples of the style. 'Handbag' house was popular in the USA and Europe in the early 90s, its name referring to the practice in nightclubs of groups of women dancing around their purses and handbags to avoid theft. The form itself could be identified by its feel good melodies, handclaps, piano vamps, its allusions to disco and the prominence of female and upbeat vocals. Such music often found its way into the national charts on both sides of the Atlantic, with C & C Music Factory's hits or Black Box's 'Ride On Time' the most successful representatives of this style. 'Ambient' house, a seemingly paradoxical style, tried to take house in a more mellow direction by slowing the tempo considerably, using less aggressive percussion sounds and taking inspiration from dub and reggae. The Orb, Andy Weatherall, Future Sound Of London, Beloved, José Padilla and KLF were all early pioneers of this sound. The latter's 1990 collection, Chill Out, is often considered the classic ambient house album. 'Tribal' house was effectively a 'deep' form of house, occasionally using African rhythms and vocal sounds, heavy bass and samples from other musical forms. The US DJ, Danny Tenaglia became known for his 'tribal' sets in New York in the early 90s. A recent European hybrid, 'tech-house' is essentially a blend of house and techno, combining the former's essential exuberance with the latter's more pounding, aggressive sounds.

These often tricky distinctions aside, house music's essence remains its 4/4 tempo and its use of electronics. In 15 years, it has become the sound of Saturday night around the world. Like hip-hop, it rose from urban hedonism and parties, embraced cheap technology and has become ubiquitous in the commercial world – a byword for youth. House is now used everywhere: as the accompaniment to the aerobics class or as the incidental music for television sports programmes. Its heart, however, remains firmly in the disco.

## HOUSE OF LOVE

After a short spell with the ill-fated, glam rock-inspired Kingdoms, UK-born vocalist and guitarist Guy Chadwick teamed up with drummer Pete Evans, guitarist Terry Bickers, bass player Chris Groothuizen and vocalist/guitarist Andrea Heukamp to form UK band the House Of Love. Throughout 1986, the quintet played at small pubs and despatched a demo tape to Creation Records, which, after constant play in the office, attracted the attention of label head Alan McGee. He financed the recording of their debut single, the sparkling 'Shine

On', which was released in May 1987 (the song eventually became a Top 20 hit when it was re-released three years later). A follow-up, 'Real Animal', was also issued, but sold relatively poorly. After touring extensively under tough conditions, Heukamp decided to leave the band. Continuing as a quartct, the House Of Love spent the spring of 1988 recording their debut album, which cost an astonishingly meagre £8,000 to complete. A pilot single, 'Christine', was rightly acclaimed as one of the best UK independent singles of the year. Its shimmering guitar work was exemplary and indicated the enormous potential of the ensemble. The debut album did not disappoint and was included in many critics' nominations for the best record of 1988.

Already, the House Of Love was tipped as the band most likely to succeed in 1989 and the release of the excellent 'Destroy The Heart' reinforced that view. Speculation was rife that they would sign to a major label and eventually Phonogram secured their signatures. In keeping with their 60s/guitar-based image, the band's releases were subsequently issued on the newly revived Fontana Records label. A torturous period followed. The first two singles for the label, 'Never' and 'I Don't Know Why I Love You', both stalled at number 41, while the album suffered interminable delays. By Christmas 1989, guitarist Terry Bickers had quit over what was euphemistically termed a personality clash. He was immediately replaced by Simon Walker, and early the following year the band's long-awaited £400,000 second album, *Fontana*, appeared to mixed reviews. As Chadwick later acknowledged: 'We'd staked everything on the first album.' Extensive touring followed, ending with the departure of Walker, tentatively replaced by original member Andrea Heukamp, who returned from Germany.

Thereafter, Chadwick suffered a long period of writer's block while the departing Bickers enjoyed acclaim in Levitation. Although the House Of Love lost ground to newly revered guitar bands such as the Stone Roses, they re-emerged in October 1991 with an acclaimed EP featuring the excellent 'The Girl With The Loneliest Eyes'. In 1992, the band's long-awaited new album, *Babe Rainbow*, was released to a degree of critical acclaim, but the impression of underachievement was hard to avoid. Following 1993's *Audience With The Mind* the band collapsed, Chadwick re-emerging a year later with the Madonnas. By 1997, he was signed to Setanta Records as a solo artist, releasing the 'This Strength' single in November and *Lazy, Soft & Slow* the following year.

● ALBUMS: *The House Of Love* (Creation/Relativity 1988) ★★★★, *Fontana* (Fontana/PolyGram 1990) ★★★, *Babe Rainbow* (Fontana 1992) ★★★, *Audience With The Mind* (Fontana 1993) ★★.

● COMPILATIONS: *A Spy In The House Of Love* (Fontana 1990) ★★, *Best Of* (Fontana/Mercury 1998) ★★★★, *The John Peel Sessions 1988:1989* (Strange Fruit 2000) ★★★, *1986–1988: The Creation Recordings* (PLR 2001) ★★★.

**HOUSEMARTINS**

Formed in 1984, this UK pop band originally comprised Paul Heaton (b. 9 May 1962, Birkenhead, Merseyside, England; vocals, guitar), Stan Collimore (b. 6 April 1962, Hull, Humberside, England; bass), Ted Key (guitar), and Hugh Whitaker (drums). After signing to Go! Discs, the quartet humorously promoted themselves 'the fourth best band from Hull'. Their modesty and distinctly plain image disguised a genuine songwriting talent, which quickly emerged. During late 1985, Key departed and was replaced by Norman Cook (b. 31 July 1963, Brighton, Sussex, England). By 1986, the band achieved their first UK hit with their third release, the infectious 'Happy Hour', which climbed to number 3. Their UK Top 10 debut album *London 0 Hull 4* displayed a wit, freshness and verve that rapidly established them as one of Britain's most promising bands. In December 1986, their excellent a cappella version of 'Caravan Of Love' gave them a deserved UK number 1 hit.

Early in 1987, the Housemartins received a coveted BPI award as the Best Newcomers of the year. In the summer, they underwent a line-up change, with David Hemingway (b. 20 September 1960, Hull, England) replacing drummer Hugh Whitaker. An acclaimed EP, *Five Get Over Excited* followed, after which the band displayed their left-wing political preferences by performing at the Red Wedge concerts. After securing another Top 20 hit with the catchy 'Me And The Farmer', the quartet issued their final studio album, the self-mocking *The People Who Grinned Themselves To Death*. Although still at the peak of their powers, the band split in June 1988, announcing that they had only intended the Housemartins to last for three years. The power of the original line-up was indicated by the subsequent successes of offshoot projects such as Heaton and Hemingway's Beautiful South and Cook's DJ alias Fatboy Slim. Collimore has gone on to become a successful children's book writer. In 1993 Hugh Whitaker was charged and sentenced to six years' imprisonment for wounding with intent and three arson attacks on a business acquaintance.

● ALBUMS: *London 0 Hull 4* (Go! Discs 1986) ★★★★, *The People Who Grinned Themselves To Death* (Go! Discs 1987) ★★.

● COMPILATIONS: *Now That's What I Call Quite Good!* (Go! Discs 1988) ★★★★.

● FURTHER READING: *The Housemartins, Tales From Humberside*, Nick Swift.

**HOUSTON, WHITNEY**

b. 9 August 1963, Newark, New Jersey, USA. This pop and soul singer followed the traditions of her mother Cissy Houston and cousin Dionne Warwick by beginning her vocal career in gospel. There was much diversity in her early performances, however. These included engagements as backing singer with established acts, such as Chaka Khan, as well as lead vocals on the Michael Zager Band's single 'Life's A Party'. She also appeared as a model in various magazines, and as an actress in television shows such as *Give Me A Break*. By 1983, she had entered a worldwide contract with Arista Records, and the following year had her first commercial success when 'Hold Me', a duet with Teddy Pendergrass, crept into the US Top 50. However, the rest of that year was taken up with the recording of a debut album. Clive Davis, the head of Arista, who had taken a strong personal interest in the vocalist, insisted on selecting the best songwriters and producers in search of the definitive debut album. *Whitney Houston* was finally released in March 1984, from which time it would begin its slow stalking of the album charts, topping them early the next year. Its steady climb was encouraged by the success of the singles 'You Give Good Love' and 'Saving All My Love For You', which hit numbers 3 and 1, respectively. The latter single also saw her on top of the charts in the UK and much of the rest of the world. The disco-influenced 'How Will I Know' and the more soul-flavoured 'Greatest Love Of All', both topped the US charts in rapid succession. Her domination was acknowledged by a series of prestigious awards, notably a Grammy for 'Saving All My Love For You' and an Emmy for Outstanding Individual Performance In A Variety Program On US TV.

'I Wanna Dance With Somebody (Who Loves Me)', released in 1987, topped the charts on both sides of the Atlantic, paving the way for *Whitney* to become the first album by a female artist to debut at number 1 on the US album chart, a feat it also achieved in the UK. The album included a version of 'I Know Him So Well', sang as a duet with her mother Cissy, and the ballad 'Didn't We Almost Have It All' which became her fifth successive US number 1 shortly afterwards. However, even this was surpassed when 'So Emotional' and 'Where Do Broken Hearts Go' continued the sequence, breaking a record previously shared by the Beatles and the Bee Gees. In 1988, she made a controversial appearance at Nelson Mandela's 70th Birthday Party, where other acts accused her of behaving like a prima donna. By September, 'Love Will Save The Day' had finally broken the winning sequence in the USA where it could only manage number 9. Another series of awards followed, including Pop Female Vocal and Soul/R&B Female Vocal categories in the American Music Awards, while rumours abounded of film offers alongside Robert De Niro and Eddie Murphy. Houston's recording of the title track to the 1988 Olympics tribute, *One Moment In Time*, restored her to US Top 5 prominence and topped the UK singles chart. The follow-up 'I'm Your Baby Tonight' put her back on top of the US singles chart. Despite the relatively modest success of the album of the same name (number 3 in the US charts), 'All The Man That I Need' compensated by becoming her ninth number 1. She became permanently enshrined in the hearts of the American public, however, when she took the microphone to perform 'The Star Spangled Banner' at Super Bowl XXV in Miami. The public response ensured that the version emerged as a single shortly afterwards. She also performed the song at Houston as she welcomed back US troops returning from the Gulf War. Such open displays of patriotism did not endear Houston to all. Her remarkably rich voice also caused some debate,

with some critics claiming that her masterful vocal technique is not equalled by her emotional commitment to her music.

In July 1992, Houston married singer Bobby Brown (the relationship would prove tempestuous). The same year she made a credible acting debut in the movie *The Bodyguard*. Four songs recorded by her were lifted from the phenomenally successful soundtrack album – cover versions of Dolly Parton's powerful 'I Will Always Love You', which topped the US chart for 14 weeks and the UK charts for nine, and Chaka Khan's 'I'm Every Woman', and 'I Have Nothing' and 'Run To You'. Houston spent most of the 90s concentrating on her acting career, but made a surprise return to the studio for 1998's *My Love Is Your Love*. Enlisting the songwriting help of Missy 'Misdemeanor' Elliott, Diane Warren and Wyclef Jean, the album was a confident attempt by Houston to reclaim ground lost to the new diva superstars Mariah Carey and Celine Dion. 'When You Believe', a duet with Carey taken from the animated DreamWorks movie *The Prince Of Egypt*, was a transatlantic hit. With the album selling poorly, however, Houston's fortunes were revived by the US number 2 single, 'Heartbreak Hotel', and the atypical and hard-hitting 'It's Not Right But It's Okay', a US/UK Top 5 hit single.

● ALBUMS: *Whitney Houston* (Arista 1985) ★★★★, *Whitney* (Arista 1987) ★★★★, *I'm Your Baby Tonight* (Arista 1990) ★★★, with various artists *The Bodyguard* film soundtrack (Arista 1992) ★★★, *The Preacher's Wife* film soundtrack (Arista 1996) ★★, *My Love Is Your Love* (Arista 1998) ★★★.
● COMPILATIONS: *Whitney: The Greatest Hits* (Arista 2000) ★★★★, *Love, Whitney* (Arista 2001) ★★★.
● VIDEOS: *The Greatest Hits* (Arista 2000).
● FILMS: *The Bodyguard* (1992), *The Preacher's Wife* (1996).

## HUE AND CRY

Brothers Patrick (b. 10 March 1964, Coatbridge, Strathclyde, Scotland) and Gregory Kane (b. 11 September 1966, Coatbridge, Strathclyde, Scotland) formed Hue And Cry in 1986. Patrick writes the lyrics and provides the vocals, while his brother concentrates on writing music, and plays piano and keyboards. Although they initially used session players both on stage and in the studio, some of their most powerful work has been where their sound is stripped down to voice and piano. Their first single, 'I Refuse', was released in 1986 and flopped, but the following year the soul-fired 'Labour Of Love' gave them a UK Top 10 hit. They received much attention for the memorable single 'Looking For Linda' (the true story of a woman who left home to buy a packet of cigarettes and ended up on a southbound train heading away from her old life). The brothers' jazz affinities shone through on *Remote*, which featured contributions from the Brecker Brothers, Ron Carter, Jon Faddis, and Tito Puente among others. *Stars Crash Down* featured contributions from fellow Scots Eddi Reader and Ewan Vernal, and James Prine from Deacon Blue, but following its release the duo parted company with their long-term label Circa. *Truth And Love*, produced and largely performed by Greg Kane, was released on the brothers' short-lived Fidelity label.

By this point, both brothers had established busy schedules away from the band. Always one of the more articulate of personalities within the pop world, Patrick has served as both an outspoken television presenter and music journalist. He was also elected the Rector of Glasgow University (narrowly edging out Tony Benn). A firm socialist, he turned his back on the Labour Party and gave very vocal support to the Scottish Nationalist Party. Certainly, he refuses to accept the boundaries between music and politics, as the lyrics to the single 'Peaceful Face' demonstrate: 'The future I see, The century comes and it goes, And my child will be there to bear all its woes'. He has been instrumental in forming the Artists For An Independent Scotland organization which is supported by other Scottish 'celebrities' and rock stars such as Fish. Gregory Kane, meanwhile, is an in-demand soundtrack composer.

The brothers continue to record as Hue And Cry, with their experimental edge and jazz leanings long since having taken precedence over any commercial considerations. *Piano & Voice* and *Jazz Not Jazz* were bold projects that worked because of the strength of Pat Kane's voice, even when tackling syrupy standards such as 'Send In The Clowns'. The duo's second album for Linn Records, 1999's *Next Move*, assimilated elements of urban R&B and drum 'n' bass into their smooth jazz sound.

● ALBUMS: *Seduced And Abandoned* (Circa 1987) ★★★, *Remote* (Circa 1988) ★★★, *Stars Crash Down* (Circa 1991) ★★★, *Truth And Love* (Fidelity 1992) ★★, *Showtime!* (Permanent 1994) ★★, *Piano & Voice* (Permanent 1995) ★★★, *JazzNotJazz* (Linn 1996) ★★★, *Next Move* (Linn 1999) ★★★.
● COMPILATIONS: *The Bitter Suite* remix album (Circa 1989) ★★★, *Labours Of Love: The Best Of Hue And Cry* (Circa 1993) ★★★.

## HUGHES, GLENN

b. 21 August 1952, Cannock, Staffordshire, England. Hughes left school at the age of 15 to follow his dream of becoming a musician. He began playing lead guitar with the News in 1967, where he also sang, emulating his heroes Otis Redding and Wilson Pickett. Later he switched to bass guitar, inspired by James Jamerson from the Tamla/Motown Records 'house band'. These influences, married to a love of rock 'n' roll, led him to form Trapeze in 1968 with Dave Holland (drums) and Mel Galley (guitar). Trapeze signed to the Moody Blues' record label, Threshold Records, and released three albums up to 1973, when Hughes was offered a job with a new Birmingham band, Electric Light Orchestra. However, he declined and in June joined Deep Purple instead. It was with this band that Hughes made his mark in the UK with his superb singing on *Burn*, where he joined with, and some believe outclassed, their new vocalist David Coverdale. Hughes' influence over the band became a major factor in Ritchie Blackmore's decision to quit, and his association with Deep Purple continued until

1976 when he re-formed Trapeze with the original line-up, although this venture failed to tour or record. When they finally began a US tour, Hughes walked out halfway through. The band continued without him while their leader disappeared from public view. Two years later, he resurfaced with a solo album before again dropping out of sight.

In 1982 Hughes joined with Pat Thrall (guitar, ex-Pat Travers Band) and Quiet Riot drummer Frankie Banali to form Hughes/Thrall, who released one album to a poor reception (although this set went on to achieve 'legendary' status and became one of the most sought-after rock albums of the 80s). After the project fell apart, Hughes worked for a time with Gary Moore, but little came of the collaboration. In 1985, he reunited with Mel Galley and a host of stars to record as the supergroup Phenomena. Although the ensuing concept album was considered obsolete by rock critics, it did serve to put Hughes back on the map, and Tony Iommi, looking for a replacement for Ian Gillan in Black Sabbath, contacted him. Hughes spent less than a year with the band but recorded some fine vocals for *Seventh Star*. He then returned to obscurity and suffered personal problems, but help from an unusual quarter was at hand. Bill Drummond of the KLF was keen to experiment with blending rock and dance music (he had already gained infamy in such matters with Extreme Noise Terror), and in 1991 he coaxed Hughes back into the limelight for the hit single 'America – What Time Is Love?'. This success reanimated the vocalist's efforts and he set about resurrecting his solo career with a series of fine releases on the SPV labels. He also launched his own Pink Clouds Records label.

● ALBUMS: *Play Me Out* (Safari 1977) ★★★, *Blues* (Roadrunner 1992) ★★★, *From Now On ...* (Empire/Zero Corporation 1994) ★★, *Burning Japan Live* (Zero Corporation/SPV/Shrapnel 1994) ★★★, *Feel* (Zero Corporation/SPV 1995) ★★★, *Addiction* (Zero Corporation/SPV/Shrapnel 1996) ★★★, *The Way It Is* (SPV/Shrapnel 1999) ★★★, *Return Of Crystal Karma* (SPV 2000) ★★★, *A Soulful Christmas* (Pink Cloud 2000) ★★★, *Building The Machine* (SPV/DNA 2001) ★★★.
● COMPILATIONS: *From The Archives Volume 1: Incense & Peaches* (Pink Cloud 2000) ★★★.

## HUMAN LEAGUE

The history of the Human League is essentially that of two radically different UK bands, one experimental and arcane, the other melodic and commercial. The first incarnation of the Human League formed in the summer of 1978 with a line-up comprising Ian Craig Marsh (b 11 November 1956, Sheffield, England; synthesizer), Martyn Ware (b. 19 May 1956, Sheffield, England; synthesizer), Phil Oakey (b. 2 October 1955, Sheffield, England; vocals) and Addy Newton. The latter left soon after the band was named Human League and was replaced by Adrian Wright (b. 30 June 1956, Sheffield, England), who was credited as 'visual director'.

Early in 1978, the band was signed to Robert Last's Edinburgh-based independent label Fast Product.

Their first single was the unusual 'Being Boiled', which sold 16,000 copies and resulted in them securing a tie-in deal with Virgin Records. Their debut, *Reproduction*, sold steadily, while the EP *Holiday, '80*, won them an appearance on the prestigious television show *Top Of The Pops*. By this point, Philip Oakey's pierced nipples and geometric haircut had made him the focal point of the band. This led to some friction within the Human League, which was not overcome by the chart success of their second album, *Travelogue*. Matters culminated at the end of 1980 with the shock departure of Marsh and Ware, who went on to found BEF and its offshoot Heaven 17. In return for a percentage of royalties on future releases, Marsh and Ware allowed Oakey to retain the name Human League.

Instead of recruiting experienced musicians as replacements Oakey, somewhat bizarrely, chose two teenage girls, whom he discovered at a Sheffield discotheque. Susanne Sulley (b. 22 March 1963, Sheffield, England) and Joanne Catherall (b. 16 September 1962, Sheffield, England) had absolutely no knowledge of the music business, had never sung professionally and were busy at school studying for A-levels when Oakey made his offer. The new line-up was completed by bass player Ian Burden (b. 24 December 1957, Sheffield, England) and former Rezillos guitarist Jo Callis (b. 2 May 1955, Glasgow, Scotland). The new band contrasted radically with the cold, remote image of the original Human League and pursued a pure pop Holy Grail, which delivered a series of UK hits during 1981. 'Boys And Girls', 'The Sound Of The Crowd', 'Love Action' and 'Open Your Heart' paved the way for the band's celebrated pop album, *Dare!*, which sold over five million copies. An extraordinary year ended with the excellent Christmas chart-topper, 'Don't You Want Me', the biggest-selling UK single of 1981. The song was particularly notable for its use of a double point of view, which was brilliantly captured in the accompanying video with Oakey and Catherall trading perspectives on a fragmenting relationship. The track went on to become a number 1 in the USA, spearheading a British invasion of 'new pop' artists.

The Human League then took a long sabbatical, interrupted only by a couple of further hits with 'Mirror Man' and '(Keep Feeling) Fascination' and a mini-album of dance remixes. The 1984 comeback album, *Hysteria*, met a mixed response, although the attendant singles, 'The Lebanon', 'Life On Your Own' and 'Louise', all reached the UK Top 20. Oakey ended 1984 by teaming up with disco producer Giorgio Moroder for a surprisingly successful single ('Together In Electric Dreams') and album. A further two years passed before the next Human League album, *Crash*, and, along the way, Wright and Callis departed. Several of the tracks on the new album were composed by producers Jimmy Jam and Terry Lewis, among them the sublime US number 1 hit, 'Human'.

Another four years passed before, in 1990, the Human League returned with a new album, which met a cool response. Following a lengthy break from the public eye, and just when the world had

seemingly buried them, they returned five years later with *Octopus* and a series of sparkling hit singles. Much of the freshness and simplicity of *Dare!* was present in the new collection. Singles such as the UK Top 10 hit 'Tell Me When' indicated a strong grasp of how repeated hooklines in pop songs can creep into the subconscious – and cannot be resisted. A new chapter began in 2001 with another career relaunch and a favourable critical reception for *Secrets*. Despite their erratic career, the Human League has shown a remarkable ability to triumph commercially and aesthetically, and usually at the least predictable moments.

● ALBUMS: *Reproduction* (Virgin 1979) ★★, *Travelogue* (Virgin 1980) ★★, *Dare!* (Virgin/A&M 1981) ★★★★, *Love And Dancing* (Virgin/A&M 1982) ★★★, *Hysteria* (Virgin/A&M 1984) ★★, *Crash* (Virgin/A&M 1986) ★★★, *Romantic?* (Virgin/A&M 1990) ★★, *Octopus* (East West 1995) ★★★, *Secrets* (Papillon/Ark 21 2001) ★★★★.

● COMPILATIONS: *Human League's Greatest Hits* (Virgin/A&M 1988) ★★★★, *Greatest Hits* (Virgin 1995) ★★★, *Soundtrack To A Generation* (Disky 1998) ★★★.

● VIDEOS: *Greatest Video Hits* (Warners 1995).

● FURTHER READING: *The Story Of A Band Called The Human League*, Alaska Ross and Jill Furmanovsky. *The Human League: Perfect Pop*, Peter Nash.

## HUNNINGALE, PETER

b. *c*.1962, London, England. Hunningale, aka Mr Honey Vibes, established his reputation in the lovers rock idiom. He began his musical career playing bass as part of the Vibes Corner Collective, which also featured Barrington Levine, Jimmy Simpson, Ray Simpson and Fitzroy Blake. In 1982, he released his debut as a singer, 'Slipping Away'/'Swing And Dine', which sold respectably on LGR Records. 'Got To Know You'/'Money Money' was then issued on his own Street Vibes label, which he co-founded with long-term collaborator Blake (it is now run in association with Tippa Irie and Crucial Robbie). In 1987, he topped the UK reggae chart with 'Be My Lady', regarded by many as his debut. The success of this single and his debut album led to a prolific period that included the singles 'Falling', 'It's My Turn', 'If You Want It' and 'Mr Vibes'. The popularity of combination hits from Jamaica inspired Hunningale and Tippa Irie to team up for 'Raggamuffin Girl' in 1989, which went straight to number 1 in the UK reggae charts, and was voted Best British Reggae Record by *Echoes* newspaper at the close of the year; the single led to a long and fruitful partnership with Irie. With this success behind them, the duo embarked on two album collaborations – *The New Decade* for Island Records and *Done Cook And Currie* for Rebel MC's Tribal Base label. The former collection was produced by Hunningale himself and featured two songs popular on the UK sound system circuit, 'Shocking Out' and 'Dibi Dibi'. He also produced and played all the instruments on *Done Cook And Currie*, which produced another major domestic reggae hit with 'Inner City'. His second solo album, *Mr Vibes*, followed in the same year. Hunningale's next collaboration with Irie came in 1993, this time a single, 'Shouting For The Gunners', to celebrate their mutual fondness for the London football club Arsenal. The following year's *Mr Government* was a more roots-flavoured offering, released on the Mad Professor's Ariwa Sounds label, after which Hunningale worked with Crucial Robbie once more on a version of Desmond Dekker's '007'.

Throughout Hunningale's career awards have been bestowed upon him, including Best Newcomer in 1987, Best Reggae Vocalist Of The Year in 1989 and 1991 and in the mid-90s he made a rare television appearance after winning additional accolades in the Black Music Association Awards. Hunningale also demonstrated his versatility when he performed in the reggae musical *Johnny Dollar* and secured his independence with the inauguration of the Street Vibes label. As well as recording many hits in the UK, Hunningale also worked with legendary Jamaican producer Gussie Clarke, which resulted in 'Love Like This'.

Hunningale's outstanding achievements continued in 1995 when Lloyd 'Musclehead' Francis' production of his hit 'Baby Please' knocked his Gussie P production of 'Perfect Lady' from the number 1 position in the reggae chart. The same year, Hunningale recorded a version of 'Declaration Of Rights' in a reunion with Tippa Irie, which featured on his *Nah Give Up* compilation, alongside such reggae chart hits as 'Trust Me' and 'Sorry'. Hunningale displayed his honeyed voice on songs including 'Out In The Country', 'Candy', 'Crazy Love', 'How Could I Leave' and 'Love Is Here To Stay'. A series of popular duets with Dennis Brown, Lloyd Brown and Janet Lee Davis, performing 'Cupid', 'Lonely Girl' and 'We Can Work It Out', respectively, all met with approval. His distinguished career has also seen him work with artists such as the Original Pioneers, Maxi Priest (writing the title track to his *Best Of Me* hit album), Chosen Few, Trevor Hartley, Double Trouble, Tinga Stewart and B.B. Seaton, as well as many others, either as musician, producer or writer. Late in 1996 Hunningale performed as part of the combination Passion, which also included Glamma Kid and Nerious Joseph, among others. 'Share Your Love', their version of Teddy Riley's R&B hit, 'No Diggity', spent over eight weeks at number 1 on the reggae chart.

● ALBUMS: *In This Time* (Level Vibes 1987) ★★★, with Tippa Irie *The New Decade* (Mango/Island 1991) ★★★★, *Mr Vibes* (Street Vibes 1992) ★★★, with Tippa Irie *Done Cook And Currie* (Tribal Base 1992) ★★★, *Mr Government* (Ariwa Sounds 1994) ★★★, *Back To The Old Skool* (Discotex 1998) ★★★.
● COMPILATIONS: *Nah Give Up* (Kalymazoo 1995) ★★★★, *Reggae Max* (Jet Star 1996) ★★★.

## HURLEY, STEVE

Formerly a DJ at Chicago station WBMX, Steve 'Silk' Hurley's first recordings, like many of his peers, were originally cut specifically to augment his DJ repertoire. One such track, 'Music Is The Key', got a particularly warm reception, and Hurley (b. 9 November 1962, Chicago, Illinois, USA) borrowed money from his father and placed it on his friend Rocky Jones' DJ International label. It made number 9 in the US dance charts, though no royalties were forthcoming. He was similarly dismayed when his 'I Can't Turn Around' was hijacked by Farley Jackmaster Funk, and turned into 'Love Can't Turn Around', with new vocals by Daryl Pandy in 1985. It became a hit without any of the credit being extended to Hurley. However, his reward was just around the corner. After recording the mighty 'Baby Wants To Ride' with Jamie Principle he scored the first house number 1 with 'Jack Your Body' on 24 January 1987. Later he would create Kym Sims' 'Too Blind To See It', and was invited to remix Roberta Flack's 'Uh Uh Ooh Ooh Look Out' – which he saw as a great personal achievement. Other remix projects came thick and fast, including Paula Abdul (the *Vibeology* EP), Yasmin ('Sacrifice'), Simply Red ('Something Got Me Started'), Ce Ce Peniston ('We Got A Love Thang') and Rodeo Jones ('Get Wise'). At one time in the 90s it seemed that a dozen such remixes were appearing on the market at the same time, and in truth they were all relatively similar, albeit polished and accomplished. Hurley had few complaints, raking in the money at a reported $20,000 per throw and working with heroes like Stevie Wonder. In addition, he established his own production company ID (signed to Sony in the UK and Europe, its remix roster including Chicago DJ Ralphi Rosario and Juan Atkins). A previous dance venture, JM Silk (formed with famous house vocalist Keith Nunnally) had proved ill fated.
● ALBUMS: *Work It Out* (Atlantic 1989) ★★★.

## HÜSKER DÜ

Formed in Minneapolis, Minnesota, USA, in 1979, this punk trio comprised guitarist/vocalist Bob Mould (b. 16 October 1960, Malone, New York, USA), bass player Greg Norton, and drummer Grant Hart. Their melding of pop and punk influences inspired thousands of UK, US and European bands. Indeed, it is hard to think of a single other band having such a profound impact on modern alternative music as this trio.

Taking their name, which means 'Do you remember?', from a Norwegian board game, they started out as an aggressive hardcore thrash band before challenging that genre's restrictions and expanding to other musical formats. Their primary strength, like so many other truly great bands, was in having two songwriting partners (Mould and Hart) who for the entirety of their career fully complemented each other. Their first single, 'Statues', was released on the small Reflex label in 1981. The same year, a debut album, *Land Speed Record*, arrived on New Alliance Records, followed by an EP, *In A Free Land*. *Everything Falls Apart* in 1982 saw them back on Reflex. By the advent of their second EP, *Metal Circus* (now on SST Records), Hüsker Dü had become a critics' favourite in the USA – a rapport that was soon to be exported to their UK brethren. *Zen Arcade* in 1984 brought about a stylistic turning point – a two-record set, it followed a single storyline about a young boy leaving home and finding life even more difficult on his own. A 14-minute closing song, 'Reoccurring Dreams', in which it was revealed that the boy's entire ordeal had been a dream, broke all the rules of punk. A non-album cover version of the Byrds' 'Eight Miles High' followed, and a 1985 album, *New Day Rising*, maintained the trio's reputation as a favourite of critics and college radio stations, with its irresistible quicksilver pop songs. After *Flip Your Wig* the band signed with Warner Brothers Records (there were several other interested parties), with whom they issued *Candy Apple Grey* in 1986 and *Warehouse: Songs And Stories*, another double set, the following year. In December 1987, Hart was dismissed from the group (though there are many conflicting versions of events leading up to this juncture), which summarily disbanded. Mould and Hart continued as solo artists, before Mould formed the equally rumbustious Sugar in 1991.

● ALBUMS: *Land Speed Record* (New Alliance 1981) ★★, *Everything Falls Apart* (Reflex 1982) ★★, *Metal Circus* mini-album (Reflex/SST 1983) ★★★, *Zen Arcade* (SST 1984) ★★★★, *New Day Rising* (SST 1985) ★★★, *Flip Your Wig* (SST 1985) ★★★★, *Candy Apple Grey* (Warners 1986) ★★★★, *Warehouse: Songs And Stories* (Warners 1987) ★★★★, *The Living End* 1987 recording (Warners 1994) ★★★.

● COMPILATIONS: *Everything Falls Apart And More* (Warners 1993) ★★★★.

## I, LUDICROUS

Offbeat indie band I, Ludicrous comprising Will Hung (b. David Rippingale, 4 November 1956, London, England; vocals) and John Procter (b. 9 May 1957, Epsom, England; instruments). The duo first met in 1981 while working for Finsbury Data Services in London. Their mutual passion for the Fall and Crystal Palace Football Club cemented the partnership. They had additionally been involved in various failed punk bands over the years, but only formed a group together in February 1985. After witnessing a performance by John Cooper Clarke and Nico at the Cricketers in Kensington, London, the duo decided they could do much better than the third support, a talentless comedian. Their debut gig was dreamed up as support to performance artist friend Max Couper, with Procter providing a musical soundtrack to Hung's off-the-cuff observations on the day he had endured. This intention soon metamorphosed into a songwriting partnership, which after just three gigs secured them a contract with Kaleidoscope Records. Armed only with a Casio keyboard and Littlewoods mail-order guitar, their central appeal lay in the monotone delivery of unlikely narratives about 'Lunch With The Geldofs' or 'Preposterous Tales'. The latter was their first release, on a flexi-disc that accompanied *Blah Blah Blah* fanzine in April 1987. It was received warmly by disc jockey John Peel, who offered them a Radio 1 session, while his favourite band, the Fall, invited them to support at London's Astoria venue. Their debut album, *It's Like Everything Else*, duly emerged in September 1987 to glowing and/or confused reviews. 'Quite Extraordinary' followed in 1988 as their first single, but then the band was hamstrung by a series of business problems. The collapse of Red Rhino distribution led to a contract with the tiny Rodney Rodney! label, but this failed to give the requisite push to either *A Warning To The Curious* or *Light And Bitter*, their next two albums. Forced to finance their own output, the duo offered a new album in 1992, *Idiots Savants*, while the attendant single, 'We Stand Around', was Single Of The Week in the *New Musical Express* in September 1992. None of this was enough to allow the participants to give up their many and various day jobs, however, though the release of occasional singles and live tapes, including 1994's 'Hats Off To Eldorado' and 2000's 'Approaching 40', has confirmed I, Ludricous' continued wry presence in the UK music industry's underbelly.

● ALBUMS: *It's Like Everything Else* (Kaleidoscope 1987) ★★★, *A Warning To The Curious* (Rodney Rodney! 1989) ★★★, *Light And Bitter* (Rodney Rodney! 1990) ★★★, *Idiots Savants* (I, Ludicrous 1992) ★★★.

## ICE-T

b. Tracy Marrow, 16 February 1958, Newark, New Jersey, USA. One of the most outspoken rappers to emerge from the 80s west coast hip-hop scene, and one of the founding fathers of gangsta rap, Ice-T boasts (sometimes literally) a violent past in which he was shot twice – once while involved in an armed robbery. His name, fittingly, is taken from black exploitation author Iceberg Slim, and his backing on record provided by Afrika Islam and DJ Aladdin's hardcore hip-hop. His first record was actually 'The Coldest Rapper' in 1983, which was improvised over a Jimmy Jam And Terry Lewis rhythm, and made him the first Los Angeles hip-hop artist. Unfortunately he was subsequently held under contract by mogul Willie Strong for several years. Disillusioned, he made his money from petty and not so petty crime, and appeared in the breakdance movie Breakin', which included his 'Reckless' cut on the soundtrack. He followed it with the faddish 'Killers' single. The breakthrough, however, came with 'Ya Don't Know', which was widely credited with being the first west coast hip-hop artefact (although the honour was undoubtedly Ice-T's, the real beneficiary should have been the obscure 'The Coldest Rapper' cut).

Four LPs in just three years created something of a stir in the USA, based as they were largely on Ice-T's experiences as a gang member in Los Angeles. In 1989, he reached the lower end of the UK charts with 'High Rollers', but did better the following year teaming up with Curtis Mayfield on a remake of 'Superfly'. He married Darlene, the model who normally appeared semi-clad on his record sleeves, and admitted to owning a pit-bull terrier affectionately titled Felony. For a time, too, he delighted in inviting journalists to his luxury Beverly Hills home to show them his personal armoury of semi-automatic weapons. Success also enabled him to start his own record company, Rhyme Syndicate. Ice-T's vision of the black man as sophisticated and articulate (being hard as nails is, of course, de rigueur) ranks him among the most potent forces in contemporary black culture. His refusal to engage in a white liberal agenda (he was the first rap artist to have warning stickers placed on his album sleeves) irritated many, but helped to establish him as an authentic spokesperson for dispossessed black youth. His 1987 debut, Rhyme Pays, featured an Uzi emblazoned on the cover, an image that served as a particularly effective mission statement: hardcore raps on street violence and survival being the order of the day. By the time of its follow-up, there was demonstrably greater imagination displayed in terms of backing music. Like many of his west coast brethren, Ice-T had rediscovered funk. Notable tracks included 'Girls L.G.B.N.A.F.', which the PMRC later discovered stood for 'Let's Get Butt Naked And Fuck'. Their reaction to this (arguably among the least offensive statements on Ice-T's records) was so overheated that the debate heavily informed his follow-up set. However, his crowning glory came with 1991's OG (an acronym for Original Gangster that has since passed into rap's lexicon), which ranks alongside the best work of Ice Cube, Public Enemy

or N.W.A. in terms of sustained intensity, yet managed to maintain a little more finesse than his previous work.

In 1991, with appealing irony, Ice-T starred as a cop in the movie New Jack City. He had earlier contributed the title track to the LA gangster movie Colors. He also appeared with former N.W.A. and solo artist Ice Cube in the Walter Hill movie Looters (renamed Trespassers due to its release at the same time as the LA riots), as well as Surviving The Game and cult comic hero movie Tank Girl. His other soundtrack credits include Dick Tracy.

Ice-T's hobbies during the early 90s included his own thrash metal outfit, Body Count, who released an album in 1992 and stirred up immeasurable controversy via one of its cuts, 'Cop Killer'. The furore led to the termination of his major-label recording contract, and it was little wonder that Ice-T was targeted on right-wing assassination lists discovered by the police in 1993. His album from that year, Home Invasion, saw him take on the mantle of agent provocateur in the young white male's home, a theme reinforced in its cover and title – Ice-T was a threat in your neighbourhood, with another manifesto of spiteful intent ('I'm takin' your kids' brains, You ain't getting them back, I'm gonna fill 'em with hard drugs, big guns, bitches, hoes and death'). Then he went and spoiled all the good work by writing a book, the Ice-T Opinion, which was so full of dumb ideas that it largely discredited such achievements. On 22 March 1994, he introduced UK television station Channel 4's Without Walls, a documentary on the rise of the blaxploitation movies. Ice-T's own recording career in the late 90s was sidetracked by his movie commitments, although he managed to find the time to record 1999's poorly received 7th Deadly Sin. The following year he began appearing as Detective Odafin 'Fin' Tutuola in Law & Order: Special Victims Unit, a role for which he is now more widely known than his pioneering musical exploits over the previous 15 years. His own life would make an excellent documentary subject, although, as he notes in Home Invasion's 'Ice Muthafuckin' T', 'Every fucking thing I write, Is going to be analysed by somebody white'.

● ALBUMS: Rhyme Pays (Sire 1987) ★★★, Power (Sire 1988) ★★, The Iceberg/Freedom Of Speech ... Just Watch What You Say (Sire/Warners 1989) ★★★, OG (Original Gangster) (Sire/Warners 1991) ★★★★, Home Invasion (Rhyme Syndicate/Priority 1993) ★★★, VI: Return Of The Real (Rhyme Syndicate/Priority 1996) ★★, 7th Deadly Sin (Roadrunner 1999) ★★.

● COMPILATIONS: The Classic Collection (Excello/Rhino 1993) ★★★, Greatest Hits: The Evidence (Atomic Pop 2000) ★★★★.

● VIDEOS: OG: The Original Gangster Video (Sire 1991).

● FURTHER READING: The Ice Opinion, Ice-T and Heidi Seigmund.

● FILMS: Breakin' (1984), Rappin' (1985), Listen Up: The Lives Of Quincy Jones (1990), New Jack City (1991), Ricochet (1991), Trespass (1992), Who's The Man (1993), CB4 (1993), Surviving The Game (1994),

The Legend Of Dolemite (1994), Mr Payback: An Interactive Movie (1995), Tank Girl (1995), Johnny Mnemonic (1995), Mean Guns (1997), Below Utopia (1997), Rhyme & Reason (1997), The Deli (1997), Crazy Six (1998), Stealth Fighter (1999), Sonic Impact (1999), Point Doom (1999), Pimps Up, Ho's Down (1999), The Heist (1999), The Alternate (1999), Luck Of The Draw (2000), Lost Angeles (2000), Guardian (2000), Gangland (2000), 3000 Miles To Graceland (2001), Deadly Rhapsody (2001), 'R Xmas (2001), Ticker (2001), Out Kold (2001), Ablaze (2001), Stranded (2001), Kept (2001), Crime Partners 2000 (2001), Tracks (2002).

## ICEHOUSE

This Australian rock band was formed as Flowers in the late 70s by classically trained songwriter and multi-instrumentalist Iva Davies (b. Ivor Davies, 22 May 1955). Influenced by Roxy Music and David Bowie, Flowers' other members included Keith Welsh (bass), John Lloyd (drums), and Michael Hoste (keyboards). The first single, 'Can't Help Myself' was a Top 10 hit in 1980. The following year the band signed to Chrysalis Records, touring the UK and North America. Its name was changed to Icehouse (the title of the debut album) to avoid confusion with a US outfit called Flowers. Despite further Australian success with 'Love In Motion' and 'Great Southern Land', Davies disbanded the group in 1982 to concentrate on the solo Primitive Man. However, he was persuaded to re-form Icehouse the next year with British musicians Andy Qunta (keyboards) and ex-Killing Joke member Guy Pratt (guitar). The new line-up also included Lloyd, Hoste and leading Australian guitarist Robert Kretschmer. Almost immediately, Icehouse had a UK hit with 'Hey Little Girl', which was accompanied by a striking video directed by Russell Mulcahy. After touring Europe in support of David Bowie, Davies took the band off the road for a further two years. During this time, he composed scores for Mulcahy's feature movie Razorback and (with Kretschmer and Graeme Murphy) for a ballet for the Sydney Dance Company. The band returned in 1986 with the tougher 'No Promises' and the glam-rock flavoured 'Baby You're So Strange' from Measure For Measure. In 1987, there were more Australian hits with 'Crazy' and 'Electric Blue' (co-written by John Oates of Hall And Oates), both of which reached the US Top 20 the following year. Although failing to reach this commercial peak again, Davies continued to record with Icehouse before lapsing into relative silence in the mid-90s. He returned in 1999, reworking 'Great Southern Land' into a new classical composition entitled 'The Ghost Of Time'. The piece was performed at the Sydney Opera House to celebrate the new millennium.

● ALBUMS: as Flowers Icehouse (Regular/Chrysalis 1980) ★★★, Primitive Man (Regular/Chrysalis 1982) ★★, Sidewalk (Regular/Chrysalis 1984) ★★, Measure For Measure (Regular/Chrysalis 1986) ★★★, Man Of Colours (Regular/Chrysalis 1987) ★★★, Code Blue (Regular 1990) ★★★★, Big Wheel (Diva 1993) ★★, The Berlin Tapes (Diva 1995) ★★★, The Ghost Of Time (Diva 1999) ★★★.

● COMPILATIONS: Love In Motion (Chrysalis 1983) ★★★, Great Southern Land (Regular/Chrysalis 1989) ★★★, Masterfile (Massive 1992) ★★★, Full Circle remixes (Massive 1994) ★★★, The Singles: A Sides And Selected B Sides 3-CD box set (Diva 1996) ★★★, No Promises (Diva 1997) ★★★.

● VIDEOS: Live At The Ritz (Chrysalis 1987), Live In Concert (Music Club 1989), Masterfile (Massive 1993).

## ICICLE WORKS

Emerging from the profligate network of Liverpudlian bands that existed during the punk rock and new wave era, the Icicle Works were formed by Ian McNabb (b. 3 November 1960, Liverpool, Merseyside, England; vocals, guitar), Chris Layhe (bass), and Chris Sharrock (drums). McNabb was formerly in City Limits with the near-legendary Edie Shit (b. Howie Mimms), and Sharrock played with the Cherry Boys (who also included Mimms at one point). Taking their name from a science fiction novel – The Day The Icicle Works Closed Down – they made their recording debut with a six-track cassette, Ascending, released on the local Probe Plus emporium in 1981. The band then founded their own Troll Kitchen label on which they prepared 'Nirvana', their premier single. Gaining support from BBC disc jockey John Peel, they came to the attention of Beggars Banquet Records, initially through their Situation 2 offshoot. Their second single, 'Birds Fly (Whisper To A Scream)', was an 'indie' hit, but they had to wait for the next effort, 'Love Is A Wonderful Colour', to breach the UK Top 20. The subject matter was typically subverted by McNabb's irony and cynicism ('When love calls me, I shall be running swiftly, To find out, just what all the fuss is all about').

Teaming up with producer Ian Broudie (ex-Big In Japan) helped the Icicle Works to a string of singles successes over the ensuing years, including 'Hollow Horse' and 'Understanding Jane', with their sound gradually shifting from subtle pop to harder rock territory. In 1986, they recruited Dave Green on keyboards, but the following year the band was turned upside down when both Sharrock and Layhe left within a short space of time. Sharrock joined the La's and later drummed for World Party. Layhe's role was taken by former Black bass player Roy Corkhill, while the drummer's stool was claimed by Zak Starkey, whose father Ringo Starr formerly drummed for another Liverpool band. This line-up prospered for a short time but in 1989 McNabb assembled a new band. Retaining only Corkhill, he added Mark Revell on guitar, Dave Baldwin on keyboards, and Paul Burgess on drums. The band signed a new contract with Epic Records and released one album before McNabb left to go solo. One of England's most underrated and natural lyricists, McNabb's cult status has continued into the new millennium, while his time with the Icicle Works has left a rich legacy of songwriting.

● ALBUMS: The Icicle Works (Beggars Banquet 1984) ★★★, The Small Price Of A Bicycle (Beggars Banquet 1985) ★★★, If You Want To Defeat Your Enemy Sing His Song (Beggars Banquet 1987) ★★★, Blind (Beggars Banquet 1988) ★★★, Permanent Damage

(Epic 1990) ★★★, *BBC Radio One Live In Concert* 1987 recording (Windsong 1994) ★★.
● COMPILATIONS: *Seven Singles Deep* (Beggars Banquet 1986) ★★, *The Best Of The Icicle Works* (Beggars Banquet 1992) ★★★★.

## IDOL, BILLY

b. William Michael Albert Broad, 30 November 1955, Stanmore, Middlesex, England. While studying English Literature at Sussex University, Broad became involved with the 'Bromley contingent' followers of the Sex Pistols. Inspired by the energy of punk, he formed his own group, Chelsea, in 1976. The original outfit was short-lived and Billy Idol, as he was now known, next founded Generation X. This band lasted from 1976 to 81, after which Idol launched his solo career in New York and recorded *Don't Stop*, which featured a revival of Tommy James And The Shondells' UK number 1 'Mony Mony'. Through 1982–84, Idol's career blossomed and his acerbic vocal style and lively stage act brought a string of hits including 'Hot In The City' (US number 23), 'Eyes Without A Face' (US number 4/UK number 18), 'White Wedding' (UK number 6), 'Rebel Yell' (UK number 6 when reissued) and 'To Be A Lover' (US number 6). With his album sales increasing each year, Idol actually became an idol and turned an old hit to advantage by taking a live version of 'Mony Mony' to number 1 in the USA in 1987.
Despite his legendary excessive lifestyle, Idol appeared in several charity shows. In 1988, he took part in Neil Young's Bridge School Benefit concert and the following year guested in the charity performance of the Who's *Tommy* in London. After being auditioned for a part in Oliver Stone's *The Doors*, Idol almost emulated its central character by suffering an early death. A motorcycle crash in February 1990 seriously damaged his leg, but he recovered remarkably quickly and the same May hit the number 2 slot in America with 'Cradle Of Love' (taken from the Andrew Dice Clay movie *The Adventures Of Ford Fairlaine*). However, he soon found himself back in trouble, this time with the Los Angeles courts when, in 1992, he was put on probation for two years and fined $2,700 for an assault on a 'fan'. This all added fuel to the rebel image but by now Idol had become far more successful than most of the punk founders with whom he rubbed shoulders back in 1977. His attempt to rebrand his image on 1993's *Cyberpunk* was a notable commercial and critical failure, and the following year Idol narrowly escaped death for a second time when he overdosed. He laid low until the end of the decade when he made a cameo appearance in the Adam Sandler comedy *The Wedding Singer*. Idol's comeback was confirmed in the new millennium thanks to a highly entertaining *Behind The Music* documentary for the VH1 channel, and an accompanying live CD recorded with guitarist Steve Stevens.
● ALBUMS: *Billy Idol* (Chrysalis 1981) ★★★, *Don't Stop* (Chrysalis 1981) ★★★, *Rebel Yell* (Chrysalis 1984) ★★★★, *Whiplash Smile* (Chrysalis 1986) ★★★, *Charmed Life* (Chrysalis 1990) ★★, *Cyberpunk*

(Chrysalis 1993) ★★, *VH-1 Storytellers* (Capitol 2002) ★★★.
● COMPILATIONS: *Vital Idol* (Chrysalis 1986) ★★★, *Idol Songs: 11 Of The Best* (Chrysalis 1988) ★★★★, *Greatest Hits* (Capitol 2001) ★★★★.
● VIDEOS: *VH-1 Storytellers* (Warner Music Vision 2002).
● FURTHER READING: *Billy Idol: Visual Documentary*, Mike Wrenn.
● FILMS: *The Doors* (1991), *The Wedding Singer* (1998).

## IGLESIAS, JULIO

b. Julio José Iglesias de la Cueva, 23 September 1943, Madrid, Spain. Iglesias studied law at Madrid University and played football (goalkeeper) for Real Madrid before suffering severe injuries in a 1963 car accident. While recuperating, he learned guitar and began to write songs. After continuing his studies in Cambridge, England, he entered the 1968 Festivalde la Canción in Benidorm. Performing his own composition 'La Vida Sigue Igual' ('Life Continues All The Same'), he won first prize and soon afterwards signed a recording contract with the independent Discos Columbia where Ramon Arcusa became his producer. Iglesias represented Spain in the Eurovision Song Contest, subsequently recording the song 'Gwendolyne' in French, Italian, and English. During the next few years, he toured widely in Europe and Latin America, scoring international hits with 'Manuela' (1974) and 'Hey' (1979). His global reach was increased in 1978 when he signed to CBS Records International and soon had hits in French and Italian. The first big English-language success came in 1982 when his version of 'Begin The Beguine' topped the UK charts. This was followed by the multi-language compilation album *Julio*, which sold a million copies in America. Co-produced by Arcusa and Richard Perry, *1100 Bel Air Place* was aimed directly at American audiences and included duets with Willie Nelson ('To All The Girls I've Loved Before') and Diana Ross ('All Of You'). A later duet (and international hit) was 'My Love' with Stevie Wonder in 1988. Iglesias won the *Billboard* Latin album of the year award in 1996 for *La Carreterra*. By the end of the 90s, Iglesias had sold in excess of 220 million albums in seven languages, making him one of the most successful artists ever in the history of popular music. His sons Enrique and Julio Jnr. have also enjoyed success as recording artists.
● ALBUMS: *Yo Canto* (Columbia 1969) ★★★, *Todos Los Dias Un Dia* (Columbia 1969) ★★★, *Soy* (Columbia 1970) ★★, *Gwendolyne* (Columbia 1970) ★★, *Como El Alamo Al Camino* (Columbia 1971) ★★, *Rio Rebelde* (Columbia 1972) ★★, *Asi Nacemos* (Columbia 1973) ★★, *A Flor De Piel* (Columbia 1974) ★★, *El Amor* (Columbia 1975) ★★, *A Mexico* (Columbia 1975) ★★, *America* (Columbia 1976) ★★, *En El Olympia* (Columbia 1976) ★★, *A Mis 33 Años* (Columbia 1977) ★★, *Mi Vida En Canciones* (Columbia 1978) ★★, *Emociones* (Columbia 1979) ★★, *Hey!* (Columbia 1980) ★★, *De Niña A Mujer* (Columbia 1981) ★★, *Begin The Beguine* (Columbia 1981) ★★★, *Momentos* (Columbia 1981) ★★, *En*

*Concierto* (Columbia 1982) ★★, *Amor* (Columbia 1982) ★★, *Julio* (Columbia 1983) ★★★, *1100 Bel Air Place* (Columbia 1984) ★★★, *Libra* (Columbia 1985) ★★, *Un Hombre Solo* (Columbia 1987) ★★, *Non Stop* (Columbia 1988) ★★, *Sentimental* (Columbia 1988) ★★, *Raices* (Columbia 1989) ★★, *Starry Night* (Columbia 1990) ★★★, *Calor* (Columbia 1992) ★★, *La Carreterra* (Columbia 1995) ★★★, *Tango* (Columbia 1996) ★★, *Noche De Cuatro Lunas* (Columbia 2000) ★★★.
● COMPILATIONS: *My Life: The Greatest Hits* (Columbia 1998) ★★★.
● FURTHER READING: *Julio!*, Jeff Rovin.
● FILMS: *La Vida Sigue Igual* (1969), *Me Olvidé De Vivir* (1980).

## IMAGINATION

One of the most successful British funk bands of the early 80s, Imagination was formed by the idiosyncratically named Leee John (b. John Lesley McGregor, 23 June 1957, Hackney, London, England; vocals), Ashley Ingram (b. 27 November 1960, Northampton, England; guitar) and Errol Kennedy (b. Montego Bay, West Indies). John (of St. Lucian descent) was educated in New York, where he also became a backing vocalist for the Delfonics and Chairmen Of The Board. He met Ingram, who played bass for both bands, and they formed a duo called Fizzz. Back in England, John, who had already appeared on *Junior Showtime* as a child, enrolled at the Anna Scher Theatre School where he studied drama. Kennedy was an experienced singer with Jamaican bands and learned the drums through the Boys Brigade and later the Air Training Corps band. He had also spent some time in the soul group Midnight Express. Kennedy met John and Ingram in early 1981, after which they formed Imagination as a pop/soul three-piece. They made an immediate impact with their debut 'Body Talk', and further Tony Swain-produced hits followed, including UK Top 5 entries with 'Just An Illusion' and 'Music And Lights'. However, the run of hits dried up by 1984, when John returned to acting. He had already appeared in the UK science fiction serial, *Dr. Who*, in 1983. Having switched to RCA Records in 1986, Imagination made a minor comeback in 1988 with 'Instinctual'. By this point Kennedy had been replaced by Peter Royer, and the departure of Ingram in 1990 left the charismatic Leee John as the sole remaining original member. Although periodically returning to Imagination, John has subsequently concentrated on solo releases and songwriting projects. He enjoyed two big club hits in the late 90s with 'The Mighty Power Of Love' and 'Call On Me'.
● ALBUMS: *Body Talk* (R&B/MCA 1981) ★★★, *In The Heat Of The Night* (R&B/MCA 1982) ★★★, *Night Dubbing* (R&B 1983) ★★, *Scandalous* (R&B 1983) ★★, *Trilogy* (R&B 1986) ★★, *Closer* (RCA 1987) ★★★, *Like It Is: Revised And Remixed Classics* (Sony 1989) ★★★ *Fascination Of The Physical* (New Music 1992) ★★.
● COMPILATIONS: *The Very Best Of Imagination* (Music Club 2000) ★★★.

## IMMACULATE FOOLS

UK pop band originally comprising two sets of brothers from Kent, Kevin Weatherill (vocals, guitar) and Paul Weatherill (bass, vocals), Andy Ross (guitar) and Peter Ross (drums). They made their debut with 'Nothing Means Nothing' in September 1984, before hitting the UK Top 60 with 'Immaculate Fools' in January 1985. Afterwards they spent much time touring the continent where they enjoyed more popularity, especially in Spain. Further singles included 'Hearts Of Fortune' and 'Save It' in 1985. Their second album, *Dumb Poet*, was well received by critics (including a five-star review in *Sounds* magazine), though it did not recapture their earlier chart success. It spawned the singles 'Tragic Comedy' and 'Never Give Less Than Anything'. Following the departure of the Ross brothers, Barry Wickens, Paul Skidmore and Ian Devlin joined in time for *Another Man's World*, but by then impetus had been lost, and the UK media proved less sympathetic to the band's summery, fey pop songs. The band moved to Spain where they continued to be fêted as superstars up until their eventual demise in 1997. The Weatherill brothers were joined by Wickens, Brian Betts (guitar), and Nick Thomas (drums) on their two final albums, *Woodhouse* and *Kiss And Punch*.
● ALBUMS: *Hearts Of Fortune* (A&M 1985) ★★★★, *Dumb Poet* (A&M 1987) ★★★, *Another Man's World* (Discos CBS 1990) ★★★, *The Toy Shop* (Sony 1992) ★★★★, *Woodhouse* (Magic Sponge/Cooking Vinyl 1994) ★★★, *Kiss And Punch* (Cooking Vinyl 1996) ★★★.
● COMPILATIONS: *The Best* (A&M 1987) ★★★★, *No Gods ... No Masters* (Snapper 1998) ★★★.
● VIDEOS: *Searching For Sparks* (Channel 5 1987).

## IN TUA NUA

This septet from Dublin, Eire, combined traditional Irish instrumentation (pipes and whistles) with commercial instruments. Unlike the Pogues or the Saw Doctors, however, they used this musical platform to play in the style of a rock act. Led by vocalist Leslie Dowdall, other members included Brian O'Brien (pipes), Martin Colncy, Vinnie Kilduf and Steve Wickham (fiddle). Discovered by Bono of U2 they were originally signed to Island Records but later moved to Virgin Records. Their singles included 'Comin' Thru', 'Take My Hand' (their Island debut in 1984), a cover version of Jefferson Airplane's 'Somebody To Love' (1985), 'Seven Into The Sea' (1986), 'Heaven Can Wait' (1987) and 'The Long Acre' (1988). Only 'All I Wanted' (1989) gave them a hit, and a minor breakthrough at that. They gigged with Bob Dylan at the Irish Self Aid show, before Wickham left in 1986 to join the Waterboys. He was replaced on violin by Angela De Burca. *The Long Acre* was produced by Don Dixon of R.E.M. fame, but by 1990 In Tua Nua had elected to call it a day. O'Brien later worked as a soloist on the hit dance show, *Riverdance*.
● ALBUMS: *Vaudeville* (Virgin 1987) ★★★, *The Long Acre* (Virgin 1988) ★★★.

## INCANTATION

This UK instrumental band found success playing South American panpipe music and ethnic instruments such as whistles, armadillo shells, llama toenails, condor bones and nose flutes. Formed in 1982 and signed initially to Beggars Banquet Records subsidiary Coda Records, they were led by Mike Taylor (quena, zamponas, bombo, chajchas, vocals) and Tony Hinnigan (quena, zamponas, bombo, caja, guitar, tiple). The other members of the band included Forbes Henderson, Simon Rogers, Chris Swithinbank, Sergio Avila and Mauricio Venegas. Their distinctive sound earned them a surprise UK Top 20 hit in 1982 with 'Cacharpaya (Andes Pumpsa Daesi)', which was used in the popular BBC Television natural history programme *Flight Of The Condor*. Afterwards, Incantation's commercial fortunes dwindled, though their albums continued to sell modestly to the folk/world community. Their innovative music was also heard on the soundtracks of the movies *The Mission*, *Patriot Games*, *Clear And Present Danger*, and *Legends Of The Fall*.

After a four-year break, Taylor and Hinnigan reformed Incantation in 1993. They recorded for the Cooking Vinyl Records label, including a reworking of 'Cacharpaya'. Taylor parted company with Hinnigan in 1996, ending an association that had spanned nearly 25 years. The latter continued to lead a new line-up of Incantation for touring purposes, in addition to working with composers James Horner and Michael Nyman on soundtrack scores.

● ALBUMS: *On The Wing Of A Condor* (Coda 1982) ★★★★, *Dance Of The Flames* (Coda 1983) ★★★, *Virgins Of The Sun* (Coda 1984) ★★★, *Panpipes Of The Andes* (Coda 1986) ★★★, *The Meeting* (Hiam 1987) ★★★, *On Gentle Rocks* (PDI 1992) ★★★, *Sergeant Early's Dream & Ghost Dances (Music From The Ballet Rambert)* (Cooking Vinyl 1994) ★★★, *Incantation* (Cooking Vinyl 1995) ★★★.
● COMPILATIONS: *The Best Of Incantation: Music From The Andes* (Coda 1985) ★★★★, *Geoglyph: The Very Best Of Incantation* (Cooking Vinyl 1998) ★★★★.

## INDIGO GIRLS

This US duo comprises Amy Ray (b. 12 April 1964, Decatur, Georgia, USA; vocals, guitar) and Emily Saliers (b. 22 July 1963, New Haven, Connecticut, USA; vocals, guitar), who had met aged 10 and 11 while at school in Decatur, Georgia, USA. Soon they started to perform together, initially as the B Band, then Saliers And Ray. Their first cassette, *Tuesday's Children*, mainly consisted of cover versions. They changed their name to Indigo Girls while at Emory University in Atlanta. Their early releases were on their own label, J. Ellis Records, named after an English teacher on whom they shared a crush. These commenced with a single, 'Crazy Game', in 1985, followed by an EP the following year, produced by Frank French of Drivin' N' Cryin'. An album, *Strange Fire*, produced by John Keane, featured re-recorded versions of their strongest early songs, 'Crazy Game' and 'Land Of Canaan'.

Ray And Saliers signed to Epic Records in 1988, and their first release for the label featured, among others, Michael Stipe of R.E.M. and the Irish group Hothouse Flowers. *Indigo Girls* was produced by Scott Litt, and included Saliers' composition 'Closer To Fine', later recorded by the UK's Wonder Stuff. The duo toured heavily throughout the USA to promote the album, in addition to playing support dates to Neil Young and R.E.M. *Indigo Girls* achieved gold status in September 1989, and the duo won a Grammy Award as the Best Contemporary Folk Group of 1989. *Strange Fire* was reissued towards the end of that year, but with an additional track, 'Get Together', made famous by the Youngbloods. In addition to playing an AIDS research benefit in Atlanta, Georgia, in 1989, the duo were also asked by Paul Simon to perform at a fund-raising event in 1990 for the Children's Health Fund, a New York-based project founded by the singer. *Nomads*Indians*Saints* included the excellent Emily Saliers song 'Hammer And A Nail', which also featured Mary-Chapin Carpenter on backing vocals. Litt was once again recalled as producer, with R.E.M.'s Peter Buck also guesting, but the album lacked something of its predecessors' impact. *Rites Of Passage* repaired much of the damage, with a full musical cast including guest vocals by Jackson Browne, the Roches and David Crosby, drums from Budgie (Siouxsie And The Banshees) and production by Queensrÿche veteran Peter Collins. Traditional songs such as 'The Water Is Wide' as well as a cover version of Dire Straits' 'Romeo And Juliet' made it the Indigo Girls' broadest and finest set to date.

Touring and vacations preceded work on *Swamp Ophelia* at the end of 1993. The sessions saw the duo swap acoustic for electric guitars for the first time on 'Touch Me Fall', and while touring they took a break to appear in a new recording of Andrew Lloyd Webber's musical, *Jesus Christ Superstar*, with Saliers as Mary Magdalene and Ray as Jesus Christ. Their late 90s albums *Shaming Of The Sun* and *Come On Now Social* broke no new ground, although the duo's songwriting remained as dependable as ever.

● ALBUMS: as the B Band *Tuesday's Children* cassette only (Unicorn 1981) ★★, *Blue Food* cassette only (J Ellis 1985) ★★★, *Strange Fire* (Indigo 1987) ★★, *Indigo Girls* (Epic 1989) ★★★, *Nomads*Indians*Saints* (Epic 1990) ★★★, *Indigo Girls Live: Back On The Bus, Y'All* mini-album (Epic 1991) ★★, *Rites Of Passage* (Epic 1992) ★★★★, *Swamp Ophelia* (Epic 1994) ★★★, *Shaming Of The Sun* (Epic 1997) ★★★, *Come On Now Social* (Epic 1999) ★★★, *Become You* (Daemon/Epic 2002) ★★★.
Solo: Amy Ray *Color Me Grey* cassette only (No Label 1985) ★★, *Stag* (Daemon 2001) ★★★.
● COMPILATIONS: *1200 Curfews* (Epic 1995) ★★★, *Retrospective* (Epic 2000) ★★★★.
● VIDEOS: *Watershed* (Columbia Music Video 1995).

## INGRAM, JAMES

b. 16 February 1956, Akron, Ohio, USA. A singer, composer and multi-instrumentalist, Ingram moved to Los Angeles in the early 70s where he played keyboards for Leon Haywood, and formed his own group, Revelation Funk. He also served as demo singer for various publishing companies, an occupation that led to his meeting and working with Quincy Jones. Ingram's vocals were featured on the US Top 20 singles, 'Just Once' and 'One Hundred Ways', taken from *The Dude* (1981), Jones' last album for A&M Records. Signed to Jones' own Qwest Records label, Ingram had a US number 1 in April 1982, duetting with Patti Austin on 'Baby, Come To Me', which became the theme for the popular television soap *General Hospital*. In the same year, he released *It's Your Night*, an album that eventually spawned the US hit single 'Yah Mo B There' (number 19, December 1983), on which he was joined by singer-songwriter Michael McDonald. Ingram made the US Top 20 again the following September when he teamed up with Kenny Rogers and Kim Carnes for 'What About Me?'.

Ingram's subsequent albums, *Never Felt So Good*, produced by Keith Diamond, and *It's Real*, on which he worked with Michael Powell and Gene Griffin, failed to live up to the promise of his earlier work, although he continued to feature on the singles chart. 'Somewhere Out There', a duet with Linda Ronstadt recorded for Steven Spielberg's animated movie *An American Tail*, reached US number 2 in December 1986, and provided Ingram with his first UK Top 10 single the following July. 'I Don't Have The Heart', meanwhile, topped the US chart in August 1990. The same year Ingram was featured, along with Al B. Sure!, El DeBarge and Barry White, on 'The Secret Garden (Sweet Seduction Suite)', from Quincy Jones' *Back On The Block*. In 1994, Ingram recorded 'The Day I Fall In Love' with Dolly Parton. Ingram has also served as a backing singer for several other big-name artists, such as Luther Vandross and the Brothers Johnson. His compositions include 'P.Y.T. (Pretty Young Thing)', which he wrote in collaboration with Quincy Jones for Michael Jackson's 1982 smash hit album *Thriller*.

● ALBUMS: *It's Your Night* (Qwest 1983) ★★★, *Never Felt So Good* (Qwest 1986) ★★★, *It's Real* (Warners 1989) ★★, *Always You* (Warners 1993) ★★.
● COMPILATIONS: *Greatest Hits: The Power Of Great Music* (Qwest 1991) ★★★★, *Forever More (Love Songs, Hits & Duets)* (Private Music 1999) ★★★.

## INSPIRAL CARPETS

During the late-80s UK music scene, the city of Manchester and its surrounds spawned a host of exciting new bands and the Inspiral Carpets were at the head of the pack alongside Happy Mondays, James, the Stone Roses and 808 State. The band was formed in Oldham by school friends Graham Lambert (guitar) and Stephen Holt (vocals). They were joined by drummer Craig Gill and performed in their hometown Oldham with various other members until they were joined by organist Clint Boon and bass player David Swift. Boon, whose Doors-influenced playing later became the band's trademark, met the other members when they began rehearsing at his studio in Ashton-under-Lyne. Their debut EP, *Planecrash*, was released by the independent label Playtime, and they were consequently asked to record a John Peel session for BBC Radio 1.

In 1988, there was an acrimonious split between the

band and label and between the various members. Holt and Swift were replaced by Tom Hingley and Martin Walsh, formerly with local bands Too Much Texas and the Next Step, respectively. The band formed their own label, Cow Records, and after a string of well-received singles signed a worldwide contract with Mute Records. 'This Is How It Feels' was a hit and *Life* was critically acclaimed for its mixture of sparkling pop and occasional experimental flashes. Further singles had less impact and *The Beast Inside* received a mixed response, some critics claiming the band were becoming better known for their merchandise, like T-shirts and promotional milk bottles. The T-shirts bearing the immortal words 'Cool as Fuck!' inevitably aroused considerable controversy, particularly when a fan was arrested for causing offence by wearing such a garment. Afterwards the band journeyed onwards without ever arousing the same level of interest, though both *Revenge Of The Goldfish* and *Devil Hopping* had their moments. 'Bitch's Brew', from the former, stronger album, was a classy stab at Rolling Stones-styled sweeping pop revival, though elsewhere too many songs continued to be dominated by Boon's organ, which, once a powerful novelty, now tended to limit the band's songwriting range. The band was released from Mute Records in 1995 with their former company issuing an epitaph in the shape of *The Singles*. Boon set up the highly enjoyable the Clint Boon Experience, while Hingley recorded a solo album and started his own record label Newmemorabilia.
● ALBUMS: *Life* (Mute 1990) ★★★, *The Beast Inside* (Mute 1991) ★★★, *Revenge Of The Goldfish* (Mute 1992) ★★★, *Devil Hopping* (Mute 1994) ★★★.
● COMPILATIONS: *The Singles* (Mute 1995) ★★★, *Radio 1 Sessions* (Strange Fruit 1999) ★★★.

## INXS

Formed in 1977 as the Farriss Brothers in Sydney, Australia, INXS originally comprised the three Farriss brothers Tim (b. 16 August 1957; guitar), Jon (b. 18 August 1961; drums) and Andrew (b. 27 March 1959; keyboards), Michael Hutchence (b. 22 January 1960, Lain Cove, Sydney, Australia, d. 22 November 1997, Sydney, Australia; lead vocals), Kirk Pengilly (b. 4 July 1958; guitar, saxophone, vocals) and Garry Beers (b. 22 June 1957; bass, vocals). The band moved to Perth, Western Australia to develop their own distinctive rock sound, which incorporated both black dance music and white soul influences. INXS began its recording career in 1980 with a single, 'Simple Simon'/'We Are The Vegetables' on the independent Deluxe label. Over the next three years, half a dozen singles reached the lower Top 40 in Australia, but the second album, *Underneath The Colours* sold well, and the next *Shabooh Shoobah* reached the Top 5. It was with the 'Original Sin' single of early 1985 and its accompanying album, *The Swing*, that the band finally hit the top of the charts in Australia. The album and single generated interest in the band from the USA, Europe and South America, and the follow-up album, *Listen Like Thieves*, consolidated their worldwide success, except in the UK where critics savaged the band, but it would not be long before sales finally took off there as well.

In 1986, Hutchence made his acting debut in the movie *Dogs In Space*. One song from the film, 'Rooms For The Memory', earned him a solo Australian Top 10 single. The band toured the USA and Europe constantly, and MTV aired their videos; as a result, *Kick* achieved over one million sales on advance orders in the USA alone and the band finally gained a number 1 US hit with 'Need You Tonight' in January 1988. The band's success could be attributed to many factors, including an unchanged line-up from the beginning, the sultry good looks of vocalist Hutchence, unstinting touring schedules, diverse songwriters in the band and consistently fresh production with a new producer for each album. After *Kick* and before the release of *X*, all the members had a 12-month break and became involved with other projects – Hutchence with Max Q; Andrew Farriss in production work with Jenny Morris; and Garry Beers joined a loose collection of friends for a tour and recording as Absent Friends.

Hutchence's much publicized, fleeting romance with Kylie Minogue brought the band's name to the attention of a whole new generation of potential fans. INXS' 1993 set, *Full Moon, Dirty Hearts*, included a Hutchence/Chrissie Hynde (the Pretenders) duet on 'Kill The Pain', and the single 'The Gift'. The video of the latter was banned by MTV, formerly INXS' greatest ally, due to its use of Holocaust and Gulf War footage. Hutchence embarked on a highly publicized relationship with Paula Yates, being cited in her divorce from Bob Geldof. Over the next few years, until his untimely death in 1997, Hutchence and Geldof were at loggerheads over the custody of the latter's children with Yates. Hutchence was found hanged in his hotel room in Sydney, Australia, on 22 November 1997. Yates died almost three years later, completing the tragic cycle. The remaining members of INXS resumed live work in 2001.

● ALBUMS: *INXS* (Deluxe 1980) ★★, *Underneath The Colours* (RCA 1981) ★★, *Shabooh Shoobah* (Mercury 1982) ★★★, *The Swing* (Mercury 1984) ★★★, *Listen Like Thieves* (Mercury 1985) ★★★, *Kick* (Mercury 1987) ★★★, *X* (Mercury 1990) ★★, *Live Baby Live* (Mercury 1991) ★★, *Welcome To Wherever You Are* (Mercury 1992) ★★★, *Full Moon, Dirty Hearts* (Mercury 1993) ★★★, *Elegantly Wasted* (Mercury 1997) ★★.
Solo: Max Q *Max Q* (Mercury 1989) ★★★. Absent Friends *Here's Looking Up Your Address* (Roo Art 1990) ★★.
● COMPILATIONS: *The Greatest Hits* (Mercury 1994) ★★★★, *Shine Like It Does: The Anthology (1979–1997)* (Rhino 2001) ★★★★.
● VIDEOS: *Truism* (PMI/EMI 1991), *The Best Of INXS* (PMI/EMI 1994).
● FURTHER READING: *INXS: The Official Story Of A Band On The Road*, St John Yann Gamblin (ed.). *The Final Days Of Michael Hutchence*, Mike Gee.

## IOVINE, JIMMY

b. 11 March 1953, Brooklyn, New York, USA. One of the leading record producers of the 80s, Iovine found his first studio job through songwriter Ellie Greenwich, and by 1973 he was an engineer at the Record Plant in New York City. There he worked on tracks by John Lennon, Southside Johnny And The Asbury Jukes and Bruce Springsteen. His first assignment as producer was for New Jersey band Flame in 1977, but his first hit album was *Easter* by Patti Smith, which included 1978's UK Top 5/US Top 20 single 'Because The Night'. Iovine was now established as a top-grade producer and during the 80s he worked with numerous major rock acts. In 1979, he began his association with Tom Petty for whom he produced three albums. There was later work with Dire Straits (*Making Movies*) and with Stevie Nicks on her first two solo albums. In 1983, he was called in for the U2 live recording *Under A Blood Red Sky*, followed by movie tie-in *Rattle And Hum*. Often co-producing with the artist, Iovine's other credits include work with Simple Minds (*Once Upon A Time*), Alison Moyet (*Raindancing*), Shakespears Sister, the Eurythmics (*We Too Are One*) and Gene Loves Jezebel. He renewed his partnership with Patti Smith in 1988, co-producing *Dream Of Life* with her husband Fred 'Sonic' Smith. In 1990, Iovine began a new career in A&R, setting up the Interscope label with Ted Fields. During its first year of operation, the company had hits from Marky Mark And The Funky Bunch, Primus, and Gerardo. New signings including Bush, No Doubt, and the Wallflowers helped propel Interscope into the mainstream in the latter part of the decade. The label also enjoys a strong association with rap and Latin music.

## IRON MAIDEN

Formed in London, England, in 1976, Iron Maiden was from the start the brainchild of Steve Harris (b. 12 March 1957, Leytonstone, London, England; bass), formerly a member of pub rockers Smiler. Named after a medieval torture device, the music was suitably heavy and hard on the senses. The heavy metal scene of the late 70s was widely regarded as stagnant, with only a handful of bands proving their ability to survive and produce music of quality. It was at this time that a new breed of young British bands began to emerge. This movement, which began to break cover in 1979 and 1980, was known as the New Wave Of British Heavy Metal, or NWOBHM. Iron Maiden was one of the foremost bands in the genre, and many would say its definitive example. Younger and meaner, the NWOBHM bands dealt in faster, more energetic heavy metal than any of their forefathers (punk being an obvious influence).

There were several line-up changes in the Iron Maiden ranks in the very early days, and come the release of their debut EP, the band featured Harris, Dave Murray (b. 23 December 1958, London, England; guitar), Paul Di'Anno (b. 17 May 1959, Chingford, London, England; vocals) and Doug Sampson (drums). The band made its live debut at the Cart & Horses Pub in Stratford, east London, in 1977, before honing its sound on the local pub circuit over the ensuing two years. Unable to solicit a response from record companies, the band sent a three-track tape, featuring 'Iron Maiden', 'Prowler' and 'Strange World', to Neal Kay, DJ at north London's hard rock disco, the Kingsbury Bandwagon Soundhouse. Kay's patronage of Iron Maiden won them an instant welcome, which prompted the release of *The Soundhouse Tapes* on the band's own label.

In November 1979, the band added second guitarist Tony Parsons to the line-up for two tracks on the *Metal For Muthas* compilation, but by the time the band embarked on sessions for their debut album, he had been replaced by Dennis Stratton (b. 9 November 1954, London, England), and Sampson by Clive Burr (b. 8 March 1957; drums, ex-Samson). A promotional single, 'Running Free', reached number 34 on the UK charts and brought an appearance on BBC Television's *Top Of The Pops*. Refusing to mime, they became the first band since the Who in 1973 to play live on the show. *Iron Maiden* was a roughly produced album, but reached number 4 in the UK album listings on the back of touring stints with Judas Priest and enduringly popular material such as 'Phantom Of The Opera'. *Killers* boasted production superior to that of the first album, and saw Dennis Stratton replaced by guitarist Adrian Smith (b. 27 February 1957). In its wake, Iron Maiden became immensely popular among heavy metal fans, inspiring fanatical devotion, aided by blustering manager Rod Smallwood and apocalyptic mascot Eddie (the latter had been depicted on the cover of 'Sanctuary' standing over Prime Minister Margaret Thatcher's decapitated body).

The release of *Number Of The Beast* was crucial to the development of the band. Without it, Iron Maiden might never have gone on to be such a force in the heavy metal arena. The album was a spectacular success, the sound of a band on the crest of a wave. It was also the debut of former infantryman and new vocalist Bruce Dickinson (b. Paul Bruce Dickinson, 7 August 1958, Worksop, Nottinghamshire, England), replacing Paul Di'Anno (who went on to front Dianno, Paul Di'Anno's Battlezone and Killers). Formerly of Samson, history graduate Dickinson made his live debut with Iron Maiden on 15 November 1981. Singles such as 'Run To The Hills' and 'The Number Of The Beast' were big UK chart hits, Iron Maiden leaving behind their NWOBHM counterparts in terms of success, just as the movement itself was beginning to peter out. *Piece Of Mind* continued their success and was a major hit in the UK (number 3) and USA (number 14). Clive Burr was replaced by Nicko McBrain on the sessions, formerly drummer with French metal band Trust, who had supported Iron Maiden on their 1981 UK tour (he had also played in Streetwalkers). *Piece Of Mind* was not dissimilar to the previous album, showcasing the strong twin-guitar bite of Murray and Smith, coupled with memorable vocal lines and a sound that perfectly suited their air-punching dynamic. Single offerings, 'Flight Of Icarus' and 'The Trooper', were instant hits, as the band undertook two massive tours, the four-month *World Piece* jaunt in 1983, and a *World Slavery* retinue, which included four sell-out dates at London's Hammersmith Odeon a year later. With the arrival of *Powerslave* in November, some critics accused Iron Maiden of conforming to a self-imposed writing formula, and playing safe with tried and tested ideas. Certainly, there was no significant departure from the two previous albums, but it was nonetheless happily consumed by the band's core supporters, who also purchased in sufficient quantities to ensure UK chart hits for 'Aces High' and 'Two Minutes To Midnight'. *Live After Death* was a double-album package of all their best-loved material, recorded live on their gargantuan 11-month world tour. By this time, Iron Maiden had secured themselves an unassailable position within the metal hierarchy, their vast popularity spanning all continents.

*Somewhere In Time* was a slight departure: it featured more melody than previously, and heralded the use of guitar synthesizers. Their songwriting still shone through and the now obligatory hit singles were easily attained in the shape of 'Wasted Years' and 'Stranger In A Strange Land'. Reaching number 11 in the USA, this was another million-plus seller. Since the mid-80s Iron Maiden had been staging increasingly spectacular live shows, with elaborate lighting effects and stage sets. The *Somewhere In Time* tour (seven months) was no exception, ensuring their continued fame as a live band, which had been the basis for much of their success. A period of comparative inactivity preceded the release of *Seventh Son Of A Seventh Son*, which was very much in the same vein as its predecessor. A concept album, it retained its commercial edge (giving the band their second UK number 1 album) and yielded hit singles in 'Can I Play With Madness', the surprisingly sensitive 'The Evil That Men Do' and 'The Clairvoyant'. After another exhausting mammoth world trek, the band announced their intention to take a well-earned break of at least a year. Speculation abounded that this signalled the dissolution of the band, exacerbated by Dickinson's solo project, *Tattooed Millionaire*, his book, *The Adventures Of Lord Iffy Boatrace*, and EMI Records' policy of re-releasing Iron Maiden's single catalogue in its entirety (on 12-inch).

After a considerable hiatus, news of the band surfaced again. Steve Harris felt that the direction pursued on the last two albums had been taken as far as possible, and a return to the style of old was planned. Unhappy with this game plan, Adrian Smith left to be replaced by Janick Gers (b. Hartlepool, Teeside, England), previously guitarist with White Spirit and Ian Gillan (he had also contributed to Dickinson's solo release). The live show was also scaled down in a return to smaller venues. *No Prayer For The Dying* was indeed much more like mid-period Iron Maiden, and was predictably well-received, bringing enormous UK hit singles with 'Holy Smoke' and 'Bring Your Daughter To The Slaughter'. The latter, previously released in 1989 on the soundtrack to *A Nightmare On Elm Street 5*, had already been awarded the Golden Raspberry Award for Worst Song that year. Nevertheless, it gave Iron Maiden their first ever UK number 1. The obligatory world tour followed.

Despite being denounced as 'Satanists' in Chile, 1992 also saw the band debut at number 1 in the UK charts with *Fear Of The Dark*, which housed another major single success in 'Be Quick Or Be Dead' (number 2). However, it was Dickinson's swansong with the band, who invited demo tapes from new vocalists following the lead singer's announcement that he would depart following current touring engagements. His eventual replacement was Blaze Bayley (b. 1963, Birmingham, West Midlands, England) from Wolfsbane. His debut album was *The X-Factor*, and on this and at live gigs (which they only resumed in November 1995), he easily proved his worth. This was a daunting task, having had to learn Iron Maiden's whole catalogue and win over patriotic Dickinson followers. In February 1999 it was announced that Dickinson and Smith (who had formed Psycho Motel in the interim) had rejoined the band, restoring the classic 80s line-up. To the great delight of their loyal fans, an excellent new studio album, *Brave New World*, was not long in following.

● ALBUMS: *Iron Maiden* (EMI 1980) ★★★, *Killers* (EMI 1981) ★★, *Number Of The Beast* (EMI 1982) ★★★★, *Piece Of Mind* (EMI 1983) ★★★, *Powerslave* (EMI 1984) ★★, *Live After Death* (EMI 1985) ★★★, *Somewhere In Time* (EMI 1986) ★★★, *Seventh Son Of A Seventh Son* (EMI 1988) ★★★★, *No Prayer For The Dying* (EMI 1990) ★★★, *Fear Of The Dark* (EMI 1992) ★★★, *A Real Live One (Volume One)* (EMI 1993) ★★★, *A Real Dead One* (EMI 1993) ★★, *Live At Donington '92* (EMI 1993) ★★, *The X Factor* (EMI 1995) ★★★, *Virtual XI* (EMI 1998) ★★★, *Brave New World* (EMI 2000) ★★★★, *Rock In Rio* (EMI 2002) ★★★.

● COMPILATIONS: *The Best Of The Beast* (EMI 1996) ★★★, *Ed Hunter* (EMI 1999) ★★★★.

● VIDEOS: *Live At The Rainbow* (PMI/EMI 1984), *Behind The Iron Curtain Video EP* (PMI/EMI 1986), *Live After Death* (PMI/EMI 1986), *Run To The Hills* (Video Collection 1987), *Twelve Wasted Years* (PMI/EMI 1987), *Maiden England* (PMI/EMI 1989), *The First Ten Years (The Videos)* (PMI/EMI 1990), *Raising Hell* (PMI/EMI 1993), *Donington Live 1992* (PMI/EMI 1994), *Rock In Rio* (Sanctuary 2002).

● FURTHER READING: *Running Free: The Official Story Of Iron Maiden*, Garry Bushell and Ross Halfin. *Iron Maiden: A Photographic History*, Ross Halfin. *What Are We Doing This For?*, Ross Halfin. *Run To The Hills, Iron Maiden: The Official Biography*, Mick Wall, *The Iron Maiden Companion*, Marco Gamba and Nicola Visintini.

## ISHAM, MARK

b. 7 September 1951, New York City, New York, USA. Born into a musical family that encouraged him to learn the piano, violin, and trumpet at an early age, Mark Isham began studying the jazz trumpet while at high school and then explored electronic music while in his early 20s. For a time he pursued parallel careers as a classical, jazz and rock musician, performing, for instance, with the San Francisco Opera, the Beach Boys and Pharoah Sanders, but by the early 70s, he concentrated his efforts on jazz. As co-leader of pianist Art Lande's Rubisa Patrol, he recorded two albums on ECM Records in the late 70s, continuing his partnership with Lande through to the late 80s. Together with guitarist Peter Mannu, synthesizer player Patrick O'Hearn and drummer Terry Bozzio, he set up the Group 87 ensemble in 1979, releasing a self-titled debut album in 1980 and *A Career In Dada Processing* four years later. At the same time, Isham continued his links with rock music, recording and touring as part of Van Morrison's band, where his trumpet and flügelhorn set off the saxophone of Pee Wee Ellis to good effect. During the 80s, Isham developed his compositional skills, using a synthesis of brass, electronics, and his own plaintive trumpet to produce a very visual, narrative form of music. He recalls that 'my mother once told me that, as a kid, even before I really played music, I tried to tell stories with music. So, whether it's in the vocabulary of heavy metal or Stravinsky, the thread has to do with images.' Isham has taken that thread into film music, scoring the Academy Award-winning documentary *The Times Of Harvey Milk*, the movie *Mrs. Soffel* (both recorded on *Film Music*), and writing music to accompany children's fairytales. His other feature credits include *Trouble In Mind*, *The Moderns*, *Everybody Wins*, *Reversal Of Fortune*, *Little Man Tate*, *Billy Bathgate*, *A Midnight Clear*, *Sketch Artist*, *Cool World*, *A River Runs Through It*, *The Public Eye*, *Of Mice And Men*, *Nowhere To Run*, *Fire In The Sky*, *Made In America*, *Romeo Is Bleeding*, *Short Cuts*, *The Getaway*, *The Browning Version*, *Mrs. Parker And The Vicious Circle*, *Quiz Show*, *Timecop*, *Nell*, *The Net*, *Kiss The Girls*, *Blade*, *Galapagos: The Enchanted Voyage*, *Rules Of Engagement*, *Men Of Honor*, *Gotti* and *The Majestic*. His television scores include *Chicago Hope* and *EZ Streets*, the latter receiving an Emmy.

Throughout his career, Isham has remained a prolific session man, whose work encompasses recordings with artists as varied as saxophonist Dave Liebman, guitarist David Torn, singer-songwriters Bruce Springsteen, Joni Mitchell, Suzanne Vega, Tanita Tikaram and Marianne Faithfull, and the Rolling Stones. His own recordings have encompassed acoustic and electric jazz, electronica, orchestral scores, children's music, and new age. In the latter category, Isham received a 1990 Grammy for Best New Age Performer for that year's self-titled album. Isham is blessed with an instantly memorable trumpet sound, one that is burnished, resonant, in places lush but which can, at times, be bleakly powerful, relying on minimalist fragments to achieve its subdued effect.

● ALBUMS: *Vapor Drawings* (Windham Hill 1983) ★★★★, with Lande *We Begin* (ECM 1987) ★★★, *Castalia* (Virgin 1988) ★★★★, *Tibet* (Windham Hill 1989) ★★★, *Mark Isham* (Virgin 1990) ★★★★, *Songs My Children Taught Me* (Windham Hill 1991) ★★★, *Blue Sun* (Columbia 1995) ★★★, *Miles Remembered: The Silent Way Project* (Columbia 1999) ★★★★.

● COMPILATIONS: *Film Music* (Windham Hill 1987) ★★★★, *A Windham Hill Retrospective* (Windham Hill 1998) ★★★★.

● FILMS: *Made In Heaven* (1987).

## IT BITES

Formed in Egremont, Cumbria, England in 1982, this rock/pop band had all played together in various guises previously, usually in cover bands. Singer Francis Dunnery spent time with a punk outfit called Waving At Trains, having previously worked as an engineer. The rest of the band's *curriculum vitae* ranged from bricklayer to factory worker. The band's stable line-up comprised Dunnery (vocals, guitar), John Beck (keyboards), Dick Nolan (bass), and Bob Dalton (drums). Their first release was the strictly amateur 'All In Red', but under the wing of Virgin Records they hit in July 1986 with 'Calling All The Heroes', which reached UK number 6. Unjustly assumed to be strictly for teenagers, they were continually marketed as such by their record company. They demonstrated considerable talent with 'Whole New World', which surprisingly stalled outside the UK Top 50. It Bites, however, wanted to be a rock band. This fact was born out by some of their stated influences (10cc to Led Zeppelin to Can) and a tour with Robert Plant. Later albums were more blues-based, and included 'green' material such as 'Murder Of The Planet Earth'. Dunnery went on to a solo career following the band's demise.

● ALBUMS: *The Big Lad In The Windmill* (Virgin/Geffen 1986) ★★★, *Once Around The World* (Virgin/Geffen 1988) ★★, *Eat Me In St Louis* (Virgin/Geffen 1989) ★★, *Thank You And Goodnight* (Virgin 1991) ★★.

● COMPILATIONS: *Calling All The Heroes: The Best Of It Bites* (EMI 1998) ★★★.

## IT'S IMMATERIAL

This pop duo, based in Liverpool, England, first emerged in 1980 with the low-key single 'Young Man (Seeks An Interesting Job)'. Further independent singles followed, before they enjoyed an unlikely UK chart hit in 1986 with 'Driving Away From Home (Jim's Tune)', and an album with the enduring catchphrase title of *Life's Hard And Then You Die*. Following 'Eds Funky Diner' and the impeccably strange 'Space (He Called From The Kitchen)', they disappeared from view for some time, before principal duo John Campbell (ex-Yachts) and Jarvis Whitehead re-emerged with a second album for Siren Records in 1990. As before, the music was of a subdued, understated nature, with wry wit in the manner of an indie Pet Shop Boys. Other members of the band included, at various times, Henry Priestman of the Christians, Paul Barlow (drums), Julian Scott (bass), Mick Dempsey (percussion), Brenda Airturo (percussion), Brenda Kenny (percussion) and Gillian Miller (backing vocals).

● ALBUMS: *Life's Hard And Then You Die* (Siren/Virgin 1985) ★★★, *Song* (Siren/Virgin 1990) ★★.

## JACKSON, FREDDIE

b. 2 October 1956, Harlem, New York City, New York, USA. A singer-songwriter, who was especially successful in the late 80s, Jackson was brought up in Harlem, and sang at the White Rock Baptist church while he was still a young child. Later, he worked in a bank before joining the group LJE, along with the singer, songwriter and producer Paul Laurence. In the early 80s, Jackson moved to California and became lead singer with the R&B vocal/instrumental group Mystic Merlin. He sang on their *Full Moon*, which featured the popular soul/dance track 'Mr Magician'. In 1984, Jackson returned to the east coast where he was spotted singing in a New York club by Melba Moore. After serving as a backing vocalist for Moore, Evelyn 'Champagne' King, and others, Jackson signed a solo contract with Capitol Records, and issued *Rock Me Tonight* in 1985. Both the album, and its title track, 'Rock Me Tonight (For Old Times Sake)', which Jackson had written with Paul Laurence, made the US Top 20, and also did well in the UK. Subsequent singles from *Rock Me Tonight*, such as 'You Are My Lady' and 'He'll Never Love You (Like I Do)', proved to be ideally suited for the burgeoning soul club scene on both sides of the Atlantic. In 1986, Jackson duetted with Melba Moore on 'A Little Bit More' from her album *A Lot Of Love*, and issued his own *Just Like The First Time*, which included three more successful dance sides, 'Have You Ever Loved Somebody', 'Tasty Love', and 'Jam Tonight'. Jackson's subsequent albums did not fare so well, and were sometimes criticized for their 'sameness'. Nevertheless, *Don't Let Love Slip Away* contained two UK hits, 'Nice 'N' Slow' and 'Crazy (For Me)', and *Time For Love* was given extra interest by the inclusion of guest artists such as Audrey Wheeler, Will Downing and Najee. *Here It Is* was the sole product of an abortive stay on RCA Records. Jackson's songwriting activities, mostly in collaboration with Paul Laurence, resulted in numbers such as 'Trust Me' for Lilo Thomas, 'Keepin' My Lover Satisfied' for Melba Moore, and 'Jam Song' for Howard Johnson. After an extended lay-off, Jackson returned to the studio to record 1999's *Life After 30*.

● ALBUMS: *Rock Me Tonight* (Capitol 1985) ★★★, *Just Like The First Time* (Capitol 1986) ★★★, *Don't Let Love Slip Away* (Capitol 1988) ★★, *Do Me Again* (Capitol 1990) ★★★, *Time For Love* (Capitol 1992) ★★, *Here It Is* (RCA 1994) ★★★, *At Christmas* (Orpheus 1994) ★★, *Private Party* (Scotti Bros 1995) ★★, *Life After 30* (Orpheus 1999) ★★★, *Live In Concert* (Town Sound 2000) ★★.

● COMPILATIONS: *The Greatest Hits Of Freddie Jackson* (Capitol 1993) ★★★, *For Old Times Sake: The Freddie Jackson Story* (EMI 1996) ★★★★, *Anthology*

(The Right Stuff 1998) ★★★, *The Very Best Of Freddie Jackson* (EMI 2001) ★★★, *The Very Best Of Classic Freddie* (Disky 2002) ★★★.

## JACKSON, JERMAINE

b. Jermaine LaJuane Jackson, 11 December 1954, Gary, Indiana, USA. Jermaine was one of five brothers who formed the Jackson Five in 1962. Besides playing bass, he acted as vocal counterpoint to his younger brother Michael Jackson, a musical relationship that continued after the group was signed to Motown Records in 1968. Jermaine contributed occasional lead vocals to their albums in the early 70s, and his performance of 'I Found That Girl' on *Third Album* was one of their most affecting ballads. Like his brothers Michael and Jackie Jackson, Jermaine was singled out by Motown for a solo career, and he had an immediate US Top 10 hit with a revival of Shep And The Limeliters' doo-wop classic 'Daddy's Home', in 1972. Later releases were less favourably received, but he consolidated his position within the company in 1973 with his marriage to Hazel, the daughter of Motown boss Berry Gordy (the marriage survived until 1987). His new family connections entailed a stark conflict of interest when the other members of the Jackson Five decided to leave the label in 1975. Given the choice of deserting either his brothers or his father-in-law, he elected to remain with Motown, where his solo releases were subsequently given a higher priority than before. Despite heavy promotion, Jermaine's late 70s recordings failed to establish him as a distinctive soul voice, and he faced constant critical comparisons with the Jacksons' work on Epic. His career was revitalized by the intervention of Stevie Wonder, who wrote and produced the 1979 US/UK Top 10 hit 'Let's Get Serious', which successfully echoed the joyous funk of Wonder's own recordings. The gentle soul of 'You Like Me Don't You' brought him another hit in 1981, while the US Top 20 single 'Let Me Tickle Your Fancy' the following year featured an unlikely collaboration with new wave band Devo.

Jackson's increased public profile won him a more generous contract with Motown in the early 80s. He formed his own production company, launching Michael Lovesmith as a recording artist and overseeing the career development of Syreeta. This increased freedom was not enough to keep him at Motown, and in 1983 he signed with Arista Records. The following year, he was reconciled with his brothers: he joined the Jacksons on the *Victory* album and tour, and his own *Jermaine Jackson* featured a sparkling duet with Michael Jackson on 'Tell Me We're Not Dreaming'. Two US Top 20 hits, 'Dynamite' and 'Do What You Do', helped maintain his commercial profile, with the latter also reaching the UK Top 10. He subsequently collaborated with Pia Zadora on the theme from the movie *Voyage Of The Rock Aliens*, and with Whitney Houston on his 1986 project *Precious Memories*. In that same year, Jermaine formed his own label, WORK Records, and accepted an offer to portray the late Marvin Gaye in a biopic that was never completed. He continued to work with the Jacksons and as a soloist, although his later projects were overshadowed by the media circus surrounding his brother Michael at the peak of his fame in the late 80s and early 90s, a subject touched upon in Jermaine's 'Word To The Badd!!'.

● ALBUMS: *Jermaine* (Motown 1972) ★★, *Come Into My Life* (Motown 1973) ★★, *My Name Is Jermaine* (Motown 1976) ★★, *Feel The Fire* (Motown 1977) ★★, *Frontiers* (Motown 1978) ★★, *Let's Get Serious* (Motown 1980) ★★★, *Jermaine* (Motown 1980) ★★, *I Like Your Style* (Motown 1981) ★★, *Let Me Tickle Your Fancy* (Motown 1982) ★★, *Jermaine Jackson* (US) *Dynamite* (UK) (Arista 1984) ★★★, *Precious Moments* (Arista 1986) ★★, *Don't Take It Personal* (Arista 1989) ★★, *You Said* (La Face 1991) ★★.
● COMPILATIONS: *Greatest Hits & Rare Classics* (Motown 1991) ★★★, *Dynamite: The Encore Collection* (BMG 1999) ★★★, *Arista Heritage* (Arista 2000) ★★★, *Ultimate Collection* (Hip-O 2001) ★★★★.
● FILMS: *Voyage Of The Rock Aliens* (1988).

## JACKSON, JOE

b. 11 August 1954, Burton-upon-Trent, Staffordshire, England. Having learned violin and piano as a teenager in Portsmouth, Jackson gained a place to study piano, percussion, composition and orchestration at London's Royal College of Music. After leaving college in 1974 he joined the covers band Edward Bear. The line-up of Jackson, Mark Andrews (vocals) and Graham Maby (bass) changed their name to Arms & Legs and released three unsuccessful singles on the MAM Records label. Jackson returned to Portsmouth in 1977, where he worked as musical director to local cabaret act Koffee 'N' Kreme and began working on his own demo material. Joined by Maby, Gary Sanford (guitar) and Dave Houghton (drums), he was signed up by A&M Records in the summer of 1978. His accomplished debut, 'Is She Really Going Out With Him?', was not an immediate hit; however, by the time *Look Sharp!* was released, the song had become one of the stand-out numbers of his live shows, and reached the UK charts, albeit some months after first nudging the US Top 20. Jackson's first two albums revealed a confident writer of thoughtful lyrics, coupled with exciting new wave energy. 'Is She Really Going Out With Him?' has a classic opening line, containing humour, irony and jealousy: 'Pretty women out walking with gorillas down my street'. While *Look Sharp!* and *I'm The Man* (featuring the UK Top 5 hit 'It's Different For Girls') were power-pop, the subsequent *Beat Crazy* (the last album to be recorded by the original line-up of the Joe Jackson Band) began a trend of changing musical direction, which Jackson relished. *Jumpin' Jive*, although superb, was a throwback to the music of the 40s; on this album he covered classic songs by Cab Calloway and Louis Jordan.

One of Jackson's most satisfying works came in 1982 with *Night And Day*. The album was recorded in New York, where Jackson settled following his marriage break-up. The songs are introspective but positive; the hauntingly hummable UK/US Top 10 hit 'Steppin' Out', with its mantric bass line and crisp piano, is a superbly crafted pop song that won him many new admirers. *Body And Soul* came close to repeating the success, with 'You Can't Get What You Want (Till You Know What You Want)' entering the US Top 20. *Big World*, minus the long-standing services of Graham Maby, was a three-sided direct to two-track disc recorded live at the Roundabout Theatre, New York City. However, the songs had less commercial appeal and Jackson's fortunes began to decline. The instrumental *Will Power*, although faultlessly recorded with a high standard of musicianship, put Jackson in a musical netherworld. He had come so far musically, in such a short time, his followers found it hard to keep up with him. A live album and the film soundtrack to *Tucker* both arrived in 1988 and despite the critical plaudits, following the commercial failure of *Blaze Of Glory*, his contract with A&M was not renewed.

It was inconceivable that a talent as great as Jackson's would be without a contract for long, and by early 1991 he was signed to Virgin Records. *Laughter & Lust* was released to little commercial success, with Jackson finding himself in the difficult position of still being viewed as part of the new wave pop movement, yet having developed way beyond those realms. A serious musician who needs to be allowed to work without the constraints of commercial considerations, Jackson's subsequent recordings left behind all remnants of power-punk. Having demonstrated that film scores and orchestral works are well within his boundaries, he was signed to Sony Classical in 1997. The same year's *Heaven & Hell* served as a prelude to his first symphony, released in 1999. The recording won the 2001 Grammy Award for Best Pop Instrumental Album.

● ALBUMS: *Look Sharp!* (A&M 1979) ★★★★, *I'm The Man* (A&M 1979) ★★★★, *Beat Crazy* (A&M 1980) ★★, *Joe Jackson's Jumpin' Jive* (A&M 1981) ★★★★, *Night And Day* (A&M 1982) ★★★★, *Mike's Murder* film soundtrack (A&M 1983) ★★, *Body And Soul* (A&M 1984) ★★★★, *Big World* (A&M 1986) ★★, *Will Power* (A&M 1987) ★★★, *Tucker* film soundtrack (A&M 1988) ★★, *Blaze Of Glory* (A&M 1989) ★★, *Laughter & Lust* (Virgin 1991) ★★, *Night Music* (Virgin 1994) ★★★, *Heaven & Hell* (Sony Classical 1997) ★★★★, *Symphony No. 1* (Sony Classical 1999) ★★★★, with Graham Maby, Gary Burke *Summer In The City* (Manticore/Sony Classical 2000) ★★★, *Night And Day II* (Manticore/Sony Classical 2000) ★★★, *Two Rainy Nights* (Great Big Island 2002) ★★★.

● COMPILATIONS: *Stepping Out: The Very Best Of Joe Jackson* (A&M 1990) ★★★, *Greatest Hits* (A&M 1996) ★★★, *This Is It: The A&M Years* (A&M 1997) ★★★★, *Master Series* (PolyGram 1997) ★★★, *The Collection* (Spectrum 2001) ★★★, *Steppin' Out: The Very Best Of Joe Jackson* (A&M 2001) ★★★★, *The Best Of Joe Jackson: The Millennium Collection* (A&M 2001) ★★★★.

● VIDEOS: *The Big World Sessions* (A&M Video 1986), *Live In Tokyo* (A&M Video 1988), *Stepping Out The Videos: The Very Best Of Joe Jackson* (A&M Video 1990), *Laughter & Lust Live* (Warner Music Video 1992), *Two Rainy Nights* (Great Big Island 2002).

● FURTHER READING: *A Cure For Gravity: A Musical Journey*, Joe Jackson.

## JACKSON, LATOYA

b. 29 May 1956, Gary, Indiana, USA. As a member of the singing Jackson family, LaToya served her apprenticeship as a backing vocalist to the Jacksons group along with her sisters, Rebbie and Janet Jackson. LaToya embarked on a solo career in 1980, signing to the Polydor Records label. Despite the family connection, LaToya's solo career found difficulty in emulating the success of her younger sister Janet; her highest single chart position was with the US number 56, 'Heart Don't Lie' (1984) on her new label, Private I/Epic. A later label change to RCA Records did not alter her fortunes. She later exacerbated poor family relations with a nude spread in *Playboy* magazine, a somewhat scurrilous autobiography in 1991 and by refusing to sanction the 1992 ABC mini-series *The Jacksons: An American Dream*. Driven on by her manager/husband Jack Gordon, her sporadic recording career nevertheless failed to cash in on the attention. A multi-million-dollar contract to appear at the Moulin Rouge in Paris ended acrimoniously after only four months in summer 1992. Much more successful was the release of her *Playboy* video two years later. Further misguided career choices included a Nashville-recorded country album and a selection of Motown covers recorded in Scandinavia. Jackson divorced Jack Gordon in 1997 and began patching up relations with her estranged family. She settled down in Las Vegas to begin a new career.

● ALBUMS: *LaToya Jackson* (Polydor 1980) ★★★, *My Special Love* (Polydor 1981) ★★, *Heart Don't Lie* (Private I 1984) ★★★, *Imagination* (Private I 1986) ★★, *LaToya Jackson* aka *You're Gonna Get Rocked* (RCA 1988) ★★★, *No Relations* (Pump 1991) ★★, *Bad Girl* (Teldec 1993) ★★, *From Nashville To You* aka *My Country Collection* (Mar-Gor 1993) ★, *Stop! In The Name Of Love* (CMC 1995) ★★, *Bal Du Moulin Rouge Paris* (BCI 2001) ★★.

● FURTHER READING: *LaToya Jackson: Growing Up In The Jackson Family*, LaToya Jackson with Patricia Romanowski.

## JACKSON, MICHAEL

b. Michael Joseph Jackson, 29 August 1958, Gary, Indiana, USA. Jackson has spent almost his entire life as a public performer. He was a founder member of the Jackson Five at the age of four, soon becoming their lead vocalist and frontman. Onstage, he modelled his dance moves and vocal styling on James Brown, and portrayed an absolute self-confidence on stage that belied his shy, private personality. The Jackson Five were signed to Motown Records at the end of 1968; their early releases, including US chart-toppers 'I Want You Back', 'ABC', 'The Love You Save' and 'I'll Be There', illustrated his remarkable maturity. Although Michael was too young to have experienced the romantic situations that were the subject of his songs, he performed with total sincerity, showing all the hallmarks of a great soul artist. Ironically, his pre-adolescent vocal work carried a conviction that he often failed to recapture later in his career.

When MGM Records launched the Osmonds as rivals to the Jackson Five in 1970, and singled out their lead singer, 13-year-old Donny Osmond, for a solo career, Motown felt duty bound to reply in kind. Michael Jackson's first release as a solo performer was the aching ballad 'Got To Be There', a major transatlantic hit. A revival of Bobby Day's rock 'n' roll novelty 'Rockin' Robin' reached number 2 on the US chart in 1972, while the sentimental film theme 'Ben' topped the chart later in the year. Motown capitalized on Jackson's popularity with a series of hurried albums, which mixed material angled towards the teenage market with a selection of the label's standards. They also stockpiled scores of unissued tracks, which were released in the 80s to cash in on the success of his Epic recordings.

As the Jackson Five's sales slipped in the mid-70s, Michael's solo career was put on hold, and he continued to reserve his talents for the group after they were reborn as the Jacksons in 1976. He re-entered the public eye with a starring role in the film musical The Wiz, collaborating on the soundtrack album with Quincy Jones. Their partnership was renewed in 1979 when Jones produced Off The Wall, a startlingly successful collection of contemporary soul material that introduced the world to the adult Michael Jackson. In his new incarnation, Jackson retained the vocal flexibility of old, but added a new element of sophistication and maturity. The album topped the charts in the USA and UK, and contained two US number 1 singles, 'Don't Stop 'Til You Get Enough' (for which Jackson won a Grammy Award) and 'Rock With You'. Meanwhile, Motown capitalized on his commercial status by reissuing a recording from the mid-70s, 'One Day In Your Life', which duly topped the UK charts in summer 1981.

Jackson continued to tour and record with the Jacksons after this solo success, while media speculation grew about his private life. He was increasingly portrayed as a figure trapped in an eternal childhood, surrounded by toys and pet animals, and insulated from the traumas of the real world. This image was consolidated when he was chosen to narrate an album based on the 1982 fantasy movie ET – The Extra Terrestrial. The record was quickly withdrawn because of legal complications, but still won Jackson another Grammy Award.

In 1982, Thriller, Jackson's second album with Quincy Jones, was released, and went on to become one of the most commercially successful albums of all time. It also produced a run of successful hit singles, each accompanied by a promotional video that widened the scope of the genre. 'The Girl Is Mine', a duet with Paul McCartney, began the sequence in relatively subdued style, setting the scene for 'Billie Jean', an effortless mix of disco and pop that was a huge transatlantic chart-topper and spawned a series of answer records from other artists. The accompanying video was equally spectacular, portraying Jackson as a master of dance, a magician who could transform lives, and a shadowy figure who could lived outside the everyday world. Its successor, 'Beat It', also topped the US chart and helped establish another precedent, with its determinedly rock-flavoured guitar solo by Eddie Van Halen making it the first black record to receive

rotation airplay on the MTV video station. Its promotional film involved Jackson at the centre of a choreographed street battle, a conscious throwback to the set pieces of West Side Story. However, even this was a modest effort compared to 'Thriller', a rather mannered piece of disco-funk accompanied by a stunning long-form video that placed Jackson in a parade of Halloween horrors. This promo clip spawned a follow-up, The Making Of 'Thriller', which in turn sold more copies than any other home video to date.

The Thriller album and singles won Jackson a further seven Grammies; amidst this run of hits, Jackson slotted in 'Say Say Say', another duet with Paul McCartney which topped the US singles chart for six weeks. He accepted the largest individual sponsorship deal in history from Pepsi-Cola in 1983; the following year, his involvement in the Jacksons' 'Victory Tour' sparked the greatest demand for concert tickets in the history of popular music. Jackson had by now become an almost mythical figure, and like most myths he attracted hyperbole. A group of Jehovah's Witnesses announced that he was the Messiah; he was said to be taking drugs to change his skin colour to white; it was claimed that he had undergone extensive plastic surgery to alter his appearance; and photographs were published that suggested he slept in a special chamber to prevent himself ageing. More prosaically, Jackson began 1985 by co-writing and performing on the USA For Africa benefit single 'We Are The World', another international number 1. He then spent $47.5 million in purchasing the ATV Music company, who controlled the songs of John Lennon and Paul McCartney, thus effectively sabotaging his musical relationship with his erstwhile partner. Later that year he took part in Captain Eo, a short film laden with special effects that was only shown at the Disneyworld amusement park; he also announced plans to write his autobiography.

The book was delayed while he recorded Bad, another collaboration with Quincy Jones that finally appeared in 1987. It produced five US number 1 singles, among them the title track, which again set fresh standards with its promotional video. The album suffered by comparison with his previous work, however, and even its multi-million sales were deemed disappointing after the phenomenal success of Thriller. In musical terms, Bad certainly broke no fresh ground; appealing though its soft funk confections were, they lacked substance, and represented only a cosmetic advance over his two earlier albums with Jones. Unabashed, Jackson continued to work in large scale. He undertook a lengthy world concert tour to promote Bad, utilizing stunning visual effects to capture the atmosphere of his videos. At the same time, he published his autobiography, Moonwalker, which offered little personal or artistic insight; neither did the alarmingly expensive feature film that accompanied it, and which buttressed his otherworldly image.

The long-awaited Dangerous arrived at the end of 1991 and justifiably scaled the charts. This was a tour de force of gutsy dance-orientated pop, with Teddy Riley contributing to a number of tracks. Although the customarily sweet pop was sharpened to a hard point, it still displayed the unmistakable Jackson sound. By maintaining a leisurely working schedule, Jackson had guaranteed that every new project was accompanied by frenzied public anticipation. As a result, the lead-off single 'Black Or White' became a huge transatlantic number 1, topping the US charts for seven weeks.

Until 1992, Jackson's refusal to undergo probing interviews had allowed the media to portray him as a fantasy figure, a hypochondriac who lived a twilight existence cut off from the rest of humanity. He attempted to dispel this image, and succeeded to a degree, with a carefully rehearsed interview with US chat host Oprah Winfrey in 1992. The televised show was shown all over world, during which viewers saw his personal funfair in the back garden, and watched as Jackson spoke of his domineering father. However, the unthinkable happened in 1993, just as Jackson's clean image was at its peak. Allegations of sexual abuse were made by one of Jackson's young friends and the media had a riotous time. Jackson's home was raided by police while he was on tour in the Far East and the artist, clearly disturbed, cancelled a number of performances due to dehydration. No charges were made, and things began to quieten down until November 1993, when Jackson left the USA and went into hiding. Additionally, he confessed to being addicted to painkillers and was seeking treatment. After this admission, Jackson's long-time sponsors Pepsi-Cola decided to pull out of their contract with the now damaged career of the world's most popular superstar.

The media were handed more bait when Jackson married Lisa Marie Presley in May 1994, perhaps in an attempt to rebuild his image. The marriage collapsed 19 months later, giving further rise to allegations that it was merely a set-up to improve his soiled image. He did, however, enhance his reputation with *HIStory: Past, Present And Future – Book 1*. One half of the double set chronicled his past hits, but there was the equivalent of a new album forming the second half. Lyrically, the new material was strong, and Jackson very cleverly gave himself a forum to respond to his critics, most notably on the US Top 5 hit 'Scream' (a duet with his sister Janet Jackson). Although not breaking any new ground musically, the sound was refreshingly varied and, as ever, highly polished, with R. Kelly contributing the transatlantic chart-topper 'You Are Not Alone'. The downside of this return was a sickening display of self-aggrandizement at the UK's 1996 BRIT Awards. Controversy surrounded Jarvis Cocker (of Pulp), who invaded the stage in protest while Jackson, dressed in Messiah-white, was surrounded by, among others, worshipping children and a rabbi.

It appears that, despite the allegations of child abuse and the constant media attacks, particularly surrounding his unexpected second marriage to Debbie Rowe (which ended in October 1999) and the birth of three children, Jackson's fans are destined to remain loyal to the 'King of Pop'. In 2001 the singer celebrated his 30th anniversary as a solo artist, reuniting with the Jackson Five on stage and

breaking a long recording silence in August with his new single, 'You Rock My World'. The attendant *Invincible* paired Jackson with hotshot urban producer Rodney Jerkins, but was let down by a surfeit of weak ballad material. The album went straight to the top of the US and UK charts following its November release, although long-term sales indicate Jackson's commercial heyday has well and truly passed.

● ALBUMS: *Got To Be There* (Motown 1971) ★★★, *Ben* (Motown 1972) ★★★, *Music And Me* (Motown 1973) ★★★, *Forever, Michael* (Motown 1975) ★★★, *Off The Wall* (Epic 1979) ★★★★★, *One Day In Your Life* (Motown 1981) ★★★, *Thriller* (Epic 1982) ★★★★★, *ET - The Extra Terrestrial* (MCA 1983) ★★, *Farewell My Summer Love* 1973 recording (Motown 1984) ★★★, *Looking Back To Yesterday* (Motown 1986) ★★★, *Bad* (Epic 1987) ★★★, *Dangerous* (Epic 1991) ★★★★, *IIIStory: Past, Present And Future – Book 1* (Epic 1995) ★★★★, *Blood On The Dance Floor – HIStory In The Mix* (Epic 1997) ★★★, *Invincible* (Epic 2001) ★★.

● COMPILATIONS: *The Best Of Michael Jackson* (Motown 1975) ★★★, *Michael Jackson 9 Single Pack* (Epic 1983) ★★★, *The Michael Jackson Mix* (Stylus 1987) ★★★, *Anthology* (Motown 1993) ★★★★, *The Best Of Michael Jackson: The Millennium Collection* (Polydor 2000) ★★★★, *Love Songs* (Motown 2002) ★★★.

● VIDEOS: *Moonwalker* (CBS 1988), *The Making Of Thriller* (Vestron Music Video 1986), *The Legend Continues* (Video Collection 1988), *Dangerous – The Short Films* (SMV 1993), *HIStory, Volume 1* (SMV 1995), *HIStory On Film, Vol. 2* (SMV 1997).

● FURTHER READING: *Michael Jackson*, Stewart Regan. *The Magic Of Michael Jackson*, no editor listed. *Michael Jackson*, Doug Magee. *The Michael Jackson Story*, Nelson George. *Michael In Concert*, Phyl Garland. *Michael Jackson: Body And Soul: An Illustrated Biography*, Geoff Brown. *Michael!: The Michael Jackson Story*, Mark Bego. *On The Road With Michael Jackson*, Mark Bego. *Sequins & Shades: The Michael Jackson Reference Guide*, Carol D. Terry. *Michael Jackson: Electrifying*, Greg Quill. *Moonwalk*, Michael Jackson, *Michael Jackson: The Magic And The Madness*, J. Randy Taraborrelli. *Michael Jackson : The Man In The Mirror*, Todd Gold. *Live And Dangerous*, Adrian Grant. *Michael Jackson: The King Of Pop*, Lisa D. Campbell. *Michael Jackson: In His Own Words*, Michael Jackson. *The Visual Documentary*, Adrian Grant. *Michael Jackson Unauthorized*, Christopher Andersen. *The Many Faces Of Michael Jackson*, Lee Pinkerton.

● FILMS: *The Love Machine* (1971), *Save The Children* (1973), *Free To Be ... You & Me* (1974), *The Wiz* (1978), *Captain EO* (1986), *Moonwalker* (1988), *HIStory* (1994), *Ghosts* aka *Michael Jackson's Ghosts* (1997).

## JACKSON, MILLIE

b. 15 July 1944, Thompson, Georgia, USA. A former model, Millie Jackson's controversial singing career began professionally in 1964 at a club in Hoboken, New Jersey, USA. Her first recordings followed in 1970; over the next three years she made several excellent, if traditional, soul singles, which included two US R&B Top 10 entries, with 'Ask Me What You Want' and 'My Man, A Sweet Man'. 'Hurts So Good', a song from a pseudo-feminist 'blaxploitation' movie, *Cleopatra Jones*, was Jackson's biggest hit to date, reaching US number 24, but her subsequent direction was more fully shaped in 1974 with the release of *Caught Up*. With backing from the Muscle Shoals rhythm section, the tracks included a fiery interpretation of '(If Loving You Is Wrong) I Don't Want To Be Right'. The accompaniment intensified the sexual element in her work as Millie embraced either the pose of adulteress or of wronged wife. A further collection, *Still Caught Up*, continued the saga, but Jackson's style later verged on self-parody as she progressed down an increasingly blind alley. The raps became longer and more explicit, and two later albums, *Feelin' Bitchy* and *Live & Uncensored*, required warning stickers for public broadcast.

Despite excursions into C&W and a collaboration with Isaac Hayes, Jackson seemed unable to abandon her 'bad mouth' role, exemplified in 80s titles such as 'Sexercise Pts 1 & 2' and 'Slow Tongue (Working Your Way Down)'. Despite her strong cult following, the only occasion on which Jackson made any significant impact on the US or UK pop singles market was in 1985 when duetting with Elton John on 'Act Of War', which reached the UK Top 40. She continued to enjoy a string of US R&B hits, including 'Hot! Wild! Unrestricted! Crazy Love' and 'Love Is A Dangerous Game', but a creative nadir was reached with 1989's *Back To The S\*\*t!*, which featured Jackson sitting on a toilet on the front cover. In the early 90s, Jackson wrote the play *Young Man, Older Woman*, which with a run of four years proved more successful than her concurrent music releases. By the end of the decade Jackson had begun to establish herself as a leading radio host, with this work taking precedence over her recording career.

Millie Jackson possesses one of soul's outstanding voices, yet sadly chooses to limit its obvious potential in favour of her trademark lewd rapping. Nearly all of Jackson's Spring albums saw CD release in the 90s on the UK Ace's Southbound label.

● ALBUMS: *Millie Jackson* (Spring 1972) ★★★, *It Hurts So Good* (Spring 1973) ★★★, *Caught Up* (Spring 1974) ★★★★, *Soul Believer* (Spring 1974) ★★★, *Still Caught Up* (Spring 1975) ★★★, *Free And In Love* (Spring 1976) ★★★, *Lovingly Yours* (Spring 1977) ★★★, *Feelin' Bitchy* (Spring 1977) ★★★★, *Get It Out 'Cha System* (Spring 1978) ★★★, *A Moment's Pleasure* (Spring 1979) ★★★, with Isaac Hayes *Royal Rappin's* (Polydor 1979) ★★, *Live & Uncensored* (Spring 1979) ★★★, *For Men Only* (Spring 1980) ★★★, *I Had To Say It* (Spring 1981) ★★, *Just A Lil' Bit Country* (Spring 1981) ★★, *Live & Outrageous (Rated XXX)* (Spring 1982) ★★, *Hard Times* (Spring 1982) ★★, *E.S.P. (Extra Sexual Persuasion)* (Sire 1984) ★★, *An Imitation Of Love* (Jive 1986) ★★★, *The Tide Is Turning* (Jive 1988) ★★★, *Back To The S\*\*t!* (Jive 1989) ★★, *Young Man, Older Woman* (Jive 1991) ★★, *Rock N Soul* (Ichiban 1994) ★★, *It's Over!??* (Ichiban 1995) ★★, *Not For Church Folk!* (Weird Wrekuds 2001) ★★★.

● COMPILATIONS: *The Best Of Millie Jackson* (Spring 1976) ★★★★, *The Very Best! Of Millie Jackson* (Jive 1994) ★★★, *Totally Unrestricted! The Millie Jackson Anthology* (Atlantic/Rhino 1997) ★★★★, *21 Of The Best (1971-1983)* (Southbound 1998) ★★★★, *Between The Sheets* (7N 1999) ★★★★, *Sex And Soul* (7N 1999) ★★★, *Essentials* (Bellmark 2001) ★★★.

## JAGGER, MICK

b. Michael Philip Jagger, 26 July 1943, Dartford, Kent, England. The celebrated singer of the Rolling Stones, Jagger has become less a pop star than a media icon. Initially a shy, middle-class student at the London School of Economics, his love of blues, distinctive vocal style and charismatic stage persona marked him out as an original. The image of Jagger has arguably been as crucial to the ultimate long-term success of the Rolling Stones as the quality of their songwriting and musicianship. The antithesis of the pretty-boy lead vocalists of the era, Jagger's surly demeanour, rubber lips and scarecrow body were initially greeted with bemusement by the pin-up pop magazines of the time. What Jagger did was to reinforce those apparent pop star deficiencies and, with remarkable effect, transform them into commodities. The lascivious stage presence was emphasized to such a degree that Jagger became both an appealing and strikingly odd-looking pop star. His self-reconstruction even extended as far as completely altering his accent. In mid-60s television interviews Jagger came across as an urbane, well-spoken university student, but as the decade progressed pseudo-cockney inflexions infiltrated his speech, ultimately creating the multi-mouthed media monster of the present – a figure equally at home talking yobbish platitudes to the gutter press and high-brow after-dinner conversation to the quality monthlies.

Jagger's capacity to outrage the elder members of the community in the 60s was perfected in his highly energetic dervish stage persona, anti-authoritarian stance and unromantic songwriting. In songs such as '(I Can't Get No) Satisfaction', 'Get Off Of My Cloud', '19th Nervous Breakdown' and 'Have You Seen Your Mother Baby, Standing In The Shadow?' Jagger gave short shrift to sex, women, religion and even life itself. He was, undoubtedly, one of rock's most underrated and nihilistic lyricists. The force of his negative catechism was, of course, complemented by the musical contribution of Keith Richards, the architect behind the Rolling Stones' most memorable melodies. Jagger was also assisted by the quality of his players, especially Bill Wyman, Charlie Watts, Brian Jones and later, Mick Taylor. From the mid-60s onwards the rebellion implicit in Jagger's lyrics was reflected in increasingly bizarre real life situations. From urinating against an East London garage wall to saturnalian drug sessions and short-term imprisonment, Jagger came to embody the changing social values and bohemian recklessness that characterized the rock culture of the 60s. It must also be said that he performed a similar role in the 70s when his broken marriage, jet-set romances, cafe society fraternization and millionaire seclusion in exotic climes typified the bloated complacency of the musical elite of the period.

The barometer of his time, Jagger yet resisted the temptation to branch out from the Rolling Stones into too many uncharted areas. A desultory appearance in the movie *Ned Kelly* revealed that his powers of mimicry did not extend as far as a convincing Australian/Irish accent. By contrast, the extraordinary *Performance* captured the combined innocence and malevolence of Jagger's pop persona to striking effect in the guise of an east end gangster and decadent rock star The experiment was not repeated. Jagger was even less concerned about expressing himself in a literary form, unlike John Lennon, Pete Townshend and others of his generation. The most articulate of the Rolling Stones has frankly admitted that he can not even remember sufficient details of his life to pen a ghosted biography.

That peculiar combination of indolence and disinterest may have kept the Rolling Stones together as a performing unit, for Jagger studiously avoided customary rock star solo outings for virtually 25 years. When he finally succumbed to the temptation in the late 80s, the results were insubstantial. Apart from a small handful of tracks, most notably the driving 'Just Another Night' (a US Top 20 hit in 1985), the albums *She's The Boss* and *Primitive Cool* proved disappointing and no doubt contributed to his decision to take the Rolling Stones back on the road at the end of the decade. He also teamed-up with Tina Turner for a Live Aid performance and with David Bowie for a charity cover version of Martha And The Vandellas' 'Dancing In The Street'. Jagger's third solo album, 1993's *Wandering Spirit*, left his critics once again unmoved. The addition of Courtney Pine and Billy Preston could not produce a significant hit album.

Jagger once stated that he would retire before middle age for fear that the Rolling Stones might become an anachronistic parody of themselves. These days such fears appear to have been banished as the band are still recording and undertake regular high-grossing US and European stadium tours. Away from the band the new millennium saw a blitz of Jagger-related stories, including his high-profile separation from Jerry Hall, his production debut on the movie *Enigma* and a credible new solo album, *Goddess In The Doorway*.

● ALBUMS: *She's The Boss* (CBS/Columbia 1985) ★★, *Primitive Cool* (CBS/Columbia 1987) ★★, *Wandering Spirit* (Atlantic 1993) ★★, *Goddess In The Doorway* (Virgin 2001) ★★★.
● FURTHER READING: *Mick Jagger: The Singer, Not The Song*, J. Marks. *Mick Jagger And The Stones*, Tim Dowley. *Jagger Unauthorised*, Christopher Andersen. *Mick Jagger: Primitive Cool*, Christopher Sandford.
● FILMS: *Tonite Let's All Make Love In London* aka *The London Scene* (1967), *Sympathy For The Devil* aka *One Plus One* (1968), *Performance* (1970), *Gimme Shelter* (1970), *Ned Kelly* (1970), *Burden Of Dreams* (1982), *Freejack* (1992), *Bent* (1997), *The Man From Elysian Fields* (2001).

## JAGUAR

This band was formed in Bristol, England, in late 1979, with an original line-up comprising Rob Reiss (vocals), Garry Pepperd (guitar), Jeff Cox (bass) and Chris Lovell (drums). Early demos led to the band having a track included on the *Heavy Metal Heroes* compilation album. The unit subsequently attracted the attention of Neat Records, who released two Jaguar singles, 'Back Street Woman' and 'Axe Crazy', in 1981 and 1982, respectively. The band quickly gained popularity with their New Wave Of British Heavy Metal-rooted speed metal. 'Axe Crazy' was the first single release to feature new vocalist Paul Merrell (ex-Stormtrooper), who replaced Reiss. Merrell's powerful melodic voice was in fine form for the band's debut album, *Power Games*, again released on Neat in 1983. This was well received, with excellent vocal and guitar work complementing the high-speed power-metal rhythms. The band quickly gained a strong following in Europe, especially in the Netherlands, where they toured extensively. However, this all changed with a drastic shift in musical style on their next album. After switching labels to Roadrunner Records, *This Time* was released in 1984. This saw the band slow down considerably, proffering instead melodic rock, accompanied by the guest keyboards of Larry Dawson. It was an ill-conceived gambit that lost the band many fans. Shortly after its release, drummer Lovell was replaced by Gary Davies and keyboard player Gareth Johnson was added to the line-up. Owing to the adverse press reaction the album received, the band folded in 1985.

Merrell, Pepperd and Johnson later worked as the Arena, while Cox released an album with guitarist Fred Hale as the Lost Boyz. Following the re-release of their debut album in 1998, Pepperd and Cox revived the Jaguar name with new recruits Jamie Manton (vocals) and Nathan Cox (drums). The studio album *Wake Me* was released in March 2000, but shortly afterwards Jeff Cox elected to leave the band. He was replaced by Darren Furze.
● ALBUMS: *Power Games* (Neat/Banzai 1983) ★★★★, *This Time* (Roadrunner 1984) ★★, *Wake Me* (Neat 2000) ★★.
● COMPILATIONS: *Power Games: The Anthology* (Sanctuary 2002) ★★★.

## JAH WOBBLE

b. John Wardle, London, England. An innovative bass player, Wobble began his career with Public Image Limited. Previously he had been known as one of the 'four Johns' who hung around Malcolm McLaren's 'Sex' boutique. Heavily influenced by the experimental rhythms of bands like Can, his input to PiL's *Metal Box* collection inspired in turn many novice post-punk bass players. By August 1980 he had become one of the many instrumentalists to fall foul of Lydon in PiL's turbulent career, and set about going solo. He joined forces with his hero Holger Czukay and U2's the Edge for *Snake Charmer*, and recorded with the Human Condition, a group specializing in free-form jazz and dub improvization. However, when they disbanded, the mid-80s quickly became wilderness years for Wobble: 'The biggest kickback I have had was from sweeping the platform at Tower Hill station. It was a scream. You felt like getting on the intercom and saying "The next train is the Upminster train, calling at all stations to Upminster and by the way, I USED TO BE SOMEONE!"'.

When he began listening to North African, Arabic and Romany music, Wobble was inspired to pick up his bass once more. It was 1987 when he met guitarist Justin Adams, who had spent much of his early life in Arab countries. Their bonding resulted in Wobble putting together Invaders Of The Heart, with producer Mark Ferda on keyboards. After tentative live shows they released *Without Judgement* in the Netherlands, where Wobble had maintained cult popularity. As the late 80s saw a surge in the fortunes of dance music and rhythmic expression, Invaders Of The Heart and Wobble suddenly achieved a surprise return to the mainstream. This was spearheaded by 1990's 'Bomba', remixed by Andrew Weatherall on the fashionable Boy's Own Records. Wobble was in demand again, notably as collaborator on Sinéad O'Connor's *I Do Not Want What I Haven't Got* and Primal Scream's 'Higher Than The Sun'. This was quickly followed by Invaders Of The Heart's *Rising Above Bedlam*, in turn featuring contributions from O'Connor (the club hit, 'Visions Of You') and Natacha Atlas. Wobble's creative renaissance continued into the 90s, with Invaders Of The Heart slowly building a formidable live reputation and releasing a series of infectious, upbeat albums for Island Records. He collaborated with Brian Eno on 1995's *Spinner*, and has also released a series of concept albums on his own 30 Hertz label, exploring subjects as diverse as William Blake and Celtic poetry. Wobble also teamed up with ex-PiL bandmate Martin Atkins, Geordie Walker (ex-Killing Joke), and Chris Connelly (ex-Ministry) in the Damage Manual.

● ALBUMS: *The Legend Lives On ... Jah Wobble In 'Betrayal'* mini-album (Virgin 1980) ★★, with Holger Czukay *On The Way To The Peak Of Normal* (EMI 1982) ★★★★, *Jah Wobble's Bedroom Album* (Lago 1983) ★★, with Czukay, the Edge *Snake Charmer* (Island 1983) ★★★, with Czukay, Jaki Liebezeit *Full Circle* (Virgin 1983) ★★★, with Ollie Manland *Neon Moon* (Island 1985) ★★★, with Manland *Tradewinds* (Lago 1986) ★★★, *Psalms* (Wob 1987) ★★★, with Invaders Of The Heart *Without Judgement* (KK 1989) ★★★★, with Invaders Of The Heart *Rising Above Bedlam* (Oval 1991) ★★★★, with Invaders Of The Heart *Take Me To God* (Island 1994) ★★★★, with Eno *Spinner* (All Saints 1995) ★★★, *Heaven & Earth* (Island 1995) ★★★, *The Inspiration Of William Blake* (All Saints 1996) ★★★, with Invaders Of The Heart *The Celtic Poets* (30 Hertz 1997) ★★★, *Requiem* (30 Hertz 1997) ★★★, *The Light Programme* (30 Hertz 1997) ★★, *Umbra Sumus* (30 Hertz 1998) ★★★, with Zi Lan Liao *The Five Tone Dragon* (30 Hertz 1998) ★★★, *Deep Space* (30 Hertz 1999) ★★, with Invaders Of The Heart *Full Moon Over The Shopping Mall* (30 Hertz 1999) ★★, with Deep Space *Beach Fervour Spare* (30 Hertz 2000) ★★★, with Invaders Of The Heart *Molam Dub* (30 Hertz 2000) ★★, with Evan Parker *Passage To Hades* (30 Hertz 2001) ★★★, with Bill Laswell *Radioaxiom: A Dub Transmission* (Palm Pictures 2001) ★★★★, with Temple Of Sound *Shout At The Devil* (30 Hertz 2002) ★★★.

● COMPILATIONS: *30 Hertz: A Collection Of Diverse Workings From A Creative Genius* (Eagle 2000) ★★★★, *The Early Years* (30 Hertz 2001) ★★★.

## JAMES, RICK

b. James Johnson, 1 February 1948, Buffalo, New York, USA. The nephew of Temptations vocalist Melvin Franklin, James pioneered a crossover style between R&B and rock in the mid-60s. In 1965, he formed the Mynah Birds in New York with two future members of the Buffalo Springfield, Neil Young and Bruce Palmer, plus Goldie McJohn, later with Steppenwolf. Motown Records signed the band as a riposte to the British wave of R&B artists then dominating the charts, before their career was aborted when James was arrested for draft evasion. Resuming his career in Britain in the early 70s, James formed the funk combo Main Line. Returning to the USA, he assembled a like-minded group of musicians to perform a dense, brash brand of funk, influenced by Sly Stone and George Clinton. Signed to Motown in 1977, initially as a songwriter, he rapidly evolved a more individual style, which he labelled 'punk funk'. His first single, 'You And I', typified his approach, with its prominent bass riffs, heavy percussion and sly, streetwise vocals. The record reached the US Top 20 in summer 1978 and topped the specialist soul charts – a feat that its follow-up, 'Mary Jane', came close to repeating, though the song's blatant references to marijuana cut short any hopes of radio airplay. James chose to present himself as a social outlaw, with outspoken views on drugs and sex. In a move subsequently echoed by Prince, he amassed a stable of artists under his control at Motown, using the Stone City Band as his backing group, and the Mary Jane Girls as female pawns in his macho master plan. He also produced records by actor Eddie Murphy, vocalist Teena Marie, Val Young, and Process And The Doo-Rags.

James' own recordings, predominantly in the funk vein, continued to corner the disco market, with 'Give It To Me Baby' and 'Super Freak', on which he was joined by the Temptations, achieving notable sales in 1981. M.C. Hammer sampled the latter track on his huge 1990 hit, 'U Can't Touch This'. Both tracks came from *Street Songs*, a Grammy-nominated record that catapulted James into the superstar bracket. Secure in his commercial standing, he revealed that he preferred recording ballads to the funk workouts that had made his name, and his drift towards a more conservative image was heightened when he duetted with Smokey Robinson on the hit single 'Ebony Eyes', and masterminded the Temptations' reunion project in 1983.

James' flamboyant lifestyle took its toll on his health and he was hospitalized several times between 1979 and 1984. His career continued unabated, and he had major hits in 1984 and 1985 with the more relaxed '17' and 'The Glow'. The latter also provided the title for a highly acclaimed album, which reflected James' decision to abandon the use of drugs, and move towards a more laid-back soul style. He was angered by constant media comparisons of his work with that of Prince, and cancelled plans to star in an autobiographical film called *The Spice Of Life* in the wake of the overwhelming commercial impact of his rival's *Purple Rain*. After releasing *The Flag* in 1986, James ran into serious conflict with Motown over the status of his spin-off acts. When they refused to release any further albums by the Mary Jane Girls, James left the label, signing to Reprise Records, where he immediately achieved a soul number 1 collaborating with Roxanne Shanté on 'Loosey's Rap'.

James' drug problems had not disappeared and following years of abuse he was jailed in 1991, together with his girlfriend Tanya Hijazi, for various offences including dealing cocaine, assault and torture. The King Of Funk confessed to *Rolling Stone* that at least by being in prison he 'could not do drugs'. He was released in 1996, and made his recording comeback the following year.

● ALBUMS: *Come Get It!* (Gordy 1978) ★★★, *Bustin' Out Of L Seven* (Gordy 1979) ★★★, *Fire It Up* (Gordy 1979) ★★★, *Garden Of Love* (Gordy 1980) ★★, *Street Songs* (Gordy 1981) ★★★★, *Throwin' Down* (Gordy 1982) ★★★, *Cold Blooded* (Gordy 1983) ★★, *Glow* (Gordy 1985) ★★, *The Flag* (Gordy 1986) ★★, *Wonderful* (Reprise 1988) ★★, *Urban Rapsody* (Higher Source 1997) ★★★.

● COMPILATIONS: *Reflections: All The Great Hits* (Gordy 1984) ★★★★, *Greatest Hits* (Motown 1993) ★★★, *Bustin' Out: The Best Of Rick James* (Motown 1994) ★★★, *Greatest Hits* (Spectrum 1996) ★★★, *The Ultimate Collection* (Motown 1997) ★★★★, *The Best Of Rick James: The Millennium Collection* (Universal 2000) ★★★★, *Anthology* (Motown 2002) ★★★.

## JANE'S ADDICTION

This innovative, art-rock quartet was formed in Los Angeles, USA, in 1986, by vocalist Perry Farrell (b. Perry Bernstein, 29 March 1959, Queens, New York City, New York, USA). He had formerly starred in the Cure-influenced Psi Com, from whose ranks would also emerge Dino Paredes, while it is rumoured that two other former members joined the Hare Krishna sect. With the addition of guitarist Dave Navarro (b. David Michael Navarro, 7 June 1967, Santa Monica, California, USA), bass player Eric Avery and drummer Stephen Perkins, Jane's Addiction incorporated elements of punk, rock, folk and funk into a unique and unpredictable soundscape. They debuted with a live album on the independent Triple X label, recorded at Hollywood's Roxy venue, which received widespread critical acclaim, despite a throwaway cover version of Lou Reed's 'Rock 'n Roll' and Farrell's limited stage banter, largely consisting of profanities. Drawing inspiration from the Doors, PiL, the Velvet Underground and Faith No More, they set about delivering a hypnotic and thought-provoking blend of intoxicating rhythms, jagged and off-beat guitar lines and high-pitched vocals of mesmeric intensity. Their third album, 1987's *Ritual De Lo Habitual*, was a work of depth and complexity that required repeated listening to reveal its hidden melodies, subtle nuances and enigmatic qualities. It included the video-friendly shoplifting narrative, 'Been Caught Stealing'. In the USA, because of censorship of the album's provocative front cover (as

with earlier work, featuring a Farrell sculpture), it was released in a plain envelope with the text of the First Amendment written on it.

Farrell, meanwhile, instigated the Lollapalooza concert series, which from its inception in 1990 became something of a cultural phenomenon on a par with the rise of MTV. Despite widespread media coverage, Jane's Addiction never achieved the commercial breakthrough that their talents deserved, and Farrell dissolved the band in 1992. On his decision to defect to Porno For Pyros, taking drummer Perkins and bass player Martyn Le Noble with him, Farrell concluded, 'What it really boiled down to was, I wasn't getting along with them. I'm not saying whose fault it was. Even though I *know* whose fault it was.' The subject of these slurs, Navarro, went on to join the Red Hot Chili Peppers in 1994. In the summer of 1997 the original band, minus Avery who was replaced by the Red Hot Chili Peppers' Flea, reunited to record together. Two new tracks appeared on a compilation of live material, demos and out-takes. Both Farrell and Navarro released solo albums in 2001 before announcing another Jane's Addiction reunion tour. Le Noble took Avery's place this time around.

● ALBUMS: *Jane's Addiction* (Triple X 1987) ★★★, *Nothing's Shocking* (Warners 1988) ★★★★, *Ritual De Lo Habitual* (Warners 1991) ★★★.

● COMPILATIONS: *Live And Rare* (Warners 1991) ★★, *Kettle Whistle* (Warners 1997) ★★★.

● VIDEOS: *The Fan's Video: Soul Kiss* (Warner Reprise Video 1988), *Gift* (Warner Reprise Video 1993).

● FURTHER READING: *Perry Farrell: The Saga Of A Hypester*, Dave Thompson.

## JAPAN

Formed in London, England in early 1974, Japan comprised David Sylvian (b. David Batt, 23 February 1958, Beckenham, Kent, England; vocals), his brother Steve Jansen (b. Steve Batt, 1 December 1959, Beckenham, Kent, England; drums), Richard Barbieri (b. 30 November 1957; keyboards) and Mick Karn (b. Anthony Michaelides, 24 July 1958, London, England; saxophone). A second guitarist, Rob Dean, was added to the line-up when the band won a recording contract with the German record company Ariola-Hansa. During the same period, they joined forces with manager Simon Napier-Bell. Japan's derivative pop style hampered their prospects during 1978, and they suffered a number of hostile reviews. Eminently unfashionable in the UK punk era, they first found success in Japan. After three albums with Ariola-Hansa, they switched to Virgin Records in 1980 and found their fortunes dramatically improving thanks to the surge of popularity in the new romantic movement. Japan's androgynous image made them suddenly fashionable and they registered a UK Top 20 single with 'Quiet Life', and Top 10 hits with 'Ghosts' and a cover version of Smokey Robinson And The Miracles' 'I Second That Emotion'. Their album, *Tin Drum*, was also well received. Disagreements between Karn and Sylvian undermined the band's progress, just as they were achieving some long-overdue success and they split in late 1982. The members diversified into collaborative work and solo careers, reuniting (minus Dean) in 1991 for a project under the moniker of Rain Tree Crow.

● ALBUMS: *Adolescent Sex* (Ariola-Hansa 1978) ★★, *Obscure Alternatives* (Ariola-Hansa 1978) ★★, *Quiet Life* (Ariola-Hansa 1980) ★★★, *Gentlemen Take Polaroids* (Virgin 1980) ★★★, *Tin Drum* (Virgin 1981) ★★★, *Oil On Canvas* (Virgin 1983) ★★.

● COMPILATIONS: *Assemblage* (Hansa 1981) ★★★, *Exorcising Ghosts* (Virgin 1984) ★★★, *The Other Side Of Japan* (Receiver 1991) ★★★, *In Vogue* (Camden 1996) ★★★, *The Masters* (Eagle 1997) ★★★.

● FURTHER READING: *A Tourist's Guide To Japan*, Arthur A. Pitt.

## JARREAU, AL

b. 12 March 1940, Milwaukee, Wisconsin, USA. Singing a highly sophisticated form of vocalese, Jarreau's style displays many influences. Some of these come from within the world of jazz, notably the work of Jon Hendricks, while others are external. He customarily uses vocal sounds that include the clicks of African song and the plosives common in oriental speech and singing patterns. This range of influences makes him both hard to classify and more accessible to the wider audience for crossover music. More commercially successful than most jazz singers, Jarreau's work in the 70s and 80s consistently appealed to young audiences attuned to fusions in popular music. By the early 90s, when he was entering his 50s, his kinship with youth culture was clearly diminishing, but his reputation was by this time firmly established.

Although Jarreau sang from childhood, it was many years before he decided to make singing his full-time occupation. He attended Ripon College in Wisconsin, and after graduating with a Bachelor of Science degree in psychology moved onto the University of Iowa to complete a Master's degree in Vocational Rehabilitation. Jarreau settled in San Francisco and began working as a rehabilitation counsellor, but continued to sing in small west coast clubs, working with George Duke and eventually achieving enough success to change careers. By the mid-70s he was becoming well known in the USA, and, via a recording contract with Warner Brothers Records and a European tour, greatly extended his audience. He earned the first of five US Grammy Awards in 1977 for Best Jazz Vocal Performance. The following year's *All Fly Home* earned the singer a second Grammy. His real breakthrough came with 1981's *Breakin' Away*, which sold a million copies and was garlanded with Grammy Awards for Best Male Pop Vocalist and Best Male Jazz Vocalist. Further R&B and pop hits followed, including 'We're In This Love Together' and the theme tune to the hit television series *Moonlighting*. Jarreau has consistently attempted to update his style, teaming up with Chic's Nile Rodgers for 1986's *L Is For Lover* and Narada Michael Walden for 1992's *Heaven And Earth*. The latter received a Grammy Award for Best R&B Vocal Performance. In 1996, he appeared in the Broadway production of *Grease* and released a compilation album. He subsequently signed a deal with GRP Records, releasing *Tomorrow Today* in March 2000.

● ALBUMS: *1965* (Bainbridge 1965) ★★★, *We Got By* (Reprise 1975) ★★★, *Glow* (Reprise 1976) ★★, *Look To The Rainbow: Live In Europe* (Warners 1977) ★★★, *All Fly Home* (Warners 1978) ★★★★, *This Time* (Warners 1980) ★★★, *Breakin' Away* (Warners 1981) ★★★★, *Jarreau* (Warners 1983) ★★★, *High Crime* (Warners 1984) ★★, *In London* (Warners 1984) ★★★, *You* (Platinum 1985) ★★★, *L Is For Lover* (Warners 1986) ★★★, *Heart's Horizon* (Reprise 1988) ★★★, *Heaven And Earth* (Reprise 1992) ★★★★, *Tenderness* (Warners 1994) ★★, *Tomorrow Today* (GRP 2000) ★★★★, *All I Got* (GRP 2002) ★★★.

● COMPILATIONS: *Best Of Al Jarreau* (Warners 1996) ★★★★, *Early Gold And New Spins* (Cleopatra 2000) ★★★, *Expressions* (Prism 2001) ★★★.

## JASON AND THE SCORCHERS

This country/rock 'n' roll styled US band was formed by Jason Ringenberg (b. 22 November 1958, Kewanee, Illinois, USA; vocals, guitar, harmonica) who left his parents' farm in Sheffield, Illinois in 1981 to travel to Nashville. There he teamed up with Warner Hodges (b. 4 June 1959, Nashville, Tennessee, USA; guitar) and Jeff Johnson (b. Nashville, Tennessee, USA; bass). Another original member was Jack Emerson, who went on to become the band's manager. Hodges' parents provided the band's pedigree, having been country musicians who toured with Johnny Cash. The band recruited Peter Baggs (b. 22 March 1962, Nashville, Tennessee, USA; drums) and became Jason And The Nashville Scorchers, with the prefix later dropped, playing fast country rock ('cowpunk' was the description coined in the UK). Their first EP for the Praxis label was 1982's *Reckless Country Soul* (USA only), followed by the mini-album *Fervor* a year later. This brought them well-deserved attention in the press and was subsequently re-released in 1984 on EMI Records. It was notable for the inclusion of Bob Dylan's 'Absolutely Sweet Marie', while a subsequent single tackled the Rolling Stones' '19th Nervous Breakdown'. *Lost & Found* included a cover version of Hank Williams' 'Lost Highway'; the combination of these three tracks gives a useful insight into the band's influences and sound.

After moving increasingly towards hard rock with *Thunder And Fire* in 1989, the Scorchers split up when that album failed to bring the expected commercial breakthrough. While guitarist Hodges quit the music business in disgust, Ringenberg took time to gather himself for an assault on the country market. His raunchy solo debut, *One Foot In The Honky Tonk* (released by Liberty Records and credited to 'Jason'), proved too traditional for country radio. He subsequently re-formed his old band, recording prolifically for Mammoth Records before setting up his own Courageous Chicken label. In 2000 Ringenberg released his second solo album, *A Pocketful Of Soul*.

● ALBUMS: as Jason And The Nashville Scorchers *Fervor* (Praxis 1983) ★★★, *Lost & Found* (EMI 1985) ★★★, *Still Standing* (EMI 1986) ★★★, *Thunder And Fire* (A&M 1989) ★★★, *A Blazing Grace* (Mammoth

1995) ★★★, as Jason And The Nashville Scorchers *Reckless Country Soul* 1982 recordings (Mammoth 1996) ★★★★, *Clear Impetuous Morning* (Mammoth 1996) ★★★, *Midnight Roads & Stages Seen* (Mammoth 1998) ★★★, *Rock On Germany* (Courageous Chicken 2001) ★★★.

● COMPILATIONS: *Essential Jason And The Scorchers: Are You Ready For The Country* (EMI 1992) ★★★★, *Both Sides Of The Line* (EMI 1996) ★★★★, *Wildfires + Misfires: Two Decades Of Outtakes And Rarities* (Courageous Chicken/Yep Roc 2002) ★★★.

● VIDEOS: *Midnight Roads And Stages Seen* (Mammoth 1998).

## JAY, NORMAN

b. London, England. Perhaps hyperbolically described as a clubland 'legend', Jay is certainly a hugely popular and highly respected figure in dance music. As a DJ, his style encompasses many forms of black music, including soul, funk, disco, hip-hop and garage. Perhaps his enduring popularity (the UK's *Muzik* magazine called him a 'man of the people') lies in this rare democratic approach to his playlist. Another factor is his foresight and innovation: Jay was listening to early Chicago house records and staging warehouse parties three years before the UK's acid house explosion of 1988. He is also the 'DJ's DJ', with many contemporary superstar DJ's citing him as an early influence.

Jay was born in the early 60s to West Indian parents. He had DJing ambitions even at the tender age of eight and first 'played out' at his cousin's tenth birthday party. As he matured, he was inspired by the American R&B of the late 60s, especially the sound of Sly And The Family Stone, Aretha Franklin and James Brown. By the late 70s, he had become an almost obsessive collector of US black music, collecting Motown Records, Stax Records, Atlantic Records, Salsoul and jazz recordings. He witnessed the disco phenomenon first-hand while visiting family in New York. One of his relatives was a successful Brooklyn DJ and Jay stayed for several months, visiting the seminal Paradise Garage and forming friendships with Larry Levan, Timmy Regisford, Tee Scott and then later, David Morales, Tony Humphries and Little Louie Vega before they had been heard of in the UK. Jay was inspired to take up DJing more seriously and began to build the Good Times sound system with his brother Joey to play at the Notting Hill Carnival. With his reputation and audiences growing steadily, he and Gordon Mac started a pirate radio station, Kiss FM (named after its US predecessor) in 1985.

Jay's reputation and influence attracted many talented DJs to the station, several of whom have since become household names: Jonathon More and Matt Black (Coldcut), Jazzie B. (Soul II Soul), Dr. Bob Jones, Danny Rampling, Trevor Nelson, Gilles Peterson and his partner and protégé, the ubiquitous Judge Jules. Jay and Jules were the originators of the rare groove scene, staging warehouse parties as Shake And Fingerpop and Family Funktion respectively, and playing a mixture of classics and early house records. The arrival of acid house brought dance music to a much larger audience and by 1990, Kiss FM had received a license to broadcast legally. Jay also established the UK's first garage-style club, High On Hope, playing host to US talent such as Tony Humphries, Marshall Jefferson, Blaze, Ten City and Adeva. PolyGram Records sought the skills of Jay and Gilles Peterson to launch their new subsidiary, Talkin' Loud Records, whose early signings included Omar, Bryan Powell, the Young Disciples, Galliano and Incognito. Jay has played all over the world and is often hired for celebrity parties, fashion shows and film premieres and has won numerous awards. *The Face* magazine once described him as a 'clubland institution'.

● COMPILATIONS: with Gilles Peterson *Journeys By DJ: Desert Island Mix* (JDJ 1997) ★★★★, *Philadelphia 1973–1981* (Harmless 1999) ★★★★, *Good Times With Joey And Norman Jay* (Nuphonic 2000) ★★★★, *Good Times 2 With Joey And Norman Jay* (Nuphonic 2001) ★★★★.

## JAZZ BUTCHER

From Northampton, England, and formed in 1982, Jazz Butcher served as a vehicle for the idiosyncratic, melodic songwriting talents of Pat Fish (b. Patrick Huntrods; guitar, vocals), otherwise known as the Jazz Butcher. Although early line-ups were erratic – including Rolo McGinty and Alice Thompson (both later to emerge in the Woodentops), and ex-Bauhaus bass player David J. – the one constant member during most of the early years was lead guitarist Max Eider, whose light jazz/blues feel gave an eloquence to even the most heavy-handed of tunes. In terms of style, there was a large nod in the direction of Lou Reed and Jonathan Richman, while the songs' subject matter dealt with the diverse traumas of everyday life, taking in the joys and woes of small-town living ('Living In A Village'), drink ('Soul Happy Hour'), fear and paranoia ('Death Dentist'), love ('Only A Rumour'/'Angels'), the virtues of public transport ('Grooving In The Bus Lane'), film noir and Vladimir Ilyich Lenin.

The classic Jazz Butcher line-up, including Max Eider, Felix Ray (bass) and Owen Jones (drums), underwent a major upheaval in 1987 with the departure of Eider, resulting in the unit's disintegration. By the time of *Fishcotheque*, Fish was working virtually alone, but for a new partner in guitarist Kizzy O'Callaghan. The Jazz Butcher (Conspiracy) model of the band was rebuilt to comprise Fish, O'Callaghan, Laurence O'Keefe (bass), Paul Mulreany (drums) and Alex Green (saxophone), and saw the band undergoing a change of label, moving from Glass to Creation Records. Subsequent albums saw an increasing use of cut-up film/television dialogue, and continued to garner encouraging reviews. *Illuminate* included the anti-Conservative government tract 'Sixteen Years'. It also saw some critics scoff at the way in which Creation's perseverance with the Jazz Butcher mirrored the British public's unwillingness to change administration. While the Jazz Butcher found a large audience in Europe, and America, substantial success in his homeland continued to elude him, and he decided to play his farewell concerts at the end of 1996. He subsequently drummed with the

Stranger Tractors. Fish re-formed the band with Max Eider and Owen Jones for a Hamburg reunion concert in February 1999, captured for posterity on *Glorious & Idiotic*. They were joined by Peter Crouch (guitar), Kathie McGinty (vocals) and Pat Beirne (mouth organ) on the new studio recording, *Rotten Soul*.

● ALBUMS: *The Jazz Butcher In Bath Of Bacon* (Glass 1983) ★★★, *A Scandal In Bohemia* (Glass 1984) ★★★★, as the Jazz Butcher Conspiracy *Sex And Travel* (Glass 1985) ★★★, as the Jazz Butcher And His Sikkorskis From Hell *Hamburg* (Rebel 1985) ★★★, as the Jazz Butcher Conspiracy *Distressed Gentlefolk* (Glass 1986) ★★★★, *Fishcotheque* (Creation 1988) ★★★, *Big Planet, Scarey Planet* (Creation/Genius 1989) ★★★, *Cult Of The Basement* (Creation/Rough Trade 1990) ★★★, *Condition Blue* (Creation/Sky 1991) ★★★, *Western Family: The Jazz Butcher Conspiracy In America And Canada 1992* (Creation 1993) ★★★, as the Jazz Butcher Conspiracy *Waiting For The Love Bus* (Creation/TriStar 1993) ★★★, *Illuminate* (Creation 1995) ★★★★, as the Jazz Butcher Conspiracy *Glorious & Idiotic* (ROIR 2000) ★★★, as the Jazz Butcher Conspiracy *Rotten Soul* (Vinyl Japan 2000) ★★★.

● COMPILATIONS: *The Gift Of Music* (Glass 1984) ★★★, *Bloody Nonsense* (Big Time 1986) ★★★, *Big Questions* (Glass 1987) ★★★, *Edward's Closet* (Creation 1991) ★★★, *Unconditional* (PolyGram 1992) ★★★, as the Jazz Butcher Conspiracy *Draining The Glass 1982–86* (Fire 1996) ★★★★, as the Jazz Butcher Conspiracy *¡Excellent! The Violent Years* (Creation 1997) ★★★★, as the Jazz Butcher Conspiracy *Cake City* (Vinyl Japan 2001) ★★★.

## JEFFERSON, MARSHALL

One of the legends of Chicago house music, Jefferson (b. 19 September 1959, Chicago, Illinois, USA) claims to have invented the familiar 'squelch' of the Roland TR 303 (a claim hotly countered by DJ Pierre). Jefferson's reputation rests more squarely on records such as Phuture's acid house classic 'Acid Trax', Reggie Hall's 'Music', Richard Rogers' mighty 'Can't Stop Loving You', Ce Ce Rogers' epic 'Someday' and his own 1986 house anthem 'Move Your Body'. Afterwards he would move on to helm production for Ten City, but was criticized at the time of their arrival for what some critics observed to be a fixation with nostalgia in the latter's soulful grooves. Jefferson preferred the description deep house, and was quick to proclaim the death knell for acid house. Nevertheless, Ten City hit with singles like 'Devotion', 'That's The Way Love Is' and 'Right Back To You', with Byron Stingily's distinctive vocals providing an excellent outlet for Jefferson's studio craft. He has also worked with Tyrrel Corporation and Kym Mazelle ('I'm A Lover') amongst many others, and recorded as Jungle Wonz ('Time Marches On', 'The Jungle') and Truth ('Open Your Eyes'). In 1994, Jefferson recorded only the second track under his own name, 'I Found You', for Centrestage Records, as well as continuing to produce artists of the calibre of Tom Jones, System 7 and Keith Thompson. A highly sought after remixer and DJ, Jefferson did find the time to record under his own name on 1997's *Day Of The Onion*.

● ALBUMS: *Day Of The Onion* (EFA 1997) ★★★.

● COMPILATIONS: *Past Classics* (Fierce 1998) ★★★★, *Les Parrains De La House* (Mirakkle 1998) ★★★, *Welcome To The World Of Marshall Jefferson* (MN2S 2001) ★★★★.

## JELLYBEAN

b. John Benitez, 7 November 1957, the Bronx, New York City, New York, USA. This renowned Manhattan club DJ made his mark as one of the US post-disco dance music scene's most favoured remixers/producers. From the mid-80s onwards he ventured into the pop mainstream, working with Whitney Houston, the Eurythmics, Sting, Sheena Easton, Billy Joel, Michael Jackson, Paul McCartney, Julio Iglesias, and Rubén Blades among others. Eventually he would earn his own record contract, though his *modus operandi* did not change, maintaining instead a largely supervisory role on his output. Jellybean's debut release under his own name was the 1984 EP, *Wotupski!?!*, which carried two minor dance classics, 'The Mexican' and 'Sidewalk Talk'. The latter, a US Top 20 hit featuring the vocals of Catherine Buchanan, was penned by Madonna (Benitez had significantly enhanced his own personal reputation by working on tracks for her earlier, including her breakthrough hit 'Holiday'). The million-selling *Just Visiting This Planet* featured the US Top 20 hit, 'Who Found Who' (featuring Elisa Fiorillo), and the producer enjoyed a string of UK Top 20 hits, including the aforementioned 'Who Found Who', 'The Real Thing' (featuring Steven Dante), 'Jingo', and 'Just A Mirage' (featuring Adele Bartel). It would not be until 1991's *Spillin' The Beans*, however, that Jellybean would actually record his own voice, alongside guest vocalists like Niki Harris, who, ironically, had last been seen on Madonna's tour. In 1995 Benitez founded H.O.L.A. Recordings (Home Of Latino Artists), an independent record company promoting bilingual Latin dance artists. He also runs the Jellybean Recordings label.

● ALBUMS: *Just Visiting This Planet* (Chrysalis 1987) ★★★, *Rocks The House!* (Chrysalis 1988) ★★★, *Spillin' The Beans* (Atlantic 1991) ★★.

● COMPILATIONS: *Jellybean's House Party* (Jellybean 2000) ★★★, *Jellybean's Latin House Party* (Jellybean 2000) ★★★.

## JENNINGS, WILL

b. 27 June 1944, Kilgore, East Texas, USA. Jennings is one of the leading lyric writers of recent times, and is best known for his work with the Crusaders, B.B. King, Jimmy Buffett and Steve Winwood. He moved to Tyler when he was 12 and at that time took up the trombone as he had become fascinated with traditional jazz. As a teenager Jennings played guitar in rock bands, the most notable was Blue Mountain Marriage. He then became a literature teacher at the University of Wisconsin, Eau Claire. He moved to Nashville in 1971 and co-wrote four songs with Troy Seals for Dobie Gray's *Drift Away*. During the 70s he composed further material for country artists but had his first pop success co-writing with Richard

Kerr. Together they composed 'Somewhere In The Night' for Barry Manilow and 'I Know I'll Never Love This Way Again' and 'No Night So Long' for Dionne Warwick. Next, Jennings forged a partnership with Joe Sample of the Crusaders to create the big hits 'Street Life' and 'One Day I'll Fly Away', recorded by Randy Crawford. He continued to write with Sample and King used their songs for three albums, *Midnight Believer*, *Take It Home* and *There's Always One More Time*. One of his biggest selling pop-soul ballads, however, was 'Didn't We Almost Have It All', co-written with Michael Masser for Whitney Houston.

Jennings' most fruitful long-lasting collaboration has been with Steve Winwood, whom he met in 1981 following an introduction by Chris Blackwell. Their first success together was the US hit 'While You See A Chance', from *Arc Of A Diver*. Jennings co-composed a number of tracks from that album and subsequently wrote the lyrics for many tracks on further Winwood solo releases, including the hymn-like 'There's A River', 'Talking Back To The Night', 'And I Go', 'Back In The High Life', 'I Will Be Here', 'Valerie' and the US hit singles, 'Higher Love' (1986) and 'Roll With It' (1988).

Jennings met country star Jimmy Buffett in 1982 and wrote two albums with him, *Riddle In The Sand* and *Last Mango In Paris*. The anthem of the movie *An Officer And A Gentlemen* 'Up Where We Belong' was written with Buffy Saint-Marie and was a worldwide hit for Joe Cocker and Jennifer Warnes and is Jenning's most lucrative copyright. He received a BMI Award with Eric Clapton for 'Tears In Heaven' in 1996. He also struck up a friendship and musical partnership with Roy Orbison, writing a number of songs including 'Wild Hearts Run Out Of Time' from the Nicolas Roeg movie *Insignificance*. Chart hits and Academy and BAFTA Awards continued into the 90s as Jennings was commissioned to write songs for movies and established artists. In 1998, he co-wrote (with James Horner) Celine Dion's chart-topping 'My Heart Will Go On', the theme tune to the phenomenally successful movie *Titanic*.

Jennings' success is now self-perpetuating and he is one of the most sought-after writers of the past two decades. He is humble about working with talented musicians like Winwood and Sample and yet he paints their music with colourful romantic lyrics. Jennings states 'a great piece of (popular) music is so important, it deserves the very best I can write to it'. All this is maintained with a down-to-earth attitude, painful modesty, a love of flat caps, British poetry and literature.

## JESUS AND MARY CHAIN

Formed in East Kilbride, Scotland, this indie quartet originally comprised William Reid (vocals, guitar), Jim Reid (vocals, guitar), Douglas Hart (bass) and Murray Dalglish (drums). In the summer of 1984 they moved to London and signed to Alan McGee's label, Creation Records. Their debut, 'Upside Down', complete with trademark feedback, fared well in the independent charts and was backed with a version of Syd Barrett's 'Vegetable Man'. In November 1984, Dalglish was replaced on drums by Primal Scream

vocalist Bobby Gillespie. By the end of the year, the band was attracting considerable media attention due to the violence at their gigs and a series of bans followed. Early the following year, the band signed to the WEA Records label Blanco y Negro.

The Reid brothers publicly delighted in the charms of amphetamine sulphate, which gave their music a manic edge. Live performances usually lasted 20 minutes, which brought more controversy and truculence from traditional gig habitués, who felt short-changed. 'Never Understand' further underlined comparisons with the anarchic school of 1977 in general and the Sex Pistols in particular, but the band surprised many by later issuing the more pop-orientated 'Just Like Honey'. By October 1985, Gillespie had returned to his former band, Primal Scream. One month later, the Reid Brothers issued their highly acclaimed debut, *Psychocandy*. Full of multi-tracked guitar distortion, underscored with dark melodies, many critics proclaimed it one of rock's great debuts. The following August the band reached UK number 13 with the melodic 'Some Candy Talking', which received curtailed radio play when it was alleged that the subject matter concerned heroin. During the same period, the band found a new drummer, John Moore, and parted from their manager, Alan McGee. Further hits with 'April Skies' (number 8) and 'Happy When It Rains' (number 25) preceded their second album, *Darklands*. Again fawned over by the press, though not to quite the same extent as their debut, it was followed by a tempestuous tour of Canada and America, during which one brother was briefly arrested then acquitted on a charge of assaulting a fan. In the spring of 1988, a compilation of the band's various out-takes was issued. This assuaged demand before the arrival of *Automatic* at the turn of the decade. The band was effectively just a duo for this record, with programmed synth drums as backing to the usual barrage of distortion and twisted lyrics (the best example of which was the single, 'Blues From A Gun'). The follow-up *Honey's Dead* also housed a powerful lead single in 'Reverence', which peaked at UK number 10 in spring 1992.

After this, the Reid brothers changed tack for *Stoned & Dethroned*, with the feedback all but gone in favour of an acoustic, singer-songwriter approach. Self-produced and recorded at home, its more reflective texture was embossed by the appearance of guest vocalists Shane MacGowan and Hope Sandoval (Mazzy Star). The album was poorly received commercially and critically, resulting in the band being dropped by Warners. They rejoined Creation Records at the end of 1997 and issued 'Cracking Up', their debut single of the new era, in March 1998. It was followed by *Munki*, on which the Reid brothers experimented with a motley collection of different styles. The band officially split up the following year with William Reid electing to work on his Lazycame solo project and Jim Reid forming Freeheat.

● ALBUMS: *Psychocandy* (Blanco y Negro/Reprise 1985) ★★★★, *Darklands* (Blanco y Negro/Warners 1987) ★★★, *Automatic* (Blanco y Negro/Warners 1989) ★★, *Honey's Dead* (Blanco y Negro/Def American 1992) ★★★, *Stoned & Dethroned* (Blanco y

Negro/American 1994) ★★★, *Munki* (Creation 1998) ★★★.

● COMPILATIONS: *Barbed Wire Kisses* (Blanco y Negro/Warners 1988) ★★★, *The Sound Of Speed* (Blanco y Negro 1993) ★★★, *The Complete John Peel Sessions* (Strange Fruit 2000) ★★★, *21 Singles 1984–1998* (Warners/Rhino 2002) ★★★★.

● FURTHER READING: *The Jesus And Mary Chain: A Musical Biography*, John Robertson.

## JETS

A family act originally from the Polynesian island of Tonga, the Jets are eight of the 14 children of Mike and Vake Wolfgramm. The family moved to Salt Lake City, Utah, USA but eventually settled in Minneapolis, Minnesota. The oldest boy, Leroy, began showing musical interest as a young child and joined a club act including some of his uncles when he was aged 11. Leroy and several of his sisters formed their first group, Quasar, in 1978, performing as a Polynesian act at restaurants in the Midwest. In 1984 the group signed with Don Powell, once a manager of the Jacksons. They eventually grew to eight, featuring Leroy, Eddie, Rudy, Haini, Kathi, Moana and Elizabeth Wolfgramm, the last providing lead vocals on many of their hits. The eighth member, Eugene, left the group in 1988 to form a duo, Boys Club, with Joe Pasquale, earning them a US Top 10 hit that same year with 'I Remember Holding You'. The Jets' first US Top 5 hit, 'Crush On You' in 1986, which was later a 1987 Top 5 hit in the UK, made them teen sensations. The group continued their success in the USA with four further Top 10 hits, 'You Got It All' (number 3), 'Cross My Broken Heart' (number 7), 'Rocket 2 U' (number 6) and 'Make It Real' (number 4), but their albums did not fare as well. By the end of the 80s the appeal of the Jets had lessened considerably. Leroy, Haini and Rudy continued to lead the Jets in the following decade, adopting a more gospel-orientated approach on albums such as 1997's *Love Will Lead The Way*.

● ALBUMS: *The Jets* (MCA 1986) ★★★, *Christmas With The Jets* (MCA 1986) ★★★, *Magic* (MCA 1987) ★★★, *Believe* (MCA 1989) ★★, *Love People* (Liberty Park 1994) ★★, *Love Will Lead The Way* (Shadow Mountain 1997) ★★★.

● COMPILATIONS: *The Best Of The Jets* (MCA 1990) ★★★, *Then & Now* (K-Tel 1998) ★★★, *The Best Of The Jets: The Millennium Collection* (MCA 2001) ★★★.

## JETT, JOAN, AND THE BLACKHEARTS

b. Joan Marie Larkin, 22 September 1960, Philadelphia, Pennsylvania, USA. Jett was one of the most successful US female singers to emerge from the rock scene of the 70s. She spent most of her childhood in the Baltimore, Maryland area, where she learned guitar as a child, playing along to favourite rock 'n' roll records. In 1972, her family relocated to Los Angeles, where she became enamoured with artists including David Bowie, Suzi Quatro, T. Rex and Gary Glitter. At the age of 15 she began infiltrating the Los Angeles rock scene and formed her first band. Producer Kim Fowley took the band under his wing and named it the Runaways, procuring a record contract with Mercury Records.

They recorded three punk-tinged hard rock albums that were unsuccessful in the USA but hits in Japan, where they recorded a live album. Also successful in England, they recorded their swan-song, *And Now ... The Runaways*, in that country in 1979.

After the dissolution of the Runaways, Jett moved to New York and teamed up with producer Kenny Laguna, who became her manager. Laguna had previously been involved with a number of 60s bubblegum hits. He produced Jett's first solo album, which was released on the European Ariola label. When no US label picked it up, they issued it on their own Blackheart Records and the album sold well, becoming one of the bestselling US independent releases of that era. This led to a contract with Neil Bogart's Boardwalk Records, who reissued it as *Bad Reputation* (a title inspired by the less than enthusiastic industry response to Jett after the Runaways), and saw it reach number 51 in the US charts. With her band the Blackhearts (guitarist Ricky Byrd, bass player Gary Ryan and drummer Lee Crystal), Jett recorded *I Love Rock-N-Roll* in late 1981, produced by Laguna and Ritchie Cordell. The title track, originally an obscure b-side for UK band the Arrows, became a major hit, largely owing to a big push from MTV, and spent seven weeks at number 1 in the USA in early 1982 (it also reached the UK Top 5). The follow-up single, a cover version of Tommy James And The Shondells' 'Crimson And Clover', was itself a US Top 10 hit, reaching number 7 in 1982. Also on the album was an update of a Jett song from the Runaways era, 'You're Too Possessive'.

With Neil Bogart's death, the band signed to MCA Records, which then distributed Blackheart Records. However, subsequent outings on that label were not nearly as successful as the Boardwalk releases. *Glorious Results Of A Misspent Youth* again retreated to Jett's past with the Runaways, this time on a revision of 'Cherry Bomb'. *Good Music* saw some intriguing collaborations, with members of the Beach Boys and Darlene Love guesting, and an unlikely rap duet with Scorpio of Melle Mel And The Furious 5. The album also saw the departure of Lee Crystal and Gary Ryan, the former permanently replaced by Thommy Price. Jett, meanwhile, found time to make a second movie appearance (following *We're All Crazy Now*), playing Michael J. Fox's sister in *Light Of Day*; and also sang the Bruce Springsteen-penned theme. *Up Your Alley* brought another US Top 10 hit with 'I Hate Myself For Loving You', before 1990's *The Hit List*, an album of cover versions, which included a duet with Ray Davies on 'Celluloid Heroes'. *Notorious* saw her collaborate with Paul Westerberg of the Replacements on the co-written 'Backlash', but by the advent of *Pure And Simple*, Byrd was no longer a permanent member of the band. This set saw a guest appearance from L7 on a track entitled 'Activity Grrrl', emphasizing Jett's influence on a new generation of female rockers (by this time, Jett had also produced Bikini Kill, in addition to late 70s LA punk band the Germs). The following year, Jett recorded a live album with the Seattle punk band the Gits. She revived the Blackhearts name for 1999's *Fetish*, a collection of previously released material, new songs and live tracks.

● ALBUMS: *Joan Jett* aka *Bad Reputation* (Blackheart/ Ariola/Boardwalk 1980) ★★★, *I Love Rock-N-Roll* (Boardwalk/Epic 1981) ★★★★, *Album* (Blackheart/ MCA 1983) ★★★, *Glorious Results Of A Misspent Youth* (Blackheart/MCA 1984) ★★★, *Good Music* (Blackheart/Epic 1986) ★★★, *Up Your Alley* (Blackheart/CBS 1988) ★★★, as Joan Jett *The Hit List* (Blackheart/CBS 1990) ★★★, *Notorious* (Blackheart/Epic 1991) ★★★, *Pure And Simple* (Blackheart/Warners 1994) ★★★.
● COMPILATIONS: *Flashback* (Blackheart 1993) ★★★, *Fit To Be Tied: Great Hits By Joan Jett And The Blackhearts* (Mercury 1997) ★★★, *Fetish* (Blackheart 1999) ★★, *Essential* (BCI 2000) ★★★.
● VIDEOS: *The Jett Age* (Blackheart 1992), *The Jett Age Part II* (Blackheart 1995).
● FILMS: *Urgh! A Music War* (1981), *Cool Cats: 25 Years Of Rock 'N Roll Style* (1983), *DuBEAT-e-o* aka *We're All Crazy Now* (1984), *Light Of Day* (1987), *Talking About The Weather* (1994), *Not Bad For A Girl* (1996), *Boogie Boy* (1997), *By Hook Or By Crook* (2001), *The Sweet Life* (2002).

## JIMMY JAM AND TERRY LEWIS

Based in Minneapolis, Minnesota, USA, Jimmy 'Jam' Harris (b. James Harris III, 6 June 1959, Minneapolis, Minnesota, USA) and Terry Lewis (b. 21 November 1956, Minneapolis, Minnesota, USA) are prolific producers of contemporary R&B and pop. The two first worked together in the early 80s as members of Time (formerly Flyte Time). Subsequently, Harris (keyboards) and Lewis (bass) became black music's most consistently successful production duo. They formed their own record label, Tabu, in 1980, which enjoyed enormous success with artists such as the S.O.S. Band throughout the 80s. Among the other early bands and artists to benefit from the duo's writing and production skills were Change, Cherrelle, the Force M.D.'s, Johnny Gill and the former Time singer Alexander O'Neal. Their greatest success, however, came as the creative catalysts behind Janet Jackson's career. The first album they recorded with her, 1986's *Control*, included five US Top 10 singles. The follow-up, 1989's *Janet Jackson's Rhythm Nation 1814*, was even more successful, with Jackson becoming the first artist in history to have culled from one album seven Top 5 US singles. In 1990 Jam And Lewis recorded once again with Time, who had re-formed to make *Pandemonium*, which was released on Prince's Paisley Park Records. Though the reunion was not widely regarded as a success, the duo's productions remained in the higher reaches of the charts. Their continued association with Jackson (1993's *Janet* and 1997's *The Velvet Rope*) was never surpassed commercially but many others benefited from their expertise, including Boyz II Men, Mary J. Blige, Vanessa Williams and Michael Jackson. Their pioneering work in the genre of urban R&B that became known as swingbeat, was juxtaposed with productions for other artists ranging from the Human League to Yolanda Adams and Sounds Of Blackness. In the 90s they also established a new record label, Perspective Records, distributed by A&M Records.

## JIVE BUNNY AND THE MASTERMIXERS

A throwback to the medley craze of the early 80s, with a similarly repetitive disco beat cushioning the samples, Jive Bunny were solely responsible for making recent generations believe that rock and pop classics of yesteryear are only 10 seconds long. A UK male production/mixing group comprising John Pickles and disc jockey Ian Morgan, they became UK chart-toppers with their first three singles 'Swing The Mood', 'That's What I Like' and 'Let's Party' during 1989. This equalled the record held by Gerry And The Pacemakers (1963) and Frankie Goes To Hollywood (1984). The idea was conceived by Pickles, previously the owner of an electrical shop. The concept for 'Swing The Mood' had originally come from an ex-miner living in Norway called Les Hemstock. John's son Andrew Pickles also helped out. They also appeared on 'It Takes Two Baby', by DJs Liz Kershaw and Bruno Brookes in December 1989. Subsequent hits scored progressively lower chart placings, doubtless to the relief of many. 'That Sounds Good To Me' (number 4), 'Can Can You Party' (number 8), 'Let's Swing Again' (number 19) and 'The Crazy Party Mixes' (number 13) completed their run of Top 20 chart entries. They have subsequently disappeared up their own bobtails, although new Jive Bunny albums have continued to appear with monotonous regularity. Pickles became highly successful as head of Music Factory, which controls a number of dance music labels such as Trax, Defcon and Energize.
● ALBUMS: *Jive Bunny: The Album* (Telstar 1989) ★★★, *It's Party Time* (Telstar 1990) ★★, *Christmas Party* (Crimson 1997) ★★, *Rock The Party* (Music Club 1998) ★★, *Hop Around The Clock: The Ultimate Non Stop Party Album* (Global 1998) ★★, *Spectacular Christmas Party!* (Metro 2000) ★★, *Hits Of The Year* (Metro 2000) ★★, *School Disco* (Metro 2002) ★★.
● COMPILATIONS: *The Best Of Jive Bunny And The Mastermixers* (Music Collection 1995) ★★★.

## JOBOXERS

This pop-soul outfit achieved minor fame in the early 80s with a sound built on fast beats and imagery from the film *On The Waterfront*. JoBoxers comprised Dig Wayne (b. 20 July 1958, USA; vocals), Rob Marche (b. 13 October 1962, Bristol, England; guitar), Dave Collard (b. 17 January 1961, Bristol, England; keyboards), Chris Bostock (b. 23 November 1962, Bristol, England; bass) and Sean McLusky (b. 5 May 1961, Bristol, England; drums). All except Wayne were former members of Vic Godard And The Subway Sect (from 1981 onwards), the last incarnation of a punk band who ended their career by backing Goddard's affected crooning. As JoBoxers they first attracted attention after appearing on the BBC television's *Oxford Roadshow* in 1982. Signed to RCA Records, in February 1983 they released 'Boxer Beat', which was a Top 5 hit in the UK. The follow-up 'Just Got Lucky' also went into the Top 10 and reached the US Top 40, but subsequent singles such as 'Johnny Friendly' and 'Jealous Love' did less well. The band split early in 1986, with Wayne going on to a brief solo career (one album, *Square Business*, 1987) with a band that featured Dave Collard of JoBoxers and Mark Reilly (ex-Matt Bianco). After their demise McLusky gained a reputation as a promoter on the club scene.

● ALBUMS: *Like Gangbusters* (RCA 1983) ★★, *Skin And Bone* (RCA 1985) ★★.

● COMPILATIONS: *Essential Boxerbeat* (BMG 1996) ★★★.

## JOBSON, RICHARD

b. 6 October 1960, Dunfermline, Fife, Scotland. Jobson was born the brother of John, a striker for Meadowbank Thistle Football Club, for whom Richard was also on the books. After a four-year tenure with the Skids (1977–81), Jobson moved on to join the Armoury Show, which failed to repeat the success of any of its illustrious personnel's former bands. With their demise, Jobson toured the UK with Scottish acting company Poines Plough. Turning to poetry, he hit the road once more, falling between two schools in terms of critical reception. On one side, rock critics viewed the move suspiciously, castigating him as pretentious, while the poetry critics reacted with venom to the vulgar intrusion of a rock singer. Placed in its proper context, Jobson was capable of writing good poetry, but was too much at the whim of his own indulgence. The worst example of this was his infamous live rendition of Sylvia Plath's 'Daddy'.

Jobson continued to release albums throughout the 80s, the best of which was *16 Years Of Alcohol*, also the title of a book that described his alcohol problems. He also suffers from epilepsy. *Badman*, released on Parlophone Records in 1988, was produced by Ian Broudie. Although the imagery was typically grandiose, it did include a sprightly cover version of Everything But The Girl's 'Angel'. Meanwhile, Jobson had chanced upon further careers in television and fashion. He appeared variously as the pop correspondent on BBC Television's *The Garden Party*, as presenter of *01 For London*, and in regional arts programmes and the opinion show *Biteback*. On top of this came his highly paid, and some might say unlikely, stint as a fashion model. Most notable was a series of car adverts, for which he also composed the music. In the mid-90s he moved into film production, working on *Just Another Day In London*, *Tube Tales* and *Heartlands*.

● ALBUMS: *The Ballad Of Etiquette* (Cocteau 1981) ★★, *An Afternoon In Company* (Les Disques Du Crepuscule 1982) ★★, *Ten-Thirty On A Summer Night* (Les Disques Du Crepuscule 1982) ★★, *The Right Man* (Les Disques Du Crepuscule 1986) ★★, *16 Years Of Alcohol* (Les Disques Du Crepuscule 1987) ★★★, *Badman* (Parlophone 1988) ★★★.

● FURTHER READING: *A Man For All Seasons*, Richard Jobson.

## JOEL, BILLY

b. William Martin Joel, 9 May 1949, the Bronx, New York City, New York, USA. Joel, a classically trained pianist who grew up in Long Island, joined his first group, the Echoes, in 1964. Three years later he left them in favour of the Hassels, a popular Long Island act signed to United Artists Records. Joel appeared on both of their albums, *The Hassels* and *Hour Of The Wolf*, before breaking away with drummer Jon Small to form Attila. The duo completed a self-titled album before moving in separate directions. A demo of Joel's original compositions led to the release of his 1971 debut, *Cold Spring Harbor*, but its progress was marred by insufficient promotion. However, when 'Captain Jack', a new song recorded for a radio broadcast, became an 'underground' hit, Columbia Records traced Joel to California and signed him to a long-term contract. The title track to *Piano Man*, became a US Top 30 single in 1973 and sowed the seeds of a highly successful recording career. However, Joel refused to bow to corporate demands for commercially minded material and despite enjoying hits with two subsequent albums, *Streetlife Serenade* and *Turnstiles*, it was not until 1977 that his fortunes flourished with the release of *The Stranger*, which eventually surpassed Simon And Garfunkel's *Bridge Over Troubled Water* as Columbia's bestselling album. Its best-known track, the US Top 5 hit 'Just The Way You Are', later won two Grammy Awards for Song Of The Year and Record Of The Year. This romantic ballad has since become a standard, and was a major UK hit for Barry White in 1978. Joel's 1979 album, *52nd Street*, spawned another smash single, 'My Life' while the singer's first US number 1, 'It's Still Rock 'N' Roll To Me' came from a subsequent release, *Glass Houses*. Joel's image as a popular, uncontroversial figure was shaken with *The Nylon Curtain*, which featured two notable 'protest' compositions, 'Allentown' and 'Goodnight Saigon'. However he returned to simpler matters in 1984 with *An Innocent Man*, which included the US number 1 'Tell Her About It' and the effervescent bestseller 'Uptown Girl', a tribute to his then wife, model Chrissie Brinkley. This memorable single topped the UK charts and confirmed the artist's status as an international performer. Further transatlantic hits from the album included the title track, 'The Longest Time', 'Leave A Tender Moment Alone' and 'Keeping The Faith'.

Although his output from the mid-80s onwards has been less prolific, Joel has continued to score the occasional hit single, maintaining his standing in the pop world. Most notable of these were the US Top 10 hits 'You're Only Human (Second Wind)', 'Modern Woman' and 'A Matter Of Trust', 1989's US chart-topper 'We Didn't Start The Fire' and 1993's 'River Of Dreams'. In 1990 he won the Grammy's Living Legends Award, and the following year was awarded an honorary doctorate at Fairfield University, Connecticut. Further awards included *Billboard*'s Century Award in 1994 and induction into the Rock And Roll Hall Of Fame in 1999.

Joel's back catalogue continues to sell in thousands and by the turn of the new millennium many had reached multi-platinum status in the USA. He is also the third bestselling solo artist in US recording history, behind Garth Brooks and Elton John. A perfectionist by nature, he also indicated a desire to pursue a wider musical style, and in 1997 announced that he would not be writing any pop songs in the foreseeable future, concentrating instead on classical scores. His first classical release,

*Fantasies & Delusions*, was performed by pianist Richard Joo.

● ALBUMS: *Cold Spring Harbor* (Family 1971) ★★, *Piano Man* (Columbia 1973) ★★, *Streetlife Serenade* (Columbia 1974) ★★, *Turnstiles* (Columbia 1976) ★★★, *The Stranger* (Columbia 1977) ★★★★, *52nd Street* (Columbia 1978) ★★★, *Glass Houses* (Columbia 1980) ★★★, *Songs In The Attic* (Columbia 1981) ★★★, *The Nylon Curtain* (Columbia 1982) ★★★, *An Innocent Man* (Columbia 1983) ★★★, *The Bridge* (Columbia 1986) ★★★, *Kohuept* (Columbia 1987) ★★, *Storm Front* (Columbia 1989) ★★★, *River Of Dreams* (Columbia 1993) ★★★★, *2000 Years: The Millennium Concert* (Columbia 2000) ★★★, *Fantasies & Delusions: Music For Solo Piano* (Sony Classical 2001) ★★★.

● COMPILATIONS: *Greatest Hits Volumes I & II* (Columbia 1985) ★★★★, *Greatest Hits Volume III* (Columbia 1997) ★★★, *The Complete Hits Collection 1973-1997* 4-CD box set (Columbia 1997) ★★★★, *The Ultimate Collection* (Columbia 2001) ★★★★.

● VIDEOS: *Live From Long Island* (CBS-Fox 1985), *The Video Album Volume 1* (CBS-Fox 1986), *The Video Album Volume II* (CBS-Fox 1986), *Live From Leningrad, USSR* (Sony Music Entertainment 1987), *Eye Of The Storm* (CBS 1990), *Live At Yankee Stadium* (CBS 1990), *A Matter Of Trust* (Sony Music Entertainment 1991), *Shades Of Grey* (Maritime Music 1993), *Greatest Hits Volume III: The Video* (Sony Music Entertainment 1997), *The Essential Video Collection* (Sony Music Entertainment 2001).

● FURTHER READING: *Billy Joel: A Personal File*, Peter Gambaccini.

## JOHANSEN, DAVID

b. 9 January 1950, Staten Island, New York, USA. Johansen gained recognition in the early 70s as lead singer of the New York Dolls. A R&B/rock group taking inspiration from the likes of the Rolling Stones, the New York Dolls' street attitude and outrageous sense of dress thrust them into the glitter/glam scene, although their music had little in common with others of that nature. Johansen joined his first band, the Vagabond Missionaries, in high school. At the age of 17 he moved to Manhattan, New York, and briefly worked with a band called Fast Eddie And The Electric Japs. The New York Dolls came together in late 1971 and quickly built a devoted audience at New York clubs such as the Mercer Arts Center and Max's Kansas City. They recorded two albums for Mercury Records and held on until late 1976. After their demise they became an inspiration to numerous artists, from the newly forming punk bands such as the Sex Pistols, to Kiss, to the Smiths.

Johansen launched a solo career in 1978, recording for Blue Sky Records. Less flamboyant than the New York Dolls' records, this was a solid rock effort stressing Johansen's lyrical acumen. He released three other rock/R&B-orientated solo albums for Blue Sky and one for Passport Records before shifting career directions once again. In 1983 Johansen began booking small cabaret concert dates under the name Buster Poindexter, performing a slick, tightly arranged set of vintage R&B numbers,

show tunes, and jump blues. Dressing in a formal tuxedo and playing the lounge lizard, Buster Poindexter built a following of his own, until Johansen the rocker literally ceased to exist; he completely gave up his rock act to pursue the new image full-time. He recorded albums as Buster Poindexter, including *Buster Poindexter* (1987) and *Buster Goes Berserk* (1989), the first yielding a chart and club hit in a cover version of Arrow's 1984 soca dance tune, 'Hot Hot Hot'. He was still popular as Poindexter in the 90s, touring with a 10-piece band and packing clubs, his repertoire now including Caribbean-flavoured music, salsa (1997's *Spanish Rocket Ship*) torch songs and blues, as well as early R&B. He also launched an acting career in the late 80s, appearing in movies including *Scrooged* and *Married To The Mob*. Johansen's venture into blues also bore fruit with his band the Harry Smiths, releasing two fine albums in the new millennium.

● ALBUMS: *David Johansen* (Blue Sky 1978) ★★★, *In Style* (Blue Sky 1979) ★★★, *Here Comes The Night* (Blue Sky 1981) ★★, *Live It Up* (Blue Sky 1982) ★★★★, *Sweet Revenge* (Passport 1984) ★★★, as Buster Poindexter *Buster Poindexter* (RCA 1987) ★★★, as Buster Poindexter *Buster Goes Berserk* (RCA 1989) ★★, *The David Johansen Group Live* 1978 recording (CBS 1993) ★★★, as Buster Poindexter *Buster's Happy Hour* (Rhino 1994) ★★★, as Buster Poindexter *Spanish Rocket Ship* (PolyGram 1997) ★★★, *David Johansen And The Harry Smiths* (Chesky 2000) ★★★★, with the Harry Smiths *Shaker* (Chesky 2002) ★★★.

● COMPILATIONS: *Crucial Music: The David Johansen Collection* (Columbia/Relativity 1990) ★★★, *From Pumps To Pompadour: The David Johansen Story* (Rhino 1995) ★★★★, *Looking Good* (Sony 1996) ★★★.

● FILMS: *Light Years* voice only (1986), *Candy Mountain* (1987), *Scrooged* (1988), *Married To The Mob* (1988), *Let It Ride* (1989), *Tales From The Darkside: The Movie* (1990), *Freejack* (1992), *Desire And Hell At Sunset Motel* (1992), *Mr. Nanny* (1993), *Naked In New York* (1994), *Car 54, Where Are You?* (1994), *Burnzy's Last Call* (1995), *Cats Don't Dance* voice only (1997), *The Deli* (1997), *Nick And Jane* (1997), *The Tic Code* (1998), *200 Cigarettes* (1999), *Crooked Lines* (2001), *Campfire Stories* (2001), *God Is On Their Side* (2002).

## JOHNNY HATES JAZZ

Purveyors of super-slick pop, this UK band derived their unusual name from a friend called Johnny who, literally, did not like jazz. The line-up featured Calvin Hayes (b. England; keyboards/drums), Mike Nocito (b. 5 August 1963, Wiesbaden, Germany; guitar/bass) and Clark Datchler (b. England; vocals/keyboards), the son of former Stargazers member Fred Datchler. Datchler was later replaced by multi-instrumentalist Phil Thornalley (b. 5 January 1964, Worlington, Suffolk, England; vocals/guitar, ex-Cure). The connection between all four was RAK Records, the label owned by Hayes' father, Mickie Most. Thornalley co-wrote the band's unsuccessful RAK single, 1986's 'Me And My Foolish Heart', but he could not front the band as he was producing Robbie Nevil. Hayes brought in ex-Hot Club team-mate Datchler and some expensive suits, and at the end of the year the new line-up signed to Virgin Records. 'Shattered Dreams' (the Datchler-penned follow-up) was a UK Top 5 hit during 1987, and fared even better in the US where it narrowly failed to top the *Billboard* singles chart. Three further Top 20 hits followed during the next year: 'I Don't Want To Be A Hero', 'Turn Back The Clock' and 'Heart Of Gold'. The band's first album topped the UK charts, but they were unable to sustain that level of commercial appeal. Datchler would go on to resume a largely unsuccessful solo career in 1988, releasing singles like 'Crown Of Thorns' and the albums *Raindance* (1990) and *Fishing For Souls* (1992). The Thornalley-led line-up released one further album before disbanding. Thornalley's subsequent songwriting and production career has included successful work for Bryan Adams and Natalie Imbruglia.

● ALBUMS: *Turn Back The Clock* (Virgin 1988) ★★, *Tall Stories* (Virgin 1991) ★★.
● COMPILATIONS: *The Very Best Of Johnny Hates Jazz* (Virgin 1993) ★★★.
● VIDEOS: *The Video Singles* (Virgin Music Video 1988).

## JONES, GRACE

b. Grace Mendoza, 19 May 1948, Spanish Town, Jamaica, West Indies (1952 and 1954 have also been listed as her year of birth). Six feet of style, looks and attitude, Jones moved to New York City in 1964, then became a successful Paris model, appearing on the covers of *Vogue*, *Elle* and *Der Stern*. After a flirtation with acting, she made some unexceptional disco records that sold on the strength of her image and her explicit stage show. Both were carefully crafted by her boyfriend, French artist Jean-Paul Goude. *Warm Leatherette* marked a major stylistic development. Recorded at Compass Point, Nassau, it featured top Jamaican session men Sly And Robbie, new wave material and the half-spoken delivery style that became the Grace Jones trademark. Her first hit was a cover version of the Pretenders' 'Private Life' which made the UK Top 20 in 1980. On *Nightclubbing* she turned her hand to writing, producing quality songs such as 'Pull Up To The Bumper'. In 1984 she diversified into movies, taking on Arnold Schwarzenegger in *Conan The Destroyer*. The following year she played alongside Roger Moore in the James Bond movie *A View To A Kill*. A return to the recording studios with writer/producer Trevor Horn (on his ZTT Records label) provided her with the UK number 12 hit single, 'Slave To The Rhythm'. An album of extended versions and megamixes also sold well. In 1986 the compilation *Island Life* was a big UK success, with 'Pull Up To The Bumper' (number 12) and 'Love Is The Drug' (number 35) reaching the UK charts the second time around. Subsequent releases struggled to retain this commercial ascendancy, and Jones slipped from view during the 90s. Although Chris Blackwell of Island Records had faith in her as a musical artist the public always saw her as a personality. Her striking looks, outspoken nature and media coverage buried her musical aspirations and talent.

● ALBUMS: *Portfolio* (Island 1977) ★★, *Fame* (Island 1978) ★★, *Muse* (Island 1979) ★★, *Warm Leatherette* (Island 1980) ★★★, *Nightclubbing* (Island 1981) ★★★, *Living My Life* (Island 1982) ★★★, *Slave To The Rhythm* (ZTT 1985) ★★★, *Inside Story* (Manhattan 1986) ★★, *Bullet Proof Heart* (Capitol 1990) ★★.
● COMPILATIONS: *Island Life* (Island 1985) ★★★, *Private Life: The Compass Point Sessions* 2-CD set (Island 1998) ★★★, *Best Of Grace Jones: Island Life 2* (Universal 2002) ★★.
● FURTHER READING: *Grace Jones: Ragged But Right*, Dolly Carlisle.
● FILMS: *Gordon's War* (1973), *Attention Les Yeux* aka *Let's Make A Dirty Movie* (1975), *Armee Der Liebenden Oder Revolte Der Perversen* (1979), *Deadly Vengeance* (1981), *Conan The Destroyer* (1984), *A View To A Kill* (1985), *Mode En France* (1985), *Vamp* (1986), *Straight To Hell* (1987), *Siesta* (1987), *Boomerang* (1992), *Cyber Bandits* (1995), *McCinsey's Island* (1998), *Palmer's Pick Up* (1999).

## JONES, HOWARD

b. John Howard Jones, 23 February 1955, Southampton, Hampshire, England. Coming to prominence as a synthesizer-pop maestro in the mid-80s, Jones had been trying to succeed as a musician for almost 15 years. His childhood saw him on the move from country to country but by the time he reached his teens he was settled in High Wycombe, England. He joined his first band in 1976 and over the next few years played in Warrior, the Bicycle Thieves, and Skin Tight. In 1974 he went to music college in Manchester and after graduation he began performing solo in his home town. He soon introduced dancer Jed Hoile to enliven his act by improvizing dance to his songs. Jones was offered a session by BBC disc jockey John Peel which led to tours with OMD and China Crisis. WEA Records signed him in the summer of 1983 and in September he charted in the UK Top 5 with his first single 'New Song'. He won several Best New Artist awards and followed-up with transatlantic hits like 'What Is Love?' (UK number 2), 'Hide And Seek', 'Pearl In The Shell', 'Like To Get To Know You Well' (UK number 4), 'Things Can Only Get Better' (US number 5), 'Look Mama', 'Life In One Day', 'No One Is To Blame' (US number 4) and 'You Know I Love You ... Don't You?'. His debut album *Human's Lib* topped the UK charts. Although he performed most of the music on his recordings in 1985 he formed a touring band with his brother Martin on bass, and Trevor Morais on drums.

As the 80s drew to a close, Jones singles success grew more sporadic, although 'Everlasting Love' reached the US Top 20 in 1989, and 'The Prisoner' and 'Lift Me Up' also reached the American charts. Jones even joined the unplugged trend with *Live Acoustic America* in 1996. He continues to record sporadically, although *Angels & Lovers* only gained a release in Japan. A revamped version of the album, featuring three new tracks, was released in other countries as *People*. Jones continues to play to a devoted following in mainland Europe, and in 2000 signed a new recording contract with Germany's Seven Days Music label.

● ALBUMS: *Human's Lib* (WEA/Elektra 1984) ★★★★, *Dream Into Action* (WEA/Elektra 1985) ★★★, *One To One* (WEA/Elektra 1986) ★★, *Cross That Line* (WEA/Elektra 1989) ★★★, *In The Running* (WEA/Elektra 1992) ★★★, *Working In The Backroom* (Dtox 1993) ★★★, *Live Acoustic America* (Plump 1996) ★★★, *Angels & Lovers* (Pony Canyon 1997) ★★, *People* (Dtox/Ark 21 1998) ★★, *Perform.OO* aka *Metamorphosis* (Seven Days Music/Avex 2000) ★★★, *Pefawm* (Dtox 2000) ★★, *The Peaceful Tour Live* (Dtox/Cleopatra 2002) ★★.

● COMPILATIONS: *The 12 Album* (WEA/Elektra 1984) ★★, *The Best Of Howard Jones* (WEA/Elektra 1993) ★★★★, *What Is Love?* (Pickwick 1993) ★★★, *The Essentials* (Rhino 2002) ★★★★, *Greatest Hits* (Masters 2002) ★★★.

## JONES, STEVE

b. 3 September 1955, London, England. Formerly the provider of the guitar behind Johnny Rotten's sneer in the Sex Pistols, Jones' basic but powerful style was then employed as part of the underachieving Professionals (with former Sex Pistol member Paul Cook). Prior to that he had worked with the Avengers in the USA. He later played a substantial role in the creation of two records: Iggy Pop's *Blah Blah Blah* (1986) and ex-Duran Duran member Andy Taylor's *Thunder* (1987). His first solo venture, however, was a lacklustre affair, with Jones' rough Cockney voice spread thinly over a set that mingled rock numbers with, to the horror of old punks, ballads. The worst offender in this category was the comical version of 'Love Letters'. A capable, fluent man with a rhythm guitar, given a microphone Jones came across as forced and inarticulate, a situation not helped by the clumsy moralism of tracks such as 'Drugs Suck'. Undeterred, Jones proceeded to make the same mistakes a second time with *Fire And Gasoline*. Co-produced and co-written with Ian Astbury of the Cult, and with a vocal contribution from Guns N'Roses' Axl Rose on the Sex Pistols revival track 'Did You No Wrong', it offered further evidence of Jones' decline. Billy Duffy of the Cult even managed to outgun the old stager with his solo on 'Get Ready'. Collectively, the albums offer a sad footnote to the career of one of rock and pop's most influential guitarists. Jones has since worked as part of the Neurotic Outsiders, alongside John Taylor (ex-Duran Duran) and Duff McKagan and Matt Sorum of Guns N'Roses, with the band releasing a self-titled album for Madonna's Maverick label in 1996. He has also played with the Sex Pistols on their occasional reunion tours, and worked with Bob Dylan, Insane Clown Posse and Buckcherry.

● ALBUMS: *Mercy* (Gold Mountain/MCA 1987) ★★, *Fire And Gasoline* (Gold Mountain/MCA 1989) ★★.

## JORDAN, STANLEY

b. 31 July 1959, Chicago, Illinois, USA. Having absorbed a certain amount of theory from an early training on the piano, Jordan taught himself the guitar while in his teens, and performed with the numerous pop and soul groups working around Chicago in the mid-70s. However, winning a prize at the 1976 Reno Jazz Festival inspired Jordan to devote some time to a serious study of music. Studying electronic music, theory, and composition at Princeton University, his reputation quickly spread and he soon found himself playing with Dizzy Gillespie and Benny Carter. In 1982 he recorded his first album: *Touch Sensitive* was a relatively uninspiring solo collection which registered poor sales. Three years later, Jordan's second album *Magic Touch* became a huge commercial success. Produced by Al Di Meola, it featured Onaje Allen Gumbs, Charnett Moffett, and Omar Hakim, while retaining some unaccompanied tracks. Since *Magic Touch*, Jordan's band has become a regular feature of the major international jazz festivals. He is commonly known for his development of a complex technique of 'hammering-on', which has enabled him to accompany himself with bass lines and chords.

● ALBUMS: *Touch Sensitive* (Tangent 1982) ★★, *Magic Touch* (Blue Note 1985) ★★★★, *Standards Volume 1* (Blue Note 1986) ★★★, *Flying Home* (EMI Manhattan 1988) ★★★, *Cornucopia* (Blue Note 1990) ★★★, *Stolen Moments* (Blue Note 1991) ★★★★, *Bolero* (Arista 1994) ★★★, *Live In New York* (Blue Note 1998) ★★.

● COMPILATIONS: *The Best Of Stanley Jordan* (Blue Note 1995) ★★★★.

● FILMS: *Blind Date* (1987).

## JOSEF K

This Edinburgh, Scotland-based band formed in the ashes of punk as TV Art and were influenced by New York bands such as Television, Talking Heads and the Velvet Underground. The original trio of Paul Haig (b. 1960, Scotland; vocals), Malcolm Ross (guitar) and Ron Torrance (drums) were joined briefly by Gary McCormack (later with the Exploited), before a more permanent bass player was found in David Weddell. After a name change inspired by Franz Kafka's 1925 novel *The Trial*, Josef K recorded a 10-track demo before committing 'Chance Meeting' to release on Steven Daly's Absolute label, in late 1979. Daly, who was also the drummer for Orange Juice, was the co-founder of Postcard Records, and thus signed Josef K to the newly formed label. 'Radio Drill Time' was more frantic than their debut, dominated by hectic, awkward chords and Haig's thin, nasal voice. After numerous support slots, 1980 ended with the more low-key, melodic sound of 'It's Kinda Funny'. The single fared well and Josef K were all set to release their debut, *Sorry For Laughing*, during the early months of 1981. However, unhappy with its production, the band scrapped it at the test pressing stage and moved to a Belgian studio, in conjunction with the Les Disques Du Crepescule label. The 1981 session yielded a re-recorded title track (also the strongest single), which joined tracks from the unreleased album as a session for BBC radio disc jockey John Peel, while the band returned to Belgium to work on their album. Back at Postcard, they drafted in Malcolm's brother Alistair to play trumpet on a new version of 'Chance Meeting', issued just two months later, coinciding with a full session for Peel. *The Only Fun In Town* emerged in July to a mixed reception. Its frantic, trebly live sound appeared hurried, and betrayed the fact that it had been recorded in just six days. Josef K announced their demise soon afterwards, prompted by Malcolm Ross' invitation to join Orange Juice. Les Disques Du Crepuscule issued Josef K's farewell single, 'The Missionary', in 1982, while other tracks surfaced on various compilations.

After Ross had joined Orange Juice, Haig worked with Rhythm Of Life before embarking on a solo career. In the late 80s, Scottish label Supreme International Editions followed the excellent 'Heaven Sent' with *Young And Stupid*, a collection of Peel session material and tracks from the unreleased *Sorry For Laughing*. Then, in 1990, the entire recorded history of Josef K (plus tracks from their original demo) was compiled on to two definitive CDs by Les Temps Moderne.

● ALBUMS: *The Only Fun In Town* (Postcard 1981) ★★★, *Crazy To Exist* (LTM 2002) ★★★.
● COMPILATIONS: *Young And Stupid* (Supreme International 1989) ★★★, *The Only Fun In Town/Sorry For Laughing* (Les Temps Moderne 1990) ★★★, *Sorry For Laughing & Rare Live* (Japan 1993) ★★★, *Endless Soul* (Marina 1998) ★★★.

## JOY DIVISION

Originally known as Warsaw, this Manchester post-punk outfit comprised Ian Curtis (b. 15 July 1956, Macclesfield, Cheshire, England, d. 18 May 1980, England; vocals), Bernard Dicken/Albrecht (b. 4 January 1956, Salford, Manchester, England; guitar, vocals), Peter Hook (b. 13 February 1956, Manchester, England; bass) and Steven Morris (b. 28 October 1957, Macclesfield, Cheshire, England; drums). Borrowing their name from the prostitution wing of a concentration camp, Joy Division emerged in 1978 as one of the most important bands of their era. After recording a regionally available EP, *An Ideal For Living*, they were signed to Manchester's recently formed Factory Records and placed in the hands of producer Martin Hannett. Their debut, *Unknown Pleasures*, was a raw, intense affair, with Curtis at his most manically arresting in the insistent 'She's Lost Control'. With its stark, black cover, the album captured a band still coming to terms with the recording process, but displaying a vision that was piercing in its clinical evocation of an unsettling disorder. With Morris' drums employed as a lead instrument, backed by the leaden but compulsive bass lines of Hook, the sound of Joy Division was distinctive and disturbing.

By the time of their single 'Transmission', the quartet had already established a strong cult following, which increased after each gig. Much of the attention centred on the charismatic Curtis, who was renowned for his neurotic choreography, resembling a demented marionette on wires. By the autumn of 1979, however, Curtis' performances were drawing attention for a more serious reason. On more than one occasion, he suffered an epileptic seizure and blackouts onstage, and the illness seemed to worsen with the band's increasingly

demanding live schedule. On 18 May 1980, the eve of Joy Division's proposed visit to America, Ian Curtis was found hanged. The verdict was suicide. A note was allegedly found bearing the words: 'At this moment I wish I were dead. I just can't cope any more.' The full impact of the tragedy was underlined shortly afterwards, for it quickly became evident that Curtis had taken his life at the peak of his creativity. While it seemed inevitable that the band's posthumously released work would receive a sympathetic reaction, few could have anticipated the quality of the material that emerged in 1980. The UK Top 20 single 'Love Will Tear Us Apart' was probably the finest of the year, a haunting account of a fragmented relationship, sung by Curtis in a voice that few realized he possessed. The attendant album, *Closer*, was faultless, displaying the band at the zenith of their powers. With spine-tingling cameos such as 'Isolation' and the extraordinary 'Twenty-Four Hours', the album eloquently articulated a sense of despair, yet simultaneously offered a therapeutic release. Instrumentally, the work showed maturity in every area and is deservedly regarded by many critics as the most brilliant rock album of the 80s. The following year, a double album, *Still*, collected the remainder of the band's material, most of it in primitive form. Within months of the Curtis tragedy, the remaining members sought a fresh start as New Order. In 1995 Curtis' widow, Deborah, published a book on her former husband and the band, while a compilation album and a re-released version of 'Love Will Tear Us Apart' were back on the shelves on the 15th anniversary of his death.

● ALBUMS: *Unknown Pleasures* (Factory 1979) ★★★★, *Closer* (Factory 1980) ★★★★★, *Still* (Factory 1981) ★★★, *Preston 28 February 1980* (Burning Airlines 1999) ★★★, *Les Bains Douches 18 December 1979* (Burning Airlines 2001) ★★.
● COMPILATIONS: *Substance 1977-1980* (Factory 1988) ★★★★, *Peel Sessions* (Strange Fruit 1990) ★★★, *Permanent* (London 1995) ★★★★, *Heart And Soul* 4-CD box set (London 1997) ★★★, *The Complete BBC Recordings* (Strange Fruit 2000) ★★★.
● VIDEOS: *Here Are The Young Men* (Factory 1982).
● FURTHER READING: *An Ideal For Living: An History Of Joy Division*, Mark Johnson. *Touching From A Distance*, Deborah Curtis. *New Order & Joy Division*, Claude Flowers.

## JUDAS PRIEST

This enduring heavy metal outfit was formed in Birmingham, England, in 1969, by guitarist K.K. Downing (b. Kenneth Downing) and close friend, bass player Ian Hill. As another hopeful, struggling young rock band, they played their first gig in Essington in 1971 with a line-up completed by Alan Atkins (vocals) and John Ellis (drums). The name Judas Priest came from Atkins' previous band (who took it from a Bob Dylan song, 'The Ballad Of Frankie Lee And Judas Priest') before he joined up with Hill and Downing. Constant gigging continued, with Alan Moore taking over on drums, only to be replaced at the end of 1971 by Chris Campbell. Most of 1972 was spent on the road in the UK, and in 1973 both Atkins and Campbell departed, leaving the nucleus of Hill and Downing (in 1991 Atkins released a debut solo album that included 'Victim Of Changes', a song he co-wrote in Judas Priest's infancy). At this point, their fortunes took a turn for the better. Vocalist and ex-theatrical lighting engineer Rob Halford (b. 25 August 1951, Walsall, England) and drummer John Hinch, both from the band Hiroshima, joined the unit. More UK shows ensued as their following grew steadily, culminating in the addition of second guitarist Glenn Tipton (b. 25 October 1948; ex-Flying Hat Band).

In 1974 Judas Priest toured abroad for the first time in Germany and the Netherlands, and returned home to a record contract with the small UK label Gull. The band made their vinyl debut with *Rocka Rolla* in September 1974. Disappointed with the recording, the band failed to make any impact, and Hinch left to be replaced by the returning Alan Moore. In 1975 the band's appearance at the Reading Festival brought them to the attention of a much wider audience. *Sad Wings Of Destiny* was an improvement on the debut, with production assistance from Jeffrey Calvert and Max West. However, despite good reviews, their financial situation remained desperate, and Alan Moore left for the second and final time. A worldwide contract with CBS Records saved the day, and *Sin After Sin* was a strong collection, with Simon Philips sitting in for Moore. The band then visited America for the first time with drummer Les Binks, who appeared on *Stained Class*, an album that showed Priest at a high watermark in their powers. *Killing Machine* yielded the first UK hit single, 'Take On The World', and featured shorter, punchier, but still familiar, rock songs. The formidable *Unleashed In The East* was recorded on the 1979 Japanese tour, and in that year, Binks was replaced on drums by Dave Holland of Trapeze.

After major tours with both Kiss and AC/DC, Judas Priest's popularity began to gather momentum. *British Steel* smashed into the UK Top 5, and included the Top 20 singles 'Breaking The Law' and 'Living After Midnight'. After appearing at the 1980 Donington Festival, they began recording *Point Of Entry*. It provided the hit single 'Hot Rockin', and was followed by sell-out UK and US tours. The period surrounding *Screaming For Vengeance* was phenomenally successful for the band. The hit single 'You've Got Another Thing Comin'' was followed by a lucrative six-month US tour, with the album achieving platinum status in the USA. *Defenders Of The Faith* offered a similar potent brand of headstrong metal to *Screaming For Vengeance*. *Turbo*, however, proved slightly more commercial and was poorly received, Judas Priest's traditional metal fans reacting with indifference to innovations that included the use of synthesized guitars. *Ram It Down* saw a return to pure heavy metal by comparison, but now the band's popularity had begun to wane. Scott Travis (b. Norfolk, Virginia, USA; ex-Racer X) replaced Dave Holland for the return to form that was *Painkiller*. Although no longer universally popular, Judas Priest were still a major live attraction and remained the epitome of

heavy metal, with screaming guitars matched by screaming vocalist, and the protagonists clad in studs and black leather.

The band was taken to court in 1990 following the suicide of two fans in December 1985. Both CBS Records and Judas Priest were accused of inciting suicide through the 'backwards messages' in their recording of the Spooky Tooth classic, 'Better By You, Better Than Me'. They were found not guilty in June 1993 after a long court battle, Downing admitting: 'It will be another 10 years before I can even spell subliminal.' Soon afterwards, Halford became disheartened with the band and decided to quit. He had temporarily fronted an Ozzy Osbourne-less Black Sabbath and recorded 'Light Comes Out Of The Black' with Pantera for the *Buffy The Vampire Slayer* soundtrack, as well as working on his Fight project. He debuted his new band, the electronic rock outfit Two in 1996, and later formed the highly successful Halford.

Judas Priest returned to recording with 1997's *Jugulator*, featuring new vocalist Tim 'Ripper' Owens (b. Akron, Ohio, USA). Owens had spent several years performing in Judas Priest tribute bands, and was recruited after performing just one song at an audition in London.

● ALBUMS: *Rocka Rolla* (Gull 1974) ★★, *Sad Wings Of Destiny* (Gull 1976) ★★, *Sin After Sin* (Columbia 1977) ★★★, *Stained Class* (Columbia 1978) ★★★, *Killing Machine* (UK) *Hell Bent For Leather* (US) (Columbia 1978) ★★, *Live – Unleashed In The East* (Columbia 1979) ★★★★, *British Steel* (Columbia 1980) ★★★★, *Point Of Entry* (Columbia 1981) ★★★, *Screaming For Vengeance* (Columbia 1982) ★★★, *Defenders Of The Faith* (Columbia 1984) ★★★, *Turbo* (Columbia 1986) ★★, *Priest ... Live!* (Columbia 1987) ★★, *Ram It Down* (Columbia 1988) ★★★, *Painkiller* (Columbia 1990) ★★★, *Jugulator* (SPV 1997) ★★★, *Concert Classics* (Ranch Life 1998) ★★, *Meltdown: '98 Live* (SPV 1998) ★★, *Demolition* (SPV 2001) ★★.

● COMPILATIONS: *Best Of* (Gull 1978) ★★, *Hero Hero* (Telaeg 1987) ★★, *Collection* (Castle 1989) ★★★, *Metal Works '73–'93* (Columbia 1993) ★★★★, *Living After Midnight* (Columbia 1997) ★★★.

● VIDEOS: *Fuel Of Life* (Columbia Music Video 1986), *Judas Priest Live* (Virgin Vision 1987), *Painkiller* (Sony Music Video 1990), *Metal Works '73–'93* (Columbia Music Video 1993), *Classic Albums: British Steel* (Eagle Vision 2001), *Judas Priest Live In London* (SPV 2002).

● FURTHER READING: *Heavy Duty*, Steve Gett.

## JUDDS

Freshly divorced, Naomi Judd (b. Diana Ellen Judd, 11 January 1946, Ashland, Kentucky, USA) moved with her daughters Wynonna (b. Christina Ciminella, 30 May 1964, Ashland, Kentucky, USA) and Ashley from California back to Morrill, Kentucky, where she worked as a nurse in a local infirmary. Outside working and school hours, she and the children would sing anything from bluegrass to showbiz standards for their own amusement. However, when Wynonna nurtured aspirations to be a professional entertainer, her mother lent her encouragement, to the extent of moving the family to Nashville in 1979.

Naomi's contralto subtly underlined Wynonna's tuneful drawl. While tending a hospitalized relation of RCA Records producer Brent Maher, Naomi elicited an audition in the company's boardroom. With a hick surname and a past that read like a Judith Krantz novel, the Judds – so the executives considered – would have more than an even chance in the country market. An exploratory mini-album, which contained the show-stopping 'John Deere Tractor', proved the executives correct when, peaking at number 17, 'Had A Dream' was the harbinger of 1984's 'Mama He's Crazy', the first of many country chart-toppers for the duo. The Judds would also be accorded a historical footnote as the earliest commercial manifestation of the form's 'new tradition' – a tag that implied the maintenance of respect for C&W's elder statesmen. This was shown by the Judds' adding their voices to *Homecoming*, a 1985 collaboration by Jerry Lee Lewis, Roy Orbison, Johnny Cash and Carl Perkins (who later co-wrote Naomi and Wynonna's 1989 smash, 'Let Me Tell You About Love'). The Judds' repertoire also featured revivals of Ella Fitzgerald's 'Cow-Cow Boogie', Elvis Presley's 'Don't Be Cruel' and Lee Dorsey's 'Working In A Coal Mine'. Self-composed songs included Naomi's 1989 composition 'Change Of Heart', dedicated to her future second husband (and former Presley backing vocalist) Larry Strickland. Maher too contributed by co-penning hits such as 1984's Grammy-winning 'Why Not Me', 'Turn It Loose', 'Girls Night Out' and the title track of the Judds' second million-selling album, *Rockin' With The Rhythm Of The Rain*. The team relied mainly on songsmiths such as Jamie O'Hara ('Grandpa (Tell Me 'Bout The Good Old Days)'), Kenny O'Dell ('Mama He's Crazy'), Mickey Jupp, Graham Lyle and Troy Seals ('Maybe Your Baby's Got The Blues') and Paul Kennerley ('Have Mercy', 'Cry Myself To Sleep').

Most Judds records exhibited an acoustic bias – particularly on the sultry ballads selected for *Give A Little Love*. They also demonstrated a penchant for star guests that included the Jordanaires on 'Don't Be Cruel', Emmylou Harris on 'The Sweetest Gift' (*Heartland*), Mark Knopfler on his 'Water Of Love' (*River Of Time*) and Bonnie Raitt playing slide guitar on *Love Can Build A Bridge*. In 1988, the pair became the first female country act to found their own booking agency (Pro-Tours) but a chronic liver disorder forced Naomi to retire from the concert stage two years later. Naomi and Wynonna toured America in a series of extravagant farewell concerts, before Wynonna was free – conveniently, cynics said – to begin her long-rumoured solo career. This she did in style, with a remarkable album that touched on gospel, soul and R&B, and confirmed her as one of the most distinctive and powerful female vocalists of her generation.

In 1999, Wynonna reunited with her mother for a New Year's Eve concert in Phoenix, Arizona. The following year the duo recorded four new tracks for a bonus disc issued with Wynonna's *New Day Dawning*, and undertook a multi-city tour. The results were issued as *Reunion Live*. Often excellent but overly cloying, the album celebrated the achievements of the past rather than the possibilities

for the future.

● ALBUMS: *The Judds: Wynonna & Naomi* mini-album (Curb/RCA 1984) ★★, *Why Not Me?* (Curb/RCA 1984) ★★★, *Rockin' With The Rhythm Of The Rain* (Curb/RCA 1985) ★★★, *Give A Little Love* (Curb/RCA 1986) ★★★, *Heartland* (Curb/RCA 1987) ★★★, *Christmas Time With The Judds* (Curb/RCA 1987) ★★, *River Of Time* (Curb/RCA 1989) ★★★, *Love Can Build A Bridge* (Curb/RCA 1990) ★★★, *Reunion Live* (Curb 2000) ★★.

● COMPILATIONS: *Greatest Hits* (Curb/RCA 1988) ★★★★, *Collector's Series* (Curb/RCA 1993) ★★★, *Greatest Hits, Volume 2* (Curb/RCA 1991) ★★★, *The Judds Collection 1983-1990* 3-CD box set (RCA 1991) ★★★, *Number One Hits* (Curb 1995) ★★★, *The Essential Judds* (RCA 1995) ★★★★, *The Judds Collection* (Curb/The Hit 1996) ★★★, *Number One Hits* (Curb 2000) ★★★.

● VIDEOS: *Their Final Concert* (RCA 1992), *The Farewell Tour* (RCA 1994).

● FURTHER READING: *The Judds: Unauthorized Biography*, Bob Millard. *Love Can Build A Bridge*, Naomi Judd.

## JUNGLE BROTHERS

Rap innovators and precursors to the sound later fine-tuned by De La Soul, P.M. Dawn et al. Following on from Afrika Bambaataa, the Jungle Brothers: Mike G (b. Michael Small, Harlem, New York City, New York, USA), DJ Sammy B (b. Sammy Burwell, Harlem, New York City, New York, USA) and Afrika Baby Bambaataa (b. Nathaniel Hall, Brooklyn, New York City, New York, USA) were unafraid of cross-genre experimentation. The most famous demonstration being their version of Marvin Gaye's 'What's Going On', though their incorporation of house music on 'I'll House You' is another good example. They made their debut for Warlock/Idlers Records in October 1987, before signing to Gee Street Records. As part of the Native Tongues coalition with Queen Latifah, A Tribe Called Quest and others, they sought to enhance the living experiences of black men and women by educating them about their role in history and African culture. In many ways traditionalists, the Jungle Brothers carefully traced the lines between R&B and rap, their admiration of James Brown going beyond merely sampling his rhythms (including the basis of their name – which shares the godfather of soul's initials).

A second album was slightly less funky and more soul-based, particularly effective on cuts like 'Beyond This World'. It has been argued that the Jungle Brothers' failure to break through commercially had something to do with the fact that they were initially signed to a New York dance label, Idlers. More likely is the assertion that audiences for macho skulduggery greatly outnumbered those for which intelligent, discursive hip-hop was a worthwhile phenomenon in the late 80s. By the time of their second major label set, 1993's *J Beez Wit The Remedy*, they had unfortunately succumbed to the former. They surprisingly charted again in 1998 with the Stereo MC's' remix of 'Jungle Brother', taken from the one-dimensional *Raw Deluxe*. The big beat influence was carried over to the following year's

*VIP*, which featured creative input from Alex Gifford of the Propellerheads.

● ALBUMS: *Straight Out The Jungle* (Idlers/Warlock 1988) ★★★, *Done By The Forces Of Nature* (Warners 1989) ★★★★, *J Beez Wit The Remedy* (Warners 1993) ★★, *Raw Deluxe* (Gee Street 1997) ★★, *VIP* (Gee Street 1999) ★★★.
● COMPILATIONS: *Beyond This World: Best And Rare* (East West 2001) ★★★★.

### JUNIOR
(see Giscombe, Junior)

### JUSTIFIED ANCIENTS OF MU MU
Also known as the JAMS, this coalition saw UK mavericks Bill Drummond (b. William Butterworth, 29 April 1953, South Africa) and Jimmy Cauty (b. 1956, Devon, England) engage in some startlingly imaginative methods of undermining the prevailing pop ethos. Drummond had cut his teeth in the Liverpool scene of the early 80s and played a large part in setting up Zoo Records. By 1987, he was working with Cauty and exploiting the techniques of sampling and computers. Their liberal use of other artists' material within the framework of their own songs resulted in a court case with Abba, following which all remaining copies of the JAMS' album, *1987 (What The Fuck Is Going On?)*, were legally bound to be destroyed. However, a handful of copies escaped annihilation and ended up on sale for £1,000 each. The following year the duo switched guises to become the Timelords, enjoying a worldwide hit with 'Doctorin' The Tardis', with Gary Glitter. A manual on how to have a number 1 single was succeeded by work on their own film. By this time Drummond and Cauty were calling themselves the KLF and enjoying yet more global success with the 'Stadium House' trilogy of singles. In 1991, the JAMS moniker was reactivated for 'It's Grim Up North', a UK Top 10 single that owed several musical moments to composer William Blake. Subsequently, Drummond and Cauty promptly slipped back into KLF mode to record with country singer Tammy Wynette, before staging acts of art terrorism under the K Foundation banner.

● ALBUMS: *1987 (What The Fuck Is Going On?)* (KLF Communications 1987) ★★★, *Who Killed The JAMS?* (KLF Communications 1987) ★★★.
● COMPILATIONS: *The History Of The JAMS aka The Timelords* (TVT 1989) ★★★.

### KAJAGOOGOO
Formed in Leighton Buzzard, Hertfordshire, England, this fresh-faced quartet comprised Nick Beggs (b. 15 December 1961; vocals/bass), Steve Askew (guitar), Stuart Crawford (vocals/synthesizer) and lead singer Chris Hamill (b. 19 December 1958, Wigan, Lancashire, England), better known as the anagrammatic Limahl. Emerging at a time when the 'new pop' of Duran Duran, Adam Ant, Culture Club and Spandau Ballet was in the ascendant, Kajagoogoo was perfectly placed to reap instant chart rewards. Their debut single, 'Too Shy', had an irresistibly hummable, pop melody and reached number 1 in the UK in early 1983. Significantly, the record was co-produced by Nick Rhodes, from their 'rivals' Duran Duran. Both bands relied on a strong visual image, but Kajagoogoo lacked the depth or staying power of their mid-80s contemporaries. They enjoyed two further hits, 'Ooh To Be Ah' and 'Hang On Now', before internal friction prompted Limahl's departure for a solo career. Kajagoogoo struggled on with Beggs taking lead vocals on the hits 'Big Apple' and 'The Lion's Mouth'. By 1985, however, they were suffering from diminishing chart returns and after briefly abbreviating their name to Kaja, they broke up early the following year. Beggs subsequently joined the Christian folk band Iona and, in 1993, was hired by Phonogram Records UK as A&R manager. Askew runs his own recording studio.

● ALBUMS: *White Feathers* (EMI 1983) ★★, *Islands* (EMI 1984) ★★.
● COMPILATIONS: with Limahl *Too Shy: The Singles And More* (EMI 1993) ★★, *The Very Best Of Kajagoogoo* (EMI 1996) ★★, with Limahl *Best Of The 80's* (Disky 2000) ★★.

### KAMEN, MICHAEL
b. 15 April 1948, New York City, New York, USA. A former member of the 60s band the New York Rock 'n' Roll Ensemble, Kamen is a prolific composer, conductor, and arranger working predominantly in the world of film. After studying at the Juilliard School of Music, Kamen contributed some music to the off-beat rock Western movie *Zachariah* in 1971. Later in the 70s, he wrote the complete scores for *The Next Man*, *Between The Lines*, and *Stunts*. During the 80s he scored and co-composed the music for several movies with some of contemporary pop music's most illustrious names, such as Eric Clapton (*Lethal Weapon*, *Homeboy*, and *Lethal Weapon II*), George Harrison (*Shanghai Surprise*), David A. Stewart (*Rooftops*), and Herbie Hancock (*Action Jackson*). Subsequently, Kamen scored some of the period's most entertaining and diverting UK and US movies, which included *Venom*, *Pink Floyd – The Wall*, *Angleo*, *My Love*, *The Dead Zone*, *Brazil*

(supposedly his favourite score), *Mona Lisa*, *Riot*, *Sue And Bob, Too*, *Someone To Watch Over Me*, *Suspect*, *Die Hard* and *Die Hard II*, *Raggedy Rawney*, *Crusoe*, *For Queen And Country*, *The Adventures Of Baron Munchausen*, *Dead-Bang* (with Gary Chang), *Road House*, *Renegades*, and *Licence To Kill*, Timothy Dalton's second attempt to replace Connery and Moore as James Bond.

In the early 90s Kamen composed the music for *The Krays* and *Let Him Have It*, two movies that reflected infamous criminal incidents in the UK. His subsequent soundtrack work has included *Nothing But Trouble*, *Hudson Hawk*, *The Last Boy Scout*, *Company Business*, *Blue Ice*, *Lethal Weapon 3*, *Shining Through*, *Blue Ice*, *Splitting Heirs*, *Last Action Hero*, *The Three Musketeers*, *Circle Of Friends*, *Don Juan De Marco*, and *X-Men*. In several instances, besides scoring the films, Kamen served as musical director, music editor, and played keyboards and other instruments. In 1991, he provided the music for the smash hit Kevin Costner movie, *Robin Hood: Prince Of Thieves*, and, with lyricists Bryan Adams and Mutt Lange, composed the closing number, '(Everything I Do) I Do It For You'. Adams' recording of the song enjoyed phenomenal success, staying at the top of the UK chart for an unprecedented 16 weeks. It was nominated for an Academy Award, and Kamen received two Grammys and a special Ivor Novello Award. Three years later the trio of songwriters repeated their success with 'All For Love', which was recorded by Adams, together with Sting and Rod Stewart, and turned up at the end of *The Three Musketeers* and at the top of the UK chart. Kamen has also composed music for television films such as *Liza's Pioneer Diary*, *S*H*E*, *Shoot For The Sun*, and television mini-series such as *The Duty Men* (theme: 'Watching You' (with Sashazoe)), *Band Of Brothers*, and *Edge Of Darkness*. The theme from the latter, written with Eric Clapton, gained another Ivor Novello Award (1985). He has written a guitar concerto for Clapton, a saxophone concerto for David Sanborn, and composed several scores for the Joffrey Ballet and the La Scala Opera Company.

● ALBUMS: with David Sanborn *Concerto For Saxophone* (Warners 1990) ★★★, plus Original Soundtracks.

● COMPILATIONS: *Michael Kamen's Opus* (London 1998) ★★★.

## KANTÉ, MORY

b. 29 March 1950, Albadania, Guinea. One of the great preservers and modernizers of the traditional music of west Africa's Mandinka people, Kanté also achieved major recognition in Europe in the 80s, where from his Paris base he fused the ancient sounds of the kora (west African harp) with black American dance music.

Kanté was born into a family of famous griots (musician-historians who combine entertainment with tribal history and lore), and at the age of 15, he was sent to Bamako, Mali to stay with his aunt and learn both the kora technique and the detailed tribal history that he would need if he was to become a professional griot. In 1971 he joined the Rail Band, then Mali's leading group, who for years were resident at the city's Station Hotel, where they entertained both the residents of Bamako and travellers who had completed the long train journey from Dakar in Senegal. During his seven years as guitarist and balafonist with the band, he recorded the celebrated album *L'Exil De Soundjata*, *Le Fondateur De L'Empire Mandingue*, an epic history of the reign of the Malian king and empire builder, Soundjata. As the second singer, he was widely perceived to be chief rival of Salif Keita during his time in the Rail Band, and this led directly to Keita's decision to join the Ambassadors.

In 1977, now proficient on the cora (a large harp/lute) and anxious to broaden his musical horizons, and expand his audience, Kanté left Bamako for the more prosperous and populous city of Abidjan in neighbouring Cote D'Ivoire, where he formed a 35-piece band, Les Milieus Branches, and began introducing elements of black American dance music into his arrangements. He was assisted in these early experiments by the producer Abdouaye Soumare, who had briefly worked with Stevie Wonder in the USA. With Soumare, Kanté recorded the album *Courougnégné*, a blueprint for his and other Mandinka musicians' cross-cultural fusions later in the decade. The album was a huge success in Mali, Senegal and Cote D'Ivoire, and also amongst the West African expatriate community in Paris. Encouraged by the French sales, Kanté moved to Paris with a slimmed-down version of Les Milieus Branches, and continued the stylistic innovations set out on *Courougnégné*. In 1984, he released the superb *À Paris*, which spread his name beyond France and Francophone West Africa to the UK and USA. In 1985, he collaborated with other African musicians on the Tam Tam Pour L'Ethiopie project (a pan-African fund-raising effort for Ethiopia, based on the Band Aid principle).

Kanté's biggest success to date came in 1988, when his single, 'Ye Ke Ye Ke', an inspired fusion of Mandinka kora and black American house music, enjoyed major chart success throughout Europe and West Africa. In 1990, the similarly inspired and sublime album *Touma* further developed this direction, including input from South African guitarist, and Paul Simon collaborator, Ray Chipika Phiri, plus Carlos Santana. The following year he presented his Symphony of Guinea with 130 griot musicians for the inaugural ceremony of the Grande Arche de la Défence in Paris. He also set about creating Nongo Village, a musical township for the promotion of Mande culture, in the Conakry region of his homeland. In 2000 a remixed version of 'Ye Ke Ye Ke' was featured in *The Beach*, and the following year Kanté duetted with UK singer Shola Ama on his new studio recording, *Tamala (Le Voyageur)*.

● ALBUMS: *Mory Kanté & Rail Band* (Syllart 1977) ★★, *Courougnégné* (Ebony/Barclay 1981) ★★★, *N'Diarabi* (Balani/Mélodie 1982) ★★★, *À Paris* (Aboudou Lassissi/Barclay 1984) ★★★★, *10 Cola Nuts* (Barclay 1986) ★★★, *Akwaba Beach* (Barclay 1988) ★★★★, *Touma* (Barclay 1990) ★★★★, *Nongo Village* (Barclay 1994) ★★★, *Tatebola* (Mory Kanté/Misslin 1996) ★★★, *Tamala (Le Voyageur)* (Sono/Next 2001) ★★★.

## KARN, MICK

b. Anthony Michaelides, 24 July 1958, London, England. Formerly the bass player with early '80s UK art-pop band Japan, Karn released his debut solo album after that band's dissolution in 1982. Featuring several session musicians in addition to Karn on vocals, bass, keyboards and synthesizers, it reached number 74 in the UK charts. In June 1983 he joined Ultravox's Midge Ure for a one-off single, 'After A Fashion', which reached number 39 in the UK charts. In the following year he formed Dali's Car with former Bauhaus singer Pete Murphy and Paul Vincent Lawford, before resuming his solo career in 1986. 'Buoy' was credited to Mick Karn featuring David Sylvian (his former Japan colleague), and preceded the release of his second album, *Dreams Of Reason Produce Monsters*. Afterwards Karn concentrated on session work, his long list of clients including Kate Bush and Joan Armatrading, and his 'secondary' career as a sculptor. His work has been exhibited in galleries in London, as well as Tokyo, Osaka and Sapporo in Japan and Turin in Italy. A long-delayed third collection, 1993's *Bestial Cluster*, was followed the next year by *Beginning To Melt*, which paired him with two former Japan members, Steve Jansen and Richard Barbieri, in addition to respected guitarist David Torn, to whose solo work Karn had previously contributed. Karn reunited with Barbieri and Jansen as JBK on 1999's _ism.

● ALBUMS: *Titles* (Virgin 1982) ★★★, *Dreams Of Reason Produce Monsters* (Virgin 1987) ★★★, *Bestial Cluster* (CMP 1993) ★★★, with Richard Barbieri, Steve Jansen *Beginning To Melt* (Medium Productions 1994) ★★★, with Terry Bozzio, David Torn *Polytown* (CMP 1994) ★★★, *Tooth Mother* (CMP 1995) ★★★, *Each Eye A Path* (Medium 2001) ★★★.

## KATRINA AND THE WAVES

This UK pop band enjoyed a major transatlantic hit with 'Walking On Sunshine' in 1985, but were also well-known for their original version of 'Going Down To Liverpool', which was successfully covered by the Bangles. The band consisted of Katrina Leskanich (b. Topeka, Kansas, USA; vocals), Kimberley Rew (guitar), Vince De La Cruz (b. Texas, USA; bass) and Alex Cooper (drums). Leskanich and De La Cruz are Americans, but came to Britain during 1976 when their military fathers served in the UK. Based at Feltwell, Norfolk, the sight of the air force base, Rew and Cooper were both graduates of Cambridge University. Rew was formerly in the Soft Boys and after leaving them released the solo *The Bible Of Bop*, in 1982. Many of the songs he wrote for his solo career were carried over into Katrina And The Waves, where he became the chief songwriter. The band was formed in 1982 but their first two albums were only released in Canada. They followed up 'Walking On Sunshine' with 'Sun Street', which was their last UK hit, although they remained a popular act on the college circuit for some time thereafter and 'That's The Way' reached the US Top 20 in 1989. By the 90s, their albums were only being released in Germany and it appeared that the band's future was in serious doubt. Although it caused some surprise Katrina And The Waves were nominated by the

British public as the UK entry for the 1997 Eurovision Song Contest. The mantric chorus of 'Love Shine A Light' appealed to the judges and it became the clear winner; obligatory chart success followed, with the single reaching UK number 3. Leskanich left the band in 1999 to work as a presenter on BBC Radio 2, but continued to record as a solo artist. Rew recorded the solo *Tunnel Into Summer* before rejoining the Soft Boys in 2001.

● ALBUMS: *Walking On Sunshine* (Attic 1983) ★★★, *Katrina And The Waves 2* (Attic 1984) ★★★, *Katrina And The Waves* (Capitol 1985) ★★★, *Waves* (Capitol 1986) ★★, *Break Of Hearts* (SBK 1989) ★★, *Pet The Tiger* (Virgin 1991) ★★, *Edge Of The Land* (Polydor Germany 1993) ★★★, *Turn Around* (Polydor Germany 1994) ★★★, *Walk On Water* (Eternal 1997) ★★.

● COMPILATIONS: *Roses* (Polydor Canada 1995) ★★★, *Anthology* (One Way 1995) ★★★, *Walking On Sunshine: The Greatest Hits* (EMI 1999) ★★★★.

## KBC BAND

The potential of three ex-Jefferson Airplane colleagues playing together once again was enormous. With petty arguing and ego problems behind them the KBC Band announced an album to the world in 1987. Marty Balin (b. Martyn Jerel Buchwald, 30 January 1942, Cincinnati, Ohio, USA; vocals), Jack Casady (b. 13 April 1944, Washington DC, USA; bass) and Paul Kantner (b. 17 March 1941, San Francisco, California, USA; guitar/vocals) released a self-titled album that sounded jaded on release. Somehow, lyrically addressing political themes such as Lebanon and Nicaragua did not work (in 'America') and Marty Balin's old epic ballad's paled against the new ('Mariel'). The addition of Keith Crossan (saxophone, guitar, vocals), Tim Gorman (guitar/vocals), Darrell Verdusco (drums) and Mark 'Slick' Aguilar (lead guitar/vocals) gave the unit a full AOR sound. The album probably charted in the USA on the strength of their names (number 75) and even produced a minor hit single with 'It's Not You, It's Not Me' (number 89). The unit disbanded shortly afterwards.

● ALBUMS: *KBC Band* (Arista 1987) ★★.

## KELLY FAMILY

The phenomenal popularity of Irish Americans the Kelly Family, a group of siblings specialising in simple folk, pop and rock tunes, has occurred swiftly but their appeal should not be underestimated: they have achieved platinum status in Germany, Switzerland and Austria, where their concert appearances regularly draw crowds of 20,000 plus. The family father and mentor is Dan Kelly (b. Daniel Jerome Kelly, USA, d. 5 August 2002, Berlin, Germany), who left America in 1966 with his wife Barbara Ann and four children, Danny, Caroline, Paul and Kathy, to settle in southern Spain. Kelly, who worked as an antiques dealer in Toledo, gave up his profession in 1972 to begin singing with his children, who by this point were already well known for their appearances at local fiestas. This first version of the Kelly Family specialised in traditional folk singing, and in 1975 the group made their

Spanish television debut under the name of the Kelly Kids. They toured Europe as street musicians, and owing to their burgeoning popularity signed a recording contract with Polydor Records. 'Who'll Come With Me (David's Song)' reached number 1 in Holland and Belgium in 1980, but the group found it difficult to progress beyond cult status in the video dominated era of the early 80s.

Barbara Ann died of breast cancer in 1981, but the family persevered and formed their own label, Kel-Life Records. Their own publishing company, Kel-Fam, was also established, which now licenses their recordings to various companies worldwide. The Kellys then returned to street busking in Paris, France, then the USA and Germany, building an audience through their dedicated, high-energy performances. The ranks were systematically swelled by younger members of the family, with each member invited to interchange instruments to keep the act fresh (a tradition maintained to this day in their spectacular stage show). Dan Kelly suffered a debilitating stroke in 1990, leaving his children to go out on tour on their own. He had recovered enough by 1994 to appear with the group on stage in Dortmund. By this point the Kelly Family were no longer just street musicians but a phenomenally successful business. *Over The Hump* sold over 4.5 million copies in Europe alone, while their own television special attracted millions of viewers. By the late 90s, the family was dividing their time between a house in southern Ireland and the palatial Schloss Gymnich in Germany.

The line-up of the Kelly Family in the new millennium comprises Patricia (b. Maria Patricia Kelly, 25 November 1969, Gamonal, Spain), Jimmy (b. Victor James Kelly, 18 February 1971, Gamonal, Spain), Paddy (b. Michael Patrick Kelly, 5 December 1977, Dublin, Eire), Maite (b. 4 December 1979, Berlin, Germany), Angelo (b. 23 December 1981, Pamplona, Spain) and Joey (b. Joseph Maria Kelly, 20 December 1972, Gamonal, Spain). The latter is the main subject of idol worship by the group's fans, and is also a noted endurance athlete. His description of the Kelly's sound: 'Clean, honest rock, and good enough to be on stage with anyone from Metallica to the Rolling Stones' goes some way to justifying their international status, though it is hard to equate a group who are regularly showered in cuddly toys while on stage with either of those bands. The patriarch Daniel Kelly died in August 2001 in Berlin after a long illness.

● ALBUMS: *The Kelly Family* (Polydor 1979) ★★★, *Lieder Der Welt* (Polydor 1979) ★★★, *Ein Vogel Kann Im Käfig Nicht Fliegen* (Polydor 1980) ★★, *Christmas All Year* (Polydor 1981) ★★, *Wonderful World!* (Polydor 1981) ★★, *Live* (Kel-Life 1988) ★★, *Keep On Singing* (Kel-Life 1989) ★★★, *New World* (Kel-Life 1990) ★★★, *Honest Workers* (Kel-Life 1991) ★★★, *Street Life* (Kel-Life 1992) ★★, *Wow* (Kel-Life 1993) ★★★, *Christmas For All* (Kel-Life 1993) ★★, *Over The Hump* (Kel-Life 1994) ★★★, *Almost Heaven* (Kel-Life 1996) ★★, *Growin' Up* (Kel-Life 1997) ★★, *From Their Hearts* (Kel-Life 1998) ★★, *Live Live Live* (Kel-Life 1998) ★★, *La Patata* (Kel-Life 2002) ★★★.

● COMPILATIONS: *The Very Best: Over 10 Years* (Kel-Life 1993) ★★★, *The Bonus Tracks Album* (Kel-Life 1999) ★★, *Best Of The Kelly Family* (Kel-Life 1999) ★★★, *Best Of The Kelly Family 2* (Kel-Life 1999) ★★★.

● VIDEOS: *A Long Time Ago With Mom* (Kel-Life 1981), *Searching For The Magic Golden Harp* (Kel-Life 1981), *Christmas All Year* (Kel-Life 1982), *Live* (Kel-Life 1988), *Street Life* (Kel-Life 1992), *Tough Road Volume One* (Kel-Life 1994), *Tough Road Volume Two* (Kel-Life 1994), *Backstage: Tough Road Volume Three* (Kel-Life 1995), *Live At Loreley* (Kel-Life 1995), *Over The Hump* (Kel-Life 1996), *Live In East Germany* (Kel-Life 1996), *Crossroads 1* (Kel-Life 1996), *Almost Heaven* (Kel-Life 1997), *Stadium Tour* (Kel-Life 1997), *Growin' Up: The Concert In East Europe Volume One* (Kel-Life 1998), *Growin' Up: The Concert In East Europe Volume Two* (Kel-Life 1998), *Making The Videos Volume One* (Kel-Life 1998), *Making The Videos Volume Two* (Kel-Life 1999), *Best Of The Kelly Family Volume One* (Kel-Life 1999), *Best Of The Kelly Family Volume Two* (Kel-Life 2000).

## KERSHAW, NIK

b. Nicolas David Kershaw, 1 March 1958, Bristol, Somerset, England. Diminutive singer-songwriter Kershaw shone brightly for a couple of years in the mid-80s UK charts before taking a more behind the scenes role in later decades.

Son of a flautist father and opera singing mother, Kershaw's first foray into the arts was as a 13-year-old student actor planning to go into repertory when he finished training. However, around 1974 he learned guitar and played Deep Purple cover versions in a school band called Half Pint Hogg (the name doubtless related to Kershaw's stature). Leaving school in 1976, he started work at the Department of Employment (and later the Co-op) but spent his evenings performing in the jazz-funk outfit Fusion. Fellow members were Reg Webb (keyboards), Ken Elson (bass), and Alan Clarke (drums). Signed to Plastic Fantastic Records and later to Telephone Records, they released one single and an album respectively. The album, *'Til I Hear From You*, contained an early version of the track 'Human Racing', which Kershaw later re-recorded. When Fusion folded, Kershaw linked with Nine Below Zero's manager Micky Modern, who helped him sign to MCA Records. The UK chart hits started to come in 1983 when his debut – 'I Won't Let The Sun Go Down On Me' – reached a modest number 47. However, early the next year the follow-up 'Wouldn't It Be Good' reached the Top 5. This perfect pop song justifiably gave Kershaw a high profile. That summer a reissue of his debut gave him his biggest success (number 2) and for the next 12 months a succession of his pleasant, simple tunes paraded through the upper reaches of the UK chart. Kershaw was backed by the Krew whose nucleus was Dennis Smith, Keiffer Airey (brother of Don Airey), Tim Moore, Mark Price and Kershaw's wife, Sheri. The first two albums featured guest appearances from Don Snow (ex-Squeeze) and Mark King of Level 42. In 1985, Elton John – a big Kershaw fan – asked him to play guitar on his single 'Nikita'.

Although the first two albums had been successes,

the third (*Radio Musicola*) proved a relative failure, and despite regular comebacks Kershaw's performing career declined. In the 90s, Kershaw returned as a songwriter of note behind other acts, notably Chesney Hawkes' massive hit 'The One And Only'. After a long absence, Kershaw returned to recording in 1998. He delighted his fans with *15 Minutes*, an assured collection of songs with all the right hooks (notably the excellent 'Somebody Loves You' and 'Your Brave Face'). The critics were less enamoured, and the album was unfairly dismissed. Similarly, the follow-up *To Be Frank* contained some very good songs, clever lyrics and at least one great chord change per song. Kershaw remains a quality songwriter, but appears unable to find a new audience to appreciate his art.

● ALBUMS: *Human Racing* (MCA 1984) ★★★, *The Riddle* (MCA 1984) ★★★, *Radio Musicola* (MCA 1986) ★★, *The Works* (MCA 1990) ★★, *15 Minutes* (Eagle 1999) ★★★★, *To Be Frank* (Eagle 2001) ★★★★.
● COMPILATIONS: *The Collection* (MCA 1991) ★★★★, *The Essential* (Spectrum 2000) ★★★★.
● FURTHER READING: *Spilling The Beans On ... Making It In Music*, Nik Kershaw.

## KEVORKIAN, FRANÇOIS

b. 10 January 1954, Rodez, France. Kevorkian is one of the original school of influential DJ-producers such as Walter Gibbons, Jellybean and Larry Levan that emerged from New York during disco's heyday in the mid-70s. He has since gone on to produce and remix a range of diverse artists including the Smiths, Adam Ant, Kraftwerk, Pet Shop Boys, Jean-Michel Jarre, Depeche Mode, Yazoo, Cure, Cult, Erasure, Ashford And Simpson, Diana Ross, Can, the Eurythmics, Gloria Estefan and U2 among many others.

Kevorkian drummed with various bands while studying biochemical engineering for a year at Lyon before being expelled, and then pharmacy at Strasbourg at the insistence of his parents. Kevorkian began DJing at a local bar in Strasbourg where the owner preferred him to play ambient, background music rather than music for dancing – with no mixer, Kevorkian would simply play one record after another. He relocated to New York City in September 1975 to pursue a career as a drummer. Falling on hard times during the winter, Kevorkian took a part-time job at the club, Galaxy 21, where he was hired to play 'fill in' drums to accompany the DJ. The DJ at the club was the legendary Walter Gibbons, who was not pleased to have to compete with a percussionist. Gibbons would play increasingly fast records and tracks with drum solos to try to outdo Kevorkian. Fortunately, Kevorkian knew the solos and was able to keep up. This experience proved something of an education for him: as he played drums with the records, he was also learning about what Gibbons was doing with them. When the club eventually closed, Kevorkian moved to work at Experiment Four, where the resident DJ was Jellybean. The two quickly became friends and Jellybean allowed Kevorkian to use his four-track reel-to-reel tape recorder to cut and splice tracks in a very primitive way (using scissors and sticky tape) to make medleys of popular tracks at the time, extending their drum breaks and repeating certain sections. His reworking of 'Happy Song And Dance' by Rare Earth became a New York club favourite. Kevorkian's technique was imitated by several others in the following years – notably the house pioneer, Frankie Knuckles.

Kevorkian subsequently secured a regular spot at the club New York, New York in 1977, where he met and befriended Larry Levan. Shortly after this, Kevorkian took an A&R job at the seminal disco label, Prelude, and began working with Levan at the label's studios. He also worked on remixes for the labels West End and Salsoul. Kevorkian's mix of 'Push Push (In The Bush)' by Musique achieved gold sales status and he also produced dancefloor successes such as 'You're The One For Me', 'Music, Part 1' and 'Keep On' for another Prelude band, D-Train. Kevorkian's other productions that have become club classics include 'I Hear Music In The Streets' by Musique, 'Body Music' by the Strikers, 'Gonna Get Over You' by France Joli, and Sharon Redd's 'You Got My Love' and 'Beat The Street'. The explosion in 'dance versions' and remixes coupled with the increasing popularity of the 12-inch single during the 80s led to Kevorkian's 'magic touch' being sought by many popular artists wanting to make their music more accessible to a club audience. He set up his own label in 1987, Wave, and opened his own recording studios, Axis in 1995. In 1990, Kevorkian briefly returned to DJing for several sell-out performances with Larry Levan in Japan. In 1997, he released *FK EP* and *Hypnodelic* on his Wave label. In the same year, he also mixed the compilations *Prelude: The Sound Of New York* and *The Best Of Wave, Volume 1*. Kevorkian remains an in-demand producer and remixer and is cited by many of today's 'superstar DJs' as an important inspiration.

● ALBUMS: *FK EP* (Wave 1997) ★★★★, *Hypnodelic* (Wave 1997) ★★★★.
● COMPILATIONS: *The Best Of Wave, Volume 1* (Wave 1997) ★★★★, *Essential Mix* (ffrr 2000) ★★★★.
● FURTHER READING: *Love Saves The Day*, Tim Lawrence.

## KHAN, CHAKA

b. Yvette Marie Stevens, 23 March 1953, Great Lakes Naval Training Station, Illinois, USA. Having sung with several Chicago club bands, including Lyfe, Lock And Chains and Baby Huey And The Babysitters, Chaka Khan became acquainted with Ask Rufus, a group formed from the remnants of hit group the American Breed. When Khan replaced original singer Paulette McWilliams, the line-up truncated its name to Rufus and as such released a succession of superior funk singles. Khan's stylish voice was the group's obvious attraction and in 1978 she began recording as a solo act. 'I'm Every Woman' topped the US R&B chart that year while subsequent releases, 'What Cha' Gonna Do For Me' (1981) and 'Got To Be There' (1982), consolidated this position. However, a 1984 release, 'I Feel For You', established the singer as an international act when it reached number 3 in the USA and number 1 in the UK pop charts. This exceptional performance was written by

Prince and featured contributions from Stevie Wonder and Melle Mel. It led to a platinum-selling album and won Khan a Grammy for Best R&B Female Performance. Khan continued to forge a successful career, working with David Bowie and Robert Palmer, and duetting with Steve Winwood on his international smash, 'Higher Love'. In 1985 she enjoyed two Top 20 UK chart entries with 'This Is My Night' and 'Eye To Eye', while four years later a remix of 'I'm Every Woman' reached the Top 10 in the UK. She collaborated with Gladys Knight, Brandy and Tamia on the minor hit single 'Missing You' in 1996, taken from the Queen Latifah movie Set It Off. She formed her own label Earth Song, in 1998, debuting with the Prince-produced Come 2 My House.

● ALBUMS: Chaka (Warners 1978) ★★★, Naughty (Warners 1980) ★★★, What Cha' Gonna Do For Me (Warners 1981) ★★★, Echoes Of An Era (Elektra 1982) ★★★, Chaka Khan (Warners 1982) ★★★, I Feel For You (Warners 1984) ★★★, Destiny (Warners 1986) ★★, CK (Warners 1988) ★★★, Life Is A Dance – The Remix Project (Warners 1989) ★★, The Woman I Am (Warners 1992) ★★★, Come 2 My House (Earth Song/NPG 1998) ★★★.

● COMPILATIONS: Epiphany: The Best Of Chaka Khan Volume 1 (Reprise 1996) ★★★★, I'm Every Woman: The Best Of (Warners 1999) ★★★.

● VIDEOS: The Jazz Channel Presents Chaka Khan (Image Entertainment 2001).

## KID CREOLE AND THE COCONUTS

b. Thomas August Darnell Browder, 12 August 1950, Montreal, Quebec, Canada. A relatively exciting entry into the UK charts at the height of new romanticism in the early 80s, Kid Creole And The Coconuts introduced many to the dynamic pulse of Latin pop. Darnell, who was raised in the Bronx, New York City, originally formed Dr. Buzzard's Original Savannah Band in the 70s with his brother Stony Browder Jnr. They would go on to create the Coconuts with the aid of 'Sugar Coated' Andy Hernandez (aka Coati Mundi), plus several multi-instrumentalists and a singing/dancing troupe led by his wife Adriana Kaegi. The group's fusion of salsa with disco pop was conducted with immense flair on their 1980 debut, Off The Coast Of Me. The follow-up album introduced a concept also pursued by three subsequent collections – namely a search by Kid and the Coconuts for Mimi, with nods to the various geographical stop-off points on the journey. The theme was not laboured, however, and proved entirely secondary to the bristling musical energy and zest beneath the surface. The Coconuts then hit a rich commercial vein with Tropical Gangsters (known as Wise Guy outside the UK). Three Top 10 chart placings followed for the album's singles; 'I'm A Wonderful Thing, Baby', 'Stool Pigeon' and 'Annie, I'm Not Your Daddy', the latter missing the top spot by just one place.

Their live shows at this time were among the most propulsive and enchanting of the period, with outlandish dancing and cod theatricals garnishing the Latin beats. Afterwards the band's commercial profile declined, but there was no similar qualitative

discount. Doppelganger returned to the grand theme as its premise – this time the cloning of Kid Creole by evil scientist King Nignat. Again such considerations proved secondary to the gripping music, particularly effective on 'The Lifeboat Party', which crept inside the UK Top 50. Elsewhere the selections spanned reggae, soul, scat jazz, and funk, all flavoured by the familiar salsa rumble. The Coconuts also released an album of their own at this time, based on the dynamics of their powerful stage revue, while Hernandez released a solo album under his assumed title Coati Mundi. Kid Creole had become King Creole by the advent of In Praise Of Older Women, but this was another full-bodied work, and certainly far superior to 1987's I, Too, Have Seen The Woods. This introduced female vocalist Haitia Fuller on shared lead vocals, but the more laboured material made it a disappointing chapter. More promising was Private Waters In The Great Divide, a return to form with inspired lyrics and buckets of the type of sexual innuendo that Creole has made his own. Subsequent albums have been released in the Japanese and European markets, although the unit remains a popular live act. In 1999, Kid Creole appeared in the West End production of Oh! What A Night.

● ALBUMS: Off The Coast Of Me (Ze 1980) ★★★, Fresh Fruit In Foreign Places (Ze 1981) ★★★, Tropical Gangsters aka Wise Guy (Ze 1982) ★★★, Doppelganger (Ze 1983) ★★★, In Praise Of Older Women And Other Crimes (Sire 1985) ★★★, I, Too, Have Seen The Woods (Sire 1987) ★★, Private Waters In The Great Divide (Columbia 1990) ★★, You Shoulda Told Me You Were ... (Columbia 1991) ★★, To Travel Sideways (Ascot/Hot 1994) ★★, Kiss Me Before The Light Changes (Victor/Hot 1994) ★★, The Conquest Of You (SPV 1997) ★★, Live (Brilliant 2000) ★★★.

● COMPILATIONS: Cre-Ole: The Best Of Kid Creole & The Coconuts (Ze 1984) ★★★★, Redux (Sire 1992) ★★★★, The Best Of Kid Creole And The Coconuts (Island 1996) ★★★★, Wonderful Thing (Spectrum 2000) ★★★.

● VIDEOS: Live: The Leisure Tour (Embassy 1986).

## KILLDOZER

Killdozer were formed in Madison, Wisconsin, USA, and the music of the area was regularly celebrated in their primal country blues. The original line-up featured Michael Gerald (bass, vocals), plus the brothers Dan (guitar) and Bill Hobson (drums). From their formation, the trio released a steady stream of albums that often highlighted their distaste at what they saw as the social and political malaise of their native country. They were just as likely to turn the spotlight on small-town weirdness, however, or their singer's rampant confusion about the state of the world. In a respite from this angst, For Ladies Only was a project dedicated to cover versions of classic songs of the 70s, including 'One Tin Soldier' and 'Good Lovin' Gone Bad'. Guitarist Paul Zagoras was recruited during the 90s in place of Bill Hobson, during which time Killdozer's formidable output was restrained somewhat due to Gerald sitting accountancy exams (he is a former mathematics teacher). However, the band bounced straight back to form with albums in 1994 and 1995, both featuring further bizarre anecdotes. Dan Hobson left in 1995 and was replaced by Erik Tunison, with second guitarist Jeff Ditzenburg also added to the line-up. The band broke up at the end of the following year with the aptly named 'Fuck You, We Quit' tour. Gerald went on to study Admiralty Law in New York.

● ALBUMS: *Intellectuals Are The Shoeshine Boys Of The Ruling Elite* (Bone Air 1984) ★★★, *Snakeboy* (Touch & Go 1985) ★★★, *Burl* mini-album (Touch & Go 1986) ★★★, *Little Baby Buntin'* (Touch & Go 1987) ★★★, *Twelve Point Buck* (Touch & Go 1988) ★★★, *For Ladies Only* (Touch & Go 1989) ★★★, *Uncompromising War On Art Under The Dictatorship Of The Proletariat* (Touch & Go 1994) ★★★, *God Hears Pleas Of The Innocent* (Touch & Go 1995) ★★★, *The Last Waltz* (Man's Ruin 1997) ★★★.

● VIDEOS: *Little Baby Buntin' Live* (Jettisoundz 1990).

## KILLING JOKE

This immensely powerful post-punk UK band combined a furious rhythm section with near-psychotic performances from Jaz Coleman (b. Jeremy Coleman, Cheltenham, England; vocals, keyboards). The band came about when Coleman, of Egyptian descent, was introduced to Paul Ferguson, then drumming for the Matt Stagger Band. Coleman joined as a keyboard player, before they both left to form their own group. This first incarnation added Geordie (b. K. Walker, Newcastle, England; guitar) and Youth (b. Martin Glover, 27 December 1960, Africa; bass), who had made his first public appearance at the Vortex in 1977 with forgotten punk band the Rage. After relocating to Notting Hill Gate they paid for a rehearsal studio and borrowed money from Coleman's girlfriend to release the *Almost Red EP*. Picked up by UK disc jockey John Peel, the band provided a session that would become the most frequently requested of the thousands he has commissioned. Via Island Records the band were able to set up their own Malicious Damage label, on which they released 'Wardance' in February 1980, notable for its remarkably savage b-side, 'Psyche'. A succession of fine, aggressive singles followed, alongside live appearances with Joy Division. They were in a strong enough position to negotiate a three-album contract with EG, which allowed them to keep the name Malicious Damage for their records. After the release of a typically harsh debut album, the band were banned from a Glasgow gig when council officials took exception to posters depicting Pope Pius giving his blessing to two columns of Hitler's Brown Shirts (a genuine photograph). It was typical of the black humour that pervaded the band, especially on their record sleeves and graphics. After the recording of the third album was completed, the band disintegrated when Coleman's fascination with the occult led him to the conclusion that the apocalypse was imminent, and he fled to Iceland. He was followed later by Youth. When Youth returned it was to begin work with Ferguson on a new project, Brilliant. However, having second thoughts, Ferguson became the third

Joker to flee to Iceland, taking bass player Paul Raven (ex-Neon Hearts) with him. Brilliant continued with Youth as the only original member. The Killing Joke output from then on lacks something of the menace that had made them so vital. However, *Night Time* combined commercial elements better than most, proffering the UK number 16 hit single 'Love Like Blood' (February 1985). While *Outside The Gate* was basically a Coleman solo album wrongly credited to the band, they returned with their best album for years with 1990's *Extremities, Dirt & Various Repressed Emotions*, which saw the drumming debut of Martin Atkins (b. 3 August 1959, Coventry, England; ex-Public Image Limited). Regardless, the band broke up once more with bitter acrimony flying across the pages of the press the same year. While his former co-conspirators pronounced Killing Joke dead, Coleman pledged to continue under the name. He did just that after a brief sojourn into classical/ethnic music via a collaborative project with Anne Dudley which resulted in *Songs From The Victorious City* released on China Records in 1991. *Pandemonium* saw Youth return to join Geordie and Coleman, with the addition of new drummer Geoff Dugmore. This saw a revitalized Killing Joke, notably on 'Exorcism', recorded in the King's Chamber of the Great Pyramid in Cairo. They were welcomed back by a wide cross-section of critics (or at least, those whom Coleman had not physically assaulted at some point) and friends. Indeed, bands claiming Killing Joke as a direct influence ranged from the Cult, Ministry and Skinny Puppy to Metallica and Soundgarden, while many noticed an uncanny similarity between the band's 'Eighties' and Nirvana's 'Come As You Are'. *Pandemonium* yielded two UK Top 40 singles, 'Millennium' and the title track, and sold in excess of 100,000 copies in the USA where they signed to Zoo Records. The next Killing Joke album, 1996's *Democracy*, took a cynical snipe at the build-up to election year in the UK.

Meanwhile, Coleman's secondary career had evolved. In addition to scoring a second symphony alongside Youth and arranging classical interpretations of the music of Pink Floyd, Led Zeppelin and the Who, he became composer in residence for the New Zealand Symphony Orchestra (the country where he spends most of his time). It led to him being hailed by conductor Klaus Tennstedt as 'the new Mahler'. In 1999, he collaborated with poet Hinewehi Mohi as Oceania, a project inspired by New Zealand's native Maori culture. Youth has become one of the UK's top dance music remixers and producers, also recording with acts as diverse as Bananarama and Crowded House.

● ALBUMS: *Killing Joke* (Malicious Damage/EG 1980) ★★★★, *what's THIS for ... !* (Malicious Damage/EG 1981) ★★★, *Revelations* (Malicious Damage/EG 1982) ★★★, *Ha! EP10* (Malicious Damage/EG 1982) ★★★, *Fire Dances* (EG 1983) ★★★★, *Night Time* (EG/Polydor 1985) ★★★, *Brighter Than A Thousand Suns* (EG/Virgin 1986) ★★★, *Outside The Gate* (EG/Virgin 1988) ★★★, *Extremities, Dirt & Various Repressed Emotions* (Noise International/RCA 1990) ★★★★, *Pandemonium* (Big

Life/Zoo 1994) ★★★, *BBC In Concert* (Strange Fruit/Windsong 1995) ★★★, *Democracy* (Zoo 1996) ★★★, *No Way Out But Forward Go* 1985 live recordings (Burning Airlines 2001) ★★★.

● COMPILATIONS: *An Incomplete Collection* (EG 1990) ★★★, *Laugh? I Nearly Bought One!* (EG/Caroline 1992) ★★★, *Wilful Days* (Blue Plate 1995) ★★★.

## KING

This Coventry, England-based act was formed in 1983 after the break-up of ska revivalists the Reluctant Stereotypes of which Paul King (vocals) was a member. The remainder of King comprised Tony Wall (bass), Mick Roberts (keyboards), James Lantsbery (guitar) and ex-Members Adrian Lillywhite (drums). They made their debut supporting the Mighty Wah! and signed to CBS Records. Despite extensive touring and a sizeable following, their first three singles and *Steps In Time* sold poorly. The break came late in 1984 when they supported Culture Club and reached a whole new teen audience. 'Love And Pride' was released early next year, and made number 2 in the UK chart, while the album went to number 6. The hits continued throughout the year, most notably with the Top 10 hit, 'Alone Without You', but King abruptly disbanded in 1986. Paul King pursued a solo career, releasing *Joy* in 1987, which at best gave him a minor UK hit with 'I Know'. The band will probably be remembered as much for their trademark spray-painted Dr. Martens boots and Paul King's affable personality than for their engaging pop songs. Paul King later became a video disc jockey for MTV.

● ALBUMS: *Steps In Time* (CBS 1984) ★★★, *Bitter Sweet* (CBS 1985) ★★.

## KING JAMMY

b. Lloyd James, Kingston, Jamaica, West Indies. Jammy, the undisputed king of computerized, digital reggae music for the 80s, was interested in little else but the sound system business from a very early age. He began by building amplifiers and repairing electrical equipment from his mother's house in the Waterhouse area of downtown Kingston, and was soon playing live with his own sound system. His prowess earned him a deserved local reputation and as Prince Jammy, he built equipment for many Waterhouse sounds. He was even acknowledged by the legendary King Tubby, another Waterhouse resident, with whom Jammy often worked.

In the early 70s Jammy left Jamaica to work in Canada, where his reputation had preceded him, and he was soon working in live stage shows, and employed in various studio activities and sound system work. He stayed for a few years but returned to Kingston and set up his first studio (with extremely limited facilities) at his in-laws' home in Waterhouse. At the same time Tubby's top engineer, Phillip Smart, left for New York and Jammy joined Tubby's team. It was during his time with Tubby that Jammy met the most influential people in reggae; he acknowledges, in particular, the inspiration provided by Bunny Lee and Yabby You. Jammy was continually expanding his own studio and sound system and in the late 70s he began to release his own productions, including the debut Black Uhuru album, coming into contact with many rising dancehall artists such as Half Pint, Junior Reid and Echo Minott.

Jammy's constant involvement with the grassroots side of the business gave him a keen sense of what was currently happening in reggae, and also allowed him to anticipate new trends. In 1985 he recorded a youth singer called Wayne Smith with a tune called 'Under Me Sleng Teng', which was to alter irrevocably the nature, and revolutionize the sound, of reggae music. The basis for 'Sleng Teng' was a Casio 'Music Box' and one of the 'rock' rhythms from the box was adapted and slowed down to become a 'reggae' rhythm. The shockwaves were scarcely believable and before long there were over 200 different versions of the rhythm available, as every producer and artist jumped on to the bandwagon. More than anything else, it opened the music to young independent producers and artists, since expensive studio time and 'real' musicians were no longer a prerequisite for recording: digital reggae ruled, and Jammy, the originator, rode the crest of the wave. His records and sound system dominated and controlled reggae music for the remainder of the decade and on into the 90s. Bobby Digital, now an established producer in his own right, was brought into Jammy's camp and he soon became the right-hand man in the set-up, with Steely And Clevie providing the rhythms. Both were established musicians with a real feeling for the new sound, and a bewildering array of 7-inch and 12-inch singles and albums were released every month. Most were massive Jamaican hits and with the help of long-time associate Count Shelly, the records were released simultaneously in New York and London while Jammy administered the business in Jamaica. Countless artists made their debut on the Jammys label, but veteran singers and vocal groups were all keen to play their part in the new sound. There was no one to rival him and in 1987, Jammy won the coveted Rockers Award for Best Producer.

Jammy's subsequent output has not been as prolific by his standards. In 1995, he revived his most innovative tune on *Sleng Teng Extravaganza '95*, featuring the modish stars updating the rhythm with their own interpretations. It is impossible to overstate his contribution to Jamaican music, because, as the top producer throughout the digital era, he has altered the sound of reggae music without ever losing touch with its foundation – the sound system.

● ALBUMS: with Dry And Heavy *In The Jaws Of The Tiger* (Green Tea 2001) ★★★.

● COMPILATIONS: various artists *Superstar Hit Parade Volumes 1-7* (Greensleeves 1984-92) ★★★★, *Ten To One* (Jammys 1985) ★★★★, *Sleng Teng Extravaganza Volumes 1 & 2* (Jammys 1986) ★★★, *A Man And His Music Volumes 1, 2 & 3* (RAS 1991) ★★★★, *Sleng Teng Extravaganza '95* (Greensleeves 1995) ★★★.

● FURTHER READING: *King Jammy's*, Beth Lesser.

## KING'S X

Initially known as the Edge and specializing in Top 40 cover versions, Doug Pinnick (bass, vocals), Ty Tabor (guitar) and Jerry Gaskill (drums) relocated to Houston, Texas, USA, in 1985, and were taken under the wing of ZZ Top video producer, Sam Taylor. Under Taylor's guidance, they concentrated on their own material and changed their name to King's X. After recording demos and being turned down by several major record companies in the USA, they finally secured a contract with the independent Megaforce label. *Out Of The Silent Planet*, with its unique sound and offbeat approach, emerged in 1988 to widespread critical acclaim. Fusing Beatles-style harmonies with hard rock and blues riffs, they encompassed a variety of genres that defied simple pigeonholing. *Gretchen Goes To Nebraska* was an even greater triumph, building on previous strengths, but adding depth in both a technical and lyrical sense. Preferring the 'positive' tag to that of Christian rockers, *Faith, Hope, Love*, released in 1990, scaled even greater heights with its state-of-the-art production and inspired compositions. The band moved to Atlantic Records in the early 90s and continued to produce acclaimed albums, including 1996's *Ear Candy*. They ended their association with Atlantic in the late 90s, moving to Metal Blade for a series of albums beginning with 1998's *Tape Head*. Pinnick also recorded as Poundhound, releasing the wonderfully titled *Massive Grooves From The Electric Church Of Psychofunkadelic Grungelism Rock Music*.

● ALBUMS: *Out Of The Silent Planet* (Megaforce 1987) ★★★, *Gretchen Goes To Nebraska* (Megaforce 1989) ★★★★, *Faith, Hope, Love* (Megaforce 1990) ★★★★, *King's X* (Atlantic 1992) ★★★★, *Dogman* (Atlantic 1994) ★★★, *Ear Candy* (Atlantic 1996) ★★★★, *Tape Head* (Metal Blade 1998) ★★★, *Please Come Home ... Mr. Bulbous* (Metal Blade 2000) ★★★, *Manic Moonlight* (Metal Blade 2001) ★★★.

● COMPILATIONS: *Best Of Kings X* (Atlantic 1998) ★★★★.

## KING, EVELYN 'CHAMPAGNE'

b 1 July 1960, the Bronx, New York City, New York, USA. A former office cleaner at Gamble And Huff's Sigma Sound studios, King was overheard singing Sam Cooke's 'A Change Is Gonna Come' by Theodore Life, a member of the company's writing and production staff. He coached the aspiring singer on recording technique and was instrumental in preparing King's career. Her debut single, 'Shame', was released in 1977 and after considerable success on the dance/club circuit – since regarded as a classic of its kind – it finally broke into the national pop charts the following year, reaching the US Top 10/UK Top 40. Evelyn's second hit, 'I Don't Know If It's Right', became the artist's second gold disc and she later enjoyed international hits with 'I'm In Love' (1981) and 'Love Come Down' (1982). After a disappointing period during the mid-80s, her 1988 set *Flirt* was generally considered to be a return to form. Although her recording career has since gone into the doldrums, King remains a popular performer on the soul/dance music scene.

● ALBUMS: *Smooth Talk* (RCA 1977) ★★★, *Music Box* (RCA 1979) ★★★, *Call On Me* (RCA 1980) ★★★, *I'm In Love* (RCA 1981) ★★★, *Get Loose* (RCA 1982) ★★★, *Face To Face* (RCA 1983) ★★, *So Romantic* (RCA 1984) ★★, *A Long Time Coming* (RCA 1985) ★★, *Flirt* (EMI 1988) ★★★, *Girl Next Door* (EMI 1989) ★★★, *I'll Keep A Light On* (Expansion 1995) ★★★.

● COMPILATIONS: *Love Come Down: The Best Of Evelyn 'Champagne' King* (RCA 1993) ★★★, *Let's Get Funky* (Camden 1997) ★★★, *Greatest Hits* (BMG 2001) ★★★.

## KITARO

b. Masanori Takahashi, 4 February 1953, Toyohashi, Japan. Soon after graduating from high school, Takahashi formed a rock band, the Far East Family Band, who released two albums and toured around the world. He was converted to synthesizer music after meeting Klaus Schulze of Tangerine Dream in 1972. The inspiration for Kitaro's new music came from visits to Asian countries including, in particular, India and the remoter reaches of his Japanese homeland. His 1978 debut, *Tenkai*, a suite for synthesizer, prompted NHK (the Japanese broadcasting company) to commission Kitaro to write a score for the lengthy television documentary, *Silk Road*. This atmospheric, meditative piece full of simple melodies and unhurried tempos earned the composer national and international recognition. As a resident of a small village in the Nagano prefecture in central Japan, Kitaro was able to pursue his work in contemplative surroundings, as reflected in his music.

For much of the 80s Kitaro's distribution outlet in the west was handled by Polydor Records and the Kuckuck (Line) labels. However, in 1986 he signed a major deal with Geffen Records confirming his status as one of the world's leading new age artists. The following year's *The Light Of The Spirit* was produced by Mickey Hart and earned a nomination for a Grammy Award. Kitaro relocated to Boulder, Colorado, USA in 1989 where he established his own Mochi House studio. In 1993, his score for Oliver Stone's *Heaven & Earth* earned a Golden Globe for the Best Original Soundtrack. In the mid-90s Kitaro signed a new recording deal with the Domo label. His releases for the label have included the seasonal *Peace On Earth*, the score for the Broadway production *Cirque Ingenieux*, and the award-winning soundtrack to *The Soong Sisters*.

● ALBUMS: *Tenkai* aka *Astral Voyage* (Victor/Polydor 1978) ★★★, *Dai-Chi* aka *Full Moon Story* or *From The Full Moon Story* (Invitation/Polydor 1979) ★★★, *Oasis* (Pony Canyon 1979) ★★★, *Silk Road 1* (Pony Canyon 1980) ★★★★, *Silk Road 2* (Pony Canyon 1980) ★★★, *Tunhuang* (Pony Canyon/Polydor 1981) ★★★, *Ki* (Canyon/Kuckuck 1981) ★★★, *Tonkó* (Polydor 1981) ★★★, *Queen Millennia* aka *Millennia* (Polydor 1982) ★★★, *Live At Budokan* (Polydor 1982) ★★, *In Person* 1980 recording (Canyon 1983) ★★, *Tenjiku* aka *India* or *Silk Road 4* (Polydor 1983) ★★★, *Silver Cloud* (Polydor 1984) ★★★, *Towards The West* (Polydor 1986) ★★★, *Tenku* (Geffen 1986) ★★★, *The Light Of The Spirit* (Geffen 1987) ★★★★, *Kojiki*

(Geffen 1990) ★★★, *Live In America* (Geffen 1991) ★★, *Dream* (Geffen 1992) ★★★, *Heaven & Earth* film soundtrack (Geffen 1993) ★★★★, *Mandala* (Domo 1994) ★★★, *An Enchanted Evening* (Domo 1995) ★★★, *Peace On Earth* (Domo 1996) ★★★, *Kitaro's World Of Music Featuring Yu-Xiao Guang* (Domo 1996) ★★★, *Cirque Ingenieux* (Domo 1997) ★★★, *The Soong Sisters* film soundtrack (Domo 1997) ★★★★, *Gaia* (Domo 1998) ★★★, *Thinking Of You* (Domo 1999) ★★★, *Ancient* (Domo 2000) ★★★, *An Ancient Journey* (Domo 2001) ★★★.

● COMPILATIONS: *Silk Road* (Kuckuck 1980) ★★★, *Best Of Kitaro* (Kuckuck 1981) ★★★★, *Ten Years* (Geffen 1988) ★★★, *Best 16 Hits* (Pony Canyon 1989) ★★★, *Super Best* (Pony Canyon 1992) ★★★, *The Best Of Kitaro* (Geffen 1993) ★★★, *Tokusen 2* (Sound Design 1994) ★★★, *The World Of Kitaro* (Domo 1996) ★★★, *The Best Of Kitaro 2* (Universal 1998) ★★★★, *Best Of Kitaro Volume 2* (Domo 1999) ★★★, *Asian Café* (BMG 2002) ★★★.

● VIDEOS: *The Light Of The Spirit* (Geffen 1987), *Live In America* (Geffen 1991), *An Enchanted Evening* (Domo 1995), *An Enchanted Evening Volume II* (Domo 1995), *Live In U.S.A.* (Pony Canyon 1995).

# KLF

Since 1987 the KLF (Kopyright Liberation Front) have operated under a series of guises, only gradually revealing their true nature to the public at large. Their principal spokesman is Bill Drummond (b. William Butterworth, 29 April 1953, South Africa), who had already enjoyed a chequered music industry career. As co-founder of the influential Zoo label in the late 70s, he introduced and later managed Echo And The Bunnymen and the Teardrop Explodes. Later he joined forces with Jimmy Cauty (b. 1956, Devon, England), an artist of various persuasions and a member of Brilliant in the mid-80s. Their first project was undertaken under the title JAMS (Justified Ancients Of Mu Mu – a title lifted from Robert Shea and Robert Anton Wilson's conspiracy novels dealing with the *Illuminati*). An early version of 'All You Need Is Love' caused little reaction compared to the provocatively titled album that followed – *1987 (What The Fuck Is Going On?)*. It liberally disposed of the works of the Beatles, Led Zeppelin *et al* with the careless abandon the duo had picked up from the heyday of punk. One of the disfigured supergroups, Abba, promptly took action to ensure the offending article was withdrawn.

In the wake of the emerging house scene the duo's next move was to compromise the theme tune to well-loved British television show *Dr Who*, adding a strong disco beat and Gary Glitter yelps to secure an instant UK number 1 with 'Doctorin' The Tardis'. Working under the title Timelords, this one-off coup was achieved with such simplicity that its originators took the step of writing a book: *How To Have A Number One The Easy Way*. After the throwaway send-up of Australian pop, 'Kylie Said To Jason', and Disco 2000's 'Uptight', the duo branched out into ambient music. Cauty, alongside Alex Paterson, played a significant part in creating arguably the leading exponents of the genre, the Orb, while as the KLF they released *Chill Out*, an ambient house

recording that is now recognised as a classic. Back in the pop charts the duo enjoyed worldwide success with their Stadium House Trilogy. The first instalment, 'What Time Is Love (Live At Transcentral)', reached the UK Top 5 in autumn 1990. The duo reached their commercial peak at the start of 1991 when the soulful house of '3 AM Eternal' topped the UK charts and broke into the US Top 5. The final instalment, 'Last Train To Transcentral', reached UK number 2 and the attendant *The White Room* was also a bestseller. Further releases followed from the myriad of names employed by the duo (JAMS – 'Down Town', 'It's Grim Up North'; Space – *Space*), but perhaps the most startling was the KLF's 'Justified And Ancient', featuring the unmistakable voice of country legend Tammy Wynette. The song revealed the KLF at the peak of their creative powers, selling millions of records worldwide while effectively taking the mickey. They were voted the Top British Group by the BPI. Instead of lapping up the acclaim, the KLF, typically, rejected the comfort of a music biz career, and deliberately imploded at the ceremony. There they performed an 'upbeat' version of '3AM Eternal', backed by breakneck-speed punk band Extreme Noise Terror, amid press speculation that they would be bathing the ceremony's assembled masses with pig's blood. They contented themselves instead with (allegedly) dumping the carcass of a dead sheep in the foyer of the hotel staging the post-ceremony party, and Drummond mock machine-gunning the assembled dignitaries. They then announced that the proud tradition of musical anarchy they had brought to a nation was at a close: the KLF were no more. Although a remix of 'America: What Time Is Love?' subsequently became another huge hit, their only new recording in 1992 came with a version of 'Whatever Will Be, Will Be (Que Sera, Sera)' (naturally renamed 'K Sera Sera', and recorded with the Soviet Army Chorale), which, they insisted, would only see the light of day on the advent of world peace.

The KLF returned to their rightful throne, that of England's foremost musical pranksters, with a stinging art terrorist racket staged under the K Foundation banner. In late 1993, a series of advertisements began to appear in the quality press concerning the Turner Prize art awards. While that body was responsible for granting £20,000 to a piece of non-mainstream art, the K Foundation (a new vehicle for Messrs Drummond and Cauty) promised double that for the worst piece of art displayed. The Turner short list was identical to that of the KLF's. More bizarre still, exactly £1,000,000 was withdrawn from the National Westminster bank (the biggest cash withdrawal in the institution's history), nailed to a board and paraded in front of a select gathering of press and art luminaries. The money was eventually returned to their bank accounts (although members of the press pocketed a substantial portion), while the £40,000 was awarded to one Rachel Whiteread, who also won the 'proper' prize. The K Foundation later cemented its notoriety by burning the aforementioned one million pounds, an event captured on home video.

Since that time, Drummond and Cauty have made several pseudonymous returns to the singles charts, including the 1996 tribute to footballer Eric Cantona, 'Ooh! Aah! Cantona', as 1300 Drums Featuring The Unjustified Ancients Of Mu, and in 1997 as 2K for the charmingly titled 'Fuck The Millennium'. Urban guerrillas specializing in highly original shock tactics, the KLF offer the prospect of a brighter decade should their various disguises continue to prosper.

● ALBUMS: *Towards The Trance* (KLF Communications 1988) ★★★★, *The What Time Is Love Story* (KLF Communications 1989) ★★★★, *The White Room* (KLF Communications/Arista 1990) ★★★, *Chill Out* (KLF Communications/Wax Trax! 1990) ★★★★.

● VIDEOS: *Stadium House* (PMI 1991).

● FURTHER READING: *Justified And Ancient: The Unfolding Story Of The KLF*, Pete Robinson. *Bad Wisdom*, Mark Manning and Bill Drummond.

## KNOPFLER, MARK

b. 12 August 1949, Glasgow, Scotland. This homely ex-teacher was Dire Straits' main asset through his skill as a composer, a tuneful if detached vocal style – and a terse, resonant fretboard dexterity admired by Eric Clapton and Chet Atkins, both of whom sought his services for studio and concert projects in the 80s. Courted also by movie directors to score incidental music, Knopfler inaugurated a parallel solo career in 1983 with David Puttnam's film *Local Hero* from which an atmospheric tie-in album sold moderately well with its single 'Going Home' (the main title theme) a minor UK hit (which was incorporated into the band's stage act). Further film work included soundtracks to *Cal*, Bill Forsyth's *Comfort And Joy* and with Dire Straits' Guy Fletcher, *The Princess Bride*. After he and the band's drummer Pick Withers played on Bob Dylan's *Slow Train Coming*, Knopfler was asked to produce the enigmatic American's *Infidels* in 1983. Further commissions included diverse acts such as Randy Newman, Willy DeVille (*Miracle*), Aztec Camera (*Knife*) and Tina Turner, for whom he composed the title track of *Private Dancer*. Knopfler was also in demand as a session guitarist, counting Steely Dan (*Gaucho*), Phil Lynott (*Solo In Soho*), Van Morrison (*Beautiful Vision*) and Bryan Ferry (*Boys And Girls*) among his clients. By no means confining such assistance to the illustrious, he was also heard on albums by Sandy McLelland And The Backline and Kate And Anna McGarrigle (*Love Over And Over*).

For much of the later 80s, Knopfler was preoccupied with domestic commitments and, in 1986, he was incapacitated by a fractured collar bone following an accident at a celebrity motor race during the Australian Grand Prix. In 1989, however, he and old friends Brendan Croker and Steve Phillips formed the Notting Hillbillies for an album and attendant tour, but neither this venture nor several nights backing Clapton during a 1990 Albert Hall season indicated an impending schism in Dire Straits' ranks. Throughout the first half of the 90s Knopfler sessioned on countless albums and, with Dire Straits finally winding down, it was only in 1996 that his 'official' solo career was announced. The debut *Golden Heart* featured support from slide blues guitarist Sonny Landreth, singer songwriter Paul Brady, the Chieftains and Vince Gill. Knopfler then returned to soundtrack work with contributions to the movies *Wag The Dog*, *Metroland* and *A Shot At Glory*. His belated follow-up album, *Sailing To Philadelphia*, featured contributions from Van Morrison and James Taylor, but Knopfler's underrated writing skills really shone through on the tracks 'Baloney Again' and 'Silvertown Blues'.

● ALBUMS: *Local Hero* film soundtrack (Vertigo/Warners 1983) ★★★, *Cal* film soundtrack (Vertigo/PolyGram 1984) ★★★, *Comfort And Joy* (Vertigo 1984) ★★, *The Princess Bride* film soundtrack (Vertigo/Warners 1987) ★★, *Last Exit To Brooklyn* film soundtrack (Vertigo/Warners 1989) ★★, with Chet Atkins *Neck And Neck* (Columbia 1990) ★★★, *Golden Heart* (Vertigo/Warners 1996) ★★★, *Wag The Dog* mini-album film soundtrack (Vertigo/PolyGram 1998) ★★, *Sailing To Philadelphia* (Mercury/Warners 2000) ★★★, *A Shot At Glory* film soundtrack (Mercury 2001) ★★★.

● COMPILATIONS: *Screenplaying* (Vertigo/Warners 1993) ★★★.

● FURTHER READING: *Mark Knopfler: An Unauthorised Biography*, Myles Palmer. *Mark Knopfler*, Wolf Marshall.

## KOOL AND THE GANG

Originally formed as a quartet, the Jazziacs, by Robert 'Kool' Bell (b. 8 October 1950, Youngstown, Ohio, USA; bass), Robert 'Spike' Mickens (b. Jersey City, New Jersey, USA; trumpet), Robert 'The Captain' Bell - later known by his Muslim name Amir Bayyan (b. 1 November 1951, Youngstown, Ohio, USA; saxophone, keyboards) and Dennis 'D.T.' Thomas (b. 9 February 1951, Jersey City, New Jersey, USA; saxophone). Based in Jersey City, this aspiring jazz group opened for acts such as Pharoah Sanders and Leon Thomas. They were later joined by Charles 'Claydes' Smith (b. 6 September 1948, Jersey City, New Jersey, USA; guitar) and 'Funky' George Brown (b. 5 January 1949, Jersey City, New Jersey, USA; drums), and as the Soul Town Band, moderated their early direction by blending soul and funk, a transition completed by 1969 when they settled on the name Kool And The Gang. The group crossed over into the US pop chart in 1973 and initiated a run of 19 stateside Top 40 hits on their own De-Lite label starting with 'Funky Stuff', a feat consolidated the following year with a couple of Top 10 hits, 'Jungle Boogie' and 'Hollywood Swinging'. They continued to enjoy success, although their popularity momentarily wavered in the latter half of the 70s as the prominence of disco strengthened.

In 1979 the Gang added vocalists James 'J.T.' Taylor (b. 16 August 1953, Laurens, South Carolina, USA) and Earl Toon Jnr., with Taylor emerging as the key member in a new era of success for the group, which coincided with their employment of an outside producer. Eumire Deodato refined the qualities already inherent in the group's eclectic style and together they embarked on a series of highly successful international hits including 'Ladies Night'

(1979), 'Too Hot' (1980) and the bubbling 'Celebration', a 1980 platinum disc and US pop number 1 – later used by the media as the homecoming theme for the returning American hostages from Iran. Outside the USA they achieved parallel success and proved similarly popular in the UK where 'Get Down On It' (1981), 'Joanna' (1984) and 'Cherish' (1985) each reached the Top 5. The arrival of Taylor also saw the group's albums achieving Top 30 status in their homeland for the first time, with *Celebrate!* reaching the Top 10 in 1980.

Their longevity was due, in part, to a settled line-up. The original six members remained with the group into the 80s and although newcomer Toon left, Taylor blossomed into an ideal frontman. This core was later supplemented by several auxiliaries, Clifford Adams (trombone) and Michael Ray (trumpet). This idyllic situation was finally undermined by Taylor's departure in 1988 and he was replaced by three singers, former Dazz Band member Skip Martin plus Odeen Mays and Gary Brown. Taylor released a solo album in 1989, *Sister Rosa*, while the same year the group continued recording with the album *Sweat*. The compilation set *The Singles Collection* captures one of the most engaging and successful of soul/funk catalogues. Taylor rejoined in 1995, but subsequent releases indicated a group well past their sell-by date.

● ALBUMS: *Kool And The Gang* (De-Lite 1969) ★★, *Live At The Sex Machine* (De-Lite 1971) ★★, *Live At P.J.s* (De-Lite 1971) ★★, *Music Is The Message* (De-Lite 1972) ★★, *Good Times* (De-Lite 1973) ★★★, *Wild And Peaceful* (De-Lite 1973) ★★★, *Light Of Worlds* (De-Lite 1974) ★★★, *Spirit Of The Boogie* (De-Lite 1975) ★★, *Love And Understanding* (De-Lite 1976) ★★, *Open Sesame* (De-Lite 1976) ★★, *The Force* (De-Lite 1977) ★★, *Everbody's Dancin'* (1978) ★★, *Ladies' Night* (De-Lite 1979) ★★★, *Celebrate!* (De-Lite 1980) ★★★, *Something Special* (De-Lite 1981) ★★, *As One* (De-Lite 1982) ★★, *In The Heart* (De-Lite 1983) ★★★★, *Emergency* (De-Lite 1984) ★★, *Victory* (Curb 1986) ★★, *Forever* (Mercury 1986) ★★, *Sweat* (Mercury 1989) ★★, *Kool Love* (Telstar 1990) ★★, *State Of Affairs* (Curb 1996) ★★, *All The Best* (Curb 1998) ★★, *Gangland* (Eagle 2001) ★★.

● COMPILATIONS: *The Best Of Kool And The Gang* (De-Lite 1971) ★★, *Kool Jazz* (De-Lite 1974) ★★, *Kool And The Gang Greatest Hits!* (De-Lite 1975) ★★★, *Spin Their Top Hits* (De-Lite 1978) ★★★★, *Kool Kuts* (De-Lite 1982) ★★★, *Twice As Kool* (De-Lite 1983) ★★★★, *The Singles Collection* (De-Lite 1988) ★★★★, *Everything's Kool And The Gang: Greatest Hits And More* (Mercury 1988) ★★★★, *Great And Remixed 91* (Mercury 1992) ★★★, *The Collection* (Spectrum 1996) ★★★, *Greatest Hits* (PolyGram 1998) ★★★★, *The Very Best Of Kool & The Gang* (Mercury 1999) ★★★★, *The Best Of Kool & The Gang: The Millennium Collection* (PolyGram 2000) ★★★★, *Kool Funk Essentials 1970–1977* (Singular 2001) ★★.

## KORGIS

The Korgis comprised two former members of Stackridge, James Warren (bass/guitar/vocals) and Andy Davis (drums/guitar), plus Phil Harrison (keyboards/percussion), and Stuart Gordon (guitar/violin). This UK quartet reached the English Top 20 with their debut record 'If I Had You', but had problems when their next two singles failed. When their self-titled album also failed to make an impact it seemed they would end up as one-hit-wonders. However, 'Everybody's Gotta Learn Sometime', a classy love song, reached the UK Top 5 and US Top 20 and was followed by a minor UK hit with 'If It's Alright With You Baby'. By 1983 the band had been dropped by their label Rialto and were basically down to a core of just Warren, who carried the name on for a few more years and a number of one-off record deals. European success continued on a limited basis but at home the Korgis' success had ended. Warren released a solo album, *Burning Questions*, in 1986. The unit of Warren and Davis reformed in 1990 with the addition of John Baker (b. 2 April 1961, Bath, Avon, England; guitar, keyboards, vocals; ex-Graduate). They recorded an album of new material together with a new version of 'Everybody's Gotta Learn Sometime'. During their career the band never performed live, so it came as a surprise when they announced their first tour in the summer of 1993. The Korgis disbanded for the second time shortly afterwards.

● ALBUMS: *The Korgis* (Rialto 1979) ★★★, *Dumb Waiters* (Rialto 1980) ★★★, *Sticky George* (Rialto 1981) ★★, *Burning Questions* (Sonet 1986) ★★, *This World's For Everyone* (Dureco 1992) ★★.

● COMPILATIONS: *The Best Of The Korgis* (Rialto 1983) ★★★, *The Best Of And The Rest Of The Korgis* (Rialto 1990) ★★★, *Archive Series* (Rialto 1997) ★★★, *Klassics: The Best Of The Korgis* (Music Club 2001) ★★★.

## KRAFTWERK

The word 'unique' is over-used in music, but Kraftwerk have a stronger claim than most to the tag. Ralf Hütter (b. 20 August 1946, Krefeld, Germany; organ) and woodwind student Florian Schneider-Esleben (b. 7 April 1947, Düsseldorf, Germany; woodwind) met while they were studying improvised music in Düsseldorf, Germany. They drew on the influence of experimental electronic forces such as composer Karlheinz Stockhausen and Tangerine Dream to create minimalist music on synthesizers, drum machines and tape recorders. Having previously recorded an album in 1970 with Organisation (*Tone Float*), Hütter and Schneider-Esleben formed Kraftwerk and recorded their debut album with drummers Andreas Hohmann and Klaus Dinger. Guitarist Michael Rother and bass player Eberhard Krahnemann were subsequently recruited for live performances at art galleries. Hütter briefly left the line-up, but returned in time for the recording of a second self-titled album. During the recording of *Kraftwerk 2*, Dinger and Rother left to form Neu!. Produced by Conny Plank (later to work with Ultravox and the Eurythmics), the bleak, spartan music provoked little response.

After releasing a duo set, *Ralf Und Florian*, Hütter and Schneider-Esleben were joined by Wolfgang Flür (electronic drums) and Klaus Roeder (guitar/violin/keyboards). *Autobahn* marked Kraftwerk's breakthrough and established them as purveyors of hi-tech, computerized music. The title track, running at more than 22 minutes, was an attempt to relate the monotony and tedium of a long road journey. An edited version reached the Top 10 in the US and UK charts. In 1975, Roeder was replaced by Karl Bartos, who played on *Radioactivity*, a concept album based on the sounds to be found on the airwaves. *Trans Europe Express* and *The Man-Machine* were pioneering electronic works which strongly influenced a generation of English new wave acts like the Human League, Tubeway Army (Gary Numan), Depeche Mode and OMD, while David Bowie claimed to have long been an admirer. The *New Musical Express* said of *The Man-Machine*: 'It is the only completely successful visual/aural fusion rock has produced so far.'

Kraftwerk spent three years building their own Kling Klang studios in the late 70s, complete with, inevitably, scores of computers. The single 'The Model', from *The Man-Machine*, gave the band a surprise hit when it topped the UK charts in 1982, and it led to a trio of hits, including 'Showroom Dummies' and 'Tour De France', a song that was featured in the movie *Breakdance* and became the theme for the cycling event of the same name in 1983. *Electric Cafe* was a disappointment, but Kraftwerk were now cited as a major influence on a host of electro artists from Afrika Bambaataa to the respected producer Arthur Baker. Bambaataa and Baker's pioneering 1982 'Planet Rock' single was built around samples of both 'Trans Europe Express' and 'Numbers' (from 1981's *Computer World*).

Hütter and Schneider-Esleben have remained enigmatically quiet ever since *Electric Cafe*. In 1990, a frustrated Flür departed to be replaced by Fritz Hijbert (Flür later collaborated with Mouse On Mars under the name of Yamo). Kraftwerk's best known songs were collected together in 1991 on the double, *The Mix*, aimed chiefly at the dance music market by EMI Records. 'I think our music has to do with emotions. Technology and emotion can join hands . . .' said Hütter in 1991. They made a surprise return to live performance with a headline appearance at the UK's Tribal Gathering in the summer of 1997. In December 1999, Hütter and Schneider-Esleben recorded a new single, 'Expo 2000', to promote the Expo 2000 European Business Conference in Hannover.

● ALBUMS: *Kraftwerk* (Philips 1970) ★★, *Kraftwerk 2* (Philips 1971) ★★, *Ralf Und Florian* (Philips/Vertigo 1973) ★★★, *Autobahn* (Philips/Vertigo 1974) ★★★★, *Radioaktivität* aka *Radioactivity* (Kling Klang/Capitol 1975) ★★★, *Trans Europe Express* (Kling Klang/Capitol 1977) ★★★★★, *Die Mensch Maschine* aka *The Man-Machine* (Kling Klang/Capitol 1978) ★★★★, *Computerwelt* aka *Computer World* (Kling Klang/EMI 1981) ★★★★, *Electric Cafe* (Kling Klang/EMI 1986) ★★★, *Concert Classics* 1975 recording (Ranch Life 1998) ★★★.
● COMPILATIONS: *Kraftwerk* a UK compilation of the first two releases (Vertigo 1972) ★★, *The Best Of Kraftwerk: Exceller 8* (Vertigo 1975) ★★★, *Highrail* (Fontana 1979) ★★★, *Elektro Kinetik* (Vertigo 1981) ★★★, *The Mix* (Kling Klang/EMI 1991) ★★★★.
● FURTHER READING: *Kraftwerk: Man, Machine And Music*, Pascal Bussy. *From Düsseldorf To The Future (With Love)*, Tim Barr. *Kraftwerk: I Was A Robot*, Wolfgang Flür.

## KRAUSE, DAGMAR

b. 4 June 1950, Hamburg, Germany. Vocalist Krause began performing in Hamburg's thriving underground scene during the late 60s. She subsequently joined Peter Blegvad and Anthony Moore in Slapp Happy, a 70s *avant garde* attraction which drew heavily on European musical traditions. Krause's dispassionate vocals were among the trio's many attributes and her intonation proved ideal when the trio joined forces with the politically orientated Henry Cow. Moore and Blegvad took Slapp Happy out of the collective in 1975, but Krause opted to remain with the former act until its disintegration later in the decade. The singer recorded the remarkable concept album *Babble* with UK artist Kevin Coyne in 1979, and worked with Chris Cutler and Fred Frith in the Art Bears, and Cutler and Lindsay Cooper in News From Babel. She subsequently embarked on a solo career with *Angebot Und Nachfrage* (*Supply & Demand: Songs By Brecht/Weill & Eisler*), a collection of Bertolt Brecht/Kurt Weill and Hanns Eisler's theatrical songs. *Panzerschlacht: Die Lieder Von Hanns Eisler* (*Tank Battles: The Songs Of Hanns Eisler*) revealed the artist's continued infatuation with the cabaret of Germany's Weimar Republic. She rejoined Blegvad and Moore in 1997 to record a new Slapp Happy album, *Ça Va*. The following year she teamed up with French-Canadian composer Marie Goyette to record *A Scientific Dream And A French Kiss*.
● ALBUMS: with Kevin Coyne *Babble* (Virgin 1979) ★★★★, *Angebot Und Nachfrage* aka *Supply & Demand: Songs By Brecht/Weill & Eisler* (Hannibal 1986) ★★★★, *Panzerschlacht: Die Lieder Von Hanns Eisler* aka *Tank Battles: The Songs Of Hanns Eisler* (Island 1988) ★★★, *Radio Session* (Voiceprint 1993) ★★★★, with Marie Goyette *A Scientific Dream And A French Kiss* (Resurgence 1998) ★★★.

## KROKUS

Formed in Solothurn, Switzerland, Krokus appeared in 1974 playing symphonic rock similar to Yes, Genesis and Emerson, Lake And Palmer. After four years and two rather lacklustre albums, they switched to a hard rock style and dropped the frills in favour of a back-to-basics approach in the mode of AC/DC. The band originally comprised Chris Von Rohr (vocals), Fernando Von Arb (guitar), Jörg Nägeli (bass), Tommy Kiefer (guitar) and Freddy Steady (drums). The songs were formulaic numbers based on simple riffs and predictable choruses that were chanted repeatedly. With Von Rohr's voice lacking the necessary vocal range, he stepped down to become the bass player in favour of new arrival 'Maltezer' Marc (b. Marc Storace, Malta; ex-Tea). Nägeli occasionally played keyboards and subsequently took over the technical side of the band.

*Metal Rendez-vous* was the turning point in the band's career; released in 1980, it was heavier than anything they had done before and coincided with the resurgence of heavy metal in Britain. They played the Reading Festival in 1980 and were well received, and their next two albums continued with an aggressive approach, though they streamlined their sound to make it more radio-friendly. *Hardware* and *One Vice At A Time* both reached the US and UK album charts. Before *Headhunter* materialized, a series of personnel changes took place, with the replacement of Kiefer with ex-roadie Mark Kohler and Steve Pace taking over drums from Freddy Steady. Produced by Tom Allom, *Headhunter*'s high-speed, heavy-duty approach propelled it to number 25 in the *Billboard* album charts. Kohler took over bass from the departed Von Rohr (he returned briefly in the late 80s) and Jeff Klaven replaced the temporarily absent Pace on *The Blitz*, an erratic album that reached number 31 on the US chart mainly on the strength of its predecessor. Tommy Keiser (ex-Cobra) was brought in on bass on the follow-up *Change Of Address*, with Kohler returning to his role as rhythm guitarist. Despite a switch of labels to MCA Records, there was a continuing downward trend in the band's fortunes during the late 80s, with their personnel in a constant state of flux. Von Arb and the other members subsequently put the band on hold to work on solo projects.

The band's music progressed little during the 90s, still relying heavily on the legacy of AC/DC and the Scorpions. Peter Tanner took over from Storace on lead vocals for their first album of the new decade, *Stampede*. The line-up at this point comprised sole remaining founder member Von Arb, Many Maurer (bass), Tony Castell (guitar), and Peter Haas (drums). Von Arb successfully fought a lymphoma scare to record 1995's *To Rock Or Not To Be* with Maurer and Krokus stalwarts Storace, Kohler and Freddy Steady. Yet another round of personnel changes preceded 1999's *Round 13*, with Von Arb and Maurer joined by Haas, Carl Sentance (vocals) and Chris Lauper (guitar). Dave Stettler replaced Lauper the following year. Storace returned to the line-up in 2002.

● ALBUMS: *Krokus* (Phonogram 1975) ★★, *To You All* (Phonogram 1977) ★★, *Pain Killer* aka *Pay It In Metal* (Phonogram/Mercury 1978) ★★, *Metal Rendezvous* (Ariola 1980) ★★★, *Hardware* (Ariola 1981) ★★★, *One Vice At A Time* (Ariola 1982) ★★★, *Headhunter* (Ariola/Arista 1983) ★★★, *The Blitz* (Ariola/Arista 1984) ★★, *Change Of Address* (Arista 1986) ★★, *Alive And Screamin'* (Arista 1986) ★★, *Heart Attack* (MCA 1988) ★★, *Stampede* (Phonag 1991) ★★, *To Rock Or Not To Be* (Phonag 1995) ★★, *Round 13* (Phonag/Angel Air 1999) ★★.
● COMPILATIONS: *Early Days '75 – '78* (Phonogram 1980) ★★, *The Best Of Krokus: Stayed Awake All Night* (Arista 1987) ★★★, *The Dirty Dozen: The Very Best Of Krokus 1979 – 1983* (Ariola 1993) ★★★, *The Definitive Collection* (Arista 2000) ★★★★.

## L.A. GUNS

This US hard rock band was originally formed in 1983 by guitarist Tracii Guns, vocalist Axl Rose, and drummer Rob Gardner. All three members subsequently appeared in the original line-up of Guns N'Roses, before Guns left to re-form his own band with two members of Faster Pussycat, Paul 'Mars' Black (vocals) and Mick Cripps (bass), Nickey Alexander (drums) and Robert Stoddard (guitar; ex-Dogs D'Amour). Further line-up changes saw Cripps replaced by Kelly Nickels (ex-Faster Pussycat) and Black by ex-Girl vocalist Phil Lewis. Working on material that was a hybrid of metal, glam and blues-based rock 'n' roll, they signed with PolyGram Records in the USA the following year. However, with new drummer Steve Riley (ex-W.A.S.P.) arriving too late to appear on their self-titled debut, the band continued to use the services of Nickey Alexander (formerly 'Nicky Beat' of punk legends the Weirdos). *Cocked & Loaded* was a marked improvement on its predecessor; the band had matured as songwriters and Lewis' vocals were stronger and more convincing. *Hollywood Vampires* saw them diversifying musically, but retaining the essential energy and rough edges for which they had become renowned. Touring as support to Skid Row in Europe, it at last looked as though Guns would no longer have to look longingly at the phenomenal success his former band had achieved in his absence. However, it was not to be. As the band disintegrated, Guns went on to form a new outfit, Killing Machine, while Lewis formed Filthy Lucre. However, L.A. Guns were soon re-formed when both these bands failed. *Vicious Circle*, featuring new drummer Michael 'Bones' Gershima, continued the vampiric metaphors of the band's previous album with the track 'Crystal Eyes', a song also included on *Hollywood Vampires*. Greeted as a strong return, it was arguably the best recorded work to date by either Guns or Lewis, but following its release the band fell apart again. Lewis, Cripps and Gershima were the first to leave, with Nickels following shortly before the recording of *American Hardcore*. Guns and the returning Riley were joined on this album by Johnny Crypt (bass) and 'Roxy' Chris Van Dahl (vocals). Nickels returned to the line-up for 1999's *Shrinking Violet*, which also featured new singer Jizzy Pearl. The original quintet reunited on the same year's *Greatest Hits And Black Beauties*, which featured new songs and re-recorded versions of some of their old material. The following year they re-recorded *Cocked & Loaded* in its entirety. Nickels was absent from their first proper studio album of the new millennium, *Man In The Moon*.

● ALBUMS: *L.A. Guns* (Vertigo 1988) ★★, *Cocked & Loaded* (Vertigo 1989) ★★★, *Hollywood Vampires* (Polydor 1991) ★★★, *Vicious Circle* (Polydor 1994)

★★★★, *American Hardcore* (CMC 1996) ★★★, *Shrinking Violet* (Axe Killer 1999) ★★, *Greatest Hits And Black Beauties* (US) *The Very Best Of* (UK) (Deadline/Zebra 1999) ★★★, *Live: A Nite On The Strip* (Deadline 2000) ★★, *Cocked & Re-Loaded* (Deadline 2000) ★★★, *Man In The Moon* (Spitfire 2001) ★★★, *Waking The Dead* (Spitfire 2002) ★★★.
● COMPILATIONS: *Hollywood A Go Go* (Mercury 1996) ★★★.
● VIDEOS: *One More Reason* (PolyGram Music Video 1989), *Love, Peace & Geese* (PolyGram Music Video 1990).

## LA'S

The La's were originally formed by artist/musician Mike Badger (b. 18 March 1962) in 1984 in Liverpool, Merseyside, England, but his departure in 1986 left a line-up comprising songwriter Lee Mavers (b. 2 August 1962, Huyton, Liverpool, England; guitar/vocals), John Power (b. 14 September 1967; bass), Paul Hemmings (guitar) and John Timson (drums). Early demo tapes resulted in their signing with Go! Discs in 1987. After a well-received debut single, 'Way Out', which hallmarked the band's effortless, 60s-inspired pop, they took a year out before issuing the wonderfully melodic 'There She Goes'. When this too eluded the charts, the La's, far from disillusioned, returned to the studio for two years to perfect tracks for their debut album. The line-up also changed, with Lee's brother Neil (b. 8 July 1971, Huyton, Liverpool, England) taking up drums and ex-Marshmellow Overcoats guitarist Cammy (b. Peter James Camell, 30 June 1967, Huyton, Liverpool, England) joining the line-up. In the meantime, 'There She Goes' became a massive underground favourite, prompting a reissue two years on (after another single, 'Timeless Melody'). In late 1990, it reached the UK Top 20. *The La's* followed that same month, an invigorating and highly musical collection of tunes that matched, and some would argue outstripped, the Stone Roses' more garlanded debut. Its comparative lack of impact could be put down to Mavers' truculence in the press, verbally abusing Go! Discs for insisting on releasing the record and disowning its contents: 'That's the worst LP I've ever heard by anyone.' Comparisons with the best of the 60s, notably the Byrds and the Beach Boys, stemmed from the band's obsession with real instruments, creating a rootsy, authentic air.

After 'Feelin'' was drawn from the album, the La's set about recording tracks for a new work and spent much of summer 1991 touring America and Japan. Little was then heard of the band for the next four years, which took few acquainted with Mavers' studio perfectionism by surprise. The delays proved too much for Power, however, who departed to set up the highly successful Cast (Mavers has subsequently expressed his extreme dislike for the band). Back in the notoriously insular La's camp, rumours continued to circulate of madness and drug addiction. A collaboration with Edgar Summertyme of the Stairs was vaunted, but no public assignments were forthcoming. Mavers finally performed a solo acoustic set in 1995, in support of Paul Weller, which went so badly awry that he had the plug pulled on

him. In April, he spoke to the *New Musical Express* about a 'second' La's album. Sessions were undertaken in the west London studio owned by Rat Scabies of the Damned, with Mavers playing all the instruments. Predictably, no material from the sessions has ever been released.
● ALBUMS: *The La's* (Go! Discs 1990) ★★★★.
● COMPILATIONS: *Lost La's 1984–1986: Breakloose* (Viper 1999) ★★★, *Lost La's 1986–1987: Callin' All* (Viper 2001) ★★★.

## LABELLE, PATTI

b. Patricia Louise Holte, 24 May 1944, Philadelphia, Pennsylvania, USA. The lead singer of LaBelle began her solo career in 1976 when her former group, who had originally begun recording in the early 60s as the Blue Belles, disbanded. Although her first releases showed promise, she was unable to regain the profile enjoyed by LaBelle and at the beginning of the 80s, Patti agreed to tour with a revival of the stage play *Your Arms Too Short To Box With God*. The production reached Broadway in 1982 and, with Al Green as a co-star, became one of the year's hits. The following year's 'If Only You Knew' rose to the top of the US R&B charts. Having made her film debut as a blues singer in *A Soldier's Story* (1984), Patti LaBelle teamed up with Bobby Womack on the magnificent duet, 'Love Has Finally Come At Last'. Two tracks from 1984's box-office smash *Beverly Hills Cop*, 'New Attitude' (US Top 20) and 'Stir It Up', also proved popular. 'On My Own', a sentimental duet with Michael McDonald, was a spectacular international hit in 1986. This million-selling, US chart-topping single confirmed LaBelle's return. Although some commentators criticize her almost operatic delivery, Patti LaBelle remains a powerful and imposing performer. She made a return to the US stage in 1989, performing in various states with the 'lost' Duke Ellington musical *Queenie Pie*, and continued to release strong albums throughout the 90s.
● ALBUMS: *Patti LaBelle* (Epic 1977) ★★★, *Tasty* (Epic 1978) ★★★, *It's Alright With Me* (Epic 1979) ★★★, *Released* (Epic 1980) ★★★, *The Spirit's In It* (Philadelphia International 1981) ★★★, *I'm In Love Again* (Philadelphia International 1983) ★★★, *Patti* (Philadelphia International 1985) ★★★, *The Winner In You* (MCA 1986) ★★★, *Be Yourself* (MCA 1989) ★★, *This Christmas* (MCA 1990) ★★★, *Burnin'* (MCA 1991) ★★★, *Live!* (MCA 1992) ★★, *Gems* (MCA 1994) ★★★, *Flame* (MCA 1997) ★★★, *Live! One Night Only* (MCA 1998) ★★, *When A Woman Loves* (MCA 2000) ★★★.
● COMPILATIONS: *Best Of Patti LaBelle* (Epic 1982) ★★★, with the Blue Belles *Over The Rainbow: The Atlantic Years* (Ichiban 1994) ★★★, *Greatest Hits* (MCA 1996) ★★★★, *You Are My Friend: The Ballads* (Epic 1997) ★★★, with the Blue Belles *The Best Of The Early Years* (Hip O 1999) ★★★, *The Best Of Patti LaBelle: The Millennium Collection* (MCA 1999) ★★★★, *Love Songs* (Sony 2001) ★★★, *Greatest Love Songs* (Hip-O 2002) ★★★★.
● VIDEOS: *Live In New York* (MCA Music Video 1991), *Live! One Night Only* (MCA Music Video 1998).
● FURTHER READING: *Don't Block The Blessings ... Revelations Of A Lifetime*, Patti LaBelle with Laura B.

Randolph. *LaBelle Cuisine: Recipes To Sing About*, Patti LaBelle with Laura B. Randolph. *Patti's Pearls: Lessons In Living Genuinely, Joyfully, Generously*, Patti LaBelle and Laura Randolph Lancaster.
● FILMS: *A Soldier's Story* (1984), *Sing* (1989).

## LADYSMITH BLACK MAMBAZO

The success of Paul Simon's album *Graceland* did much to give the music of black South Africa international recognition in the mid-80s, and in particular gave a high profile to the choral group Mambazo and their captivating a cappella Zulu music (iscathamiya). Founded by Joseph Shabalala (b. 28 August 1941, Ladysmith, South Africa) in 1960, the group's name referred to Shabalala's home-town of Ladysmith, while also paying tribute to the seminal 50s choral group Black Mambazo (black axe) led by Aaron Lerole (composer of the 1958 UK hit 'Tom Hark' by his brother Elias [Lerole] And His Zig Zag Flutes).

The group began working professionally in 1971, with a version of ingoma ebusukuk ('night music'), which Shabalala dubbed 'cothoza mfana' ('walking on tiptoe', an accurate description of Mambazo's ability to follow choruses of thundering intensity with split-second changes into passages of delicate, whisper-like intimacy). Until 1975, most of Mambazo's album output concentrated on traditional folk songs, some of them with new lyrics that offered necessarily coded, metaphorical criticisms of the apartheid regime. After 1975, and Shabalala's conversion to Christianity, religious songs were added to the repertoire – although, to non-Zulu speakers, the dividing line will not be apparent.

In 1987, following the success of *Graceland*, the group's Warner Brothers Records debut album *Shaka Zulu*, produced by Paul Simon, reached the UK Top 40, and also sold substantially in the USA and Europe. In 1990, *Two Worlds One Heart* marked a radical stylistic departure for the group through its inclusion of tracks recorded in collaboration with George Clinton and the Winans. On 10 December 1991, as the result of what was described as a 'roadside incident' in Durban, South Africa, Joseph's brother and fellow founder member was shot dead. The group were back on a major label for 1997's *Heavenly*, which featured Dolly Parton singing lead vocals on a cover version of 'Knockin' On Heaven's Door'. Bolstered by the appearance of 'Inkanyezi Nezazi' on a Heinz television commercial, the following year's best of compilation was a surprise bestseller in the UK, climbing to number 2 in October 1998. In a tragic echo of his brother's death, Shabalala's wife Nellie was shot dead on 15 May 2002 near Durban. She had been the leader of her own church choir, the Women Of Mambazo.
● ALBUMS: *Amabutho* (BL 1973) ★★★, *Isitimela* (BL 1974) ★★★, *Amaqhawe* (BL 1976) ★★★, *Ulwandle Oluncgwele* (BL 1977) ★★★, *Umthombo Wamanzi* (BL 1982) ★★★, *Ibhayibheli Liyindlela* (BL 1984) ★★★, *Induku Zethu* (Shanachie 1984) ★★★, *Inala* (Shanachie 1986) ★★★, *Ezulwini Siyakhona* (Shanachie 1986) ★★★, *Shaka Zulu* (Warners 1987) ★★★★, *Journey Of Dreams* (Warners 1988) ★★★★,

with Danny Glover *How The Leopard Got His Spots* (Windham Hill 1989) ★★★, *Two Worlds One Heart* (Warners 1990) ★★★★, *Inkanyezi Nezazi* (Flame Tree 1992) ★★★, *Liph' Iqiniso* (Flame Tree 1994) ★★★, *Gift Of The Tortoise* (Flame Tree 1995) ★★★, *Thuthukani Ngoxolo (Let's Develop In Peace)* (Shanachie 1996) ★★★, *Heavenly* (A&M 1997) ★★, *In Harmony* (Wrasse 1999) ★★.
● COMPILATIONS: *Classic Tracks* (Shanachie 1991) ★★★★, *Best Of Ladysmith Black Mambazo* (Shanachie 1992) ★★★★, *Spirit Of South Africa* (Nascente 1997) ★★★★, *The Star And Wiseman: The Best Of Ladysmith Black Mambazo* (PolyGram 1998) ★★★, *Gospel Songs* (Wrasse 1999) ★★★★, *The Chillout Sessions* (Wrasse 2002) ★★.

## LAMB, ANNABEL

Although this UK pop vocalist is relegated to the one-hit wonder category, her unusual vocal delivery of the Doors' hit 'Riders On The Storm' created considerable interest and made the UK Top 30 in 1983. The brooding, breathy vocal style was used to great effect on this and subsequent releases. Her backing musicians included Robin Langridge (keyboards), Steve Greetham (bass), Chris Jarrett (guitar) and Jim Dvorak (trumpet). The hybrid of jazz, rock and reggae consistently produced by Wally Brill found only a loyal coterie of fans. Though little was heard of Lamb in the mainstream press following 1988's *Justice*, she has remained a popular live artist and in the mid-90s recorded a new studio album, which was released in the UK in 1998.
● ALBUMS: *Once Bitten* (A&M 1983) ★★★, *The Flame* (A&M 1984) ★★★, *When Angels Travel* (RCA 1986) ★★★, *Brides* (RCA 1987) ★★★, *Justice* (Metronome 1988) ★★★, *Flow* (Way Out West 1998) ★★★.
● COMPILATIONS: *Heartland* (A&M 1988) ★★★★.

## LAMBRETTAS

This Brighton, England-based band comprised Jez Bird (vocals, guitar), Doug Saunders (guitar, vocals), Mark Ellis (bass, vocals) and Paul Wincer (drums). Together with Secret Affair, the Merton Parkas and the Chords, they were part of the UK's short-lived mod revival of 1979–80. After securing a contract with Elton John's Rocket Records, they had 'Go Steady' included on the label's compilation *499 2139*, alongside fellow mod hopefuls the Act, the Escalators, Les Elite and the Vye. A month later, in November 1979, the same version of 'Go Steady' was released as a single, with little success, but drew much attention from the growing mod audiences. Success arrived with 'Poison Ivy', a catchy remake of the Leiber And Stoller-penned classic, reaching number 7 in the UK charts during 1980, eight places higher than the Coasters' original version of 1959. Their popularity continued with follow-up singles entering the charts, 'D-a-a-ance' climbed to number 12 and 'Another Day (Another Girl)' just managed to scrape into the UK Top 50, reaching number 49. The latter was originally called 'Page Three', but threatened legal action by the *Sun* newspaper persuaded the band to rethink the title. Their long-playing debut, *Beat Boys In The Jet Age*, peaked at number 28 and was also their last glimpse of the charts. Successive releases, 'Steppin' Out', 'Good Times', 'Anything You Want', 'Decent Town' and 'Somebody To Love', had little impact on either critics or record-buying public, and by the time they issued *Ambience* in 1981, the mod revival was dead and buried and the band quickly folded. In 1985, Razor Records unearthed the Lambrettas' back catalogue, releasing a compilation of their singles, entitled *Kick Start*.

● ALBUMS: *Beat Boys In The Jet Age* (Rocket 1980) ★★★, *Ambience* (Rocket 1981) ★★.
● COMPILATIONS: *Kick Start* (Razor 1985) ★★★.

## LANDSBOROUGH, CHARLIE

b. Charles Alexander Landsborough, 26 October 1941, Wrexham, Clwyd, Wales. Landsborough's family came from Birkenhead and he has spent his life on Merseyside. After several jobs, he trained as a teacher, but music has been the mainstay of his life. He was part of a local beat group, the Top Spots, but developed his own style by writing gentle, melodic, romantic ballads, albeit influenced by the American singer-songwriter Mickey Newbury. Because of his teaching commitments and transport problems with 'unreliable cars', Landsborough remained little known outside Merseyside for the first years of his recording career. His main strength is as a songwriter. Foster And Allen entered the UK charts with the astute reflections of 'I Will Love You All My Life', and Roly Daniels put 'Part Of Me' into the Irish charts. The repertoire of many Irish country artists includes 'The Green Hills Are Rolling Still', while 'Heaven Knows', which suggests that people should be colour-coded according to their deeds, has been recorded by George Hamilton IV. His breakthrough came in the mid-90s with the track 'What Colour Is The Wind', which was featured on Pat Kenny's Dublin-based chat show. The album of the same name rose to the top of the Irish album charts, and marked the emergence of Landsborough as one of the UK's leading country acts. His 1999 album *Still Can't Say Goodbye* even broke into the pop Top 40. Landsborough does not stray from his niche of astute social or romantic observations and, sooner or later, a big-name artist will convert one of his songs into a standard. The most likely contenders are 'No Time At All' and 'I Will Love You All My Life'.

● ALBUMS: *Heaven Knows* (Ritz 1989) ★★★ *Songs From The Heart* (Ritz 1992) ★★★, *What Colour Is The Wind* (Ritz 1994) ★★★, *With You In Mind* (Ritz 1996) ★★★, *Further Down The Road* (Ritz 1997) ★★★, *Still Can't Say Goodbye* (Ritz 1999) ★★★, *Live From Dublin* (Ritz 2000) ★★★, *Once In A While* (Telstar 2001) ★★★, *Movin' On* (Telstar 2002) ★★★.
● COMPILATIONS: *The Collection* (Ritz) ★★★, *The Very Best Of Charlie Landsborough* (Ritz 1998) ★★★.
● VIDEOS: *An Evening With Charlie Landsborough* (Ritz Video 1995), *Shine Your Light: The Charlie Landsborough Story* (Ritz Video).

## LANOIS, DANIEL

b. 19 September 1951, Hull, Quebec, Canada. This esteemed producer rose to fame during the late 80s through his contribution to major releases by Peter Gabriel (*So*) and U2 (*The Unforgettable Fire* and *The Joshua Tree*). He subsequently produced *Robbie Robertson*, the widely-acclaimed 'comeback' album by the former leader of the Band, and in 1989 undertook a similar role on Bob Dylan's *Oh Mercy*, widely-regarded as the artist's finest work in several years. Lanois' love of expansive, yet subtle, sound, reminiscent of 'new age' styles, combines effectively with mature, traditional rock, as evinced on the artist's own album, *Acadie*. Drawing inspiration from French-Canadian heritage – Lanois used both his native country's languages, sometimes within the same song – he created a haunting tapestry combining the jauntiness of New Orleans' music with soundscape instrumentals. Contributions by Brian Eno and the Neville Brothers, the latter of whom Lanois also produced, added further weight to this impressive collection. Lanois and Eno co-produced U2's two aforementioned multi-million-selling studio albums and their combined influence helped give the band's sound new dimensions. He was instrumental in redirecting Emmylou Harris' career with *Wrecking Ball* in 1995 and toured with her, leading his own band during the autumn of that year. He produced Dylan's excellent *Time Out Of Mind* in 1997.

● ALBUMS: *Acadie* (Opal 1989) ★★★★, *For The Beauty Of Wynona* (Warners 1993) ★★★, *Cool Water* (ITM 1994) ★★★.

## LASWELL, BILL

b. 12 February 1955, Salem, Illinois, USA. Laswell started playing guitar but later switched to bass. He was, he has said, more interested in being in a band than in playing music, but in the 70s he became more committed and has since organized some of the most challenging bands in recent popular music, including Material, Curlew (with Tom Cora, Nicky Skopelitis and George Cartwright), Praxis, Arcana (with Derek Bailey and Tony Williams) and Last Exit (with Sonny Sharrock, Peter Brötzmann and Ronald Shannon Jackson). For the Material album, *The Third Power*, he assembled a band including Shabba Ranks, the Jungle Brothers, Herbie Hancock, Sly And Robbie and Fred Wesley. Laswell and Hancock had already worked together, in Last Exit (on *The Noise Of Trouble*) and on two Hancock albums which he produced: on *Future Shock* in particular the 'backing band' was effectively Material.
Laswell has established several adventurous record labels, including OAO, Celluloid and Axiom. The latter was formed in 1990 to facilitate the release of Laswell's experiments in ambient and techno. His collaborations in this field include work with such artists as Pete Namlook, Klaus Schulze, Buckethead and DJ Spooky. In the late 90s, Laswell began to explore drum 'n' bass, including the trance dub vehicle Sacred System. He also inaugurated his 'reconstruction and mix translation' series, applying the concept to such artists as Bob Marley, Miles Davis and Santana. In addition, he has produced for a wide range of people, including Iggy Pop, Motörhead, Laurie Anderson, Fela Kuti, Gil Scott-Heron, Yellowman, Afrika Bambaataa, Yoko Ono, Public Image Limited, Mick Jagger, Nona Hendryx,

James 'Blood' Ulmer and Manu Dibango.

● ALBUMS: *Baselines* (OAO/Celluloid 1984) ★★★, with Peter Brötzmann *Lowlife* (Celluloid 1987) ★★★, *Hear No Evil* (Virgin 1988) ★★★, with Pete Namlook *Psychonavigation* (FAX/Subharmonic 1994) ★★★★, with Jonah Sharp *Visitation* (Subharmonic 1994) ★★★, with Tetsu Inoue *Cymatic Scan* (FAX/Subharmonic 1994) ★★★, *Outer Dark* (FAX 1994) ★★★, with Namlook *Outland* (FAX 1994) ★★★★, with Terre Thaemlitz *Web* (Subharmonic 1995) ★★★, with Nicholas James Bullen *Bass Terror* (Subsonic/Sub Rosa 1995) ★★★, with M.J. Harris *Somnific Flux* (Subharmonic 1995) ★★★, with Atom Heart, Tetsu Inoue *Second Nature* (FAX/Sub Meta 1995) ★★★, *Silent Recoil* (Low 1995) ★★★, with Namlook *Psychonavigation 2* (FAX/Subharmonic 1995) ★★★★, with Sacred System *Chapter One (Book Of Entrance)* (ROIR 1996) ★★★, with Namlook, Klaus Schulze *The Dark Side Of The Moog IV* (FAX/Ambient World 1996) ★★★, with Haruomi Hosono *Interpieces Organization* (Teichiku/Baidis 1996) ★★★, with Namlook *Outland 2* (FAX 1996) ★★★, *Oscillations* (Sub Rosa 1996) ★★★, with Namlook, Schulze *The Dark Side Of The Moog V* (FAX 1996) ★★★, with Namlook *Psychonavigation III* (FAX 1997) ★★★, *City Of Lights* (Sub Rosa 1997) ★★★, with Namlook, Schulze *The Dark Side Of The Moog VI* (FAX 1997) ★★★, with Style Scott *Bill Laswell Meets Style Scott Inna Dub Meltdown* (WordSound 1997) ★★★, *Dreams Of Freedom: Ambient Translations Of Bob Marley In Dub* (Axiom/Island 1997) ★★★★, with Sacred System *Sacred System: Chapter Two* (ROIR 1997) ★★★, *Panthalassa: The Music Of Miles Davis 1969–1974* (Sony/Columbia 1997) ★★★★, with Namlook *Outland 3* (FAX 1998) ★★★, *Oscillations 2* (SubRosa 1998) ★★★, with Percy Howard, Charles Hayward, Fred Frith *Meridiem* (Materiali Sonori 1998) ★★★, *Jazzonia* (Douglas 1998) ★★★, with Namlook, Schulze *The Dark Side Of The Moog VII* (FAX 1998) ★★★, *Invisible Design* (Tzadik 1999) ★★★, with Namlook *Psychonavigation 4* (FAX 1999) ★★★, *Imaginary Cuba: Deconstructing Havana* (Wicklow/ BMG 1999) ★★★★, *Broken Vessels* film soundtrack (VelVel/Koch 1999) ★★★, *Permutation* (Ion 1999) ★★★, *Dub Chamber 3* (ROIR 2000) ★★★, with Namlook *Outland 4* (FAX 2000) ★★★, *Emerald Aether: Shape Shifting* (Shanachie 2000) ★★★★, *Lo-Def Pressure* (Sub Rosa 2000) ★★★, with Toshinori Kondo *Life/Space/Death* (MusicDeli/Spiritual Nature 2000) ★★★, *Cyclops* aka *Points Of Order* (Cyclops/Points Of Order 2001) ★★★, with Jah Wobble *Radioaxiom: A Dub Transmission* (Palm Pictures 2001) ★★★★, *Divine Light: The Music Of Carlos Santana* (Sony 2001) ★★★★, *Points Of Order* (Interrhythmic 2002) ★★★.

● COMPILATIONS: *Material & Friends* (Celluloid 1984) ★★★★, *Deconstruction: The Celluloid Recordings* (Celluloid/Metronome 1994) ★★★★, *Ambient Compendium* (M.I.L. Multimedia 1996) ★★★, *Filmtracks 2000* (Tzadik 2001) ★★★★.

## LAUPER, CYNDI

b. Cynthia Anne Stephanie Lauper, 22 June 1953, Queens, New York City, New York, USA. Starting her career as a singer in Manhattan's clubs, Lauper began writing her own material when she met pianist John Turi in 1977. They formed Blue Angel and released a self-titled album in 1980 which included raucous versions of rock classics as well as their own numbers. She split with Turi and in 1983 began working on what was to become her multi-million-selling solo debut, *She's So Unusual*. It made number 4 in the USA and provided four hit singles the exuberant 'Girls Just Want To Have Fun' (US/UK number 2), which became a cult anthem for independent young women; 'Time After Time' (US number 1/UK number 3, later covered by Miles Davis on *You're Under Arrest* and by the jazz duo Tuck And Patti), 'She Bop' (US number 3, which broached the unusual subject of female masturbation) and 'All Through The Night' (US number 4, written by Jules Shear). The album also featured Prince's 'When You Were Mine'. At the end of 1984 *Billboard* magazine placed Lauper first in the Top Female Album Artists and she was awarded a Grammy as Best New Artist. Her image was one that adapted, for the American market, something of a colourful 'punk' image that would not offend parents too much but at the same time retain a sense of humour and rebelliousness that would appeal the youth. Pundits in the UK claimed to have seen through this straight away, yet they acknowledged Lauper's talent nonetheless. *True Colors* did not have the same commercial edge as its predecessor, yet the title track still provided her with an US number 1 and a Top 20 hit in the UK. The follow-up, 'Change Of Heart' (written by Essra Mohawk and featuring the Bangles), reached US number 3 in November 1986. In 1988, Lauper took a role as a beautician in the poorly received film, *Vibes*. She made a brief return to the charts in 1990 with the US/UK Top 10 single 'I Drove All Night' from *A Night To Remember*. Another lacklustre film appearance in *Off And Running* was not seen in the UK until two years later. Seen in some quarters as little more than a visual and vocal oddity, Lauper has nevertheless written several magnificent pop tunes ('Time After Time' is destined to become a classic) and, in 1985, boosted her credibility as a singer when she performed a stirring duet with Patti LaBelle at LaBelle's show at the Greek Theater in Los Angeles. Lauper was joined by her former writing partners Ron Hyman and Eric Bazilian for *Hat Full Of Stars*, a successful mix of soul/pop/hip-hop with a smattering of ethnic/folk. A reworked version of her biggest hit, retitled 'Hey Now (Girls Just Want To Have Fun)', reached number 4 in the UK charts in September 1994. The singer gave birth to a baby boy on 19 November 1997. The following year she recorded the seasonal album *Merry Christmas ... Have A Nice Life*, her final release for Sony Records.

● ALBUMS: as Blue Angel *Blue Angel* (Polydor 1980) ★★★, *She's So Unusual* (Portrait 1983) ★★★★, *True Colors* (Portrait 1986) ★★★, *A Night To Remember* (Epic 1989) ★★, *Hat Full Of Stars* (Epic 1993) ★★, *Sisters Of Avalon* (Epic 1997) ★★★, *Merry Christmas ... Have A Nice Life* (Epic 1998) ★★★.

● COMPILATIONS: *The Best Remixes* (Epic 1989) ★★★, *Twelve Deadly Cyns ... And Then Some* (Epic 1994) ★★★★, *Time After Time: The Best Of Cyndi*

Lauper (Epic 2001) ★★★★.
● VIDEOS: *Twelve Deadly Cyns ... And Then Some* (Epic 1994).
● FILMS: *Vibes* (1988), *Off And Running* aka *Moon Over Miami* (1991), *Life With Mikey* (1993), *Mrs. Parker And The Vicious Circle* (1994), *The Bel Air Witch Project* (1999), *The Opportunists* (2000).

## LEGENDARY PINK DOTS

This London, England-based experimental outfit was formed in 1981, based around lyricist and singer Edward Ka-Spel and keyboard player Phillip Knight aka the Silver Man, who emerged as part of the burgeoning do-it-yourself scene of the late 70s. Performing what they described as 'psychedelic' music – in an 'exploratory sense, rather than nostalgia' – they released their first album, *Brighter Now*, on the small Birmingham independent label In Phaze Records, eventually running through two other homes before settling with Play It Again Sam. The band emigrated to the Netherlands in 1985, after Ka-Spel had become disenchanted with his native country's reaction to *The Tower* ('a really important album to me'). A series of recordings continued to fare better on the continent than in the UK, while Ka-spel recorded the latest of several solo albums with Steve Stapleton of Nurse With Wound. He also branched out with a side project, the Maria Dimension, and worked with Skinny Puppy (as Teargarden for the 1987 album, *Tired Eyes Slowly Burning*). Ka-Spel, now known as The Prophet Qa'Sepel, maintained his prolific recording schedule into the following decade, despite the market for his marginalized electronic pop songs having barely enlarged since the early 80s.
● ALBUMS: *Brighter Now* (In Phaze/New Europeans 1982) ★★★, *Curse* (In Phaze 1983) ★★★, *Faces In The Fire* (Play It Again Sam 1984) ★★★, *The Tower* (In Phaze 1984) ★★★★, *The Lovers* (Ding Dong 1985) ★★★, *Asylum* (Play It Again Sam 1985) ★★★, *Island Of Jewels* (Play It Again Sam 1986) ★★★, *Any Day Now* (Play It Again Sam/Wax Trax! 1987) ★★★, *The Golden Age* (Play It Again Sam/Wax Trax! 1988) ★★★, *Greetings 9* (Materiali Sonori 1989) ★★, *Crushed Velvet Apocalypse* (Play It Again Sam/Wax Trax! 1990) ★★★★, *Four Days* (Mirrordot/Terminal Kaleidoscope 1990) ★★, *The Maria Dimension* (Play It Again Sam/Caroline 1991) ★★★★, *The Shadow Weaver* (Play It Again Sam/Wax Trax! 1992) ★★★, *Malachai (Shadow Weaver Part 2)* (Play It Again Sam/Caroline 1993) ★★★, *9 Lives To Wonder* (Play It Again Sam 1994) ★★, *From Here You'll Watch The World Go By* (Soleilmoon 1995) ★★★, *Remember Me This Way* (Soleilmoon 1996) ★★★, *Hallway Of The Gods* (Soleilmoon 1997) ★★★, *Nemesis Online* (Soleilmoon 1998) ★★★, *Live At The Metro* (SPV Poland 1999) ★★, *Farewell, Milky Way* 1994 recording (Cacciocavallo/Soleilmoon 2000) ★★★, *A Perfect Mystery* (Cacciocavallo/Soleilmoon 2000) ★★★, *Synesthesia* (SPKR 2002) ★★.
● COMPILATIONS: *Stone Circles: A Legendary Pink Dots Anthology* (Play It Again Sam/Wax Trax! 1987) ★★★, *The Legendary Pink Box* 3-LP box set (Play It Again Sam 1989) ★★★, *Chemical Playschool 8+9* (TeKa/World Serpent 1995) ★★★, *Canta Mientras*

*Puedas* (Play It Again Sam/Soleilmoon 1996) ★★★, *Lullabies For The New Dark Ages* 4-CD box set (Soleilmoon 1996) ★★★, *Under Triple Moons* (ROIR 1997) ★★★, *Stained Glass Soma Fountains* (Soleilmoon 1997) ★★★, *Chemical Playschool 10* (Soleilmoon 1997) ★★★, *Poi Poka Mozhesh* (Brudenia 1999) ★★★, *A Guide To The Legendary Pink Dots Vol. 1: The Best Ballads* (SPV Poland 2000) ★★★, *Chemical Playschool 11/12/13* (Soleilmoon 2001) ★★★.
● VIDEOS: *Live In Texas, April 20, 1989* (Videophile 1989).

## LENNON, JULIAN

b. John Charles Julian Lennon, 8 April 1963, Liverpool, England. To embark on a musical career in the same sphere as his late father was a bold and courageous move for Julian Lennon. The universal fame of John Lennon brought the inevitable comparisons, which quickly became more a source of irritation than pride. This awful paradox must have hampered the now low-profile career of a young star who began by releasing a commendable debut album in 1984. The album was produced by Phil Ramone and utilised a healthy mix of different musical styles. At times, Julian's voice uncannily and uncomfortably mirrored that of John's, but he was soon scaling the US and UK pop charts with excellent compositions such as 'Valotte' and the reggae-influenced 'Too Late For Goodbyes'. Lennon was nominated for a Grammy in 1985 as the Best New Act, but success may have come too soon, and he indulged in the usual excesses and was hounded by the press, merely to find out what club he frequented and whom he was dating.
*The Secret Value Of Daydreaming* was a poor album of overdone rock themes and was critically ignored. Lennon licked his wounds and returned in 1989 with *Mr. Jordan* and a change of style. The soul/disco 'Now You're In Heaven' was a lively comeback single, and the album showed promise. 1991 saw Lennon return to the conventional activities of recording and promotion with the release of a single embracing 'green' issues, 'Salt Water' supported by an imaginative video and a heavy promotion schedule. On this album, Julian Lennon seemed to be making a career on his own terms, rather than those dictated by the memories of his father. By 1995, Virgin had released Lennon from his contract, and he joined a touring production of the play *Mr Holland's Opus* for which he sang the title song. After many years of legal wrangles, Lennon received a financial settlement from his father's estate and the executor Yoko Ono. The sum of £20 million is alleged to have been agreed. Lennon was quoted as saying he needed the money to relaunch his rock career. He subsequently broke a seven-year silence with *Photograph Smile*. The album was released on his label and was issued on the same day as his half-brother Sean's debut. The first single 'Day After Day' was a fabulous song but was virtually ignored by the media as they fawned over young Sean. The album was varied and much more like his father's mid-period Beatles' work. Sadly, due to his past over-indulgence, Julian needs to court the media favourably before his recent work is properly

listened to. *Photograph Smile* is an outstanding record of great maturity that was virtually ignored.

● ALBUMS: *Valotte* (Virgin 1984) ★★★, *The Secret Value Of Daydreaming* (Virgin 1986) ★★, *Mr Jordan* (Virgin 1989) ★★, *Help Yourself* (Virgin 1991) ★★, *Photograph Smile* (Music From Another Room 1998) ★★★★.

● COMPILATIONS: *Behind The Music: The Julian Lennon Collection* (Rhino 2001) ★★★.

## LES MISÉRABLES

According to Alain Boublil, who wrote the book (with Claude-Michel Schönberg) and original lyrics for this show, it all began one night in London when he saw the Artful Dodger on stage in the 1978 West End revival of Lionel Bart's *Oliver!* From then on, he became obsessed with the image of young Gavroche, and all the other wonderful characters in Victor Hugo's classic novel, *Les Misérables*. Boublil's subsequent musical adaptation, in collaboration with composer Schönberg and poet Jean-Marc Natel, was originally released as a bestselling double album before being staged in Paris by Robert Hossein at the 4,500-seater Palais des Sports. As with so many other musicals in the past two decades, the key moment in the development of *Les Misérables* came when producer Cameron Mackintosh announced his involvement. After hearing the recording, he set about the immense task of adapting it into something suitable for British audiences, with the aid of directors Trevor Nunn and John Caird, journalist and lyricist Herbert Kretzmer, and Oxford Professor of Poetry James Fenton. (The latter's work was later rejected, although he still retains a credit and a percentage of the gross.)

The result, a co-production between Mackintosh and the Royal Shakespeare Company, opened at the Barbican Theatre on 8 October 1985. It was one hour longer than the Paris show, and had six new songs and a 20-minute prologue. The year is 1815, and an embittered Jean Valjean (Colm Wilkinson) is released on a ticket of leave after 19 years in prison. Eight years later, Valjean has broken his parole. He now owns a factory and has become Mayor, but is forced to sack one of his workers, Fantine (Patti LuPone), because she has borne an illegitimate child. Meanwhile, hot on Valjean's trail throughout the piece, is policeman Javert (Roger Allam). Fantine is dead, and her daughter Cosette (a role shared between a child and soprano Rebecca Caine) has been abused for several years by the Thénardiers (Alun Armstrong and Susan Jane Tanner). Valjean inveigles her away to Paris, where, several years later, there is great political unrest. Cosette is now a young woman, and in love with Marius (Michael Ball), one of a band of students preparing for the revolution. The barricades go up, and the revolutionaries face an army warning they must surrender or die. The Thénardiers' daughter, Eponine (Frances Ruffelle), is killed, as is the urchin Gavroche along with the rest of the rebels, including their leader Enjolras (David Burt). Valjean refuses the opportunity to dispose of Javert, and escapes with the injured Marius. Shattered by Valjean's enlightened attitude, Javert throws himself into the Seine. Cosette nurses Marius back to health, and after they are married – just before the old man's death – she learns of the debt she owes to Valjean. Highlights of the sung-through score included Valjean's thrilling 'Who Am I?' and his Act 2 show-stopper, 'Bring Him Home', Fantine's 'I Dreamed A Dream', Marius' poignant 'Empty Chairs At Empty Tables', along with 'Dog Eats Dog', delivered by Alun Armstrong's repellent Thénardier ('a sewer rat with wit'). The remainder of the highly dramatic and emotional numbers were 'At The End Of The Day', 'Lovely Ladies', 'Come To Me', 'Confrontation', 'Castle On A Cloud', 'Master Of The House', 'Look Down', 'Stars', 'Little People', 'Red And Black', 'Do You Hear The People Sing?', 'I Saw Him Once', 'In My Life', 'One Day More', 'On My Own', 'The Attack', 'A Little Fall Of Rain', 'Drink With Me To Days Gone By', 'Soliloquy', 'Wedding Chorale', 'Beggars At The Feast' and 'Finale'.

Critical reaction was not favourable ('Victor Hugo on the garbage dump . . . few glimmers of fun . . . Hugo-ago-go . . push-button emotionalism at the expense of character and content'), although *The Times* had no reservations about John Napier's set 'that assembly of rotting timber and ironwork, locking together like two ungainly monsters to form the Gorbeau tenement or the barricades'. Mackintosh hesitated before transferring the show to the West End, but after learning that the Barbican box office was constantly under siege, he went ahead, opening at the Palace Theatre, on the 4 December 1985. A New York production made its debut at the Broadway Theatre on 12 March 1987 to an entirely different critical reception (Clive Barnes: 'This is magnificent, red-blooded, two-fisted theatre'). Wilkinson and Ruffelle reprised their roles, and also in the cast were Terrence Mann (Javert), David Bryant (Marius), Judy Kuhn (Cosette), Michael Maguire (Enjolras), Randy Graff (Fantine), and Jennifer Butt and Leo Burmester (Thénardiers). The show scooped the Tony Awards, winning for Best Musical, Book, Score, Director (Nunn and Caird), Featured Actress (Ruffelle), Featured Actor (Maguire), Sets (Napier), and Lighting (David Hersey).

Since that time, *Les Misérables* has been seen by more that 40 million people, grossing over $1.6 billion worldwide. Ironically, the only country to resist its appeal has been France, where a 1991 staging at the Théâtre de Mogador was withdrawn after only seven months. In January 1994, the show overtook *Jesus Christ Superstar* as the third-longest-running musical (after *Cats* and *Starlight Express*) in the history of the London musical theatre. A 10th anniversary concert performance was presented at London's Royal Albert Hall on 8 October 1995. It featured the Royal Philharmonic Orchestra, and a company of over 250 performers from many of the worldwide productions, with principals: Colm Wilkinson (Jean Valjean), Philip Quast (Javert), Ruthie Henshall (Fantine), Jenny Galloway (Madame Thénardier), Alun Armstrong (Thénardier), Lea Salonga (Eponine), Michael Ball (Marius), Michael Maguire (Enjolras), and Judy Kuhn (Cosette). Towards the end of 1996, as the New

York production neared its own 10th anniversary, there was much anger and indignation when Mackintosh sacked most of the cast on the grounds that the production had got 'flabby', and the actors had simply outgrown the student-aged characters. Generous pay-offs soon quelled a potentially inflammable situation that the press dubbed the 'Bloodbath On Broadway'. Other changes were made to the Broadway show (which moved to the Imperial Theatre in October 1990), and they were incorporated into the London production when it closed for a week in September 1997. *Les Misérables* now has its own Internet website, magazine (*Barricade*) and about 30 different cast albums.

The best remembered of all the films based on Victor Hugo's novel would appear to be the 1935 version starring Fredric March and Charles Laughton. The latest was released in 1998, with Liam Neeson, Geoffrey Rush, Uma Thurman, and Claire Danes.

## LET'S ACTIVE

Ostensibly the vehicle for veteran US all-rounder Mitch Easter, Let's Active issued three melodic albums during the mid-80s. Easter previously played alongside various members of the dB's in the Sneakers in the late 70s, and also worked with the H-Bombs and the Cosmopolitans. His first solo outing graced *Shake To Date*, a UK compilation of material from the US Shake label, in 1981. In between 'discovering' R.E.M. and then producing their early work, Easter eventually set up Let's Active. *Cypress* did not emerge until 1984, and featured Easter joined by Faye Hunter (bass) and Sam Romweber (drums). The songwriting skills were evident (and the debt to John Lennon and Paul McCartney was clear), but the album lacked bite, and despite the band supporting Echo And The Bunnymen on tour it did not sell. Almost two years later, Let's Active found that bite with *Big Plans For Everybody*, aided by drummers Eric Marshall and Rob Ladd, and Angie Carlson (guitar, keyboards, vocals). Promoted by 'In Little Ways', the album seemed the perfect encapsulation of Easter's aims: superb production, an ingenious blend of instrumentation and, above all, strong songs. Easter's commitments elsewhere delayed the third Let's Active album for nearly three years, and as such, *Every Dog Has His Day* (with John Heames now in the ranks) was slightly disappointing.

● ALBUMS: *Cypress* (I.R.S. 1984) ★★, *Big Plans For Everybody* (I.R.S. 1986) ★★★★, *Every Dog Has His Day* (I.R.S. 1988) ★★★.

## LEVAN, LARRY

b. Lawrence Philpot, 18 July 1954, Brooklyn, New York, USA, d. 8 November 1992, New York City, New York, USA. Levan deserves acknowledgement as a hugely innovative and influential DJ, and many cite him as the true originator of modern dance music in all its forms. Contemporary DJs including Paul Oakenfold, Judge Jules and Norman Jay cite him as an inspirational figure. Levan began his career DJing at The Gallery and later the Continental Baths in New York City, before moving on to the Paradise Garage in SoHo, from where garage music takes its

name. He DJed there every weekend from 1976 until the club's closure in 1987, playing an eclectic and seamless blend of disco, soul, gospel, rock and reggae to an ecstatically receptive audience, a scenario that bore a striking resemblance to the acid house phenomenon of the late 80s. Levan's production credits included the Peech Boys' 'Don't Make Me Wait', Taana Gardner's 'Heartbeat', Instant Funk's 'I Got My Mind Made Up' and Skyy's 'First Time Around'. He also remixed Gwen Guthrie's 'Ain't Nothing Goin' On But The Rent'. Like many of the period's experimenters and pleasure-seekers, Levan fell victim to a considerable appetite for drugs, particularly cocaine and heroin. The closure of the Paradise Garage in 1987 depressed him greatly and his intake of narcotics increased. He died of heart failure at the age of 38, leaving a legacy which would help to form garage, house and their derivative styles.

● COMPILATIONS: *Larry Levan Live At The Paradise Garage* (Strut 2000) ★★★★.

## LEVEL 42

Formed in 1980 as an instrumental jazz/funk unit, heavily influenced by the music of Stanley Clarke, this UK band originally comprised Mark King (b. 20 October 1958, England; bass/vocals), Phil Gould (b. 28 February 1957, England; drums), Rowland 'Boon' Gould (b. 14 March 1955, England; guitar) and Mike Lindup (b. 17 March 1959; keyboards). By the release of their debut single, 'Love Meeting Love', King was urged to add vocals to give the band a more commercial sound. Their Mike Vernon-produced album was an exciting collection of funk and modern soul orientated numbers that made the UK Top 20. Cashing in on this unexpected success, their previous record company issued a limited edition album of early material, which their new record company Polydor Records repackaged the following year. Word had now got round that Level 42 were one of the most exciting new bands of the 80s, the focal point being Mark King's extraordinary bass-slapping/thumb technique, which even impressed the master of the style, Stanley Clarke. Most of their early singles were minor hits until 'The Sun Goes Down (Living It Up)' in 1984 made the UK Top 10. Their worldwide breakthrough came with *World Machine*, a faultless record that pushed their style towards straight, quality pop. King's vocals were mixed up-front and the group entered a new phase in their career as their fans left the dance floor for the football stadiums. This also coincided with a run of high-quality hit singles between 1985 and 1987, notably, 'Something About You', 'Leaving Me Now', 'Lessons In Love', the autobiographical 'Running In The Family' and the immaculate tear-jerker 'It's Over'. Both *Running In The Family* and *Staring At The Sun* were major successes, although the latter had no significant hit singles. After the release of the former, the band changed its line-up drastically with Boon and Phil Gould replaced by Alan Murphy (b. 18 November 1953, d. 19 October 1989, London, England) and Gary Husband (b. 14 June 1960, Leeds, Yorkshire, England) respectively. Murphy tragically died of pneumonia a year after the release of *Staring*

*At The Sun*. Veteran jazz guitarist Allan Holdsworth (b. 6 August 1946, Leeds, England) filled in for the recording of *Guaranteed*. Jakko Jakszyk (b. 8 June 1958) joined in 1991, adding a stronger sound to the band's live performances.

Despite the return of Phil Gould on drums on *Forever Now*, Level 42's career had faltered by the mid-90s as both their recording and public activity took a lower profile, and Mark King took life easy from his base in the Isle of Wight. They announced their split in 1994, playing their last show at the Royal Albert Hall, London on 14 October. King later acquired the rights to the name and resumed touring in 2002. Level 42 should be remembered for briefly bringing quality jazz/funk music to the foreground by blending it with catchy pop melodies, albeit with 80s over crisp production.

● ALBUMS: *Level 42* (Polydor 1981) ★★★, *Strategy* (Elite 1981) ★★★, *The Early Tapes: July–August 1980* (Polydor 1981) ★★, *The Pursuit Of Accidents* (Polydor 1982) ★★★, *Standing In The Light* (Polydor 1983) ★★★, *True Colours* (Polydor 1984) ★★★★, *A Physical Presence* (Polydor 1985) ★★, *World Machine* (Polydor 1985) ★★★★, *Running In The Family* (Polydor 1987) ★★★, *Staring At The Sun* (Polydor 1988) ★★, *Guaranteed* (RCA 1991) ★★, *Forever Now* (RCA 1994) ★★.

Solo: Mark King *Influences* (Polydor 1993) ★★, *One Man* (Eagle 1998) ★★.

● COMPILATIONS: *Level Best* (Polydor 1989) ★★★★, *The Remixes* (Polydor 1992) ★★★, *The Very Best Of Level 42* (Polydor 1998) ★★★.

● VIDEOS: *Live At Wembley* (Channel 5 1987), *Family Of Five* (Channel 5 1988), *Level Best* (Channel 5 1989), *Fait Accompli* (PolyGram Music Video 1989).

● FURTHER READING: *Level 42: The Definitive Biography*, Michael Cowton.

### LeVert

From Philadelphia, Pennsylvania, USA, contemporary R&B band LeVert derived their name from the surname of brothers Sean and Gerald LeVert (b. 13 July 1966, Cleveland, Ohio, USA), the offspring of O'Jays founder Eddie LeVert. The predominantly vocal trio additionally included school friend Marc Gordon. Their 1985 debut album, *I Get Hot*, produced the US R&B hit 'I'm Still', but marketing at the small independent Tempre Records failed to satisfy their ambitions. A year later, they signed to Atlantic Records and struck number 1 in the US R&B charts with '(Pop, Pop, Pop) Goes My Mind', taken from *Bloodline*. The similarity of Gerald's voice to that of his father's was unmistakable, yet LeVert were undoubtedly a product of the 80s with their advanced production techniques and layered rhythms. The follow-up album, *Bloodline*, went gold and yielded a further substantial crossover pop hit with 'Casanova'. *Just Coolin'*, accompanied by a successful single of the same title, kept up the commercial momentum, but failed to match the impact of the group's earlier work. With Gerald freelancing as a producer for several other R&B acts, *Rope-A-Dope* again achieved gold status, despite apparent creative stagnation. The group was put on temporary hold when Gerald

announced the launch of a solo career in 1991, but he returned in time for *For Real Tho'*. However, with their lead singer's busy schedule taking centre stage, it appeared for some time that LeVert's absence would become permanent, until the release of *The Whole Scenario* in 1997. Gerald subsequently returned to his increasingly successful solo career.

● ALBUMS: *I Get Hot* (Tempre 1985) ★★★, *Bloodline* (Atlantic 1986) ★★★, *The Big Throwdown* (Atlantic 1987) ★★★, *Just Coolin'* (Atlantic 1988) ★★★, *Rope-A-Dope* (Atlantic 1990) ★★, *For Real Tho'* (Atlantic 1992) ★★, *The Whole Scenario* (Atlantic 1997) ★★★.

● COMPILATIONS: *The Best Of LeVert* (Rhino 2001) ★★★★.

### LEWIS, HUEY, AND THE NEWS

This highly successful AOR band was formed in Marin County, California, USA in 1980 by ex-Clover members Huey Lewis (b. Hugh Anthony Cregg III, 5 July 1950, New York City, New York, USA; vocals, harmonica) and Sean Hopper (keyboards). They recruited guitarist and saxophonist Johnny Colla, Mario Cipollina (bass), Bill Gibson (drums) and Chris Hayes (lead guitar), all fellow performers at a regular jam session at local club Uncle Charlie's. Their debut album was produced by Bill Schnee and released by Chrysalis Records, and a single from it, 'Do You Believe In Love' reached the US Top 10 in 1982 aided by a tongue-in-cheek video. The band's easy-going rock/soul fusion reached its peak with *Sports*, which provided five US Top 20 hits in 1983 and 1984. Among them were the Chinn And Chapman and song 'Heart & Soul', 'The Heart Of Rock & Roll', 'If This Is It' and 'I Want A New Drug'. Lewis sued Ray Parker Jnr. over the latter song, claiming it had been plagiarised for the *Ghostbusters* theme. Between 1985 and 1986, three Huey Lewis & The News singles headed the US charts. They were 'The Power Of Love' (chosen as the theme tune for Robert Zemeckis' movie *Back To The Future*), the Hayes-Lewis composition 'Stuck With You' and 'Jacob's Ladder', written by Bruce Hornsby. 'Perfect World' (1988) from the fifth album was also a success although *Hard At Play* did less well. Lewis' status with AOR audiences was underlined when he was chosen to sing the national anthem at the American Bowl in the 80s.

The band maintained a lower musical profile in the 90s, with Lewis electing to concentrate on his acting career instead. A beautiful a cappella cover version of Curtis Mayfield's 'It's All Right', released in June 1993, was followed by *Four Chords And Several Years Ago*, a tour of the band's musical mentors. The band's comeback album, the soulful *Plan B*, was released in July 2001.

● ALBUMS: *Huey Lewis & The News* (Chrysalis 1980) ★★, *Picture This* (Chrysalis 1982) ★★★★, *Sports* (Chrysalis 1983) ★★★★, *Fore!* (Chrysalis 1986) ★★, *Small World* (Chrysalis 1988) ★★, *Hard At Play* (EMI 1991) ★★, *Four Chords And Several Years Ago* (Elektra 1994) ★★★, *Plan B* (Silvertone 2001) ★★★.

● COMPILATIONS: *The Heart Of Rock & Roll: The Best Of Huey Lewis & The News* (Chrysalis 1992) ★★★, *Time Flies: The Best Of Huey Lewis & The News* (East West 1996) ★★★, *The Heart Of Rock & Roll*

(EMI Gold 2000) ★★★, *Classic Masters* (EMD 2002) ★★★.

## LILLYWHITE, STEVE

b. England. Lillywhite was one of the UK's leading record producers in the 80s, best known for his work with the Pogues and U2. He started out as a tape operator for Phonogram Records in 1972. After producing the demo tapes that won Ultravox a contract with Island Records, he joined the company as a staff producer. Lillywhite specialized in producing late 70s new wave bands such as Eddie And the Hot Rods, Siouxsie And the Banshees (the hit 'Hong Kong Garden' and *The Scream*), the Members, Penetration, XTC and the Buzzards before he was approached to supervise Peter Gabriel's third solo album, released in 1980. By the early 80s, Lillywhite was widely recognized as one of the most accomplished of younger producers. Now a freelance, Island brought him in to work on U2's debut *Boy*. He also produced the band's next two albums, *October* and *War*. In addition he worked with artists as varied as singer-songwriter Joan Armatrading, stadium rockers Simple Minds, art-punks Psychedelic Furs and the Rolling Stones (1986's *Dirty Work*). In 1988, Lillywhite produced contrasting albums by the Pogues (*If I Should Fall From Grace With God*) and Talking Heads (*Naked*). He continued his association with the Pogues on their 1988 follow-up, *Peace And Love*, and worked on Talking Heads vocalist David Byrne's 1989 solo effort *Rei Momo*. Lillywhite also has production credits with English singer Kirsty MacColl, whom he married in 1984, Morrissey, the Dave Matthews Band and Phish.

## LIMAHL

b. Christopher Hamill, 19 December 1958, Wigan, Lancashire, England Limahl (an anagram of his surname) came to prominence as lead vocalist with Kajagoogoo. His rancorous exit from the group in 1983 was caused partly by guitarist Nick Beggs' increasing control over the outfit's destiny. However, a flamboyant performer and a friend of BBC pop presenter Paul Gambaccini, Limahl was well placed for solo success that began with 'Only For Love' in the UK Top 20. After a relative flop with 1984's 'Too Much Trouble', he touched number 4 with the movie title theme, 'Never Ending Story'. This Giorgio Moroder opus was also Limahl's only US chart entry. Apart from *Don't Suppose* flitting briefly into the UK charts, he has since been absent from the commercial scene in nearly all territories. He continues to perform live and appear in musical theatre.
● ALBUMS: *Don't Suppose* (EMI 1984) ★★.

## LINX

One of the leading lights in the brief but high-profile Brit-funk movement of the early 80s (with Light Of The World, its spin-offs Beggar And Co, Imagination and Freeez), Linx were based around the duo of David Grant (b. 8 August, 1956, Kingston, Jamaica, West Indies; vocals) and Sketch Martin (b. Antigua, West Indies; bass), and completed by Bob Carter (keyboards) and Andy Duncan (drums). Grant's family moved to the UK in the late 50s and he grew up in north London. Sketch was taken to the UK when he was four, and was based in West Ham, east London. They met while working in a hi-fi shop. Grant later opened a record shop with his cousin, and became a junior reporter on a local paper, before working at Island Records' press office. Martin worked for the civil service, a film company, and the Performing Rights Society. They had their debut single, 'You're Lying', released as a private pressing (1,000 copies) and sold through a specialist funk shop before Chrysalis Records picked up on it and enabled it to be a hit. They were the first of the Brit-funk bands to make an impression in the USA, when 'You're Lying' made the R&B charts. Further singles included 'Intuition' and 'So This Is Romance'. The video for 'Intuition' featured the late Bertice Reading, while their stage performances harked back to the best traditions of the Glitter Band and Adam And The Ants by employing twin drummers. Grant moved on to a solo career with Chrysalis and had hit duets with Jaki Graham. He moved to Polydor Records in 1987 then Fourth & Broadway in 1990.
● ALBUMS: *Intuition* (Chrysalis 1981) ★★★, *Go Ahead* (Chrysalis 1981) ★★.
● COMPILATIONS: *The Best Of David Grant And Linx* (Chrysalis 1993) ★★★.

## LISA LISA AND CULT JAM

Formed in Harlem, New York, USA, this R&B trio comprising Lisa Lisa (b. Lisa Velez, 15 January 1967, New York City, New York, USA; vocals), Mike Hughes (guitar) and Alex 'Spanador' Moseley (guitar) was put together and produced by rap crew Full Force. The trio was signed to Columbia Records in 1985 and recorded their debut single, 'I Wonder If I Take You Home', only a week after forming. The single, which rose to the Top 10 in the US R&B charts and the national UK Top 20, was produced, written and recorded with the complete Full Force aggregation – only in concert did Lisa Lisa work strictly in the reduced trio format. Lisa Lisa And Cult Jam continued to achieve US Top 10 singles in the national and dance charts throughout the late 80s, including two number 1 hits in 1987, 'Head To Toe' and 'Lost In Emotion'. Their self-titled 1985 debut was only moderately successful, but 1987's *Spanish Fly* reached the US Top 10. In 1989, their third album, *Straight To The Sky*, stalled at number 77 and produced no hit singles. All three albums were written, arranged and produced by Full Force. *Straight Outta Hell's Kitchen* divided the production duties between Full Force and C & C Music Factory, but was even less successful. Lisa Lisa embarked on a solo career, releasing 1994's *LL 77*, before diversifying into acting and television presenting.
● ALBUMS: *Lisa Lisa & Cult Jam With Full Force* (Columbia 1985) ★★★★, *Spanish Fly* (Columbia 1987) ★★★★, *Straight To The Sky* (Columbia 1989) ★★★, *Straight Outta Hell's Kitchen* (Columbia 1991) ★★.
● COMPILATIONS: *Past, Present & Future* (Thump 1996) ★★★, *Super Hits* (Columbia 1997) ★★★★, *Let The Beat Hit 'Em* (Connoisseur 2001) ★★★★.

## LITTLE ANGELS

This UK heavy rock quintet was formed in Scarborough, Yorkshire, England, during 1985, originally under the title Mr Thrud. Comprising Tony Jepson (vocals), Bruce John Dickinson (b. 10 May 1968, Berwick-upon-Tweed, Scotland; guitar), Mark Plunkett (bass), Jimmy Dickinson (keyboards) and Dave Hopper (drums), they were a youthful outfit, whose energy and enthusiasm in the live setting won them a loyal fanbase in their native north-east. Following a series of independent releases, notably 1987's seven-track debut *Too Posh To Mosh*, they attracted the attention of Polydor Records. *Don't Prey For Me*, which featured new drummer Michael Lee, included a dozen gems of melodic, but roughshod, rock 'n' roll, characterized by Jepson's raucous and charismatic vocals. The big-budget follow-up, mixed by the Steve Thompson/Michael Barbiero partnership, was a disappointment. Abandoning their roots, this set saw them make a concerted attempt to break into the American FM radio market. Internal disputes began to manifest themselves in 1991. Drummer Michael Lee secretly auditioned for the Cult, and was ejected from the band as a result. His replacement was Mark Richardson. *Jam* regained much of the lost ground in 1993, entering the UK charts at number 1 and winning their first support slot on Van Halen's European tour. However, having found their niche, they nevertheless elected to go their separate ways in 1994. The Dickinsons moved on to b.l.o.w., while Richardson joined Skunk Anansie.

● ALBUMS: *Too Posh To Mosh* (Powerstation 1987) ★★★★, *Don't Prey For Me* (Polydor 1989) ★★★★, *Young Gods* (Polydor 1991) ★★, *Jam* (Polydor 1993) ★★★, *Little Of The Past* (Polydor 1994) ★★★.
● COMPILATIONS: *Too Posh To Nosh* (Castle 1994) ★★★.
● VIDEOS: *Big Bad Video* (Polydor 1991).

## LITTLE STEVEN

b. Steven Van Zandt, 22 November 1950, Boston, Massachusetts, USA. From a professional beginning in Stell Mill (with Bruce Springsteen) and similar New Jersey bar bands, Van Zandt toured as backing guitarist to the Dovells before passing briefly through the ranks of Southside Johnny And The Asbury Jukes whose first three albums he supervised. He also contributed several compositions to these, some written with Springsteen, with whose E Street Band he served on and off from 1975 to 1984 when, without rancour, he was replaced by Nils Lofgren. Overcoming inhibitions about his singing, Van Zandt, also known as 'Miami Steve' or 'Little Steven', next led Little Steven And The Disciples Of Soul, a 12-piece that made its stage debut at London's Marquee Club with personnel that included the Asbury Jukes horn section and, on bass Jean Beauvoir (ex-Plasmatics). Theirs was a body of recorded work that, lyrically, reflected Van Zandt's increasing preoccupation with world politics. This was exemplified by 'Solidarity' (from 1984's *Voice Of America*), which was covered by Black Uhuru. After a fact-finding expedition to

South Africa, he masterminded Sun City, a post-Live Aid project that raised over $400,000 for anti-apartheid movements in Africa and the Americas via an album (credited to Artist United Against Apartheid), single and concert spectacular featuring Bob Dylan, Lou Reed, Ringo Starr, Springsteen and other big names. To a less altruistic end, his reputation as a producer snowballed through his efforts on records by such as Gary 'U.S.' Bonds (with Springsteen), Lone Justice and Ronnie Spector, as well as his own gradually more infrequent offerings. Without a record contract for most of the 90s, Van Zandt's profile was raised at the end of the decade when he landed the role of Silvo Dante in HBO's acclaimed Mafia drama series, *The Sopranos*, and toured with the reunited E-Street Band. He also released *Born Again Savage*, which contained material recorded with Adam Clayton and Jason Bonham in the mid-90s.

● ALBUMS: as Little Steven And The Disciples Of Soul *Men Without Women* (EMI America 1982) ★★★, *Voice Of America* (EMI America 1984) ★★★, *Freedom No Compromise* (Manhattan 1987) ★★★, *Revolution* (RCA 1989) ★★★, *Born Again Savage* (Renegade Nation 1999) ★★.
● COMPILATIONS: *Greatest Hits* (EMI 1999) ★★★.
● FILMS: *American Flyers* (1985).

## LIVE AID

(see Band Aid/Live Aid)

## LIVING COLOUR

This US rock band was originally formed by Vernon Reid (b. 22 August 1958, London, England; guitar), Muzz Skillings (bass) and William Calhoun (b. 22 July 1964, Brooklyn, New York, USA; drums). Reid had studied performing arts at Manhattan Community College, having moved to New York at the age of two. His first forays were in experimental electric jazz with Defunk, before he formed Living Colour as a trio in 1984. Both Skillings and Calhoun were experienced academic musicians, having studied and received acclaim at City College and Berklee College Of Music, respectively. The line-up was completed by the induction of vocalist Corey Glover (b. 6 November 1964, Brooklyn, New York, USA), who had just finished a role in Oliver Stone's movie *Platoon*, and whom Reid had originally encountered at a friend's birthday party. Their first major engagement came when Mick Jagger saw them performing at CBGB's and invited them to the studio for his forthcoming solo album. Jagger's patronage continued as he produced two demos for the band, which secured them a contract with Epic Records. Their debut, *Vivid*, earned them early critical acclaim and rose to number 6 in the US charts. Fusing disparate black musical formats such as jazz, blues and soul, alongside commercial hard rock, its diversity was reflected in the support slots the band acquired to promote it, Cheap Trick, Robert Palmer and Billy Bragg among them. Musically, the band was most closely aligned to the first of that trio, although their political edge mirrored the concerns of Bragg.

In 1985, Reid formed the *Black Rock Coalition*

pressure movement alongside journalist Greg Tate, and Living Colour grew to be perceived as their nation's most articulate black rock band. Two subsequent singles, 'Cult Of Personality' (which included samples of John F. Kennedy's speeches and won a Grammy Award) and 'Open Letter (To A Landlord)', were both provocative but intelligent expressions of urban concerns. The ties with the Rolling Stones remained strong, with Reid collaborating on Keith Richards' solo album. They also joined the Rolling Stones on their Steel Wheels tour. After sweeping the boards in several Best New Band awards in such magazines as *Rolling Stone*, *Time's Up* was released in 1990, and afforded another Grammy Award. Notable contributions, apart from the omnipresent Jagger, included Little Richard on the controversial 'Elvis Is Dead'.

In 1991 worldwide touring established Living Colour as a highly potent force in mainstream rock. Following Skillings' departure, bass player Doug Wimbish (b. 22 September 1956, Hartford, Connecticut, USA) from Tackhead joined them for *Stain*, which added a sprinkling of studio gimmickry on a number of tracks. The band announced its dissolution early in 1995; Vernon Reid stated: '. . . Living Colour's sense of unity and purpose was growing weaker and fuzzier, I was finding more and more creative satisfaction in my solo projects. Finally it became obvious that I had to give up the band and move on'. An excellent retrospective, *Pride*, was released following their demise. Reid released an impressive solo debut in 1996. Calhoun's jazz quintet issued their debut *Live At The Blue Note* in 2000.

● ALBUMS: *Vivid* (Epic 1988) ★★★★, *Time's Up* (Epic 1990) ★★★★, *Stain* (Epic 1993) ★★★, *Dread* Japanese live release (Epic 1993) ★★★.
● COMPILATIONS: *Pride* (Epic 1995) ★★★★, *Super Hits* (Epic 1998) ★★★, *Play It Loud!* (Sony 1998) ★★★.

## LIVING IN A BOX

This Sheffield, England-based pop band comprised Richard Darbyshire (b. 8 March 1960, Stockport, Cheshire, England; vocal/guitars, ex-Zu Zu Sharks), Marcus Vere (b. 29 January 1962; keyboards) and Anthony Critchlow (drums). Their first single, the self-referential, 'Living In A Box' was a UK Top 10 and US Top 20 hit in the spring of 1987 and further successes followed over the next two years, most notably, 'Blow The House Down' and 'Room In Your Heart'. Meanwhile, vocalist Darbyshire guested on Jellybean's *Jellybean Rocks The House*. Having enjoyed a hit album with their self-titled debut, the band consolidated their success with *Gatecrashing*. However, they sundered in 1990 as their chart fortunes declined. Darbyshire subsequently launched an abortive solo career with Virgin Records. He enjoyed more success as a songwriter for other acts.

● ALBUMS: *Living In A Box* (Chrysalis 1987) ★★★, *Gatecrashing* (Chrysalis 1989) ★★★.
● COMPILATIONS: *The Best Of* (Disky 1999) ★★★, *The Very Best Of Living In A Box* (EMI 2000) ★★★.

## LL COOL J

b. James Todd Smith, 14 January 1968, St. Albans, Queens, New York City, USA. Long-running star of the rap scene, LL Cool J found fame at the age of 16, his pseudonym standing for 'Ladies Love Cool James'. As might be inferred by this, LL is a self-professed lady-killer in the vein of Luther Vandross or Barry White, yet he retains a superior rapping agility.

Smith started rapping at the age of nine, after his grandfather bought him his first DJ equipment. From the age of 13 he was processing his first demos. The first to respond to his mail-outs was Rick Rubin of Def Jam Records, then a senior at New York University, who signed him to his fledgling label. The first sighting of LL Cool J came in 1984 on a 12-inch, 'I Need A Beat', which was the label's first such release. However, it was 'I Just Can't Live Without My Radio', which established his gold-chained, bare-chested B-boy persona. The song was featured in the *Krush Groove* movie, on which the rapper also performed. In its wake, he embarked on a 50-city US tour alongside the Fat Boys, Whodini, Grandmaster Flash and Run-DMC. The latter were crucial to LL Cool J's development: his *modus operandi* was to combine their beatbox cruise control with streetwise B-boy raps, instantly making him a hero to a new generation of black youth. As well as continuing to tour with the trio, he would also contribute a song, 'Can You Rock It Like This', to Run-DMC's *King Of Rock*. His debut album too, would see Rubin dose the grooves with heavy metal guitar breaks first introduced by Run-DMC. LL Cool J's other early singles included 'I'm Bad', 'Go Cut Creator Go', 'Jack The Ripper' and 'I Need Love' (the first ballad rap, recorded with the Los Angeles Posse), which brought him a UK Top 10 score. Subsequent releases offered a fine array of machismo funk-rap, textured with personable charm and humour.

Like many fellow rappers, LL Cool J's career has not been without incident. Live appearances in particular have been beset by many problems. Three people were shot at a date in Baltimore in December 1985, followed by an accusation of 'public lewdness' after a 1987 show in Columbus, Ohio. While playing rap's first concert in Cote d'Ivoire, Africa, fights broke out and the stage was stormed. Most serious, however, was an incident in 1989 when singer David Parker, bodyguard Christopher Tsipouras and technician Gary Saunders were accused of raping a 15-year-old girl who attended a backstage party after winning a radio competition in Minneapolis. Though LL Cool J's personal involvement in all these cases was incidental, they undoubtedly tarnished his reputation. He has done much to make amends, including appearances at benefits including Farm Aid, recording with the Peace Choir, and launching his *Cool School Video Program*, in an attempt to encourage children to stay at school. Even Nancy Reagan invited him to headline a 'Just Say No' concert at Radio City Music Hall.

Musically, LL Cool J is probably best sampled on his 1990 set, *Mama Said Knock You Out*, produced by the omnipresent Marley Marl, which as well as the familiar sexual braggadocio included his thoughts on the state of rap past, present and future. The album went triple platinum, though the follow-up, *14 Shots To The Dome*, was a less effective attempt to recycle the formula. Some tracks stood out: 'A Little Something', anchored by a sample of King Floyd's soul standard 'Groove Me', being a good example. Like many of rap's senior players, he has also sustained an acting career, with appearances in *The Hard Way* and *Toys*, playing a cop in the former and a military man in the latter. *Phenomenon* and 2000's US chart-topping *G.O.A.T.* celebrated Cool's remarkable longevity on the rap scene, and featured guest appearances from Keith Sweat and Ralph Tresvant on the former, and Method Man and Redman on the latter.

● ALBUMS: *Radio* (Columbia 1985) ★★★, *Bigger And Deffer* (Def Jam 1987) ★★, *Walking With A Panther* (Def Jam 1989) ★★★, *Mama Said Knock You Out* (Def Jam 1990) ★★★★, *14 Shots To The Dome* (Def Jam 1992) ★★★, *Mr. Smith* (Def Jam 1995) ★★★, *Phenomenon* (Def Jam 1997) ★★★★, *G.O.A.T. Featuring James T. Smith: The Greatest Of All Time* (Def Jam 2000) ★★★.

● COMPILATIONS: *All World Greatest Hits* (Def Jam 1996) ★★★.

● FILMS: *Krush Groove* (1985), *Wildcats* aka *First And Goal* (1986), *The Hard Way* (1991), *Toys* (1992), *Out-Of-Sync* (1995), *Touch* (1997), *B\*A\*P\*S* (1997), *Caught Up* (1998), *Woo* (1998), *Halloween H20: Twenty Years Later* aka *Halloween 7* (1998), *Deep Blue Sea* (1999), *In Too Deep* (1999), *Any Given Sunday* (1999), *Charlie's Angels* (2000), *Rollerball* (2002).

## LLOYD WEBBER, ANDREW

b. 22 March 1948, London, England. The 'Sir Arthur Sullivan' of the rock age was born the son of a Royal College of Music professor and a piano teacher. His inbred musical strength manifested itself in a command of piano, violin and French horn by the time he had spent a year at Magdalen College, Oxford, where he penned *The Likes Of Us* with lyricist (and law student) Tim Rice. As well as his liking for modern composers such as Hindemith, Ligeti and Penderecki, this first musical also revealed a captivation with pop music that surfaced even more when he and Rice collaborated in 1967 on *Joseph And The Amazing Technicolor Dreamcoat*, a liberal adaptation of the scriptures. Mixing elements of psychedelia, country and French *chanson*, it was first performed at a London school in 1968 before reaching a more adult audience, via fringe events, the West End theatre (starring Paul Jones, Jess Conrad and Maynard Williams), an album, and, in 1972, national television.

In the early 70s, Lloyd Webber strayed from the stage, writing the music scores for two British films, *Gumshoe* and *The Odessa File*. His next major project with Rice was the audacious *Jesus Christ Superstar* which provoked much protest from religious groups. Among the studio cast were guest vocalists Michael D'Abo, Yvonne Elliman, Ian Gillan and Paul Raven (later Gary Glitter), accompanied by a symphony orchestra under the baton of André Previn – as well as members of Quatermass and the Grease Band. Issued well before its New York opening in 1971, the

tunes were already familiar to an audience that took to their seats night after night as the show ran for 711 performances. A less than successful film version was released in 1973. After the failure of *Jeeves* in 1975 (with Alan Ayckbourn replacing Rice) Lloyd Webber returned to form with *Evita*, an approximate musical biography of Eva Peron, self-styled 'political leader' of Argentina. It was preceded by high chart placings for its album's much-covered singles, most notably Julie Covington's 'Don't Cry For Me Argentina' and 'Oh! What A Circus' from David Essex.

*Evita* was still on Broadway in 1981 when *Cats*, based on T.S. Eliot's *Old Possum's Book Of Practical Cats*, emerged as Lloyd Webber's most commercially satisfying work so far. It was also the composer's second musical without Rice, and included what is arguably his best-known song, 'Memory', with words by Eliot and the show's director, Trevor Nunn. Elaine Paige, previously the star of *Evita*, and substituting for the injured Judi Dench in the feline role of Grizabella, took the song into the UK Top 10. Subsequently, it became popular for Barbra Streisand, among others. With *Song And Dance* (1982), which consisted of an earlier piece, *Tell Me On Sunday* (lyrics by Don Black), and *Variations* composed on a theme by Paganini for his cellist brother, Julian, Lloyd Webber became the only theatrical composer to have three works performed simultaneously in both the West End and Broadway. Two items from *Song And Dance*, 'Take That Look Off Your Face' and 'Tell Me On Sunday' became hit singles for one of its stars, Marti Webb. Produced by Cameron Mackintosh and Lloyd Webber's Really Useful Company, it was joined two years later by *Starlight Express* (lyrics by Richard Stilgoe), a train epic with music which was nicknamed 'Squeals On Wheels' because the cast dashed around on roller skates pretending to be locomotives. Diversifying further into production, Lloyd Webber presented the 1983 comedy *Daisy Pulls It Off*, followed by *The Hired Man*, *Lend Me A Tenor* and Richard Rodgers and Lorenz Hart's *On Your Toes* at London's Palace Theatre – of which he had become the new owner.

Like Sullivan before him, Lloyd Webber indulged more personal if lucrative artistic whims in such as *Requiem*, written for his father, which, along with *Variations*, became a bestselling album. A later set, *Premiere Collection*, went triple platinum. A spin-off from *Requiem*, 'Pie Jesu' (1985), was a hit single for Paul Miles-Kington and Sarah Brightman, the composer's second wife. She made the UK Top 10 again in the following year, with two numbers from Lloyd Webber's *The Phantom Of The Opera* (adapted from the Gaston Leroux novel), duetting with Steve Harley on the title theme, and later with Cliff Richard on 'All I Ask Of You'. The original 'Phantom', Michael Crawford, had great success with his recording of another song hit from the show, 'The Music Of The Night'. Controversy followed, with Lloyd Webber's battle to ensure that Brightman re-created her role of Christine in the Broadway production in 1988. His US investors capitulated, reasoning that future Lloyd Webber creations were guaranteed box office smashes before their very conception. Ironically, *Aspects Of Love* (lyrics by Charles Hart and Don Black), which also starred Brightman (by now Lloyd Webber's ex-wife), was rated as one of the failures (it did not recoup its investment) of the 1990/1 Broadway season, although it eventually ran for over 300 performances. In London, the show, which closed in 1992 after a three-year run, launched the career of Michael Ball, who had a UK number 2 with its big number, 'Love Changes Everything'.

In April 1992, he intervened in the Tate Gallery's attempt to purchase a Canaletto. Anxious, that it should remain in Britain, he bought the picture for £10 million. He was reported as commenting 'I'll have to write another musical before I do this again'. That turned out to be *Sunset Boulevard*, a stage adaptation of Billy Wilder's 1950 Hollywood classic, with Lloyd Webber's music, and book and lyrics by Don Black and Christopher Hampton. It opened in London on 12 July 1993 with Patti LuPone in the leading role of Norma Desmond, and had its American premiere in Los Angeles five months later, where Desmond was played by Glenn Close. Legal wrangles ensued when Lloyd Webber chose Close to star in the 1994 Broadway production instead of LuPone (the latter is said to have received 'somewhere in the region of $1 million compensation'), and there was further controversy when he closed down the Los Angeles production after having reservations about the vocal talents of its prospective new star, Faye Dunaway. She too, is said to have received a 'substantial settlement'. Meanwhile, *Sunset Boulevard* opened at the Minskoff Theatre in New York on November 17 with a record box office advance of $37.5 million. Like *Cats* and *The Phantom Of The Opera* before it, the show won several Tony Awards, including best musical, score and book. Lloyd Webber was living up to his rating as the most powerful person in the American theatre in a list compiled by *TheaterWeek* magazine.

Lloyd Webber's knighthood in 1992 was awarded for services to the theatre, not only in the US and UK, but throughout the world – at any one time there are dozens of his productions touring, and resident in main cities. Among his other show/song honours have been Drama Desk, Grammy, Laurence Olivier, and Ivor Novello Awards. *Cats*, together with *Starlight Express* and *Jesus Christ Superstar*, gave Lloyd Webber the three longest-running musicals in British theatre history for a time, before the latter show was overtaken by *Les Misérables*. He is also the first person to have a trio of musicals running in London and New York. *Jesus Christ Superstar* celebrated its 20th anniversary in 1992 with a UK concert tour, and other Lloyd Webber highlights of that year included a series of concerts entitled *The Music Of Andrew Lloyd Webber* (special guest star Michael Crawford), a smash hit revival of *Joseph And The Amazing Technicolor Dreamcoat* at the London Palladium, and the recording, by Sarah Brightman and José Carreras, of Lloyd Webber and Don Black's Barcelona Olympic Games anthem 'Friends For Life' ('Amigos Para Siempre').

Since those heady days, Lloyd Webber admirers have waited in vain for another successful theatrical project, although there has been no shortage of personal kudos. He was inducted into the Songwriters Hall of Fame, presented with the Praemium Imperiale Award for Music, became the first recipient of the ASCAP Triple Play Award, and in 1996 received the Richard Rodgers Award for Excellence in the Musical Theatre. In the same year, a revised version of his 1975 flop, *Jeeves*, entitled By Jeeves, was well received during its extended West End season, but a new work, *Whistle Down The Wind* (lyrics: Jim Steinman, book: Patricia Knop), failed to transfer to Broadway following its Washington premiere. After being extensively reworked, it played for two and a half years in London's West End. A revival of *Jesus Christ Superstar* re-opened the old Lyceum, just off the Strand, and a film version of *Evita*, starring Madonna, was finally released, containing a new Lloyd Webber–Rice song, 'You Must Love Me', for which they won Academy Awards.

Elevated to the peerage in 1997, Baron Lloyd-Webber of Sydmonton disclosed that the New York and London productions of *Sunset Boulevard*, which both closed early in that year, 'lost money massively overall', and that his Really Useful Group had reduced its staff and suffered substantial financial setbacks. On the brighter side, in January 1996 the West End production of his most enduring show, *Cats*, took over from *A Chorus Line* as the longest-running musical of all time, and in June 1997, the show's New York production replaced *A Chorus Line* as the longest-running show (musical or play) in Broadway history. The New York production finally closed on 10 September 2000 after a run of 7,485 performances and the West End production closed on its 21st anniversary on 11 May 2002.

Early in 1998, Lloyd Webber was honoured with *Variety*'s first British Entertainment Personality Of The Year Award, and two years later he became the largest West End theatre owner, when, with backing from City financiers, he bought the Stoll Moss group of 10 theatres, including the London Palladium and Theatre Royal, Drury Lane, for £87.5 million. In the same month, Lloyd Webber's latest effort, *The Beautiful Game*, opened in the West End. Written with comedian/author Ben Elton, it won the London Critics Circle Award for Best Musical. In 2002, Lloyd Webber shrewdly tapped into the fashionable Anglo-Indian market with his new musical *Bombay Dreams*, a colourful extravaganza set against the backdrop of India's famous film industry. The script was provided by actress/author Meera Syal, lyrics by Don Black and the music by composer A.R. Rahman. The show opened at London's Apollo Victoria Theatre on 19 June.

● ALBUMS: *Masterpiece: Live From The Great Hall Of The People, Beijing* (Eagle 2002) ★★★.

● COMPILATIONS: *The Very Best Of ... Broadway Collection* (Polydor 1996) ★★★, *Gold* (Polydor 2001) ★★★, *Now & Forever* 5-CD box set (Decca Broadway 2002) ★★★.

● VIDEOS: *The Premier Collection Encore* (PolyGram Music Video 1994), *Andrew Lloyd Webber: Celebration* (PolyGram Music Video 1998).

● FURTHER READING: *Andrew Lloyd Webber*, G. McKnight. *Fanfare: The Unauthorized Biography Of*

*Andrew Lloyd Webber*, J. Mantle. *Andrew Lloyd Webber: His Life And Works*, M. Walsh. *Cats On A Chandelier: The Andrew Lloyd Webber Story*, Michael Coveney.

## LOGGINS, KENNY

b. 7 January 1948, Everett, Washington, USA. Loggins, who began his career as a staff writer for Wingate Music, came to prominence as a member of Loggins And Messina from 1972 to 77. After separating from Jim Messina, he set out on a solo recording career, specialising in rock ballads such as 'Whenever I Call You "Friend"', a 1978 US Top 5 hit which was co-written by Melissa Manchester and had harmony vocals by Stevie Nicks. In 1979, Loggins enjoyed a Top 20 hit with 'This Is It' and co-wrote the Doobie Brothers' million-selling US chart-topper 'What A Fool Believes' with the band's singer, Michael McDonald. The US Top 20 hit 'Don't Fight It', meanwhile, was a collaboration with Journey singer Steve Perry. During the 80s, Loggins came to prominence as a writer and performer of theme songs for the new breed of Hollywood action movies. Beginning with 1980's Top 10 hit 'I'm Alright' (from *Caddyshack*) and 1984's chart-topping title song from *Footloose* (also a UK Top 10 hit), he reached his commercial peak with the soundtrack of *Top Gun* in 1986. As well as co-writing several of the songs used in the movie, Loggins recorded the US number 2 hit, 'Danger Zone'. This was followed by music for 1988's *Caddyshack II*, including another US Top 10 hit, 'Nobody's Fool'. He had a minor hit with 'Conviction Of The Heart' in 1991, taken from his 'divorce' album, *Leap Of Faith*. Six years later he concurrently released an album and book detailing his remarriage. His most successful recordings in recent years have been two children's albums named after his first ever hit song, 'House At Pooh Corner', which the Nitty Gritty Dirt Band took into the US charts in 1971.

● ALBUMS: *Celebrate Me Home* (Columbia 1977) ★★★, *Nightwatch* (Columbia 1978) ★★★, *Keep The Fire* (Columbia 1979) ★★★★, *Alive* (Columbia 1980) ★★★, *High Adventure* (Columbia 1982) ★★★, *Vox Humana* (Columbia 1985) ★★, *Back To Avalon* (Columbia 1988) ★★, *Leap Of Faith* (Columbia 1991) ★★, *Outside From The Redwoods - An Acoustic Afternoon* (Columbia 1993) ★★★, *Return To Pooh Corner* (Sony Wonder 1994) ★★★, *The Unimaginable Life* (Sony 1997) ★★, *December* (Sony 1998) ★★★, *More Songs From Pooh Corner* (Sony Wonder 2000) ★★★.

● COMPILATIONS: *At His Best* (Hollywood 1992) ★★★, *Yesterday, Today, Tomorrow: The Greatest Hits Of Kenny Loggins* (Columbia 1997) ★★★.

● VIDEOS: *Alive* (CBS/Fox 1981), *Outside From The Redwoods* (Sony Music Video 1993), *Return To Pooh Corner* (Sony Wonder 1996).

● FURTHER READING: *The Unimaginable Life: Lessons Learned On The Path Of Love*, Kenny And Julia Loggins.

## LONE JUSTICE

US country-rockers fronted by Maria McKee (b. 17 August 1964, Los Angeles, California, USA) who was the half-sister of Love's Bryan MacLean. When she was just three years old, her brother would take her to the various clubs along Los Angeles' Sunset Strip and she was befriended by the likes of Frank Zappa and the Doors. When she grew up, she and MacLean formed a duo initially called the Maria McKee Band, but later changed to the Bryan MacLean Band to cash in on *his* slightly higher profile. Heavily immersed in country music, McKee formed the first incarnation of Lone Justice with Ryan Hedgecock (guitar), Don Heffington (drums) and Marvin Etzioni (bass). The band earned a recording contract with Geffen Records at the recommendation of Linda Ronstadt. McKee's talents were also admired by artists such as Bob Dylan, U2's Bono, who offered them a support slot on tour, and Tom Petty, who donated songs to the first album. One of these, 'Ways To Be Wicked', while not achieving any notable chart status, was responsible for bringing the band to the attention of the UK audience via an imaginative black-and-white, cut-up-and-scratched video. The band's more established line-up transmuted to that of expatriate Brit Shayne Fontayne (guitar), Bruce Brody (keyboards), Gregg Sutton (bass) and Rudy Richman (drums). They were managed by the respected producer Jimmy Iovine. In 1985, former Undertones singer Feargal Sharkey had a UK number 1 hit with McKee's 'A Good Heart'. Lone Justice split suddenly in 1987 with McKee going on to a solo career, taking only Brody with her from Lone Justice.

● ALBUMS: *Lone Justice* (Geffen 1985) ★★★, *Shelter* (Geffen 1987) ★★, *Radio One Live In Concert* 1986 recording (Windsong 1993) ★★.

● COMPILATIONS: *This World Is Not My Home* (Geffen 1999) ★★★.

## LONG RYDERS

Formed in November 1981, the Long Riders (as they were then known) initially included three ex-members of the Unclaimed - Sid Griffin (b. Kentucky, USA; guitar, vocals), Barry Shank (bass, vocals) and Matt Roberts (drums). Steve Wynn completed this early line-up, but the guitarist was replaced by Stephen McCarthy on leaving to form the Dream Syndicate. Griffin and McCarthy remained at the helm throughout the group's turbulent history. As part of Los Angeles' 'paisley underground' movement, the Long Ryders' history is linked with not only that of the Dream Syndicate, but also that of other guitar-orientated bands such as Rain Parade, (early) Bangles, Green On Red and Blood On The Saddle. A mini-album, *The Long Ryders*, was completed with Des Brewer (bass) and Greg Sowders (drums), although by the time the quartet secured a permanent contract, Tom Stevens had joined in place of Brewer. *Native Sons*, an excellent set influenced by Buffalo Springfield and Gram Parsons, suggested a promising future, but the Long Ryders were unable to repeat its balance of melody and purpose. They withered on record company indecision and, unable to secure a release from their contract, the group broke up in 1987. Griffin moved on to a dual career leading the Coal Porters and working as a music journalist.

● ALBUMS: *The Long Ryders* aka *10.5.60* mini-album

(PVC 1983) ★★★, *Native Sons* (Frontier/Zippo 1984) ★★★★, *State Of Our Union* (Island 1985) ★★★, *Two-Fisted Tales* (Island 1987) ★★, *BBC Radio One In Concert* (Windsong 1994) ★★★.
● COMPILATIONS: *Metallic B.O.* early recordings (Overground 1990) ★★, *Best Of The Long Ryders* (PolyGram 1998) ★★★★.

## LOOSE TUBES

Appearing on the London scene in 1984 this big (20-piece plus) band appealed to (and reflected) the new, smart young audience jazz was attracting at the time, and seemed likely to prove a considerable 'crossover' success. It was run as a collective, although trombonist Ashley Slater acted as 'frontman' and Django Bates (b. Leon Bates, 2 October 1960, Beckenham, Kent, England) emerged as a main writer for the band. Characterized by clever arrangements, technically slick soloing and an urbane stage-presence, Loose Tubes was acclaimed by many critics and created interest in jazz among sections of the public that had not previously paid the genre any attention. It spawned several other successful units, which indulged in various styles (funk, African, soca, bebop and so on), including Human Chain, Pig Head Son, Lift, the Iain Ballamy Quartet, the Steve Berry Trio, the Tim Whitehead Band, Parker Bates Stubbs and the Julian Argüelles Quartet. By the early 90s the parent group had disbanded – although reunions should never be ruled out. Slater later enjoyed commercial success collaborating with DJ Norman Cook as Freakpower.
● ALBUMS: *Loose Tubes* (Loose Tubes 1984 ★★★★, *Delightful Precipice* (Loose Tubes 1986) ★★★, *Open Letter* (Editions EG 1988) ★★★.

## LORA LOGIC

London, England-based art student Susan Whitby originally adopted the pseudonym Lora Logic during her stint as saxophonist in X-Ray Spex. After leaving that group following their debut single, she soon re-emerged in 1978 with her own outfit, Essential Logic, who quickly recorded a couple of hard-edged EPs, *Aerosol Burns* and *Wake Up*. One album was recorded, *Beat Rhythm News* (1979), before Lora commenced on a series of solo recordings in 1981. Her quirky, occasionally arresting, vocals were in evidence on her sole album, *Pedigree Charm*, and she can be heard on a number of recordings by other artists including the Raincoats, Stranglers, Swell Maps and Red Crayola. Logic later joined the Hare Krishna cult, just like X-Ray Spex's Poly Styrene before her. She returned to music in the mid-90s to play with the re-formed X-Ray Spex. She revived the Essential Logic moniker in the new millennium, teaming up with Gary Valentine (guitar), Dave Jones (bass) and Nick Pretzell (drums) to record a four-track mini-album.
● ALBUMS: *Pedigree Charm* (Rough Trade 1982) ★★★.

## LORDS OF THE NEW CHURCH

This rock band was made up of several well-known personalities, and was often described as a punk 'supergroup'. The personnel comprised Brian James

(b. 18 February 1961; guitar, ex-Damned), Stiv Bators (b. Stivin Bators, 22 October 1949, Cleveland, Ohio, USA, d. 5 June 1990, Paris, France; vocals, ex-Dead Boys), Dave Tregunna (b. 1954, Derby, England; bass, ex-Sham 69) and drummer Nicky Turner (b. 4 May 1959; ex-Barracudas). When Jimmy Pursey left Sham 69, the rest of the band had continued in the Wanderers, drafting in Stiv Bators. It was at this point that James contacted Bators with a view to setting up a group. Miles Copeland took on their management, their name coming from his original suggestion, Lords Of Discipline. They made their live debut in Paris in 1981. Their debut vinyl, 'New Church', helped to increase criticisms about the band's apparent blasphemy, hardly dispelled when the album appeared with lines such as: 'Greed and murder is forgiven when in the name of the Church'. The self-titled debut premiered an authentic rock band with dark shades, flirting with apocalyptic and religious imagery. The single, 'Dance With Me', from *Is Nothing Sacred?*, gained several MTV plays with a video directed by Derek Jarman. Unfortunately, its success was scuppered after mistaken allegations about paedophilia saw it taken off air. Their final studio album, *Method To Our Madness*, revealed a band treading water with stifled heavy rock routines. They did not split officially until 1989, but before that Tregunna had departed for Cherry Bombz, while Alistair Simmons contributed some guitar. Bators died the following year after being struck by a car in Paris. James and Tregunna revived the Lords Of The New Church name in 2002, touring Europe and the USA.
● ALBUMS: *Lords Of The New Church* (I.R.S./Illegal 1982) ★★, *Is Nothing Sacred?* (I.R.S. 1983) ★★★, *Method To Our Madness* (I.R.S. 1984) ★★, *Live At The Spit* 1982 recording (Illegal 1988) ★★, *The Lords Prayers I* (Pilot 2002) ★★, *The Lords Prayers I* (Pilot 2002) ★★.
● COMPILATIONS: *Killer Lords* (I.R.S./Illegal 1985) ★★★.
● VIDEOS: *Holy War* (JE 1994), *Live From London* (K-Tel 2000).

## LORI AND THE CHAMELEONS

Formed in 1979 in Liverpool, England, this band was a vehicle for the evocative teenage singer Lori Larty. With backing, production and songwriting provided by former Big In Japan alumni David Balfe and Bill Drummond, Lori emerged with an appealing, almost spoken-word tribute to Japan (the country), entitled 'Touch'. A sparkling arrangement, the disc entered the bottom of the UK charts and appeared to signal the emergence of a new talent. The concept of the group appeared to revolve vaguely around exotic, travelogue pop, with each song title referring to a specific geographical location: Japan, Peru, Russia and the Ganges River in India. The second single, 'The Lonely Spy', boasted another impressive, atmospheric vocal from Lori and an astonishing backing that emulated the bombastic scores associated with *James Bond* films. After four superb tracks, which represented some of the best UK pop of the period, the group ceased operating. The journeyman Troy Tate reappeared in the Teardrop

Explodes, while Drummond turned to management and was later the brains behind a series of pseudonymous groups including the Justified Ancients Of Mu Mu (JAMS) and the Timelords who later emerged as the very successful KLF. Lori, meanwhile, spurned imminent pop success by returning to art college and effectively retiring from the music business. Her fleeting career provided as much mystery and instant appeal as the extraordinary discs on which she appeared.

## LOS LOBOS

Los Lobos are the undisputed leaders of the Tex-Mex brand of rock 'n' roll, which is Latin-based Chicano music built around accordion and guitar. They were formed in 1973 in Los Angeles by Cesar Rosas (b. 26 September 1954; vocals, guitar, mandolin), David Hidalgo (b. 6 October 1954; vocals, guitar, accordion), Luis (Louie) Pérez (b. 29 January 1953; drums, guitar, quinto), and Conrad Lozano (b. 21 March 1951; vocals, bass, guitarron). Their mixture of Clifton Chenier zydeco and Richie Valens rock was a totally refreshing new sound. Their debut album came in 1978 with the self-financed *Just Another Band From East LA*, and although not a hit it was a critical success. The line-up was bolstered in 1983 by multi-instrumentalist Steve Berlin (b. 14 September 1955). The reviewers welcomed the following year's *How Will The Wolf Survive?*, with open arms, but still it only made moderate sales. The superb title track vocal has an uncanny resemblance to Steve Winwood, although it was not representative of the style of the whole album. The band continued to receive excellent reviews of their stage act, but it was not until 1987 that they found commercial success. Following their major contribution to the film soundtrack *La Bamba* the title single was released. It became an international number 1 and the first song in Spanish to top the pop charts. *La Pistola Y El Corazón* was a deliberate attempt to go back to their roots following their recent overwhelming profile. *Kiko* in 1992 was an excellent record, moving them back to a varied rock approach with delightful hints of Cajun, straight rock and even soul music. *Colossal Head* in 1996 featured ex-Attractions drummer Pete Thomas. Hidalgo and Perez have also recorded with their sideline project, the Latin Playboys, while Rosas worked with the all-star Tex-Mex outfit Los Super Seven and released his solo debut, *Soul Disguise*. The main group re-formed for their Hollywood Records debut, *This Time*.
● ALBUMS: *Del Este De Los Angeles* aka *Just Another Band From East LA* (New Vista 1978) ★★★, *And A Time To Dance* (Slash 1983) ★★★, *How Will The Wolf Survive?* (Slash 1984) ★★★★, *By The Light Of The Moon* (Slash 1987) ★★★★, *La Pistola Y El Corazón* (Slash 1988) ★★★, *The Neighborhood* (Slash 1990) ★★★★, *Kiko* (Slash 1992) ★★★★, with Lalo Guerrero *Papa's Dream* (Warners 1995) ★★★, *Colossal Head* (Warners 1996) ★★★, *This Time* (Hollywood 1999) ★★★★, *Good Morning Aztlán* (Mammoth 2002) ★★★.
● COMPILATIONS: various artists *Si Se Puede!* (Pan American 1976) ★★★, *Just Another Band From East L.A.: A Collection* (Slash/Warners 1993) ★★★★, *El*

*Cancionero Mas Y Mas: La Historia De La Banda Del Este De Los Angeles* 4-CD box set (Rhino/WEA 2000) ★★★★.

## LOTUS EATERS

Rising from the ashes of the Wild Swans, Liverpool, England's Lotus Eaters enjoyed instant commercial success with a fragrant pop song, 'The First Picture Of You', their debut single reaching UK number 15 in July 1983. Revolving around Peter Coyle (vocals) and Jem Kelly (guitar), plus Alan Wills (drums), Gerard Quinn (keyboards) and Phil (bass), the rhythm section was later replaced by Michael Dempsey (bass) and Steve Creese (drums). However, the band never managed to regain their Top 20 status, despite four catchy follow-ups: 'You Don't Need Someone New' later in 1983, 'Set Me Apart' and 'Out On Your Own' (both 1984) and a final attempt, 'It Hurts' (1985). Those who appreciate well-crafted, quality melodic pop should look no further than their debut album, *No Sense Of Sin*. Coyle and Kelly later reactivated the Wild Swans but were again unable to sustain significant interest. They made a surprise return to the studio in the new millennium to record a second Lotus Eaters album, *Silentspace*.
● ALBUMS: *No Sense Of Sin* (Sylvan 1984) ★★★, *Silentspace* (Vinyl Japan 2001) ★★★.
● COMPILATIONS: *The First Picture Of You* (Vinyl Japan 1998) ★★★.

## LOVE AND ROCKETS

This *avant garde* UK rock band formed at Christmas 1985 from the ashes of Bauhaus. When David Jay (aka David J) had finished working with the Jazz Butcher on the *Sex And Travel* and *A Scandal In Bohemia* albums, he linked up once more with old colleague Daniel Ash, who had been working with Tones On Tail. Kevin Haskins also came with Ash, forming the band's nucleus of David Jay (vocals, bass, keyboards), Daniel Ash (vocals, guitar, keyboards) and Haskins (drums, keyboards). Early singles included 'Kundiluni Express', concerning Tantric meditation, and a cover of the Temptations' 'Ball Of Confusion'. The band's 1985 debut, *Seventh Dream Of Teenage Heaven*, was a celebration of the rituals of youth, based loosely on their own experiences of going to rock concerts to see bands such as Roxy Music. Like all of the post-Bauhaus projects, the band failed to cultivate a UK audience to rival their previous standing. However, they had a Top 5 hit single in the USA in 1989 with the hard-rocking 'So Alive', where their work still sells moderately well. Both Ash and David J concentrated on their solo careers, before Love And Rockets returned with *Hot Trip To Heaven*, a bold, dance-oriented record. Following the *Glittering Darkness* EP, the band jettisoned the ambient dance approach for the *Sweet F.A.* album, which featured the moderately successful single, 'Sweet Lover Hangover'. Beggars Banquet Records dropped the band in 1997, and following one further release the members elected to return to their solo careers.
● ALBUMS: *Seventh Dream Of Teenage Heaven* (Beggars Banquet 1985) ★★, *Express* (Beggars Banquet 1986) ★★★, *Earth Sun Moon* (Beggars

Banquet 1987) ★★★, *Love And Rockets* (Beggars Banquet 1988) ★★★, *Hot Trip To Heaven* (American 1994) ★★★, *Sweet F.A.* (Beggars Banquet 1996) ★★★, *Lift* (Red Ant 1998) ★★★.

## LOVERBOY

Canadian hard rock outfit formed in 1978 by Mike Reno (b. Joseph Michael Rynoski, 8 January 1955, New Westminster, British Columbia, Canada; vocals), Paul Dean (b. 19 February 1946, Vancouver, British Columbia, Canada; guitar), Doug Johnston (b. 19 December 1957, Vancouver, British Columbia, Canada; keyboards), Scott Smith (b. Donald Scott Smith, 13 February 1955, d. November 2000, California, USA; bass) and Matthew Frenette (b. 7 March 1954, Calgary, Alberta, Canada; drums). Reno was formerly with Moxy, and Dean and Frenette had been members of Streetheart, a melodic AOR/heavy rock band. With this pedigree, Loverboy was signed up by Columbia Records in March 1980. Producer Bruce Fairbairn helped them to record a self-titled album that was to set Loverboy's standard for years to come. It was an US styled melodic hard rock collection that also dipped into reggae and jazz moods. Buoyed by the US hit singles 'Turn Me Loose' (number 35) and 'The Kid Is Hot Tonite' (number 55), *Loverboy* went platinum. After touring, the band re-entered the studio, with Fairbairn again producing, to record the follow-up, *Get Lucky*. The album lived up to its name by selling over three million copies, helped by the US Top 30 success of 'Working For The Weekend' and 'When It's Over'. The only territory where the band had failed to take off was Europe. After further touring Fairbairn produced the multi-platinum *Keep It Up* in 1983, from which 'Hot Girls In Love' reached US number 11. Loverboy's inviting blend of melodic AOR had been honed to a fine art, the album's success keeping the band on the road for nearly two years. On *Lovin' Every Minute Of It* they were joined by Tom Allom, best known for his work with Judas Priest. The result was a musically tougher album that proved to be the band's least successful, though it still sold well over a million copies. The title track, written by Def Leppard producer Robert John 'Mutt' Lange, broke into the US Top 10, as did 'This Could Be The Night'. 'Heaven In Your Eyes', taken from the soundtrack of *Top Gun*, reached US number 12 later in the year. Fairbairn had by now made his name as the producer of Bon Jovi, but returned to the helm for Loverboy's *Wildside*, released in 1987, and one of their most cohesive albums. Bryan Adams, Richie Sambora and Jon Bon Jovi all co-wrote various tracks. This was followed by a marathon two-year tour, the band's longest yet. They did, however, take a break for two months to record tracks with producer Bob Rock before supporting Def Leppard on their European tour in the spring of 1988. Afterwards, Loverboy returned home to Canada and an uncertain future. Dean and Reno announced plans to record solo and this left the rest of the band in limbo. In 1989, the *Big Ones* compilation was released by Columbia. The album contained three new tracks that had been recorded with Bob Rock. Later that year, Dean released a solo effort assisted

by Loverboy drummer Frenette and Jon Bon Jovi on harmonica. The parent band re-formed for a benefit gig in 1992, and the following May resumed playing as a full-time unit. Several US tours followed before Johnson decided to leave the band in December 1996. The remaining quartet released a new album on the CMC International label in 1997. Scott Smith died in a boating accident in November 2000. Loverboy carried on with Streetheart bass player Spider Sinnaeve.

● ALBUMS: *Loverboy* (Columbia 1980) ★★★, *Get Lucky* (Columbia 1981) ★★★, *Keep It Up* (Columbia 1983) ★★★, *Lovin' Every Minute Of It* (Columbia 1985) ★★★, *Wildside* (Columbia 1987) ★★★, *Six* aka *VI* (CMC 1997) ★★.

● COMPILATIONS: *Big Ones* (Columbia 1989) ★★★★, *Classics* (Columbia 1994) ★★★, *Temperature's Rising* (Sony 1995) ★★★, *Super Hits* (Sony 1997) ★★★, *Live, Loud And Loose. (1982-1986)* (Columbia 2001) ★★★.

● VIDEOS: *Loverboy In Concert* (Vestron Video 1985), *Any Way You Look At It* (CBO 1986).

## LOVETT, LYLE

b. Lyle Pearce Lovett, 1 November 1957, Klein, Texas, USA. Singer-songwriter Lovett grew up 25 miles north of Houston in the rural Klein community (an area largely populated by farmers of German extraction), which was named after his grandfather, Adam Klein. During his teenage years, as Houston's borders expanded, Lovett was exposed to more urban influences, and attended Texas A&M University where he studied journalism and then German. During this period (late 70s), he began writing songs; his early heroes included Guy Clark (who later wrote a dedication on the sleeve of Lovett's first album), Jerry Jeff Walker and Townes Van Zandt. Having visited Europe (to improve his German) in the late 70s, he met a local country musician named Buffalo Wayne (who apparently took his name from his favourite western heroes), and remained in touch after returning to Texas – when Wayne was organizing an event in Luxembourg in 1983, he booked Lovett, and also on the bill was an American band from Phoenix whose members included Matt Rollings (keyboards) and Ray Herndon (guitar), who were later involved with Lovett's albums.

Lovett worked the same Texas music circuit as Nanci Griffith, singing on two of her early albums, *Once In A Very Blue Moon* (1984, which included one of his songs, 'If I Were The Woman You Wanted') and *Last Of The True Believers* (1985), on the cover of which he is pictured. When Guy Clark heard a demo tape by Lovett in 1984, he passed it on to Tony Brown of MCA Records, and by 1986, Lovett had signed to MCA/Curb. His self-titled debut album was idiosyncratic, to say the least, including both the song covered by Griffith and 'Closing Time', which was covered by Lacy J. Dalton, as well as a fine song he co-wrote with fellow singer-songwriter Robert Earl Keen Jnr., 'This Old Porch'. However, his acceptance was slow in US country music circles, and Lovett first received substantial critical acclaim when the album was eventually released in Europe.

The follow-up, *Pontiac*, was released in 1987 after Lovett had successfully toured Europe backed only by cellist John Hagen. The album made it clear that Lovett was rather more than a folk or country artist, with songs such as the surreal 'If I Had A Boat' and 'She's Hot To Go', while guests on the album included Emmylou Harris. By this time, Lovett was talking about both recording and touring with what he called His Large Band, with several saxophone players and a female backing singer, Francine Reed, as well as a regular rhythm section, and his third album, released in 1989, was indeed titled *Lyle And His Large Band*. Including an insidiously straight cover version of the Tammy Wynette standard 'Stand By Your Man', and a version of the R&B oldie 'The Glory Of Love', this again delighted critics by its very humour and eclecticism, but further confused record buyers, especially in the USA, who were unsure whether this was a country or jazz record or something quite different.

At this point Lovett moved away from Nashville, where he was regarded as too weird, and as a result, his fourth album, produced by Los Angeles heavyweight George Massenburg, was not released until early 1992. Its title, *Joshua Judges Ruth* (three consecutive books in the Old Testament, but meaning something very different if read as a phrase), was symptomatic of Lovett's intelligence, but perhaps equally so of his idiosyncratic approach. As usual, critics loved it, although it included hardly any traces of country music, and seemed to portray him as a Tom Waits-like figure – ultra-sophisticated, but somewhat off the wall. In 1992, Lovett was chosen as the opening act for many of the dates on the first world tour during the 90s by Dire Straits. This exposed him to a huge international audience, but seems to have done little to extend his cult following. In the same year, Lovett met Hollywood actress Julia Roberts on the set of *The Player*, a high-grossing movie, in which Lovett played the role of detective DeLongpre. They married in June 1993; the following year their marriage was floundering, and by 1995 it was over.

Lovett resumed his career as one of the sharpest and wittiest songwriters to come out of America in recent times. He performed 'You've Got A Friend In Me' with Randy Newman for the soundtrack of the hugely successful movie *Toy Story*. *The Road To Ensenada* mixed Lovett's razor wit with pathos. Long-standing observers of Lovett's lyrics will read much into this album and pontificate for hours about their relevance to his relationship with Roberts. On *Step Inside This House*, Lovett performed revelatory cover versions of 21 favourite Texan songs.

● ALBUMS: *Lyle Lovett* (MCA/Curb 1986) ★★★★, *Pontiac* (MCA/Curb 1987) ★★★★, *Lyle Lovett And His Large Band* (MCA/Curb 1989) ★★★, *Joshua Judges Ruth* (MCA/Curb 1992) ★★★★, *I Love Everybody* (MCA/Curb 1994) ★★★★, *The Road To Ensenada* (MCA/Curb 1996) ★★★, *Step Inside This House* (MCA/Curb 1998) ★★★, *Live In Texas* (MCA/Curb 1999) ★★★★.

● COMPILATIONS: *Anthology Volume One: Cowboy Man* (MCA 2001) ★★★★.

● FILMS: *The Player* (1992), *Short Cuts* (1993), *Luck,*

*Trust & Ketchup: Robert Altman In Carver Country* (1993), *Prêt-à-Porter* aka *Ready To Wear* (1994), *Bastard Out Of Carolina* (1996), *Fear And Loathing In Las Vegas* (1998), *The Opposite Of Sex* (1998), *Cookie's Fortune* (1999), *3 Days Of Rain* (2000), *The New Guy* (2002).

## LUDUS

Founded in 1978, this Manchester, England-based quartet was consistently fronted by the enigmatic lyricist/vocalist Linder Sterling aka Linda Mulvey (b. Liverpool, England). The backing was provided by Arthur Cadmon (b. Peter Sadler, Stockport, England), formerly of Manicured Noise and originally the musical genius behind the group. The line-up was completed by bass player Willie Trotter (b. Manchester, England) and drummer Phil 'Toby' Tolman (ex-Ed Banger And The Nosebleeds). With their jazz-influenced forays and Linder's strong, sloganeering, elliptical feminist lyrics, the band were one of the most interesting of the Manchester new wave of the late 70s. The departure of Cadmon and later Trotter, replaced by Ian Devine (b. Ian Pincombe), saw them change direction, though the jazz influence remained. Sterling, a former girlfriend of Howard Devoto and designer of the striking sleeve art for the Buzzcocks' 'Orgasm Addict', later became a well-publicized confidante of Morrissey and established herself as one of the UK's leading visual artists. In spite of some inspired moments, the band almost wilfully avoided the mainstream, although their final singles for Les Disques Du Crepuscule, including 'Sordide Sentimental', displayed a certain pop sensibility via the keyboards and production of former Magazine member Dave Formula. As manager Richard Boon concluded: 'Ludus were totally improvisational and their set list would read: "bass, drums, voice, next number". There was something self-limiting about Linder. Any time she seemed on the brink of a breakthrough, even if that meant selling 50 extra records, she would retreat, just like the poet Stevie Smith.' Ian Devine teamed up in 1989 with ex-Weekend singer Alison Statton to form Devine And Statton.

● ALBUMS: *The Seduction* (New Hormones 1980) ★★★, *Pickpocket* (New Hormones 1981) ★★★.

● COMPILATIONS: *Nue Au Soleil* (Les Disques Du Crepuscule/Interior 1987) ★★★, *The Damage* (LTM 2002) ★★★.

## LYNCH, RAY

b. 3 July 1943, Utah, USA. One of the most prominent and influential of the new age musicians of the 80s, Lynch's initial training was on piano, before he switched to classical guitar at age 12 after hearing Andrés Segovia's work. Later he moved to Barcelona, Spain, studying guitar technique for three years under Eduardo Sainz de la Maza. His studies continued back in America with a three-year course at the University of Texas, learning composition of symphonic and chamber music. Some of these scores were later performed by the Dallas Symphony Orchestra. He also joined a group of madrigal singers as an auxiliary lutist. This led to an invitation to join the Renaissance Quartet in New York. He consequently relocated to the east coast and spent seven years performing with the Quartet and other sympathetic 'early music' groups, with interest in medieval and baroque music undergoing something of a revival.

Purchasing a 125-acre farm in Maine, Lynch concurrently toured the country giving virtuoso solo performances, until he found something lacking in his life and dropped everything to move to California. His recording career was well under way at this point, having started in 1983 with *The Sky Of The Mind*, a reflective piece of mood music, with Tibetan bells merging with classically formed song structures. *Deep Breakfast* became a certified Platinum album in the aftermath, mainly on the strength of the accompanying hit single, 'Celestial Soda Pop'. The five year delay before *No Blue Thing* engendered a much expanded sound, with evocative melodies fashioning a full, adroit range of moods and atmospherics. It quickly became a runaway success in US new age circles, staying on *Billboard*'s genre chart for 122 weeks. Lynch also won *Billboard*'s award for New Age Album Of The Year, an honour that the same record was awarded again the following year. 1993's *Nothing Above My Shoulders But The Evening* reflected on the trials of the human spirit, with Lynch commenting: 'The mind filters out so much of our humanity. Great art, if we participate fully in it, gives us permission to feel, and creates a space in which we can feel at a depth not ordinarily allowed.'

● ALBUMS: *The Sky Of Mind* (Ray Lynch Productions 1983) ★★★, *Deep Breakfast* (Ray Lynch Productions 1984) ★★★, *No Blue Thing* (Windham Hill 1989) ★★★★, *Nothing Above My Shoulders But The Evening* (Windham Hill 1993) ★★★.
● COMPILATIONS: *Best Of Volume One* (Windham Hill 1998) ★★★★.

## LYNNE, JEFF

b. 30 December 1947, Birmingham, England. Lynne's long and varied musical career began in 1966 when he joined the Nightriders, a popular beat group still reeling from the loss of their leader, Mike Sheridan, and guitarist, Roy Wood. Having completed all contractual obligations, the band took the name, Idle Race and, under Lynne's guidance, became a leading exponent of classic late 60s pop. Frustrated at a lack of commercial success, the artist opted to join the Move in 1970, where he was teamed with the aforementioned Wood. Lynne's contributions to the unit's late-period catalogue included the riff-laden 'Do Ya', but this era is also marked by the duo's desire to form a more experimental outlet for their talents. This resulted in the launch of the Electric Light Orchestra, or ELO, of which Lynne took full control upon Wood's early and sudden departure. ELO gradually developed from cult favourites into one of the 70s leading recording acts, scoring international success with several platinum-selling albums, including *A New World Record* and *Out Of The Blue*. Lynne's dual talents as a composer and producer ensured the band's status but sensing an artistic sterility, he abandoned his creation in 1986. The artist then assumed an

increasingly backroom role, but won praise for his production work with George Harrison (*Cloud Nine*), Randy Newman (*Land Of Dreams*) and Roy Orbison (*Mystery Girl*). He also contributed his distinctive production qualities to much of Tom Petty's output during this period.

Lynne's work with Orbison coincided with his position as 'Otis Wilbury' in the Traveling Wilburys, an informal 'supergroup' completed by Orbison, Harrison, Tom Petty and Bob Dylan. This particularly prolific period was also marked by his work with Brian Wilson on the ex-Beach Boys' first long-awaited solo album. In 1990, Lynne also unveiled his own solo debut, *Armchair Theatre*, on which his gifts for pop melody remained as sure as ever. In the mid-90s, Lynne gained a measure of success (and some criticism) for his production of the Beatles lost tapes, notably 'Free As A Bird' and 'Real Love'. He co-produced Paul McCartney's excellent *Flaming Pie* in 1997. In 2001, he returned to the ELO moniker and released a new album.
● ALBUMS: *Armchair Theatre* (Reprise 1990) ★★★.
● COMPILATIONS: *Message From The Country (The Jeff Lynne Years 1968-1973)* (Harvest 1979) ★★★.

## LYNOTT, PHIL

b. Philip Parris Lynott, 20 August 1949, Birmingham, West Midlands, England, d. 4 January 1986, Eire. Having enjoyed considerable success in Thin Lizzy, Lynott first recorded solo in 1980, the same year that he married Caroline Crowther, daughter of UK television celebrity Leslie Crowther. Lynott's first single, 'Dear Miss Lonely Hearts', reached number 32 in the UK charts and was followed by an album, *Solo In Soho*. A tribute to Elvis Presley, 'King's Call' also reached number 35. Lynott had to wait until 1982 for his next hit, 'Yellow Pearl', which reached the UK Top 20 after being used as the theme tune to television show *Top Of The Pops*. In the summer of 1983, Thin Lizzy broke up and it was widely anticipated that Lynott would go on to solo fame. A new group, Grand Slam, failed to develop and Lynott's subsequent solo single, 'Nineteen', did not sell. The last notable instalment in his career came in May 1985 when he partnered Gary Moore on the number 5 hit, 'Out In The Fields'. He played his last gig with Grand Slam at the Marquee in London on 3 December 1985. At the turn of the following year, he suffered a drug overdose and, following a week in a coma, died of heart failure, exacerbated by pneumonia.
● ALBUMS: *Solo In Soho* (Vertigo 1980) ★★★, *The Phillip Lynott Solo Album* (Vertigo 1982) ★★, *Live In Sweden 1983* (Zoom Club 2002) ★★★.
● COMPILATIONS: *Soldier Of Fortune: The Best Of Phil Lynott And Thin Lizzy* (Telstar 1987) ★★★, *I Am Just A Cowboy* (Ozit 2000) ★★★.
● FURTHER READING: *Phillip Lynott: The Rocker*, Mark Putterford. *Songs For While I'm Away*, Phillip Lynott, *My Boy: The Phillip Lynott Story*, Philomena Lynott.

# M

M was the brainchild of former art school student and folk singer Robin Scott (b. 1 April 1947, Croydon, Surrey, England), who released an album for the Head Records label in 1969. He later worked as manager of the R&B band Roogalator and formed the Do It label to release an album by them. Do It later found critical success with the band Adam And The Ants. Scott moved to Paris in 1978, where he produced the Slits and several French bands. It was here that he got the idea for the band M, whose name was taken from the signs for the Paris Metro. Their debut single 'Moderne Man' was not successful and was released at the same time as a single by Comic Romance in which Scott also featured. However M's quirky and hook-laden second single 'Pop Muzik' was a massive hit both in the UK (number 2) and the USA (number 1) as well as across Europe. As a gimmick, some copies of the single featured both a and b-sides on the one playing surface with the listener taking pot luck as to which groove the needle dropped on to. An album was released to capitalize on the hit and, as well as the singles, also featured a re-recording of the track 'Cowboys And Indians' – previously the b-side of the 'Comic Romance' single. The album was recorded using session musicians Wally Badarov (keyboards), Gary Barnacle (saxophone/flute), Philip Gould (drums), Julian Scott (bass, ex-Roogalator), and Betty Vinchon (vocals). Among the musicians on the second album was Level 42's Mark King. After a couple of minor hit follow-ups, M's career slipped into rapid decline with subsequent singles (including a release on Stiff Records) failing to chart. Only a 1989 remix of 'Pop Musik' returned the name of M to the charts. Meanwhile, Scott worked with Ryûichi Sakamoto on two albums and recorded an unreleased album with African artists.

● ALBUMS: *New York, London, Paris, Munich* (Sire/MCA 1979) ★★★, *The Official Secrets Act* (Sire/MCA 1980) ★★★, *Famous Last Words* (Sire 1982) ★★.

● COMPILATIONS: *Pop Muzik: The Very Best Of M* (Music Club 1996) ★★★.

## MAAL, BAABA

b. 12 November 1953, Podor, Senegal. Vocalist and guitarist Maal had humble origins, growing up in the sparsely populated town of Podor, where his father worked in the fields, but also had the honour of calling worshippers to the mosque using song. The influence of Islam would remain central to his son's activities too, both father and son being members of the Fulani community, which originally brought the Muslim religion to the area. His mother was also a musician, writing her own songs, though the influence of imported western sounds (via transistor radio) such as Otis Redding and James Brown, then reggae ambassador Jimmy Cliff, would also have a profound influence. After winning a scholarship to the Ecole Des Beaux Arts in Dakar, the capital of Senegal, he travelled widely throughout Senegal and neighbouring Mali and Mauritania, studying the traditional music of the area. 'It's very important for young modern musicians in Africa to do a lot of research. To know what is African music. You cannot say you are doing African music if you don't know exactly where this music comes from.' He spent a further two years of academic study at the Paris Conservatoire, learning European theory and composition, before returning to Dakar in the early 80s to form Le Daande Lenol ('the voice of the race'). This group was formed with his long-standing friend, musical accomplice, and family 'griot', Mansour Seck.

In 1982 Maal released the first of seven cassette-only albums which would, by mid-decade, establish him as a potential rival to Youssou N'Dour, the reigning king of Senegalese youth music. Disc jockey John Peel described *Djam Leelii*, as like 'listening to Muddy Waters for the first time'. The music employed the Pekan songs of Northern fishermen, Gumbala chants of ancient warriors and Dilere weaving tunes. Most pervasively, the musical framework was based on the Yela songs of indigenous women pounding grain – taught to him by his mother. In 1985, he signed to the Paris-based label Syllart, releasing the superb albums: *Wango* and *Taara*.

In 1991 Maal moved to London-based Island Records subsidiary, Mango, ensuring his continued growth as an international artist. His debut for Mango, *Baayo*, featured a typically acoustic line-up, with Maal and Seck joined by Sayan Sissokho (guitar), Malick Sow (xalam) and Yakhoba Sissokho (kora). The emphasis here was on the experiences of his childhood, a delightful portrait of West African life which justified the award of several critical accolades. *Lam Toro*, dedicated to his mother, provided a more modern Senegalese sound, with synthesizers and programmed percussion. It was later released in remixed form. *Firin' In Fouta* was well received by the critics and introduced freeform jazz and reggae beats in an impressive marriage of the new and the old. It was partially based on a return journey to Podor when Maal made recordings of the traditional singers and musicians he had heard in his youth, mixing these into the final recording in Dakar. *Nomad Soul* featured an array of guest vocalists (Sinéad O'Connor, Luciano) and producers (Eno, Howie B.), but Maal's unique talent still shone through. He returned to his acoustic roots on *Missing You (Mi Yeewnii)*, focusing on the rich musical heritage of West Africa.

● ALBUMS: with Mansour Seck *Dannibe* cassette only (1982) ★★★, with Mansour Seck *Vol. 2: Pindi Pinaal* cassette only (1983) ★★★, with Mansour Seck *Vol. 3: Taan Farba Baggel* cassette only (1983) ★★★, with Mansour Seck *Djam Leelii* cassette only (1983) ★★★★, with Wandama *Vol. 2: Yela* cassette only (1984) ★★★, *Yewende* cassette only (Studio 2000

1984) ★★★, with Wandama *Vol. 3: Bibbe Leydi Ngoume* cassette only (1984) ★★★, with Wandama *Vol. 4* cassette only (Studio 2000 1985) ★★★, with Wandama *Vol. 5* cassette only (Studio 2000 1985) ★★★, with Le Daande Lenol *Suka Naayo* cassette only (Studio 2000 1987) ★★★, with Le Daande Lenol *Wango* cassette only (Syllart 1988) ★★★★, *Taara* (Melodie/Syllart 1990) ★★★★, *Ndilane* cassette only (Studio 2000 1990) ★★★★, *Baayo* (Mango 1991) ★★★, *Nouvelle Generation* (Studio 2000 1991) ★★★, *Olel* cassette only (1992) ★★★, *Thiayo* cassette only (1992) ★★★, *Lam Toro* (Mango 1992) ★★, *Lam Toro: The Remix Album* (Mango 1992) ★★, *Tono* cassette only (Mbaye Gueye 1994) ★★★, *Tiim Timol* cassette only (Studio 2000 1994) ★★★, *Firin' In Fouta* (Mango 1995) ★★★★, *Live En Allemagne* cassette only (Mbaye Gueye 1995) ★★★, *Nomad Soul* (Mbaya Gueye/Palm Pictures 1998) ★★★, *Live At The Royal Festival Hall* (Palm Pictures 1999) ★★★★, *Laamdo* cassette only (Origines 2000) ★★★, *Missing You (Mi Yeewnii)* (Palm Pictures 2001) ★★★★.

● VIDEOS: *Live At The Royal Festival Hall* (Palm Pictures 1999).

## MacColl, Kirsty

b. 10 October 1959, England, d. 18 December 2000, Mexico. The daughter of the celebrated folk singer Ewan MacColl, Kirsty enjoyed success in her own right as an accomplished songwriter and pop vocalist. Originally signed to Stiff Records as a 16-year-old after they heard her singing with punk outfit the Drug Addix, she was most unfortunate not to secure a massive hit with the earnest 'They Don't Know'. Many years later, the television comedienne Tracey Ullman took an inferior rendition of the song to number 2 in the UK charts. MacColl had to wait until 1981 for her first chart hit. A change of label to Polydor Records brought her deserved UK Top 20 success with the witty 'There's A Guy Works Down The Chip Shop Swears He's Elvis'. Her interest in country and pop influences was discernible on her strong debut, *Desperate Characters*.

In 1984, MacColl married producer Steve Lillywhite, and in the same year she returned to the charts with a stirring cover version of Billy Bragg's 'A New England'. During the next couple of years, she gave birth to two children, but still found herself in demand as a backing singer. She guested on recordings by a number of prominent artists, including Simple Minds, the Smiths, the Rolling Stones, Talking Heads, Robert Plant, Van Morrison and Morrissey. In December 1987, MacColl enjoyed her highest ever chart placing at number 2 when duetting with Shane MacGowan on the Pogues' evocative vignette of Irish emigration, 'Fairytale Of New York'. In 1989, she returned to recording solo with the highly accomplished *Kite*. The album included the powerful 'Free World' and an exceptionally alluring cover version of the Kinks' 'Days', which brought her back to the UK Top 20. Smiths' guitarist Johnny Marr guested on several of the album's tracks and appeared on the excellent follow-up released in 1991. *Electric Landlady*, an amusing pun on Jimi Hendrix's *Electric Ladyland*, was another strong album that demonstrated MacColl's diversity and songwriting talent. The haunting, dance-influenced 'Walking Down Madison' gave her another Top 40 UK hit. Her career was sympathetically compiled on *Galore*, which demonstrated a highly accomplished singer, even though four albums in 15 years was hardly the sign of a prolific artist. MacColl returned over five years later with the sparkling Latin American collection, *Tropical Brainstorm*. Her revived career was cut short by a tragic accident in December. The singer was hit and killed by a speedboat while swimming with her children off the coast of Mexico. She had recently finished recording a series on Cuba for BBC Radio 2.

● ALBUMS: *Desperate Characters* (Polydor 1981) ★★★, *Kite* (Virgin 1989) ★★★★, *Electric Landlady* (Virgin 1991) ★★★, *Titanic Days* (ZTT 1994) ★★, *Tropical Brainstorm* (V2 2000) ★★★★.
● COMPILATIONS: *Galore* (Virgin 1995) ★★★★, *What Do Pretty Girls Do?* (Hux 1998) ★★★, *The One And Only* (Metro 2001) ★★★.

## Mackintosh, Cameron

b. 17 October 1946, Enfield, Middlesex, England. 'The Czar of theatrical producers' – that is what the American magazine *TheaterWeek* called him in 1993 when they rated him number 3 in their list of the 100 Most Powerful People in American Theater. The son of a Maltese-born mother and a Scottish father, Mackintosh attended a small public school in Bath and became obsessed by the musical theatre at the age of eight after being taken to see a production of Julian Slade's *Salad Days* at Bristol Old Vic in 1954. After leaving school, where he was known as Darryl F. Mackintosh, he attended the Central School for Speech and Drama for a year before becoming an assistant stage manager at the Theatre Royal, Drury Lane when *Camelot* was running. His first forays into producing came with some budget-priced touring shows before he moved into the West End in 1969 with a revival of *Anything Goes*. It proved to be a disaster and was withdrawn after 27 performances. *Trelawny* (1972) and *The Card* (1973) fared better, and, after a number of provincial productions of varying degrees of profitability, Mackintosh's breakthrough finally came in 1976 with *Side By Side By Sondheim*.

During the next few years he mounted successful revivals of *Oliver!*, *My Fair Lady* and *Oklahoma!*, before his meeting with Andrew Lloyd Webber resulted in *Cats* in 1981. The show transformed the lives of both men, and became the prototype for future productions which overthrew the old style of musical and provided a simple and vivid theatrical experience that did not rely on big name stars, and was easily exportable. In the 80s Mackintosh went from strength to strength with *Song And Dance*, *Les Misérables*, *The Phantom Of The Opera*, and *Miss Saigon* (1989). In 1990, the latter show provided an example of just how powerful Mackintosh had become when American Equity initially objected to the casting of Jonathan Pryce in the Broadway production 'because it would be an affront to the Asian community'. After the producer threatened to withdraw the show altogether – and one or two others as well – capitulation was more or less immediate. The incident did nothing to improve the producer's ruthless (he prefers 'relentless') reputation with the New York theatre community, many of whom object to his dictatorial attitude and 'flashy' marketing methods. For some reason he deliberately did not use those ploys when his London hit, *Five Guys Named Moe*, transferred to Broadway, and that may well be one of the reasons for its relatively poor showing.

In 1992, Mackintosh was involved with a rare flop which some say marked the beginning of his decline. *Moby Dick* ('a damp squib . . . garbage') is reported to have cost him £1 million and a great deal of pride during its 15-week run, and he hinted at the time that he may be past his peak. However, the highly impressive monetary facts continued to emerge: a personal salary of over £8 million in 1991, the 39th richest man in Britain, and the acquisition of a substantial stake in two West End theatres, the Prince of Wales and the Prince Edward. His love of musicals – that is all he seems to be interested in producing – has caused Mackintosh to divert some of his reported £300 million wealth to a number of extremely worthy causes. As well as numerous donations to small theatrical projects, he provided £2 million to endow Oxford University's first professorship in drama and musical theatre, and his £1 million gift to the Royal National Theatre has enabled it to mount highly acclaimed revivals of *Carousel* and *Sweeney Todd*, the first two in a series of five classic musicals. It is not all philanthropy: Mackintosh is reported to retain the rights to the productions when they are eventually produced in the commercial sector. His kudos have included the 1991 *Observer* Award for Outstanding Achievement, and the prestigious Richard Rodgers Award for Excellence In Musical Theatre (1992). Previous recipients have been Harold Prince, Julie Andrews and Mary Martin. In 1994, Mackintosh's major revival of *Oliver!* opened at the London Palladium, starring Jonathan Pryce, and in 1995 his production company, Cameron Mackintosh Limited, earned a Queen's Award for Export Achievement. Two years earlier, for the benefit of an awe-struck journalist, he had attempted to remember all the musicals he had running in various parts of the world. They included six *Cats*, 20 *Phantom Of The Opera*, 12 *Les Misérables*, seven *Miss Saigon*, four *Five Guys Named Moe*, two *Follies* . . . et cetera, et cetera, as Yul Brynner used to say.

In July 1996, following on from *Les Misérables* and *Miss Saigon*, a third collaboration between Mackintosh and the creative team of Alain Boublil and Claude-Michel Schönberg, entitled *Martin Guerre*, opened in London. However, it failed to live up to its illustrious predecessors, and folded after a 20-month run. On a rather smaller scale, Mackintosh's *The Fix*, a 'daring new musical', also incurred the critics' wrath when presented at the Donmar Warehouse in 1997. Mackintosh received a knighthood for 'services to the musical theatre' in the 1995 New Year Honours List, and three years later was presented with the Bernard Delfont Award

by the Variety Club of Great Britain. In June 1998, two charity performances of *Hey Mr Producer! The Musical World Of Cameron Mackintosh* at London's Lyceum Theatre saluted the impresario's 30 years in showbusiness. Later in the year, he was supervising the Sondheim revue *Putting It Together* (Mark II, with Carol Burnett) in Los Angeles, *Martin Guerre* (Mark III) in Yorkshire, England, and the US premiere of George Stiles and Anthony Drewe's Vivian Ellis Award-winning musical, *Just So* (Mark numerous), at Goodspeed, Connecticut.

● ALBUMS: *Hey Mr Producer!* 2-CD set (First Night 1998) ★★★.
● VIDEOS: *Hey Mr Producer!* (VCI 1998).
● FURTHER READING: *Hey Mr Producer!: The Musicals Of Cameron Mackintosh*, Sheridan Morley and Ruth Leon.

## MADNESS

This highly regarded UK ska/pop band evolved from the London-based Invaders in the summer of 1979. Their line-up comprised Suggs (b. Graham McPherson, 13 January 1961, Hastings, Sussex, England; vocals), Mark Bedford (b. 24 August 1961, London, England; bass), Mike Barson (b. 21 April 1958, London, England; keyboards), Chris Foreman (b. 8 August 1958, London, England; guitar), Lee Thompson (b. 5 October 1957, London, England; saxophone), Chas Smash (b. Cathal Smythe, 14 January 1959; vocals, trumpet) and Dan Woodgate (b. 19 October 1960, London, England; drums). After signing a one-off contract with 2-Tone they issued 'The Prince', a tribute to blue beat maestro Prince Buster (whose song 'Madness' had inspired the band's name). The single reached the UK Top 20 and the follow-up, 'One Step Beyond' (a Buster composition), did even better, peaking at number 7, the first result of their new contract with Stiff Records. An album of the same title revealed Madness' charm, with its engaging mix of ska and exuberant pop, a fusion they humorously dubbed 'the nutty sound'. Over the next two years the band enjoyed an uninterrupted run of UK Top 10 hits, including 'My Girl', *Work Rest And Play* (EP), 'Baggy Trousers', 'Embarrassment', 'The Return Of The Los Palmas Seven', 'Grey Day', 'Shut Up' and 'It Must Be Love' (originally a hit for its composer, Labi Siffre). Although Madness appealed mainly to a younger audience and were known as a zany, fun-loving band, their work occasionally took on a more serious note. Both 'Grey Day' and 'Our House' showed their ability to write about working-class family life in a fashion that was piercingly accurate, yet never patronizing. At their best, Madness were the most able commentators on London life since the Kinks in the late 60s. An ability to tease out a sense of melancholy beneath the fun permeated their more mature work, particularly on the 1982 album *The Rise And Fall*. That same year Suggs married singer Bette Bright and the band finally topped the charts with their twelfth chart entry, 'House Of Fun' (which concerned teenage sexuality and the purchase of prophylactics). More UK hits followed, including 'Wings Of A Dove' and 'The Sun And The Rain', but in late 1983 the band suffered a serious setback when founding member Barson quit. They continued to release some exceptional work in 1984 including 'Michael Caine' and 'One Better Day'. At the end of that year, they formed their own label, Zarjazz. Its first release was Feargal Sharkey's 'Listen To Your Father' (written by the band), which reached the UK Top 30.

Madness continued to enjoy relatively minor hits by previous standards with the contemplative 'Yesterday's Men', the exuberant 'Uncle Sam' and a cover version of the former Scritti Politti success, 'The Sweetest Girl'. In the autumn of 1986, they announced that they were splitting-up. Seventeen months later, they reunited as a four-piece under the name The Madness, but failed to emulate previous successes. One of Mark Bedford's projects was a collaboration with ex-Higsons member Terry Edwards in Butterfield 8. Lee Thompson and Chris Foreman later worked under the appellation the Nutty Boys, relcasing onc album, Crunch, in 1990, and played to capacity crowds in London clubs and pubs.

In June 1992 the original Madness re-formed for two open-air gigs in Finsbury Park, London, which resulted in Madstock, a 'live' document of the event. The band's renewed public image was rewarded with four chart entries during the year; three reissues, 'It Must Be Love', 'House Of Fun' and 'My Girl', and 'The Harder They Come'. In 1993, a 'musical about homelessness', One Step Beyond, by Alan Gilbey, incorporated 15 Madness songs when it opened on the London fringe – further evidence, as if any were needed, of the enduring brilliance of Madness' irresistible songcraft. Following further Madstock concerts, the original line-up returned to the studio in the late 90s to record new material. 'Lovestruck' indicated their enduring popularity when it entered the UK singles chart at number 10 in July 1999. A credible new album, Wonderful, followed in September, containing in addition to 'Lovestruck', the rousing 'Johnny The Horse' and a guest appearance by Ian Dury (to whom the album is dedicated) on 'Drip Fed Fred'. Madness have no enemies; they are a rich part of the UK's musical heritage.

● ALBUMS: One Step Beyond (Stiff 1979) ★★★★, Absolutely (Stiff 1980) ★★★, Madness 7 (Stiff 1981) ★★★, The Rise And Fall (Stiff 1982) ★★★★, Keep Moving (Stiff 1984) ★★★, Mad Not Mad (Zarjazz 1985) ★★, as the Madness The Madness (Virgin 1988) ★★, Madstock (Go! Discs 1992) ★★★, Wonderful (Virgin 1999) ★★★.

● COMPILATIONS: Complete Madness (Stiff 1982) ★★★, Utter Madness (Zarjazz 1986) ★★★, The Peel Sessions (Strange Fruit 1986) ★★, Divine Madness (Virgin 1992) ★★★★, The Business: The Definitive Singles Collection (Virgin 1993) ★★★★, The Heavy Heavy Hits (Virgin 1998) ★★★★, The Lot box set (Virgin 1999) ★★★.

● VIDEOS: Complete Madness (Stiff 1984), Utter Madness (Virgin Vision 1988), Complete And Utter Madness (Virgin Vision 1988), Divine Madness (Virgin Vision 1992).

● FURTHER READING: A Brief Case Of Madness, Mark Williams. Total Madness, George Marshall.

## MADONNA

b. Madonna Louise Ciccone, 16 August 1958, Bay City, Michigan, USA. An icon for female pop stars thanks to her proven ability to artistically reinvent herself while retaining complete control of her career, Madonna is also one of the most commercially successful artists in the history of popular music. The young Ciccone excelled at dance and drama at high school and during brief periods at colleges in Michigan and North Carolina. In 1977, she went to New York, studying with noted choreographer Alvin Ailey and taking modelling jobs. Two years later, Madonna moved to France to join a show featuring disco singer Patrick Hernandez. There she met Dan Gilroy and, back in New York, the pair formed club band the Breakfast Club. Madonna played drums and sang with the band before setting up Emmy in 1980 with Detroit-born drummer and former boyfriend, Steve Bray. Together, Madonna and Bray created club tracks which led to a recording deal with Sire Records. With leading New York disc jockey Mark Kamins producing, she recorded 'Everybody', a US club hit in 1982. Madonna broke out from the disco scene into mainstream pop with 'Holiday', written and produced by Jellybean. It reached the US Top 20 in late 1983 and was a Top 10 hit across Europe the following year.

By now, her tough, raunchy persona was coming across to international audiences and the attitude was underlined by the choice of Tom Kelly and Billy Steinberg's catchy 'Like A Virgin' as a 1984 single. The track provided the singer with the first of her subsequent 11 US number 1s. The follow-up, 'Material Girl', included a promotional video which introduced one of Madonna's most characteristic visual styles, the mimicking of Marilyn Monroe's 'blonde bombshell' image. By the time of her appearance at 1985's Live Aid concert and her high-profile wedding to actor Sean Penn on 16 August the same year, Madonna had become an internationally recognized superstar, known to millions of tabloid newspaper readers without any interest in her music. Among the fans of her work were a growing number of 'wannabees', teenage girls who aped her independent and don't-care stance.

From 1985 to 87, Madonna turned out a stream of irresistibly catchy transatlantic Top 5 singles. 'Crazy For You', her second US chart-topper, was co-written by ex-Carpenters collaborator John Bettis, while she co-wrote her first UK number 1, 'Into The Groove', with Steve Bray. These were followed by 'Dress You Up', 'Live To Tell', and the transatlantic chart-topper, 'Papa Don't Preach'. 'True Blue', 'Open Your Heart' and 'La Isla Bonita' were further successes taken from 1986's True Blue. Like an increasing number of her songs, 'Who's That Girl' (her second transatlantic number 1) and 'Causing A Commotion' were tied in to a movie – in this instance, a poorly received comedy in which she starred with Sir John Mills. Madonna's film career had begun with a minor role in the b-movie A Certain Sacrifice before she starred in the acclaimed Desperately Seeking Susan. The following year she appeared with husband Penn in her first real failure, Shanghai Surprise. She separated from Penn in 1988, the same year she appeared on Broadway in David Mamet's play *Speed The Plow*. Back on the music scene, the singer continued to attract controversy when, in 1989, the video for 'Like A Prayer' (her third transatlantic chart-topper), with its links between religion and eroticism, was condemned by the Vatican and caused Pepsi-Cola to cancel a sponsorship deal with the star. The resulting publicity helped the album of the same title – co-produced with new collaborator Patrick Leonard – to become a global bestseller.

In 1990, her career reached a new peak of publicity and commercial success. She starred with Warren Beatty in the blockbuster movie *Dick Tracy*, while the extravagant costumes and choreography of the Blond Ambition world tour were the apotheosis of Madonna's uninhibited melange of sexuality, song, dance and religiosity. The tour was commemorated by the following year's documentary movie, *Truth Or Dare*. Among her hits of the early 90s were the transatlantic number 1 'Vogue', devoted to a short-lived dance craze, 'Hanky Panky', 'Justify My Love' (co-written with Lenny Kravitz), 'Rescue Me' and 'This Used To Be My Playground' (from the soundtrack of *A League Of Their Own*).

Madonna's reputation as a strong businesswoman, in control of each aspect of her career, was confirmed in 1992 when she signed a multi-million-dollar deal with the Time-Warner conglomerate, parent company of Sire. This guaranteed the release of albums, films and books created by her own Maverick production company. The publication of her graphic and erotic book *Sex* put her back on top of the charts, though this time it was in the bestselling book lists. The book was an unprecedented success, selling out within hours and needing an immediate reprint. The attendant *Erotica* marked a slight creative downturn, and was her first album since her debut not to generate a US number 1 single. She returned to form on *Bedtime Stories*, on which she teamed up with Soul II Soul producer Nellee Hooper, who wrote the title track in conjunction with Björk. 'Take A Bow' returned the singer to the top of the US singles chart, while the rest of the album boasted songs that combined, by her own description, pop, R&B, hip-hop and Madonna. The 1995 compilation of her slower material, *Something To Remember*, featured the excellent new song, 'You'll See'.

In 1996, her need to shock had mellowed considerably with a credible movie portrayal of Eva Peron in Alan Parker's *Evita*. Later that year she became 'with child' on 14 October with the birth of Lourdes Maria Ciccone Leon. She returned to music with March 1998's *Ray Of Light*, one of her finest recordings to date. Collaborating with producer William Orbit, Madonna positively revelled in a new found musical freedom. Her voice had also matured into a rich and expressive instrument. The album generated several transatlantic hit singles, including 'Frozen' (a UK chart-topper), 'Ray Of Light', 'Drowned World (Substitute For Love)', 'The Power Of Good-bye' and 'Nothing Really Matters'. 'Beautiful Stranger', taken from the soundtrack to the Mike Myers' movie *Austin Powers: The Spy Who Shagged Me*, reached number 2 in the UK charts in June 1999. Another soundtrack, for the movie *The Next Best Thing*, co-written and co-produced by Madonna and Orbit, was released on the singer's Maverick label. It featured her new single, a reworking of Don McLean's classic 'American Pie'. She worked with Orbit and French dance producer Mirwais on her next collection, *Music*, the title track of which was a transatlantic chart-topper in September 2000. Shortly before the release of the album, on 11 August, the singer gave birth to her second child, Rocco. On 22 December, she married the UK film director Guy Ritchie in Scotland and managed once again to grab most of the newspaper headlines. Madonna is without doubt an artist with 'star quality', and no other female singer in the pop arena has been as prominent or as successful.

● ALBUMS: *Madonna* (Sire 1983) ★★★, *Like A Virgin* (Sire 1984) ★★★, *True Blue* (Sire 1986) ★★★★, *Who's That Girl* film soundtrack (Sire 1987) ★★, *You Can Dance* remix album (Sire 1987) ★★★, *Like A Prayer* (Sire 1989) ★★★★, *I'm Breathless* (Sire 1990) ★★★, *Erotica* (Maverick 1992) ★★★, *Bedtime Stories* (Maverick 1994) ★★★★, *Evita* film soundtrack (Warners 1996) ★★★, *Ray Of Light* (Maverick/Warners 1998) ★★★★, *Music* (Maverick/Warners 2000) ★★★.

● COMPILATIONS: *The Immaculate Collection* (Sire 1990) ★★★★★, *Best Of The Rest Volume 2* (Sire 1993) ★★★, *Something To Remember* (Maverick 1995) ★★★★, *The Early Years: Give It To Me* (Sanctuary 2001) ★★★, *GHV2* (Maverick 2001) ★★★★.

● VIDEOS: *The Virgin Tour* (Warner Music Video 1986), *Ciao Italia – Live From Italy* (Sire 1988), *Immaculate Collection* (Warner Music Video 1990), *Justify My Love* (Warner Music Video 1991), *The Real Story* (Wienerworld Video 1991), *Madonna Video EP* (Warner Music Video 1991), *In Bed With Madonna* (Video Collection 1991), *Madonna: The Unauthorised Biography* (MIA Video 1994), *Ray Of Light* (Warner Home Video 1998), *The Video Collection 93:99* (Warner Vision 1999), *What It Feels Like For A Girl* (Warner Reprise Video 2001), *Drowned World Tour 2001* (Warner Music Vision 2001).

● FURTHER READING: *Madonna: Her Story*, Michael McKenzie. *Madonna: The New Illustrated Biography*, Debbi Voller. *Madonna: In Her Own Words*, Mick St Michael. *Madonna: The Biography*, Robert Matthew-Walker. *Madonna*, Marie Cahill. *Madonna: The Style Book*, Debbi Voller. *Like A Virgin: Madonna Revealed*, Douglas Thompson. *Sex*, Madonna. *Madonna Unauthorized*, Christopher Anderson. *I Dream Of Madonna: Women's Dreams Of The Goddess Of Pop*, Kay Turner (compiler). *The I Hate Madonna Handbook*, Ilene Rosenzweig. *Madonna: The Girlie Show*, Glenn O'Brien. *Deconstructing Madonna*, Fran Lloyd. *Live!*, no author listed. *The Madonna Scrapbook*, Lee Randall. *Madonna: An Intimate Biography*, J. Randy Taraborrelli. *Madonna: Queen Of The World*, Douglas Thompson. *Madonna*, Andrew Morton. *Madonna Style*, Carol Clerk.

● FILMS: *A Certain Sacrifice* (1979), *Desperately Seeking Susan* (1985), *Vision Quest* (1985), *Shangai Surprise* (1986), *Who's That Girl?* (1987), *Bloodhounds*

Of Broadway (1989), Dick Tracy (1990), Madonna: Blond Ambition World Tour '90 (1990), Madonna: Truth Or Dare (1991), A League Of Their Own (1992), Shadows And Fog (1992), Body Of Evidence (1993), Dangerous Game (1993), Blue In The Face (1995), Four Rooms (1995), Girl 6 (1996), Evita (1996), The Next Best Thing (2000), Swept Away (2002).

## MAGNUM

This Birmingham, England-based pomp rock outfit was formed in 1972 by Tony Clarkin (guitar), Bob Catley (vocals), Kex Gorin (drums) and Dave Morgan (bass). They remained unsigned, undertaking various engagements, including acting as Del Shannon's backing band, until 1978, when they were signed by Jet Records. By this time, Morgan had departed, to be replaced by Colin 'Wally' Lowe, and Richard Bailey had joined as keyboard player. Between 1978 and 1980, Magnum released three albums to a moderate degree of success, and toured relentlessly with Judas Priest, Blue Öyster Cult, and Def Leppard. Chase The Dragon was released in 1982, with new keyboard player Mark Stanway, and gave them their first Top 20 album; it featured the grandiose pomp of 'Sacred Hour' and 'The Spirit', both of which still feature in their current live set. Following the release of Eleventh Hour, problems beset the band: Clarkin became ill, and a dispute with Jet Records ensued. The band fragmented as a result, but the troubles were soon resolved, and a number of low-key club dates persuaded them to continue. FM Revolver Records signed the band in 1985 for On A StoryTeller's Night. Its Top 40 success, along with a highly successful tour of the UK, prompted Polydor Records to offer a long-term contract. Vigilante, which featured new drummer Mickey Barker (ex-Pyewackett), was the first release under the new contract, and was produced by Queen's Roger Taylor.

The backing of a major label paid immediate dividends with a Top 30 album and a sell-out UK tour. This success was taken one step further with Wings Of Heaven (1988), their first gold album and UK Top 10 hit. Top 40 single success came with 'Days Of No Trust', 'Start Talkin' Love' and 'It Must Have Been Love'. Numerous compilation albums, including Mirador and Anthology, were released, along with reissues of their now extensive back-catalogue from Jet Records. A two-year gap between official releases resulted in the Keith Olsen-produced Goodnight L.A., and again Top 40 success was achieved with a single, 'Rocking Chair', the album also enjoying Top 10 status. Extensive touring promoted Goodnight L.A. and several shows were recorded for a double live set, The Spirit. A new contract with EMI Records began with 1994's Rock Art. After years of struggle and setbacks, Magnum's popularity had been achieved the hard way, by dint of constant touring and a series of high-quality albums, but Clarkin and Catley left the group in 1996 to work on their Hard Rain project. They reunited with their former colleagues to record 2002's well-received Breath Of Life.

● ALBUMS: Kingdom Of Madness (Jet 1978) ★★★, Magnum II (Jet 1979) ★★★, Marauder (Jet 1980) ★★★, Chase The Dragon (Jet 1982) ★★★, The Eleventh Hour (Jet 1983) ★★★, On A StoryTeller's Night (Polydor 1985) ★★★, Vigilante (Polydor 1986) ★★★, Wings Of Heaven (Polydor 1988) ★★★★, Goodnight L.A. (Polydor 1990), Invasion – Magnum Live (Receiver 1990) ★★★, The Spirit (Polydor 1991) ★★★, Sleepwalking (Polydor 1992) ★★★, Rock Art (EMI 1994) ★★★, Firebird (Spectrum/PolyGram 1995) ★★★, Breath Of Life (SPV 2002) ★★★.

● COMPILATIONS: Anthology (Raw Power 1986) ★★★★, Collection (Castle 1990) ★★★★, Box Set (Castle 1992) ★★★, Chapter And Verse: Best Of (Polydor 1993) ★★★, Uncorked (Jet 1994) ★★★, Long Days Black Nights: The Alternative Anthology 3-CD set (Sanctuary 2002) ★★★.

● VIDEOS: Magnum Live: The Sacred Hour (Embassy 1985), On The Wings Of Heaven (Polydor 1988), From Midnight To LA (Channel 5/PolyGram 1990), On A Storyteller's Night (Hendring 1991)

## MAISONETTES

Based in Birmingham, England, this 60s-influenced pop outfit reached number 7 in the UK chart in 1983 with 'Heartache Avenue' a particularly memorable song with strong influences of 60s soul music. The band was formed by Lol Mason (vocals), Elaine Williams (vocals), Denise Ward (vocals), Mark Tibbenham (keyboards), and Nick Parry (drums). Mason, the driving force behind the band, was no stranger to chart success, having previously been the singer with City Boy. Two follow-up singles, 'Where I Stand' and 'Say It Again', and an album, all for the Birmingham independent label Ready Steady Go!, flopped, and the band broke up.

● ALBUMS: For Sale (Ready Steady Go! 1983) ★★.

## MALMSTEEN, YNGWIE

b. Lars Johann Yngwie Lannerback, 30 June 1963, Stockholm, Sweden. This Swedish guitar virtuoso was the originator of the high-speed, technically precise, neo-classical style that developed during the 80s. Influenced by Jimi Hendrix, Ritchie Blackmore and Eddie Van Halen, Malmsteen first picked up a guitar at the age of five and had formed his first band, Powerhouse, by the time he entered his teens. At age 14 he formed Rising, named after Rainbow's second album, and recorded a series of demo tapes. One of these was picked up by producer and guitar specialist Mike Varney. Malmsteen was persuaded by Varney to relocate to Los Angeles and join Ron Keel's Steeler as lead guitarist, and went straight into the studio to record the band's debut album. Following this, he was approached by Kiss, UFO and Ozzy Osbourne, but declined their offers in favour of teaming up with Graham Bonnet in a new group called Alcatrazz. This association lasted for one studio album and a live set, recorded in Japan.

After the dissolution of that band, Malmsteen was immediately offered a solo contract by Polydor Records, just as his reputation and stature were beginning to escalate. He released the self-produced Rising Force, utilizing ex-Jethro Tull drummer Barriemore Barlow, vocalist Jeff Scott Soto and keyboard player Jens Johansson. This comprised a mixture of new songs and reworked demo material that had been available for several years. Deciding to work within a band framework once more, but this time exercising tight control, Malmsteen formed Rising Force with Soto and Johansson, plus bass player Marcel Jacob and drummer Anders Johansson. This basic formation recorded two albums, the second of which, 1986's *Trilogy*, saw Soto replaced by ex-Ted Nugent vocalist Mark Boals. The album showcased Malmsteen's amazing virtuosity and ability to combine speed with melody.

Following an 18-month break after a serious road accident involving Malmsteen, Rising Force was resurrected with ex-Rainbow vocalist Joe Lynn Turner. Produced by Jeff Glixman and mixed by the Thompson/Barbiero team, *Odyssey* was released in 1988 to widespread acclaim. At last Malmsteen's guitar pyrotechnics were anchored within commercial hard rock structures. The guitar solos, for once, were economical, and did not detract from the songs. The album reached number 40 on the US *Billboard* album chart and brought many new fans to the guitarist. Eager to capitalize on this success, Malmsteen then issued a disappointing and self-indulgent live album recorded in Leningrad. The momentum was lost and Joe Lynn Turner was dismissed, to be replaced with a Swedish vocalist, Goran Edman. *Eclipse* emerged in 1990 with weak vocals and an unusually restrained Malmsteen on guitar, and it appeared that he was suppressing his real desires and talents in the search for commercial success. *Fire & Ice* debuted at number 1 in the Japanese charts. The follow-up *The Seventh Sign* introduced new vocalist Michael Vescera, and was the first release of a new recording contract with the Japanese label Pony Canyon. Malmsteen switched back to his old flamboyant style on *Inspiration*, a collection of cover versions featuring vocals by Turner, Boals and Soto. In 1996, Malmsteen joined with Soto as Human Clay to issue their self-titled debut. The following year he recruited new vocalist Mats Leven to record *Facing The Animal*, and began work on his first concerto. The latter was released in 1998 by Pony Canyon's classical imprint. Boals returned as lead singer on the Rising Force albums *Alchemy* and *War To End All Wars*. Malmsteen remains at his best when he is in control; his amazing technique is what the listener wants to hear.

● ALBUMS: *Yngwie Malmsteen's Rising Force* (Polydor 1984) ★★★, with Rising Force *Marching Out* (Polydor 1985) ★★★, with Rising Force *Trilogy* (Polydor 1986) ★★★, with Rising Force *Odyssey* (Polydor 1988) ★★★, *Trial By Fire: Live In Leningrad* (Polydor 1989) ★★, *Eclipse* (Polydor 1990) ★★, *Fire & Ice* (WEA 1992) ★★, *The Seventh Sign* (Pony Canyon 1994) ★★★, *I Can't Wait* mini-album (Pony Canyon 1994) ★★★, *Magnum Opus* (Pony Canyon/Viceroy 1995) ★★, *Inspiration* (Pony Canyon/Foundation 1996) ★★★, *Facing The Animal* (Pony Canyon/Mercury 1997) ★★, *Concerto For Electric Guitar And Orchestra In E Flat Minor Op. 1* (Canyon Classics 1998) ★★, *Live!!* (Pony Canyon/Dream Catcher 1998) ★★, with Rising Force *Alchemy* (Pony Canyon 1999) ★★, with Rising Force *War To End All Wars* (Pony Canyon/Spitfire 2000) ★★★, with Rising Force

*Attack!!* (Pony Canyon 2002) ★★★.

● COMPILATIONS: *The Yngwie Malmsteen Collection* (Polydor 1991) ★★★★, *Anthology 1994-1999* (Pony Canyon 2000) ★★★, *The Best Of 1990-1999* (Dream Catcher 2000) ★★★, *Archives* 8-CD box set (Pony Canyon 2001) ★★★.

● VIDEOS: *Yngwie Malmsteen's Rising Force Live '85* (PolyGram Music Video 1985), *Trial By Fire: Live In Leningrad* (PolyGram Music Video 1989), *The Yngwie Malmsteen Video Collection* (PolyGram Music Video 1992), *Live At Budokan* (Pony Canyon 1994), *Live!!* (Pony Canyon 1998).

## MAN JUMPING

Once described by Brian Eno as the most interesting band in the world, Man Jumping evolved out of the co-operative band Lost Jockey. Lost Jockey had been set up in 1980 to perform the music of American Minimalist/Systems composers (Steve Reich, Philip Glass, Terry Riley), together with works by members of the ensemble, such as Andrew Poppy and Orlando Gough (b. 24 August 1953, Brighton, Sussex, England; keyboards). Growing to over 30 musicians, it became unmanageable and collapsed in 1983 after producing two excellent albums: *Hoovering The Beach* (1981) and the 10-inch *Lost Jockey* (1982). The remaining members, Andy Blake (b. 10 January 1955, Devizes, Wiltshire, England; saxophone/flute), John Lunn (b. 13 May 1956, Glasgow, Scotland; bass/keyboards), Gough, Schaun Tozer (b. 16 September 1955, Rochford, Essex, England; keyboards), Charlie Seaward (7 October 1953, Salisbury, Wiltshire, England; keyboards/flute) and Glyn Perrin (21 October 1955, London, England; keyboards/cello), decided to pull a more viable unit out of the ashes, planning a more varied repertoire with the emphasis on original pieces. Martin Ditcham (b. 22 February 1951, Ilford, Essex, England) came in on drums and percussion (replaced in 1986 by Simon Limbrick, from the Lumiere Theatre Company). They had problems getting their recordings promulgated (A&R people liked their mix of Systems, funk, jazz, Afro and the 'classical' *avant garde*, but did not know how to label or, consequently, market it) and the band started doing live gigs in late 1985. The following summer they opened the Covent Garden Music Festival with a free open-air concert, and took part in the Summerscope season at London's South Bank Centre. The band and individual members also performed much fine work with dance companies such as Second Stride (*Weighing The Heart*) and the London Contemporary Dance Theatre (*Unfolding Field*). The excellent *Jump Cut* was reissued in 1999 on the Shaping Invisible label.

● ALBUMS: *Jump Cut* (Cocteau 1984) ★★★★, *World Service* (Editions EG 1987) ★★.

## MANOWAR

This traditionalist heavy metal quartet from the USA (whose motto is 'Death To False Metal') was formed in 1981 by bass player Joey DeMaio (a former Black Sabbath roadie) and ex-Shakin' Street and Dictators guitarist Ross 'The Boss' Funicello. Recruiting vocalist Eric Adams and drummer Donnie Hamzik, they decided on an approach that was to be the total antithesis of melodic AOR. Dressed in animal skins, they delivered a brutal series of riffs that were characterized by Adams' barbaric vocals and the dense bass work of Demaio. They debuted in 1982 with *Battle Hymns*, a milestone in the metal genre. With subject material firmly centred on fighting, bloodshed, death and carnage, they came across as a turbo-charged hybrid of Ted Nugent and Black Sabbath. The album was notable for an amazing version of the 'William Tell Overture', played as an electric bass solo, while the voice of actor Orson Welles appeared on 'Dark Avenger'. *Battle Hymns* failed to sell, however, and with the press treating the band as an absurd joke, they were dropped by their record company in 1982. They subsequently signed to Megaforce (Music For Nations in the UK), using their own blood on the contract, their veins opened via a ceremonial dagger. Scott Columbus took over the drum-stool on *Into Glory Ride*, another intensely heavy, chest-beating collection of metal epics. They built up a small yet loyal cult following, but were generally panned by the rock mainstream. Their UK tours in 1983 and 1984 attracted poor audiences, but they had more success in Europe. *Sign Of The Hammer*, featured some excellent guitar work from Ross The Boss and contained their most accessible compositions to date, including the archetypal metal boast, 'All Men Play On 10'. Once again it flopped, and after a rethink they returned two years later with *Fighting The World* (in the meantime, they had entered *The Guinness Book Of Records* as the world's loudest band). On this album, they incorporated elements borrowed from Kiss and Judas Priest into their songwriting, but although it was aimed at the rock mainstream, it failed to win many new fans. *Kings Of Metal* was released in 1988 and met with a similar fate. Disillusioned, Ross The Boss quit the same year with Scott Columbus following suit in 1990 (Ross was replaced by Death Dealer, aka David Shankle, Columbus by Kenny 'Rhino' Earl). Karl Logan replaced Shankle on 1996's *Louder Than Hell*, which also featured the returning Columbus. Now veterans of the metal scene, Manowar remain colourful, flamboyant and rather kitsch but in the age of nu-metal appear rather outdated.

● ALBUMS: *Battle Hymns* (Capitol/Liberty 1982) ★★★★, *Into Glory Ride* (Megaforce 1983) ★★★, *Hail To England* (Music For Nations 1984) ★★★★, *Sign Of The Hammer* (10 1984) ★★★, *Fighting The World* (Atlantic 1987) ★★★, *Kings Of Metal* (Atlantic 1988) ★★, *The Triumph Of Steel* (Atlantic 1992) ★★, *Louder Than Hell* (Geffen 1996) ★★★, *Hell On Wheels* (Geffen 1997) ★★, *Hell On Stage Live* (Nuclear Blast/Metal Blade 1999) ★★, *Warriors Of The World* (Nuclear Blast 2002) ★★★.

● COMPILATIONS: *The Hell Of Steel* (Atlantic 1994) ★★★, *Anthology* (Connoisseur 1997) ★★★.

● VIDEOS: *Hell On Earth Part 1* (Metal Blade 2000).

## MARC AND THE MAMBAS

Formed by Marc Almond (b. Peter Marc Almond, 9 July 1956, Southport, Lancashire, England), Marc And The Mambas was a pseudonym that the singer employed for his more arcane and adventurous work. Weary of the restrictions that came with his pop star role in Soft Cell, the Mambas project enabled him to attempt more daring and original ideas without compromise. With the assistance of Annie Hogan, Almond completed *Untitled* in which he unveiled spirited revivals of material by artists such as Lou Reed and Jacques Brel. By 1983, Almond was plunging far deeper into the Marc And The Mambas project, despite the continued success of Soft Cell. This phase culminated in the release of a double album, *Torment And Toreros*. This was unquestionably Almond's most extreme and personal recording, full of melodrama with a revealing glimpse into the singer's darker side. When the album received a poor review in one music paper, Almond was so despondent and incensed that he announced his retirement. What that comment actually meant was the imminent dissolution of Marc And The Mambas and a final return to Soft Cell. When they, too, collapsed at the end of 1983, Almond embarked on a solo career, although his first post-Soft Cell recording, *Vermin In Ermine* was credited to Marc And The Willing Sinners and featured several musicians who had joined in the Mambas experiment.

● ALBUMS: *Untitled* (Some Bizzare 1982) ★★, *Torment And Toreros* (Some Bizzare 1983) ★★.

## MARIE, TEENA

b. Mary Christine Brockert, 5 March 1957, Santa Monica, California, USA. A singer, songwriter, multi-instrumentalist, arranger and producer, Teena Marie is remembered as one of the few white artists to sustain a consistent career in the US soul market. Spotted by Motown Records' Berry Gordy in the 70s, he linked her up with funk star and labelmate Rick James, and her early career strongly reflected their joint influences. The highly commercial 1979 debut album, *Wild And Peaceful*, saw her backed by James and the Stone City Band on a set that included their hit duet, 'I'm A Sucker For Your Love'. She returned the favour by partnering James on 'Fire And Desire' on his *Street Songs* album in 1981. Afterwards, Marie took increasing control of her career and songwriting, singing both ballads and funk. She achieved great success on the R&B charts, while both 'I Need Your Lovin'' and 'Square Biz' reached the Top 20 of the US *Billboard* pop charts in 1980 and 1981, respectively. In the UK, 'Behind The Groove', a surprise disco smash at number 6 in the singles chart, led to confusion in public minds over her and the similarly titled Kelly Marie (it also, accidentally, picked up on the prevalent UK disco trend for songs with 'Groove' in the title). However, her greatest success followed her move to Epic Records, which some saw as an assertion of her independence (her legal battle with Motown ended with the US courts passing a law named after the singer), with the number 4-peaking US hit, 'Lovergirl'. Afterwards, her chart career declined. *Emerald City* was a funky outing, notable particularly for Stevie Ray Vaughan's guitar solo on 'You So Heavy'. Demonstrating her talent for modernizing her technique with the advent of each new instalment in R&B's

development, *Ivory* was co-produced by Soul II Soul's Jazzie B. The singer now records for her own Sarai label.

● ALBUMS: *Wild And Peaceful* (Gordy 1979) ★★★, *Lady T* (Gordy 1980) ★★★, *Irons In The Fire* (Gordy 1980) ★★★, *It Must Be Magic* (Gordy 1981) ★★★★, *Robbery* (Epic 1983) ★★★, *Starchild* (Epic 1984) ★★★, *Emerald City* (Epic 1986) ★★★, *Naked To The World* (Epic 1988) ★★★, *Ivory* (Epic 1990) ★★★★, *Passion Play* (Sarai 1994) ★★.

● COMPILATIONS: *Greatest Hits* (Motown 1985) ★★★, *Greatest Hits* different track-listing to Motown issue (Epic 1991) ★★★, *I Need Your Lovin': The Very Best Of Teena Marie* (Motown 1994) ★★★★, *Motown Milestones: The Best Of Teena Marie* (Motown 1996) ★★★, *Lovergirl: The Teena Marie Story* (Sony 1997) ★★★, *Funk Biz* (Sony 1998) ★★★, *Love Songs* (Sony 2000) ★★★, *Ultimate Collection: I Just Want To Be Your Lovergirl* (PolyGram 2000) ★★★, *The Best Of Teena Marie: The Millennium Collection* (Universal 2001) ★★★★.

## MARILLION

Front-runners of the short-lived UK progressive rock revival of the early 80s, Marillion survived unfavourable comparisons with Genesis to become a popular melodic rock band, notching up several successful UK singles plucked from their grandiose concept albums.

The band was formed in Aylesbury, Buckinghamshire, originally as Silmarillion, a name taken from the novel by J.R.R. Tolkien. The original line-up comprised Doug Irvine (bass), Mick Pointer (b. 22 July 1956, England; drums), Steve Rothery (b. 25 November 1959, Brampton, South Yorkshire, England; guitar) and Brian Jellyman (keyboards). After recording the instrumental demo, 'The Web', the band recruited Fish (b. Derek William Dick, 25 April 1958, Dalkeith, Edinburgh, Scotland; vocals) and Diz Minnett (bass), and began building a strong following through almost continuous gigging. Before recording their debut, 'Market Square Heroes', Jellyman and Minnett were replaced by Mark Kelly (b. 9 April 1961, Dublin, Eire; keyboards) and Pete Trewavas (b. 15 January 1959, Middlesbrough, Cleveland, England; bass). Fish wrote all the lyrics for *Script For A Jester's Tear* and became the focal point of the band, often appearing on stage in garish make-up, echoing the style, both visually and vocally, of Genesis' singer Peter Gabriel. In 1983, Pointer was sacked and replaced for brief stints by Andy Ward of Camel, then John Martyr and Jonathan Mover, before the arrival of Ian Mosley (b. 16 June 1953, London, England), a veteran of many progressive rock bands, including Curved Air and the Gordon Giltrap band. Marillion's second album, *Fugazi*, embraced a more straightforward hard rock sound and yielded two hits, 'Assassing' and 'Punch And Judy'. The chart-topping *Misplaced Childhood* was the band's biggest-selling album – surprisingly so, as it featured an elaborate concept, being virtually one continuous piece of music based largely on Fish's childhood experiences. 'Kayleigh', a romantic ballad extracted from this mammoth work, reached number 2 in the UK charts, and 'Lavender'

followed it into the Top 5 four months later. *Clutching At Straws* was less successful and, by 1988, Fish was becoming increasingly dissatisfied with the band's musical development and left to pursue a solo career. The live double album *The Thieving Magpie* was his last recorded contribution, and provided a fitting overview of Marillion's past successes.

The band acquired Steve Hogarth (b. 14 May 1959, Kendal, England), formerly of the Europeans, who made his debut on *Seasons End*, proving himself equal to the daunting task of fronting a well-established band. The 90s found Marillion as popular as ever, with the ghost of Fish receding into the background. With Hogarth fronting the band, consistent success continued, including Top 30 chart status for 'Sympathy', 'The Hollow Man' and 'Beautiful'. The best of their more recent albums is 1995's *Afraid Of Sunlight*, which tackled the subject of fame, with references to the recently deceased Nirvana vocalist, Kurt Cobain, John Lennon and O.J. Simpson, the former American footballer who at the time was on trial for murder. The band's first studio work of the new millennium, *Anoraknophobia*, was funded by fans who paid for the record a year before its release, a novel venture which raised a few eyebrows in the music industry.

● ALBUMS: *Script For A Jester's Tear* (EMI/Capitol 1983) ★★★, *Fugazi* (EMI/Capitol 1984) ★★★, *Real To Reel* mini-album (EMI 1984) ★★, *Misplaced Childhood* (EMI/Capitol 1985) ★★★★, *Brief Encounter* mini-album (Capitol 1986) ★, *Clutching At Straws* (EMI/Capitol 1987) ★★★, *The Thieving Magpie (La Gazza Ladra)* (EMI/Capitol 1988) ★★, *Seasons End* (EMI/Capitol 1989) ★★★, *Holidays In Eden* (EMI 1991) ★★★, *Brave* (EMI/I.R.S. 1994) ★★★, *Afraid Of Sunlight* (EMI/I.R.S. 1995) ★★★★, *Made Again* (EMI/Intact 1996) ★★, *This Strange Engine* (Intact/Velvel 1997) ★★★, *Radiation* (Raw Power/Velvel 1998) ★★, *Marillion.com* (Intact 1999) ★★★, *Anoraknophobia* (Racket 2001) ★★★, *Anorak In The UK Live* (EMI 2002) ★★★.

● COMPILATIONS: *B'Sides Themselves* (EMI 1988) ★★, *A Singles Collection 1982-1992* UK title *Six Of One, Half-Dozen Of The Other* US title (EMI/I.R.S. 1992) ★★★, *Essential Collection* (EMI 1996) ★★★, *The Best Of Both Worlds* (EMI 1997) ★★★★, *Kayleigh: The Essential Collection* (EMI 1998) ★★★, *The CD Singles '82-'88* (EMI 2000) ★★★, *Refracted!* (Racket 2001) ★★.

● VIDEOS: *Recital Of The Script* (EMI 1983), *1982–86 The Videos* (EMI 1986), *Live From Loreley* (EMI 1987), *From Stoke Row To Ipanema* (EMI 1990), *A Singles Collection* (EMI 1992), *Brave The Movie* (EMI 1995), *The EMI Singles Collection* (EMI 2002).

● FURTHER READING: *Marillion: In Words And Pictures*, Carol Clerk. *Market Square Heroes: The Authorized Story Of Marillion*, Mick Wall. *Marillion: The Script*, Clive Gifford.

## MARILYN

b. Peter Robinson, 3 November 1962, Kingston, Jamaica, West Indies. Marilyn launched his UK singing career on the coattails of his friend Boy George as England's second cross-dressing pop star. Much photographed in the teenage press, he became a major celebrity in 1983 with the release of 'Calling

Your Name', which became a number 4 hit in the UK charts (many critics suggested it sounded like a Culture Club offcut). The tabloids turned on him with barely-concealed venom. As Marilyn complained later, 'You just expect that, after Danny La Rue and Quentin Crisp and God knows who else, that people would be able to accept someone with a bit of make-up. England is like such a bunch of old drag-queens anyway. If you pick up a history book . . . I'm quite tame compared to a lot of people.' Afterwards, however, a succession of further singles for Mercury Records attained ever-decreasing chart positions. The gospel-flavoured 'Cry And Be Free' reached 31 in February 1984. Exactly a year later 'You Don't Love Me' reached UK number 40. His record company dispatched him to Detroit, Michigan, to work with producer Don Was. However, when he arrived there he found nobody had paid for a room for him to stay in. Without personal funds, he cut his famous blonde hair (which gave him his name) and ceased to wear make-up, abandoning the image that had brought him his initial success. Despite this 'Baby You Left Me' (one of two tracks recorded with Was) failed to re-ignite his career, and the only time he is heard of now is in 'Where Are They Now' features.

● ALBUMS: *Despite Straight Lines* (Virgin 1985) ★★.

## MARINE GIRLS

This UK quartet was formed by four Hertfordshire school friends: Jane Fox (bass, vocals), her sister Alice (vocals, percussion), Tracey Thorn (b. 26 September 1962; guitar, vocals) and the soon-to-depart Gina (percussion, vocals). The Marine Girls recorded their home-made *Beach Party* in a garden shed. Musically competent, within limitations, their lyrics showed remarkable strength and eloquence in dealing with the age-old problems of difficult boyfriends, new love and loneliness, often using the symbolic context of the sea and all its mysteries. With initial encouragement from the Television Personalities, the album was released by the Whaam! label and was later picked up by Cherry Red Records, who signed the group for a second album. By this time, Thorn had left school to go to Hull University, where she struck up a romantic and artistic relationship with Cherry Red stablemate Ben Watt. They recorded the Cole Porter song 'Night And Day' under the name of Everything But The Girl. Thorn had also released a solo album in 1982, *A Distant Shore*, which was well received by the critics and public. Pursuing a parallel career as a Marine Girl and as a duettist with Watt at first proved comfortable, but with the increasing popularity and media attention of Everything But The Girl, an amicable split with the Fox sisters came in late 1983, after the release of the successful *Lazy Ways*. Continuing their seaside/oceanic fixation, the sisters formed Grab Grab The Haddock, which produced two fine EPs on CherrGrab Grab The Haddocky Red before folding in 1986. The line-up of was notable for the inclusion of Lester Noel, who later joined Norman Cook in Beats International.

● ALBUMS: *Beach Party* (Whaam! 1981) ★★, *Lazy Ways* (Cherry Red 1983) ★★★.

## MARLEY, ZIGGY, AND THE MELODY MAKERS

b. David Marley, 17 October 1968, Kingston, Jamaica, West Indies. 'Ziggy' Marley, one of Bob Marley's four children with his wife Rita Marley, started his career as one of the Melody Makers with siblings Sharon, Cedella and Stephen, whose appearance at their father's funeral in 1981 marked their introduction to the rest of the world. The following year, 'What A Plot', released on Rita's label, was a big hit, and Ziggy's lead vocals sounded uncannily similar to his late father's. The Melody Makers were allowed the time and space to mature and practise before committing themselves needlessly to vinyl – unlike so many of their Jamaican counterparts, where recording activities were an economic necessity – and by the late 80s they were a headline act, especially in the USA. Their *Play The Game Right* debut, the only album to be credited simply to the Melody Makers, included one notable excerpt from their father's songbook, 'Children Playing In The Street', which he had originally written for them. Despite their tender years, the record stands up to repeated listening and suggests that Marley's maturity and wisdom were hereditary. The album to confirm this was *Conscious Party*. Produced by Chris Frantz and Tina Weymouth from Talking Heads, and featuring an inspired selection of backing musicians, the set boasted high-calibre material such as 'Tomorrow People' and 'We Propose', which would not have disgraced any Wailers album. *One Bright Day* was a similarly delightful collection, comprising slick dance reggae with articulate rebuttals of the South African apartheid system.

The Melody Makers have resisted the obvious temptation to re-record too many of their father's songs, and instead have forged a career in their own right. In his excellent book *Bob Marley – Conquering Lion Of Reggae*, Stephen Davis illustrates the group's popularity in America by detailing a short exchange between two youngsters after seeing Bob Marley on video; one's question, 'Who's that?', is met with the cursory response, 'Ziggy Marley's father'. In his own lifetime, Bob and the Wailers did not break the American market with the same level of success as the Melody Makers. They are also very popular in Jamaica – and not just because of Ziggy's lineage, though his ability to sing over his father's songs as 'specials' for some of Kingston's top sound systems, adapting the lyrics for each particular system, has made him widely popular. Ziggy And The Melody Makers have transcended the 'famous parent' tag to become stars in their own right, following on from their father's tradition without ever leaning on it too heavily. As Bob once remarked: 'All a my family are music'.

● ALBUMS: *Play The Game Right* (EMI 1985) ★★★, *Hey World* (EMI 1986) ★★, *Conscious Party* (Virgin 1988) ★★★★, *One Bright Day* (Virgin 1989) ★★★★, *Jahmekya* (Virgin 1991) ★★★, *Joy & Blues – Ghetto Youths United* (Virgin 1993) ★★★, *Free Like We Want 2 B* (Elektra 1995) ★★★, *Fallen Is Babylon* (Elektra 1997) ★★★, *Spirit Of Music* (Elektra 1999) ★★★, Live (Elektra 2000) ★★★.

● COMPILATIONS: *Time Has Come: The Best Of*

*Ziggy Marley And The Melody Makers* (EMI/ Manhattan 1988) ★★★★, *The Best Of Ziggy Marley 1988-1993* (Virgin 1997) ★★★, *Classic Masters* (EMD 2002) ★★★.
● VIDEOS: *Ziggy Marley & The Melody Makers Live!* (Aviva 2001).

## MARRS
A collaboration between two 4AD Records bands, Colourbox and AR Kane, which, though a one-off, was enough to set the independent, dance music and national charts alight during autumn 1987. 'Pump Up The Volume' was augmented on the a-side by UK champion scratch mixer C.J. Mackintosh and London disc jockey/journalist Dave Dorrell. Primarily aimed at the dance market, the record was originally mailed to the 500 most influential regional club and dance DJs on an anonymous white label, in order that it received exposure six weeks prior to its stock version. On official release, it entered the charts at number 35, a figure attained on 12-inch sales only. Daytime radio play ensured the single was the next week's highest climber, rising 24 places to number 11. The following two weeks it stayed at number 2 before reaching the number 1 spot on 28 September 1987. Originally the idea of 4AD supremo Ivo, the single featured samples of James Brown, a practice already common in hip-hop that would soon come into vogue for an avalanche of dance tracks: 'We've used a lot of rhythms and time signatures from old records, classic soul records, but mixed that with modern electronic instruments and AR Kane's guitar sound', was how the single was described. The single was never followed up, apparently due to acrimony between the involved personnel over finance, which was a great shame. As such, the MARRS discography is a brief but blemishless one. Dorrell would go on to manage Bush while Mackintosh returned to the club circuit.

## MARSALIS, BRANFORD
b. 26 August 1960, Breaux Bridge, Louisiana, USA. With their father, Ellis Marsalis, a bop pianist, composer and teacher, it is not surprising that his sons Branford, Jason, Delfeayo and Wynton Marsalis all took up music in childhood. Branford Marsalis' first instrument was the alto saxophone, which he played during his formative years and while studying at Berklee College Of Music. In 1981, he played in Art Blakey's Jazz Messengers and the following year began a spell with a small band led by Wynton. During this period, Marsalis switched instruments, taking up both soprano and tenor saxophones. He also played on record dates with leading jazzmen such as Miles Davis and Dizzy Gillespie. After three years in his brother's band, he began a period of musical searching. Like many young musicians of his era, Marsalis often played in jazz-rock bands, including that led by Sting. He also formed his own small group with which he toured and recorded. By the late 80s he had established a reputation as a leading post-bop jazz saxophonist, but also enjoyed status in fusion and even classical circles (*Romances For Saxophone*).
Like most jazzmen, Marsalis drew early inspiration

from the work of other musicians, amongst them John Coltrane, Ben Webster, Wayne Shorter, Ornette Coleman and especially Sonny Rollins. In some of his recordings these influences have surfaced, leading to criticisms that he has failed to develop a personal style. Closer attention reveals that these stylistic acknowledgements are merely that and not an integral part of his musical make up. His 90s work, including 1993's *I Heard You Twice The First Time* and 1997's *The Dark Keys*, showed a strong leaning towards the blues, with both John Lee Hooker and B.B. King featuring on the former. Perhaps of more significance to Marsalis' development as a musician is the fact that his career appears fated to be constantly compared to and contrasted with that of his virtuoso brother Wynton. This has often resulted in his being overshadowed, which is unfortunate because Branford Marsalis had proved himself to be an inventive soloist with considerable warmth. His best work contains many moments of powerful emotional commitment. In the mid-90s he relocated to Hollywood for a spell on Jay Leno's *The Tonight Show*.
● ALBUMS: *Scenes In The City* (Columbia 1983) ★★★★, with Wynton Marsalis *Black Codes (From The Underground)* (Columbia 1985) ★★★, *Royal Garden Blues* (Columbia 1986) ★★★, *Random Abstract* (Columbia 1987) ★★★★, *Renaissance* (Columbia 1987) ★★★, *Trio Jeepy* (Columbia 1988) ★★★★, *Crazy People Music* (Columbia 1990) ★★★★, *The Beautiful Ones Are Not Yet Born* (Columbia 1992) ★★★★, *I Heard You Twice The First Time* (Columbia 1993) ★★★, *Bloomington* (Columbia 1993) ★★★, *Buckshot La Fonque* (Columbia 1994) ★★★★, with Ellis Marsalis *Loved Ones* (Columbia 1996) ★★★, *The Dark Keys* (Columbia 1996) ★★★★, *Requiem* (Columbia 1999) ★★★, *Contemporary Jazz* (Columbia 2000) ★★★, with the Orpheus Chamber Orchestra *Creation* (Sony Classical 2001) ★★★, *Footsteps Of Our Fathers* (Marsalis/Rounder 2002) ★★★★.
● COMPILATIONS: *Popular Songs: The Best Of Wynton Marsalis* (Sony 2001) ★★★★.
● VIDEOS: *Steep* (Sony 1989), *The Music Tells You* (Sony 1993).

## MARSALIS, WYNTON
b. 18 October 1961, New Orleans, Louisiana, USA. Marsalis took up the trumpet at the age of six, encouraged by his father, Ellis Marsalis, a pianist, composer and teacher. His brothers, Jason, Delfeayo and Branford Marsalis are also musicians. Before entering his teenage years he was already studying formally, but had simultaneously developed an interest in jazz. The range of his playing included performing with a New Orleans marching band led by Danny Barker, and playing trumpet concertos with the New Orleans Philharmonic Orchestra. Marsalis later extended his studies at two of the USA's most prestigious musical education establishments, Berkshire Music Center at Tanglewood and the Juilliard School of Music in New York City. By the age of 19, he was already a virtuoso trumpeter, a voracious student of jazz music, history and culture, and clearly destined for great things. It

was then that he joined Art Blakey's Jazz Messengers, perhaps the best of all finishing schools for post-bop jazzmen. During the next two years he matured considerably as a player, touring and recording with Blakey and also with other leading jazzmen, including Herbie Hancock and Ron Carter. He also made records under his own name and, encouraged by his success, decided to form his own permanent group. In this he was joined by his brother Branford. During 1983, he again worked with Hancock. The following year he recorded in London with Raymond Leppard and the National Philharmonic Orchestra, playing concertos by Haydn, Hummell and Leopold Mozart – a side-step that led to his becoming the unprecedented recipient of Grammy Awards for both jazz and classical albums. He next toured Japan and Europe, appearing at many festivals, on television and making many recording sessions.

By 1991, and still only just turned 30, Marsalis had become one of the best-known figures on the international musical stage. His prolific output reached new heights in 1999, when he recorded nine albums of classical and jazz music, a collection of film music, and released a 7-CD box set documenting his septet's appearances at New York's Village Vanguard in the early 90s. Insofar as his classical work is concerned, Marsalis has been spoken of in most glowing terms. In his jazz work his sublime technical ability places him on a plateau he shares with very few others. Nevertheless, despite such extraordinary virtuosity, the emotional content of Marsalis' work often hints only lightly at the possibilities inherent in jazz. Sometimes, the undeniable skill and craftsmanship are displayed at the expense of vitality. If compared to, for instance, Jon Faddis, eight years his senior, or Clifford Brown, who died at the age of only 26, then there is clearly some distance to go in his development as a player of emotional profundity.

● ALBUMS: *Wynton Marsalis* (Columbia 1981) ★★★★, *Think Of One* (Columbia 1982) ★★★★, with Branford and Ellis Marsalis *Fathers And Sons* (Columbia 1982) ★★★, *Think Of Me* (Columbia 1983) ★★★, *Hot House Flowers* (Columbia 1984) ★★★★, *Black Codes (From The Underground)* (Columbia 1985) ★★★★, *J Mood* (Columbia 1986) ★★★★, *Live At Blues Alley* (Columbia 1987) ★★★★, *Marsalis Standard Time, Volume 1* (Columbia 1987) ★★★★, *The Majesty Of The Blues* (Columbia 1988) ★★★, *Crescent City Christmas Card* (Columbia 1989) ★★★, *Tune In Tomorrow* soundtrack (Columbia 1989) ★★★, *Marsalis Standard Time, Volume 2: Intimacy Calling* (Columbia 1991) ★★★, *Marsalis Standard Time, Volume 3: The Resolution Of Romance* (Columbia 1991) ★★★, *Soul Gestures In Southern Blue, Vol. 1: Thick In The South* (Columbia 1991) ★★★, *Soul Gestures In Southern Blue, Vol. 2: Uptown Ruler* (Columbia 1991) ★★★, *Soul Gestures In Southern Blue, Vol. 3: Levee Low Moan* (Columbia 1991) ★★★, *Blue Interlude* (Columbia 1992) ★★★, *Citi Movement (Griot New York)* 2-CD set (Columbia 1993) ★★★, *Resolution To Swing* (Columbia 1993) ★★★, *Marsalis Standard Time, Vol. 4: Plays Monk* (Columbia 1993) ★★★, *Joe's Cool Blues* (Columbia 1994) ★★★, *In This House, On This Morning* (Columbia 1994) ★★★, *Live In Swing Town* (Jazz Door 1994) ★★★, with the Lincoln Center Jazz Orchestra *Blood On The Fields* (Columbia 1997) ★★★★, *Jump Start & Jazz* (Sony Classical 1997) ★★★, *Marsalis Standard Time, Vol. 5: The Midnight Blues* (Columbia 1998) ★★★, with the Lincoln Center Jazz Orchestra *Big Train* (Columbia 1999) ★★★★, *Mr. Jelly Lord: Standard Time, Vol. 6* 1993 recording (Columbia 1999) ★★★★, *Reeltime* (Sony 1999) ★★★, *Live At The Village Vanguard* 7-CD box set (Columbia 1999) ★★★★, *Sweet Release And Ghost Story: Two More Ballets* (Sony Classical 1999) ★★, *Selections From The Village Vanguard Box* (Columbia 2000) ★★★★, *The Marciac Suite* (Columbia 2000) ★★★.
● COMPILATIONS: *Popular Songs: The Best Of Wynton Marsalis* (Columbia 2001) ★★★★.
● VIDEOS: *The London Concert* (Sony Classical 1994), *Marsalis On Music* (Sony 1995).
● FURTHER READING: *Sweet Swing Blues On The Road*, Wynton Marsalis and Frank Stewart. *Skain's Domain*, Leslie Gourse.

## MARSHALL, KEITH

Marshall was originally the guitarist for UK glam rock band Hello. When the band finally collapsed, he turned to singing and walked straight into a successful solo career in Germany with his first single 'Remember Me'. It was followed by another three chart contenders including the 1981 worldwide hit, 'Only Crying'. While Germany continued to hold him dear, Marshall was not content to spend the rest of his career rewriting his greatest hit and has continued to move on musically, releasing records mainly in Europe, leaving the UK with only the occasional single.
● ALBUMS: *Keith Marshall* (Arrival 1981) ★★.
● COMPILATIONS: *Tonight We Dance* (Arrival 1988) ★★★.

## MARX, RICHARD

b. 16 September 1963, Chicago, Illinois, USA. This singer/songwriter began his career at the age of five, singing on US advertising jingles written by his father. This became his professional vocation until he moved to Los Angeles and worked as a session vocalist in the studio for Lionel Richie, Madonna and Whitney Houston. He also established himself as a songwriter, co-writing Kenny Rogers 1984 hit 'What About Me?', and providing material for Chicago, Vixen and Freddie Jackson. Afterwards, Marx embarked on a solo career in his own right, enjoying a string of hits in the late 80s, including 'Don't Mean Nothing' (US number 3, 1987), 'Should've Known Better' (US number 3, 1987), 'Endless Summer Nights' (US number 2, 1988). Three successive US number 1 singles in 1988–89 ('Hold On To The Nights', 'Satisfied' and 'Right Here Waiting'), and the hit albums *Richard Marx* and *Repeat Offender* (a US chart-topper) proved the commercial effectiveness of his big ballad formula. Marx married Cynthia Rhodes of Animotion in January 1989. The following decade saw Marx struggling to repeat his earlier success on the pop charts. He did enjoy a UK Top 5 hit in 1992 with 'Hazard', while the 1994 ballad 'Now And Forever', featured on the soundtrack of *The*

*Getaway*, topped the US Adult Contemporary chart for 11 weeks. Marx also established himself as an in-demand songwriter and producer, and in 1999 started his own record company.

● ALBUMS: *Richard Marx* (EMI-Manhattan 1987) ★★★, *Repeat Offender* (EMI-Manhattan 1989) ★★, *Rush Street* (Capitol 1991) ★★★, *Paid Vacation* (Capitol 1994) ★★★, *Flesh And Bone* (Capitol 1997) ★★★, *Days In Avalon* (Signal 21 2000) ★★★.

● COMPILATIONS: *Greatest Hits* (Capitol 1997) ★★★, *The Essential* (EMI Gold 2000) ★★★.

## MATT BIANCO

This UK jazz/pop act was formed in 1984 by ex-Blue Rondo A La Turk members Mark Reilly (b. 20 February 1960, High Wycombe, Buckinghamshire, England; lead vocals) and Daniel White (b. 26 August 1959, Hertfordshire, England; keyboards), with Basia (b. Basha Trzetrzelewska, 30 September 1959, Jaworzno, Galica, Poland; vocals). They emerged in the latter part of the UK jazz/pop scene in the early 80s, alongside other acts such as Sade and Animal Nightlife. Signed to the WEA Records distributed YZ label, they achieved a run of UK hits in 1984 with the breezy, samba-laced 'Get Out Of Your Lazy Bed' (number 15), 'Sneaking Out The Back Door'/'Matt's Mood' (number 44), 'Half A Minute' (number 23). The following year a cover version of Georgie Fame's 'Yeh Yeh' reached number 13. The initial employment of various session musicians was abandoned in favour of a full-time band, taking on keyboard player Mark Fisher (who already had connections to them in the capacity of songwriter), plus bass player Kito Poncioni (b. Rio, Brazil). Basia left after the release of 1984's debut album, *Whose Side Are You On*, to forge her own solo career and was replaced by Jenni Evans. Daniel White also left around this time. Basia and White recorded *Time And Tide* together and, because of White's contractual problems the album, and various singles from it, came out as Basia solo releases. By now Matt Bianco was, in pop terms, unfashionable, but Reilly's fascination, and adeptness with fusing Latin rhythms to pop, gave the band their biggest UK hit in 1988 with the number 11 single, 'Don't Blame It On That Girl/Wap-Bam-Boogie'. Increasingly driven to cater for a select audience, the band continued to produce specialized, quality pop music into the following decade, enjoying particular success in Japan.

● ALBUMS: *Whose Side Are You On* (WEA 1984) ★★★★, *Matt Bianco* (WEA 1986) ★★★, *Indigo* (WEA 1988) ★★★, *Samba In Your Casa* (East West 1991) ★★, *Another Time, Another Place* (JVC Victor/ZYX 1993) ★★★, *Gran Via* (JVC Victor/ZYX 1995) ★★★, *World Go Round* (JVC Victor 1998) ★★★★, *Rico* (JVC Victor 2000) ★★★.

● COMPILATIONS: *The Best Of Matt Bianco* (WEA 1990) ★★★★, *Yeah Yeah* (Warners 1993) ★★★, *A/Collection* (JVC Victor/Interchord 1998) ★★★★.

## MAY, DERRICK

b. USA. If one name crops up again and again in discussions of techno, it is that of Derrick 'Mayday' May. Alongside Juan Atkins, Carl Craig and Kevin Saunderson, May is regarded as one of the kings of the Detroit sound. Inspired by Yello and Kraftwerk, he began to make electronic music with Atkins and Saunderson while studying with them at Belleville High, Detroit. Recording either as Mayday or Rhythim Is Rhythim (occasionally in conjunction with Carl Craig) and generally on his own Transmat Records label, he went on to carve out a new vein in dance music that synthesized the advances of the electro movement with the more challenging end of the house movement – a music that defined 'techno'. Early cuts such as 'Nude Photo' and 'The Dance', both on Transmat, were inspirational to many. However, it was the release of 'Strings Of Life' in 1987, which, with its wide appeal to the house music fans of the late 80s, simultaneously brought May his deserved acclaim and Detroit techno to European club-goers.

May has never proved prolific in his recordings. After the success of 'Strings Of Life' he largely fled the dance scene, aside from a remix of Yello's 'The Race'. Rhythim Is Rhythim did not follow-up 'Strings Of Life' until 1990, when 'The Beginning' was released. May went on to cut three disappointing tracks on System 7's debut album, before Network released *Innovator: Soundtrack For The Tenth Planet* in 1991, a six-track EP that comprised some of May's definitive moments to date. In the same year, May was responsible for what Carl Craig has called the finest remix ever, Sueño Latino's 'Sueño Latino', itself a reworking of Manuel Goettsching's epic 'E2-M4'. It was followed in 1992 by *Relics*, a double album of Transmat's finest moments, heavily featuring Rhythim Is Rhythim, which coincided with a re-release of 'Strings Of Life' on the Belgium label Buzz, this time in a drumless version reminiscent of May's 'Sueño Latino' remix. More recently, Transmat has been revived following its signing to Sony. This has resulted in the long-awaited release of Rhythim Is Rhythim's 1991 recordings, 'Kao-tic Harmony' and 'Icon', and the Japanese (and subsequent American) release of a comprehensive Derrick May retrospective, *Innovator*, which contains all May's work for the Transmat label including remixes and tracks released for the first time.

● COMPILATIONS: *Relics: A Transmat Compilation* (Buzz 1992) ★★★★, *Mayday Mix – Derrick May* (MOS 1997) ★★★, *Innovator* (Transmat 1997) ★★★★, with System 7 *Mysterious Traveller* (A-Wave 2002) ★★★★.

## MAZE (FEATURING FRANKIE BEVERLY)

Frankie Beverly (b. 6 December 1946, Philadelphia, Pennsylvania, USA) had an apprenticeship in several Philadelphia groups. One such unit, Frankie Beverly And The Butlers, recorded several well-received singles in the 60s, but never managed to attract more than local play. By the early 70s, however, impressed by Santana and Sly And The Family Stone, he formed a self-contained band, Raw Soul, and they moved to San Francisco where they became the house band at a local club, the Scene. Discovered by a girlfriend of Marvin Gaye, the group subsequently supported the singer in concert, and it was he who suggested they change their name in deference to their now cooler sound. The septet, which featured

Wayne aka Wuane Thomas (guitar), Sam Porter (keyboards), Robin Duhe (bass), Roame Lowry (congas, vocals), McKinley Williams (percussion, vocals), Joe Provost (drums) plus Beverly, thus became Maze. Their debut album was issued in January 1977, the first of eight albums for Capitol Records. Their third album, 1979's *Inspiration* featured new drummer Ahaguna Sun, who in turn was replaced by Billy Johnson on the follow-up *Joy And Pain*. This album also featured two further personnel changes, with keyboard player Kevin Burton and guitarist Ron Smith brought in to the line-up. The excellent *Live In New Orleans* set saw Burton replaced by Phillip Woo. This line-up went on to record one of Maze's finest studio outing, 1983's *We Are One*.

The band consistently hit the R&B charts during this period, although only 'Workin' Together' (1978), 'Feel That You're Feelin'' (1979), 'Southern Girl' (1980), 'Running Away' (1981) and 'Love Is The Key' (1983) managed to break into the Top 10. Maze finally reached the top of the R&B charts in 1985 with 'Back In Stride', taken from the same year's *Can't Stop The Love* which was recorded with new musicians Wayne Thomas (guitar), Wayne Linsey and Sam Porter (both keyboards), Tony St. James and Ricky Lawson (both drums), and additional bass player Randy Jackson. A final album for Capitol was recorded live in Los Angeles, and featured yet another drummer, Mike White.

Their debut for Warner Brothers Records, *Silky Soul*, featured the nucleus of Beverly, Williams, Lowry and Duhe joined by occasional band members Woo, Linsey and William Bryant (keyboards), Smith (guitar), Jackson (bass), and Lawson (drums). The album generated their second R&B chart-topper 'Can't Get Over You', while the title track reached the Top 5. White and Sonny Emery joined the Maze personnel for their second Warners album, *Back To Basics*. Although they are no longer a fixture on the charts, Maze remain one of soul's most consistent live attractions.

● ALBUMS: *Maze Featuring Frankie Beverly* (Capitol 1977) ★★★★, *Golden Time Of Day* (Capitol 1978) ★★★★, *Inspiration* (Capitol 1979) ★★★, *Joy And Pain* (Capitol 1980) ★★★, *Live In New Orleans* (Capitol 1981) ★★★★, *We Are One* (Capitol 1983) ★★★★, *Can't Stop The Love* (Capitol 1985) ★★★, *Live In Los Angeles* (Capitol 1986) ★★★★, *Silky Soul* (Warners 1989) ★★★, *Back To Basics* (Warners 1993) ★★★.

● COMPILATIONS: *LifeLines: The Greatest Hits Of Maze Featuring Frankie Beverly* (Capitol 1989) ★★★★, *Southern Girl* (CEMA 1995) ★★★, *Anthology* (Capitol 1996) ★★★★, *Greatest Slow Jams* (Capitol 1998) ★★★★.

● VIDEOS: *Live In New Orleans* (Capitol 2001).

## McDONALD, MICHAEL

b. 2 December 1952, St. Louis, Missouri, USA. McDonald has one of the most effortless and powerful voices in modern soul/rock. For a period in the 80s he also became a major, although not always completely consistent, hit songwriter. He recorded an abortive solo session for Bell Records in the early 70s, but found greater fame as a guest vocalist with Steely Dan and as a member of the Doobie Brothers. McDonald was instrumental in steering the latter's sound towards highly commercial soul-based rock. Following his departure from the Doobie Brothers in 1982, McDonald embarked on a popular solo career. He had already won a Grammy for the Doobie Brothers hit, co-written with Kenny Loggins, 'What A Fool Believes', but during the 80s he had his compositions recorded by numerous artists, including Aretha Franklin, Millie Jackson and Carly Simon. He almost made the top of the US charts in 1982 with the soulful 'I Keep Forgettin' (Every Time You're Near)'. His 'Yah Mo B There', recorded with James Ingram in 1984, is a modern soul classic – it is not often that a white singer is able to write and sing in a predominantly black music genre with such conviction and integrity. The 1985 album *No Lookin' Back* was a dance favourite, and was followed the next year by his epic US number 1 duet with Patti LaBelle, 'On My Own'. During that year, he enjoyed an international hit with the theme from the movie *Running Scared*, the graceful 'Sweet Freedom'. His commercial profile declined in the 90s and with Reprise Records losing interest he joined the re-formed Doobie Brothers. In 1999, McDonald inaugurated the Ramp Records label with the support of actor Jeff Bridges and Chris Pelonis. The following February he released *Blue Obsession*, an album originally scheduled for release on his old label.

● ALBUMS: *If That's What It Takes* (Warners 1982) ★★★★, *No Lookin' Back* (Warners 1985) ★★★, *Lonely Talk* (Warners 1989) ★★★, *Take It To Heart* (Reprise 1990) ★★★, *Blink Of An Eye* (Reprise 1993) ★★, *Blue Obsession* (Ramp 2000) ★★★, *In The Spirit: A Christmas Album* (MCA 2001) ★★.

● COMPILATIONS: *That Was Then: The Early Recordings Of Michael McDonald* (Arista 1982) ★★, *Sweet Freedom: Best Of Michael McDonald* (Warners 1986) ★★★, *The Very Best Of Michael McDonald* (Rhino 2001) ★★★★.

● VIDEOS: *A Gathering Of Friends* (Aviva International 2001).

## McFERRIN, BOBBY

b. 11 March 1950, New York City, New York, USA. To call Bobby McFerrin a jazz vocalist is hardly to do him justice, for when McFerrin performs – he usually appears solo in lengthy concerts – he uses his entire body as a sound-box, beating noises out of his slender frame while emitting a constant accompaniment of guttural noises, clicks and popping sounds. To all this he adds a vocal technique that owes a slight debt to the bop vocalist Betty Carter and her daring swoops and scat vocals.

McFerrin was brought up in a musical family – both his parents are opera singers, his father performing on the film soundtrack of *Porgy And Bess* in 1959 – but his main jazz influence came from Miles Davis' *Bitches Brew*. Training as a pianist at the Juilliard School of Music and later at Sacramento State College, he worked first as an accompanist, then as a pianist and singer during the 70s. He came to public notice in 1979, when he performed in New York with the singer Jon Hendricks, but it was his unaccompanied appearance at the 1981 Kool Jazz Festival that brought him widespread acclaim. By 1983, he had perfected his solo style of wordless, vocal improvisations. His debut album contained a dramatic reworking of Van Morrison's 'Moondance', while *The Voice* mixed his fondness for pop classics – this time, the Beatles' 'Blackbird' – with more adventurous pieces, notably the self-descriptive 'I'm My Own Walkman'. The 1988 album *Simple Pleasures* shows off his wide range with its mixture of pop classics and self-composed material. The highlight of the album was his idiosyncratic version of Cream's 'Sunshine Of Your Love', complete with a vocal electric guitar. That recording also spawned a huge hit single, 'Don't Worry Be Happy', which was featured in the popular movie *Cocktail*. It reached number 1 in the USA and number 2 in the UK. Further success came when Cadbury's chocolate used 'Thinkin' About Your Body' in a major advertising campaign (substituting the word 'chocolate' for 'body'). This moved him away from a jazz audience although *Paper Music* was an impressive venture, with McFerrin attempting the music of Bach, Mozart and Mendelssohn. He moved back to his jazz roots when he joined forces with Yellowjackets on *Bang!Zoom*, arguably his finest album to date. McFerrin is a true original, blessed with a remarkable vocal ability that goes beyond the usual limitations of the human voice.

● ALBUMS: *Bobby McFerrin* (Elektra Musician 1982) ★★★, *The Voice* (Elektra Musician 1984) ★★★, *Spontaneous Inventions* (Blue Note 1986) ★★★, *Simple Pleasures* (EMI Manhattan 1988) ★★★, *Medicine Music* (EMI Manhattan 1990) ★★★, *Hush* (Columbia 1991) ★★★, with Chick Corea *Play* (Blue Note 1992) ★★★, *Paper Music* (Sony 1995) ★★★, *The Mozart Sessions* (Sony 1996) ★★★, *Bang!Zoom* (Blue Note 1996) ★★★, *Circle Songs* (Sony 1997) ★★★, *Beyond Words* (Blue Note 2002) ★★★.

## McGEE, ALAN

b. 29 September 1960, Glasgow, Scotland. After leaving school at the age of 17, McGee became an electrician. His friendship with future Primal Scream founders Bobby Gillespie and Robert Young established important early connections, before he relocated to London where he worked as a clerk for British Rail. He also joined up with another future member of Primal Scream, Andrew Innes, in the Laughing Apple, and set up his own Autonomy label and the fanzine *Communication Blur*. He also promoted gigs for his nomadic club, the Living Room, booking acts such as the Nightingales and the Television Personalities. To his surprise, he found that he was making a profit, so elected to release records and formed the label Creation Records in 1983. During the early phase of the label's history, McGee issued singles by artists such as the Loft, the Pastels, Primal Scream, the Jasmine Minks and his own venture, Biff Bang Pow!. After signing the Jesus And Mary Chain in 1984, McGee's credibility as a manager and label owner escalated dramatically. He stayed with the band for two, often stormy, years and along the way issued some fascinating product

by Felt, the Bodines and the Weather Prophets. The ill-fated tie-up with Warner Brothers Records, Elevation Records, encouraged McGee to pursue the independent route with more vigour. During the latter half of the 80s, the Creation roster extended to include Nikki Sudden, Momus, Clive Langer and, most crucially, the House Of Love. After one album and two excellent singles, the latter signed to Phonogram.

After 1988, McGee turned increasingly to dance music for inspiration. Initial releases by Love Corporation, Hynotone, JBC and DJ Danny Rampling were not commercial successes, but the new direction was sound. Ironically, it was former psychedelic outfit Primal Scream who embraced the dance culture most effectively, providing the label with hits such as 'Loaded' and 1991's epochal *Screamadelica*. Further success followed as Creation entered its most productive phase during the mid-90s, with the critically acclaimed and bestselling My Bloody Valentine, Ride, Teenage Fanclub, Boo Radleys and, biggest of all, Oasis. The label entered a troubled period in the late 90s, however, and was stunned by the departure of McGee and Green in November 1999, followed by Oasis' announcement that their new album would be released through their own label. McGee launched his new label, Poptones, the following summer. The label hit financial problems in late 2001 giving credence to the rumour that McGee had lost interest. Despite these recent problems, his genuine love of music and thrust for innovation made McGee one of the most influential music business entrepreneurs to emerge in the UK during the 90s.

● FURTHER READING: *Alan McGee & The Story Of Creation Records: This Ecstasy Romance Cannot Last*, Paolo Hewitt. *The Creation Records Story: My Magpie Eyes Are Hungry For The Prize*, David Cavanagh.

## McLAREN, MALCOLM

b. 22 January 1946, London, England. After a tempestuous childhood, during which he was reared by his eccentric grandmother, McLaren spent the mid- to late 60s at various art colleges. In 1969 he became romantically involved with fashion designer Vivienne Westwood and they subsequently had a son together, Joseph. Malcolm was fascinated by the work of the Internationale Situationist, a Marxist/Dadaist group which espoused its doctrines through sharp political slogans such as 'be reasonable – demand the impossible'. Their use of staged 'situations', designed to gain the attention of and ultimately enlighten the proletariat, impressed McLaren, and would significantly influence his entrepreneurial career.

In 1971, he opened the shop Let It Rock in Chelsea's Kings Road, which catered for Teddy Boy fashions. Among the shop's many visitors were several members of the New York Dolls, whose management McLaren took over in late 1974. It was to prove an ill-fated venture, but McLaren did spend some time with them in New York and organized their 'Better Dead Than Red' tour. After returning to the UK, he decided to find a new, young group whose power, presence and rebelliousness equalled that of the

New York Dolls. The result was the Sex Pistols, whose brief spell of public notoriety ushered in the era of punk. McLaren was at the peak of his powers during this period, riding the wave of self-inflicted chaos that the Sex Pistols spewed forth. The highlights included McLaren taking sizeable cheques from both EMI Records and A&M Records, who signed then fired the group in quick succession. The creation of the tragic caricature Sid Vicious, the conflict with Johnny Rotten, the involvement with Great Train Robber Ronnie Biggs and, finally, a self-glorifying film *The Great Rock 'n' Roll Swindle* were all part of the saga.

Following the Sex Pistols' demise, McLaren launched Bow Wow Wow, heavily promoting the 14-year-old singer Annabella Lwin. Although their recordings were highly original for the period, the dividends proved unimpressive and the group split. In the meantime, McLaren had served as 'advisor' to and let slip through his hands 80s stars such as Adam Ant and Boy George (Culture Club). Eventually, he decided to transform himself into a recording star, despite the fact that he could not sing (ample evidence of which had appeared on his *Great Rock 'n' Roll Swindle* out-take, 'You Need Hands'). His singular ability to predict trends saw him assimilating various styles of music, from the Zulu tribes in Africa to the ethnic sounds of the Appalachian Mountains. The arduous sessions finally came to fruition with *Duck Rock*, which featured two UK Top 10 singles, 'Buffalo Girls' and 'Double Dutch'. The work pre-empted rock's interest in world music, as exemplified on *Graceland* by Paul Simon.

McLaren next persisted with the music of urban New York and was particularly interested in the 'scratching' sounds of street hip-hop disc jockeys. *Would Ya Like More Scratchin'* again anticipated the strong dance culture that would envelop the UK pop scene in the late 80s. Ever restless, McLaren moved on to a strange fusion of pop and opera with *Fans*, which featured a startling version of 'Madam Butterfly' that became a UK Top 20 hit. Following his experimental forays in the music business, McLaren relocated to Hollywood for a relatively unsuccessful period in the film industry. Nothing substantial emerged from that sojourn, but McLaren remains as unpredictable and innovative as ever. *Paris*, and the subsequent ambient remix album, proved more popular in Europe than the UK.

● ALBUMS: *Duck Rock* (Island 1983) ★★★★, *D'Ya Like Scratchin'?* (Island 1984) ★★★, *Fans* (Island 1984) ★★★, *Swamp Thing* (Island 1985) ★, as Malcolm McLaren And The Bootzilla Orchestra *Waltz Darling* (Epic 1989) ★★, as Malcolm McLaren Presents The World Famous Supreme Team Show *Round The Outside! Round The Outside!* (Virgin 1990) ★★, *Paris* (Disques Vogue 1994) ★★★, *The Largest Movie Houses In Paris (The Ambient Remixes)* (World Attractions 1996) ★★, *Buffalo Gals Back To Skool* (Virgin 1998) ★★★.

● FURTHER READING: *Starmakers & Svengalis: The History Of British Pop Management*, Johnny Rogan. *The Wicked, Wicked Ways Of Malcolm McLaren*, Craig Bromsberg.

## MEAT PUPPETS

Formed in Tempe, Arizona, USA, Curt Kirkwood (b. 10 January 1959, Wichita Falls, Texas, USA; guitar, vocals), Cris Kirkwood (b. 22 October 1960, Amarillo, Texas, USA; bass, vocals) and Derrick Bostrom (b. 23 June 1960, Phoenix, Arizona, USA; drums) made their debut in 1981 with a five-track EP, *In A Car*. *Meat Puppets*, released the following year on the influential hardcore label SST Records, offered a mix of thrash punk with hints of country, captured to perfection on the alternative cowboy classic, 'Tumbling Tumbleweeds'. Their affection for roots music was fully realized on *Meat Puppets II*, a captivating set marked by dramatic shifts in mood and Curt Kirkwood's uncertain, but expressive, vocals. *Meat Puppets II* hauled country back to the campfire. *Up On The Sun* showed the trio moving further from their punk roots, embracing instead neo-psychedelic melodies. This evolution was enhanced further on *Mirage*, yet another critically acclaimed set. Having proclaimed an affection for ZZ Top, Curt Kirkwood introduced a more direct, fuzz-toned sound on *Huevos*, which was recorded in one marathon 72-hour session. Kirkwood shunned using a traditional plectrum, using instead a quarter dollar coin. Viewed by many long-time fans as a sell-out, *Huevos*' commercial appeal continued on *Monster*, the trio's heaviest, most 'traditional' set to date. Memorable hooklines were combined with hard-rock riffs and despite the qualms of those preferring the band's early work, the set was lauded as one of 1989's leading independent releases.

Surprisingly the Meat Puppets then disbanded, re-forming in 1991, buoyed by continued interest in their work and a contract with London Records. Subsequent releases kept interest in the band alive, and in 1993 the Kirkwood brothers joined Nirvana on their now-legendary MTV *Unplugged* appearance. Three songs from *Meat Puppets II*; 'Lake Of Fire', 'Plateau' and 'Oh Me', were immortalized during this affectionate collaboration. The following year's *Too High To Die* proved to be the most commercial and successful album of their long career. *No Joke!* was less successful, and following its release the band began to disintegrate. Curt Kirkwood was the only remaining original member present on 2000's desultory *Golden Lies*.

● ALBUMS: *Meat Puppets* (SST 1982) ★★, *Meat Puppets II* (SST 1983) ★★★, *Up On The Sun* (SST 1985) ★★★, *Mirage* (SST 1987) ★★★★, *Huevos* (SST 1987) ★★★, *Monsters* (SST 1989) ★★★, *Forbidden Places* (London 1991) ★★★, *Too High To Die* (London 1994) ★★★, *No Joke!* (London 1995) ★★★, *Live In Montana 1988* recording (Rykodisc 1999) ★★★, *Golden Lies* (Breaking/Atlantic 2000) ★★, *Live At Maxwell's* (DCN 2002) ★★.

● COMPILATIONS: *No Strings Attached* (SST 1990) ★★★.

## MEKONS

Although initially based in Leeds, England, the Mekons made their recording debut for the Edinburgh-based Fast Product label in January 1978. Recorded by Andy Corrigan (vocals), Mark White (vocals), Ros Allen (bass), Jon Langford (drums, later guitar, vocals), Ken and Tong, 'Never Been In A Riot', the outlet's first release, was the subject of effusive music press praise, and its joyous amateurism set the standard for much of the band's subsequent work. Having completed a second single, 'Where Were You', the Mekons were signed to Virgin Records where a line-up of Langford, Carrigan, White, Allen, Kevin Lycett (guitar) and Tom Greenhalgh (guitar) completed *The Quality Of Mercy Is Not Strnen*. This unusual title was drawn from the axiom that, if you gave a monkey a typewriter and an infinite amount of time, it would eventually produce the complete works of Shakespeare, a wry comment on the band's own musical ability.

The Mekons' enthusiasm, particularly in a live setting, is undoubtedly infectious and has contributed greatly to their long career (after a brief break-up in 1982). Despite numerous personnel changes (over 30 different members), they have retained a sense of naïve adventurism, embracing country, folk, world music and roots material in their customarily ebullient manner. By the 90s three of the core members of the band (Greenhalgh, Langford and Sarah Corina, Greenhalgh's violinist partner who joined in 1991) had relocated to Chicago, Illinois, USA, where the band enjoyed a loose recording contract with Quarterstick Records. This followed an unfortunate major label coalition with A&M Records. Other important contributors to the Mekons' legacy include Sally Timms, vocalist and full-time member since the late 80s, who has released several solo albums and is based in New York, accordion player Rico Bell, and drummer Steve Goulding (ex-Graham Parker And The Rumour), a part-time journalist who has worked with Pig Dog Pondering. Langford also worked with Goulding on his part-time country band, Jon Langford And The Pine Valley Cosmonauts, who issued an album in Germany in 1994, and released records with his own country rock side project, the Waco Brothers. He has also had numerous exhibitions of his paintings.

The Mekons' first release for over three years, 1996's *King Of The Pirates*, was a bizarre collaboration with American writer Kathy Acker. *Me* was another challenging, conceptual work that bemused and amused in equal measures, but the Mekons' devoted followers were rewarded by the follow-up *Journey To The End Of The Night*'s seamless fusion of the band's eclectic musical tastes.

● ALBUMS: *The Quality Of Mercy Is Not Strnen* (Virgin 1979) ★★★, *Mekons* aka *Devil Rats And Piggies A Special Message From Godzilla* (Red Rhino 1980) ★★★, *Fear And Whiskey* (Sin 1985) ★★★, *The Edge Of The World* (Sin 1986) ★★★, *The Mekons Honky Tonkin'* (Sin/Cooking Vinyl 1987) ★★★, *So Good It Hurts* (Sin/Cooking Vinyl 1988) ★★★, *Rock N' Roll* (Blast First/A&M 1989) ★★★, *The Curse Of The Mekons* (Blast First/Mute 1991) ★★★, *I Love Mekons* (Quarterstick/Touch And Go 1993) ★★★, *Retreat From Memphis* (Quarterstick 1994) ★★★, with Kathy Acker *Pussy, King Of The Pirates* (Scout 1996) ★★★, *Mekons United* CD/Novel (Quarterstick 1996) ★★, *Me* (Quarterstick 1998) ★★★, *Journey To The End Of The Night* (Quarterstick 2000) ★★★★, *Oooh!* (Quarterstick 2002) ★★★.

● COMPILATIONS: *It Falleth Like Gentle Rain From Heaven: The Mekons Story* (CNT Productions 1982) ★★★, *New York* cassette only (ROIR 1987) ★★★, *Original Sin* (Rough Trade/TwinTone 1989) ★★★, *I Have Been To Heaven And Back: Hen's Teeth And Other Lost Fragments Of Unpopular Culture Vol. 1* (Quarterback 1999) ★★★, *Where Were You?: Hen's Teeth And Other Lost Fragments Of Unpopular Culture Vol. 2* (Quarterback 1999) ★★★, *New York On The Road 86–87* (ROIR 2001) ★★★.
● FURTHER READING: *Mekons United*, no author listed.

## MEL AND KIM

One of Stock, Aitken and Waterman's acts, Mel (b. Melanie Susan Appleby, 11 July 1966, London, England, d. 19 January 1990) and sister Kim (b. Kim Appleby, 28 August 1961, London, England) were two East End, London girls with a neat line in pop dance routines. They both started their careers as models – a fact which would come back to haunt them when topless pictures of Mel turned up in *Playboy* and *Penthouse* magazines. Picked up by the Stock, Aitken and Waterman team, they saw 'Showing Out (Get Fresh At The Weekend)' reach number 3 in the UK during 1986, and the following year they gave their mentors their first chart-topper as producers with 'Respectable'. The girls even stayed on top of the charts when the charity single 'Let It Be', by Ferry Aid, to which they contributed, supplanted 'Respectable'. The group was now such hot property that their name was hijacked at Christmas 1987 by Mel Smith and Kim Wilde for their version of 'Rockin' Around The Christmas Tree'. The title track of their debut album (the initials *F.L.M.* stood for Fun, Love And Money) and 'That's The Way It Is' continued their string of UK Top 10 singles, but the hit records stopped when Mel was taken away from the 1988 Montreux Festival in a wheelchair. The official report was that she had a slipped disc, while press speculation intimated that it was something more serious. In late 1988, Kim smiled bravely in interviews and said that her sister was well on the way to recovery. However, the news soon broke that Mel was undergoing treatment for spinal cancer and she, too, showed her courage by allowing the press to publish pictures of her even though she was suffering the side effects of chemotherapy. Mel died in January 1990 from pneumonia. Kim carried on with the solo single, 'Don't Worry', and her self-titled debut album.
● ALBUMS: *F.L.M.* (Supreme 1987) ★★★.
● COMPILATIONS: *The Best Of Mel & Kim* (Disky 1998) ★★★.

## MELLE MEL AND THE FURIOUS 5

Melle Mel (b. Melvin Glover, New York City, New York, USA) was a typical black 'ghetto child' whose interest in music originally stemmed from the Beatles. He soon embraced the earliest sounds of hip-hop in the mid 70s, becoming a breakdancer with the D-Squad. As a DJ with his brother Kid Creole he was influenced by others in the profession like Klark Kent and Timmy Tim who used to talk rhymes while playing music. The pair started their own brand of rapping and around 1976 set up with another DJ, Grandmaster Flash – who gave Melle Mel his new name. Flash already had one MC – Cowboy – with him, and so the new team became Grandmaster Flash and the 3MCs. Over the next couple of years they were joined by Scorpio and then Rahiem. Spurred by the success Of 'Rapper's Delight' by the Sugarhill Gang, Flash's team recorded 'Super Rappin'' for Enjoy Records. Another flop single 'We Rap Mellow', under the name Younger Generation, was followed by a move to Sugarhill Records as Grandmaster Flash And The Furious Five. Together they recorded one of rap's greatest standards, 'The Message'. This 1982 UK Top 10 hit, with featured vocalist Melle Mel, was a hugely significant record which took hip-hop away from braggadocio into social commentary.

Subsequent releases over the next few years came out under a wide variety of names and the battle for best billing plus squabbles with management and record company eventually led to the group splitting in two in 1984. A deep rift between Flash and Mel came about because, according to the latter: 'We'd known that Sugarhill was crooks when we first signed with 'em, so the plan had always been to build it up to a certain point where . . . they couldn't keep on taking the money that they was taking! That's what I'd been banking on, but those that left didn't seem to see it the same way.' Mel retained Cowboy and Scorpio and recruited another of his brothers King Louie III plus Tommy Gunn, Kami Kaze, and Clayton Savage. Flash had inaugurated a $5 million court action against Sylvia Robinson's Sugarhill label to attain full rights to the Grandmaster Flash name, which he lost. The group's new operating title was thus Grandmaster Melle Mel And The Furious Five. The name was forced on the band by Sugarhill, though it infuriated Flash and Mel himself was unhappy with it. Singles like 1984's 'Beat Street Breakdown Part 1', and 'We Don't Work For Free' would fail to break the upper echelons of the charts, though Mel did appear on the intro to Chaka Khan's worldwide smash 'I Feel For You'. There was also a UK Top 10 hit in 1985 with 'Step Off', after which his popularity cooled.

By 1987 the mutual lack of success encouraged the separated parties to reunite as Grandmaster Flash, Melle Mel And The Furious Five for a Paul Simon hosted charity concert in New York. The intervening years between then and Mel's appearance on Quincy Jones' 'Back On The Block' were lost to drug addiction – painfully ironic, considering that Mel's best known record remains 'White Lines (Don't Do It)', an anti-drug blockbuster which was credited to Grandmaster Flash And Melle Mel. It first hit the charts in 1983 and re-entered on several occasions. Originally targeted specifically at cocaine, it was revamped in 1989 by Sylvia Johnson because of the crack boom. Its pro-abstinence stance was not physically shared by the protagonists. When Mel was in the studio in 1982, laying down the vocal track, he admits that the 'only thing I was thinking about in that studio was listening to the record, joking and getting high'. In 1994 news broke that Mel was back and fighting fit (taking the trouble to perform press-

ups for interviewers to prove the point), and working on a new album with former Ice-T collaborator Afrika Islam. He also linked with Flash for his 'Mic Checka' radio show, but the 1997 comeback album, *Right Now*, proved a disappointing collection.

● ALBUMS: *Work Party* (Sugarhill 1984) ★★★, as Grandmaster Mele-Mel And Scorpio *Right Now* (Straight Game 1997) ★★.

● COMPILATIONS: *Stepping Off* (Sugarhill 1985) ★★★.

## MELLENCAMP, JOHN

b. 7 October 1951, Seymour, Indiana, USA. Mellencamp survived an early phase as a glam-rocker to become one of America's most successful mainstream rock singers of the past two decades. He played in local band Trash with guitarist Larry Crane, who remained with Mellencamp throughout the 80s. In 1976, David Bowie's manager Tony de Fries signed him to a recording deal with MainMan. Mellencamp's name was changed to Johnny Cougar and he was given a James Dean-style image. The rush-released *Chestnut Street Incident*, comprised mainly of cover versions, did not chart. He left MainMan and moved back to Indiana, formed the Zone and recorded the self-penned *The Kid Inside*. Shortly afterwards he signed to Riva Records, owned by Rod Stewart's manager Billy Gaff who presented the singer as the next Bruce Springsteen. His first chart action came courtesy of *John Cougar*, which included the US Top 30 single 'I Need A Lover' in December 1979. Cougar and his band toured constantly, a strategy which paid off in 1982 when *American Fool* headed the US album chart (USA sales by 1996 were 5 million) while both 'Hurts So Good' and 'Jack And Diane' were million-sellers.

The following year the singer became John Cougar Mellencamp, eventually dropping the 'Cougar' part in 1989. Many of his songs were now dealing with social problems, and Mellencamp was one of the organisers of the Farm Aid series of benefit concerts. His straight-ahead rock numbers also brought a string of big hits in the second half of the 80s. Among the most notable were 'Small Town', 'R.O.C.K. In The USA', 'Paper In Fire' (1987) and 'Cherry Bomb' (1988). *Lonesome Jubilee* used fiddles and accordions to illustrate bleak portraits of America in recession, while 'Pop Singer' from *Big Daddy* expressed Mellencamp's disillusionment with the current state of the music business. He took time off to concentrate on painting but returned with *Whenever We Wanted*, which recaptured the muscular rock sound of his earlier albums.

In 1992, Mellencamp directed and starred in the movie *Falling From Grace*. He continued to hit the US charts with amazing rapidity and, up until early 1991, he had charted 21 singles in the US Hot 100 of which nine were Top 10, with one number 1, 'Jack And Diane' in 1982. Despite the relative failure of 1993's *Human Wheels*, Mellencamp made a strong comeback with *Dance Naked* and the attendant Top 10 cover version of Van Morrison's 'Wild Night'. Mellencamp suffered a major heart attack shortly after the release of *Dance Naked*, and following this scare was sidelined for over a year. He returned in

1996 with *Mr. Happy Go Lucky*, on which his sound was augmented by the work of noted dance music producer Junior Vasquez. A more traditional self-titled set, his first for new label Columbia Records, was released in 1998, earning Mellencamp his best reviews in years. In 2000, Mellencamp teamed up with novelist Stephen King to write a full-length ghost story stage musical.

● ALBUMS: *Chestnut Street Incident* (MainMan 1976) ★★, *The Kid Inside* (Castle 1977) ★★, *A Biography* (Riva 1978) ★★, *John Cougar* (Riva 1979) ★★★, *Nothing Matters And What If It Did* (Riva 1981) ★, *American Fool* (Riva 1982) ★★★, *Uh-Huh* (Riva 1983) ★★★, *Scarecrow* (Riva 1985) ★★★, *The Lonesome Jubilee* (Mercury 1987) ★★★, *Big Daddy* (Mercury 1989) ★★★, *Whenever We Wanted* (Mercury 1991) ★★★, *Human Wheels* (Mercury 1993) ★★★, *Dance Naked* (Mercury 1994) ★★★, *Mr. Happy Go Lucky* (Mercury 1996) ★★★, *John Mellencamp* (Columbia 1998) ★★★★, *Cuttin' Heads* (Columbia 2001) ★★★.

● COMPILATIONS: *Early Years* (Rhino 1986) ★★, *The John Cougar Collection* (Castle 1986) ★★★, *The Best That I Could Do 1978–1988* (Mercury 1997) ★★★, *Rough Harvest* (Mercury 1999) ★★★.

● VIDEOS: *John Cougar Mellencamp: Ain't That America* (Embassy 1984).

● FURTHER READING: *American Fool: The Roots And Improbable Rise Of John Cougar Mellencamp*, Torgoff. *Mellencamp: Paintings And Reflections*, John Mellencamp.

● FILMS: *Falling From Grace* (1992).

## MEN AT WORK

Formed in Melbourne, Australia, in 1979, by singer Colin James Hay (b. 29 June 1953, Scotland – emigrated to Australia aged 14) and guitarist Ron Strykert (b. 18 August 1957, Australia), initially as an acoustic duo. With the later addition of Greg Ham (b. 27 September 1953, Australia), John Rees (bass) and Jerry Speiser (drums), Men At Work performed for two years in small, inner-suburban pubs before being discovered and signed by CBS Records executive Peter Karpin. In 1981, the first single, 'Who Can It Be Now?', was an enormous Australian hit, soon followed by 'Down Under' and *Business As Usual*. The band's success surprised and infuriated home critics, who had written them off as derivative and insipid. Blessed with three songwriters and supported by videos which showcased the band's sense of humour, and with added exposure as a support act to Fleetwood Mac, Men At Work were able to achieve two US number 1 hits in 1982 with 'Who Can It Be Now?' and 'Down Under'. *Business As Usual* also climbed to the top of the US album charts the same year, spending a remarkable 15 weeks in the peak position. The band also won the 1982 Best New Artist Grammy. Success followed in the UK where 'Down Under' reached number 1 in early 1983, accompanied by *Business As Usual* topping the charts. By now, Men At Work could comfortably claim to be the world's most successful Australian pop band. The follow-up *Cargo*, sold well in the US, reaching number 3, and provided two Top 10 singles in 'Overkill' and 'It's A Mistake'. Despite the album reaching the Top 10 in the UK, single success there

was harder to sustain, with three singles reaching Top 40 status only. The band's third album, *Two Hearts*, sold less well although it did achieve gold status in the USA, peaking at number 50.

The original personnel had by now disintegrated, leaving Hay as the sole surviving member. The break-up in 1985 followed arguments over management and writing, and each member followed his own path. Hay recorded a solo album in 1987, *Looking For Jack*, which reached the lower end of the US album chart. *Wayfaring Sons*, released on MCA in 1990 and credited to the Colin Hay Band, used Celtic music as its base. Hay continued to release albums in the 90s, but in 1996 reunited with Ham under the Men At Work banner. The new line-up released a live album recorded during a sold-out Brazilian tour.

● ALBUMS: *Business As Usual* (Epic 1981) ★★★, *Cargo* (Epic 1983) ★★★, *Two Hearts* (Epic 1985) ★★, *Brazil 96* (Sony 1996) ★★★.

● COMPILATIONS: *Puttin' In Overtime* (Sony 1995) ★★★, *Contraband: The Best Of Men At Work* (Columbia 1996) ★★★★, *Super Hits* (Sony 2000) ★★★.

● VIDEOS: *Live In San Francisco Or Was It Berkeley?* (CBS-Fox 1984).

## MEN WITHOUT HATS

Formed in Montreal, Canada, in 1980, this act was the brainchild of Ivan Doroschuk (vocals). An independent EP, *Folk Of The 80s*, created overseas cult interest to the extent that it was reissued on Britain's Stiff Records, along with an edit of its 'Antarctica' track as a single. Composer Doroschuk fronted the most permanent line-up of the band with his brothers Stefan (guitar, violin) and Colin Doroschuk (keyboards), plus Allan McCarthy (d. 1995; drum programming). Produced by manager Marc Durand, *Rhythm Of Youth* reached number 13 in the US in the wake of 'Safety Dance', 1983's global hit single (US number 3, UK number 6) born of a truce between electro-pop and medieval jollity that carried an anti-nuclear message over into an arresting video. A sure sign of its impact was a parody by 'Weird Al' Yankovic. No more hits came the band's way, but their recordings still received a fair critical consideration. Ivan and Colin Doroschuk later set up their own Uforia label.

● ALBUMS: *The Safety Dance* (Statik 1982) re-released as *Rhythm Of Youth* (Backstreet/MCA 1983) ★★★, *Folk Of the 80s (Part III)* (MCA 1984) ★★★, *Pop Goes The World* (Mercury 1987) ★★, *The Adventures Of Women & Men Without Hate In The 21st Century* (Mercury 1989) ★★, *Sideways* (Mercury 1991) ★★★.

● COMPILATIONS: *Collection* (Oglio 1996) ★★★, *Greatest Hits* (Aquarius 1997) ★★★★.

## MERCURY, FREDDIE

b. Frederick Bulsara, 5 September 1946, Zanzibar, d. 24 November 1991, London, England. Best known as the flamboyant lead singer of the multi-million-selling UK group Queen, Mercury also branched out into extra-curricular musical activities. In 1973, while Queen were about to release their debut album, Mercury recorded a revival of the Beach

Boys' 'I Can Hear Music' under the glam rock name Larry Lurex. It was not until late 1984 that he again attempted a solo work, this time with the UK Top 20 hit 'Love Kills', from the Giorgio Moroder soundtrack to the film *Metropolis*. A second solo single, 'I Was Born To Love You', reached the UK Top 20 early the next year. A solo album and some lowly placed solo singles followed. In 1986, Mercury contributed some tracks to the cast recording of Dave Clark's musical *Time*. His greatest solo success, however, came in 1987, with a kitsch revival of the Platters' 'The Great Pretender', which reached the UK Top 5. Later that year, Mercury emphasized his love of opera by teaming up with Monserrat Caballe for the grandiloquent 'Barcelona', another Top 10 success. An album of the same title was also successful and, in late 1988, the operatic duo played a major show at the Avinguda De Maria Cristina Stadium in Barcelona. Mercury retained a low profile thereafter, and, following much speculation over his health, in November 1991 he finally admitted that he was suffering from AIDS. Within 48 hours, on 24 November, he died from bronchial pneumonia at his Knightsbridge home. A major concert was arranged in April 1992 at London's Wembley stadium. Known as the Freddy Mercury Aids Benefit, it attracted the largest ever worldwide viewing audience when televised live.

● ALBUMS: *Mr Bad Guy* (Columbia 1985) ★★, with Monserrat Caballe *Barcelona* (Polydor 1988) ★★.

● COMPILATIONS: *Solo* 10-CD/2-DVD box set (Parlophone 2000) ★.

● FURTHER READING: *Freddie Mercury: This Is The Real Life*, David Evans & David Minns. *The Show Must Go On: The Life Of Freddie Mercury*, Rick Sky. *A Kind Of Magic: A Tribute To Freddie Mercury*, Ross Clarke. *Mercury And Me*, Jim Hutton with Tim Wapshott. *Freddie Mercury: More Of The Real Life*, David Evans and David Minns. *Mercury: The King Of Queen*, Laura Jackson. *Freddie Mercury: The Definitive Biography*, Lesley Ann Jones. *Living On The Edge: The Freddie Mercury Story*, David Bret. *Freddie Mercury*, Peter Freestone with David Evans.

## METALLICA

The most consistently innovative metal band of the late 80s and 90s was formed in 1981 in California, USA, by Lars Ulrich (b. 26 December 1963, Copenhagen, Denmark; drums) and James Alan Hetfield (b. 3 August 1963, USA; guitar/vocals) after each separately advertised for fellow musicians in the classified section of American publication *The Recycler*. They recorded their first demo, *No Life Til' Leather*, with Lloyd Grand (guitar), who was replaced in January 1982 by David Mustaine (b. 13 September 1961, La Mesa, California, USA), whose relationship with Ulrich and Hetfield proved unsatisfactory. Jef Warner (guitar) and Ron McGovney (bass) each had a brief tenure with the band. At the end of 1982 Clifford Lee Burton (b. 10 February 1962, USA, d. 27 September 1986; bass, ex-Trauma) joined the band, playing his first live performance on 5 March 1983. Mustaine departed to form Megadeth and was replaced by Kirk Hammett (b. 18 November 1962, San Francisco, California, USA; guitar). Hammett,

who came to the attention of Ulrich and Hetfield while playing with rock band Exodus, played his first concert with Metallica on 16 April 1983.

The Ulrich, Hetfield, Burton and Hammett combination endured until disaster struck the band in the small hours of 27 September 1986, when Metallica's tour bus overturned in Sweden, killing Cliff Burton. During those four years, the band put thrash metal on the map with the aggression and exuberance of their debut, *Kill 'Em All*, the album sleeve of which bore the legend 'Bang that head that doesn't bang'. This served as a template for a whole new breed of metal, though the originators themselves were quick to dispense with their own rule book. Touring with New Wave Of British Heavy Metal bands Raven and Venom followed, while Music For Nations signed them for European distribution. Although *Ride The Lightning* was not without distinction, notably on 'For Whom The Bell Tolls', it was 1986's *Master Of Puppets* that offered further evidence of Metallica's appetite for the epic. Their first album for Elektra Records in the USA (who had also re-released its predecessor), this was a taut, multi-faceted collection that both raged and lamented with equal conviction.

After the death of Burton, the band elected to continue, the remaining three members recruiting Jason Newsted (b. 4 March 1963; bass) of Flotsam And Jetsam. Newsted played his first concert with the band on 8 November 1986. The original partnership of Ulrich and Hetfield, however, remained responsible for Metallica's lyrics and musical direction. The new line-up's first recording together was *The $5.98 EP – Garage Days Re-Revisited* – a collection of cover versions including material from Budgie, Diamond Head, Killing Joke and the Misfits, which also served as a neat summation of the band's influences to date. Sessions for *And Justice For All* initially began with Guns N'Roses producer Mike Clink at the helm. A long and densely constructed effort, this 1988 opus included an appropriately singular spectacular moment in 'One' (a US Top 40/UK Top 20 single), while elsewhere the barrage of riffs somewhat obscured the usual Metallica artistry. The songs on 1991's US/UK chart-topper *Metallica* continued to deal with large themes – justice and retribution, insanity, war, religion and relationships. Compared to *Kill 'Em All* nearly a decade previously, however, the band had grown from iconoclastic chaos to thoughtful harmony, hallmarked by sudden and unexpected changes of mood and tempo. The MTV-friendly 'Enter Sandman' broke the band on a stadium level and entered the US Top 20. The single also reached the UK Top 10, as did another album track, 'Nothing Else Matters'.

Constant touring in the wake of the album ensued, along with a regular itinerary of awards ceremonies. There could surely be no more deserving recipients, Metallica having dragged mainstream metal, not so much kicking and screaming as whining and complaining, into a bright new dawn when artistic redundancy seemed inevitable (the album was certified as having sold thirteen million copies in the USA alone by June 2001).

The follow-up *Load* entered the US charts at number 1. The album marked a change in image for the band, who began to court the alternative rock audience. The following year's *Reload* collected together more tracks recorded at the *Load* sessions, and featured 60s icon Marianne Faithfull on the first single to be released from the album, 'The Memory Remains'. *Garage Inc.* collected assorted cover versions, and broke the band's run of US number 1 albums when it debuted at number 2 in December 1998. The following year's *S&M*, recorded live with the San Francisco Symphony Orchestra, evoked the worst excesses of heavy rock icons Deep Purple. In January 2001, Newsted announced he was leaving after almost 15 years service with the band.

● ALBUMS: *Kill 'Em All* (Megaforce 1983) ★★★, *Ride The Lightning* (Megaforce 1984) ★★★, *Master Of Puppets* (Elektra 1986) ★★★★, *And Justice For All* (Elektra 1988) ★★★, *Metallica* (Elektra 1991) ★★★★, *Live Shit: Binge & Purge* 3-CD/video set (Elektra 1993) ★★★★, *Load* (Mercury 1996) ★★★★, *Reload* (Vertigo 1997) ★★★, *Garage Inc.* (Vertigo 1998) ★★★, *S&M* (Vertigo 1999) ★★.

● VIDEOS: *Cliff 'Em All* (Channel 5 1988), *2 Of One* (Channel 5 1989), *A Year And A Half In The Life Of Metallica* (PolyGram Music Video 1992), *Metal Up Your Ass: The Interview Sessions* (Startalk 1996), *Cunning Stunts* (PolyGram Music Video 1998), *S&M* (Elektra Entertainment 1999), *Classic Albums: Metallica* (Eagle Vision 2001).

● FURTHER READING: *A Visual Documentary*, Mark Putterford. *In Their Own Words*, Mark Putterford. *Metallica Unbound*, K.J. Doughton. *Metallica's Lars Ulrich: An Up-Close Look At The Playing Style Of ...*, Dino Fauci. *Metallica Unbound*, K.J. Doughton. *Metallica Live!*, Mark Putterford. *Metallica: The Frayed Ends Of Metal*, Chris Crocker. *The Making Of: Metallica's Metallica*, Mick Wall and Malcolm Dome. *From Silver To Black*, Ross Halfin.

## METEORS

The Meteors were the first UK band to combine punk's energy with raw 50s rockabilly and invent a new musical form – psychobilly. In the USA, the Cramps had discovered a similar formula, but theirs was less violent and more dramatic. Together, they influenced a whole movement and an accompanying youth culture during the 80s, and have endured into the new millennium.

In the late 70s, P. Paul Fenech (vocals, guitar) and Nigel Lewis (double bass, vocals) were churning out rockabilly and rock 'n' roll standards in acts such as the Southern Boys and, as a duo, Rock Therapy. Around 1980, drummer Mark Robertson was recruited, coinciding with a name change to Raw Deal, and they appeared on Alligator Records' *Home Grown Rockabilly* compilation. After a name change to the Meteors, the band issued a debut EP, *Meteor Madness*, jammed with compulsive, raw rockabilly, with lyrics drawing inspiration from graveyards and vampiric legend, all performed in a crazed, headlong amphetamine rush to the end of the song. 'Radioactive Kid' followed suit, and *In Heaven* was issued on their Lost Souls label. Around the same time, the Meteors recorded an EP featuring a cover version of the Electric Prunes' 'Get Me To The World On Time' under the guise of the Clapham South Escalators. Robertson left soon afterwards and was replaced by Woody, but after releasing demos, Lewis also departed to form the Tall Boys. Fenech was left to soldier on, bringing in electric bass player Mick White and Russell Jones for August 1982's 'Mutant Rock'. Another personnel change (Steve 'Ginger' Meadham joining on drums) preceded the Meteors' second album, *Wreckin' Crew*, early in 1983, featuring the previous single, a wild cover version of John Leyton's 'Johnny Remember Me'. That same year saw another departure, with White forming his own psychobilly act, the Guana Batz. His position was filled by Rick Ross for a national tour, captured on *Live*. Unfortunately, Ross left for the USA and in his place came Ian 'Spider' Cubitt, to record *Stampede*, 'I'm Just A Dog' and 'Fire, Fire'. *Monkey's Breath*, featuring new bass player Neville Hunt, surfaced in September 1985, alongside a cover version of Creedence Clearwater Revival's 'Bad Moon Rising'.

After two more unofficial offerings (*Live II* and *Live And Loud*), the Meteors covered Jan And Dean's 'Surf City' and completed *Sewertime Blues*. *Don't Touch The Bang Bang Fruit* featured a cover version of the Stranglers' 'Go Buddy Go'. By this time, Spider's place had been filled by Toby 'Jug' Griffin and Austin H. Stones briefly deputized on bass. Lee Brown (ex-Pharaohs) took on a more permanent role on bass, in time for another punk cover version in the Ramones' 'Somebody Put Something In My Drink'. Hot on its heels came *Only The Meteors Are Pure Psychobilly*, featuring new recordings of old 'classics'. Newer material was included on *Mutant Monkey And The Surfers From Zorch* later that year, although 'Rawhide' proved to be another popular cover. Even more powerful was *Undead, Unfriendly And Unstoppable*, which benefited from new drummer Mark Howe. The release of 'Please Don't Touch' proved that, despite waves of imitators, the Meteors were still the most vibrant psychobilly band around.

Despite further personnel changes, Fenech continued to lead the Meteors into the following decade. Several studio albums complemented the band's enduring live reputation, so it was something of a surprise when, in the new millennium, Fenech announced they would be ceasing live performances. The final line-up of the Meteors, with Fenech joined by Wolfgang Hordemann and Shaun Berry, played their farewell concert on 18 November 2000 in Germany.

● ALBUMS: *In Heaven* (Lost Soul 1981) ★★★, *Wreckin' Crew* (ID 1983) ★★★, *Live* (Wreckin' 1983) ★★★, *Stampede* (Mad Pig 1984) ★★★, *The Curse Of The Mutants* (Dojo 1984) ★★★, *Monkey's Breath* (Mad Pig 1985) ★★★, *Live II* (Dojo 1986) ★★, *Live And Loud* (Link 1986) ★★, *Sewertime Blues* (Anagram 1987) ★★★, *Night Of The Werewolf* (Dojo 1987) ★★★, *Don't Touch The Bang Bang Fruit* (Anagram 1987) ★★★, *Only The Meteors Are Pure Psychobilly* (Anagram 1988) ★★★, *The Mutant Monkey And The Surfers From Zorch* (Anagram 1988) ★★★, *Undead, Unfriendly And Unstoppable* (Anagram 1989) ★★★,

*Psycho Down* (Cleopatra 2001) ★★, *Live Styles Of The Sick And Shameless* (Anagram 2002) ★★.
● COMPILATIONS: *Teenagers From Outer Space* (Big Beat 1986) ★★★, *The Best Of ...* (Anagram 1993) ★★★, *Graveyard Stomp* (Reactive 1998) ★★★, *Peel Sessions (1983–1985)* (Raucous 1999) ★★★.

## METHENY, PAT

b. 12 August 1954, Kansas City, Missouri, USA. Although classed as a jazz guitarist, Metheny has bridged the gap between jazz and rock music in the same way that Miles Davis did in the late 60s and early 70s. Additionally, he played a major part in the growth of jazz's popularity among the younger generation of the 80s. Throughout his career, his extraordinary sense of melody has prevented his work from becoming rambling or self-indulgent.

His first musical instrument was a French horn, and surprisingly he did not begin with the guitar until he was a teenager. His outstanding virtuosity soon had him teaching the instrument at the University Of Miami and the Berklee College Of Music in Boston. He joined Gary Burton in 1974, and throughout his three-album stay, he contributed some fluid Wes Montgomery-influenced guitar patterns. Manfred Eicher of ECM Records saw the potential and initiated a partnership that lasted for 10 superlative albums. He became, along with Keith Jarrett, ECM's biggest-selling artist, and his albums regularly topped the jazz record charts. Metheny has also been one of the few jazz artists to make regular appearances in the pop album charts, such is the accessibility of his music.

His early albums, *Bright Size Life* (featuring the late Jaco Pastorius), and *Watercolors* showed a man who was still feeling his way. His own individual style matured with *Pat Metheny Group* in 1978. Together with his musical partner (and arguably, his right arm), the brilliant keyboard player Lyle Mays, whose quiet presence at the side of the stage provided the backbone for much of Metheny's work, he initiated a rock band format that produced album after album of melodious jazz/rock. Following a major tour with Joni Mitchell and Pastorius (*Shadows And Light*), Metheny released *New Chautauqua*, on which he demonstrated an amazing dexterity on the 12-string guitar. The album made the US Top 50. He returned to the electric band format for *American Garage*, which contained the country-influenced '(Cross The) Heartland'. The double set *80/81* featured Michael Brecker, Jack DeJohnette, Charlie Haden and Dewey Redman, and was more of a typical jazz album, featuring in particular the moderately *avant garde* 'Two Folk Songs'. Nevertheless, the record still climbed the popular charts. During this time, Metheny constantly won jazz and guitarist polls. Mays' keyboards featured prominently in the band structure, and he received co-authorship credit for the suite *As Falls Wichita, So Falls Wichita Falls*.

Metheny had by now become fascinated by the musical possibilities of the guitar synthesizer or synclavier. He used this to startling effect on *Offramp*, notably on the wonderfully contagious and sexual 'Are You Going With Me?'. The double set *Travels* showed a band at the peak of its powers,

playing some familiar titles with a new freshness. The short piece 'Travels' stands as one of his finest compositions; the low-level recording offers such subtle emotion that it becomes joyously funereal. *Rejoicing* was a modern jazz album demonstrating his sensitive interpretations of music by Horace Silver and Ornette Coleman. *First Circle* maintained the standard and showed a greater leaning towards Latin-based music, though still retaining Metheny's brilliant ear for melody. In 1985, he composed the score for the movie *The Falcon And The Snowman*, which led to him recording 'This Is Not America' with David Bowie. The resulting UK Top 20/US Top 40 hit brought Metheny many new young admirers. The concert halls found audiences bedecked in striped rugby shirts, in the style of their new hero. Ironically, at the same time, following a break with ECM, Metheny turned his back on possible rock stardom and produced his most perplexing work, *Song X*, with free-jazz exponent Ornette Coleman. Reactions were mixed in reviews of this difficult album – ultimately the general consensus was that it was brilliantly unlistenable. He returned to more familiar ground with *Still Life (Talking)* and *Letter From Home*, although both experimented further with Latin melody and rhythm. Metheny enjoyed a particularly creative and productive time from 1989–90. *Reunion* was a superb meeting with his former boss Gary Burton. A few months later he recorded *Question And Answer* with Dave Holland and Roy Haynes. Additionally he was heavily featured, along with Herbie Hancock, on the excellent DeJohnette album, *Parallel Realities*.

Metheny continued into the 90s with *Secret Story*, an album of breathtaking beauty featuring gems such as 'Above The Treetops' and the poignant 'The Truth Will Always Be'. Although the album may have made jazz purists cringe, it was a realization of all Metheny's musical influences. His second live album, *The Road To You*, did not have the emotion of *Travels*. It was something to keep the fans quiet before he unleashed an exciting recording with John Scofield, the guitarist who most regularly shared the honours with Metheny at the top of the jazz polls. The follow-up, *Zero Tolerance For Silence*, could only be described as astonishing. For many the wall-of-sound guitar was a self-indulgent mess, and after repeated plays the music did not get any easier, but it needed to be appreciated what a bold move this thrash metal outing was. Metheny also found himself reviewed in the Heavy Metal press for the first (and last) time. *We Live Here* was a return to more traditional ground, and restored Metheny to his familiar position at the top of the jazz charts. It won a Grammy in 1996 for the best contemporary jazz album.

In the late 90s, Metheny recorded acclaimed duet albums with Haden and Jim Hall. His 1999 offering *A Map Of The World* was a set piece of evocative beauty. The album, a series of 28 pieces inspired by the motion picture *A Map Of The World*, was misunderstood as being merely a movie soundtrack. It ranks as one of his finest works; delicate in parts, emotional in places, especially where the music is enriched by a full orchestra. On this album

Metheny's dexterity as a guitarist takes second place to his brilliance as a composer. The subsequent trio album with Larry Grenadier (bass) and Bill Stewart (drums) was of an equally high standard. The attendant *Trio – Live* compiled the results of Metheny's first live trio work since the early 90s. Metheny is able to comfortably move between the pop jazz that made his name and pure jazz. He is one of the very few artists who can do it with such success and modesty.

● ALBUMS: *Bright Size Life* (ECM 1976) ★★★★, *Watercolors* (ECM 1977) ★★★, *Pat Metheny Group* (ECM 1978) ★★★★, *New Chautauqua* (ECM 1979) ★★★★, *American Garage* (ECM 1979) ★★★★, *80/81* (ECM 1980) ★★★, with Lyle Mays *As Falls Wichita, So Falls Wichita Falls* (ECM 1981) ★★★★, *Offramp* (ECM 1982) ★★★★, *Travels* (ECM 1983) ★★★★, with Charlie Haden, Billy Higgins *Rejoicing* (ECM 1983) ★★★, *First Circle* (ECM 1984) ★★★, *The Falcon And The Snowman* film soundtrack (EMI America 1985) ★★, with Ornette Coleman *Song X* (Geffen 1986) ★★★, *Still Life (Talking)* (Geffen 1987) ★★★★, *Letter From Home* (Geffen 1989) ★★★, with Gary Burton *Reunion* (Geffen 1989) ★★★★, *Question And Answer* (Geffen 1990) ★★★★, *Secret Story* (Geffen 1992) ★★★★, *The Road To You: Recorded Live In Europe* (Geffen 1993) ★★★, with John Scofield *I Can See Your House From Here* (Blue Note 1994) ★★★, *Zero Tolerance For Silence* (Geffen 1994) ★, *We Live Here* (Geffen 1995) ★★★★, *Quartet* (Geffen 1997) ★★★, *Beyond The Missouri Sky (Short Stories By Charlie Haden & Pat Metheny)* (Verve 1997) ★★★★, *Imaginary Day* (Warners 1997) ★★★★, with Derek Bailey, Gregg Bendian, Paul Wertico *The Sign Of 4* 3-CD set (Knitting Factory Works 1997) ★★★★, with Burton, Chick Corea, Roy Haynes, Dave Holland *Like Minds* (Concord Jazz 1998) ★★★★, *Jim Hall & Pat Metheny* (Telarc 1999) ★★★, *A Map Of The World* (Warners 1999) ★★★★, *Trio 99–00* (Warners 2000) ★★★★, *Trio – Live* (Warners 2000) ★★★★, *Speaking Of Now* (Warners 2002) ★★★.

● COMPILATIONS: *Works* (ECM 1983) ★★★★, *Works II* (ECM 1988) ★★★★.

● VIDEOS: *More Travels* (Geffen 1993).

## MEZZOFORTE

Until the arrival of the Sugarcubes, jazz-fusion band Mezzoforte was Iceland's best-known musical export. The group was formed in 1977 at a Reykjavik high school by Fridrik Karlsson (b. 24 April 1960; guitar), Eythór Gunnarsson (b. 9 September 1961; keyboards), Jóhann Ásmundsson (b. 30 March 1961; bass), and Gunnlaugur Briem (b. 8 September 1962; drums). They signed a recording contract with local label Steinar, and with the assistance of Stefán S. Stefánsson (saxophone) recorded their debut album. Bjorn Thorarensen (keyboards) joined in time for the recording of the band's second long-player. Kristinn Svavarsson (saxophone) was featured on the exuberant 'Garden Party', which was a Top 20 hit in the UK in 1983. The tune was covered in the USA by Herb Alpert who performed it at half-speed, reportedly because he had learned the piece from a 45 rpm single accidentally played at 33. The follow-up, 'Rockall', was only a minor hit but it was adopted

as a signature tune by radio chart shows in the Netherlands and UK. For a brief period, the group was based in London and in the mid-80s Mezzoforte played the European jazz festival circuit with vocalists Chris Cameron and Noel McCalla, formerly with Moon and Mike Rutherford's group. In 1990, Karlsson released a solo album featuring singer Ellen Kristjansdóttir and members of Mezzoforte. Further Mezzoforte releases took a back seat to the members' outside projects, although the band was officially still in existence at the turn of the new millennium.

● ALBUMS: *Mezzoforte* (Steinar 1979) ★★★, *Í Hakanum* (Steinar 1980) ★★★, *Surprise Surprise* (Steinar 1983) ★★, *Live At The Dominion* (Steinar 1984) ★★★, *Observations* (Steinar 1984) ★★★, *Rising* (Steinar 1985) ★★, *No Limits* (Steinar 1986) ★★★, *Playing For Time* (Steinar 1989) ★★★, *Daybreak* (Steinar 1993) ★★★, *Monkey-Fields* (Steinar 1995) ★★★.

● COMPILATIONS: *Catching Up With Mezzoforte* (Steinar 1983) ★★★, *The Saga So Far* (Steinar 1985) ★★★, *Fortissimos* (Steinar 1991) ★★★★.

## MICHAEL, GEORGE

b. Georgios (Yorgos) Kyriacos Panayiotou, 25 June 1963, Finchley, London, England. Michael first served his pop apprenticeship in the million-selling duo Wham!, the most commercially successful, teen-orientated band of the 80s. His solo career was foreshadowed in 1984's UK chart-topper 'Careless Whisper', a song about a promiscuous two-timer with the oddly attractive line: 'Guilty feet have got no rhythm'. By the time Wham! split in 1986, Michael was left with the unenviable task of reinventing himself as a solo artist. The balladeering 'Careless Whisper' had indicated a possible direction, but the initial problem was one of image. As a pin-up pop idol, Michael had allowed himself to become a paste-board figure, best remembered for glorifying a hedonistic lifestyle and shoving shuttlecocks down his shorts in concert. The rapid transition from dole queue reject to Club Tropicana playboy had left a nasty taste in the mouths of many music critics. Breaking the Wham! icon was the great challenge of Michael's solo career, and his finest and most decisive move was to take a sabbatical before recording an album, to allow time to put his old image to rest. In the meantime, he cut 1986's UK chart-topper 'A Different Corner', a song stylistically similar to 'Careless Whisper' and clearly designed to show off his talent as a serious singer-songwriter. Enlivening his alternate image as a blue-eyed soul singer, he teamed up with Aretha Franklin the same year for the uplifting 'I Knew You Were Waiting (For Me)', a transatlantic chart-topper. Michael's re-emergence came in 1988, resplendent in leather and shades and his customary designer stubble. A pilot single, 'I Want Your Sex' was banned by daytime radio stations and broke his string of number 1s in the UK. The transatlantic chart-topper *Faith* followed, and was not only well-received but sold in excess of 10 million copies. The album spawned four US number 1 singles, with the title track, 'Father Figure', 'One More Try' and 'Monkey' all reaching the top. Equally adept at soul workouts and ballads, and regarded by some as one of the best new pop songwriters of his era, Michael seemed set for a long career. In 1990, he released his second album, *Listen Without Prejudice, Vol. 1*, a varied work which predictably sold millions and topped the UK album chart. The first single from the album, 'Praying For Time', reached number 1 in the USA. In the UK, however, the comeback single was surprisingly only a Top 10 hit. Still dissatisfied with his media image, Michael announced that he would cease conducting interviews in future and concentrate on pursuing his career as a serious songwriter and musician.

A duet with Elton John on 'Don't Let The Sun Go Down On Me' revived his UK chart fortunes, reaching number 1 in December 1991, and also topping the US charts. In 1992, the *Sunday Times* announced his arrival as one of the richest men in the UK. Although Michael, with some help from Queen and Lisa Stansfield, topped the UK charts with the *Five Live* EP in summer 1993, a court clash with his record label Sony dominated his activities in the following two years. The case, which was eventually estimated to have cost him $7 million, saw Michael arguing that his contract rendered him a 'pop slave' and demanding to be released from it. Mr Justice Jonathan Parker ruled in Sony's favour and Michael stated he would appeal, and also insisted that he would never again record for the label. In July 1995, it looked likely that Michael had managed to free himself from Sony – but only at the cost of $40 million. The buy-out was financed by David Geffen's new media empire, DreamWorks, and Virgin Records, who were also reputed to have paid him an advance of £30 million for two albums. The first was *Older*, one of the decade's slickest productions. Although it became a huge success there was no great depth to the songs underneath the immaculate production. The album yielded two UK chart-toppers, 'Jesus To A Child' and 'Fastlove'.

Michael announced the formation of his own record label Aegean Records, in February 1997. On April 7 1998, he was arrested for 'lewd behaviour' in a toilet cubicle at the Will Rogers Memorial Park in Beverly Hills, California. Michael later confirmed his long-rumoured homosexuality and was sentenced to perform community service. He bounced back with an excellent single, 'Outside', which entered the UK charts at number 2 in October 1998. The *Ladies & Gentlemen* compilation was a bestseller, topping the UK chart for 8 weeks. His duet with Mary J. Blige on a cover version of Stevie Wonder's 'As' broke into the UK Top 5 in March 1999. At the end of the year, Michael released *Songs From The Last Century*, a motley selection of cover versions that drew a bemused response from most critics.

The singer returned to the charts in March 2002 with the one-off single 'Freeek!', which was accompanied by a risqué £1 million video. He courted controversy again a few months later, baiting US President George W. Bush and UK Prime Minister Tony Blair with 'Shoot The Dog'. The single's poor chart showing (only reaching number 12) indicated Michael's commercial star was very much on the wane.

● ALBUMS: *Faith* (Epic 1987) ★★★★, *Listen Without Prejudice, Vol. 1* (Epic 1990) ★★★, *Older* (Virgin 1996) ★★★, *Songs From The Last Century* (Aegean/Virgin 1999) ★★.
● COMPILATIONS: *Ladies & Gentlemen: The Best Of George Michael* (Epic 1998) ★★★★.
● CD-ROM: *Older/Upper* (Aegean/Virgin 1998) ★★★.
● VIDEOS: *Faith* (CMV Enterprises 1988), *George Michael* (CMV Enterprises 1990), *The Video Selection* (SMV 1998).
● FURTHER READING: *Wham! (Confidential) The Death Of A Supergroup*, Johnny Rogan. *George Michael: The Making Of A Super Star*, Bruce Dessau. *Bare*, George Michael with Tony Parsons. *In His Own Words*, Nigel Goodall. *Older: The Unauthorised Biography Of George Michael*, Nicholas and Tim Wapshott.

## MICHIGAN AND SMILEY

Papa Michigan (b. Anthony Fairclough) and General Smiley (b. Erroll Bennett) began their career in the early 80s at Studio One under the direction of Coxsone Dodd. The duo recorded their number 1 hit 'Rub A Dub Style' over the original master tape for Alton Ellis' 'I'm Just A Guy', followed by the equally popular 'Nice Up The Dance'. Although Dodd released hits in the dancehall style, the sessions proved to be his swan-song before relocating to New York. The duo were able to overcome this setback by recording at Tuff Gong Studio the classic 'One Love Jamdown', produced by Jahmet Enwright, which was released as a double a-side with Freddie McGregor's 'Jogging'. Michigan And Smiley gave a dynamic performance at the annual Reggae Sunsplash Festival in 1981, which led to a debut appearance in the UK where they topped the bill at the *Black Echoes* Reggae Awards Show. In 1982, Henry 'Junjo' Lawes productions dominated the dancehall, introducing current DJs to a wider audience without attenuating the sound. Michigan And Smiley recorded a grim warning to prospective philanderers, 'Diseases', and the song inspired Yellowman to record an identical version alongside his sparring partner, Fathead. Throughout the 80s Michigan And Smiley sustained attention in the album charts with the releases *Step By Step*, *Sugar Daddy*, *Back In The Biz* and *Reality Must Rule Again*. The duo enjoyed a revival in the 90s when some of their earlier hits resurfaced through VP in the USA.
● ALBUMS: *Rub A Dub Style* (Studio One 1980) ★★★★, *Downpression* (Greensleeves 1982) ★★★, with Eek A Mouse *Live At Reggae Sunsplash* (Sunsplash 1982) ★, *Up Town/Downtown* (VP 1995) ★★.

## MICRODISNEY

This incendiary pop/folk band was formed in Cork, Eire, in 1980. There was little cohesion in their early formations: 'We used to be much more frenzied in those days, a Fall-type mess, and our line-up was always changing. Originally Sean [O'Hagan] was going to play guitar and I [Cathal Coughlan] was going to recite poetry, then one week it was guitar, bass, drums, then guitar keyboard and violin, then we had a drum machine . . .' After settling on the more traditional formation of drums, guitars, bass and keyboards, the band began releasing singles which were eventually collected together on 1984's *We Hate You White South African Bastards*. The title was typically inflammatory, and in direct opposition to that of the same year's long-playing debut, *Everybody Is Fantastic*. An early clue to their subversive nature, on the surface Microdisney were purveyors of accessible and restrained pop music. This attracted Virgin Records, but the band had a dark edge in Coughlan's bitter lyricism. Their Virgin debut, 'Town To Town', dented the lower regions of the UK charts and was quickly followed by *Crooked Mile*. However, Microdisney elected to bite the hand that fed them with the near-hit 'Singer's Hampstead Home', which thinly masked an attack on Virgin's fallen idol, Boy George. They bowed out with *39 Minutes*, by which time the vitriol was really flowing, counterbalanced as ever by O'Hagan's delicate country guitar. Despite critical acclaim, Microdisney's sales had remained disappointingly in the cult bracket. O'Hagan went on to form the High Llamas, while Coughlan's Fatima Mansions did much to spice up the late 80s and early 90s.

● ALBUMS: *Everybody Is Fantastic* (Rough Trade 1984) ★★★, *We Hate You White South African Bastards* mini-album (Rough Trade 1984) ★★, *The Clock Comes Down The Stairs* (Rough Trade 1985) ★★★, *Crooked Mile* (Virgin 1987) ★★★, *39 Minutes* (Virgin 1988) ★★★.

● COMPILATIONS: *Peel Sessions* (Strange Fruit 1989) ★★★★, *Big Sleeping House* (Virgin 1995) ★★★★.

## MIDNIGHT OIL

Formed in Sydney, New South Wales, Australia, in 1975, and then known as Farm, this strident band has pioneered its own course in Australian rock without relying on the established network of agencies and record companies. The original nucleus of the band comprised Martin Rotsey (guitar), Rob Hirst (drums) and Jim Moginie (guitar). They were later joined by law student Peter Garrett (lead vocals). The outfit became notorious for always insisting on total control over its recorded product and media releases, including photos, and when booking agencies denied the band gigs, the members organized their own venues and tours, taking advantage of the band's large following on the alternative rock scene.

Joined by Dwayne 'Bones' Hillman (bass) in 1977 and changing their name to Midnight Oil, the band took a couple of album releases to refine its songwriting style, principally by Moginie and Hirst. As *Head Injuries* went gold in Australia, the imposing shaven-headed Garrett, who had by now received his law degree, began to make known his firm views on politics. Having signed a worldwide contract with CBS/Columbia Records, it was *10,9,8,7,6,5,4,3,2,1*, that saw the band gain mainstream radio airplay. Featuring songs about the environment, anti-nuclear sentiments, anti-war songs and powerful anthems of anti-establishment, it also propelled the band into the international market place. They performed at many charity concerts, promoting Koori (Australian aborigines) causes in Australia and the loquacious

Garrett almost gained a seat in the Australian parliament in 1984 while standing for the Nuclear Disarmament Party. The following album saw the band tour the USA and Europe, and *Rolling Stone* writers voted the album one of the best of 1989, despite a low profile there. While many regard *Red Sails In The Sunset* as their best work, subsequent albums have been equally highly regarded. The band's peak chart positions in the UK and USA were achieved with 1987's *Diesel And Dust*, the album reaching UK number 19 and US number 21. The band continued its antagonistic attitude towards major industrial companies in 1990, by organizing a protest concert outside the Manhattan offices of the Exxon oil company, who were responsible for the Valdez oil slick in Alaska. Although recent studio releases have failed to reach the peaks of previous albums, Midnight Oil remains a powerful live act.

● ALBUMS: *Midnight Oil* (Powderworks 1978) ★★, *Head Injuries* (Powderworks 1979) ★★★, *Place Without A Postcard* (Columbia 1981) ★★★, *10,9,8,7,6,5,4,3,2,1* (Columbia 1982) ★★★, *Red Sails In The Sunset* (Columbia 1985) ★★★★, *Diesel And Dust* (Columbia 1987) ★★★★, *Blue Sky Mining* (Columbia 1990) ★★★★, *Scream In Blue-Live* (Columbia 1992) ★★★, *Earth And Sun And Moon* (Columbia 1993) ★★★, *Breathe* (Columbia 1996) ★★★, *Redneck Wonderland* (Columbia 1998) ★★★, *Capricornia* (Liquid 8 2002) ★★★.

● COMPILATIONS: *20,000 Watts R.S.L.: The Collection* (Columbia 1997) ★★★★.

● FURTHER READING: *Strict Rules*, Andrew McMillan.

## MIGHTY LEMON DROPS

This UK independent label pop band broke through in 1985 with the highly touted 'Like An Angel'. The band featured Paul Marsh (vocals, guitar), David Newton (guitar), Tony Linehan (bass) and Keith Rowley (drums), who had all enjoyed chequered careers in numerous Wolverhampton outfits. Newton had previously played with Active Restraint in 1982, which also included Marsh and Linehan. They in turn played regularly alongside Another Dream, and both bands featured on single releases by local label Watchdog Video And Records. Newton and Neal Cook of Another Dream put together the Wild Flowers, alongside Dave Atherton (also ex-Another Dream; guitar, keyboards), Pete Waldron (bass) and Dave Fisher (drums). After a further single and a support to Simple Minds, Newton moved on once more, forming the Mighty Lemon Drops with Marsh and Linehan. The temporary drummer was Martin Gilks (later with the Wonder Stuff), before Keith Rowley stepped in full-time. As part of the *New Musical Express*' 'C-86' generation, they were snapped up by Chrysalis Records. Despite the charm of several singles in an Echo And The Bunnymen vein, they failed to translate independent chart success into hits. Although they were dropped by Chrysalis after three albums (after which Linehan was replaced by Marcus Williams), they remained favourites on the US college circuit. This was not enough to sustain them, and they broke up in the early 90s leaving a compilation of live

tracks and demos on Overground Records.
● ALBUMS: *Happy Head* (Chrysalis 1986) ★★★, *Out Of Hand* mini-album (Chrysalis 1987) ★★, *World Without End* (Chrysalis 1988) ★★★, *Laughter* (Chrysalis 1989) ★★★, *Sound* (Sire 1991) ★★★, *All The Way - Live In Cincinnati* (Overground 1993) ★★.
● COMPILATIONS: *Roller Coaster: The Best Of Mighty Lemon Drops 1986–1989* (EMI 1997) ★★★.

## MIKE AND THE MECHANICS

Mike Rutherford (b. 2 October 1950, Guildford, Surrey, England; bass) formed the Mechanics in 1985, during a pause in the career of Genesis while vocalist Phil Collins was engrossed in his solo career. The line-up comprised Paul Carrack (b. 22 April 1951, Sheffield, Yorkshire, England; vocals/keyboards, ex-Ace), Paul Young (b. 17 June 1947, Wythenshawe, Lancashire, England, d. 17 July 2000, Altrincham, Cheshire, England; vocals, ex-Sad Café), Peter Van Hooke and Adrian Lee. Van Hooke was already an accomplished session musician, having played or toured with many singers, from Van Morrison to Rod Argent. The band's first UK Top 30 hit came with 'Silent Running (On Dangerous Ground)' in 1986, which was used as the theme to the movie *On Dangerous Ground*. They enjoyed greater success in the USA where the single reached number 6, and its follow-up, 'All I Need Is A Miracle', climbed one place higher. In early 1989, the band reached US number 1 and UK number 2 with the Rutherford/B.A. Robertson-penned 'The Living Years', an personal song expressing Rutherford's regret at the lack of communication he had with his father while he was alive. The attendant album reached number 2 on the UK charts and number 13 in America. With the exception of the UK number 13 single 'Word Of Mouth', further chart success eluded the band. Quality singles such as the highly emotive 'A Time And Place' and 'Everybody Gets A Second Chance' failed to make the UK Top 50, a sobering thought for future songwriters with high hopes of chart success. *Beggar On A Beach Of Gold* was preceded by the lively UK Top 20 single 'Over My Shoulder'; unfortunately this proved to be the album's only ingot. The title track was written by B.A. Robertson and was a Top 40 hit in the UK in 1995. Pedestrian cover versions of the Miracles' 'You Really Got A Hold On Me' and Stevie Wonder's 'I Believe (When I Fall In Love It Will Be Forever)' added nothing and the album, although competent, did not break any new ground. The band continues to be as fluid as possible, with a new album appearing in July 1999, although the death of Young the following year was a great shock.
● ALBUMS: *Mike + The Mechanics* (WEA 1985) ★★, *Living Years* (WEA 1988) ★★★★, *Word Of Mouth* (Virgin 1991) ★★★, *Beggar On A Beach Of Gold* (Virgin 1995) ★★, *Mike And The Mechanics* (Virgin 1999) ★★★.
● COMPILATIONS: *Hits* (Virgin 1996) ★★★.
● VIDEOS: *Hits* (Warner Music Vision 1996).

## MILKSHAKES

This UK, Chatham, Kent-based band were originally conceived in the late 70s by the Pop Rivets roadies Mickey Hampshire and Banana Bertie as Mickey And The Milkshakes. Often appearing on the same circuit as fellow Medway town bands the Dentists and the Prisoners, they performed as a 'psychobilly' outfit, supporting the Pop Rivets from time to time with Wreckless Eric cover versions. Pop Rivets leader Billy Childish then began writing with Hampshire and in 1980 formed a new version of Mickey And The Milkshakes. Eventually settling on a line-up of Childish and Hampshire (guitars, vocals), Russ Wilkins (bass) and Bruce Brand (drums), they started recording a string of albums featuring various R&B classics plus original material. After the first album they truncated their name. Later on, when John Agnew replaced Wilkins, they began to refer to themselves as Thee Milkshakes. In addition to their normal activities of gigging and recording, they also acted as the backing band to an all-girl vocal trio called the Delmonas. As prolific releasers of album material, The(e) Milkshakes were only modestly successful with singles, achieving two UK Independent Top 20 hits with 'Brand New Cadillac' (1984) and 'Ambassadors Of Love' (1985). The band split in 1984 (although Milkshake material continued to be released long after), with Childish going on to form the equally productive Thee Mighty Caesars.
● ALBUMS: as Mickey And The Milkshakes *Talkin' 'Bout Milkshakes* (Milkshakes 1981) ★★★, as The(e) Milkshakes *Fourteen Rhythm And Beat Greats* (Milkshakes 1982) ★★★, *After School Session* (Upright 1983) ★★, *The Milkshakes IV (The Men With The Golden Guitars)* (Milkshakes 1983) ★★, *Sing And Play 20 Rock And Roll Hits Of The 50s & 60s* (Big Beat 1984) ★★, *Nothing Can Stop These Men* (Milkshakes 1984) ★★, *In Germany* (Wall City 1984) ★★★, *They Came, They Saw, They Conquered* (Pink Dust/Enigma 1984) ★★★, *Thee Knights Of Trashe* (Milkshakes 1984) ★★★, with the Prisoners *The Last Night At The M.I.C. Club* (Empire 1984) ★★★, with the Prisoners *Thee Milkshakes Vs The Prisoners Live* (Media Burn 1986) ★★★, *The 107 Tapes* (Media Burn 1986) ★★★, *The Milkshakes' Revenge!* (Hangman 1987) ★★★, *Live From Chatham* (Hangman 1988) ★★★, *Still Talking 'Bout* (Vinyl 1991) ★★★.
● COMPILATIONS: *Showcase* (Brain Eater 1984) ★★★, *19th Nervous Shakedown* (Big Beat 1990) ★★★.

## MILLI VANILLI

This infamous pop duo comprised Rob Pilatus (b. 8 June 1965, New York, USA, d. 3 April 1998, Frankfurt, Germany) who was brought up in an orphanage, and Fabrice Morvan, who was training to be a trampoline athlete until a fall damaged his neck. Based in Germany, they worked as dancers for various German groups, before forming their own duo combining rap and soul, taking their name from a New York club. They enjoyed huge international hits between 1988 and 1989 with 'Girl You Know It's True' (US number 2/UK number 3), 'Baby Don't Forget My Number' (US number 1), 'Girl I'm Gonna Miss You' (US number 1/UK number 2) and 'Blame It On The Rain' (US number 1) before suffering a major backlash when they were exposed as frontmen for a 'group' fabricated by Boney M producer Frank Farian. The duo had apparently been chosen for their looks and were effectively locked out of the studio when recording took place. After handing back music industry awards (including a Best New Artist Grammy), they promised to return with a new contract and their own voices. However, Farian re-launched the group in 1991 as the Real Milli Vanilli, using Brad Howell, Johnny Davis and Charles Shaw, the singers from the original studio sessions. Pilatus, who had already spent time in jail for parole violation, died of an overdose in Frankfurt, Germany in April 1998, marking a sordid end to the Milli Vanilli story.

● ALBUMS: *Girl You Know It's True* (Arista 1988) ★★, *Two X Two* remix album (Arista/Cooltempo 1989) ★.

## MINOGUE, KYLIE

b. 28 May 1968, Melbourne, Australia. Coming from a stage family, Minogue passed an audition for the Australian soap opera, *Neighbours*, which eventually led to her recording debut with Little Eva's hit 'The Loco-Motion'. When the television series was successfully screened in Britain, prolific hit producers Stock, Aitken and Waterman intervened to mould Minogue's attractive, wholesome, anodyne image to their distinctive brand of radio-centred pop. The first UK single, 'I Should Be So Lucky', reached number 1 in early 1988, presaging an impressive chart run of instantly hummable UK hits, including 'Got To Be Certain' (number 2), 'Je Ne Sais Pas Pourquoi' (number 2), 'Hand On Your Heart' (number 1), 'Wouldn't Change A Thing' (number 2), 'Never Too Late' (number 4), 'Tears On My Pillow' (number 1), 'Better The Devil You Know' (number 2), 'Step Back In Time' (number 4), 'What Do I Have To Do' (number 6) and 'Shocked' (number 6). With solo success enhanced by duets with co-star Jason Donovan, including the UK number 1 'Especially For You', Minogue emerged as one of the most successfully marketed acts of the late 80s and early 90s, with books and movies, including *The Delinquents*. In 1991, the former soap star drastically changed her girl-next door image and adopted a sexier persona, which won her even more media coverage – particularly when she became romantically involved with INXS lead singer, Michael Hutchence.

Further hit singles included a duet with Keith Washington on 'If You Were With Me Now' and 'Give Me Just A Little More Time' (number 2). Surprisingly, she even won some acclaim in the music press and found herself championed as an unlikely 'pop goddess', signing to dance music label Deconstruction Records in 1994. She enjoyed another UK hit single the same year with the mature 'Confide In Me'. In 1996 she recorded a single, 'Where The Wild Roses Grow', with Nick Cave and the following year was working in the recording studio with the Manic Street Preachers. The original title for *Impossible Princess* had to be changed, as it was felt that it clashed with the death of Princess Diana. Not to be confused with her 1994 self-titled release, *Kylie Minogue* was a much grungier album than expected, but marked a downturn in Minogue's

commercial fortunes that resulted in her being dropped by Deconstruction. She signed a new deal with Parlophone Records in 1999, and returned to the top of the UK charts the following July with the infectious dance single, 'Spinning Around'. *Light Years* saw Minogue firmly back in the disco pop bracket, an area to which she is clearly best suited. She returned to the top of the UK singles chart in September 2001 with the highly catchy 'Can't Get You Out Of My Head' (written by former Mud guitarist Rob Davis and Cathy Dennis). A sparkling new album followed to delight her fans. Minogue's renaissance continued in America, with 'Can't Get You Out Of My Head' breaking into the Top 10 and *Fever* rapidly ascending the charts.

● ALBUMS: *Kylie* (PWL 1988) ★★★, *Enjoy Yourself* (PWL 1989) ★★★, *Rhythm Of Love* (PWL 1990) ★★★★, *Let's Get To It* (PWL 1991) ★★, *Kylie Minogue i* (Deconstruction 1994) ★★, *Kylie Minogue ii* (Deconstruction 1998) ★★★, *Light Years* (Parlophone 2000) ★★★★, *Fever* (Parlophone/Capitol 2001) ★★★★.

● COMPILATIONS: *The Kylie Collection* (Mushroom 1988) ★★★, *Kylie's Remixes* (Alfa/PWL 1989) ★★, *Remixed And Official 1990* (PWL 1990) ★★, *Kylie's Remixes Vol. 2* (PWL 1992) ★★, *Celebration: Greatest Hits* (PWL 1992) ★★★, *Greatest Remix Hits Vol. 1* (WEA/Mushroom 1993) ★★★, *Kylie Non Stop History 50 + 1* (Mushroom 1993) ★★★, *Greatest Remix Hits Vol. II* (WEA/Mushroom 1993) ★★★, *Greatest Remix Hits Vol. 3* (Mushroom 1998) ★★★, *Greatest Remix Hits Vol. 4* (Mushroom 1998) ★★, *Hits+* (Deconstruction 2000) ★★★.

● VIDEOS: *On A Night Like This: Live In Sydney* (Parlophone 2001).

● FURTHER READING: *Kylie Minogue: An Illustrated Biography*, Sasha Stone. *The Superstar Next Door*, Sasha Stone. *Kylie Naked: A Biography*, Jenny Stanley-Clarke. *Kylie's Secrets*, Virginia Blackburn.

● FILMS: *The Delinquents* (1989), *Street Fighter* (1994), *Hayride To Hell* (1995), *Misfit* (1996), *Bio-Dome* (1996), *Diana & Me* (1997), *Cut* (2000), *Sample People* (2000), *Moulin Rouge!* (2001).

## MINT JULEPS

This UK a cappella soul group from London's east end, consisted of sisters Debbie, Lizzie, Sandra and Marcia Charles, plus their friends Debbie and Julie. They all formerly worked together at the Half Moon Young People's Theatre, where they decided to form a group. They played at various benefits and toured with Sister Sledge and Billy Bragg, and worked as backing singers for Bob Geldof, the Belle Stars and Dr. Feelgood. They signed to Stiff Records, and were managed by former Darts members Rita Ray and Rob Fish. The Mint Juleps recorded vocal versions of Neil Young's 'Only Love Can Break Your Heart', Robert Palmer's 'Every Kinda People', and the original 'Girl To The Power Of 6' (produced by Trevor Horn). They later moved away from a cappella into a style of lightweight rap in the same vein as Salt-N-Pepa. They appeared on the ex-Grateful Dead drummer Mickey Hart's *Mystery Box* in 1996.

● ALBUMS: *One Time* (Stiff 1985) ★★★.

## MINUTEMEN

Formed in 1980 in San Pedro, California, USA, and originally known as the Reactionaries, this influential hardcore trio initially comprised David Boon (guitar, vocals), Mike Watt (bass) and Frank Tonche (drums), but the latter was replaced by George Hurley prior to recording. Although the trio donated tracks to several independent compilations, notably for the pivotal Radio Tokyo Tapes and the Posh Boy and New Alliance labels, their association with SST Records resulted in some of the genre's most impressive recordings. The unfettered rage of their early work was less apparent on *Buzz Or Howl Under The Influence Of Heat* and *Project: Mersh EP* ('mersh' is San Pedro slang for 'commercial'), but *Double Nickels On The Dime* and *3-Way Tie (For Last)* showed an undeterred passion and commitment. The Minutemen came to a premature end in 1986 following the death of David Boon. Watt and Hurley decided to drop the group's name, and in its place formed fIREHOSE with guitarist Ed Crawford.
● ALBUMS: *The Punch Line* (SST 1981) ★★, *What Makes A Man Start Fires?* (SST 1983) ★★, *Buzz Or Howl Under The Influence Of Heat* (SST 1983) ★★★, *Double Nickels On The Dime* (SST 1984) ★★★, *The Politics Of Time* (New Alliance 1984) ★★★, *Just A Minute Men* (Virgin Vinyl 1985) ★★★, *Project: Mersh EP* (SST 1985) ★★★, *3-Way Tie (For Last)* (SST 1985) ★★★, *Ballot Result* (SST 1987) ★★★.
● COMPILATIONS: *My First Bells 1980–1983* cassette (SST 1985) ★★★, *Post-Mersh, Vol. 1* (SST 1987) ★★, *Post-Mersh, Vol. 2* (SST 1987) ★★★, *Post-Mersh, Vol. 3* (SST 1989) ★★★.

## MISFITS

Like the 13th Floor Elevators in the 60s and the New York Dolls in the early 70s, this US punk band was swiftly surrounded in a cloak of mythology and cult appeal. Long after their demise (they played their last live gig in 1983), their obscure US-only records were fetching large sums of money in collecting circles, among those fascinated by the band's spine-chilling mix of horror-movie imagery and hardcore. The Misfits were formed in New Jersey, New York, in 1977 by Jerry Only (bass) and Glenn Danzig (b. 23 June 1959, Lodi, New Jersey, USA; vocals) and, like many aspiring new wave acts, played in venues such as CBGB's, adding guitarist Bobby Steele and drummer Joey Image. Later that year, 'Cough Cool' became their first single on their own Plan 9 label. A four-track EP, *Bullet* (in a sleeve showing John F. Kennedy's assassination), was recorded before their debut album, and was followed by 'Horror Business'. A third single, 'Night Of The Living Dead', surfaced in 1979, the reference to the classic George A. Romero movie revealing the Misfits' continued fascination with blood-and-guts horror. Then came an EP, *Three Hits From Hell*, recorded in 1980, but not issued until the following April, and a seasonal October single, 'Halloween'. Having lost Steele to the Undead, replaced by Jerry's brother Doyle, Googy (aka Eerie Von) stepped in on drums during a European tour with the Damned as Image's narcotic problems worsened. The Misfits rounded off 1981 by recording the seven-track mini-album *Evilive*,

originally sold through the band's Fiend fan club, which also secured a German 12-inch release.
The band's only original UK release was a 12-inch EP, *Beware*. Other Misfits releases included several patchy albums that failed to capture their live impact: 1982's *Walk Among Us*, *Earth A.D.* (aka *Wolfsblood*) and the posthumous brace, *Legacy Of Brutality* and *Misfits*. Danzig issued his first solo single in 1981, 'Who Killed Marilyn?', later forming Samhain with Misfits drummer Eerie Von. He was subsequently venerated in heavy metal magazines in the late 80s as his eponymous Danzig vehicle gained ground. The other Misfits mainstays, brothers Jerry and Doyle, formed the hapless Kryst The Conqueror, who released one five-song EP with the help of Skid Row guitarist David Sabo. An ambitious 4-CD set was issued in 1996 in the shape of a coffin, and the following year the band re-formed, with Danzig replaced by Michale Graves, releasing an album for Geffen Records. Two years later they signed with Roadrunner Records.
● ALBUMS: *Walk Among Us* (Ruby 1982) ★★★, *Evilive* mini-album (Plan 9 1982) ★★★, *Earth A.D./Wolfsblood* (Plan 9 1983) ★★★, *American Psycho* (Geffen 1997) ★★★, *Famous Monsters* (Roadrunner 1999) ★★★.
● COMPILATIONS: *Legacy Of Brutality* (Plan 9 1985) ★★★, *The Misfits* (Plan 9 1986) ★★★★, *Evilive* expanded version of 1981 mini-album (Plan 9 1987) ★★★, *The Misfits* 4-CD box set (Caroline 1996) ★★★★, *Static Age* (Caroline 1997) ★★★★, *Cuts From The Crypt* (Roadrunner 2001) ★★★.

## MISSION

This UK rock band evolved from the Sisters Of Mercy, when Wayne Hussey (b. Jerry Wayne Hussey, 26 May 1958, Bristol, England) and Craig Adams split from Andrew Eldritch. They quickly recruited drummer Mick Brown (ex-Red Lorry, Yellow Lorry) and guitarist Simon Hinkler (ex-Artery). The original choice of title was the Sisterhood, which led to an undignified series of exchanges in the press between the band and Eldritch. In order to negate their use of the name, Eldritch put out a single under the name Sisterhood on his own Merciful Release label. Thus, the name the Mission was selected instead. After two successful independent singles on the Chapter 22 label, they signed to Mercury Records in the autumn of 1986. Their major label debut, 'Stay With Me', entered the UK singles charts while the band worked on their debut album. *God's Own Medicine* was the outcome, revealing a tendency towards straightforward rock, and attracting criticism for its bombast. A heavy touring schedule ensued, with the band's offstage antics attracting at least as much attention as their performances. A particularly indulgent tour of America saw Adams shipped home suffering from exhaustion. His temporary replacement on bass was Pete Turner.
After headlining the Reading Festival, they began work on a new album under the auspices of Led Zeppelin bass player John Paul Jones as producer. *Children* was even more successful than its predecessor, reaching number 2 in the UK album

charts, despite the customary critical disdain. 1990 brought 'Butterfly On A Wheel' as a single, providing further ammunition for accusations that the band were simply dredging up rock history. In February, the long-delayed third album, *Carved In Sand*, was released, revealing a more sophisticated approach to songwriting. During the world tour to promote the album, both Hinkler and Hussey became ill because of the excessive regime. Hinkler departed suddenly when they reached Toronto, leaving Dave Wolfenden to provide guitar for the rest of the tour. On their return, Paul Etchell took over the position on a more permanent basis. Over the Christmas period, members of the band joined with Slade's Noddy Holder and Jim Lea to re-record 'Merry Xmas Everybody' for charity.

After signing to Vertigo Records, Hussey, Adams and Brown recorded the dance music-influenced *Masque*, which featured songs co-written with Miles Hunt of the Wonder Stuff. However, numerous personnel difficulties then blighted the band's progress. Craig Adams returned to Brighton, while Hussey and Brown brought in bass player Andy Cousin (ex-Sisters Of Mercy), keyboard player Rik Carter and guitarist Mark Gemini Thwaite. A reflective Hussey, promoting the *Sum & Substance* compilation, conceded: 'We had an overblown sense of melodrama. It was great – pompous songs, big grand statements. We've never attempted to do anything that's innovative'. The band returned to a guitar-based sound for two subsequent releases on their own label. Soon after the release of *Blue* the band announced they were splitting-up. They played their final show on 26 October at a festival in South Africa. They resurrected the Mission name in 2002 to record the surprisingly strong new studio album, *Aura*.

● ALBUMS: *God's Own Medicine* (Mercury 1986) ★★, *The First Chapter* (Mercury 1987) ★★★, *Children* (Mercury 1988) ★★★, *Carved In Sand* (Mercury 1990) ★★★, *Grains Of Sand* (Mercury 1990) ★★, *Masque* (Vertigo 1992) ★★★, *Live: No Snow, No Show For The Eskimo* (Windsong 1993) ★★, *Neverland* (Equator 1995) ★★, *Blue* (Equator 1996) ★★, *Aura* (Playground 2002) ★★★★.
● COMPILATIONS: *Magnificent Pieces* 4-CD box set (PHCR 1991) ★★★, *Sum And Substance* (Vertigo 1994) ★★★, *Salad Daze: Radio 1 Sessions* (Nighttracks 1994) ★★, *Tower Of Strength* (Spectrum 2000) ★★★★.
● VIDEOS: *Crusade* (Channel 5 1987), *From Dusk To Dawn* (PolyGram Music Video 1988), *South America* (MISH Productions 1989), *Waves Upon The Sand* (PolyGram Music Video 1991), *Sum And Substance* (PolyGram Music Video 1994).
● FURTHER READING: *The Mission: Names Are For Tombstones Baby*, Martin Roach with Neil Perry.

## MISSION OF BURMA

Once cited as 'the ultimate collision of punk and pop', this Boston, Massachusetts, USA-based band were compared by other commentators to the UK's art terrorists Wire. Certainly, they invoked a similar level of rapture among US critics and, much like Wire, self-consciously avoided the glare of the mainstream. The original line-up of Clint Conley (bass, vocals), Peter Prescott (drums, vocals) and Roger Miller (guitar, vocals) were greatly influential for a number of more commercially viable outfits. They formed in 1979, when Miller and Conley moved to Boston from Ann Arbor and New York, respectively. They briefly put together Moving Parts before joining with resident Bostonian Prescott. Burma kicked off with supports for the UK's Gang Of Four. These went well and the Leeds funksters continued to sponsor them early in their development. They would split in March 1983, due to Miller's aggravated tinnitus, after a career that embraced well-defined but chaotic live and recorded work. Through a series of reissues on the venerated underground label, Taang! Records, critics have now reassessed their historical importance. Among their staunchest admirers are R.E.M., who regularly covered 'Academy Fight Song' in their live sets during the 90s.

Miller went on to record as a solo artist and with his non-touring band Birdsongs Of The Mesozoic, while Prescott formed Volcano Suns and then Kustomized. Conley produced Yo La Tengo's debut before leaving the music business to work as a television producer. In a surprise move, the trio announced they would re-form to play several US shows in January 2002.

● ALBUMS: *Signals, Calls, And Marches* (Ace Of Hearts 1981) ★★★, *Vs.* (Ace Of Hearts 1982) ★★★★, *The Horrible Truth About Burma* (Ace Of Hearts 1985) ★★★, *Forget* (Taang! 1988) ★★★, *Let There Be Burma* (Taang! 1990) ★★★.
● COMPILATIONS: *Mission Of Burma* (Rykodisc 1988) ★★★★.
● VIDEOS: *Live At The Bradford* (Atavistic 1992).

## MO-DETTES

Despite the name, the timing of their appearance on the music scene and the fact that they covered the Rolling Stones' 'Paint It Black', the Mo-Dettes were not modettes and disliked anyone who said they were. They were originally formed for a one-off gig at the Acklam Hall, supporting the Vincent Units. Their line-up was built around Kate Korus (b. Katherine Corris, New York, USA; guitar), who played with the Castrators before lasting just three gigs with the earliest line-up of the Slits. She left (to be replaced by Viv Albertine) and attempted to form several bands. Korus took a long time finding musicians with whom she was happy, but eventually she came across (on the set of *The Great Rock 'n' Roll Swindle* where both had non-acting jobs) drummer June Miles-Kingston (the sister of Bob Kingston of Tenpole Tudor) and bass player Jane Crockford. Crockford had previously played in the Banks Of Dresden with Richard Dudanski. Through a mutual friend they met Ramona Carlier, a singer from Switzerland whose experience to date had been backing vocals at a few sessions, plus a one-off party gig with a band called the Bomberettes, and had been in England about a year. The first product of their labours was 'White Mice' – on their own Mode label through Rough Trade Records. Ramona left late in 1981 to start a solo career, and was replaced by Sue Slack. Soon after, Korus left to be replaced by Melissa Ritter. The final split came shortly afterwards in

1982, owing to further internal friction. Miles-Kingston moved on to Fun Boy Three's backing band, before she produced a solo single for Go! Discs, joined the Communards and sang on various sessions. Kate Korus also released a single with Jennie McKeown of the Belle Stars.

● ALBUMS: *The Story So Far* (Mode 1980) ★★.
● COMPILATIONS: *Loved By Thousands ... Hated By Millions* (Bullet Proof 1995) ★★.

## MODERN ENGLISH

Formed in Colchester, Essex, England, in 1977 by Robbie Grey (vocals), Gary McDowell (guitar, vocals), and Michael Conroy (bass, vocals), and originally known as the Lepers. Richard Brown (drums) and Stephen Walker (keyboards) were subsequently added to the line-up of this durable indie rock band. A debut single, 'Drowning Man' was released in 1980 on the Limp Records label. The band's full-length *Mesh & Lace*, released in suitably arty packaging by 4AD Records a year later, drew heavily on the gloom rock sound already patented by bands such as Joy Division, and had little originality or focus. The follow-up *After The Snow*, recorded by the same line-up, was a minor revelation, as they introduced warmth and strong guitar harmonies (most notably on the minor classic 'I Melt With You'), rejecting the tinny bleakness of the debut. It was well received in the USA, and the band relocated to New York to consolidate a popularity encouraged by college radio. *Richochet Days* had a crisper production but less creative experimentation. By *Stop Start*, released by Sire Records in 1986, Walker and Brown had left, and Aaron Davidson (keyboards, guitar) had joined. The band had tried too hard for commercial approval and was left with an unspecific rock/pop sound that caused them to split soon afterwards. Grey returned to England to form a new outfit, but reconvened Modern English in 1990 with Davidson and Conroy. They released *Pillow Lips* on the TVT label, but to little interest. Grey subsequently put the band on hold to study and travel. In 1995, he re-formed Modern English with Matthew Shipley (keyboards) and Steven Walker (guitar), and recorded *Everything's Mad* for the Imago label. The band continues to tour extensively on the US club circuit, and in 2001 signed a new recording contract with A.P.G. Music.

● ALBUMS: *Mesh & Lace* (4AD 1981) ★★, *After The Snow* (4AD/Sire 1982) ★★★★, *Richochet Days* (4AD/Sire 1984) ★★★, *Stop Start* (Sire/Beggars Banquet 1985) ★★, *Pillow Lips* (TVT 1990) ★★, *Everything's Mad* (Imago 1996) ★★★.
● COMPILATIONS: *Best Of Modern English: Life In The Gladhouse 1980-1984* (4AD 2001) ★★★.

## MODERN ROMANCE

From the remnants of UK punk band, the Leyton Buzzards, crawled singer Geoffrey Deanne (b. 10 December 1954, London, England) and bass player David Jaymes (b. 28 November 1954, Woodford, Essex, England). After becoming involved in the London club scene (alongside luminaries like Steve Strange), they formed a company called Business Art

Productions with manager Brian O'Donoughue. Signed to WEA Records, they released 'Tonight'. This flopped, so in late 1980, Jaymes and Deanne formed a new line-up featuring Deanne and Jaymes, the latter's brother Robbie (b. 3 October 1962; keyboards), Paul Gendler (b. 11 August 1960; guitar) and Andy Kyriacou (b. 19 April 1958; drums, ex-Linx; Central Line). John Du Prez (b. 14 December 1946, Sheffield, Yorkshire, England) also featured on trumpet. Through their club connections they came across the Latin-American music salsa, which was set to be all the craze in the summer of 1981. They quickly recorded 'Everybody Salsa', which gave them their first UK Top 20 hit. It was followed by other successful material in a similar vein; 'Ay Ay Ay Ay Moosey' (number 10), 'Queen Of The Rapping Scene' (number 37) and 'Cherry Pink And Apple Blossom White' (number 15). At this point Deanne left to release several solo singles and write for camp club act Divine. Former fireman Michael J. Mullins (b. 9 November 1956) was his replacement. Their hit run continued in 1983, with 'Best Years Of Our Lives' (number 4), 'High Life' (number 8), 'Don't Stop That Crazy Rhythm' (number 14) and 'Walking In The Rain' (number 7). A cover of Baltimora's 'Tarzan Boy' the following year fared less well. They disbanded shortly afterwards. David Jaymes released a solo single in 1988, while Deanne went on to write comedy scripts. John Du Prez moved to Hollywood where he composed film scores for hit movies such as *Personal Services* and *A Fish Called Wanda*.

● ALBUMS: *Adventures In Clubland* (WEA 1981) ★★, *Trick Of The Light* (WEA 1983) ★★, *Move On* (RCA 1985) ★★.
● COMPILATIONS: *Party Tonight!* (Ronco 1983) ★★★.

## MOLLY HATCHET

This Lynyrd Skynyrd-style, blues-rock boogie outfit emerged from the US deep south. The name derived from a tale of a woman in seventeenth-century Salem who beheaded her lovers with an axe after sleeping with them. The initial line-up comprised guitarists Dave Hlubek, Steve Holland and Duane Roland, plus bass player Banner Thomas, vocalist Danny Joe Brown and drummer Bruce Crump. Their debut album, produced by Tom Werman (of Cheap Trick and Ted Nugent fame), was an instant success, with its three-pronged guitar onslaught and gut-wrenching vocals. Brown was replaced by Jimmy Farrar in 1980, before the recording of *Beatin' The Odds*. Farrar's vocals were less distinctive than Brown's, and an element of their identity was lost during the time that Farrar fronted the band. Nevertheless, commercial success ensued, with both *Beatin' The Odds* and *Take No Prisoners* peaking on the *Billboard* album chart at numbers 25 and 36, respectively.

In 1982, Danny Joe Brown rejoined the band in place of the departed Farrar, while Thomas was replaced by Riff West on bass. *No Guts ... No Glory* emerged and marked a return to their roots: explosive guitar duels, heart-stopping vocals and steadfast rock 'n' roll. Surprisingly, the album flopped and Hlubek insisted on a radical change in

direction. Steve Holden quit and keyboard player John Galvin was recruited for the recording of *The Deed Is Done*. This was a lightweight pop-rock album, largely devoid of the band's former trademarks. Following its release, the band retired temporarily to lick their wounds and reassess their future. In 1985, *Double Trouble Live* was unveiled, with a return to former styles. It included versions of their best-known songs, plus a Lynyrd Skynyrd tribute in the form of 'Freebird'. Founder-member Dave Hlubek departed, to be replaced by Bobby Ingram. The band signed a new contract with Capitol Records and returned with 1989's *Lightning Strikes Twice*. This leaned away from their southern roots towards highly polished AOR. It featured cover versions of Paul Stanley's 'Hide Your Heart' and 'There Goes The Neighbourhood', but was poorly received by fans and critics alike. Brown, meanwhile, continued to be plagued by illness as the result of diabetes. He eventually left the band in 1996 as they embarked on another recording comeback with a line-up comprising Ingram, Galvin, Phil McCormack (vocals), Bryan Bassett (guitar), Andy McKinney (bass) and Mac Crawford (drums). The revived band, now with additional keyboard player Tim Donovan and with Russ Maxwell and Sean Shannon replacing Bassett and Crawford, has continued to tour and record with great success.
● ALBUMS: *Molly Hatchet* (Epic 1978) ★★★, *Flirtin' With Disaster* (Epic 1979) ★★★, *Beatin' The Odds* (Epic 1980) ★★, *Take No Prisoners* (Epic 1981) ★★, *No Guts ... No Glory* (Epic 1983) ★★★, *The Deed Is Done* (Epic 1984) ★★, *Double Trouble Live* (Epic 1985) ★★, *Lightning Strikes Twice* (Capitol 1989) ★★, *Devil's Canyon* (SPV/Mayhem 1996) ★★, *Silent Reign Of Heroes* (SPV/CMC 1998) ★★, *Live At The Agora Ballroom* 1979 recording (Phoenix 1999) ★★★, *Kingdom Of XII* (SPV/CMC 2000) ★★.
● COMPILATIONS: *Greatest Hits* (Epic 1985) ★★★, *Cut To The Bone* (Sony 1995) ★★★, *Super Hits* (Epic 1998) ★★★.

## MONEY, EDDIE

Legend has it that Brooklyn native Eddie Mahoney (b. 2 March 1949, New York, USA) was a New York police officer when first discovered by promoter Bill Graham (he was, in fact, a NYPD typist). Nevertheless, under Graham's managerial wing, Mahoney became Eddie Money and produced two hit singles in 'Baby Hold On' and 'Two Tickets To Paradise' from his self-titled debut, to begin a career that saw him maintain arena-headlining status in America with a series of consistently fine R&B-flavoured AOR records. His 1978 release *Life For The Taking* produced two more hits, 'Rock And Roll The Place' and 'Maybe I'm A Fool', as Money built a strong live reputation that freed him from the constraining need for radio or MTV airplay to sell albums or concert tickets, although the hits continued to come. The mid-80s release *Where's The Party?* saw a slight dip in form, but Money stormed back with perhaps his best 80s album, *Can't Hold Back*, producing three huge hits in the title track, 'I Wanna Go Back' and 'Take Me Home Tonight', where his warm, soulful vocals were augmented by Ronnie

Spector. His first release of the 90s, *Right Here*, saw Money move away from the keyboard-dominated sound of preceding albums towards the rootsier feel of his early work, producing another hit with a cover version of Romeo's Daughter's 'Heaven In The Backseat'.
Money's commercial fortunes waned during the 90s, and by the middle of the decade the singer had been dropped by Columbia Records. He resurfaced on the CMC International label at the end of the decade, releasing a new studio album, *Ready Eddie*.
● ALBUMS: *Eddie Money* (Columbia 1977) ★★★, *Life For The Taking* (Columbia 1978) ★★★, *Playing For Keeps* (Columbia 1980) ★★, *No Control* (Columbia 1982) ★★★, *Where's The Party?* (Columbia 1984) ★★, *Can't Hold Back* (Columbia 1986) ★★★, *Nothing To Lose* (Columbia 1988) ★★, *Right Here* (Columbia 1991) ★★★, *Unplug It In* (Columbia 1992) ★★, *Shakin' With The Money Man* (CMC 1997) ★★, *Ready Eddie* (CMC 1999) ★★.
● COMPILATIONS: *Greatest Hits: The Sound Of Money* (Columbia 1989) ★★★★, *Good As Gold* (Sony 1996) ★★★, *Super Hits* (Sony 1997) ★★★, *Greatest Hits Live* (BMG 1998) ★★, *The Best Of Eddie Money* (Columbia 2001) ★★★★.

## MONOCHROME SET

Any all-encompassing classification of the Monochrome Set's music would be difficult. During a sporadic career that has spanned as many musical styles as it has record labels, they have been on the verge of breaking to a wider audience on a number of occasions. Formed in the UK during late 1976, Andy Warren (bass), Lester Square (guitar) and Bid (guitar, vocals) were playing in the B-Sides with Adam Ant. When the B-Sides became Adam And The Ants, Bid and Lester Square left. They formed the Monochrome Set in January 1978, later joined by Warren in 1979 after his role on the debut Ants album. With Jeremy Harrington (bass, ex-Gloria Mundi) and J.D. Haney (drums, ex-Art Attacks), the band issued singles during 1979–80 for Rough Trade Records, including 'He's Frank', 'Eine Symphonie Des Graeuns', 'The Monochrome Set' and 'He's Frank (Slight Return)', each completely different in style and content. Their debut, *Strange Boutique*, skirted the UK charts. After the title track came further singles '405 Lines' and 'Apocalypso', and a second album, *Love Zombies*. Lex Crane briefly sat in on drums before ex-Soft Boys member Morris Windsor joined for the release of the brilliant sex satire 'The Mating Game', in July 1982, followed by 'Cast A Long Shadow' and the memorable *Eligible Bachelors*.
By this time Carrie Booth had joined on keyboards while Nick Wesolowski took up the drums and Foz (b. James Foster) the guitar soon after. *Volume, Contrast, Brilliance ...* compiled their Rough Trade recordings and selected BBC Radio 1 sessions, and coincided with another indie hit, 'Jet Set Junta' (like many Monochrome Set compositions deflating class/monetary division). 'Jacob's Ladder' seemed a sure-fire hit for 1985, but like 'Wallflower' later that year and the charming *The Lost Weekend*, eluded the charts. Disheartened, the band split and it was left to

Cherry Red Records' El subsidiary to issue a sympathetic retrospective, *Fin*, a year later. Various collections filtered out over the next three years (*Colour Transmission* featured much of the DinDisc material, while *Westminster Affair* highlighted their earliest recordings).

In December 1989, the band re-formed, with Bid, Lester and Warren joined by Orson Presence on guitar and keyboards, marking their return with *Dante's Casino*. From there on, they have concentrated primarily on their cult following in the Far East, with frequent tours there. Their most recent album was 1995's *Trinity Road*. One-time guitarist Foz resurfaced in the late 90s with David Devant And His Spirit Wife.

● ALBUMS: *Strange Boutique* (DinDisc 1980) ★★, *Love Zombies* (DinDisc 1980) ★★, *Eligible Bachelors* (Cherry Red 1982) ★★★, *The Lost Weekend* (Blanco y Negro 1985) ★★★, *Fin* live (El 1986) ★★★, *Dante's Casino* (Vinyl Japan 1990) ★★★, *Jack* (Honeymoon 1991) ★★, *The Monochrome Set Live* (Demon 1993) ★★★, *Charade* (Cherry Red 1993) ★★★, *Misère* (Cherry Red 1994) ★★★, *Trinity Road* (Cherry Red 1995) ★★★.

● COMPILATIONS: *Volume, Contrast, Brilliance ... Sessions & Singles Vol. 1* (Cherry Red 1983) ★★★, *Colour Transmission* (Virgin 1987) ★★★, *Westminster Affair* (Cherry Red 1988) ★★, *What A Whopper!* (Cherry Red 1991) ★★★, *Black & White Minstrels* (Cherry Red 1995) ★★★, *Tomorrow Will Be Too Long: The Best Of The Monochrome Set* (Caroline 1995) ★★★, *Chaps* (Snapper 1997) ★★★.

● VIDEOS: *Destiny Calling* (Visionary 1994).

## MOORE, CHRISTY

b. 7 May 1945, Prosperous, Co. Kildare, Eire. Moore's beginnings were fairly typical for a solo folk performer in the 60s: playing the club circuit in Eire, subsequently doing likewise in England while in between working on building sites and road gangs. Influenced by the American styles of Woody Guthrie, Bob Dylan and the British folk giant, Ewan MacColl, Moore performed in the UK folk clubs alongside the rising stars of the period. It was in England, in 1969, that he recorded his first album, *Paddy On The Road*, a collaboration with Dominic Behan. His first solo album led to the formation of the inspired traditional outfit Planxty, with whom he stayed until 1974. He became involved in the mid-70s with the Anti-Nuclear Roadshow, which featured performers, environmental activists and politicians. The 'Roadshow' established Moore's reputation as a campaigning and political performer and the ensemble's success made a heavy contribution to undermining the plans for an Irish nuclear power programme.

After a brief reunion with Planxty in the late 70s, Moore and fellow Planxty member Donal Lunny split in 1981 to form the innovative Moving Hearts. Despite the band taking a similar ideologically agit-prop stance, Moore eventually felt uncomfortable within a group set-up and, in 1982, returned to solo work. Since that time, he has continued to mix traditional songs with contemporary observations of social and political aspects of Irish life, and has addressed the political problems of Central America and South Africa. His songs are notable not only for their spiky commentary but also an engaging humour. Christy Moore's standing in Irish folk music is unparalleled, and his influence has spilled over into the field of pop and rock, winning critical favour, respect and debt, from such contemporary pop performers as the Pogues, Elvis Costello, Billy Bragg and U2.

● ALBUMS: *Paddy On The Road* (Mercury 1969) ★★★, *Prosperous* (Trailer 1972) ★★★, *Whatever Tickles Your Fancy* (Polydor 1975) ★★★, *Christy Moore* (Polydor 1976) ★★★, *The Iron Behind The Velvet* (Tara 1978) ★★★, *Live In Dublin* (Tara 1979) ★★★, *The Time Has Come* (WEA 1983) ★★★, *Ride On* (WEA 1984) ★★★, *The Spirit Of Freedom* 1983 recording (WEA 1985) ★★★, *Ordinary Man* (WEA 1985) ★★★, *Nice 'N' Easy* (Polydor 1986) ★★★, *Unfinished Revolution* (WEA 1987) ★★★, *Voyage* (WEA 1989) ★★★, *Smoke & Strong Whiskey* (Newberry 1991) ★★★, *King Puck* (Grapevine 1993) ★★★, *Live At The Point* (Grapevine 1994) ★★★, *Graffiti Tongue* (Grapevine 1996) ★★★★, *Traveller* (Columbia 1999) ★★★, *This Is The Day* (Columbia 2001) ★★★.

● COMPILATIONS: *The Christy Moore Folk Collection* i (Tara 1972) ★★★, *The Christy Moore Folk Collection* ii (Tara 1978) ★★★, *The Christy Moore Folk Collection* iii (Tara 1978) ★★★, *The Christy Moore Collection '81–'91* (WEA 1991) ★★★★, *Collection Part Two* (Grapevine 1997) ★★★.

● VIDEOS: *Christy* (SMV 1995).

● FURTHER READING: *One Voice: My Life In Song*, Christy Moore.

## MORRISSEY

b. Steven Patrick Morrissey, 22 May 1959, Davyhulme, Manchester, England. Morrissey began his career with the vague intention of succeeding as a music journalist. Unemployed in Manchester during the late 70s, he frequently wrote letters to the music press and was eventually taken on by *Record Mirror* as a freelance local reviewer. During this period, he also ran a New York Dolls fan club and wrote a booklet about them. Another small illustrated volume, *James Dean Is Not Dead*, briefly catalogued the career of another Morrissey obsession. Two other projects, on girl groups and minor film stars, failed to reach the printed page. In the meantime, Morrissey was attempting unsuccessfully to progress as a performer. He had played a couple of gigs with local band the Nosebleeds and failed a record company audition with a relaunched version of Slaughter And The Dogs. In 1982, he was approached by Wythenshawe guitarist Johnny Maher (later Marr) with the idea of forming a songwriting team. They soon developed into the Smiths, the most important and critically acclaimed UK band of the 80s.

Morrissey's arch lyrics, powerful persona and general news worthiness made him a pop figure whose articulacy was unmatched by any of his contemporaries. By the late summer of 1987, the Smiths had disbanded, leaving Morrissey to pursue a solo career. Early the following year he issued his first post-Smiths single, 'Suedehead', with Vini Reilly (Durutti Column) filling the guitarist's spot. The track was irresistibly commercial and reached the UK Top 5. The subsequent *Viva Hate* hit number 1 in the UK album charts soon after, indicating a long and successful future with EMI Records. A further UK Top 10 single with the John Betjeman-influenced 'Everyday Is Like Sunday' reiterated that point. In spite of his successes, Morrissey was initially keen on promoting a Smiths reunion but the closest this reached was the equivalent of a farewell concert in the unlikely setting of Wolverhampton Civic Hall. On 22 December 1988, Morrissey performed alongside former Smiths Andy Rourke, Mike Joyce and Craig Gannon for a 1,700 capacity audience, many of whom had queued for days in order to gain admittance to the venue. The following year brought several problems. Although he continued to release strong singles such as 'The Last Of The Famous International Playboys' and 'Interesting Drug', both reviews and chart placings were slightly less successful than expected. By the time of 'Ouija Board, Ouija Board', Morrissey suffered the most disappointing reviews of his career and, despite its charm, the single only reached number 18.

Financial wrangles and management changes, which had characterized the Smiths' career, were repeated by Morrissey the soloist. A projected album, *Bona Drag*, was delayed and eventually cancelled, although the title served for a formidable hits and b-side compilation. In the meantime, Morrissey concentrated on the singles market, issuing some fascinating product, most notably the macabre 'November Spawned A Monster' and controversial 'Piccadilly Palare'. In March 1991, Morrissey issued the long-awaited *Kill Uncle*, a light yet not unappealing work, produced by Clive Langer and Alan Winstanley. By this time, the artist had not toured since the heyday of the Smiths, and there were some critics who wondered whether he would ever perform again. That question was answered in the summer and winter of 1991 when the singer embarked on a world tour, backed by a rockabilly band, whose raw energy and enthusiasm brought a new dimension to his recently understated studio work. The fruits of this collaboration were revealed on *Your Arsenal*, a neat fusion of 50s rockabilly influences and 70s glam rock. The presence of former David Bowie acolyte Mick Ronson as producer added to its impetus.

During 1992, Morrissey again hit the headlines when he issued a bitter attack on author Johnny Rogan. Prior to the publication of a book on the Smiths, which he had yet to read, Morrissey decreed: 'Personally, I hope Johnny Rogan ends his days very soon in an M3 pile-up.' The much publicized and long-running dispute merely served to focus attention on the book and heighten appreciation of his Smiths work. *Beethoven Was Deaf*, a live album that disappeared after only two weeks in the charts, was a dismal failure. However, Morrissey was now beginning to cultivate a following in the USA substantially beyond the cult devotees who had followed the Smiths in that country. This offered welcome succour at a time when UK critics were

predicting his imminent downfall. Then came the Madstock disaster – a live appearance in support of a re-formed Madness that saw Morrissey bedecked in a Union Jack – which, when combined with song titles such as 'Bengali In Platforms' and 'The National Front Disco', saw a huge debate rage in the media over the artist's interpretation of 'Englishness'. *Vauxhall And I*, a chilling treatise of pained reflection proved Morrissey's most outstanding release to date, reaching number 1 in the UK. With the more sedate production of Steve Lillywhite, this was the closest the artist had come to matching his lyricism with the right material components since the Smiths. Indeed, as *Select* magazine decreed: 'If he keeps making albums like this, you won't want the Smiths back.' However, it was to be his last album with EMI/HMV Records, apart from the much criticized compilation *The World Of Morrissey*. Meanwhile, a collaboration with Siouxsie on the single 'Interlude' fell outside the UK Top 20.

Morrissey next moved to BMG Records as they chose to revive another old label, this time RCA-Victor Records for 1995's *Southpaw Grammar*. This set opened with 'The Teachers Are Afraid Of The Pupils', an arresting 11-minute update to the Smiths' 'The Headmaster Ritual', which placed the secondary school teacher in the role of victim. Critics were not overly impressed and the album disappeared from the play lists and people's minds after a few weeks. Morrissey made the headlines in 1997 with the long-standing court case over Mike Joyce's claim on royalties. The judge ruled against Morrissey and Marr. This must have been his absolute nadir; even his tracker-dog biographer Rogan was able to confront him at the courtrooms. Ploughing on, Morrissey released the delayed *Maladjusted* for new label Island Records, although he was forced to omit a track that allegedly attacked Joyce and Rourke.

● ALBUMS: *Viva Hate* (HMV/Sire 1988) ★★★★, *Kill Uncle* (HMV/Sire 1991) ★★, *Your Arsenal* (HMV/Sire 1992) ★★★★, *Beethoven Was Deaf* (HMV 1993) ★★, *Vauxhall And I* (Parlophone/Sire 1994) ★★★★, *Southpaw Grammar* (RCA Victor/Reprise 1995) ★★★, *Maladjusted* (Island 1997) ★★★.
● COMPILATIONS: *Bona Drag* (HMV/Sire 1990) ★★★★, *The World Of Morrissey* (Parlophone/EMI 1995) ★★, *Suedehead: The Best Of* (EMI 1997) ★★★, *The CD Singles '88–'91* (EMI 2000) ★★★, *The CD Singles '91–'95* (EMI 2001) ★★★, *The Best Of Morrissey* (Rhino 2001) ★★★★.
● VIDEOS: *Hulmerist* (PMI/EMI 1990), *Live In Dallas* (Warner Music Video 1992), *Introducing Morrissey* (Warner Music Video 1996), *¡Oye Esteban!* (Reprise 2000).
● FURTHER READING: *Morrissey In His Own Words*, John Robertson. *Morrissey Shot*, Linder Sterling. *Morrissey & Marr: The Severed Alliance*, Johnny Rogan. *Peepholism: Into The Art Of Morrissey*, Jo Slee. *Landscapes Of The Mind*, David Bret.

## MORSE, STEVE

Instrumental rock guitarist Steve Morse (b. 28 July 1954, Hamilton, Ohio, USA) took his primary influence, like so many others, from the Beatles.

Expanding his listening to include prevalent rock bands such as the Yardbirds, Jimi Hendrix and Led Zeppelin, as well as a nascent interest in country music, Morse moved with his family to Georgia at the age of 13. There he was captivated by a live concert by classical guitarist Juan Mercadal, and he persuaded the artist to give him lessons. He went on to study with Mercadal at the University of Miami, while also assembling his first band, Dixie Dregs (aka the Dregs). Inspired by a campus performance from John McLaughlin's original Mahavishnu Quartet, he dedicated himself to exploring the conventions and frontiers of instrumental rock music. The Dregs, essentially a vehicle for these experiments, went on to record eight albums of bright, impressive fusion. Morse qualified as a pilot during this time, and flying remains his greatest passion outside of music. He formed the Steve Morse Band with the Dregs drummer Rod Morgenstein and bass player Jerry Peek. Their 1984 debut, The Introduction, continued to mine a particularly adept blend of instrumental rock fusion, with a guest role for guitarist Albert Lee. There was more of a vocal presence for Stand Up, which featured appearances from two other renowned guitarists, Eric Johnson and Peter Frampton. After a brief spell with Kansas Morse recorded his first 'solo' collection, High Tension Wires, which also included a reunion of the original Dixie Dregs on the track 'Leprechaun Promenade'. By the advent of Southern Steel, the Steve Morse Band was a core team of Morse, his Dixie Dregs colleague Dave LaRue (bass), and Van Romaine (drums).

In addition to his work with his own band, Morse recorded and toured with the re-formed Dixie Dregs throughout the 90s. The acclaim surrounding Morse has rarely died down throughout his career – Guitar Player magazine made him ineligible for their Best Overall Guitarist poll after he won it five times in succession. He has also collaborated with artists including Eddie Van Halen, Steve Howe and Lynyrd Skynyrd, and accepted an invitation to join Deep Purple for a spell in 1994. The Steve Morse Band's sixth album, Structural Damage, revealed an undiminished talent, and included the Celtic-influenced 'Sacred Ground' and the cinematic 'Dreamland'. The solo project, Major Impacts, saw Morse recording in the style of different guitarists who had influenced his playing.

● ALBUMS: The Introduction (Elektra 1984) ★★★, Stand Up (Elektra 1986) ★★★, High Tension Wires (MCA 1989) ★★★, Southern Steel (MCA 1991) ★★★★, Coast To Coast (MCA 1993) ★★★, Structural Damage (High Street 1995) ★★★★, StressFest (High Street 1996) ★★★, Major Impacts (Magna Carta 2000) ★★★, Split Decision (Magna Carta 2002) ★★★.
● VIDEOS: Highlights (Warner Music 1995).

## MOTELS

Formed in Berkeley, California, in the early 70s, the early line-up of the Motels, originally known as the Warfield Foxes, comprised Martha Davis (b. 15 January 1951, Berkeley, California, USA; vocals), Dean Chamberlain (guitar), Robert Newman (drums) and Richard D'Andrea (bass). Relocating to Los Angeles, the band recorded a demo tape for Warner Brothers Records in 1975, but internal disagreements led to their break up. A new line-up, comprising Jeff Jourard (guitar), his brother Martin (keyboards, saxophone), Michael Goodroe (bass) and UK session drummer Brian Glascock (ex-Toe Fat), assembled for appearances at Hollywood's Whiskey club throughout July 1978, attracting a modicum of music industry interest in the process. In 1979, their stunning debut album was issued by Capitol Records. Like its remaining tracks, the hit ballad 'Total Control' was produced by John Carter and composed by central figure Davis, whose eclectic tastes included blues, Broadway musicals and Stravinsky. Her onstage presence was 'exceptionally charismatic', wrote The Los Angeles Times, wrongly predicting that she 'could become one of the most influential female performers in rock'. Her boyfriend, Tim McGovern, replaced Jeff Jourard during sessions for Careful, with a sleeve adorned with a print of a Dougie Fields painting.

Though the singles 'Whose Problem?' and 'Days Are O.K.' flitted into the US and UK charts, they fared well in regional charts in Australasia, a territory where the band made its strongest impact. Their albums and tie-in singles tended to hover around the lower half of the UK Top 40 after All Four One, at number 16, marked the Motels' commercial zenith. Guy Perry replaced McGovern on guitar shortly before the release of the album, which had to be re-recorded after Capitol had rejected the original tapes. In their homeland they enjoyed two Top 10 hits with 'Only The Lonely' (1982) and 'Suddenly Last Summer' (1983). Little Robbers utilised session drummer David Platshon, with Glascock relegated to percussion, but promotion of the album was put on hold while Davis recovered from a cancer scare. Following one further album, Davis announced the end of the Motels in early 1987. She embarked on an abortive solo career, and later worked as a songwriter. She established a new line-up of the Motels in 1998.

● ALBUMS: Motels (Capitol 1979) ★★★★, Careful (Capitol 1980) ★★★, All Four One (Capitol 1982) ★★★, Little Robbers (Capitol 1983) ★★, Shock (Capitol 1985) ★★.
Solo: Martha Davis Policy (Capitol 1987) ★★★.
● COMPILATIONS: No Vacancy: The Best Of The Motels (Capitol 1990) ★★★★, Anthologyland (Oglio 2001) ★★★★, Classic Masters (EMD 2002) ★★★.

## MÖTLEY CRÜE

This heavy rock band was formed in 1980 by Nikki Sixx (b. Frank Ferranno, 11 December 1958, San Jose, California, USA; bass) and consisted of former members of several other Los Angeles-based outfits. Tommy Lee (b. Thomas Bass, 3 October 1962, Athens, Greece; drums) was recruited from Suite 19; Vince Neil (b. Vince Neil Wharton, 8 February 1961, Hollywood, California, USA; vocals) from Rocky Candy; while Sixx himself had recently left London. Mick Mars (b. Bob Deal, 3 April 1956, Terra Haute, Indiana, USA; guitar) was added to the line-up after Sixx and Lee answered an advertisement announcing 'Loud, rude, aggressive guitarist available'. Their first single, 'Stick To Your Guns'/'Toast Of The Town', was issued in 1981 on their own Leathür label, followed by their self-produced debut, *Too Fast For Love*. The band signed to Elektra Records in 1982, and the album was remixed and reissued that August. The following year they recorded a new set, *Shout At The Devil*, with producer Tom Werman. He stayed at the helm for the two albums that broke them to a much wider audience in the USA, *Theatre Of Pain* (which sold more than two million copies) and *Girls, Girls, Girls*, which achieved the highest entry (number 2) for a heavy metal album on *Billboard*'s album chart since *The Song Remains The Same* by Led Zeppelin in 1976. These albums refined the raw sound of earlier releases, without hiding the influence that Kiss and Aerosmith exerted on their work. This change in style, which saw Mötley Crüe experimenting with organs, pianos and harmonicas in addition to their traditional instruments, was described as a move from 'club-level metal glam' to 'stadium-size rock 'n' roll'. The band were not without their setbacks, however. In December 1984, Vince Neil was involved in a major car crash in which Hanoi Rocks drummer Razzle was killed. The subsequent *Theatre Of Pain* was dedicated to his memory, and this grim incident helped to inform the mood of the recording. Three years later, Nikki Sixx came close to death after a heroin overdose following touring with Guns N'Roses. Feuds with that same band, particularly between Neil and Axl Rose, later provided the band with many of their column inches in an increasingly disinterested press. They survived to appear at the Moscow Peace Festival in 1989 before more than 200,000 people, and then issue *Dr. Feelgood*, which gave them their first US number 1 chart placing. The album also yielded two US Top 10 singles with the title track and 'Without You'.

Vince Neil was unexpectedly ejected from the band's line-up in 1992, establishing the Vince Neil Band shortly thereafter. His replacement for 1994's self-titled album was John Corabi (ex-Scream), although the band's problems continued with a record label/management split and a disastrous North American tour. Neil was working with the band again in autumn 1996. Lee became the focus of much press attention as a result of his explosive marriage to actress Pamela Anderson. Corabi was sacked in 1996 and the following year instigated litigation against the band members for damages arising from non-payment of monies owed to him. This action was taken as *Generation Swine* was released. Lee eventually left the band in 1999 to concentrate on his new outfit Methods Of Mayhem. He was replaced by Randy Castillo (d. 26 March 2002), who debuted on the following year's *New Tattoo*. The compulsively readable biography, *The Dirt*, was published in May 2001. The band's future was put on hold the following year after Castillo's untimely death.

● ALBUMS: *Too Fast For Love* (Leathür 1981) ★★, *Shout At The Devil* (Elektra 1983) ★★, *Theatre Of Pain* (Elektra 1985) ★★, *Girls, Girls, Girls* (Elektra 1987) ★★★, *Dr. Feelgood* (Elektra 1989) ★★★, *Mötley Crüe* (Elektra 1994) ★★★, *Generation Swine* (Elektra 1997)

★★★, *New Tattoo* (Motley 2000) ★★.
● COMPILATIONS: *Raw Tracks* (Elektra 1988) ★★★, *Decade Of Decadence '81–'91* (Elektra 1991) ★★★★, *Greate$t Hit$* (Motley 1998) ★★★, *Live: Entertainment Or Death* (Motley 1999) ★★★, *Supersonic & Demonic Relics* (Motley 1999) ★★.
● VIDEOS: *Uncensored* (WEA Music Video 1987), *Dr. Feelgood, The Videos* (Warner Music Video 1991), *Decade Of Decadence '81–'91* (Warner Music Video 1992), *Lewd Crüed & Tattooed* (Aviva International 2001).
● FURTHER READING: *Lüde, Crüde And Rüde*, Sylvie Simmons and Malcolm Dome. *The Dirt: Confessions Of The World's Most Notorious Rock Band*, Tommy Lee, Mick Mars, Vince Neil and Nikki Sixx with Neil Strauss.

## MOTÖRHEAD

In 1975, Lemmy (b. Ian Kilmister, 24 December 1945, Stoke-on-Trent, Staffordshire, England; vocals, bass) was sacked from Hawkwind after being detained for five days at Canadian customs on possession charges. The last song he wrote for them was entitled 'Motörhead', and, after ditching an earlier suggestion, Bastard, this became the name of the band he formed with Larry Wallis of the Pink Fairies on guitar and Lucas Fox on drums. Together they made their debut supporting Greenslade at the Roundhouse, London, in July. Fox then left to join Warsaw Pakt, and was replaced by 'Philthy' Phil Taylor (b. 21 September 1954, Chesterfield, England; drums), a casual friend of Lemmy's with no previous professional musical experience. Motörhead was a four-piece band for less than a month, with Taylor's friend 'Fast' Eddie Clarke (b. 5 October 1950, Isleworth, Middlesex, England) of Continuous Performance as second guitarist, until Wallis returned to the Pink Fairies.

The Lemmy/Taylor/Clarke combination lasted six years until 1982, in which time they became one of the most famous trios in hard rock. With a following made up initially of Hells Angels (Lemmy had formerly lived with their president, Tramp, for whom he wrote the biker epic 'Iron Horse'), the band made their official debut with the eponymous 'Motörhead'/'City Kids'. A similarly titled debut album charted, before the band moved over to Bronze Records. *Overkill* and *Bomber* firmly established the band's *modus operandi*, a fearsome barrage of instruments topped off by Lemmy's hoarse invocations. They toured the world regularly and enjoyed hits with 'Ace Of Spades' (one of the definitive heavy metal performances, it graced a 1980 album of the same name that saw the band at the peak of their popularity) and the number 5 single 'Please Don't Touch' (as Headgirl). Their reputation as the best live band of their generation was further enhanced by the release of *No Sleep 'Til Hammersmith*, which entered the UK charts at number 1. In May 1982 Clarke left, citing musical differences, and was replaced by Brian Robertson (b. 12 September 1956, Glasgow, Scotland), who had previously played with Thin Lizzy and Wild Horses. This combination released *Another Perfect Day*, but this proved to be easily the least popular of all

Motörhead line-ups. Robertson was replaced in November 1983 by Wurzel (b. Michael Burston, 23 October 1949, Cheltenham, England; guitar) – so-called on account of his scarecrow-like hair – and Philip Campbell (b. 7 May 1961, Pontypridd, Wales; guitar, ex-Persian Risk), thereby swelling the Motörhead ranks to four.

Two months later and, after a final appearance on UK television's *The Young Ones*, Taylor left to join Robertson in Operator, and was replaced by ex-Saxon drummer Pete Gill. Gill remained with the band until 1987 and played on several fine albums including their GWR debut *Orgasmatron*, the title track of which saw Lemmy's lyric-writing surpass itself. By 1987 Phil Taylor had rejoined Motörhead, and the line-up remained unchanged for five years, during which time Lemmy made his acting debut in the *Comic Strip* film *Eat The Rich*, followed by other celluloid appearances including the role of a taxi driver in *Hardware*.

In 1991, the band signed to Epic Records, releasing the acclaimed *1916*. The following year's *March Or Die* featured the American Mikkey Dee (ex-King Diamond) on drums and guest appearances by Ozzy Osbourne and Slash (Guns N'Roses). The title track revealed a highly sensitive side to Lemmy's lyrical and vocal scope in the way it dealt with the horrors of war. The idiosyncratic Lemmy singing style, usually half-growl, half-shout, and with his neck craned up at 45 degrees to the microphone, remained in place. On a more traditional footing, they performed the theme song to the horror movie *Hellraiser 3*, and convinced the film's creator, Clive Barker, to record his first promotional video with the band. Lemmy also hammed his way through insurance adverts, taking great delight in his press image of the unreconstructed rocker. Wurzel left the band and formed Wykeaf in 1996. His former bandmates have continued to release albums on a regular basis for the SPV label.

● ALBUMS: *Motörhead* (Chiswick 1977) ★★★, *Overkill* (Bronze 1979) ★★★, *Bomber* (Bronze 1979) ★★★, *On Parole* (United Artists 1979) ★★★, *Ace Of Spades* (Bronze 1980) ★★★★, *No Sleep 'Til Hammersmith* (Bronze 1981) ★★★★, *Iron Fist* (Bronze 1982) ★★★★, *What's Words Worth?* 1978 recording (Big Beat 1983) ★★★, *Another Perfect Day* (Bronze 1983) ★★, *Orgasmatron* (GWR 1986) ★★★★, *Rock'N'Roll* (GWR 1987) ★★★, *Eat The Rich* film soundtrack (GWR 1987) ★★★, *No Sleep At All* (GWR 1988) ★★★, *Blitzkreig On Birmingham Live '77* (Receiver 1989) ★★, *The Birthday Party* (GWR 1990) ★★, *1916* (Epic 1991) ★★★, *March Or Die* (Epic 1992) ★★★, *Bastards* (ZYX 1993) ★★★, *I* (SPV 1996) ★★, *Overnight Sensation* (SPV 1996) ★★★, *Snake Bite Love* (SPV 1998) ★★★, *Live On The King Biscuit Flower Hour* 1983 recording (King Biscuit 1998) ★★, *Everything Louder Than Everyone Else* (SPV 1999) ★★, *We Are Motörhead* (SPV 2000) ★★, *Hammered* (SPV 2002) ★★, *What's Wordsworth?* 1978 recording (Ace 2002) ★★.

● COMPILATIONS: *No Remorse* (Bronze 1984) ★★★★, *Anthology* (Raw Power 1986) ★★, *Born To Lose* (Castle 1986) ★★, *Dirty Love* (Receiver 1990) ★★, *Welcome To The Bear Trap* (Castle 1990) ★★, *Best*

*Of Motörhead* (Action Replay 1990) ★★, *Lock Up Your Daughters* (Receiver 1990) ★★, *From The Vaults* (Knight 1990) ★★, *Meltdown* 3-CD box set (Castle 1991) ★★★, *All The Aces* (Castle 1993) ★★, *The Best Of Motörhead* (Castle 1993) ★★★★, *Protect The Innocent* 4-CD box set (Essential 1997) ★★★, *Born To Lose, Live To Win: The Bronze Singles 1978–1983* 10-CD box set (Castle 1999) ★★★★, *The Best Of Motörhead* (Metal-Is 2000) ★★★★, *The Chase Is Better Than The Catch: The Singles A's & B's* (Castle 2001) ★★★, *Over The Top: The Rarities* (Castle 2001) ★★★, *Motörhead* (Ace 2001) ★★★, *The Bronze Age* 4-CD box set (Sanctuary 2002) ★★★★, *Keep Us On The Road: Live 1977* (Castle/Sanctuary 2002) ★★.

● VIDEOS: *Live In Toronto* (Avatar 1984), *Deaf Not Blind* (Virgin Vision 1984), *The Birthday Party* (Virgin Vision 1986), *The Best Of Motörhead* (Castle Music Pictures 1991), *Everything Louder Than Everything Else* (Sony Music Video 1991), *25 & Alive: Boneshaker* (SPV 2001).

● FURTHER READING: *Motörhead: Born To Lose, Live To Win*, Alan Burridge. *Motörhead*, Giovanni Dadomo. *Lemmy: In His Own Words*, Harry Shaw. *Motörheadbangers: Diary Of The Fans Volume 1*, Alan Burridge.

## MOVING PICTURES

Formed in Sydney, Australia in 1980, Moving Pictures had a monster single, 'What About Me?', in early 1982 which went to number 1 in Australia and made the US Top 30. The band comprised Alex Smith (vocals), Ian Lees (bass), Garry Frost (guitar, vocals), Charlie Cole (keyboards, trumpet, vocals), Andrew Thompson (saxophone) and Mark Meyer (drums), Moving Pictures' debut album featured strong ballads, but its rock-orientated live act was successfully captured on their second album which was a minor success. The band continued for several more years releasing a series of unsuccessful singles and another album before disbanding. The band would probably have achieved more success in the USA had its label Elektra Records not struck difficulties just as the band first charted. Guitarist Garry Frost later formed 1927, which also had an excellent response from Australian radio and the public.

● ALBUMS: *Days Of Innocence* (EMI 1982), ★★★ *Matinee* (Wheatley/EMI 1983) ★★★, *Last Picture Show* (Wheatley 1987) ★★.

● COMPILATIONS: *Ultimate Collection* (EMI 2000) ★★★.

## MOYET, ALISON

b. Genevieve Alison-Jane Moyet, 18 June 1961, Basildon, Essex, England. The former singer of the synthesizer duo Yazoo (known as Yaz in the USA), Moyet embarked on a solo career in 1983, after critics had consistently praised her outstanding natural blues voice. The debut *Alf* was a superb recording produced and co-written by Tony Swain and Steve Jolley. 'Love Resurrection' (number 10), 'All Cried Out' (number 8) and 'Invisible' (number 21) were all UK hits in 1984, while the album made number 1 and took root in the charts for nearly two years. 'Invisible' also provided her with a debut US

Top 40 single.

In 1985, Moyet abandoned pop and toured with a jazz band led by John Altman, performing standards which included a version of Billie Holiday's 'That Ole Devil Called Love', which became her biggest UK hit to date, climbing to number 2 in April. The tour was not well received and following her performance with Paul Young at the Live Aid concert, little was seen or heard of Moyet. During this time she gave birth to a daughter and experienced the break-up of her marriage. She returned in 1987 with the UK number 3 hit 'Is This Love?', while the attendant *Raindancing* narrowly missed the number 1 position. Moyet enjoyed two further UK single successes with the driving 'Weak In The Presence Of Beauty' (number 6) and a sensitive cover version of a standard previously associated with Dick Haymes and Kitty Lester, 'Love Letters' (number 4).

Once again Moyet disappeared, giving birth to another child but experiencing another bout of lack of self-confidence. She returned in 1991, embarking on a UK tour and releasing a new album. *Hoodoo* was a diverse record that broke Moyet away from the mould she was anxious to escape. It was artistically satisfying, although commercially pedestrian and effectively enabled this highly talented singer to start again. Another lengthy hiatus was broken by the release of *Essex* in 1994, but this album failed to redress the balance with material that was nowhere near as strong as her outstanding voice deserved. Her cover version of Jules Shear's 'Whispering Your Name' did return Moyet to the UK Top 20. There was a reminder of the quality of her past songs on a well-compiled retrospective, which reached number 1 in the UK album chart in 1995.

After a long period away from the public eye, Moyet returned to prominence in August 2001 when she made her debut as Mama Morton on the London stage in *Chicago*, playing alongside actress Denise Van Outen. The following year she signed a new recording contract with Sanctuary Records and released her first studio album in eight years, *Hometime*.

● ALBUMS: *Alf* (CBS/Columbia 1984) ★★★★, *Raindancing* (CBS/Columbia 1987) ★★, *Hoodoo* (Columbia 1991) ★★★, *Essex* (CBS 1994) ★★, *Hometime* (Sanctuary 2002) ★★★.

● COMPILATIONS: *Singles* (Columbia 1995) ★★★, *The Essential* (Sony 2001) ★★★★.

## MR. MISTER

Although formed in Phoenix, Arizona, USA soft metal artists Mr. Mister were based in Los Angeles and were the brainchild of Richard Page (bass/ vocals) and Steve George (b. 20 May 1955; keyboards) who had previously played together in the Pages. They were both also experienced session men, working alongside REO Speedwagon and John Parr. The line-up was completed when Steve Farris (guitar) and Pat Mastelotto (drums) joined in 1982. Their debut in 1984, *I Wear The Face*, provided the minor US hit 'Hunters Of The Night'. The album was released in the UK two years later. The next album broke the band by scaling the top of the charts in

1985 and delivering two US number 1 singles in 'Broken Wings' and 'Kyrie'. Its release coincided with a marathon Tina Turner support tour. Both singles also made the UK Top 20. After one more album Farris left and was replaced by the well-known session guitarist Buzzy Feiten. A fourth album was denied a release by RCA, and in 1989 the band elected to call it a day.

● ALBUMS: *I Wear The Face* (RCA 1984) ★★, *Welcome To The Real World* (RCA 1985) ★★★, *Go On* (RCA 1987) ★★.

● COMPILATIONS: *Broken Wings* (Camden 1998) ★★★, *The Best Of ... Mr. Mister* (Buddha 2001) ★★★.

## MTV

The first television channel entirely devoted to music was launched in the USA in 1981. MTV was also *the* major influence on the growth of music video during the 80s. Although there had been numerous US rock television shows since *American Bandstand* in the 50s, the immediate predecessor of MTV was *Popclips*, a 30-minute show combining comedy with music videos. It was produced by Michael Nesmith's Pacific Arts company in 1981 for the Nickelodeon cable television channel. On 1 August that year, Nickelodeon's owners Warner Amex Satelite Entertainment Company (WASEC) launched MTV (Music Television) with Buggles' 'Video Killed The Radio Star' as its first offering. Headed at the outset by Robert Pittman, the 24-hour station hired five V-Js (video-jockeys) from radio and the theatre to announce the videos. Starting from a small audience base, the station used 'I Want My MTV' promotional spots by artists such as Pete Townshend, David Bowie, Mick Jagger and Pat Benatar to increase its reach. (In 1986, Dire Straits affectionately parodied the slogan in 'Money For Nothing', which duly won that year's MTV Award for best video.) Soon, MTV plays for their promotional videos were boosting record sales for bands like the Human League ('Don't You Want Me'), Duran Duran ('Hungry Like The Wolf', 'Rio') and the US success in 1983/4 of such UK artists as Haircut 100 and A Flock Of Seagulls was widely attributed to MTV airplay. The inaugural MTV Video Music Awards was held on 14 September 1984 (the Cars' 'You Might Think' was the Video Of The Year).

The impact of MTV led to the formation of specialist cable channels for black music (Black Entertainment TV) and country (the Nashville Network). A direct competitor, Cable Music Channel, launched by Ted Turner failed to dislodge MTV from its pre-eminence. Meanwhile, the growth in television video programming and its influence on the charts forced record companies to produce accompanying videos for almost every new single they issued. By 1984, MTV Networks (as WASEC was now renamed) was making annual profits of six million dollars and it began a programme of international expansion with outlets in Japan (1984), Australia (1987) and Brazil (1990). Opened on 1 August 1987, MTV Europe had built up a reach of 30 million households in 28 countries by the early 90s, and operated its own programming policy, using videos by local artists as well as programmes imported from the

USA. In 1991, MTV Asia was launched from Hong Kong as a satellite channel, also with a pledge to feature local acts. Expansion in the USA took the form of the creation of VH-1, devoted to album and adult-orientated rock, in 1985, shortly before MTV Networks was purchased by Viacom Ltd. In February 1987, Sumner Redstone purchased the controlling interest in Viacom.

The channel's range of shows now covered alternative music (*120 Minutes*), heavy metal (*Headbanger's Ball*), and hip-hop (*Yo! MTV Raps*). In January 1990, *MTV Unplugged*, a showcase for acoustic sets by established bands, was premiered. Further expansion included the launch, in 1991, of the animation series Liquid Television (spawning the inimitable cartoon characters Beavis And Butt-Head), MTV Latino (1993), MTV Online (1994), MTV Interactive (1994), and M2: Music Television aka MTV2 (1996). On January 11 2001, MTV went dark for the first time in its history to run a scroll listing the names of victims of hate crime. The list ran continuously and without commercial breaks for 17 hours. In August, the network celebrated its 20th anniversary. It is now distributed to more than 340 million households worldwide.

● FURTHER READING: *MTV Unplugged: First Edition*, Sarah Malarkey (ed.).

## MUDHONEY

Mudhoney, forged from a host of hobbyist bands, can lay claim to the accolade 'godfathers of grunge' more legitimately than most – whether or not they desire that title. The band comprises Mark Arm (b. 21 February 1962, California, USA; vocals), Steve Turner (b. 28 March 1965, Houston, USA; guitar), Matt Lukin (b. 16 August 1964, Aberdeen, Washington, USA; bass) and Dan Peters (b. 18 August 1967, Seattle, Washington, USA; drums). Arm and Turner were both ex-Green River, the band that also gave birth to Pearl Jam, and the less serious Thrown-Ups. Lukin was ex-Melvins, and Peters ex-Bundles Of Hiss. Mudhoney were the band that first took the sound of Sub Pop Records to wider shores. In August 1988, they released the fabulous 'Touch Me I'm Sick' single, one of the defining moments in the evolution of 'grunge', followed shortly by their debut mini-album. Contrary to popular belief, Turner chose the name *Superfuzz Bigmuff* after his favourite effects pedals rather than any sexual connotation. Early support included the admiration of Sonic Youth who covered their first a-side, while Mudhoney thrashed through Sonic Youth staple 'Halloween' on the flip-side of a split single. The first album was greeted as a comparative disappointment by many, though there were obvious stand-out tracks ('When Tomorrow Hits'). The EP *Boiled Beef And Rotting Teeth* contained a cover version of the Dicks' 'Hate The Police', demonstrating a good grasp of their 'hardcore' heritage. They had previously demonstrated an ability to choose a sprightly cover tune when Spacemen 3's 'Revolution' had appeared on the b-side to 'This Gift'. Mudhoney also holds other UK cult artists such as Celibate Rifles and Billy Childish in high esteem. Members of the former helped in production of the band, while on trips to England they have invited the latter to join as support. It was Mudhoney's patronage that led to Childish's Thee Headcoats releasing material through Sub Pop.

Meanwhile, Mudhoney's shows were becoming less eye-catching, and progressively close to eye-gouging. Early gigs in London saw Arm invite every single member of the audience on to the stage, with the resultant near-destruction of several venues. *Every Good Boy Deserves Fudge* was a departure, with Hammond organ intruding into the band's accomplished rock formula. It demonstrated their increasing awareness of the possibilities of their own songwriting. The band members all have middle-class backgrounds, and while Arm is an English graduate, Turner has qualifications in anthropology. After much speculation, Mudhoney became the final big players in the Sub Pop empire to go major when they moved to Warner Brothers Records, though many argue that none of their efforts thus far have managed to reproduce the glory of 'Touch Me I'm Sick' or other highlights of their independent days. *My Brother The Cow*, however, revealed a band nearly back to its best. Released after extensive worldwide touring with Pearl Jam, highlights included 'Into Your Schtick', which reflected on the passing of one-time friend Kurt Cobain. Jack Endino's production, meanwhile, added lustre and managed effectively to capture the band's always compelling live sound.

Mark Arm also plays with the trashy Australian garage rock band Bloodloss, who released their major label debut, *Live My Way*, in 1995. He returned to Mudhoney for their 1998 release, *Tomorrow Hit Today*. Another hiatus ensued before the band returned in 2002 with the excellent *Since We've Become Translucent*.

● ALBUMS: *Superfuzz Bigmuff* mini-album (Sub Pop 1988) ★★★, *Mudhoney* (Sub Pop 1989) ★★, *Every Good Boy Deserves Fudge* (Sub Pop 1991) ★★★, *Piece Of Cake* (Reprise 1993) ★★★, *Five Dollar Bob's Mock Cooter Stew* mini-album (Reprise 1993) ★★, *My Brother The Cow* (Reprise 1995) ★★★, *Tomorrow Hit Today* (Reprise 1998) ★★★, *Since We've Become Translucent* (Sub Pop 2002) ★★★★.

● COMPILATIONS: *Superfuzz Bigmuff Plus Early Singles* (Sub Pop 1991) ★★★, *March To Fuzz: Best Of & Rarities* (Sub Pop 2000) ★★★.

● VIDEOS: *Absolutely Live* (Pinnacle 1991), *No. 1 Video In America This Week* (Warner Music Video 1995).

## MURRAY, PAULINE, AND THE INVISIBLE GIRLS

Following the demise of Penetration, Murray (b. 8 March 1958, Durham, England) departed, with bass guitarist Robert Blamire, to form a new group. Producers Martin Hannett and Steve Hopkins were claimed to be the 'Invisible' members, while the actual line-up consisted of John Maher (ex-Buzzcocks), Dave Rowbotham and Dave Hassell. The Invisible Girls would also act as studio and road band for John Cooper Clarke, and included among its ranks Pete Shelley, Karl Burns (the Fall), Bill Nelson, Vini Reilly (Durutti Column) and numerous others. A self-titled album and single, 'Dream

Sequence', announced the arrival of Pauline Murray And The Invisible Girls in 1980, and gained strong critical support. The album featured guest appearances from Wayne Hussey (ex-Dead Or Alive, Sisters Of Mercy, the Mission) in addition to the previously mentioned Invisible luminaries. Despite this fine collection, the band split after two subsequent single releases from it: 'Searching For Heaven' and 'Mr. X'. Blamire went into production work while Murray took two years away from the music industry: 'I just . . . retreated from music really, just backed right out and decided what I wanted to do. Which took about a year to two years . . . I think Penetration to the Invisible Girls was such a vast leap that it lost everyone. It lost us as well'. Blamire and Murray reunited in the similarly short-lived Pauline Murray And The Storm, before retiring from the music business at the start of the following decade.

● ALBUMS: *Pauline Murray And The Invisible Girls* (Illusive 1981) ★★★.
● COMPILATIONS: *Storm Clouds* (Cat And Mouse 1989) ★★★.

## MUSICAL YOUTH

Formed at Duddeston Manor School, Birmingham, England, this pop/reggae-influenced group featured two sets of brothers, Kelvin and Michael Grant and Junior and Patrick Waite (b. *c.*1969, d. 18 February 1993). The latter pair's father, Frederick Waite, was a former member of Jamaican group the Techniques, and sang lead with Junior at the start of the group's career in the late 70s. Although schoolboys, the group managed to secure gigs at certain Birmingham pubs and released a single, 'Political'/'Generals', on local label 021 Records. An appearance on BBC disc jockey John Peel's evening show brought further attention to the group and they were signed to MCA Records. By that time, founding father Frederick Waite had backed down to be replaced by Dennis Seaton as lead singer. During the winter of 1982, the group issued one of the fastest-selling singles of the year in 'Pass The Dutchie'. Based on the Mighty Diamonds' 'Pass The Kouchie' (a song about marijuana), the title had been subtly altered to feature the patois 'dutchie' (literally a 'cooking pot'). The infectious enthusiasm of the group's performance captured the public's imagination and propelled the record to number 1 in the UK charts. A US Top 10 hit also followed. The catchy follow-up, 'Youth Of Today', also reached the UK Top 20 and early in 1983 'Never Gonna Give You Up' climbed to number 6. Minor successes with 'Heartbreaker' and 'Tell Me Why' were succeeded by a surprise collaboration with Donna Summer on the UK Top 20 hit 'Unconditional Love'. A revival of Desmond Dekker's '007' saw them back in the Top 30, but after one final hit with 'Sixteen', they fell from commercial grace and subsequently split up in 1985 when Seaton left the band. Plans to re-form were scotched when Patrick Waite, who had gone on to a career of juvenile crime, died of natural causes while awaiting a court appearance on drug charges. The Grant brothers remain involved in music, while Seaton released a solo set in 1989 before going on to

form his own band, XMY.
● ALBUMS: *The Youth Of Today* (MCA 1982) ★★★, *Different Style* (MCA 1983) ★★.
Solo: Dennis Seaton *Imagine That* (Bellaphon 1989) ★★.
● FURTHER READING: *Musical Youth: Their Own Story*, no editor listed.

## MUTE RECORDS

Daniel Miller's brainchild was originally set up for a single under the guise of the Normal. 'T.V.O.D.'/ 'Warm Leatherette' became the first Mute single in early 1978, a pioneering utilization of electronics that paved the way for Mute's alignment with synthesized and hi-tech sounds. Several hundred albums later, Mute's singular artistic identity and experimental approach still cut a distinctive chord through an apathetic music industry. Along with Factory Records and Rough Trade Records, Mute has demonstrated an ability to combine aesthetic autonomy with survival. Among the label's early group roster were Fad Gadget, DAF and Depeche Mode. It was the success of the latter that convinced many that a post-punk independent label could succeed in producing a consistent chart act. Despite the offers made to the group from major labels, Depeche Mode resisted any temptation to move – a tribute to Miller's business acumen and his faith in Depeche Mode's artistic growth. The label has also been greatly assisted by ex-Depeche Mode member Vince Clarke's series of projects from Yazoo through to Erasure. Owing to Depeche Mode and Erasure's continuing international success, Mute has been able to finance less commercial acts such as Laibach, Crime And The City Solution, Diamanda Galas and Nitzer Ebb. The label's acquisition of the back catalogues of Cabaret Voltaire, Can and Throbbing Gristle also ensured the continued availability of these seminal artists' output. In the 90s a subsidiary operation dealing with dance music, Novamute Records, was established, dealing with forerunning experimental artists such as Moby. On a more conventional front the parent label also signed the Inspiral Carpets, but the long-standing artist to best combine critical and commercial approbation has undoubtedly been Nick Cave. In 2002 Mute was sold to EMI Records for a reported £23 million with Miller still in charge of creative policy.
● COMPILATIONS: *International* (Mute 1991) ★★★.

## MY BLOODY VALENTINE

It took several years for My Bloody Valentine to capture their groundbreaking hybrid of ethereal melodies and studio-orientated, discordant sounds that proved so influential on the independent scene of the late 80s. Their roots lay in Dublin, where singer/guitarist Kevin Shields joined drummer Colm O'Ciosoig in the short-lived Complex. Forming My Bloody Valentine in 1984, the pair moved to Berlin, joined by vocalist Dave Conway (vocals) and Tina (keyboards). A mini-album, *This Is Your Bloody Valentine*, on the obscure German Tycoon label in 1984, made little impression (although it was later reissued in the UK), so the band returned to London and recruited bass player Debbie Googe. The 12-inch

EP *Geek!* (and the accompanying, 'No Place To Go') emerged on Fever in mid-1986, and, like their debut, was strongly influenced by the Cramps and the Birthday Party. Later that year, the band signed with Joe Foster's fledgling Kaleidoscope Sound label for *The New Record By My Bloody Valentine* EP, which revealed a new influence, the Jesus And Mary Chain.

A switch to the Primitives' label Lazy, produced 'Sunny Sundae Smile' (1987), which meshed bubblegum pop with buzzsaw guitars, a formula that dominated both the mini-album, *Ecstasy*, and 'Strawberry Wine', released later that year. The departure of Conway signalled a change in musical direction, reinforced by the arrival of vocalist Bilinda Butcher. A further move to Creation Records allowed for a drastic reappraisal in recording techniques, first apparent on the formidable *You Made Me Realise* EP in 1988. Enticing melodic structures contrasted with the snarling, almost unworldly collage of noise, developed more fully that year on My Bloody Valentine's pivotal *Isn't Anything*, from which was drawn the barrage of guitars, 'Feed Me With Your Kiss'. At last, the band had unearthed a completely new sound, and following the album's release their status mushroomed. The release of an EP, *Glider* (1990), alongside a remix from the in-demand DJ Andrew Weatherall, flirted with both dance music and the charts while 'Tremelo' (1991) must rank as arguably the most extreme piece of music to reach the UK Top 30. To quote the band, it 'sounded like it was being played through a transistor radio'.

My Bloody Valentine's increasing maturity saw the meticulously produced *Loveless* album reinforce their reputation as one of the prime influences on the late 80s UK independent scene – one to which bands such as Slowdive, Lush and Chapterhouse owed a great deal. However, the massive studio bills run up during that time saw My Bloody Valentine leave Creation, moving instead to Island Records. At this point, another agonising gestation period was embarked upon, allegedly due to difficulty installing equipment in their purpose-built studio in south London. Shields contributed to the 1996 Experimental Audio Research album *Beyond The Pale*. O'Ciosoig and Googe eventually tired of waiting for their errant leader, forming Clear Spot and Snowpony respectively. Shields became a semi-permanent member of Primal Scream, contributing to their albums *Xtrmntr* and *Evil Heat*.

● ALBUMS: *This Is Your Bloody Valentine* mini-album (Tycoon 1984) ★★, *Ecstasy* mini-album (Lazy 1987) ★★, *Isn't Anything* (Creation 1988) ★★★★★, *Loveless* (Creation 1991) ★★★★.

## N'DOUR, YOUSSOU

b. 1959, Dakar, Senegal. Born in the Medina, or 'old town', district of Dakar, N'Dour is the son of Ndeye Sokhna Mboup, herself a well-known traditional musician, who gave him his grounding in the traditional music of the Wolof people. His first public performances came with two local music and drama groups, including Sine Dramatic, which he joined in 1972. The following year he made his first public appearance with a modern band, singing with Orchestre Diamono. In 1975, he toured the Gambia with the band, returning after his parents complained he was too young to start a life on the road. In 1976 N'Dour took the first steps in a career which would establish him as one of Senegal's greatest musical pioneers, joining the Star Band, who were the houseband at Dakar's leading night spot, the Miami Club. With them N'Dour began to forge the fusion of western electric instrumentation and traditional Wolof rhythms and lyrics that became known as mbalax.

In 1979, N'Dour left the Star Band, and set up Etoile De Dakar, which in 1982 he re-formed as Super Etoile De Dakar. The mature mbalax style emerged at this time, as N'Dour added a variety of western instrumentation to the tough, multi-rhythmic Wolof folk songs that he was reinterpreting: a base of rolling, flamenco-like guitars, fuzz-box guitar solos and stabbing, Stax-like horns. Slowly, the sound developed. Ten cassette releases, starting with *Tabaski* in 1981, displayed an increasing fullness and power of arrangement. The lyrical subject matter ranged from folk tales to celebrations of life in Dakar, and the problems faced by migrants to the cities. In Senegal, N'Dour's reputation increased. His prowess as a praise singer attracted rich and famous patrons, all of them keen to be immortalized in his songs and willing to pay large sums of money for the privilege. Poorer people, particularly the urban youth, identified with his pride in his Wolof roots while also enjoying the rock and soul edges his instrumentation and arrangements brought to the music.

Outside Senegal his music received wider attention with the western release of two classic albums, *Immigrés* (1985) and *Nelson Mandela* (1986), which attracted sustained critical praise and significant sales in the USA, UK and France. In 1987 N'Dour was invited to support Peter Gabriel on a lengthy USA tour, returning to Dakar with an Akai sampler with which to record and further explore the traditional sounds of Senegal. The results were to be heard on *The Lion* and its 1990 follow-up *Set*. Both were realized via a new contract with Virgin Records, though he was later unceremoniously 'released' from the contract. For purists in the West, the albums showed rather too much western influence. His Senegalese audience, however, received them with huge enthusiasm. Books and videos on N'Dour followed, cementing his position as the pre-eminent African musical export of the 90s. While *Eyes Open*, despite several enchanting songs, led some to believe N'Dour had lost his edge, *The Guide* pronounced his talent undiminished. Collaborating with Jacob Desvarieux, Branford Marsalis and others, it was the first album to be conceived, recorded and produced in Senegal. Taken from it, '7 Seconds', a duet with Neneh Cherry, reached number 3 in the UK charts in 1994, only furthering N'Dour's status as a genuine crossover artist. He subsequently concentrated on his home market, releasing several cassette only albums and appearing live every weekend at his Thiossane club. *Joko*, his long awaited return to the international fold, was released in February 2000.

● ALBUMS: *Show A Abidjan* (ED 1983) ★★, *Diongoma* (MP 1983) ★★★, *Immigrés* (Celluloid/Earthworks 1984) ★★★★, *Nelson Mandela* (ERT 1985) ★★★★, *The Lion* (Virgin 1989) ★★★, *Set* (Virgin 1990) ★★, *Eyes Open* (40 Acres 1992) ★★, *Wommat: The Guide* (Columbia 1994) ★★★★, with Yandé Codou Sène *Gainde – Voices From The Heart Of Africa* (World Network 1995) ★★★, *Lii!* cassette only (Jololi 1997) ★★★, *Spécial Fin D'Année* (Jololi 1999) ★★★★, *Joko (The Link)* (Columbia/Nonesuch 2000) ★★★★, *Le Grand Bal Vols. 1 & 2* (Jololi 2000) ★★★, *Ba Tay* (Jololi 2002) ★★★.

● COMPILATIONS: *Hey You! The Best Of* (Music Club 1993) ★★★, *Live: Bir Sorano Juin '93, Vols. 1 & 2* (Studio 1993) ★★★, *7 Seconds: The Best Of Youssou N'Dour* (Columbia/Legacy 2002) ★★★★.

# N.W.A.

The initials stand for Niggers With Attitude, which was the perfect embodiment of this Los Angeles crew's outlook. They comprised Dr. Dre (b. Andre Young, 18 February 1965, South Central, Los Angeles, California, USA), DJ Yella (b. Antoine Carraby, Compton, Los Angeles, California, USA), MC Ren (b. Lorenzo Patterson, Compton, Los Angeles, California, USA) and Eazy-E (b. Eric Wright, 7 September 1963, Compton, California, USA, d. 26 March 1995, Los Angeles, California, USA). Founder-member Ice Cube (b. O'Shea Jackson, 15 June 1969, Crenshaw, South Central Los Angeles, California, USA), arguably the most inspiring of the rapping crew, departed for a solo career after financial differences with the band's manager (which would later be recorded in a highly provocative song that attacked him for, amongst other things, being Jewish). However, all the band's members had long CVs: Dr. Dre had DJed for World Class Wreckin' Crew, and had produced Ice Cube's first band, CIA. Both Eazy-E and DJ Yella had recorded and produced several rap discs under their own names, the former funding his Ruthless Records label, allegedly, through illegal activities. Other early members of the posse included Arabian Prince and D.O.C.
N.W.A.'s first single was 'Boyz 'N The Hood', marking out their lyrical territory as guns, violence and 'bitches'. Though *N.W.A. And The Posse* was their

debut album, they only performed four of the raps on it, and to all intents and purposes, *Straight Outta Compton* counts as their first major release. For those attracted to the gangsta rappers first time round, this was more of the same, only sharper and more succinct. A landmark release, in its aftermath rap became polarized into two distinct factions; traditional liberal (reflecting the ideas of Martin Luther King) and a black militancy redolent of Malcolm X, albeit much less focused and reasoned. In 1989, the FBI investigated *Straight Outta Compton*'s infamous 'Fuck Tha Police', after which Ice Cube left the group. It set a precedent for numerous actions against N.W.A., including the first time anyone in the music industry had received a threatening letter from the FBI. *Efil4zaggin* (Niggaz4life spelt backwards), which made US number 1, also surpassed the outrage factor of its predecessor by addressing gang rape and paedophilia, in addition to the established agenda of oral sex, cop killing and prostitution. Musically, it contained furious blasts of raggamuffin and 70s funk, but that was somehow secondary. It did reveal some humour in the band, i.e. on 'Don't Drink That Wine' (which jokingly encourages drug abuse instead), or lines like, 'Why do I call meself a nigger, you ask me? Because my mouth is so muthafuckin' nasty, Bitch this bitch that nigger this nigger that, In the meanwhile my pockets are getting fat.' However, such wit was stretched paper-thin over a clutch of expletives and obscenities. The UK government used the Obscene Publications Act to seize copies but were forced to return them following legal action. Ultimately the BPI withdrew their support from Island Marketing's successful action. Counsel for the defence was Geoffrey Robertson QC, who had played a similar role in the infamous *Oz* trial of 1971. Expert testimony from Wendy K of Talkin' Loud Records, rap author David Toop and psychologist Guy Cumberbatch of Aston University swung the case. This prompted a variety of statements from British MPs outlining their intention to toughen up the law. However, even the anti-censorship lobby had to concede that N.W.A.'s by turns ludicrous ('Find 'Em Fuck 'Em And Flee') and dangerous ('To Kill A Hooker') songs blurred the generally positive influence of the rap movement.
As the decade progressed it became obvious that the remaining members of N.W.A. were spending more time on their solo projects, Dr. Dre, in particular, going on to enjoy huge success both as an influential artist and producer with Death Row Records, the phenomenally successful label he co-founded with Marion 'Suge' Knight. His acrimonious parting from Eazy-E over monies owed through Ruthless Records was celebrated in records by both artists. The latter succumbed to AIDS and died in 1995 through complications following a collapsed lung after having been hospitalized for some time. Yella has been quiet, co-production credits on Ruthless and promoting his own pornographic website aside, while Ren released a number of disappointing solo albums.
● ALBUMS: *N.W.A. And The Posse* (Ruthless 1987) ★★★, *Straight Outta Compton* (Ruthless 1989)

★★★★★, *Efil4zaggin* (Ruthless 1991) ★★.
● COMPILATIONS: *Greatest Hits* (Virgin 1996) ★★★, *The N.W.A. Legacy Volume 1, 1988–1998* (Priority/Virgin 1999) ★★★★, *The N.W.A. Legacy Volume 2* (Priority/Virgin 2002) ★★★.

## NAKED RAYGUN

Formerly Negro Commander, a band whose life span extended to a single show, Chicago, Illinois, USA's Naked Raygun were their city's premier hardcore band of the early 80s. Despite appearances to the contrary, their name was chosen prior to the election of US President Ronald Reagan. Dropping bass player Marco Pezzati for Camilo Gonzalez of the Wayouts at the same time as they lost their original name, the rest of the band comprised Jeff Pezzati (vocals) and Santiago Durango (guitar). No drummer featured in the original line-up until Jim Colao was recruited. Santiago then moved on to Big Black and Arsenal, and was replaced by John Haggerty who had already played saxophone at early shows. Their recording career had begun with the documentary 1981 Chicago live compilation, *Busted At Oz*, released on Autumn Records (it also featured the Effigies and Strike Under, from whom later members would come). New drummer Eric Spicer (ex-DVA) was drafted in 1983 as the group began to take shape. 'The old line-up didn't have a common, long-term goal. We just had practices, we just played some songs we had in our heads . . . We never talked about records, we played any show in Chicago we could get . . .'
They played their first New York date at Gildersleeves later that year. It had taken the band three years to complete their first tour, after which they announced two further tours in 1984. Their first record release had been 1983's cacophonous *Basement Screams* EP on Ruthless Records (run by Big Black and the Effigies, and entirely different to the label of the same name operated by rapper Eazy-E). However, their debut album was a vastly superior artefact in showcasing their talents, with individual songs of great quality including 'Surf Combat' and 'Gear', while 'Metastasis' benefited from Pezatti's trademark malevolent vocal inflections. The jazzy intonations of 'Libido', meanwhile, served as an early indication of a willingness to change their mode of address. In 1986, Pierre Kezdy deputized for Camilo on bass, and their *All Rise* album of that year proved to be their finest moment. The group moved from Homestead Records to set up their own Sandpunder label, before another shift to Caroline Records. Their admiration for the work of the Buzzcocks was compounded when they were joined onstage by a drunken Steve Diggle on their 1989 UK tour to promote *Understand?*. After an emotional final gig at Chicago's Maxwell's venue Haggerty left (to join Pegboy) to be replaced by Bill Stephens (ex-Product 19). However, his contribution to 1990's *Raygun ... Naked Raygun* failed to fill the gap adequately, and Naked Raygun subsequently ground to a halt.
● ALBUMS: *Throb Throb* (Homestead 1985) ★★★, *All Rise* (Homestead 1986) ★★★★, *Jettison* (Caroline 1988) ★★★, *Understand?* (Caroline 1989) ★★★, *Raygun ... Naked Raygun* (Caroline 1990) ★★.

● COMPILATIONS: *Huge Bigness: Selected Tracks From The Collected Works, 1980–1992* (Quarterstick 1999) ★★★.

## NAPALM DEATH

This quintet from Birmingham, England, was formed in 1981. Dispensing with their original style by the mid-80s, they then absorbed punk and thrash metal influences to create the new subgenera of grindcore, arguably the most extreme of all musical forms. Side one of their debut album featured Justin Broadrick (guitar), Mick Harris (drums) and Nick Bullen (bass, vocals), but by side two this had switched to Bill Steer (guitar), Jim Whitely (bass) and Lee Dorrian (vocals), with Harris the only survivor from that first inception (though that, too, had been subject to numerous changes). Broadrick went on to join Head Of David and Godflesh. *Scum* largely comprised sub-two-minute blasts of metallic white noise, overridden by Dorrian's unintelligible vocal tirade. The lyrics dealt with social and political injustices, but actually sounded like somebody coughing up blood.
Their main advocate was Radio 1 disc jockey John Peel, who had first picked up on *Scum*, playing the 0.75 second-long track 'You Suffer' three times before inviting them to record a session for the programme in September 1987. This came to be acknowledged as one of the 'Classic Sessions' in Ken Garner's 1993 book on the subject, and introduced new bass player Shane Embury (also Unseen Terror, who split after one album in 1988). Elsewhere, Napalm Death were the subject of derision and total miscomprehension. They were, however, the true pioneers of the 'blast-snare' technique – whereby the tempo of a given beat is sustained at the maximum physical human tolerance level. They went on to attract a small but loyal cult following on the underground heavy metal scene. *From Enslavement To Obliteration*, consisting of no less than 54 tracks on the CD, was a state-of-the-artless offering that easily bypassed previous extremes in music. However, following a Japanese tour in 1989 Dorrian elected to leave the band to put together Cathedral. Despite the gravity of the split, replacements were found in vocalist Mark 'Barney' Greenway (ex-Benediction) and US guitarist Jesse Pintado (ex-Terrorizer).
To maintain their profile the band embarked on the European Grindcrusher tour (in their wake, grindcore had developed considerably and found mass acceptance among the rank and file of the metal world) with Bolt Thrower, Carcass and Morbid Angel, before playing their first US dates in New York. A second guitarist, Mitch Harris (ex-Righteous Pigs), was added in time for *Harmony Corruption*, which, along with the 12-inch 'Suffer The Children', saw Napalm Death retreat to a more pure death metal sound. During worldwide touring in 1992, sole surviving original member Mick Harris became disillusioned with the band and vacated the drum-stool for Danny Herrera, a friend of Pintado's from Los Angeles. A fourth album, *Utopia Banished*, celebrated the band's remarkable survival instincts, while the heady touring schedule continued unabated.

By 1993, the band had played in Russia, Israel, Canada and South Africa in addition to the more familiar European and US treks. A cover version of the Dead Kennedys' 'Nazi Punks Fuck Off' issued as a single, reinstated their political motives. As *Fear, Emptiness, Despair* confirmed, however, they remain the antithesis of style, melody and taste – the punk concept taken to its ultimate extreme, and a great band for all the difficulty of listening to them. Both *Diatribes* and *Inside The Torn Apart* represented business as usual. Harris has recorded two albums with Eraldo Bernocchi, 1997's *Overload Lady* and the following year's *Total Station*, and collaborated with Embury as Meathook Seed. In 1999, Napalm Death released the covers EP *Leaders Not Followers* for their new label, Dream Catcher Records. It was followed a year later by the typically uncompromising *Enemy Of The Music Business*.

● ALBUMS: *Scum* (Earache 1986) ★★, *From Enslavement To Obliteration* (Earache 1988) ★★★, *The Peel Sessions* mini-album (Strange Fruit 1989) ★★★, *Harmony Corruption* (Earache/Combat 1990) ★, *Live Corruption* (Earache 1990) ★, *Utopia Banished* (Earache/Relativity 1992) ★★, *Fear, Emptiness, Despair* (Earache/Columbia 1994) ★★, *Diatribes* (Earache 1996) ★★, *Inside The Torn Apart* (Earache 1997) ★★, *Breed To Breathe* mini-album (Earache 1997) ★★, *Bootlegged In Japan* (Earache 1998) ★★, *Words From The Exit Wound* (Earache 1998) ★★★, *Leaders Not Followers* mini-album (Dream Catcher/Relapse 1999) ★★, *Enemy Of The Music Business* (Dream Catcher/Spitfire 2000) ★★★.

● COMPILATIONS: *Death By Manipulation* (Earache/Relativity 1991) ★★, *The Complete Radio One Sessions* (Strange Fruit/Fuel 2000) ★★★.

● VIDEOS: *Live Corruption* (Fotodisk 1990), *The DVD* (Earache 2001).

## NELSON, BILL

b. William Nelson, 18 December 1948, Wakefield, West Yorkshire, England. Although originally noted for his innovative guitar work with Be-Bop Deluxe, Nelson's solo releases actually form the majority of his total output. *Northern Dream* was a dreamy, acoustic debut, released in 1971 after he had already spent several years playing throughout his home county with pre-progressive rock outfits such as the Teenagers, Global Village and Gentle Revolution. He fronted Be-Bop Deluxe for most of the 70s before responding to punk and techno-rock forces by assembling Bill Nelson's Red Noise. *Sound On Sound*, released in 1979, was an agitated but confused debut from Red Noise and afterwards Nelson returned to solo work. The 1980 single 'Do You Dream In Colour?' provided his highest UK solo chart placing at number 52. It was released on his own label, Cocteau Records. Following a short-lived contract with Mercury Records he continued to release introspective, chiefly home-recorded albums on the Cocteau label, which Nelson founded in 1980 with his former manager Mark Rye. He was in demand as a producer and worked on sessions with many new wave bands including the Skids and A Flock Of Seagulls.

Surprisingly, after the demise of Be-Bop Deluxe,

Nelson showed little inclination to use the guitar and preferred to experiment with keyboards and sampled sounds, composing thematic pieces that have been used in films and plays. He recorded backing music for the Yorkshire Actors Company's version of both *Das Kabinet* and *La Belle Et La Bette*, issued later as albums. Many of his releases throughout the 80s were of a whimsical, self-indulgent nature and missed the input of other musicians. Numerous albums were issued via his fan club and the quality was rarely matched by the prolificacy, which twice ran to four-album boxed sets, *Trial By Intimacy* and *Demonstrations Of Affection*. In 1991 he moved markedly towards a stronger and more defined melodic style with *Luminous* on Manchester's independent label, Imaginary, and also spoke of returning to his first love, the guitar. *Practically Wired (Or How I Became ... Guitar Boy!)* was Nelson's first guitar instrumental album, while the following year's *After The Satellite Sings* flirted with drum 'n' bass. In the mid-90s, Nelson set up the Populuxe label to facilitate the release of his recordings. He also records with Roger Eno and Kate St. John as Channel Light Vessel.

● ALBUMS: *Northern Dream* (Smile 1971) ★★★, as Bill Nelson's Red Noise *Sound On Sound* (Harvest 1979) ★★★, *Quit Dreaming And Get On The Beam* (Mercury 1981) ★★★★, *Sounding The Ritual Echo* (Mercury 1981) ★★★, *Das Kabinet* (Cocteau 1981) ★★★, *The Love That Whirls (Diary Of A Thinking Heart)* (Cocteau/PVC 1982) ★★★, *La Belle Et La Bete* (Cocteau/PVC 1982) ★★★, *Chimera* mini-album (Mercury 1983) ★★★, *Savage Gestures For Charms Sake* (Cocteau 1983) ★★★, *Vistamix* expanded re-release of *Chimera* (Portrait 1984) ★★★, *A Catalogue Of Obsessions* (Cocteau 1984) ★★★, *The Summer Of God's Piano* (Cocteau 1984) ★★★, as Bill Nelson's Orchestra Arcana *Iconography* (Cocteau 1986) ★★, *Getting The Holy Ghost Across* (UK) *On A Blue Wing* (US) (Portrait 1986) ★★★, *Chamber Of Dreams* (Cocteau 1986) ★★★, *Map Of Dreams* television soundtrack (Cocteau 1987) ★★★, *Chance Encounters In The Garden Of Lights* (Cocteau 1987) ★★★, as Bill Nelson's Orchestra Arcana *Optimism* (Cocteau 1988) ★★, *Pavilions Of The Heart And Soul* (Cocteau 1989) ★★★, *Demonstrations Of Affection* (Cocteau 1989) ★★★, *Altar Pieces* cassette only (The Orpheus Organisation 1990) ★★★, *Simplex* (Cocteau 1990) ★★★, *Luminous* (Imaginary 1991) ★★★, *Blue Moons & Laughing Guitars* (Virgin Venture/Caroline 1992) ★★★, *Crimsworth (Flowers, Stones, Fountains And Flames)* (Resurgence 1995) ★★★, *Practically Wired (Or How I Became ... Guitar Boy!)* (All Saints/Gyroscope 1995) ★★★, *After The Satellite Sings* (Resurgence/Gyroscope 1996) ★★★, with Culturemix *Culturemix With Bill Nelson* (Resurgence 1996) ★★★, *Buddha Head* (Populuxe/Blueprint 1997) ★★★, *Electricity Made Us Angels* (Populuxe/Blueprint 1997) ★★★, *Deep Dream Decoder* (Populuxe/Resurgence 1997) ★★★, *Atom Shop* (Discipline 1998) ★★★, *Simplex* (Lenin 2001) ★★, *Noise Candy* 6-CD box set (Lenin 2002) ★★★.

● COMPILATIONS: *Trial By Intimacy (The Book Of Splendours)* 4-LP box set (Cocteau 1984) ★★★, *The Two Fold Aspect Of Everything* (Cocteau 1984) ★★★,

*The Strangest Things Sampler* (Cocteau 1989) ★★★, *Duplex: The Best Of Bill Nelson* (Cocteau 1989) ★★★, *Demonstrations Of Affection* 4-CD box set (Cocteau 1990) ★★★, *My Secret Studio: Music From The Great Magnetic Back Of Beyond* 4-CD box set (Resurgence/Gyroscope 1995) ★★★, *Confessions Of A Hyperdreamer (My Secret Studio, Volume 2)* (Populuxe/Resurgence 1997) ★★★, *What Now, What Next?* (Discipline 1998) ★★★, *Whistling While The World Turns* (Lenin 2000) ★★★.

## NEVILLE BROTHERS

The Neville Brothers represent the essence of 40 years of New Orleans music distilled within one family unit. The Nevilles comprise Art (b. Arthur Lanon Neville, 17 December 1937, New Orleans, Louisiana, USA; keyboards, vocals), Charles (b. 28 December 1938, New Orleans, Louisiana, USA; saxophone, flute), Aaron Neville (b. 24 January 1941, New Orleans, Louisiana, USA; vocals, keyboards) and Cyril (b. 10 January 1948, New Orleans, Louisiana, USA; vocals). Each member is also a capable percussionist.

They have, individually and collectively, been making an impression on R&B, rock 'n' roll, soul, funk and jazz since the early 50s. Art Neville was the leader of the Hawkettes, whose 1954 Chess Records hit 'Mardi Gras Mambo' has become a New Orleans standard, reissued every year at Mardi Gras time. From 1957 he released solo singles on Specialty Records, and in the early 60s, both he and Aaron worked (separately) for the legendary producer Allen Toussaint. Aaron had emerged from vocal group the Avalons, and although he had a minor R&B hit in 1960 with Toussaint's 'Over You', it was not until 1967 that he achieved fame with the soul ballad 'Tell It Like It Is', a million-seller that reached number 2 in the charts. Charles Neville, meanwhile, had been working – on the road and back home as part of the Dew Drop Inn's house band – with many legendary names: B.B. King, Bobby Bland and Ray Charles, among them. In 1968, Art formed the Meters, one of the Crescent City's most innovative and respected outfits. Featuring Leo Nocentelli (guitar), George Porter (bass), Joseph Modeliste (drums) and, later, Cyril Neville (percussion), they were New Orleans' answer to Booker T. And The MGs, and besides their own albums, they could be heard on early 70s releases by Paul McCartney, Robert Palmer, LaBelle and Dr. John.

*The Wild Tchoupitoulas* was a transitional album, featuring the Meters' rhythm section and all four Neville Brothers; by 1978 they were officially a group. Despite a considerable 'cult' following, particularly among fellow musicians, it took them until 1989 and the release of the Daniel Lanois-produced *Yellow Moon*, to find a wider audience. A single, 'With God On Our Side', was extracted and became a minor hit; Aaron, duetting with Linda Ronstadt, achieved his greatest chart success since 'Tell It Like It Is', when 'Don't Know Much' reached US and UK number 2 and won them the first of two Grammy Awards. In 1990, as a band, they released *Brother's Keeper* and appeared on the soundtrack of the movie *Bird On A Wire*. *Family Groove* was a more

pedestrian offering, but was followed by a compelling live set that played to the group's strengths. *Mitakuye Oyasin Oyasin* was a new studio album that featured Aaron's strong cover version of Bill Withers' 'Ain't No Sunshine'. It was followed in 1999 by the excellent *Valence Street*.

● ALBUMS: as the Wild Tchoupitoulas *The Wild Tchoupitoulas* (Antilles 1976) ★★★, *The Neville Brothers* (Capitol 1978) ★★★, *Fiyo On The Bayou* (A&M 1981) ★★★★, *Neville-ization* (Spindletop 1982) ★★★★, *Neville-ization II* (Spindletop 1984) ★★★, *Uptown* (EMI America 1987) ★★, *Live At Tipitina's Volume 2* (Demon 1988) ★★★, *Yellow Moon* (A&M 1989) ★★★★, *Brother's Keeper* (A&M 1990) ★★★★, *Family Groove* (A&M 1992) ★★★, *Live On Planet Earth* (A&M 1994) ★★★, *Mitakuye Oyasin Oyasin/All My Relations* (A&M 1996) ★★★, *Valence Street* (Columbia 1999) ★★★.

● COMPILATIONS: *Treacherous: A History Of The Neville Brothers 1955–1985* (Rhino 1987) ★★★★, *Legacy: A History Of The Nevilles* (Charly 1990) ★★★★, *Treacherous Too!* (Rhino 1991) ★★★, *With God On Our Side* 2-CD set (A&M 1997) ★★★, *Greatest Hits* (A&M 1998) ★★★★, *The Best Of The Neville Brothers: Uptown Rulin'* (A&M 1999) ★★★★.

● VIDEOS: *Tell It Like It Is* (BMG Video 1990).

● FURTHER READING: *The Brothers*, Neville Brothers with David Ritz.

## NEVILLE, AARON

b. 24 January 1941, New Orleans, Louisiana, USA. Neville began performing in the Hawkettes, a group that also featured his brother Art Neville. Aaron was signed to Minit Records as a solo artist, but despite a minor hit with 'Over You' (1960), he remained largely unknown until the release of 'Tell It Like It Is' (1966). This simple, haunting ballad showcased the singer's delicate delivery while the song's slogan-like title echoed the sentiments of the rising Black Power movement. Sadly, the single's outlet, Par-Lo, went bankrupt, and despite subsequent strong releases, Neville was unable to repeat its commercial success. In 1978, following the break-up of the Meters, Aaron joined Art, Cyril and Charles in the Neville Family Band, later renamed the Neville Brothers. He continued a parallel solo career and in 1989 enjoyed an international hit with 'Don't Know Much', a duet with Linda Ronstadt. *Warm Your Heart* was a strong collection, but subsequent albums have failed to do justice to Neville's astonishing voice.

● ALBUMS: *Tell It Like It Is* (Par-Lo 1967) ★★, *Orchid In The Storm* mini-album (Demon 1986) ★★★, *Warm Your Heart* (A&M 1991) ★★★, *The Grand Tour* (A&M 1993) ★★★, *Soulful Christmas* (A&M 1993) ★★, *The Tattooed Heart* (A&M 1995) ★★, *To Make Me Who I Am* (A&M 1997) ★★, *Devotion* (Chordant 1999) ★★★.

● COMPILATIONS: *Like It 'Tis* (Minit 1967) ★★, *Humdinger* (Stateside 1986) ★★, *Make Me Strong* (Charly 1986) ★★★, *Show Me The Way* (Charly 1989) ★★★, *Greatest Hits* (Curb 1990) ★★★, *My Greatest Gift* (Rounder 1990) ★★★, *The Best Of Aaron Neville: The Millennium Collection* (A&M 2002) ★★★★.

● FURTHER READING: *The Brothers*, Neville Brothers with David Ritz.

## NEW EDITION

Upbeat US teenage pop stars New Edition were formed by Maurice Starr, who modelled them on the Jackson Five. He recruited five handsome young men, Bobby Brown (b. 5 February 1969, Boston, Massachusetts, USA), Ralph Tresvant (b. 16 May 1968, Boston, Massachusetts, USA), Michael Bivins (b. 10 August 1968, Boston, Massachusetts, USA), Ricky Bell (b. 18 September 1967, Boston, Massachusetts, USA) and Ronnie DeVoe (b. 17 November 1967, Boston, Massachusetts, USA), who originally performed high-quality mainstream pop with soul overtones. As their careers progressed, however, they began to incorporate the sound and style of hip-hop, inadvertently becoming forerunners for the 'New Jack Swing' (aka swingbeat) hybrid that Teddy Riley then developed. Following the success of 1983's *Candy Girl*, New Edition fired Starr, who then repeated the trick and earned a good deal of money by masterminding the career of New Kids On The Block. The first rap exchanges occurred on *New Edition*, their MCA Records debut, where the quintet proved particularly effective on tracks such as 'School'.

Shortly afterwards, Brown left for a hugely successful solo career that still embraced hip-hop as well as harmonic soul ballads. New Edition continued with an idiosyncratic album of doo-wop cover versions, before the arrival of Johnny Gill for *Heart Break*, which was produced by Jimmy Jam And Terry Lewis. With sales and interest slumping, the remaining members set out on more successful solo projects. Bell Biv DeVoe comprised the adventures of the three named founder-members, while both Gill and Tresvant followed the solo trail. A total reverse in their fortunes occurred in 1996, when their first album in many years entered the *Billboard* album chart at number 1, a remarkable comeback.

● ALBUMS: *Candy Girl* (Streetwise 1983) ★★, *New Edition* (MCA 1984) ★★★, *All For Love* (MCA 1985) ★★★, *Christmas All Over The World* (MCA 1985) ★★, *Under The Blue Moon* (MCA 1986) ★★, *Heart Break* (MCA 1988) ★★★, *Home Again* (MCA 1996) ★★★.
● COMPILATIONS: *New Edition's Greatest Hits* (MCA 1991) ★★★★, *Lost In Love: The Best Of Slow Jams* (MCA 1998) ★★★, *All The Number Ones* (Universal 2000) ★★★★.

## NEW KIDS ON THE BLOCK

Formed in 1984, this pop group from Boston, Massachusetts, USA, featured Joe McIntyre (b. 31 December 1972, Needham, Massachusetts, USA), Jordan Knight (b. 17 May 1970, Worcester, Massachusetts, USA), Jonathan Knight (b. 29 November 1968, Worcester, Massachusetts, USA), Daniel Wood (b. 14 May 1969, Boston, Massachusetts, USA) and Donald Wahlberg (b. 17 August 1969, Boston, Massachusetts, USA). They were discovered by producer/writer Maurice Starr, who had previously moulded the career of New Edition. It was Starr who presented his protégés with a rap song titled 'New Kids On The Block' from which they took their name. Their self-titled album, released in 1986, fused rap and pop and brought them popularity among a predominantly white teenage audience. However, it was not until summer 1988 that they broke through to the US charts with the Top 10 hit 'Please Don't Go Girl'. In 1989, they became the biggest-selling group in America, enjoying Top 10 hits with 'You Got It (The Right Stuff)', 'Didn't I (Blow Your Mind)', 'Cover Girl' and 'This One's For The Children', and topping the charts with 'I'll Be Loving You (Forever)' and 'Hangin' Tough'. 'You Got It (The Right Stuff)' and a reissue of 'Hangin' Tough' climbed to number 1 in the UK, thereby establishing the quintet as an act of international teen appeal. The following year's US number 1 'Step By Step' became their most successful single, and was followed by another Top 10 hit, 'Tonight'. The attendant *Step By Step* topped both the Sand UK album charts, although it sold less than their debut album. In 1992, they shortened their name to NKOTB, but failed to match the commercial success they enjoyed between 1989 and 1990, even though *Face The Music* (recorded without Starr) credibly reinvented them as a stylish urban R&B outfit. The group disbanded in June 1994 to concentrate on solo careers.

● ALBUMS: *New Kids On The Block* (Columbia 1986) ★★, *Hangin' Tough* (Columbia 1988) ★★★, *Merry, Merry Christmas* (Columbia 1989) ★, *Step By Step* (Columbia 1990) ★★, *No More Games/The Remix Album* (Columbia 1990) ★★, *Face The Music* (Columbia 1994) ★★★.
● COMPILATIONS: *H.I.T.S* (Columbia 1991) ★★★, *Greatest Hits* (Sony 1999) ★★★.
● FURTHER READING: *New Kids On The Block: The Whole Story By Their Friends*, Robin McGibbon. *New Kids On The Block*, Lynn Goldsmith.

## NEW MODEL ARMY

With their roots embedded in the punk era, New Model Army were formed in Bradford, Yorkshire, England, in 1980, and immediately outlined their manifesto by naming themselves after the Sir Thomas Fairfax/Oliver Cromwell revolutionary army. The band was formed by Justin 'Slade The Leveller' Sullivan (b. Buckinghamshire, England; guitar, vocals), a former platform sweeper and Mars bar production-line worker, with the help of Jason 'Moose' Harris (bass, guitar) and Robb Heaton (b. Cheshire, England; drums, guitar). Their brand of punk folk/rock attracted a loyal cult following, much of which shared the band's grievances towards the Tory government policies of the 80s. This was best executed on their debut album, which combined militant themes such as 'Spirit Of The Falklands' and 'Vengeance' (a vitriolic anthem about getting even with one's trespassers) with the haunting lament for childhood 'A Liberal Education'. The band's championing of traditional working-class ethics saw an unexpected boost for a dying art and trade – that of the clog.

New Model Army made their first public appearance at Scamps Disco in Bradford in October 1980. After releasing singles on Abstract Records, enjoying a number 2 UK independent chart hit with 'The Price' in 1984, they formed an unlikely alliance with the multinational EMI Records, which saw the band acquire a higher profile and a significantly increased recording budget. They eventually broke through to a wider audience with 'No Rest', which peaked at number 28 on the UK singles chart in 1985 – a position they were never to beat in an impressive run of 12 UK chart singles between 1985 and 1991. With often-inflammatory lyrics, the band has never compromised their beliefs for commercial gain. They ran into trouble with BBC Television's *Top Of The Pops* show for donning T-shirts with the (albeit laudable) slogan 'Only Stupid Bastards Use Heroin'. This attracted some derision from 'anarcho-punk' traditionalists Conflict, who replied with their own motif: 'Only Stupid Bastards Help EMI'. They subsequently continued to release high-quality albums, with considerable crossover potential, always maintaining credibility with their original fanbase.

In December 1991, New Model Army left EMI, eventually finding a new home on Epic Records. Their first single for the label revealed few concessions to the mainstream: 'Here Comes The War' featured a picture of a charred body, and a pull out poster instructing the user in how to prepare a nuclear bomb. In 1994, a dance remix of 'Vengeance' was released as a protest against the Criminal Justice Bill. After a lengthy absence the band reconvened for 1998's *Strange Brotherhood*.

● ALBUMS: *Vengeance* (Abstract 1984) ★★★, *No Rest For The Wicked* (EMI 1985) ★★★, *The Ghost Of Cain* (EMI 1986) ★★, *New Model Army* mini-album (EMI 1987) ★★, *Radio Sessions 83 – 84* (Abstract 1988) ★★, *Thunder And Consolation* (EMI 1989) ★★★, *Impurity* (EMI 1990) ★★★, *Raw Melody Men* (EMI 1990) ★★★, *The Love Of Hopeless Causes* (Epic 1993) ★★★, *BBC Radio One: Live In Concert* (Windsong 1994) ★★, *Strange Brotherhood* (EMI 1998) ★★★, *& Nobody Else* (Attack 1999) ★★★, *Eight* (Attack 2000) ★★.

● COMPILATIONS: *The Independent Story* (Abstract 1987) ★★★, *History* (EMI 1992) ★★★, *B-Sides & Abandoned Tracks* (EMI 1998) ★★★, *All Of This: The 'Live' Rarities* (EMI 1999) ★★, *Lost Songs* (Attack 2002) ★★.

● VIDEOS: *History: The Videos 85–90* (PMI 1993).

## New Musik

This UK synth-pop band comprised Tony Mansfield (guitar, keyboards, vocals), Tony Hibbert (bass), Phil Towner (drums) and Clive Gates (keyboards). They came to prominence after a minor UK hit in 1979 with 'Straight Lines', and three bigger hits during 1980 on the GTO label, 'Living By Numbers', 'The World Of Water' and 'Sanctuary'. Mansfield regarded their debut *From A To B* as rudimentary, but the succeeding *Anywhere* fared less well, despite its evident maturity. The change in style also took its toll on the band, with the departures of Hibbert and Towner soon after its release. They were replaced by electronic percussionist Cliff Venner for the band's final and rather uninspired *Warp*. Full of empty electronic dance tracks it was notable for a daring attempt at the Beatles' 'All You Need Is Love'. However, sales were very poor and they soon disbanded. Mansfield went on to produce hits for Captain Sensible, Mari Wilson, Naked Eyes and worked on A-Ha's debut album, *Hunting High And Low*.

● ALBUMS: *From A To B* (GTO 1980) ★★★, *Anywhere* (GTO 1981) ★★★, *Warp* (GTO 1982) ★★.

● COMPILATIONS: *Sanctuary* (Epic 1981) ★★★.

## New Order

When Joy Division's Ian Curtis committed suicide in May 1980 the three remaining members, Bernard Sumner (b. Bernard Dicken/Albrecht, 4 January 1956, Salford, Manchester, England; guitar, vocals), Peter Hook (b. 13 February 1956, Manchester, England; bass) and Stephen Morris (b. 28 October 1957, Macclesfield, Cheshire, England; drums) continued under the name New Order. Sumner took over vocal duties and the trio embarked on a low-key tour of the USA, intent on continuing as an entity independent of the massive reputation Joy Division had achieved shortly before their demise. Later that same year they recruited Morris' girlfriend, Gillian Gilbert (b. 27 January 1961, Manchester, England; keyboards, guitar), and wrote and rehearsed their debut, *Movement*, which was released the following year. Their first single, 'Ceremony', penned by Joy Division, was a UK Top 40 hit in the spring of 1981, and extended the legacy of their previous band. Hook's deep, resonant bass line and Morris' crisp, incessant drumming were both Joy Division trademarks. The vocals, however, were weak, Sumner clearly at this stage feeling uncomfortable as frontman.

The band's desire to explore new electronic technology, and their immersion in acid house culture, was becoming apparent in their music, most notably on an extended version of b-side 'Everything's Gone Green' and May 1982's Top 30 single 'Temptation'. Their support for the new club culture was evinced by their joint ownership of Manchester's Haçienda club, which was opened in Whitworth Street in May 1982 and went on to become the most famous dance music venue in England. Much was made, in 1983, of the band 'rising from the ashes' of Joy Division in the music press, when *Power, Corruption & Lies* was released. Their experimentation with electronic gadgetry was fully realized and the album contained many surprises and memorable songs. The catchy bass riff and quirky lyrics of 'Age Of Consent' made it an instant classic, while the sign-off line on the otherwise elegiac 'Your Silent Face', 'You've caught me at a bad time/So why don't you piss off', showed that Sumner no longer felt under any pressure to match the poetic, introspective lyricism of Ian Curtis. As well as redefining their sound they clearly now relished the role of 'most miserable sods in pop'. 'Blue Monday', released at this time in 12-inch format only, went on to become the biggest-selling 12-inch single of all time in the UK.

In 1983 'disco' was a dirty word in the independent fraternity and 'Blue Monday', which combined an infectious dance beat with a calm, aloof vocal, was a brave step into uncharted territory. As well as influencing a legion of UK bands, it would be retrospectively regarded as a crucial link between the disco of the 70s and the dance/house music wave at the end of the 80s. New Order had now clearly established themselves, and throughout the 80s and into the 90s they remained the top independent band in the UK, staying loyal to Manchester's Factory Records. Their subsequent collaboration with 'hot' New York hip-hop producer Arthur Baker spawned the anti-climactic 'Confusion' (1983) and 'Thieves Like Us' (1984). Both singles continued their preference for the 12-inch format, stretching in excess of six minutes, and stressing their lack of concern for the exposure gained by recording with mainstream radio in mind. *Low-Life* appeared in 1985 and remains their most consistently appealing album to date. While the 12-inch version of *Low-Life*'s 'The Perfect Kiss' was a magnificent single, showing the band at their most inspired and innovative, the collaboration with producer John Robie on the single version of 'Sub-Culture' indicated that their tendency to experiment and 'play around' could also spell disaster. Their next album, 1986's *Brotherhood*, although containing strong tracks such as 'Bizarre Love Triangle', offered nothing unexpected. It was not until the UK Top 5 single 'True Faith' in 1987, produced and co-written by Stephen Hague hot on the heels of his success with the Pet Shop Boys, and accompanied by an award-winning Phillipe Decouffle video, that New Order found themselves satisfying long-term fans and general public alike. The following year Quincy Jones' remix of 'Blue Monday' provided the group with another Top 5 hit.

If the recycling of old songs and proposed 'personal' projects fuelled rumours of a split, then 1989's UK number 1 *Technique* promptly dispelled them. The album, recorded in Ibiza, contained upbeat bass- and drums-dominated tracks that characterized the best of their early output. Its most striking feature, however, was their flirtation with the popular Balearic style, as in the hit single 'Fine Time', which contained lines such as 'I've met a lot of cool chicks, But I've never met a girl with all her own teeth', delivered in a voice that parodied Barry White's notoriously sexist, gravelly vocals of the 70s. Meanwhile, the band had changed significantly as a live act. Their reputation for inconsistency and apathy, as well as their staunch refusal to play encores, was by now replaced with confident, crowd-pleasing hour-long sets. In the summer of 1990 they reached the UK number 1 position with 'World In Motion', accompanied by the England World Cup Squad, with a song that earned the questionable accolade of best football record of all time, and caused a band member to observe, 'this is probably the last straw for Joy Division fans'.

Rather than exploiting their recent successes with endless tours, New Order unexpectedly branched out into various spin-off ventures. Hook formed the hard-rocking Revenge, Sumner joined former Smiths guitarist Johnny Marr in Electronic and Morris/Gilbert recorded an album under the self-effacing title the Other Two. The extra-curricular work prompted persistent rumours that New Order had irrevocably split, but no official announcement or press admission was forthcoming. In the summer of 1991, the band announced that they had reconvened

for a new album, to be produced by Stephen Hague, which was eventually released in 1993. *Republic* consequently met with mixed reviews reflecting critical confusion about their status and direction. While retaining the mix of rock and dance music successfully honed on *Technique*, the tone was decidedly more downbeat, even sombre. Sadly, it arrived too late to help the doomed Factory label.

Following a headlining appearance at that year's Reading Festival, the band's membership returned to varied solo projects, with Hook forming the critically praised Monaco in 1996. In 1998, after five years silence, the four members reconvened for live appearances and to record new material. The first new track to appear, 'Brutal', was featured on the soundtrack of *The Beach*. The band returned to the UK charts in August 2001 with the Top 10 single, 'Crystal'. A new studio album, *Get Ready*, followed in October.

● ALBUMS: *Movement* (Factory 1981) ★★★, *Power, Corruption & Lies* (Factory 1983) ★★★, *Low-Life* (Factory/Qwest 1985) ★★★★, *Brotherhood* (Factory/Qwest 1986) ★★★★, *Technique* (Factory/Qwest 1989) ★★★, *Republic* (London 1993) ★★★★, *Get Ready* (London/Reprise 2001) ★★★.
● COMPILATIONS: *Substance* (Factory/Qwest 1987) ★★★★, *The Peel Sessions* (Strange Fruit 1990) ★★★, *Live In Concert* (Windsong 1992) ★★★, *(The Best Of) New Order* (London 1995) ★★★★★, *(The Rest Of) New Order* (London 1995) ★★★.
● VIDEOS: *Taras Schevenko* (Factory 1983), *Pumped Full Of Drugs* (Factory 1986), *Academy* (Palace Video 1989), *Substance 1989* (Factory/Virgin 1989), *New Order Story* (PolyGram Video 1993), *(The Best Of) New Order* (PolyGram Video 1994), *New Order 3 16* (Warner Music Vision 2001).
● FURTHER READING: *New Order & Joy Division: Pleasures And Wayward Distractions*, Brian Edge. *New Order & Joy Division: Dreams Never End*, Claude Flowers.

# NEW ROMANTICISM

New romanticism emerged in the UK music scene in the early 80s as a direct backlash against the austerity of the punk movement. At various times it became a catch-all term for quite disparate bands working within the pop world, and consequently works better as a description of a specific time rather than sound or style. Where punk railed against life on England's council estates, the new romantics celebrated glamour, ostentatious clothes and hedonism. The coming of age of the video as a promotional tool was important to the development of new romanticism, as were the outlandish haircuts (A Flock Of Seagulls), the frilled shirts (Duran Duran, Spandau Ballet) and the fact that men could be seen wearing mascara (practically everyone involved). Guitars, though present, were subordinate to synthesizers. The movement's early fulcrum was Stevo, whose *Some Bizzare Album* compilation in 1980 introduced such artists as Classix Nouveaux, Blancmange, Depeche Mode and Soft Cell. Centred on London clubs such as Blitz, this new gaggle of groups was at first termed 'futuristic'. The Human League had been active for some time in Sheffield but in a new incarnation perfectly amalgamated simple song ideas with basic keyboard skills to define the essential new romantic blueprint. Adam And The Ants were historically linked with punk, as were, more obliquely, Culture Club, though both found a place on the fringe of the movement as a platform for major chart success. If the most obvious historical ancestor of new romanticism was David Bowie, then Japan were his closest living relatives, aping even his fascination with the Orient. The two biggest stars were undoubtedly Duran Duran and Spandau Ballet. The former wrote classic pop hooks with casual ease for much of the period, though Spandau Ballet were always more visually than aurally appealing, despite the occasional winning single (the melodrama of 'Gold' was resonant enough for P.M. Dawn to make it rap's first new romantic sample). Of less enduring fame or substance were Classix Nouveaux, Visage and A Flock Of Seagulls, despite the latter breaking through in the American market. Nevertheless, several exceptional singles were left behind that effectively defined the times, and it was to no great surprise that the movement was revisited in 1995 with the development of the 'Romo' scene.

● FURTHER READING: *Like Punk Never Happened – Culture Club And The New Pop*, Dave Rimmer.

## NEW WAVE OF BRITISH HEAVY METAL

The names speak for themselves – Iron Maiden, Def Leppard, Saxon, Samson, Venom, Diamond Head, Girlschool and Praying Mantis. These represented only a handful of the bands who found success during the period 1979 to 1981. The phrase was first coined by Geoff Barton at UK magazine *Sounds*, but much credit is also owing to DJ Neal Kay, whose help in giving bands such as Iron Maiden and Praying Mantis (as well as many others) their first break was crucial. EMI Records were quick off the mark and with Kay's help, they produced the compilation album *Metal For Muthas*, which put many bands on the road to fame, and others, including Toad The Wet Sprocket, on the road to obscurity. Well over 200 bands emerged during this period and many released records on their own labels – even more never made it past the rehearsal stage, while others remained strictly 'bedroom' bands. This enthusiasm also helped to revitalize older bands and some, including Gillan and Motörhead, became spearheads for the movement. However, by 1981 the corporate machine began to eat up the talent and American influences crept in, destroying the movement's identity. If, as has often been stated, the movement started with Iron Maiden's *Soundhouse Tapes* EP in 1979, then it would be equally true to suggest that the final nail in its coffin came in September 1981, when Paul Di'Anno left that band. Just like punk in 1977, the ideas and attitude fell victim to clean living and commerciality.

● COMPILATIONS: *Metal For Muthas Volume 1* (EMI 1980) ★★★, *Metal For Muthas Volume 2 Cut Loud* (EMI 1980) ★★, *Brute Force* (MCA 1980) ★★, *New Electric Warriors* (Logo 1980) ★★★, *The N.W.O.B.H.M. '79 Revisited* (Vertigo 1990) ★★,

*N.W.O.B.H.M. Rarities Vol. 1* (British Steel/Cherry Red 1998) ★★★, *N.W.O.B.H.M. Rarities Vol. 2* (British Steel/Cherry Red 1998) ★★★, *N.W.O.B.H.M. Rarities Vol. 3* (British Steel/Cherry Red 1998) ★★★.

## NEWTON, JUICE

b. Judy Kaye Cohen, 18 February 1952, Lakehurst, New Jersey, USA. This singing daughter from a military family spent most of her childhood in Virginia. While completing a formal education in California, she fronted Dixie Peach, a country rock combo that was renamed Silver Spur for their RCA Records albums in the mid-70s. Despite assistance from top Los Angeles session musicians, immediate solo success was dogged by Bonnie Tyler's version of 'It's A Heartache' eclipsing Newton's own, though she gained a US country hit by proxy when the Carpenters covered her self-composed 'Sweet Sweet Smile' in 1978. Two years later, she arrived in *Billboard*'s Top 5 with a revival of Chip Taylor's 'Angel Of The Morning' (her only UK hit) and then 'Queen Of Hearts' (also a hit for Dave Edmunds), while the *Juice* album containing both peaked at number 22. She enjoyed more hits in the pop charts with 'Love's Been A Little Hard On Me', *Quiet Lies* and a 1983 overhaul of the Zombies' 'Tell Her No', but it was the country market that came to provide the bulk of her success. After an encouraging response when she performed 'The Sweetest Thing I've Ever Known' at 1981's annual Country Radio Seminar, this old Silver Spur track was remixed for a single to become a country number 1 the following year. Other genre successes included a reworking of Brenda Lee's 'Break It To Me Gently', Dave Loggins' 'You Make Me Want To Make You Mine', 'Hurt' and a duet with Eddie Rabbitt, 'Born To Each Other'. She later married polo star Tom Goodspeed and concentrated on the nightclub circuit.

● ALBUMS: with Silver Spur *Juice Newton And Silver Spur* (RCA 1975) ★★★, with Silver Spur *After The Dust Settles* (RCA 1977) ★★★, with Silver Spur *Come To Me* (Capitol 1977) ★★, *Well Kept Secret* (Capitol 1978) ★★★, *Take A Heart* (Capitol 1979) ★★★, *Juice* (Capitol 1981) ★★★★, *Quiet Lies* (Capitol 1982) ★★★, *Dirty Looks* (Capitol 1983) ★★★, *Can't Wait All Night* (RCA 1984) ★★★, *Old Flame* (RCA 1986) ★★★, *Emotion* (RCA 1987) ★★★, *Ain't Gonna Cry* (RCA 1989) ★★, *The Trouble With Angels* (River North 1998) ★★, *American Girl* (Renaissance 2000) ★★★, *Every Road Leads Back To You* (Image 2002) ★★★.

● COMPILATIONS: *Collection* (EMI 1983) ★★★, *Greatest Hits* (Capitol 1984) ★★★★, *Greatest Country Hits* (Curb 1990) ★★★.

## NICKS, STEVIE

b. Stephanie Nicks, 26 May 1948, Phoenix, Arizona, USA. When Stevie Nicks joined Fleetwood Mac in January 1975, she not only introduced her talents as a singer and songwriter, but provided a defined focal point during the group's live appearances. A former vocalist with Fritz, a struggling San Francisco band, Nicks moved to Los Angeles with her boyfriend and fellow ex-member Lindsey Buckingham. Together they recorded *Buckingham-Nicks*, a promising but largely neglected album, at the Second City Studio in

Van Nuys. The collection was subsequently used to demonstrate the facilities to Mick Fleetwood. By coincidence, both Nicks and Buckingham were in a nearby room and were introduced to the Fleetwood Mac drummer when he showed interest in their work. Within weeks the duo were invited to join his band to replace the departing Bob Welch. Their arrival brought a change in Fleetwood Mac's commercial fortunes. Nicks provided many of their best-known and successful songs, including the atmospheric 'Rhiannon' and the haunting 'Dreams'. The latter was one of several excellent compositions that graced the multi-million-selling *Rumours*, although the album itself signalled the collapse of two in-house relationships, including that of Buckingham and Nicks.

In 1980, following the release of Fleetwood Mac's much-maligned *Tusk*, the singer began recording a solo album. *Bella Donna*, released the following year, achieved platinum sales and remained on the *Billboard* album chart for over two years. It also spawned two US Top 10 singles in 'Stop Draggin' My Heart Around', a duet with Tom Petty and 'Leather And Lace', which featured former Eagles drummer, Don Henley. A second selection, *The Wild Heart*, followed in 1983 and this bestseller also produced two major hits in 'Stand Back' and 'Nightbird'. Her third album, *Rock A Little*, was less successful, artistically and commercially, and following its release Nicks entered the Betty Ford Clinic to be treated for drug dependency. She then rejoined Fleetwood Mac for *Tango In The Night*, which marked the departure of Lindsey Buckingham. Although his absence has created more space within the band's framework, a revitalized Nicks continued her solo activities, as exemplified by 1989's *The Other Side Of The Mirror*. She rejoined Buckingham in Fleetwood Mac when the *Rumours* line-up reconvened in 1997. A solo box set was released the following year. The star-studded but anodyne *Trouble In Shangri-La* returned Nicks to the US Top 10 in 2001

● ALBUMS: with Lindsey Buckingham *Buckingham-Nicks* (Polydor 1973) ★★, *Bella Donna* (Warners 1981) ★★★★, *The Wild Heart* (Warners 1983) ★★★, *Rock A Little* (Modern 1985) ★★, *The Other Side Of The Mirror* (EMI 1989) ★★★, *Street Angel* (EMI 1994) ★★, *Trouble In Shangri-La* (Warners 2001) ★★.

● COMPILATIONS: *Timespace: The Best Of Stevie Nicks* (EMI 1991) ★★★, *The Enchanted Works Of Stevie Nicks* 3-CD box set (Atlantic 1998) ★★★.

● VIDEOS: *In Concert* (CBS-Fox 1983), *Live At Red Rocks* (Sony Entertainment 1987), *I Can't Wait* (Weaver-Finch 1996).

## NIGHTINGALES

After a series of low-key UK school bands, Robert Lloyd (b. 1959, Cannock, Staffordshire, England) formed the Prefects - one of the earliest punk bands - who toured with the Clash. They split up in 1979 and Lloyd assembled the Nightingales using the best of the musicians who had passed through the ranks of the Prefects. The first of many subsequent line-ups comprised Lloyd, Alan and Paul Apperley, Joe Crow and Eamonn Duffy. They were ably championed by BBC Radio 1 disc jockey John Peel,

for whom Lloyd recorded more sessions under various guises than any other artist. The Nightingales' debut single, 'Idiot Strength', was released in 1981 on the band's own Vindaloo label in association with Rough Trade Records. Joe Crow then departed and his replacements, Nick Beales and Andy Lloyd, brought a totally different sound to the band. Cherry Red Records picked them up and the band's career began in earnest. Lloyd soon established himself as one of the more interesting lyricists on the independent chart. Most of his tirades were draped in humour: 'I'm too tired to do anything today, but tomorrow I'll start my diet, and answer some of my fan mail ('Elvis: The Last Ten Days'). The lack of success of subsequent releases led Lloyd and friends to the new Red Flame label started by Dave Kitson, the promoter of the Moonlight Club in London's Hampstead. Still unhappy with the way record companies were handling his band's career, Lloyd decided to reactivate the Vindaloo label. Ironically, this led to the demise of the Nightingales as Lloyd needed to spend more time as songwriter, producer and label boss for his relatively successful roster of artists such as We've Got A Fuzzbox And We're Gonna Use It and comedian Ted Chippington. When Fuzzbox toured America, taking the Nightingales' keyboard player with them, Lloyd dissolved the band and concentrated on a solo career. The Nightingales' legacy was wrapped up in 1991 with a compilation album for Mau Mau Records with sleeve-notes written by a still devoted John Peel.

● ALBUMS: *Pigs On Purpose* (Cherry Red 1982) ★★★, *Hysterics* (Red Flame 1983) ★★★, *In The Good Old Country Ways* (Vindaloo 1986) ★★★, *The Peel Sessions EP* (Strange Fruit 1988) ★★★.

● COMPILATIONS: *Just A Job* (Vindaloo 1983) ★★★, *What A Scream* (Mau Mau 1991) ★★★, *Pissed & Potless: The Definitive Nightingales Collection* (Cherry Red 2001) ★★★.

## NINE BELOW ZERO

A powerful and exciting UK R&B band of the late 70s, the group took its name from a song by Sonny Boy 'Rice Miller' Williamson and was led by guitarist/singer Dennis Greaves and virtuoso harmonica player Mark Feltham. With Peter Clark (bass, vocals) and Kenny Bradley (drums), Feltham recorded the EP *Packed Fair And Square* (1979). This led to a recording contract with A&M Records and a live recording at London's Marquee Club where Nine Below Zero had a residency. The producer was Glyn Johns. With Stix Burkey replacing Bradley, the second album included some original songs while *Third Degree* was a minor UK hit. The band dissolved in the mid-80s as Feltham concentrated on session work and Greaves went on to a solo career and became a member of the Truth. However, Feltham revived Nine Below Zero at the end of the decade, signing a new recording contract with the China label. By the mid-90s they were recording with the mighty A&M when roots blues was experiencing a small rebirth and at the end of the decade they had settled down with Indigo, a small specialist blues label which would seem to be better suited to their particular aspirations. The band is excellent in a live setting, and continues to work in the UK and Europe at festivals and small clubs. The 2000 line-up featured the ever-present Greaves together with Billy 'Boy' Miskimmin (harmonica), and the rhythm section who worked with the late Rory Gallagher, Gerry McAvoy (bass) and Brendan O'Neill (drums).

● ALBUMS: *Live At The Marquee* (A&M 1980) ★★★★, *Don't Point Your Finger* (A&M 1981) ★★★, *Third Degree* (A&M 1982) ★★★★, *Live At The Venue* (China 1990) ★★★, *Off The Hook* (China 1992) ★★★, *Live In London* (Indigo 1995) ★★★, *Ice Station Zero* (A&M 1996) ★★, *Covers* (Zed 1997) ★★, *Give Me No Lip Child* (Indigo 2000) ★★★★.

## NITZER EBB

This electronic-based UK band was formed by Douglas McCarthy (b. 1 September 1967, Chelmsford, Essex, England; vocals, guitar) and Bon Harris (b. Vaughan David Harris, 12 August 1965, Chelmsford, Essex, England; percussion, vocals, guitar). Frustrated by their environment at school in Chelmsford, and inspired by bands such as D.A.F., Bauhaus and the Birthday Party, they began their first experiments with synthesizers and drum machines in 1983. They were joined in their strictly amateur pursuits by schoolmate David Gooday. They had summoned enough experience and confidence to release their first single the next year, 'Isn't It Funny How Your Body Works', on Power Of Voice Communications. They were nothing if not prolific, releasing a further five singles over the next 12 months, which led to a contract with the premier UK independent stable, Mute Records, and Geffen Records in the USA. Their first album reached the shelves in 1987, *That Total Age*, home to surging minimalist aggression, and the beginning of a long-term relationship with producer Flood, who would remix the single 'Join In The Chant'. On Gooday's departure Julian Beeston (b. 27 September 1967) was enrolled. After a lengthy European trek with Depeche Mode, the band recorded *Belief*, and in 1989 followed up their world tour with *Showtime*. Their third album revealed a swing in attitude, with music that was less confrontational and more consumer-friendly. This was particularly true in the USA, where the single 'Fun To Be Had' peaked at number 2 on the dance chart. Nitzer Ebb's later albums confirmed their popularity with fans and a previously reluctant press. As McCarthy puts it: 'With the advent of *Ebbhead*, I think we've managed to twist listenability around to our way of thinking'. McCarthy and Harris were joined on 1995's *Big Hit* by percussionist Jason Payne. Nitzer Ebb was then put on hold as the members worked on solo projects.

● ALBUMS: *That Total Age* (Mute/Geffen 1987) ★★, *Belief* (Mute/Geffen 1989) ★★, *Showtime* (Mute/Geffen 1990) ★★★, *Ebbhead* (Mute/Geffen 1991) ★★★, *Big Hit* (Mute/Geffen 1995) ★★★.

## No FX

No FX was formed in Berkeley, California, USA, in 1983. Immediately, it was obvious that they were one of the few bands on the hardcore scene to embrace humorous lyrical fare to genuinely

amusing effect. The original trio of Fat Mike (b. Mike Burkett; vocals, bass), Eric Melvin (guitar, vocals) and Erik Ghint (b. Erik Sandin; drums) was joined by guitarist Dave Cassilas in 1987. They set their agenda with their debut EP for Mystic Records, *The P.M.R.C. Can Suck On This*. Afterwards, they addressed accusations about being on this most unfashionable of labels (which was completely injudicious in releasing material by any hardcore band that came its way) with the *So What If We're On Mystic!* EP. It was via a contract with Epitaph Records and the *Ribbed* album that No FX became a productive unit in terms of worldwide sales. New guitarist Steve Kidwiler featured on both *S&M Airlines* and *Ribbed*, the latter an unblemished collection of genuinely funny songs, notably the male-hygiene-bonding epic, 'Shower Days'. The full musicianship and clean production only helped to illuminate their witty, everyday intrigues, with lyrics written by Fat Mike, a graduate of San Francisco University. El Hefe (b. Aaron Abeyta; guitar, trumpet) replaced Kidwiler in 1991, making his debut on *The Longest Line* EP. With the breakthrough of acts such as the Offspring and Rancid, No FX, significantly older than either, became a mainstream act by the mid-90s, though in truth they had not altered musical direction since their inception. Instead, each album offered increasingly savage witticisms and a disciplined but flexible musical attack, able to vary pace from anything between outright thrash and ska. The band has also released several EPs and albums on Fat Mike's own Fat Wreck Chords label.

● ALBUMS: *Liberal Animation* (Fat Wreck Chords 1988) ★★, *S&M Airlines* (Epitaph 1989) ★★, *Ribbed* (Epitaph 1990) ★★★, *White Trash Two Heebs And A Bean* (Epitaph 1992) ★★★, *Punk In Drublic* (Epitaph 1994) ★★, *I Heard They Suck Live!!* (Fat Wreck Chords 1995) ★★, *Heavy Petting Zoo* (Epitaph 1996) ★★, *So Long And Thanks For All The Shoes* (Epitaph 1997) ★★, *Pump Up The Valuum* (Epitaph 2000) ★★★.

● COMPILATIONS: *Maximum RockNRoll* (Mystic 1992) ★★, *45 Or 46 Songs That Weren't Good Enough To Go On Our Other Records* (Fat Wreck Chords 2002) ★★.

● VIDEOS: *10 Years Of Fuckin' Up* (Fat Wreck Chords 1994).

## NOMI, KLAUS

b. Klaus Sperber, 1944, Bavaria, Germany, d. 6 August 1983, New York, USA. Famed for his Mephistophelean make-up and piercing tenor voice, Sperber claimed erroneously to have worked in the 70s as both a professional opera singer and as David Bowie's dresser. Brought up in West Berlin he developed his love of opera as a child extra in various productions and, following a spell at the Berlin Music School, as an usher at the Berlin (Deutsche) Opera. Sperber moved to New York in the early 70s where he worked as a Cordon Bleu pastry chef, but also began developing his Klaus Nomi alter ego. He also appeared in Anders Grafstrom's underground classic, *The Long Island Four*. By 1979, Nomi was touring in Europe and the

USA as a highly idiosyncratic cabaret act, performing barely recognizable electronic reworkings of everything from Saint Saens' 'Samson And Delilah' and Donna Summer's 'I Feel Love' to Chubby Checker's 'The Twist'. An appearance on *Saturday Night Live* on December 15 backing David Bowie introduced his startling image to a wider public.

In 1980, he signed to RCA Records and released a version of Elvis Presley's 'Can't Help Falling In Love' as a single. He worked with Man Parrish, the New York electro and hi-NRG producer, on his self-titled debut album. Nomi was well received in the US, becoming a regular guest on *Saturday Night Live* and starring in the movie *Urgh! A Music War*. In England, his openness about his homosexuality and outrageous dress sense aligned him with the New Romantic movement. He seemed to be playing upon his goofball appeal with American audiences on his second album, *Simple Man*, which included a version of 'Ding Dong! The Witch Is Dead' from *The Wizard Of Oz*. The record closed with Henry Purcell's 'Death' leading into an arrangement of John Dowland's 'If My Complaints Could Passion Move' – an oblique and moving eulogy to the first victims of AIDS. The disease took his own life the following year – Nomi was one of the first celebrity victims of the disease. Several posthumous compilation albums have been released, and a recording of one of his early concert performances appeared in Germany.

● ALBUMS: *Klaus Nomi* (RCA 1981) ★★★, *Simple Man* (RCA 1982) ★, *Klaus Nomi Encore!* (RCA 1983) ★★, *In Concert* (RCA 1986) ★★★,
● COMPILATIONS: *Collection* (RCA 1990) ★★★, *Eclipsed: The Best Of Klaus Nomi* (Razor & Tie 1999) ★★★.
● FILMS: *Mr. Mike's Mondo Video* (1979), *Urgh! A Music War* (1981).

## NOTTING HILLBILLIES

On 31 May 1986, Mark Knopfler (b. 12 August 1949, Glasgow, Scotland) played a low-key gig at the Grove pub in Holbeck, Leeds, with old friends Steve Phillips (b. Nicholas Stephen Phillips, 18 February 1948, London, England) and Brendan Croker (b. 15 August 1953, Bradford, Yorkshire, England). They were billed as the Notting Hillbillies and each received the princely sum of £22 for their performance. Phillips first met Knopfler in 1968 when both interviewed a local blues and country guitarist (also called Steve Phillips) for the *Yorkshire Post*. As both journalists played guitar they formed the Duolian String Pickers duo and played together during the late 60s. They split when Knopfler went to university in 1970. When he finished studying three years later he went to London and eventually formed Dire Straits. Meanwhile, Phillips formed the Steve Phillips Juke Band to play rockabilly. In 1976, Croker met Phillips and when the Juke Band split they toured as Nev And Norriss. Four years later, Phillips temporarily retired from music to concentrate on art, and Croker eventually formed the 5 O'Clock Shadows.

In 1986, Knopfler, flushed with success through Dire Straits, decided the time was right to do something a little different and all three musicians came together.

Dire Straits manager Ed Bicknell was recruited as drummer (he had previously played in Mogul Thrash) and with backing musicians such as Guy Fletcher (guitar), Paul Franklin (pedal steel) and Marcus Cliff (bass, of the 5 O'Clock Shadows), they set out on a tour. They made just one album before returning to concentrate on their main bands.

● ALBUMS: *Missing ... Presumed Having A Good Time* (Vertigo 1990) ★★.
● VIDEOS: *Notting Hillbillies: Missing* (Channel 5 1990).

## NWOBHM

(see New Wave Of British Heavy Metal)

## NYLONS

Formed in Toronto, Canada, in 1978, the Nylons' original line-up comprised four erstwhile actors: Paul Cooper (tenor), Marc Connors (d. March 1991, baritone), Dennis Simpson (bass) and Claude Morrison (tenor), although Simpson was quickly replaced by Ralph Cole who in turn was replaced by Arnold Robinson (b. Wilmington, North Carolina, USA). The latter had spent several years in Sonny Turner's Platters (aka Sounds Unlimited). Originally harmonizing a cappella, their material was one third original, one third classic doo-wop and one third contemporary pop covers. Their 1982 debut album featured bare rhythmic accompaniment underpinning the group's elegant harmonies. *One Size Fits All* housed the single 'Silhouettes', which gained a number of plays on mainstream US radio. The Tokens' 'The Lion Sleeps Tonight' and Steam's 'Na Na Hey Hey Kiss Him Goodbye' were reprised on *Seamless* and *Happy Together*, respectively, and again sold well in their domestic market, while the latter single also breached the US charts at number 12 in 1987. Their version of the Turtles' 'Happy Together' (which gave their fourth album its title), peaked at number 75 in the US charts. Paul Cooper departed in 1991 to be replaced by Micah Barnes, but by the following year Marc Connors had died from viral pneumonia, prompting a further line-up shuffle, with Billy Newton-Davis stepping into the breach. A new deal with BMG in Canada and Scotti Bros in the USA ensued before further line-up changes brought in Garth Mosbaugh for Barnes and Gavin Hope for Newton-Davis in 1994, then Mark Cassius for Hope three years later. Despite the personnel changes, the Nylons remain a highly popular touring unit worldwide.

● ALBUMS: *The Nylons* (Attic 1982) ★★★, *One Size Fits All* (Attic 1982) ★★★, *Seamless* (Attic 1984) ★★★, *Happy Together* (Attic 1987) ★★, *Rockapella* (Attic 1989) ★★, *Four On The Floor* (Attic 1991) ★★, *Live To Love* (BMG 1992) ★★, *Harmony – The Christmas Songs* (BMG 1994) ★★, *Because ...* (BMG 1994) ★★★, *Run For Cover* (BMG 1995) ★★, *Fabric Of Life* (Shoreline 1997) ★★★, *Wish For You* (Lightyear 2000) ★★★.
● COMPILATIONS: *Illustrious: A Collection Of Classic Hits* aka *Perfect Fit* (Attic 1993) ★★★.

## O'CONNOR, HAZEL

b. 16 May 1955, Coventry, England. O'Connor's introduction to showbusiness involved working as a dancer and started with a minor movie role in *Girls Come First*. At the close of the 70s, she signed to the Albion label and issued the single 'Ee-I-Adio', which failed to sell. Her profile increased when she appeared in the film *Breaking Glass*, a melodramatic portrayal of a fictional rock star. O'Connor's aggressive singing style and confrontational appearance was used to good effect on the Tony Visconti-produced 'Eighth Day' (complete with 'robotic' intonation) which reached the UK Top 5 in 1980. The following year, she registered two further Top 10 singles, 'D-Days' and the uncharacteristic ballad 'Will You'. Various disputes with her record company and management slowed down her career. In 1984, she recorded *Smile* for RCA Records but the record sold poorly and the label declined to renew her option. O'Connor subsequently appeared in the musical *Girlfriends* in 1987, before relocating to Los Angeles to pursue her acting career. She moved to Co Wicklow, Ireland in 1990. In the late 90s she was touring her one-woman musical show, *Beyond Breaking Glass*.

● ALBUMS: *Breaking Glass* film soundtrack (A&M 1980) ★★, *Sons And Lovers* (A&M 1980) ★★, *Glass Houses* (A&M 1980) ★★, *Cover Plus* (Albion 1981) ★★, *Smile* (RCA 1984) ★★, *Live In Berlin* (Start 1997) ★.

● FURTHER READING: *Hazel O'Connor: Uncovered Plus*, Hazel O'Connor.

● FILMS: *Breaking Glass* (1980).

## O'DONNELL, DANIEL

b. 12 December 1961, Kincasslagh, County Donegal, Eire. O'Donnell is without doubt the biggest-selling act in history in the musical genre known as 'Country 'n' Irish'. His success can be attributed to the fact that he is a clean-cut and gimmick-free vocalist with leanings towards sentimental MOR material. In musical terms what O'Donnell records is unadventurous, yet his immense popularity makes it clear that his output has been brilliantly targeted.

O'Donnell first emerged in the UK in 1985, although by this point he was already popular in Ireland. His first attempts at singing came when he worked as a backing vocalist in the band that backed his sister, folk/country singer Margo, during the early 80s, and his popularity among the female audiences quickly increased. After a handful of early recordings (later released after he came to fame as 'The Boy From Donegal'), he signed to Michael Clerkin's Ritz Records, an Irish label based in London, and *Two Sides Of Daniel O'Donnell* was released in 1985. It was

promoted by the first in a continuing series of nationwide UK tours that attracted capacity audiences (largely composed of fans of artists such as the late Jim Reeves – O'Donnell usually features in his stage show a medley of songs connected with Reeves).

In 1986, came a second O'Donnell release, *I Need You*, which the following March became his first album to reach the UK country charts. That year's album *Don't Forget To Remember* (featuring a cover version of the hit by the Bee Gees as its title track) was O'Donnell's first to enter the UK country chart at number 1, a feat he repeated with his five subsequent original albums, although the next one to be released in chronological terms, *The Boy From Donegal*, consisted mainly of material recorded in 1984 before he signed to Ritz, and was released in the UK by Prism Leisure. In 1988, Ritz licensed O'Donnell's next release, *From The Heart*, to Telstar Records, a television marketing company, and as well as entering the UK country chart at number 1, the album also reached the UK pop album chart in the autumn of that year, while a video, *Daniel O'Donnell Live In Concert*, was released. The following year brought *Thoughts Of Home*, an album and video that were both heavily advertised on television by Telstar – the album made the Top 40 of the pop chart and the video became O'Donnell's first to reach the UK Music Video chart; once again, all his subsequent video releases have featured in the latter chart, which the original *Live In Concert* also entered in the wake of *Thoughts From Home*.

By 1990, O'Donnell was back with an album, *Favourites*, and a companion video, *TV Show Favourites*, which was composed of material filmed for a hugely successful Irish television series. However, of far greater interest in 1990 was the news that he was making an album in Nashville with noted producer Allen Reynolds (who had enjoyed major success with Don Williams, Crystal Gayle, Kathy Mattea and latterly, Garth Brooks). Released in late 1990, *The Last Waltz* was somewhat closer to genuine country music than its predecessors, and once again entered the UK country album charts at the top and charted strongly in the UK pop equivalent. During 1991, it was decided that nearly all of O'Donnell's album catalogue was MOR rather than country, and at a stroke, the UK country album chart – in which O'Donnell usually occupied the majority of the Top 10 places – hardly featured his albums at all. This produced an avalanche of complaints (including one from a nun) and public demonstrations urging that the decision be reversed and his albums be reinstated in the country list, which eventually occurred in late 1991. Another release, *The Very Best Of Daniel O'Donnell*, a compilation composed partly of previously released items along with some newly recorded material, continued O'Donnell's remarkable success story. His imported albums have sold prodigiously in areas with populations of Irish extraction, and several concert appearances, including one at New York's Carnegie Hall in 1991, have been commercial triumphs.

During the 90s O'Donnell attempted to conquer the

gospel market, although both *Songs Of Inspiration* and *I Believe* proved to be lacklustre collections. In April 1998, O'Donnell finally broached the UK Top 10 with the charity single 'Give A Little Love', achieving the biggest hit of his career. 'The Magic Is There' and 'The Way Dreams Are' came close to repeating the success, debuting at number 16 and 18 respectively. O'Donnell ended his long association with Ritz in 2001, signing to the newly formed Rosette Records label.

● ALBUMS: *Two Sides Of Daniel O'Donnell* (Ritz 1985) ★★★, *I Need You* (Ritz 1986) ★★★, *Don't Forget To Remember* (Ritz 1987) ★★★, *The Boy From Donegal* 1984 recording (Ritz 1987) ★★★, *From The Heart* (Telstar 1988) ★★★, *Thoughts Of Home* (Telstar 1989) ★★★, *Favourites* (Ritz 1990) ★★★, *The Last Waltz* (Ritz 1990) ★★★, *Follow Your Dream* (Ritz 1992) ★★★, *A Date With Daniel Live* (Ritz 1993) ★★★, *Especially For You* (Ritz 1994) ★★★, *Christmas With Daniel* (Ritz 1994) ★★, with Mary Duff *Timeless* (Ritz 1996) ★★★, *Songs Of Inspiration* (Ritz 1996) ★★, *I Believe* (Ritz 1997) ★★★, *Love Songs* (Ritz 1998) ★★★, *Faith & Inspiration* (Ritz 2000) ★★★, *Live, Laugh, Love* (Rosette 2001) ★★★.

● COMPILATIONS: *The Very Best Of Daniel O'Donnell* (Ritz 1991) ★★★★, *The Classic Collection* (Ritz 1995) ★★★★, *Irish Collection* (Ritz 1996) ★★★, *Greatest Hits* (Ritz 1999) ★★★, *Heartbreakers* (Music Club 2000) ★★★.

● VIDEOS: *Live In Concert* (Ritz 1988), *Thoughts Of Home* (Telstar Video 1989), *TV Show Favourites* (Ritz 1990), *An Evening With Daniel O'Donnell* (Ritz 1990), *Follow Your Dream* (Ritz 1992), *And Friends Live* (Ritz 1993), *Just For You* (Ritz 1994), *Christmas With Daniel O'Donnell* (Ritz 1996), *The Gospel Show: Live From The Point* (Ritz 1998), *Give A Little Love* (Ritz 1998), *The Daniel O'Donnell Show* (Rosette 2001).

● FURTHER READING: *Danny Boy: A Life Of Daniel O'Donnell*, Andrew Vaughan. *Daniel O'Donnell: My Story*, Daniel O'Donnell with Eddie Rowley.

## O'HARA, MARY MARGARET

b. Toronto, Ontario, Canada. O'Hara's meagre recorded output is the source of much dismay among fans of her mesmerising songs and astonishing soprano voice. After graduating from Ontario Art College in the mid-70s, she began singing with the rock bands Dollars and Songship. The latter renamed themselves Go Deo Chorus on O'Hara's suggestion, and soon developed a reputation as a powerful live act. O'Hara was the band's focal point as both chief songwriter and a highly eccentric lead singer. Although she left the band in 1983, a demo tape featuring several of her songs came to the attention of Virgin Records. The following year they signed O'Hara as a solo artist. Things soon began to go awry after such an auspicious start, however, as fraught sessions for her debut album saw O'Hara falling out with producers and her record company owing to her highly unconventional approach to recording. The situation was rescued by the intervention of composer Michael Brook, who stepped in and mixed the songs to both artist and record company's satisfaction. *Miss America* was finally released in 1988. The album's

stunning fusion of jazz, soul and pop earned O'Hara widespread acclaim, with critics comparing her unconventional song structures and swooping vocals to the work of singers such as Tim Buckley and Van Morrison. Although there was not a bad track on the album, 'Keeping You In Mind' and the hypnotic 'You Will Be Loved Again' stood out in particular. The four-track *Christmas E.P.*, including her own 'Christmas Evermore', followed in 1991, but since that release, O'Hara's solo career has remained on extended hold. She has appeared as guest vocalist on albums by artists including the Henrys (with whom she frequently sings live), Morrissey, This Mortal Coil, Walkabouts and Holly Cole, and also contributed to the Kurt Weill and Vic Chesnutt tribute albums. O'Hara, who is the sister of television comedienne Catherine O'Hara, has also worked in film as an actress and soundtrack composer.

● ALBUMS: *Miss America* (Virgin 1988) ★★★★, *Christmas E.P.* mini-album (Virgin 1991) ★★★, *Apartment Hunting* film soundtrack (Maplemusic 2002) ★★★.

● FILMS: *The Hunter* (1980), *Candy Mountain* (1987), *The Events Leading Up To My Death* (1992), *Apartment Hunting* (1999).

## O'NEAL, ALEXANDER

b. 15 November 1953, Natchez, Mississippi, USA. O'Neal was one of the best-known soul crooners of the late 80s. In 1978, he joined Flyte Tyme with future producers Jimmy Jam And Terry Lewis. The group (as Time) became the backing band for Prince, although O'Neal was soon dismissed for insubordination. During the early 80s, he began a solo career as a vocalist, making his first recordings with Jam and Lewis producing in 1984. The resulting album was issued by the local Tabu label, and contained R&B hits with 'A Broken Heart Can Mend', 'Innocent' (a duet with Cherrelle) and 'If You Were Here Tonight'. The latter reached the UK Top 20 in 1986, after Cherrelle's 'Saturday Love' (which featured O'Neal) had been an even bigger success there. His career was interrupted by treatment for drug and alcohol addiction, but O'Neal broke through to the mainstream US audience in 1987/8 with his second album and the singles 'Fake', 'Criticize' and 'Never Knew Love Like This', another collaboration with Cherrelle. He remained very popular in the UK with live performances (including a Prince's Trust concert) and a BBC Television special, and 'Criticize' reaching the Top 5.

When, in 1991, O'Neal released his first album of new material for three years, it went straight into the UK Top 5. Jam and Lewis were again the producers. O'Neal's popularity steadily waned during the mid-to-late 90s, and by the time of 1996's *Lovers Again* (released in America in 1998) he was no longer working with Jam And Lewis. After an extended hiatus from the recording scene, O'Neal returned in 2002 with *Saga Of A Married Man*.

● ALBUMS: *Alexander O'Neal* (Tabu 1985) ★★★, *Hearsay* (Tabu 1987) ★★★★, *My Gift To You* (Tabu/A&M 1988) ★★★, *All True Man* (Tabu/Epic 1991) ★★★★, *Love Makes No Sense* (Tabu/A&M

1993) ★★★★, *Lovers Again* (One World/Ichiban Premier 1996) ★★★, *Saga Of A Married Man* (Zinc/Eagle 2002) ★★★.
● COMPILATIONS: *All Mixed Up* (Tabu 1987) ★★★, *This Thing Called Love: The Greatest Hits Of Alexander O'Neal* (Tabu 1992) ★★★★, *The Best Of Alexander O'Neal* (Tabu/Motown 1995) ★★★.

## OCEAN, BILLY

b. Leslie Sebastian Charles, 21 January 1950, Trinidad, West Indies. Raised in England, Ocean worked as a session singer simultaneously with his employment at the Dagenham Ford Motor Company plant, before being signed by the GTO label as a solo artist. His early UK hits included the number 2 singles 'Love Really Hurts Without You' (1976) and 'Red Light Spells Danger' (1977), two purposeful, if derivative, performances. The singer's subsequent releases fared less well, and for four years between 1980 and 1984, Ocean was absent from the UK charts. Paradoxically, it was during this period that he began to win an audience in America. Ocean moved there at the turn of the decade and several R&B successes prepared the way for 'Caribbean Queen (No More Love On The Run)', his first national US pop number 1. Now signed to the Jive Records label, this million-selling 1984 single introduced an impressive run of hits, including two more US chart toppers, 'There'll Be Sad Songs (To Make You Cry)' (1986) and 'Get Outta My Dreams, Get Into My Car' (1988). Despite securing a UK number 1 in 1986 with 'When The Going Gets Tough, The Tough Get Going' (which was featured in the movie *The Jewel Of The Nile*), Ocean's luck in Britain constantly fluctuated. However, his popular appeal secured him three UK Top 5 albums during this period, including the *Greatest Hits* collection in 1989. 'When The Going Gets Tough, The Tough Get Going' was later a UK hit for Irish boy band Boyzone.
● ALBUMS: *Billy Ocean* (GTO 1977) ★★, *City Limit* (GTO 1980) ★★, *Nights (Feel Like Getting Down)* (GTO 1981) ★★★, *Inner Feelings* (GTO 1982) ★★★, *Suddenly* (Jive 1984) ★★★, *Love Zone* (Jive 1986) ★★, *Tear Down These Walls* (Jive 1988) ★★, *Time To Move On* (Jive 1993) ★★, *L.I.F.E.* (Jive 1997) ★★.
● COMPILATIONS: *Greatest Hits* (Jive 1989) ★★★, *Lover Boy* (Spectrum 1993) ★★★.

## ODYSSEY

Formed in New York City, vocalists Lillian, Louise and Carmen Lopez were originally known as the Lopez Sisters. Their parents came from the Virgin Islands, but they were born and raised in Stamford, Connecticut, USA. Carmen left the group in 1968 and was replaced by Tony Reynolds (b. Manila), who, after the group's first album, was replaced by Bill McEachern. Odyssey's 1977 release, 'Native New Yorker', reached the US Top 20, but the song proved more popular in the UK where it peaked at number 5. It was not until 1980 that Odyssey appeared again in the UK chart with the first of several UK hits. 'Use It Up And Wear It Out' topped the chart in June of that year, while the beautiful, soulful ballad, 'If You're Looking For A Way Out', gave them their third Top 10 hit. Two more effortless pop/soul offerings,

'Going Back To My Roots' (1981) and 'Inside Out' (1982), reached the Top 5. However, the lack of sustained success at home hampered the group's wider progress and they latterly broke up.
● ALBUMS: *Odyssey* (RCA 1977) ★★★, *Hollywood Party Tonight* (RCA 1978) ★★★, *Hang Together* (RCA 1980) ★★★, *I Got The Melody* (RCA 1981) ★★, *Happy Together* (RCA 1982) ★★, *A Piping Journey* (Mannick Music 1987) ★★.
● COMPILATIONS: *Best Of Odyssey* (RCA 1981) ★★★, *Magic Touch Of Odyssey* (Telstar 1982) ★★, *Magic Moments With Odyssey* (RCA 1984) ★★★, *Greatest Hits* (Stylus 1987) ★★★, *Greatest Hits* (RCA 1990) ★★★.

## OMD

This UK synthesizer pop duo was formed by Paul Humphreys (b. 27 February 1960, Liverpool, England) and Andy McCluskey (b. 24 June 1959, Liverpool, England). Originally combining in school band Equinox they moved on through VCL XI and Hitlerz Underpantz, and finally the Id. When that band broke up in 1978, McCluskey spent a short time with Dalek I Love You before he and Humphreys, together with Paul Collister, performed live in October 1978 under their full title Orchestral Manoeuvres In The Dark. Tony Wilson of Factory Records became interested in the band, releasing their debut 'Electricity'. It was quickly re-released when Virgin Records subsidiary DinDisc signed them. Its success subsequently allowed the band the chance to build their studio. They replaced their four-track recorder ('Winston') with real personnel Malcolm Holmes (ex-Equinox and the Id) and Dave Hughes (Dalek I Love You). 'Red Frame/White Light' (1980) was released as a single to preface the band's first, self-titled album. Their breakthrough, however, came with the re-recorded 'Messages' and was followed by the UK Top 10 hit 'Enola Gay', and its familiar nuclear war sentiments. *Organisation* followed, with Martin Cooper replacing Dave Hughes shortly afterwards. The more sophisticated *Architecture & Morality* showed a new romanticism, particularly in the UK Top 5 singles 'Souvenir', 'Joan Of Arc' and 'Maid Of Orleans'. *Dazzle Ships* (1983) was a flawed attempt at progression, highlighting dilemmas forced on them by popularity and DinDisc's collapse (the band transferred to Virgin). *Junk Culture* faced similar critical disdain, despite boasting the presence of the Top 5 single, 'Locomotion'. *Crush* was a less orchestrated and more commercial affair, featuring the return of political commentary alongside the permanent insertion of Graham and Neil Weir into the line-up. The band enjoyed a surprise US Top 5 hit in 1986 with 'If You Leave', taken from the soundtrack of the movie *Pretty In Pink*. *The Pacific Age* was premiered on another of the band's frequent worldwide touring endeavours, but it was obvious from its chart position that their domestic popularity was slipping. The six-piece line-up was proving too cumbersome and the Weir brothers departed shortly afterwards. The rift was compounded when Holmes and Cooper and, more importantly, Humphreys, joined the list of departures. McCluskey retained the name and, after a long restorative period, resurfaced in 1991 with the UK number 3 hit 'Sailing On The Seven Seas', and the Top 10 follow-up 'Pandora's Box'. The resultant album harked back to the era of *Architecture & Morality* with the use of choral effects. Meanwhile, Humphreys, Holmes and Cooper formed a new band under the name the Listening Pool.

McCluskey continued to release records under the OMD moniker into the 1990s, though failing to match the commercial success he enjoyed with Humphries during the mid-80s. He enjoyed more reward in the new millennium as the musical mastermind behind girl group, Atomic Kitten.

● ALBUMS: *Orchestral Manoeuvres In The Dark* (DinDisc 1980) ★★★, *Organisation* (DinDisc 1980) ★★★, *Architecture & Morality* (DinDisc 1981) ★★★, *Dazzle Ships* (Virgin 1983) ★★, *Junk Culture* (Virgin 1984) ★★★, *Crush* (Virgin 1985) ★★★, *The Pacific Age* (Virgin 1986) ★★, *Sugar Tax* (Virgin 1991) ★★, *Liberator* (Virgin 1993) ★★★, *Universal* (Virgin 1996) ★★★.

● COMPILATIONS: *The Best Of OMD* (Virgin 1988) ★★★★, *The OMD Singles* (Virgin 1998) ★★★★, *The Peel Sessions 1979–1983* (Virgin 2000) ★★★, *Navigation: The OMD B-Sides* (Virgin 2001) ★★★.

● FURTHER READING: *Orchestral Manoeuvres In The Dark*, Mike West.

## ORANGE JUICE

Formed in Scotland at the end of the 70s, this engaging and, in some quarters, revered, pop band comprised Edwyn Collins (b. 23 August 1959, Edinburgh, Scotland; vocals, lead guitar), James Kirk (vocals, rhythm guitar), David McClymont (bass) and Steven Daly (drums). They began their career on the cult independent label Postcard Records, where they issued some of the best pop records of the early 80s, including 'Blue Boy' and 'Falling And Laughing'. Collins' coy vocal and innocent romanticism gave them a charm that was matched by strong musicianship. After signing to Polydor Records they issued *You Can't Hide Your Love Forever*, a highly accomplished effort that augured well for the future. At that point, the band suffered an internal shake-up with Kirk and Daly replaced by Malcolm Ross and Zeke Manyika. *Rip It Up* was another strong work, and the insistent title track reached the UK Top 10. Further musical differences saw the band reduced to Collins and Manyika as they completed an energetic mini-album, *Texas Fever*, and an eponymous third album, which included the wistful 'What Presence?'. Collins subsequently recorded a couple of singles with Paul Quinn, after which he embarked on a solo career that only began to fulfil its early promise in the mid-90s. Ross joined the line-up of Roddy Frame's Aztec Camera. Manyika also spawned solo projects on Polydor and Parlophone Records.

● ALBUMS: *You Can't Hide Your Love Forever* (Polydor 1982) ★★★, *Rip It Up* (Polydor 1982) ★★★★, *Texas Fever* mini-album (Polydor 1984) ★★★, *The Orange Juice* (Polydor 1984) ★★★, *Ostrich Churchyard* (Postcard 1992) ★★.

● COMPILATIONS: *In A Nutshell* (Polydor 1985)

★★★, *The Very Best Of Orange Juice* (Polydor 1992) ★★★★, *The Heather's On Fire* (Postcard 1993) ★★★.

● VIDEOS: *Dada With Juice* (Hendring Music Video 1989).

## OSBORNE, JEFFREY

b. 9 March 1948, Providence, Rhode Island, USA. The son of a jazz trumpeter, Osborne sang with L.T.D (Love, Togetherness And Devotion) from 1970 until its disbandment 12 years later. However, he remained subject to the L.T.D. contract with A&M Records for whom he recorded five albums as a solo artist. Under George Duke's supervision, the first of these contained the singles 'I Really Don't Need No Light' and 'On The Wings Of Love' which both reached the US Top 40. The latter was a 'sleeper' hit in the UK, after 'Don't You Get So Mad' and the title track of *Stay With Me Tonight* had made headway there. *Don't Stop* featured a duet with Joyce Kennedy – duplicated on her *Lookin' For Trouble*, which was produced by Osborne. *Emotional* was a strong album, as were the subsequent singles, one of which, 'You Should Be Mine (The Woo Woo Song)', reached US number 13. For two years, Osborne chose, perhaps unwisely, to rest on his laurels, although 'Love Power', a duet with Dionne Warwick, climbed to US number 12 in 1987. He returned with the solo set *One Love – One Dream* (co-written with Bruce Roberts). In 1990, Osborne transferred to Arista Records. Airplay for his increasingly predictable output was no longer automatic, however, and he was unable to restore his commercial profile. He left Arista in 1994 and recorded a Christmas album in 1997. He resurfaced in 2000 with a new album for Windham Hill Records.

● ALBUMS: *Jeffrey Osborne* (A&M 1982) ★★★, *Stay With Me Tonight* (A&M 1983) ★★★, *Don't Stop* (A&M 1984) ★★★, *Emotional* (A&M 1986) ★★★, *One Love – One Dream* (A&M 1988) ★★, *Only Human* (Arista 1990) ★★★, *Something Warm For Christmas* (Modern 1997) ★★, *That's For Sure* (Private/Windham Hill 2000) ★★★.

● VIDEOS: *The Jazz Channel Presents Jeffrey Osborne* (Image Entertainment 2001).

## OSBOURNE, OZZY

b. John Osbourne, 3 December 1948, Aston, Birmingham, England. In January 1979 this highly individual and by now infamous vocalist and songwriter left Black Sabbath, a band whose image and original musical direction he had helped to shape. His own band was set up with Lee Kerslake, formerly of Uriah Heep, on drums, Rainbow's Bob Daisley (bass) and Randy Rhoads (b. Randall William Rhoads, 6 December 1956, Santa Monica, California, USA, d. 19 March 1982), fresh from Quiet Riot, on guitar. Rhoads' innovative playing ability was in much evidence on the debut, *Blizzard Of Oz*. By the time of a second album, Daisley and Kerslake had left to be replaced by Pat Travers drummer Tommy Aldridge and Rudy Sarzo (bass).

Throughout his post-Black Sabbath career, Osborne has courted publicity, most famously in 1982 when he had to undergo treatment for rabies following an onstage incident when he bit off the head of a bat. In the same year, his immensely talented young guitarist, Rhoads, was killed in an air crash. In came Brad Gillis but, so close was Rhoads' personal as well as musical relationship to Osbourne, many feared he would never be adequately replaced. *Talk Of The Devil* was released later in 1982, a live album that included Sabbath material. Following a tour that saw Sarzo and Gillis walk out, Osbourne was forced to rethink the line-up of his band in 1983 as Daisley rejoined, along with guitarist Jake E. Lee. Aldridge left following the release of *Bark At The Moon*, and was replaced by renowned virtuoso drummer Carmine Appice (b. 15 December 1946, Staten Island, New York, USA). This combination was to be short-lived, however, Randy Castillo replacing Appice, and Phil Soussan taking on the bass guitar. Daisley appeared on *No Rest For The Wicked*, although Black Sabbath bass player Geezer Butler played on the subsequent live dates. The album also featured talented young guitarist and songwriter Zakk Wylde (b. Jersey City, New Jersey, USA), who would form an important part of the Osbourne set-up for the next seven years.

The late 80s were a trying time for Osbourne. He went on trial in America for allegedly using his lyrics to incite youngsters to commit suicide; he was eventually cleared of these charges. His wife, Sharon (daughter of Don Arden), also became his manager, and helped Osbourne to overcome the alcoholism that was the subject of much of his work. His lyrics, however, continued to deal with the grimmest of subjects, including the agony of insanity. However, in later years Osbourne has kept to contemporary issues, rejecting to a certain extent the satanic, werewolf image he constructed around himself during the early 80s. In March 1989, he enjoyed a US Top 10 hit with a duet with Lita Ford, 'Close My Eyes Forever'. He embarked on a 'farewell' tour in 1992, but broke four bones in his foot which inhibited his performances greatly. He also donated $20,000 to the Daughters Of The Republic Of Texas appeal to help restore the Alamo, and performed his first concert in the city of San Antonio since being banned for urinating on a wall of the monument in 1982.

Predictably, neither retirement nor atonement sat too comfortably with the man, and by late 1994 he was announcing the imminent release of a new solo album, recorded in conjunction with Steve Vai. He also teamed up with Therapy? to sing lead vocals on the track 'Iron Man' for the Black Sabbath tribute album, *Black Nativity*. Far less likely was his pairing with Miss Piggy of *The Muppet Show* on 'Born To Be Wild', for a bizarre Muppets compilation album. He also confessed that his original partner on his 1992 Don Was-produced duet with actress Kim Basinger, 'Shake Your Head', was Madonna, although he had not actually recognized her. Other strange couplings included one with the Scottish comedian Billy Connolly and the popular UK boxer Frank Bruno on the 'Urpney Song', written by Mike Batt for the cartoon series *Dreamstone*.

Osbourne's 1995 release *Ozzmosis* was one of the strongest of his career, and was a major commercial success. The line-up on the album was Geezer Butler (bass), Rick Wakeman (keyboards), Wylde (guitar), and Deen Castronovo (drums). Osbourne subsequently inaugurated the Ozz-Fest, a heavy metal tour package featuring himself and other hard rock bands. The tour proved to be a huge success and remains an ongoing and lucrative concern. At the end of the 90s, Osbourne also rejoined the original line-up of Black Sabbath for a series of highly successful live shows. His first studio album of the new millennium, *Down To Earth*, was released in 2001. He became a household figure the following year when his dysfunctional family life was featured on the MTV reality television show, *The Osbournes*. This endearing 10-part series garnered some of the channel's highest viewing figures.

Osbourne is one hard-rocker who has tried every excess known and has survived. Amazingly, his work continues to sound inspired and exciting.

● ALBUMS: *Blizzard Of Oz* (Jet 1980) ★★★, *Diary Of A Madman* (Jet 1981) ★★★, *Talk Of The Devil* (Jet 1982) ★★★, *Bark At The Moon* (Jet 1983) ★★, *The Ultimate Sin* (Epic 1986) ★★, *Tribute* (Epic 1987) ★★★, *No Rest For The Wicked* (Epic 1988) ★★, *Just Say Ozzy* (Epic 1990) ★★, *No More Tears* (Epic 1991) ★★★, *Live & Loud* (Epic 1993) ★★, *Ozzmosis* (Epic 1995) ★★★★, *Down To Earth* (Epic 2001) ★★★, *Live At Budokan* (Epic 2002) ★★.

● COMPILATIONS: *Ten Commandments* (Priority 1990) ★★, *The Ozz Man Cometh* (Epic 1997) ★★★★, *The Osbourne Family Album* (Epic 2002) ★★★.

● VIDEOS: *The Ultimate Ozzy* (Virgin Vision 1987), *Wicked Videos* (CIC Videos 1988), *Bark At The Moon* (Hendring Music Video 1990), *Don't Blame Me* (Sony Music Video 1992), *Live & Loud* (Sony Music Video 1993), *Ozzy Osbourne: The Man Cometh* (SMV 1997).

● FURTHER READING: *Ozzy Osbourne*, Garry Johnson. *Diary Of A Madman: The Uncensored Memoirs Of Rock's Greatest Rogue*, Mick Wall. *Ozzy Unauthorized*, Sue Crawford.

## OTTAWAN

This European disco duo consisted of Annette (b. 1960, Guadeloupe Islands, West Indies) and Patrick (b. 1956, Guadeloupe Islands, West Indies). Patrick moved to Paris in 1966 and Annette in 1976. He was already a star in France when they met and formed Ottawan. 'D.I.S.C.O.' was a hit on the continent in 1979 and was requested by returning holiday makers who helped make it a UK hit in 1980. Only the combined efforts of the Police ('Don't Stand So Close To Me') and Barbra Streisand ('Woman In Love') managed to hold Ottawan at number 2 for three weeks. The follow-ups, all in a very similar vein, were 'You're OK', 'Hands Up (Give Me Your Heart)' (which reached number 3), and 'Help, Get Me Some Help!'. By this time their audience was growing tired of their material, and Ottawan disbanded.

● ALBUMS: *Ottawan* (Carrere 1980) ★.

● COMPILATIONS: *Ottawan's Greatest Hits* (Carrere 1981) ★, *The Very Best Of Ottawan* (Carrere 1993) ★.

## OYSTERBAND

The Oysterband biographical entry was withdrawn at the strong suggestion of band member John James.

● ALBUMS: *Jack's Alive* (Pukka 1980) ★★, *English Rock 'N' Roll – The Early Years 1800–1850* (Pukka 1982) ★★★★, *Lie Back And Think Of England* (Pukka 1983) ★★★, *20 Golden Tie-Slackeners* (1984) ★★★, *Liberty Hall* (Pukka 1985) ★★★, *Step Outside* (Cooking Vinyl 1986) ★★★, *Wide Blue Yonder* (Cooking Vinyl 1987) ★★★, with June Tabor *Freedom And Rain* (Cooking Vinyl 1990) ★★★, *Deserters* (Cooking Vinyl 1992) ★★★★, *Holy Bandits* (Cooking Vinyl 1993) ★★★★, *The Shouting End Of Life* (Cooking Vinyl 1995) ★★★, *Deep Dark Ocean* (Cooking Vinyl 1997) ★★★, *Alive And Acoustic* (Running Man 1998) ★★★, *Here I Stand* (Running Man 1999) ★★★.
● COMPILATIONS: *Trawler* (Cooking Vinyl 1994) ★★★★, *Granite Years (Best Of ... 1986 To '97)* (Cooking Vinyl 2000) ★★★★.

## OZRIC TENTACLES

Predominantly a 80s UK festival band playing a mixture of progressive rock and 60s extended-jam music, Ozric Tentacles was originally a name conjured up by the band for a psychedelic breakfast cereal. Their original line-up featured Ed Wynne (guitar), his brother Roly Wynne (bass), Nick 'Tig' Van Gelder (drums), Gavin Griffiths (guitar) and Joie 'Ozrooniculator' Hinton (keyboards). They met around an open campfire at Stonehenge in 1982. By the following year a second synthesizer player, Tom Brookes, had joined. They started gigging in clubs such as the 'Crypt' in Deptford, south-east London. There they met their second percussionist, Paul Hankin. They soon became regulars at another psychedelic 'head' venue, the Club Dog, at the George Robey pub in Finsbury Park, north London. The band's long existence has seen a number of shifts in personnel. In 1984 Griffiths left to form the Ullulators, and Brookes left a year later. Hinton remained but also played for the aforementioned Ullulators and the Oroonies. The next major change arrived in 1987 when Merv Peplar replaced Van Gelder. Later Steve Everitt replaced Brookes on synthesizers, while Marcus Carcus and John Egan added extra percussion and flute.

Considering their lengthy career it might appear that the band have had a relatively sporadic, and recent, recording output. However, much of their work from the mid-80s onwards was made available on six cassette-only albums. Into the early 90s, with the British neo-hippie, new-age travellers receiving a higher media profile and their role in organizing music festivals becoming increasingly important, bands such as the Ozric Tentacles and the Levellers benefited greatly and began to widen their audience. Hinton and Peplar left the band in 1994 and devoted their energies to their dance side project, Eat Static. New members Rad and Seaweed were featured on the meandering instrumental albums *Become The Other* and *Curious Corn*. Do not be put off by the trappings; this band can really play as a musically solid unit and occasionally reach glorious heights.

● ALBUMS: *Erpsongs* cassette only (Dovetail 1985) ★★, *Tantric Obstacles* cassette only (Dovetail 1986) ★★, *Live Ethereal Cereal* cassette only (Dovetail 1986) ★★★, *There Is Nothing* cassette only (Dovetail 1986) ★★★, *Sliding Gliding Worlds* cassette only (Dovetail 1988) ★★★, *The Bits Between The Bits* cassette only (Dovetail 1989) ★★, *Pungent Effulgent* (Dovetail 1989) ★★★★, *Erpland* (Dovetail 1990) ★★★★, *Strangeitude* (Dovetail 1991) ★★★, *Live Underslunky* (Dovetail 1992) ★★★, *Jurassic Shift* (Dovetail 1993) ★★★★, *Aborescence* (Dovetail 1994) ★★, *Become The Other* (Dovetail 1995) ★★, *Curious Corn* (Snapper 1997) ★★★, *Spice Doubt* (Snapper 1998) ★★, *Floating Seeds Remixed* (Snapper 1999) ★★★, *Waterfall Cities* (Stretchy/Phoenix Rising 1999) ★★★★, *Swirly Termination* (Snapper 2000) ★★★, *Hidden Step* (Stretchy/Phoenix Rising 2000) ★★★, *Live At The Pongmasters Ball* (Snapper 2002) ★★★.
● COMPILATIONS: *Vitamin Enhanced* 6-CD box set of the first six albums (Dovetail 1993) ★★★.

# P

## PABLO

b. Pablo Lubadika Porthos, 1952, Inongo, Zaire. Vocalist and guitarist Pablo first came to the attention of European African music enthusiasts in the early 80s, following the release of Island Records' soukous compilation album, *Sound D'Afrique*, and the tracks 'Mbanda' and 'Madeleina'. By this time, he was already a major star in Zaire, having worked during the 70s with such bands as Orchestre Kara, Kim Bantous and Lovy Du Zaire. He was also featured on Sam Mangwana's first major hit, 'Georgette Eckins'. Having been invited to join Les Quatre Etoiles in 1984, he declined, preferring to pursue a solo career as a vocalist, and a session career as a guitarist. His first UK release was *Pablo Pablo Pablo* in 1985, but afterwards he would concentrate almost exclusively on session work in Paris.
● ALBUMS: *Idie* (AMR 1981) ★★★, *Concentration* (Syllart 1982) ★★★, *Revient En Force* (COSIC 1983) ★★★, *En Action* (Darl 1984), *Pablo Pablo Pablo* (Globestyle 1985) ★★★, with Tutu *Safula* (BIZ 1987) ★★★.
● COMPILATIONS: *Okominiokolo* (Sterns 1993) ★★★★.

## PAIGE, ELAINE

b. Elaine Bickerstaff, 5 March 1951, Barnet, Hertfordshire, England. An actress and singer, often called the first lady of contemporary British musical theatre, Elaine Paige was trained at the Aida Foster Stage School in Golders Green, north London. She had already appeared in several stage musicals in the 60s and 70s, including *The Roar Of The Greasepaint-The Smell Of The Crowd*, *Hair* (her first West End show), *Maybe That's Your Problem*, *Rock Carmen*, *Jesus Christ Superstar*, *Grease* and *Billy*, before she was chosen to portray Eva Peron in Tim Rice and Andrew Lloyd Webber's *Evita* in 1978. Although Julie Covington had sung the part on the original concept album and had a UK number 1 hit in 1977 with 'Don't Cry For Me Argentina', Paige went on to make the role her own. In spite of the disappointment of being unable to play the part on Broadway (because of American union rules), *Evita* made Paige into a star almost overnight. She won a Society Of West End Theatres Award for her Outstanding Performance, and was also voted Show Business Personality Of The Year. In the 80s she starred in *Cats* (as Grizabella, singing 'Memory'), *Abbacadabra*, *Chess*, and a West End revival of Cole Porter's *Anything Goes*.
She topped the UK singles chart in 1985 with a number from *Chess*, 'I Know Him So Well', on which she duetted with Scottish singer Barbara Dickson. Her first solo album, released four years earlier, featured a variety of songs, mostly with lyrics by

Tim Rice. It was recorded with the assistance of Stuart Elliott (ex-Cockney Rebel), Ian Bairnson and David Paton from Pilot, and Mike Moran. As well as a version of Paul Simon's 'How The Heart Approaches What It Yearns', there was a rare Paul McCartney instrumental ('Hot As Sun') with words by Rice. Two of Paige's albums, 1983's *Stages* and 1985's *Love Hurts*, reached the UK Top 10. Her most unusual album, consisting entirely of cover versions of Queen songs, was released in 1988. In 1989, she turned her attention to straight acting, making two films for the BBC, including the acclaimed *Unexplained Laughter*, with Diana Rigg. She had previously worked in television programmes such as *Crossroads*, *Lady Killers*, *Ladybirds*, *A View Of Harry Clark*, and *Tales Of The Unexpected*, as well as musical specials such as *Elaine Paige In Concert*.
In 1990, her long-term personal relationship with Tim Rice dissolved and she threw herself into her work. She embarked on concert tours of Europe, the Middle East, Scandinavia and the UK, most recently accompanied by a 26-piece symphony orchestra. In 1993, she was highly acclaimed for her powerful and dramatic performance as the legendary Edith Piaf in Pam Gems' play with music, *Piaf*, at the Piccadilly Theatre in London. In May 1995, she took over from Betty Buckley in the leading role of Norma Desmond in the West End hit musical *Sunset Boulevard*, and later in the year received an OBE in the Queen's Birthday Honours List. In 1996, she finally appeared on Broadway when she replaced Betty Buckley in the New York production of *Sunset Boulevard*. Returning to the West End two years later, she made a daring career move by successfully taking on the role of the duplicitous widow Celimene in Molière's scathing comedy, *The Misanthope*, before starring in a hit revival of Richard Rodgers and Oscar Hammerstein II's *The King And I* at the London Palladium in 2000.
● ALBUMS: with Peter Oliver *Barrier* (Euro Disk 1978) ★★, *Elaine Paige* (Warners 1982) ★★★, *Stages* (K-Tel 1983) ★★, *Cinema* (K-Tel 1984) ★★, *Sitting Pretty* (Warners 1985) ★★, *Love Hurts* (Warners 1985) ★★, *Christmas* (Warners 1986) ★★★, *The Queen Album* (Siren 1988) ★★, *Love Can Do That* (RCA 1991) ★★, with Barbara Dickson *Together* (RCA 1992) ★★★, *Romance And The Stage* (RCA 1993) ★★, *Piaf* (Warners 1995) ★★★, *Encore* (Warners 1995) ★★★, *Performance* (BMF 1996) ★★★, and Original Cast recordings.
● COMPILATIONS: *Memories: The Best Of Elaine Paige* (Telstar 1987) ★★★, *The Collection* (Pickwick 1990) ★★★, with Barbara Dickson *The Best Of Elaine Paige And Barbara Dickson* (Telstar 1992) ★★★, *On Reflection: The Very Best Of Elaine Paige* (Telstar 1998) ★★★.

## PALE FOUNTAINS

Formed in Liverpool in the early 80s by songwriter Michael Head (b. 28 November 1961, Liverpool, England; guitar, vocals) and Chris McCaffrey (bass) with Thomas Whelan (drums) and Andy Diagram, formerly of Dislocation Dance and the Diagram Brothers. Having been assimilated into the early 80s' 'quiet pop'/'Bossa Nova' movement, Pale Fountains also drew upon such influences as the Beatles, the Mamas And The Papas and Love, but were probably better known for wearing short baggy trousers. Previously on the Operation Twilight label, the band attempted to break into the big time when they signed to Virgin Records. Despite this lucrative move, this highly touted band never broke out of their cult status. Their highest national chart position was the UK Top 50 'Thank You' in 1982. They split following 1985's *From Across The Kitchen Table*, with Head going on to form Shack with his brother John.

● ALBUMS: *Pacific Street* (Virgin 1984) ★★★, *From Across The Kitchen Table* (Virgin 1985) ★★★.
● COMPILATIONS: *Longshot For Your Love* (Marina 1998) ★★★.

## PARR, JOHN

b. 18 November 1954, Nottingham, England. This UK vocalist, guitarist, composer and producer specialized in highly melodic AOR. He enjoyed a brief period of transatlantic success in the mid-80s, with his recordings for Atlantic Records compared to Rick Springfield and Eddie Money. Parr broke into the US Top 30 at the end of 1984 with 'Naughty Naughty', following which he composed the themes for the movies *American Anthem* and *St. Elmo's Fire*. The second of these singles topped the US chart and made the UK Top 10 in summer 1985. Parr also duetted with Meat Loaf on 'Rock 'N' Roll Mercenaries', but this failed to embellish either artist's profile, stopping just short of the Top 30. Two solo albums, his self-titled debut in 1985 and *Running The Endless Mile* in 1986, both fared poorly with the critics. Parr has continued to record albums and remains an in demand movie theme composer. His finest moment remains the energetic 'St. Elmo's Fire (Man In Motion)'.

● ALBUMS: *John Parr* (Atlantic 1984) ★★★, *Running The Endless Mile* (Atlantic 1986) ★★, *Man With A Vision* (Blue Martin 1992) ★★, *Under Parr* (Blue Martin 1996) ★★.

## PASSIONS

This English post-punk band, with definite pop leanings, was formed in June 1978 and comprised Barbara Gogan (b. Dublin, Eire; vocals, guitar), Mitch Barker (vocals), Clive Timperley (guitar, vocals), Claire Bidwell (bass, vocals) and Richard Williams (drums). All save Timperley had featured in Rivers Of Passion, while all except Bidwell had spent time in the various incarnations of the Derelicts between 1974 and 1976. During this time, Timperley also played with Joe Strummer's 101ers. Gogan left her Dublin home at the age of 18 and settled in France within a Marxist commune. She came to London in 1972 and moved into a 'squat' near Ladbroke Grove, where she became involved with the Derelicts, a loose collection of like-minded left-wingers. Evolving into the Passions, they released their first single, 'Needles And Pins', on the tiny Soho label, also home of the Nips and the Inmates. They lost Barker in 1979 when a broken leg halted his musical activities. Continuing as a four-piece they signed to Fiction Records for their debut album and one single,

'Hunted'. Bidwell left in July 1980 to form Schwarze Kapelle and then joined the Wall. David Agar, once a member of the fledgling Spandau Ballet, replaced her. Three days later, they were dropped by Fiction but fell immediately on their feet with a contract for Polydor Records. The Passions finally found success in 1981 with their second single for the label, 'I'm In Love With A German Film Star'. It would be their only hit, despite the eloquence and strength of later material. Timperley left to run a health shop in December 1981, while the recruitment of Kevin Armstrong (ex-Local Heroes SW9) on guitar and Jeff Smith (ex-Lene Lovich band) on keyboards failed to put the brakes on their commercial slide. Armstrong himself left in August 1982 to be replaced by Steve Wright.

● ALBUMS: *Michael And Miranda* (Fiction 1980) ★★, *Thirty Thousand Feet Over China* (Polydor 1981) ★★★, *Sanctuary* (Polydor 1982) ★★.
● COMPILATIONS: *Passion Plays* (Polydor 1985) ★★★.

## PASTELS

Formed in Glasgow, Scotland, in 1982, the Pastels were one of the prime movers in the 80s 'shambling'/'anorak' independent scene that influenced later luminaries such as the Flatmates and Talulah Gosh. Group leader Stephen Pastel (b. Stephen McRobbie, Scotland; guitar, vocals) went to great lengths to distance the Pastels from their past idolaters, and they later served as a major influence on Scottish bands such as Teenage Fanclub (whose Norman Blake is a fan club member and later played in the Pastels) and Captain America/Eugenius. However, their history has been characterized by the kind of lethargy that has doomed them to mere cultism: 'I just find careerism and naked ambition really ugly'.

The Pastels themselves were motivated by a conglomeration of the Monkees and the Ramones. The early line-up also comprised Brian Superstar (b. Brian Taylor; guitar) and Chris Gordon (drums), but the latter's early departure signalled a recurring instability in the group's rhythm section. Their first release on the Television Personalities' Whaam! label, the *Songs For Children* EP, was the beginning of an unsettled relationship with a variety of labels including Glass, Rough Trade Records, and Creation Records. Appearances on various compilations, not least a prestigious slot on the seminal *C86* collection ('Breaking Lines') from the *New Musical Express* increased their standing in the independent market, while their music combined ambitious vision with naïve ability. A settled line-up – McRobbie, Superstar, Aggi Wright (vocals), Martin Hayward (bass) and Bernice Swanson (drums) – completed two albums, *Up For A Bit With The Pastels* and *Sittin' Pretty*, wherein the group matured from the charming innocence of early releases to embrace a myriad of contrasting styles held together by McRobbie's committed vision. Material ranged from the buoyant 'Nothing To Be Done' to the lengthy 'Baby Honey' and 'Ditch The Fool', as the Pastels expanded their musical horizons with the temporary aid of Eugene Kelly (ex-Vaselines), Norman Blake and David Keegan, formerly of the Shop Assistants and McRobbie's partner in the pivotal 53rd & 3rd Records label. By the early 90s, Keegan had become a full-time member of the Pastels. Following a series of alterations, the Pastels re-emerged centred around McRobbie, Wright (now on bass) and Katrina Mitchell (drums), the latter pursuing a concurrent path as a member of Melody Dog. Against the odds, this trio was still in place for 1995's *Mobile Safari*, an enjoyable collection of ragamuffin odes to life in and outside of an underachieving indie band, punctuated by songs such as 'Yoga' and 'Classic Lineup'. Their 1997 release, *Illumination*, received lacklustre reviews from an increasingly disinterested music press.

● ALBUMS: *Up For A Bit With The Pastels* (Glass 1987) ★★★, *Sittin' Pretty* (Chapter 22 1989) ★★★, *Mobile Safari* (Domino 1995) ★★★, *Illumination* (Domino 1997) ★★, *Illuminati* remixes (Domino 1998) ★★★.

● COMPILATIONS: *Suck On The Pastels* (Creation 1988) ★★★, *1986-1993 Truckload Of Trouble* (Seed 1993) ★★★★.

## PEARL HARBOR AND THE EXPLOSIONS

Formed in San Francisco, California, in 1979, this much-touted attraction was centred on vocalist Pearl Harbor (b. 1958, Germany, of a Filipino mother), who, as Pearl E. Gates, had previously been a dancer in the Tubes' live show. She subsequently joined Jane Dornacker in Leila And The Snakes, before taking the group's rhythm section – Hilary Stench (bass) and John Stench (drums) – into this new act. Their act continued the theatricality of the Tubes, but Gates was more interested in conventional rock 'n' roll. To this end, she recruited Peter Bilt (guitar) and formed Pearl Harbor And The Explosions in October 1978. They specialized in old-fashioned rock 'n' roll/rockabilly spiced with 'new wave' energy. Their debut single 'Drivin'' (which was later covered by Jane Aire And The Belvederes) came out on the independent 415 Records label and became a cult hit. Its success encouraged Warner Brothers Records to sign the band. Their self-titled debut was a strong, promising work, but the band failed to complete a follow-up. They split in June 1980 leaving Pearl to continue with a solo album, *Don't Follow Me, I'm Lost Too*, under her new name Pearl Harbour. The album was produced by Nicky Gallagher (former member of Ian Dury's Blockheads). *Pearls Galore!*, a belated but far superior follow-up, was her last solo release for several years. The Stench brothers joined ex-Jefferson Airplane guitarist Jorma Kaukonen in Vital Parts, before embarking on an association with cult *avant garde* act Chrome.

● ALBUMS: *Pearl Harbor And The Explosions* (Warners 1979) ★★★, as Pearl Harbour *Don't Follow Me, I'm Lost Too* (Warners 1980) ★★, as Pearl Harbour *Pearls Galore!* (Island 1984) ★★★, as Pearl Harbour *Here Comes Trouble* (Shattered 1995) ★★★.

## PENGUIN CAFÉ ORCHESTRA

This collection of accomplished musicians was inaugurated to cater for the musical eclecticism of leader Simon Jeffes (b. 19 February 1949, Sussex, England, d. 11 December 1997, Somerset, England). In its history the orchestra has included: founding members Jeffes, Helen Liebmann (cello), and Steve Nye (keyboards), along with Geoffrey Richardson (viola), Neil Rennie (ukulele), Bob Loveday (violin), Ian Maidman (percussion, bass), Peter McGowan (violin), Stephen Fletcher (piano), Julia Segovia (percussion), Barbara Bolte (oboe), Jill Streater (oboe), and Annie Whitehead (trombone). After spending his childhood in Canada, Jeffes returned to England and studied classical guitar at the Royal Academy with Julian Byzantine and Gilbert Biberian. Disillusioned with the contemporary classical scene, he found inspiration in ethnic music: 'A friend gave me a tape of African things . . . listening to it was like rediscovering the reason we play music – not to become professional, but because we are moved to do it.' Jeffes nurtured a desire to create an ensemble capable of fusing musics from around the world, of different styles and cultures – literally an Utopian dream which came to him, allegedly, while suffering from food poisoning in the south of France in 1972.

After working on the fringes of the pop world, involving himself with production work with groups such as Caravan and Camel, Jeffes found a champion for his musical vision in Brian Eno. The Orchestra recorded their 1976 debut album on Eno's esoteric Obscure label. Jeffes continued his studio work, being hired at various points by the Clash and Malcolm McLaren with Sid Vicious, alongside work with the Yellow Magic Orchestra and Baaba Maal. A follow-up did not appear until almost five years later, and using esoteric song titles such as 'The Ecstasy Of Dancing Fleas' and 'Cutting Branches For A Temporary Shelter' they betrayed a degree of pretentiousness. The music however, swayed between a studied seriousness and a sense of jolliness. The orchestra also drew criticism over the years on account of being *too* clever and employing a dry approach to their music – an observation often levelled at classically trained musicians seen to be straying outside their boundaries.

A growing interest in world music during the 80s meant that Jeffes' work began to find a wider audience, and in 1988 the Royal Ballet adapted eight Penguin Café Orchestra compositions for *'Still Life'* At The Penguin Café. During the 90s Jeffes moved to Somerset and built himself a new studio. One track recorded there, 'Telephone And Rubber Band' (from 1995's *Concert Program*), received regular airplay as the theme to Mercury's One-2-One television commercials. Diagnosed with a brain tumour, Jeffes died in December 1997.

● ALBUMS: *Music From The Penguin Café* (Obscure/Caroline 1976) ★★★, *Penguin Café Orchestra* (Editions EG/Caroline 1982) ★★★, *Broadcasting From Home* (Editions EG/Caroline 1984) ★★★, *Signs Of Life* (Editions EG/Caroline 1987) ★★★★, *When In Rome ... Recorded Live At The Royal Festival Hall* (Editions EG/Caroline 1988) ★★★, *Union Café* (Zopf/Windham Hill 1993) ★★★, *Concert Program* (Zopf/Windham Hill 1995) ★★★.

● COMPILATIONS: *Preludes, Airs And Yodels: A Penguin Café Primer* (Virgin 1996) ★★★★, *Piano*

*Music* (Zopf 2000) ★★★, *A Brief History* (Zopf 2001) ★★★★, *A History* 4-CD box set (Zopf 2001) ★★★★.

## PEPSI AND SHIRLIE

Former backing singers to Wham!, Lawrie 'Pepsi' Demacque (b. 10 December 1958, Paddington, London, England) and Shirlie Holliman (b. 18 April 1962, Watford, Hertfordshire, England) embarked on a solo career after that group's break-up in 1986. This connection was put to great use in the UK teenage magazine market where their pop/dance style appealed to suburban audiences. Signing to Polydor Records, the duo achieved two UK Top 10 singles in 1987 with 'Heartache' (number 2) and 'Goodbye Stranger' (number 9). Later singles fared less well and *Change* was released over three years after their debut. Though it included one song George Michael had written for them, 'Someday', it seemed that Pepsi And Shirlie's following had moved on. The album failed to chart and no single success resulted. Their attempts to rehabilitate their image to that of club divas in 1993 fooled no one. Demacque went on to appear in several London musicals, in addition to finding regular employment as a session singer. Holliman married Martin Kemp of Spandau Ballet.
● ALBUMS: *All Right Now* (Polydor 1987) ★★★, *Change* (Polydor 1991) ★★.

## PERFECT DISASTER

Having tested the water as Orange Disaster, then the Architects Of Disaster, these calamitously inclined types finally settled on the Perfect Disaster in 1984, as the original rhythm section departed to form Fields Of The Nephilim. The initial UK-based line-up consisted of Phil Parfitt, Allison Pates, John Saltwell and Malcolm Catto, although personnel changes were to plague the band's career. Ignored by the British music scene, the Perfect Disaster took their twisted, broody guitar sound to France for their self-titled debut album in 1985. There followed a couple of years of blank struggle on both sides of the English Channel before the band signed to Fire Records at home and released the critically acclaimed *Asylum Road*. Prior to this, Saltwell and Pates both left, disillusioned, to be replaced by bass player Josephine Wiggs (b. Josephine Miranda Cordelia Susan Wiggs, 26 February 1965, Letchworth, Hertfordshire, England) and long-term guitarist Dan Cross. In 1989 better prospects lurked over the horizon: the *Up* album, which stretched splendidly from fiery two-chord blasts to near-suicidal ramblings, coincided with prestigious live shows with the likes of the Jesus And Mary Chain. The band's initial inspiration, based upon singer Parfitt's spell working at a Victorian mental institution, looked set to reap rewards. The public, alas, did not share the critics' enthusiasm for the band. The *Heaven Scent* album continued the Perfect Disaster's foray into the darker side of alternative music, but rumours of the band's demise, which persisted throughout 1991, were finally confirmed. Wiggs left to spend more time on the Breeders, a side project that also involved Tanya Donelly from Throwing Muses and Kim Deal of the Pixies, allowing John Saltwell to return on bass, and Jon Mattock was borrowed from Spacemen 3 to contribute the drumming for *Heaven Scent*. Parfitt would go on to write alongside Jason Pierce (Spiritualized) before forming Oedipussy.
● ALBUMS: *The Perfect Disaster* (Kampa 1985) ★★, *Asylum Road* (Fire 1988) ★★★, *Up* (Fire 1989) ★★★★, *Heaven Scent* (Fire 1990) ★★★.

## PET SHOP BOYS

Formed by Neil Tennant (b. 10 July 1954, North Shields, Northumberland, England; vocals) and Chris Lowe (b. 4 October 1959, Blackpool, Lancashire, England; keyboards) in 1981, this highly inventive UK duo owes their long-term career to the ability to bridge melodic pop and dance music with intelligence and style.

Lowe studied as an architect and had previously played in cabaret act, One Under The Eight, while Tennant was employed as a journalist on the UK pop magazine *Smash Hits*. After writing and recording demos, they came under the wing of New York dance producer Bobby 'O' Orlando. In the summer of 1984, they issued the Orlando-produced 'West End Girls', which passed unnoticed. After being dropped from Epic Records, they were picked up by Parlophone Records the following year. A second single 'Opportunities (Let's Make Lots Of Money)' also failed but a re-recording of 'West End Girls', produced by Stephen Hague, began selling in late 1985. In January 1986, this hypnotic single topped the charts in the UK and repeated the feat later in the USA. The duo's debut *Please*, 'Love Comes Quickly', a remixed version of 'Opportunities (Let's Make Lots Of Money)' and 'Suburbia' consolidated their position in the UK during 1986. The following year, the duo returned to number 1 with the Cat Stevens' influenced 'It's A Sin'. By this time, they were critically fêted as one of the more interesting bands of their time, with an engaging love of pop irony, camp imagery, and arch wordplay. The quality of their melodies was also evident in the successful collaboration with Dusty Springfield, 'What Have I Done To Deserve This?' which reached number 2 in both the UK and the USA.

By the end of the year the duo were back at the top in their home country with a cover version of the Elvis Presley hit, 'Always On My Mind', also a US Top 5 single. After releasing the well-received *Actually*, the duo appeared in the documentary film, *It Couldn't Happen Here*, which co-starred *Carry On* actress, Barbara Windsor. The film was given the cold shoulder by reviewers and was seen as a mild hiccup in the duo's fortunes. A fourth UK number 1 with 'Heart' was followed by a production and songwriting credit on Eighth Wonder's hit single, 'I'm Not Scared'. *Introspective* spawned further UK Top 10 hits in 'Domino Dancing', 'Left To My Own Devices' and 'It's Alright'. Having previously eschewed live tours (they had hitherto performed one-off concerts only), the Pet Shop Boys made their debut in Japan and the Far East, before finally reaching the UK. In typical manner, the show's concept took them as far away from the traditional pop concert as possible and incorporated the use of actors, dancers and film.

A surprise collaboration in 1989 with Liza Minnelli gave her a UK Top 10 hit with 'Losing My Mind'. The duo's own inventive wit was again in evidence on the UK Top 5 hit 'So Hard', the laconic 'Being Boring' (a rare failure that only reached number 20), and an odd fusion of U2's 'Where The Streets Have No Name' and Frankie Valli's 'Can't Take My Eyes Off You'. The attendant *Behaviour* was a downbeat, slightly disappointing album. In 1991, the duo issued one of the best compilations of the era, *Discography*. Despite Tennant's continued involvement with Johnny Marr and Bernard Sumner in Electronic, the duo insisted that the Pet Shop Boys were only taking a short break.

The UK Top 10 hit 'Can You Forgive Her' was a fine trailer to 1993's *Very*, a superb collection that tinkered with the duo's sound to incorporate contemporary dance music sounds. Later in the year, they enjoyed a UK number 2 hit with a bold cover version of the Village People's gay anthem, 'Go West'. *Alternative* was an excellent double CD of b-sides, which fully demonstrated their pioneering sound in 'leftfield dance pop'. *Bilingual* experimented with Latin rhythms, and featured two further UK Top 10 singles, 'Before' and 'Se A Vide E (That's The Way Life Is)'. The duo's long-awaited new album, *Nightlife*, was premiered by the single 'I Don't Know What You Want But I Can't Give It Any More'. Despite a rare lapse of taste on the camp 'New York City Boy', the album highlighted their remarkable creativity on tracks such as 'Happiness Is An Option' and the bittersweet single 'You Only Tell Me You Love Me When You're Drunk', which put them back in the UK Top 10 in January 2000.

Tennant and Lowe subsequently collaborated with writer Jonathan Harvey on the West End musical, *Closer To Heaven*, which opened at the Arts Theatre in May 2001. The show earned some particularly harsh reviews from theatre critics, and despite attracting a cult audience closed after only four months. The duo returned to the charts in 2002 with *Release*. The album featured a more guitar-orientated sound, notably on the powerful 'I Get Along'.

● ALBUMS: *Please* (Parlophone 1986) ★★★★, *Disco* (Parlophone 1986) ★★★, *Actually* (Parlophone 1987) ★★★★, *Introspective* (Parlophone 1988) ★★★, *Behaviour* (Parlophone 1990) ★★★, *Very* (Parlophone 1993) ★★★★, *Disco 2* (Parlophone 1994) ★★, *Bilingual* (Parlophone 1996) ★★★, *Bilingual Remixed* (Parlophone 1997) ★★★, *Nightlife* (Parlophone 1999) ★★★★, *Release* (Parlophone/Sanctuary 2002) ★★★.
● COMPILATIONS: *Discography: The Complete Singles Collection* (Parlophone 1991) ★★★★★, *Alternative* (Parlophone 1995) ★★★★, *Essential Pet Shop Boys* (EMI 1998) ★★★.
● VIDEOS: *Highlights: Pet Shop Boys On Tour* (PMI 1990), *Videography: The Singles Collection On Video* (PMI 1991), *Performance* (PMI 1992), *Projections* (PMI 1993), *Various* (PMI 1994), *Discovery: Live In Rio* (PMI 1995), *Somewhere: Pet Shop Boys In Concert* (Game Entertainment 1997), *Montage: The Nightlife Tour* (PMI 2001).
● FURTHER READING: *Pet Shop Boys, Literally*, Chris Heath. *Pet Shop Boys: Introspective*, Michael Crowton. *Pet Shop Boys Versus America*, Chris Heath and Pennie Smith.
● FILMS: *It Couldn't Happen Here* (1987).

## PETRA

One of the first US Christian hard rock bands, Petra are an excellent musical unit who have never been swayed by passing trends and have adhered resolutely to their own ideals and beliefs. Petra specialize in a varied musical approach, with their stadium rock sound incorporating elements of the Eagles, Joe Walsh, Kansas and Deep Purple. They have released well over a dozen high-quality albums to date, with their popularity having gradually waned from its peak in 1984.

The band was formed in 1972 by Bob Hartman (b. 26 December 1949, Byron, Ohio, USA; guitar), Greg Hough (guitar/vocals), John DeGroff (bass), and Bill Glover (drums, releasing their self-titled debut album in 1974. Greg X. Volz (b. 12 January 1950, Peoria, Illinois, USA; vocals) was added to the line-up on 1977's *Come And Join Us*. Mark Kelly (b. 28 June 1956, Enid, Oklahoma, USA; bass), John Slick (b. 28 September 1953, Fort Wayne, Indiana, USA; keyboards) and Louie Weaver (b. 13 July 1951, Nashville, Tennessee, USA; drums) joined the new look line-up in 1981. A series of strong selling albums introduced the band to a wider audience. They appeared in the US Top 12 best-attended bands list in *Performance* magazine, while 1983's *Not Of This World* sold in excess of a quarter of a million units. John Lawry replaced Slick on 1985's *Beat The System*, and John Schlitt (b. 3 February 1950, Lincoln, Illinois, USA; ex-Head East) was recruited as the new lead vocalist on 1986's *Back To The Street*. The band adopted a heavier direction thereafter, with Ronny Cates replacing Kelly on 1988's *On Fire!*. David Lichens (guitar) and Jim Cooper (keyboards) joined and departed in the mid-90s, while Lonnie Chapin (b. Oregon, USA; bass), Pete Orta (b. 26 August 1971, USA; lead guitar) and Kevin Brandow (guitar) played on *God Fixation* and *Double Take*, alongside long-standing members Weaver and Schlitt. Hartman is still part of the organization although he no longer tours, instead he prefers to take a role as writer and producer.

● ALBUMS: *Petra* (Myrrh 1974) ★★, *Come And Join Us* (Myrrh 1977) ★★, *Washes Whiter Than* (Star Song 1979) ★★, *Never Say Die* (Star Song 1981) ★★★, *More Power To Ya* (Star Song 1982) ★★★, *Not Of This World* (Kingsway 1983) ★★★, *Beat The System* (Kingsway 1984) ★★★, *Captured In Time & Space* (Star Song 1986) ★★, *Back To The Street* (Star Song 1986) ★★, *This Means War!* (Star Song 1987) ★★★, *On Fire!* (Star Song 1988) ★★★, *Petra Praise: The Rock Cries Out* (Dayspring 1989) ★★★, *Beyond Belief* (Dayspring 1990) ★★★, *Unseen Power* (Word 1991) ★★★, *Wake-Up Call* (Word 1993) ★★★, *No Doubt* (Word 1995) ★★★, *Petra Praise 2: We Need Jesus* (Word 1997) ★★★, *God Fixation* (Word 1998) ★★, *Double Take* (Word 2000) ★★★, *Revival* (Word 2001) ★★★.
● COMPILATIONS: *Means Rock* (Star Song 1989) ★★★, *War & Remembrance* (Star Song 1990) ★★★, *Petrafied: The Best Of Petra* (CBS 1991) ★★★★,

*Petraphonics* (Star Song 1992) ★★★, *Power Praise* (Word 1993) ★★★, *Rock Block* (Sparrow 1995) ★★★, *The Early Years Vol. 1* (Star Song 1996) ★★★.
● VIDEOS: *Captured In Time And Space* (Sony 1989).

## PETTY, TOM, AND THE HEARTBREAKERS

The Heartbreakers were formed from the ashes of Petty's first professional band, Mudcrutch, in 1971. In addition to Tom Petty (b. 20 October 1953, Florida, USA; guitar) the band comprised; Mike Campbell (b. 1 February 1954, Florida, USA; guitar), Benmont Tench (b. 7 September 1954, Gainesville, Florida, USA; keyboards), Stan Lynch (b. 21 May 1955, Gainesville, Florida, USA; drums) and Ron Blair (b.16 September 1952, Macon, Georgia, USA; bass). Armed with a Rickenbacker guitar and a Roger McGuinn voice, their debut album gained greater acceptance in England, a country where anything Byrds-like would find an audience. McGuinn in fact later recorded 'American Girl' (and did a fine Petty impersonation). The tight-structured rock formula of the first album showed great promise and eventually it made a substantial impression on the US charts, over a year after release. Having received rave reviews following his visit to Europe, he released a highly praised second collection, *You're Gonna Get It*. Petty was able to appeal both to the new wave and lovers of American west coast rock with his songs. *Damn The Torpedoes* followed a lengthy legal battle during which time he filed for bankruptcy. His cash flow soon improved as the album was only kept from the top of the US charts by Pink Floyd, and it went on to reach platinum status.

Petty's subsequent albums have been similarly satisfying although not as successful. In 1981, he duetted with Stevie Nicks on 'Stop Draggin' My Heart Around', complete with an MTV-style video, and in 1983 he was one of the artists to encourage Del Shannon to record again, producing his album *Drop Down And Get Me*. In 1985, he had another major hit with 'Don't Come Around Here No More' aided by an imaginative and award-winning *Alice in Wonderland* video depicting him as the Mad Hatter. During the recording of *Southern Accents*, Petty smashed his hand (in anger) on the recording console and had to have a metal splint permanently fixed, as the bones were too badly broken. Petty's outburst failed to stop the album becoming another million-seller. That same year he played Live Aid in Philadelphia. The following year he reunited with Nicks for a remake of the Searchers' 'Needles And Pins'. His association with Bob Dylan prospered as they toured and wrote together. The live album *Pack Up The Plantation* delighted old fans, but failed to break any new ground. In 1988, Jeff Lynne and Petty struck up a friendship and together with George Harrison, Roy Orbison and Dylan, they formed the highly successful Traveling Wilburys supergroup. Lynne's high-tech and over-crisp production was in evidence on 1989's *Full Moon Fever* (a solo project) and *Into The Great Wide Open*, but fortunately the strength of Petty's songs won through. Both albums showcased Petty's great gift for combining melody with irresistible middle eights, and acknowledged influential bands including the Beatles, the Byrds

and the Searchers.

A greatest hits album was released in 1993 and became a huge hit in his homeland. It served as an introduction to a younger audience who had seen Petty cited as a major influence on many 90s guitar-based rock bands. This new wave of success inspired Petty to deliver the beautiful *Wildflowers*, probably his most satisfying album. On this overtly acoustic and mellow collection, Petty's lower and more mature vocal delivery gave his lyrics a chance to be heard clearly. Seasoned session drummer Steve Ferrone replaced the long-serving Stan Lynch, and with Howie Epstein (bass) transformed the permanent nucleus of Petty, Tench and Campbell into an unbeatable live band. Lynch has become a hugely successful songwriter, now based in Nashville. Petty has succeeded in a fickle marketplace by playing honest, unpretentious catchy rock with irresistible hooklines. He is one of the most durable American artists of the past three decades, and when motivated is still capable of being creative and not dwelling on past glories.
● ALBUMS: *Tom Petty And The Heartbreakers* (Shelter 1976) ★★★, *You're Gonna Get It* (Shelter 1978) ★★★★, *Damn The Torpedoes* (MCA 1979) ★★★★, *Hard Promises* (MCA 1981) ★★★★, *Long After Dark* (MCA 1982) ★★★, *Southern Accents* (MCA 1985) ★★★★, *Pack Up The Plantation: Live!* (MCA 1985) ★★★, *Let Me Up (I've Had Enough)* (MCA 1987) ★★★★, *Full Moon Fever* (MCA 1989) ★★★★, *Into The Great Wide Open* (MCA 1991) ★★★★, *Wildflowers* (Warners 1994) ★★★★, *She's The One* (Warners 1996) ★★★, *Echo* (Warners 1999) ★★★.
● COMPILATIONS: *Greatest Hits* (MCA 1993) ★★★★, *Playback* 6-CD box set (MCA 1995) ★★★★, *Anthology: Through The Years* (Universal 2000) ★★★★.
● VIDEOS: *Playback* (MCA Music Video 1995), *High Grass Dogs: Live From The Fillmore* (Warner Reprise Video 1999).

## PHD

This UK pop duo comprised Jim Diamond (b. 28 September 1951, Glasgow, Scotland; vocals), Tony Hymas (keyboards). Their debut album included the single 'I Won't Let You Down', which initially failed to chart. Convinced that the band had potential an extra push from WEA Records was put behind the record and finally it paid off when the single reached number 3 in the UK charts in 1982 and repeated its success in Europe. However, they found life hard afterwards with their second and final album, which did not sell as well. The duo went their separate ways, with Diamond signing a solo deal with A&M Records and enjoying further chart success.
● ALBUMS: *PhD* (Warners 1981) ★★, *Is It Safe ?* (Warners 1983) ★★.

## PIGBAG

Pigbag will be forever linked with their debut single, and only hit, 'Papa's Got A Brand New Pigbag' (a play on words on the mid-60s James Brown classic, 'Papa's Got A Brand New Bag'). A quirky but nevertheless catchy funk/soul instrumental, the single was first released in May 1981, but took almost

a year to reach the charts, peaking at number 3. Word had it that their label, Y, had deleted the single and then reactivated it when the demand was sufficient. The band had formed around the Gloucestershire and Avon region from the ashes of hardline militant funk act the Pop Group; Simon Underwood (bass) joined up with James Johnstone (guitar, keyboards), Ollie Moore (saxophone), Chip Carpenter (drums) and Roger Freeman (percussion). By the time of their hit, Pigbag had already issued two further singles, 'Sunny Day' and 'Getting Up'. The debut album, *Dr Heckle And Mr Jive*, subsequently reached the UK Top 20. Despite shrewd promotion, Pigbag's heyday was short-lived. 'Big Bean' peaked at number 40 and 'Hit The "O" Deck' failed to make any impact. After a live album, the band broke up, although 'Papa's Got A Brand New Pigbag' was later re-recorded in 1987, to coincide with *The Best Of Pigbag*. Johnstone later surfaced in ambient dance duo Infinite Wheel.
● ALBUMS: *Dr Heckle And Mr Jive* (Y 1982) ★★, *Lend An Ear* (Y 1983) ★★, *Pigbag – Live* (Y 1983) ★★.
● COMPILATIONS: *Favourite Things* (Y 1983) ★★, *Discology: The Best Of Pigbag* (Kaz 1987) ★★★, *The BBC Sessions* (BBC Music 1998) ★★★.

## PiL
(see Public Image Limited)

## PINE, COURTNEY
b. 18 March 1964, London, England. Like many of his generation of young, black, UK jazz musicians, Pine came from a reggae and funk background. Pine is a dazzling performer on many instruments, notably saxophone, clarinet, flute and keyboards. He had been a member of Dwarf Steps, a hard-bop band consisting of Berklee College Of Music graduates, before joining reggae artists Clint Eastwood And General Saint. His interest in jazz was fostered when he participated in workshops run by John Stevens. In 1986, he deputized for Sonny Fortune in Elvin Jones' band, and was involved in setting up the Jazz Warriors. He came to wider public notice as a result of playing with Charlie Watts' Orchestra, George Russell's European touring band and with Art Blakey at the Camden Jazz Festival. Blakey invited him to join the Jazz Messengers, but Pine decided to stay in Britain. In 1987, he played at the Bath Festival with the Orchestre National de Jazz. By that time, his reputation had spread far beyond jazz circles, and his first album was a massive seller by jazz standards. He appeared before a huge worldwide audience at the Nelson Mandela 70th Birthday Concert at Wembley, backing dancers IDJ, and was the main subject of a number of television arts programmes about jazz in the late 80s, his smart image and articulate seriousness about his music enabling him to communicate with many people who had never before given jazz a hearing. Pine became much in demand for film and television, and appeared, for example, on the soundtrack of Alan Parker's *Angel Heart* and over the titles of BBC Television's *Juke Box Jury*. His quartet comprised young American luminaries Kenny Kirkland, Charnett Moffett and Marvin 'Smitty' Smith.

Many of Pine's admirers feel that in some ways his high media profile has hindered his development, but his talent, dedication and level-headedness have ensured that he has never been diverted by the hype, and his most recent work illustrates an emotional depth matching his undoubted technical brilliance. He has also continued to play in reggae and other pop contexts (*Closer To Home*), and is a frequent collaborator with UK soul singer Mica Paris. *Modern Day Jazz Stories* showed a strong rap/hip-hop influence and featured a funky support trio of Ronnie Burrage, Moffett and Geri Allen. *Underground* delved further into hip-hop rhythms with support from DJs Sparky and Pogo. Pine has done much to make jazz palatable for a younger audience, and as such is one of the UK's best ambassadors of the genre.
● ALBUMS: *Journey To The Urge Within* (Island 1986) ★★★, *Destiny's Song And The Image Of Pursuance* (Island 1988) ★★★, *The Vision's Tale* (Island 1989) ★★★, *Within The Realms Of Our Dreams* (Island 1991) ★★★, *Closer To Home* (Island 1992) ★★★, *To The Eyes Of Creation* (Island 1992) ★★★★, *Modern Day Jazz Stories* (Antilles 1996) ★★, *Underground* (Talkin' Loud 1997) ★★★, *Another Story* (Talkin' Loud 1998) ★★, *Back In The Day* (Blue Thumb 2000) ★★★.

## PIXIES
This highly influential alternative rock band was formed in Boston, Massachusetts, USA, by roommates Charles Thompson IV aka Black Francis (b. Long Beach, California, USA; vocals/guitar) and Joey Santiago (guitar). A newspaper advertisement, requiring applicants for a 'Hüsker Dü/Peter, Paul And Mary band', solicited bass player Kim Deal (b. 10 June 1961, Dayton, Ohio, USA) who in turn introduced drummer David Lovering. Originally known as Pixies In Panoply, the quartet secured a recording contract on the UK independent label 4AD Records on the strength of a series of superior demo tapes. Their debut release, 1987's *Come On Pilgrim*, introduced the band's abrasive, powerful sound and Francis' oblique lyrics. *Surfer Rosa*, produced by Big Black's Steve Albini, exaggerated the savage fury of its predecessor and the set was acclaimed Album Of The Year in much of the UK rock press. A new partnership with producer Gil Norton resulted in the superlative *Doolittle*, which emphasized the quartet's grasp of melody, yet retained their drive. This thrilling collection scaled the UK Top 10, aided and abetted by the band's most enduring single, 'Monkey Gone To Heaven'. The Pixies were now a highly popular attraction and their exciting live performances enhanced a growing reputation, establishing clear stage favourites in 'Debaser', 'Cactus', 'Wave Of Mutilation' and 'Bone Machine'. *Bossanova*, which reached number 3 on the UK album chart yet only number 70 in their homeland, showed an undiminished fire with a blend of pure pop ('Allison') and sheer ferocity ('Rock Music'). It also featured the UK Top 30 single, 'Velouria'. The band found themselves the darlings of the rock press and was once again widely applauded for recording one of the top albums of the year. Kim Deal,

meanwhile, attracted glowing reviews for her offshoot project, the Breeders. *Trompe Le Monde* was, if anything, an even harsher collection than those that had preceded it, prompting some critics to describe it as the 'Pixies' heavy metal album'. Following the renamed Frank Black's departure for a solo career in early 1993 the band effectively folded, but their reputation continues to outshine any of the membership's concurrent or subsequent projects. Released in 1997, the excellent CD compilation *Death To The Pixies* confirmed the band's enduring influence, one that is greater in the UK and Europe than the USA.

● ALBUMS: *Come On Pilgrim* (4AD 1987) ★★★, *Surfer Rosa* (4AD 1988) ★★★★, *Doolittle* (4AD/Elektra 1989) ★★★★, *Bossanova* (4AD/Elektra 1990) ★★★, *Trompe Le Monde* (4AD/Elektra 1991) ★★★, *The Pixies* 1987 recordings (spinART 2002) ★★★.
● COMPILATIONS: *Death To The Pixies 1987–1991* (4AD 1997) ★★★★, *Pixies At The BBC* (4AD/Elektra 1998) ★★★, *Complete B-Sides* (4AD 2001) ★★★★.

## PLASMATICS

Formed in 1979 in New York City, USA, the Plasmatics was a theatrical hardcore band that incorporated into its performances such violent acts as blowing up Cadillacs and chainsawing guitars in half. Assembled by and masterminded by former pornography entrepreneur Rod Swenson, the original personnel of the group included vocalist Wendy O. Williams (b. 1949, d. 6 April 1998, Starrs, Connecticut, USA) a former star of sex shows, who wore see-through lingerie, but for the most part, appeared topless with strategically placed masking tape. The remainder of the band comprised Richie Stotts (guitar), who wore a blue mohawk haircut and a pink tutu on stage, Wes Beech (guitar), Stu Deutsch (drums) and Chosei Funahara (bass, later replaced by Jean Beauvoir).

After releasing two EPs on the independent Vice Squad label in 1979, the Plasmatics signed with Stiff Records in the USA and the UK, releasing *New Hope For The Wretched* in 1980. It was largely panned by the critics but sold as a cult item due to the band's extensive press coverage, as did such singles as 'Butcher Baby' and 'Monkey Suit'. A second album, *Beyond The Valley Of 1984*, was issued on Stiff in 1981, as was an EP, *Metal Princess*. In 1982, the Plasmatics signed to Capitol Records and released *Coup D'État*, but by then had evolved into an outright heavy metal outfit and lost most of their novelty appeal. Williams and Beauvoir went on to record solo albums following the Plasmatics' mid-80s break-up. In April 1998, Williams was found dead from a self-inflicted gunshot wound.

● ALBUMS: *New Hope For The Wretched* (Stiff 1980) ★★, *Beyond The Valley Of 1984* (Stiff 1981) ★★★, *Coup D'État* (Capitol 1982) ★★.

## PLIMSOULS

One of a group of bands from Los Angeles, California, USA, playing power-pop in the mid-80s, the Plimsouls comprised Peter Case (b. 5 April 1954, USA; vocals, guitar, ex-Nerves), plus Lou Ramirez (drums), Dave Pahoa (bass) and Eddie Munoz (lead guitar). Formed in 1979, they originally worked as Tone Dogs before changing names and earning a strong local live reputation. This culminated in the low-budget recording in 1980 of a debut EP, *Zero Hour*, on the band's own Beat Records which captured their live energy despite its lo-fi recording quality. Their love of 60s pop was more fully realized on *The Plimsouls*, whose vibrant pop tunes were given a clearer production. However, disappointed by record sales the band's relationship with Planet deteriorated, and they signed to Geffen Records. Again the band stayed long enough to produce only a single recording, the widely acclaimed *Everywhere At Once*, which included 'A Million Miles Away', issued as a 12-inch single while the band were between labels. One of the album's most enduring tracks, 'How Long Will It Take?', seemed to amplify the Plimsouls' long-standing role as commercial underachievers, and they broke up shortly afterwards. Case went on to a solo career while the Plimsouls' original legacy was wrapped up with the 1988 release by French label Fan Club of a 1981 live gig. In 1997, the band re-formed and released *Kool Trash*.

● ALBUMS: *The Plimsouls* (Planet 1981) ★★★, *Everywhere At Once* (Geffen 1983) ★★★★, *Gangrene Tambourines* (Fan Club 1984) ★★, *One Night In America* 1981 recording (Fan Club 1988) ★★★, *Kool Trash* (Musidisc/Shaky City 1997) ★★★.

## POGUES

The London punk scene of the late-70s inspired some unusual intermingling of styles and the Pogues (then known as Pogue Mahone) performed punky versions of traditional Irish folk songs in pubs throughout the capital. They were fronted by singer Shane MacGowan (b. 25 December 1957, Kent, England) and also included Peter 'Spider' Stacy (tin whistle), Jem Finer (banjo, mandolin), James Fearnley (guitar, piano accordion), Cait O'Riordan (bass) and Andrew Ranken (drums). MacGowan had spent his late teen years singing in a punk group called the Nipple Erectors (aka the Nips) which also featured Fearnley. After several complaints the band changed their name (Pogue Mahone is 'kiss my arse' in Gaelic) and soon attracted the attention of the Clash who asked them to be their opening act. Record companies were perturbed by the band's occasionally chaotic live act where they would often fight onstage and Stacy kept time by banging his head with a beer tray. In 1984 Stiff Records signed them and recorded *Red Roses For Me*, which contained several traditional tunes as well as excellent originals such as 'Streams Of Whiskey' and 'Dark Streets Of London'. It announced a major songwriting talent in MacGowan's evocative descriptions of times and places he had often visited first-hand. Elvis Costello produced *Rum, Sodomy & The Lash* on which Philip Chevron, formerly a guitarist with the Radiators From Space, replaced Finer who was on 'paternity leave'.

The Pogues soon established themselves as a formidable and unique live act and the record entered the UK Top 20. There were further changes when the multi-instrumentalist Terry Woods (a co-founder of Steeleye Span) joined, and Cait O'Riordan was replaced by Darryl Hunt. O'Riordan later married Elvis Costello. The Pogues' intrinsically political stance resulted in the video that accompanied the single 'A Pair Of Brown Eyes' having to be re-edited because the band was filmed spitting on a poster of Prime Minister Margaret Thatcher. 'We represent the people who don't get the breaks. People can look at us and say, "My God, if that bunch of tumbledown wrecks can do it, so can I",' explained Chevron in a press interview. The band would later have their protest ballad, 'Birmingham Six', banned from airplay. The album on which this appeared, *If I Should Fall From Grace With God*, was produced by Steve Lillywhite and embraced Middle Eastern and Spanish sounds. It sold more than 200,000 copies in the USA and 'Fairytale Of New York', a rumbustious but poignant duet by MacGowan and Lillywhite's wife, Kirsty MacColl, was a Christmas number 2 hit in the UK in 1987.

In the autumn of 1989, there were fears for the future of the Pogues when MacGowan's heavy drinking led to him pulling out of several shows. He was due to join the band in the USA for a prestigious tour with Bob Dylan when he collapsed at London's Heathrow Airport. He missed all the support spots with Dylan and the band played without him. 'Other groups in a situation like that would've either said, "Let's get rid of the guy" or "Let's split up", but we're not the sort to do that. We're all part of each other's problems whether we like it or not,' said Chevron. *Peace And Love* featured songs written by nearly every member of the band and its eclectic nature saw them picking up the hurdy-gurdy, the cittern and the mandola. Its erratic nature drew criticism from some quarters, mainly from original fans who preferred the early folk-punk rants. While the other members were clearly strong players, it was widely accepted that MacGowan was the most talented songwriter. His output had always been highly sporadic but there were now fears that the drinking that fuelled his earlier creativity may have slowed him to a standstill. In an interview in 1989 he said he had not been 'dead straight sober' since he was 14 and that he drank in quantity because 'it opened his mind to paradise'. It was announced in September 1991 that MacGowan had left the band and been replaced by the former Clash singer Joe Strummer. This relationship lasted until June the following year when Strummer stepped down and the lead vocalist job went to Spider Stacy. MacGowan later re-emerged with his new band, the Popes, while his erstwhile colleagues continued to tour heavily, recording competent new material that lacked the flair of old. The Pogues eventually called it a day in August 1996. They reunited with the errant MacGowan in December 2001 to play several live dates.

● ALBUMS: *Red Roses For Me* (Stiff 1984) ★★★, *Rum, Sodomy & The Lash* (Stiff 1985) ★★★★, *If I Should Fall From Grace With God* (Stiff 1988) ★★★★, *Peace And Love* (Warners 1989) ★★★, *Hell's Ditch* (Pogue Mahone 1990) ★★★, *Waiting For Herb* (PM 1993) ★★, *Pogue Mahone* (Warners 1995) ★★, *Streams Of Whiskey* 1991 recording (Sanctuary 2002) ★★.

● COMPILATIONS: *The Best Of The Pogues* (PM 1991) ★★★★, *The Rest Of The Best* (PM 1992) ★★★, *The Very Best Of ...* (Warners 2001) ★★★★.
● VIDEOS: *Live At The Town And Country* (Virgin 1988), *Completely Pogued* (Start 1988), *Poguevision* (WEA 1991).
● FURTHER READING: *The Pogues: The Lost Decade*, Ann Scanlon. *Poguetry: The Lyrics Of Shane MacGowan*, John Hewitt and Steve Pyke (illustrators). *Shane MacGowan: Last Of The Celtic Soul Rebels*, Ian O'Doherty. *A Drink With Shane MacGowan*, Victoria Mary Clarke and Shane MacGowan. *Life & Music ... Shane MacGowan*, Joe Merrick.

## POISON

This heavy metal band was formed in Pennsylvania, USA, in the spring of 1983 by Bret Michaels (b. Bret Sychak, 15 March 1962, Harrisburg, Pennsylvania, USA; vocals) and Rikki Rockett (b. Alan Ream, 8 August 1959, Pennsylvania, USA; drums). They were soon joined by Bobby Dall (b. Harry Kuy Kendall, 2 November 1958, Miami, Florida, USA; bass) and Matt Smith (guitar). Legend has it that Slash from Guns N'Roses also auditioned at one point. The quartet played local clubs as Paris, before moving to Los Angeles and changing their name. It was at this point that Smith left the band and was replaced by C.C. DeVille (b. Bruce Anthony Johannesson, 14 May 1963, Brooklyn, New York, USA; guitar). Poison were signed by Enigma Records in 1985. The following year's debut album went double platinum in America and produced three hits, with 'Talk Dirty To Me' reaching the US Top 10. *Open Up And Say ... Ahh!* gave them their first US number 1, 'Every Rose Has Its Thorn'. Four other singles were also released, including a cover version of 'Your Mama Don't Dance' which was a major US hit for Loggins And Messina in 1972.

Poison were originally considered a 'glam band' because of the make-up they wore, but by the release of 1990's *Flesh & Blood* this image had been toned down dramatically. That year they also played their first UK shows. Fans declared their love of songs such as the US Top 5 singles, 'Unskinny Bop' and 'Something To Believe In', when the band made their official UK debut in front of 72,500 people at the Donington Festival on 18 August 1990. The following year saw the release of a live album, but shortly afterwards DeVille was replaced on guitar by the much-travelled Richie Kotzen. *Native Tongue* added brass with the Tower Of Power Horns and established the band alongside Bon Jovi as purveyors of image-conscious, hard melodic rock. As well as many supporters, this inevitably also saw them pilloried by more purist elements in heavy metal fandom. In 1994, Michaels' face appeared on the newsstands once more when he dated *Baywatch* star Pamela Anderson, before being unceremoniously 'dumped'. Blues Saraceno replaced Kotzen and helped the band record *Crack A Smile*. Due to problems with their record company, however, the album was shelved and a greatest hits set was released instead. The same year Michaels began an acting career, taking a major role in *A Letter*

From Death Row, which he also wrote and co-produced. A companion solo album was also released, and at the same time, DeVille rejoined the band. Poison's 1999 reunion tour was successful enough to warrant Capitol Records releasing Crack A Smile with extra tracks added from a 1990 MTV Unplugged session. Shortly afterwards the band released the live Power To The People on their own CMI label.

● ALBUMS: Look What The Cat Dragged In (Capitol 1986) ★★★, Open Up And Say ... Ahh! (Capitol 1988) ★★★★, Flesh & Blood (Capitol 1990) ★★★★, Swallow This Live (Capitol 1991) ★★★, Native Tongue (Capitol 1993) ★★★, Crack A Smile – And More! (Capitol 2000) ★★★★, Power To The People (CMI 2000) ★★★.
● COMPILATIONS: Poison's Greatest Hits 1986–1996 (Capitol 1996) ★★★.
● VIDEOS: Sight For Sore Ears (Enigma Music Video 1989), Flesh, Blood & Videotape (Capitol Music Video 1991), 7 Days Live (Capitol Music Video 1994), Greatest Video Hits (Capitol Video 2001).

## POLICE

The reggae-influenced minimalist pop sound of this highly talented UK trio was one of the musical high points of the late 70s and early 80s. Their individual talent and egos ultimately overcame them and they fragmented, although each of the strong-willed former members has never ruled out the possibility of a rematch.

The Police's line-up featured Stewart Copeland (b. 16 July 1952, Alexandria, Egypt; drums, percussion, vocals), Andy Summers (b. Andrew Somers, 31 December 1942, Poulton Le Fylde, Lancashire, England; guitar) and Sting (b. Gordon Sumner, 2 October 1951, Wallsend, Tyne And Wear, England; bass, vocals). Masterminded by Miles Copeland, ex-Curved Air member Stewart Copeland and ex-Last Exit bass player Sting first came together with the vastly experienced Summers in Mike Howlett's Strontium 90 project. The trio bonded so well that original guitarist Henry Padovani (b. Corsica, France) was given no alternative but to leave. He had previously played on their independent chart hit 'Fall Out', released on Miles Copeland's Illegal label. Summers, a former session musician with Zoot Money, Dantalian's Chariot, Eric Burdon And The New Animals, Soft Machine and Kevin Ayers, blended instantly with Copeland's back-to-front reggae drum technique and Sting's unusual and remarkable voice. Summers added a sparse clean guitar utilizing a flanger with echo, a sound he arguably invented and most certainly popularized; he spawned many imitators during his career with the Police. The mixture of such unusual styles gave them a totally fresh sound that they honed and developed over five outstanding albums; each record was a step forward both in musical content and sales. Astonishingly, their A&M Records debut 'Roxanne' failed to chart when first released, but this now-classic tale of a prostitute was a later success on the back of 'Can't Stand Losing You'. Their heavily reggae-influenced Outlandos D'Amour and Regatta De Blanc dominated the UK charts for most of 1979 and contained such chart-toppers as 'Message In A Bottle'

and 'Walking On The Moon'. Sting's simple but intelligently written lyrics were complete tales. Zenyatta Mondatta was their big breakthrough in America, Europe, Japan, and indeed, the rest of the world. The band's third UK number 1, 'Don't Stand So Close To Me', a tale of the temptations of being a schoolteacher (Sting's previous occupation), was closely followed by the lyrically rich yet simply titled 'De Do Do Do, De Da Da Da'. The following year, having now conquered the world, they released Ghost In The Machine, which contained Sting's most profound lyrics to date and was enriched by Hugh Padgham's fuller production. The major hit singles from this album were the thought-provoking 'Spirits In The Material World', 'Invisible Sun', a brooding atmospheric comment on Northern Ireland, and the joyous Caribbean carnival sound of 'Every Little Thing She Does Is Magic', which provided their fourth UK number 1.

Following yet another multi-million seller, the band relaxed in 1982 to concentrate on solo projects. Copeland resurrected his Klark Kent alter ego, releasing Klark Kent, and wrote the music for the movie Rumblefish. Summers had a book of photographs published to coincide with an exhibition of his camera work, and also recorded an album with Robert Fripp. Sting appeared in the film adaptation of Dennis Potter's Brimstone And Treacle and had the UK gutter press speculate on his sexual preferences. The Police reconvened in 1983 and released the carefully crafted Synchronicity; almost as if they knew this would be their last album. The package was stunning, a superb album containing numerous potential hit singles, and a series of expertly made accompanying videos. The obsessive 'Every Breath You Take', probably their greatest song, stayed at number 1 in the UK for four weeks, and for twice as many weeks in the USA, while the album stayed at the top for an astonishing 17 weeks. The collection varies from gentle songs such as 'Tea In The Sahara' and 'Wrapped Around Your Finger', to the mercurial energy of 'Synchronicity II'.

The trio played their final live shows in June 1986, sharing top billing with U2 on Amnesty International's 25th anniversary tour. A month later they reconvened for the final time to record an updated version of 'Don't Stand So Close To Me' for the compilation album Every Breath You Take: The Singles. Several greatest hits packages and a live album have periodically rekindled interest in the band. To finish on such a high and to retire as undefeated champions must leave each member with a good feeling. In retrospect, it is better to have produced five excellent albums than a massive catalogue of indifferent collections. Like the Beatles, they never outstayed their welcome, and thus will always be fondly remembered.

● ALBUMS: Outlandos D'Amour (A&M 1978) ★★★★, Regatta De Blanc (A&M 1979) ★★★★, Zenyatta Mondatta (A&M 1980) ★★★, Ghost In The Machine (A&M 1981) ★★★, Synchronicity (A&M 1983) ★★★★, Live! 1979 recording (A&M 1995) ★★.
● COMPILATIONS: Every Breath You Take: The Singles (A&M 1986) ★★★★, Greatest Hits (A&M 1992) ★★★★, Message In A Box 3-CD box set (A&M

1993) ★★★, *Every Breath You Take: The Classics* (A&M 1995) ★★★★, *The Very Best Of Sting & The Police* (A&M 1997) ★★★★.
● VIDEOS: *Around The World* (Thorn EMI Video 1981), *Synchronicity Concert* (PolyGram Video 1983), *Every Breath You Take: The Videos* (PolyGram Video 1986), *Outlandos To Synchronicities: A History Of The Police Live!* (PolyGram Video 1995).
● FURTHER READING: *The Police Released*, no editor listed. *Message In A Bottle*, Rossetta Woolf. *The Police: L'Historia Bandido*, Phil Sutcliffe and Hugh Fielder. *The Police: A Visual Documentary*, Miles. *The Police*, Lynn Goldsmith. *Complete Guide To The Music Of The Police And Sting*, Chris Welch.

## POP GROUP

This seminal UK punk act operated from Bristol, Avon, in the late 70s, combining abstracted funk with chaos and expressionist vocals courtesy of Mark Stewart. The topics under consideration – starvation, war, exploitation – were similar to those expounded by anarcho-punks Crass, but the Pop Group's music was much more sophisticated. Their records proved both inspirational and intolerable, some of the most extreme music to have been pressed on to vinyl. Their masterpiece was 1980's *For How Much Longer Must We Tolerate Mass Murder*. Unable to maintain such a pitch of intensity, the band splintered into different projects. Bass player Simon Underwood left to form Pigbag, a welcome relief from the drabness punk conformity had created, with its riot of bright shirts, ethnic rhythms and James Brown references. Guitarist and saxophonist Gareth Sager went on to form the irrepressible Rip Rig And Panic. Only singer Mark Stewart kept to his bleak viewpoint, forming Mark Stewart And The Maffia with the rhythm team from Sugarhill Records and working with producer Adrian Sherwood. Guitarist John Waddington formed Maximum Joy and drummer Bruce Smith moved through Rip Rig And Panic to work as a session musician with artists including Terence Trent D'Arby and Soul II Soul.
● ALBUMS: *Y* (Radar 1979) ★★★, *For How Much Longer Must We Tolerate Mass Murder* (Rough Trade 1980) ★★★★, *We Are Time* (Rough Trade 1980) ★★.
● COMPILATIONS: *We Are All Prostitutes* (Radar 1998) ★★★.

## POP WILL EAT ITSELF

This UK band took its name from the headline of an article on Jamie Wednesday (later Carter USM) by writer David Quantick in the *New Musical Express*. Having previously rehearsed and gigged under the names From Eden and Wild And Wondering, the band emerged as Pop Will Eat Itself in 1986 with a line-up comprising Clint Mansell (b. 7 November 1963, Coventry, England; vocals, guitar), Adam Mole (b. 1962, Stourbridge, England; keyboards), Graham Crabb (b. 10 October 1964, Streetly, West Midlands, England; drums, later vocals) and Richard March (b. 4 March 1965, York, Yorkshire, England; bass).
Making their live debut at the Mere, Stourbridge Art College, their first recording was the privately issued EP *The Poppies Say Grr*, which was named as Single Of The Week in the *New Musical Express*. BBC Radio

sessions followed and the band appeared in the independent charts with the follow-up EPs *Poppiecock* and *The Covers*. Already known for their hard pop and vulgarisms, they ran into trouble with the release of 'Beaver Patrol', which was criticized for its puerile sexism. Their debut album, *Box Frenzy*, followed in late 1987 and displayed their odd mix of guitar pop with sampling. The insistent 'There Is No Love Between Us Anymore' was their most impressive single to date and augured well for the future, as did 'Def Con One' in 1988. During that year, they were invited to play in the USSR, and soon afterwards signed to the major RCA Records. 'Can U Dig It' and 'Wise Up Sucker' were minor successes, as was their second album. A world tour sharpened their approach and during 1990, they achieved mainstream acclaim with 'Touched By The Hand Of Cicciolina', a paean addressed to the Italian porn star-turned-politician. Two further hit singles, 'X,Y & Zee' and '92 Degrees', followed in 1991. The band recruited a full-time (human) drummer in 1992 when Fuzz (b. Robert Townshend, 31 July 1964, Birmingham, England; ex-Pig Bros; General Public) joined, but following *Weird's Bar & Grill* a year later, RCA dropped them. Now effectively despised by the media, Pop Will Eat Itself continued despite expectations that this might signify the end of the band, forging a new contract with Infectious Records. The results of the latter contract hardly endeared them to critics, though the title of the 1995 remix collection *Two Fingers My Friends!*, at least underlined their tenacity and self-sufficiency. Crabb left in 1994, releasing an album as Golden Claw Musics. March went on to form big beat mavericks Bentley Rhythm Ace, while Mansell established himself as a soundtrack composer on movies such as *Pi* and *Requiem For A Dream*.
● ALBUMS: *Box Frenzy* (Chapter 22 1987) ★★, *Now For A Feast!* early recordings (Rough Trade 1989) ★★★, *This Is The Day, This Is The Hour, This Is This!* (RCA 1989) ★★★, *The Pop Will Eat Itself Cure For Sanity* (RCA 1990) ★★, *The Looks Or The Lifestyle* (RCA 1992) ★★★, *Weird's Bar & Grill* (RCA 1993) ★★, *Dos Dedos Mes Amigos* (Infectious 1994) ★★★, *Two Fingers My Friends!* remixes (Infectious 1995) ★★★.
● COMPILATIONS: *There Is No Love Between Us Anymore* (Chapter 22 1992) ★★★, *16 Different Flavours Of Hell* (RCA/BMG 1993) ★★★, *Wise Up Suckers* (BMG 1996) ★★★.

## POSTCARD RECORDS

After the impetus of punk's initial onslaught, like-minded individuals in every corner of Britain set about creating their own musical identity. If they could not play music, they went one better and founded their own label. Alan Horne set about realizing his ambition in late 70s Glasgow, Scotland when he discovered local favourites Orange Juice. Here was a band that could be harnessed, and Horne set about creating Postcard Records with lead singer Edwyn Collins as the 'Sound Of Young Scotland'. Orange Juice's 'Falling And Laughing' was issued early in 1980, housed in distinctive fold-around, hand-coloured sleeves, with a free flexi-disc. Much of the Postcard label's appeal would stem from the precious nature of its roster and the presentation of its releases as vital and desirable artefacts. To do this, Horne needed more than one band and after losing the Fire Engines, opted for manic Edinburgh act Josef K. Postcard's second release was also arguably their finest; Orange Juice's 'Blue Boy'. Their debut had caused a stir, certainly, but this formidable single, awash with frenetic guitarwork and an unforgettably passionate melody, sent the critics reeling. Josef K's 'Radio Drill Time' was less accessible and more frenzied, but an aura already surrounded the label. Next came the Go-Betweens, an obscure Australian outfit whom Horne met while they were touring the UK. They promptly recorded 'I Need Two Heads', which became the fourth Postcard single, but this was to prove their only single for the label. Josef K's more relaxed 'It's Kinda Funny' and another Orange Juice classic, 'Simply Thrilled Honey', saw out 1980, and Horne took the end of year opportunity to redesign the label's image. The spartan brown labels (with a drum-beating pussycat) were replaced by a checked design to reflect the new sleeves, portraying a collage of Scottish national dress. In the meantime, Josef K hit a stumbling block. They were unhappy with the sound on their debut *Sorry For Laughing*, and eventually scrapped it before it reached the shops. Postcard instead relied on Orange Juice for 'Poor Old Soul', before introducing a new signing early in 1981, Aztec Camera. Fronted by the 16-year-old Roddy Frame, their debut, 'Just Like Gold', was more traditional than other Postcard material, but nonetheless endearing. Josef K teamed up with Belgian label Les Disques Du Crepescule for 'Sorry For Laughing' (the title track to the abandoned album), and followed this with 'Chance Meeting', a re-recording of their first single. By this time, mid-1981, Postcard was basking in the critical sunshine and Orange Juice succumbed to a seductive offer from Polydor Records. Their next single, 'Wan Light', was abandoned and from this point on, Postcard fell apart. Josef K finally took the plunge with a re-recorded album, *The Only Fun In Town*, and Aztec Camera continued to ply their acoustic sensibilities with 'Mattress Of Wire', but Horne soon moved on to pastures new, leaving numerous projects on the shelf. In addition to the first long-player from Aztec Camera, Horne had allocated numbers to singles from the Bluebells (later to enjoy commercial success at London Records), the Jazzateers (who joined Rough Trade Records) and Secret Goldfish (reputedly an Orange Juice pseudonym). Aztec Camera and the Go-Betweens also moved to Rough Trade, and Josef K split up, while Horne eventually re-surfaced managing the labels Win and Swamplands.

## POWER STATION

This commercial rock band started out as a Tony Thompson (drums, ex-LaBelle; Chic) solo project, but came to be viewed as a spin-off from Duran Duran. Andy Taylor (b. 16 February 1961, Wolverhampton, England; guitar) saw it as a cross between Chic and the Sex Pistols, and was joined by fellow Duran Duran member John Taylor (b. Nigel

John Taylor, 20 June 1960, Birmingham, West Midlands, England; bass) and vocalist Robert Palmer (b. Alan Palmer, 19 January 1949, Batley, Yorkshire, England). Thompson's Chic partner Bernard Edwards (b. 31 October 1952, Greenville, North Carolina, USA, d. 18 April 1996, Tokyo, Japan) handled production duties. Palmer had previously met the Duran Duran members at a MENCAP charity concert. They hit almost immediately with 'Some Like It Hot' and a cover version of T. Rex's 'Get It On'. Both tracks reached the US Top 10. Then, after a subsequent minor hit with 'Communication' marking their third success of 1985, they split. Their single album was recorded at the Power Station Studio in New York, from which they took their name. Palmer did not want to tour, so he was replaced by former Silverhead and Detective vocalist Michael Des Barres. Following the band's quick exit John Taylor returned to Duran Duran while his namesake Andy went on to a solo career. He invited Steve Jones to guest on his debut solo album, fulfilling the prophecy of his stated ambition that Power Station should fuse the Sex Pistols and Chic by eventually working with members of both. The reunion in 1996 was unexpected as major problems were encountered during the recording sessions for the second coming. Bernard Edwards, who produced the first album and stepped in after John Taylor jumped ship mid-way, died during recording. *Living In Fear*, although well produced was a record out of its time. Very much a creation of the 80s, the Power Station's new songs sounded dated in the context of 90s alternative rock and pop. The public voted by keeping their hands out of their wallets.

● ALBUMS: *The Power Station* (Parlophone 1985) ★★★, *Living In Fear* (Chrysalis 1996) ★★.

## PRAYING MANTIS

Formed in London, England, in 1977, Praying Mantis were at the forefront of the New Wave Of British Heavy Metal. The original line-up comprised Tino 'Troy' Neophytou (guitar, vocals), Pete Moore (guitar, vocals), Tino's brother Chris 'Troy' Neophytou (bass, vocals) and Chris Hudson (drums). Through early demo recordings, the band attracted the attention of heavy-metal club DJ Neal Kay, who helped them to release an independent three-track EP, *The Soundhouse Tapes Part 1*, a title also used by Iron Maiden for their first release. Praying Mantis' career can be closely linked with Iron Maiden during those early years as, in addition to both bands appearing on the *Metal For Muthas* compilation released by EMI Records in 1980, they also toured England together. By now Bob Angelo and Mick Ransome had replaced Moore and Hudson in the line-up. Signing to Arista Records and replacing Angelo (who joined Weapon in July 1981) and Ransome with guitarist/vocalist Steve Carroll and ex-Ten Years After drummer Dave Potts, the band's debut, *Time Tells No Lies*, was released in 1981. It was not well received, owing to the lacklustre production and basic melodic rock sound. The band decided a line-up change was needed, replacing Carroll with ex-Grand Prix vocalist Bernie Shaw and recruiting keyboard player Jon Bavin. This line-up went on to record 'Turn The

Tables' for a compilation album released on the Jet Records label. Through a lack of media interest the band metamorphosed into Stratus, who specialized in standard melodic rock and also featured ex-Iron Maiden drummer Clive Burr.

To celebrate the 10th anniversary of the NWOBHM the band re-formed early in 1990 to tour Japan as part of the British All Stars. This new line-up consisted of founder members Tino and Chris Troy, ex-Iron Maiden vocalist Paul Di'Anno, ex-Iron Maiden guitarist Dennis Stratton and ex-Weapon drummer Bruce Bisland. The Troys, Stratton and Bisland continued under the Praying Mantis banner, recruiting a series of lead vocalists including Colin Peel, Gary Barden and Tony O'Hora. They enjoy particular acclaim in the Far East and are still recording new studio material.

● ALBUMS: *Time Tells No Lies* (Arista 1981) ★★, *Live At Last* (Pony Canyon/Zoom 1990) ★★★, *Predator In Disguise* (Pony Canyon/Under One Flag 1991) ★★★, *A Cry For The New World* (Pony Canyon/Under One Flag 1993) ★★, *To The Power Of Ten* (Pony Canyon 1995) ★★★, *Captured Alive In Tokyo City* (Pony Canyon/Zoom 1996) ★★, *Forever In Time* (Pony Canyon 1998) ★★, *Nowhere To Hide* (Pony Canyon 2000) ★★★.

● COMPILATIONS: *Demorabilia* (Pony Canyon 1999) ★★.

## PREFAB SPROUT

The intricate tales and thoughts in the lyrics of songwriter Paddy McAloon indicate a major songwriter. His Bob Dylan imagery and Elvis Costello bluntness helped make Prefab Sprout one of the most refreshing pop bands of the late 80s and beyond.

Prefab Sprout was formed in 1982 by Paddy McAloon (b. 7 June 1957, Durham, England; guitar, vocals), Martin McAloon (b. 4 January 1962, Durham, England; bass), Wendy Smith (b. 31 May 1963, Durham, England; vocals, guitar) and Neil Conti (b. 12 February 1959, London, England). Following a self-pressed single 'Lions In My Own Garden', Paddy attracted the attention of the independent label Kitchenware. They had further hits in the UK independent charts and their debut *Swoon* made the national chart. *Swoon* was a wordy album featuring songs with many chord changes that ultimately concentrated on lyrics rather than melody. Later that year the excellent 'When Love Breaks Down' failed to excite the singles-buying public. A remixed version by Thomas Dolby was released the following year, but once again failed.

When *Steve McQueen* was issued in 1985, the band became media darlings, with Paddy McAloon coming near to overexposure. The album was a critical success, featuring hummable songs with fascinating lyrics, and it made a respectable showing in the charts. At the end of the year, 'When Love Breaks Down' was issued for a third time and finally became a hit. In the USA, *Steve McQueen* was forcibly retitled *Two Wheels Good*. A striking work, the album included a tribute to Faron Young and the arresting 'Goodbye Lucille #1' (aka 'Johnny Johnny'). *From Langley Park To Memphis* in 1988 was a major success

worldwide; Paddy McAloon had now refined his art to produce totally accessible yet inventive pop music. The album represented a courageous change of direction with McAloon employing strings and composing melodies that recalled the great show musical writers of the pre-rock 'n' roll era. 'Nightingales' was very much in this vein, and the work ended with the strikingly melodramatic 'Nancy (Let Your Hair Down For Me)' and 'The Venus Of The Soup Kitchen'. Already the band had reached the stage of having superstar guests 'turning up on the album'. Both Stevie Wonder (harmonica solo on 'Nightingales') and Pete Townshend put in appearances. 'The King Of Rock 'N' Roll' became their biggest UK hit to date. *Protest Songs* was a collection scheduled to appear before their previous album and its success was muted by the continuing sales of both *Steve McQueen* and *From Langley Park To Memphis*. McAloon unleashed *Jordan: The Comeback* in 1990, and for many critics it was the album of the year. All McAloon's talents had combined to produce a concept album of magnificence. Over 64 minutes in length, the album boasted 19 tracks, full of striking melodies and fascinatingly oblique lyrics. The ghost of Elvis Presley haunted several of the songs, most notably the elegiac 'Moon Dog'.

McAloon spent the next few years tinkering with various new projects, paying the bills by writing songs for actor/singer Jimmy Nail. A new album, *Andromeda Heights*, finally appeared in 1997. Sophisticated mood music, it met with a polite response from critics still entranced by McAloon's intricate musical and lyrical conceits. Another lengthy gap ensued before *The Gunman And Other Stories* was released. This time McAloon had donned cowboy boots and a Stetson hat.

● ALBUMS: *Swoon* (Kitchenware 1984) ★★★, *Steve McQueen* (Kitchenware 1985) ★★★★, *From Langley Park To Memphis* (Kitchenware 1988) ★★★, *Protest Songs* (Kitchenware 1989) ★★★, *Jordan: The Comeback* (Kitchenware 1990) ★★★★, *Andromeda Heights* (Columbia 1997) ★★★, *The Gunman And Other Stories* (Columbia 2001) ★★★.

● COMPILATIONS: *A Life Of Surprises: The Best Of* (Kitchenware 1992) ★★★★, *38 Carat Collection* (Columbia 1999) ★★★★.

● VIDEOS: *A Life Of Surprises: The Video Collection* (SMV 1987).

● FURTHER READING: *Myths, Melodies & Metaphysics, Paddy McAloon's Prefab Sprout*, John Birch.

## PRETENDERS

Chrissie Hynde (b. 17 September 1951, Akron, Ohio, USA) came to England to seek her fortune in 1973. After meeting with *New Musical Express* writer and future boyfriend Nick Kent, she joined the paper and gained entrance into the world of rock. During her pre-Pretenders days she worked at Malcolm McLaren's shop, SEX, played with Chris Spedding in France, and moved back to America where she formed a band called Jack Rabbit. She returned to punk-era London in 1976, forming the short-lived Berk Brothers and achieving a brief period of tabloid notoriety as part of the Moors Murderers, a non-existent band set up as a publicity stunt by the notorious punk icon Steve Strange. By the time she assembled the Pretenders in 1978, Hynde had gained a great deal of experience. The classic Pretenders line-up comprised Pete Farndon (b. 2 June 1952, Hereford, England, d. 14 April 1983; bass), James Honeyman-Scott (b. 4 November 1956, Hereford, England, d. 16 June 1982, London, England; guitar) and Martin Chambers (b. 4 September 1951, Hereford, England; drums, who replaced Gerry Mackleduff). They were signed to Dave Hill's Real Records, which was soon co-opted by Sire Records. Their debut single was a Nick Lowe-produced cover version of the Kinks' 'Stop Your Sobbing'. It scraped into the UK Top 40 in February 1979, having received critical praise and much interest. 'Kid' and the superb 'Brass In Pocket' followed. The latter was accompanied by a black-and-white video with Hynde portrayed as a waitress, and reached the number 1 position in the UK in November. It was their chart-topping debut album that eventually put them on the road to becoming one of the decade's most important bands. *Pretenders*, a *tour de force* of articulate pop, remains their finest work. In addition to their previous singles, the album included the reggae-styled 'Private Life' (later recorded by Grace Jones), the frenetic 'Precious', the Byrds-like 'Talk Of The Town' (a UK Top 10 single) and the beautiful ballad 'Lovers Of Today'.

Throughout 1980, the band became a major stadium attraction in the USA, and it was in America that Hynde met and fell in love with her musical idol, the Kinks' Ray Davies. *Pretenders II* was released in 1982. It was another collection of melodious rock played with new-wave enthusiasm. Standout tracks were 'Message Of Love', the brilliantly confessional 'The Adulteress', and another Davies chestnut, 'I Go To Sleep' (a UK number 7 single the previous November), first recorded by the Applejacks in 1964. During the turbulent month of June, Pete Farndon, whose drug abuse had been a problem for some time, was fired. Two days later Honeyman-Scott was found dead from a deadly concoction of heroin and cocaine. Nine months later Hynde gave birth to a daughter by Ray Davies. Two months after this happy event, tragedy struck again. Pete Farndon was found dead in his bath from a drug overdose.

The new full-time Pretenders were Robbie McIntosh on lead guitar, and bass player Malcolm Foster. They set about recording a third album and the band ended the year with another UK Top 20 hit single, the Christmassy '2000 Miles'. *Learning To Crawl* was released at the beginning of another successful year, and climbed to number 5 on the US album chart. The album was erratic, but it did contain some gems, notably the epic 'Thin Line Between Love And Hate', the powerful 'Middle Of The Road' and the melodic, yet poignant tribute to Honeyman-Scott, 'Back On The Chain Gang' (the band's first US Top 10 single). The band embarked on another US tour, but Hynde refused to be parted from her baby daughter who accompanied her, while Davies and his band were touring elsewhere. In May 1984, following a whirlwind affair, Hynde married Jim Kerr of Simple

Minds. Back with the Pretenders she appeared at Live Aid at the JFK stadium in Philadelphia, and would enjoy success in August 1985 under her own name duetting with UB40 on the UK chart-topping reggae remake of Sonny And Cher's 'I Got You Babe'. Following the birth of another daughter (Jim Kerr was the father this time), Hynde dismantled the band for a period. A number of musicians were used to record *Get Close*, including a soon to depart Chambers, McIntosh, bass player T.M. Stevens, keyboard player Bernie Worrell, and drummer Blair Cunningham (ex-Haircut 100). The Jimmy Iovine-produced album was released at the end of 1987 but received a mixed reception. Two tracks, 'Don't Get Me Wrong' and 'Hymn To Her', had already charted in the UK Top 10 the previous year.

A troubled tour of America saw Worrell and Stevens sacked, McIntosh quitting, and Foster and keyboard player Rupert Black reinstated. Ex-Smiths member Johnny Marr also played several dates, but subsequent attempts by Hynde to record with the mercurial guitarist foundered. In 1988 a solo Hynde performed with UB40 at the Nelson Mandela Concert and the subsequent duet, 'Breakfast In Bed', was a UK Top 10 hit in June. Hynde's marriage to Kerr collapsed before 1990's *Packed!*, recorded with drummer Cunningham, bass player John McKenzie, and guitarists Billy Bremner and Dominic Miller. The album proved to be another critical and commercial success, demonstrating her natural gift for writing tight, melodic rock songs.

Hynde subsequently spent much of her time campaigning for animal rights and environmental issues, before returning with a new album in 1994. *Last Of The Independents* saw Hynde reunited with drummer Martin Chambers, alongside Adam Seymour (guitar) and Andy Hobson (bass). In March 1995, in the company of Cher, Neneh Cherry and Eric Clapton, Hynde topped the UK charts with the charity single 'Love Can Build A Bridge'. The same year's *The Isle Of View* saw Hynde performing an acoustic set of Pretenders material backed by a string quartet. She returned to the band format with 1999's ¡*Viva El Amor!*, a passionate record that spoke volumes about Hynde's undying commitment to rock music.

● ALBUMS: *Pretenders* (Real/Sire 1980) ★★★★, *Pretenders II* (Real/Sire 1981) ★★★★, *Learning To Crawl* (Real/Sire 1984) ★★★★, *Get Close* (WEA/Sire 1986) ★★, *Packed!* (WEA/Sire 1990) ★★, *Last Of The Independents* (WEA 1994) ★★★, *The Isle Of View* (WEA 1995) ★★★, ¡*Viva El Amor!* (WEA 1999) ★★★.
● COMPILATIONS: *The Singles* (WEA/Sire 1987) ★★★★, *Greatest Hits* (WEA 2000) ★★★★.
● VIDEOS: *The Isle Of View* (Warner Music Vision 1995).
● FURTHER READING: *Pretenders*, Miles. *The Pretenders*, Chris Salewicz. *The Pretenders: With Hyndesight*, Mike Wrenn.

## PRIEST, MAXI

b. Max Elliot, 10 June 1962, Lewisham, London, England. Former carpenter Maxi Priest established himself as a hugely successful crossover reggae artist in the late 80s. Named by his mother after her fondness for Max Bygraves, Elliot took his new name upon his conversion to Rastafarianism (from Priest Levi, one of the figureheads of the 12 tribes of Israel). He made his initial music industry breakthrough by employing his artisan's skills in building sound systems. He went on to tour with Saxon International, the UK's premier reggae assembly, where he rubbed shoulders with Peter King, Phillip Papa Levi, Smiley Culture and Asher Senator. He made his name and reputation as a 'singing' DJ, vocalizing improvised observations over prime 70s roots music, but he soon progressed to a more soulful style that was captured by producer Paul Robinson (aka Barry Boom) on his debut, You're Safe. After recording this album, he began a run of hits in 1986 with 'Strollin' On', 'In The Springtime' and 'Crazy Love'. In 1987, he gained a minor hit single with a cover version of Robert Palmer's 'Some Guys Have All The Luck'. However, most successful was his 1988 cover version of Cat Stevens' 'Wild World', though it owed more of a debt to the Jimmy Cliff reggae version. Further chart appearances followed with 'Close To You', 'Peace Throughout The World' and 'Human Work Of Art'. Bona Fide included contributions from, among others, Soul II Soul, a group undoubtedly influenced by Priest's mellow but evocative brand of lovers rock. In 1996, Priest enjoyed a UK Top 20 hit with 'That Girl', in combination with Shaggy.

● ALBUMS: You're Safe (Virgin 1985) ★★, Intentions (Virgin 1986) ★★, Maxi (10 1987) ★★, Bona Fide (10 1990) ★★★, Fe Real (10 1992) ★★, Man With The Fun (Virgin 1996) ★★, Live In Concert 1986 recording (Strange Fruit 1999) ★★★, Combination (Virgin 1999) ★★★.
● COMPILATIONS: The Best Of Me (10 1991) ★★★.

# PRINCE
b. Prince Rogers Nelson, 7 June 1958, Minneapolis, Minnesota, USA. A prodigiously talented singer-songwriter, multi-instrumentalist and producer, Prince was named after the Prince Roger Trio, of whom his father, pianist John Nelson, was a member. After running away from his mother and stepfather, he briefly joined up with John, who bought him his first guitar. He was later adopted by the Andersons, and became a close friend of Andre Anderson (later Andre Cymone). Prince was already conversant with piano and guitar and had written his own material from an early age. Together with Anderson he joined the latter's cousin, Charles Smith, in a junior high school band titled Grand Central. As Prince progressed to high school, Grand Central became Champagne, and he introduced original material into his sets for the first time. His musical development continued with the emergence of 'Uptown', a musical underground scene that included Flyte Time, as well as other important influences including Jellybean Johnson, Terry Lewis and Alexander O'Neal. Prince's first demos were recorded in 1976 with Chris Moon, who gave him guidance in the operation of a music studio, and free reign to experiment at weekends. Moon also introduced him to backer Owen Husney, after which Prince provided interested parties with a superior-quality demo. Husney and his partner Levinson set about a massive 'hyping' campaign, the results of which secured him a long-term, flexible contract with Warner Brothers Records after a great deal of scrambling among the majors.

Debuting with Prince For You, Prince sent shock waves through his new sponsors by spending double his entire advance on the production of a single album. It sold moderately (USA number 163), with the single 'Soft And Wet' making a big impact in the R&B charts. The album's blend of deep funk and soul was merely an appetizer in comparison to his later exploits, but enough to reassure his label that their investment had been a solid one. By 1979 Prince had put together a firm band (his debut had been recorded almost exclusively by himself). This featured Cymone (bass), Gayle Chapman and Matt Fink (both keyboards), Bobby Z (drummer) and Dez Dickerson (guitar). Despite lavishing considerably less time and money on it than its predecessor, Prince nevertheless charted (US number 22) and boasted two successful singles, 'Why You Wanna Treat Me So Bad?' and 'I Wanna Be Your Lover'. A succession of live dates promoting the new album Dirty Mind saw Lisa Coleman replacing Chapman. The album was the first fully to embody Prince's sexual allure, and the phallic exhortations on his Fender Telecaster and explicit material such as 'Head' appalled and enticed in equal proportions. Artists such as Rick James, whom Prince supported in 1980, were among those who mistrusted Prince's open, androgynous sexuality. Returning to Minneapolis after an aborted UK tour, Cymone departed for a solo career while former members of Flyte Time and others released a self-titled album under the band name the Time. It transpired later that their songs had been written by Prince, who was the motivation behind the entire project.

Prince was nothing if not prolific, and both Controversy and 1999 followed within 12 months. Controversy attempted to provide a rationale for the sexual machinations that dominated Dirty Mind, falling unhappily between the two stools of instinct and intellect. It was a paradox not entirely solved by 1999, a double album that had enough strong material to make up two sides of excellence but no more. The promotional tour featured a special revue troupe: Prince And The Revolution headlined above the Time and Vanity 6 (an all-girl Prince creation). The single 'Little Red Corvette' was lifted from the album and was the first to gain significant airplay on MTV. The song was almost entirely constructed for this purpose, using a strong 'white' metaphor as leverage. After internal disputes with the Time, Prince began work on the Purple Rain movie, a glamorized autobiographical piece in which he would star. The potent social commentary of 'When Doves Cry' was lifted from the soundtrack and became the first Prince song to grace the top of the US charts. 'Let's Go Crazy' and 'Purple Rain' (numbers 1 and 2, respectively) further established him as a figurehead for the 80s. The latter saw him turn his hand to Jimi Hendrix pyrotechnics and textures in the song. After the end of a huge and successful tour, Prince returned to the studio for a duet with Apollonia, the latest in a seemingly endless succession of female protégés. He also found time to revitalize the career of Scottish pop singer Sheena Easton by composing her US Top 10 effort 'Sugar Walls'.

When *Around The World In A Day* emerged in 1985, it topped the US charts for a three-week run, despite a deliberate lack of promotion. Drowning in quasi-psychedelia and 60s optimism, it was a diverting but strangely uneventful, almost frivolous, jaunt. It preceded the announcement that Prince was retiring from live appearances. Instead, he had founded the studio/label/complex Paisley Park in central Minneapolis, which would become the luxurious base for his future operations. As work began on a second movie, *Under The Cherry Moon*, 'Kiss' was released to become his third US number 1. Held one place beneath it was the Bangles' 'Manic Monday', written by Prince under one of his numerous pseudonyms, in this case, Christopher.

Prince quickly overturned his decision not to perform live, and set out on the *Parade* tour to promote the number 1 album of the same name. Unfortunately, although 'Kiss' and 'Girls And Boys' represented classic Prince innuendo, the rest of the album lacked focus. The shows, however, were spectacular even by Prince standards, but his backing band the Revolution were nevertheless disbanded at the end of the tour. In 1987, Prince instituted a new line-up for the latest live engagements. While retaining the backbone of the Revolution (Fink, Leeds, Brooks and Safford) he added Sheila E., Marco Weaver, and Seacer. The new album was to be a radical departure from the laconic, cosseted atmosphere that pervaded *Parade*. 'Sign 'O' The Times', the title track, was a hard-hitting testimony to urban dystopia, drug-related violence and human folly. The vast majority of tracks on the double album revisited the favoured territory of sex and sensuality. The follow-up album would elaborate on the darker shades of *Sign 'O' The Times'* apocalyptic vision. However, *The Black Album* was recalled by Prince before it reached the shops. Combining primal funk slices with sadistic overtones, Prince's decision to suspend it ensured that it would become the 80s' most coveted bootleg. The mythology surrounding its non-release has it that *The Black Album* was the work of Prince's 'dark' side – 'Spooky Electric'. This was given credence by the subsequent *Lovesexy*, apparently the result of the pre-eminence of 'Camille' – Prince's 'good' side. Playing both albums side by side certainly reveals a sharp dichotomy of approach.

Prince's next tour, meanwhile, saw the inclusion of a huge Pink Cadillac as a mobile part of the set. Exhausted musicians testified to the difficulty of backing their leader, rushing from orchestrated stadium performances to private club dates where entire sets would be improvised, all of which Prince, naturally, took in his stride. 1989 closed with a duet with Madonna, who, alongside Michael Jackson, was the only artist able to compete with Prince in terms of mass popularity. The following year was dominated by the soundtrack album for the year's biggest movie, *Batman*. If the album was not his

greatest artistic success, it proved a commercial smash, topping the US charts for six weeks. He had also written and produced an album for singer Mavis Staples. At first glance it seemed an unlikely combination, but Prince's lyrics tempered the sexual with the divine in a manner that was judged acceptable by the grand lady of gospel. In February 1990 Sinéad O'Connor recorded a version of Prince's composition 'Nothing Compares 2 U', which topped both the US and UK charts. In September, he released *Graffiti Bridge*, which accompanied a movie release of the same title. The album was composed entirely of Prince compositions of which he sang just over half – other guests included Tevin Campbell, Mavis Staples and the Time. Both album and movie were critical and commercial failures, however. *Graffiti Bridge* was his first commercial let down for some time, peaking at number 6 in the USA (although it made number 1 in the UK).

Prince, as usual, was already busy putting together new projects. These included his latest backing outfit, the New Power Generation, featuring Tony M (rapper), Rosie Gaines (vocals), Michael Bland (drums), Levi Seacer (guitar), Kirk Johnson (guitar), Sonny T (bass) and Tommy Barbarella (keyboards). They were in place in time for the sessions for *Diamonds And Pearls*, a comparatively deliberate and studied body of work. The album was released in October 1991, and showcased the new backing band. Greeted by most critics as a return to form, the New Power Generation were considered his most able and vibrant collaborators since the mid-80s. Taken from it, 'Cream' became a US number 1. 1992's 'Money Don't Matter 2 Night' featured a video directed by filmmaker Spike Lee, while 'Sexy MF' was widely banned on UK radio because of its suggestive lyrics. Both 'Sexy MF' and 'My Name Is Prince' were included on the *Love Symbol Album* – which introduced the cryptic 'symbol' that he would legally adopt as his name in June 1993. Much of the attention subsequently surrounding the artist concerned his protracted battle against his record company, Warner Brothers. His behaviour became increasingly erratic – speaking only through envoys, he appeared at the 1995 BRIT Awards ceremony with the word 'slave' written across his forehead as a protest. In October he abandoned the symbol moniker and from that point was known as 'The Artist Formerly Known As Prince'. Naturally, this produced enough running gags to fill a book and his credibility was in serious danger. In 1995, he released *The Gold Experience*, a return to the raunchy funk of his 80s prime in tracks such as 'Pussy Control' and 'I Hate You'. It also included the smoothly accessible 'The Most Beautiful Girl In The World', his bestselling single for many years.

Following the release of *Chaos And Disorder* in July 1996, Prince sacked the New Power Generation and announced that he would not be touring, preferring to spend more time with his wife and new baby (who tragically died months after birth). He celebrated his release from the Warner Brothers contract with the sprawling *Emancipation*. Another 4-CD set, *Crystal Ball*, was initially sold over the Internet before being released to distributors. The first three CDs compiled previously unreleased tracks, while the all-acoustic fourth CD, *The Truth*, featured 12 strong new songs recorded the previous year. Although the artist has yet to provide the definitive album of which he is so obviously capable, the continued flow of erratic, flawed gems suggests that the struggle will continue to captivate his audience. In May 2000, Prince announced he had reverted to using his original moniker. Sighs of relief echoed around the world.

● ALBUMS: *Prince – For You* (Warners 1978) ★★★, *Prince* (Warners 1979) ★★★, *Dirty Mind* (Warners 1980) ★★★, *Controversy* (Warners 1981) ★★★, *1999* (Warners 1982) ★★★★, *Purple Rain* film soundtrack (Warners 1984) ★★★★, *Around The World In A Day* (Paisley Park 1985) ★★★, *Parade – Music From Under The Cherry Moon* film soundtrack (Paisley Park 1986) ★★★, *Sign 'O' The Times* (Paisley Park 1987) ★★★★, *Lovesexy* (Paisley Park 1988) ★★★, *Batman* film soundtrack (Warners 1989) ★★★, *Graffiti Bridge* (Paisley Park 1990) ★★, *Diamonds And Pearls* (Paisley Park 1991) ★★★, *Symbol* (Paisley Park 1993) ★★★, *Come* (Paisley Park 1994) ★★, *The Gold Experience* (Warners 1995) ★★★, *Chaos And Disorder* (Warners 1996) ★★, *Emancipation* (New Power Generation 1996) ★★, *Crystal Ball* 4-CD set (New Power Generation 1998) ★★★, *New Power Soul* (NPG 1998) ★★, *Rave Un2 The Joy Fantastic* (Arista/NPG 1999) ★★★, *The Rainbow Children* (NPG 2001) ★★★.

● COMPILATIONS: *The Hits: Volume I & II* (Paisley Park/Warners 1993) ★★★★, *The Vault ... Old Friends 4 Sale* (Warners 1999) ★★★★, *The Very Best Of Prince* (Rhino 2001) ★★★★.

● VIDEOS: *Double Live* (PolyGram Music Video 1986), *Prince And The Revolution; Live* (Channel 5 Video 1987), *Sign O' The Times* (Palace Video 1988), *Lovesexy Part 1* (Palace Video 1989), *Lovesexy Part 2* (Palace Video 1989), *Get Off* (Warner Music Video 1991), *Prince: The Hits Collection* (Warner Music Video 1993), *3 Chains O' Gold* (Warner Reprise 1994), *Billboards* (Warner Vision 1994).

● FURTHER READING: *Prince: Imp Of The Perverse*, Barney Hoskyns. *Prince: A Pop Life*, Dave Hill. *Prince By Controversy*, The 'Controversy' Team. *Prince: A Documentary*, Per Nilsen. *Prince: An Illustrated Biography*, John W. Duffy. *Prince*, John Ewing. *Dancemusicsexromance – Prince: The First Decade*, Per Nilsen.

## PROCLAIMERS

This Scottish folk duo, who specialize in belligerent harmonies, comprises identical twins Craig and Charlie Reid from Auchtermuchty. They had an early UK hit in 1987 with the Gerry Rafferty-produced 'Letter From America'. Follow-ups included the typically boisterous 'Make My Heart Fly' and 'I'm Gonna Be (500 Miles)'. Pete Wingfield was brought in to produce *Sunshine On Leith*, after which they took a two-year sabbatical. Writing for the third album was disrupted, however, when they spent much energy and money ensuring that their beloved, debt-ridden Hibernian Football Club did not close down. In common with many fans, they are now shareholders. They reappeared in 1990 with the *King Of The Road* EP. The title track, a cover version of the old Roger Miller song, came from the movie

*The Crossing*. Other tracks on the EP, which reached the UK Top 10, included the folk/country classic 'The Long Black Veil'. On the back of the unexpected success of 'I'm Gonna Be (500 Miles)', which reached the US Top 5 in 1993 after featuring prominently in the Johnny Depp movie *Benny & Joon*, their comeback album *Hit The Highway* enjoyed commercial success in America. Following that, the duo once again disappeared from the public's immediate view and seven years were to pass before their next album was released.

● ALBUMS: *This Is The Story* (Chrysalis 1987) ★★★, *Sunshine On Leith* (Chrysalis 1988) ★★★★, *Hit The Highway* (Chrysalis 1994) ★★★, *Persevere* (Nettwerk 2001) ★★★.

● COMPILATIONS: *The Best Of* (Chrysalis 2002) ★★★★.

● VIDEOS: *The Best Of ... Videos* (EMI 2002).

## PROPAGANDA

This Euro pop/synthesizer unit left their native Germany to arrive in England in 1983. Propaganda originally comprised founder members Ralf Dörper (b. 11 January 1960, Düsseldorf, Germany; keyboards, ex-Die Krupps) and DJ Andreas Thein, with Susanne Freytag (b. 3 September 1957, Düsseldorf, Germany; vocals), Claudia Brücken (b. 7 December 1963, Berchenz, Germany; vocals, ex-Toppolinos) and Michael Mertens (b. 23 October 1953, Stendahl, Germany; percussion, ex-Düsseldorf Symphony Orchestra). They found an early advocate in Paul Morley of ZTT Records, and their first release, 'Dr. Mabuse', rallied well in the UK charts, reaching number 27. However, due to the label, and Trevor Horn's commitment to Frankie Goes To Hollywood, the follow-up would not be released until over a year later by which time Thein had departed. 'Duel'/'Jewel' was more successful still as Brücken moved permanently to England to wed Morley. The band's first live performance in June 1985 saw their line-up bolstered by Derek Forbes (ex-Simple Minds) on bass and Steve Jansen (ex-Japan) on drums. *A Secret Wish* and the single from it, 'P:Machinery', emerged a month later. Their European tour saw another line-up shuffle with Brian McGee (also ex-Simple Minds) taking over drums, and Kevin Armstrong on guitar, alongside Brücken, Mertens, Freytag and Forbes. Dörper had departed on the advent of the tour (he later rejoined Die Krupps).

Tensions within the band were exacerbated by Brücken's relationship with Morley and by the start of 1986 the band had become involved in a huge legal battle with ZTT, with Brücken deciding to stay with her husband's label. She formed Act with Thomas Leer in 1987, recording a solitary album, *Laughter, Tears And Rage*. When the litigation had finished in 1988, the new Propaganda line-up featured only Mertens from the original line-up. Besti Miller, an American expatriate based in Germany, was recruited as lead singer, with Forbes and McGee completing the line-up. They released *1234* in 1990, with contributions from old hands Freytag and Dörper, as well as Howard Jones and David Gilmour. Meanwhile, Brücken had embarked on a solo career releasing *Love: And A Million Other Things*.

● ALBUMS: *A Secret Wish* (ZTT 1985) ★★★, *Wishful Thinking* (ZTT 1985) ★★★, *1234* (Virgin 1990) ★★.

● COMPILATIONS: *Outside World* (ZTT 2002) ★★★.

## PSYCHEDELIC FURS

Until the recruitment of a drummer (Vince Ely) in 1979, Richard Butler (b. 5 June 1956, Kingston-upon-Thames, Surrey, England; vocals), Roger Morris (guitar), John Ashton (b. 30 November 1957; guitar, ex-Photon), Duncan Kilburn (woodwinds) and Tim Butler (b. 7 December 1958; bass) had difficulties finding work. The band was also dogged by an unprepossessing sullenness in interview, an equally anachronistic name – inspired by the 1966 Velvet Underground track, 'Venus In Furs' – and Richard Butler's grating one-note style. It was not until a session on John Peel's BBC Radio 1 programme that they were invested with hip credibility – and a CBS Records recording contract. Under Steve Lillywhite's direction, their bleak debut album was followed by minor singles chart entries with 'Dumb Waiter' and 'Pretty In Pink', both selections from 1981's more tuneful and enduring *Talk Talk Talk*. Creeping even closer to the UK Top 40, 'Love My Way' was the chief single from *Forever Now*, produced in the USA by Todd Rundgren.

On replacing Ely with Philip Calvert (ex-Birthday Party) in 1982, the outfit traded briefly as just 'the Furs' before *Mirror Moves* emitted a UK Top 30 hit with 'Heaven' (which was underpinned with a fashionable disco rhythm). Lucrative too were 'Ghost In You' and a re-recording of 'Pretty In Pink' for inclusion on 1986's movie of the same title. That same year, they appeared at the mammoth Glastonbury Festival – which, to many of their fans, remains the most abiding memory of the Psychedelic Furs as performers. By 1990, Ashton, the Butler brothers and hired hands were all that remained of a band that had become mostly a studio concern. Three years later the band were just a very fond memory, with Richard Butler moving on to recapture 'the spark of surprise' with new outfit Love Spit Love. The two Butlers and John Ashton re-formed the Psychedelic Furs at the end of the decade.

● ALBUMS: *Psychedelic Furs* (Columbia 1980) ★★★, *Talk Talk Talk* (Columbia 1981) ★★★, *Forever Now* (Columbia 1982) ★★★, *Mirror Moves* (Columbia 1984) ★★★, *Midnight To Midnight* (Columbia 1987) ★★, *Book Of Days* (Columbia 1989) ★★, *World Outside* (Columbia 1991) ★★, *Radio 1 Sessions* (Strange Fruit 1997) ★★★.

● COMPILATIONS: *All Of This And Nothing* (Columbia 1988) ★★★★, *Crucial Music: The Collection* (Columbia 1989) ★★★, *Should God Forget: A Retrospective* (Columbia/Legacy 1997) ★★★, *Greatest Hits* (Columbia/Legacy 2001) ★★★.

## PSYCHIC TV

This somewhat misrepresented UK *avant garde* collective have seen their aural experimentalism overshadowed by their connections with the literary underworld, or simply the underworld itself. They were formed by Genesis P-Orridge (b. Neil Megson; ex-Pork Dukes and Throbbing Gristle) and Peter Christopherson (ex-Throbbing Gristle). The line-up also included Geoff Rushton (former editor of *Stabmental* fanzine). However, Christopherson and Rushton soon left to form Coil. P-Orridge has been portrayed in much of the media as a deranged and dangerous madman. He had first come to the attention of the media and authorities as the organizer of the 'Prostitution' exhibition at London's ICA gallery in the late 70s. His shock tactics continued with his work in Throbbing Gristle and Psychic TV, and much use was made of fascinating/disturbing slide and film back-projection at gigs. Alternatively, Genesis has repeatedly been revealed as a most personable and charming a character as any the music industry has thrown up, albeit a little mischievous. P-Orridge takes his inspiration from the works of the Marquis De Sade, Charles Manson and particularly William Burroughs. Burroughs reciprocated the respect, and stated of Psychic TV that they provided 'the most important work with communication that I know of in the popular medium'. This is central to the band, and the philosophical congregation that backs them, the Temple Ov Psychick Youth. Their use of guerrilla tactics in the information war follows on from Throbbing Gristle's work, and makes use of broad readings of situationist and deconstructionist thought. P-Orridge's respect for 60s stars Brian Wilson and Brian Jones was revealed with two minor UK chart singles in 1986. The surprisingly poppy 'Godstar' celebrated the former Rolling Stones guitarist, while the tribute to Wilson was a cover version of 'Good Vibrations'. In an ambitious project, from 1986 the group aimed to issue 23 live albums on the 23rd of each month (23 being a statistically symbolic number), each recorded in a different country on their world tour. After walking out of their contract with Some Bizzare Records (who released their debut single 'Just Driftin'), the group no longer involved themselves with the business concerns of music, such as promotion. Their ranks were swelled by a variety of members, including John Gosling (ex-Zos Kia), Alex Ferguson (ex-Alternative TV), Daniel Black, Matthew Best, Dave Martin and many others. They also branched out into other media such as film and literature (making recordings of Burroughs' speeches available for the first time).

Although the mainstream music press continually paints a black picture of Psychic TV's music (and activities), it can at times be surprisingly bright and accessible. Conventional society's inability to come to terms with Psychic TV's message was demonstrated early in 1992 when police seized videos, books and magazines from Genesis P-Orridge's Brighton home after a performance art video was, it was claimed, shown out of context on a television programme about child abuse. The Orridges fled to California, where they collaborated with Timothy Leary and became heavily involved in the US dance music scene. Their most important collaborator during this decade has been multi-instrumentalist Larry Thrasher.

● ALBUMS: *Force The Hand Of Chance* (Some Bizzare 1982) ★★★, *Themes/Cold Dark Matter* (Temple 1982) ★★★, *Dreams Less Sweet* (Some Bizzare 1983) ★★★, *25 December 1984 – A Pagan Day* (Temple 1984) ★★★, *Berlin Atonal Vol. 1* (Atonal 1984) ★★★, *Berlin Atonal Vol. 2* (Atonal 1984) ★★★, *Those Who Do Not* (Gramm 1984) ★★★, *N.Y. Scum Haters* (Temple 1984) ★★★, *Themes 2* (Temple 1985) ★★★, *Mouth Of The Night* (Temple 1985) ★★★, *Descending* (Sordide Sentimental 1985) ★★, *Live In Tokyo* (Temple 1986) ★★★, *Live In Paris* (Temple 1986) ★★★, *Live In Heaven* (Temple 1987) ★★★, *Live In Glasgow* (Temple 1987) ★★★, *Themes 3* (Temple 1987) ★★★, *Live En Suisse* (Temple 1987) ★★★, *Live In Gottingen* (Temple 1987) ★★★, *Live In Toronto* (Temple 1987) ★★★, *Temporary Temple* (Temple 1987) ★★★, *Album 10* (Temple 1988) ★★★, *Allegory & Self* (Temple 1988) ★★★, *Jack The Tab* (Castalia 1988) ★★★, *Tekno Acid Beat* (Temple 1988) ★★★, *Live At The Mardi Gras* (Temple 1988) ★★★, *Live At Thee Circus* (Temple 1988) ★★★, *Live At Thee Ritz* (Temple 1988) ★★, *Kondole* (Temple 1989) ★★★, *Live At Thee Pyramid* (Temple 1989) ★★★, *Bregenz* (Temple 1989) ★★, *A Real Swedish Live Show* (Temple 1989) ★★★, *Towards Thee Infinite Beat* (Temple/Wax Trax! 1990) ★★★, *Beyond Thee Infinite Beat* remixes (Temple/Wax Trax! 1990) ★★★, *At Stockholm* (Psychick Sweden 1990) ★★★, *Live At The Berlin Wall i* (Temple 1990) ★★, *Live At The Berlin Wall ii* (Temple 1990) ★★, *Direction Ov Travel* (Temple 1991) ★★★, with various artists *Ultrahouse: The L.A. Connection* (Wax Trax! 1991) ★★★, *Peak Hour* (Temple 1993) ★★★, *Al-Or-Al: Thee Transmutation Ov Mercury* (Dossier 1994) ★★, *Ultradrug* (Visionary 1994) ★★, *A Hollow Cost* (Visionary/Invisible 1994) ★★★, *Electric Newspaper Issue One* (Dossier 1994) ★★, *Blinded Eye In Thee Pyramids* (Tempus 1994) ★★★, *Ambient Indoctrination* (ITC 1994) ★★, *Stations Ov Thee Cross/Breathe* (ITC 1994) ★★, *Sirens* remixes (Visionary 1995) ★★, *Cathedral Engine* (Dossier 1995) ★★★, *Electric Newspaper Issue Two* (Dossier 1995) ★★, *Electric Newspaper Issue Three* (Dossier 1995) ★★, *Thee Fractured Garden: Discourses Ov Innocence Devoured* (Invisible 1995) ★★★, *Trip Reset* (Cleopatra 1996) ★★★★, *Cold Blue Torch* (Cleopatra 1996) ★★★, *Spatial Memory* (Dossier 1996) ★★★, *Electric Newspaper Issue Four* (Invisible 1997) ★★★, *Sulphur: Low Seed Replication* remixes (NER/World Serpent 1997) ★★, *Were You Ever Bullied At School ... Do You Want Revenge?* (Cold Spring 2000) ★★.
● COMPILATIONS: *High Jack: The Politics Of Ecstasy* (Wax Tax! 1990) ★★★, *Splinter Test 1* (Caroline 1994) ★★★, *Splinter Test 2* (Caroline 1994) ★★★, *Tarot Ov Abomination* (Caroline 1994) ★★★, *Stained By Dead Horses* (Caroline 1994) ★★★, *Sugarmorphosis* (Caroline 1994) ★★★, *Hex Sex: The Singles Pt. One* (Cleopatra 1994) ★★★★, *Godstar: The Singles Pt. Two* (Cleopatra 1995) ★★★★, *Beauty From Thee Beast: Thee Best Ov Psychic TV And Genesis P-Orridge* (Visionary 1995) ★★★★, *Origin Of The Species* (Invisible 1998) ★★★, *Best Ov Psychic TV: Time's Up* (Cleopatra 1999) ★★★★, *Origin Of The Species Volume Too!* (Invisible 1999) ★★★, *Origin Of The Species III* (Invisible 2002) ★★★.

● VIDEOS: *Thee 1st Transmissions: Thee Temple Ov Psychick Youth* (Temple/Fresh Sounds 1982), *Psychic TV: Live In Berlin* (Atonal 1984), *Interview 4-11-88* (Videophile 1988), *Psychick Television: 8Transmissions8* (Jettisoundz 1988), *Joy* (Jettisoundz 1989), *P.T.V: Maple Syrup* (Jettisoundz 1991), *The Hafler Trio & Thee Temple Ov Psychick Youth: Dreamachine* (Staalplaat 1991), *Genesis P-Orridge: Exile & Exhileration* (Visionary 1992), *PTV-Black* (Visionary/Cleopatra 1993), *Beauty From Thee Beast: Thee Best Ov Psychic TV And Genesis P-Orridge* (Visionary 1995), *Thee Majesty/Genesis P-Orridge: Relocating The Sacred* (Punkcast 2001), *Time's Up Live* (DVD 2002).
● FURTHER READING: *Esoterrorist: Selected Essays 1980–1988*, Genesis P-Orridge. *A Comprehensive Collective Ov Lyrics 1981–90*, Vittore Baroni. *Thee Psychick Bible*, Genesis P-Orridge. *Painful But Fabulous: The Life And Art Of Genesis P-Orridge*, Genesis P-Orridge, Douglas Rushkoff, and Carl Abrahamsson.

## PUBLIC ENEMY

Hugely influential and controversial New York, USA-based rap act, frequently referred to as 'The Black Sex Pistols', Public Enemy's legacy extends beyond rap, and has attained a massive cultural significance within black communities. The effect on the consciousness (and consciences) of white people is almost as considerable.

Public Enemy were initially viewed either as a radical and positive avenging force, or a disturbing manifestation of the guns 'n' violence-obsessed, homophobic, misogynist, anti-Semitic attitudes of a section of the black American ghetto underclass. The crew's origins can be traced to 1982 and the Adelphi University, Long Island, New York. There college radio DJ Chuck D. (b. Carlton Douglas Ridenhour, 1 August 1960, Roosevelt, Long Island, New York City, USA) and Hank Shocklee were given the chance to mix tracks for the college station, WBAU, by Bill Stephney. Together they produced a collection of aggressive rap/hip-hop cuts under the title *Super Special Mix Show* in January 1983. They were eventually joined by Flavor Flav (b. William Drayton, 16 March 1959, Roosevelt, Long Island, New York City, USA), who had previously worked alongside Chuck D. and his father in their V-Haul company in Long Island, and rang the station incessantly until he too became a host of their show. In 1984, Shocklee and Chuck D. began mixing their own basement hip-hop tapes, primarily for broadcast on WBAU, which included 'Public Enemy Number 1', from which they took their name.

By 1987 they had signed to Rick Rubin's Def Jam Records (he had first approached them two years earlier) and increased the line-up of the group for musical and visual purposes – Professor Griff 'Minister Of Information' (b. Richard Griffin), DJ Terminator X (b. Norman Rogers) and a four-piece words/dance/martial arts back-up section (Security Of The First World). Shocklee and Chuck D. were also to be found running a mobile DJ service, and managed Long Island's first rap venue, the Entourage. The sound of Public Enemy's debut, *Yo!*

*Bum Rush The Show*, was characteristically hard and knuckle bare, its title track a revision of the original 'Public Enemy Number 1' cut. With funk samples splicing Terminator X's turntable sequences, a guitar solo by Living Colour's Vernon Reid (on 'Sophisticated Bitch'), and potent raps from Chuck D. assisted by Flav's grim, comic asides, it was a breathtaking arrival. That Public Enemy were not only able to follow-up, but also improve on that debut set with *It Takes A Nation Of Millions To Hold Us Back*, signified a clear division between them and the gangsta rappers. Their nearest competitors, N.W.A., peaked with *Straight Outta Compton*, their idea of progress seemingly to become more simplistically hateful with each subsequent release. Public Enemy, on the other hand, was beginning to ask questions, and if America's white mainstream audience chose to fear rap, the invective expressed within 'Black Steel In The Hour Of Chaos', 'Prophets Of Rage' and 'Bring The Noise' gave them excellent cause.

That anxiety was cleverly exploited in the title of the band's third set, *Fear Of A Black Planet*. Despite their perceived antagonistic stance, they proved responsive to some criticism, evident in the necessary ousting of Professor Griff in 1989 for an outrageous anti-Semitic statement made in the US press. He would subsequently be replaced by James Norman, then part-time member Sister Souljah. *Fear Of A Black Planet*, their first record without Griff's services, nevertheless made use of samples of the news conferences and controversy surrounding his statements, enhancing the bunker mentality atmosphere which pervaded the project. The single, '911 Is A Joke', an attack on emergency service response times in ghetto areas, became the subject of a barely credible Duran Duran cover version, strangely confirming Public Enemy's mainstream standing. *Apocalypse 91 ... The Enemy Strikes Black* was almost as effective, the band hardly missing a beat musically or lyrically with black pride cuts like 'I Don't Wanna Be Called Yo Nigga' and 'Bring The Noise', performed with thrash metal outfit Anthrax. In September 1990, it was revealed that they actually appeared in an FBI report to Congress examining 'Rap Music And Its Effects On National Security'. Despite their popularity and influence, or perhaps because of it, there remained a large reservoir of antipathy directed towards the band within sections of the music industry (though more thoughtful enclaves welcomed them; Chuck D. would guest on Sonic Youth's 1990 album, *Goo*, one of several collaborative projects). Either way, their productions in the late 80s and early 90s were hugely exciting – both for the torrents of words and the fury of the rhythm tracks, and in the process they have helped to write rap's lexicon. 'Don't Believe The Hype' (1988) became as powerful a slogan in the late 80s/early 90s as 'Power To The People' was almost 20 years earlier. Similarly, the use of 'Fight The Power' in Spike Lee's 1989 movie *Do The Right Thing* perfectly expressed suppressed anger at the Eurocentric nature of American culture and history. In the 90s several members of the band embarked on solo careers, while Hank Shocklee and his brother

Keith established Shocklee Entertainment in 1993, a production firm and record label. Public Enemy released their first album in three years in 1994 with *Muse Sick-N-Hour Mess Age*, though touring arrangements were delayed when Terminator X broke both his legs in a motorcycle accident. The album was released on 4 July – American Independence Day. Again, it proved practically peerless, with cuts like 'So Watcha Gone Do Now' putting the new breed of gangsta rappers firmly in their place. Following its release, Flav was charged with possession of cocaine and a firearm in November 1995, while Chuck D. became a noted media pundit.

In 1998, the original line-up of Public Enemy regrouped for a new album, which also served as the soundtrack for Spike Lee's *He Got Game*. Public Enemy terminated their 12-year association with Def Jam shortly afterwards, a series of disagreements ending with an argument over the band's decision to post their new single, 'Swindler's Lust', on the Internet. They then signed up with an Internet record company, Atomic Pop, and became the first mainstream band to release an album online.

● ALBUMS: *Yo! Bum Rush The Show* (Def Jam 1987) ★★★, *It Takes A Nation Of Millions To Hold Us Back* (Def Jam 1988) ★★★★, *Fear Of A Black Planet* (Def Jam 1990) ★★★★, *Apocalypse '91 ... The Enemy Strikes Black* (Def Jam 1991) ★★★, *Muse Sick-N-Hour Mess Age* (Def Jam 1994) ★★★, *He Got Game* film soundtrack (Def Jam 1998) ★★★, *There's A Poison Goin On ...* (Atomic Pop 1999) ★★★★, *Revolverlution* (SlamJamz/In The Paint 2002) ★★★.

● COMPILATIONS: *Greatest Misses* features six 'new' tracks (Def Jam 1992) ★★★★, *Twelve Inch Mixes* (Def Jam 1993) ★★★.

● VIDEOS: *Public Enemy Live From House Of Blues* (Aviva International 2001).

● FURTHER READING: *Fight The Power – Rap, Race And Reality*, Chuck D. with Yusuf Jah.

## PUBLIC IMAGE LIMITED

Public Image Ltd (PiL) was the 'company' formed by John Lydon (b. 31 January 1956, Finsbury Park, London, England) when he left behind both the Sex Pistols and his previous moniker, Johnny Rotten, in January 1978. With Lydon on vocals, classically trained pianist and early Clash guitarist Keith Levene on guitar, reggae-influenced bass player Jah Wobble (b. John Wardle, London, England) and Canadian drummer Jim Walker (ex-Furies), the band were put together with the working title of the Carnivorous Buttock Flies. By the time the debut single – the epic 'Public Image' – was released in its newspaper sleeve in September, they had adopted the less ridiculous name. Their live debut followed in Brussels on 12 December, and they played the UK for the first time on Christmas Day. In January 1979, ex-101ers and Raincoats drummer Richard Dudanski replaced Walker, who went on to punk band the Straps. The *Metal Box* set came out later that year as a set of 12-inch records housed in tin 'film' cans (it was later reissued as a normal album). One of the most radical and difficult albums of its era, its conception and execution was a remarkable blend of Lydon's antagonism and Levene's climatic guitar. The single, 'Death Disco', also reached the UK charts. With Dudanski leaving, Fall drummer Karl Burns was enlisted until Martin Atkins (b. 3 August 1959, Coventry, England) from Mynd, joined in time to tour the USA in the spring of 1980. A live album, *Paris Au Printemps*, was recorded, after which both Wobble and Atkins left. Wobble went on to record solo material and work briefly in 1987 for London Transport as a train guard, while Atkins formed Brian Brain.

In May 1981, Lydon and Levene, augmented by hired musicians, played from behind an onstage screen at the New York Ritz. The crowd failed to grasp the concept and 'bottled' the band. After *Flowers Of Romance*, Pete Jones (b. 22 September 1957) became bass player and Atkins returned on drums. Around this time subsidiary members Dave Crowe and Jeanette Lee, who had been with the band since the beginning in business roles, both departed and the group started a new era as Lydon decided to settle in Los Angeles. In 1983 Jones left as the hypnotic 'This Is Not A Love Song' became a Top 5 hit, and Levene also departed as it was climbing the chart.

In a relatively quiet period when Lydon collaborated with Afrika Bambaataa on the Time Zone single 'World Destruction', PiL released only the 1984 album *This Is What You Want, This Is What You Get*, and another set of live recordings from foreign fields. Lydon also made his first feature film appearance in *Order Of Death* (1983). They returned to the forefront with 1986's *Album*, from which came 'Single' aka 'Rise', featuring the drumming talents of Ginger Baker. The album included numerous guest/session musicians such as Steve Vai, Ryûichi Sakamoto and Tony Williams. The next year, Lydon assembled a permanent band once again, this time drawing on guitarists John McGeoch (b. 28 May 1955, Greenock, Strathclyde, Scotland) and Lu Edmunds, American bass player Allan Dias, and drummer Bruce Smith. Edmunds was forced to leave in 1989 because he was suffering from tinnitus (Ted Chau was a temporary replacement), and Smith left in 1990 as the band fell into inactivity once more. The three remaining members came back to life in 1990 when Virgin Records issued a *Greatest Hits ... So Far* compilation, confidently touting the new single 'Don't Ask Me' – Lydon's nod to the environmental problems of the world.

After several years and countless collaborators, Lydon has remained the *enfant terrible* of the music industry, a constant irritant, and occasional source of brilliance: 'I've learned to manipulate the music business. I have to deal with all kinds of stupid, sycophantic people. I've just learned to understand my power. Everyone should learn that, otherwise they lose control'. PiL then recruited new drummer Mike Joyce (ex-Smiths; Buzzcocks), but Lydon concentrated more on his autobiography and other musical projects (such as the Leftfield collaboration 'Open Up') than PiL in the 90s. He also released a critically derided solo album in 1997.

● ALBUMS: *Public Image* (Virgin 1978) ★★★, *Metal Box* (UK) *Second Edition* (US) (Virgin 1979) ★★★★, *Paris Au Printemps* (Virgin 1980) ★★, *Flowers Of Romance* (Virgin 1981) ★★, *Live In Tokyo* (Virgin 1983) ★★, *Commercial Zone* (PiL/Virgin 1983) ★★, *This Is What You Want, This Is What You Get* (Virgin 1984) ★★★, *Album* (Virgin 1986) ★★★, *Happy?* (Virgin 1987) ★★★, *9* (Virgin 1989) ★★, *That What Is Not* (Virgin 1992) ★★.

● COMPILATIONS: *Greatest Hits ... So Far* (Virgin 1990) ★★★, *Plastic Box* 4-CD box set (Virgin 1999) ★★★.

● VIDEOS: *Live In Tokyo* (Virgin Video 1983), *Videos* (Virgin Video 1986).

● FURTHER READING: *Public Image Limited: Rise Fall*, Clinton Heylin.

## PYLE, ARTIMUS, BAND

Having replaced original drummer Bob Burns in Lynyrd Skynyrd in 1975, Pyle (b. Thomas Delmer Pyle, 15 July 1948, Kentucky, USA) spent two years touring and recording with that band before the fateful air crash in October 1977 that killed Steve Gaines and Ronnie Van Zant. He then formed the Artimus Pyle Band (APB) in the late 70s with a line-up consisting of Darryll Otis Smith (vocals), John Boerstler (guitar), Steve Brewington (bass) and Steve Lockhart (guitar, keyboards). The band continued in the Lynyrd Skynyrd tradition, playing a mixture of souped-up rock 'n' roll and heavy rock with a pronounced southern flavour. However, in the process he knocked several of the rough edges off his former band's sound. Despite the presence of numerous colleagues and co-writers, their self-titled debut and the follow-up collection (as APB, with Lockhart replaced by Russ Milner and new vocalist Karen Blackmon) failed to inspire sales beyond a loyal clique of diehard Lynyrd Skynyrd fans. *Nightcaller* in particular was an obvious attempt to penetrate AOR radio without the songwriting substance necessary to do so. Lacking any real hope of a commercial breakthrough, it was no surprise that Pyle put his band on hold in the mid-80s and elected to return to the re-formed Lynyrd Skynyrd. He revived APB in the following decade and has established the band as a leading southern rock attraction.

● ALBUMS: *A.P.B.* (MCA 1982) ★★★, as APB *Nightcaller* (MCA 1983) ★★, *Live From Planet Earth* (Last Resort 2000) ★★★.

## Q MAGAZINE

At once iconoclastic and orthodox, Q has changed the nature of UK-based rock journalism and become a pillar of the UK music business since its appearance in 1986. In the hands of founding editors David Hepworth and Mark Ellen and designer Andy Cowles it rapidly established a strong identity at a time when established journals such as *Melody Maker* and *New Musical Express* were losing theirs. Hepworth and Ellen persuaded ambitious publishers EMAP that an up-market mélange of rock, lifestyle, films and books would work, and set about creating Q. The monthly publication interval and new power of desktop publishing removed the restrictions that confined their rivals. With great good fortune, they secured an interview with Paul McCartney for the first issue, after which UK circulation grew steadily from an initial 41,000 to 173,000 by the end of 1990. A period of stagnation followed, due partly to the advent of the recession, and partly to the appearance of *Vox* from rival publisher IPC (home of *NME*). From mid-1992 onwards, the upward trend was resumed as *Vox* proved to be a poor imitator, and Q had reached worldwide sales of over 215,000 by mid-1996. Between 1992 and summer 1995, Q was edited by Danny Kelly, before Andrew Collins took over the post and led the magazine into a increasingly strong position. In the course of the magazine's growth, it shed or diluted some of the peripheral coverage to concentrate on rock. Inevitably, Q's success also led to some compromise in the tone and range of its content. Record companies recognized its influence on the CD market with a resulting increase in the correspondence between featured artists and their CD releases. Nevertheless, the magazine continued to succeed in attracting buyers across a wide range of musical tastes, even those whose primary interest is not the music but the personality.

A huge shadow was cast over the magazine's lengthy success when the popular John Bauldie, one of the original important cogs (he was sub-editor, writer, reviewer, Bob Dylan expert and Bolton Wanderers fan), was tragically killed in a freak helicopter accident in October 1996. Towards the end of the decade, the magazine underwent its first design revamp. A glut of editors passed through the magazine in the first two years of the new millennium, with incumbent Andy Pemberton replaced by Andrew Harrison, John McKie and then Danny Eccleston in the space of a few months. The magazine has also experienced a slight decline in circulation which has settled at around the 200,000 mark, although with regular ABC fluctuations it still leads any rival by a considerable.

The founders went on to establish *Mojo* in 1993 from the same offices, aimed at the slightly older reader. The original production and editorial team can look back with the knowledge that from issue 1 they got it absolutely right. Quite apart from the editorial content, they immediately succeeded with the design and format: both logo and original typography were sound and have required only one major revamp. Although similar magazines have encroached upon its once hallowed territory (*Uncut* and *Classic Rock* in particular), Q remains at the helm.

## Q-TIPS

Fronted by Paul Young (b. 17 January 1956, Luton, Bedfordshire, England), the Q-Tips were one of the most renowned live groups on the UK club circuit in the early 80s, playing an estimated 800 gigs in under three years. The group was formed in 1979 by Young and other ex-members of Streetband, John Gifford (guitar, vocals) and Mick Pearl (bass, vocals). In place of their former outfit's rock sound, Q-Tips was organized as a classic soul group with an experienced brass section of Tony Hughes (trumpet) and saxophonists Steve Farr and Stewart Blandamer, who had worked with Johnny Wakelin's Kinshasa Band, Jimmy James And The Vagabonds and the Flirtations. Other members were Barry Watts (drums) and veteran Ian Kewley (keyboards) from Samson and latterly hard rock outfit Limey. With matching suits and arrangements out of the Tamla/Motown and Stax Records songbooks, Q-Tips were seen as part of a mod revival. After releasing a frantic version of Joe Tex's 'SYSLJFM (The Letter Song)' on the independent Shotgun label, the group signed to Chrysalis Records and covered the Miracles' 'Tracks Of My Tears'. By this time, Gifford had been replaced by Garth Watt-Roy, whose career had included spells with Greatest Show On Earth, Fuzzy Duck, Marmalade and Limey. The debut album included Blandamer originals such as 'A Man Can't Lose' as well as cover versions, but its lack of sales led to Chrysalis dropping the group. They signed to Rewind Records, who chose a version of Boudleaux Bryant's 'Love Hurts' as a single. Although this failed to sell, it brought Young to the notice of CBS Records, who signed him as a solo artist at the start of 1982. This was the signal for the break-up of Q-Tips, and they disbanded after a farewell tour and the release of a live album. *Live At Last* included 'Broken Man', the first song co-written by Young and Kewley, who would continue their partnership during the first phase of the singer's solo career. The Q-Tips briefly reunited in 1993.

● ALBUMS: *Q-Tips* (Chrysalis 1980) ★★★, *Live At Last* (Rewind 1982) ★★★, *BBC Radio 1 Live In Concert* (Windsong 1991) ★★.

## QUARTERFLASH

This band from Portland, Oregon, USA were most renowned for October 1981's US number 3 hit single, 'Harden My Heart'. This track, which also reached the UK Top 50, was a prime example of the band's AOR sound, delivering passionate guitars, wailing saxophone, emotive vocals, and an enormous chorus. Originally known as Seafood Mama,

Quarterflash boasted the talents of husband-and-wife team Rindy Ross (vocals, saxophone) and Marv Ross (guitar). The other members of the band were Jack Charles (vocals, guitar), Rich Gooch (bass), Rick DiGiallonardo (keyboards) and Brian Willis (drums). They had two further US Top 20 singles with 'Find Another Fool' (number 16, February 1982) and 'Take Me To Heart' (number 14, June 1983). They recorded three strong albums, although their 1981 debut met with most commercial success, reaching number 8 in America. Quarterflash split-up in 1985 after the release of *Back Into Blue*, but the Rosses re-formed the band in 1990 much to the delight of classic AOR fans. Joined by Doug Fraser (guitar), Sandin Wilson (bass), Mel Kubik (keyboards) and Gregg Williams (drums), they recorded a new studio album, *Girl In The Wind*. Six years later, on 11 August, they played their final show in Portland.

● ALBUMS: *Quarterflash* (Geffen 1982) ★★★, *Take Another Picture* (Geffen 1983) ★★★, *Back Into Blue* (Geffen 1985) ★★★, *Girl In The Wind* (Epic 1991) ★★.

● COMPILATIONS: *Harden My Heart ... The Best Of Quarterflash* (Geffen 1997) ★★★.

## QUEEN LATIFAH

b. Dana Owens, 18 March 1970, East Orange, New Jersey, USA. Rap's first lady, Queen Latifah, broke through in the late 80s with a style that picked selectively from jazz and soul traditions. The former Burger King employee maintained her early commitment to answer the misogynist armoury of her male counterparts, and at the same time impart musical good times to all genders. After working as the human beatbox alongside female rapping crew Ladies Fresh, she was just 18 years old when she released her debut single, 'Wrath Of My Madness', in 1988. A year later, her debut long-player enjoyed fevered reviews: an old, wise head was evident on the top of her young shoulders. Production expertise from Daddy-O, KRS-One, DJ Mark The 45 King and members of De La Soul doubtlessly helped as well. By the time of her third album, she had moved from Tommy Boy Records to a new home, Motown Records, and revealed a shift from the soul and ragga tones of *Nature Of A Sista* to sophisticated, sassy hip-hop.

She subsequently embarked on a career as an actor, notably in the hit streetwise black comedy, *Living Single*, where she played magazine boss Khadijah James. Her movie credits already include *Juice*, *Jungle Fever* and *House Party 2*. As if that were not enough, she additionally set up her own Flavor Unit record label and management company in 1993, as an outlet for new rap acts as well as her own recordings. The first release on it, 'Roll Wit Tha Flava', featured an all-star cast including Naughty By Nature's Treach, Fu-Schnickens' Chip-Fu, Black Sheep's Dres and D-Nice. She also guested on the Shabba Ranks single, 'Watcha Gonna Do'. Previous collaborations had included those with De La Soul ('Mama Gave Birth To The Soul Children', in that band's infancy) and Monie Love (the agenda-setting 'Ladies First').

Queen Latifah represents an intelligent cross-section of hip-hop influences. Though she is a forthright advocate of her race's struggle, she is also the daughter of and brother to policemen. *Black Reign*, in fact, is dedicated to the death of that same brother: 'I see both sides. I've seen the abuse and I've been the victim of police who abuse their authority. On the other side you've got cops getting shot all the time, you got people who don't respect them at all'. While a little too strident to live up to the Arabic meaning of her name (Latifah equates to delicate and sensitive), Queen Latifah remains one of the most positive role models for young black women (and men) in hip-hop culture: 'Aspire to be a doctor or a lawyer, but not a gangster'. As one of the singles lifted from *Black Reign* advocated: 'UNITY (Who You Calling A Bitch?)'. Following a lengthy hiatus owing to acting commitments, Latifah returned to recording with 1998's *Order In The Court*.

● ALBUMS: *All Hail The Queen* (Tommy Boy 1989) ★★★★, *Nature Of A Sista* (Tommy Boy 1991) ★★★, *Black Reign* (Motown 1993) ★★★, *Order In The Court* (Flavor Unit 1998) ★★★.

● COMPILATIONS: *She's A Queen: A Collection Of Hits* (Universal 2002) ★★★★.

● FILMS: *Jungle Fever* (1991), *House Party 2* (1991), *Juice* (1992), *Who's The Man* (1993), *My Life* (1993), *Set It Off* (1996), *Hoodlum* (1997), *The Wizard Of Oz* (1998), *Living Out Loud* (1998), *Sphere* (1998), *The Bone Collector* (1999), *Bringing Out The Dead* voice only (1999), *The Country Bears* (2002), *Brown Sugar* (2002), *Chicago* (2002).

## QUEENSRŸCHE

Queensrÿche were formed in Seattle, USA, by Geoff Tate (vocals), Chris DeGarmo (guitar), Michael Wilton (guitar), Eddie Jackson (bass), and Scott Rockenfield (drums), from the ashes of club circuit band the Mob and, in Tate's case, the Myth. Immediately, Tate offered them a distinctive vocal edge, having studied opera – he had turned to hard rock because of the lyrical freedom it offered. A four-track demo tape recorded in the basement of Rockenfield's parents' house in June 1982 led to record store owners Kim and Diana Harris offering to manage the band. The tape itself took on a life of its own, circulating throughout the north-west of America, and in May 1983 the band launched their own 206 Records label to house the songs on a self-titled 12-inch EP (lead track, 'Queen Of The Reich', had long since given them their name). The EP caused quite a stir in rock circles and led to EMI Records offering them a seven-album contract. The record was quickly re-released and grazed the UK Top 75, although the band's sound was still embryonic and closer to Britain's New Wave of British Heavy Metal than the progressive rock flavour that would become their hallmark.

Their first full album for EMI, *The Warning*, was comparatively disappointing, failing to live up to the promise shown on the EP, particularly in the poor mix, which was the subject of some concern for both the record company and band. Only 'Road To Madness' and 'Take Hold Of The Flame', two perennial live favourites, met expectations. *Rage For Order* followed in 1986 and saw the band creating a more distinctive style, making full use of modern technology, yet somehow the production (this time from Neil Kernon) seemed to have over-compensated. Although a dramatic improvement, and the first genuine showcase for Tate's incredible vocal range and the twin guitar sound of DeGarmo and Wilton, the songs emerged as clinical and neutered. 1988 saw the Peter Collins-produced *Operation: Mindcrime*, a George Orwell-inspired concept album that was greeted with enthusiastic critical acclaim on its release. With some of the grandiose futurism of earlier releases dispelled, and additional orchestration from Michael Kamen, worldwide sales of over one million confirmed this as the album to lift the band into rock's first division. In the wake of its forerunner, there was something positively minimal about *Empire*, which boasted a stripped-down but still dreamlike rock aesthetic best sampled on the single 'Silent Lucidity', a Top 10 US hit in November 1991, which was also nominated for a Grammy. The album itself earned a Top 10 placing in America.

Only single releases broke a four-year recording gap between *Empire* and 1994's *Promised Land*, the most notable of which was 1993's 'Real World', included on the soundtrack to the Arnold Schwarzenegger flop *Last Action Hero*. Although a more personal and reflective set, *Promised Land* continued the band's tradition of dramatic song structures, this time without Kamen's arranging skills. Well over a decade into a career that at first seemed of limited appeal, Queensrÿche's popularity continued to grow. However, they stumbled with 1997's *Hear In The New Frontier*, which experimented with a less grandiose style that confused both critics and record buyers. DeGarmo left the band the following year and was replaced by Kelly Gray. The new line-up made a short-lived move to Atlantic Records, resulting in 1999's studio set *Q2K*. Gray left following the release of 2001's *Live Evolution*.

● ALBUMS: *The Warning* (EMI 1984) ★★, *Rage For Order* (EMI 1986) ★★, *Operation: Mindcrime* (EMI 1988) ★★★★, *Empire* (EMI 1990) ★★★, *Promised Land* (EMI 1994) ★★★, *Hear In The New Frontier* (EMI 1997) ★★★, *Q2K* (Atlantic 1999) ★★★, *Live Evolution* (Sanctuary 2001) ★★.
● COMPILATIONS: *Queensrÿche* includes *Queensrÿche* and *Prophecy* EPs (EMI 1988) ★★★.
● VIDEOS: *Live In Tokyo* (PMI 1985), *Video Mindcrime* (PMI 1989), *Operation Livecrime* (PMI 1991/93), *Building Empires* (PMI 1993), *Live Evolution* (Sanctuary 2001), *Empire* (EMI 2002).

## QUIET RIOT

This US heavy metal band had their 'five minutes' of fame in 1983 with a remake of the Slade song, 'Cum On Feel The Noize', and a US number 1 album, *Metal Health* – the first metal album to reach that position in the US charts. However, they were unable to maintain that momentum with subsequent releases. The band formed in 1975 with lanky vocalist Kevin DuBrow, Randy Rhoads (b. Randall William Rhoads, 6 December 1956, Santa Monica, California, USA, d. 19 March 1982; guitar), Drew Forsyth (drums) and Kelly Garni (bass), taking their name from a

suggestion made by Status Quo's Rick Parfitt. They recorded two albums that were released only in Japan, and with Rudy Sarzo replacing Garni in 1978. Rhoads left the following year to join Ozzy Osbourne and was later tragically killed in a plane crash in March 1982. At that point, the band briefly split up with some members joining the vocalist in a band called DuBrow, and Sarzo also working with Osbourne. Quiet Riot regrouped around DuBrow, Sarzo, guitarist Carlos Cavazo and drummer Frankie Banali and signed to the Pasha label for their breakthrough album and single in 1983, their musical and visual style fashioned after the harder-rocking glam acts of the 70s. Friction within the band followed their quick success and resultant publicity affected sales of the 1984 follow-up, *Condition Critical*, which reached number 15 in the US charts but was considered disappointing. Sarzo was replaced by Chuck Wright in 1985. The new line-up recorded another album in 1986, which reached number 31 but showed a marked decline in creativity. DuBrow and Wright were subsequently ejected from the band and a self-titled 1988 release, with new vocalist Paul Shortino (ex-Rough Cutt) and Sean McNabb on bass, barely scraped the charts. The band then split-up, with Banali going on to work with W.A.S.P. In the early 90s, DuBrow, Banali and Cavazo reunited with the addition of new bass player Kenny Hillery, to record *Terrified*, the first of a series of lacklustre new releases. Wright returned in place of Hillery on 1995's *Down To The Bone*, but two years later the classic line-up was reunited when Sarzo was brought back on board. *Alive And Well* featured new material and re-recorded versions of some of the band's 80s hits. A new studio album, *Guilty Pleasures*, was released two years later.

● ALBUMS: *Quiet Riot* (Columbia Japan 1977) ★★, *Quiet Riot II* (Columbia Japan 1978) ★★, *Metal Health* (Pasha 1983) ★★★, *Condition Critical* (Pasha 1984) ★★, *QRIII* (Pasha 1986) ★, *Quiet Riot* (Pasha 1988) ★, *Terrified* (Moonstone 1993) ★★, *Down To The Bone* (Kamikaze 1995) ★★, *Alive And Well* (Axe Killer 1999) ★★, *Guilty Pleasures* (Bodyguard 2001) ★★.
● COMPILATIONS: *Winners Take All* (Sony 1990) ★★★, *The Randy Rhoads Years* (Rhino 1993) ★★★, *Greatest Hits* (Sony 1996) ★★★, *Super Hits* (Sony 1999) ★★★, *The Collection* (Connoisseur 2000) ★★★.

# R

## R. CAJUN AND THE ZYDECO BROTHERS

R. Cajun was formed in 1979 by Chris Hall, a former member of Shufflin' Sam and a keen enthusiast of Cajun music. The original line-up was Chris Hall (b. 2 July 1952, Sheffield, Yorkshire, England; accordion, vocals), Tony Dark (fiddle), Alf Billington (guitar, vocals), and Veronica Matthews (triangle). The following year, Trevor Hopkins (bass) joined the line-up, but was soon replaced by Beeds (b. 13 October 1947, Derby, Derbyshire, England; guitar, harmonica). The line-up, which started to make some impact on the folk circuit in 1982, consisted of Hall, Billington, John Squire (fiddle, guitar, mandolin), who joined that year, as did Jan Hall (b. 17 January 1953, Sheffield, Yorkshire, England; triangle, percussion). *Bayou Rhythms* included the Zydeco Brothers, Graham Jones (bass) and Neil 'Freddy' Hopwood (b. 23 April 1947, Lichfield, Staffordshire, England; drums). Hopwood had formerly been a member of Dr. Strangely Strange and the Sutherland Brothers bands. The album contained some infectious pieces such as 'Cajun Two-Step', and 'Bayou Pom Pom Special', as well as standards such as 'Jambalaya' and 'Deportees', and quickly established them as a popular group at festivals. In 1984, Dave Blant (b. 27 November 1949, Burton Upon Trent, Staffordshire, England; bass, vocals) joined, replacing Graham Jones. Having previously left the group, Tony Dark re-joined them in 1986, in turn replacing John Squire. The same year, Clive Harvey (b. 27 November 1945, Watford, Hertfordshire, England; guitar, vocals) was added. It was this line-up that recorded *Pig Sticking In Arcadia*. Three years later, Dark again left the group, to be replaced by Derek Richardson (fiddle), then Dave 'Mitch' Proctor (b. 8 December 1952, Heanor, Derbyshire, England; fiddle) joined in 1990, replacing Richardson.

Despite the various personnel changes, the overall sound of the group has remained remarkably constant. Their blend of Cajun and zydeco, apart from being unusual, has added to the band's original sound and style. They continue playing festivals, both at home and abroad, where they are equally popular. Chris Hall is the co-owner of Swamp, an organization that runs Bearcat Records and the UK's top Cajun venue, The Swamp Club, in Derby. John Elliott (guitar, vocals) replaced Clive Harvey in 1998.

● ALBUMS: *Bayou Rhythms* (Moonraker 1984) ★★★, *Pig Sticking In Arcadia* (Discethnique 1987) ★★★, *Out Of The Swamp* (Bearcat 1990) ★★★, *Don't Leave The Floor* (Bearcat) ★★★, *No Known Cure* (Bearcat 1993) ★★★, *That Cajun Thing* (Bearcat 1995) ★★★, *Get Up Get Down* (Bearcat 2000) ★★★.

## R.E.M.

R.E.M. played their first concert in Athens, Georgia, USA, on 19 April 1980. Their line-up consisted of four drop-outs from the University of Georgia; Michael Stipe (b. 4 January 1960, Decatur, Georgia, USA; vocals), Peter Buck (b. 6 December 1956, Berkeley, California, USA; guitar), Mike Mills (b. 17 December 1958, Orange County, California, USA; bass) and Bill Berry (b. 31 July 1958, Duluth, Minnesota, USA; drums). Without the charisma of Stipe and his eccentric onstage behaviour, hurling himself about with abandon in between mumbling into the microphone, they could easily have been overlooked as just another bar band, relying on the harmonious guitar sound of the Byrds for their inspiration. Acquiring a healthy following among the college fraternity in their home-town, it was not long before they entered the studio to record their debut single, 'Radio Free Europe', to be released independently on Hibtone Records. This was greeted with considerable praise by critics who conceded that the band amounted to more than the sum of their influences. Their country/folk sound was contradicted by a driving bassline and an urgency that put the listener more in mind of the Who in their early mod phase. Add to this the distinctive voice of Stipe and his inaudible, perhaps even non-existent, lyrics, and R.E.M. sounded quite unlike any other band in the USA in the post-punk era of the early 80s.

Newly signed to I.R.S. Records, they gained further favourable notices for August 1982's mini-album, *Chronic Town*, produced by Mitch Easter. Their eagerly awaited full-length debut arrived in April 1983. With production duties handled by Easter and Don Dixon, *Murmur* surpassed all expectations, and was eventually made Album Of The Year by *Rolling Stone* magazine. As in the USA, the band earned a devoted cult following in Europe, largely comprised of college students. *Reckoning* appeared the following year and was permeated by a reckless spontaneity that had been missing from their earlier work. Recorded in only 12 days, the tracks varied in mood from frustration, as on 'So. Central Rain (I'm Sorry)', to the tongue-in-cheek sing along '(Don't Go Back To) Rockville'. The songs were accessible enough but, as would be the case for most of the 80s, the singles culled from R.E.M.'s albums were generally deemed uncommercial by mainstream radio programmers. However, their cult reputation benefited from a series of flop singles on both sides of the Atlantic. Although received enthusiastically by critics, the Joe Boyd-produced *Fables Of The Reconstruction* was a stark, morose album that mirrored a period of despondency within the band. Peter Buck summed it up in the 90s – 'If we were to record those songs again, they would be very different'.

*Lifes Rich Pageant*, produced by Don Gehman, showed the first signs of a politicization within the band that would come to a head and coincide with their commercial breakthrough in the late 80s. Stipe's lyrics began to dwell increasingly on the prevailing amorality in the USA and question its inherited ethics, while retaining their much vaunted obliqueness. Tracks such as 'These Days' and

'Cuyahoga' were rallying cries to the young and disaffected; although the lyrics were reflective and almost bitter, the music was the most joyous and uplifting the band had recorded to date. This ironic approach to songwriting was typified by 'It's The End Of The World As We Know It (And I Feel Fine)', from 1987's equally impressive *Document*, which intentionally trivialized its subject matter with a witty and up-tempo infectiousness. In a similar vein was 'The One I Love', a deliberately cold and detached dismissal of an ex-lover that was, nevertheless, completely misinterpreted as romantic by countless record-buyers who pushed the single up to number 9 on the *Billboard* Hot 100 chart. The album was produced by Scott Litt, who would continue to work with the band over the next few years.

R.E.M.'s major label debut *Green* arrived the following year and sold slowly but steadily in the USA. The attendant single 'Stand' reached US number 6 in January 1989, while 'Orange Crush' entered the UK Top 30 the same June. Apart from demonstrating their environmental awareness, particularly on 'You Are The Everything', the album laid more emphasis on Stipe's vocals and lyrics. This, to the singer's dismay, led to his elevation as 'spokesman for a generation', particularly with the apparent self-revelation of 'World Leader Pretend'. Already hero-worshipped by adoring long-term fans who saw him as both pin-up and creative genius, Stipe insisted: 'Rock 'n' roll is a joke, people who take it seriously are the butt of the joke'. The world tour that coincided with the album's release saw R.E.M. making a smooth transition from medium-size venues to the stadium circuit, owing as much to Stipe's individual choreography as to the elaborate, projected backdrops.

After a break of two years, during which Berry, Buck and Mills collaborated with singer Warren Zevon as the Hindu Love Gods, the band re-emerged with *Out Of Time*. Their previous use of horns and mandolins to embroider songs did not prepare their audience for the deployment of an entire string section, nor were the contributions from B-52's singer Kate Pierson and Boogie Down Productions' KRS-One expected. Ostensibly the band's first album to contain 'love' songs, it was unanimously hailed as a masterpiece and topped both the US and UK album charts. The accompanying singles from the album, 'Losing My Religion' (US number 4/UK number 19), 'Shiny Happy People' (US number 10/UK number 6), 'Near Wild Heaven' (UK number 27) and 'Radio Song' (UK number 28), gave them further hits.

*Automatic For The People* was released in October 1992 to universal favour, reaching the top of the charts in the UK and USA. The album produced a number of memorable singles including the moody 'Drive' (US number 28/UK number 11), the joyous Andy Kaufman tribute 'Man On The Moon' (US number 30/UK number 18) with its classic Elvis Presley vocal inflections from Stipe and an award-winning accompanying monochrome video, 'The Sidewinder Sleeps Tonite' (UK number 17) and 'Everybody Hurts' (US number 29/UK number 7). *Monster* showed the band in grunge-like mode, not letting any accusations of selling out bother them, and certainly letting fans and critics alike know that they had not gone soft. 'What's The Frequency, Kenneth?' (UK number 9) started a run of hit singles taken from the album and further awards were heaped upon them.

Following the collapse of Bill Berry in Switzerland while on a major tour in 1995, the band was forced to rest. Berry was operated on for a ruptured aneurysm and made a full recovery. In August 1996, the band re-signed with Warner Brothers Records for the largest recording contract advance in history: $80 million was guaranteed for a five-album contract. *New Adventures In Hi-Fi* was released in September. Recorded mostly during soundchecks during the ill-fated *Monster* tour, it was nevertheless another excellent collection. From the epic chord changes of 'Be Mine' to the cool understated calm of 'How The West Was Won And Where It Got Us', it showed the band's remarkable creative depth. 'E-Bow The Letter', featuring Patti Smith, also provided the band with a UK Top 5 single.

In October 1997, Bill Berry shocked the music world by announcing his intention to leave R.E.M. after 17 years with the band; the remaining members were quick to confirm that they would be continuing without him, using the adage 'a three-legged dog can still walk'. Although there was no official replacement on drums, with the rest of the band electing to continue R.E.M. as a three-piece, ex-Screaming Trees drummer Barrett Martin contributed to sessions for 1998's *Up*, which also featured new producer Pat McCarthy. Introduced by the single 'Daysleeper' (a UK Top 10 hit), this album was the band's most adventurous recording since the mid-80s. The following year they provided the soundtrack for the Andy Kaufman biopic *Man On The Moon*, which included the excellent new track, 'The Great Beyond'. *Reveal* delighted fans and critics with sharp lyrics and some classic Buck chord changes. Even the guitarist's minor air-rage incident on route to London (he was acquitted of any criminal charges in March 2002) could not taint the plaudits the album received. They earned further praise the following year when they contributed the track 'All The Right Friends' to the soundtrack of Cameron Crowe's *Vanilla Sky*.

The critical praise heaped upon R.E.M. has been monumental, but despite all this attention they have remained painfully modest and reasonably unaffected, and, despite the loss of Berry, still appear united. They are one of the most important and popular bands to appear over the past three decades, and although their commercial heyday appears to have passed they still retain massive credibility.

● ALBUMS: *Chronic Town* mini-album (I.R.S. 1982) ★★★, *Murmur* (I.R.S. 1983) ★★★★, *Reckoning* (I.R.S. 1984) ★★★, *Fables Of The Reconstruction* (I.R.S. 1985) ★★★, *Lifes Rich Pageant* (I.R.S. 1986) ★★★★, *Document* (I.R.S. 1987) ★★★, *Green* (Warners 1988) ★★★★, *Out Of Time* (Warners 1991) ★★★★, *Automatic For The People* (Warners 1992) ★★★★★, *Monster* (Warners 1994) ★★★, *New Adventures In Hi-Fi* (Warners 1996) ★★★★, *Up* (Warners 1998) ★★★,

*Reveal* (Warners 2001) ★★★★.
● COMPILATIONS: *Dead Letter Office* (I.R.S. 1987) ★★★, *Eponymous* (I.R.S. 1988) ★★★★, *The Best Of R.E.M.* (I.R.S. 1991) ★★★, *In The Attic: Alternative Recordings 1985–1989* (Capitol/EMI 1997) ★★★.
● VIDEOS: *Athens, Ga – Inside/Out* (A&M Video 1987), *Succumbs* (A&M Video 1987), *Pop Screen* (Warner Reprise Video 1990), *Tourfilm* (Warner Reprise Video 1990), *This Film Is On* (Warner Reprise Video 1991), *Parallel* (Warner Reprise Video 1995), *Roadmovie* (Warner Reprise Video 1996).
● FURTHER READING: *REMarks: The Story Of R.E.M.*, Tony Fletcher. *R.E.M.: Behind The Mask*, Jim Greer. *R.E.M.: File Under Water, The Definitive Guide To 12 Years Of Recordings And Concerts*, Jon Storey. *REMnants: The R.E.M. Collector's Handbook*, Gary Nabors. *It Crawled From The South: An R.E.M. Companion*, Marcus Gray. *Talk About The Passion: R.E.M. An Oral History*, Denise Sullivan. *R.E.M. The "Rolling Stone" Files: The Ultimate Compendium Of Interviews*, no editor listed. *R.E.M. Documental*, Dave Bowler and Bryan Dray. *R.E.M. Inside Out*, Craig Rosen. *The R.E.M. Companion*, John Platt (ed.). *Adventures In Hi-Fi: The Complete R.E.M.*, Rob Jovanovic and Tim Abbott.

## RAIN

This indie band originated in Liverpool, England, in the late 80s and adopted the heritage of harmony pop in the vein of the Byrds. Rain was initially notable by dint of having three good harmony singers to back up their Rickenbacker guitar sound. Ned Clark (guitar, vocals), Colin Murphy (guitar, vocals), Martin Campbell (bass), and Tony McGuigan (drums) formed the band at the Merseyside Trade Union Community And Unemployed Resource Centre in Liverpool, set up with a £100,000 grant. Their original locale was the severely depressed Huyton area, but eight months later they were signed to CBS Records and worked on album sessions with Nick Lowe. After a debut single, 'Lemonstone Desired', they courted controversy with the provocative nudity featured on the cover of 'Taste Of Rain'. Their sole album was honed by months of rehearsal with guest appearances by Green On Red and blues musician Joe Louis Walker. (NB: not to be confused with the Manchester-based band of the same name featuring Paul Arthurs, Tony McCarroll and Paul McGuigan, who later found fame with Oasis.)
● ALBUMS: *A Taste Of Rain* (Columbia 1991) ★★★.

## RAIN PARADE

Part of Los Angeles, California, USA's rock renaissance of the early 80s, the Rain Parade drew from late 60s influences to forge a new brand of psychedelia-tinged rock. After a promising debut single, 'What She's Done To Your Mind', on their own Llama label, the band – David Roback (vocals, guitar, percussion), brother Steven (vocals, bass), Matthew Piucci (vocals, guitar, sitar), Will Glenn (b. William Cooper Glenn, 1957, d. 16 March 2001, California, USA; keyboards, violin) and Eddie Kalwa (drums) – issued *Emergency Third Rail Power Trip* to critical acclaim in 1983, followed by the excellent 'You Are

My Friend' in 1985. Such was their impetus that the Rain Parade signed with Island Records, despite the loss of key figure David Roback (who then formed Opal with partner and bass player Kendra Smith, eventually re-emerging in Mazzy Star). His replacement, John Thoman, arrived alongside new drummer Mark Marcum in time for *Beyond The Sunset*, drawn from live performances in Japan. A second studio set, *Crashing Dream*, emerged later in the year, but some of the original Rain Parade's otherworldly, evocative nature had been lost. Piucci would go on to form Gone Fishin' and the Hellenes. He would also record an album with Neil Young's Crazy Horse. Steven Roback and Thoman formed Viva Saturn, while Glenn joined Mazzy Star. The latter succumbed to cancer in March 2001.
● ALBUMS: *Emergency Third Rail Power Trip* (Enigma 1983) ★★★★, *Explosions In The Glass Palace* mini-album (Zippo 1984) ★★★★, *Beyond The Sunset* (Restless 1985) ★★★, *Crashing Dream* (Island 1985) ★★★.
● COMPILATIONS: *Demolition* (090 1990) ★★★.

## RAINCOATS

This female outfit epitomized the experimental approach that characterized much of punk's aftermath. The band was formed at Hornsey Art College, London, in 1976 by Gina Birch and Ana Da Silva. Augmented by Vicky Aspinall and manager Shirley O'Loughlin, they were originally joined by Palmolive (b. Paloma Romero) before she left to concentrate on the Slits. This line-up was merely a nucleus for a flexible structure that involved numerous other musicians. As Birch recalls: 'We didn't exactly ignore the audience, but for us, playing was an emotional thing. We would struggle, we would cry, we didn't really know what we were doing half the time.' The Raincoats' debut, 'Fairytale In The Supermarket', appeared on Rough Trade Records (a label that shared their groundbreaking stance) in 1979. It would sell a healthy 25,000 copies. A self-titled album that same year boasted a similarly distinctive sound, and both were revered by critics and a hardcore of admirers alike. *Odyshape* followed in 1981, but was less direct than their debut. Two further singles, a cover version of Sly Stone's 'Running Away' in 1982, and 'Animal Rhapsody' a year later, both hinted at unfulfilled potential. The Raincoats eventually delivered their swan song in 1984 with *Moving*. However, as fitting an epitaph as any can be found on *The Kitchen Tapes*, on the ROIR label, originally released in 1983.
The Raincoats may have remained of historical interest only had not one of their biggest fans, Kurt Cobain of Nirvana, tracked down Ana Da Silva to an antique shop in Notting Hill, London. In exchange for a customized original of the band's debut album, Cobain offered the Raincoats the chance to re-form and support Nirvana on upcoming UK dates (he would also write sleeve-notes for the CD reissues of their albums). Thus the 1994 model Raincoats, who featured Da Silva with Birch, joined by violinist Anne Wood and drummer Steve Shelley (a stand-in on loan from Sonic Youth). Palmolive was said to have departed for a life of religious evangelicalism in

Texas, while Aspinall was busy running a dance label. The new line-up issued *Looking In The Shadows* in 1996. Original members Da Silva and Birch were augmented by ex-Bratmobile Heather Dunn (drums) and Anne Wood (violin).

● ALBUMS: *The Raincoats* (Rough Trade 1979) ★★★, *Odyshape* (Rough Trade 1981) ★★, *The Kitchen Tapes* cassette only (ROIR 1983) ★★★, *Moving* (Rough Trade 1984) ★★★, *Looking In The Shadows* (Geffen 1996) ★★★.

● COMPILATIONS: *Fairytales* (Tim/Kerr 1995) ★★★.

## RAMONE, PHIL

b. USA. One of his country's most venerable and talented producers, Phil Ramone's interests in music began at the age of three, when he undertook violin and piano lessons. A child prodigy, his studies of classical violin brought him to world renown before he was even a teenager, including a command performance for Queen Elizabeth of England aged just 10. During his adolescence he was enticed away from classical music by pop and rock 'n' roll, leading to his first job as an engineer in New York, where he cut his musical teeth. In this discipline he worked on landmark recordings such as Arlo Guthrie's 'Alice's Restaurant', João and Astrud Gilberto's 'The Girl From Ipanema', Wings' 'Uncle Albert/Admiral Halsey' and B.J. Thomas' 'Raindrops Keep Fallin' On My Head'. His production work is even more extensive, encompassing work with Billy Joel, Frank Sinatra, Paul Simon, Julian Lennon, Barbra Streisand, Gloria Estefan, Bob Dylan, Dionne Warwick, Sinéad O'Connor, Peter, Paul And Mary and Chicago. His soundtrack work on films, his other great passion, include *Midnight Cowboy*, *Flashdance* and *A Star Is Born*. His theatrical commissions include *Hair* and *Promises, Promises*, while producing cast albums of productions including *Little Shop Of Horrors* and *Starlight Express*.

Ramone's most distinctive quality is his ability to combine a love of music's essence with a keen interest in emerging technology – he was one of the earliest and most vocal acolytes of compact discs when they were first introduced in the 80s. Indeed, the first CD single ever released, Billy Joel's 'The Stranger', was a Ramone production. Despite accruing substantial wealth from his production work, in the 90s he showed no signs of slowing down, working with Johnny Mathis, Patricia Kaas, Michael Crawford, Barry Manilow and many others in 1995 and 1996. By this time, he had received eight Grammies for his work, a mark exceeded by only one other producer, Quincy Jones. In the late 90s, Ramone wholeheartedly embraced the Internet, working with Lucent Technology on downloadable music files and setting up N2K Encoded Music.

## RANK AND FILE

Formed in Austin, Texas, USA in 1981, Rank And File comprised former members of the Dils, Chip Kinman (guitar, vocals) and Tony Kinman (bass, vocals), and ex-Nuns guitarist/vocalist Alejandro Escovedo (b. San Antonio, Texas, USA). Drummer Slim Evans completed the line-up featured on *Sundown*, an

exemplary blend of new wave and country. The album included 'Amanda Ruth', later recorded by the Everly Brothers. The Kinman brothers then took control of the band and, having moved to Austin, Texas, completed *Long Gone Dead* with session musicians, including Jeff Ross (guitar), Richard Greene (fiddle) and Stan Lynch, drummer with Tom Petty And The Heartbreakers. The new set emphasized the duo's love of pop melody, but the contents were still infused with a country feel. A long hiatus ensued, but their third album proved a major disappointment, lacking the verve and charm of its predecessors. Rank And File was then disbanded with the Kinmans later founding Blackbird. Escovedo reappeared leading the acclaimed True Believers before embarking on a solo career.

● ALBUMS: *Sundown* (Slash 1982) ★★★★, *Long Gone Dead* (Slash 1984) ★★★, *Rank And File* (Rhino 1987) ★★.

## RATT

This heavy metal band was formed in Los Angeles, California, USA, by Stephen Pearcy (vocals), Robbin Crosby (b. 4 August 1959, San Diego, California, USA, d. 6 June 2002, Los Angeles, California, USA; guitar), Warren DeMartini (guitar), Juan Croucier (bass), and Bobby 'The Blotz' Blotzer (drums). They evolved out of 70s band Mickey Ratt, transmuting into their present form in 1983, with a hint of pop about their brand of metal similar to Cheap Trick or Aerosmith. They released a self-titled mini-album in 1983 on a local label, and struck up a close personal friendship with members of Mötley Crüe, which no doubt helped them to sign to Atlantic Records the following year. They made their breakthrough with their first full album, *Out Of The Cellar*, which stayed in the *Billboard* Top 20 for six months and spawned the hit single 'Round And Round'. Ratt toured with Ozzy Osbourne before joining a Billy Squier jaunt where they were apparently 'thrown off' because they were more popular than the headline act. Their subsequent output saw them follow a familiar heavy metal route, with accusations over sexist videos contrasting with their ability to sell out concert halls and produce recordings that regularly received platinum discs. *Detonator* featured several songs co-written with Desmond Child and proved their most adventurous recording to date.

Ratt split-up with the departure of Pearcy in 1992. The singer unveiled his new outfit, Arcade, the following year. However, he was reunited with his former colleagues in 1997 to record the poorly received *Collage*. A major label deal followed, and 1999's self-titled album, featuring new bass player Robbie Crane, was a marked improvement. Crosby died of complications from AIDS in June 2002.

● ALBUMS: *Ratt* (Time Coast 1983) ★★, *Out Of The Cellar* (Atlantic 1984) ★★★, *Invasion Of Your Privacy* (Atlantic 1985) ★★, *Dancing Undercover* (Atlantic 1986) ★★, *Reach For The Sky* (Atlantic 1988) ★★★, *Detonator* (Atlantic 1990) ★★★, *Collage* (De Rock 1997) ★★, *Ratt* (Portrait/Columbia 1999) ★★★.

● COMPILATIONS: *Ratt & Roll 8191* (Atlantic 1991) ★★★.

● VIDEOS: *The Video* (Atlantic 1986).

## RAVE

Usually an illicit one-off gathering for late night enjoyment of pre-recorded dance music in the late 80s/early 90s, often in disused warehouses and factories and later in the open air. A musical definition of rave is more problematic. Descending from the acid house sound and ethos, the sound tended to be fast techno and hardcore records, pitched between 125 and 140 beats-per-minute and often released on tiny independent labels with little background information. Some of rave's established anthems included Toxic Two's 'Rave Generator' and Human Resource's 'Dominator'. Like other forms of dance music, rave had its favoured DJs and remixers. However, arguably the most recognisable and popular of the rave acts were Liam Howlett's Prodigy. Other acts venerated include Altern 8, Bizarre Inc., Bassheads and early K Klass material.

● FURTHER READING: *Altered State: The Story Of Ecstasy Culture And Acid House*, Matthew Colin. *Energy Flash: A Journey Through Rave Music And Dance Culture*, Simon Reynolds. *Adventures In Wonderland: A Decade Of Club Culture*, Sheryl Garratt.

## REA, CHRIS

b. 4 March 1951, Middlesbrough, Cleveland, England. Rea is a singer-songwriter and guitarist with a wide following throughout Europe. Of Irish/Italian parentage, he grew up in the north-east of England where his family owned an ice cream parlour. Rea's first group was Magdalene, a local band in which he replaced David Coverdale, who had joined Deep Purple. As Beautiful Losers, the band won a national talent contest in 1975 but remained unsuccessful. Rea went solo, signing to Magnet Records where Gus Dudgeon produced his first album. With a title referring to a suggested stage-name for Rea, it included the impassioned 'Fool (If You Think It's Over)', which reached the Top 20 in the US and was later covered successfully in the UK by Elkie Brooks. With Britain in the grip of punk and new wave, Rea's earliest supporters were in Germany, and throughout the first part of the 80s he steadily gained in popularity across the Continent through his gruff, bluesy singing and rock guitar solos, notably the instrumental track, 'Deltics'. His backing group was led by experienced keyboards player Max Middleton. Rea's most successful record at this time was 'I Can Hear Your Heartbeat' from *Water Sign*. In Britain, the breakthrough album proved to be *Shamrock Diaries*. Both it and 'Stainsby Girls' (a slice of nostalgia for the northern England of his adolescence) reached the Top 30 in 1985. Two years later, *Dancing With Strangers* briefly went to number 2 in the UK charts although the gritty 'Joys Of Christmas' was commercially unsuccessful.

In 1988, WEA Records acquired Rea's contract through buying Magnet, and issued a compilation album, which sold well throughout Europe. The album reached the Top 5 in the UK and suddenly Rea was fashionable, something that this unpretentious artist has been trying to live down ever since. This was followed by his first UK number 1 hit *The Road To Hell*, one of the most successful albums of the late

80s. The powerful title track told of an encounter with the ghost of the singer's mother and a warning that he had betrayed his roots. Like its predecessor, *Auberge* topped the UK chart while its title track reached the UK Top 20. 'Julia', a track from *Espresso Logic,* became his twenty-seventh UK hit in November 1993.

Rea has remained loyal to his roots, refusing to join the rock *cognoscenti*, but seriously overreached himself with 1996's misguided film project, *La Passione*. He sensibly returned to easily accessible, crafted MOR on *The Blue Cafe*. The following year he took the lead role in Michael Winner's black comedy *Parting Shots*, and released the disappointing *The Road To Hell Part 2*. In summer 2000, Rea enjoyed an unlikely club hit in Ibiza with José Padilla's remix of 'All Summer Long', taken from *King Of The Beach*. The following year he underwent a life-threatening operation that removed his pancreas and duodenum. After recovery Rea returned to his blues roots on *Dancing Down The Stony Road*.

● ALBUMS: *Whatever Happened To Benny Santini?* (Magnet 1979) ★★★, *Deltics* (Magnet 1979) ★★, *Tennis* (Magnet 1980) ★★, *Chris Rea* (Magnet 1982) ★★, *Water Sign* (Magnet 1983) ★★, *Wired To The Moon* (Magnet 1984) ★★, *Shamrock Diaries* (Magnet 1985) ★★★, *On The Beach* (Magnet 1986) ★★★★, *Dancing With Strangers* (Magnet 1987) ★★★★, *The Road To Hell* (Warners 1989) ★★★★, *Auberge* (Atco 1991) ★★★★, *God's Great Banana Skin* (East West 1992) ★★★, *Espresso Logic* (East West 1993) ★★★, *La Passione* film soundtrack (East West 1996) ★★, *The Blue Cafe* (East West 1998) ★★★, *The Road To Hell Part 2* (East West 1999) ★★, *King Of The Beach* (East West 2000) ★★★, *Dancing Down The Stony Road* (Jazzy Blue 2002) ★★★★.

● COMPILATIONS: *New Light Through Old Windows* (Warners 1988) ★★★, *The Very Best Of* (East West 2001) ★★★★.

● FILMS: *La Passione* (1996), *Parting Shots* (1999).

## REDD KROSS

This Los Angeles, California, USA band was formed in 1979. Redd Kross melded elements of 70s glam-rock, 60s psychedelia and 80s heavy metal to become a popular 'alternative' act in the 80s. Originally called the Tourists, the band changed its name to Red Cross (they were later forced to change the spelling after the International Red Cross organization threatened to sue). At the beginning, the band consisted of 15-year-old Jeff McDonald as singer, his 11-year-old brother Steve on bass, Greg Hetson on guitar and Ron Reyes on drums. After gaining local recognition opening for such hardcore outfits as Black Flag, Red Cross made its first recordings in 1980 for a compilation album on the punk label Posh Boy Records. Shortly afterwards Hetson left to form the Circle Jerks and Reyes joined Black Flag. The band signed with manager John Silva, who went on to manage Nirvana and Sonic Youth following introductions by members of Redd Kross. Other musicians came and went throughout the band's history, the McDonald brothers being the only mainstay. The band's popularity grew steadily, particularly among those who listened to college radio stations, and by the end of the 80s they had recorded three albums in addition to the debut. Some featured cover versions of songs by such influences as the Rolling Stones and Kiss, while elsewhere the band's originals crossed 70s punk with the bubblegum hits of the 60s.

Redd Kross resurfaced in the autumn of 1990 with *Third Eye*, their first album for a major label, Atlantic Records. However, it was 1993's *Phaseshifter* that brought about their commercial breakthrough, with the band continuing to record catchy post-punk homages to 70s kitsch, a ploy that was still proving popular by the time of 1997's exuberant *Show World*.
● ALBUMS: *Born Innocent* (Smoke 7 1982) ★★, *Teen Babes From Monsanto* (Enigma 1984) ★★★, *Neurotica* (Big Time 1987) ★★★, *Third Eye* (Atlantic 1990) ★★, *Phaseshifter* (This Way Up/Mercury 1993) ★★★, *Show World* (This Way Up 1997) ★★★★.

## REPLACEMENTS

This pop-punk band was formed in Minneapolis, Minnesota, USA, in 1979, with Paul Westerberg (b. 31 December 1960, Minneapolis, USA; guitar, vocals), Tommy Stinson (b. 6 October 1966, San Diego, California, USA; bass), Bob Stinson (b. 17 December 1959, Mound, Minnesota, USA, d. 18 February 1995; guitar) and Chris Mars (b. 26 April 1961, Minneapolis, USA; drums). Originally the Impediments, their early shambolic, drunken gigs forced a name change to secure further work. Their debut album for the local Twin/Tone label showcased their self-proclaimed power trash style, earning comparisons with hardcore legends Hüsker Dü. Subsequent albums saw the Replacements diversifying to encompass influences from folk, country and blues, without straying far from their winning formula of rock 'n' roll married to the raw passion of punk rock. Beloved by critics on both sides of the Atlantic, the band appeared on the verge of mainstream success in America with the release of *Pleased To Meet Me*. Bob Stinson was replaced by Slim Dunlap and Westerberg was at the height of his songwriting powers on the suicide anthem 'The Ledge', and the achingly melodic 'Skyway'. Greater success somehow eluded them and *All Shook Down* was a largely subdued affair, hinting at an impending solo career for Westerberg. However, it was Mars who became the first ex-Replacement to record following the band's dissolution in 1990. Westerberg would go on to sing under his own name, while Tommy Stinson formed his own bands, Bash And Pop and then Perfect. Dunlap reappeared on Dan Baird's debut solo album. Bob Stinson died in 1995 of a suspected drug overdose. The 1997 double CD compilation included unreleased material and rarities.
● ALBUMS: *Sorry Ma, Forgot To Take Out The Trash* (Twin/Tone 1981) ★★, *Hootenanny* (Twin/Tone 1983) ★★★, *Let It Be* (Twin/Tone 1984) ★★★★, *The Shit Hits The Fans* cassette only (Twin/Tone 1985) ★★, *Tim* (Sire 1985) ★★★, *Pleased To Meet Me* (Sire 1987) ★★★★, *Don't Tell A Soul* (Sire 1989) ★★★, *All Shook Down* (Sire 1990) ★★★.
● COMPILATIONS: *Boink!!* (Glass 1986) ★★★, *All For Nothing/Nothing For All* (Reprise 1997) ★★★.

## RESIDENTS

Despite a recording career spanning four decades, the Residents have successfully – and deliberately – achieved an air of wilful obscurity. Mindful of the cult of personality, they studiously retain an anonymity and refuse to name personnel, thus ensuring total artistic freedom. The most common disguise worn by the members for their multi-media stage show is a giant eyeball mask. Their origins are shrouded in mystery and mischief, although common currency agrees the outfit was founded in Shrieveport, Louisiana, USA. They later moved to San Mateo, California, where a series of home-recorded tapes was undertaken. In 1971, they collated several of these performances and sent the results to Hal Haverstadt of Warner Brothers Records, who had signed Captain Beefheart. No name had been included and thus the rejected package was returned marked 'for the attention of the residents', which the collective accepted as a sign of distinction.

In 1972 the various members resettled in San Francisco where they launched Ralph Records as an outlet for their work. *Meet The Residents* established their unconventional style, matching bizarre reconstructions of 60s pop favourites with ambitious original material. Critics drew comparisons with the Mothers Of Invention, but any resemblance was purely superficial as the Residents drew reference from a wider variety of sources and showed a greater propensity to surprise. *The Third Reich Rock 'N' Roll* contained two suites devoted to their twisted vision of contrasting cover versions, whereas *Not Available* comprised material they did not wish to release. It had been recorded under the Theory Of Obscurity, whereby a record should not be issued until its creators had forgotten its existence, but appeared as a stopgap release during sessions for the ambitious *Eskimo*. *The Commercial Album* consisted of 40 tracks lasting exactly 1 minute and contrasted the Residents' next project, the *Mole Trilogy*, which comprised *Mark Of The Mole*, *The Tunes Of Two Cities* and *The Big Bubble*. The collective undertook extensive live appearances in the USA and Europe to promote this expansive work, which in turn spawned several in-concert selections and an EP devoted to music played during the shows' intermission. Their subsequent *American Composers Series* included *George And James*, a homage to George Gershwin and James Brown, *Stars & Hank Forever*, a celebration of Hank Williams and John Phillip Sousa, and *The King And Eye*, an album of Elvis Presley hits. If this suggests a paucity of original material, it is worth recalling that the Residents' strength lies in interpretation and use of cultural icons as templates for their idiosyncratic vision. The collective have continued to mine this vision into the new millennium, increasingly drawing on digital technology to pursue their aims. The religious-themed *Wormwood: Curious Stories From The Bible* demonstrates that the Residents have not lost the capacity to shock.
● ALBUMS: *Meet The Residents* (Ralph 1974) ★★★★, *The Third Reich 'N' Roll* (Ralph 1976) ★★★, *Fingerprince* (Ralph 1977) ★★★, *Not Available* (Ralph

1978) ★★★, *Duck Stab/Buster And Glen* (Ralph 1978) ★★★★, *Eskimo* (Ralph 1979) ★★★, *The Commercial Album* (Ralph/Pre 1980) ★★★★, *Mark Of The Mole* (Ralph 1981) ★★★, *The Tunes Of Two Cities* (Ralph 1982) ★★, *Intermission* mini-album (Ralph 1982) ★★, with Renaldo And The Loaf *Title In Limbo* (Ralph 1983) ★★★, *The Mole Show Live At The Roxy* (Ralph 1983) ★★, *George And James* (Ralph/Korova 1984) ★★★, *Whatever Happened To Vileness Fats?* (Ralph 1984) ★★, *Assorted Secrets* cassette only (Ralph 1984) ★★, *The Census Taker* (Episode 1985) ★★, *The Big Bubble* (Ralph 1985) ★★, *The 13th Anniversary Show* (Ralph 1986) ★★, *Live In The USA/The 13th Anniversary Tour* (Ralph 1986) ★★, *Stars & Hank Forever* (Ralph 1986) ★★, *For Elsie* (Cryptic 1987) ★★, *The 13th Anniversary Show: Live In Holland* (Torso 1987) ★★, *God In Three Persons* (Rykodisc 1988) ★★, *God In Three Persons: Original Soundtrack Recording* (Rykodisc 1988) ★★, *The King And Eye* (Enigma 1989) ★★, *Buckaroo Blues & Black Barry* cassette only (Ralph 1989) ★★, *Stranger Than Supper* (UWEB 1990) ★★★, *Cube-E: Live In Holland* (Enigma 1990) ★★, *Freak Show* (Ralph 1990) ★★★, *Daydream B-Liver* (UWEB 1991) ★★, *Our Finest Flowers* (East Side Digital 1992) ★★, *Poor Kaw-Liga's Pain* (EuroRalph 1994) ★★, *Gingerbread Man* (EuroRalph/East Side Digital 1994) ★★, *Hunters* (Milan 1995) ★★, *Have A Bad Day* (EuroRalph/East Side Digital 1996) ★★, *Pollex Christi* (Ralph 1997) ★★, *Live At The Fillmore* (Ralph 1998) ★★, *Residue Deux* (East Side Digital 1998) ★★, *Wormwood: Curious Stories From The Bible* (EuroRalph/East Side Digital 1998) ★★★, *Roadworms: The Berlin Sessions* (East Side Digital 2000) ★★★, *Icky Flix: Original Soundtrack* (East Side Digital 2001) ★★★, *Demons Dance Alone* (East Side Digital 2002) ★★★.
● COMPILATIONS: *Nibbles* (Virgin 1979) ★★★, *Residue* (Ralph 1983) ★★, *Ralph Before '84 Volume 1* (Korova 1984) ★★★, *Ralph Before '84 Volume 2* (Ralph 1985) ★★★, *Heaven?* (Rykodisc 1986) ★★★, *Hell!* (Rykodisc 1986) ★★★, *Liver Music* (UWEB 1990) ★★★, *Uncle Willie's Highly Opinionated Guide To The Residents* (Ralph 1993) ★★★, *Our Tired, Our Poor, Our Huddled Masses* (EuroRalph/Rykodisc 1997) ★★★★, *Residue Deux* (EuroRalph/East Side Digital 1998) ★★, *Petting Zoo* (East Side Digital 2002) ★★★.
● VIDEOS: *Ralph Volume One* (Ralph 1984), *The Mole Show/Whatever Happened To Vileness Fats?* (Ralph 1986), *Video Voodoo* (Ralph 1987), *The Eyes Scream* (Palace/Torso 1991), *Twenty Twisted Questions* (Ralph 1993), *Freak Show* (Ralph 1995), *Disfigured Night* (Cryptic Corporation 1997), *Icky Flix* (East Side Digital 2001).
● FURTHER READING: *Meet The Residents: America's Most Eccentric Band*, Ian Shirley.

## REVILLOS

Formed in March 1979 by Eugene Reynolds and Fay Fife, previously vocalists with Scottish band the Rezillos. HiFi Harris (guitar), Rocky Rhythm (drums) and three backing singers – Jane White, Jane Brown and Tricia Bryce – completed the group's original line-up, but within months the latter trio had been replaced by Babs and Cherie Revette. The Revillos made their debut with 'Where's The Boy For Me' in 1979, but although this exciting performance recalled the best of the previous group, it failed to emulate their success. Internal friction undermined the unit's undoubted potential – guitarists, bass players, and singers were replaced with regularity as Reynolds, Fife and Rhythm pursued their uncompromising vision. An album, *Rev-Up*, captured the Revillos' enchanting mixture of girl-group, beat and science fiction, but they were subsequently dropped by their record company. Undeterred, the band inaugurated Superville for ensuing releases and embarked on two gruelling tours of the USA and Canada, which they financed themselves. However, an anticipated contract failed to materialize and this ebullient act later disintegrated. They briefly re-formed in the mid-90s to tour Japan, captured on a 15-song live set.
● ALBUMS: *Rev-Up* (Dindisc 1980) ★★★, *Attack* (Superville 1983) ★★, *Live And On Fire In Japan* (Vinyl Japan 1995) ★★, *Totally Alive!* (Captain Oi! 2002) ★★.
● COMPILATIONS: *Motorbike Beat* (Mau Mau 1995) ★★★, *From The Freezer* (Damaged Goods 1996) ★★, *Wireless Recordings* (BBC Vinyl Japan 1999) ★★★.

## RICHIE, LIONEL

b. 20 June 1949, Tuskegee, Alabama, USA. Richie grew up on the campus of Tuskegee Institute, where he formed a succession of R&B groups in the mid-60s. In 1968, he became the lead singer and saxophonist with the Commodores. They signed to Atlantic Records in 1968 for a one-record contract, before moving to Motown Records, being schooled as support act to the Jackson Five. The Commodores became established as America's most popular soul group of the 70s, and Richie was responsible for writing and singing many of their biggest hits, specializing in romantic, easy-listening ballads such as 'Easy', 'Three Times A Lady' and 'Still'. His mellifluous vocal tones established him as the most prominent member of the group, and by the late 70s he had begun to accept songwriting commissions from other artists. He composed Kenny Rogers' 1980 number 1 'Lady', and produced his *Share Your Love* the following year. Also in 1981, Richie duetted with Diana Ross on the theme song for the movie *Endless Love*. Issued as a single, the track topped the UK and US charts, and became one of Motown's biggest hits to date.
The success of 'Endless Love' encouraged Richie to branch out into a fully-fledged solo career in 1982. His debut, *Lionel Richie*, produced another chart-topping single, 'Truly', which continued the style of his ballads with the Commodores. In 1983, he released *Can't Slow Down*, which catapulted him into the first rank of international superstars, eventually selling more than 15 million copies worldwide. The set also won two Grammy Awards, including Album Of The Year. It spawned the number 1 hit 'All Night Long', a gently rhythmic dance number that was promoted by a startling video, produced by Michael Nesmith. Several more Top 10 hits followed, the most successful of which was 'Hello', a sentimental love song that showed how far Richie had moved from his R&B roots. Now described by one critic as 'the black

Barry Manilow', Richie wrote and performed a suitably anodyne theme song, 'Say You, Say Me', for the movie *White Nights* – winning an Oscar for his pains. He also collaborated with Michael Jackson on the charity single 'We Are The World' by USA For Africa. In 1986, he released *Dancing On The Ceiling*, another phenomenally popular album that produced a run of US and UK hits. The title track, which revived the sedate dance feel of 'All Night Long', was accompanied by another striking video, a feature that has played an increasingly important role in Richie's solo career. The critical consensus was that this album represented nothing more than a consolidation of his previous work, though Richie's collaboration with the country group Alabama on 'Deep River Woman' did break new ground.

Since then, his ever more relaxed schedule has kept his recording and live work to a minimum. He broke the silence in 1996 with *Louder Than Words*, on which he resisted any change of style or the musical fashion hopping of the past decade. Instead, he stayed with his chosen path of well-crafted soul music, which in the intervening years has become known as 'Urban R&B'. *Time* featured several more of Richie's trademark ballads, but was disappointingly bland. *Renaissance*, a more up-tempo collection initially only available on the European market, was a marked improvement.

● ALBUMS: *Lionel Richie* (Motown 1982) ★★★, *Can't Slow Down* (Motown 1983) ★★★★, *Dancing On The Ceiling* (Motown 1986) ★★★, *Back To Front* (Motown 1992) ★★, *Louder Than Words* (Mercury 1996) ★★, *Time* (Mercury 1998) ★★, *Renaissance* (Mercury/Island 2000) ★★★.
● COMPILATIONS: *Truly: The Love Songs* (Motown 1998) ★★★.
● VIDEOS: *All Night Long* (RCA/Columbia 1986), *Dancing On The Ceiling* (Hendring Music Video 1988).
● FURTHER READING: *Lionel Richie: An Illustrated Biography*, David Nathan.
● FILMS: *The Preacher's Wife* (1996).

## RILEY, MARC, AND THE CREEPERS

b. 10 July 1961, Manchester, England. Riley started playing in a band when he was aged 15, 'then I sort of wormed my way into the Fall when I was 16'. He left in 1983 to form the Creepers, with Eddie Fenn (drums), Paul Fletcher (guitar) and Pete Keogh (bass). The last two were later replaced by Mark Tilton (guitar) and Phil Roberts (bass). The records that followed were full of hard-hitting humour and remained as opinionated as those of Riley's former boss, Mark E. Smith (who apparently wrote the sarcastic 'Middle Mass' about Riley). Examples included the anti-Paul Weller rallying cry, 'Bard Of Woking'. Riley formed In Tape Records with keyboard player Jim Khambatta, who also managed the Creepers. Starved of commercial success, and burdened by his heritage, Riley disbanded the Creepers in 1987 and formed the Lost Soul Crusaders before developing a career in radio. Riley currently broadcasts on BBC Radio One as DJ Mark Radcliffe's sidekick.

● ALBUMS: *Cull* (In Tape 1984) ★★, *Gross Out* (In Tape 1984) ★★, *Fancy Meeting God!* (In Tape 1985) ★★, *Warts 'n' All* (In Tape 1985) ★★, as the Creepers *Miserable Sinners* (In Tape 1986) ★★, as the Creepers *Rock 'N' Roll Liquorice Flavour* (Red Rhino 1987) ★★.
● COMPILATIONS: *Sleeper: A Retrospective* (Bleed 1989) ★★★.

## RIP RIG AND PANIC

Evolving out of Bristol's the Pop Group, Rip Rig And Panic was formed in 1981 as a conceptual musicians' collective, taking its name from an album by Rahsaan Roland Kirk. The group's prime movers were multi-instrumentalist and songwriter Gareth Sager, jazz trumpeter Don Cherry's step-daughter Neneh Cherry (b. Neneh Mariann Karlsson, 10 March 1964, Stockholm, Sweden; vocals), Cherry's partner and drummer Bruce Smith, Sean Oliver (d. March 1990; bass) and Mark Springer (piano). Powerful and disturbing live, their playful, anarchic jazz-funk was well captured on the irreverent 1981 debut album *God*, which appeared as two 45rpm discs, but was too radical for daytime airplay or significant sales. They performed at the first WOMAD festival in 1982 shortly before Cherry returned to Sweden to have her first baby. Sean Oliver's sister Andrea temporarily took over vocals, and Louis Moholo joined on drums. The equally experimental second album, *I Am Cold*, appeared in 1982, followed by the more accessible *Attitude* in 1983. Unwilling to compromise further, but feeling the strain of constant innovation, they split in 1985, only to realign as the smaller outfit Float Up CP, and, briefly, God Mother And Country, before Cherry went on to a successful solo career, with Andrea Oliver contributing to some of her songs. Sean Oliver, who went on to co-write Terence Trent D'Arby's 'Wishing Well', died of sickle-cell anaemia in 1990. Sager formed Head, while Springer released a solo album before going on to work on film and television soundtracks. He returned to solo recording with 1998's *Eye*.

● ALBUMS: *God* (Virgin 1981) ★★★, *I Am Cold* (Virgin 1982) ★★★, *Attitude* (Virgin 1983) ★★★, as Float Up CP *Kill Me In The Morning* (Upside 1985) ★★.

## RIVER CITY PEOPLE

Tim Speed (b. 17 November 1961, Chester, Cheshire, England; guitar/vocals), Paul Speed (b. 27 October 1964, Chester, Cheshire, England; drums) and Dave Snell (bass), were all studying at Liverpool Polytechnic in 1987 when they got together with Siobhan Maher (b. 11 January 1964, Liverpool, England; vocals), who had previously played with Snell in Peep Show and was now working as a researcher for the BBC. After the fortuitous break of an all-expenses-paid video for '(What's Wrong With) Dreaming', commissioned by the British independent television programme, *The Chart Show*, they signed to EMI Records and found themselves recording in Los Angeles with producer Don Gehman. The results of this collaboration were heard on their debut, *Say Something Good*, released in September 1989, which spawned a number of successful pop-rock singles: '(What's Wrong With)

Dreaming?', 'Walking On Ice' and the double a-side hit 'Carry The Blame'/'California Dreamin'', the latter being a remake of the classic Mamas And The Papas track, which reached number 13 in the UK charts. Between extensive touring throughout the UK and abroad, they recorded their follow-up *This Is The World*. Released in October 1991 and recorded at Peter Gabriel's Real World Studios, it demonstrated a new 'harder edge' but retained their more sensitive side, so evident on 'Say Something Good'. River City People disbanded soon afterwards, with Maher going on to work with Debbi Peterson (ex-Bangles) in Kindred Spirit and the Speed brothers resurfacing in Speed at the end of the 90s.

● ALBUMS: *Say Something Good* (EMI 1989) ★★★★, *This Is The World* (EMI 1991) ★★★.

## ROACHFORD

This UK soul/funk band is led by Andrew Roachford (vocals/keyboards/percussion), and features Chris Taylor (drums), Hawi Gondwe (guitars) and Derrick Taylor (bass). Andrew Roachford performed from the age of 14 when he played in London's Soho jazz clubs. The band was assembled in 1987, and by early 1988 was touring with Terence Trent D'Arby and the Christians, gaining a reputation for excellent live shows. Strong live support was instrumental to their breakthrough and CBS Records beat many other labels to sign the band. Two singles and an album came out in late 1988, but it was not until early 1989 that 'Cuddly Toy' was re-released to become a UK Top 5 hit. It was closely followed by the minor hit, 'Family Man'. The self-titled album was also rediscovered and the band started to make inroads into the American market, with 'Cuddly Toy' breaking into the Top 30. Sessions for their second album took place in Britain and at Prince's Paisley Park studios. None of the singles released from 1994's *Permanent Shade Of Blue* managed to break into the UK Top 20, but the album was an acclaimed fusion of blues and funk stylings. After a three-year hiatus, Roachford returned with the more mainstream-orientated *Feel*, to mixed reviews.

● ALBUMS: *Roachford* (Columbia 1988) ★★★, *Get Ready!* (Columbia 1991) ★★★, *Permanent Shade Of Blue* (Columbia 1994) ★★★★, *Feel* (Columbia 1997) ★★.

● COMPILATIONS: *The Roachford Files* (Columbia 2000) ★★★★.

## ROBERTSON, ROBBIE

b. Jaime Robbie Robertson, 5 July 1943, Toronto, Ontario, Canada. Robertson's professional career began in 1960 when he replaced guitarist James Evans in Ronnie Hawkins' backing group, the Hawks. Robertson's rough, but exciting style prevails on several of Hawkins' releases, including 'Matchbox', 'Bo Diddley' and 'Who Do You Love', the last of which boasts an arresting solo. The group then left Hawkins and by 1964 was barnstorming tiny American venues, firstly as the Canadian Squires, then as Levon And The Hawks. They recorded a handful of singles including Robertson's 'The Stones I Throw', which showed the genesis of a remarkable compositional talent. The compulsive

backing the Hawks had provided on sessions by blues singer John Hammond led to their association with Bob Dylan. Their emphatic drive underscored Robertson's raging guitar work and helped complete the one-time folk singer's transformation from acoustic sage to electric guru. Robertson's songwriting blossomed during their relationship. His lyrics assumed a greater depth, suggesting a pastoral America, while the music of the group, now dubbed simply the Band, drew its inspiration from a generation of rural styles, both black and white, as well as contemporary soul music peers. Such skill resulted in a body of work that, by invoking the past, created something familiar, yet original.

The Band broke up in 1976 following a farewell concert at San Francisco's Winterland Ballroom. The event was captured in the celebratory film *The Last Waltz*, directed by Martin Scorsese, which in turn inspired Roberston's cinematic ambitions. *Carny*, which he also produced, provided his only starring role to date, although he maintained a working relationship with Scorsese by scoring several of his movies, including *Raging Bull* and *The Color Of Money*. A 1983 collaboration, *King Of Comedy*, was notable for Robertson's solo track, 'Between Trains'. This understated performance was the prelude to the artist's 'comeback' album. *Robbie Robertson*, released in 1987, was an exceptional collection and offered a full, state-of-the-art production, and notable guest contributions by U2, Peter Gabriel, Daniel Lanois and the late Gil Evans, as well as his former Band colleagues Rick Danko and Garth Hudson. Such appearances enhanced a work that compared favourably with Robertson's previous recordings and included two exceptional compositions in 'Fallen Angel' and 'Broken Arrow'.

This artistic rebirth boded well for the 90s, although *Storyville* was a disappointing album for those expecting a repeat of his solo debut. Robertson was not part of the reformation of the Band in 1993. His most interesting project to date (although uncommercial) was in 1994 with the Red Road Ensemble, a group of native Americans. Robertson is passionate about their continuing plight and much of his time in the mid-90s was spent working on their behalf. In 1995, he collaborated with Scorsese again on the soundtrack for *Casino*. *Contact From The Underworld Of Redboy* was a bold fusion of native American tribal chants and contemporary dance beats, with featured collaborators including Howie B., Marcus De Vries, Rita Coolidge and Leonard Peltier, a political prisoner whose vocal contribution to the track 'Sacrifice' was recorded in prison. Robertson also achieved a surprise hit in gay clubs with the Howie B. track 'Take Your Partner By The Hand'. He joined DreamWorks Records in the capacity of A&R director in 1998.

● ALBUMS: *Robbie Robertson* (Geffen 1987) ★★★★, *Storyville* (Geffen 1991) ★★★, with the Red Road Ensemble *Music For The Native Americans* (Capitol 1994) ★★★, *Contact From The Underworld Of Redboy* (Capitol 1998) ★★★★.

● COMPILATIONS: *Classic Masters* (Capitol 2002) ★★★.

● FILMS: *Eat The Document* (1972), *The Last Waltz*

(1978), *Carny* (1980), *Visiting Hours* (1982), *The Crossing Guard* (1995), *Dakota Exile* narrator (1996), *Wolves* narrator (1999).

## ROCHES

Sisters Maggie (b. 26 October 1951, Detroit, Michigan, USA) and Terre Roche (b. 10 April 1953, New York City, New York, USA) began singing a mixture of traditional, doo-wop and barbershop quartet songs in New York clubs in the late 60s. Their first recording was as backing singers on Paul Simon's 1972 album, *There Goes Rhymin' Simon*. Through Simon, the duo recorded an album for CBS Records in 1975 that attracted little attention. The following year, the Roches became a trio with the addition of the distinctive voice of younger sister Suzzy Roche (b. New York City, New York, USA) to Terre's soprano and Maggie's deep alto. With Maggie's compositions, by turns whimsical and waspish, featuring strongly they became firm favourites on New York's folk club scene. A Warner Brothers Records recording contract followed and Robert Fripp produced the self-titled second album, which included compositions by each of the sisters and remains their strongest recording to date. Among the many lyrical extravaganzas were Maggie's best-known song of infidelity 'The Married Men' (later covered by Phoebe Snow), Terre's poignant and autobiographical 'Runs In The Family' and 'We', the trio's a cappella opening number at live performances. The highly commercial 'Hammond Song' was arguably the star track (featuring a fine Fripp solo). *Nurds*, another Fripp production featured the extraordinary 'One Season' wherein the trio manages to sing harmony almost a cappella but totally (and deliberately) out of tune. (Harmony vocalists will appreciate that this is extremely difficult). *Keep On Doing*, maintained a high standard including a refreshing burst of Handel's 'Hallelujah Chorus' and Maggie's tragic love song 'Losing You'. If the Roches ever had strong desires on the charts, *Another World* was potentially the album to do it. Featuring a full rock-based sound, this remains an undiscovered gem including the glorious title track and a cover of the Fleetwoods' 'Come Softly To Me'. Throughout the 80s, the Roches continued to perform in New York and appeared occasionally at European folk festivals. They also wrote and performed music for theatre productions and the 1988 movie *Crossing Delancy*. *Speak* went largely unnoticed in 1989. Their next album was a memorable Christmas gift, *Three Kings*. Containing traditional Yuletide songs and carols it displayed clearly the Roches exceptional harmony. *A Dove* in 1992 featured the 'Ing' Song' a brilliant lyrical exercise with every word ending with ing.

The Roches remain a highly original unit with a loyal cult following. Quirky is a description the Roches would probably squirm at, but no other word better describes their style. 'My Winter Coat' from *Can We Go Home Now?* is a perfect example; few artists would attempt an eight-minute song about a coat. The album also featured several songs informed by the death of the sisters' father from Alzheimer's Disease. Suzzy Roche released her debut solo album in 1997.

● ALBUMS: *Seductive Reasoning* (Columbia 1975) ★★, *The Roches* (Warners 1979) ★★★★, *Nurds* (Warners 1980) ★★★, *Keep On Doing* (Warners 1982) ★★★, *Another World* (Warners 1985) ★★★, *No Trespassing* (Rhino 1986) ★★, *Crossing Delancy* film soundtrack (Varèse Sarabande 1988) ★★★, *Speak* (MCA/Paradox 1989) ★★★, *Three Kings* (MCA 1990) ★★★, *A Dove* (MCA 1992) ★★, *Will You Be My Friend* (Baby Boom 1994) ★★, *Can We Go Home Now?* (Rykodisc 1995) ★★★, Suzzy And Maggie Roche *Zero Church* (Red House 2002) ★★★.

## ROCKET 88

This part-time attraction was drawn from the ranks of the UK's finest R&B/jazz musicians. Formed in 1979, the unit revolved around singer/guitarist Alexis Korner, bass player/vocalist Jack Bruce and three members of the Rolling Stones' circle, Ian Stewart (piano), Bill Wyman (bass) and Charlie Watts (drums). The unit took its name from a 1951 recording by Jackie Brenson, often cited as the first rock 'n' roll single, although the music offered by this *ad hoc* collective invoked the earlier boogie-woogie style of Meade 'Lux' Lewis. Their lone album, recorded live in Hannover, Germany, included versions of 'St. Louis Blues' and 'Roll 'Em Pete' and, while undeniably low-key, was nonetheless an enthralling glimpse into the artistic preferences of musicians freed from perceived commercial restraints. Korner's premature death ended speculation that Rocket 88 might blossom into a full-time commitment. Not to be confused with the US band Rocket 88s, led by pianist Mitch Woods.

● ALBUMS: *Rocket 88* (Atlantic 1981) ★★★.

## ROLLINS, HENRY

b. Henry Garfield, 13 February 1961, Washington, DC, USA. Vocalist Rollins quickly returned to action following the break-up of hardcore legends Black Flag, releasing *Hot Animal Machine*, followed by the *Drive By Shooting* EP (under the pseudonym Henrietta Collins And The Wife Beating, Child Haters). The Rollins Band was eventually formed in 1987 with Chris Haskett (guitar), Andrew Weiss (bass) and Sim Cain (drums). The group developed their own brand of hard rock with blues and jazz influences, over several studio and live albums, building a considerable following with their heavy touring schedule. Rollins' lyrics deal with social and political themes, often unashamedly exorcizing personal demons from a troubled childhood. The sight of the heavily muscled and tattooed frontman on stage, dripping sweat and roaring out his rage, is one of the most astonishing, memorable sights in hard rock music, topping off an enthralling live act. Their commercial rise began with the opening slot on the first Lollapalooza tour, exposing the band to huge audiences for the first time. *The End Of Silence* was a deserved success, and contained some of Rollins' most strikingly introspective lyrics. 'Just Like You' narrated his difficulty in dealing with his similarities to an abusive father: 'You should see the pain I go through, When I see myself I see you'. Rollins' spoken word and publishing activities (his regime is one that allows for little more than a few hours' sleep each night) also drew major media interest.

An accomplished and experienced spoken word performer with several albums to his credit, Rollins' often hilarious style is in direct contrast to his musical persona, and he has drawn comparisons to Lenny Bruce, Bill Hicks and Dennis Leary (although, in contrast, he implores his audience not to destroy themselves with poisons like alcohol and tobacco). Despite the humour there is a serious edge to his words, best animated in the harrowing story of the murder of his best friend, Joe Cole, within feet of him. Rollins' workaholic frame also levers his own publishing company, 2.13.61 (after his birth date), which has grown from small beginnings in 1984 to publish a wide range of authors, including Rollins' own prolific output. He also has a music publishing enterprise Human Pittbull and co-owns a record label (Infinite Zero) with Rick Rubin dedicated to classic punk reissues – Rollins himself having graduated from the infamous late 70s Washington DC 'straight edge' scene and bands such as SOA. He has additionally broken into film acting, appearing in *The Chase* and *Johnny Mnemonic*.

Back with the Rollins Band, *Weight*, produced by long-time soundman Theo Van Rock, saw the first personnel change since the band's inception with Melvin Gibbs replacing Weiss, and adding a funkier spine to the band's still intense core. *Come In And Burn*, released in 1997, was adjudged a largely uninspiring collection. Rollins released a further spoken word recording, *Think Tank*, in 1998 and pursued new acting opportunities, including an appearance in David Lynch's *Lost Highway*.

● ALBUMS: *Hot Animal Machine* (Texas Hotel 1986) ★★, *Big Ugly Mouth* spoken word (Texas Hotel 1987) ★★★, *Sweat Box* spoken word (Texas Hotel 1989) ★★, *The Boxed Life* spoken word (Imago 1993) ★★★, as the Rollins Band *Live* (Eksakt 1987) ★★★, *Life Time* (Texas Hotel 1988) ★★★, *Do It* (Texas Hotel 1988), *Hard Volume* (Texas Hotel 1989) ★★★, *Turned On* (Quarterstick 1990) ★★★, *The End Of Silence* (Imago 1992) ★★★, *Weight* (Imago 1994) ★★★, *Get In The Van* (Imago 1994) ★★★, *Everything* (Thirsty Ear 1996) ★★, *Come In And Burn* (DreamWorks 1997) ★★, *Think Tank* spoken word (DreamWorks 1998) ★★★, with the Rollins Band *Live In Australia 1990* (Buddha 1999) ★★★, *Get Some Go Again* (DreamWorks 2000) ★★★, *A Rollins In The Wry* spoken word (Quarterstick 2001) ★★★, with the Rollins Band *Nice* (Sanctuary/SPV 2001) ★★★, *The Only Way To Know For Sure* (Sanctuary 2002) ★★★.
● VIDEOS: *You Saw Me Up There* (Sanctuary 2001).
● FURTHER READING: *High Adventures In The Great Outdoors* aka *Bodybag*, Henry Rollins. *Pissing In The Gene Pool*, Henry Rollins. *Bang!*, Henry Rollins. *Art To Choke Hearts*, Henry Rollins. *One From None*, Henry Rollins. *Black Coffee Blues*, Henry Rollins. *Letters To Rollins*, R.K. Overton. *Get In The Van: On The Road With Black Flag*, Henry Rollins. *Eye Scream*, Henry Rollins. *See A Grown Man Cry, Now Watch Him Die*, Henry Rollins. *The Portable Henry Rollins*, Henry Rollins. *Solipist*, Henry Rollins. *Do I Come Here Often? (Black Coffee Blues Pt. 2)*, Henry Rollins.

*Turned On: A Biography Of Henry Rollins*, James Parker. *Smile, You're Traveling, (Black Coffee Blues Pt. 3)*, Henry Rollins.
● FILMS: *The Right Side Of My Brain* (1985), *Jugular Wine: A Vampire Odyssey* (1994), *The Chase* (1994), *Johnny Mnemonic* (1995), *Heat* (1995), *Lost Highway* (1997), *Jack Frost* aka *Frost* (1998), *You Saw Me Up There* (1998), *Morgan's Ferry* (1999), *Live Freaky Die Freaky* voice only (1999), *Desperate But Not Serious* (1999), *Scenes Of The Crime* (2001), *Past Tense* (2001).

## ROOMFUL OF BLUES

Formed in the Boston, Massachusetts area in 1967, Roomful Of Blues quickly established first a national reputation in the USA with their very authentic-sounding, big band swing, and then broke through on the international scene in the 80s. The act honed their first-hand knowledge of the music by playing with many of the originators, as well as making numerous recordings in their own right. They also recorded behind 'Big' Joe Turner, Eddie 'Cleanhead' Vinson and Earl King. The main successful alumni include the act's founder members Duke Robillard (b. Michael Robillard, 4 October 1948, Woonsocket, Rhode Island, USA; guitar) and pianist Al Copley, alongside Ronnie Earl (b. Ronald Earl Horvath, 1953, New York City, USA), vocalist Curtis Salgado and saxophonist Greg Piccolo. The longest-serving members of the band are Rich Lataille (b. 29 October 1952, Providence, Rhode Island, USA; saxophone), who joined in 1970, and Bob Enos (b. 4 July 1947, Boston, Massachusetts, USA; trumpet) who was recruited in 1981. Another long-serving member is Chris Vachon (b. 4 October 1957, South County, Rhode Island, USA; guitar), who joined in 1990. Despite the many personnel changes, Roomful Of Blues continues to work regularly, although their impact has lessened due to the many similar acts that have followed in their wake. Hopes for a new era of interest in Roomful Of Blues rose in 1994 when they signed a three-album contract with the Bullseye Blues label under the leadership of Carl Querfurth (b. 3 February 1956, Camden, New Jersey, USA; trombone).

A stable line-up ensued for the excellent *Turn It On! Turn It Up!*. Upon its release on 13 October 1995, the Governor of Rhode Island announced an official annual Roomful Of Blues day for the state of Rhode Island. Members of the band during this period included John 'JR' Rossi (b. 13 November 1942; drums), Doug James (b. Douglas James Schlecht, 1953, Turlock, California, USA; saxophone), Matt McCabe (b. 6 June 1955, Devon, England; keyboards), Sugar Ray Norcia (b. 6 June 1954, Westerly, Rhode Island, USA; vocals, harmonica) and Kenny 'Doc' Grace (b. 11 March 1951, Providence, Rhode Island, USA; bass). Querfurth, Norcia and Rossi were replaced by John Wolf, McKinley 'Mac' Odom and Mike Warners respectively at the start of 1998. Ray Gennari (trombone) was recruited the following year, while another slew of personnel changes saw Thomas Enright (bass), Chris Lemp (drums) and Hank Walther (keyboards) joining in 2000.
● ALBUMS: *The First Album* (Island 1977) ★★, *Let's*

*Have A Party* (Antilles 1979) ★★, *Hot Little Mama* (Blue Flame 1981) ★★★, *Eddie 'Cleanhead' Vinson And Roomful Of Blues* (Muse 1982) ★★★★, *Blues Train/Big Joe Turner & Roomful Of Blues* (Muse 1983) ★★★, *Dressed Up To Get Messed Up* (Rounder 1984) ★★★, *Live At Lupo's Heartbreak Hotel* (Rounder 1986) ★★★, with Earl King *Glazed* (Black Top 1988) ★★★, *Dance All Night* (Rounder 1994) ★★★, *Turn It On! Turn It Up!* (Bullseye Blues 1995) ★★★★, *Under One Roof* (Bullseye Blues 1997) ★★★, *There Goes The Neighborhood* (Bullseye Blues 1998) ★★, *Watch You When You Go* (Bullseye 2001) ★★★.
● COMPILATIONS: *Roomful Of Blues With Joe Turner/Roomful Of Blues With Eddie Cleanhead Vinson* (32 Blues 1997) ★★★★, *Swingin' & Jumpin'* (32 1999) ★★★, *Blues'll Make You Happy Too* (Bullseye Blues 2000) ★★★★.

## ROTH, DAVID LEE

b. 10 October 1954, Bloomington, Indiana, USA. Roth, the former lead vocalist with US hard rockers Van Halen, first expressed his desire to go solo during a period of band inactivity during 1985. He subsequently recorded a mini-album, *Crazy From The Heat*, featuring a varied selection of material that was a departure from the straight metal approach of Van Halen. The album was favourably reviewed and after much speculation, he finally broke ranks in the autumn of 1985. Roth soon found himself in the US Top 3 with an unlikely cover version of the Beach Boys' 'California Girls' (complete with a suitably tacky video), and an even stranger version of 'I Ain't Got Nobody'. This bizarre change must have baffled and bemused his fans, but he soon assembled an impressive array of musicians, notably guitar virtuoso Steve Vai, bass player Billy Sheehan (ex-Talas) and drummer Greg Bissonette to record *Eat 'Em And Smile*. This featured an amazing selection of blistering rockers and offbeat, big production numbers. It proved that Roth was still a great showman; the album was technically superb and infused with an irreverent sense of 'Yankee' humour.

*Skyscraper*, released two years later, built on this foundation, but focused more on an elaborately produced hard rock direction. Billy Sheehan departed shortly after its release to be replaced by Matt Bissonette. Brett Tuggle on keyboards was also recruited to expand the line-up to a five-piece and add an extra dimension to their sound. Steve Vai left in 1989 to pursue a solo career, but was only temporarily missed as Jason Becker stepped in, a new six-string whizz kid of the Yngwie Malmsteen school of guitar improvisation. *A Little Ain't Enough* emerged in 1991 and, although technically faultless, it tended to duplicate ideas from Roth's previous two albums. *Your Filthy Little Mouth* saw him relocate to New York. This time, amid the histrionics about girls and cars, were odes to the Los Angeles riots, and the unutterably horrible pseudo-reggae of 'No Big 'Ting'. In 1996, following Sammy Hagar's departure (sacking) from Van Halen, Lee Roth was falsely rumoured to be rejoining the band he had left 10 years earlier. Two years later, Roth published his wonderfully salacious autobiography and formed the

hard-rocking DLR Band.
● ALBUMS: *Crazy From The Heat* (Warners 1985) ★★★, *Eat 'Em And Smile* (Warners 1986) ★★, *Skyscraper* (Warners 1988) ★★, *A Little Ain't Enough* (Warners 1991) ★★, *Your Filthy Little Mouth* (Warners 1994) ★★, *DLR Band* (Wawazat 1998) ★★★.
● COMPILATIONS: *The Best Of David Lee Roth* (Rhino 1997) ★★★.
● VIDEOS: *David Lee Roth* (WEA 1987).
● FURTHER READING: *Crazy From The Heat*, David Lee Roth.

## ROUGH TRADE RECORDS

Initially based near west London's Portobello Road, the Rough Trade retail shop opened in February 1976, just months prior to the rise of the punk rock phenomenon. Owned by Geoff Travis (b. 2 February 1952, Stoke Newington, London, England), it was an important outlet for punk and independent releases from the UK and USA. Travis' empathy for this musical revolution helped build the shop's reputation as a leading source for import material, British independent releases, complementary reggae releases and as a selling point for the proliferation of music fanzines. The demand for outlets generated by bands inspired the formation of a distribution network and label, and the Rough Trade record label was launched two years later with the release of 'Paris Maquis' by Metal Urbain, which anticipated the industrial style flourishing later in the decade. Subsequent releases by reggae artist Augustus Pablo and *avant garde* act Cabaret Voltaire confirmed Rough Trade's reputation as an outlet for diverse talent. Stiff Little Fingers, Young Marble Giants, Aztec Camera, the Raincoats, the Go-Betweens, the Fall, Scritti Politti and the Pop Group maintained the company's reputation as purveyors of challenging music, while a succession of excellent recordings by the Smiths combined perception with popular acclaim, making them the company's biggest asset for much of its history. The label also became the natural outlet for several US acts, ranging from the guitar-orientated Feelies, Dream Syndicate, the idiosyncratic Jonathan Richman and Camper Van Beethoven, to the experimental styles of Pere Ubu and the offbeat country/folk of Souled American. Many defections to major labels, most notably Aztec Camera and Scritti Politti, underlined the pitfalls bedevilling independent outlets and in 1984, under the aegis of the giant Warner Brothers Records corporation, Travis established Blanco Y Negro on which acts who preferred the security of a major company could nonetheless enjoy the intimacy of an independent. Jesus And Mary Chain, Everything But The Girl and Dinosaur Jr were among the new label's signings, confirming Travis as one of Britain's most astute executives. Rough Trade Records continued to serve as the natural outlet for independently minded acts throughout the 80s, but the defection to EMI Records of the aforementioned Smiths was a significant loss. Hopes were then pinned on the Sundays, but the collapse of the Rough Trade distribution network in 1991 put the label's fate in jeopardy. A trimming-down of staff and operations found the company steadying its position, but although recordings by artists such as Robert Wyatt suggested a long-term future as a haven for adventurism, the Rough Trade network collapsed shortly afterwards. The shop, which had become an independent entity in January 1983, continued to flourish, establishing several new branches (including franchise stores in Tokyo and Paris), a mail-order business, and a limited-edition vinyl label (For Us Records). Travis bought back the record label name in the late 90s, and demonstrated that he had lost none of his old flair by financing releases by acclaimed new artists such as Eileen Rose, David Kitt, and Jeb Loy Nichols.

● COMPILATIONS: *Wanna Buy A Bridge?* (Rough Trade 1980) ★★★, *Rough Trade Shops: 25 Years* 4-CD box set (Mute 2001) ★★★★, *Rough Trade Shops: Electronic 01* (Mute 2002) ★★★★.

## RUBIN, RICK

b. Frederick Rubin, Long Island, New York, USA. In the early 80s Rubin was studying at New York University, listening not only to the punk and rap sounds of his youth but also the newer rap and go-go sounds. His first production job was 'It's Yours' by T. La Rock (1984), but it was not until he formed Def Jam Records with Russell Simmons, boss of the Rush rap management agency, that he was able to create the rap/metal, black/white synthesis that Rubin had in mind. Encouraging a New York Jewish hardcore outfit called the Beastie Boys to experiment with rap was a shrewd move, especially when 'Rock Hard', complete with AC/DC sample, encouraged Columbia Records to invest in Def Jam. It was the idea of uniting Simmons' brother's act Run-DMC with Rubin's adolescent heroes Aerosmith that really put Def Jam on the map. 'Walk This Way' and its parent album, *Raising Hell* did more to introduce black rap to a white audience than anything before or since. For several years, the label could do no wrong, presenting a roster encompassing the rap of LL Cool J and Public Enemy, the soul of Oran 'Juice' Jones and the speed metal of Slayer. However, towards the end of the 80s, things began to fall apart. The Beastie Boys jumped ship, Public Enemy were veering more and more from the racial melting-pot idealism that Rubin advocated, and he and Simmons were having disagreements over A&R policy. Rubin left to form Def American (later American Recordings), and a production career which came up with some fine records (by the likes of the Red Hot Chili Peppers, Johnny Cash and his old idols AC/DC) but nothing as groundbreaking as the early Def Jam material. He did, however, keep to his production credo; 'The less going on in a record, and the clearer and more in-your-face it is, the better.' This delight in frill-free intensity is carried through in Rubin's recent project, the Infinite Zero collaboration with Henry Rollins, re-releasing long-lost obscurities by the likes of Devo, Gang Of Four, Tom Verlaine and Suicide's Alan Vega.

● FURTHER READING: *The Men Behind Def Jam: The Radical Rise Of Russell Simmons And Rick Rubin*, Alex Ogg.

## RUN-DMC

This New York, USA-based rap crew comprises Joseph 'Run' Simmons (b. 24 November 1966, Queens, New York City, New York, USA; the brother of Russell Simmons, their Rush Management boss), Darryl 'D.M.C.' McDaniels (b. 31 May 1964, Queens, New York City, New York, USA) and DJ 'Jam Master Jay' (b. Jason Mizell, 21 January 1965, Queens, New York City, New York, USA). The trio originally came together as Orange Crush in the early 80s, becoming Run-DMC in 1982 after graduating from St. Pascal's Catholic School. They had known each other as children in the Hollis district of New York City, Mizell and McDaniels even attending the same kindergarten.

After circulating demos the trio signed to Profile Records for an advance of $2,500, immediately scoring a US underground hit with 'It's Like That'. However, it was the single's b-side, 'Sucker M.C.'s', which created the stir. It single-handedly gave birth to one of rap's most prevalent terms, and almost became a genre in its own right. Many critics signpost the single as the birth of modern hip-hop, with its stripped down sound (no instruments apart from a drum machine and scratching from a turntable, plus the fashion image of the B-boy: street clothing, chiefly sportswear, and street language). In the wake of the single's success, their debut album went gold in 1984, the first time the honour had been bestowed upon a rap act. They cemented their position as hip-hop's men of the moment with furious touring, and appearances on the *Krush Groove* movie, a fictionalised account of the life of Russell Simmons, who was now joint-head of Def Jam Records with Rick Rubin. They also took a hand at the prestigious King Holliday (a Martin Luther King tribute) and Sun City (Artists Against Apartheid) events.

Run-DMC broke further into the mainstream on both sides of the Atlantic in 1986 when, via Rubin's auspices, they released the heavy metal/rap collision 'Walk This Way' (featuring Steve Tyler and Joe Perry of Aerosmith). Its distinctive video caught the imagination of audiences on both sides of the Atlantic, and the single rocketed into the US Top 5. The partnership had been predicted by earlier singles, 'Rock Box' and 'King Of Rock', both of which fused rap with rock. By 1987, *Raising Hell* had sold three million copies in the US, becoming the first rap album to hit the R&B number 1 mark, the first to enter the US Top 10, and the first to go platinum. Run-DMC also became the first rap act to have a video screened by MTV, the first to feature on the cover of *Rolling Stone*, and the first non-athletes to endorse Adidas products (a sponsorship deal which followed rather than preceded their 'My Adidas' track). Sadly, a projected collaboration with Michael Jackson never took place, though they did duet with Joan Rivers on her television show, and held street seminars to discuss inter-gang violence.

Subsequent efforts failed to maintain their position at the forefront of rap, as their audience flocked to the hardcore political sounds of Public Enemy and N.W.A. Both *Tougher Than Leather* and *Back From Hell* contained a few tough-like-the-old-times tracks

('Beats To The Ryhme', 'Pause') among the fillers. The former album was tied to a disastrous film project of similar title. In the 90s Daniels and Simmons experienced religious conversion, after the former succumbed to alcoholism and the latter was falsely accused of rape in Cleveland. Singles continued to emerge sporadically, notably 'What's It All About', which even sampled the Stone Roses' 'Fool's Gold'. Despite an obvious effort to make 1993's *Down With The King* their major comeback album, with production assistance offered by Pete Rock, EPMD, the Bomb Squad, Naughty By Nature, A Tribe Called Quest, even Rage Against The Machine, and guest appearances from KRS-One and Neneh Cherry, it was hard to shake the view of Run-DMC as a once potent, now spent force. Unsurprisingly, this was not their own outlook, as Simmons was keen to point out: 'The Run-DMC story is an exciting story. It's a true legend, its the sort of life you want to read about'. The album also enjoyed a respectable commercial run and, true to form, the trio enjoyed an unexpected UK chart-topper five years later with a Jason Nevins remix of 'It's Like That'. Their extended studio hiatus was ended in April 2001 with the release of the star-studded *Crown Royal*.

● ALBUMS: *Run-D.M.C.* (Profile 1984) ★★★★, *King Of Rock* (Profile 1985) ★★★★, *Raising Hell* (Profile 1986) ★★★★, *Tougher Than Leather* (Profile 1988) ★★★, *Back From Hell* (Profile 1990) ★★★, *Down With The King* (Profile 1993) ★★★, *Crown Royal* (Profile 2001) ★★★.

● COMPILATIONS: *Together Forever: Greatest Hits 1983-1991* (Profile 1991) ★★★★, *Together Forever: Greatest Hits 1983-1998* (Profile 1998) ★★★★.

● VIDEOS: *Kings Of Rap* (Visual Entertainment 1998).

● FURTHER READING: *Run-DMC*, B. Adler.

● FILMS: *Krush Groove* (1985), *Tougher Than Leather* (1988).

## RUNRIG

This premier Scottish band has emerged from a folk background to enjoy a strong commercial profile in the pop charts, and is arguably the most popular act north of Carlisle. By combining national and cultural pride with stadium rock appeal, Runrig have helped alert the world to Scottish popular music and traditions without a hint of compromise. The band made its debut – as the Run Rig Dance Band – at the Kelvin Hall, Glasgow in 1973. Initially a trio comprising of brothers Rory MacDonald (b. 27 July 1949, Dornoch, Sutherland, Scotland; guitar/bass/vocals, ex-Skyevers), Calum MacDonald (b. 12 November 1953, Lochmaddy, North Uist, Scotland; drums/vocals) and Blair Douglas (accordion), the band was viewed as a part-time venture, 'Something to do during the holidays,' as Calum later stated.

Donnie Munroe (b. 2 August 1953, Uig, Isle Of Skye, Scotland; vocals/guitar) joined the following year as the band took on a more serious perspective. At this point their repertoire comprised of cover versions – Creedence Clearwater Revival was a particular favourite – and traditional material played in a folk/rock manner, reminiscent of Horslips and Fairport Convention. Although the MacDonald

siblings were writing material, Runrig demurred from playing them live until 1978 and the release of *Play Gaelic*. Issued on the Scottish Lismor Records label, this pastoral set introduced newcomer Robert MacDonald (no relation) who had replaced Blair Douglas. A higher profile ensued and, with the extra credibility of an album behind them, the band set up their own label, Ridge Records. Malcolm Jones (b. 12 July 1959, Inverness, Scotland; guitar, mandolin, accordion) replaced Robert MacDonald who was unwilling to turn professional (sadly, he died of cancer in 1986). *Highland Connection* introduced a greater emphasis on electric styles and in 1980 Iain Bayne (b. 22 January 1960, St. Andrews, Fife, Scotland) took over as the drummer, freeing Calum to concentrate on vocals and percussion. By the release of *Recovery*, produced by Robert Bell of the Blue Nile, it was clear the band was more than just another folk/rock act. The music retained its rural feel and traditions, with many songs being sung in Gaelic, but the sound took Runrig outside the narrow bounds of the traditional arena.

English keyboard player Richard Cherns joined the band for its first European tour, but left following the release of *Heartland*. He was replaced by Peter Wishart (b. 9 March 1962, Dunfermline, Fife, Scotland), who was briefly a member of Big Country in 1981. Runrig performed successful concerts in Canada and East Berlin in 1987 and played support to U2 at Murrayfield, Edinburgh, Scotland. After the release of *The Cutter & The Clan*, the band signed to Chrysalis Records, who immediately re-released the album. Chart success followed in 1989 with *Searchlight* almost making the Top 10 in the UK charts. Constant touring – the secret of Runrig's appeal – ensued and in 1990, the *Capture The Heart* EP entered the UK Top 50. A television broadcast of a live performance elicited huge response from viewers to the extent that five concerts at Glasgow's Royal Concert Hall sold out. A subsequent video, *City Of Lights*, reached the Top 10-selling videos in the UK. The highly acclaimed *The Big Wheel* reached number 4 in the UK charts, and an open-air concert at Loch Lomond was attended by 45,000 people. The *Hearthammer* EP broached the UK Top 30 in September 1991, followed by the Top 50 single 'Flower Of The West' and *Amazing Things*, which confirmed their crossover appeal by reaching number 2 in the UK album charts. The band was also to be found performing the singles 'Wonderful' and 'The Greatest Flame' on BBC Television's *Top Of The Pops*.

Following an extensive tour the band bounced back into the pop charts when 'An Ubhal As Airde (The Highest Apple)', which was used as the music for a Carlsberg television advertisement, reached number 18 in the UK charts in May 1995. Donnie Munro stood as a Labour candidate in the 1997 General Election, and subsequently left the band to pursue a political career (he has released solo material). The band celebrated their 25th anniversary in 1998 by releasing a collection of their Gaelic material. Later in the year, Bruce Guthro (b. 31 August 1961, Cape Breton, Nova Scotia, Canada) was recruited as the band's new vocalist. He made his recording debut on the following year's *In Search Of Angels*.

● ALBUMS: *Play Gaelic* (Neptune/Lismor 1978) ★★★, *Highland Connection* (Ridge 1979) ★★★, *Recovery* (Ridge 1981) ★★★, *Heartland* (Ridge 1985) ★★★, *The Cutter & The Clan* (Ridge 1987) ★★★, *Once In A Lifetime* (Chrysalis 1988) ★★★, *Searchlight* (Chrysalis 1989) ★★★, *The Big Wheel* (Chrysalis 1991) ★★★★, *Amazing Things* (Chrysalis 1993) ★★★, *Transmitting Live* (Chrysalis 1994) ★★★, *Mara* (Chrysalis 1995) ★★, *In Search Of Angels* (Ridge 1999) ★★★, *Live At Celtic Connections 2000* (Ridge 2000) ★★★, *The Stamping Ground* (Ridge 2001) ★★★.

● COMPILATIONS: *Long Distance: The Best Of Runrig* (Chrysalis 1996) ★★★★, *Beat The Drum* (EMI 1998) ★★★★, *The Gaelic Collection 1973–1998* (Ridge 1998) ★★★, *BBC Session And Live At The Royal Concert Hall, Glasgow '96* (EMI 1999) ★★★.

● VIDEOS: *City Of Lights* (PolyGram Video 1990), *Wheel In Motion* (PolyGram Video 1992), *Runrig Live At Stirling Castle: Donnie Munro's Farewell* (PolyGram Video 1997), *Live In Bonn* (2000).

● FURTHER READING: *Going Home: The Runrig Story*, Tom Morton.

## RUSH

This Canadian heavy rock band was formed by Geddy Lee (b. Gary Lee Weinrib, 29 July 1953, Willowdale, Toronto, Canada; keyboards, bass, vocals), Alex Lifeson (b. Alex Zivojinovich, 27 August 1953, British Columbia, Canada; guitar) and John Rutsey (drums). From 1969 to 1972 they performed in Toronto playing a brand of Cream-inspired material, honing their act on the local club and bar circuit. In 1973, they recorded a version of Buddy Holly's 'Not Fade Away' as their debut release, backing it with 'You Can't Fight It', for their own label, Moon Records. Despite failing to grab the attention as planned, the band pressed ahead with the recording of a debut album, which was remixed by Terry 'Broon' Brown (he would continue to work with the band until 1984's *Grace Under Pressure*.) With no bite from the majors, once again this arrived via Moon, with distribution by London Records. The quality of their live appointments improved, picking up support slots with the New York Dolls in Canada and finally crossing the US border to play gigs with ZZ Top.

Eventually Cliff Burnstein of Mercury Records (who would later also sign Def Leppard) heard the band and reissued their debut. At this point Neil Peart (b. 12 September 1952, Hamilton, Ontario, Canada; drums, ex-Hush), who was to be the main songwriter of the band, replaced Rutsey, and Rush undertook their first full tour of the USA. Rush's music by this point was typified by Lee's oddly high-pitched voice, a tremendously powerful guitar sound, especially in the early years, and a recurrent interest in science fiction and fantasy from the pen of Neil Peart. Later he would also conceptualize the work of authors such as John Barth, Gabriel Garcia Marquez, and John Dos Passos. This approach reached its zenith in the band's 1976 concept album, *2112*, based on the work of novelist/philosopher Ayn Rand, which had as its central theme the concept of individual

freedom and will. Including a 20-minute title track that lasted all of side one, it was a set which crystallized the spirit of Rush for both their fans and detractors. However, the band's most popular offering, *A Farewell To Kings*, followed by *Hemispheres* in 1978, saw Peart finally dispense with his 'epic' songwriting style. By 1979, Rush were immensely successful worldwide, and the Canadian Government awarded them the title of official Ambassadors of Music.

As the 80s progressed, Rush streamlined their image to become sophisticated, clean-cut, cerebral music-makers. Some early fans denigrated their determination to progress musically with each new album, though in truth the band had thoroughly exhausted its earlier style. They enjoyed a surprise hit single in 1980 when 'The Spirit Of Radio' broke them out of their loyal cult following, and live shows now saw Lifeson and Lee adding keyboards for a fuller sound. Lee's vocals had also dropped somewhat from their earlier near-falsetto. The best-recorded example of the band from this period is the succinct *Moving Pictures* from 1981, a groundbreaking fusion of technological rock and musical craft that never relies on the former at the expense of the latter. However, their career afterwards endured something of a creative wane, with the band at odds with various musical innovations. Despite this, live shows were still exciting events for the large pockets of fans the band retained all over the world, and in the powerful *Hold Your Fire* in 1987 they proved they were still able to scale former heights.

In 1994, the band agreed to a break for the first time in their career, during which Lifeson worked on his Victor side project. They returned in 1996 with *Test For Echo*. Often criticized for lyrical pretension and musical grandstanding – unkind critics have suggested that Rush is exactly what you get if you let your drummer write your songs for you – they nevertheless remain Canada's leading rock attraction, and have clearly found strength and unity following an extended hiatus owing to the deaths of Peart's daughter and wife (the drummer's *Ghost Rider: Travels On The Healing Road* details his grief and the healing process). The post-tragedy *Vapor Trails*, released in 2002, is one of their strongest albums in many years.

● ALBUMS: *Rush* (Moon 1974) ★★, *Fly By Night* (Moon 1975) ★★, *Caress Of Steel* (Mercury 1975) ★★, *2112* (Mercury 1976) ★★★, *All The World's A Stage* (Mercury 1976) ★★, *A Farewell To Kings* (Mercury 1977) ★★★, *Hemispheres* (Mercury 1978) ★★, *Permanent Waves* (Mercury 1980) ★★★★, *Moving Pictures* (Mercury 1981) ★★★★, *Exit: Stage Left* (Mercury 1981) ★★★, *Signals* (Mercury 1982) ★★★, *Grace Under Pressure* (Mercury 1984) ★★, *Power Windows* (Mercury 1985) ★★, *Hold Your Fire* (Mercury 1987) ★★, *A Show Of Hands* (Mercury 1989) ★★★, *Presto* (Atlantic 1989) ★★, *Roll The Bones* (Atlantic 1991) ★★, *Counterparts* (Mercury 1993) ★★, *Test For Echo* (Atlantic 1996) ★★, *Vapor Trails* (Atlantic 2002) ★★★★.

● COMPILATIONS: *Archives* 3-CD set (Mercury 1978) ★★★, *Rush Through Time* (Mercury 1980) ★★,

*Chronicles* (Mercury 1990) ★★★★, *Retrospective 1 (1974-1980)* (Mercury 1997) ★★★, *Retrospective 2 (1981-1987)* (Mercury 1997) ★★★, *Different Stages: Live* 3-CD set (East West 1998) ★★★.
● VIDEOS: *Exit ... Stage Left* (RCA/Columbia Video 1981), *Through The Camera Eye* (RCA/Columbia Pictures 1985), *Grace Under Pressure Tour* (PolyGram Music Video 1986), *A Show Of Hands* (PolyGram Music Video 1989), *Chronicles* (Anthem Music Video 1990).
● FURTHER READING: *Rush*, Brian Harrigan. *Rush Visions: The Official Biography*, Bill Banasiewicz. *Rush, Tribute, Merely Players*, Robert Telleria. *Ghost Rider: Travels On The Healing Road*, Neil Peart.

## RUSH, JENNIFER
b. Heidi Stern, 29 September 1960, New York City, New York, USA. Rush studied piano, violin and singing before starting her pop career. She went to Europe in 1969, when her father, the opera singer Maurice Stern, took an engagement at the Flensburg Opera in northern Germany. She subsequently settled in Wiesbaden, Germany, but moved back to America in the early 70s. A return to Germany came at the beginning of the 80s, working as a secretary for the US Army in Harlaching, Bavaria. Her career in popular music was hallmarked by the spectacular success of 'The Power Of Love', an emphatic MOR ballad that became a major worldwide hit. It reached number 1 in the UK charts in June 1985, re-entering the Top 60 nearly 18 months later in December 1986. Further success arrived via duets with Elton John ('Flames Of Paradise', her only US Top 40 hit) and Michael Bolton, before teaming up with Placido Domingo, in many ways a salute to her operatic roots, for the 1989 hit, 'Till I Loved You'. She also enjoyed solo success with '25 Lovers', 'Ring Of Ice' and 'I Come Undone'. By the 90s, she had become a fixture on AOR radio in the USA, with each of her albums selling strongly. She has over 50 gold records to date, and numerous platinum albums (four of which went 'double platinum').
● ALBUMS: *Jennifer Rush* (CBS 1985) ★★★, *Movin'* (CBS 1985) ★★, *Heart Over Mind* (CBS 1987) ★★★, *Passion* (CBS 1988) ★★, *Wings Of Desire* (CBS 1989) ★★, *Jennifer Rush* (EMI Electrola 1992) ★★, *Out Of My Hands* (EMI Electrola 1995) ★★, *Credo* (EMI Electrola 1997) ★★.
● COMPILATIONS: *Best Of Jennifer Rush* (Sony 1999) ★★★.

## RUTHERFORD, MIKE
b. 2 October 1950, Guildford, Surrey, England. While working in Genesis, guitarist Rutherford enjoyed a solo career broken into two distinct phases. His 1980 debut was a concept album based on Peter C. Brown's novel, featuring vocalist Noel McCalla, formerly with Moon who made two albums for Epic Records in the mid-70s. Neither *Smallcreep's Day* nor the follow-up, *Acting Very Strange*, were commercially successful. Rutherford resumed his solo activity in 1985, under the name Mike And The Mechanics. He had two new songwriting partners – producer Chris Neil and former hitmaker B.A. Robertson. The band employed twin lead vocalists in

Paul Carrack (ex-Ace; Squeeze) and Paul Young from Sad Café. The new formation created two US hit singles, 'Silent Running (On Dangerous Ground)' and 'All I Need Is A Miracle' and a million-selling album. The same line-up was retained for *Living Years*, whose title track was both an international bestseller and an Ivor Novello award winner. Co-written by Rutherford and Robertson it was strongly autobiographical in its theme of the death of a parent. During the late 80s and 90s, Mike And The Mechanics was also a touring band, with the addition of Peter Van Hooke (drums) and Adrian Lee (bass).
● ALBUMS: *Smallcreep's Day* (Charisma 1980) ★★, *Acting Very Strange* (Warners 1982) ★★.

# S

## S.O.S. BAND

Formed in Atlanta, Georgia, USA, in 1977, the S.O.S. Band enjoyed a long run of hits on the US R&B charts during the 80s. The group originally consisted of Mary Davis (vocals, keyboards), Jason 'T.C.' Bryant (keyboards), Billy R. Ellis (saxophone) and James Earl Jones III (drums). They performed regularly, as Sounds Of Santa Monica, at Lamar's Regal Room in Atlanta where they were discovered by Milton Lamar, the club's owner, who later became their manager. The group signed to the independent Tabu Records and soon added new members Willie 'Sonny' Killebrew (saxophone, flute), John Simpson III (bass, keyboards) and Bruno Speight (guitar). The group then changed its name to the S.O.S. Band and teamed up with songwriter/producer Sigidi Adullah. Performing in the then popular funk style, the band began to amass a catalogue of US hits in 1980, with 'Take Your Time (Do It Right) Part 1' rising to number 1 on the R&B chart and number 3 on the national pop chart. Abdul Ra'oof (trumpet, percussion, vocals) was added to the line-up following the release of the band's self-titled debut. They returned to the pop singles chart four more times throughout their career, but never again came close to that initial position despite teaming up with producers Jimmy Jam And Terry Lewis in the mid-80s. On the R&B chart, however, they were mainstays through 1987, returning to the Top 10 four more times – in 1983 with 'Just Be Good To Me' (number 2) and 'Tell Me If You Still Care' (number 5), in 1984 with 'Just The Way You Like It' (number 6), and in 1986 with 'The Finest' (number 2). Five S.O.S. Band albums also charted in the USA, the debut, S.O.S., faring the best at number 12. There were a number of personnel changes throughout the decade, with vocalist Davis leaving for a solo career in 1987. She reunited with Ra'oof and Bryant in the mid-90s for a reunion tour.
● ALBUMS: S.O.S. (Tabu 1980) ★★, Too (Tabu 1981) ★★, S.O.S. III (Tabu 1982) ★★, On The Rise (Tabu 1983) ★★★, Just The Way You Like It (Tabu 1984) ★★★, Sands Of Time (Tabu 1985) ★★★, Diamonds In the Raw (Tabu 1989) ★★, One Of Many Nights (Arista 1991) ★★★.
● COMPILATIONS: The Way You Like It (Columbia 1988) ★★★, The Best Of The S.O.S. Band (Tabu 1995) ★★★.

## SADE

b. Helen Folasade Adu, 16 January 1959, Ibadan, Nigeria. Sade's sultry jazz-tinged vocals made her one of the most successful international stars of the 80s. Of mixed Nigerian/English parentage, Sade grew up in Clacton, Essex, England, writing songs as a teenager. While an art student in London, she joined Arriva, where she met guitarist Ray St. John with whom she composed 'Smooth Operator'. From 1981–83, Sade fronted the funk band Pride, leaving the following year to form her own band with ex-Pride members Stewart Matthewman (saxophone), Andrew Hale (keyboards) and Paul Denman (bass). The line-up was completed by drummer Paul Cook. The group gained a following on the London club scene and in 1984 its first single, the lilting 'Your Love Is King' was a UK Top 10 hit. The Robin Millar-produced Diamond Life broke her into the US market on the back of the Top 5 hit single 'Smooth Operator', and went on to become one of the biggest-selling debut albums of the decade.

Sade received the Grammy Award for Best New Artist in 1985. The same year's Promise, with all songs written by group members, rose to the top of both the UK and US charts and generated further transatlantic hit singles, 'The Sweetest Taboo' and 'Never As Good As The First Time'. Sade also contributed music to the soundtrack of Julien Temple's Absolute Beginners, a 1986 film in which she had a cameo role as Athene Duncannon. With ex-Wham! backing singer Leroy Osbourne added to the group, Sade began a world tour in 1988 to coincide with the release of her third album, from which 'Paradise' headed the R&B chart in the USA. Sade took her time in delivering Love Deluxe. Although it was another mature work, and included two excellent hit singles in 'No Ordinary Love' and 'Feel No Pain', the fickle British public proved lukewarm. The album briefly dented the UK top 30, while in the USA it was a million-seller, peaking at number 3.

A greatest hits package was released in 1994, while the male members of the band recorded separately as Sweetback. In 1996, Sade gave birth to her first child. She made her long-awaited return to the music scene in November 2000 with the single 'By Your Side' and Lovers Rock, enjoying particular success on the US market. She was awarded an OBE in 2002's New Year's Honours List.
● ALBUMS: Diamond Life (Epic/Portrait 1984) ★★★★, Promise (Epic/Portrait 1985) ★★★★, Stronger Than Pride (Epic 1988) ★★★★, Love Deluxe (Epic 1992) ★★, Lovers Rock (Epic 2000) ★★★★, Lovers Live (Epic 2002) ★★★.
● COMPILATIONS: The Best Of Sade (Epic 1994) ★★★★.
● VIDEOS: Diamond Life (SMV 1985), Life Promise Pride Love (SMV 1993), Sade Live (SMV 1994), Lovers Live (Epic 2002).
● FILMS: Absolute Beginners (1986).

## SAKAMOTO, RYÛICHI

b. 17 January 1952, Tokyo, Japan. Sakamoto studied composition and electronic music at Tokyo College of Arts and took a Master of Arts degree in 1976 before forming the Yellow Magic Orchestra with Haruomi Hosono and Yukihiro Takahashi two years later. It was with the YMO that he first achieved international recognition with 'Computer Game (Theme From The Invaders)' reaching number 17 in the UK charts in 1980. Sakamoto's first solo album (aside from a rare jazz release) was recorded in 1978, but not widely distributed until 1982 and only then in Holland. The first easily available recording was *B-2 Unit*, made while he was still a member of the Yellow Magic Orchestra in 1980 with the help of Andy Partridge (XTC) and Dennis Bovell. Singer Robin Scott was given equal billing on *The Left Handed Dream*, with US session guitarist Adrian Belew also featured. *The End Of Asia* was recorded with Danceries, a Japanese classical ensemble, which specialized in recreating medieval music. Working alongside David Sylvian (to whose work Sakamoto became a key contributor), he scored two UK hit singles with 'Bamboo Houses' (1982) and 'Forbidden Colours' (1983).

Since the mid-80s, Sakamoto has established a successful career as a solo recording artist, a film composer and an actor. His evocative soundtrack to Nagisa Oshima's *Merry Christmas, Mr. Lawrence* – in which he made his acting debut – received critical acclaim; his contribution to the soundtrack of Bernardo Bertolucci's *The Last Emperor* (with David Byrne and Cong Su) earned him an Academy Award. In September 1985, at the Tsukaba Expo, he collaborated with Radical TV on a spectacular live performance of *TV WAR*, a science fiction show involving music, video and computer graphics. He has constantly attracted a variety of leading musicians in studio work, varying from Iggy Pop to Brian Wilson and Robbie Robertson and was assisted by Thomas Dolby on *Illustrated Musical Encyclopedia* and the single 'Field Work' (1986). He also contributed to Public Image Limited's *Album* and Arto Lindsay's *Esperanto*.

Sakamoto's solo albums have consistently displayed a hi-tech integration of western pop music with traditional music from Japan, the Middle East and Africa. After releasing *Beauty*, which incorporated Okinawan music, Sakamoto toured the USA and Europe and established his international fame with his highly eclectic style. He conducted and arranged the music at the opening ceremony for the 1992 Barcelona Olympic Games. *Discord* marked his first attempt at orchestral composition, and was marketed as a multimedia package. In 1999, his composition 'Energy Flow' was used in a television advertisement in Japan. Its popularity took the song to the top of the charts. It was included on *BTTB*, an endearing collection of solo piano pieces. Sakamoto also released *Cinemage*, which featured reworkings of themes from his film soundtracks.

● ALBUMS: *Thousand Knives Of* (Nippon Columbia 1978) ★★★, with Kazumi Watanabe *Tokyo Joe* (Nippon Columbia 1978) ★★, with the Kakutogi Session *Summer Nerves* (CBS 1979) ★★, *B-2 Unit* (Alfa/Island 1980) ★★★, with Robin Scott *Hidari Ude No Yume* aka *Left Handed Dream* (Alfa 1981) ★★★, with Danceries *The End Of Asia* (Denon 1982) ★★★, *Merry Christmas, Mr. Lawrence* film soundtrack (London/Virgin 1983) ★★★, *Avec Piano* aka *Coda* (London 1983) ★★★, *Ongakuzukan* aka *Illustrated Musical Encyclopedia* (Midi/Virgin 1984) ★★★★, *Esperanto* (Midi 1985) ★★★, *Futurista (Miraiha-Yaro)* (Midi 1986) ★★★, *Koneko Monogatari (A Kitten's Story)* aka *The Adventures Of Chatran* film soundtrack (Midi 1987) ★★★, *Neo Geo* (CBS 1987) ★★★, *Aile De Honnêamise (Oneamisu No Tsubasa)* (Midi 1987)

★★★, *Media Bahn Live* (Midi 1987) ★★★, with David Byrne, Cong Su *The Last Emperor* film soundtrack (Virgin 1988) ★★★, *Playing The Orchestra* (Virgin 1988) ★★★, *Beauty* (Virgin 1990) ★★★★, *The Handmaid's Tale* film soundtrack (GNP/Crescendo 1990) ★★★, *Heartbeat* (Virgin 1992) ★★★, *Wild Palms* film soundtrack (Capitol 1993) ★★★, *Little Buddha* film soundtrack (Virgin 1993) ★★★, *Sweet Revenge* (Elektra 1994) ★★★, *Smoochy* (Güt/For Life 1995) ★★★, *Music For Yohji Yamamoto Collection 1995* (Gütbounce 1996) ★★★, *1996* (Güt/For Life 1996) ★★★, *Discord* (Güt/For Life 1997) ★★★, with Yoshiuki Sahashi *Stalker* film soundtrack (Güt/For Life 1997) ★★★, *Snake Eyes* film soundtrack (Hollywood 1998) ★★★, *Love Is The Devil* film soundtrack (Asphodel 1998) ★★★, *Music From The Motion Picture Snake Eyes* (Hollywood 1998) ★★, *BTTB* (WEA/Sony Classical 1998) ★★★, *Cinemage* (Sony Classical 2000) ★★★, *Gohatto* film soundtrack (Warners 2000) ★★★, *L.O.L.* (Warners 2000) ★★★, *Zero Landmine* (Warners 2001) ★★★, *Casa* (WPC 2001) ★★★, *Casa Live In Tokyo 2001* (WPC 2001) ★★★, *Comica* (WPC 2002) ★★★.

● COMPILATIONS: *Favorite Visions* (Better Days 1983) ★★★, *Best Selection* (Alfa 1986) ★★★, *Grupo Musicale* (Midi) ★★★, *Better Days Of Ryûichi Sakamoto* (Nippon Columbia 1992) ★★★, *Soundtracks* (Virgin 1993) ★★★, *Grupo Musicale II* (Midi 1993) ★★★, *Virgin Tracks (Best Of)* (Virgin 1993) ★★★, *The Best Of Güt Years 1994-1997* (Güt/For Life 2000) ★★★.

● VIDEOS: *Elephantism* (WPC 2002).

● FURTHER READING: *Otowo Miru, Tokiwo Kiku (Seeing Sound And Hearing Time)*, Ryûichi Sakamoto and Shôzô Omori. *Seldom-Illegal*, Ryûichi Sakamoto.

● FILMS: *Merry Christmas, Mr. Lawrence* (1983), *The Last Emperor* (1987), *New Rose Hotel* (1998).

## SAMSON

This UK heavy metal band first took shape in summer 1977 by guitarist Paul Samson, and over the course of its long history has been dogged by line-up changes, management disputes and record company problems. These have often occurred at critical points in the band's career, just as major success seemed imminent.

The first incarnation of the band comprised Paul Samson (guitar, vocals), Chris Aylmer (bass) and Clive Burr (b. 8 March 1957; drums), and debuted with the single 'Telephone' in September 1978. 'Mr. Rock & Roll' followed in February 1979, by which point Burr had been replaced by the masked Thunderstick (b. Barry Graham). The singles' high-energy, blues-based rock placed Samson among the leading lights of the New Wave Of British Heavy Metal movement, as did their debut long-player *Survivors*. New vocalist Bruce Bruce (b. Paul Bruce Dickinson, 7 August 1958, Worksop, Nottinghamshire, England; vocals) was added to the line-up in July of that year, and a recording contract with the RCA Records subsidiary Gem followed. *Head On* and *Shock Tactics* were well received at the time and remain minor classics of the new metal genre.

In 1981, Bruce Bruce and Thunderstick departed,

with the former assuming his real name Bruce Dickinson and joining former Samson drummer Clive Burr in Iron Maiden. Thunderstick formed a new group under his own name. Nicky Moore (ex-Tiger) and Mel Gaynor (ex-Light Of The World) stepped in on vocals and drums, respectively, but Gaynor soon moved on and Pete Jupp was brought in as a replacement. *Before The Storm* and *Don't Get Mad, Get Even*, released by new label Polydor Records, are Samson's most accomplished works, with Moore's gritty and impassioned vocals giving the band a sound that was both earthy and honest. Chris Aylmer left in 1984 and was replaced by ex-Diamond Head bass player Merv Goldsworthy, and an additional guitarist Dave Colwell was also brought in, but the band split up soon afterwards, dismayed at increasing pressure from their record company to conform to an American style soft rock direction. The excellent live set *Thank You And Goodnight ...* was followed by *Head Tactics*, a collection of remixes from *Head On* and *Shock Tactics*. Moore worked with Uli Roth's Electric Sun before forming Mammoth with John McCoy, Aylmer joined Rogue Male, and Jupp helped form FM. Paul Samson, who also worked with John McCoy, formed Paul Samson's Empire with Colwell, Kevin Riddles (bass), Mark Brabbs (drums) and Sam Bluitt (vocals), although the latter was soon replaced by Mick White. *Joint Forces*, featuring material recorded by Samson and Moore in late 1984 and early 1985, was used to launch the new Castle Communications Records label, Raw Power.

Paul Samson and White re-formed Samson in 1987, recruiting Charlie Mack (drums), Dave Boyce (bass), and Toby Sadler (keyboards; ex-Airrace). A mini-album *And There It Is* was released prior to the sacking of White, who was replaced in February 1989 by Peter Scallan. Paul Samson reunited with Thunderstick on a series of American dates later in the year, and completed work on *Refugee*, a classy, if slightly dated, collection of bluesy, hard rock numbers. He also gigged with the Rogues, alongside Tony Tuohy (drums), Gerry Sherwin (bass) and Rik Anthony (vocals), which evolved into the new line-up of Samson with the return of Aylmer in place of Sherwin. Following the release of *Nineteen Ninety-Three* the band was put on hold once more, with Paul Samson going on to work with Ric Lee's Breakers, the Richard Black Project and form Metallic Blue with bass player Ian Ellis. He reunited with Thunderstick and Aylmer in 1999 to celebrate the '20th Anniversary' of Samson, playing at August's *Metal Crusade 99* festival in Tokyo.

● ALBUMS: *Survivors* (Laser 1979) ★★★, *Head On* (Gem 1980) ★★★, *Shock Tactics* (RCA 1981) ★★★, *Before The Storm* (Polydor 1982) ★★★★, *Don't Get Mad, Get Even* (Polydor 1984) ★★★★, *Thank You And Goodnight ...* (Razor 1985) ★★★★, *Joint Forces* (Raw Power 1986) ★★★, *Refugee* (Communique 1990) ★★★, *Live At Reading '81* (Raw Fruit 1990) ★★★, *Live At The Marquee* (Magnum 1994) ★★, *Nineteen Ninety-Three* (Magnum 1995) ★★, *Live In London 2000* (Zoom Club 2001) ★★.

● COMPILATIONS: *Head Tactics* (Capitol 1986) ★★★, *Pillars Of Rock* (Connoisseur 1990) ★★★, *Burning Emotion: The Best Of 85–90* (Magnum 1995)

★★★, *The BBC Sessions* (High Vaultage 1997) ★★★, *Past Present & Future* (Zoom Club 1999) ★★★, *The Anthology* (Sanctuary 2002) ★★★.

● VIDEOS: *Biceps Of Steel* (RCA 1980).

## SANBORN, DAVID

b. 30 July 1945, Tampa, Florida, USA. Sanborn's virtuosity has now spanned four decades, taking him from being a band member (with the seminal Paul Butterfield) to a leading session player for artists such as David Bowie, James Taylor and Stevie Wonder. His is the alto saxophone solo on Bowie's 'Young Americans'. He grew up in St. Louis and played with some of the finest Chicago school bluesmen, including Albert King. Nowadays, under his own name, Sanborn records and performs regularly. His blistering alto saxophone style competes somewhere between Junior Walker and Dick Heckstall-Smith, and is all the more remarkable because for many years as a child he suffered from polio and had breathing difficulties. Sanborn does not flirt with his instrument; he blows it hard. His solo debut was in 1975 with *Taking Off*. Over the next decade he produced a series of albums that were all successful, and won a Grammy award for *Voyeur*. In 1987, *A Change Of Heart* proved to be a big hit in the jazz charts, although much of it was in the rock style, notably the unrelenting and powerful 'Tintin' along with the pure funk of 'High Roller'. *Close-Up* featured a sensitive (though raucous) reading of the Diana Ross and Marvin Gaye hit 'You Are Everything'. That was to be his last pop influenced album to date and in 1991 Sanborn made his first ever 'pure jazz album' and achieved the esteem of the jazz reviewers. *Another Hand* and more recently *Pearls* have lifted Sanborn to the peak of his already lengthy career. The latter album was lodged at the top of the *Billboard* Jazz chart for many weeks in 1995. He signed a major new contract with Verve Records in December 2000.

● ALBUMS: *Taking Off* (Warners 1975) ★★, *David Sanborn* (Warners 1976) ★★, *Promise Me The Moon* (Warners 1977) ★★★, *Heart To Heart* (Warners 1978) ★★★, *Hideaway* (Warners 1979) ★★★, *Voyeur* (Warners 1980) ★★★★, *As We Speak* (Warners 1981) ★★★, *Backstreet* (Warners 1982) ★★★, *Straight To The Heart* (Warners 1984) ★★★★, *Double Vision* (Warners 1986) ★★★, *A Change Of Heart* (Warners 1987) ★★★, *Close-Up* (Reprise 1988) ★★★, *Another Hand* (Elektra 1991) ★★★★, *Upfront* (Elektra 1992) ★★★, *Hearsay* (Elektra 1994) ★★★, with Tim Berne *Diminutive Mysteries* (JMT 1993) ★★★★, *Pearls* (Elektra Musician 1995) ★★★★, *Songs From The Night Before* (Warners 1996) ★★★, *Inside* (Elektra 1999) ★★★.

● COMPILATIONS: *Love Songs* (Warners 1995) ★★★, *The Best Of David Sanborn* (Warners 1996) ★★★★, *The Essentials* (Rhino 2002) ★★★★.

## SATRIANI, JOE

Satriani, who grew up in Long Island, New York, USA, is a skilled guitarist responsible for teaching the instrument to, among others, Kirk Hammett of Metallica, and Steve Vai. After travelling abroad extensively in his youth he returned to the USA to form the Squares. This project folded in 1984 through an abject lack of commercial recognition, giving Satriani the opportunity to concentrate on his experimental guitar playing. The outcome of this was the release of an EP, *Joe Satriani*. Following a spell with the Greg Kihn band, appearing on *Love And Rock 'N' Roll*, Satriani released *Not Of This Earth*, an album that was less polished than its successor, *Surfing With The Alien*. Despite offering no vocal accompaniment, this set was a major seller and brought mainstream respect to an artist often felt to be too clinical or technical for such reward. In 1988 he was joined more permanently by Stuart Hamm (bass) and Jonathan Mover (drums), also working for a spell on Mick Jagger's late 80s tour.

Never afraid to push his considerable musical skills to the limit, Satriani has played the banjo and harmonica on his albums, as well as successfully attempting vocals on *Flying In A Blue Dream*. In 1993, Satriani released *Time Machine*, a double CD that contained a mixture of new and previously unreleased tracks dating back to 1984, and also live material from his 1993 Extremist world tour. The guitarist then replaced Ritchie Blackmore in Deep Purple in 1994, while maintaining his own solo recording career with further albums.

● ALBUMS: *Not Of This Earth* (Relativity 1986) ★★★, *Surfing With The Alien* (Relativity 1987) ★★★★, *Dreaming 11* (Relativity 1988) ★★★, *Flying In A Blue Dream* (Relativity 1989) ★★★, *Time Machine* (Relativity 1993) ★★★, *Joe Satriani* (Epic 1995) ★★★, with Eric Johnson, Steve Vai *G3 Live In Concert* (Epic 1997) ★★★★, *Crystal Planet* (Epic 1998) ★★★, *Engines Of Creation* (Epic 2000) ★★★, *Live In San Francisco* (Epic 2001) ★★, *Strange Beautiful Music* (Epic 2002) ★★★.

● COMPILATIONS: *The Extremist* (Relativity 1992) ★★★.

● VIDEOS: *Reel Satriani* (Dream Catcher 1998), *Live In San Francisco* (Epic Music Video 2001).

## SAUNDERSON, KEVIN

b. 9 May 1964, Brooklyn, New York City, New York, USA. Alongside his Belleville High School contemporaries, Derrick May and Juan Atkins, Saunderson is a legendary Detroit techno pioneer. He has used many recording names such as the Reese Project, Tronik House, Reese, Essaray, E-Dancer, Kreem, Inter-City and Reese And Santonio but it is undoubtedly his more commercial collaboration with Paris Grey (b. Shanna Jackson, 5 November 1965, Glencove, Illinois, USA) as Inner City that has achieved the most recognition and success. Saunderson moved to Detroit with his family in the mid-70s, meeting May and Atkins at Belleville. After studying telecommunications for two years at Eastern Michigan University, he quit to join May and Atkins in pursuit of a musical career. The three men founded the music collective Deep Space Soundworks in 1981, and later Detroit's Music Institute, which quickly became the focal point for the city's underground club movement. Saunderson worked as a DJ, then moved into producing records before establishing his own label, KMS Records, in 1986.

As house and techno grew in popularity, so did demand for Saunderson's releases. His first release would be 'Triangle Of Love' on Atkins' Metroplex imprint, before breaking through with 'The Sound'. His first big success arrived in 1988 with 'Big Fun'. The basic track was recorded in a makeshift studio in the basement of his apartment, but Saunderson was looking for a female vocalist to finish it off. His friend Terry 'Housemaster' Baldwin suggested Chicago-based singer, Paris Grey. Grey flew to Detroit to record the track, which did not resurface until months later when the UK's Neil Rushton visited Detroit, looking to compile an album for Virgin Records that would showcase the city's new techno sound. 'Big Fun' was included on *Techno ? The New Dance Sound Of Detroit*, and became an international hit when it was released as a single. The follow-up 'Good Life' was an even bigger hit (reaching the UK Top 5) and finally prompted Grey to leave her job as a sales assistant in a Chicago store. Their debut, *Paradise*, was a landmark in the development of the Detroit sound and wore its influences on its sleeve, with a particular nod to white, European bands such as Kraftwerk, Can, and Depeche Mode. Saunderson has subsequently released numerous singles, remixes and productions, balancing his commercial work with Inner City and the soul-inspired Reese Project, with the harder-edged techno of Tronik House, E-Dancer and Kreem. He has also remained in demand as a DJ.

● COMPILATIONS: *Faces & Phases* (Planet E 1997) ★★★★, *X-Mix Transmission From Deep Space Radio* (Studio !K7 1998) ★★★, *KSO1* (Trust The DJ 2002) ★★★.

## SAXON

Formed in the north of England in the late 70s, Saxon were originally known as Son Of A Bitch and spent their early days paying dues in clubs and small venues up and down the UK, with Peter 'Biff' Byford (vocals), Graham Oliver (guitar), Paul Quinn (guitar), Steve Dawson (bass) and Pete Gill (drums) building a strong live reputation. After the name switch they signed a contract with French label Carrere, better known for its disco productions than its work with heavy metal bands. During the late 70s, many young metal bands were emerging in a UK scene that became known as the New Wave Of British Heavy Metal. These bands challenged the supremacy of the old guard of heavy metal bands, and Saxon was at the head of this movement along with Iron Maiden and Diamond Head. The first album was a solid, if basic, heavy rock outing, but the release of *Wheels Of Steel* turned the tide. Saxon's popularity soared, earning themselves two UK Top 20 hits with 'Wheels Of Steel' and '747 (Strangers In The Night)'. They capitalized on this success with the release in the same year of *Strong Arm Of The Law*, another very heavy, surprisingly articulate, metal album. A further Top 20 hit arrived with 'And The Bands Played On', drawn from the following year's *Denim And Leather*, which also produced 'Never Surrender'.

Saxon toured the USA to great acclaim and appeared

at the Donington Festival. By the time of 1982's *The Eagle Has Landed*, which gave Saxon their most successful album, reaching the UK Top 5, the band was at its peak. That same year, Pete Gill was replaced by drummer Nigel Glockler, who had previously worked with Toyah (Gill joined Motörhead in 1984). At this point Saxon counted among rivals only the immensely popular Iron Maiden. The release of *Power And The Glory* enforced their credentials as a major rock band. The follow-up, *Innocence Is No Excuse*, was a more polished and radio-friendly production but it stalled just inside the Top 40. It heralded an uncertain time for the band and a resulting slide in their popularity. The departure of Steve Dawson contributed to their malaise. *Rock The Nations* was as punishing as old, but the chance to recapture former glories had now expired.

In 1990, Saxon returned to the public eye with a UK tour that featured a set-list built on their popular older material. *Solid Ball Of Rock* was their most accomplished album for some time, but in early 1995 Oliver, Dawson and Gill played live together while contesting the rights to the name Saxon with Byford. The issue was soon resolved, however, and Byford was back in place for *Dogs Of War*, with Oliver having taken his leave. A workmanlike record harking back to the band's mid-80s propensity for epic choruses, it was neither awful nor progressive. Oliver, Dawson and Gill formed Son Of A Bitch before winning the right to adopt the Oliver/Dawson Saxon moniker. Byford and Quinn remain at the helm of the official Saxon.

● ALBUMS: *Saxon* (Saxon Carrere 1979) ★★★, *Wheels Of Steel* (Saxon Carrere 1980) ★★★, *Strong Arm Of The Law* (Carrere 1980) ★★★, *Denim And Leather* (Carrere 1981) ★★★, *The Eagle Has Landed* (Carrere 1982) ★★★, *Power And The Glory* (Carrere 1983) ★★★, *Crusader* (Carrere 1984) ★★★, *Innocence Is No Excuse* (Parlophone 1985) ★★, *Rock The Nations* (EMI 1986) ★★, *Destiny* (EMI 1988) ★★★, *Rock 'N' Roll Gypsies* (Roadrunner 1990) ★★, *Solid Ball Of Rock* (Virgin 1991) ★★★, *Dogs Of War* (HTD/Virgin 1995) ★★, *Metalhead* (SPV 1999) ★★, *Killing Ground* (SPV 2001) ★★★.
Solo: Steve Dawson *Pandemonium Circus* (Angel Air 2002) ★★★.
● COMPILATIONS: *Anthology* (Raw Power 1988) ★★★, *Back On The Streets* (Connoisseur 1990) ★★★, *Greatest Hits Live* (Essential 1990) ★★, *Best Of* (EMI 1991) ★★★★, *BBC Sessions/Live At The Reading Festival '86* (EMI 1998) ★★★, *Diamonds And Nuggets* (Angel Air 2000) ★★★, *Coming To The Rescue* (Snapper 2002) ★★★.
● VIDEOS: *Live Innocence* (PMI/EMI 1986), *Power & The Glory – The Video Anthology* (PMI/EMI 1989), *Saxon Live* (Spectrum/PolyGram 1989), *Greatest Hits Live* (Castle Music Pictures 1990).

## SCHENKER, MICHAEL

b. 10 January 1955, Savstedt, Germany. Schenker began his musical career in 1971 at the age of 16, when, along with brother Rudolf, he formed the Scorpions. After contributing impressive guitar work on the band's *Lonesome Crow* debut, he was offered the chance to replace Bernie Marsden in UFO. Schenker joined the group in June 1973 and their resultant musical direction swung to hard rock. *Phenomenon*, released in 1974, featured the metal classics 'Doctor, Doctor' and 'Rock Bottom', with Schenker's performance on his Gibson 'Flying V' hammering home the band's new identity. A series of strong albums followed before Schenker eventually quit in 1978 after the recording of *Obsession*. The split had been predicted for some time following personal conflicts between Schenker and vocalist Phil Mogg. The guitarist moved back to Germany and temporarily rejoined the Scorpions, contributing to *Lovedrive*, released in 1979. Soon afterwards he formed his own band, the Michael Schenker Group, which was later abbreviated to MSG. MSG's personnel remained in a constant state of flux, with Schenker hiring and firing musicians seemingly at will. In 1991, Schenker also took time out between MSG albums to contribute to the Contraband project, a one-off collaboration between members of Shark Island, Vixen, Ratt and L.A. Guns. Schenker has continued to play with both the Scorpions and UFO, while recording with further line-ups of his own group.

● ALBUMS: *Thank You* (Positive Energy 1993) ★★★, *Thank You With Orchestra* (Positive Energy 1999) ★★★, *The Unforgiven World Tour* (SPV 1999) ★★★, *Adventures Of The Imagination* (SPV 2000) ★★★, *Dreams And Expressions* (Michael Schenker 2000) ★★★, *The Odd Trio* (Michael Schenker 2000) ★★★, *Thank You 2* (SPV 2002) ★★★, *Thank You 3* (SPV 2002) ★★★.

## SCHNEIDER, JOHN

b. 8 April 1960, Mount Kisco, Westchester County, New York, USA. Schneider, a gifted musician and actor, has appeared in musicals from the age of 14. He played Bo Duke in the long-running US television series about a disaster-prone hillbilly family, *The Dukes Of Hazzard*, from 1979 to 85. He is featured on the 1982 cast album of the same name. In 1981, he had his first US hit (pop chart number 14, country number 4) with a revival of Elvis Presley's 'It's Now Or Never', and proved himself to be one television star who could sing. However, despite other successes on the US country chart, he was not accepted as a bona fide artist by country disc jockeys. In 1984, the disc jockeys were given unmarked copies of 'I've Been Around Enough To Know', and many of them played the record believing it to be by George Strait. Schneider's identity was revealed and the single topped the US country chart. He had further number 1s with 'Country Girls', 'What's A Memory Like You (Doing In A Love Like This)?' and 'You're The Last Thing I Needed Tonight'. Schneider, however, unlike most country stars, did not care for touring and his final US Top 10 country hit was in 1987 with 'Love, You Ain't Seen The Last Of Me', at a time when he was planning just that. He returned to acting and was in a successful series, *Grand Slam*, in 1990.

● ALBUMS: *Now Or Never* (Scotti Bros 1981) ★★★, *White Christmas* (Scotti Bros 1981) ★★, *Quiet Man* film soundtrack (Scotti Bros 1982) ★★, *Too Good To*

*Stop Now* (MCA 1984) ★★★, *Trying To Outrun The Wind* (MCA 1985) ★★★, *A Memory Like You* (MCA 1986) ★★★, *Take The Long Way Home* (MCA 1986) ★★★, *You Ain't Seen The Last Of Me!* (MCA 1987) ★★★.
● COMPILATIONS: *Greatest Hits* (MCA 1987) ★★★.
● FILMS: *Smokey And The Bandit* (1977), *Eddie Macon's Run* (1983), *Cocaine Wars* (1986), *The Curse* (1987), *Speed Zone!* (1989), *Come The Morning* (1993), *Exit To Eden* (1994), *The Little CHP* (1995), *Snow Day* (2000), *Lightning: Fire From The Sky* (2001).

## SCRITTI POLITTI

Founded by a group of Leeds, England-based art students in 1978, by the time of their first single, 'Skank Bloc Bologna', the nucleus of Scritti Politti was Green Gartside (b. 'Green' Strohmeyer-Gartside, 22 June 1956, Cardiff, Wales; vocals, guitar – who refuses to reveal his actual first name), Matthew Kay (keyboards, manager) and Tom Morley (drums) and Nial Jinks (bass, departed 1980). At this stage, the group was explicitly political (Green had been a Young Communist and the band's Italian-derived name translates roughly as 'political writing'), encouraging listeners to create their own music in the face of the corporate record industry. Gartside also gained a reputation for convoluted wordplay within his lyrics. This early *avant garde* phase gave way to a smooth sound that brought together elements of pop, jazz, soul and reggae on songs such as 'The Sweetest Girl' (with Robert Wyatt on piano) and 'Asylums In Jerusalem'/'Jacques Derrida', which appeared on their debut album for Rough Trade Records, produced by Adam Kidron. Morley quit the group in November 1982, by which time Gartside *was* Scritti Politti. *Songs To Remember* became Rough Trade's most successful chart album; number 1 in the UK independent and, in the national chart, peaking at number 12 (beating Stiff Little Fingers' previous effort at number 14). After moving on to Virgin Records, Green linked up with New York musicians David Gamson (keyboards, programming) and Fred Maher (drums), who formed the basis of the group that made a series of UK hits in the years 1984–88. Produced by Arif Mardin, these included 'Wood Beez (Pray Like Aretha Franklin)' (number 10), 'Absolute' (number 17), and 'The Word Girl' (number 6).
A three-year silence was broken by 'Oh Patti (Don't Feel Sorry For Loverboy)' (number 13), lifted from *Provision*, and boasting a trumpet solo by Miles Davis. Gartside again maintained a low profile for two years after 'First Boy In This Town (Love Sick)', failed to break into the UK Top 60 in late 1988. He returned in 1991 with a revival of the Beatles' 'She's A Woman', featuring leading reggae star Shabba Ranks, reaching number 20, while another Jamaican star, Sweetie Irie, guested on a version of Gladys Knight And The Pips' 1967 hit, 'Take Me In Your Arms And Love Me'. Gartside's extended lay-off was eventually broken with the release of 1999's eclectic *Anomie & Bonhomie*. The album reflected Gartside's infatuation with hip-hop, and featured guest appearances from Mos Def and Meshell Ndegéocello.
● ALBUMS: *Songs To Remember* (Rough Trade 1982) ★★★, *Cupid & Psyche 85* (Virgin 1985) ★★★, *Provision* (Virgin 1988) ★★, *Anomie & Bonhomie* (Virgin 1999) ★★★.
● VIDEOS: *Scritti Politti* (Virgin 1985).

## SEALS, DAN

b. 8 February 1948, McCamey, Texas, USA. Leaving successful pop duo England Dan And John Ford Coley was, at first, a disastrous career move for Dan Seals. His management left him with unpaid tax bills and mounting debts and he lost his house, his van, and his money. He says, 'I was bankrupt, separated and living at friends' places. My kids were with friends. It was a real bad time.' Furthermore, the two albums that he made for Atlantic Records as a solo artist, *Stones* and *Harbinger*, had little impact. However, Kyle Lehning, who produced his hits with England Dan And John Ford Coley, never lost faith and helped to establish him on the US country charts with 'Everybody's Dream Girl' in 1983. Further country hits followed and he had a US number 1 hit with 'Meet Me In Montana', a duet with Marie Osmond, in 1985. Seals then had an extraordinary run of nine consecutive US number 1 country singles: the dancing 'Bop', the rodeo story 'Everything That Glitters (Is Not Gold)', 'You Still Move Me', 'I Will Be There', 'Three Time Loser', the wedding song 'One Friend', 'Addicted' and 'Big Wheels In The Moonlight', many of which he wrote himself. Two further number 1 hits in 1990 included a reworking of soul singer Sam Cooke's 'Good Times'. *Won't Be Blue Anymore* sold half a million copies in the USA, while another big-selling record, *On The Front Line*, included an exquisite duet with Emmylou Harris, 'Lullaby'. Seals signed to Warner Brothers Records in 1991, but *Walking The Wire* was a commercial failure and he has since concentrated on touring. The two volumes of *In A Quiet Room* feature acoustic versions of Seals' best-known songs.
● ALBUMS: as England Dan *Stones* (Atlantic 1980) ★★, as England Dan *Harbinger* (Atlantic 1981) ★★, *Rebel Heart* (Liberty 1983) ★★★, *San Antone* (EMI America 1984) ★★★, *Won't Be Blue Anymore* (EMI America 1985) ★★★, *On The Front Line* (EMI America 1986) ★★★, *Rage On* (Capitol 1988) ★★★, *On Arrival* (Capitol 1990) ★★★, *Walking The Wire* (Warners 1992) ★★, *Fired Up* (Warners 1994) ★★, *In A Quiet Room* (Intersound 1995) ★★★, *In A Quiet Room II* (Serengeti 1998) ★★★, *Make It Home* (Lightyear 2002) ★★★.
● COMPILATIONS: *The Best Of Dan Seals* (Capitol 1987) ★★★★, *Classics Collection Volume 1* (Liberty 1988) ★★★, *Early Dan Seals* (Liberty 1991) ★★★, *Greatest Hits* (Liberty 1991) ★★★, *Classics Collection Volume 2* (Liberty 1992) ★★★, *Best Of Dan Seals* (Curb 1994) ★★★, *Certified Hits* (Capitol 2001) ★★★.

## SECRET AFFAIR

Led by Ian Page (b. Ian Paine, England; vocals, trumpet, piano, organ), and Dave Cairns (b. England; guitar, vocals), Secret Affair, one of the most creative neo-mod groups of the late 70s, emerged out of the lightweight UK new wave band

New Hearts, who folded in 1978 having released two lacklustre singles. The Secret Affair line-up was completed by Dennis Smith (bass, vocals, ex-Advertising) and Chris Bennett (drums, ex-Alternative TV). Bennett was quickly replaced by Seb Shelton (ex-Young Bucks). They debuted supporting the Jam (as the New Hearts had once done), but made their name at the Bridge House Tavern in Canning Town, London, centre of the mod revival. They appeared on the *Mods Mayday* live compilation but then set up their own I-Spy label through Arista Records. Subsequently they toured with Purple Hearts and Back To Zero under the banner 'March Of The Mods'. Their first single, 'Time For Action', was an immediate success for both band and label, featuring Chris Gent (of the Autographs) on saxophone. They also signed Squire to the I-Spy label. Further singles in differing styles charted and the debut album was well received, particularly the epic title track which referred to their fan following. However, Shelton left late in 1980 to join the Up-Set, then Dexys Midnight Runners, and was replaced by Paul Bultitude. After two singles from the final Secret Affair album failed commercially, they disbanded. Dave Cairns went on to form the duo Flag, with Archie Brown, his former colleague from the Young Bucks. He subsequently formed another band called Walk On Fire with Dennis Smith. Page, who now writes fantasy books, formed Ian Page and Bop whose single 'Unity Street' created some interest. Bultitude joined Mari Wilson's Wilsations and later founded the Dance Network label. Smith threw in his lot with Nik Kershaw's Krew, and Seb Shelton went on to manage, among others, the Woodentops.

● ALBUMS: *Glory Boys* (I-Spy 1979) ★★★, *Behind Closed Doors* (I-Spy 1980) ★★★, *Business As Usual* (I-Spy 1982) ★★, *Live At The Bridge* (Receiver 1997) ★★★.

● COMPILATIONS: *Time For Action: The Very Best Of Secret Affair* (Camden 1997) ★★★.

## SELECTER

When Coventry, England's Specials needed a b-side for their own debut, 'Gangsters', they approached fellow local musician Neol Davies. With the assistance of John Bradbury aka Prince Rimshot (drums), and Barry Jones (trombone), Davies concocted the instrumental track 'The Selecter'. Released on the Specials' own 2-Tone label, the single took off with both sides receiving airplay. This meant that a band had to be formed to tour. Bradbury was busy drumming for the Specials and Jones had returned to his newsagent business so Davies assembled the Selecter Mk II. This consisted of Pauline Black (vocals), Davies (guitar), Crompton Amanor (drums, vocals), Charles H. Bainbridge (drums), Gappa Hendricks, Desmond Brown (keyboards) and Charlie Anderson (bass). Anderson claims the original ska superstar, Prince Buster, among his ancestors.

The Selecter's 1980 debut album featured the renowned ska trombonist Rico Rodriguez. Like many of the bands who first found fame on 2-Tone, the Selecter departed for pastures new – in this case 2-Tone's distributors, Chrysalis Records. They managed a string of successful UK singles such as 'On My Radio', 'Three Minute Hero', and 'Missing Words'. Black left in 1981 and recorded the single 'Pirates Of The Airwaves' with Sunday Best, before concentrating on acting. She would reappear to the general public as hostess of the children's pop/games show *Hold Tight*. However, more impressive performances included a one-woman show, *Let Them Call It Jazz*, plus portrayals of Cleopatra and Billie Holiday, the latter bringing her the *Time Out* Award for Best Actress in 1990.

Black rejoined the Selecter on tour in 1991 as signs of a ska revival in London gained ground, though she also found time to host Radio 5's *Black To The Future* and complete her first novel, *The Goldfinches*. A phone call from Doug Trendle (aka Buster Bloodvessel from Bad Manners) had prompted the Selecter's re-formation, which culminated in the release of their first new material for over a decade in 1994. Davies, who had fallen out with the other band members, went on to work with Horace Panter (ex-Specials) and Anthony Harty (ex-Style Council) in Box Of Blues. In 1997, the Selecter supported one-time ska revivalists No Doubt on a US stadium tour. They continue to perform as a revitalised unit, with Black's voice having improved with the patina of age.

● ALBUMS: *Too Much Pressure* (2-Tone 1980) ★★★★, *Celebrate The Bullet* (Chrysalis 1981) ★★★, *Out On The Streets: Live In London* (Triple X 1992) ★★, *The Happy Album* (Triple X 1994) ★★★, *Hairspray* (Triple X 1995) ★★★, *Live At Roskilde Festival* (Magnam Music 1997) ★★, *Cruel Britannia* (Madfish/Snapper 1998) ★★, *Perform The Trojan Songbook* (Receiver 1999) ★★★, *My Perfect World: Live* (Receiver 1999) ★★, *Perform The Trojan Songbook Vol. 2* (Receiver 2000) ★★★.

● COMPILATIONS: *Prime Cuts* (Magnum 1995) ★★★, *Selecterized: The Best Of The Selecter 1991–1996* (Dojo 1997) ★★★, *BBC Sessions/Live At The Paris Theatre '79* (EMI 1998) ★★★, *Too Much Pressure* (Harry May 1999) ★★★.

## SEX GANG CHILDREN

This London-based post-punk/gothic band were briefly in vogue in the early 80s. They were built around vocalist Andi Sex Gang, who talked himself into support slots for which he needed quickly to assemble a new band. He eventually settled on Dave Roberts (bass), Terry McLeay (guitar) and Rob Stroud (drums), who played their first gig under the name Panic Button. The name Sex Gang Children was taken from a William Burroughs book and was actually on a list of names with which fellow King's Road fashion victim Boy George was toying. It later transpired that Boy George had in turn taken it from Malcolm McLaren's original suggestion for a moniker for the band that would become Bow Wow Wow. By 1982, a number of bands in the same mould began breaking through in the capital. Sex Gang Children's first vinyl release was a 12-inch titled 'Beasts', produced by Nicky Garrett (ex-UK Subs), after which Tony James (Generation X, later Sigue Sigue Sputnik) began to take an interest in the band. Their most fondly remembered release, 'Into The Abyss', closed

1982, with their debut vinyl long-player arriving early the next year. The single lifted from it, 'Sebastiane', featured Jinni Hewes from Marc And The Mambas on violin. Andi then performed a debut with Marc Almond ('The Hungry Years') for the compilation *The Whip*, which also included a contribution from Roberts' other band, Car Crash International. Stroud left to join Pink And Black (featuring future All About Eve bass player Andy Cousins), and was replaced by Nigel Preston (d. 7 May 1992; ex-Theatre Of Hate). He stayed long enough to record the single 'Mauritia Mayer', before he took part in a bizarre 'drummers' swap with Ray Mondo of the Cult. Events took a further strange turn when the latter was deported back to Sierra Leone for passport irregularities after a US tour. Roberts also departed, leaving Andi and McLeay to recruit Cam Campbell (bass), and Kevin Matthews (drums). However, only one single, 'Deiche', was released before the band disintegrated and Andi set out on a solo career, renaming his backing musicians the Quick Gas Gang. He released *Blind!* and *Arco Valley*, before reuniting with Roberts in 1992 to record a new studio album. He continued to lead Sex Gang Children throughout the decade and into the new millennium, releasing several new studio albums as well as pursuing a parallel solo career.

● ALBUMS: *Naked* cassette only (Sex Gang Children 1982) ★★★, *Song And Legend* (Illuminated 1983) ★★★, *Beasts* (Illuminated 1984) ★★, *Ecstasy And Vendetta Over New York* cassette only (ROIR 1984) ★, *Re-enter The Abyss (The 1985 Remixes)* (Dojo 1985) ★, *Nightland (Performance USA 83)* (Arkham House 1986) ★★, *Play With Children* (Cleopatra 1992) ★★★, *Medea* (Cleopatra 1993) ★★★, *Live In Paris '84* (Dressed To Kill) ★★, *Veil* (Dressed To Kill 1999) ★★★, *The Wrath Of God* (Livid 2001) ★★, *Bastard Art* (Dressed To Kill 2002) ★★★.

Solo: Andi Sexgang *Blind!* (Illuminated 1985) ★★★, *Arco Valley* (Jungle 1989) ★★★, *God On A Rope* (Cleopatra 1993) ★★★, *Western Songs For Children* (Triple X 1995) ★★, with Mick Rossi *Gabriel And The Golden Horn* (Hollows Hill 1999) ★★, *Last Of England* (Dressed To Kill 1999) ★★★, *Faithfull Covers* (Dressed To Kill 2000) ★★★.

● COMPILATIONS: *The Hungry Years: The Best Of Sex Gang Children* (Receiver 1991) ★★★, *Dieche* (Cleopatra 1993) ★★★, *Shout & Scream: The Definitive Sex Gang Children* (Age Of Panik 1997), *Welcome To My World* (Receiver 1998) ★★★, *Pop Up* (Dressed To Kill 1999) ★★, *Anthology* (Dressed To Kill 2000) ★★★, *The Dark Archives Volume 1* (Triple X 2000) ★★★, *Demonstration!* (Dressed To Kill 2000) ★★, *The Legends Collection* (Dressed To Kill 2001) ★★★, *Fall: The Complete Singles* (Pilot 2001) ★★★.

## SHACK

Formed in 1986 by brothers Michael (b. 28 November 1961, Liverpool, England) and John Head (b. 4 October 1965, England), Shack emerged from the ashes of the Pale Fountains. Having had their fingers burnt by the major record companies – the Pale Fountains reached number 46 in the UK charts with 'Thank You', but were generally misunderstood by their employers – Shack joined up with independent label the Ghetto Recording Company. Experts at the cleverly understated melodic guitar pop song, 1988 saw the release of their acclaimed debut album, *Zilch*, which was produced by Ian Broudie. Yet instead of persevering with their commercial instincts, Shack laid low until reappearing with a single in 1991. A planned second album was finally issued in 1995, after the master tapes had been destroyed in a studio fire and the DAT of the sessions went missing. Bass player Pete Wilkinson joined Cast while the Heads went on to back ex-Love singer Arthur Lee. They resurfaced in 1997 with *The Magical World Of The Strands*, a superb collection of downbeat, melodic indie pop recorded as the Strands. Having been barely credited for their originality at the time (much of what Shack were doing in 1990 could be heard in the wave of mid-90s guitar-based indie bands), the Head brothers received some much deserved critical support when they returned in 1999 with the wondrous Shack album, *HMS Fable*.

● ALBUMS: *Zilch* (Ghetto 1988) ★★★, *Water Pistol* (Marina 1995) ★★★★, *HMS Fable* (London 1999) ★★★★.

## SHAKATAK

One of the original benefactors of the early 80s UK jazz/funk boom, alongside contemporaries Level 42, Shakatak originally comprised Bill Sharpe (keyboards), Steve Underwood (bass), Keith Winter (guitar), Roger Odell (drums), and Nigel Wright (keyboards, synthesizers). Between 1980 and 1987, Shakatak had 14 UK chart singles. Beginning with their chart debut, 1980's 'Feels Like The First Time' on Polydor Records, the string of hits included 'Easier Said Than Done' (1981), 'Night Birds' (1982), 'Dark Is The Night' (1983) and 'Down On The Street' (1984). By this point, a number of personnel changes had taken place, with Underwood replaced by George Anderson in 1982 and the introduction of female lead vocalist, Jill Saward, on 1984's *Down On The Street*. This understated group proved their reputation as one of the finest purveyors of classy jazz/funk with the successful compilation, *Coolest Cuts*.

The latter half of the 80s showed Shakatak leaving behind the demands of instant pop chart hits and allowing themselves to mature, honing their jazz influences and building on their enormous popularity in Japan. The band released several exclusive instrumental albums for the Japanese market during this period (later compiled on *Perfect Smile* and *Open Your Eyes*), but parted company with founder member Winter due to ill health. During the 90s, Shakatak consolidated their reputation in both Europe and the USA, where they regularly place albums high on the *Billboard* Contemporary Jazz chart.

All the members have released solo material, the most successful of which was Sharpe's collaboration with Gary Numan on the one-off single 'Change Your Mind', in 1985. On reaching the UK Top 20, it was not until four years later that the duo released a full album, *Automatic*. In 1999, Sharpe collaborated with producer Don Grusin on the Latin-jazz project, *State Of The Heart*.

● ALBUMS: *Drivin' Hard* (Polydor 1981) ★★★,

*Nightbirds* (Polydor 1982) ★★★★, *Invitations* (Polydor 1982) ★★★, *Out Of This World* (Polydor 1983) ★★★, *Down On The Street* (Polydor 1984) ★★★, *Live!* (Polydor 1985) ★★, *Day By Day/City Rhythm* (Polydor 1985) ★★★, *Into The Blue* Japan only (Polydor 1986) ★★★, *Golden Wings* Japan only (Polydor 1987) ★★★, *Never Stop Your Love* aka *Manic & Cool* (Polydor 1987) ★★★★, *Da Makani* Japan only (Polydor 1988) ★★★, *Niteflite* Japan only (Polydor 1989) ★★★, *Turn The Music Up* (Polydor 1989) ★★★★, *Fiesta* Japan only (Polydor 1990) ★★★, *Bitter Sweet* (Polydor 1991) ★★★, *Utopia* Japan only (Polydor 1991) ★★★, *Street Level* (Inside Out 1993) ★★★, *Under The Sun* (Inside Out 1993) ★★★, *The Christmas Album* (Inside Out 1993) ★★★, *Full Circle* (Inside Out 1994) ★★★, *Let The Piano Play* (Inside Out 1997) ★★★, *Live At Ronnie Scott's* (Indigo 1998) ★★★★, *View From The City* aka *Magic* (Inside Out/Instinct 1999) ★★★, *Under Your Spell* (Inside Out 2001) ★★★.

● COMPILATIONS: *Coolest Cuts* (Polydor 1988) ★★★★, *Greatest Grooves* (Connoisseur 1990) ★★★★, *Perfect Smile* (Polydor 1990) ★★★, *Night Moves* (Pickwick 1990) ★★★, *Open Your Eyes* (Polydor 1991) ★★★, *The Remix Best Album* (Polydor 1991) ★★, *The Collection Vol. 1* (Spectrum 1998) ★★★, *Shinin' On* (Instinct 1998) ★★★, *Jazz In The Night* (Inside Out 1999) ★★★, *The Collection Vol. 2* (Spectrum 2000) ★★★, *The Magic Of Shakatak* (Inside Out 2000) ★★★★.

## SHARKEY, FEARGAL

b. Sean Feargal Sharkey, 13 August 1958, Londonderry, Northern Ireland. Sharkey first found fame as the lead singer of the Undertones, whose singles provided some of the best punk-pop of the late 70s. The band eventually fell apart in 1983, after which Sharkey teamed up with Vince Clarke in the short-lived Assembly. The plaintive 'Never Never' was a Top 5 hit for the duo and highlighted the power of Sharkey's distinctive, quavering vocal style. In 1984, Sharkey recorded the underrated 'Listen To Your Father' for Madness' label Zarjazz and this was followed in 1985 by his biggest success, 'A Good Heart'. This insistent tune, written by Maria McKee, established him as a potential major act by reaching number 1 in the UK charts. The Top 5 follow-up 'You Little Thief' was equally distinctive and Sharkey's debut album, produced by David A. Stewart was well received. Sharkey subsequently moved to America, where he recorded the disappointing *Wish*. A long-delayed third album, *Songs From The Mardi Gras*, continued Sharkey's slow drift away from the mainstream, although it did spawn a surprise UK Top 20 hit, 'I've Got News For You'. By 1993, Sharkey had established himself as A&R Manager for Polydor Records. He has continued to work in this side of the industry, holding the post of Managing Director for EXP Ltd before being appointed a member of the Radio Authority in 1998. He turned down the opportunity to join his former colleagues when the Undertones re-formed in the late 90s.

● ALBUMS: *Feargal Sharkey* (Virgin 1985) ★★★, *Wish* (Virgin 1987) ★★, *Songs From The Mardi Gras* (Virgin 1991) ★★★.

## SHELTON, RICKY VAN

b. 12 January 1952, Danville, near Lynchburg, Virginia, USA. Shelton was raised in a church-going family and he learned to love gospel music. His brother worked as a musician and through travelling with him, he also acquired a taste for country music. He worked as a pipe fitter but his fiancée Bettye realized his singing potential, and in 1984, suggested that they went to Nashville where she had secured a personnel job. In 1986, he impressed producer Steve Buckingham during a club performance, and his first recording session for Columbia Records yielded a US Top 30 country hit in 'Wild-Eyed Dream'. He then made the country Top 10 with one of his best records, the dramatic story-song 'Crimes Of Passion'. In 1987, Shelton had a US country number 1 by reviving a song from a Conway Twitty album, 'Somebody Lied'. The following year he had another number 1 with Harlan Howard's 'Life Turned Her That Way', which, unlike Merle Tillis, he performed in its original 4/4 tempo. His revival of an obscure Roger Miller song, 'Don't We All Have The Right', also went to number 1, giving him five country hits from his first album. He went on to enjoy US country number 1s with revivals of 'I'll Leave This World Loving You', Ned Miller's 'From A Jack To A King' and a new song, 'Living Proof'.

Although Shelton has much in common with his hard-nosed contemporaries, he succumbed to a middle-of-the-road album of familiar Christmas songs and is the author of a series of bestselling children's books about a duck called Quacker. He recorded a duet of 'Sweet Memories' with Brenda Lee, while 'Rockin' Years' with Dolly Parton was a number 1 country single in 1991. The following year Shelton recorded an album of semi-spiritual material, *Don't Overlook Salvation*, as a gift to his parents, before enjoying more hits with the new recordings included on *Greatest Hits Plus*. In the mid-90s, Shelton lost ground, unable to achieve the hits with the same regularity. He recorded an ironic song, 'Still Got A Couple Of Good Years Left', which became a US country Top 50 hit in 1993, but left Columbia shortly afterwards. Shelton's independent label releases, *Making Plans* and *Fried Green Tomatoes*, demonstrate that he is still a viable musical force even if his commercial heyday appears to be over.

● ALBUMS: *Wild-Eyed Dream* (Columbia 1987) ★★★, *Loving Proof* (Columbia 1988) ★★★, *Ricky Van Shelton Sings Christmas* (Columbia 1989) ★★, *RVS III* (Columbia 1990) ★★★, *Backroads* (Columbia 1991) ★★★, *Don't Overlook Salvation* (Columbia 1992) ★★★, *A Bridge I Didn't Burn* (Columbia 1993) ★★★, *Love And Honor* (Columbia 1994) ★★★, *Making Plans* (Vanguard 1997) ★★★, *Fried Green Tomatoes* (Audium 2000) ★★★, *Blue Christmas* (Audium 2000) ★★.

● COMPILATIONS: *Greatest Hits Plus* (Columbia 1992) ★★★, *Super Hits* (Columbia 1995) ★★★★, *Super Hits* (Sony 1996) ★★★, *Super Hits Volume 2* (Sony 1996) ★★★, *16 Biggest Hits* (Sony 1999) ★★★★.

## SHOCKED, MICHELLE

b. Michelle Johnston, 24 February 1962, Dallas, Texas, USA. This roots singer/songwriter's music draws on frequently tough experiences of a nomadic lifestyle. Her childhood had been divided between a religiously inclined mother (Catholic then Mormon), and her estranged father, a some-time mandolin player. She originally came to prominence in 1986 via a Walkman recorded gig, taped around a campfire, complete with crickets on backing vocals. The album was released on Cooking Vinyl Records, and went on to top the UK independent charts. *Short Sharp Shocked*, her first release for major label Mercury Records, highlighted more varied and less self-conscious stylings than the more mainstream Suzanne Vega/Tracy Chapman school. *Captain Swing* was her 'big band' record, where she was joined once more by Dwight Yoakam's producer/guitarist Pete Anderson, as well as a plethora of famous extras (Fats Domino, Bobby Bland, Randy Newman). Despite songs with titles like 'God Is A Real Estate Developer', its jazzy rhythms and swishing brass made it her most commercially accessible. The album's title was taken from the nineteenth-century leader of a farm labourer's revolt, the type of subject matter that put her in good company with touring companion Billy Bragg. The recording of *Arkansas Traveller* was completed by travelling across the US and further a field with a portable studio. Hence musicians like Taj Mahal, Doc Watson, Levon Helm, Clarence 'Gatemouth' Brown and Hothouse Flowers made their contributions in Ireland, Australia and elsewhere. Shocked had spent time researching the origins of American music and in particular the black-faced minstrel legacy, which she attacked with her own traditional songs.

In the summer of 1995, Shocked filed a suit to be released from her contract with PolyGram Records following a number of accusations from both parties. *Kind Hearted Woman*, which Shocked had been selling at her gigs since 1994, was finally given a general release two years later. The independently produced follow-up was recorded with Fiachna O'Braonain of Hothouse Flowers. *Deep Natural*, released in 2002 on Shocked's Mighty Sound label, originally came with a bonus disc featuring many of the album's tracks reworked as dub instrumentals.

● ALBUMS: *The Texas Campfire Tapes* (Cooking Vinyl 1986) ★★★, *Short Sharp Shocked* (Mercury/Cooking Vinyl 1988) ★★★, *Captain Swing* (Mercury/Cooking Vinyl 1989) ★★, *Arkansas Traveller* (Mercury/London 1992) ★★★, *Kind Hearted Woman* (Mood Swing/Private 1994) ★★★, with Fiachna O'Braonain *Artists Make Lousy Slaves* (Private 1996) ★★★, *Good News* (Mood Swing 1998) ★★★, *Deep Natural* (Mighty Sound 2002) ★★★.
● COMPILATIONS: *Mercury Poise: 1988-1995* (Mercury 1996) ★★★.

## SHONEN KNIFE

Japanese sisters Atsuko Yamano (b. 22 February c.1960, Osaka, Japan) and Naoko Yamano (b. 18 December c.1961, Osaka, Japan) with Michie Nakatani (b. 8 October c.1961, Osaka, Japan) play buzzsaw, distinctly Ramones-derived, pop. Shonen Knife means 'Boy Knife', the brand name of a small Japanese pocket knife. They formed in December 1981, their sporadic recording career starting in

Osaka on the Japanese label Zero with 1982's *Burning Farm EP*. The band then relocated to the west coast of America after a compilation cassette released by Calvin Johnson of Beat Happening had attracted some interest. There they came to the attention of US punk pop fans in general, and Nirvana in particular. The latter took them under their wing with support slots, which brought them international recognition. By this time, however, they had long been a cult delicacy in American punk circles, made evident when 30 bands each contributed to an album's worth of cover versions of Shonen Knife songs (*Every Band Has A Shonen Knife Who Loves Them*). Although their charm may be limited in the long term, a suitable epitaph for their appeal came from Nirvana's Kurt Cobain: 'They play pop music, pop, pop, pop music.' After a three-year gap, they attempted a comeback with *Brand New Knife*. Michie Nakatani left following the release of 1998's *Happy Hour*.

● ALBUMS: *Burning Farm* mini-album (Zero 1982) ★★★, *Yamano Atchan* mini-album (Zero 1984) ★★★, *Pretty Little Baka Guy* mini-album (Zero 1986) ★★★, *712* (Nippon Crown 1991) ★★★, *Let's Knife* (MCA Victor 1992) ★★★, *Rock Animals* (August Records 1993) ★★, *Brand New Knife* (MCA/Big Deal 1996) ★★★, *Happy Hour* (Universal 1998) ★★, *Strawberry Sound* (Universal 2000) ★★★, *Heavy Songs* (Warners 2002) ★★★.
● COMPILATIONS: *Shonen Knife* (Giant 1990) ★★★, *The Birds And The B Sides* (Virgin America 1996) ★★★, *Millennium Edition* (Universal 2001) ★★★.

## SHRIEKBACK

This art-funk outfit originally evolved around a three-man nucleus of ex-Gang Of Four member Dave Allen (bass), Carl Marsh (guitar, vocals; ex-Out On Blue Six), plus Barry Andrews (b. 12 September 1956, West Norwood, London, England; keyboards, vocals), previously with XTC, Robert Fripp's League Of Gentlemen and Restaurant For Dogs. The trio fused funk and rock with a unique and complex rhythmic approach, creating a distinctive and influential sound. The first fruits of this project came in 1982 with the *Tench* EP and then 'Sexthinkone' on the Y label, but it was the next two singles, 'My Spine (Is the Bassline)' (1982) and 'Lined Up' (1983), which established the band's trademark complex rhythms and chanted vocals. 'Working On The Ground' helped secure a contract with Arista Records, who released *Jam Science* in 1984. The album, which featured drummer Martyn Barker, also spawned two excellent singles, 'Hand On My Heart' and 'Mercy Dash'. The following year saw the release of *Oil And Gold*, which included 'Nemesis' and 'Fish Below The Ice'. Although more commercially based, the band had lost that hard, infectious funk vein that was previously so predominant. Marsh left the band before a move to Island Records yielded *Big Night Music* early in 1987, accompanied by 'Gunning For The Buddha' a month earlier. 'Get Down Tonight' followed in 1988, presaging the album *Go Bang!*, which featured only Andrews and Barker from the early line-up (Dave Allen went on to work with King Swamp and Low Pop Suicide). New members included Michael Cozzi (guitar) and Sarah and

Wendy Partridge (vocals), but Andrews and Barker ended the band shortly afterwards.

Those looking for an introduction to Shriekback might opt for *The Infinite*, a collection of the Y singles released on the Kaz label. Since then, there have been several further compilations, with the definitive *Priests And Kanibals* drawing from the band's work on Y, Arista and Island. In 1992, inspired by the UK's burgeoning dance music scene, Allen, Andrews and Barker re-formed to record *Sacred City*, which also included contributions from Underworld's Karl Hyde. Barker and Andrews subsequently fronted various line-ups of the band for sporadic live work. *Naked Apes & Pond Life*, the majority of which had actually been recorded back in 1995, was finally released in early 2000.

● ALBUMS: *Care* (Y 1983) ★★★★, *Jam Science* (Arista 1984) ★★★, *Oil And Gold* (Arista 1985) ★★★, *Big Night Music* (Island 1987) ★★★, *Go Bang!* (Island 1988) ★★, *Sacred City* (World Domination/Shriek 1992) ★★★, *Naked Apes & Pond Life* (Mauve/Mushroom 2000) ★★★.

● COMPILATIONS: *The Best Of Shriekback: The Infinite* (Kaz 1985) ★★★★, *The Best Of Shriekback Volume Two: Evolution* (Kaz 1988) ★★★, *The Dancing Years* (Island 1990) ★★★, *Natural History: The Very Best Of Shriekback* (Essential 1994) ★★★, *Priests And Kanibals: The Best Of* (Arista 1994) ★★★★, *Aberrations 1981-1984* (Weatherbox 2001) ★★★.

● VIDEOS: *Jungle Of The Senses* (Island Visual Arts 1987)

## SIBERRY, JANE

b. 12 October 1955, Toronto, Ontario, Canada. This singer/composer stands outside the traditional boundaries of folk music, being compared to artists such as Laurie Anderson, Joni Mitchell and Suzanne Vega. Having graduated from the University of Guelph with a degree in Microbiology, Siberry began by performing on the local coffee house circuit in Canada. Her first, independently produced album was released in 1980 and followed by a Canadian tour. She financed the project by earning tips working as a waitress. *No Borders Here* included 'Mimi On The Beach', an underground hit at home in Canada. *The Speckless Sky* went gold in Canada, and won two CASBYS, Canada's People Choice Award, for both album and producer of the year. Siberry made her first live appearance in Europe, following the release of *The Walking*, at the ICA in London. *The Walking* marked her recording debut for Reprise Records. Having recorded her earlier production demos in a 16-track studio located in an apple orchard near Toronto, she decided to record the whole of *Bound By The Beauty* at Orchard Studio. For the task, a 24-track unit was parachuted into the studio. The album was mixed by Kevin Killen, known for work with both Kate Bush and Peter Gabriel and was greeted with considerable critical acclaim. The belated follow-up, 1993's *When I Was A Boy*, saw her work with Brian Eno on two tracks. Commenting on its distinctive title and character, she noted: 'I think this record is more whole in a funny way . . . It is also more masculine. Before, my work has always had a sense of graciousness and

hospitality, like the good mother. I don't think I could be called a female singer/songwriter with this record'. In 1996, after one further record for Warners, Siberry launched her own Sheeba label, on which she has pursued her increasingly esoteric muse.

● ALBUMS: *Jane Siberry* (Street 1980) ★★★, *No Borders Here* (Open Air 1984) ★★★, *The Speckless Sky* (Reprise 1985) ★★★, *The Walking* (Duke Street 1987) ★★, *Bound By The Beauty* (Reprise 1989) ★★★★, *When I Was A Boy* (Reprise 1993) ★★★, *Maria* (Warners 1995) ★★★, *Teenager* (Sheeba 1996) ★★★, *A Day In The Life* (Sheeba 1997) ★★, *Tree: Music For Films And Forests* (Sheeba 1997) ★★, *Lips: Music For Saying It* (Sheeba 1998) ★★, *Child: Music For the Christmas Season* (Sheeba 1999) ★★, *Hush* (Sheeba 2000) ★★★, *City* (Sheeba 2001) ★★★.

● COMPILATIONS: *Summer In The Yukon* (Reprise 1992) ★★★, *A Collection 1984-1989* (Duke Street 1993) ★★★, *New York Trilogy* 4-CD box set (Sheeba 1999) ★★★, *Love Is Everything: The Jane Siberry Anthology* (Rhino 2002) ★★★★.

## SIGUE SIGUE SPUTNIK

These UK punk/glam revivalists engineered themselves a briefly prosperous niche in the mid-80s. The creation of Tony James (ex-Chelsea; Generation X), Sigue Sigue Sputnik artlessly copied the shock tactics of Sex Pistols manager Malcolm McLaren. Instead of taking on board the Pistols' nihilism, James poached from cyberpunk novels and films (particularly Ridley Scott's *Blade Runner*) for their image. This consisted of dyed hair piled high, bright colours and an abundance of eyeliner. James had also recruited clothes designer Martin Degville (b. 27 January 1961, England; vocals), Neal X (b. Neil Whitmore; guitar), Ray Mayhew (drums) and Chris Kavanagh (b. 4 June 1964; drums), taking pride in their apparent lack of musical experience. Taking their name from a Moscow street gang, they set about a publicity campaign that resulted in EMI Records, understandably keen not to let the next Sex Pistols slip through their hands again, signing them for a reported £4 million. The figure, however, was deliberately exaggerated in order to provoke publicity. Their first single was 'Love Missile F1-11', which soared to number 3 in the UK charts in February 1986. However, although '21st Century Boy' also made the Top 20, and a debut album sold advertising space between tracks, James' moneymaking ruse soon ended. Despite an avalanche of intentionally lurid press, the band dissolved, and Tony James subsequently, albeit briefly, joined the Sisters Of Mercy in 1991. Kavanagh would go on to Big Audio Dynamite, though James would make another attempt at resurrecting Sigue Sigue Sputnik later in the 90s. Degville recorded the dreadful solo set *World War Four* in 1991. He reunited with James and Whitmore in the late 90s, buoyed by Sigue Sigue Sputnik's continued popularity on the Internet. The trio recorded a new album *Piratespace* and toured during 2001.

● ALBUMS: *Flaunt It* (Parlophone/Manhattan 1986) ★★, *Dress For Excess* (Parlophone 1989) ★, *Piratespace* (Sputnikworld 2001) ★★.

● COMPILATIONS: *The First Generation* (Jungle 1990) ★★, *21st Century Boys* (EMI 2001) ★★.
● FURTHER READING: *Ultra*, no author listed.

## SIMPLE MINDS

Timeless and epochal, Simple Minds was formed in January 1978 by Jim Kerr (b. 9 July 1959, Glasgow, Scotland; vocals), Charlie Burchill (b. 27 November 1959, Glasgow, Scotland; guitar), Tony Donald (bass) and Brian McGee (drums). They rose out of the ashes of Glasgow punk outfit Johnny And The Self-Abusers who, in true anarchic fashion, deliberately folded on the day their debut single 'Saints And Sinners' was released. A second guitarist Duncan Barnwell and keyboard player Michael MacNeil (b. 20 July 1958, Glasgow, Scotland) were recruited through newspaper advertisements, before Derek Forbes (b. 22 July 1956, Glasgow, Scotland) replaced a disaffected Donald. The numerous upheavals of this initial era were completed with Barnwell's departure. During this time, they did manage to record an impressive demo that caught the attention of *New Musical Express* writer Ian Cranna. This key exposure gave them immediate notoriety, and they quickly established themselves as one of Scotland's hottest new attractions. Kerr soon charmed other music journalists with his charisma and precocious banter.

Simple Minds were subsequently signed to Zoom Records, an Edinburgh-based independent label marketed by Arista Records and run by Bruce Findlay, who shortly afterwards became the band's full-time manager. 'Life In A Day', the band's debut single, broached the UK charts in March 1979 while the attendant John Leckie-produced album reached number 30. Critics were divided over its merits, although a consensus deemed the set derivative. Within weeks, the quintet began decrying their creation and embarked on a more radical direction. *Real To Real Cacophony* unfolded within the recording studio in an attempt to regain an early spontaneity and while this largely experimental collection was a commercial flop, it reinstated the band's self-respect and won unanimous music press approbation. *Empires And Dance* was released in September 1980. The set fused the flair of its predecessor to a newly established love of dance music and reflected influences garnered during European tours. It included 'I Travel', a pulsating travelogue which became a firm favourite throughout the club circuit and helped engender a new sense of optimism in the band's career.

Now free of Arista, Simple Minds were signed to Virgin Records in 1981, and paired with producer Steve Hillage. The resultant sessions spawned two albums, *Sons And Fascination* and *Sister Feelings Call*, which were initially released together. It became the band's first UK Top 20 entrant, spawning three minor hit singles with 'The American', 'Love Song' and 'Sweat In Bullet' and began Simple Minds' transformation from cult to popular favourites. This very success unnerved Brian McGee, who abhorred touring. In August 1981 he was replaced by former Slik and Skids drummer Kenny Hyslop (b. 14 February 1951, Helensburgh, Strathclyde, Scotland),

although the newcomer's recorded contribution was confined to 'Promised You A Miracle'. This powerful song reached number 13 in Britain, and proved popular in Europe and Australia where the band enjoyed an almost fanatical following. Although Mike Ogletree joined on Hyslop's departure, a former musician, Mel Gaynor (b. 29 May 1960, London, England), eventually became the quintet's permanent drummer. All three musicians were featured on *New Gold Dream (81, 82, 83, 84)*, which peaked at number 3 in the UK album chart. Here the band began harnessing a more commercial sound, and they achieved a series of hits with the attendant singles, 'Glittering Prize' and 'Someone Somewhere (In Summertime)'. A sixth collection, *Sparkle In The Rain*, united the quintet with producer Steve Lillywhite, inspiring comparisons with his other protégés, U2. 'Waterfront', a brash, pulsating grandiose performance, and 'Speed Your Love To Me', prefaced its release, with the album entering the UK chart at number 1. The set also featured 'Up On The Catwalk', a further Top 30 entrant, and a cover version of Lou Reed's 'Street Hassle', a long-established group favourite.

Kerr's profile reached an even wider audience when he married Pretenders' singer Chrissie Hynde in 1984, but their relationship could not survive the rigours of constant touring and being in different parts of the world. The following year Simple Minds, with new bass player John Giblin, chose to record in America under the aegis of Jimmy Iovine and Bob Clearmountain. It was during this period that the band contributed 'Don't You (Forget About Me)' to the soundtrack of the movie *The Breakfast Club*. The quintet remained ambivalent about the song, which was written by Keith Forsey and Steve Schiff, but it paradoxically became a US number 1 when issued as a single. Although the band initially vetoed a worldwide release, they reneged in the light of this achievement whereupon the record became a massive international hit and confirmed their world-beating status. However, the track did not appear on the ensuing *Once Upon A Time* that, despite international success, drew considerable criticism for its bombastic approach. Three tracks, 'Alive & Kicking', 'Sanctify Yourself' and 'All The Things She Said' nonetheless reached the UK Top 10, with the former also making US number 3, while a concurrent world tour, documented on *Live In The City Of Light*, was one of the year's major events. The proceeds of several dates were donated to Amnesty International, reflecting a growing politicization within the band. They had also been one of the many highlights of 1985's legendary *Live Aid* concert, with Kerr clearly relishing the moment.

In 1988, Simple Minds were a major inspiration behind the concert celebrating Nelson Mandela's 70th birthday, but although a new composition, 'Mandela Day', was recorded for the event, Simple Minds refused to release it as a single, fearful of seeming opportunistic. The song was later coupled with 'Belfast Child', a lengthy, haunting lament for Northern Ireland based on a traditional folk melody, 'She Moved Through The Fair'. This artistically ambitious work topped the UK singles chart in

February 1989 and set the tone for the band's subsequent album, *Street Fighting Years*, their first studio set in four years. Although it provided the band with their fourth UK chart-topping album in a row and achieved platinum status within five days, sales then dropped rather dramatically, reflecting the uncompromising nature of its content. Two further singles entered the UK Top 20, 'This Is Your Land' and 'Kick It In', while *The Amsterdam EP*, which included a cover version of Prince's 'Sign 'O' The Times', reached number 18 at the end of the year. This contradictory period closed with the rancorous departure of Giblin and MacNeil, the latter replaced by Peter Vitesse, and the ending of the band's ten-year association with Bruce Findlay and Schoolhouse Management.

Simple Minds entered the 90s with only Kerr and Burchill remaining from the original line-up. Gaynor, Vitesse and new bass player Malcolm Foster (b. 13 January 1956, Gosport, Hampshire, England) completed the line-up on *Real Life*, which saw the band re-introducing more personal themes to their songwriting after the political concerns of previous albums. The new material, including the Top 10 single 'Let There Be Love', recaptured the band's trademark grand, epic sound. Kerr married Patsy Kensit in January 1992, although the couple would split-up only a few years later. During the same year, Gaynor left the band, leaving Kerr and Burchill to complete their next album with a host of session players. The highly commercial 'She's A River' preceded 1995's *Good News From The Next World*, the band's final album for Virgin. After another lengthy hiatus, Kerr, Burchill and a returning Forbes released *Néapolis*, an album that marked a determined effort to recreate the edgy, electronic style of their early 80s work. While not always successful, it did at least indicate a band once again willing to take a few chances. In 2001, they were signed by Eagle Records, and released *Neon Lights*, an album of cover versions including 'The Needle And The Damage Done' (Neil Young) and 'All Tomorrow's Parties' (the Velvet Underground). A new studio album followed in 2002.

● ALBUMS: *Life In A Day* (Zoom 1979) ★★, *Real To Real Cacophony* (Arista 1979) ★★★, *Empires And Dance* (Arista 1980) ★★, *Sons And Fascination/Sister Feelings Call* (Virgin 1981) ★★★, *New Gold Dream (81, 82, 83, 84)* (Virgin/A&M 1982) ★★★★, *Sparkle In The Rain* (Virgin/A&M 1984) ★★★★, *Once Upon A Time* (Virgin/A&M 1985) ★★★★, *Live In The City Of Light* (Virgin/A&M 1987) ★★, *Street Fighting Years* (Virgin/A&M 1989) ★★, *Real Life* (Virgin/A&M 1991) ★★★, *Good News From The Next World* (Virgin 1995) ★★★, *Néapolis* (Chrysalis 1998) ★★★, *Neon Lights* (Eagle 2001) ★★, *Cry* (Eagle/Red Ink 2002) ★★★.

● COMPILATIONS: *Themes For Great Cities: Definitive Collection 79–81* US only (Stiff 1981) ★★, *Celebration* (Arista 1982) ★★★, *Glittering Prize 81/92* (Virgin/A&M 1992) ★★★★, *The Early Years: 1977–1978* (Mindmood 1998) ★★, *Original Gold* (Disky 1999) ★★★, *The Best Of Simple Minds* (Virgin 2001) ★★★.

● VIDEOS: *Verona* (Virgin Music Video 1990), *Glittering Prize 81/92* (Vision Video 1992).

● FURTHER READING: *Simple Minds: The Race Is The Prize*, Alfred Bos. *Simple Minds: Glittering Prize*, Dave Thomas. *Simple Minds*, Adam Sweeting. *Simple Minds: Street Fighting Years*, Alfred Bos. *Simple Minds: A Visual Documentary*, Mike Wrenn.

## SIMPLY RED

This soul-influenced UK band revolves around the central figure of vocalist Mick Hucknall (b. 8 June 1960, Denton, Greater Manchester, England). Hucknall's first musical outing was with the punk-inspired Frantic Elevators, who recorded a handful of singles, including the impressive ballad 'Holding Back The Years'. When they split up in 1983, the vocalist formed Simply Red with a fluid line-up that included Ojo, Mog, Dave Fryman and Eddie Sherwood. After signing to Elektra Records the band had a more settled line-up featuring Hucknall, Tony Bowers (bass), Fritz McIntyre (b. 2 September 1958; keyboards), Tim Kellett (brass), Sylvan Richardson (guitar) and Chris Joyce (drums). Their 1985 debut *Picture Book* climbed to number 2 in the UK charts, while their enticing cover version of the Valentine Brothers' 'Money's Too Tight To Mention' was a Top 20 hit. Although the band registered a lowly number 66 with the follow-up 'Come To My Aid', they rediscovered the hit formula with a sterling re-recording of the minor classic 'Holding Back The Years', which peaked at UK number 2. The song went on to top the US charts, ushering in a period of international success. Their next album, *Men And Women*, included collaborations between Hucknall and former Motown Records composer Lamont Dozier. Further hits followed with 'The Right Thing', 'Infidelity' and a reworking of the Cole Porter standard, 'Ev'ry Time We Say Goodbye'. Having twice reached number 2 in the album charts, Simply Red finally scaled the summit in 1989 with the accomplished *A New Flame*. The album coincided with another hit, 'It's Only Love', which was followed by a splendid reworking of Harold Melvin And The Blue Notes' 'If You Don't Know Me By Now', which climbed to number 2 in the UK and topped the US chart.

In the early 90s, Simply Red (now effectively Hucknall and various backing musicians) consolidated their position as one of the most accomplished blue-eyed soul outfits to emerge from the UK in recent years. The 1991 album *Stars* pursued hip-hop-inspired rhythms, alongside their usual soul style. It topped the UK charts over a period of months, outselling much-hyped efforts by Michael Jackson, U2, Dire Straits and Guns N'Roses. The follow-up *Life* was also a bestseller, although it showed little sign of creative development. The album did feature the wonderful 'Fairground', however, which provided Hucknall with his first ever UK chart-topping single. The band returned to the charts in 1996 and 1997 with cover versions of Aretha Franklin's 'Angel' and Gregory Isaacs' 'Night Nurse'. Their fifth consecutive UK number 1 album, *Blue*, featured several other covers (including two takes of the Hollies' 'The Air That I Breathe') and marked a return to the smooth soul style of *A New Flame*. The disappointing *Love And The Russian*

*Winter*, which was pilloried in the press, broke the band's run of UK chart-toppers.

● ALBUMS: *Picture Book* (Elektra 1985) ★★★★, *Men And Women* (Warners 1987) ★★, *A New Flame* (Warners 1989) ★★★, *Stars* (East West 1991) ★★★★, *Life* (East West 1995) ★★★, *Blue* (East West 1998) ★★★, *Love And The Russian Winter* (East West 1999) ★★.

● COMPILATIONS: *Greatest Hits* (East West 1996) ★★★, *It's Only Love* (East West 2000) ★★★.

● VIDEOS: *Greatest Video Hits* (Warner Music Vision 1996), *Simply Red: Live At The Lyceum* (Warner Music Vision 1998).

● FURTHER READING: *Simply Mick: Mick Hucknall Of Simply Red. The Inside Story*, Robin McGibbon and Rob McGibbon. *The First Fully Illustrated Biography*, Mark Hodkinson.

## SINITTA

b. Sinitta Renay Malone, 19 October 1966, Seattle, Washington, USA. The daughter of singer Miquel Brown, Sinitta's brand of manufactured disco-pop was aided by competent studio production and songwriting assistance by a variety of talent, namely the Stock, Aitken and Waterman team, plus, at various times, Ralf Rene Maue, Paul Hardcastle and James George Hargreaves. Though she was born in America, Sinitta attended boarding school in Britain from an early age. In 1980, she gained a part in *The Wiz*, and later stage appearances included a part in the David Essex musical, *Mutiny*. Her pop career was launched when 'So Macho'/'Cruising, which had originally stalled at UK number 47 in March 1986, climbed to the number 2 position three months later. Sinitta's pleasant appearance went a long way in securing, for a while, constant coverage in the British teen pop magazines. This was reflected her run of UK hits on the Fanfare label in the latter half of the 80s, distinguished by three further Top 10 singles, 'Toy Boy' (number 4, July 1987), 'Cross My Broken Heart' (number 6, March 1988) and 'Right Back Where We Started From' (number 4, June 1989). A cover version of the 1973 Robert Knight hit 'Love On A Mountain Top' reached number 20 in October 1989. Although her run of hit singles had begun to dry up, she signed a major label deal with Arista Records in 1992. 'Shame Shame Shame' stalled at number 28 in July, however. In early 1993, she released *The Supreme EP*, which as the name suggests featured a collection of Supremes cover versions. She subsequently concentrated on the theatre and A&R work, and found religion, but returned to the pop scene at the end of the decade.

● ALBUMS: *Sinitta!* (Fanfare 1987) ★★, *Wicked!* (Fanfare 1989) ★★.

## SIOUXSIE AND THE BANSHEES

Siouxsie Sioux (b. Susan Dallion, 27 May 1957, London, England) was part of the notorious 'Bromley contingent', including Steve Severin (b. Steven Bailey, 25 September 1955), which followed the Sex Pistols in their early days. Siouxsie had also taken part in the 100 Club Punk Festival, singing an elongated version of 'The Lord's Prayer' with a group that included Sid Vicious on drums. The fledgling singer also achieved some minor fame after a verbal exchange with television presenter Bill Grundy, which unwittingly prompted the Sex Pistols' infamous swearing match on the *Today* programme. Within months of that incident Siouxsie put together her backing group the Banshees, featuring Pete Fenton (guitar), Severin (bass) and Kenny Morris (drums). Siouxsie flirted with Nazi imagery, highlighted by black make-up and frequently exposed breasts. By mid-1977 Fenton was replaced by John McGeoch (b. 28 May 1955, Greenock, Strathclyde, Scotland), and the group supported Johnny Thunders And The Heartbreakers as well as recording a session for the BBC disc jockey John Peel. By 1978, Siouxsie And The Banshees had signed to Polydor Records (the last of the important punk bands of the era to be rounded up by a major) and released their first single, the sublime 'Hong Kong Garden', which reached the UK Top 10. *The Scream* soon followed, produced by Steve Lillywhite. Less commercial offerings ensued with 'The Staircase (Mystery)' and 'Playground Twist', which were soon succeeded by *Join Hands*. During a promotional tour, Morris and McKay abruptly left, to be replaced by former Slits drummer Budgie (b. Peter Clark, 21 August 1957) and temporary Banshee Robert Smith, on leave from the Cure. Siouxsie's Germanic influences were emphasized on the stark 'Mittageisen (Metal Postcard)', which barely scraped into the Top 50. Both 'Happy House' and 'Christine' were more melodic offerings, deservedly bringing greater commercial success. After the success of *Kaleidoscope*, the band embarked on a world tour, including a concert behind the 'Iron Curtain'. Another Top 10 album, *Juju*, was followed by some extra-curricular activities. Siouxsie and Budgie formed an occasional offshoot group, the Creatures, who enjoyed success in their own right (1983's bizarre cover version of Mel Tormé's 'Right Now' reached number 14 in the UK charts), as well as recording an album. Smith and Severin also recorded successfully together as the Glove.

After the string-accompanied *A Kiss In The Dreamhouse*, the band reconvened in the autumn of 1983 to play a concert for Italy's Communist Party. A highly commercial version of the Beatles' 'Dear Prudence' provided them with their biggest UK hit, peaking at number 3. Early in 1984, the evocative 'Swimming Horses' maintained their hit profile, while further personnel changes ensued with the enlistment of John Carruthers from Clock DVA. He was replaced in turn by Jon Klein. Regular albums during the mid-80s showed that Siouxsie And The Banshees had established a loyal cult following and could experiment freely in the studio without a significant loss of commercial appeal. Having already enjoyed success with a cover version, the band then tackled Bob Dylan's 'This Wheel's On Fire', which reached the UK Top 20. An entire album of cover versions followed, though *Through The Looking Glass* received the most awkward reviews of the band's career. A change of direction with *Peep Show* saw the band embrace a more sophisticated sound, maintaining the eastern nuances of yore but doing so within an elaborate musical scheme. They returned to the charts in 1991 with the evocative 'Kiss Them For Me' and *Superstition*, an album of light touch but contrastingly dense production.

Their greatest achievement of the 90s, arguably, was the much-delayed *The Rapture*. Adding musical adventurism (notably the heavily orchestrated three movements of the title track) to familiar but entertaining refractions from their earlier career ('Not Forgotten'), the approach of middle age had evidently not weakened their resolve. Some criticism was received that the album was a sell-out and the band announced in April 1996 that they were 'going out with dignity'. Siouxsie and Budgie continued as the Creatures, while Severin recorded *Visions*, an album of instrumental electronica only available via the Internet. Contrary to their previous statements, the Banshees re-formed in 2002 to play a series of live shows across the USA.

● ALBUMS: *The Scream* (Polydor 1978) ★★★, *Join Hands* (Polydor 1979) ★★★, *Kaleidoscope* (Polydor 1980) ★★★, *Juju* (Polydor 1981) ★★★, *A Kiss In The Dreamhouse* (Polydor 1982) ★★★, *Nocturne* (Polydor 1983) ★★★, *Hyaena* (Polydor 1984) ★★★, *Tinderbox* (Polydor 1986) ★★★, *Through The Looking Glass* (Polydor 1987) ★★, *Peep Show* (Polydor 1988) ★★★, *Superstition* (Polydor 1991) ★★★, *The Rapture* (Polydor 1995) ★★★.

● COMPILATIONS: *Once Upon A Time: The Singles* (Polydor 1981) ★★★★, *The Peel Sessions* (Strange Fruit 1991) ★★★, *Twice Upon A Time: The Singles* (Polydor 1992) ★★★.

● VIDEOS: *Greetings From Zurich* (Polydor 1993).

● FURTHER READING: *Siouxsie And The Banshees*, Mike West. *Entranced: The Siouxsie & The Banshees Story*, Brian Johns.

● FILMS: *Jubilee* (1978).

## SISTERS OF MERCY

A post-punk UK rock outfit whose flirtations with gothic imagery have dogged the public and media perception of them throughout an eclectic career. The Sisters Of Mercy formed in Leeds, Yorkshire, England, in 1980, when Leeds and Oxford University drop-out Andrew Eldritch (b. Andrew Taylor, 15 May 1959, England; vocals) teamed up with Gary Marx (b. Mark Pairman, England; guitar) and a drum machine. After releasing 'The Damage Done' (on which Eldritch plays drums and guitar, and Marx sings) on their own Merciful Release label, the band expanded to include Ben Gunn (guitar) and Craig Adams (bass) for supports with Clash, Psychedelic Furs and the Birthday Party. A cult reputation in the north of England was augmented by excellent press, and further enhanced by the release of their third single 'Alice'. A magnificent gothic dance saga, together with the subsequent 'Temple Of Love' (which reached number 2 on the UK singles chart), it hallmarked the band's early musical character.

In-between these two landmark 45s Gunn left to be replaced by Wayne Hussey (b. Jerry Wayne Hussey, 26 May 1958, Bristol, England). WEA Records picked up the distribution for Merciful Release as the band's reputation continued to grow throughout 1983 and 1984. Despite the release of their debut album, the following year brought a creative watershed.

Continuing rivalries between Marx and Eldritch forced the former to depart. This was only a stopgap treaty, with the band announcing a final split in July 1985 after a concert at the Royal Albert Hall (captured for posterity on the *Wake* video). The rest of the year witnessed extraordinary legal wrangles between Eldritch on one hand and Adams and Hussey on the other, each claiming use of the name Sisters Of Mercy. Eldritch went as far as releasing a record (*Gift*) under the title Sisterhood simply to prevent Adams and Hussey from adopting this halfway-house title. The duo eventually settled on the Mission as their new home, while Eldritch moved to Germany.

Still operating under the Sisters Of Mercy title, Eldritch recruited Patricia Morrison (b. 14 January 1962; ex-Gun Club) and fashioned a more dance-orientated sound on hit singles 'This Corrosion' (UK number 7) and 'Dominion' (UK number 13), and the Top 10 album *Floodland*. A two-year spell of inactivity was broken in 1990 with the Top 20 single 'More', showcasing another new line-up; Tony James (ex-Sigue Sigue Sputnik; bass), Tim Bricheno (b. 6 July 1963, Huddersfield, Yorkshire, England; guitar, ex-All About Eve) and Andreas Bruhn (guitar). *Vision Thing* indulged Eldritch's penchant for deep-rooted, esoteric metaphor, which occasionally makes his lyrics futile and impenetrable. They undertook a loss-making, aborted tour with Public Enemy in 1991, though this did little to dampen the confidence of the self-confessed 'world's greatest lyricist'. A remixed version of 'Temple Of Love', recorded with Israeli singer Ofra Haza, propelled the band into the UK Top 5 the following summer. New guitarist Adam Pearson featured on the following year's single, 'Under The Gun', released to promote a greatest hits set. Eldritch's prolonged wrangles with East West Records subsequently kept the band out of the recording studio, although their erstwhile frontman remained active as a remixer on the dance music scene. Supported by various musicians he has kept the Sisters Of Mercy active as a live outfit.

● ALBUMS: *First And Last And Always* (Merciful Release/Elektra 1985) ★★★, *Floodland* (Merciful Release/Elektra 1987) ★★★, *Vision Thing* (Merciful Release/Elektra 1990) ★★.

● COMPILATIONS: *Some Girls Wander By Mistake* (Merciful Release/East West 1992) ★★, *A Slight Case Of Overbombing: Greatest Hits Volume One* (Merciful Release/East West 1993) ★★★.

● VIDEOS: *Wake: In Concert At The Royal Albert Hall* (PolyGram Music Video 1986), *Shot* (Warner Music Vision 1989), *Shot Rev 2.0* (Warner Music Vision 1993).

● FURTHER READING: *Sisters Of Mercy Discography: Heartland*, Andrew James Pinell.

## SKINNY PUPPY

Industrial band Skinny Puppy, from Vancouver, Canada, are widely regarded as a forceful influence on the development of the genre in the late 80s, counting Nine Inch Nails' Trent Reznor among their loudest advocates. The principals behind the band were cEVIN Key (as this multi-instrumentalist prefers to call himself) and Nivek Ogre (b. Kevin

Ogilvie), the band's singer and lyricist, who is not related to their producer, Dave Ogilvie (later a full-time member of the band). They met in 1983, and quickly discovered a mutual taste in esoteric film music.

Skinny Puppy's first release was a cassette, *Back And Forth*, before the *Remission* EP, released on the Canadian label Nettwerk Records in 1904. This introduced their dark electronics, textured by synthesizers, samples and tape loops. It was followed by *Bites*, again reminiscent of Throbbing Gristle and Cabaret Voltaire's early experimentation and aural shock tactics. A more homespun component was the strong dance rhythms and sequences, which, while stopping some way short of convention, helped make these recordings more accessible. It featured Wilhelm Schroeder as collaborator, with one track, 'Assimilate', produced by Severed Heads' Tom Ellard. *Mind: The Perpetual Intercourse* continued previous threads but with superior production. It also introduced Dwayne Goettel (b. 1965, d. 23 August 1995) on keyboards and electronics, Schroeder's replacement, and formerly of another industrial unit named Psyche. His contribution to *Cleanse Fold And Manipulate* helped improve the band's aesthetic, though the appeal of the results was largely limited to an underground fanbase. The follow-up chose a slightly altered lyrical tack, with Ogre expanding on his environmental concerns ('Human Disease (S.K.U.M.M.)') and issue songs ('VX Gas Attack' marking a pre-Gulf War riposte to Saddam Hussein and Iraq). The anti-vivisection theme was also relocated to the stage, where Ogre would dramatize the roles of test animal, lab technician, and consumer. Al Jourgensen of Ministry joined for the sessions that produced *Rabies*, adding metallic guitar runs to help bring Skinny Puppy to the attention of other musical sub-genres. *Too Dark Park* refined previous lyrical concerns, to produce a set of bunker-mentality belligerence and stark minimalism. *Last Rights* was to have featured spoken extracts from the 60s LSD-celebrity Timothy Leary, but although he gave permission his management blocked their use at the last moment. Its substitution with 40 seconds of silence caused a major fault on several thousand copies.

Members of Skinny Puppy were involved in a number of side projects. Key worked with former pen pal Edward Ka-Spel of the Legendary Pink Dots as the more pop-orientated Tear Garden. Various members of Skinny Puppy, including long-standing collaborator Alan Nelson, also played with Hilt, whose debut album was released in 1989. In 1990, a compilation of 12-inch versions was released, including Adrian Sherwood's remix of 'Addiction'. Goettel died from a heroin overdose in August 1995. The band had recently completed an album for Rick Rubin's American Records, with the provisional title of *The Process*. Goettel had also formed a spin-off project, Download (also the title of a song from *Last Rights*), and an EP was released, posthumously, on the German label Off Beat Records. In interviews to promote the new album at the beginning of 1996, the remaining members announced their decision not to continue with the band. Download was formed by some of the ex-members the same year.

● ALBUMS: *Back And Forth* cassette only (Skinny Puppy 1983) ★★★, *Bites* (Nettwerk 1985) ★★★, *Mind: The Perpetual Intercourse* (Nettwerk/Capitol 1987) ★★★, *Cleanse Fold And Manipulate* (Nettwerk/Capitol 1987) ★★★, *VIVsectVI* (Nettwerk/Capitol 1988) ★★★, *Rabies* (Nettwerk/Capitol 1989) ★★★, *Too Dark Park* (Nettwerk/Capitol 1990) ★★★, *Ain't It Dead Yet* live album (Nettwerk/Capitol 1991) ★★★, *Last Rights* (Nettwerk/Capitol 1992) ★★★, *The Process* (Subconscious/American 1995) ★★★.
● COMPILATIONS: *Bites And Remission* (Nettwerk 1987) ★★★, *Twelve Inch Anthology* (Nettwerk 1990) ★★★, *Back And Forth Series Two* (Nettwerk 1993) ★★, with Teargarden *Bouquet Of Black Orchids* (Play It Again Sam 1994) ★★★, *Brap* (Off Beat 1996) ★★★, *The Singles Collect* (Nettwerk 2000) ★★★, *B-Sides Collect* (Nettwerk 2000) ★★★.
● VIDEOS: *Ain't It Dead Yet?* (Capitol 1992).

## SKY

This UK instrumental outfit, devoted to fusing classical, jazz and rock music, was founded in 1979 by virtuoso guitarist John Williams (b. 24 April 1941, Melbourne, Victoria, Australia). Having already played concerts at Ronnie Scott's jazz club, Williams formed Sky with rock guitarist Kevin Peek, classical percussionist Tristran Fry, ex-Curved Air keyboards player Francis Monkman (b. 9 June 1949, Hampstead, London, England) and Herbie Flowers, a versatile session bass player and composer of the novelty UK number 1 'Grandad'. The quintet made an instant impact in Britain with their debut album, which mixed original compositions with inventive adaptations of classical pieces. The follow-up even headed the UK chart in 1980, aided by 'Toccata', a Top 5 hit single taken from a theme by Bach. European and Japanese concert tours were equally successful. In 1981, Monkman was replaced by Steve Gray for the recording of the jazzier *Sky 3*. The follow-up, *Sky 4: Forthcoming*, was an uneven collection comprised solely of interpretations of classical pieces. *Cadmium ...* was more pop-orientated, containing the Alan Tarney compositions 'A Girl In Winter' and 'Return to Me'. After its release Williams left the group, which continued to record as quartet with guest musicians until 1987 when it folded. They reunited for one-off appearances at the London Palladium in 1990 and a television concert in 1991. A proper relaunch took place the following year with Richard Durrant replacing Kevin Peek, but since 1994's UK tour the members have concentrated on other projects.

● ALBUMS: *Sky* (Ariola 1979) ★★★, *Sky 2* (Ariola Hansa 1980) ★★★, *Sky 3* (Ariola 1981) ★★★, *Sky 4: Forthcoming* (Ariola 1982) ★★, *Five Live* (Ariola 1983) ★★, *Cadmium ...* (Ariola 1983) ★★, *The Great Balloon Race* (Epic 1985) ★★★, *Mozart* (UK) *The Mozart Album* (USA) (Epic 1987) ★★.
● COMPILATIONS: *Masterpieces* (Telstar 1984) ★★★, *Classic Sky* (BMG 1989), *The Best Of Sky* (Freestyle 1994) ★★★, *The Very Best Of Sky* (Crimson 1998) ★★★, *Squared* (Recall 1999) ★★★.
● VIDEOS: *Sky At Westminster Abbey: Commemorating 20 Years Of Amnesty International* (BBC Video 1982).

## SLAYER

This intense death/thrash metal quartet was formed
in Huntington Beach, Los Angeles, USA, during
1982. Comprising Tom Araya (b. Thomas Araya, 6
June 1961, Valparaiso, Chile; bass, vocals), Kerry
King (b. 3 June 1964, Los Angeles, California, USA;
guitar), Jeff Hanneman (b. 31 January 1964,
Oakland, California, USA; guitar) and Dave
Lombardo (b. 16 February 1963, Havana, Cuba;
drums), they made their debut in 1983, with a track
on the compilation *Metal Massacre III*. This led to
Metal Blade signing the band and releasing their first
two albums. *Show No Mercy* and *Hell Awaits* were
undiluted blasts of pure white metallic noise. The
band played at breakneck speed with amazing
technical precision, but the intricacies of detail were
lost in a muddy production. Araya's lyrics dealt with
death, carnage, Satanism and torture, but were
reduced to an indecipherable guttural howl. Rick
Rubin, producer and owner of the Def Jam Records
label teamed up with the band in 1986 for the
recording of *Reign In Blood*. Featuring 10 tracks in
just 28 minutes, it took the concept of thrash to its
ultimate conclusion. The song 'Angel Of Death'
became notorious for its references to Joseph
Mengele, the Nazi doctor who committed atrocities
against humanity (ironic, given that Araya has non-
Aryan origins). They themselves admitted to a right-
wing stance on matters of society and justice, despite
being the subject of virulent attacks from that
quarter over the years.

*Hell Awaits* saw Rubin achieve a breakthrough in
production with a clear and inherently powerful
sound, and opened up the band to a wider audience.
*South Of Heaven* represented Slayer applying the
brakes and introducing brain-numbing bass riffs
similar to Black Sabbath, but was delivered with the
same manic aggression as before. The guitars of
Hanneman and King screamed violently and Araya's
vocals were comprehensible for the first time.
*Seasons In The Abyss* pushed the band to the forefront
of the thrash metal genre, alongside Metallica. A
state-of-the-art album in every respect, although
deliberately commercial, it is the band's most
profound and convincing statement. A double live
album followed, recorded in London, Lakeland, and
San Bernadino between October 1990 and August
1991. It captured the band at their brutal and
uncompromising best and featured definitive
versions of many of their most infamous numbers.
However, it saw the permanent departure of
Lombardo after many hints of a separation, with ex-
Forbidden drummer Paul Bostaph (b. 4 March 1964,
San Francisco, California, USA; stepping in. 
Lombardo went on to form Grip Inc., working with
Death leader Chuck Schuldiner. In 1994, the band
worked alongside Ice-T on a cover version of the
Exploited's 'Disorder' for the *Judgement Night*
soundtrack, before unveiling their sixth studio
album, *Divine Intervention*. Bostaph was replaced by
Jon Dette (ex-Testament) on *Undisputed Attitude*, a
covers album that demonstrated the band's punk
influence and featured a particularly inspired version
of the Stooges' 'I Wanna Be Your Dog'. Bostaph
rejoined the band for 1998's *Diabolus In Musica*

● ALBUMS: *Show No Mercy* (Metal Blade 1983) ★★,
*Live Undead* (Metal Blade 1985) ★★, *Hell Awaits*
(Metal Blade 1985) ★★, *Reign In Blood* (Def Jam
1986) ★★★★, *South Of Heaven* (Def Jam 1988) ★★★,
*Seasons In The Abyss* (Def American 1990) ★★★,
*Live: Decade Of Aggression* (Def American 1991)
★★★★, *Divine Intervention* (American 1994) ★★★,
*Undisputed Attitude* (American 1996) ★★★, *Diabolus
In Musica* (American 1998) ★★★★, *God Hates Us All*
(American 2001) ★★★.
● VIDEOS: *Live Intrusion* (American Visuals 1995).

## SLY AND ROBBIE

Sly Dunbar (b. Lowell Charles Dunbar, 10 May 1952,
Kingston, Jamaica, West Indies; drums) and Robbie
Shakespeare (b. 27 September 1953, Kingston,
Jamaica, West Indies; bass) have probably played on
more reggae records than the rest of Jamaica's many
session musicians put together. The pair began
working together as a team in 1975 and they quickly
became Jamaica's leading, and most distinctive,
rhythm section. They have played on numerous
releases, including recordings by U-Roy, Peter Tosh,
Bunny Wailer, Culture and Black Uhuru, while
Dunbar also made several solo albums, all of which
featured Shakespeare. They have constantly sought
to push back the boundaries surrounding the music
with their consistently inventive work.

Dunbar, nicknamed 'Sly' in honour of his fondness
for Sly And The Family Stone, was an established
figure in Skin Flesh And Bones when he met
Shakespeare. Dunbar drummed his first session for
Lee Perry as one of the Upsetters; the resulting
'Night Doctor' was a big hit both in Jamaica and the
UK. He next moved to Skin Flesh And Bones, whose
variations on the reggae-meets-disco/soul sound
brought them a great deal of session work and a
residency at Kingston's Tit For Tat club. Sly was still
searching for more, however, and he moved on to
another session group in the mid-70s, the
Revolutionaries. This move changed the course of
reggae music through the group's work at Joseph
'Joe Joe' Hookim's Channel One Studio and their
pioneering rockers sound. It was with the
Revolutionaries that he teamed up with bass player
Shakespeare, who had undergone a similar
apprenticeship with session bands, notably Bunny
Lee's Aggrovators. The two formed a friendship that
turned into a musical partnership that was to
dominate reggae music throughout the remainder of
the 70s and into the 80s.

Known simply as Sly And Robbie (and occasionally
Drumbar And Basspeare), they not only formed
their own label, Taxi, which produced many hit
records for scores of well-known artists but also
found time to do session work for just about every
important name in reggae. They toured extensively
as the powerhouse rhythm section for Black Uhuru
and, as their fame spread outside of reggae circles,
they worked with Grace Jones, Bob Dylan, Ian Dury
and Joan Armatrading, among a host of other rock
stars. In the early 80s, they were among the first to
use the burgeoning 'new technology' to musical
effect; they demonstrated that it could be used to its
full advantage without compromising their

musicianship in any way. In a genre controlled by producers and 'this week's star', reggae musicians have rarely been accorded their proper respect, but the accolades heaped on Sly And Robbie have helped to redress the balance.

Sly And Robbie's mastery of the digital genre, coupled with their abiding love of and respect for the music's history, placed them at the forefront of Kingston's producers of the early 90s. Their 'Murder She Wrote' cut for Chaka Demus And Pliers set the tone for 1992, while 'Tease Me' for the same duo, built around a sample from the Skatalites' 60s hit 'Ball Of Fire', was another significant UK chart success in 1993 – this was quite remarkable for a team whose successful career had already spanned three decades. They achieved further commercial (if not artistic) success with 1997's celebrity-packed *Friends*, with guest singers including Maxi Priest, Ali Campbell (UB40) and Mick Hucknall (Simply Red) brought in to cover reggae standards. Hucknall's bland cover version of Gregory Isaacs' 'Night Nurse' reached the UK charts the same year. Sly And Robbie were one of the first artists to move with Chris Blackwell when he founded the Palm Pictures label in 1998. The following year they collaborated with leading producer Howie B. on *Drum & Bass Strip To The Bone*.

● ALBUMS: *Disco Dub* (Gorgon 1978) ★★, *Gamblers Choice* (Taxi 1980) ★★★, *Raiders Of The Lost Dub* (Mango/Island 1981) ★★★, *60s, 70s Into The 80s* (Mango/Island 1981) ★★★, *Dub Extravaganza* (CSA 1984) ★★★, *A Dub Experience* (Island 1985) ★★★, *Language Barrier* (Island 1985) ★★★, *Electro Reggae* (Island 1986) ★★★, *The Sting* (Taxi 1986) ★★★, *Rhythm Killers* (4th & Broadway 1987) ★★★★, *Dub Rockers Delight* (Blue Moon 1987) ★★★, *The Summit* (RAS 1988) ★★★, *Two Rhythms Clash* (RAS 1989) ★★★, *Silent Assassin* (4th & Broadway 1989) ★★★, *Taxi Christmas* (RAS 1991) ★★★, *Remember Precious Time* (RAS 1992) ★★★, *Friends* (East West 1997) ★★, *Drum & Bass Strip To The Bone By Howie B* (Palm Pictures 1998) ★★★, *Dub Fire* (NYC Music 2000) ★★★, with Monty Alexander *Monty Meets Sly And Robbie* (Telarc 2000) ★★★.

● COMPILATIONS: *Present Taxi* (Taxi 1981) ★★★★, *Crucial Reggae* (Taxi 1984) ★★★, *Taxi Wax* (Taxi 1984) ★★★, *Taxi Gang* (Taxi 1984) ★★★, *Reggae Greats* (Island 1985) ★★★, *Taxi Connection Live In London* (Taxi 1986) ★★★, *Taxi Fare* (Taxi 1987) ★★★, *Two Rhythms Clash* (RAS 1990) ★★★, *DJ Riot* (Mango/Island 1990) ★★★, *Hits 1978–90* (Sonic Sounds 1991) ★★★★, *Present Sound Of Sound* (Musidisc 1994) ★★★, *Present Ragga Pon Top* (Musidisc 1994) ★★★, *Gold Dubs: Ultimate Reggae Collection* (Fine Tune 2000) ★★★, *Duble Trouble* (Artists Only 2000) ★★★, *Ultimate Collection: In Good Company* (Hip-O 2001) ★★★★, *Good Dubs: The Prime Of Sly & Robbie* (Music Club 2001) ★★★.

● VIDEOS: *Strip To The Bone* (Palm Pictures 1999).

## SMILEY CULTURE

b. David Emmanuel, London, England. The son of a Jamaican father and South American mother, Smiley Culture gained his nickname at school, where his method of chatting up girls was simply to ask for a smile. He served his apprenticeship with a number of local sounds before hitting the big time with south London's Saxon sound system, the home of a formidable amount of British reggae talent, including Maxi Priest, Tippa Irie and Phillip Papa Levi. His live reputation attracted the attention of record producers and his first recording for Fashion Records, 'Cockney Translation', featuring Smiley slipping effortlessly from Jamaican patois to a south London accent, touched a nerve and sold an unprecedented 40,000 copies. His follow-up, 'Police Officer', again featuring the cockney and 'yardy' voices, did even better and reached the national Top 20 in early 1985. Appearances on BBC Television's *Top Of The Pops* followed – a first for a reggae DJ – and Smiley became a 'star'. A major recording contract with Polydor Records followed. As well as hosting his own Channel 4 television show, *Club Mix*, Smiley also found time for a cameo appearance in the movie *Absolute Beginners*, singing Miles Davis' 'So What'. He continued to record, including some interesting collaborations with American hip-hop artists, before setting up his own management company and working extensively in advertising.

Smiley Culture is important in that he was among the first UK-based reggae artists to challenge the Jamaicans and succeed. The British public also took him to their hearts, while the lyrics of 'Cockney Translation' have been used by teachers and lecturers to illustrate the effects and influence of immigration on the English language.

● ALBUMS: *The Original* (Fashion 1985) ★★★, *Tongue In Cheek* (Polydor 1986) ★★★.

● FILMS: *Absolute Beginners* (1986).

## SMITHEREENS

Influenced by the 60s pop of the Beatles, Beach Boys and the Byrds, the Smithereens formed in New Jersey, USA, in 1980. Members Jim Babjak (guitar) and Dennis Diken (drums) had played together since 1971; Mike Mesaros (bass) was recruited in 1976, and finally Pat DiNizio (vocals). After recording two EPs, they backed songwriter Otis Blackwell ('Great Balls Of Fire') on two obscure albums. In 1986, the band signed to Enigma Records and released their first full album, *Especially For You*, which fared well among both college radio and mainstream rock listeners, as did the single 'Blood And Roses'. After a lengthy tour, the Smithereens recorded their second album, *Green Thoughts*, in 1988, this time distributed by Capitol Records. *Smithereens 11* was their biggest selling album, reaching number 41 in the US chart. The band's music was also featured in several movie soundtracks including the teen-horror movie *Class Of Nuke 'Em High*. Their career faltered in 1991 with the poorly received *Blow Up* (US number 120), leaving critics to ponder whether the band had run out of ideas, a belief that gained credence with 1994's lacklustre *A Date With The Smithereens*. With the band unable to secure a new recording contract, DiNizio took the opportunity to release a pleasant solo debut in 1997. The Smithereens subsequently signed to Koch Records, and returned to the studio to record material featured on *God Save The Smithereens*.

● ALBUMS: *Especially For You* (Enigma 1986) ★★★,

*Green Thoughts* (Capitol 1988) ★★★★, *Smithereens 11* (Enigma 1990) ★★★★, *Blow Up* (Capitol 1991) ★★, *A Date With The Smithereens* (RCA 1994) ★★, *God Save The Smithereens* (Koch 1999) ★★★.
Solo: Pat DiNizio *Songs & Sounds* (Velvel 1997) ★★★.
● COMPILATIONS: *Blown To Smithereens* (Capitol 1995) ★★★★, *Attack Of The Smithereens* (Capitol 1995) ★★, *The Best Of The Smithereens* (CEMA 1999) ★★★.

## SMITHS

Acclaimed by many as the most important UK band of the 80s, the Smiths were formed in Manchester, England during the spring of 1982. Morrissey (b. Steven Patrick Morrissey, 22 May 1959, Davyhulme, Manchester, England) and Johnny Marr (b. John Maher, 31 October 1963, Ardwick, Manchester, England) originally combined as a songwriting partnership, and only their names appeared on any contract bearing the title 'Smiths'. Morrissey had previously played for a couple of months in the Nosebleeds and also rehearsed and auditioned with a late version of Slaughter And The Dogs. After that, he wrote reviews for *Record Mirror* and penned a couple of booklets on the New York Dolls and James Dean. Marr, meanwhile, had played in several Wythenshawe groups including the Paris Valentinos, White Dice, Sister Ray and Freaky Party. By the summer of 1982, the duo decided to form a group and recorded demos with drummer Simon Wolstencroft and a recording engineer named Dale. Wolstencroft subsequently declined an offer to join the Smiths and in later years became a member of the Fall. Eventually, Mike Joyce (b. 1 June 1963, Fallowfield, Manchester, England) was recruited as drummer, having previously played with the punk-inspired Hoax and Victim. During their debut gig at the Ritz in Manchester, the line-up was augmented by go-go dancer James Maker, who went on to join Raymonde and later RPLA.
By the end of 1982, the band had appointed a permanent bass player. Andy Rourke (b. Manchester, England) was an alumnus of various previous groups with Marr. After being taken under the wing of local entrepreneur Joe Moss, the band strenuously rehearsed and after a series of gigs, signed to Rough Trade Records in the spring of 1983. By that time, they had issued their first single on the label, 'Hand In Glove', which failed to reach the Top 50. During the summer of 1983, they became entwined in the first of several tabloid press controversies when it was alleged that their lyrics contained references to child molesting. The eloquent Morrissey, who was already emerging as a media spokesperson of considerable power, sternly refuted the rumours. During the same period, the band commenced work on their debut album with producer Troy Tate, but the sessions were curtailed, and a new set of recordings undertaken with John Porter. In November 1983, they issued their second single, 'This Charming Man', a striking pop record that infiltrated the UK Top 30. Following an ill-fated trip to the USA at the end of the year, the quartet began 1984 with a new single, the notably rockier 'What Difference Does It Make?', which took them to

number 12. *The Smiths* ably displayed the potential of the band, with Morrissey's oblique, genderless lyrics coalescing with Marr's spirited guitar work. The closing track of the album was the haunting 'Suffer Little Children', a requiem to the child victims of the 60s Moors Murderers. The song later provoked a short-lived controversy in the tabloid press, which was resolved when the mother of one of the victims came out on Morrissey's side.
A series of college gigs throughout Britain established the band as a cult favourite, with Morrissey displaying a distinctive image, complete with National Health spectacles, a hearing aid and bunches of gladioli. A collaboration with Sandie Shaw saw 'Hand In Glove' transformed into a belated hit, while Morrissey dominated music press interviews. His celibate stance provoked reams of speculation about his sexuality, and his ability to provide good copy on subjects as diverse as animal rights, royalty, Oscar Wilde and 60s films, made him a journalist's dream interviewee. The singer's celebrated miserabilism was reinforced by the release of the autobiographical 'Heaven Knows I'm Miserable Now', which reached number 19 in the UK. Another Top 20 hit followed with 'William, It Was Really Nothing'. While the Smiths commenced work on their next album, Rough Trade issued the interim *Hatful Of Hollow*, a bargain-priced set that included various flip-sides and radio sessions. It was a surprisingly effective work which captured their inchoate charm.
By 1984, the Smiths found themselves fêted as Britain's best band by various factions in the music press. The release of the sublime 'How Soon Is Now?' justified much of the hyperbole and this was reinforced by the power of their next album, *Meat Is Murder*. This displayed Morrissey's increasing tendency towards social commentary, which had been indicated in his controversial comments on Band Aid and the IRA bombings. The album chronicled violence at schools ('The Headmaster Ritual'), adolescent thuggery ('Rusholme Ruffians'), child abuse ('Barbarism Begins At Home') and animal slaughter ('Meat Is Murder'). The proselytizing tone was brilliantly complemented by the musicianship of Marr, Rourke and Joyce. Marr's work on such songs as 'The Headmaster Ritual' and 'That Joke Isn't Funny Anymore' effectively propelled him to a position as one of Britain's most respected rock guitarists. Despite releasing a milestone album, the band's fortunes in the singles charts were relatively disappointing. 'Shakespeare's Sister' received a lukewarm response and stalled at number 26, amid ever-growing rumours that the band was dissatisfied with their record label. Another major UK tour in 1985 coincided with various management upheavals, which dissipated the band's energies.
A successful trek across the USA was followed by the release of the plaintive summer single 'The Boy With The Thorn In His Side', which, despite its commerciality, only reached number 23. A dispute with Rough Trade delayed the release of the next Smiths album, which was preceded by the superb 'Big Mouth Strikes Again', another example of Marr

at his best. During the same period, Rourke was briefly ousted from the band due to his flirtation with heroin. He was soon reinstated, however, along with a second guitarist, Craig Gannon, who had previously played with Aztec Camera, the Bluebells and Colourfield. In June 1986, *The Queen Is Dead* was issued and won immediate critical acclaim for its diversity and unadulterated power. The range of mood and emotion offered on the album was startling to behold, ranging from the epic grandeur of the title track to the overt romanticism of 'There Is A Light That Never Goes Out' and the irreverent comedy of 'Frankly, Mr Shankly' and 'Some Girls Are Bigger Than Others'. A superb display of Morrissey/Marr at their apotheosis, the album was rightly placed alongside *Meat Is Murder* as one of the finest achievements of the decade.

A debilitating stadium tour of the USA followed and during the band's absence, they enjoyed a formidable Top 20 hit with the disco-denouncing 'Panic'. The sentiments of the song, coupled with Morrissey's negative comments on certain aspects of black music, provoked further adverse comments in the press. That controversy was soon replaced by the news that the Smiths were to record only one more album for Rough Trade, and intended to transfer their operation to the major label EMI Records. Meanwhile, the light pop of 'Ask' contrasted with riotous scenes during the band's 1986 UK tour. At the height of the drama, the band almost suffered a fatality when Johnny Marr was involved in a car crash. While he recuperated, guitarist Craig Gannon was fired, a decision that prompted legal action. The band ended the year with a concert at the Brixton Academy supported by fellow Mancunians the Fall. It was to prove their final UK appearance.

After another hit with 'Shoplifters Of The World Unite' they completed what would prove to be their final album. The glam rock-inspired 'Sheila Take A Bow' returned the Smiths to the Top 10 and their profile was maintained with the release of another sampler album, *The World Won't Listen*. Marr was growing increasingly disenchanted with the band's musical direction, however, and privately announced that he required a break. With the band's future still in doubt, press speculation proved so intense that an official announcement of a split occurred in August 1987. *Strangeways, Here We Come*, an intriguing transitional album, was issued posthumously. The work indicated the different directions towards which the major protagonists were progressing during their final phase.

A prestigious television documentary examining the band's career followed on *The South Bank Show*, and a belated live album, *Rank*, was issued the following year. The junior members Rourke and Joyce initially appeared with Brix Smith's Adult Net and backed Sinéad O'Connor, before Joyce joined the Buzzcocks. Morrissey pursued a solo career, while Marr moved from the Pretenders to The The and Electronic, as well as appearing on a variety of sessions for artists as diverse as Bryan Ferry, Talking Heads, Billy Bragg, Kirsty MacColl, the Pet Shop Boys, Stex and Banderas. In 1992, there was renewed interest in the Smiths following the furore surrounding Johnny

Rogan's controversial biography of the band, and Warner Brothers Records' acquisition of their back catalogue from Rough Trade. In 1996, the long-standing legal action taken by Mike Joyce was resolved with Morrissey and Marr losing their case. Joyce was awarded damages of £1 million, and Morrissey subsequently lost his appeal.

● ALBUMS: *The Smiths* (Rough Trade 1984) ★★★, *Meat Is Murder* (Rough Trade 1985) ★★★★, *The Queen Is Dead* (Rough Trade 1986) ★★★★, *Strangeways, Here We Come* (Rough Trade 1987) ★★★, *Rank* (Rough Trade 1988) ★★.
● COMPILATIONS: *Hatful Of Hollow* (Rough Trade 1984) ★★★, *The World Won't Listen* (Rough Trade 1987) ★★★, *Louder Than Bombs* (Rough Trade 1987) ★★★, *The Peel Sessions* (Strange Fruit 1988) ★★, *Best ... I* (WEA 1992) ★★★, *Best ... II* (WEA 1992) ★★, *Singles* (WEA 1995) ★★★★, *The Very Best Of* (WEA 2001) ★★★★.
● VIDEOS: *The Complete Picture* (WEA 1993).
● FURTHER READING: *The Smiths*, Mick Middles. *Morrissey & Marr: The Severed Alliance*, Johnny Rogan. *The Smiths: The Visual Documentary*, Johnny Rogan. *The Smiths: All Men Have Secrets*, Tom Gallagher, M. Chapman and M. Gillies. *The Smiths And Beyond: Images*, Kevin Cummins.

## SNIPER

This Japanese heavy metal band was formed in 1981 by guitarist Mansanori Kusakabe. Enlisting the services of Shigehisa Kitao (vocals), Romy Murase (bass) and Shunji Itoh (drums), their brand of heavy metal drew strongly on the styles of UFO and Deep Purple. Debuting with the single 'Fire' in 1983, they contributed 'Crazy Drug' to the *Heavy Metal Forces* compilation album the following year. Their first album was recorded live at the Electric Ladyland Club in Nagoya in 1984 and featured new recruit Ravhun Othani (ex-Frank Marino Band) as a second guitarist. The album was a limited edition of 1,000, which sold out, only to be re-pressed twice, with similar success. The band disintegrated shortly after its release, but was resurrected in 1985 by Kusakabe. The new line-up included Noburu Kaneko (vocals), Takeshi Kato (keyboards), Tsukasa Shinohara (bass) and Toshiyuki Miyata (drums). They produced *Quick And Dead*, but it made little impact outside Japan. A proposed tour of Holland to support it was cancelled and the band soon faded from view.
● ALBUMS: *Open The Attack* (Electric Ladyland 1984) ★★★, *Quick And Dead* (Megaton 1985) ★★.

## SOFT BOYS

When Syd Barrett gave up music for art, another Cambridge musician emerged to take on his mantle. Robyn Hitchcock (b. 3 March 1953, London, England) started out as a solo performer and busker before becoming a member of B.B. Blackberry And The Swelterettes, then the Chosen Few, the Worst Fears, and Maureen And The Meatpackers. It was with the last-named that Hitchcock first recorded (in 1976), although the results were not released until much later. His next group, Dennis And The Experts, became the Soft Boys in 1976. The Soft Boys' first recording session was in March 1977, by which point the line-up was Hitchcock (vocals, guitar, bass), Alan Davies (guitar), Andy Metcalfe (bass), and Morris Windsor aka Otis Fagg (drums). The original sessions remain unreleased but the same line-up also recorded a three-track EP – known as the *Give It To The Soft Boys* – for the local Cambridge label Raw Records. This was released in the autumn of 1977, after which Davies left and Kimberley Rew was installed on guitar, harmonica, and vocals. The Soft Boys, now signed to Radar Records, released the single '(I Wanna Be An) Anglepoise Lamp', but it was not considered representative of their innovative live work. Forming their own Two Crabs label they released *Can Of Bees* in 1979, after which they replaced Metcalfe with Matthew Seligman (ex-Camera Club). Jim Melton, who had been playing harmonica for a while, also left. Their remaining releases came on the Armageddon label and included *Underwater Moonlight*, an album that is considered one of Hitchcock's finest moments.

The Soft Boys broke up early in 1981 and Hitchcock went on to enjoy an erratic solo career, recruiting along the way Metcalfe and Windsor to form the Egyptians. Rew joined Katrina And The Waves and wrote the classic 'Going Down To Liverpool' (later a hit single for the Bangles), while Seligman joined Local Heroes SW9 and continued to contribute to Hitchcock's solo efforts. The Soft Boys have periodically re-formed to play reunion gigs, including an extensive transatlantic tour in 2001. During the same year, Matador Records released a superb expanded edition of *Underwater Moonlight*. Hitchcock, Rew, Seligman and Windsor recorded a new studio album for the label the following year.

● ALBUMS: *A Can Of Bees* (Two Crabs 1979) ★★★, *Underwater Moonlight* (Armageddon 1980) ★★★★, *Two Halves For The Price Of One* (Armageddon 1981) ★★★, *Invisible Hits* (Midnight Music 1983) ★★★, *Live At The Portland Arms* cassette only (Midnight Music 1987) ★★★, *Underwater Moonlight ... And How It Got There* (Matador 2001) ★★★★, *Nextdoorland* (Matador 2002) ★★★.
● COMPILATIONS: *Raw Cuts* mini-album (Overground 1989) ★★, *1976–81* (Rykodisc 1993) ★★★★.

## SOFT CELL

Formed in Leeds, England, in 1980 this electro-pop duo features vocalist Marc Almond (b. Peter Marc Almond, 9 July 1956, Southport, Lancashire, England) and synthesizer player Dave Ball (b. 3 May 1959, Blackpool, Lancashire, England). The art school twosome came to the attention of Some Bizzare Records entrepreneur Stevo following the release of their self-financed EP *Mutant Moments*. He duly included their 'Girl With The Patent Leather Face' on the compilation *Some Bizzare Album* and negotiated a licensing deal with Phonogram Records in Europe and Sire Records in the USA. Their debut single, 'Memorabilia', produced by Mute Records boss Daniel Miller, was an underground hit, paving the way for the celebrated 'Tainted Love'. Composed by the Four Preps' Ed Cobb and already well known as a northern soul club favourite by Gloria Jones, 'Tainted Love' topped the UK charts, became the bestselling

British single of the year and remained in the US charts for an astonishing 43 weeks. Produced by the former producer of Wire, Mike Thorne, the single highlighted Almond's strong potential as a torch singer, a role that was developed on subsequent hit singles including 'Bedsitter, 'Say Hello Wave Goodbye', 'Torch' and 'What'.

Almond's brand of erotic electronic sleaze could only partially be realized in the Soft Cell format and was more fully developed in the offshoot Marc And The Mambas. Implicit in Soft Cell's rise was a determined self-destructive streak, which meant that the group was never happy with the pop machinery of which it had inevitably become a part. The title of *The Art Of Falling Apart*, indicated how close they were to ending their hit collaboration. At the end of 1983, the duo announced their proposed dissolution and undertook a final tour early the following year, followed by a farewell album, *This Last Night In Sodom*.

Almond embarked on a solo career, while Ball would eventually become one half of the Grid. The duo reunited in the late 90s and began working on new studio material, some of which appeared on a 2002 compilation set. The remainder featured on the first Soft Cell album in almost 20 years, *Cruelty Without Beauty*.

● ALBUMS: *Non-Stop Erotic Cabaret* (Some Bizzare 1981) ★★★★, *Non-Stop Ecstatic Dancing* (Some Bizzare 1982) ★★, *The Art Of Falling Apart* (Some Bizzare 1983) ★★★, *This Last Night In Sodom* (Some Bizzare 1984) ★★★, *Cruelty Without Beauty* (Cooking Vinyl 2002) ★★★.
● COMPILATIONS: *The Singles 1981–85* (Some Bizzare 1986) ★★★★, *Their Greatest Hits* (Some Bizzare 1988) ★★★, *Memorabilia: The Singles* (Polydor 1991) ★★★, *Say Hello To Soft Cell* (Spectrum 1996) ★★, *The Twelve Inch Singles* 3-CD set (Some Bizzare 2001) ★★★, *The Very Best Of Soft Cell* (Mercury 2002) ★★★★.
● FURTHER READING: *Soft Cell*, Simon Tebbutt. *The Last Star: A Biography Of Marc Almond*, Jeremy Reed. *Tainted Life: The Autobiography*, Marc Almond.

## SONIC YOUTH

A product of New York's experimental 'No-Wave' scene, Sonic Youth first recorded under the auspices of *avant garde* guitarist Glenn Branca. Thurston Moore (b. 25 July 1958, Coral Gables, Florida, USA; guitar), Lee Ranaldo (b. 3 February 1956, Glen Cove, New York, USA; guitar) and Kim Gordon (b. 28 April 1953, Rochester, New York, USA; bass) performed together on Branca's *Symphony No. 3*, while the band debuted in its own right on his Neutral label. *Sonic Youth* was recorded live at New York's Radio City Music Hall in December 1981 and featured original drummer Richard Edson. Three further collections, *Confusion Is Sex*, *Sonic Death* and a mini-album, *Kill Yr Idols*, completed the quartet's formative period, which was marked by their pulsating blend of discordant guitars, impassioned vocals and ferocious, compulsive drum patterns, courtesy of newcomer Jim Sclavunos, or his replacement, Bob Bert. *Bad Moon Rising* was the first Sonic Youth album to secure a widespread release in both the USA and Britain.

This acclaimed set included the compulsive 'I'm Insane' and the eerie 'Death Valley '69', a collaboration with Lydia Lunch, which invoked the horror of the infamous Charles Manson murders.

Bob Bert was then replaced by Steve Shelley (b. 23 June 1962, Midland, Michigan, USA), who has remained with the line-up ever since. In 1986, the band unleashed *EVOL*, which refined their ability to mix melody with menace, particularly on the outstanding 'Shadow Of A Doubt'. The album also introduced the band's tongue-in-cheek fascination with Madonna. 'Expressway To Yr Skull' was given two alternative titles, 'Madonna, Sean And Me' and 'The Cruxifiction Of Sean Penn'. Later in the year the band were joined by Mike Watt from fIREHOSE in Ciccone Youth, which resulted in a mutated version of 'Into The Groove(y)' and 1989's *Ciccone Youth*, which combined dance tracks with experimental sounds redolent of German groups Faust and Neu. Sonic Youth's career continued with the highly impressive *Sister*, followed in 1988 by *Daydream Nation*, a double set that allowed the band to expand themes when required. Once again, the result was momentous. The instrumentation was powerful, recalling the intensity of the Velvet Underground or Can, while the songs themselves were highly memorable.

In 1990, Sonic Youth left the independent circuit by signing with the Geffen Records stable, going on to establish a reputation as godfathers to the alternative US rock scene with powerful albums such as *Goo*, *Dirty* and *A Thousand Leaves*. The independently released *Syr* mini-albums, meanwhile, document the band's restless experimentalism. Jim O'Rourke, a collaborator since 1997, joined the band as a full-time member on 2002's *Murray Street*. The album took its name from the New York street where the band's studio, Echo Canyon, is located.

In keeping with Sonic Youth's legendary reputation, Thurston Moore was instrumental in the signing of Nirvana to Geffen Records, while Kim Gordon was similarly pivotal in the formation of Hole. Steve Shelley would also work closely with Geffen on a number of acts. Successive stints on Lollapalooza tours helped to make Sonic Youth the nation's best-known underground band, while the group's members continued to collaborate on music and soundtrack projects to a degree that ensured the continuation of an already vast discography. Moore also runs his own underground record label, Ecstatic Peace!.

● ALBUMS: *Confusion Is Sex* (Neutral 1983) ★★★, *Kill Yr Idols* mini-album (Zensor 1983) ★★, *Sonic Death: Sonic Youth Live* cassette only (Ecstatic Peace! 1984) ★★, *Bad Moon Rising* (Homestead 1985) ★★★, *EVOL* (SST 1986) ★★★★, *Sister* (SST 1987) ★★★★, *Daydream Nation* (Blast First 1988) ★★★★, *Goo* (Geffen 1990) ★★★, *Dirty* (Geffen 1992) ★★★★, *Experimental Jet Set, Trash And No Star* (Geffen 1994) ★★★, *Washing Machine* (Geffen 1995) ★★★, *Made In USA* film soundtrack 1986 recording (Rhino/Warners 1995) ★★, *Syr 1* mini-album (Syr 1997) ★★★, *Syr 2* mini-album (Syr 1997) ★★★, with Jim O'Rourke *Syr 3* mini-album (Syr 1997) ★★★, *A Thousand Leaves* (Geffen 1998) ★★★★, *Goodbye 20th Century* (Syr

1999) ★★, *NYC Ghosts & Flowers* (Geffen 2000) ★★★, *Murray Street* (Geffen 2002) ★★★.

● COMPILATIONS: *Screaming Fields Of Sonic Love* (Blast First 1995) ★★★.

● VIDEOS: *Goo* (DGC 1991).

● FURTHER READING: *Confusion Is Next: The Sonic Youth Story*, Alec Foege.

## SPACEMEN 3

Spacemen 3 were instigated in Rugby, Warwickshire, England, in 1982 by Sonic Boom (b. Pete Kember, 19 November 1965) and regional soulmate Jason Pierce (also, strangely enough, b. 19 November 1965). Augmented by the rhythm section of Rosco and Pete Baines, it took Spacemen 3 four full years to blossom on to record. Initially crying shy of sounding too much like the Cramps, the band carefully evolved into one-chord wonders, masters of the hypnotic, blissed out groove. Such was their languid approach to working, and so dream inspiring was their music, Spacemen 3 made a habit of sitting down for the entirety of their gigs. *Playing With Fire* included the intensely repetitive blast of 'Revolution'. The free live album given away with the first 2000 copies of the previous album featured superior versions of some of their recorded live material. By this time Baines and Rosco had formed what was tantamount to a Spacemen 3 spin-off in the Darkside, allowing Will Carruthers and John Mattock to step into their places, and although this was the peak of the band's career, fundamental problems were still inherent. Sonic Boom made no secret of his drug dependency, having replaced heroin with methadone, and he and Jason Pierce were gradually growing apart to the point where they were chasing different goals. The relationship became so strained that *Recurring*, although still a Spaceman 3 effort, saw the two forces working separately, side one being attributed to Boom, and side two to Pierce. By this stage Boom had embarked upon a solo career and Pierce was working with Mattock and Carruthers in another band, Spiritualized, a situation that further fanned the flames. When *Recurring* finally saw the light of day, Spaceman 3's creative forces refused even to be interviewed together – a petty demise to what was, for some time, a creatively intense band.

● ALBUMS: *Sound Of Confusion* (Glass 1986) ★★, *The Perfect Prescription* (Glass 1987) ★★★, *Performance* (Glass 1988) ★★, *Playing With Fire* (Fire 1989) ★★★, *Dreamweapon: An Evening Of Contemporary Sitar Music* (Fierce 1990) ★★, *Recurring* (Fire 1991) ★★★, *For All The Fucked Up Children Of This World We Give You Spacemen 3* first recording session (Sympathy For The Record Industry 1995) ★, *Live In 89* (Orbit 1995) ★★.

● COMPILATIONS: *Taking Drugs To Make Music To Take Drugs To: The Northampton Demos* (Bomp 1990) ★★★, *Translucent Flashbacks (The Glass Singles)* (Fire 1995) ★★★.

## SPANDAU BALLET

Evolving from a school group, the Makers, these leading UK New Romantics formed in 1979 with a line-up comprising Gary Kemp (b. 16 October 1959, Islington, London, England; guitar), his brother

Martin Kemp (b. 10 October 1961, Islington, London, England; bass), Tony Hadley (b. Anthony Patrick Hadley, 2 June 1960, Islington, London, England), John Keeble (b. 6 July 1959, Islington, London, England; drums), and Steve Norman (b. 25 March 1960, Islington, London, England; rhythm guitar/saxophone/percussion). Another school colleague, Steve Dagger, became the band's long-standing manager. Spandau Ballet originally came to prominence as part of the new romantic scene revolving around a handful of fashionable London clubs, at which the habitués would dress in outlandish clothes and make-up. Such was the interest in this unknown band that the group was offered a contract by Island Records' proprietor Chris Blackwell. This was rejected and, instead, the band set up their label, Reformation. During early 1980, they were filmed for a television documentary and soon after licensed their label through Chrysalis Records. Their powerful debut, the harrowing 'To Cut A Long Story Short' reached the UK Top 5. With their kilts and synthesizers, it was easy to assume that the band were just part of a passing fashion and over the next year their singles 'The Freeze' and 'Musclebound' were average rather than exceptional. The insistent 'Chant Number 1 (I Don't Need This Pressure On)' revealed a more interesting soul/funk direction, complete with added brass and a new image. The single reached the UK Top 3, but again was followed by a relatively fallow period with 'Paint Me Down' and 'She Loved Like Diamond' barely scraping into the charts. The band completed a couple of albums and employed various producers, including Trevor Horn for 'Instinction' and Tony Swain and Steve Jolley for 'Communication'.

By 1983, the band had begun to pursue a more straightforward pop direction and pushed their lead singer as a junior Frank Sinatra. The new approach was demonstrated most forcibly on the irresistibly melodic 'True', which topped the UK charts for several weeks. The album of the same name repeated the feat, while the follow-up 'Gold' reached number 2. The obvious international appeal of a potential standard like 'True' was underlined when the song belatedly climbed into the US Top 5 the same year.

During the mid-80s, Spandau Ballet continued to chart regularly with such hits as 'Only When You Leave', 'I'll Fly For You', 'Highly Strung', 'Round And Round', 'Fight For Ourselves' and 'Through The Barricades'. A long-running legal dispute with Chrysalis forestalled the band's progress until they signed to CBS Records in 1986. The politically conscious Through The Barricades and its attendant hit singles, 'Fight For Yourselves' and the title track, partly re-established their standing. Their later work, however, was overshadowed by the acting ambitions of the Kemp brothers, who appeared to considerable acclaim in the London gangster film, The Krays. Martin Kemp later found greater fame with the role of Steve Owen in the long-running UK television soap opera EastEnders. Hadley embarked on a largely low-key solo career, and although his voice remained as strong as ever, his material has lacked any distinction. In May 1999, Hadley, Norman, and

Keeble lost their fight to reclaim a share of £1 million in royalties from the band's songwriter Gary Kemp. They continue to tour although they are unable to use the Spandau Ballet name.

● ALBUMS: *Journey To Glory* (Reformation 1981) ★★, *Diamond* (Reformation 1982) ★, *True* (Reformation 1983) ★★★, *Parade* (Reformation 1984) ★★, *Through The Barricades* (Reformation 1986) ★★★, *Heart Like A Sky* (CBS 1989) ★★.

● COMPILATIONS: *The Singles Collection* (Chrysalis 1985) ★★★, *The Best Of Spandau Ballet* (Chrysalis 1991) ★★★, *Gold: The Best Of Spandau Ballet* (Chrysalis 2000) ★★★, *Reformation* 3-CD set (Chrysalis 2002) ★★★.

## SPEAR OF DESTINY

Formed from the ashes of Theatre Of Hate in early 1983, Spear Of Destiny took their name from the mythological weapon that pierced the body of Christ, and was supposedly acquired over the years by Attila The Hun, Napoleon, and Hitler. This helped the band to attract quite a volume of destructive commentary in the press. The original line-up featured mainstay Kirk Brandon (b. 3 August 1956, Westminster, London, England; vocals, guitar), Chris Bell (drums), Lasettes Ames (saxophone), and Stan Stammers (bass, ex-Theatre Of Hate). They signed to CBS Records, but maintained their own label design, 'Burning Rome', which had appeared on previous Theatre Of Hate releases. The first single, 'Flying Scotsman', arrived in 1983, and was featured on *Grapes Of Wrath* alongside the relentless single 'The Wheel'. Critical response to the band was divided. By July, Bell and Ames had left, for reasons described by Bell as personal and religious. Brandon and Stammers brought in former Theatre Of Hate saxophonist John Lennard (b. Canada; ex-Diodes) and Nigel Preston (ex-Theatre Of Hate; Sex Gang Children). A third line-up added Alan St. Clair (guitar) and Neil Pyzor (keyboards, saxophone, ex-Case), Dolphin Taylor (drums, ex-Tom Robinson Band; Stiff Little Fingers) and Nicky Donnelly (saxophone, ex-Case). This formation recorded *One Eyed Jacks*, arguably the band's best album, and the singles 'Rainmaker', 'Liberator' and 'Prisoner Of Love'. The latter signalled a change in direction that would be more fully realized on the follow-up album. When *World Service* arrived, there was considerable disappointment from fans and critics alike. Having built an enviable reputation as a lyricist of considerable vigour, tracks such as 'Mickey' seemed grotesque and clumsy.

Further personnel changes became commonplace, and by 1987 the band had switched from Epic to Virgin Records for *Outland*, with the line-up now comprising Pete Barnacle (drums), Volker Janssen (keyboards) and Chris Bostock (bass) alongside Brandon. The summer of that year saw Brandon incapacitated for six months with an ankle injury that left him unable to walk, an affliction from which he still carries a limp. However, the band was soon back in the charts with 'Never Take Me Alive', and a support tour with U2. By December 1990, old colleague Stan Stammers returned on bass, alongside new drummer and guitarist Bobby Rae Mayhem and

Mark Thwaite. In 1991, Brandon was touring once more under the joint Theatre Of Hate/Spear Of Destiny banner, but by 1996 he had dropped the name of his latest band 10:51 and reverted to Theatre Of Hate. He embarked on unsuccessful litigation with Boy George that year over allegations of a homosexual relationship, revealed in George's autobiography. Judgement went against him and he was ordered to pay part of the substantial costs. Brandon subsequently returned to record the new studio album, *Religion*.

● ALBUMS: *Grapes Of Wrath* (Burning Rome/Epic 1983) ★★, *One Eyed Jacks* (Burning Rome/Epic 1984) ★★★★, *World Service* (Burning Rome/Epic 1985) ★★, *Outland* (10 1987) ★★, *The Price You Pay* (Virgin 1988) ★★, *S.O.D.'s Law* (Virgin 1992) ★★, *Live At The Lyceum* (Diablo 1993) ★★, *BBC Radio 1 Live In Concert* 1987 recording (Windsong 1994) ★, *Religion* (Eastworld 1997) ★★, *Live '83; The Preacher* (Receiver 2000) ★★.

● COMPILATIONS: *The Epic Years* (Epic 1987) ★★★, *The Collection* (Castle 1992) ★★★, *Time Of Our Lives: The Best Of Spear Of Destiny* (Virgin 1995) ★★★, *Psalm 1* (Eastworld 1999) ★★, *Psalm 2* (Eastworld 1999) ★★, *Psalm 3* (Eastworld 1999) ★★.

## SPINAL TAP

The concept for Spinal Tap – a satire of a fading British heavy metal band – was first aired in a late 70s television sketch. Christopher Guest (b. Christopher Haden-Guest, 5 February 1948, New York, USA), formerly of parody troupe *National Lampoon*, played the part of lead guitarist Nigel Tufnell, while Harry Shearer (b. 23 December 1943, Los Angeles, California, USA) played bass player Derek Smalls, and Michael McKean (b. 17 October 1947, New York, USA) played vocalist David St. Hubbins. Their initial sketch also featured Loudon Wainwright III and drummer Russ Kunkel, but these true-life musicians dropped out of the project on its transformation to full-length movie. *This Is Spinal Tap*, released in 1984, was not a cinematic success, but it has since become highly popular through the medium of video. Its portrayal of a doomed US tour is ruthless, exposing incompetence, megalomania and sheer madness, but in a manner combining humour with affection. However, rather than incurring the wrath of the rock fraternity, the movie has been lauded by musicians, many of whom, unfathomably, claim inspiration for individual scenes. Contemporary UK comedy team the Comic Strip mined similar themes for their creation, Bad News.

Spinal Tap reunited as a 'real' band and undertook an extensive tour in 1992 to promote *Break Like The Wind*, which featured guest appearances by Jeff Beck, Nicky Hopkins and Slash (Guns N'Roses). A remastered version of the original album was released in autumn 2000, along with an Internet only album downloadable from the band's Tapster site. At this stage, it seems that Spinal Tap's jokes at heavy metal's expense are too deeply rooted in truth ever to wear thin.

● ALBUMS: *This Is Spinal Tap* (Polydor 1984) ★★★, *Break Like The Wind* (MCA 1992) ★★★, *Back From*

*The Dead* (Tapster 2000) ★★★.

● VIDEOS: *This Is Spinal Tap* (Polydor 1984), *The Return Of Spinal Tap* (Second Sight 1992).

● FURTHER READING: *Inside Spinal Tap*, Peter Occhiogrosso. *This Is Spinal Tap: The Official Companion*, Karl French.

● FILMS: *This Is Spinal Tap* (1984).

## SPLODGENESSABOUNDS

The origins of this UK band are heavily tinged with apocrypha. Max Splodge (then a drummer) replaced Gerry Healy in Alien Sex Fiend in 1978 and stayed for a few months before forming a duo called the Faber Brothers with guitarist Pat Thetic Von Dale Chiptooth Noble. They performed at Butlins Holiday Camp in Bognor, Sussex, but were sacked and returned to London to start a band. As Splodgenessabounds, they started gigging in March 1979 and though various members came and went, the line-up briefly comprised Max Splodge (vocals), his girlfriend Baby Greensleeves (vocals), Pat Thetic (guitar), Miles Runt Flat (guitar), Donkey Gut (b. Winston Forbe; keyboards), Whiffy Archer (paper and comb), Desert Island Joe Lurch Slythe and a dog. Robert Rodent joined on bass in early 1980 and Flat left. They came to the public's attention when, to the eternal annoyance of publicans everywhere, they had a freak hit with 'Two Pints Of Lager And A Packet Of Crisps Please' in 1980. Other memorable songs in their repertoire included 'I've Got Lots Of Famous People Living Under The Floorboards Of My Humble Abode', 'Simon Templar', and a savage reworking of Rolf Harris' 'Two Little Boys'. Max Splodge was also appeared in the play *Camberwell Beauty*. After falling out with Deram Records in 1982, the band signed to Razor under the shortened title Splodge, where they released *In Search Of The Seven Golden Gussets*, a tribute to mythical items of ladies underwear. By this time, the line-up included the following miscreants; Ronnie Plonker (guitar), Smacked Arse O'Reardon (bass), Poodle (drums) and Tone Tone The Garden Gnome (guitar). Max later recorded solo on Neat releasing the Tony James (Sigue Sigue Sputnik) single 'Phut Phut Splodgenik', before joining the Angelic Upstarts. He revived Splodgenessabounds in the late 90s, recording new studio albums for the Captain Oi! Label with various personnel.

● ALBUMS: *Splodgenessabounds* (Deram 1981) ★★★, *In Search Of The Seven Golden Gussets* (Razor 1982) ★★, *Live And Loud!!* (Link 1988) ★, *I Don't Know* (Captain Oi! 2000) ★★★, *The Artful Splodger* (Captain Oi! 2001) ★★.

## SPYRO GYRA

Formed in 1975 by saxophonist Jay Beckenstein (b. 14 May 1951, New York City, New York, USA) and pianist Jeremy Wall, the original Spyro Gyra comprised Chet Catallo (electric guitar), David Wolford (electric bass), Eli Konikoff (drums), and Gerardo Velez (percussion). After a modest start in Buffalo, New York, and an album on a small independent label, Beckenstein's hard work and commitment through countless changes of personnel resulted in appearances at major international jazz festivals in the 80s, and several gold albums. In addition to having numerous hits in the USA, the band found considerable success in the UK with the infectious 'Morning Dance'. The band's mainstream treatment of a mixture of funk, Latin, and jazz remains popular today. They remain, however, an enigma; their following is considerable and stays stable after more than 20 years together. In terms of their music, they have never challenged the jazz world to take them seriously. Similarly, they are too clever musically to be taken into the mainstream of easy listening. They fit well into the GRP Records family with its high standard of technical excellence and accessible music. The line-up in the late 90s comprised Julio Fernandez (guitar), Tom Schuman (keyboards), Joel Rosenblatt (drums), Scott Ambush (bass), in addition to the guiding force, Beckenstein. He released his solo debut, *Eye Contact*, in 2000.

● ALBUMS: *Spyro Gyra* (Infinity 1978) ★★, *Morning Dance* (Infinity 1979) ★★★★, *Catching The Sun* (MCA 1980) ★★, *Carnival* (MCA 1980) ★★★, *Freetime* (MCA 1981) ★★, *Incognito* (MCA 1982) ★★, *City Kids* (MCA 1983) ★★, *Access All Areas* (MCA 1984) ★★, *Alternating Currents* (GRP 1985) ★★, *Breakout* (MCA 1986) ★★, *Stories Without Words* (MCA 1987) ★★, *Rites Of Summer* (GRP 1988) ★★, *Point Of View* (MCA 1989) ★★★, *Fast Forward* (GRP 1990) ★★, *Three Wishes* (GRP 1992) ★★, *Dreams Beyond Control* (GRP 1993) ★★★, *Love And Other Obsessions* (GRP 1994) ★★, *Heart Of The Night* (GRP 1996) ★★, *20/20* (GRP 1997) ★★★, *Road Scholars* (GRP 1998) ★★, *Got The Magic* (Windham Hill 1999) ★★★, *In Modern Times* (Heads Up 2001) ★★★.

● COMPILATIONS: *The Collection* (GRP 1991) ★★★.

● VIDEOS: *Graffiti* (GRP 1992).

## SQUEEZE

Formed in Deptford, London, England, in 1974, Squeeze came to prominence in the late 70s riding on the new wave created by the punk movement. Original members Chris Difford (b. 4 November 1954, London, England; guitar, lead vocals), Glenn Tilbrook (b. 31 August 1957, London, England; guitar, vocals), and Jools Holland (b. Julian Holland, 24 January 1958, Deptford, London, England; keyboards) named the band after a disreputable Velvet Underground album. With the addition of Harry Kakoulli (bass), and original drummer Paul Gunn replaced by session drummer Gilson Lavis (b. 27 June 1951, Bedford, England), Squeeze released an EP, *Packet Of Three*, in 1977 on the Deptford Fun City label. It was produced by former Velvet Underground member John Cale. The EP's title in itself reflected the preoccupation of the band's main songwriters, Chris Difford and Glenn Tilbrook, with England's social underclass. It led to a major contract with A&M Records and a UK Top 20 hit in 1978 with 'Take Me I'm Yours'. Minor success with 'Bang Bang' and 'Goodbye Girl' that same year was followed in 1979 by two number 2 hits with 'Cool For Cats' and 'Up The Junction'.

Difford's lyrics were by now beginning to show an acute talent in capturing the flavour of contemporary south London life with a sense of the tragi-comic. This began to flower fully with the release of 1980's *Argybargy*, which spawned the singles 'Another Nail In My Heart' (UK Top 20) and the sublime 'Pulling Mussels (From The Shell)'. The set was Squeeze's most cohesive album to date; having finally thrown off any remaining traces of a punk influence, they now displayed some of the finest 'kitchen sink' lyrics since Ray Davies' peak. The album also featured the band's new bass player, John Bentley (b. 16 April 1951). In 1980, Holland left for a solo career that included performing and recording with his band, Jools Holland And The Millionaires (which displayed his talent for the 'boogie-woogie' piano style) and hosting the UK television show *The Tube*. His replacement was singer/pianist Paul Carrack (b. 22 April 1951, Sheffield, Yorkshire, England), formerly with pub-rock band Ace. He appeared on *East Side Story*, which was co-produced by Elvis Costello. Carrack stamped his mark on the album with his excellent performance on 'Tempted' and with the success of 'Labelled With Love', a UK Top 5 hit, the album became the band's most commercial to date. Carrack departed soon afterwards to join Carlene Carter's group, and was replaced by Don Snow (b. 13 January 1957, Kenya; ex-Sinceros). The follow-up, *Sweets From A Stranger*, was an uneven affair, although it did spawn the superb 'Black Coffee In Bed'.

At the height of their success, amid intense world tours, including selling out New York's Madison Square Garden, Difford And Tilbrook dissolved the band. However, the duo continued to compose together, releasing an album in 1984. The following year they re-formed the band with Lavis, the returning Holland, and a new bass player, Keith Wilkinson. *Cosi Fan Tutti Frutti* was hailed as a return to form, and, although not supplying any hit singles, the tracks 'King George Street', 'I Learnt How To Pray' and Difford/Holland's 'Heartbreaking World' stood out. In 1987 Squeeze achieved their highest position in the UK singles chart for almost six years when 'Hourglass' reached number 16 and subsequently gave the band their first US Top 40 hit, climbing one place higher. '853-5937' repeated the transatlantic success, breaking into the Top 40 a couple of months later. The accompanying album, *Babylon And On*, featured contributions from the Soft Boys' Andy Metcalfe (horns, keyboards).

After the release of 1989's *Frank*, which contained one of the most sensitive lyrics ever written by a man about menstruation ('She Doesn't Have To Shave'), Holland departed once again to concentrate on television work. With Matt Irving joining as a second keyboard player, Squeeze released a live album, *A Round And A Bout*, on their old Deptford Fun City label in 1990, before signing a new recording contract with Warner Brothers Records. The release of *Play* confirmed and continued Chris Difford and Glenn Tilbrook's reputation as one of the UK's finest songwriting teams, with 'Gone To The Dogs' and 'Wicked And Cruel' particularly resonant of earlier charms. *Some Fantastic Place* saw them reunited with A&M Records, although there was some critical carping about their insistence on a group format that did not always augur well for their more adroit and sober compositions. *Ridiculous* was their strongest album in years, showing them back to writing sharp, humorous yet provocative lyrics on the up-tempo tracks and poignant love songs on the ballads. The lively 'Electric Trains', for example, managed to make the unlikely pairing of Julie Andrews and Jerry Garcia in one lyric! 'Grouch Of The Day' cleverly delivered self-deprecating honesty, while the minor hit 'This Summer' has the wonderful lyric: 'nights we spent out of control like two flags wrapped around a pole'. This was a tremendous set of songs that strangely missed the record-buying public by a mile, leaving many to wonder if they had fallen into cult obscurity in the same manner as those other outstanding craftsmen of the classic English pop single, Andy Partridge of XTC and Ray Davies of the Kinks. Like Davies and Partridge, Difford and Tilbrook were still writing perfect hooks and middle eights mixed with intelligent, interesting, and often bitingly accurate observations of life.

Following the demise of A&M Records, Squeeze issued *Domino* on their own Quixotic Records label. They displayed the material to the music market place in Cannes at the annual MIDEM festival in January 1999 by playing a blistering set. With little fanfare, the album was issued in the UK, and proved to be yet another gem, rife with great songs and melody. Featuring Holland's younger brother Chris on keyboards, Hilaire Penda (bass) and Ash Soan (drums), this version of Squeeze sounded as good as any previous incarnation. Stand-out tracks included the painfully observant tale of the result of family divorce, 'To Be A Dad', and the honest confession of infidelity, 'Sleeping With A Friend'. Difford and Tilbrook proved they were still capable of writing top-notch material from their hearts, without pandering to musical trends. Sadly, these prized upholders of the great English pop song tradition disbanded Squeeze not long afterwards. Tilbrook released his solo debut, *The Incomplete Glenn Tilbrook*, in May 2001.

● ALBUMS: *Squeeze* (A&M 1978) ★★★, *Cool For Cats* (A&M 1979) ★★★★, *Argybargy* (A&M 1980) ★★★★, *East Side Story* (A&M 1981) ★★★★, *Sweets From A Stranger* (A&M 1982) ★★, *Cosi Fan Tutti Frutti* (A&M 1985) ★★★, *Babylon And On* (A&M 1987) ★★★, *Frank* (A&M 1989) ★★★, *A Round And A Bout* (Deptford Fun City/I.R.S. 1990) ★★, *Play* (Reprise 1991) ★★, *Some Fantastic Place* (A&M 1993) ★★★, *Ridiculous* (A&M/Ark 21 1995) ★★★★, *Domino* (Quixotic/Valley 1998) ★★★★.

Solo Glenn Tilbrook *The Incomplete Glenn Tilbrook* (Quixotic 2001) ★★★.

● COMPILATIONS: *Singles 45's And Under* (A&M 1982) ★★★★, *Greatest Hits* (A&M 1992) ★★★, *Excess Moderation* (A&M 1996) ★★★, *Piccadilly Collection* (A&M 1996) ★★★, *Six Of One* box set (A&M 1997) ★★★★, *Up The Junction* (Spectrum 2000) ★★★, *Big Squeeze: The Very Best Of Squeeze* (Universal 2002) ★★★★.

## STAR SOUND

The credit for the Star Sound phenomenon arguably belongs to an unknown European bootlegger who created a medley of songs by original artists for use in discotheques during 1980. One of the tunes in the sequence was Shocking Blue's 'Venus' and its appearance so outraged publisher William van Kooten that he was determined to record a rival legal version. Producer Jaap Eggermont, formerly a drummer in Golden Earring, elected to retain 'Venus' followed by the Archies' 'Sugar Sugar' and a wealth of Beatles oldies. Three Fab Four soundalikes, Bas Muys, Okkie Huysdens and Hans Vermoulen took on the roles of John Lennon, Paul McCartney and George Harrison, respectively. In the UK, the track was titled 'Stars On 45' and credited to Star Sound, but in the USA, where the medley reached the top of the charts, Stars On 45 were the registered artists and the song sub-title was the longest in chart-topping history: 'Medley: Intro/Venus/Sugar Sugar/No Reply/I'll Be Back/Drive My Car/Do You Want To Know A Secret/We Can Work It Out/I Should Have Known Better/Nowhere Man/You're Going To Lose That Girl/Stars On 45'. In the UK, 'Stars On 45, Volume 2' featured a medley of Abba songs and, like its predecessor, reached number 2. Before long, the idea was ruthlessly milked and other record companies took note by releasing medley tributes by such artists as the Beach Boys and Hollies. A decade later, the medley art was resurrected and perfected by the multi-chart-topping Jive Bunny And The Mastermixers.

● ALBUMS: *Stars On 45* (CBS 1981) ★★, *Stars On 45 – Volume 2* (CBS 1981) ★★, *Stars Medley* (CBS 1982) ★★.

● COMPILATIONS: *The Very Best Of Stars On 45* (Music Club 1994) ★★, *Greatest Stars On 45, Vol. 1* (Victor 2000) ★★, *Greatest Stars On 45, Vol. 2* (Victor 2000) ★★.

## STARLIGHT EXPRESS

Andrew Lloyd Webber is quoted as saying that this show, which was nick-named 'Squeals On Wheels' by one unkind critic, started out in 1975 as an entertainment intended for children. In 1983 he rewrote it for the benefit of his own children, Imogen and Nicholas, and then, with the help of lyricist Richard Stilgoe, it became the full-blown musical which opened at the Apollo Victoria in London on 27 March 1984. The theatre's interior had to be completely re-designed to accommodate a series of racetracks, gantries, ramps, and bridges which encircled and dominated the auditorium. More than 20 roller skaters, pretending to be trains, zoom along the tracks enacting a story in which, after a number of races, Rusty (Ray Shell), a shy little steam engine, triumphs over Greaseball (Jeff Shankley) the flashy diesel locomotive, and gets hitched up to his favourite carriage, Pearl (Stephanie Lawrence). The high-tech effects, plus Arlene Phillips' imaginative choreography and Trevor Nunn's direction, created what seemed almost like a giant computer game. The loudly amplified score contained elements of rock, blues, country, and many other influences, in songs such as 'Call Me Rusty', 'Only He (Has The Power To Move Me)', 'Pumping Iron', 'U.N.C.O.U.P.L.E.D', 'AC-DC', 'Right Place, Right Time', 'One Rock 'N' Roll Too Many' and 'Light At The End Of The Tunnel'. The show proved to be a consistently popular attraction, and, in April 1992, became the second longest-running British musical after *Cats*. Later in the year the production was revised and rechoreographed, and five new songs added, before it resumed its record-breaking journey. One member of the new cast, Lon Satton, had played Poppa the old steam locomotive since the first night in 1984. *Starlight Express* was also reworked for its Broadway run which began in March 1987 and lasted for 761 performances. In September 1993, a 90-minute edition of the show opened at the Las Vegas Hilton, the first major legitimate production ever to play the US gambling capital. In March 2001, as the London version of *Starlight Express* entered its eighteenth year, it was reported that it had been seen by eight million people at the Apollo Victoria, and grossed over £446 million worldwide.

## STEELY AND CLEVIE

This Jamaican studio 'band' comprises Wycliffe 'Steely' Johnson and Cleveland 'Clevie' Browne (pronounced 'Brown-ie'). Every five years or so, Jamaica produces a rhythm section that dominates reggae. In the 70s, it was brothers, Carlton and Aston 'Familyman' Barrett, who drove the Upsetters and Bob Marley's Wailers. The late 70s/early 80s belonged to Sly And Robbie, but by 1986 reggae required a team fully conversant with computerized music: Steely And Clevie fulfilled that role.

Wycliffe 'Steely' Johnson first surfaced with Sugar Minott's Youth Promotion organization, playing keyboards on Minott's classic *Ghetto-ology* (1978). After a period with the Generation Gap, he joined the Roots Radics, earning a reputation for hard work and innovation. When the Radics became *the* band for the new dancehall music of the early 80s, it gave Steely a perfect understanding of a minimal, raw-basics kind of reggae. Drummer Clevie began playing as part of the Browne Bunch in the 70s with brothers Dalton and Danny Browne. During the late 70s, he played sessions at Studio One, backing Freddie McGregor, and played with the In Crowd. In the early 80s McGregor hired Clevie for his road group, known as the Studio One Band, and on tour, Clevie came into contact with equipment that was not yet *de rigueur* in Jamaican studios; he consequently became interested in drum machines, while his fellow-drummers declared them an abomination. Prior to that, Clevie had recorded tracks with Bob Marley in 1979, when the singer was using a primitive drum machine in the studio. In the mid-80s Clevie's brothers, Danny and Dalton, were the musical pulse of the Bloodfire Posse, the first all-electronic reggae group. By the time digital music arrived, Clevie was ready for it.

At some point in the late 70s, Steely and Clevie met during sessions for Augustus Pablo at Lee Perry's Black Ark studio, working on Hugh Mundell's *Africa Must Be Free By 1983*. The pair's relationship was enhanced by contrasting characters – Clevie the studious, mild musician, and Steely the louder, ragga character. When they took up residence as house band at King Jammy's studio in 1986, they were clearly on the verge of something new and exciting.

Jammy's was the engine of mid-80s reggae; from there, Steely And Clevie worked with everyone, cutting 10 singles a week at its peak in 1987 and a stream of albums from various artists such as Cocoa Tea, Dennis Brown, Admiral Bailey and Lieutenant Stitchie. Jammy's produced the best ragga sounds on the island at the time, and although producer King Jammy received the praise, much of the work was done by Steely and Clevie, engineers Bobby Digital and Squingie Francis, and the arranger, Mikey Bennett. They also gigged for most of the other influential producers in Jamaica; hence, they knew virtually everyone when they began their own label – Steely And Clevie – in 1988. They immediately hit with a debut release from Johnny P., making the DJ a star. The formula of brash, unusual beats and strong melodies also worked for Foxy Brown, relaunched Tiger's career, produced hits for Anthony Red Rose, Anthony Malvo and Little Twitch, and revived older acts Dillinger and Johnny Osbourne. Sessions for Gussie Clarke helped to establish his studio as the major technological force in late 80s reggae, and Steely And Clevie cut a series of inimitable 'one rhythm' albums on their own label: *Limousine*, *Bursting Out*, *Real Rock Style* and *Can't Do The Work*. Broader attention followed with work for former Soul II Soul singer Caron Wheeler, Maxi Priest, Aswad and J.C. Lodge.

● COMPILATIONS: *Bursting Out* (S&C 1988) ★★★★, *At The Top* (Black Solidarity 1988) ★★★, *Can't Do The Work* (S&C 1989) ★★★★, *Limousine* (S&C 989) ★★★, *Real Rock Style* (S&C/Jet Star 1989) ★★★★, *Godfather* (VP 1990) ★★★, *Lion Attack* (VP 1990) ★★★, *Poco In The East* (S&C 1990), *More Poco* (VP 1990) ★★★, *Girl Talk* (VP 1991) ★★★, *Present Soundboy Clash* (Profile 1991) ★★★, *Play Studio One Vintage* (Heartbeat 1992) ★★★★, *High Gear* (VP 1997) ★★★, *Dubbist* (Prestige 2002) ★★★.

## STEPHENSON, MARTIN

b. 27 July 1961, County Durham, England. This singer-songwriter's reputation has been bolstered by virtue of countless searing live performances throughout the UK. His early love of literature and music led to the formation of the first Daintees line-up in his early teens. With a regular turnover of staff and lack of proper gigs, the band nevertheless became something of a busking sensation, on the evidence of which Newcastle record label Kitchenware sent them into the studio. After two singles, notable among which was 1982's intoxicating 'Roll On Summertime', a debut album was embarked upon. The Daintees line-up at this time comprised Stephenson (guitar, vocals), Anthony Dunn (bass, acoustic guitar, vocals), John Steel (keyboards, harmonica, bass, vocals) and Paul Smith (drums, percussion). *Boat To Bolivia*, released in 1986, was praised by the *New Musical Express* because it 'builds bridges between love and hate, between cradle and grave, between folk and pop, between the past and present'. The candidness and honesty of Stephenson's lyrics were best portrayed on 'Caroline' and 'Crocodile Cryer'. He also revealed his appreciation of the folk/blues rag guitar style with 'Tribute To The Late Reverend Gary Davis' as well as regular live performances of Van Dyke Parks' 'High Coin'.

A lengthy hiatus delayed the arrival of the follow-up until 1988. *Gladsome, Humour & Blue* contained the superb 'Wholly Humble Heart'. Once again, reviews were excellent, and Stephenson enhanced an already impressive reputation for hearty live shows. *Salutation Road* proved to be the songwriter's most politicized work, prefaced by the single 'Left Us To Burn', which directly attacked Margaret Thatcher. Two further albums with the Daintees were released by the Kitchenware label, before Stephenson embarked on a solo career with a series of acclaimed releases for Demon Records. In the new millennium, he released a series of mail-order-only acoustic projects. He also records and tours with his swing outfit the Toe-Rags and, from time to time, a new line-up of the Daintees.

● ALBUMS: with the Daintees *Boat To Bolivia* (Kitchenware 1986) ★★★★, with the Daintees *Gladsome, Humour & Blue* (Kitchenware 1988) ★★★, with the Daintees *Salutation Road* (Kitchenware 1990) ★★★★, with the Daintees *The Boy's Heart* (Kitchenware 1992) ★★★, with the Daintees *High Bells Ring Thin* (Kitchenware 1993) ★★★, *Yogi In My House* (Demon 1995) ★★★, *Sweet Misdemeanour* (Demon 1995) ★★★, *Beyond The Leap, Beyond The Law* (Demon 1997) ★★★, with the Toe-Rags *When It's Gone – It's Gone* (Get Rhythm 1998) ★★★, *Martin Stephenson* (Floating World 1999) ★★★, with the Toe-Rags *Red Man's In Town* (Real To Reel 1999) ★★★, *Lilac Tree* (Own Label 2000) ★★★, *The Church & The Minidisc* (Own Label 2000) ★★★, *The Disciples Of Merle & Doc* (Own Label 2000) ★★★, with the Daintees *Live In The 21st Century* (Fresh Ear 2001) ★★★, *The Incredible Shrinking Band* (Barbaraville 2001) ★★★, *Collective Force* (Force 2002) ★★★.

● COMPILATIONS: *There Comes A Time: The Best Of Martin Stephenson And The Daintees* (Kitchenware 1993) ★★★★.

● FURTHER READING: *Janus*, Martin Stephenson and Pete McAdam.

## STEVENS, SHAKIN'

b. Michael Barratt, 4 March 1948, Ely, South Glamorgan, Wales, the youngest of 12 children. A rock 'n' roll singer in the style of the early Elvis Presley, Stevens brought this 50s spirit to a long series of pop hits during the 80s. In the late 60s, he became lead singer with a Welsh rock revival group, the Backbeats, who immediately changed their name to Shakin' Stevens And The Sunsets. During 1970-73, the band recorded unsuccessful albums for Parlophone Records, CBS Records and Dureco Records in Holland, where the Sunsets had a large following. In 1976, they recorded a cover version of the Hank Mizell hit 'Jungle Rock' before disbanding. Shakin' Stevens now began a solo career, and his debut single was 'Never', in March 1977. He appeared on stage in Jack Good's West End musical *Elvis*, which won a number of awards. He also appeared on Good's stage revival of his pioneering television series *Oh Boy!*, and had further exposure on television with the same revival, which was later known as *Let's Rock*. His recording career still did

not take off, and following the disappointing *Shakin' Stevens* for Track Records he signed a more lucrative contract with Epic Records under the guidance of his new manager Freya Miller. Three singles followed; Roy Head's 'Treat Her Right', Jody Reynolds' death song 'Endless Sleep', in the style of 50s UK rocker Marty Wilde, and 'Spooky', produced by ex-Springfields member Mike Hurst, but there was still no chart action. A change of producer to Stuart Colman in 1980 brought Stevens' first Top 20 hit, 'Marie Marie', first recorded by the Blasters, and the following year Colman's infectious rockabilly arrangement of the 1954 Rosemary Clooney number 1 'This Ole House' topped the UK chart and became a huge international success.

Over the next seven years, Stevens had 32 Top 40 hits in the UK, and similar popularity followed in Europe and beyond (he was the first artist to go double platinum in Sweden), although he made almost no impact in the USA. Among his hits were three further chart-toppers – a revival of Jim Lowe's 1956 song 'Green Door' (1981), Stevens' own composition 'Oh Julie' (1982) and 'Merry Christmas Everyone' (1985). With an audience equally divided between young children and the middle-aged, his other recordings included brief excursions into soul (the Supremes' 'Come See About Me' in 1987) and MOR ballads (the Bing Crosby/Grace Kelly film theme 'True Love', 1988). He duetted with fellow Welsh artist Bonnie Tyler on 'A Rockin' Good Way (To Mess Around And Fall In Love)' (1984), which was first recorded in 1960 by Dinah Washington and Brook Benton.

At the dawn of the 90s, even though he was hugely popular in Europe, there were signs that Stevens' hold over his UK audiences was faltering. Although the Pete Hammond-produced 'I Might' reached the UK Top 20, his subsequent records in 1990/1 made little impact. A major promotion for the compilation *The Epic Years* (billed as 'Shaky') failed to dent the UK Top 50. 1993 started badly for Stevens, as litigation with his former band the Sunsets was resolved, it was alleged that Dave Edmunds and Shaky had to pay out £500,000 in back royalties. In 1995, he decided to take some time out, to review his career and business affairs. He returned to touring in 1999 and to the recording studio the following year.

● ALBUMS: with the Sunsets *A Legend* (Parlophone 1970) ★★, with the Sunsets *I'm No J.D.* (Columbia 1971) ★★★, with the Sunsets *Rockin' And Shakin'* (Contour 1972) ★★, with the Sunsets *Shakin' Stevens And The Sunsets* (Emerald 1973) ★★, *Shakin' Stevens* (Track 1977) ★★, *Take One!* (Epic 1979) ★★★, *This Ole House* (Epic 1981) ★★★, *Shaky* (Epic 1981) ★★★★, *Give Me Your Heart Tonight* (Epic 1982) ★★, *The Bop Won't Stop* (Epic 1983) ★★, *Lipstick, Powder And Paint* (Epic 1985) ★★★, *Let's Boogie* (Epic 1987) ★★, *A Whole Lotta Shaky* (Epic 1988) ★★, *Rock 'N' Roll* (Telstar 1990) ★★, *Merry Christmas Everyone* (Epic 1991) ★.

● COMPILATIONS: *Greatest Hits* (Epic 1984) ★★★, with the Sunsets *The Collection* (Castle 1986) ★★, *The Track Years* (MFP 1986) ★★, with the Sunsets *Good Rockin' Tonight* (Pickwick 1987) ★★, with the

Sunsets *Outlaw Man* (Spectrum 1988) ★★, *The Epic Years* (Epic 1992) ★★★, *Greatest Hits* (Rhino 1995) ★★★★, *The Very Best Of Shakin' Stevens* (Epic 1999) ★★★.
● VIDEOS: *Shakin' Stevens Video Show Volume 1 & 2* (CMV 1989).

## STEVO

b. Steven Pearse, 26 December 1962, Dagenham, Essex, England. One of the most outspoken, adventurous and original discoverers of arcane talent, Stevo came to the fore of the British music scene during the early 80s. A misfit and underachiever at school, he was virtually illiterate and underwent a self-improving course that coincided with his rise to prominence in the music industry. Originally a disc jockey, he compiled an 'electronic music' and 'futurist' chart for the music press that led to him being bombarded with roughly-hewn demos from unknown artists. During 1980, Stevo packaged the best of this material as the *Some Bizzare Album* (its misspelling was unintentional but apposite). Among the artists included were Throbbing Gristle, Classix Nouveaux, Clock DVA, Cabaret Voltaire, Blancmange, Depeche Mode, Soft Cell and The The. The latter two artists came under Stevo's management and joined his innovative Some Bizzare Records label. Stevo received instant recognition for his brusque behaviour and eccentric business dealings. After the chart-topping success of Soft Cell, major record companies anxious to license his acts were forced to endure the teenage entrepreneur's strange whims, which included signing a contract in the pouring rain while sitting on one of the lions in Trafalgar Square. With similar eccentricity, the contract for the hand of Psychic TV included a clause demanding a year's supply of baby food. It said much for Stevo's power and persuasion that he managed to license so many wilfully uncommercial acts to the major labels. His strength lay in an ability to capture innovative acts at an early stage when they were merely regarded as weird. In the case of Soft Cell and later The The, Stevo showed that he had the ear to nurture potentially major artists. Many other acts were a testament to his love of the unusual. Berlin's Einstürzende Neubauten decried conventional rock instruments in favour of industrial sounds, and the scream of clanging metal as percussion could also be heard via Test Department. The unremitting aural depravity of Foetus threatened to complete Stevo's journey into the darker areas of the soul, and with commercial acts on the wane the future of his label was perpetually in doubt. In the 90s, however, Stevo continued to stalk the musical boundaries with a stream of new signings including Stex, Tim Hutton, Kandis King and Vicious Circle.
● FURTHER READING: *Starmakers And Svengalis: The History Of British Pop Management*, Johnny Rogan.

## STEWART, DAVE, AND BARBARA GASKIN

One of the surprise hits of the early 80s was a UK number 1 cover version of Leslie Gore's 'It's My Party' by two former members of several UK progressive bands. Dave Stewart (b. 30 December 1950, Waterloo, London, England) was originally organist in Uriel in late 1967 (with Steve Hillage). When Hillage left, Stewart and Uriel's other members Clive Brooks and Mont Campbell formed Egg who released a couple of albums in the late 60s and early 70s. At the same time, Stewart often guested on keyboards with Steve Hillage's new band Khane. In 1973, he replaced David Sinclair in Hatfield And The North who included a female backing group, the Northettes, consisting of Barbara Gaskin (b. Hatfield, England; ex-Spirogyra), Amanda Parsons, and Ann Rosenthal. Hatfield And The North metamorphosed into National Health in 1975 but eventually folded later in the decade. Stewart formed his own record label Broken Records and recorded a cover version of the Jimmy Ruffin hit, 'What Becomes Of The Broken Hearted', featuring Colin Blunstone on vocals. The record (and label) were picked up by Stiff Records and became a Top 20 UK hit. For the follow-up, Stewart chose his former Hatfield And The North colleague (and by now, lover) Barbara Gaskin to sing lead with Northette Amanda Parsons on backing vocals. The record – 'It's My Party' – reached number 1. Subsequent singles 'Johnny Rocco' and 'The Siamese Cat Song' (from *Lady And The Tramp*) flopped, though 'Busy Doin' Nothin' (from *A Connecticut Yankee In The Court Of King Arthur*) made the Top 50. 'Leipzig' and 'I'm In A Different World' were further failures, but in 1986 they returned with another oldie – Little Eva's 'The Loco-Motion', which scraped into the charts. The duo has continued to record material for their Broken Records label, and remain especially popular in Japan.
● ALBUMS: *The Big Idea* (Broken/Rykodisc 1989) ★★★, *Spin* (Broken 1991) ★★★.
● COMPILATIONS: *Up From The Dark* (Rykodisc 1986) ★★★, *Broken Records: The Singles* (Midi 1987) ★★★, *As Far As Dreams Can Go* (Midi 1988) ★★★, *Selected Tracks* (Musidisc 1993) ★★★.

## STING

b. Gordon Sumner, 2 October 1951, Wallsend, Tyne & Wear, England. Sting's solo career began in 1982, two years before the break-up of the Police, for whom he was lead singer and bass player. In that year he starred in the film *Brimstone And Treacle* and from it released a version of the 30s ballad, 'Spread A Little Happiness', composed by Vivian Ellis. Its novel character and Sting's own popularity ensured Top 20 status in Britain. While continuing to tour and record with the Police, he also co-wrote and appeared on the Dire Straits hit 'Money For Nothing' and sang harmonies on Phil Collins' *No Jacket Required*. By 1985, however, the other members of the Police were pursuing solo interests and Sting formed a touring band, the Blue Turtles. It included leading New York jazz figures such as Branford Marsalis (alto saxophone), Kenny Kirkland (keyboards) and Omar Hakim (drums). The group recorded his first solo album at Eddy Grant's studio in Jamaica before Marsalis and Sting performed at the Live Aid concert with Phil Collins. *The Dream Of The Blue Turtles* found Sting developing the more cerebral lyrics found on the final Police album, *Synchronicity*. It also brought him three big international hits with 'If You Love Somebody Set Them Free' (UK number 26, US number 3), 'Fortress Around Your Heart' (UK number 49, US number 8), and 'Russians' (UK number 12, US number 16).

In 1985, Michael Apted directed *Bring On The Night*, an in concert film about Sting and his touring band (a live album was also released). Following a tour with the Blue Turtles, Sting recorded 1987's *Nothing Like The Sun* (a title taken from a Shakespeare sonnet) with Marsalis and Police guitarist Andy Summers plus guests Rubén Blades, Eric Clapton and Mark Knopfler. The album was an instant success internationally and contained 'They Dance Alone (Gueca Solo)', Sting's tribute to the victims of repression in Argentina, in addition to a notable recording of Jimi Hendrix's 'Little Wing'. This track featured one of the last orchestral arrangements by the late Gil Evans. The same year Sting took part in Amnesty International's *Human Rights Now!* tour and devoted much of the following two years to campaigning and fund-raising activity on behalf of environmental causes, notably highlighting the plight of the Indians of the Brazilian rainforest. He set up his own label, Pangaea, in the late 80s to release material by jazz and *avant garde* artists. In August 1990, a track from *Nothing Like The Sun*, 'An Englishman In New York' (inspired by English eccentric Quentin Crisp), reached number 15 in the UK charts after being remixed by Ben Liebrand.

In 1991, Sting released the autobiographical *The Soul Cages* from which 'All This Time' reached number 5 on the US *Billboard* charts. He continued in a similar vein with *Ten Summoner's Tales*, which contained further high quality hit singles including 'If I Ever Lose My Faith In You' and 'Fields Of Gold'. 'All For Love', a collaboration with Bryan Adams and Rod Stewart for the movie *The Three Musketeers*, topped the US charts in November 1993, and reached number 2 in the UK the following January. The compilation *Fields Of Gold* highlighted Sting's considerable accomplishment as one of the finest quality songwriters to appear out of the second UK 'new wave' boom (post-1977). The collection featured two new tracks, 'When We Dance' and 'This Cowboy Song', the former providing Sting with his highest charting UK solo single when it reached number 9 in October 1994.

Sting spent a traumatic time during the summer of 1995 when he had to testify in court after accusing his accountant of stealing vast sums of his income. The outcome was in the singer's favour and the accountant Keith Moore was jailed for six years. *Mercury Falling* was very much a marking-time album, not as strong as *Ten Summoner's Tales* but good enough to satisfy his fans and placate most reviewers. The title track of his new album, *Brand New Day*, proved he was still capable of achieving hit singles when it reached UK number 13 in September 1999. The album lacked the punch of his more recent work, but struck a chord in America where it enjoyed a long residency on the charts. Similarly low-key and slightly subdued was *All This Time*, a live album recorded on the fateful 11 September

2001. The inclusion of stellar jazz musicians such as Christian McBride and Jason Rebello could not rescue this lacklustre album.

● ALBUMS: *Dream Of The Blue Turtles* (A&M 1985) ★★★, *Bring On The Night* (A&M 1986) ★★, *Nothing Like The Sun* (A&M 1987) ★★★★, *Nado Como El Sol* mini-album (A&M 1988) ★★★, *The Soul Cages* (A&M 1991) ★★★, *Acoustic Live In Newcastle* mini-album (A&M 1991) ★★★, *Ten Summoner's Tales* (A&M 1993) ★★★★, *Mercury Falling* (A&M 1996) ★★★, *Brand New Day* (A&M 1999) ★★★, *All This Time* (A&M 2001) ★★.

● COMPILATIONS: *Fields Of Gold 1984–1994* (A&M 1994) ★★★★, *The Best Of Sting/The Police* (A&M 1997) ★★★★.

● VIDEOS: *Bring On The Night* (A&M Sound Pictures 1987), *Sting: The Videos* (A&M Sound Pictures 1988), *The Soul Cages Concert* (A&M Video 1991), *Live At The Hague* (PolyGram Music Video 1991), *Unplugged* (A&M Video 1992), *Ten Summoner's Tales* (A&M Video 1993), *The Best Of Sting: Fields Of Gold 1984–94* (A&M Video 1994), *The Brand New Day Tour: Live From The Universal Amphitheatre* (PolyGram Music Video 2000), *All This Time* (Universal 2002).

● FURTHER READING: *Sting: A Biography*, Robert Sellers. *The Secret Life Of Gordon Sumner*, Wensley Clarkson. *Complete Guide To The Music Of: The Police And Sting*, Chris Welch. *Demolition Man*, Christopher Sandford.

● FILMS: *Quadrophenia* (1979), *Radio On* (1980), *Artemis '81* (1980), *Brimstone And Treacle* (1982), *Dune* (1984), *Plenty* (1985), *Bring On The Night* (1985), *Stormy Monday* (1988), *Julia Julia* (1988), *Lock, Stock And Two Smoking Barrels* (1998).

## STOCK, AITKEN AND WATERMAN

Modelling themselves on the Motown Records hit factory of the 60s, Mike Stock (b. 3 December 1951, England), Matt Aitken (b. 25 August 1956, England) and Pete Waterman (b. 15 January 1947, Coventry, England) were the most successful team of UK writer/producers during the 80s. Waterman had been a soul disc jockey, promoter, producer and remixer (Adrian Baker's 'Sherry', Susan Cadogan's 1975 Top 5 UK hit 'Hurts So Good'). In 1984, he joined forces with Stock and Aitken, members of pop band Agents Aren't Aeroplanes. The trio first designed records for the thriving British disco scene, having their first hits with singles by Divine ('You Think You're A Man', UK number 16, July 1984), Dead Or Alive ('You Spin Me Round (Like A Record)', UK number 1, March 1985) and Sinitta ('So Macho', 1986). The team specialized in designing songs for specific artists and they gained further UK number 1s in 1987 with 'Respectable' by Mel And Kim and Rick Astley's 'Never Gonna Give You Up'. In that year, too, they released a dance single under their own names, 'Roadblock' reaching UK number 13. A follow-up, 'Mr. Sleaze', reached number 3 as the b-side to Bananarama's 'Love In The First Degree' in October.

In 1988, SAW, as they were now referred to, launched their own PWL label and shifted their attention to the teenage audience. Their main vehicles were Australian soap opera stars Kylie Minogue and Jason

Donovan. Minogue's 'I Should Be So Lucky' was the first of over a dozen Top 10 hits in four years and the epitome of the SAW approach, a brightly produced, tuneful and highly memorable song. Donovan had similar success both with SAW compositions like 'Too Many Broken Hearts' and revivals (Brian Hyland's 'Sealed With A Kiss'). The Stock, Aitken Waterman formula was applied to other artists such as Sonia, Brother Beyond, Big Fun, Donna Summer and the May 1989 charity single 'Ferry 'Cross The Mersey', but by 1991, a change of direction was apparent. Following Astley's example, Jason Donovan had left the fold in search of artistic freedom. Equally significantly, the SAW team was sundered by the departure of its main songwriter Matt Aitken. Stock and Aitken became independent producers, while Waterman stayed busy as PWL branched into three new labels, PWL America, PWL Continental and PWL International. He found even greater success as producer of Steps and as a celebrity judge on the hit television series, Pop Idol.

● COMPILATIONS: *Hit Factory* (PWL 1987) ★★★, *Hit Factory, Volume 2* (PWL 1988) ★★★, *Hit Factory, Volume 3* (PWL 1989) ★★★, *The Best Of Stock, Aitken and Waterman* (PWL 1990) ★★★.

● VIDEOS: *Roadblock* (Touchstone Video 1988).

● FURTHER READING: *I Wish I Was Me*, Pete Waterman.

## STONE ROSES

A classic case of an overnight success stretched over half a decade, the UK band Stone Roses evolved through a motley collection of Manchester-based non-starters such as the Mill, the Patrol, and English Rose before settling down as Stone Roses in 1985. Acclaimed for their early warehouse gigs, at this time the line-up consisted of Ian Brown (b. Ian George Brown, 20 February 1963, Ancoats, Gt. Manchester, England; vocals), John Squire (b. 24 November 1962, Broadheath, Gt. Manchester, England; guitar), Reni (b. Alan John Wren, 10 April 1964, Manchester, England; drums), Andy Couzens (guitar) and Pete Garner (bass).

In their home-town, at least, the band had little trouble in working up a following, in spite of their predilection for juxtaposing leather trousers with elegant melodies. In 1987, guitarist Andy Couzens left, later to form the High, and Pete Garner followed soon after, allowing Gary 'Mani' Mounfield (b. 16 November 1962, Crumpsall, Gt. Manchester, England) to take over bass guitar. By this time, the band had already made a low-key recording debut with the ephemeral 45, 'So Young'. By the end of the year the reconstituted foursome were packing out venues in Manchester, but finding it difficult to attract attention in the rest of the country. A contract with the Silvertone Records label in 1988 produced 'Elephant Stone', and showed its makers to have grasped the essence of classic 60s pop. A year later, they had carried it over the threshold of the independent scene and into the nation's living rooms. When the follow-up, 'Made Of Stone', attracted media attention, the Stone Roses' ball started rolling at a phenomenal pace. Their debut album was hailed in all quarters as a guitar/pop

classic, and as the Manchester 'baggy' scene infiltrated Britain's consciousness, Stone Roses – alongside the funkier, grubbier Happy Mondays – were perceived to be leaders of the flare-wearing pack.

By the close of 1989, the Roses had moved from half-filling London's dingiest clubs to playing to 7,500 people at Alexandra Palace. Having achieved such incredible success so quickly, when the band vanished to work on new material, the rumour mongers inevitably came out in force. In 1990, 'One Love' reached the UK Top 10, but aside from this singular vinyl artefact, the media was mainly concerned with the band's rows with a previous record company, who had reissued old material accompanied by a video made without the band's permission. This resulted in the band vandalizing the company's property, which in turn led to a much publicized court case. As if this was not enough, Stone Roses were back in court when they tried to leave Silvertone, who took an injunction out against their valuable protégés. This prevented any further Stone Roses material from being released, even though the band eventually won their case and signed to Geffen Records for a reported $4 million. At the end of 1991, their eagerly awaited new product was still stuck somewhere in the pipeline while, in true Stone Roses fashion, after their live extravaganzas at Spike Island, Glasgow, London and Blackpool, plans were afoot for a massive open-air comeback gig the following spring. It never happened that year, or the next. In fact, the Stone Roses' absence from the limelight – initially through contractual problems with Silvertone and management squabbles – then seemingly through pure apathy, became something of an industry standing joke. Had their debut album not had such a huge impact on the public consciousness they would surely have been forgotten.

Painstaking sessions with a series of producers finally saw the immodestly titled *Second Coming* released in 1995. It was announced in an exclusive interview given to *The Big Issue*, the UK magazine dedicated to helping the homeless, much to the chagrin of a slavering British music press. Almost inevitably, it failed to meet expectations, despite the fact that the US market was now opening up for the band. They also lost drummer Reni, who was replaced within weeks of its release by Robbie Maddix, who had previously played with Manchester rapper Rebel MC. Promotional gigs seemed less natural and relaxed than had previously been the case, while Silvertone milked the last gasp out of the band's legacy with them to compile a second compilation album (from only one original studio set). The tour they undertook in late 1995 dispelled any further gossip about loss of form or break-ups and nudged them back into the minds of critics who were beginning to see the band in a less than favourable light. In interview, it was clear that Squire was becoming disenchanted; he would not always show a united front, admitting that they had lost much by having such a gap between releases. It was, therefore, not too great a shock when he announced his departure in April 1996. Squire's carefully worded official statement read: 'It is with great regret that I feel compelled to announce my decision to leave. I believe all concerned will benefit from a parting of the ways at this point and I see this as the inevitable conclusion to the gradual social and musical separation we have undergone in the past few years. I wish them every success and hope they go on to greater things.'

This left Ian Brown and company faced with deciding on a concrete plan of action or becoming another memorable rock legend. They chose the former and only commented on Squire's departure at the 1996 Reading Festival, where they were headlining. Speaking positively, Brown said that Squire had been a barrier for the band playing live. With new members Aziz Ibrahim (guitar) and Nigel Ippinson (keyboards), they planned to be much more active. The press reports were a different matter. Most sources confirmed that Brown's vocals were so off-key it was excruciating to have to listen. They made the right decision in October 1996 by announcing their demise. Mani joined Primal Scream full-time and ex-guitarist John Squire was retained by their record company Geffen, going on to form the Seahorses. Brown, meanwhile, embarked on a solo career. Too much was against the Stone Roses to survive together either creatively or socially.

● ALBUMS: *The Stone Roses* (Silvertone 1989) ★★★★★, *Second Coming* (Geffen 1995) ★★★.

● COMPILATIONS: *Turns Into Stone* (Silvertone 1992) ★★★, *The Complete Stone Roses* (Silvertone 1995) ★★★, *Garage Flower* (Silvertone 1996) ★★, *The Remixes* (Silvertone 2000) ★★.

● VIDEOS: *The Complete Stone Roses* (Wienerworld 1995).

● FURTHER READING: *The Stone Roses And The Resurrection Of British Pop*, John Robb. *Breaking Into Heaven: The Rise And Fall Of The Stone Roses*, Mick Middles.

## STRAIT, GEORGE

b. 18 May 1952, Poteet, Texas, USA. Strait, the second son of a schoolteacher, was raised in Pearsall, Texas. When his father took over the family ranch, he developed an interest in farming. Strait heard country music throughout his youth but the record that cemented his love was Merle Haggard's *A Tribute To The Best Damn Fiddle Player In The World (Or, My Salute To Bob Wills)*. Strait dropped out of college to elope with his girlfriend, Norma, and then enlisted in the US Army. While there, he began playing country music. While at university studying agriculture, he founded the Ace In The Hole band (his 1989 US country number 1, 'Ace In The Hole', was not about his band, nor did it feature them). In 1976, he briefly recorded for Pappy Daily's D Records in Houston, one title being 'That Don't Change The Way I Feel About You'. Starting in 1977, Strait made trips to Nashville, but he was too shy to do himself justice. Disillusioned, he considered a return to Texas but his wife urged him to persevere. A club owner he had worked for, Erv Woolsey, was working for MCA Records; he signed him to the label and then became his manager.

In 1981, Strait's first single, 'Unwound', made number 6 in the US country charts. After two further hits, 'Fool Hearted Memory', from *The Soldier*, a movie in which he had a cameo role, went to number 1. Strait was unsure about the recitation on 'You Look So Good In Love', but it was another chart-topper and led to him calling a racehorse Looks Good In Love. Strait's run of 18 US country number 1 hits also included 'Does Fort Worth Ever Cross Your Mind?' (1985), 'Nobody In His Right Mind Would've Left Her' (1986), 'Am I Blue' (1987), 'Famous Last Words Of A Fool' (1988) and 'Baby's Gotten Good At Goodbye' (1989). Strait was a throwback to the 50s honky-tonk sound of country music. He used twin fiddles and steel guitar and his strong, warm delivery was similar to that of Haggard and Lefty Frizzell. He made no secret of his influences, recording a fine tribute to Frizzell, 'Lefty's Gone'. Strait suffered a personal tragedy when his daughter, Jennifer, died in a car accident in 1986. Managing to compose himself, *Ocean Front Property* became the first album to enter *Billboard*'s country music chart at number 1, and it included another classic single, 'All My Ex's Live In Texas', which also demonstrated his love of western swing. The white-Stetsoned Strait, who also manages to run a large farm, became one of the USA's top concert attractions, winning many awards from the Country Music Association, but it was only in 1989 that he became their Entertainer Of The Year.

After the impressive *Chill Of An Early Fall*, Strait enjoyed a major commercial success with a starring role in the movie *Pure Country*. The magnificent box set *Strait Out Of The Box* demonstrates how consistent he has been over the years. Among the previously unissued tracks is a bizarre duet of 'Fly Me To The Moon', featuring that well-known honky tonk singer Frank Sinatra. A box set retrospective often indicates that a career is nearing its end, but *Lead On* in 1994 and *Clear Blue Sky* in 1996 were as good as anything he has recorded, the latter making its debut at number 1 on the *Billboard* country chart. The title track also became his twenty-sixth US country number 1. *Carrying Your Love With Me*, another excellent collection, put Strait up there with the leading male country artists of the 90s – even though the creases on his jeans are dangerously straight. His status was confirmed when he picked up awards for best male artist and best album at the 1997 CMA Awards. *Always Never The Same* confirmed Strait's enormous popularity, debuting at number 6 on the mainstream *Billboard* 200 in March 1999.

● ALBUMS: *Strait Country* (MCA 1981) ★★★★, *Strait From The Heart* (MCA 1982) ★★★, *Right Or Wrong* (MCA 1983) ★★★, *Does Fort Worth Ever Cross Your Mind?* (MCA 1984) ★★★★, *Something Special* (MCA 1985) ★★, *No. 7* (MCA 1986) ★★★, *Merry Christmas Strait To You!* (MCA 1986) ★★★, *Ocean Front Property* (MCA 1987) ★★★★, *If You Ain't Lovin' (You Ain't Livin')* (MCA 1988) ★★★★, *Beyond The Blue Neon* (MCA 1989) ★★★, *Livin' It Up* (MCA 1990) ★★, *Chill Of An Early Fall* (MCA 1991) ★★★★, *Holding My Own* (MCA 1992) ★★★, *Pure Country* film soundtrack (MCA 1992) ★★★, *Easy Come, Easy Go*

(MCA 1993) ★★★, *Lead On* (MCA 1994) ★★★★, *Clear Blue Sky* (MCA 1996) ★★★★, *Carrying Your Love With Me* (MCA 1997) ★★★★, *One Step At A Time* (MCA 1998) ★★★, *Always Never The Same* (MCA 1999) ★★★★, *Merry Christmas Wherever You Are* (MCA 1999) ★★, *George Strait* (MCA 2000) ★★★, *Road Less Traveled* (MCA 2001) ★★★.

● COMPILATIONS: *Greatest Hits* (MCA 1985) ★★★★, *Greatest Hits, Volume 2* (MCA 1987) ★★★★, *Strait Out Of The Box* 4-CD box set (MCA 1995) ★★★★, *The Very Best Of George Strait, Vol. 2 (1988-1993)* (Universal 1998) ★★★★, *Latest Greatest Straitest Hits* (MCA 2000) ★★★, *20th Century Masters The Millennium Collection* (MCA 2002) ★★★★.

● VIDEOS: *The Man In Love With You* (MCA Music Video 1994), *Pure Country* (MCA Music Video 1995), *Live!* (MCA Music Video 1997).

● FURTHER READING: *George Strait: The Story Of Country's Living Legend*, Mark Bego.

● FILMS: *The Soldier* (1982), *Pure Country* (1992)

## STRAWBERRY SWITCHBLADE

This colourful duo, comprising Jill Bryson (vocals, guitar) and Rose McDowall (vocals, guitar), emerged as a product of the late 70s Glasgow, Scotland punk scene. Their appearance in polka-dotted frocks with frills, ribbons, flowers and cheap jewellery unfortunately distracted attention from their songwriting. Despite sounding like a happy pop band, their lyrics expressed sadness. The debut single in 1983, 'Trees And Flowers', was written as a result of Bryson's agoraphobia. Signed to the independent Ninety-Two Happy Customers label (under the aegis of producers David Balfe and Bill Drummond) this melancholy song was given a pastoral feel by the oboe playing of former Ravishing Beauties member Kate St. John. With added studio assistance from Roddy Frame (guitar) of Aztec Camera and Madness' Mark Bedford (bass), the single reached number 4 in the UK Independent chart. The duo found national success in late 1984 with the chirpy 'Since Yesterday' and were fêted by the music media. An over-produced debut album, far removed from the simplicity of 'Trees And Flowers', entered the UK Top 30 but failed to supply the duo with the expected run of hit singles. Their last hit came in 1985 with a cover version of Dolly Parton's classic, 'Jolene'. Following their break-up, McDowall attempted to revive her career in the late 80s, for a time working under the name Candy Cane, but she met with little success. She also recorded with Felt and Psychic TV.

● ALBUMS: *Strawberry Switchblade* (Korova 1985) ★★.

## STRAY CATS

With high-blown quiffs and 50s 'cat' clothes, Brian Setzer (b. 10 April 1959, Massapequa, New York, USA; guitar/vocals), Lee Rocker (b. Leon Drucher, 1961; double bass) and Slim Jim Phantom (b. Jim McDonnell, 20 March 1961; drums) emerged from New York's Long Island as the most commercially viable strand of the rockabilly resurgence in the early 80s – though they had to migrate to England initially to find chart success. Their exhilarating

repertoire was dominated by the works of artists such as Carl Perkins and Eddie Cochran in addition to some stylized group originals, but their taste was sufficiently catholic to also acknowledge the influence of later rock 'n' roll practitioners such as Creedence Clearwater Revival and Joe Ely. Probably their most iconoclastic re-working, however, was their arrangement of the Supremes' 'You Can't Hurry Love' that appeared on the b-side of their second single, 1981's 'Rock This Town'. This shared the same UK chart position as their earlier, debut hit, 'Runaway Boys', reaching number 9. 'Stray Cat Strut', produced by Dave Edmunds, was another hit as was the trio's debut album, but 1981 closed with the comparative failure of both *Gonna Ball* and 'You Don't Believe Me'.

The band was buoyed by the US success of *Built For Speed*, however, which combined the best of the two UK albums and rocketed to number 2 on the album charts, and the belated Top 10 success of 'Rock This Town', 'Stray Cat Strut', and '(She's) Sexy + 17'. Following the release of *Rant N' Rave With The Stray Cats* the band fell apart. Rocker and Phantom amalgamated – as Phantom, Rocker And Slick – with guitarist Earl Slick with whom they appeared on a star-studded televised tribute to Carl Perkins, organized by Edmunds in 1985, and released two lacklustre albums. Setzer released a solo album before reuniting briefly with Phantom and Rocker in order to record 1986's *Rock Therapy*. A more solid reunion took place in 1988, and the trio returned to the lower reaches of the UK charts in 1989 with 'Bring It Back Again'. The attendant *Blast Off!* was a disappointment, however, and after three more albums the unit disbanded. Setzer went on to greater success in the late 90s when his 16-piece orchestra spearheaded America's swing revival. Slim Jim Phantom and Lee Rocker resurfaced as the Swing Cats.

● ALBUMS: *Stray Cats* (Arista 1981) ★★★, *Gonna Ball* (Arista 1981) ★★★, *Built For Speed* US only (EMI America 1982) ★★★, *Rant N' Rave With The Stray Cats* (EMI America/Arista 1983) ★★★, *Rock Therapy* (EMI America 1986) ★★★, *Blast Off!* (EMI 1989) ★★, *Let's Go Faster* (Liberation 1990) ★★, *Choo Choo Hot Fish* (Pump 1992) ★★, *Original Cool* (Blast Off 1993) ★★★, *Rockabilly Rules: At Their Best, Live* (Essential 1999) ★★★, *Hollywood Strut* (Cleopatra 2000) ★★★.

● COMPILATIONS: *Rock This Town: Best Of The Stray Cats* (EMI 1990) ★★★, *Greatest Hits* (EMI 1992) ★★★, *Live: Tear It Up* (Receiver 1994) ★★★, *Rock This Town: A Classic Live Collection* (Receiver 1995) ★★, *Something Else: Live* (Receiver 1995) ★★, *Archive* (Rialto 1996) ★★★, *Runaway Boys: A Retrospective '81-'92* (Capitol 1997) ★★★★, *The Best Of Stray Cats* (Capitol 1998) ★★★, *Live Struttin'* (Big Ear 1999) ★★.

## STYLE COUNCIL

UK band founded in 1983 by Paul Weller (b. John William Weller, 25 May 1958, Woking, Surrey, England) and Mick Talbot (b. 11 September 1958, London, England). Weller had been lead singer of the Jam while Talbot was the former keyboards player with the Merton Parkas, Dexys Midnight

Runners, and the Bureau. Other collaborators included drummer Steve White (b. 31 May 1965, London, England) and singer Dee C. Lee (b. Diane Sealey, 6 June 1961, London, England), whom Weller later married. Weller's avowed aim with the Style Council was to merge his twin interests of soul music and social comment. In this, his most important model was Curtis Mayfield, who later appeared on *The Cost Of Loving*. The continuing popularity of the Jam ensured that all the Style Council's releases in 1983 were UK Top 20 hits. They included 'Speak Like A Child', 'Money-Go-Round (Part 1)', 'Long Hot Summer' and 'A Solid Bond In Your Heart'. Tracey Thorn from Everything But The Girl was a guest vocalist on the debut album, *Café Bleu*. Perhaps the most effective Style Council song was the evocative 'My Ever Changing Moods', the first of three UK Top 10 hits in 1984 and their only substantial US hit. The following year spawned another big UK hit, 'Walls Come Tumbling Down', and the chart-topping album *Our Favourite Shop*.

During the mid-80s, Weller's political activism was at its height as he recorded 'Soul Deep' as the Council Collective with Jimmy Ruffin and Junior Giscombe, aimed at raising funds for the families of striking coal miners, and became a founder-member of Red Wedge, an artists support group for the Labour Party. Style Council appeared at Live Aid in 1985 and in 1986 made a short film, *JerUSAlem*, a satirical attack on the pop music industry. There were continuing UK hits, notably 'Have You Ever Had It Blue' (featured in the 1986 film *Absolute Beginners*) and 'It Didn't Matter' (1987), the band's last UK Top 10 hit. With its eclectic mix of soul, classical and pop influences, 1988's *Confessions Of A Pop Group* was less of a commercial success, and by 1990 the Style Council was defunct. Weller re-emerged the next year with a new band, the Paul Weller Movement, recording for his own Freedom High label, and subsequently became one of the most acclaimed solo artists of the 90s with albums such as *Wild Wood* and *Stanley Road*.

● ALBUMS: *Introducing The Style Council* mini-album (Polydor 1983) ★★★, *Café Bleu* (UK) *My Ever Changing Moods* (US) (Polydor/Geffen 1984) ★★★, *Our Favourite Shop* (UK) *Internationalists* (US) (Polydor/Geffen 1985) ★★★★, *Live! The Style Council, Home & Abroad* (Polydor/Geffen 1986) ★★, *The Cost Of Loving* (Polydor 1987) ★★, *Confessions Of A Pop Group* (Polydor 1988) ★★.

● COMPILATIONS: *The Singular Adventures Of The Style Council: Greatest Hits Vol. 1* (Polydor 1989) ★★★★, *Here's Some That Got Away* (Polydor 1993) ★★, *The Style Council Collection* (Polydor 1996) ★★★, *The Style Council In Concert* (Polydor 1998) ★★, *The Complete Adventures Of The Style Council* 5-CD box set (Polydor 1998) ★★★, *Greatest Hits* (Polydor 2000) ★★★★, *The Collection* (Spectrum 2001) ★★★.

● VIDEOS: *What We Did On Our Holidays* (PolyGram Music Video 1983), *Far East & Far Out: Council Meeting In Japan* (PolyGram Music Video 1984), *What We Did The Following Year* (PolyGram Music Video 1985), *Showbiz!, The Style Council Live* (PolyGram Music Video 1986), *JerUSAlem* (Palace Video 1987), *Confessions Of A Pop Group* (Channel 5 Video 1988), *The Video Adventures Of The Style Council* (Channel 5/PolyGram Music Video 1989).

● FURTHER READING: *Mr Cool's Dream - The Complete History Of The Style Council*, Ian Munn.

## SUBWAY SECT
(see Godard, Vic, And The Subway Sect)

## SUDDEN, NIKKI
Following the dissolution of premier UK art punk band Swell Maps, former lead singer and driving force Sudden (b. Nicholas Godley, 19 July 1956, London; guitar, vocals) joined the Abstract label to release *Waiting On Egypt*. He had continued to make music erratically before this. Among these recordings were sessions with Another Pretty Face (later Mike Scott's Waterboys) in Christmas 1980. His first solo single was 'Back To The Start' on Rather Records, before the release of 'Channel Steamer', which would form part of the debut album. He was pleased with the results: 'Nearly everyone I know thinks it's the best thing I've ever done and I must admit when I listen to it I get a pleasant surprise'. Also included were 'Forest Fire' and 'New York', both unreleased Swell Maps songs. The nucleus of musicians that he employed included Scott (guitar), Steve Burgess (bass), Anthony Thistlethwaite (saxophone), and Empire (ex-Television Personalities) on drums. Following *The Bible Belt* in 1983 Sudden would work extensively with Dave Kusworth as the Jacobites, releasing over half a dozen albums for Glass and Creation Records. He also wrote for several music magazines including the later issues of *Zig Zag* during this period, subsequently collaborating on projects with Roland S. Howard. His 1991 solo release, *The Jewel Thief*, saw him working with long-time fans R.E.M. In 1993, Sudden re-formed the Jacobites with Kusworth.

● ALBUMS: *Waiting On Egypt* (Abstract 1982) ★★★, *The Bible Belt* (Flicknife 1983) ★★★, with Rowland S. Howard *Kiss You Kidnapped Charabanc* (Creation 1987) ★★★, with Jeremy Gluck, Rowland S. Howard *I Knew Buffalo Bill* (Flicknife 1987) ★★, with the French Revolution *Groove* (Creation 1989) ★★★, *The Jewel Thief* (Creation 1991) ★★★, *Seven Lives Later* (Idiot Savant 1996) ★★, *Red Brocade* (Wagging Dog 2001) ★★★★.

● COMPILATIONS: *The Last Bandit: The Best Of Nikki Sudden* (Glitterhouse 2000) ★★★★.

## SUGARCUBES
This offbeat pop band was formed in Reykjavik, Iceland, on 8 June 1986, the date taken from the birth of Björk's son Sindri. The settled line-up featured Björk Gudmundsdottir (b. 21 November 1965, Reykjavik, Iceland; vocals, keyboards), Bragi Olaffson (bass), Einar Orn Benediktsson (vocals, trumpet), Margret 'Magga' Ornolfsdottir (keyboards, replacing original keyboard player Einar Mellax), Sigtryggur 'Siggi' Baldursson (drums), and Thor Eldon (guitar). Björk's stepfather was in a rock showband, and after early stage appearances she completed her first album at the age of 11. She was also the singer for prototype groups Tappi Tíkarrass

then Theyr, alongside Siggi Baldursson. The latter band shot to prominence when Jaz Coleman and Youth (Killing Joke) mysteriously appeared in Iceland in March 1982, paranoid about an impending apocalypse, and collaborated on several projects with Theyr. Björk, Benediktsson and Baldursson then went on to form Kukl, who toured Europe and released two records on the Crass label, establishing a link with the UK anarcho-punk scene that would be cemented when the band joined UK independent label One Little Indian Records.

The Sugarcubes' debut single, 'Birthday', and album, *Life's Too Good*, saw the band championed in the UK press almost immediately. In particular, praise was heaped on Björk's distinctive and emotive vocals. The Sugarcubes ran their own company in Iceland called Bad Taste, an organization that encompassed an art gallery, poetry bookshop, record label, radio station, and publishing house. Björk's ex-husband Thor Eldon, a graduate in media studies from London Polytechnic and the band's guitarist, sired their son Sindri under a government incentive scheme to boost the island's population, the financial rewards for this action allowing him to buy a pair of contact lenses. He then married Magga Ornolfsdottir (ex-the Giant Lizard), who joined the band in time for their second album. In addition, Siggi Baldursson and Bragi Olaffson, the band's rhythm section, were brother-in-laws, having married twin sisters. Most bizarre of all, however, was the subsequent marriage of Einar Benediktsson and Bragi Olaffson in Denmark in 1989, the first openly gay marriage in pop history. *Here Today, Tomorrow, Next Week*, its title taken from a line in Kenneth Graeme's book *Wind In The Willows*, was a much more elaborate album, with a full brass section on 'Tidal Wave' and strings on the single 'Planet'. However, compared with the rapturous reception granted their first album, *Here Today* took a critical pasting. Even label boss Derek Birkett conceded that it was far too deliberate. The press was also quick to seize on the fact that Benediktsson's vocal interjections detracted from the band's performance.

After much touring, the band returned to Reykjavik, where they followed their own interests for a time. Björk collaborated on the Bad Taste album *Glimg Glo*: 'Just Icelandic pop songs from the 50s with jazz influences'. Baldursson also contributed drums. Members of the band spent time as an alternative jazz orchestra. The band then played a concert for President Mitterand of France, in Reykjavik, and Björk joined 808 State on their *Ex:El* album and single, 'Oops'. The Sugarcubes' third album found them in favour with the music press and back in the charts with 'Hit', but the inevitable happened shortly afterwards, with Björk heading for a critically and commercially rewarding solo career.

● ALBUMS: *Life's Too Good* (One Little Indian 1988) ★★★★, *Here Today, Tomorrow, Next Week* (One Little Indian 1989) ★★, *Stick Around For Joy* (One Little Indian 1992) ★★★, *It's It* remixes (One Little Indian 1992) ★★.

● COMPILATIONS: *The Great Crossover Potential* (One Little Indian 1998) ★★★.

## SUGARHILL GANG

Englewood, New Jersey, USA troupe, whose 'Rapper's Delight' was hip-hop's breakthrough single and paved the way for the mainstream success of rap music in the 80s. They gave the music an identity and a calling card in the first line of the song: 'A hip-hop, The hi-be, To the hi-be, The hip-hip-hop, You don't stop rockin'. Master G (b. Guy O'Brien, 1963), Wonder Mike (b. Michael Wright, 1958) and Big Bank Hank (b. Henry Jackson, 1958) saw massive international success in 1979 with 'Rapper's Delight', based on the subsequently widely borrowed rhythm track from Chic's 'Good Times', over which the trio offered a series of sly boasts which were chatted rather than sung. Sugarhill Records boss Joe Robinson later commented on the song's elevation to commercial status: 'no 15 minute record has ever got played on the radio, so I said, what am I gonna do with this? But all I had to do with it was get one play anywhere and it broke'. Considered at the time to be something of a novelty item, 'Rapper's Delight' was significantly more than that. Sylvia and Joe Robinson had recruited the three rappers on an *ad hoc* basis. Hank was a former bouncer and pizza waiter, and brought fresh rhymes from his friend Grandmaster Caz, although the pair subsequently fell out over compensation for the use of Caz's lyrics. The backing was offered by Positive Force, a group from Pennsylvania who enjoyed their own hit with 'We Got The Funk', but became part of the Sugarhill phenomenon when 'Rapper's Delight' struck. They would go on to tour on the Sugarhill Gang's early live shows, before the Sugarhill house band took over. Smaller hits followed with 'The Love In You' (1979) and 'Kick It Live From 9 To 5' (1982), before the group faded and fell apart in the early 80s. The Sugarhill Gang was already assured of their place in hip-hop's history, even if reports that Big Bank Hank was working as a Englewood garbage man were correct.

● ALBUMS: *Rapper's Delight* (Sugarhill 1980) ★★★, *8th Wonder* (Sugarhill 1982) ★★, *Jump On It!* (Kid Rhino 1999) ★★.

● COMPILATIONS: *Rapper's Delights* (Sequel 1999) ★★★.

## SUMMERS, ANDY

b. Andrew Somers, 31 December 1942, Poulton-le-Fylde, Lancashire, England. Raised in Bournemouth, Dorset, Summers was performing in the city's clubs and coffee-bars while still a teenager. He first encountered Zoot Money in the Don Robb Band, a local cabaret attraction, and later joined the ebullient singer in his Big Roll Band. This excellent soul/R&B group became one of the leading acts of the London club circuit during the mid-60s. Summers retained his association with Money in Dantalian's Chariot and the US-based New Animals. When the latter broke up in 1968, the guitarist remained in California where he studied classical styles, joined a Latino-rock band, and acted with various Hollywood theatre groups. He returned to England in 1973 and over the next four years Summers toured with several contrasting artists, including Neil Sedaka, David Essex, Kevin Coyne and Kevin Ayers. In May

1977, he played guitar in a temporary unit, Strontium 90, which also included Sting (bass) and Stewart Copeland (drums). Summers so impressed the duo they asked him to join their full-time outfit, the Police. The guitarist remained with this hugely successful band until they split-up after the release of 1983's *Synchronicity*.

A superbly inventive musician, he did much to popularize the use of the 'flanging' effect, Summers' embarked on several projects; his finely honed skills were more fully developed on *I Advance Unmasked*, a collaboration with King Crimson's Robert Fripp. Ensuing solo albums have enhanced the guitarist's reputation for both excellence and imagination, in particular his interpretations of the music of Thelonious Monk (*Green Chimneys*) and Charles Mingus (*Peggy's Blue Skylight*).

● ALBUMS: with Robert Fripp *I Advance Masked* (A&M 1982) ★★★★, with Fripp *Bewitched* (A&M 1984) ★★★, *XYZ* (MCA 1987) ★★, *Mysterious Barricades* (Private Music 1988) ★★★, *The Golden Wire* (Private Music 1989) ★★★★, *Charming Snakes* (Private Music 1990) ★★★★, *World Gone Strange* (Private Music 1991) ★★, with John Etheridge *Invisible Threads* (Mesa 1993) ★★★, *Synaesthesia* (CMP 1996) ★★★, *The Last Dance Of Mr. X* (RCA Victor 1997) ★★★, with Victor Biglione *Strings Of Desire* (RCA Victor 1998) ★★★★, *Green Chimneys: The Music Of Thelonious Monk* (RCA Victor 1999) ★★★★, *Peggy's Blue Skylight* (RCA Victor 2000) ★★★★.

● COMPILATIONS: *A Windham Hill Retrospective* (Windham Hill 1998) ★★★★.

## SURVIVOR

This sophisticated melodic US rock band was put together by guitarists Jim Peterik (formerly of the Ides Of March) and Frankie Sullivan in 1978. Recruiting vocalist Dave Bickler, they recorded their self-titled debut as a three-piece. This featured a potpourri of ideas that had no definite direction or style. They expanded the band to a quintet in 1981, with the addition of Marc Doubray (drums) and Stephen Ellis (bass). From this point on, the band were comparable in approach to the AOR rock styles of Styx, Foreigner and Journey, but never achieved the same degree of recognition or success. Their first short-lived flirtation with glory came with the song 'Eye Of The Tiger', used as the theme to the *Rocky III* movie. The single, with its heavy drumbeat and rousing chorus, became a worldwide number 1 hit in 1982, and is still a staple of FM radio and various advertising campaigns. Unfortunately, the rest of the songs on the album of the same name were patchy in comparison. Nevertheless, the work succeeded on the strength of the title cut, peaking at numbers 2 and 12 on the US and UK album charts, respectively.

*Caught In The Game*, released the following year, was a more satisfying album. It adopted a heavier approach and featured a more up-front guitar sound from Sullivan, but did not find favour with the record-buying public. Bickler was fired at this stage and replaced by ex-Cobra vocalist Jimi Jamison, whose vocals added an extra, almost soulful dimension to the band. The resulting *Vital Signs* gave the band

their second breakthrough. It enjoyed a six-month residency on the *Billboard* album chart, reaching number 16 as its highest position, and spawned two Top 10 hits with 'High On You' and 'The Search Is Over'. They recorded 'Burning Heart' (essentially a re-tread of 'Eye Of The Tiger') as the theme song to *Rocky IV* in 1986 and achieved another international hit, reaching number 5 on the UK singles chart. Surprisingly, the song was not included on *When Seconds Count*, which pursued a heavier direction once more. The band had contracted to a three-piece nucleus of Jamison, Sullivan and Peterik at this juncture and used session musicians to finish the album. *Too Hot To Sleep* was probably the most consistent and strongest album of the band's career, featuring a collection of commercially minded, hard rock anthems. The album made little commercial impact and they finally disbanded in 1989. Bickler, Sullivan, Ellis and Doubray reunited in 1997, and were later joined by Jamison.

● ALBUMS: *Survivor* (Scotti Bros 1979) ★★, *Premonition* (Scotti Bros 1981) ★★, *Eye Of The Tiger* (Scotti Bros 1982) ★★, *Caught In The Game* (Scotti Bros 1983) ★★★, *Vital Signs* (Scotti Bros 1984) ★★★, *When Seconds Count* (Scotti Bros 1986) ★★, *Too Hot To Sleep* (Scotti Bros 1988) ★★★.

● COMPILATIONS: *Greatest Hits* (Scotti Bros 1990) ★★★, *Prime Cuts: Classic Tracks* (PolyGram 1998) ★★★, *Fire In Your Eyes: Greatest Hits* (PolyGram 2001) ★★★.

## SWEETHEARTS OF THE RODEO

Sisters Janis and Kristine Oliver grew up in California and spent much time harmonizing. In 1973, they started working as an acoustic duo, taking their name from a Byrds album. Although they mostly performed contemporary country rock songs, they also had some traditional country leanings. They both married, becoming Janis Gill and Kristine Arnold. Janis went to Nashville with her then husband, Vince Gill, who became one of the first of the 'new country' singers. Janis invited her sister to Nashville, where they won a major talent contest. In 1986, the duo recorded their first album, *Sweethearts Of The Rodeo*, which yielded five US country singles including 'Hey Doll Baby'. By and large, Kristine is the lead singer and Janis the songwriter, although their wide repertoire includes 'I Feel Fine' and 'So Sad (To Watch Good Love Go Bad)'. The long delay before Columbia Records released *Sisters* led to rumours that the duo's time at the label was drawing to a close. This was confirmed by a move to Sugar Hill Records, for whom the sisters released two albums characterised, as ever, by their beautiful harmony singing. Janis changed her name to Janis Oliver Cummins in November 2000, following her marriage to Roy Cummins. She had separated from Vince Gill in April 1997.

● ALBUMS: *Sweethearts Of The Rodeo* (Columbia 1986) ★★★, *One Time, One Night* (Columbia 1988) ★★★, *Buffalo Zone* (Columbia 1990) ★★★, *Sisters* (Columbia 1992) ★★★, *Rodeo Waltz* (Sugar Hill 1993) ★★★, *Beautiful Lies* (Sugar Hill 1996) ★★★.

● COMPILATIONS: *Anthology* (Renaissance 2000) ★★★★.

## SWING OUT SISTER

A brace of sparkling pop hits in late 1986/early 1987 marked a fine opening for UK jazz/pop trio Swing Out Sister. 'Breakout' (number 4) and 'Surrender' (number 7) preceded *It's Better To Travel*, which topped the UK album charts. 'Breakout' also provided the band with a US Top 10 single in autumn 1987. The band was formed by Corinne Drewery (vocals), Andrew Connell (keyboards) and Martin Jackson (drums). Connell had played for many years in the respected Manchester funk/new-wave band A Certain Ratio while Jackson had drummed with various Manchester bands including Magazine and the Chameleons. A management link-up saw the pair join forces with fashion designer Drewery whose father had been a member of the Nottingham-based Junco Partners. Jackson left the band soon after *It's Better To Travel* and did not play on the follow-up, *Kaleidoscope World*, although he helped program drum machines on several tracks. Connell, a grade eight pianist and fan of Burt Bacharach and Herb Alpert, injected an orchestrated, spacious element into songs like 'Forever Blue' and 'Masquerade', assisted by producer Paul O'Duffy. The album did not contain as much commercial punch as *It's Better To Travel* but was warmly received by critics and reached number 3 on the UK album chart. The duo eschewed a heavy workload and seemed to be happy releasing records intermittently on their own idiosyncratic terms, enjoying particular acclaim in Japan. In 1994, they put together a full band, featuring Derick Johnson (bass), Myke Wilson (drums), Tim Cansfield (guitar), John Thrikell (trumpet) and Gary Plumey (saxophone) for the release of *The Living Return*. After that album's acid jazz departures, *Shapes And Patterns* marked a return to the cheery pop sound of their early releases. The duo's subsequent releases have been confined to the Japanese market.

● ALBUMS: *It's Better To Travel* (Mercury 1987) ★★★★, *Kaleidoscope World* (Fontana 1989) ★★★, *Get In Touch With Yourself* (Fontana 1992) ★★★, *The Living Return* (Mercury 1994) ★★, *Shapes And Patterns* (Fontana 1997) ★★★, *Filth And Dreams* (Mercury 1999) ★★, *Somewhere Deep In The Night* (Universal 2001) ★★★★.

● COMPILATIONS: *Swing Out Singles* (Mercury 1992) ★★★★, *The Best Of Swing Out Sister* (Fontana 1996) ★★★★.

● VIDEOS: *And Why Not* (Phonogram 1987), *Kaleidoscope World* (Phonogram 1989).

## SYLVIAN, DAVID

b. David Batt, 23 February 1958, Beckenham, Kent, England. Sylvian's androgynous image and ethereal vocals made him a prominent figure in leading New Romantic band Japan. Just before their break-up in late 1982, he branched out into a new venture recording with Ryûichi Sakamoto of the Yellow Magic Orchestra (with whom he had already collaborated on a track from Japan's *Gentlemen Take Polaroids*). The duo's 'Bamboo House' reached number 30 in the UK and the collaboration continued the following July with 'Forbidden Colours', the haunting theme to the movie *Merry*

Christmas, Mr. Lawrence reaching number 16. Sylvian's own 'Red Guitar' reached number 17 the following June, but he soon gained a reputation as an uncompromising artist, intent on working at his own pace and to his own agenda. Released in June 1984, the atmospheric *Brilliant Trees* reached the UK Top 5 and was widely acclaimed. Over two years elapsed before the double album follow-up *Gone To Earth*, which fared less well. Sylvian returned to the pop fringe with 'Let The Happiness In', but his love of experimentation was still present, as collaborations with former Can member Holger Czukay on the ambient collections *Plight & Premonition* and *Flux + Mutability* emphasized. Sylvian subsequently joined former Japan colleagues (minus Dean) on a 1991 reunion project under the moniker of Rain Tree Crow. Another collaboration with Sakamoto in 1992 with 'Heartbeat (Tainai Kaiki II)' briefly dented the charts, after which Sylvian worked on an album and toured with Robert Fripp. After moving to the USA, Sylvian began work on his long overdue new solo album. *Dead Bees On A Cake* finally appeared in February 1999. Even with less than first class songs, Sylvian possesses a voice so good that it flatters anything he touches.

● ALBUMS: *Brilliant Trees* (Virgin 1984) ★★★★, *Alchemy (An Index Of Possibilities)* cassette only (Virgin 1985) ★★, *Gone To Earth* (Virgin 1986) ★★★, *Secrets Of The Beehive* (Virgin 1987) ★★★, with Holger Czukay *Plight & Premonition* (Virgin 1988) ★★★, with Holger Czukay *Flux + Mutability* (Virgin 1989) ★★★, with Russell Mills *Ember Glance* (Virgin 1991) ★★★, with Robert Fripp *The First Day* (Virgin 1993) ★★★, with Robert Fripp *Damage* (Virgin 1994) ★★★, *Dead Bees On A Cake* (Virgin 1999) ★★★, *Approaching Silence* (Virgin/Shakti 1999) ★★★.

● COMPILATIONS: *Weatherbox* 5-CD box set (Virgin 1989) ★★★, *Everything And Nothing* (Virgin 2000) ★★★★, *Camphor* (Virgin 2002) ★★★.

● VIDEOS: with Robert Fripp *Live In Japan* (VAP 1995).

● FURTHER READING: *David Sylvian: 80 Days*, D. Zornes, H. Sawyer and H. Powell. *The Last Romantic*, Martin Power.

## T'PAU

Formed in 1986, this UK band began as a songwriting partnership between vocalist Carol Decker (b. 10 September 1957, England) and guitarist Ronnie Rogers (b. 13 March 1959, Shrewsbury, England). While recording a demonstration disc, they were joined by session musicians Michael Chetwood (b. 26 August 1954, Shrewsbury, England; keyboards), Paul Jackons (b. 8 August 1961; bass) and Tim Burgess (b. 6 October 1961, Shrewsbury, England; drums). The band then signed to Virgin Records subsidiary Siren as T'Pau, the name being taken from a character in the science fiction television series *Star Trek*. Having acquired the services of producer Roy Thomas Baker, T'Pau recorded their first sessions in Los Angeles. Their first two singles failed to make any impact in the UK market, until 'Heart And Soul' abruptly established them in the US charts, where it climbed to number 4 in 1987. The song was re-promoted in Britain and repeated that chart placing. In order to bolster the line-up, lead guitarist Dean Howard was recruited and a major UK tour followed. Decker's strong, expressive vocals were highlighted on 'China In Your Hand', which topped the UK charts, a feat repeated by *Bridge Of Spies*. Further UK Top 20 hits with 'Valentine' (number 9), 'I Will Be With You' (number 14), 'Secret Garden' (number 18) and 'Whenever You Need Me' (number 16) consolidated their standing, without threatening a return to peak form. Following their break-up in 1991 Decker embarked on an abortive solo career, while Rogers returned to studio work. Decker re-formed the band for 1998's *Red*, which was released on their Gnatfish label. Decker also started an acting career, appearing in *Nine Dead Gay Guys* in 2001.

● ALBUMS: *Bridge Of Spies* (Siren 1987) ★★★, *Rage* (Siren 1988) ★★, *The Promise* (Siren 1991) ★★, *Red* (Gnatfish 1998) ★★.

● COMPILATIONS: *Heart And Soul: The Very Best Of T'Pau* (Virgin 1992) ★★★, *The Greatest Hits* (Virgin 1995) ★★★.

● VIDEOS: *View From A Bridge* (Virgin Video 1988).

## TALK TALK

Formed in 1981, this high quality UK band comprised Mark Hollis (b. Tottenham, London, England; vocals), Lee Harris (drums), Paul Webb (bass), Simon Brenner (keyboards). They were soon signed to EMI Records who were intent on moulding them into the same league as stablemates Duran Duran. In fact, they could not have been more different. They went along with their company's ideas for the first album, which produced a number of memorable UK hit singles including 'Today' (number 14, July 1982), 'Talk Talk' (number 23,

November 1982) and 'It's My Life' (number 46, January 1984). Keen to shake off the 'New Romantic' tag, they dismissed their keyboard player to make them a looser, more flexible creative unit. For the next couple of years Hollis spent the time writing new material and assembling a pool of musicians to record a second album. The format was repeated with 1986's highly accessible and mature *The Colour Of Spring*, which included the sublime UK Top 20 hit 'Life's What You Make It'. Both albums were critically acclaimed and proved that the band was a much more creative and imaginative act than their debut had suggested. *Spirit Of Eden*, however, showed their true musical preferences. A solemn six-track record, it had little commercial appeal, and no obvious hit single. It was a remarkable record deserving of a much better fate. Its poor showing led to EMI dropping the band who went on to sign a new contract with Polydor Records. It was three years before another studio album appeared, and to fill in the gap a greatest hits compilation was issued without the band's permission. It nevertheless managed to sell over a million copies and give them three more hit singles. Ironically, their biggest success so far was the EMI reissue of their previous hit, 'It's My Life', which climbed to number 13 in May 1990. *Laughing Stock* picked up where they had left off although like its predecessor it failed to match the catchy commercial appeal of *The Colour Of Spring*.

The group disbanded and it was over seven years, before Hollis broke his silence with an astonishingly quiet and delicate acoustic solo album, recorded with a single pair of microphones, which appeared to have taken his musical vision to its logical conclusion. Talk Talk deserve to be reappraised as during a particularly barren time for UK pop music they were unfairly compared to image seekers with little talent. The imaginative arrangements, ambitious songs, and distinctive vocals of Hollis were rarely off target.

● ALBUMS *The Party's Over* (EMI 1982) ★★, *It's My Life* (EMI 1984) ★★★, *It's My Mix* (EMI 1984) ★★, *The Colour Of Spring* (EMI 1986) ★★★★, *Spirit Of Eden* (Parlophone 1988) ★★★★, *Laughing Stock* (Verve 1991) ★★★, *Hammersmith* 1986 recording (Pond Life 1999) ★★★.

Solo: Mark Hollis *Mark Hollis* (Polydor 1997) ★★★.

● COMPILATIONS: *Natural History: The Very Best Of Talk Talk* (Parlophone 1990) ★★★, *History Revisited: The Remixes* (Parlophone 1991) ★★, *The Very Best Of Talk Talk* (EMI 1997) ★★★, *Asides And Besides* (EMI 1998) ★★, *The Collection* (EMI Gold 2000) ★★★, *Remixed* (EMI 2001) ★.

## TALKING HEADS

One of the most critically acclaimed bands of the post-punk era, Talking Heads pursued an idiosyncratic path of (often) uncompromising brilliance up to their acrimonious break-up in 1991. The band was formed by ex-Rhode Island School of Design, students David Byrne (b. 14 May 1952, Dumbarton, Scotland; vocals, guitar), Chris Frantz (b. Charlton Christopher Frantz, 8 May 1951, Fort Campbell, Kentucky, USA; drums) and Tina

Weymouth (b. Martina Michéle Weymouth, 22 November 1950, Coronado, California, USA; bass). In 1974, the three friends relocated to New York, living and rehearsing in Manhattan and naming themselves Talking Heads (Byrne and Frantz had originally played together as the Artistics). After making their live debut in June 1975 at the punk club CBGB's, they were approached by Seymour Stein of Sire Records, who would eventually sign them. The band's art school background, witty invention and musical unorthodoxy were evident on their intriguingly titled debut, 'Love > Building On Fire', released in December 1976. The line-up was subsequently expanded to include keyboard player/guitarist Jerry Harrison (b. Jeremiah Griffin Harrison, 21 February 1949, Milwaukee, Wisconsin, USA), a former member of Jonathan Richman's Modern Lovers.

After touring extensively, the quartet issued *Talking Heads: 77*, an exhilarating first album, which was widely praised for its verve and intelligence. The highlight of the set was the insistent 'Psycho Killer', a *tour de force* in which singer Byrne displayed his deranged vocal dramatics to the full. His wide-eyed stare, jerky movements and onstage cool reminded many commentators of Anthony Perkins, star of Hitchcock's movie *Psycho*. For their second album, the band turned to Brian Eno as producer. *More Songs About Buildings And Food* was a remarkable work, its title echoing Talking Heads' anti-romantic subject matter. Byrne's eccentric vocal phrasing was brilliantly complemented by some startling rhythm work and the songs were uniformly excellent. The climactic 'The Big Country' a satiric commentary on consumerist America, featured the scathing aside: 'I wouldn't live there if you paid me'. The album also featured one cover version, an interesting reading of Al Green's 'Take Me To The River' which became a US Top 30 hit. Eno's services were retained for the more opaque *Fear Of Music*, which included the popular 'Life During Wartime' and introduced African rhythms on the opening track 'I Zimbra'. Byrne next collaborated with Eno on the adventurous *My Life In The Bush Of Ghosts*, before the band reunited for the striking *Remain In Light*. Recorded with additional personnel including guitarist Adrian Belew, the album explored 'found voices' and African polyrhythms to great effect and boasted the superb 'Once In A Lifetime'. An edited version of this track provided one of the best UK hit singles of 1981.

During the early 80s, the band's extra-curricular activities increased and while Byrne explored ballet on *The Catherine Wheel*, Frantz and Weymouth (man and wife since the first Talking Heads album was released) enjoyed club success with their spin-off project, Tom Tom Club. The live double *The Name Of This Band Is Talking Heads* served as a stopgap until *Speaking In Tongues* appeared in the summer of 1983. As ambitious as ever, the album spawned the band's first US Top 10 single 'Burning Down The House'. While touring with additional guitarist Alex Weir (formerly of the Brothers Four), the band were captured on film by director Jonathan Demme. The edited results were released as *Stop Making Sense*, a groundbreaking concert movie which also spawned a bestselling soundtrack. The excellent *Little Creatures*,

a more accessible offering than their earlier experimental work, featured two strong singles in 'And She Was' and 'Road To Nowhere'. The latter brought the band their biggest UK chart hit (number 6) and was accompanied by an imaginative and highly entertaining video.

In 1986, Byrne moved more forcibly into movies with his directorial debut, the offbeat comedy *True Stories*. The album of the same name featured the band performing version of songs originally sung by the actors. It was two more years before the band reconvened for *Naked*. Recorded in Paris and produced by Steve Lillywhite, the work included musical contributions from keyboard player Wally Badarou and guitarists Yves N'Djock and Johnny Marr. Since then, the four members have branched out into various offshoot ventures. The single and double-album retrospectives released in autumn 1992 provide a fairly definitive assessment of their career, including some interesting rarities, but without doing justice to a band rightly regarded as one of the best and most influential of their time. In 1996, Weymouth, Frantz and Harrison launched a new album as the Heads, with guest vocalists taking the place of Byrne. In 1999, an expanded version of *Stop Making Sense* was released to promote the theatrical release of a remastered edition of the original movie. The original Talking Heads buried the hatchet for long enough to perform at their inauguration into the Rock And Roll Hall Of Fame in March 2002.

● ALBUMS: *Talking Heads: 77* (Sire 1977) ★★★★, *More Songs About Buildings And Food* (Sire 1978) ★★★★, *Fear Of Music* (Sire 1979) ★★★, *Remain In Light* (Sire 1980) ★★★★★, *The Name Of This Band Is Talking Heads* (Sire 1982) ★★★, *Speaking In Tongues* (Sire/EMI 1983) ★★★, *Stop Making Sense* (Sire/EMI 1984) ★★★★, *Little Creatures* (Sire/EMI 1985) ★★★★, *True Stories* (Sire/EMI 1986) ★★★, *Naked* (Sire/EMI 1988) ★★★, as the Heads *No Talking Just Head* (Radioactive/MCA 1996) ★★★, *Stop Making Sense: Special New Edition* (EMI 1999) ★★★★.
● COMPILATIONS: *The Best Of: Once In A Lifetime* (Sire/EMI 1992) ★★★★, *Popular Favorites: Sand In The Vaseline* (Sire/EMI 1992) ★★★★, *12x12 Original Remixes* (EMI 1999) ★★.
● VIDEOS: *Stop Making Sense* (PMI 1985), *True Stories* (PMI 1986), *Storytelling Giant* (PMI 1988), *Stop Making Sense: Special New Edition* (Palm Pictures 1999).
● FURTHER READING: *Talking Heads*, Miles. *The Name Of This Book Is Talking Heads*, Krista Reese. *Talking Heads: The Band And Their Music*, David Gans. *Talking Heads: A Biography*, Jerome Davis. *This Must Be The Place: The Adventures Of Talking Heads In The 20th Century* (US) *Fa Fa Fa Fa Fa Fa: The Adventures Of Talking Heads In The 20th Century* (UK), David Bowman.
● FILMS: *Stop Making Sense* (1984).

## TEARDROP EXPLODES

This Liverpool, Merseyside, England-based band was assembled by vocalist Julian Cope (b. 21 October 1957, Deri, Glamorgan, Wales), a former member of the near mythical Crucial Three, which had featured Ian McCulloch (later of Echo And The Bunnymen) and Pete Wylie (later of Wah!). The Teardrop

Explodes took their name from a page in a Marvel comic and originally came together in late 1978 with a line-up featuring Cope, Michael Finkler (guitar), Paul Simpson (keyboards) and Gary Dwyer (drums). After signing to Bill Drummond and Dave Balfe's Liverpool record label Zoo, they issued 'Sleeping Gas' in early 1979. It was soon followed by the eccentric but appealing 'Bouncing Babies'. By then, Simpson had left for the Wild Swans, to be replaced by Balfe, who had previously appeared in the short-lived Lori And The Chameleons. The exuberant 'Treason (It's Just A Story)' was the Teardrop Explodes' most commercial and exciting offering to date, and was unlucky not to chart. The shaky line-up next lost Finkler, who was replaced by Alan Gill, formerly of Dalek I Love You. A distribution agreement with Phonogram Records coincided with a higher press profile for Cope, which was rewarded with the minor hit 'When I Dream'. *Kilimanjaro* followed and displayed the band as one of the most inventive and intriguing of their era. A re-promoted/remixed version of 'Treason' belatedly charted, as did the stirring 'Passionate Friend'.

By late 1981, Cope was intent on restructuring the line-up; new members included Alfie Agius and Troy Tate. *Wilder* further displayed the wayward talents of Cope, bristling with ideas, unusual melodies and strong arrangements influenced by late 60s psychedelia. When the sessions for a third album broke down, Cope curtailed the band's activities and in 1984 embarked on an erratic, yet often inspired solo career. The irreverently titled *Everybody Wants To Shag The Teardrop Explodes* was posthumously exhumed for release in 1990, using the sessions for that projected third collection.

● ALBUMS: *Kilimanjaro* (Mercury 1980) ★★★, *Wilder* (Mercury 1981) ★★★★, *Everybody Wants To Shag The Teardrop Explodes* (Fontana 1990) ★★.

● COMPILATIONS: *Piano* (Document 1990) ★★★, *The Greatest Hit* (Mercury 2001) ★★★.

## TEARS FOR FEARS

School friends Roland Orzabal (b. Roland Orzabal de la Quintana, 22 August 1961, Portsmouth, Hampshire, England) and Curt Smith (b. 24 June 1961, Bath, Somerset, England) formed Tears For Fears after they had spent their teenage years in bands together, including a ska revivalist combo called Graduate who issued records on the Precision label. After Graduate split in 1981, the duo recorded demos as History Of Headaches. Their new name, Tears For Fears, was drawn from Arthur Janov's book *Prisoners Of Pain*. They signed to Phonogram Records in 1981 while other synthesizer bands, including the Human League and Depeche Mode, were breaking through into the pop field. During this time the duo was augmented by Ian Stanley on keyboards and Manny Elias on drums. Their first two singles, 'Suffer Little Children' and 'Pale Shelter', were unsuccessful but 'Mad World', produced by former Adam And The Ants drummer Chris Hughes, made number 3 in the UK charts in November 1982. Curt Smith, dressed in long overcoats and sporting a pigtail, was touted in the UK as a vaguely alternative teen idol. *The Hurting* showcased a thoughtful,

tuneful band and it topped the UK charts, supplying further Top 10 singles with 'Change' and a reissued 'Pale Shelter'. By *Songs From The Big Chair* Orzabal was handling most of the vocal duties and had taken on the role of chief songwriter. 'Shout' and 'Everybody Wants To Rule The World' were number 1 hit singles in the USA, and the album also reached number 1. The song 'Everybody Wants To Rule The World' was adopted as the theme tune for the Sport Aid famine relief event in 1986 (with a slight change in the title to 'Everybody Wants To Run The World'), giving the band massive exposure.

Tears For Fears took a lengthy break after 1985 and reappeared four years later with a highly changed sound on *The Seeds Of Love*. They shunned their earlier electronic approach and attempted to weave together huge piano and vocal chords in a style reminiscent of the Beatles. Its release was delayed many times as the pair constantly remixed the material. The album featured unknown American vocalist Oleta Adams, who the duo had discovered singing in a hotel bar in Kansas City. Orzabal later produced her debut album. Both the album and single, 'Sowing The Seeds Of Love', were Top 10 hits in the UK and USA, but the lavish arrangements did not receive the same critical approval. The chart failure of subsequent singles marked the beginning of the end for the band as a commercial force. Shortly before the release of 1992's greatest hits set, Smith left the band to begin a solo career (renaming himself Mayfield in 1998). Retaining the name of the band, Orzabal released *Elemental*, the first album to be completed after Smith's departure. A muted response greeted *Raoul And The Kings Of Spain* in 1995. Orzabal's solo debut, released six years later, was a much more satisfying release.

● ALBUMS: *The Hurting* (Mercury 1983) ★★★, *Songs From The Big Chair* (Mercury 1985) ★★★★, *The Seeds Of Love* (Fontana 1989) ★★★, *Elemental* (Mercury 1993) ★★, *Raoul And The Kings Of Spain* (Epic 1995) ★★.

Solo: Curt Smith *Soul On Board* (Mercury 1993) ★, as Mayfield *Mayfield* (Zerodisc 1998) ★. Roland Orzabal *Tom Cats Screaming Outside* (Eagle 2001) ★★★★.

● COMPILATIONS: *Tears Roll Down (Greatest Hits 82–92)* (Fontana 1992) ★★★★, *Saturnine Martial & Lunatic* (Fontana 1996) ★★★, *The Best Of Tears For Fears: The Millennium Collection* (Universal 2000) ★★★★, *The Working Hour: An Introduction To Tears For Fears* (Mercury 2001) ★★★, *Shout: The Very Best Of Tears For Fears* (Mercury 2001) ★★★.

● VIDEOS: *Scenes From The Big Chair* (4 Front Video 1991).

● FURTHER READING: *Tears For Fears*, Ann Greene.

## TECHNO

An easy definition of techno would be percussion-based electronic dance music, characterized by stripped-down drum beats and basslines. However, the real roots of techno can be traced back to the experimental musicologists like Karl Heinz Stockhausen. In terms of equipment there was no greater precedent than that set by Robert Moog, who invented the synthesizer in California, and provoked the first fears of the 'death of real music' that have shadowed electronic recordings ever since. If Chicory Tip's 'Son Of My Father' was the first to employ the Moog in 1972, then Kraftwerk were certainly the first to harness and harvest the possibilities of the synthesizer and other electronic instruments. Kraftwerk served as godfathers to UK electro pop outfits like the Human League (in their early experimental phase) and Depeche Mode. It is hard to imagine now but groups like these and even Gary Numan proved a huge influence on the US hip-hop scene and the development of New York electro in the early 80s (particularly Afrika Bambaataa's 'Planet Rock'). Nevertheless, techno as we now know it descended from the Detroit region, which specialized in a stripped-down, abrasive sound, maintaining some of the soulful elements of the Motown Records palette, over the innovations that hip-hop's electro period had engendered. Techno also reflected the city's decline, as well as the advent of technology, and this tension was crucial to the dynamics of the sound. As Kevin Saunderson recounts: 'When we first started doing this music we were ahead. But Detroit is still a very behind city when it comes to anything cultural.'

Techno as an umbrella term for this sound was first invoked by an article in *The Face* in May 1988, when it was used to describe the work of Saunderson (particularly 'Big Fun'), Derrick May (who recorded techno's greatest anthem, 'Strings Of Life') and Juan Atkins ('No UFO's'). The Detroit labels of note included May's Transmat Records, Juan Atkins' Metroplex, Saunderson's KMS Records, Underground Resistance, Planet E, Red Planet, Submerge and Accelerate. Much like house, the audience for techno proved to be a predominantly British/European one. Labels like Rising High Records and Warp Records in the UK, and R&S Records in Belgium helped build on the innovations of May, Atkins and Carl Craig. UK artists like the Prodigy and LFO took the sound to a new, less artful but more direct level. According to Saunderson, the difference between most Detroit techno and its English re-interpreters was that it lacked the 'spirituality' of the original. Had he wished to produce more controversy, he might have substituted 'blackness' – nearly all of the main Detroit pioneers were black. Most UK techno, conversely, at least until the advent of the jungle genre, were white. Most techno utilizes the establishment of a groove or movement by repetition, building a framework that does not translate easily into more conventional musical terms. Some obviously find this adjustment difficult, but the variations in texture and tempo are at least as subtle as those in rock music – often more so, due to the absence of a lyrical focus.

● FURTHER READING: *Techno Rebels: The Renegades Of Electronic Funk*, Dan Sicko.

## TECHNOTRONIC

Belgian commercial techno outfit created by producer Jo Bogaert, aka Thomas De Quincy. After playing keyboards in the indie outfit White Light in the mid-80s, Bogaert began working on his own dance music tracks, using various pseudonyms such as Nux Nemo and Acts Of Madmen. He was looking for a female rapper to sing over a backing track he had produced, before stumbling upon Ya Kid K (b. Manuela Kamosi, Zaire) in the Antwerp rap group, Fresh Beat. Kamosi had moved to Belgium from her native Zaire at 11, and later spent some time in Chicago where she was introduced to rap and deep house. With Bogaert she recorded 'Pump Up The Jam', which eventually reached number 2 in both the US and UK charts in 1989. The single was actually credited to Technotronic featuring Felly (a model who appeared on the cover). However, when *Pump Up The Jam: The Album* was released they were rebilled as Technotronic Featuring Ya Kid K. The album also featured MC Eric whose most notable contribution was the chant sequence on another hit, 'This Beat Is Technotronic'. Follow-ups included 'Get Up! (Before The Night Is Over)' with Ya Kid K, 'Rockin' Over The Beat', 'Megamix' (Bogaert on his own) and 'Turn It Up' (Technotronic Featuring Melissa And Einstein). Ya Kid K went on to perform on Hi Tek 3's 'Spin That Wheel' in 1990 (a version of which was included on Technotronic's *Trip On This* remix album) and later pursued a solo career. She was replaced by Reggie Magloire (who had previously worked with Indeep) for the album *Body To Body*. Technotronic's last chart success came in 1992 when a track from their debut album, 'Move That Body', reached US number 5 thanks to its use in a Revlon television commercial. Bogaert has continued to record sporadically with Technotronic as well as releasing the solo projects, *Different Voices* (1993) and *Millennium* (1996).

● ALBUMS: *Pump Up The Jam: The Album* (Epic/SBK 1989) ★★★, *Trip On This: The Remixes* (Epic/SBK 1990) ★★★, *Body To Body* (Epic/SBK 1991) ★★★, *Recall* (SBK 1995) ★★★.

● COMPILATIONS: *Greatest Hits* (Castle 1993) ★★★, *Pump Up The Hits* (Dance Street 1998) ★★★.

● VIDEOS: *Pump Up The Hits* (Capitol 1990).

## TELEVISION PERSONALITIES

A crass meeting of 60s pastiche and a tongue-in-cheek nod towards punk have characterized Dan Treacy's Television Personalities over their long, erratic career. Treacy teamed up with Edward Ball (b. 23 November 1959, Chelsea, London, England) back in 1977, releasing the privately pressed '14th Floor' the following year. After Ball's solo single as O Level, the pair issued what was to be seen as a pivotal artefact of the time, the EP *Where's Bill Grundy Now?* (1978). BBC disc jockey John Peel latched on to one of the tracks, 'Part Time Punks' (a cruel send-up of a rapidly decaying London scene), and this exposure attracted the interest of Rough Trade Records. Ball spent some time working on his solo projects in the early 80s, the Teenage Filmstars and the Times. Treacy, Ball and drummer Mark 'Empire' Sheppard recorded the Television Personalities' debut album, *... And Don't The Kids Just Love It*, which extended Treacy's exploration of 60s influences. From it came the whimsical 'I Know Where Syd Barrett Lives' as a single, the band's last for Rough Trade. Treacy then teamed up with Ed Ball to form the Whaam! label for Television Personalities and Times products plus other signings, including the Marine Girls. 1982, the band's busiest recording year, saw *Mummy You're Not Watching Me* share the instant appeal of their debut. 'Three Wishes' followed, and coincided with a minor psychedelic revival in London. *They Could Have Been Bigger Than The Beatles* was a surprisingly strong collection of demos and out-takes. The band were soon expanded by Mark Flunder (bass), Dave Musker (organ) and Joe Foster (12-string guitar) for a tour of Italy, with Flunder replaced by ex-Swell Maps bass player Jowe Head for a similar tour of Germany. 'A Sense Of Belonging' (1983) saw a one-off return to Rough Trade and caused a minor scandal over its sleeve. However, delays meant that *The Painted Word* was not issued until January 1985. Foster, who had played with the band on and off since 1980, and Musker soon left to work at Creation Records. With a new drummer, Jeff Bloom, Treacy set up a new label, after Whaam! folded due to pressure from pop duo Wham!. In the meantime, the German album *Chocolat-Art* captured one of their European live gigs. It was not until early 1990 that the next album emerged; *Privilege* included the catchy 'Salvador Dali's Garden Party'. The band subsequently lay low for a further two years (punctuated by a live album for Overground Records) until the release of *Closer To God*. Struggling with personal problems, Treacy did not record again until 1995's melodic *I Was A Mod Before You Was A Mod*. Ball signed with Creation as a solo artist and had his first hit in 1997 with 'Love Is Blue'. The most recent Television Personalities album *Don't Cry Baby ... It's Only A Movie* collected cover versions and original material recorded in 1994/95/

● ALBUMS: *And Don't The Kids Just Love It* (Rough Trade 1981) ★★★, *Mummy You're Not Watching Me* (Whaam! 1982) ★★★, *They Could Have Been Bigger Than The Beatles* (Whaam! 1982) ★★, *The Painted Word* (Illuminated 1985) ★★★, *Chocolat-Art* (Pastell 1985) ★★, *I Know Where Dan Treacy Lives* (HWD 1985) ★★, *Privilege* (Fire 1990) ★★★, *Camping In France* (Overground 1991) ★★, *Closer To God* (Fire 1992) ★★★, *I Was A Mod Before You Was A Mod* (Overground 1996) ★★★, *Top Gear* (Overground 1996) ★★, *Made In Japan* (Little Teddy 1996) ★★, *Don't Cry Baby ... It's Only A Movie* (Damaged Goods 1998) ★★.

● COMPILATIONS: *Yes Darling, But Is It Art? (Early Singles And Rarities)* (Fire 1995) ★★★, *Prime Time* (Nectar 1997) ★★★, *Part Time Punks: The Very Best Of Television Personalities* (Cherry Red 1999) ★★★★, *The Boy Who Couldn't Stop Dreaming* (Vinyl Japan 2000) ★★★, *Fashion Conscious* (Little Teddy 2000) ★★★.

# 10,000 MANIACS

This US band originally comprised enigmatic vocalist Natalie Merchant (b. 26 October 1963, Jamestown, New York, USA), backed by Robert Buck (b. 1958, Jamestown, New York, USA, d. 19 December 2000, Pittsburgh, Pennsylvania, USA; guitar), John Lombardo (guitar), Dennis Drew (keyboards) and Steven Gustafson (bass). Merchant, Buck, Drew, and Gustafson first started playing together in Jamestown, New York in February 1981

under the name of Still Life, adding Lombardo and changing their name shortly afterwards. The title was derived from the 1960s horror movie, 2,000 Maniacs. They initially specialized in cover versions of songs by such bands as Joy Division and Gang Of Four, but would later change from a rock-pop format to one that encompassed folk and world traditions. Drummer Jerome Augustyniak joined the line-up following the release of 1982's *Human Conflict Number Five* EP, and helped record the band's debut album, *Secrets Of The I Ching*. BBC disc jockey John Peel endorsed 'My Mother The War', and it appeared in his Festive 50 selection for 1983.

The band was signed to Elektra Records in 1985, and after a well-received UK tour recorded *The Wishing Chair* with Joe Boyd as producer. Lombardo left the band in 1986 following one more strenuous touring. There was a change of producer for *In My Tribe*, with Peter Asher stepping in, as he did with the subsequent release, *Blind Man's Zoo*. The production change obviously worked, with the highly acclaimed *In My Tribe* breaking into the US Top 40 in 1987, going gold in 1988 and platinum the following year. 'Peace Train' received a great deal of airplay, but following alleged death threat declarations to American servicemen by Yusuf Islam, formerly Cat Stevens, the writer of the song, the band insisted that any re-pressing of the album should exclude the aforementioned track. *Blind Man's Zoo* went into the US Top 20 in 1989, achieving gold status the same year. Following the release of *Blind Man's Zoo*, the band remained on the road from June to December of 1989. This consolidated their standing as a highly original outfit, albeit one utilizing several musical influences. This was superbly demonstrated in their *Our Time In Eden*, particularly the lilting 'Noah's Dove' and the punchy brass of 'Few And Far Between'. Merchant's 'Jezebel' featured string arrangements by Paul Buckmaster. *Hope Chest* was a remixed compilation of the band's first two independently released albums.

In September 1993, Merchant departed to develop her solo career, commenting 'There is no ill will between the members of the group, this is a natural passage.' Shortly afterwards, the band enjoyed their biggest US success when a cover version of Patti Smith's 'Because The Night', taken from *MTV Unplugged*, Merchant's last recording with the band, reached number 11 in the singles chart. The 10,000 Maniacs persevered by recruiting former member Lombardo and singer/violinist Mary Ramsey, with whom Lombardo had spent the intervening years recording as John And Mary. This line-up recorded two pleasant but unremarkable folk rock collections before Buck succumbed to liver disease and died in December 2000.

● ALBUMS: *Human Conflict Number Five* mini-album (Mark 1982) ★★, *Secrets Of The I Ching* (Christian Burial 1983) ★★★, *The Wishing Chair* (Elektra 1985) ★★, *In My Tribe* (Elektra 1987) ★★★★, *Blind Man's Zoo* (Elektra 1989) ★★★, *Our Time In Eden* (Elektra 1992) ★★★, *MTV Unplugged* (Elektra 1993) ★★★, *Love Among The Ruins* (Geffen 1997) ★★, *The Earth Pressed Flat* (Bar/None 1999) ★★★.

● COMPILATIONS: *Hope Chest: The Fredonia*

*Recordings 1982–1983* (Elektra 1990) ★★.
● VIDEOS: *MTV Unplugged* (Elektra 1994).

## TENPOLE TUDOR

This theatrical UK punk-pop band was led by the inimitable Edward Tudor-Pole (b. 6 December 1955, London, England), who first took to the stage at the age of nine when he appeared in *A Christmas Carol*. After a course at Chiswick Polytechnic he went to train at the Royal Academy of Dramatic Arts. In 1977, he joined a band called the Visitors which also included future *Riverside* BBC Television host Mike Andrews. Tudor-Pole formed the band Tenpole Tudor with Gary Long (drums), Dick Crippen (bass) and Bob Kingston (guitar). Kingston came from a musical family and had previously been a member of Sta-Prest with his brother Ray, himself later in the Temper. His sister June would soon become a member of the Mo-Dettes. Tudor-Pole appeared in the film *The Great Rock 'n' Roll Swindle* (Malcolm McLaren had been an early mentor) and performed 'Who Killed Bambi', which appeared on the b-side of the Sex Pistols' UK Top 10 hit 'Silly Thing'. He also helped Paul Cook and Steve Jones write the title song to the film. The first single under the band's own name was 'Real Fun', which came out on Korova Records. After signing to Stiff Records, the band released 'Three Bells In A Row'. Over the next few months they took part in the *Sons Of Stiff* tour, reached the UK charts three times, starting with the raucous Top 10 hit 'Swords Of A Thousand Men', recruited a second guitarist in the form of Munch Universe, and released two albums, before they suddenly went out of fashion once more.
In 1982, Tudor-Pole decided to dissolve the band. Crippen, Long and Kingston became the Tudors and released 'Tied Up With Lou Cool', while Tudor-Pole formed a new Cajun-style Tenpole Tudor and issued the 'Hayrick Song'. He then left Stiff and moved into jazz and swing-style bands, while also reviving his acting career. In 1985, he formed an old-style Tenpole Tudor and toured the country dressed in armour, but left the following year to concentrate on acting. He subsequently appeared on stage (*The Sinking Of The Belgrano*), film (*Straight To Hell*, *Absolute Beginners* and *Walker*) and television (in the comedy *Roy's Raiders*). He also re-formed Tenpole Tudor again in 1989, and it seemed likely that he would continue to do so at regular intervals until his acting career took off. Memorably playing the narrator in the stage play *The Road*, Tudor-Pole then took over the host's role on Channel 4 television's *The Crystal Maze*. His most recent film appearances include *Different For Girls* (1996), *Les Misérables* (1998), *Quills* (2000), and *Harry Potter And The Chamber Of Secrets* (2002).
● ALBUMS: *Eddie, Old Bob, Dick And Gary* (Stiff 1981) ★★, *Let The Four Winds Blow* (Stiff 1981) ★★.
● COMPILATIONS: *Wunderbar* (Dojo 1992) ★★, *Swords Of A Thousand Men: The Best Of* (Metro 2001) ★★★.

## THAT PETROL EMOTION

This critically lauded and highly skilled pop band's efforts to break into the mainstream were consistently thwarted despite a splendid arsenal of songs. The band was originally formed when the O'Neill brothers, Sean (b. 26 August 1957, Londonderry, Northern Ireland; guitar) and Damian (b. Stephen Damian O'Neill, 15 January 1961, Belfast, Northern Ireland; bass) parted from the fragmenting Undertones in 1983. A new approach was immediate with Sean reverting to his Irish name (having always appeared as John in his former band), and Damian switching to bass instead of guitar. They added Ciaran McLaughlin (b. 18 November 1962, Londonderry, Northern Ireland; drums), Reámann O'Gormain (b. 7 June 1961, Londonderry, Northern Ireland; guitar, ex-Bam Bam And The Calling), and, most importantly, dynamic Seattle, Washington, USA-born frontman Steve Mack (b. 19 May 1963, Greenwich Village, New York City, New York, USA; vocals).
They debuted with a single, 'Keen', on the small independent label Pink. Both that and the subsequent 'V2' (on their own Noiseanoise label) proved radical departures for those clamouring for a rerun of the Undertones, with frothing guitar and a fuller sound. There was now a political agenda too, ironic in view of the press bombardment of the Undertones as to why they did not write songs about the troubles in Northern Ireland. The questioning of British imperialism, explored through factors such as 'racist' jokes and the fate of political prisoners, would become a tenet of their music (and, more particularly, their record sleeves). Both their pop-based debut (for Demon Records) and *Babble* were dominated by frantic guitar and Mack's whole-hearted delivery. However, their one album contract with Polydor Records finished with *Babble* and they moved on to Virgin Records for the more diverse *End Of The Millennium Psychosis Blues*. This included the controversial but poignant ballad 'Cellophane', the bone-shattering disco of 'Groove Check', and the Sonic Youth-tainted 'Under The Sky'. Big Jim Paterson (trombone) and Geoff Barrett (saxophone) had been added to bolster the sound, but finances could not stretch to taking them on tour.
McLaughlin was beginning to emerge as a major songwriting force, as Sean O'Neill elected to give family matters more prominence and returned to Derry. His brother switched to guitar with John Marchini (b. April 1960, Coleraine, Northern Ireland) taking over on bass. *Chemicrazy*, which followed, was exceptionally strong, especially on singles 'Hey Venus' and 'Sensitize'. In the light of its commercial failure the band was dropped by Virgin, going on to release a final album on their Koogat label, with new bass player Brendan Kelly. However, *Fireproof*'s lack of sales again contrasted with the critical reception, and in March 1994 announcements of the band's split reached the music press (though they had already been inactive for some time). Despite constant campaigning on their behalf by the press, 'Big Decision', a direct call to political activism that reached a paltry UK number 43 in 1987, remained their biggest chart success.
● ALBUMS: *Manic Pop Thrill* (Demon 1986) ★★★, *Babble* (Polydor 1987) ★★★★, *End Of The Millennium Psychosis Blues* (Virgin 1988) ★★★, *Peel*

Sessions Album (Strange Fruit 1989) ★★★, Chemicrazy (Virgin 1990) ★★★★, Fireproof (Koogat 1993) ★★★, Final Flame 1994 live recording (Sanctuary 2000) ★★★.

## THE THE

Formed in 1979, this UK band centre around the activities of singer-songwriter Matt Johnson (b. 15 August 1961, London, England). Initially, the unit included Keith Laws and cartoonist Tom Johnston, but the line-up was continually changing and often featured Johnson alone. Following their debut at London's Africa Centre on 11 May 1979, The The's first single, 'Controversial Subject', was issued by 4AD Records. Two years later, they signed with Stevo's Some Bizzare Records and released the excellent 'Cold Spell Ahead'. Since 4AD still had a one-record option, Johnson issued Burning Blue Soul for them under his own name. Manager Stevo found it difficult to license The The's material to a major label but eventually Phonogram Records invested £8,000 in 'Uncertain Smile' (a retitled version of 'Cold Spell Ahead', produced in New York by Mike Thorne. It was an exceptionally impressive recording, but its impact was overshadowed by contractual machinations that saw Johnson move to another label, CBS Records. A projected album, The Pornography Of Despair, took longer to complete than expected and was vetoed by Johnson. The superb Soul Mining, one of 1983's most critically acclaimed albums, eventually replaced it.

By now, Johnson was already known for his uncompromising attitude and lust for perfection. Three years passed before the release of Infected, but it was well worth the wait. The album served as a harrowing commentary on the sexual, spiritual, political and economic malaise of 80s Britain. The production was exemplary and emphasized Johnson's standing as one of the most important cult artists to emerge during the decade.

In 1988, Johnson established a new version of The The featuring former Smiths guitarist Johnny Marr, bass player James Eller and drummer Dave Palmer. A worldwide tour coincided with the release of Mind Bomb, which garnered the least promising reviews of Johnson's career. The work was bombastic in tone and filled with lyrical diatribes and anti-religious rants allied to distinctly unmelodic songs. Johnson retained the new band for 1993's Dusk, a brutally honest examination of mortality that recovered some of the lost ground. The bizarre Hanky Panky saw Johnson deliver 11 cover versions of Hank Williams' songs to coincide with the publication of a new biography on the subject. After relocating to New York, Johnson left Epic after they rejected 1997's experimental Gun Sluts. He returned in February 2000 with the typically uncompromising Naked Self.

● ALBUMS: Soul Mining (Some Bizzare 1983) ★★★★, Infected (Epic 1986) ★★★★, Mind Bomb (Epic 1989) ★★, Dusk (Epic 1993) ★★★, Hanky Panky (Epic 1995) ★★, Naked Self (Nothing/ Universal 2000) ★★★.
● COMPILATIONS: 45 RPM: The Singles Of The The (Epic 2002) ★★★.

● VIDEOS: Infected (CBS-Fox 1987), Versus The World (Sony Music Video 1991), From Dawn 'Til Dusk (Sony Music Video 1993).

## THEATRE OF HATE

Formed in September 1981, this UK post-punk band originally featured Kirk Brandon (b. 3 August 1956, Westminster, London, England; vocals, ex-Pack), John Lennard (saxophone), Stan Stammers (bass), Billy Duffy (b. William Henry Duffy, 12 May 1961, Manchester, England; guitar) and Nigel Preston (d. 7 May 1992; drums). This was in fact the band's second line-up, Brandon having ditched all his former Pack, Jonathan Werner (bass), Jim Walker (drums) and Simon Werner (guitar), following the release of the first of a series of live albums and three singles. After establishing a strong live reputation for their hard, uncompromising lyrics, and harrowing, martial rhythms, the group recorded their 1982 debut album Westworld. Produced by Mick Jones of the Clash, the work proved commercial enough to infiltrate the UK Top 20. The attendant single, 'Do You Believe In The Westworld?', also gave the band their only Top 40 singles entry. Drummer Preston was replaced by Luke Rendle, while Duffy went on to form the Cult. Despite their promise and strong following, Theatre Of Hate fell apart a year after their inception with Stammers and Brandon going on to form Spear Of Destiny. Following his unsuccessful 1997 litigation against Boy George over allegations of an earlier homosexual affair, Brandon was back on the boards under the banner Kirk Brandon's Theatre Of Hate.

● ALBUMS: He Who Dares Wins Live At The Warehouse Leeds (SS 1981) ★★, Live At The Lyceum (Straight 1982) ★★, Westworld (Burning Rome 1982) ★★★★, He Who Dares Wins Live in Berlin (SS 1982) ★, Retribution (Castle 1996) ★, Love Is A Ghost: Live At The Lyceum '81 (Receiver 2000) ★★.
● COMPILATIONS: Revolution (Burning Rome 1993) ★★, Ten Years After (Burning Rome 1993) ★★, He Who Dares I & II (Dojo 1996) ★, Act 2 (Eastworld 1998) ★★, Act 4: The Sessions/Live At The Astoria (Eastworld 1998) ★★, Act 5: The Singles/He Who Dares 2 (Eastworld 1998) ★★, Propaganda: The Best Of Theatre Of Hate (Music Club 2001) ★★★, The Singles Collection (AlmaFame 2002) ★★★.

## THEN JERICO

Titled, incorrectly, after the city whose walls fell to the trumpets of the Israelites in the Bible, UK band Then Jerico managed three Top 40 hits in 1989 before breaking up. Originally comprising Mark Shaw (b. 10 June 1961, Chesterfield, Derbyshire, England; vocals), Jasper Stainthorpe (b. 18 February 1958, Tonbridge, Kent, England), Scott Taylor (b. 31 December 1961, Redhill, Surrey, England; guitar) and Steve Wren (b. 26 October 1962, Lambeth, London, England), the band formed when Shaw and Stainthorpe met in a north London studio, where the latter was working as an engineer. Stainthorpe recommended Wren though it transpired that he had already turned down an offer from Shaw two years earlier. Scott Taylor, former guitarist in Belouis Some's backing band, completed the line-up on the band's 1987 debut First (The Sound Of Music). The band received more press for Shaw's good looks than their inoffensive pop music, which was bolstered by the addition of Robert Downes (b. 7 December 1961, Cheadle Hulme, Cheshire, England; guitar) for their second album. Their biggest hit was 'Big Area' which reached number 13 in 1989. Shaw turned solo following the band's split, and released a poorly received solo album (*Almost*) in 1991 on EMI Records. He performed as Shaw Etc before re-forming Then Jerico with Michael MacNeil (ex-Simple Minds) and Andy Taylor (ex-Duran Duran) for an attempted comeback, spearheaded by 1998's *Orgasmaphobia*.

● ALBUMS: *First (The Sound Of Music)* (London 1987) ★★, *The Big Area* (London 1989) ★★★, as Then Jerico/Mark Shaw Etc. *Alive & Exposed* (Townsend 1992) ★★, *Orgasmaphobia* (Eagle 1998) ★★.

● COMPILATIONS: *Electric* (London 1995) ★★, *The Best Of Then Jerico* (London) ★★★.

## THIS MORTAL COIL

This UK band was essentially the creation of Ivo Watts-Russell, the co-owner of 4AD Records, a highly successful Wandsworth, London-based independent label. This Mortal Coil was actually a collaboration of musicians recording in various permutations, overseen and directed by Watts-Russell. The first single, an epic cover version of Tim Buckley's 'Song To The Siren', was originally intended as a b-side. However, bolstered by the considerable talents of Robin Guthrie and Elizabeth Fraser (Cocteau Twins), it saw its own release and became a near-permanent fixture in the independent charts in 1983 as a result. The album that followed set the pattern for the occasional outings to come. Featuring a selection of artists from the 4AD roster plus various outsiders, the albums included several cover versions of works by Watts-Russell's favourite songwriters (Buckley, Alex Chilton, Roy Harper, Gene Clark and Syd Barrett). At times shamefully indulgent, the series nevertheless highlighted the occasional stunning performance and breathtaking arrangement. The final This Mortal Coil outing was 1991's *Blood*, a collection which continued this tradition. In addition to label favourites Kim Deal (Pixies), Tanya Donelly (Throwing Muses/Breeders/Belly) and Heidi Berry, Caroline Crawley (Shelleyan Orphan) was also recruited. Previous incumbents included Howard Devoto and Gordon Sharp (Cindytalk). In 1998, Watts-Russell repeated the exercise with the Hope Blister.

● ALBUMS: *It'll End In Tears* (4AD 1984) ★★★, *Filigree And Shadow* (4AD 1986) ★★★, *Blood* (4AD 1991) ★★★.

● COMPILATIONS: *1983-1991* (4AD 1993) ★★★.

## THOMPSON TWINS

The origins of this UK synthesizer pop act were much less conventional than their chart material might suggest. Their name derived from the *Tin Tin* cartoon books of Hergé. Formed in 1977, the line-up featured Tom Bailey (b. 18 January 1956, Halifax, Yorkshire, England; vocals, keyboards, percussion), Peter Dodd (b. 27 October 1953; guitar) and John

Roog (guitar, vocals, percussion), who were friends living in Chesterfield when they decided to experiment with music. Several gigs later, they relocated to London where they picked up drummer Chris Bell (later Spear Of Destiny and Gene Loves Jezebel). In 1980, they released their first single, 'Squares & Triangles', on their own Dirty Discs label. After sporadic gigs, in 1981 their line-up expanded to include Joe Leeway (b. 15 November 1955, Islington, London, England; percussion, vocals), Alannah Currie (b. 28 September 1958, Auckland, New Zealand; percussion, saxophone), and Matthew Seligman (bass, ex-Soft Boys). This seven-piece became a cult attraction in the capital, where their favourite gimmick involved inviting their audience on stage to beat out a rhythmic backdrop to the songs. Their motivation was similar to that of the punk ethos: 'We were angry with the world in general – the deceit and the lies.' They signed a contract with Hansa Records in early 1981, which allowed them to set up their own label, T Records. However, when their debut *A Product Of ...* was released it showed a band struggling to make the transition from stage to studio. Producer Steve Lillywhite took them in hand for *Set*, and the Bailey-penned 'In The Name Of Love' saw them achieve their first minor hit in the UK. It did much better in the USA, staying at the top of the *Billboard* Disco charts for five weeks. Before this news filtered back, four of the band had been jettisoned, leaving just Bailey, Currie and Leeway. The cumbersome bohemian enterprise had evolved into a slick business machine, each member taking responsibility for the music, visuals or production, in a manner not dissimilar to the original Public Image Limited concept.

Reinventing their image as the Snap, Crackle and Pop characters of breakfast cereal fame, the Thompson Twins set about a sustained assault on the upper regions of the UK charts. 'Love On Your Side' was their first major hit, preceding *Quick Step & Side Kick*, their first album as a trio, which rose to number 2 in 1983. Highly commercial singles, 'We Are Detective', 'Hold Me Now', 'Doctor! Doctor!' and 'You Take Me Up', put them for a while in the first division of UK pop, and were also highly successful in the US. Further hits followed, most notably 'Lay Your Hands On Me', 'King For A Day' and the anti-heroin 'Don't Mess With Doctor Dream', and their fourth album, *Into The Gap*, topped the UK charts. However, when Leeway left at the end of 1986 the Thompson Twins became the duo their name had always implied. Bailey and Currie had been romantically involved since 1980, and had their first child eight years later. Unfortunately, success on the scale of their previous incarnation deserted them for the rest of the 80s, although their songwriting talents earned Deborah Harry a UK Top 20 hit in 1989 with 'I Want That Man'. After an unsuccessful liaison with Warner Brothers Records, Bailey and Currie formed Babble in 1994.

● ALBUMS: *A Product Of ...* (Hansa/T 1981) ★★, *Set* (T 1982) ★★, *In The Name Of Love* US only (Arista 1982) ★★, *Quick Step & Side Kick* (UK) *SideKicks* (US) (Arista 1983) ★★★★, *Into The Gap* (Arista 1984)

★★★, *Here's To Future Days* (Arista 1985) ★★, *Close To The Bone* (Arista 1987) ★★, *Big Trash* (Warners 1989) ★★, *Queer* (Warners 1991) ★★.
● COMPILATIONS: *Take Two* (Arista 1983) ★★, *Greatest Mixes: The Best Of Thompson Twins* (Arista 1988) ★★★, *The Greatest Hits* (Stylus 1990) ★★★, *The Best Of Thompson Twins* (Old Gold 1991) ★★★, *Love, Lies, And Other Strange Things: Greatest Hits* (Arista 1996) ★★★, *Singles Collection* (Camden 1996) ★★★, *Master Hits* (Arista 1999) ★★★.
● VIDEOS: *SideKicks: The Movie* (Thorn EMI 1983), *Into The Gap Live* (Arista Video 1984), *Single Vision* (Arista Video 1985),
● FURTHER READING: *The Thompson Twins: An Odd Couple*, Rose Rousse. *Thompson Twin: An '80s Memoir*, Michael White.

## THOMPSON, RICHARD
b. 3 April 1949, Totteridge & Whetstone, London, England. The talented Thompson forged his reputation as guitarist, vocalist, and composer with Fairport Convention which, although initially dubbed 'England's Jefferson Airplane', later evolved into a seminal folk-rock act through such acclaimed releases as *What We Did On Our Holidays*, *Unhalfbricking*, *Liege And Leif* and *Full House*. Thompson's sensitive compositions graced all of the above but none have been applauded more than 'Meet On The Ledge' (from *What We Did On Our Holidays*). This simple lilting song oozes with restraint, class and emotion and is one of the most evocative songs to come out of the late 60s 'underground' music scene. Thompson's innovative guitar style brought a distinctive edge to their work as he harnessed diverse influences such as Django Reinhardt, Charlie Christian, Otis Rush, James Burton and Mike Bloomfield.
The guitarist left the band in 1971 and having contributed to two related projects, *The Bunch* and *Morris On*, completed an impressive solo debut, *Henry The Human Fly*. He then forged a professional and personal partnership with singer Linda Peters. The couple, as Richard And Linda Thompson, recorded a series of excellent albums, notably *I Want To See The Bright Lights Tonight* (1974) and *Hokey Pokey* (1975), which established the artist's reputation for incisive, descriptive compositions. Thompson also collaborated with disparate vocalists such as Sandy Denny, John Martyn, Iain Matthews, Elvis Costello, and Pere Ubu's David Thomas, which in turn enhanced his already considerable reputation.
The Thompsons separated in 1982, although the guitarist had completed his second solo album, *Strict Tempo!*, a compendium of styles based on hornpipes, jigs and reels, the previous year. Thompson then recorded the acclaimed *Hand Of Kindness*, which juxtaposed traditional-styled material such as 'Devonside' with the pained introspection of 'A Poisoned Heart And A Twisted Memory' and 'The Wrong Heartbeat'. The superb concert recording *Small Town Romance* preceded Thompson's major label debut, *Across A Crowded Room*, a lesser work featuring the embittered 'She Twists The Knife Again'. In 1986, Thompson undertook extensive US

and UK tours to promote *Daring Adventures*, leading a group that included Clive Gregson and Christine Collister. The album itself included two of his most affecting ballads, 'How Will I Ever Be Simple Again' and 'Al Bowlly's In Heaven'. Thompson then completed the soundtrack to *The Marksman*, a BBC Television series, before joining John French, Fred Frith and Henry Kaiser for the experimental *Live, Love, Larf & Loaf*. In 1988, he switched outlets to Capitol Records, teaming up with *Daring Adventures* producer Mitchell Froom once again to record the over-cooked *Amnesia*. Froom's production was also a problem on the 1991 follow-up *Rumor And Sigh*, although some of the material ('Read About Love', 'I Feel So Good', 'I Misunderstood', '1952 Vincent Black Lightning') was among the finest of Thompson's career. Thompson recorded with the Golden Palominos, and performed with David Byrne during the same year.
The 1993 3-CD compilation *Watching The Dark* collected many unreleased live performances, and helped to put into perspective Thompson's remarkable contribution to rock music from his debut with Fairport Convention onwards. If *Watching The Dark* was his past, the double CD set *You? Me? Us?*, and *Mock Tudor* represent his future. In musical terms, nothing has changed; Thompson's lyrics remain as dark and bleak as ever, and the guitar playing is exemplary. Two new Thompson classics arrive in the shape of 'Cold Kisses' (on *You? Me? Us?*) and 'Dry My Tears And Move On' (on *Mock Tudor*). In other words, the future looks bright, as Thompson appears to be able to deliver time and time again without any repetition. He is one of the most important songwriters of the present day.
● ALBUMS: *Henry The Human Fly* (Island 1972) ★★★, *Strict Tempo!* (Elixir 1981) ★★★, *Hand Of Kindness* (Hannibal 1983) ★★★★, *Small Town Romance* (Hannibal 1984) ★★★★, *Across A Crowded Room* (Polydor 1985) ★★★, *Daring Adventures* (Polydor 1986) ★★★★, with John French, Fred Frith, Henry Kaiser *Live, Love, Larf & Loaf* (Rhino/Demon 1987) ★★★★, with Peter Filleul *The Marksman* film soundtrack (BBC 1987) ★★, *Amnesia* (Capitol 1988) ★★★, with French, Frith, Kaiser *Invisible Means* (Windham Hill/Demon 1990) ★★★, with Filleul *Hard Cash* film soundtrack (Special Delivery 1990) ★★★, *Sweet Talker* film soundtrack (Capitol 1991) ★★, *Rumor And Sigh* (Capitol 1991) ★★★★, *Mirror Blue* (Capitol 1994) ★★★★, with Danny Thompson *Live At Crawley 1993* (Whatdisc 1995) ★★★, *You? Me? Us?* (EMI 1996) ★★★, *Two Letter Words* 1994 recording (Fly 1996) ★★★, with Danny Thompson *Industry* (Parlophone 1997) ★★★, with Philip Pickett *The Bones Of All Men* (Hannibal 1998) ★★★, *Celtschmerz* (Flypaper 1998) ★★★, *Mock Tudor* (Capitol 1999) ★★★★.
● COMPILATIONS: *(Guitar, Vocal)* (Island 1976) ★★★★, *Live (More Or Less)* US only (Island 1977) ★★★★, *Doom & Gloom From The Tomb* cassette only (Fly 1985) ★★★, *The Guitar Of Richard Thompson* cassette only (Homespun 1986) ★★★, *Doom & Gloom II – Over My Dead Body* cassette only (Fly 1991) ★★★, *Watching The Dark* 3-CD box set (Hannibal 1993) ★★★★★, *Action Packed: The Best Of*

*The Capitol Years* (Capitol 2001) ★★★★.
● VIDEOS: *Across A Crowded Room* (Sony 1983).
● FURTHER READING: *Richard Thompson: 21 Years Of Doom & Gloom*, Clinton Heylin. *Gypsy Love Songs & Sad Refrains: The Recordings Of Richard Thompson & Sandy Denny*, Clinton Heylin. *Richard Thompson: Strange Affair, The Biography*, Patrick Humphries.

## THOR

b. Jon-Mikl Thor, Vancouver, British Columbia, Canada. This body builder turned singer who took his name from a Marvel comic character, was a former Mr. Teenage USA, Mr. Canada and Mr. North America. His band comprised a former model, Pantera (b. Rusty Hamilton; vocals), Steve Price (guitar), Keith Zazzi (bass) and Mike Favata (drums). Their debut release, *Keep The Dogs Away*, appeared in 1978. This album was an uneventful affair of basic hard rock/heavy metal which, even at the time of its release, sounded dated. Thor then took a long break until returning with the release of a mini-album, *Unchained*, in 1984. Then came Thor's most successful album, *Only The Strong*, released in 1985. Much attention was paid to Thor's live party-piece – where, by blowing into it, he expanded and burst a rubber hot-water bottle (often with the claim 'let's see Michael Jackson do this'). Other 'theatricals' included staged clashes between Norse gods, with Thor resplendent in spiked body armour, wielding a mighty (plastic) sword or bearded axe – all conducted without the tiniest trace of irony, and an almost camp machismo from the band's frontman. 1985 proved an eventful year for Thor as not only did he have two singles, 'Let The Blood Run Red' and 'Thunder On The Tundra' (both from *Only The Strong*), released, but also a live album, *Live In Detroit*. That year also saw him enter the film world, appearing in and writing the soundtrack for *Recruits*. Part of the soundtrack formed the basis for Thor's next release, *Recruits: Wild In The Streets*. That marked the temporary end of Thor's musical aspirations as he once again turned his attention to the movie business by appearing in *Zombie Nightmare* alongside original *Batman* star Adam West. He revived the Thor name occasionally during the following decade, releasing a new studio album in 1998.
● ALBUMS: *Keep The Dogs Away* (RCA 1978) ★★, *Unchained* mini-album (Albion/Ultra Noise 1984) ★★★, *Only The Strong* (Viper/Roadrunner 1985) ★★★, *Live In Detroit* (Viper/Raw Power 1985) ★★, *Recruits: Wild In The Streets* (Roadrunner 1986) ★★★, as Tritonz *The Edge Of Hell* (RCA 1986) ★★, *Thunderstruck: Tales From The Equinox* (Star 1998) ★★, *Triumphant* (ThorToen 2002) ★★.
● COMPILATIONS: *Ride Of The Chariots (An-Thor-Logy)* (Star 1997) ★★★.
● VIDEOS: *Live In London* (PolyGram 1984).

## 3 MUSTAPHAS 3

This pseudo-Balkan band did much to popularize world music in the mid- to late 80s, revealing a serious musical intent behind the elaborate mythology that saw each band member adopting 6 August as an official birthday in order to avoid confusion. Niaveti Mustapha III (b. Tim Fienburgh; flutes, German bagpipes), Hijaz Mustapha (b. Ben Mandelson, Liverpool, England; violin, bouzouki), Houzam Mustapha (b. Nigel Watson; drums), Sabah Habas Mustapha (b. Colin Bass; bass, percussion), Kemo 'Kem Kem' Mustapha (b. Kim Burton; accordion, piano), and Daoudi Mustapha (clarinet) made their UK debut in August 1982. They claimed to hail from the hard-to-locate Balkan city of Szegerley, and their major breakthrough was going from Balkan Beat Bastard Bad Boys to Godfathers Of World Music, without changing their direction. The Mustaphas were occasionally joined by Expensive Mustapha (trumpet). The humorous ensemble was first brought to public attention by BBC Radio 1 disc jockey John Peel. The band attracted a degree of criticism for not taking their music seriously, but the end product was still extremely popular with audiences both in Europe and the USA. As an indication of this, *Soup Of The Century* was number 1 in the *Billboard* World Music charts, and was voted the Best World Music/International Album For 1990 by NAIRD (National Association of Independent Record Distributors), in the USA. For *Heart Of Uncle*, on Globestyle Records, the band was joined by their sister Laura Tima Daviz Mustapha (vocals). They backed a number of other artists, such as Ofra Haza, where they sang 'Linda Linda' and managed to offend some people by singing half the lyrics in Hebrew and half in Arabic. Select members contributed to *Out On The Rolling Sea*, a 1994 tribute album to Bahamian guitarist Joseph Spence.
● ALBUMS: *From The Balkans To Your Heart – The Radio Years* (Exil 1985) ★★★, *Bam! Mustaphas Play Stereo* mini-album (Globestyle 1985) ★★★, *L'Orchestre 'Bam' De Grand Mustapha International & Party Play Local Music* mini-album (Globestyle 1986) ★★★, *Shopping* (Globestyle 1987) ★★★, *Heart Of Uncle* (Globestyle 1989) ★★★, *Soup Of The Century* (Fez-O-Phone 1990) ★★★.
● COMPILATIONS: *Friends, Fiends & Fronds* (Globestyle 1991) ★★★★, *Bam! Big Mustaphas Play Stereolocalmusic* (Ace 1997) ★★★, *Play Musty For Me* (Kartini 2001) ★★★.

## THUNDERS, JOHNNY

b. John Anthony Genzale Jnr., 15 July 1952, New York City, New York, USA, d. 23 April 1991, New Orleans, Louisiana, USA. Johnny Thunders first gained recognition as a member of the New York Dolls, an aggregation that built a reputation for its hard R&B-influenced rock sound and glam/punk appearance in the early 70s. First calling himself Johnny Volume, the guitarist joined the high school band Johnny And The Jaywalkers, then a local band called Actress, which included in their line-up two other future Dolls members, Arthur Kane and Billy Murcia. Actress evolved into the New York Dolls in late 1971. Genzale, now renamed Johnny Thunders, recorded two albums for Mercury Records with the New York Dolls. After leaving the band in 1975 along with drummer Jerry Nolan, the pair formed a new band alongside ex-Television guitarist Richard Hell called the Heartbreakers. This line-up was completed with the addition of guitarist Walter Lure.

Hell left the band soon afterwards to form the Voidoids, with Billy Wrath replacing him. Thunders and the Heartbreakers recorded prolifically for US and UK labels such as Track and Jungle Records. They achieved greater popularity in the UK, where they were accepted as peers by early punk-rock bands that had idolized the New York Dolls. Thunders earned a reputation for his shambling stage performances owing to an excess of drugs and alcohol, and he often made unscheduled guest appearances with other artists.

Thunders' first solo collection, *So Alone*, found him supported by many UK musicians, including Phil Lynott, Peter Perrett (the Only Ones), Steve Jones and Paul Cook (the Sex Pistols), Steve Marriott (Humble Pie/the Small Faces) and Paul Gray (Eddie And The Hot Rods/Damned). Thunders also recorded with ex-MC5 guitarist Wayne Kramer in a group called Gang War, and gigged with fellow junkie Sid Vicious, in the Living Dead. The Heartbreakers broke up and re-formed numerous times, recording their last album together in 1984. Thunders resurfaced in the late 80s with an album of 50s and 60s R&B/pop cover versions recorded with singer Patti Palladin. Despite the promise of all this activity Thunders was found dead in a hotel room in New Orleans, Louisiana in mysterious circumstances in 1991. He was 38. Despite Thunders' notorious drug dependency the autopsy failed to reveal the cause of death, although later reports cited a heroin overdose.

● ALBUMS: *So Alone* (Real 1978) ★★★★, *In Cold Blood* (New Rose 1983) ★★★, *Too Much Junkie Business* cassette only (ROIR 1983) ★★★, *Hurt Me* (New Rose 1984) ★★★, *Que Sera Sera* (Jungle 1985) ★★★, *Stations Of The Cross* cassette only (ROIR 1987) ★★, with Patti Palladin *Copy Cats* (Restless 1988) ★★★, with Wayne Kramer *Gang War* (Zodiac 1990) ★, *Bootlegging The Bootleggers* (Jungle 1990) ★★, *Live At Max's Kansas City '79* (ROIR 1996) ★★★, *Have Faith* (Mutiny 1996) ★★, with Sylvain Sylvain *Sad Vacation* 1984 recordings (Receiver 1999) ★★★, *Belfast Nights* (Amsterdamned 2000) ★★, *Live And Wasted: Unplugged 1990* (Receiver 2000) ★★★.

● COMPILATIONS: *Hurt Me* (Dojo 1995) ★★★, *The Studio Bootlegs* (Dojo 1996) ★★, *Born Too Loose: The Best Of Johnny Thunders* (Jungle 1999) ★★★, *You Can't Put Your Arms Around A Memory* 3-CD set (Castle 2002) ★★★.

● FURTHER READING: *Johnny Thunders: In Cold Blood*, Nina Antonia. *Johnny Thunders Discography*.

## TIFFANY

b. Tiffany Renee Darwish, 2 October 1971, Oklahoma, USA. Pop singer Tiffany, based in Norwalk, California, had immediate success with the release of the US number 1 singles 'I Think We're Alone Now' (originally a Top 5 hit for Tommy James And The Shondells in 1967) and 'Could've Been'. Both were included on the artist's 1987 debut album, recorded while she was still only 15 years old. So too was the number 7-peaking 'I Saw Him Standing There' (an utterly sexless version of the Beatles 'I Saw Her Standing There'), another bubble-gum pop treatment of a well-loved standard. The album was helped to the top of the US charts by Tiffany's

promotional tour of shopping malls – a gambit that pushed her ahead of the similarly gushing Debbie Gibson in US adolescent magazine circles The only hit on the follow-up collection, *Hold An Old Friend's Hand*, was 'All This Time' (US number 6), indicating a lessening of her grip on the teen market. The singer had also moved out of the parental home and sued her mother for emancipation. By the advent of *New Inside*, her 'mature' album, no one seemed to be interested anymore and her career as a hitmaker effectively closed with it. One further album was issued without the singer's blessing on the Asian market before she moved to Nashville in an unsuccessful attempt to break into the country market. She resurfaced in 2000 on the Los Angeles-based Eureka Records label with the Alanis Morissette-influenced *The Color Of Silence*. Two years later, she posed nude for *Playboy* magazine.

● ALBUMS: *Tiffany* (MCA 1987) ★★★, *Hold An Old Friend's Hand* (MCA 1988) ★★, *New Inside* (MCA 1990) ★, *Dreams Never Die* (MCA 1993) ★, *The Color Of Silence* (Eureka 2000) ★★.

● COMPILATIONS: *Greatest Hits* (Hip-O 1996) ★★.

● FILMS: *Jetsons: The Movie* voice only (1990).

## TIKARAM, TANITA

b. 12 August 1969, Munster, Germany. Tikaram's intense lyrics brought her instant commercial success at the age of 19. She spent her early years in Germany where her Fijian-born father was serving with the British army. In 1982, the family moved to England, settling in Basingstoke, Hampshire. Tikaram began writing songs and in November 1987 played her first gig at London's Mean Fiddler, after sending a cassette of her songs to the venue. By the time of her fourth gig, she was supporting Warren Zevon at the Hammersmith Odeon. Following an appearance on a local London television show, she was signed to Warner Brothers Records and recorded *Ancient Heart* in 1988. The producers were Rod Argent (ex-Zombies) and experienced session musician Peter Van Hooke. 'Good Tradition' and 'Twist In My Sobriety' were immediate hits in the UK and across Europe. The album was a huge success and Tikaram became a role model for artists aspiring to emulate late 60s bed-sitter singer/songwriters.

Tikaram spent most of 1989 on tour before releasing her second album, which included 'We Almost Got It Together' and 'Thursday's Child'. Although not as consistent as her debut it reached the same position in the UK album chart, number 3. *Everybody's Angel*, at Bearsville Studio in Woodstock, was co-produced with Van Hooke and Argent. Former Emerald Express violinist Helen O'Hara was among the backing musicians. 'Only The Ones We Love' with harmony vocals by Jennifer Warnes was issued in 1991, and in the same year, she made her second world tour. In 1992, the self-produced *Eleven Kinds Of Loneliness* was released to a muted reaction, and although her 1995 release had a much bigger publicity campaign it seemed that her highly commercial days were in the past. Following a three-year sabbatical during which she acted and travelled, Tikaram returned with a different image and an atmospheric new album, *The Cappuccino Songs*.

● ALBUMS: *Ancient Heart* (Warners 1988) ★★★★, *The Sweet Keeper* (East West 1990) ★★, *Everybody's Angel* (East West 1991) ★★, *Eleven Kinds Of Loneliness* (East West 1992) ★★, *Lovers In The City* (East West 1995) ★★★, *The Cappuccino Songs* (Mother 1998) ★★★.
● COMPILATIONS: *The Best Of Tanita Tikaram* (East West 1997) ★★★★.

## 'TIL TUESDAY

This Boston, Massachusetts, USA-based band are now chiefly remembered for giving birth to the talents of singer-songwriter and bass player Aimee Mann (b. 8 September 1960, Richmond, Virginia, USA). Formed in 1983, the band enjoyed a US Top 10 hit single, 'Voices Carry' two years later. Despite their early success, the band failed to follow-up on the promise of their debut, though a rueful Mann places the blame for this squarely on the shoulders of record company intransigence and politicking. The band was formed around Mann, who had previously played with the Young Snakes, Michael Hausman (drums), Robert Holmes (guitar) and Joey Pesce (keyboards).

Their debut album, titled after the hit single, was produced by Mike Thorne and announced Mann's compositional skills and lyrical assurance. There remained those, however, not convinced by the strength of her vocal delivery. *Welcome Home* replaced Thorne with Rhett Davies as producer, but the record, though flawlessly constructed, lacked the sparkle of the debut. Only Mann and Hausman remained from the original line-up by the time of 1988's *Everything's Different Now*, which utilised a Jules Shear (then Mann's paramour) song as its title track. Expressing his happiness at falling for Mann, and sung by the subject of his affections, it offered an interesting insight into their relationship when compared to the same album's '(Believed You Were) Lucky', at which stage Mann had dumped Shear but still used his music to bear her own lyric about their parting. 'The Other End (Of The Telescope)', meanwhile, was co-written and sung with Elvis Costello. However, the writing was on the wall for 'Til Tuesday, with Epic Records threatening to block any future release and not promoting the records in a satisfactory manner. The band broke up in 1988 allowing Mann to pursue a solo career, taking Hausman as her manager.
● ALBUMS: *Voices Carry* (Epic 1985) ★★★, *Welcome Home* (Epic 1986) ★★★, *Everything's Different Now* (Epic 1988) ★★★★.
● COMPILATIONS: *Coming Up Close: A Retrospective* (Sony 1996) ★★★★.

## TIMBUK 3

Formed in Madison, Wisconsin, USA, in 1978 Timbuk 3 was a duo consisting of husband and wife Pat MacDonald and Barbara Kooyman MacDonald. The pair met while attending the University of Madison and began writing and performing their songs. They went to New York City where they played on the street for tips before settling in Austin, Texas. While in Austin they became regulars at clubs such as the Hole In The Wall and the Austin

Outhouse. They recorded a demo and made an appearance on MTV's *I.R.S. The Cutting Edge*, which led to a recording contract with I.R.S. Records. Using a boombox for their rhythm section, the duo (playing acoustic and electric guitars) began making appearances on other television programmes and recorded their debut, *Greetings From Timbuk 3*, in 1986. It reached number 50 in the USA, largely on the strength of the sparkling first single, 'The Future's So Bright, I Gotta Wear Shades', a danceable novelty song that climbed to number 19 (21 in the UK). The album was a mixture of similarly light fare and darker, more serious themes, as was the 1988 follow-up, *Eden Alley*. The MacDonalds were joined by Wally Ingram (drums) following the release of *Edge Of Allegiance*, and by *Big Shot In The Dark* they had evolved into a full band with the addition of bass player Courtney Audain. Timbuk 3 eventually split up in the mid-90s following the dissolution of the MacDonalds' marriage. Pat formed Ark 21, a new record label, in 1997 and embarked on a solo career.
● ALBUMS: *Greetings From Timbuk 3* (I.R.S. 1986) ★★★★, *Eden Alley* (I.R.S. 1988) ★★★, *Edge Of Allegiance* (I.R.S. 1989) ★★★, *Big Shot In The Dark* (I.R.S. 1991) ★★★, *Espace Ornano* (Watermelon 1993) ★★, *Looks Like Dark To Me* mini-album (High Street 1994) ★★★, *A Hundred Lovers* (High Street 1995) ★★★★.
Solo: Pat MacDonald *Pat MacDonald Sleeps With His Guitar* (Ark 21 1997) ★★★, *Begging Her Graces* (Ulftone 1999) ★★★, *Degrees Of Gone* (Ulftone 2001) ★★★.
● COMPILATIONS: *Field Guide: Some Of The Best Of Timbuk 3* (I.R.S. 1992) ★★★★.
● VIDEOS: *Greetings From Eden Valley* (I.R.S. 1988).

## TIPPA IRIE

b. Anthony Henry, 1965, London, England. Raised in a south London community where the sound system business was a way of life, by the age of 13 Henry was performing with local sound systems and learning the art of chatting in rhyme by listening to Jamaican DJs on record. At 15, he was an adept MC with King Tubby's sound system in Brixton (not to be confused with the Jamaican dub maestro). Although British MCs were previously held to be inferior to their Jamaican counterparts, when dancehall took a grip on reggae in the early 80s, it coincided with the rise of the most talented 'chatters' Britain had ever produced. The live recordings of sound system sessions that swept Jamaica were soon copied in London, and Tippa found himself on three live albums in 1983, *Live At DSYC Volumes 1–3*, recorded at London's Dick Shepherd Youth Centre. They had an enormous impact, showcasing British youngsters who were proving themselves as powerful with a rhyme as their Jamaican counterparts. When Tippa joined Saxon he was alongside the best reggae rappers in Britain, including Phillip Papa Levi, Peter King, Daddy Rusty, Daddy Colonel, Sandy, and later, Smiley Culture, Asher Senator and singer Maxi Priest. It was the most powerful line-up any UK sound had ever assembled. In 1984, Saxon recorded a live album (*Coughing Up Fire*) for Greensleeves Records, who picked up Tippa for studio recordings.

'Sleng Teng Finish Already', 'Telephone' and 'It's Good To Have The Feeling You're The Best' all sold well and gained him appearances on television shows such as *Club Mix*. No one expected 'Hello Darling' to plant Tippa on *Top Of The Pops*, but the cheeky single was a smash hit. However, because it was so unexpected, it took a long time for Tippa's follow-up to arrive and, consequently, 'Heartbeat' merely scraped the charts. A further attempt at chart success came with the appropriately titled 'Panic Panic', with Tippa lost on a dance record. That year's album, *Is It Really Happening To Me?*, summed up the pressure he felt. Tippa chose to return to grass roots, and *Two Sides Of Tippa Irie* in 1987 found him more relaxed on album than previously: this was Tippa, ragga MC, not chart-climber. In 1988, he teamed with Jamaican ragga star Papa San to record *JA To UK MC Clash*, another fine, low-key album, and in 1989 issued *Ah-Me-Dis*, which also earned a debut American release on Miles Copeland's I.R.S. Records label. He eventually left Saxon in the summer of 1989. Meanwhile, the mainstream media kept one eye open for him, and he made several television appearances in 1988, including on BBC Television's current affairs programme *Panorama*, as an anti-crack spokesperson. While he might never recapture the success of 'Hello Darling', Tippa can never be entirely discounted – as long as there is a lyric in his head, he will be working.

● ALBUMS: *Is It Really Happening To Me?* (Greensleeves 1986) ★★★, *Two Sides Of Tippa Irie* (GT's 1987) ★★★, with Papa San *JA To UK MC Clash* (Fashion 1988) ★★★★, *Ah-Me-Dis* (GT's/I.R.S. 1989) ★★★, *Original Raggamuffin* (Mango/Island 1989) ★★★, with Peter Hunningale *A New Decade* (Mango/Island 1990) ★★★★, with Hunningale *Done Cook And Curry* (Tribal Bass 1991) ★★★, *Sapphire And Steel* (I.R.S. 1993) ★★★, *Rebel* (RAS 1994) ★★★, *I Miss* (Resin 2000) ★★★★.

● COMPILATIONS: *Mr. Versatile* (Jammin 1998) ★★★★.

## TOM TOM CLUB

This US outfit was formed by bass player Tina Weymouth (b. Martina Michéle Weymouth, 22 November 1950, Coronado, California, USA) and her husband, drummer Chris Frantz (b. Charlton Christopher Frantz, 8 May 1951, Fort Campbell, Kentucky, USA), as a spin-off from their main band, Talking Heads. The pair were on holiday in Nassau in the Bahamas (later buying a house there) when they met Steven Stanley, the engineer at Compass Point studios and a keyboard player. They also met Monte Browne, the guitarist with T-Connection who were recording there. The four set about rehearsing and recording together and came up with 'Wordy Rappinghood' which was a UK Top 10 hit in 1981 under the group name the Tom Tom Club, taken from the name of a hall where they practised. 'Genius Of Love' was a huge dance hit which has subsequently resurfaced as a sample in countless tracks. Franz and Weymouth were keen to stress how 'we've deliberately embraced all the types of music that Talking Heads hasn't. We like the accessibility and fun of dance music, but that's not all we do'. The

quartet stayed together on and off as a studio project utilizing various other people when necessary. These included Weymouth's two sisters Laura and Lani on vocals, plus percussionists Uziah 'Sticky' Thompson and Steve Scales, guitarists Adrian Belew and Alex Weir, keyboard players Bernie Worrell, Wally Badarou, Tyrone Downie and Raymond Jones. Their second album included a cover version of the soul classic 'Under The Boardwalk'. Frantz and Weymouth produced Ziggy Marley early in 1988, and September saw the band playing a three-week stint at CBGB's with Lou Reed and Deborah Harry as guests. They began a UK tour with guitarist Mark Roule and keyboard player Gary Pozner as the latest semi-permanent personnel. Their third album was a more rock-orientated collection, including a cover version of the Velvet Underground's 'Femme Fatale', with Lou Reed on guitar. Frantz and Weymouth recorded the fourth Tom Tom Club album, the experimental, funky *Dark Sneak Love Action*, at their own Clubhouse studio in Connecticut. The duo's production schedule took up an increasing amount of time during the 90s, but they still found time to team up with Talking Heads guitarist Jerry Harrison and record an album as the Heads in 1996. *No Talking Just Head* was warmly received by fans of the original band, which had officially split-up in 1995 (despite being effectively disbanded since 1991). Weymouth and Franz recorded the next Tom Tom Club album, *The Good The Bad And The Funky*, with soul singer Charles Pettigrew, formerly of Charles And Eddie.

● ALBUMS: *Tom Tom Club* (Sire/Island 1981) ★★★★, *Close To The Bone* (Sire/Island 1983) ★★★, *Boom Boom Chi Boom Boom* (Sire 1989) ★★, *Dark Sneak Love Action* (Sire/Reprise 1992) ★★★, *The Good The Bad And The Funky* (Rykodisc 2000) ★★★.

## TOTO

The experienced Los Angeles session team of Bobby Kimball (b. Robert Toteaux, 29 March 1947, Vinton, Louisiana, USA; vocals), Steve Lukather (b. 21 October 1957, Los Angeles, California, USA; guitar), David Paich (b. 21 June 1954, Los Angeles, California, USA; keyboards, vocals, son of Marty Paich), Steve Porcaro (b. 2 September 1957, Connecticut, USA; keyboards, vocals), David Hungate (b. Texas, USA; bass) and Jeff Porcaro (b. 1 April 1954, Hartford, Connecticut, USA, d. 5 August 1992, Holden Hills, California, USA; drums) decided in 1978 to begin functioning in their own right after years of blithe dedication to the music of others on tour and disc. A couple of Toto albums found over a million buyers each but, overall, this rather faceless band met moderate success with moderate records – penned mainly by Paich – on which polished, close-milked vocal harmonies floated effortlessly over layers of treated sound.

*Toto* (1978) was attended by a smash hit in 'Hold The Line' (US number 5, UK number 14), but the band's most commercial period was 1982/3 when the Grammy Award-winning *Toto IV* generated two international hits with the atmospheric 'Africa' (US number 1/UK number 3) and 'Rosanna' (US number 2/UK number 12), as well as the US number 10 single, 'I Won't Hold You Back'. The latter won Grammys for Record Of The Year, Best Pop Vocal Performance and Best Instrumental Arrangement (nearly 20 years later, it also provided a memorable vocal sample for DJ Roger Sanchez's chart-topping single, 'Another Chance'). The following year, Kimball and Hungate were replaced by, respectively, Dave Fergie Frederikson (b. 15 May 1951, Wyoming, Michigan, USA) and Mike Porcaro (b. 29 May 1955, USA). Sales of *Isolation* and the band's soundtrack to the science fiction movie *Dune* were poor, but some lost ground was regained when it became known that Toto were responsible for the backing track of USA For Africa's single 'We Are The World'. With a new lead singer in Joseph Williams, the band reached number 11 in the US with 'I'll Be Over You', a composition by Lukather and Randy Goodrun from 1986's *Fahrenheit*. Two years later 'Pamela', produced to the expected slick standards by Earth, Wind And Fire's George Massenburg and Little Feat's Bill Payne, reached US number 22. By then, Steve Porcaro had returned to employment in the studios from which Toto had emerged.

In 1990, Jean-Michel Byron briefly replaced Williams, before Lukather became the band's vocalist. Jeff Porcaro died in 1992 after a heart attack caused by an allergic reaction to pesticide. His replacement on subsequent UK dates was British session drummer Simon Phillips. In 1995, the band released the blues-tinged *Tambu*, which attempted to steer their sound away from mainstream pop/rock. Kimball returned in 1999, although the subsequent *Mindfields* was disappointing.

● ALBUMS: *Toto* (Columbia 1978) ★★★, *Hydra* (Columbia 1979) ★★, *Turn Back* (Columbia 1981) ★★, *Toto IV* (Columbia 1982) ★★★★, *Isolation* (Columbia 1984) ★★, *Dune* film soundtrack (Columbia 1984) ★★, *Fahrenheit* (Columbia 1986) ★★, *The Seventh One* (Columbia 1988) ★★, *Kingdom Of Desire* (Columbia 1992) ★★, *Absolutely Live* (Columbia 1993) ★, *Tambu* (Columbia 1995) ★★★, *Mindfields* (Columbia 1999) ★★.

● COMPILATIONS: *Past To Present 1977-1990* (Columbia 1990) ★★★, *Toto XX* (Columbia 1998) ★★★.

● VIDEOS: *Past To Present 1977-1990* (Sony Music Video 1990).

## TOXIC EPHEX

Arguably the finest Scottish punk/folk crossover artists of the 80s, this Aberdeen six-piece comprised Dod (vocals), Carmen (fiddle), Fred (guitars), Mikey (bass), Chizel (drums) and Frankie (rhythm guitar). Local favourites for several years before their underground popularity spread throughout the rest of Scotland and England, their endeavours in this direction were helped by support slots to the politically and musically sympathetic New Model Army and Men They Couldn't Hang. Their vinyl debut had come on the early 80s Crass Records sampler *Bullshit Detector 2*, after which they created their own delightfully titled Green Vomit Records. From that label came a split album with fellow Scottish political punk outfit Oi Polloi, then the endearing *The Adventures Of Nobby Porthole - The*

*Cock Of The North*. Staffed by mad fiddlers, snarling political vocals and diatribes against the Conservative government of the period, it also included an enchanting version of the Scottish folk standard 'Bonnie Wee Jeanie McColl'. Alas, the demise of the fondly remembered sextet came in 1991, although Carmen (dubbed by some sections of the press as 'a female Nigel Kennedy') reappeared both solo and with ceilidh specialists Old Blind Dogs.

● ALBUMS: *Mad As Fuck (Don't You Think?)* split album with Oi Polloi (Green Vomit 1987) ★★, *The Adventures Of Nobby Porthole - The Cock Of The North* (Green Vomit 1990) ★★★.

## TOY DOLLS

From Sunderland, England, the Toy Dolls is a punk trio centred around lead singer Olga (b. Michael Algar). Other personnel, at various times, comprised some five bass players, 14 drummers and 39 drivers and roadies - and that was only by the end of the 80s. The Toy Dolls have long been a cult attraction, their scampering, hyperactive anthems the absurd earning them a dedicated following. However, they achieved a UK Top 5 chart hit with a breakneck revision of 'Nellie The Elephant' in Christmas 1984. Its ludicrous nature was not out of place with their standard fare: 'Yul Brynner Was A Skinhead', 'Nowt Can Compare To Sunderland Fine-Fare', 'Geordies Gone To Jail'. They also launched attacks on UK television personalities such as Deirdre Barlow from the famous soap opera *Coronation Street* ('Deirdre's A Slag') and presenter Anne Diamond. They did little, however, to reinforce their punk street credibility by composing a new theme tune to the children's television pop show *Razamatazz*. They re-formed in the late 90s after some inactivity.

● ALBUMS: *A Far Out Disc* (Volume 1985) ★★★, *Bare Faced Cheek* (Neat 1987) ★★★, *Dig That Groove Baby* (Volume 1988) ★★★, *Idle Gossip* (Volume 1988) ★★, *Wakey Wakey* (Volume 1989) ★★, *20 Tunes Live In Tokyo* (Receiver 1990) ★★, *Fat Bob's Feet* (Receiver 1991) ★★, *One More Megabyte* (Rotten 1998) ★★, *On Stage In Stuttgart* (Receiver 1999) ★★★, *Anniversary Anthems* (Receiver 2000) ★★★.

● COMPILATIONS: *Singles 1983-84* (Volume 1986) ★★★, *Collection* (Castle 1992) ★★★, *Ten Years: The Best Of Toy Dolls* (Castle 1994) ★★★, *The History 1979-1996* (Receiver 1997) ★★★★, *The History: Part II* (Receiver 1997) ★★★, *The Wonderful World Of The Toy Dolls* (Cleopatra 1998) ★★★, *Covered In Toy Dolls* (Captain Oi! 2002) ★★★, *We're Mad! The Anthology* (Castle 2002) ★★★★.

● VIDEOS: *Idle Gossip* (Jettisoundz 1986), *We're Mad* (Jettisoundz 1988).

## TOYAH

b. Toyah Ann Willcox, 18 May 1958, Kings Heath, Birmingham, England. One of the more talented individuals to have risen under the banner of punk, Toyah roamed with the gangs of Birmingham before channelling her energy into Birmingham Old Rep Drama School. She later worked as a mime artist at the Ballet Rambert, before winning her first professional acting role in the BBC Television play

*Glitter* with Noel Edmonds and Phil Daniels, in which she sang with the band Bilbo Baggins. Her next major role was as Emma in *Tales From The Vienna Wood*. Actor Ian Charleston then took her to tea with filmmaker Derek Jarman who offered her the part of Mad in *Jubilee*. It was here she met Adam Ant and for a time the pair, plus Eve Goddard, formed a band called the Man Eaters. However, the clash of egos ensured that the band was short-lived. Toyah formed a band with Peter Bush (keyboards), Steve Bray (drums, ex-Boyfriends), and Mark Henry (bass) while acting in Vienna. At the same time, she appeared in the movie *The Corn Is Green* with Katharine Hepburn, and played Monkey in *Quadrophenia*. The band was signed to Safari in 1979 and released 'Victims Of The Riddle'. In August, Charlie Francis (ex-Patrick Fitzgerald) replaced Henry. Toyah's extravagant vocal style and arresting lyrical subject matter were particularly evident on the powerful 'Bird In Flight'. While she was appearing in *Quatermass* the band started recording *Sheep Farming In Barnet*. During a busy year, Toyah also hosted the *Look! Hear!* television series for BBC Midlands, had a minor role in *Shoestring*, and made several other acting appearances. She was considered for the leading role in *Breaking Glass*, but it was eventually offered to Hazel O'Connor. Further singles followed the release of *The Blue Meaning*, before Toyah was rewarded with the UK Top 10 success of the *Four From Toyah EP* in 1981. Of the offerings, the repetitive lisp of 'It's A Mystery' carved out her identity with both public and press. Her first UK Top 10 single, 'I Want To Be Free', came across as a petulant nursery anthem, but was attractive enough to appeal to a nation's teenagers. Toyah's biggest hit, the exuberant 'Thunder In The Mountains', peaked at number 4 at the end of 1981, the same year that *Anthem* climbed to number 2 in the UK album charts. The following year she also charted with the startling, hypnotic 'Ieya' and the raucous 'Be Loud Be Proud (Be Heard)', and enjoyed another UK Top 10 success with *The Changeling*. Subsequent albums were recorded using session musicians instead of the band. Further acting roles came with the film *The Tempest* and the stage play *Trafford Tanzi*. She became a Buddhist, married King Crimson guitarist Robert Fripp and later recorded with him. She stayed with Safari until *Minx*, after which she recorded for Epic and then EG. Her last major hit was with a Top 60 cover version of 'Echo Beach' in 1987. She has since pursued a successful career as a television presenter and stage actress.

● ALBUMS: *Sheep Farming In Barnet* (Safari 1979) ★★, *The Blue Meaning* (Safari 1980) ★★, *Toyah! Toyah! Toyah! – Live* (Safari 1980) ★★, *Anthem* (Safari 1981) ★★★, *The Changeling* (Safari 1982) ★★, *Warrior Rock: Toyah On Tour* (Safari 1982) ★★, *Love Is The Law* (Safari 1983) ★★, *Mayhem* (Safari 1985) ★★, *Minx* (Portrait 1985) ★★, with Robert Fripp *The Lady Or The Tiger* (Editions EG 1986) ★★★, *Desire* (Editions EG 1987) ★★★, *Prostitute* (Editions EG 1988) ★★★, *Ophelia's Shadow* (Editions EG 1991) ★★★, *Kneeling At The Shrine (Sunday All Over The World)* (Editions EG 1991) ★★, *Dreamchild* re-released as *Phoenix* (Cryptic 1994) ★★★, *Take The*

*Leap* Japan only (Canyon 1994) ★★, *Toyah The Acoustic Album* (Aardvark 1996) ★★★.

● COMPILATIONS: *Toyah Toyah Toyah – All The Hits* (K-Tel 1984) ★★★, *Best Of Toyah* (Connoisseur Collection 1994) ★★★, *Looking Back* (Tring 1995) ★★★, *The Very Best Of Toyah* (Nectar 1997) ★★★, *Live & More: Live Favourites And Rarities* (Connoisseur 1998) ★★, *Proud, Loud And Heard: The Best Of Toyah* (Music Club 1998) ★★★.

● VIDEOS: *Toyah! Toyah! Toyah!* (K-Tel 1984), *Good Morning Universe: Live At Theatre Royal, Drury Lane* (BBC Video 1988), *Toyah At The Rainbow* (BBC Video 1988).

● FURTHER READING: *Toyah*, Mike West. *Toyah*, Gayna Evans. *Living Out Loud*, Toyah Willcox.

● FILMS: *Jubilee* (1977), *The Tempest* (1979), *Quadrophenia* (1979), *Corn Is Green* television (1979), *Urgh! A Music War* (1981), *Murder: Ultimate Grounds For Divorce* (1984), *The Ebony Tower* television (1984), *Anchoress* (1993), *Julie And The Cadillacs* (1999).

## TRANSVISION VAMP

This UK band was founded by the media-conscious Wendy James (b. 21 January 1966, London, England) and songwriter/guitarist Nick Christian Sayer (b. 1 August 1964). The line-up was completed by the arrival of Tex Axile (b. 30 July 1963; keyboards), Dave Parsons (b. 2 July 1962; bass), and Pol Burton (b. 1 July 1964; drums). The band borrowed heavily, in terms of image and content, from a variety of sources such as T. Rex, the Clash and most notably Blondie. James was frequently compared, unusually favourably, to Blondie's former lead singer, the peroxide blonde Deborah Harry. Despite being an easy target for her detractors, James filled the space that had been long open for a British female teenage-rebel figure. On signing to MCA Records, Transvision Vamp made their initial foray on to the UK pop scene in 1987 with the single 'Revolution Baby', but it was not until the cover version of Holly And The Italians' 'Tell That Girl To Shut Up' that they made any impact on the UK chart, while the follow-up, 'I Want Your Love', reached the UK Top 5. Their first album, *Pop Art*, also reached the UK Top 5. In 1989, further single chart hits with 'Baby Don't Care' (number 3), 'The Only One' and 'Landslide Of Love' (both Top 20) paved the way for the number 1 album *Velveteen*. This run of successes halted in 1991, with the result that MCA refused to release *The Little Magnets Versus The Bubble Of Babble* in the UK. Transvision Vamp's resultant low profile led to persistent rumours of a break-up. James' sense of self-publicity and cheap outrage gave the band's name a consistently high profile, and it was no surprise when she embarked on a solo career. Parsons went on to join Bush.

● ALBUMS: *Pop Art* (MCA 1988) ★★★, *Velveteen* (MCA 1989) ★★, *The Little Magnets Versus The Bubble Of Babble* (MCA 1991) ★.

● COMPILATIONS: *Kill Their Sons* (Universal 1998) ★★.

● VIDEOS: *Kiss Their Sons* (The Video Collection 1998).

## TRAVELING WILBURYS

This supergroup was formed in 1988 by accident as George Harrison attempted to make a new solo album, after enlisting the production talent of Jeff Lynne. At short notice, only Bob Dylan's garage was available to rehearse in, and over the next few days Tom Petty and Roy Orbison dropped by and joined in. This wonderful potpourri of stars re-introduced 'having a good time' to their vocabulary and the result was not a Harrison solo but the superb debut from the Traveling Wilburys. The outing proved to be a major success, bringing out the best of each artist; in particular, this was a marvellous swan song for Roy Orbison who tragically died soon afterwards. The deliberately erroneously titled *Volume 3* was released in 1990 and received similar plaudits. The members then came under pressure to tour but were able to resist, leaving open the possibility of future collaboration if mutually convenient at some point. This has to be the climate in which the last of the great supergroups can survive.

● ALBUMS: *Volume 1* (Wilbury 1988) ★★★★, *Volume 3* (Wilbury 1990) ★★★.

## TRIFFIDS

Hailing from the isolated Western Australian city of Perth, David McComb's band, along with the Go-Betweens and Nick Cave, contributed greatly to increasing the northern hemisphere's respect for Antipodean rock, which for a long time was seldom taken seriously. The band was formed in 1980 by McComb (b. 17 February 1962, Perth, Australia, d. 2 February 1999, Melbourne, Australia; lead vocals, guitar, keyboards), his brother Robert McComb (violin, guitar, vocals), and Alsy MacDonald (b. 14 August 1961, Australia; drums, vocals). The latter had been writing and playing music with David McComb since they formed the high school band Dalsy. The Triffids' first single, 'Stand Up', was released in 1981 on the White label, after which the band relocated to Melbourne and then Sydney. Martyn Casey (bass) and Jill Birt (keyboards, vocals) replaced Will Akers and Margaret Gillard on their 1983 debut, *Treeless Plain*, released on the Australian independent Hot label.

The band's breakthrough into the European market came with 1986's *Born Sandy Devotional*, which was recorded after they had left Australia to set up base in London, England. This atmospheric set, featuring new member 'Evil' Graham Lee (pedal and lap steel guitar), was redolent at times of Bruce Springsteen and boasted the brooding 'Wide Open Road' and the desolate 'Sea Birds' and 'Stolen Property'. The follow-up found the Triffids returning to a simpler recording technique – an outback sheep-shearing shed and an eight-track recorder, producing a collection of Australian C&W/folk-blues songs. Departing from Hot, the Triffids landed a major contract with Island Records. New guitarist Adam Peters was featured on *Calenture*, their first album for Island. McComb's lyrics, which were starkly evocative of the rural Australian townships and psyche, reached new peaks on *The Black Swan*, their most musically varied set. Disillusioned by their lack of commercial success, the band called it a day

after this album, although a live set was issued posthumously. David McComb went on to work with the Blackeyed Susans and recorded an excellent country-tinged solo collection in 1994. He assembled a band, the Red Ponies, to tour Europe but ill-health curtailed his musical activities and he underwent a heart transplant in 1995. McComb subsequently enrolled at Melbourne University and performed from time to time with his new band, Costar. His untimely death in February 1999 was apparently the result of complications following a car accident.

● ALBUMS: *Treeless Plain* (Hot/Rough Trade 1983) ★★★, *Raining Pleasure* mini-album (Hot/Rough Trade 1984) ★★★, *Field Of Glass* (Hot/Rough Trade 1985) ★★★, *Born Sandy Devotional* (Hot/Rough Trade 1986) ★★★★, *In The Pines* (Hot/Rough Trade 1986) ★★★, *Calenture* (Island 1987) ★★★★, *The Black Swan* (Island 1989) ★★★, *Stockholm* (MNW 1990) ★★★.
Solo: David McComb *Love Of Will* (Mushroom 1994) ★★★★.

● COMPILATIONS: *Love In Bright Landscapes* Dutch release (Hot/Megadisc 1986) ★★★, *Australian Melodrama* (Mushroom 1994) ★★★★.

## TRIUMPH

This Canadian power-trio formed in Toronto during 1975. Comprising Rik Emmett (b. 1953, Toronto, Ontario, Canada; guitar, vocals), Gil Moore (drums) and Mike Levine (bass, keyboards), Triumph shared many similarities to Rush aside from geographical location. All three members were highly accomplished musicians who experimented with many facets of high-tech melodic rock, yet they followed a rockier road than their fellow countrymen.

Triumph's music was characterized by Emmett's high-pitched vocals and intricate guitar work, supplemented by keyboard fills and a thunderous rhythm section. Interest built slowly, but the band finally made a breakthrough with *Progressions Of Power*, their fourth album, released in 1980. *Allied Forces* and *Never Surrender* saw the pinnacle of their success, with both albums attaining gold status in the USA. *Thunder Seven*, a CD-only release, was a disjointed collection, while the live album that followed suffered from a wooden sound and flat production. In live settings, the band frequently used Rick Santers as an extra guitarist to overcome the limitations of a three-man line-up. Like Rush, their concerts were renowned for their sophisticated special effects rather than the actual music, and featured every conceivable pyrotechnic device available, plus the ultimate in computerized, laser lighting rigs. *The Sport Of Kings* saw the band move in a blatantly commercial direction, but *Surveillance* marked a return to their roots: an aggressive and well-produced hard rock album. Emmett left the band in 1988 and was replaced by guitarist Phil Xenides. The vocals were taken over by Moore, but much of Triumph's character left with Emmett.

● ALBUMS: *Triumph* (Attic 1976) ★★, *Rock & Roll Machine* (Attic/RCA 1977) ★★, *Just A Game* (Attic/RCA 1979) ★★, *Progressions Of Power* (RCA

1980) ★★★, *Allied Forces* (RCA 1981) ★★★, *Never Surrender* (RCA 1983) ★★★, *Thunder Seven* (MCA 1984) ★★, *Stages* (MCA 1985) ★★, *The Sport Of Kings* (MCA 1986) ★★, *Surveillance* (MCA 1987) ★★★, *Edge Of Excess* (Virgin 1992) ★★★, *In Concert* (King Biscuit Flower Hour 1996) ★★.

● COMPILATIONS: *Classics* (MCA 1989) ★★★★.

● VIDEOS: *Triumph Live At The US Festival* (MCA 1988), *A Night Of Triumph Live* (Emperor Entertainment 1988).

## TRUE BELIEVERS

This Austin, Texas, USA-based outfit burned brightly for a few years in the mid- to late 80s but never achieved the audience they deserved. With a brand of guitar music that combined the rudiments of garage rock with glam rock (comparisons to the Faces, Mott The Hoople and New York Dolls featured in their press coverage), they nevertheless broke up after just one album. The band's core members were Alejandro Escovedo (b. San Antonio, Texas, USA; guitar, vocals) and brother Javier (guitar, vocals). Javier had previously played with Los Angeles punk band the Zeros, while Alejandro joined the influential San Francisco band the Nuns, before forming Rank And File in Austin. Alejandro left that band in 1983 before the recording of their second album, convincing Javier to relocate to Austin and join him in the True Believers, whose line-up was completed by bass player Denny DeGorgio. They became good friends and touring buddies with Los Lobos, earning a reputation as one of the hottest live acts in Texas. In the process, they added third guitarist Jon Dee Graham, who also contributed to songwriting and vocals (many drummers passed through the ranks). The band was signed by Rounder Records in 1985, entering the studio with producer Jim Dickinson to record their debut album shortly thereafter. With glowing reviews, parent company EMI Records asked them to repeat the process with a bigger budget for their projected second album, though they insisted the band use Georgia Satellites producer Jeff Glixman. The result was barely concealed tension and hostility throughout, with DeGorgio and Kevin Foley, the then drummer, being fired. The ensuing album was denied a release. Following a management rationalization at EMI the band was one of a clutch dropped from the roster. The True Believers continued to tour with the aid of Hector Munoz (drums) and J.D. Foster (bass, vocals), but were unable to obtain the rights to their unreleased record. As a consequence, the band disintegrated in late 1987. Alejandro Escovedo has gone on to record several acclaimed roots rock sets, while his brother worked with Will And The Kill, the Lost and Sacred Hearts. Graham has subsequently recorded with members of X. The True Believers' second album was finally made public in 1994 when Rykodisc issued the unreleased tracks alongside the contents of their debut album in one CD reissue.

● ALBUMS: *True Believers* (Rounder 1986) ★★★.

● COMPILATIONS: *Hard Road* (Rykodisc 1994) ★★★.

## TUBE, THE

Though never a great ratings success, Channel 4's first music series, *The Tube*, is fondly recalled as one of British television's most exciting and pioneering music shows. It was produced by Malcolm Gerrie (formerly in charge of 'kiddie pop' show *Razzamatazz*) at Tyne Tees Television, with wife-and-husband team Andrea and Geoff Wonfor as executive producer and film director. Of fundamental importance to its success was the pairing of presenters Paula Yates and Jools Holland. The show ran from 1982 to 1986, with the laconic duo (Yates' usual flirtatious persona contrasting with Holland's easy charm) introducing a series of bands and artists who had no previous television experience. The Fine Young Cannibals, Frankie Goes To Hollywood and Paul Young were all made famous by their appearances, as the show pursued an adventurous booking policy primarily directed by researcher Chris Phipps, Chris Cowie and Geoff Brown. This allowed space for acts as diverse as Rubella Ballet, Cameo, Public Image Limited (John Lydon famously returning to the Sex Pistols' 'Anarchy In The UK') and Iggy Pop to appear. Other presenters, including Muriel Gray and Leslie Ash, and poet Mark Miwurdz also joined the team, though Yates and Holland remained the main pivots – despite the fact that the show's links were never as slick as conventional television demanded. While Yates continued to appear during the late stages of her pregnancy during the second series, Holland immortalized himself by swearing on air some weeks before the end of the *Tube*'s final series (he was 'suspended' for his errant behaviour). After the show's close, the various members of cast and crew have largely remained within the television industry – Holland presenting *Later With Jools Holland*, Yates hosting various shows before her untimely death in September 2000, Gray joining *Frocks On The Box*, Mark Miwurdz returning to his real name, Mark Hurst, and to stand-up comedy, and Ash returning to acting in *Men Behaving Badly*.

In *The Tube*'s wake Channel 4 launched a number of new pop formats, including *Club X*, *Network 7*, *Big World Cafe*, *Friday Night At The Dome* and finally the lamentable *The Word*, without ever recapturing the shambolic magic of *The Tube* – an impression reinforced by the show's repeats in the 90s. After various freelance projects (notably with U2, whose appearance on *The Tube* is among the show's most memorable moments), Malcolm Gerrie, now of Initial Film And Television, launched Channel 4's *The White Room* in 1995.

## TURNER, TINA

b. Annie Mae Bullock, 26 November 1939, Brownsville, Tennessee, USA. A singer while in her early teens, this enduring artist was a regular performer in St. Louis' nightclubs when she was discovered in 1956 by guitarist Ike Turner. She joined his group as a backing singer, but quickly became the co-star and featured vocalist, a relationship sealed two years later with their marriage. Ike And Tina Turner was a highly successful act on the R&B circuit, before expanding their audience through a controversial liaison with producer Phil Spector. They emerged as a leading pop/soul act during the late 60s/early 70s with tours in support of the Rolling Stones and hits with 'Proud Mary' (1971) and 'Nutbush City Limits' (1973). However, the relationship between husband and wife grew increasingly strained as Ike's behaviour became irrational. Tina walked out of their professional and personal relationship during a 1975 tour, incurring the wrath of concert promoters who remained unsympathetic when the singer attempted a solo act. During this time the singer appeared in Ken Russell's film of the Who's rock-opera *Tommy*, offering an outrageous portrayal of the Acid Queen; however, this acclaimed cameo failed to successfully launch Turner's solo career.

Her career was rejuvenated in 1983 when British act Heaven 17 invited her to participate in an offshoot project dubbed BEF. She contributed a suitably raucous cover version of the Temptations 'Ball Of Confusion' which, in turn, engendered a recording contract with Capitol Records. Turner's reading of Al Green's 'Let's Stay Together' reached the UK Top 10, while an attendant album, *Private Dancer*, hurriedly completed in its wake, spawned another major hit in 'What's Love Got To Do With It'. This melodramatic ballad topped the US chart, reached number 3 in England, and won two Grammys as Record Of The Year and Best Pop Vocal Performance, Female. The title track, written by Mark Knopfler, was also a transatlantic hit. Turner enhanced her popularity worldwide through a series of punishing tours, yet her energy remained undiminished.

In the mid-80s Turner accepted a role in the movie *Mad Max Beyond Thunderdome*, the theme from which, 'We Don't Need Another Hero', was another international hit. The following year she duetted with Mick Jagger at the Live Aid concert and contributed to the US charity single 'We Are The World'. Her 1985 autobiography was filmed in 1993 as *What's Love Got To Do With It*, which also gave its title to a bestselling album and an extensive worldwide tour. She released the title track from the James Bond movie *Goldeneye* in October 1995. The Bono/Edge composition had Turner sounding uncannily like Shirley Bassey (the vocalist on 'Goldfinger'). The Trevor Horn-produced *Wildest Dreams* was a further solid rock album, laying her strong R&B roots to rest. Turner returned to the UK Top 10 in October 1999, days short of her sixtieth birthday, with 'When The Heartache Is Over'. This preceded the disappointing *Twenty Four Seven*, following which Turner announced she was retiring from live performance.

Although commentators have criticised Turner's one-dimensional approach, she enjoys massive popularity. She is truly happy with her present life and talks articulately about her difficult past. The voluptuous image is kept for the stage, while a quieter Turner enjoys the fruits of her considerable success offstage. She was inducted into the Rock And Roll Hall Of Fame in 1991.

● ALBUMS: *The Country Of Tina Turner* (Connoisseur) ★★★, *Acid Queen* (United Artists 1975) ★★★, *Rough* (United Artists 1978) ★★, *Love*
*Explosion* (United Artists 1979) ★★★, *Private Dancer* (Capitol 1984) ★★★★, *Break Every Rule* (Capitol 1986) ★★★, *Live In Europe: Tina Turner* (Capitol 1988) ★★, *Foreign Affair* (Capitol 1989) ★★★, *What's Love Got To Do With It?* film soundtrack (Parlophone 1993) ★★★, *Wildest Dreams* (Parlophone/Virgin 1996) ★★★, *Twenty Four Seven* (Parlophone 1999) ★★.

● COMPILATIONS: *Simply The Best* (Capitol 1991) ★★★★, *Tina Turner: The Collected Recordings, 60s To 90s* (Capitol 1994) ★★★★.

● VIDEOS: *Nice 'N' Rough* (EMI 1982), *Private Dancer Video EP* (PMI 1985), *Private Dancer Tour* (PMI 1985), *What You See Is What You Get* (PMI 1987), *Break Every Rule* (PMI 1987), *Rio 88* (PolyGram Music Video 1988), *Foreign Affair* (PMI 1990), *Do You Want Some Action* (Channel 5 1990), *Simply The Best* (PMI 1991), *Wild Lady Of Rock* (Hendring Music Video 1992), *What's Love Live* (1994), *The Girl From Nutbush* (Strand 1995), *Wildest Dreams* (Feedback Fusion 1996), *Live In Amsterdam* (Castle Music Pictures 1997), *One Last Time Live In Concert* (Eagle Vision 2001).

● FURTHER READING: *I, Tina*, Tina Turner with Kurt Loder. *The Tina Turner Experience*, Chris Welch. *Takin' Back My Name*, Ike Turner and Nigel Cawthorne

● FILMS: *Tommy* (1975), *Sgt. Pepper's Lonely Hearts Club Band* (1978), *Mad Max Beyond Thunderdome* (1985), *What's Love Got To Do With It* (1993), *Last Action Hero* (1993).

## TV SMITH'S EXPLORERS

Formed from the punk debris of the Adverts, the Explorers saw TV Smith (b. Timothy Smith; vocals) and Tim Cross (guitar) combine with Erik Russell (guitar), Colin Stoner (bass) and John Towe (drums). After only one gig at the London Marquee in March 1980, Cross quit, and three performances later, Towe followed suit. With Mel Wesson and Dave Sinclair, respectively, stopping the musical gap, the new line-up signed to Chiswick Records. The aggressive 'Tomahawk Cruise' was voted Single Of The Week in *Sounds* music paper, but failed to chart. Over the next two years, the band recorded several singles and an album for the Epic Records subsidiary Kaleidoscope, until Smith moved on to a solo career. After recording 'War Fever' and *Channel Five*, he formed a new outfit, Cheap, though he remains best known for his work with the Adverts.

● ALBUMS: *The Last Words Of The Great Explorer* (Kaleidoscope 1981) ★★.

## 23 SKIDOO

Post-punk experimentalists who, alongside other industrial acts such as Cabaret Voltaire, A Certain Ratio and Throbbing Gristle did much to influence the course of UK dance music. Taking their name from an Aleister Crowley reference, the group was formed in London, England in 1979 by Fritz Catlin (b. Fritz Haaman; drums/percussion) and brothers Alex Turnbull (percussion) and Johnny Turnbull (guitar). Their debut single, 'Ethics', was released on the Pineapple label and featured additional members Tom Heslop (vocals) and Sam Mills (guitar). The same line-up decamped to Cabaret Voltaire's Western Works studio to record 'Last Words'/'The Gospel Comes To New Guinea' and the *Seven Songs* mini-album, that somewhat confusingly featured eight tracks. Psychic TV and Current 93's David Tibet joined the founding trio on the following year's *The Culling Is Coming*, an album of ritual music on which the band's percussion-based grooves and eastern leanings came to the fore.

Particular inspiration was drawn from the Turnbull brothers trip to Asia, where they became enamoured of Indonesian gamelan orchestras. Bass player Sketch Martin (b. Antigua, West Indies; ex-Linx) was added to the line-up for *Urban Gamelan*, a masterful fusion of industrial, funk and world music. The four members disbanded as a unit after this album but continued to work with each other on a temporary basis. They also formed Ronin Records, a label that has been instrumental in the promotion of UK hip-hop. The quartet's long-avowed intention to record a new album came to fruition with 2000's self-titled release for Virgin Records, that successfully incorporated contemporary genres such as drum 'n' bass and trip-hop into their sound.

● ALBUMS: *Seven Songs* mini-album (Fetish 1982) ★★★, *The Culling Is Coming* (Operation Twilight/Les Disques Du Crepuscule 1983) ★★★, *Urban Gamelan* (Illuminated 1984) ★★★★, *23 Skidoo* (Virgin 2000) ★★★.
● COMPILATIONS: *Just Like Everybody* (Bleeding Chin 1987) ★★★.

## TWISTED SISTER

Formed in 1976, this New York, USA-based quintet's original purpose was to provide the antidote to the disco music that was saturating the airwaves during the mid-70s. Featuring Dee Snider (b. Daniel Snider, 15 March 1955, Massapequa, Long Island, New York, USA; vocals), Eddie Ojeda (guitar), Mark 'The Animal' Mendoza (bass, ex-Dictators), Jay Jay French (guitar) and Tony Petri (drums) they had a bizarre image that borrowed ideas from Kiss, Alice Cooper and the New York Dolls. Musically they combined sexually provocative lyrics and dumb choruses with heavy-duty, metallic rock 'n' roll. A.J. Pero (ex-Cities) took over on drums before the recording of their debut, *Under The Blade*. This was picked up from the independent Secret label by Atlantic Records, following a successful UK appearance at the Reading Festival and a controversial performance on *The Tube* television show in 1982. The band never lived up to their initial promise, with successive albums simply regurgitating earlier ideas. Their greatest success was *Stay Hungry*, which cracked the Top 20 album charts on both sides of the Atlantic. It also included the hit single, 'I Am, I'm Me', which peaked at number 18 in the UK. Their audience had become bored with them by the time *Come Out And Play* was released and the tour to support it was a flop. Pero quit and returned to his former outfit, Cities; Joey 'Seven' Franco (ex-Good Rats) was drafted in as replacement. Snider steered the band in a more melodic direction on *Love Is For Suckers*. The album was still born; Atlantic terminated their contract,

and the band imploded in 1987.

Snider went on to form Desperado, with ex-Gillan guitarist Bernie Tormé (subsequently evolving, more permanently, into Widowmaker), before finding belated success as a heavy metal DJ. Twisted Sister briefly reunited to record a new song for the 1998 movie *Strangeland*, which was written by and starred Snider. Looking back on his days dressing up with his old band, Snider would conclude: 'All that flash and shit wears thin. There's gotta be something beyond it. And there wasn't with Twisted Sister'.
● ALBUMS: *Under The Blade* (Secret 1982) ★★, *You Can't Stop Rock 'N' Roll* (Atlantic 1983) ★★, *Stay Hungry* (Atlantic 1984) ★★★, *Come Out And Play* (Atlantic 1985) ★★, *Love Is For Suckers* (Atlantic 1987) ★★, *Live At Hammersmith* (Music For Nations/CMC 1994) ★★.
● COMPILATIONS: *Big Hits & Nasty Cuts: The Best Of Twisted Sister* (Atlantic 1992) ★★★, *Club Daze Volume 1: The Studio Sessions* (Spitfire 1999) ★★, *Club Daze Volume 2: Never Say Never* (Spitfire 2001) ★★, *Disco Sucks* (Snapper 2001) ★★.
● VIDEOS: *Stay Hungry* (Virgin 1984), *Come Out And Play* (Atlantic 1985).
● FILMS: *Pee-Wee's Big Adventure* (1985).

## TYGERS OF PAN TANG

This hard rock band was formed in Whitley Bay, Newcastle-upon-Tyne, England, in 1978, as part of the New Wave Of British Heavy Metal. The four-piece line-up comprised Jess Cox (vocals), Robb Weir (guitar), Richard 'Rocky' Laws (bass) and Brian 'Big' Dick (drums). Their debut EP was the first rock release on Newcastle's Neat label, and it quickly topped all the metal charts. On the back of their first flush of success, they moved to MCA Records. However, after one album, 1980's *Wild Cat*, Cox departed to be replaced by Jon Deverill (b. Cardiff, Wales; vocals), and additional member John Sykes (guitar) was recruited. Sykes left following the band's third album, *Crazy Nights*, and was replaced by former Penetration guitarist Fred Purser. *The Cage* broke the band in the USA, before two years of disputes with MCA effectively scuppered their career. Deverill and Dick recruited new members Steve Lamb (guitar), Neil Shepherd (guitar), and David Donaldson (bass) to record 1985's *The Wreck-Age*. Former vocalist Cox formed Tyger Tyger the following year in order to try to recapture the original band's past glories. Meanwhile, Deverill, Dick and Lamb carried on recording as Tygers Of Pan Tang into the late 80s before finally pulling the plug. Weir and Cox reunited in 1999 to play a live set at the Wacken Festival. A new line-up led by Weir recorded a new studio album in 2001.
● ALBUMS: *Wild Cat* (MCA 1980) ★★★, *Spellbound* (MCA 1981) ★★, *Crazy Nights* (MCA 1981) ★★, *The Cage* (MCA 1982) ★★, *The Wreck-Age* (Music For Nations 1985) ★★, *Burning In The Shade* (Zebra 1987) ★, *Live At Wacken* (Spitfire 2001) ★★, *Live At Nottingham Rock City* 1981 recording (Edgy 2001) ★★★, *Mystical* (Z 2001) ★★.
● COMPILATIONS: *The Best Of The Tygers Of Pan Tang* (MCA 1983) ★★★, *First Kill* (Neat 1986) ★★.

**TYLER, BONNIE**
b. Gaynor Hopkins, 8 June 1951, Skewen, South Wales. Tyler's powerful, melodramatic voice was a perfect vehicle for the quasi-operatic imagination of producer Jim Steinman. After winning a talent contest in 1970, Tyler sang regularly in Welsh clubs and pubs, fronting a soul band called Mumbles. A throat operation in 1976 gave her voice an extra huskiness that attracted writer/producers Ronnie Scott and Steve Wolfe. Tyler successfully recorded their compositions 'Lost In France' and 'It's A Heartache', a million-seller in the USA. 'Married Men' (from the movie *The World Is Full Of Married Men*) was only a minor hit, and in 1981 Tyler changed labels to CBS Records and was teamed with Meat Loaf producer Steinman. He created 'Total Eclipse Of The Heart', a gigantic ballad that is probably Tyler's finest performance. The single reached number 1 on both sides of the Atlantic while 'Faster Than The Speed Of Night' also topped the UK charts. In 1984 Tyler duetted with fellow Welsh singer Shakin' Stevens on 'A Rockin' Good Way' and her dramatic delivery brought commissions to record the film themes 'Holding Out For A Hero' (a Steinman song from *Footloose* which reached the UK Top 10) and 'Here She Comes' from Giorgio Moroder's score for *Metropolis*. Next, Steinman paired Tyler with Todd Rundgren on 'Loving You's A Dirty Job But Someone's Got To Do It' (1986). Songwriter Desmond Child was brought in to produce *Hide Your Heart* in 1988, and in the same year she took part in George Martin's recording of the Dylan Thomas verse drama *Under Milk Wood*.

After a two-year absence from recording, Tyler signed to German label Hansa and *Bitterblue* was a big hit across northern Europe. Among those writing and producing for the album were Nik Kershaw, Harold Faltermeyer and Moroder. Her new contract with East West brought her together with Jim Steinman for *Free Spirit*. Even he could not rescue the production on an empty album of AOR vagaries, set against a singer with a distinctive voice that demands epic material.

● ALBUMS: *The World Starts Tonight* (RCA 1977) ★★, *Natural Force* (UK) *It's A Heartache* (USA) (RCA 1978) ★★★, *Diamond Cut* (RCA 1979) ★★, *Goodbye To The Island* (RCA 1981) ★★, *Faster Than The Speed Of Night* (Columbia 1983) ★★★, *Secret Dreams And Forbidden Fire* (Columbia 1986) ★★, *Hide Your Heart* (Columbia 1988) ★★, *Bitterblue* (Hansa 1991) ★★, *Free Spirit* (East West 1995) ★★.
● COMPILATIONS: *The Very Best Of Bonnie Tyler* (RCA 1981) ★★★, *Greatest Hits* (Telstar 1986) ★★★, *The Best* (Columbia 1993) ★★★, *Greatest Hits* (Sanctuary 2001) ★★★★.
● FILMS: *Footloose* (1984).

**U2**
Indisputably one of the most popular rock acts in the world, this Irish quartet's achievements since the late 70s have been extraordinarily cohesive and consistent. U2 began their musical career at school in Dublin in 1977. Bono (b. Paul David Hewson, 10 May 1960, Dublin, Eire; vocals), The Edge (b. David Evans, 8 August 1961, Barking, Essex, England; guitar), Adam Clayton (b. 13 March 1960, Chinnor, Oxfordshire, England; bass) and Larry Mullen Jnr. (b. Laurence Mullen, 31 October 1961, Dublin, Eire; drums) initially played Rolling Stones and Beach Boys cover versions in an outfit named Feedback. They then changed their name to the Hype before finally settling on U2 in 1978. After winning a talent contest in Limerick that year, they came under the wing of manager Paul McGuinness and were subsequently signed to CBS Records Ireland. Their debut EP *U2:3* featured 'Out Of Control' (1979), which propelled them to number 1 in the Irish charts. They repeated that feat with 'Another Day' (1980), but having been passed by CBS UK, they were free to sign a deal outside of Ireland with Island Records. Their UK debut '11 O'Clock Tick Tock', produced by Martin Hannett, was well received but failed to chart. Two further singles, 'A Day Without Me' and 'I Will Follow', passed with little sales while the band prepared their first album, produced by Steve Lillywhite. *Boy*, a moving and inspired document of adolescence, received critical approbation, which was reinforced by the live shows that U2 were undertaking throughout the country. Bono's impassioned vocals and the band's rhythmic tightness revealed them as the most promising live unit of 1981. After touring America, the band returned to Britain where 'Fire' was bubbling under the Top 30. Another minor hit with the impassioned 'Gloria' was followed by the strident *October*. The album had a thrust reinforced by a religious verve that was almost evangelical in its force. In February 1983 the band reached the UK Top 10 with 'New Year's Day', a song of hope inspired by the Polish Solidarity Movement. *War* followed soon afterwards to critical plaudits. The album's theme covered both religious and political conflicts, especially in the key track 'Sunday Bloody Sunday', which had already emerged as one of the group's most startling and moving live songs. Given their power in concert, it was inevitable that U2 would attempt to capture their essence on a live album. *Under A Blood Red Sky* did not disappoint and, as well as climbing to number 2 in the UK, it brought them their first significant chart placing in the USA at number 28.

By the summer of 1984, U2 were about to enter the vanguard of the rock elite. Bono duetted with Bob Dylan at the latter's concert at Slane Castle and U2 established their own company, Mother Records, with the intention of unearthing fresh musical talent in Eire. *The Unforgettable Fire*, produced by Brian Eno and Daniel Lanois, revealed a new maturity and improved their commercial and critical standing in the US charts. The attendant single, 'Pride (In The Name Of Love)', displayed the passion and humanity that were by now familiar ingredients in U2's music and lyrics. The band's commitment to their ideals was further underlined by their appearances at Live Aid, Ireland's Self Aid, and their involvement with Amnesty International and guest spot on Little Steven's anti-Apartheid single, 'Sun City'.

During this same period, U2 embarked on a world tour and completed work on their next album. *The Joshua Tree* emerged in March 1987 and confirmed U2's standing, now as one of the most popular acts in the world. The album topped both the US and UK charts and revealed a new, more expansive sound that complemented their soul-searching lyrics. The familiar themes of spiritual salvation permeated the work and the quest motif was particularly evident on both 'With Or Without You' and 'I Still Haven't Found What I'm Looking For', which both reached number 1 in the US charts, confirming U2 as indisputably the most successful European act to cross the Atlantic for several years.

After such a milestone album, 1988 proved a relatively quiet year for U2. Bono and the Edge appeared on Roy Orbison's *Mystery Girl* and the year ended with the double-live album and film, *Rattle And Hum*. The band also belatedly scored their first UK number 1 single with the R&B-influenced 'Desire'. The challenge to complete a suitable follow-up to *The Joshua Tree* took considerable time, with sessions completed in Germany with Lanois and Eno. Meanwhile, the band members appeared on the Cole Porter tribute album *Red Hot + Blue*, performing a radical reading of 'Night And Day'. In late 1991, 'The Fly' entered the UK charts at number 1, emulating the success of 'Desire'. *Achtung Baby* was an impressive work that captured the majesty of its predecessor, yet also stripped down the sound to provide a greater sense of spontaneity. The work emphasized U2's standing as an international rock act, and although the critics were less than generous with the follow-up *Zooropa* and the dance-orientated *Pop* the band remained one of the most popular 'stadium' attractions in the world during the 90s.

In the mid-90s Bono devoted much of his time to writing songs for others. With the Edge he wrote the James Bond film theme 'Goldeneye' for Tina Turner and became involved in the Passengers project alongside the rest of U2 and Brian Eno (the 1995 release *Original Soundtracks 1* spawned a couple of memorable ballads, 'Miss Sarajevo' and 'Your Blue Room'.) He also established himself as a highly respected and shrewd political advocate for a number of causes. His verbal lashing of the French president Jacques Chirac at the 1995 MTV Awards in Paris created headlines. Obviously upset by the country's recent nuclear tests, Bono came onstage smiling to accept an award. The audience were brilliantly fooled by his perfectly delivered sarcasm:

'What a city' (cheers and applause), 'what a night' (cheers and applause), 'what a bomb' (confused laughter and applause), 'what a mistake' (mixed response), 'what a wanker you have for President' (sporadic boos). Of more particular note is the singer's tireless work in helping to solve the financial and health crisis in Africa. In 1999 he joined the Jubilee 2000 (later renamed Drop The Debt) movement, dedicated to erasing the public debt of 52 of the world's poorest countries, many of them located in Africa. In his role as a Jubilee 2000 ambassador, Bono has met with Pope John Paul II, US president George W. Bush, former US president Bill Clinton, US Treasury Secretary Paul O'Neill, and UN Secretary-General Kofi Annan. In 2002, he founded DATA (Debt, Aid, Trade for Africa)

What many critics and fans regard as the musical renaissance of U2 began in October 1998 when a re-recorded b-side, 'Sweetest Thing', reached UK number 3. The single was followed by the release of the band's first compilation album. In March 2000, the Bono-scripted movie *The Million Dollar Hotel* was released. The soundtrack included the new U2 track 'The Ground Beneath Her Feet', featuring lyrics by novelist Salman Rushdie. *All That You Can't Leave Behind* eschewed the band's preoccupation with electronica to return to the epic rock sound they championed in the late 80s. The chart-topping 'Beautiful Day' won three Grammy Awards, including Song Of The Year, the following February. The album's enduring appeal was confirmed when the band won four more awards at the following year's Grammy Awards, including Best Rock Album and Record Of The Year ('Walk On').

● ALBUMS: *Boy* (Island 1980) ★★★, *October* (Island 1981) ★★★, *War* (Island 1983) ★★★★, *Under A Blood Red Sky* (Island 1983) ★★★, *The Unforgettable Fire* (Island 1984) ★★★★, *Wide Awake In America* (Island 1985) ★★★, *The Joshua Tree* (Island 1987) ★★★★, *Rattle And Hum* (Island 1988) ★★★, *Achtung Baby* (Island 1991) ★★★★, *Zooropa* (Island 1993) ★★★, *Pop* (Island 1997) ★★★, *All That You Can't Leave Behind* (Island 2000) ★★★★.

● COMPILATIONS: *The Joshua Tree Singles* (Island 1988) ★★★, *The Best Of 1980-1990* (Island 1998) ★★★★.

● VIDEOS: *Under A Blood Red Sky (Live At Red Rocks)* (PolyGram Music Video 1983), *The Unforgettable Fire Collection* (PolyGram Music Video 1985), *Rattle And Hum* (PolyGram Music Video 1988), *Achtung Baby* (PolyGram Music Video 1992), *Zoo TV Live From Sydney* (PolyGram Music Video 1994), *PopMart: Live From Mexico City* (PolyGram Music Video 1998), *The Best Of 1980-1990* (PolyGram Music Video 1999), *Classic Albums: U2 - Joshua Tree* (Eagle Rock Entertainment 1999), *Elevation 2001: U2 Live From Boston* (Universal 2001).

● FURTHER READING: *U2: Touch The Flame. An Illustrated Documentary*, Geoff Parkyn. *Unforgettable Fire: The Story Of U2*, Eamon Dunphy. *Rattle And Hum*, Peter Williams and Steve Turner. *U2: Stories For Boys*, Dave Thomas. *U2 The Early Days: Another Time, Another Place*, Bill Graham. *U2: Three Chords & The Truth*, Niall Stokes. *Wide Awake In America*, Alan Carter. *U2: A Conspiracy Of Hope*, Dave Bowler and

Brian Dray. *U2: The Story So Far*, Richard Seal. *U2: Burning Desire – The Complete Story*, Sam Goodman. *U2 Live: A Concert Documentary*, Pimm Jal De La Perra. *Race Of Angels: The Genesis Of U2*, John Waters. *U2, The Rolling Stones File*, editors of *Rolling Stone*. *U2 At The End Of The World*, Bill Flanagan. *U2 Faraway So Close*, B.P. Fallon. *The Complete Guide To The Music Of U2*, Bill Graham. *The Making Of: U2's Joshua Tree*, Dave Thompson. *Bono: The Biography*, Laura Jackson. *Into The Heart: The Stories Behind Every Song*, Niall Stokes. *U2: The Complete Encyclopedia*, Mark Chatterton.
● FILMS: *Rattle And Hum* (1988).

## UB40

Named after the form issued to unemployed people in the UK to receive benefit, UB40 are the most long-lasting proponents of crossover reggae in the UK. The multiracial band was formed in Birmingham, England, in 1978 around the brothers Robin (b. 25 December 1954, Birmingham, England; lead guitar, vocals) and Ali Campbell (b. 15 February 1959, Birmingham, England; lead vocals, guitar), the sons of Birmingham folk club singers Lorna and Ian Campbell. Other founder-members included Earl Falconer (b. 23 January 1959, Birmingham, England; bass, vocals), Michael Virtue (b. 19 January 1957, Birmingham, England; keyboards), Brian Travers (b. 7 February 1959; saxophone), James Brown (b. 20 November 1957; drums), and Norman Hassan (b. 26 January 1958, Birmingham, England; percussion, vocals). Reggae toaster Astro (b. Terence Wilson, 24 June 1957) joined UB40 to record 'Food For Thought' with local producer Bob Lamb (former drummer with Locomotive and the Steve Gibbons band). 'King' (coupled with 'Food For Thought') was a tribute to Martin Luther King that provided UB40 with a UK Top 5 debut single in March 1980. Two further Top 10 hits followed, with 'My Way Of Thinking'/'I Think It's Going To Rain Today' and 'The Earth Dies Screaming'/'Dream A Lie'. Their long-playing debut, *Signing Off*, boasted an album sleeve with a 12-inch square replica of the notorious, bright yellow unemployment card. This image attracted a large contingent of disaffected youths as well as proving popular with followers of the 2-Tone/ska scene. The following year, UB40 formed their own label, DEP International, on which they released 'One In Ten', an impassioned protest about unemployment which still managed to return the band to the UK Top 10. *Labour Of Love*, a collection of cover versions, signalled a return to the reggae mainstream and it brought UB40's first number 1 hit single in 'Red Red Wine' (1983). Originally written by Neil Diamond, it had been a big reggae hit for Tony Tribe in 1969. The album contained further hit singles in Winston Groovy's 'Please Don't Make Me Cry', Jimmy Cliff's 'Many Rivers To Cross' and Eric Donaldson's 'Cherry Oh Baby'. The follow-up, *Geffrey Morgan ...*, a UK number 3 album, supplied UB40 with the Top 10 hit 'If It Happens Again'. 'I Got You Babe' (1986) was a different kind of cover, as Ali Campbell and Chrissie Hynde of the Pretenders duetted on a chart-topping revival of the Sonny And Cher pop hit. The same team had a further hit in 1988 with a revival of Lorna

Bennett's 1969 reggae song 'Breakfast In Bed'. Both songs, plus the number 3 hit 'Don't Break My Heart', were featured on 1985's *Baggariddim*. The follow-up *Rat In The Kitchen* included the hit title track and the African liberation anthem 'Sing Our Own Song'.

After performing 'Red Red Wine' at the 1988 Nelson Mandela Concert at Wembley, renewed promotion in the USA resulted in the single reaching the number 1 spot. Throughout the 80s, UB40 toured frequently in Europe and North America, boosting sales of their releases. They also played Russia in 1986, filming the tour for video release. Further UK Top 10 success followed at the end of the decade with versions of the Chi-Lites' 'Homely Girl' (1989) and Lord Creator's 'Kingston Town' (1990), both of which appeared on a second volume of cover versions, *Labour Of Love II* (which has subsequently sold over five million copies worldwide). In 1990, the band had separate Top 10 hits in the UK and USA, as a Campbell/Robert Palmer duet on Bob Dylan's 'I'll Be Your Baby Tonight' charted in Britain, and a revival of the Temptations' 'The Way You Do The Things You Do' was a Top 10 hit in America.

Following a quiet period the band returned in 1993 with a version of '(I Can't Help) Falling In Love With You', which reached number 1 in the UK and USA thanks to its inclusion on the soundtrack of the movie *Sliver*, and also fostered the career of new pop-reggae star Bitty McClean. The attendant *Promises And Lies* provided UB40 with their second UK chart-topping album. The following year they backed Pato Banton on his worldwide hit cover version of the Equals' 'Baby Come Back'. Litigation took place in 1995 when Debbie Banks, an amateur poet, claimed that their major hit 'Don't Break My Heart' was based upon her lyrics. She won the case and was awarded a substantial amount in back royalties. Campbell released his debut solo album the same year.

After another extended sabbatical the band returned in 1997 with a solid collection, *Guns In The Ghetto*. The following year the band backed various chatters, including Beenie Man, Lady Saw, Mad Cobra, Ninjaman and Lieutenant Stitchie, on the excellent *UB40 Present The Dancehall Album*, recorded at Ali Campbell and Brian Travers' new Jamaican studio. It was the first instalment in a series planned to showcase Jamaican reggae both old and new. *Labour Of Love III* included the band's biggest UK hit since 1993, a cover version of Johnny Osbourne's 'Come Back Darling' reaching number 10 in late 1998.

UB40 have tirelessly promoted reggae and ska, through no other motive than a love and respect for the music. They have never become star struck and as such are one of the most credible units of the modern era. They truly live up to the principle of 'the family that plays together stays together'.
● ALBUMS: *Signing Off* (Graduate 1980) ★★★★, *Present Arms* (DEP International 1981) ★★★, *Present Arms In Dub* (DEP International 1981) ★★★, *UB44* (DEP International 1982) ★★★, *Live* (DEP International 1983) ★★★, *Labour Of Love* (DEP International/A&M 1983) ★★★★, *Geffrey Morgan ...* (DEP International/A&M 1984) ★★★★, *Baggariddim* (DEP International 1985) ★★★, *Rat In The Kitchen*

(DEP International/A&M 1986) ★★★, *CCC: Live In Moscow* (DEP International/A&M 1987) ★★★, *UB40* (DEP International/A&M 1988) ★★★★, *Labour Of Love II* (DEP International/Virgin 1989) ★★★, *Promises And Lies* (DEP International/Virgin 1993) ★★★, *Guns In The Ghetto* (DEP International/Virgin 1997) ★★★, with various artists *Present The Dancehall Album* (DEP International/Virgin 1998) ★★★★, *Labour Of Love III* (DEP International/Virgin 1998) ★★★, *Cover Up* (DEP International/Virgin 2001) ★★★, with various artists *Present The Fathers Of Reggae* (DEP International/Virgin 2002) ★★★.
Solo: Ali Campbell *Big Love* (DEP International/Virgin 1995) ★★★.
● COMPILATIONS: *The Singles Album* (Graduate 1982) ★★★, *The Best Of UB40 (1980-1983)* (A&M 1985) ★★★, *The UB40 File* (Graduate 1985) ★★★, *The Best Of UB40 Volume One* (DEP International/Virgin 1987) ★★★★, *UB40 Box Set* (DEP International/Virgin 1991) ★★★★, *The Best Of UB40 Volume Two* (DEP International/Virgin 1995) ★★★, *The Very Best Of UB40 1980-2000* (DEP International/Virgin 2000) ★★★★.
● VIDEOS: *Labour Of Love* (Virgin Vision 1984), *Best Of UB40* (Virgin Vision 1987), *CCCP The Video Mix* (Virgin Vision 1987), *UB40 Live* (Virgin Vision 1988), *Dance With The Devil* (Virgin Vision 1988), *Labour Of Love II* (Virgin Vision 1990), *A Family Affair Live In Concert* (Virgin Vision 1991), *Live In The New South Africa* (PMI 1995).

## ULLMAN, TRACEY

b. 30 December 1959, Slough, Berkshire, England. A child actress who trained at the Italia Conti Stage School, Ullman made her debut in the Berlin production of *Gigi* before returning to London to appear in the stage productions of *Elvis* (with Shakin' Stevens), *Grease*, *The Rocky Horror Show*. In 1981, she won the London Theatre Critics Award for her performance as Beverly in *Four In A Million*. She later starred in the BBC television comedy series *A Kick Up The Eighties* (with Rik Mayall) and *Three Of A Kind* (with Lenny Henry and David Copperfield). Ullman secured a contract with Stiff Records and released her debut album in 1983. This collection, which climbed to number 14 in the UK chart, comprised a set of cover versions from various eras of modern pop, spawning two Top 5 singles; 'Breakaway' (Jackie DeShannon) and 'Move Over Darling' (Doris Day), and a version of Kirsty MacColl's 'They Don't Know' which reached UK number 2 and earned Ullman a US Top 10 hit in April 1984. The accompanying videos generated interest in Britain owing to the cameo appearance of Labour Party leader, Neil Kinnock. The follow-up *You Caught Me Out*, fared less well and her singing career was put on hold. More television comedy appearances in Independent television's *Girls On Top* with Dawn French, Jennifer Saunders and Ruby Wax was followed by a move to the USA, after her marriage to television producer, Allan McKeown. The couple relocated to Los Angeles, California, where Ullman established her acting career appearing alongside Meryl Streep in 1985's *Plenty*.

Two years later she inaugurated her own successful comedy series, *The Tracey Ullman Show*, which ran until 1990. The show won three Emmys, but is probably best remembered for giving Matt Groening's *The Simpsons* its first network airing. In 1991, Ullman appeared on Broadway in her one woman show, *The Big Love*. She won further Emmys for a guest appearance on *Love And War* and her cable special *Tracey Takes On New York*, and completed several acclaimed film roles. *Tracey Takes On ...* was made into a regular HBO series in 1995, which two years later earned Ullman a sixth Emmy award. She earned further acclaim for her role as Frenchy Winkler in Woody Allen's *Small Time Crooks*.
● ALBUMS: *You Broke My Heart In 17 Places* (Stiff/MCA 1983) ★★, *You Caught Me Out* (Stiff 1984) ★★.
● COMPILATIONS: *Forever: The Best Of Tracey Ullman* (Stiff 1985) ★★, *The Best Of Tracey Ullman* (Rhino 1991) ★★★.
● VIDEOS: *Tracey Takes On ... Movies, Vanity, Fame* (1998), *Tracey Takes On ... Sex, Romance, Fantasy* (1998), *Tracey Takes On ... Fern & Kay* (1998).
● FURTHER READING: *Tracey Takes On*, Tracey Ullman.
● FILMS: *Give My Regards To Broad Street* (1984), *Plenty* (1985), *Jumpin' Jack Flash* (1986), *I Love You To Death* (1990), *Happily Ever After* voice only (1990), *Robin Hood: Men In Tights* (1993), *Household Saints* (1993), *Bullets Over Broadway* (1994), *Prêt-À-Porter* aka *Ready To Wear* (1994), *I'll Do Anything* (1994), *Panic* (2000), *Small Time Crooks* (2000), *C-Scam* (2000), *Searching For Debra Winger* (2002).

## ULTRAMAGNETIC MC'S

This Bronx, New York, USA-based four-piece rap troupe incorporated the best traditions of jazz and funk in their polished, rhythmic style. Having worked with Boogie Down Productions' KRS-One among many others, the Ultramagnetic MC's earned their reputation at the forefront of rap, pioneering the use of the sampler in hip-hop. They comprised Maurice Smith (aka Moe Love; DJ), Keith Thornton (aka Kool Keith; lead MC), Trevor Randolph (aka T.R. Love; rapper and co-producer) and Cedric Miller (aka Ced Gee; MC and co-producer). The quartet emerged from posses such as The People's Choice Crew and New York City Breakers just as Kool Herc and Afrika Bambaataa's work saw hip-hop break cover. Their own backgrounds could be traced to underground basement clubs like the Audobon Ballroom, Sparkle and the Back Door.
The quartet's 1988 debut served as a direct influence on the 'Daisy Age' rap of subsequent acts such as De La Soul and P.M. Dawn, although those bands subsequently left Ultramagnetic MC's trailing in their commercial wake. Singles such as 'Give The Drummer Some' (from which, nine years later, English techno pioneers the Prodigy would sample their controversial 'smack my bitch up' lyric) showed them in their best light: call-and-response raps demonstrating individual members' self-espoused talent in the best traditions of the old school. They were not always so dextrous, however.

While *Funk Your Head Up* included the excellent single cut, 'Poppa Large', it also housed the appalling 'Porno Star'. On *The Four Horsemen*, and its attendant singles, 'Two Brothers With Checks (San Francisco, Harvey)' and 'Raise It Up', the quartet unveiled an 'intergalactic hip-hop' concept, and a new methodology (notably Kool Keith rhyming in double-speak on 'One, Two, One, Two'). More down to earth was 'Saga Of Dandy, The Devil & Day', an account of the Negro baseball league co-written with historian James Reilly.

Following the Ultramagnetic MC's split, Ced Gee and T.R. Love offered their production skills to several artists including Boogie Down Productions' landmark *Criminal Minded*, as well as Tim Dog's infamous 'Fuck Compton'. Keith collaborated with the Prodigy and set up his own Funky Ass label, recording under a variety of monikers including Dr. Octagon, Poppa Large, the Reverend Tom, Sinister 6000, Big Willie Smith and Mr. Gerbik. The quartet performed a reunion show in 1997.

● ALBUMS: *Critical Beatdown* (Next Plateau 1988) ★★★★, *Funk Your Head Up* (Mercury 1992) ★★★, *The Four Horsemen* (Wild Pitch 1993) ★★★.

● COMPILATIONS: *The Basement Tapes 1984–1990* (Tuff City 1994) ★★, *New York What Is Funky* (Tuff City 1996) ★★, *The B-Sides Companion* (Next Plateau 1997) ★★★.

## ULTRAVOX

The initial premise of Ultravox came from the 70s school of electro-rock represented by pioneers Kraftwerk and the glam rock of Brian Eno and Roxy Music. Formed in 1974, initially as Tiger Lily, the early line-up comprised Royal College Of Art student John Foxx (b. Dennis Leigh, Chorley, Lancashire, England; vocals), Steve Shears (guitar), Warren Cann (b. 20 May 1952, Victoria, British Columbia, Canada; drums), Chris Cross (b. Christopher Allen, 14 July 1952, London, England; bass) and Billy Currie (b. William Lee Currie, 1 April 1950, Huddersfield, Yorkshire, England; keyboards, synthesizer, violin). Their rise coincided with the ascendancy of the new wave although they were for the most part ignored by a rock press more concerned with the activities of the burgeoning punk scene and consequently live gigs were frequently met with indifference. Signed to Island Records in 1976, their albums made little impact on the record buying public, despite the endorsement of Brian Eno who produced their first album. However, Ultravox's influence on a growing movement of British synthesizer music, in particular Gary Numan, was later acknowledged. Shears was replaced by Robin Simon in 1978, but after *Systems Of Romance* had garnered disappointing sales, Island dropped the act, with both Simon and Foxx (who many felt was the main creative force behind the band) leaving to pursue solo careers.

Ultravox was put on hold while the remaining members took stock. On a sojourn with Visage, Currie met Midge Ure (b. James Ure, 10 October 1953, Cambuslang, Lanarkshire, Scotland; lead vocals, guitar), a former member of Slik and the Rich Kids. The duo found a compatibility of ideas and decided to revive Ultravox as a more pop-orientated quartet with Cross and Currie. Having departed from Island, the band signed to Chrysalis Records. Their new direction brought minor chart success with 'Sleepwalk' and 'Passing Strangers'. It was not until the magnificent 'Vienna' was released that Ultravox found the success that had eluded them for so long. Held at the UK number 2 spot in January and February of 1981 by Joe Dolce's inane 'Shaddap You Face' and hits from the recently murdered John Lennon, the song's moody and eerie atmosphere was enhanced by an enigmatic video that paid homage to Carol Reed's *The Third Man*. A string of UK hits followed during the next three years, including 'All Stood Still', 'The Thin Wall' and 'The Voice' (1981), 'Reap The Wild Wind' and 'Hymn' (1982), 'Visions In Blue' and 'We Came To Dance' (1983), 'Dancing With Tears In My Eyes' and 'Love's Great Adventure' (1984). Ure's anguished, melodramatic style blended well with the high-energy pop of their contemporaries, Duran Duran and Spandau Ballet, the leaders of the UK's New Romantic scene.

The band enjoyed success throughout Europe, but never quite achieved a breakthrough in the USA. While Ure's simultaneous solo work proved, for a short time, successful, the group projects became less cohesive as their vocalist achieved greater fame. Cann was replaced by Big Country's Mark Brzezicki on 1986's *U-Vox*, but by the following year Ultravox had disbanded. Billy Currie carried on with U-Vox, featuring original guitarist Simon, which faded away following another name change (to Humania). Currie eventually won a legal battle to use the Ultravox name in 1991. Cann and Cross had lost interest by this point, however, so the band was resurrected as a duo with singer Tony Fennell, releasing the poorly received *Revelation* in 1992. The follow-up *Ingenuity* featured yet another line-up, with Currie joined by Sam Blue (vocals), Vinny Burns (guitar), Gary Williams (bass), and Tony Holmes (drums). Currie has since resumed his solo career.

● ALBUMS: *Ultravox!* (Island 1977) ★★, *Ha! Ha! Ha!* (Island 1977) ★★, *Systems Of Romance* (Island 1978) ★★★, *Vienna* (Chrysalis 1980) ★★★, *Rage In Eden* (Chrysalis 1981) ★★★, *Quartet* (Chrysalis 1982) ★★, *Monument – The Soundtrack* (Chrysalis 1983) ★★, *Lament* (Chrysalis 1984) ★★★, *U-Vox* (Chrysalis 1986) ★★, *BBC Radio 1 Live In Concert* 1981 recording (Windsong 1992) ★★, *Revelation* (Deutsche Schallatten 1993) ★, *Ingenuity* (Intercord 1994) ★★, *Future Picture* (Receiver 1995) ★★.

● COMPILATIONS: *Three Into One* (Island 1980) ★★★, *The Collection* (Chrysalis 1984) ★★★, *If I Was: The Very Best Of Midge Ure & Ultravox* (Chrysalis 1993) ★★★, *Rare* (Chrysalis 1993) ★★, *Rare Volume 2* (Chrysalis 1994) ★★, *Slow Motion* (Ultravox 1994) ★★★, *Dancing With Tears In My Eyes* (EMI 1995) ★★★, *The Voice: The Best Of Ultravox* (Monument 1997) ★★★, *Extended Ultravox* (EMI 1998) ★★, *Original Gold* (Disky 1998) ★★★, *The Island Years* (Disky 1999) ★★★, *The Very Best Of Midge Ure & Ultravox* (Chrysalis 2001) ★★★.

● VIDEOS: *The Collection* (Chrysalis 1984).

● FURTHER READING: *The Past, Present & Future Of Ultravox*, Drake and Gilbert.

## UNDERTONES

Formed in Londonderry, Northern Ireland, in November 1975, this much-loved punk/pop quintet comprised Feargal Sharkey (b. Sean Feargal Sharkey, 13 August 1958, Londonderry, Northern Ireland; vocals), John O'Neill (b. John Joseph O'Neill, 26 August 1957, Londonderry, Northern Ireland; guitar), Damian O'Neill (b. Stephen Damian O'Neill, 15 January 1961, Belfast, Northern Ireland; guitar), Michael Bradley (b. 13 August 1959, Londonderry, Northern Ireland; bass) and Billy Doherty (b. William Doherty, 10 July 1958, Larne, Northern Ireland; drums). Playing on the local pub scene, the band were inspired by the punk movement to begin writing and playing their own songs. An early demo was rejected by Stiff Records, Chiswick Records and Radar Records, as the quintet continued to build a following with a series of local gigs. By 1978 the band were offered a one-off contract with the independent Belfast label Good Vibrations. Their debut EP, *Teenage Kicks*, was heavily promoted by the influential BBC disc jockey John Peel, who later nominated the lead track as his all-time favourite recording, saying that he cried when he first heard it. The band was still without a manager, so Sharkey took on responsibility for arranging a five-year contract with Sire Records (an early indication of the business acumen that would lead to A&R positions in the music industry). The label then reissued *Teenage Kicks*, which eventually climbed to number 31 in the charts on the back of their first UK tour.

By the spring of 1979, the band had entered the UK Top 20 with the infectious 'Jimmy Jimmy' and gained considerable acclaim for their debut album, which was one of the most refreshing pop records of its time. The band's genuinely felt songs of teenage angst and romance struck a chord with young listeners and ingratiated them to an older public weaned on the great tradition of early/mid-60s pop. *Hypnotised* was a more accomplished work, and featured strongly melodic hit singles in 'My Perfect Cousin' (UK number 9) and 'Wednesday Week' (UK number 11). The former was particularly notable for its acerbic humour, including the sardonic lines: 'His mother bought him a synthesizer/Got the Human League in to advise her'.

Despite a major tour of the USA, the band were unable to make an impact outside the UK and were released from their Sire contract, setting up their own label, Ardeck Records, licensed through EMI Records. The band then went to Holland to record *Positive Touch* in 1981. Of the singles taken from the album the insistent 'It's Going To Happen!' was a deserved success, but the romantic 'Julie Ocean' was not rewarded in chart terms. The Undertones' new found maturity did not always work in their favour, with some critics longing for the innocence and naïvety of their initial recordings. With *The Sin Of Pride* and attendant 'The Love Parade', the band displayed a willingness to extend their appeal, both musically with the introduction of brass, and thematically with less obvious lyrics. A growing need to explore new areas outside the restrictive Undertones banner meant the band ended their association in June 1983. The compilation *All*

*Wrapped Up*, complete with controversial sleeve, served as a fitting tribute to their passionate blend of punk and melodic pop.

Sharkey went on to team up with Vince Clarke in the short-lived Assembly, before finding considerable success as a soloist and latterly an A&R man. The O'Neill brothers subsequently formed the critically acclaimed That Petrol Emotion. The Undertones reformed on a temporary basis in the late 90s minus Sharkey, who was replaced by new singer Paul McLoon. They continue to play the occasional live show.

● ALBUMS: *The Undertones* (Sire 1979) ★★★★, *Hypnotised* (Sire 1980) ★★★★, *Positive Touch* (Ardeck 1981) ★★★★, *The Sin Of Pride* (Ardeck 1983) ★★★.
● COMPILATIONS: *All Wrapped Up* (Ardeck 1983) ★★★, *Cher O'Bowlies: The Pick Of The Undertones* (Ardeck 1986) ★★★, *The Peel Sessions Album* (Strange Fruit 1989) ★★★, *The Best Of The Undertones: Teenage Kicks* (Castle 1993) ★★★★, *True Confessions (Singles = A's + B's)* (Essential 1999) ★★★★, *The Singles Box Set* (Essential 2000) ★★★★.

## URE, MIDGE

b. James Ure, 10 October 1953, Cambuslang, Lanarkshire, Scotland. Ure worked as an apprentice engineer at the National Engineering Laboratories in East Kilbride while playing part-time with the Glasgow-based Stumble. He began his professional career as guitarist/vocalist with Salvation, a popular Glasgow-based act that evolved into Slik in 1974. By this time, he had adopted his more famous nickname, which came about by reversing the name Jim to Mij and altering the spelling! Although accomplished musicians, Slik's recording contract bound them to ill-fitting, 'teeny-bop' material, reminiscent of fellow-Scots the Bay City Rollers. Frustrated at this artistic impasse, and despite enjoying a UK chart-topping single ('Forever And Ever'), Ure opted to join the Rich Kids, a punk/pop act, centred on former Sex Pistols bass player Glen Matlock. However, despite strong support from EMI Records, the band's chemistry did not gel and they unofficially disbanded in December 1978, barely a year after inception. Ure subsequently joined the short-lived Misfits before founding Visage with Steve Strange (vocals) and Rusty Egan (drums). Ure's involvement with this informal New Romantic act was disrupted when he replaced Gary Moore in Thin Lizzy midway through an extensive US tour. His position, however, was purely temporary as he had already agreed to join Ultravox, who rose from cult status to become one of the most popular acts of the early 80s. The ever-industrious Ure also produced sessions for Steve Harley and Modern Man, collaborated with Phil Lynott ('Yellow Pearl') and Mick Karn ('After A Fashion'), and in 1982 enjoyed a UK Top 10 solo hit with his version of 'No Regrets', penned by Tom Rush and previously a hit for the Walker Brothers. Two years later he set up Band Aid with Bob Geldof. Their joint composition, the multi-million-selling 'Do They Know It's Christmas?', was inspired by harrowing film footage of famine conditions in Ethiopia and featured an all-star cast of pop contemporaries. Ure was also heavily involved in the running of 1985's spectacular rock concert, Live Aid. He resumed his solo career later in the same year with *The Gift*, which reached number 2 on the UK charts. The album spawned a number 1 single, 'If I Was'. Ure enjoyed further UK Top 30 chart success with 'That Certain Smile' (1985) and 'Call Of The Wild' (1986). During this period, Ure also worked as the musical director of the Prince's Trust charity concerts.

*Answers To Nothing*, recorded when Ultravox had eventually fizzled out in 1987, proved less successful. This effort was not followed up until three years later when the singer, now signed to Arista Records, produced *Pure* in autumn 1991. The album demonstrated that Ure had not lost his touch for melody, and he returned to the UK Top 20 with 'Cold, Cold Heart'. Although his recent work has been undistinguished and largely ignored in England, Ure continues to maintain a healthy following on the European market. *Breathe* topped the charts in Germany, with the title-track enjoying extensive media coverage when it was used on a Swatch advertisement. In March 2001, Ure was honoured by the long-running UK television series *This Is Your Life*.

● ALBUMS: with Chris Cross *The Bloodied Sword* film soundtrack (Chrysalis 1983) ★★★, *The Gift* (Chrysalis 1985) ★★★, *Answers To Nothing* (Chrysalis 1988) ★★, *Pure* (Arista 1991) ★★, *Breathe* (RCA 1996) ★★, *Move Me* (Arista/Curb 2000) ★★.

● COMPILATIONS: *If I Was: The Very Best Of Midge Ure & Ultravox* (Chrysalis 1993) ★★★, *If I Was* (Disky 1997) ★★★, *No Regrets: The Very Best Of Midge Ure* (EMI Gold 2000) ★★★, *The Very Best Of Midge Ure & Ultravox* (Chrysalis 2001) ★★★.

## VAI, STEVE

b. 6 June 1960, Long Island, New York, USA. Vai began his musical career at the age of 13, forming his first rock band, Rayge, while still at school. At this time he was tutored by Joe Satriani, who was to have a profound effect on his style for years to come. He studied jazz and classical music at the Berklee College Of Music in Boston, Massachusetts, before relocating to Los Angeles, California, in 1979. He was recruited by Frank Zappa as the lead guitarist in his backing band, while he was still only 18 years old. By 1984 he had built his own recording studio and had begun experimenting with the fusion of jazz, rock and classical music. These pieces were released as *Flex-Able* and *Flex-Able Leftovers*, and were heavily influenced by Zappa's offbeat and unpredictable style.

In 1985, Vai replaced Yngwie Malmsteen in Alcatrazz, then moved on to even greater success with David Lee Roth and later Whitesnake. *Passion And Warfare*, released in 1990, was the album that brought Vai international recognition as a solo performer. It welded together jazz, rock, funk, classical, and metal nuances within a melodic instrumental framework. It climbed to number 18 on the *Billboard* album chart, earning a gold disc in the process. The guitarist then formed Vai with Devin Townsend (vocals), T.M. Stevens (bass), Terry Bozzio (drums), recording 1993's *Sex & Religion*. The solo *Alien Love Secrets* further highlighted Vai's extraordinary style, with guitars sounding like horses on 'Bad Horsie' and a Venusian vocal on 'Kill The Guy With The Ball' created by utilizing massive EQ, his left foot and a digital whammy bar. *Fire Garden* was half-instrumental/half-vocal, and contained a bizarre mix of stunning guitar pyrotechnics, together with one of his most evocative compositions, 'Hand On Heart'. Vai takes his instrument into new realms but still makes it sound like a guitar, most of the time.

● ALBUMS: *Flex-Able* (Urantia/Akashic 1984) ★★, *Flex-Able Leftovers* (Urantia/Akashic 1984) ★★, *Passion And Warfare* (Relativity 1990) ★★★, as Vai *Sex & Religion* (Relativity 1993) ★★★, *Alien Love Secrets* (Relativity 1995) ★★★, *Fire Garden* (Epic 1996) ★★★, with Joe Satriani, Eric Johnson *G3 Live In Concert* (Epic 1997) ★★★★, *The Ultra Zone* (Epic 1999) ★★★, *Alive In An Ultra World* (Epic 2001) ★★★.

● COMPILATIONS: *The 7th Song* (Epic 2000) ★★★, *The Secret Jewel Box* 3-CD limited edition (Light Without Heat 2002) ★★★, *The Elusive Light And Sound Vol. 1* (Favored Nations 2002) ★★★.

## VAN HALEN

The origins of this, one of America's most successful heavy metal bands, date back to Pasadena, California, in 1973. Eddie Van Halen (b. 26 January

1957, Nijmegen, Netherlands; guitar, keyboards), Alex Van Halen (b. 8 May 1955, Nijmegen, Netherlands; drums) and Michael Anthony (b. 20 June 1955, Chicago, Illinois, USA; bass) who were members of the Broken Combs, persuaded vocalist David Lee Roth (b. 10 October 1954, Bloomington, Indiana, USA) to leave the Real Ball Jets and become a member. After he consented, they changed their name to Mammoth. Specializing in a mixture of 60s and 70s covers plus hard rock originals, they toured the bar and club circuit of Los Angeles virtually non-stop during the mid-70s. Their first break came when Gene Simmons (bass player of Kiss) saw one of their club gigs. He was amazed by the energy they generated and the flamboyance of their lead singer. Simmons produced a Mammoth demo, but surprisingly it was refused by many major labels in the USA. It was then discovered that the name Mammoth was already registered, so they would have to find an alternative. After considering Rat Salade, they opted for Roth's suggestion of simply Van Halen.

On the strength of Simmons' recommendation, producer Ted Templeman checked out the band, was duly impressed and convinced Warner Brothers Records to sign them. With Templeman at the production desk, Van Halen entered the studio and recorded their self-titled debut in 1978. The album was released to widespread critical acclaim and compared with Montrose's debut in 1974. It featured a unique fusion of energy, sophistication, and virtuosity through Eddie Van Halen's extraordinary guitar lines and Roth's self-assured vocal style. Within 12 months it had sold two million units, peaking at number 19 in the *Billboard* chart; over the years, this album has continued to sell and by 1996 it had been certified in the USA alone at 9 million sales. Eddie Van Halen was named as Best New Guitarist Of The Year in 1978, by *Guitar Player* magazine. The follow-up, simply titled *Van Halen II*, kept to the same formula and was equally successful. Roth's stage antics became even more sensational – he was the supreme showman, combining theatrical stunts with a stunning voice to entertaining effect. *Women And Children First* saw the band start to explore more musical avenues and experiment with the use of synthesizers. This came to full fruition on *Fair Warning*, which was a marked departure from earlier releases. *Diver Down* was the band's weakest album, with the cover versions of 60s standards being the strongest tracks. Nevertheless, the band could do no wrong in the eyes of their fans and the album, as had all their previous releases, went platinum. Eddie Van Halen was also a guest on Michael Jackson's 'Beat It', a US number 1 in February 1983. With *1984*, released on New Year's Day of that year, the band returned to form. Nine original tracks reaffirmed their position as the leading exponents of heavy-duty melodic metal infused with a pop sensibility. Spearheaded by 'Jump', a *Billboard* number 1 and UK number 7, the album lodged at number 2 in the US chart for a full five weeks during its one-year residency. This was easily his most high-profile solo outing, though his other select engagements outside Van Halen have

included work with Private Life and former Toto member Steve Lukather.

Roth upset the apple cart by quitting in 1985 to concentrate on his solo career, and ex-Montrose vocalist Sammy Hagar (b. 13 October 1947, Monterey, California, USA) eventually filled the vacancy. Retaining the Van Halen name, against record company pressure to change it, the new line-up released *5150* in June 1986. The album name was derived from the police code for the criminally insane, as well as the name of Eddie Van Halen's recording studio. The lead off single, 'Why Can't This Be Love', reached number 3 in the *Billboard* chart and number 8 in the UK, while the album became their first US number 1 and their biggest seller to date. *OU812* was a disappointment in creative terms. The songs were formularized and lacked real direction, but the album became the band's second consecutive number 1 in less than two years. *For Unlawful Carnal Knowledge*, written as the acronym *F.U.C.K.*, stirred up some controversy at the time of release. However, the music on the album transcended the juvenile humour of the title, being an immaculate collection of gritty and uncompromising rockers. The band had defined their identity anew and rode into the 90s on a new creative wave – needless to say, platinum status was attained yet again. A live album prefigured the release of the next studio set, *Balance*, with Van Halen's popularity seemingly impervious to the ravages of time or fashion. It is unusual for a greatest hits compilation to debut at number 1 but the band achieved this on the *Billboard* chart in 1996 with *Best Of Volume 1*.

Hagar departed in 1996 after rumours persisted that he was at loggerheads with the other members. Fans immediately rejoiced when it was announced that the replacement would be David Lee Roth, although not on a full-time basis. A few months later, Roth issued a statement effectively ruling out any further involvement. The vacancy went to Gary Cherone (b. 26 July 1961, Malden, Massachusetts, USA) soon after Extreme announced their formal disbanding in October 1996. The first album to feature Cherone, 1998's *Van Halen III*, was universally slated. The singer left the following year and had not been replaced by the time the band parted company with Warners in January 2002.

● ALBUMS: *Van Halen* (Warners 1978) ★★★★, *Van Halen II* (Warners 1979) ★★★★, *Women And Children First* (Warners 1980) ★★★, *Fair Warning* (Warners 1981) ★★★, *Diver Down* (Warners 1982) ★★★, *1984 (MCMLXXXIV)* (Warners 1984) ★★★★, *5150* (Warners 1986) ★★★★, *OU812* (Warners 1988) ★★★★, *For Unlawful Carnal Knowledge* (Warners 1991) ★★★, *Live: Right Here Right Now* (Warners 1993) ★★★★, *Balance* (Warners 1995) ★★★, *Van Halen III* (Warners 1998) ★★.

● COMPILATIONS: *Best Of Volume 1* (Warners 1996) ★★★★.

● VIDEOS: *Live Without A Net* (WEA 1987), *Live: Right Here Right Now* (Warner Music Video 1993), *Video Hits Volume 1* (Warner Music Video 1996).

● FURTHER READING: *Van Halen*, Michelle Craven. *Excess All Areas*, Malcolm Dome.

## VAN ZANDT, STEVEN
(see Little Steven)

## VANDROSS, LUTHER
b. Luther Ronzoni Vandross, 20 April 1951, New York City, New York, USA. Born into a family immersed in gospel and soul singing, Vandross had already formed his own group while still at school and later worked with the musical theatre workshop, Listen My Brother. This enabled him to perform at Harlem's Apollo Theatre. After a brief hiatus from the music scene in the 70s, he was invited by an old school friend and workshop colleague, Carlos Alomar, to join him in the studio with David Bowie for the recording of *Young Americans*. Vandross impressed Bowie enough to be invited to arrange the vocal parts and make a substantial contribution to the backing vocals for the album. By the time Bowie's US tour was underway, Vandross had also secured the position as opening act. His vocal talent was soon in demand and his session credits with Chaka Khan, Ringo Starr, Barbra Streisand and Donna Summer generated sufficient interest from the Cotillion label to sign him as part of a specially put-together vocal group, Luther. *Luther* and *This Close To You* (both 1976) flopped, partly owing to the use of a disco backing in favour of allowing Vandross to express his more romantic, soul style.

The singer subsequently drifted back to session work putting in outstanding performances for Quincy Jones, Patti Austin, Gwen Guthrie, Chic and Sister Sledge. This work was subsidized by his composing advertising jingles. His performance as guest singer with the studio group Change on 1980's *The Glow Of Love* earned two UK Top 20 hits in 'Glow Of Love' and 'Searching'. This led to the relaunch of a higher profile career, this time as solo artist with Epic/CBS Records. 'Never Too Much' earned him an R&B number 1 while the accompanying album reached the US Top 20. Subsequent singles, including duets with Cheryl Lynn ('If This World Were Mine') and Dionne Warwick ('How Many Times Can We Say Goodbye'), saw him strengthen his popularity with the US R&B market and gave him two further R&B number 1 hits with 'Stop To Love' (1986) and a duet with Gregory Hines, 'There's Nothing Better Than Love' (1987). Subsequent releases, including 'Here And Now' (US number 6, December 1989), 'Power Of Love/Love Power' (US number 4, April 1991) and 'Don't Want To Be A Fool' (US number 9, August 1991), crossed over to become major pop hits, establishing Vandross as one of the finest soul singers of the 80s and 90s. In 1992 Vandross collaborated with Janet Jackson, BBD and Ralph Tresvant on 'The Best Things In Life Are Free', a US number 10 and UK number 2 hit taken from the movie *Mo' Money*. 'Endless Love', a duet with Mariah Carey, reached UK number 3 in September 1994.

Vandross has won countless awards and his reputation as a producer has been enhanced by his work with Dionne Warwick, Diana Ross and Whitney Houston. A decline in sales during the mid-90s saw the termination of his Sony contract. *I Know* marked his debut for EMI Records, entering the US Top 30 in August 1998, but he subsequently relocated to Clive Davis' J Records.

● ALBUMS: *Never Too Much* (Epic 1981) ★★★, *Forever, For Always, For Love* (Epic 1982) ★★★, *Busy Body* (Epic 1983) ★★★, *The Night I Fell In Love* (Epic 1985) ★★★★, *Give Me The Reason* (Epic 1986) ★★★, *Any Love* (Epic 1988) ★★★, *Power Of Love* (Epic 1991) ★★★★, *Never Let Me Go* (Epic 1993) ★★★, *Songs* (Epic 1994) ★★★, *Your Secret Love* (Epic 1996) ★★★, *I Know* (Virgin/EMI 1998) ★★, *Luther Vandross* (J 2001) ★★★.
● COMPILATIONS: *The Best Of Luther Vandross ... The Best Of Love* (Epic 1989) ★★★★, *Greatest Hits 1981–1995* (Epic 1995) ★★★★, *One Night With You: The Best Of Love Volume 2* (Epic 1997) ★★★, *Always & Forever: The Classics* (Epic 1998) ★★★, *Greatest Hits* (Legacy 1999) ★★★, *Super Hits* (Epic 2000) ★★★, *The Essential Luther Vandross* (Epic 2002) ★★★.
● VIDEOS: *An Evening Of Songs* (Epic 1994), *Always And Forever* (Epic 1995).

## VANGELIS
b Evanghelos Odyssey Papathanassiou, 29 March 1943, Volos, Greece. A child prodigy, Vangelis gave his first public performance on the piano at the age of six, and later studied classical music, painting and film direction at the Academy of Fine Arts in Athens. In the early 60s he co-founded the formulaic beat outfit Formix, who went on to become arguably Greece's most popular group during the mid-60s pop explosion with singles such as 'Yenka Beat' and 'Geronimo Jenka'. Formix disbanded in 1967, but Vangelis continued performing session work for local singers including Aleka Kanelidou and Ricardo Credi. He formed a new group, the Papathanassiou Set, which included singer and bass player Demis Roussos, guitarist Anargyros 'Silver' Koulouris, and drummer Lucas Sideras. The group played on Greek singer George Romanos' 1968 release *In Concert And In The Studio*, and backed Vangelis on his debut solo single 'The Clock' (issued under his full name Vangelis Papathanassiou). Minus Koulouris the group moved to Paris and, as Aphrodite's Child, recorded the international hit 'Rain And Tears', based around Vangelis' interpretation of Johann Pachelbel's 'Canon'. The group enjoyed several other huge European hit singles in the late 60s, but by this time their creative mainstay Vangelis had begun to concentrate on other recordings, composing the television score for the wildlife documentary *L'Apocalypse Des Animaux* by Frederic Rossif and the soundtrack to the Jane Birkin movie *Sex Power*.

Aphrodite's Child disbanded following 1972's ambitious *666: The Apocalypse Of John*, and Vangelis turned to the newly minted synthesizer as his main compositional tool. He recorded his solo album *Fait Que Ton Rêve Soit Plus Long Que La Nuit*, a collection inspired by the student riots that took place in Paris in May 1968. Following the desultory progressive rock album *Earth*, Vangelis signed to RCA Records and moved to London. He built a studio in Marble Arch where he was able to further develop his fusion of electronic and acoustic sound. After turning down the vacant keyboard position in Yes, Vangelis recorded *Heaven And Hell*, which reached number 31 in the UK album charts in January 1976, and led to a concert at the Royal Albert Hall. The subsequent concept album *Albedo 0.39* included the voices of astronauts landing on the moon, as well as the dramatic favourite 'Pulstar'.

Returning to Greece in 1978, Vangelis collaborated with actress Irene Papas on settings of Byzantine and Greek traditional song. He moved to Polydor Records for 1979's *China*, which explored his interest in Eastern instruments and musical themes. He renewed his partnership with Rossif on the *Opera Sauvage* soundtrack for French television, before joining forces with Yes vocalist Jon Anderson, who had previously sung on *Heaven And Hell*'s closing track, 'So Long Ago, So Clear'. As Jon And Vangelis they had international success with 'I Hear You Now' (1980) and 'I'll Find My Way Home' (1981), and recorded the albums *Short Stories*, *The Friends Of Mr. Cairo* and *Private Collection*.

The following year, Vangelis resumed his activities as a film music composer with the award-winning *Chariots Of Fire*, which scooped the Oscar for Best Original Score at the 1982 Academy Awards. The title-track was a worldwide hit and prompted scores of imitation 'themes'. This was followed by impressive scores for Ridley Scott's *Blade Runner*, Costas-Gravas' *Missing*, Kurohara's *Antarctica* and Donaldson's *The Bounty*. His non-soundtrack work of this period included the dense, symphonic choral works *Soil Festivities* and *Mask*. In 1988, Vangelis signed to Arista Records, releasing *Direct*, the first in a series of improvised albums that he composed, arranged and recorded simultaneously with MIDI sequencers. In 1991, he reunited with Anderson on *Page Of Life*. The same year, Vangelis directed a spectacular outdoor event in Rotterdam to celebrate the fifth anniversary of EUREKA, the pro-technology support organisation. He was also busy working on soundtracks, with his film credits in the early 90s included Roman Polanski's *Bitter Moon* (1992) and Ridley Scott's *1492: Conquest Of Paradise* (1993).

By this time, Vangelis had signed to East West Records, who released the full remastered version of the *Blade Runner* soundtrack in 1994. In 1995, 'Conquest Of Paradise' became an unexpected German radio hit, and subsequently the single and album became number 1 bestsellers in several European countries. The same year Vangelis released a limited edition fund-raising album in honour of the artist El Greco, which was only available via Greece's national gallery, the Alexandra Soutzos Museum in Athens (although East West reissued the album in 1998). The Greco album was followed by *Voices*, which featured vocalists Stina Nordenstam, Paul Young and the Athens Opera Company. In 1996, Vangelis remixed tracks for the career-spanning compilation *Portraits*, and released *Oceanic*.

● ALBUMS: *Sex Power* film soundtrack (Philips 1970) ★★, *Fais Que Ton Rêve Soit Plus Long Que La Nuit (Poème Symphonique De Vangelis Papathanassiou)* (Reprise 1972) ★★★, *Earth* (Vertigo 1973) ★★, *L'Apocalypse Des Animaux* television soundtrack (Polydor 1973) ★★★, *Heaven And Hell* (RCA 1975) ★★★, *Albedo 0.39* (RCA 1976) ★★★, *Spiral* (RCA

1977) ★★, as Vangelis Papathanassiou *Entends-Tu Les Chiens Aboyer?* (BASF 1977) ★★, *Ignacio* film soundtrack (Egg 1977) ★★★, *Beaubourg* (RCA 1978) ★★, *China* (Polydor 1979) ★★★, *Opera Sauvage* television soundtrack (Polydor 1979) ★★★, *See You Later* (Polydor 1980) ★★, *Chariots Of Fire* film soundtrack (Polydor 1981) ★★★★, *To The Unknown Man* (RCA 1982) ★★, *Antarctica* film soundtrack (Polydor 1983) ★★★, *Soil Festivities* (Polydor 1984) ★★, *Invisible Connections* (Deutsche Grammophon 1985) ★★★, *Mask* (Polydor 1985) ★★, *Direct* (Arista 1988) ★★, *Antarctica* film soundtrack (Polydor 1988) ★★★, *The City* (East West 1990) ★★★, *1492: Conquest Of Paradise* film soundtrack (East West 1992) ★★, *Blade Runner* film soundtrack (East West 1994) ★★★, *Foros Timis Ston Greko (A Tribute To El Greco)* Greece only, reissued 1998 (Warners/East West 1995) ★★★, *Voices* (East West 1995) ★★★, *Oceanic* (East West 1997) ★★, *La Fête Sauvage* CAM 2000) ★★★.

As Jon And Vangelis: *Short Stories* (Polydor 1980) ★★★, *The Friends Of Mr. Cairo* (Polydor 1981) ★★, *Private Collection* (Polydor 1983) ★★, *Page Of Life* (Arista 1991) ★★.

● COMPILATIONS: *Best Of Vangelis* (Ariola 1975) ★★★, *The Best Of Vangelis* (RCA 1978) ★★★, *Magic Moments* cassette only (RCA 1984) ★★★, *Themes* (Polydor 1989) ★★★, *Best In Space* (RCA 1994) ★★★, *Portraits: So Long Ago, So Clear* (Polydor 1996) ★★★★, *Gift ... The Best Of Vangelis* (Camden 1996) ★★★, *Reprise 1990–1999* (East West 1999) ★★★.

As Jon And Vangelis: *The Best Of Jon And Vangelis* (Polydor 1984) ★★★.

## VAPORS

This power-pop quartet, based in Guildford, Surrey, England, came together officially in April 1979, although an earlier incarnation had existed a year earlier. The common thread was Dave Fenton, a graduate who dabbled in the legal profession before turning to music. His first band, the Little Jimmies, was formed while he studied at Nottingham University. To his rhythm guitar and vocals were added the lead guitar of Ed Bazalgette and the drums of Howard Smith, both former members of Ellery Bop. The line-up was completed by former Absolute drummer Steve Smith, who switched over to bass guitar. An early Vapors gig was watched by the Jam's Bruce Foxton, who was impressed by their gutsy pop, not unlike the Jam's own style, and invited them to appear on the *Setting Sons* tour. Foxton also became the band's manager in partnership with John Weller. After a promising but unsuccessful debut single, 'Prisoners', for United Artists Records, the follow-up, 'Turning Japanese', catapulted them to number 3 in the UK charts. In May 1980, *New Clear Days* was released. The most notable track was the single 'News At Ten', which underlined teenage insecurity with a power-pop beat that recalled the Kinks. *Magnets* was a more adventurous album, with the lyrical focus moving from the Oriental to Americana. Unfortunately, the band were receiving few plaudits for their ambitious efforts, with most critics unable to move away from the earlier Jam comparisons, which were no longer valid. The band disappeared from the scene quickly; the most recent sighting of Dave Fenton was as the landlord of a public house in Woking, Surrey, while Steve Smith joined with ex-World Domination Enterprises bass player Steve Jameson to form Cut.

● ALBUMS: *New Clear Days* (United Artists 1980) ★★★, *Magnets* (United Artists 1981) ★★★.

● COMPILATIONS: *Anthology* (One Way 1995) ★★★, *Turning Japanese: The Best Of The Vapors* (EMI 1996) ★★★, *Vaporized* (Collectables 1998) ★★★★.

## VASELINES

Formed in Bellshill, Lanarkshire, Scotland, in 1986, the Vaselines initially comprised Eugene Kelly and Frances McKee. The duo completed two singles, 'Son Of A Gun' and 'Dying For It', which balanced Kelly's abrasive guitar work with his partner's more melancholic style. McKee's quirky intonation was particularly evident on the b-side of the latter, 'Molly's Lips', a song later adopted by US band Nirvana, who maintained an affection for the Vaselines' work. James Seenan (bass) and Charles Kelly (drums) joined the pair for *Dum Dum*, which emphasized the group's irascible fascination with matters carnal, evident on titles such as 'Sex Sux (Amen)' and 'Monster Pussy'. Shop Assistants guitarist David Keegan augmented the Vaselines prior to their demise in 1987, after which Kelly briefly joined the Pastels before founding Captain America (later Eugenius) with Seenan.

● ALBUMS: *Dum Dum* (53rd & 3rd 1987) ★★★.

● COMPILATIONS: *The Way Of The Vaselines: A Complete History* (Sub Pop 1992) ★★★.

## VAUGHAN, STEVIE RAY

b. 3 October 1954, Dallas, Texas, USA, d. 27 August 1990, East Troy, Wisconsin, USA. This remarkable blues guitarist was influenced by his older brother Jimmie Vaughan (of the Fabulous Thunderbirds), whose record collection included key Vaughan motivators such as Albert King, Otis Rush and Lonnie Mack. He honed his style on his brother's hand-me-down guitars in various high school bands, before moving to Austin in 1972. He formed the Nightcrawlers with Doyle Bramhall, then Paul Ray And The Cobras, with whom he recorded 'Texas Clover' in 1974. In 1977 he formed Triple Threat Revue with vocalist Lou Ann Barton. She later fronted Vaughan's most successful project, named Double Trouble after an Otis Rush standard, for a short period after its inception in 1979. The new band also featured drummer Chris Layton and ex-Johnny Winter bass player Tommy Shannon.

Producer Jerry Wexler, an early fan, added them to the bill of the 1982 Montreux International Jazz Festival, where Vaughan was spotted and hired by David Bowie for his forthcoming *Let's Dance* (1983). Vaughan turned down Bowie's subsequent world tour, however, to rejoin his own band and record *Texas Flood* with veteran producer John Hammond. *Couldn't Stand The Weather* showed the influence of Jimi Hendrix, and earned the band its first platinum disc; in February 1985, they picked up a Grammy for their contribution to the *Blues Explosion* anthology. *Soul To Soul* saw the addition of keyboards player

Reese Wynans; Vaughan, by this point a much sought-after guitarist, could also be heard on records by James Brown, Johnny Copeland, and his mentor, Lonnie Mack. The period of extensive substance abuse that produced the lacklustre *Live Alive* led to Vaughan's admittance to a Georgia detoxification centre. His recovery was apparent on *In Step*, which won a second Grammy. In 1990, the Vaughan brothers worked together with Bob Dylan on their own *Family Style*, and as guests on Eric Clapton's American tour. Vaughan died in 1990, at East Troy, Wisconsin, USA, when, anxious to return to Chicago after Clapton's Milwaukee show, he switched helicopter seats and boarded a vehicle that crashed, in dense fog, into a ski hill. *The Sky Is Crying*, compiled by Jimmie Vaughan from album sessions, was posthumously released the following year.

Vaughan was a magnificent ambassador for the blues, whose posthumous reputation continues to increase. Plans to erect a nine-foot bronze statue to the guitarist in his hometown of Austin went ahead in October 1992. In 2001, Vaughan's former band Double Trouble (Chris Layton and Tommy Shannon) had considerable success in their own right with the chart-topping *Been A Long Time*.

● ALBUMS: *Texas Flood* (Epic 1983) ★★★★, *Couldn't Stand The Weather* (Epic 1984) ★★★★, *Soul To Soul* (Epic 1985) ★★★★, *Live Alive* (Epic 1986) ★★★, *In Step* (Epic 1989) ★★★★, as the Vaughan Brothers *Family Style* (Epic 1990) ★★★★, *The Sky Is Crying* (Epic 1991) ★★★★, *In The Beginning* 1980 recording (Epic 1992) ★★★, *Live At Carnegie Hall* (Epic 1997) ★★★, with Albert King *In Session* 1983 recording (Fantasy/Stax 1999) ★★★, *Live At Montreux 1982 & 1985* (Epic/Legacy 2001) ★★★.

● COMPILATIONS: *Greatest Hits* (Epic 1995) ★★★★, *The Real Deal: Greatest Hits 2* (Epic 1999) ★★★, *Blues At Sunrise* (Epic 2000) ★★★★, *SRV* 4-CD box set (Epic/Legacy 2000) ★★★★.

● VIDEOS: *Live At The El Mocambo* (Epic Music Video 1992), *Live From Austin Texas* (Epic Music Video 1995).

● FURTHER READING: *Stevie Ray Vaughan: Caught In The Crossfire*, Joe Nick Patoski and Bill Crawford. *The Essential Stevie Ray Vaughan*, Craig Hopkins.

## VEGA, SUZANNE

b. 12 August 1959, Sacramento, California, USA. Vega is a highly literate singer-songwriter who found international success in the late 80s and early 90s. Having moved with her parents to New York City at the age of two, Vega studied dance at the High School for the Performing Arts (as featured in the *Fame* television series) and at Barnard College, singing her own material in New York folk clubs. Signed by A&M Records in 1984, she recorded her first album with Lenny Kaye, former guitarist with Patti Smith. From this, 'Marlene On The Wall', a tale of bed-sitter angst, became a hit. In 1987 'Luka' grabbed even more attention with its evocation of the pain of child abuse told from the victim's point of view. Vega's 'Left Of Center' appeared on the soundtrack of the movie *Pretty In Pink* and she contributed lyrics for two tracks on *Songs From Liquid Days* by Philip Glass. On her third album, Vega collaborated with keyboards player and co-producer Anton Sanko, who brought a new tightness to the sound. Meanwhile, Vega's lyrics took on a more surreal and precise character, notably on 'Book Of Dreams' and 'Men In A War', which dealt with the plight of amputees. In 1990, the serendipitous 'Tom's Diner' from *Solitude Standing* became a hit in Britain after being sampled by the production duo, D.N.A. The track was remixed by Alan Coulthard for Vega's label A&M; its success led to the release of an album, *Tom's Album* (1991), devoted entirely to reworkings of the song by artists such as R.E.M. and rapper Nikki D. Vega was presumably bemused by the whole series of events. Vega's commercial presence faded during the 90s, although her critical standing continued to remain high. *Nine Objects Of Desire* was a move into a smoother sound, in her own words 'sexier and less defiant'. After a five-year absence, during which she raised her daughter and published her first book, Vega returned to the recording scene in September 2001 with *Songs In Red And Gray*.

● ALBUMS: *Suzanne Vega* (A&M 1985) ★★★★, *Solitude Standing* (A&M 1987) ★★★, *Days Of Open Hand* (A&M 1990) ★★, *99.9°F* (A&M 1992) ★★★, *Nine Objects Of Desire* (A&M 1996) ★★★, *Songs In Red And Gray* (Interscope 2001) ★★★.

● COMPILATIONS: *Tried And True: The Best Of Suzanne Vega* (A&M 1998) ★★★★.

● FURTHER READING: *The Passionate Eye: The Collected Writings Of Suzanne Vega*, Suzanne Vega.

## VELVET MONKEYS

Formed in Washington, DC, USA, the Velvet Monkeys made their recording debut in 1981 with *Everything Is Right*, a cassette collection issued on their own label. It revealed a love of pop culture from the 50s and 60s that was imbued with post-punk/hardcore love of noisy guitar patterns. This style was repeated on *Future*. They recorded the cassette-only *Big Big Sun*, a collaboration with Half Japanese, issued on Beat Happening's label K. This collection accentuated the band's leanings towards pop's *avant garde*. The Velvet Monkeys broke up in 1986 and their early incarnation is commemorated on the compilation *Rotting Corpse Au Go-Go*. Group members Don Fleming (guitar, vocals) and Jay Spiegel (drums) moved to New York, USA, where they joined Mark Kramer in B.A.L.L. When B.A.L.L. disbanded, Fleming revived the Velvet Monkeys for *Rake*, a 70s-influenced 'soundtrack' album on which he was aided by Thurston Moore (Sonic Youth), J. Mascis (Dinosaur Jr) and Julia Cafritz (ex-Pussy Galore). Fleming also enjoyed success as a producer, notably with Teenage Fanclub's *Bandwagonesque*.

● ALBUMS: *Everything Is Right* cassette only (Monkey Business 1981) ★★, *Future* (Fountain Of Youth 1983) ★★, with Half Japanese *Big Big Sun* cassette only (K 1988) ★★, *Rake* (Rough Trade 1990) ★★.

● COMPILATIONS: *Rotting Corpse Au Go-Go* (Shimmy-Disc 1989) ★★★.

## VENOM

This UK black metal band, a major influence on thrash pioneers Metallica, Slayer and Possessed, as well as the satanic fraternity, was formed in Newcastle Upon Tyne by Cronos (b. Conrad Lant; bass, vocals), Mantas (b. Jeff Dunn; guitar) and Abaddon (b. Tony Bray; drums). Their debut was 1981's legendary *Welcome To Hell*, a raw collection of brutal songs filled with dark, satanic imagery. *Black Metal* was much better in terms of playing and production, and remains Venom's best album, containing the atmospheric 'Buried Alive' amid the more customary speed bursts. *At War With Satan*, a semi-concept album, and numerous singles followed – BBC Radio 1 disc jockey Tommy Vance paid £100 to charity when Mike Read played 'Warhead' on his breakfast show for a bet – and Venom played numerous major shows worldwide (club dates were precluded by the nature of Venom's pyrotechnics, which tended to cause structural damage in enclosed spaces), proudly refusing to be anything but headliners. However, the poor *Possessed* and a spate of unofficial live and compilation releases hurt the band, and Mantas left as the *Eine Kleine Nachtmusik* live set emerged. Mike Hickey and Jimmy Clare were recruited for live commitments, and this line-up produced the commendable power metal of *Calm Before The Storm* before Cronos left, taking both guitarists for his Cronos band.

Mantas rejoined Abaddon, bringing rhythm guitarist Al Barnes and ex-Atomkraft bass player/vocalist Tony 'The Demolition Man' Dolan. *Prime Evil* harked back to the early Venom approach, albeit with rather more professionalism, and contained a good cover version of Black Sabbath's 'Megalomania'. Barnes left after 1991's *Temples Of Ice*, and the remaining trio temporarily recruited guitarist Steve 'War Maniac' White and keyboard player V.X.S. Subsequent releases failed to emulate the standards of the earlier albums, but Cronos returned to the band in 1996, replacing Dolan and restoring the founding line-up. The following year's *Cast In Stone* featured new and re-recorded material, and was followed by a world tour. After a temporary hiatus, Cronos and Mantas returned with new drummer Antton to record the excellent *Resurrection*. Venom, already the subject of a tribute album, remain among the most important of all heavy metal acts, having originated a style that became a template for much of the music's modern practitioners.

● ALBUMS: *Welcome To Hell* (Neat 1981) ★★★★, *Black Metal* (Neat 1982) ★★★★, *At War With Satan* (Neat 1984) ★★, *Possessed* (Neat 1985) ★★, *Eine Kleine Nachtmusik* (Neat 1985) ★★, *Official Bootleg* (APK 1986) ★★★, *Calm Before The Storm* (FilmTrax 1987) ★★★, *Prime Evil* (Under One Flag 1989) ★★★, *Tear Your Soul Apart* (Under One Flag 1990) ★★, *Temples Of Ice* (Under One Flag 1991) ★★, *The Waste Lands* (Under One Flag 1992) ★★, *Black Reign* (1996) ★★★, *Cast In Stone* (SPV 1997) ★★, *Resurrection* (SPV 2000) ★★★, *The Court Of Death* (Receiver 2000) ★★★, *Official Bootleg* (Cleopatra 2002) ★★★.

● COMPILATIONS: *The Singles '80 – '86* (Raw Power 1986) ★★★, *Skeletons In The Closet* (Castle 1993) ★★★, *In Memoriam: The Best Of Venom* (Griffin 1995) ★★★, *New, Live And Rare* (Caroline 1998) ★★, *Old, New, Borrowed And Blue* (Aspire 1999) ★★★, *Buried Alive* (Receiver 1999) ★★★, *Greatest Hits &*

*More* (Cleopatra 2000) ★★★, *A Triple Dose Of Venom* (Big Eye 2001) ★★★, *In League With Satan* (Essential 2002) ★★★★, *Skeletons In The Closet* (Essential 2002) ★★★, *Kissing The Beast* (Essential 2002) ★★★.

## VIOLENT FEMMES

From Milwaukee, Wisconsin, USA, the Violent Femmes was formed by Gordon Gano (b. 7 June 1963, New York, USA; vocals, guitar), Brian Ritchie (b. 21 November 1960, Milwaukee, Wisconsin, USA; bass) and Victor De Lorenzo (b. 25 October 1954, Racine, Wisconsin, USA; drums). Gano and Ritchie first teamed up for an acoustic set at the Rufus King High School, Ritchie having formerly played with Plasticland (one single, 'Mushroom Hill'/'Color Appreciation'). Joined by De Lorenzo, they recorded a debut album (through Rough Trade Records in the UK). Its rough, acoustic style failed to hide the Violent Femmes' intriguing variety of songs and lyrics, and although they later mellowed, this formed the basis of what was to follow. Two acclaimed singles, 'Gone Daddy Gone' and 'It's Gonna Rain' (both 1984), were drawn from *Violent Femmes* before *Hallowed Ground* followed a year later, a more full-bodied work that lacked the shambolic nature of their debut. *Hallowed Ground* contained, what is for many, the classic Violent Femmes composition, the macabre 'Country Death Song'. *The Blind Leading The Naked* nearly gave the band a hit single in their cover version of T. Rex's 'Children Of The Revolution' early in 1986.

There was then a long pause in the Violent Femmes' activities while Gordon Gano appeared with his side-project, the gospel-influenced Mercy Seat, and Ritchie recorded two solo sets for the SST Records label, and one for Dali-Chameleon. De Lorenzo released *Peter Corey Sent Me* in 1991 and played on Sigmund Snpek III's album, which also featured Ritchie. The release of the succinctly titled *3* re-introduced a more sophisticated Violent Femmes, although the grisly subject matter continued, while 1991's *Why Do Birds Sing?* included a savage version of the Culture Club hit 'Do You Really Want To Hurt Me?' Moving to Elektra Records and recruiting new drummer Guy Hoffman, the Violent Femmes released two further albums that failed to capture them at their potent best. An abortive deal with Interscope Records meant little was heard of the band in the late 90s. Their first new studio album in over five years, *Freak Magnet*, marked a return to the brash energy of their mid-80s heyday.

● ALBUMS: *Violent Femmes* (Slash 1983) ★★★★, *Hallowed Ground* (Slash 1984) ★★★, *The Blind Leading The Naked* (Slash 1986) ★★★, *3* (Slash 1989) ★★, *Why Do Birds Sing?* (Slash 1991) ★★, *New Times* (Elektra 1994) ★★★, *Rock!!!!!* (Elektra 1995) ★★, *Viva Wisconsin* (Cooking Vinyl/Beyond 1999) ★★★, *Freak Magnet* (Cooking Vinyl/Beyond 2000) ★★★.

● COMPILATIONS: *Debacle: The First Decade* (Slash 1991) ★★★, *Add It Up (1981–1993)* (Slash 1993) ★★★★, *Something's Wrong* (EMusic 2001) ★★★.

## VIRGIN PRUNES

This Irish performance-art/*avant garde* musical ensemble was originally formed in 1976. Fionan Hanvey, better known under his pseudonym Gavin Friday, was invited by Paul Hewson (later Bono of U2) to join a group of Dublin youths with artistic leanings who were inspired by the new wave explosion in the UK. A rough community had been formed under the title of the Village, a social club bound in secrecy. The Virgin Prunes became an official band, and an extension of the Village, by the end of 1977. Friday was joined by Guggi (b. Derek Rowen) and Dave-id (b. David Watson; vocals), Strongman (b. Trevor Rowen; bass), Dik Evans (brother of U2's The Edge; guitar) and Pod (b. Anthony Murphy; drums). Early gigs were very much performance events, with audiences bemused by the expectations placed on them. However, by the turn of the decade they had attracted strong cult support, and on the strength of the self-financed 'Twenty Tens', were signed to Rough Trade Records. Pod was the band's first casualty, opting out of their new disaffected religious stance. As a manifestation of their unconventional approach, their first album was initially released as a set of 7-, 10- and 12-inch singles, with component parts making up *A New Form Of Beauty*. After the brief tenure of Haa Lacka Binttii, Mary D'Nellon took over on drums. His instalment was in time for the band's second, and first complete album, *If I Die, I Die*. Less experimental and perverse than its predecessor, it continued nevertheless to explore the tenets of purity and beauty. At the same time, a mixed studio/live album, *Heresie*, was released, which emphasized that the performance-art aspect of the Virgin Prunes had not been totally neglected. By 1984, Guggi had become disenchanted with the music industry and departed. When Dik Evans defected for similar reasons, D'Nellon switched to guitar and Pod rejoined as drummer. *The Moon Looked Down And Laughed* witnessed another change in direction. Produced by Soft Cell's Dave Ball, it consisted largely of ballads and melodic pop, with little hint of the band's usual confrontational approach. However, following the continued lack of response from the record-buying public, Friday called a halt to his involvement with the band and embarked on a varied solo career. Subsequent releases from Strongman and D'Nellon as the Prunes failed to sustain the Virgin Prunes' original spirit of adventure.

● ALBUMS: *A New Form Of Beauty* (Rough Trade 1982) ★★★, *Heresie* (L'Invitation Au Suicide 1982) ★★, *If I Die, I Die* (Rough Trade 1982) ★★★, *The Moon Looked Down And Laughed* (Baby 1986) ★★★, *The Hidden Lie (Live In Paris 6/6/86)* (Baby 1986) ★★, as the Prunes *Lite Fantastik* (Baby 1988) ★★, as the Prunes *Nada* (Baby 1989) ★★.

● COMPILATIONS: *Over The Rainbow* (Baby 1985) ★★★, *Sons Find Devils* (Cleopatra 1998) ★★★.

● VIDEOS: *Sons Find Devils* (IKON 1985).

## VISAGE

A synthesizer 'jamming' band fronted by Steve Strange (b. Steve Harrington, 28 May 1959, Wales), with other members including Midge Ure (b. James Ure, 10 October 1953, Cambuslang, Lanarkshire, Scotland; guitar), Rusty Egan (b. 19 September 1957),

Billy Currie (b. William Lee Currie, 1 April 1950, Huddersfield, Yorkshire, England; violin), Dave Formula (keyboards), John McGeoch (b. 28 May 1955, Greenock, Strathclyde, Scotland; guitar) and Barry Adamson (b. 1 June 1958, Moss Side, Manchester, England; bass). The last three were all members of Magazine. Ure rose to fame with teenybopper stars Slik before joining the Rich Kids with whom Egan played drums. Both Egan and Ure also played in the short-lived Misfits during 1979, before Egan briefly joined the Skids and Ure linked with Thin Lizzy, then replaced John Foxx in Ultravox. Currie was also in both Ultravox and Visage, not to mention Gary Numan's band at more or less the same time.

The roots of Visage came about in late 1978 when Ure and Strange recorded a cover version of the old Zager And Evans hit 'In The Year 2525' as a demo for EMI Records, but had it turned down. The duo started recruiting instead, picking up the above-named musicians for rehearsals. The demo was hawked to Radar Records who signed them and released their first single, September 1979's 'Tar', which concerned the joys of smoking. The track was produced by Martin Rushent. Any hopes of releasing a follow-up on the label were dashed when Radar's parent company pulled the purse strings tight and wound up the label. Polydor Records picked up the band and were rewarded with a massive UK Top 10 hit in late 1980/early 1981 with 'Fade To Grey', which fitted in with the burgeoning synthesizer pop scene of the early 80s. Although the band members had other commitments, Visage made a brief effort to continue their existence. The third single, 'Mind Of A Toy', with its memorable Godley And Creme-produced video (their first), was a Top 20 hit but subsequent singles were released at greater and greater intervals and, apart from the Top 20 hits 'The Damned Don't Cry' and 'Night Train', did increasingly less well. Ure and Adamson left following the release of The Anvil, which featured saxophonist Gary Barnacle, and further personnel upheavals occurred when Currie and Formula left during the recording of Beat Boy. The band eventually fizzled out in the mid-80s, with Strange forming Strange Cruise with Wendy Wu (ex-Photos).
● ALBUMS: Visage (Polydor 1980) ★★, The Anvil (Polydor 1982) ★★, Beat Boy (Polydor 1984) ★★.
● COMPILATIONS: Fade To Grey: The Singles Collection (Polydor 1983) ★★★, Fade To Grey: Dance Mix Album (Polydor 1983) ★★, The Damned Don't Cry (Spectrum 2000) ★★★.
● VIDEOS: The Visage Videos (PolyGram Music Video 1986).
● FURTHER READING: Blitzed!, Steve Strange.

## W.A.S.P.

This theatrical shock-rock troupe was formed in 1982 in Los Angeles, USA; their name was apparently an acronym of We Are Sexual Perverts. Outrageous live performances included throwing raw meat into the audience and the whipping of a naked woman tied to a 'torture rack' as a backdrop to a primitive metal attack. The band, formed by singer Blackie Lawless (b. 4 September 1956, Staten Island, New York, USA; ex-New York Dolls, Sister) with guitarists Chris Holmes (b. 23 June 1961) and Randy Piper and drummer Tony Richards, were snapped up by Capitol Records, who then refused to release their debut single, the infamous 'Animal (F**k Like A Beast)', on legal advice. It was subsequently licensed to independent labels. W.A.S.P. was an adequate basic metal debut, although it lacked 'Animal', while The Last Command, with new drummer Steve Riley, consolidated W.A.S.P.'s status with a more refined approach, producing the excellent 'Wild Child' and 'Blind In Texas'. W.A.S.P. became a major US concert draw, albeit with a stage show much toned down from the early days. Inside The Electric Circus in 1986 continued in this vein, and saw the debut of bass player Johnny Rod (ex-King Kobra), with Lawless (up to this point the bass player) replacing Piper on rhythm guitar, while live shows saw Lawless' trademark buzzsaw-bladed codpiece replaced by a remarkable flame-throwing version.

Live ... In The Raw was a decent live set, but once again lacked 'Animal', which remained the centrepiece of W.A.S.P.'s repertoire. That song, and the band's outrageous approach, made them a constant target for the American organisation PMRC, whom Lawless successfully sued for unauthorized use of copyrighted material. As Lawless became a tireless free speech campaigner, he moved the band towards a serious stance on The Headless Children, with Quiet Riot drummer Frankie Banali replacing the L.A. Guns-bound Riley. The socio-political and anti-drug commentary was backed by vivid imagery in the live setting, but Holmes departed after the tour, the split catalyzed by his drunken appearance in the movie The Decline And Fall Of Western Civilisation Part II: The Metal Years. Lawless used session musicians to record The Crimson Idol, a Who-influenced concept effort, and toured with Rod, Doug Blair (guitar) and Stet Howland (drums). In 1993, he announced the end of W.A.S.P. after compiling the First Blood ... Last Cuts retrospective. His solo album, Still Not Black Enough, was nevertheless issued under the W.A.S.P. name. The album featured studio guitarist Bob Kulick, who also appeared on The Crimson Idol. Lawless reunited with Holmes in 1996 and elected to carry on recording and touring as W.A.S.P. Following 1997's forgettable

*Kill, Fuck, Die*, which featured new bass player Mike Duda, the release of the concert set *Double Live Assassins* served as a timely reminder that the band remains a potent live act. *Unholy Terror*, meanwhile, proved the band was still capable of producing quality work in the studio.

● ALBUMS: *W.A.S.P.* (Capitol 1984) ★★, *The Last Command* (Capitol 1985) ★★★, *Inside The Electric Circus* (Capitol 1986) ★★★, *Live ... In The Raw* (Capitol 1987) ★★, *The Headless Children* (Capitol 1989) ★★, *The Crimson Idol* (Parlophone/Capitol 1992) ★★★, *Still Not Black Enough* (Castle 1995) ★★★, *Kill, Fuck, Die* (Castle 1997) ★★, *Double Live Assassins* (CMC/Snapper 1998) ★★★, *Helldorado* (CMC/Apocalypse 1999) ★★, *The Sting* (Snapper 2000) ★★, *Unholy Terror* (Metal-Is 2001) ★★★, *Dying For The World* (Metal-Is 2002) ★★.

● COMPILATIONS: *First Blood ... Last Cuts* (Capitol 1993) ★★★, *The Best Of The Best* (Apocalypse 2000) ★★★★.

● VIDEOS: *Live At The Lyceum, London* (PMI 1984), *Videos ... In The Raw* (PMI 1988), *First Blood ... Last Visions ...* (PMI 1993), *The Sting: Live At The Key Club, L.A.* (Snapper 2001).

## WAH!

Alongside the Teardrop Explodes and Echo And The Bunnymen, Wah!, led by the freewheeling Pete Wylie (b. 22 March 1958, Liverpool, England; guitar, vocals) through its various incarnations (Wah! Heat, Wah!, Shambeko! Say Wah!, Mighty Wah!), prompted a second beat boom in Liverpool, Merseyside, England, during the early 80s. Indeed, Wylie had originally been part of the historically brief but important Crucial 3 with Julian Cope and Ian McCulloch. Whereas those bands opted for a pristine guitar pop aesthetic, Wylie and Wah! were all pop melodrama and bluster. Occasionally they lacked the technical abilities to pull off some of their grand arrangements, especially when tackling the big soul ballads, but Wylie was always a supremely entertaining frontman and amusing performer. His various collaborators included Pete Younger (bass), Rob Jones (drums), Carl 'Oddball' Washington (bass), Joe Musker (drums), Paul Barlow (drums), Henry Priestman (keyboards), Charlie Griffiths (keyboards), Jay Naughton (piano), Chris Joyce (drums), Colin Redmond (guitar), Steven Johnson (guitar), John Maher (drums), and many others, plus a brass section. Of these, Washington enjoyed the longest tenure.

The albums Wah! left behind are remarkably inconsistent, and a more informed purchase would be WEA Records' 1984 compilation of the band's singles, *The Way We Wah!*. This included 'Come Back' and 'Hope (I Wish You'd Believe Me)', plus the band's only major UK chart success, 1982's Top 3 single 'The Story Of The Blues'. Afterwards Wylie became a solo artist with the release of 1987's *Sinful* for Virgin Records. Afterwards his reputation became that of 'expert ligger', partying throughout England as a 'face about town'. When fellow Liverpudlians the Farm broke through in the 90s the good-humoured Wylie was frequently to be seen accompanying them on record and stage, and a

remixed version of 'Sinful' reached the UK Top 30 in 1991. A serious back injury sidelined Wylie for several years, but he made a triumphant return in early 2000 with the euphoric guitar pop of *Songs Of Strength & Heartbreak*, featuring the anthemic 'Heart As Big As Liverpool'. The excellent two CD set, *The Handy Wah! Whole: Songs From The Repertwah!: The Maverick Years 2000*, compiles the best of Wah! and Wylie's solo output.

● ALBUMS: *Nah! Poo! The Art Of Bluff* (Eternal 1981) ★★, as Mighty Wah! *A Word To The Wise Guy* (Beggars Banquet 1984) ★★★, as Pete Wylie *Sinful* (Virgin 1987) ★★★, *Infamy! Or I Didn't Get Where I Am Today* (Siren 1991) ★★★, as Pete Wylie Is The Mighty Wah! *Songs Of Strength & Heartbreak* (When! 2000) ★★★★.

● COMPILATIONS: *The Maverick Years '80 -'81* (Wonderful World 1982) ★★, as Mighty Wah! *The Way We Wah!* (Warners 1984) ★★★, *The Handy Wah! Whole: Songs From The Repertwah!: The Maverick Years 2000* (Essential 2000) ★★★★.

## WAITE, JOHN

b. 4 July 1952, Lancaster, Lancashire, England. Waite is a singer, bass player, and occasional harmonica player who has found greater fame and fortune in the USA than in his native land. A former art student, he began playing in bands in the late 60s and in 1976 formed the Babys with Mike Corby, Tony Brock and Walter Stocker. The Babys split in 1981 after five albums and Waite embarked on a solo career. His debut single, 'Change', was not a chart hit and he had to wait until 'Missing You' was released from his second album for a breakthrough. In the UK the record made a respectable number 9 but in the USA it went to the top. Waite formed the No Brakes band, joined by former David Bowie guitarist Earl Slick, to promote the new album, but did not scale the same heights again. Instead, he formed the ill-fated Bad English in 1989, before resuming his solo career in the mid-90s. In 1995, he had his first hit for several years with the power ballad 'How Did I Get By Without You'. The album *Temple Bar* was more in the folk-rock line and included cover versions of songs by Hank Williams and Bill Withers. *When You Were Mine* and *Figure In A Landscape*, two pleasant but unremarkable AOR collections, failed to restore Waite to the charts.

● ALBUMS: *Ignition* (Chrysalis 1982) ★★, *No Brakes* (EMI America 1984) ★★★, *Mask Of Smiles* (Capitol 1985) ★★, *Rover's Return* (EMI America 1987) ★★, *Temple Bar* (Imago 1995) ★★★, *When You Were Mine* (Pure 1997) ★★, *King Biscuit Flower Hour* (King Biscuit Flower Hour 1999) ★★, *Figure In A Landscape* (Gold Circle 2001) ★★★.

● COMPILATIONS: *Essential* (Chrysalis 1992) ★★★, *Falling Backwards: The Complete John Waite* (EMI 1996) ★★★.

## WAITRESSES

Formed in 1978 in Akron, Ohio, USA, the Waitresses were a new wave/pop band that achieved moderate popularity after relocating to the New York area in the early 80s. Led by Chris Butler (guitar, ex-Tin Huey), the other members comprised Patty

Donahue (d. 9 December 1996; vocals), Dan Klayman (keyboards), Mars Williams (saxophone), Tracy Warmworth (bass) and Billy Ficca (drums, ex-Television). After releasing an independent single on the Clone label in 1978, the Waitresses signed to the PolyGram Records subsidiary Ze Records in 1982. Their single 'I Know What Boys Like', which cast Donahue as a tease who delighted in *not* giving boys what they liked, was a popular dance hit in clubs and received substantial college radio airplay, reaching number 62 in the USA. The debut, *Wasn't Tomorrow Wonderful?*, on Polydor Records, received critical acclaim and was their highest-charting record at number 41. Their 1983 EP was issued in the USA under the title *I Could Rule The World If I Could Only Get The Parts*, and in an abbreviated UK version as *Make The Weather*. The US version featured 'Christmas Wrapping', which became a popular rap hit in clubs. Donahue briefly quit during the recording of the lacklustre *Bruiseology*, after which the band gradually fizzled out. Butler moved on to production work (Joan Osborne, Freedy Johnston) and eccentric solo projects, including a 1995 single recorded on an antique wax cylinder phonograph, and 1997's 'The Devil Glitch', a 69-minute single featuring over 500 choruses that has been confirmed by the *Guinness Book Of World Records* as the World's Longest Pop Song.

● ALBUMS: *Wasn't Tomorrow Wonderful?* (Polydor 1982) ★★★, *Bruiseology* (Polydor 1983) ★★, *King Biscuit Flower Hour* (King Biscuit Flower Hour 1997) ★★.

● COMPILATIONS: *The Best Of The Waitresses* (Polydor 1990) ★★★.

## WALKABOUTS

The Walkabouts are from Seattle, USA, and coalesced around the nucleus of Chris Eckman (vocals, guitar), a philosophy graduate, and Carla Torgerson (vocals, guitar). Two brothers, Curt (bass) and Grant Eckman (drums), were also in the band, but Curt left early on and was replaced by Michael Wells, while Glenn Slater (keyboards) joined in 1989. In 1992, Terri Moeller replaced Grant Eckman on drums and at the same time Bruce Wirth joined to provide pedal steel guitar and mandolin. The Walkabouts, who took their name from the Nicolas Roeg film *Walkabout*, were formed on the understanding that 'twisting a take on punk didn't rule out a love for Appalachian mountain music'. Early on their energized folk rock was restricted by limited budget recordings, beginning with a self-titled cassette EP in 1984. Further releases on Necessity and PopLlama followed before the band signed up to leading independent label, Sub Pop Records. *Cataract* in 1989 announced their arrival, with its fine songs including the stinging lament 'Hell's Soup Kitchen'. *Scavenger* had a bigger budget and helped the band become a major draw in America and Europe, although the subsequent *New West Motel* was only released in the latter territory. *Satisfied Mind* was an album of cover versions, taking its material from blues, country and rock. Guests on the album included Peter Buck (R.E.M.), Mark Lanegan (Screaming Trees) and Ivan Kral (Patti Smith Group), while the songs covered

included works by Nick Cave, Neil Young and Charlie Rich. *Setting The Woods On Fire*, its title taken from the Hank Williams song, was a strong collection of original material accompanied by fiddle, pedal steel guitar, mandolin and the mysterious Tiny Hat Orchestra, and saw the band court comparisons to a 90s version of Neil Young And Crazy Horse. By this time, Eckman and Torgerson had also initiated their own side project, releasing material as Chris And Carla. *Devil's Road* was their most commercial album, which alienated them from some old fans in hoping to attract many new ones. Even with the addition of the lush Warsaw Philharmonic Orchestra, their new label Virgin Records must have been slightly disappointed at the reception it was afforded. The following year's *Nighttown* covered the usual ground, boosted as ever by Torgerson's striking voice. The Walkabouts returned to independent label status for 1999's *Trail Of Stars*. Eckman and Torgerson have maintained their remarkably high standards into the new millennium, with a series of releases for the Glitterhouse label.

● ALBUMS: *The Walkabouts* cassette only (Necessity 1984) ★★, *22 Disasters* mini-album (Necessity 1985) ★★★, *See Beautiful Rattlesnake Gardens* (PopLlama Products 1988) ★★, *Cataract* (Sub Pop 1989) ★★★, *Scavenger* (Sub Pop 1991) ★★★, *New West Motel* (Sub Pop 1993) ★★★, *Satisfied Mind* (Sub Pop 1993) ★★★, *Setting The Woods On Fire* (Sub Pop 1994) ★★★, *Devil's Road* (Virgin 1996) ★★★, *Nighttown* (Virgin 1997) ★★★, *Trail Of Stars* (Grapevine 1999) ★★★, *Train Leaves At Eight* (Glitterhouse 2000) ★★★, *Ended Up A Stranger* (Glitterhouse 2001) ★★★.

● COMPILATIONS: *Death Valley Days: Lost Songs And Rarities – 1985 To 1995* (Glitterhouse 1996) ★★★.

## WALKING SEEDS

Liverpool, England's premier psychedelic 'grunge' specialists arose early in 1986 out of the ashes of the Mel-O-Tones. In between, John Neesam (drums), Frank Martin (vocals) and Bob Parker (bass, guitar) formed the Corinthians for three months, recording a seven-track demo that formed the basis of the Walking Seeds' set. The band's first EP, *Know Too Much* (1986), set the pace, fronted by the strong 'Tantric Wipeout'. By the time of the follow-up, 'Mark Chapman' (1987), Neesam had been replaced by two former members of Marshmallow Overcoat, Tony Mogan (drums) and Baz Sutton (guitar). This was followed by the extreme but patchy *Skullfuck* (the title influenced by a Grateful Dead album cover) later that year. After lying low, the band signed to Glass Records, issuing *Upwind Of Disaster, Downwind Of Atonement* in 1989. Recorded in New York, the presence of Bongwater's Mark Kramer as producer helped to bring a more defined, but nevertheless uncompromising, aura to the proceedings. Sutton left to join the La's and was briefly replaced by Andy Rowan for 1989's *Shaved Beatnik* EP (wherein the band admirably slaughtered Cream's 'Sunshine Of Your Love'). The mini-album, *Sensory Deprivation Chamber Quartet Dwarf*, was assisted by psychedelic wizard Nick 'Bevis Frond' Saloman and new bass player Lee Webster. When Glass folded, the Walking

Seeds recorded 'Gates Of Freedom' which included a b-side cover version of Pink Floyd's 'Astronomy Dominé'. This coincided with *Bad Orb ... Whirling Ball*, a more considered but still aggressively garage-like effort. The Walking Seeds tore through Bevis Frond's 'Reflections In A Tall Mirror', backed by his interpretation of the band's 'Sexorcist'. However, at this point, the band 'self-destructed', despondent about their lack of success, despite recruiting ex-Dinosaur Jr guitarist Don Fleming. A swan-song was offered in *Earth Is Hell* on the Snakeskin label, housing live material recorded in Germany earlier that year. Parker and Mogan then set up the Del-Bloods, issuing 'Black Rabbit' in 1991. The pair also surfaced in White Bitch for 'Animal Woman' and teamed up with Martin for Batloaf's 'Meat Out Of Hell' soon afterwards. Webster, meanwhile, had joined Baz Sutton in Froth that same year.
● ALBUMS: *Skullfuck* (Probe 1987) ★★, *Upwind Of Disaster, Downwind Of Atonement* (Communion 1989) ★★★, *Sensory Deprivation Chamber Quartet Dwarf* mini-album (Glass 1989) ★★, *Bad Orb ... Whirling Ball* (Shimmy-Disc 1990) ★★★, *Earth Is Hell* (Snakeskin 1990) ★★.

## WALL OF VOODOO

Formed in Los Angeles, California, USA, in 1977, in the immediate punk aftermath, Wall Of Voodoo initially comprised Stan Ridgway (b. Stanard Ridgway, 5 April 1954, Barstow, California, USA; vocals, keyboards), Bill Noland (guitar, vocals), Chas T. Gray (b. Charles Gray, bass, keyboards, synthesizer) and Joe Nanini (drums). However, by the release of 1980's self-titled EP and the following year's *Dark Continent*, Noland had been replaced by ex-Skulls member Marc Moreland (b. West Covina, USA, d. 13 March 2002, Paris, France) while Bruce Moreland had been added on bass. The latter was then dropped for *Call Of The West*, arguably the unit's finest album, on which their sense of rhythm and wash of synthesizer lines underscored Ridgway's droning, offhand vocals and film noir-influenced lyrics. The band enjoyed a minor radio hit with the album's best track, 'Mexican Radio'. Any potential this offered was sundered with Ridgway's departure in 1983. While he went on to enjoy a UK Top 5 single with 'Camouflage', Wall Of Voodoo pursued a less successful career led by new vocalist Andy Prieboy. The returning Bruce Moreland and new drummer Ned Leukhardt featured on the strong *Seven Days In Sammystown*, but subsequent albums, although of intermittent interest, lacked the adventure of their earlier work. Prieboy went on to release the solo albums *... Upon My Wicked Son* (1990) and *Sins Of Our Fathers* (1995), while Marc Moreland became a session musician and recorded a solo album under the name Department Of Crooks. He died of kidney failure in March 2002 at the age of 44.
● ALBUMS: *Dark Continent* (I.R.S. 1981) ★★★, *Call Of The West* (I.R.S. 1982) ★★★★, *Seven Days In Sammystown* (I.R.S. 1985) ★★★, *Happy Planet* (I.R.S. 1986) ★★, *The Ugly Americans In Australia* (I.R.S. 1988) ★★.
● COMPILATIONS: *Granma's House: A Collection Of* *Songs By Wall Of Voodoo* (I.R.S. 1984) ★★★, *The Index Masters* (Illegal 1991) ★★★.

## WALTERS, TREVOR

b. 1961, London, England. Walters embarked on a musical career in reggae by adding his distinct soprano voice to the Ital group. He was also recruited to sing on releases by Santic, and contributed to the hit 'Bloody Eyes'. He later recorded as part of Youth And Youth, with whom he released 'Try Love Again'. Prior to embarking on a solo career, Walters recorded the 'Back Together Again' duet with Jean Adebambo, which gave an early indication of the potential of these two fine vocalists. This release was followed by the protest song, 'They'll Never Get Away', which proved popular in the reggae charts. In 1981 Walters wrote and recorded 'Give Love A Try', which surpassed its predecessor by topping the reggae chart. In October 1981 he reached number 27 in the UK pop charts with 'Love Me Tonight'. It appeared that Walters was destined to be a one-hit-wonder in the annals of pop music, but he still attracted some derision from reggae aficionados because of his crossover success. Nevertheless, he continued releasing material that maintained a respectable profile in the reggae chart, including 'Handyman', 'Comma Comma' and, in combination with Jah Bunny, 'Lovers Medley'. The singer returned to the UK pop charts in July 1984, reaching number 9 with his rendition of Lionel Richie's 'Stuck On You'. He also covered Richie's 'Penny Lover', which, although an exemplary effort riding on a gentle lovers rock rhythm, did not chart. His crossover success inspired Polydor Records to sign him for a cover version of Andrew Gold's 'Never Let Her Slip Away'. This release remained at the lower end of the pop charts, while the follow-up, 'Love's A Lie', made no impression on any chart. The poor response, alleged to be through lack of promotion, was deemed inadequate by the company. In 1986 he enjoyed a hit with the sublime 'Love Will Find A Way', produced by Leonard Chin. In 1991, he regained his street credibility by recording with Anthony Brightly, who produced 'Can You Feel The Love' with Pure Silk. He continued to record and enjoy further hits throughout the 90s, including 'Hold' in 1998.
● ALBUMS: *Walters Gold With Love* (Adelphi 1988) ★★★.

## WANG CHUNG

This London, England-based new wave pop band was formed from the ashes of the Intellektuals and 57 Men. Originally called Huang Chung, they comprised Jack Hues (vocals/guitar), Nick Feldman (bass) and Darren Costin (drums). After four tracks featured on two 101 Records compilation albums, they released a 1980 single, 'Isn't It About Time We Were On Television?'. It was memorable enough to persuade Arista Records to sign the band in 1981. Despite an innovative first album, which used prominent saxophone, they had pared back down to a trio by their second album. They went on to achieve just one minor hit in the UK with 'Dance Hall Days' in 1984. However, they proved better suited to the US market where they enjoyed five Top

40 successes including the number 2 'Everybody Have Fun Tonight'. However, Costin left in 1985 when the band switched to A&M Records, then Geffen Records the following year. 'Hypnotise Me' was used in the 1987 movie *Innerspace*.

● ALBUMS: *Huang Chung* (Arista 1982) ★★★, *Points On A Curve* (Geffen 1904) ★★★, *To Live And Die In LA* film soundtrack (Geffen 1985) ★★, *Mosaic* (Geffen 1986) ★★★, *The Warmer Side Of Cool* (Geffen 1989) ★★.

● COMPILATIONS: *Everybody Wang Chung Tonight: Wang Chung's Greatest Hits* (Geffen 1997) ★★★★.

## WANGFORD, HANK

b. Samuel Hutt, 15 November 1940, Wangford, Suffolk, England. Wangford's father, Allen Hutt, was chief sub-editor of the communist newspaper *The Daily Worker* and president of the National Union of Journalists. His mother taught English to Russian students. Wangford studied medicine at Cambridge University and later became a doctor. He was converted to country music by Gram Parsons who attended him for treatment in 1971. After a period in the USA, Wangford became gradually more involved in country music and, despite the demands of his professional work, yearned to be a performer. When his girlfriend married his best friend, he consoled himself in a pub near the Wangford bypass in Suffolk. Here he devised the character of Hank Wangford, who would sing songs from the Wangford Hall of Pain. He says, 'Hank Wangford was a good name for the classic country star. He sings about pain, he sings about heartache, and that was good because Sam could go on living and being normal.' Starting in 1976, Wangford built a reputation on the London pub-rock circuit.

His persona was both a glorification of country music and an affectionate parody of its excesses. He formed Sincere Management (motto: 'It's in the post.') and Sincere Products ('Brought to you with no regard for quality'). Wangford generated publicity as a gynaecologist-cum-country singer, often being photographed with a Harley Street sign. His media image, however, has proved more sustainable than the lightweight music which, in fairness, is highly successful in the pub/club environment. 'Chicken Rhythm' is derived from Ray Stevens' quirky 'In The Mood', and 'Cowboys Stay On Longer' is a close cousin to David Allan Coe's 'Divers Do It Deeper'. Wangford has always been able to surround himself with talented band members, notably Andy Roberts (Brad Breath) and Melanie Harrold (Irma Cetas), who have more musical talent. His fiddler and co-singer, former member of the Fabulous Poodles and Clark Gable lookalike, Bobby Valentino, later embarked on a solo career. Wangford, with his ponytail, stubble and gap-toothed features is an engaging entertainer, creating a stage show, 'Radio Wang', and presenting two country music series for Channel 4 Television. He also works as the senior medical officer at a family planning clinic in London, and he says, 'I have had letters of referral from doctors which start "Dear Dr. Wangford", so the transmogrification is complete.'

● ALBUMS: *Live: Hank Wangford* (Cow Pie 1982) ★★, *Hank Wangford* (Cow Pie 1985) ★★★, *Rodeo Radio* (Situation 2 1985) ★★, *Stormy Horizons* (New Routes 1990) ★★, *Hard Shoulder To Cry On* (Sincere 1993) ★★, *Wake Up Dead* (Way Out West 1997) ★★★.

● FURTHER READING: *Hank Wangford, Vol. III The Middle Years*, Sam Hutt. *Lost Cowboys: From Patagonia To The Alamo*, Hank Wangford.

## WARE, MARTYN

b. 19 May 1956, Sheffield, England. A founder member of the Human League alongside Phil Oakey and Ian Craig Marsh, Ware departed after the albums *Reproduction* and *Travelogue* with Marsh to form Heaven 17. Heaven 17's career spanned several years, as did that of another Ware/Marsh offshoot, BEF (British Electronic Foundation). This 'collective' was announced with the release of *Music Of Quality And Distinction Vol. 1*, which also pointed the way to Ware's future career as a producer. Ware helped draw startling performances from some of soul and pop's foremost artists, including Chaka Khan, Mavis Staples, Billy MacKenzie (the Associates), Lalah Hathaway, Paul Jones, Green Gartside (Scritti Politti), Gary Glitter and Sandie Shaw. Most important of all was Ware's treatment of Tina Turner on 'Let's Stay Together', an international hit which lifted that artist's career out of the mire (he would subsequently produce the bestselling *Private Dancer*). Afterwards Ware produced Terence Trent D'Arby's spectacularly successful debut album. Other artists he worked with in the 90s included Paul Weller (the *Council Collective* EP project), Dan Hartman (*Circle Of Light*), Jimmy Ruffin ('The Foolish Thing To Do'), Annabella Lwin (*Naked Experience*) and Hannah Jones (*What If*). He also teamed up with fellow electronic pioneer Vince Clarke in the latter part of the decade, recording the ambitious audio-sensory albums *Pretentious* and *Spectrum Pursuit Vehicle*. The former included 'Music For Multiple Dimensions', the first piece of music commissioned by the UK's National Centre for Popular Music, while the latter comprised recordings first premiered in February 2000 at London's Roundhouse.

● ALBUMS: with Vince Clarke *Pretentious* (Mute 1999) ★★★, with Clarke *Spectrum Pursuit Vehicle* (Mute 2001) ★★★★.

## WARNES, JENNIFER

b. 3 March 1947, Seattle, Washington, USA. Warnes grew up in Orange County, California and first sang in public as a child. In 1967, her strong pop/MOR voice won a contract to appear (as Jennifer Warren) on the television series hosted by country group the Smothers Brothers. Her first recording session was a duet with Mason Williams and Warnes became part of the Los Angeles club scene. She also took a leading role in the west coast production of *Hair*. As a solo artist Warnes recorded unsuccessfully for Parrot Records and Reprise Records, where John Cale produced her 1972 album, before signing to Arista Records in 1975. There she had a Top 10 hit (and a country chart-topper) with 'Right Time Of The Night' in 1977 while 'I Know A Heartache When I See One' (1979) was also successful.

During the 80s, as well as her work as a guest vocalist, Warnes gained a reputation as a singer of film themes after 'It Goes Like It Goes' from *Norma Rae* won an Oscar for Best Original Song in 1980. She performed Randy Newman's 'One More Hour' on the soundtrack of *Ragtime* before scoring her biggest hit in 1983 with 'Up Where We Belong'. A duet with Joe Cocker, the Oscar and Grammy-winning title song from *An Officer And A Gentleman* topped the US charts. Other film songs were 'Nights Are Forever' (from *The Twilight Zone: The Movie*) and 'All The Right Moves', sung with ex-Manfred Mann's Earth Band vocalist Chris Thompson. Warnes again reached number 1 when she teamed up with Bill Medley for the *Dirty Dancing* theme, '(I've Had) The Time Of My Life' in 1987. The previous year, she recorded a much-acclaimed selection of Leonard Cohen compositions, *Famous Blue Raincoat*. Warnes had first worked with Cohen on tour in 1973 and had created vocal arrangements for his *Recent Songs*, as well as singing on his later releases. Warnes co-produced her own 1992 album for Private Music as well as co-writing most of the songs. Among the musicians contributing were Richard Thompson, Van Dyke Parks and Donald Fagen. She subsequently appeared on albums by Jackson Browne, John Prine, Tanita Tikaram and Stephen Bruton, before making a long overdue return to the studio to record *The Well*.

● ALBUMS: *I Can Remember Everything* (Parrot 1968) ★★, *See Me, Feel Me, Touch Me Heal Me* (Parrot 1969) ★★, *Jennifer* (Reprise 1972) ★★★, *Jennifer Warnes* (Arista 1977) ★★, *Shot Through the Heart* (Arista 1979) ★★, *Famous Blue Raincoat* (Cypress 1986) ★★★★, *The Hunter* (Private 1992) ★★★, *The Well* (Sin-Drome 2001) ★★★.

● COMPILATIONS: *The Best Of Jennifer Warnes* (Arista 1982) ★★★, *Just Jennifer* (Deram 1992) ★★.

## WARREN, DIANE

b. 1956, Van Nuys, California, USA. With songs performed by Aretha Franklin, Cheap Trick, Cher, Chicago, Cyndi Lauper, Dusty Springfield, Elton John, Four Tops, Gladys Knight, Gloria Estefan, Joan Jett, John Waite, Joe Cocker, Faith Hill, LeAnn Rimes, Ricky Martin, Heart, Roy Orbison, Celine Dion, the Jacksons, Tom Jones, Trisha Yearwood, Aerosmith, Roberta Flack, Tina Turner, Mark Chesnutt, the Cult and Ziggy Marley, among well over 100 others, 'Valley Girl' Warren is one of the most successful, gifted and prolific songwriters in the current music industry.

She has achieved her success despite her guitar teacher having originally pronounced her tone deaf after her father brought home her first guitar, purchased in Tijuana, Mexico. Even as a child she maintained a constant output of compositions, until her family grew so weary of their constant repetition they erected a metal shed in the back yard for her to practice in. Having gleaned her interest in music from radio and her sisters' record collections, throughout she restrained any ambitions to perform her songs, electing instead to give them to a vast and grateful army of interpreters. Warren did struggle initially however, only making songwriting a viable

living by the time she was 24. She has less than fond memories of her initial attempts to enter the music industry: 'I got a lot of stupid advice. I remember one publisher looking at a verse of one of my songs and saying, "You have nine lines in this verse, you can only have eight lines. It has to be even."' However, always in place was the dedication which has hallmarked her career: 'I've written songs on Kotex, lyrics on the palm of my hand. If I don't have a tape recorder, I'll call home and sing into my answering machine.' Legend has it that she works over 12 hours a day, often seven days a week, ensconced in a tiny office cum studio. Before she became the hottest songwriting property in the contemporary US market she was also just as determined to see her work used – one anecdote concerns her falling on her knees to persuade Cher to sing 'If I Could Turn Back Time'. It became the artist's biggest hit for 15 years, and nowadays she has no need for such powers of persuasion. Her first major break had come when Laura Branigan recorded 'Solitaire', a MOR staple. By 1985, DeBarge had taken the altogether different 'Rhythm Of The Night' to number 3 in the *Billboard* charts and Warren was established as a major songwriting source to artists from almost every genre of popular music.

Warren formed Realsongs in 1985 in response to contractual difficulties she experienced with former manager, and Laura Branigan producer, Jack White. Realsongs is administered by business colleague Doreen Dorion, who together with Ken Philips takes responsibility for placing Warren's songs with prospective artists. By now the hits were flowing freely, after the DeBarge hit had opened up a lucrative market to her. Some of her greatest compositions, such as 'Look Away' (Chicago), 'When I See You Smile' (Bad English), 'Blame It On The Rain' (Milli Vanilli), 'Love Will Lead You Back' (Taylor Dayne), 'Nothing's Gonna Stop Us Now' (Starship), 'I Get Weak' (Belinda Carlisle) and 'We're Not Making Love Anymore' (Barbra Streisand), were written between then and 1989. Her profile quickly earned her nicknames such as 'industry powerhouse' and 'hit machine'. Though she professes not to customise her material for such diverse artists, it is a source of considerable pleasure to her that critics have been unable to discern any 'house style'. Which is why she has been able to work with artists as diverse as Bette Midler and Bon Jovi. *Billboard* subsequently named Realsongs the Top Singles Publisher Of 1990. The flood of awards snowballed throughout the 90s. She received several Songwriter Of The Year awards from ASCAP and *Billboard*, and was voted Songwriter Of The Year in the Los Angeles Music Awards in 1991. Realsongs has also remained in the Top 6 Publishing Corporations assessed by *Billboard* since 1990.

By the end of the 90s Warren had over 100 million unit sales to her name, and numerous Top 10 US hits (including, at one point, holding the number 1 and 2 positions in the US singles chart via two separate artists). She had also moved heavily into movies, seeing her material aired on soundtracks including *Golden Child*, *Ghostbusters*, *License To Kill*, *White Men Can't Jump*, *Karate Kid III* and *Neverending Story III*.

Her songs have already been featured in over 50 full-length movies. A *Billboard* special feature celebrated her achievements, interviewing several of the artists who had recorded her songs. One who regularly returns to her for his repertoire is Michael Bolton: 'She is destined to achieve her appropriate status as one of the greatest songwriters in the history of music.' Grace Slick offered a more personal tribute: 'I've never met anybody who is rolling around in that much fame and money who is that real, honest and funny.' One of the few writers qualified to assess her impact on the music scene as a genuine peer was Lamont Dozier: 'She's not only a gifted songwriter, but she seems to have a sixth sense about what music lovers want to hear.' Trisha Yearwood stated 'Diane lives and breathes every song, there's this sense of mission about what she's doing'. Despite her multi-millionaire status and phenomenal success, Warren still maintains her stoic resistance to any interruption in her daunting work schedule. Warren's success and prolific output matches her with the all-time great songwriters of the great American songbook. She is already on a pedestal alongside George and Ira Gershwin and Cole Porter.

## WAS (NOT WAS)

An unlikely recording and production duo, childhood friends David Weiss (saxophone, flute, keyboards, vocals) and Don Was (b. Don Fagenson, Detroit, Illinois, USA; bass, keyboards, guitar) used a variety of singers to front their records, including Sweat Pea Atkinson, Leonard Cohen, Harry Bowens and Donny Ray Mitchell. The duo's ability to produce seamless records from the merging of unlikely source material and collaborators became a keynote in their subsequent career. Their 1981 debut album sought to imbue dance music with an intellectual credibility that it had previously lacked. While musicians were plucked from sources as varied as P-Funk and MC5, 'Tell Me That I'm Dreaming' incorporated a mutilated sample of a Ronald Reagan speech. 1983's *Born To Laugh At Tornadoes* included, bizarrely, Ozzy Osbourne rapping, and a snatch of Frank Sinatra. Because of their cutting-edge recording techniques and feel for different musics, Was (Not Was) became perennial critical favourites, especially in the UK, where they were much admired by emerging pop artists including Helen Terry, Floy Joy, Marilyn and Brother Beyond, all of whom had their albums produced by Was in the early 80s. Geffen Records rewarded their eclecticism by dropping them. They moved on to Phonogram, managing to focus much more clearly on their prospective dance market in the process. Their biggest hit was the anthemic 'Walk The Dinosaur', a transatlantic Top 10 hit, while 'Spy In The House Of Love' had similar crossover appeal. However, the music industry by know was more impressed by Don Was' numerous production credits. These included the B-52's, Iggy Pop, Bonnie Raitt and Bob Dylan, and with his production work now taking precedence, Fagenson officially parted ways with Weiss in 1993.

● ALBUMS: *Was (Not Was)* (Ze-Island 1981) ★★★, *Born To Laugh At Tornadoes* (Ze-Island 1983) ★★★, *What's Up, Dog?* (Chrysalis 1988) ★★★, *Are You Okay?* (Chrysalis 1990) ★★★.
● COMPILATIONS: *Hello, Dad ... I'm In Jail* (PolyGram 1999) ★★★★.

## WAS, DON

b. Donald Fagenson, Detroit, Illinois, USA. Growing up in Detroit in the 60s and 70s, the musical apprenticeship of Don Was came on the tough local rock and blues circuit as a working musician, where he accepted whatever work was available. However, his early ordeals proved ultimately beneficial. Detroit's unique musical melting pot continues to influence and inspire his work – and is particularly evident in his ability to cross boundaries between musical genres. As well as Fortune and Motown Records, the young Was was also exposed to the P-Funk innovations of George Clinton, a thriving jazz enclave and the guttural rock of Iggy Pop and the MC5. Together with high-school friend David Weiss, he formed Was (Not Was), later an attempt to infuse pop music with intellectual credibility, but initially a way of releasing frustration at their inability to attract girlfriends. When Weiss temporarily left the area to work as a writer for *The Herald Examiner* in Los Angeles, Was played with a number of local bands, including an ill-fated folk group who attempted to support Black Sabbath and lasted just one song before being bottled off the stage, and gypsy group the Kallao Brothers. Eventually, however, he linked up with Weiss once again, recording the first Was (Not Was) album in 1981. 'Out Come The Freaks' was the record that established the duo in Detroit and the USA, but their international breakthrough came several years later with the sublime funk of the US/UK Top 10 hit 'Walk The Dinosaur'.

Much more high-profile production work followed in the mid-80s as Was worked alongside artists such as Carly Simon, k.d. lang, the B-52's and Roy Orbison. The latter gave Was his first Grammy Award in 1988 when 'Crying', included on the soundtrack to the movie *Hiding Out*, was voted Best Country Duet. A year later, he collected no less than four Grammys, including Album Of The Year for his work on Bonnie Raitt's *Nick Of Time*. This success ensured his elevation to the status of superstar producer. Further high-profile artists embraced his uniquely innovative production methods in the late 80s and early 90s, including Iggy Pop and Bob Dylan (both of whom were long-term idols of Was), Michael McDonald, Elton John, Neil Diamond, Bob Seger, Andrew Dice Clay, the B-52's (who enjoyed their biggest hit with 'Love Shack' under his tutelage), Jackson Browne, Paula Abdul, Willie Nelson, Marianne Faithfull, Michelle Shocked, Waylon Jennings, Travis Tritt and the Rolling Stones. Indeed, his work on the latter's *Voodoo Lounge* set, as well as Raitt's *Lounging In Their Hearts*, led to his winning the Producer Of The Year Grammy in 1995.

Subsequently, Was invested much of his time in the production of movie soundtracks and documentaries, including one for BBC Television on Brian Wilson, *I Just Wasn't Made For These Times*, which won the 1995 Golden Gate Award at the San

Francisco Film Festival. He started his own film production company, whose work was first unveiled on a film short included as a bonus on an enhanced CD released by his new band, Orquestra Was. They released their debut album, *Forever's A Long, Long Time*, in 1996 on Verve Records, the first time Was had worked as a recording artist under any banner other than Was (Not Was). In keeping with his eclectic reputation, this was a typically ambitious project, comprising Hank Williams songs reinterpreted by long-standing Was (Not Was) collaborator Sweat Pea Atkinson, backed by the usual stellar cast of session musicians drawn from very different musical genres (including Merle Haggard, Herbie Hancock and Wayne Kramer). However, it is as a producer that Was is undoubtedly now best known. Alongside Phil Ramone, Was ranks as one of America's most prolific and successful contemporary producers.

## WASHINGTON, GROVER, JNR.

b. 12 December 1943, Buffalo, New York, USA, d. 17 December 1999, New York City, New York, USA. Growing up in a musical family, Washington was playing tenor saxophone before he was a teenager. He studied formally at the Wurlitzer School of Music in Buffalo and paid his dues gigging locally on tenor and other instruments in the early 60s. After military service in the late 60s he returned to his career, recording a succession of albums under the aegis of producer Creed Taylor, which effectively crossed over into the new market for jazz fusion. By the mid-70s, Washington's popular success had begun to direct the course of his music making and he moved further away from jazz. Commercially, this brought continuing successes. 'The Two Of Us', with vocals by Bill Withers, reached number 2 in the US pop charts in 1981, and *The Best Is Yet To Come* with Patti LaBelle. Over the years Washington enjoyed several gold albums, and 1980's *Winelight* sold over a million copies, achieving platinum status and gaining two Grammy Awards.

Washington's playing displayed great technical mastery, and early in his career his often blues-derived saxophone styling sometimes gave his playing greater depths than the quality of the material warranted. The fact that much of his recorded output proved to be popular in the setting of discos tended to smooth out his playing as the years passed, depleting the characteristics that had attracted so much attention at the start of his career. By the late 80s Washington was still enjoying a degree of popular success, although not at the same high level as a few years before. He worked with Ramsey Lewis and Omar Hakim in the Urban Knights during the 90s. He died in 1999, collapsing in his dressing room after taping a performance in New York for CBS' *Saturday Early Show*. He had been suffering from prostate cancer. The posthumous *Aria* featured adaptations of Puccini, Bizet, and Delibes.

● ALBUMS: *Inner City Blues* (Motown 1971) ★★, *All The King's Horses* (Motown 1972) ★★, *Soul Box* (Motown 1973) ★★, *Mister Magic* (Mister Magic 1975) ★★★, *Feels So Good* (Motown 1975) ★★★, *A*

*Secret Place* (Motown 1976) ★★★, *Live At The Bijou* (Motown 1977) ★★★, with Locksmith *Reed Seed* (Motown 1978) ★★, *Paradise* (Elektra 1979) ★★★★, *Skylarkin'* (Motown 1980) ★★★, *Winelight* (Elektra 1980) ★★★★, *Come Morning* (Elektra 1981) ★★★, *The Best Is Yet To Come* (Elektra 1982) ★★★, *Inside Moves* (Elektra 1984) ★★★, *Playboy Jazz Festival* (Elektra 1984) ★★★, with Kenny Burrell *Togethering* (Blue Note 1984) ★★, *Strawberry Moon* (Columbia 1987) ★★, *Then And Now* (Columbia 1988) ★★, *Time Out Of Mind* (Columbia 1989) ★★, *Next Exit* (Columbia 1992) ★★, *All My Tomorrows* (Columbia 1994) ★★★, *Soulful Strut* (Columbia 1996) ★★★, *Breath Of Heaven A Holiday Collection* (Sony Jazz 1997) ★★, *Aria* (Sony Classical 2000) ★★★.
● COMPILATIONS: *Baddest* (Motown 1980) ★★★, *Anthology* (Motown 1981) ★★★, *Greatest Performances* (Motown 1983) ★★★, *At His Best* (Motown 1985) ★★★, *Anthology* (Elektra 1985) ★★★, *Prime Cuts: The Columbia Years 1987-1999* (Columbia 1999) ★★★, *Millennium Collection* (Motown 2000) ★★★★, *Discovery* (Prestige 2002) ★★.

## WATERBOYS

Formed by former fanzine writer Mike Scott (b. 14 December 1958, Edinburgh, Scotland; vocals), the Waterboys evolved from Another Pretty Face, which included John Caldwell (guitar) and a frequently changing line-up from 1979 to 1981. A series of failed singles followed until Scott elected to form a new group. Borrowing the name Waterboys from a line in 'The Kids' from Lou Reed's *Berlin*, Scott began advertising in the music press for suitable personnel. Anthony Thistlethwaite (b. 31 August 1955, Leicester, England; saxophone) and Karl Wallinger (b. 19 October 1957, Prestatyn, Clwyd, Wales; keyboards, percussion, vocals) were recruited and work was completed on 'A Girl Called Johnny', a sterling tribute to Patti Smith that narrowly failed to become a big hit. The band's self-titled debut was also a solid work, emphasizing Scott's ability as a singer-songwriter. 'December', with its religious connotations, was an excellent Christmas single that again narrowly failed to chart. Augmented by musicians Kevin Wilkinson (drums), Roddy Lorimar (trumpet) and Tim Blanthorn (violin), the Waterboys completed *A Pagan Place*, which confirmed their early promise. The key track for many was 'The Big Music', which became a handy simile for Scott's soul-searching mini-epics. For the following year's *This Is The Sea*, Scott brought in a new drummer, Chris Whitten, and added a folk flavour to the proceedings courtesy of fiddler Steve Wickham. The attendant 'The Whole Of The Moon' only reached number 28 in the UK but later proved a spectacular Top 10 hit when reissued in 1990. It was a masterwork from a band seemingly at the height of its powers.

Despite their promise, the Waterboys remained a vehicle for Scott's ideas and writing, a view reinforced when Karl Wallinger left to form World Party. At this point Wickham, who had previously played with In Tua Nua, U2 and Sinéad O'Connor, took on a more prominent role. He took Scott to Eire and a long sojourn in Galway followed. Three years passed before the Waterboys released their next album, the distinctively folk-flavoured *Fisherman's Blues*. Scott's assimilation of traditional Irish music, mingled with his own spiritual questing and rock background coalesced to produce a work of considerable charm and power. Back in the ascendant, the band completed work on *Room To Roam*, which retained the folk sound, though to a lesser extent than its predecessor.

Within days of the album's release, Wickham left the band, forcing Scott to reconstruct the Waterboys' sound once more. A revised line-up featuring Thistlethwaite, Trevor Hutchinson and new drummer Ken Blevins toured the UK playing a rocking set, minus the folk music that had permeated their recent work. After signing an US/Canadian contract with Geffen Records, the Waterboys line-up underwent further changes when, in February 1992, long-serving member Thistlethwaite left the band (he has since played with the Saw Doctors and released solo albums). During the final rebuilding of the Waterboys, former Wendy And Lisa drummer Carla Azar took over the spot vacated by Ken Blevins, and Scott Thunes was recruited as the new bass player.

Mercurial and uncompromising, Scott continually steered the Waterboys through radically different musical phases, which proved consistently fascinating. Following the release of the disappointingly mainstream *Dream Harder*, Scott concentrated on his solo career for several years, before re-forming the band to record the excellent comeback album, *A Rock In The Weary Land*.

● ALBUMS: *The Waterboys* (Chicken Jazz 1983) ★★★, *A Pagan Place* (Ensign 1984) ★★★, *This Is The Sea* (Ensign 1985) ★★★★, *Fisherman's Blues* (Ensign 1988) ★★★★, *Room To Roam* (Ensign 1990) ★★★, *Dream Harder* (Geffen 1993) ★★, *A Rock In The Weary Land* (RCA/Razor & Tie 2000) ★★★★.
● COMPILATIONS: *The Best Of 1981-90* (Ensign 1991) ★★★, *The Secret Life Of The Waterboys: 1981-1985* (Ensign 1994) ★★, *The Live Adventures Of The Waterboys* (New Millennium 1998) ★★★, *The Whole Of The Moon: The Music Of Mike Scott And The Waterboys* (EMI 1998) ★★★★, *Too Close To Heaven: The Unreleased Fisherman's Blues Sessions* (RCA 2001) ★★★.

## WAX
This highly accomplished transatlantic duo featured Andrew Gold (b. 2 August 1951, Burbank, California, USA; vocals, guitar, keyboards) and Graham Gouldman (b. 10 May 1946, Manchester, England; vocals, guitar, keyboards). Gold had a successful solo career in the 70s and had met Gouldman when he worked on 10cc's last two albums. When 10cc split up in 1984, Gold teamed up with Gouldman to form Common Knowledge, but after several unsuccessful singles they decided on a complete re-launch. A change of label and name to Wax brought a US hit in 1986 with 'Right Between The Eyes'. Success in Britain came in 1987 with the catchy 'Bridge To Your Heart' (number 12), which set the duo on the right track. However, the following singles and a third album in 1989, although commercial, failed to ignite

any interest.
● ALBUMS: *Magnetic Heaven* (RCA 1985) ★★★, *American English* (RCA 1987) ★★★, *A Hundred Thousand In Fresh Notes* (RCA 1989) ★★.
● COMPILATIONS: *The Wax Files* (Dome 1997) ★★★, *common knowledge.com* (Dome 1998) ★★★.

## WEATHER GIRLS
Izora Rhodes and Martha Wash met in the San Francisco-based gospel group, NOW (News Of The World) prior to joining the backing group of rising disco star Sylvester. Dubbed Two Tons O' Fun in deference to their rotund stature, the duo recorded for the Fantasy Records label before securing a measure of infamy, as the Weather Girls, for their tongue-in-cheek release, 'It's Raining Men'. First released in the USA in 1982, the single achieved a greater success in the UK where it later peaked at number 2 in 1984 after re-entering the chart. Subsequent releases however lacked the undeniable charm of their major hit, but admirably showcased the Weather Girls' powerful voices. Ex-Spice Girls singer Geri Halliwell topped the UK charts in 2001with a cover version of 'It's Raining Men'.
● ALBUMS: *Success* (Columbia 1983) ★★★★, *Big Girls Don't Cry* (Columbia 1985) ★★, *Weather Girls* (Columbia 1988) ★★★.
● COMPILATIONS: *Super Hits* (Columbia 2000) ★★★.

## WEDDING PRESENT
Forthright and briefly fashionable indie band formed in Leeds, Yorkshire, England, in 1985, from the ashes of the Lost Pandas by David Gedge (b. 23 April 1960, Leeds, Yorkshire, England; guitar, vocals) with Keith Gregory (b. 2 January 1963, Co. Durham, England; bass), Peter Salowka (b. Middleton, Gt. Manchester, England; guitar) and Shaun Charman (b. Brighton, East Sussex, England; drums). The Wedding Present embodied the independent spirit of the mid-80s with a passion that few contemporaries could match. Furthermore, they staked their musical claim with a ferocious blend of implausibly fast guitars and lovelorn lyrics over a series of much-lauded singles on their own Reception Records label. As some cynics criticized the band's lack of imagination, *George Best* shared the merits of the flamboyant but flawed football star and reached number 47 in the UK chart. Similarly, as those same critics suggested the band were 'one-trick phonies', Pete Salowka's East European upbringing was brought to bear on the Wedding Present sound, resulting in the frenzied Ukrainian folk songs on the mini-album *Ukrainski Vistupi v Johna Peela*, so called because it was a compilation of tracks from sessions they had made for John Peel's influential BBC Radio 1 show.

Shaun Charman left the band as their debut was released, to join the Pop Guns, and was replaced by Simon Smith (b. 3 May 1965, Lincolnshire, England). Capitalizing on a still-burgeoning following, 'Kennedy' saw the band break into the Top 40 of the UK singles chart for the first time and revealed that, far from compromising on a major label, the Wedding Present were actually becoming more extreme. By their third album, *Seamonsters*, the band had forged a bizarre relationship with hardcore exponent Steve Albini (former member of the influential US outfit Big Black), whose harsh economic production technique encouraged the Wedding Present to juggle with broody lyrical mumblings and extraordinary slabs of guitar, killing the ghost of their 'jangly' beginnings. Before *Seamonsters* was released in 1991, Pete Salowka made way for Paul Dorrington, although he remained in the set-up on the business side of the band and formed the Ukrainians. In 1992, the Wedding Present undertook the ambitious project of releasing one single, every month, throughout the year. Each single charted in the UK Top 30 (admittedly in a depressed market), making the tactic a success, though the ever candid Gedge revealed that it had been done against a backdrop of record company opposition.

Their relationship with RCA Records ended following the accompanying *Hit Parade* compilations, though Island Records were quick to pick up the out-of-contract band. Keith Gregory also left the fold before *Watusi* restored the band to their previous status (reviled by certain sections of the UK media, venerated by hardcore supporters). *Mini* enhanced their place as influential (although often overlooked) indie popsters and *Saturnalia* had the *New Musical Express* reviewer Mark Beaumont gasping that 'Gedge has been one of the most consistently brilliant and grossly underrated songwriters in Britain'. High praise indeed, but in 1998 Gedge laid the band to rest and teamed up with long-time associate Sally Murrell in Cinerama.

● ALBUMS: *George Best* (Reception 1987) ★★★, *Ukrainski Vistupi V Johna Peela* mini-album (RCA 1989) ★★, *Bizarro* (RCA 1989) ★★, *Seamonsters* (RCA 1991) ★★★, *Watusi* (Island 1994) ★★★, *Mini* (Cooking Vinyl 1996) ★★, *Saturnalia* (Cooking Vinyl 1996) ★★★.

● COMPILATIONS: *Tommy* (Reception 1988) ★★★, *The BBC Sessions* (Strange Fruit 1988) ★★, *The Hit Parade Part One* (RCA 1992) ★★★, *The Hit Parade Part Two* (RCA 1993) ★★, *John Peel Sessions 1987–1990* (Strange Fruit 1993) ★★★, *Evening Sessions 1986–1994* (Strange Fruit 1997) ★★★, *Singles 1989–1991* (Manifesto 1999) ★★★, *Singles 1995–97* (Cooking Vinyl 1999) ★★.

● FURTHER READING: *The Wedding Present: Thank Yer, Very Glad*, Mark Hodkinson.

## WET WET WET

This Scottish pop band was formed in 1982 by Graeme Clark (b. 15 April 1966, Glasgow, Scotland; bass/vocals), Neil Mitchell (b. 8 June 1967, Helensburgh, Scotland; keyboards), Marti Pellow (b. Mark McLoughlin, 23 March 1966, Clydebank, Scotland), and Tom Cunningham (b. 22 June 1965, Drumchapel, Glasgow, Scotland; drums). The quartet took their name from a line in the Scritti Politti song 'Getting Having And Holding'. After frequent live performances, they recorded a promising demonstration tape, and were signed by Phonogram Records in 1985. Recordings in Memphis followed with veteran soul producer Willie Mitchell. In 1987, 'Wishing I Was Lucky' reached the UK Top

10, followed by the even more successful 'Sweet Little Mystery'. The band's agreeable blue-eyed soul was evident on their debut *Popped In Souled Out*, which climbed to number 2 in the UK album chart. Further hits followed with 'Angel Eyes (Home And Away)' and 'Temptation'. Unfortunately, the band suffered litigation at the hands of Van Morrison, who reached an out of court settlement over their use of his lyrics in part of 'Sweet Little Mystery' (also a John Martyn song title). In June 1988, Wet Wet Wet's profile was increased when they reached number 1 in the UK with a track from the various artists compilation, *Sgt Pepper Knew My Father*. Their innocuous reading of the Beatles' 'With A Little Help From My Friends' maintained their standing as 80s pin-up idols. Their reputation as one of the leading UK pop bands was enhanced in 1992 when 'Goodnight Girl' remained at the top of the charts for several weeks. Their broad appeal did not detract from the talent within, led by the confident vocals of Pellow. Their single, 'Lip Service', released in summer 1992, suggested a new interest in more dance-orientated music. Any suggestion that their commercial fortunes may be declining were blown apart by the staggering success of their cover version of the Troggs' 'Love Is All Around', the theme song to the hit movie *Four Weddings And A Funeral*, which, in 1994, stayed at the top of the UK charts for 15 weeks just one short of the record. 'Julia Says' also reached the Top 10, but subsequent releases did not achieve the same high level of commercial success. Following 1997's *10*, drummer Cunningham left the band. A more serious defection followed in May 1999, when Pellow announced he was embarking on a solo career following the admission of a drug habit. His debut, *Smile*, was released in July 2001.

● ALBUMS: *Popped In Souled Out* (Precious 1987) ★★★, *The Memphis Sessions* (Precious 1988) ★★, *Holding Back The River* (Precious 1989) ★★★, *Live* cassette only (Splash 1990) ★★, *High On The Happy Side* (Precious 1992) ★★, as Maggie Pie And The Imposters *Cloak And Dagger* (Splash 1992) ★★★, *Live At The Royal Albert Hall* (Precious 1993) ★★, *Picture This* (Mercury 1995) ★★, *10* (Mercury 1997) ★★.

Solo: Marti Pellow *Smile* (Mercury 2001) ★★.

● COMPILATIONS: *End Of Part One: Their Greatest Hits* (Precious 1993) ★★★.

● VIDEOS: *Video Singles* (Precious 1988), *Glasgow Green* (Precious 1989), *High On The Happy Side* (Precious 1992), *The Wets At The Castle* (Precious 1992), *Live At The Royal Albert Hall* (Precious 1992), *End Of Part One: Their Greatest Hits* (Precious 1993), *Picture This: All Around And In The Crowd* (Mercury 1995), *Playing Away At Home: Live At Celtic Park* (Mercury 1997).

● FURTHER READING: *Wet Wet Wet Pictured*, Mal Peachey and Simon Fowler.

## WHAM!

Generally acknowledged as the most commercially successful English pop group of the 80s, the Wham! duo first performed together in ska-influenced school band, the Executive. George Michael (b. Georgios (Yorgos) Kyriacos Panayiotou, 25 June

1963, Finchley, London, England) and Andrew Ridgeley (b. 26 January 1963, Windlesham, Surrey, England) streamlined the group and in 1982 began searching for a deal under their new name, Wham! Local boy Mark Dean was impressed with their demos and agreed to sign them to his recently formed label, Innervision. They next fell into the hands of music publishers Dick Leahy and Bryan Morrison, the former was to play a crucial part in guiding their career hereafter. After embarking on a series of 'personal appearances' at local clubs with backing singers Amanda Washbourn and Shirlie Holliman (who went on to become one half of Pepsi And Shirlie), they completed their debut single 'Wham! Rap' which had originally been intended as a disco parody. What emerged was an exhilarating dance number in its own right with intriguing double-edged lyrics. Wham! sang of soul on the dole and the need to rise above the stigma of unemployment. Although the song gained the boys some publicity, it initially failed to chart. However, the follow-up 'Young Guns' was a UK Top 10 hit in late 1982 and a remixed 'Wham! Rap' belatedly repeated that feat. A third hit, 'Bad Boys' indicated that the duo's macho, young rebel image was wearing thin, and Michael promised a change of direction in the future.

In the meantime, they required an additional tentacle to hasten their mining of gold vinyl and, after consulting Morrison/Leahy, recruited two managers, Jazz Summers and Simon Napier-Bell. Their next hit, 'Club Tropicana', was a satire on elitist London clubland but for most listeners, the parodic elements were irrelevant. Fêted by teen magazines and increasingly photographed in exotic climes, the group soon found themselves a symbol of vainglorious beach-brain hedonism and *nouveau riche* vulgarity. A chart-topping album *Fantastic* was primarily a collection of singles with a pedestrian cover of the Miracles' 'Love Machine' to show their love of Motown Records.

An acrimonious dispute with Innervision culminated in a fascinating court case, which freed the duo from their record company and they signed directly to Epic Records. They celebrated their release with their first UK number 1 'Wake Me Up Before You Go Go', quickly followed by 'Careless Whisper' (co-composed by Ridgeley, but credited to George Michael as artist). *Make It Big* zoomed to number 1 and by the end of 1984 the group had two further major successes 'Freedom' and 'Last Christmas'/'Everything She Wants'. The following year, the duo embarked on a much publicized trip to China and enjoyed considerable success in America. Rumours of an impending split were confirmed the following year but not before Wham! fired their management team over the alleged sale of their company to the owner of Sun City. Wham's act of pop euthanasia was completed on 28 June 1986 when they played a farewell concert before 72,000 fans at London's Wembley Stadium which was captured on *The Final*. Since the split George Michael's solo career blossomed, notably in the USA where he was taken more seriously as an AOR artist. Ridgeley predictably struggled to establish his own music career.

● ALBUMS: *Fantastic* (Inner Vision 1983) ★★, *Make It Big* (Epic 1984) ★★★, *The Final* (Epic 1986) ★★★.
● COMPILATIONS: *If You Were There: The Best Of Wham!* (Epic 1997) ★★★★.
● VIDEOS: *Wham! The Video* (CBS-Fox 1985), *The Best Of Wham!* (VCI 1997).
● FURTHER READING: *Wham! (Confidential) The Death Of A Supergroup*, Johnny Rogan. *Bare*, George Michael.

## WHITE LION

This US hard rock band was formed in Brooklyn, New York, during 1983, by Mike Tramp (b. Denmark; lead vocals, ex-Mabel) and Vito Bratta (guitar, ex-Dreamer). After a series of false starts, they signed to Elektra Records with Felix Robinson (bass, ex-Angel) and Dave Capozzi (drums) completing the line-up. However, the label was unhappy with the recording of *Fight To Survive* and after refusing to release the album, terminated their contract. RCA Records picked up the release option and the album finally surfaced in Japan in 1984. By this stage, James LoMenzo and Gregg D'Angelo had taken over bass and drums, respectively, on a permanent basis. The album did in fact meet with favourable reviews, some critics comparing Mike Tramp to David Lee Roth and Vito Bratta to Eddie Van Halen, others likening the songs to those of Europe, Dokken or Journey. Signing to Atlantic Records, they released *Pride*, which developed their own identity, in particular Mike Tramp's characteristically watery falsetto style. The album catapulted them from obscurity to stardom, climbing to number 11 during its year long stay on the *Billboard* album chart. It also spawned two US Top 10 hits with 'Wait' (number 8, February 1988) and 'When The Children Cry' (number 3, November 1988). *Big Game* was a disappointing follow-up. Nevertheless, it still made the US charts, peaking at number 19. *Mane Attraction*, released in 1991, saw the band recapture lost ground over the course of a strong melodic rock collection. LoMenzo and D'Angelo quit owing to 'musical differences' shortly after the album's release and were replaced by Tommy 'T-Bone' Caradonna (bass, ex-Alice Cooper) and Jimmy DeGrasso (drums, ex-Y&T). The band eventually broke-up, with Tramp going on to form Freak Of Nature.

● ALBUMS: *Fight To Survive* (Grand Slam 1984) ★★, *Pride* (Atlantic 1987) ★★★, *Big Game* (Atlantic 1989) ★★, *Mane Attraction* (Atlantic 1991) ★★.
● COMPILATIONS: *The Best Of* (Atlantic 1992) ★★★.

## WHITE, ANDY

b. 28 May 1962, Belfast, Northern Ireland. White was born into a household that brewed creative endeavour, with his father a journalist, his mother a voracious reader and his grandmother a piano player. His background also forged an awareness of socio-political matters, which resulted in his first poem ('Riots') at the age of nine. At 13, he started playing guitar, inspired by John Lennon's 'Give Peace A Chance', while his later teenage years were influenced by Northern Ireland's punk rock scene, French poetry and singer-songwriters such as Bob Dylan, Roy Harper and John Martyn. He released his debut single, 'Religious Persuasion', on Stiff Records in 1985, instantly achieving indie credibility with his blend of Dylanesque wordplay and stroppy musicianship. In 1995, White formed the loose collective Alt with Hothouse Flowers singer Liam O Maonlai and Tim Finn. A prolific recording artist with a flair for poignant poetic imagery, White has latterly bypassed the major label route to release material on his own resolutely independent label. While he may never receive mainstream popularity, his work is highly literate and intelligent. He will always find a receptive audience as long as his head and heart continue to connect.

● ALBUMS: *Rave On Andy White* (PolyGram 1986) ★★★, *Kiss The Big Stone* (PolyGram 1988) ★★★, *Himself* (Cooking Vinyl 1990) ★★★★, *Out There* (Warners 1992) ★★★★, *Destination Beautiful* (Warners 1994) ★★★, *Teenage* (Cooking Vinyl 1996) ★★★, *Speechless* (WOMAD 2000) ★★★, *Andy White* (Alt Recordings 2000) ★★★.

● COMPILATIONS: *Andywhite.compilation* (Cooking Vinyl 1998) ★★★★, *Rare* (Alt Recordings 1999) ★★★.

● FURTHER READING: *The Music Of What Happens*, Andy White.

## WIEDLIN, JANE

b. 20 May 1958, Oconomowoc, Wisconsin, USA. Wiedlin was originally the guitarist in the top US female act the Go-Go's, although she enjoyed minor success outside the band in 1983 with the Sparks collaboration, 'Cool Places'. When the split came in 1985, all five members embarked on solo careers. Wiedlin released a self-titled album that contained a minor US hit, 'Blue Kiss'. However, her heart was also set on pursuing an acting career and she made cameo appearances in *Clue* and *Star Trek 4: The Voyage Home*. A successful return to recording came in 1988 with the superb transatlantic hit 'Rush Hour'. Her energies in the 90s were directed towards her involvement in the anti-fur trade movement. This resulted in the Go-Go's re-forming briefly in 1990 at a benefit for PETA (People for the Ethical Treatment of Animals), before a full reunion took place in 1994. Wiedlin moved on to sing with FroSTed, who released their debut album *Cold* on the DGC label a year later. The record was partly co-written with fellow ex-Go-Go's member Charlotte Coffey. At the start of the new millennium, Wiedlin reunited with the Go-Go's for a US tour, and made a welcome return to her solo career with *Kissproof World*, released on her own Painful Discs label.

● ALBUMS: *Jane Wiedlin* (I.R.S. 1985) ★★★, *Fur* (EMI Manhattan 1988) ★★, *Tangled* (EMI 1990) ★★, *Kissproof World* (Painful 2000) ★★★.

● COMPILATIONS: *The Very Best Of Jane Wiedlin: From Cool Places To Worlds On Fire* (EMI 1993) ★★★.

● FILMS: *Urgh! A Music War* (1981), *Clue* (1985), *Star Trek IV: The Voyage Home* (1986), *Bill & Ted's Excellent Adventure* (1989), *Live Freaky Die Freaky* voice only (1999), *Angels!* (2000).

## WILDE, KIM

b. Kim Smith, 18 November 1960, Chiswick, London, England. The daughter of 50s pop idol Marty Wilde and Vernons Girls' vocalist Joyce Smith (née Baker), Kim was signed to Mickie Most's Rak Records in 1980 after the producer heard a demo Kim recorded with her brother Ricky. Her first single, the exuberant 'Kids In America', composed by Ricky and co-produced by Marty, climbed to number 2 in the UK charts. A further Top 10 hit followed with 'Chequered Love', while her debut *Kim Wilde* fared extremely well in the album charts. A more adventurous sound with 'Cambodia' indicated an exciting talent. By 1982, she had already sold more records than her father had done in his entire career. While 'View From A Bridge' maintained her standing at home, 'Kids In America' became a Top 30 hit in the USA. A relatively quiet period followed, although she continued to enjoy minor hits with 'Love Blonde', 'The Second Time' and a more significant success with the Dave Edmunds-produced 'Rage To Love'. An energetic reworking of the Supremes' classic 'You Keep Me Hangin' On' took her back to UK number 2 at a time when her career seemed flagging. After appearing on the Ferry Aid charity single, 'Let It Be', Wilde was back in the Top 10 with 'Another Step (Closer To You)', a surprise duet with soul singer Junior Giscombe.

Weary of her image as the girl-next-door, Wilde subsequently sought a sexier profile, which was used in the video to promote 'Say You Really Want Me'. Her more likely standing as an 'all-round entertainer' was underlined by the Christmas novelty hit 'Rockin' Around The Christmas Tree' in the company of comedian Mel Smith. In 1988, the dance-orientated 'You Came' reaffirmed her promise, and further Top 10 hits continued with 'Never Trust A Stranger' and 'Four Letter Word'. Later singles gained only lowly positions in the charts and the subsequent *Love Is* was a pale shadow of *Close*. On 1995's *Now And Forever* Wilde abandoned pop for a slick soul groove. In 1999, Wilde put her recording career behind her to present a series of television gardening shows. Two years later she returned to singing as part of an 80s package tour.

● ALBUMS: *Kim Wilde* (RAK 1981) ★★★, *Select* (RAK 1982) ★★, *Catch As Catch Can* (RAK 1983) ★★, *Teases And Dares* (MCA 1984) ★★, *Another Step* (MCA 1986) ★★, *Close* (MCA 1988) ★★★★, *Love Moves* (MCA 1990) ★★, *Love Is* (MCA 1992) ★★★, *Now And Forever* (MCA 1995) ★★.

● COMPILATIONS: *The Very Best Of Kim Wilde* (RAK 1985) ★★★, *The Singles Collection 1981-1993* (MCA 1993) ★★★, *The Gold Collection* (EMI 1996) ★★★, *The Collection* (Spectrum 2001) ★★★, *The Very Best Of Kim Wilde* (EMI 2001) ★★★.

● VIDEOS: *Video EP: Kim Wilde* (MCA 1987), *Close* (MCA 1989), *Another Step (Closer To You)* (MCA 1990), *The Singles Collection 1981-1993* (MCA 1993).

## WILSON, MARI

b. Mari MacMillan Ramsey Wilson, 29 September 1957, London, England. In the mid-80s, Mari Wilson single-handedly led a revival of the world of 50s/early 60s English kitsch. Sporting a beehive hairdo, wearing a pencil skirt and fake mink stole, her publicity photos depicted a world of long-lost suburban curtain and furniture styles, Tupperware, garish colours (often pink) and graphic designs from the period. The songs were treated in the same way, only affectionately and with genuine feeling. The whole image was the idea of Tot Taylor who, composing under the name of Teddy Johns and gifted with the ability to write pastiche songs from almost any era of popular music, also ran the Compact Organisation label. The label's sense of hype excelled itself as they immediately released a box set of Compact Organisation artists, all of which, with the exception of Wilson, failed to attract the public's attention. (Although 'model agent' Virna Lindt was a music press favourite.)

Wilson was quickly adopted by press, television and radio as a curiosity, all aiding her early 1982 singles 'Beat The Beat' and 'Baby It's True' to have a minor effect on the chart. 'Just What I Always Wanted' a Top 10 hit, fully encapsulated the Wilson style. However, it was the following year's cover of the Julie London torch-song number, 'Cry Me A River' which, despite only reaching number 27, most people have come to associate with the singer. The song also generated a revival of interest in London's recordings, resulting in many long-lost (and forgotten) albums being re-released. After touring the world with her backing vocal group, the Wilsations – which included Julia Fordham – the return home saw a slowing-down in activity. Although for the most part Wilson was out of the limelight, she provided the vocals to the soundtrack to the Ruth Ellis biopic Dance With A Stranger. In 1985, she started playing small clubs with her jazz quartet performing standards, as well as writing her own material which led to her appearance with Stan Getz at a London's Royal Festival Hall. Although still affectionately remembered for her beehive, she has been able to put that period behind her and is now taken more seriously as a jazz/pop singer, and is able to fill Ronnie Scott's club for a season.

● ALBUMS: Showpeople (Compact 1983) ★★★★, Dance With A Stranger film soundtrack (Compact 1987) ★★, The Rhythm Romance (Dino 1991) ★★★.

## WINANS

Contemporary Christian music group the Winans comprises four brothers, Marvin, Carvin, Ronald and Michael Winans, from Detroit, Michigan, USA. The family has additionally produced two well-known solo/duo gospel performers, BeBe and CeCe Winans. After having sung in gospel choirs all their lives the brothers began their professional career in the 80s. Staying close to their gospel roots but always maintaining a distinctive, jazzy sound, their reputation saw them work and perform with leading artists including Vanessa Bell Armstrong, Anita Baker and Michael McDonald, the latter pair both appearing on their 1987 album, Decision. Their two QWest albums of the early 90s, Return and All Out, saw an attempt to convert their popularity into mainstream R&B success. Even this, however, was motivated by moral concerns: 'The whole purpose was to win over young people who might have been

on the verge of going into a life of crime or going off track,' Ronald Winans told Billboard magazine in 1995. Drawn from Return, 'It's Time' peaked at number 5 on the US R&B charts in 1990 and was produced by Teddy Riley, who also rapped on the single. In consequence Return reached number 12 on the R&B album charts and was certified a gold record. However, All Out was less successful, and by 1995 and Heart And Soul the Winans had returned to their trademark gospel sound. As well as 11 other original songs it included a remake of 'The Question Is', a popular stage favourite originally featured on their 1981 debut album, Introducing The Winans. The original version been produced by gospel legend Andrae Crouch, with his nephew, Keith Crouch, playing drums. The guests on Heart And Soul included R&B star R. Kelly, as well as previous collaborators Riley, McDonald and Baker. The second generation of Winans began recording in the late 90s as Winans Phase 2.

● ALBUMS: Introducing The Winans (QWest 1981) ★★★★, Let My People Go (QWest 1985) ★★★, Decision (QWest 1987) ★★, Tomorrow (Light 1988) ★★★★, Live At Carnegie Hall (QWest 1989) ★★, Return (QWest 1990) ★★★, All Out (QWest 1993) ★★★, Heart And Soul (QWest 1995) ★★★.

● COMPILATIONS: The Very Best Of (Rhino 2002) ★★★★.

## WINSTON, GEORGE

b. 1949, Michigan, USA. Following many years of listening to music, his early heroes being Floyd Cramer, the Ventures and Booker T. And The MGs, Winston took up the piano at the age of 18. He switched to jazz after being influenced by the 'stride' piano of Fats Waller. The mysterious and enigmatic Winston stopped playing in 1977 until the music of Professor Longhair inspired him to return. Between 1980 and 1982 he recorded a trilogy of albums which have subsequently sold millions of copies. The sparse and delicate piano music of Autumn, Winter Into Spring and December gave a new dimension to solo piano recording, engineered to such perfection that the instrument truly becomes part of the room the listener is in. Not one note is wasted and he plays as if each were his last. Winston was part of the original Windham Hill Records family of artists that pioneered the USA's west coast new-age music of the early 80s. Winston kept a low profile for almost a decade until his return with Summer in 1991 continuing the tradition of his best solo work. Forest, released in 1994 won a Grammy at the 1996 awards. His tribute to pianist Vince Guaraldi (composer of 'Cast Your Fate To The Wind') became a major success in 1996. Plains was the second instalment in his landscape series, and lodged itself at the top of the New Age charts for months.

● ALBUMS: Ballads And Blues (Takoma 1972) ★★, Autumn (Windham Hill 1980) ★★★★, Winter Into Spring (Windham Hill 1982) ★★★★, December (Windham Hill 1982) ★★★★, with Meryl Streep Velveteen Rabbit (Windham Hill 1982) ★, Summer (Windham Hill 1991) ★★★, Forest (Windham Hill 1994) ★★★, Linus And Lucy: The Music Of Vince Guaraldi (Dancing Cat/Windham Hill 1996) ★★,

*Plains* (Dancing Cat/Windham Hill 1999) ★★★★.
● COMPILATIONS: *All The Seasons Of George Winston: Piano Solos* (Windham Hill 1998) ★★★.
● VIDEOS: *Seasons In Concert* (Dancing Cat Video 1997).

## WINWOOD, STEVE

b. 12 May 1948, Birmingham, England. Steve and his older brother Muff Winwood were born into a family with parents who encouraged musical evenings at their home. Steve was playing guitar with Muff and their father in the Ron Atkinson Band at the age of eight, soon after he mastered drums and piano. The multi-talented Winwood first achieved 'star' status as a member of the pioneering 60s R&B band, the Spencer Davis Group. His strident voice and full sounding Hammond Organ emitted one of the mid-60's most distinctive pop sounds. The group had a successful run of major hits in the UK and USA until their musical horizons became too limited for the musically ambitious Steve. In 1965, Winwood had previously recorded the UK turntable soul hit 'Incense' under the name of the Anglos, written by Stevie Anglo. This gave fuel to rumours of his imminent departure. It was not until 1967 that he left and went on to form Traffic, a seminal band in the development of progressive popular music. The short-lived 'supergroup' Blind Faith briefly interrupted Traffic's flow. Throughout this time his talents were sought as a session musician and he became the unofficial in-house keyboard player for Island Records.

During 1972, he was seriously ill with peritonitis and this contributed to the sporadic activity of Traffic. When Traffic slowly ground to a halt in 1974 Winwood seemed poised to start the solo career he had been threatening for so long. Instead he maintained a low profile and became a musicians' musician contributing keyboards and backing vocals to many fine albums including, John Martyn's *One World*, Sandy Denny's *Rendezvous*, George Harrison's *Dark Horse* and Toots And The Maytals *Reggae Got Soul*. His session work reads like a who's who: Jimi Hendrix, Joe Cocker, Leon Russell, Howlin' Wolf, Sutherland Brothers, Muddy Waters, Eric Clapton, Alvin Lee, Marianne Faithfull and many others. In 1976, he performed with Stomu Yamash'ta and Klaus Schulze, resulting in *Go* and *Go 2*. He also appeared on stage with the Fania All Stars playing percussion and guitar.

The eagerly anticipated self-titled solo album did not appear until 1977, and was respectfully, rather than enthusiastically, welcomed. It displayed a relaxed Winwood performing only six numbers and using first class musicians like Willy Weeks and Andy Newmark. Following its release Winwood retreated back to his 50-acre Oxfordshire farm and shunned interviews. He became preoccupied with rural life, and took up clay pigeon shooting, dog training and horse riding. It appeared to outsiders that his musical activity had all but ceased.

During the last week of 1980 the majestic *Arc Of A Diver* was released to an unsuspecting public. With his former songwriting partner Jim Capaldi now living in Brazil, Winwood had been working on lyrics supplied to him by Vivian Stanshall, George Fleming and Will Jennings. The album was an unqualified and unexpected triumph, particularly in the USA where it went platinum. The stirring single 'While You See A Chance' saw him back in the charts. He followed with the hastily put together (by Winwood standards) *Talking Back To The Night*, which became another success. Winwood, however was not altogether happy with the record and seriously contemplated retiring to become a record producer. His brother, Muff, wisely dissuaded him. Winwood began to be seen more often, now looking groomed and well preserved. Island Records were able to reap rewards by projecting him towards a younger market. His European tour in 1983 was a revelation, a super-fit Steve, looking 20 years younger, bounced on stage wearing a portable keyboard and ripped into Junior Walker's 'Roadrunner'. It was as if the 17-year-old 'Stevie' from the Spencer Davis Group had returned. His entire catalogue was performed with energy and confidence. It was hard to believe this was the same man who for years had hidden shyly behind banks of amplifiers and keyboards with Traffic.

Two years later, while working in New York on his forthcoming album his life further improved when he met his future wife Eugenia, following a long and unhappy first marriage. His obvious elation overspilled into *Back In The High Life* (1986). Most of the tracks were co-written with Will Jennings and it became his most commercially successful record so far. The album spawned three hits including the superb disco/soul cut 'Higher Love', which reached number 1 in the USA.

In 1987, his long association with Chris Blackwell and Island Records ended amidst press reports that his new contract with Virgin Records guaranteed him $13 million. The reclusive 'Midland maniac' had now become one of the hottest properties in the music business, while the world eagerly awaited the next album to see if the star was worth his transfer fee. The single 'Roll With It' preceded the album of the same name. Both were enormous successes, being a double chart-topper in the USA. The album completed a full circle. Winwood was back singing his heart out with 60s inspired soul/pop. His co-writer once again was Will Jennings, although older aficionados were delighted to see one track written with Jim Capaldi. In 1990, Winwood was involved in a music publishing dispute in which it was alleged that the melody of 'Roll With It' had been plagiarized from 'Roadrunner'.

*Refugees Of The Heart* was commercially unsuccessful, although it contained another major US hit single with the Winwood/Capaldi composition 'One And Only Man'. Following the less than spectacular performance of that album, rumours began to circulate that Traffic would be re-born and this was confirmed in early 1994. *Far From Home* sounded more like a Winwood solo album than any Traffic project, but those who love any conglomeration that has Winwood involved were not disappointed. Later that year he participated on Davey Spillane's album *A Place Among The Stones*, singing 'Forever Frozen' and later that year sang the theme song 'Reach For The Light' from the animated movie *Balto*. His next studio album, 1997's *Junction 7*, was a bitter disappointment to his legions of fans. For once, a man that had barely put a musical foot wrong in over 30 years had missed the bus.

● ALBUMS: *Steve Winwood* (Island 1977) ★★★★, *Arc Of A Diver* (Island 1980) ★★★★, *Talking Back To The Night* (Island 1983) ★★★, *Back In The High Life* (Island 1986) ★★★★, *Roll With It* (Virgin 1988) ★★★★, *Refugees Of The Heart* (Virgin 1990) ★★★, *Junction 7* (Virgin 1997) ★.

● COMPILATIONS: *Chronicles* (Island 1987) ★★★★, *The Finer Things* 4-CD box set (Island 1995) ★★★★.

● FURTHER READING: *Back In The High Life: A Biography Of Steve Winwood*, Alan Clayson. *Keep On Running: The Steve Winwood Story*, Chris Welch.

## WOMACK AND WOMACK

One of modern soul's most successful duos, comprising husband and wife team Cecil Womack (b. Cleveland, Ohio, USA) and Linda Cooke Womack. Cecil had been the youngest of the Womack Brothers, who later evolved into the Valentinos. With them, he signed to Sam Cooke's Star imprint, but Cooke's subsequent death left them homeless, and after a brief liaison with Chess Records, Bobby Womack left the group to go solo. Cecil later married singer Mary Wells, whom he managed until the couple separated. Linda, the daughter of Sam Cooke, had begun a songwriting career in 1964 at the age of 11, composing 'I Need A Woman'. She would also provide 'I'm In Love' for Wilson Pickett and 'A Woman's Gotta Have It' for James Taylor, but later forged a professional, and personal, partnership with Cecil. As she recalls: 'My father had the deepest regard for all the Womack brothers. He had talked about how talented Cecil was since I was four years old . . . We didn't actually meet until I was eight.' Together they worked extensively as a writing team for Philadelphia International Records, numbering the O'Jays and Patti LaBelle among their clients. The couple achieved a notable success with 'Love TKO', a soul hit in 1980 for Teddy Pendergrass. This melodic ballad also provided the Womacks with their first US chart entry (and was also covered by Blondie), following which the duo's fortunes prospered both in the US and UK with several excellent singles, including the club favourite, 'Love Wars' (1984) and 'Teardrops' (1988), the latter reaching the UK Top 3. They continued to write for others also, contributing 'Hurting Inside' and 'Sexy' to Ruby Turner. In the early 90s the couple journeyed to Nigeria, where they discovered ancestral ties to the Zekkariyas tribe. They consequently adopted the names Zeriiya (Linda) and Zekkariyas (Cecil), in a nod to the Afrocentricity movement.

● ALBUMS: *Love Wars* (Elektra 1983) ★★★, *Radio M.U.S.I.C. Man* (Elektra 1985) ★★★, *Starbright* (Manhattan/EMI 1986) ★★★, *Conscience* (4th & Broadway 1988) ★★, *Family Spirit* (Arista 1991) ★★, *Transformation To The House Of Zekkariyas* (Warners 1993) ★★.

● COMPILATIONS: *Greatest Hits* (Spectrum 1998) ★★★.

## WONDER STUFF

Formed in Stourbridge, West Midlands, England, in April 1986, the Wonder Stuff featured Miles Hunt (vocals, guitar), Malcolm Treece (guitar), Rob Jones (b. 1964, d. 30 July 1993, New York, USA; bass, replacing original member Chris Fradgley) and former Mighty Lemon Drops drummer Martin Gilks. The roots of the band lay in From Eden, a short-lived local group that featured Hunt on drums, Treece on guitar and Clint Mansell and Adam Mole, later of peers Pop Will Eat Itself, occupying the remaining roles.

After amassing a sizeable local following, the Wonder Stuff released their debut EP, *It's A Wonderful Day*, to favourable small press coverage in 1987. Along with the aforementioned PWEI and other Midlands hopefuls Crazyhead and Gaye Bykers On Acid, they were soon pigeonholed under the banner of 'grebo rock' by the national music press. Despite this ill-fitting description, the Wonder Stuff's strengths always lay in melodic pop songs braced against an urgent, power-pop backdrop. After an ill-fated dalliance with EMI Records' *ICA Rock Week*, a second single, 'Unbearable', proved strong enough to secure a contract with Polydor Records at the end of 1987. 'Give Give Give Me More More More' offered a minor hit the following year, and was succeeded by arguably the band's best early song. Built on soaring harmonies, 'A Wish Away' was the perfect precursor to the Wonder Stuff's vital debut, *The Eight Legged Groove Machine*, which followed later that year and established them in the UK charts. 'It's Yer Money I'm After Baby', also from the album, continued to mine Hunt's cynical furrow (further evident on the confrontational b-side, 'Astley In The Noose' – referring to contemporary chart star Rick Astley) and began a string of UK Top 40 hits. 'Who Wants To Be The Disco King?' (number 29) and the more relaxed 'Don't Let Me Down Gently' (number 19), both from 1989, hinted at the diversity of the group's second album, *Hup*. Aided by fiddle, banjo and keyboard player Martin Bell (ex-Hackney Five-O), the album contrasted a harder, hi-tech sound with a rootsy, folk feel on tracks such as 'Golden Green', a double a-side hit (number 33) when combined with a cover version of the Youngbloods' 'Get Together'.

The band's well-documented internal wrangles came to a head with the departure of Rob Jones at the end of the decade. He moved to New York to form his own band, the Bridge And Tunnel Crew, with his wife Jessie Ronson, but died of heart failure in 1993. 'Circlesquare' (number 20, May 1990) introduced new bass player Paul Clifford. A subsequent low profile was broken in April 1991 with 'The Size Of A Cow'. A UK number 5 hit, this was quickly followed by 'Caught In My Shadow' (number 18) and *Never Loved Elvis*. Once again, this third album revealed the Wonder Stuff's remorseless progression. Gone were the brash, punk-inspired three-minute classics, replaced by a richer musical content, both in Hunt's songwriting and musical performances. The extent of their popularity was emphasized in October 1991 when, in conjunction with comedian Vic Reeves, they topped the UK charts with a revival of Tommy Roe's 'Dizzy'. The band made a swift return to the

Top 10 in 1992 with the *Welcome To The Cheap Seats EP*, the title track's post-punk jig (with Kirsty MacColl on backing vocals) typifying the direction of the following year's *Construction For The Modern Idiot*. With songs now imbued with far more optimism owing to Hunt's improved romantic prospects, singles such as 'Full Of Life (Happy Now)' (number 28, 1993) and 'Hot Love Now!' (number 19, 1994) replaced previous uncertainties with unforced bonhomie. Thus, it came as something as a surprise when Hunt announced the band's dissolution to the press in July 1994 long before any grapes could sour – a decision allegedly given impetus by Polydor's insistence that the band should crack the USA (a factor in striking down the label's previous great singles band, the Jam).

The Wonder Stuff bowed out at a final gig in Stratford upon Avon, Hunt leaving the stage with a pastiche of the Sex Pistols' epigram 'Every Feel You've Been Treated?' ringing in fans' ears. Writer James Brown offered another tribute in his sleeve-notes to the compulsory posthumous singles compilations: 'It was pointed out that if the writer Hunter S. Thompson had been the presiding influence over the Beatles, they might have looked and sounded like the Wonder Stuff. Suitably abbreviated, it provided less accurate testimony than 'greatest hits', perhaps, but it was certainly more in keeping with the band's legacy.

Former members of the band (Treece, Clifford and Gilks) briefly regrouped in 1995 as Weknowwhereyoulive, with the addition of former Eat singer Ange Dolittle on vocals. Hunt also gave up his job as host of MTV's *120 Minutes* to put together a new band known as Vent 414. Following the break-up of both these ventures Hunt and Treece reunited to play live acoustic shows. The four surviving original members reunited in late 2000 to perform a number of live shows in London. Hunt subsequently began recording with the Miles Hunt Club, releasing an eponymous album in April 2002.

● ALBUMS: *The Eight Legged Groove Machine* (Polydor 1988) ★★★★, *Hup* (Polydor 1989) ★★★, *Never Loved Elvis* (Polydor 1991) ★★★, *Construction For The Modern Idiot* (Polydor 1993) ★★, *Live In Manchester* (Windsong 1995) ★★, *Cursed With Insincerity* (Eagle 2001) ★★★.
● COMPILATIONS: *If The Beatles Had Read Hunter ... The Singles* (Polydor 1994) ★★★★, *Love Bites And Bruises* (Polydor 2000) ★★★.
● VIDEOS: *Eleven Appalling Promos* (PolyGram Music Video 1990), *Welcome To The Cheap Seats* (PolyGram Music Video 1992), *Greatest Hits Finally Live* (PolyGram Music Video 1994).

## WOODENTOPS

At one point, it seemed likely that the Woodentops from Northampton, England, would be commercially successful. After the offbeat 'Plenty', a one-off single for the Food Records label in 1984, songwriter Rolo McGinty (guitar, vocals), Simon Mawby (guitar), Alice Thompson (keyboards), Frank de Freitas (bass) and Benny Staples (drums) joined Geoff Travis' Rough Trade Records and issued a string of catchy singles that fared increasingly well

commercially. The jolly 'Move Me' was followed by the menacing pace of 'Well Well Well' while 'It Will Come' seemed a likely hit. The band's critically acclaimed debut album, *Giant*, was an enticing mixture of frantic acoustic guitars and a warm yet offbeat clutch of songs. After 'Love Affair With Everyday Living' in 1986, McGinty decided on a change in direction, hardening up the Woodentops' sound and incorporating new technology within their live repertoire. The results were heard the following year on *Live Hypnobeat Live*, which relied on material from *Giant*, albeit performed live in a drastically revitalized way. *Wooden Foot Cops On The Highway* and the accompanying single, 'You Make Me Feel'/'Stop This Car', showed how far the Woodentops had progressed by early 1988, although it was to be their final album. Less uncompromising than their live project, the sound was more mature, with an emphasis on detail previously lacking. What the band failed to achieve in commercial terms was more than compensated for by the level of critical and public respect they earned. McGinty moved into deep house, recording as Pluto, Dogs DeLuxe and Bad Apples. Thompson has since become a successful writer with a number of novels published.
● ALBUMS: *Giant* (Rough Trade 1986) ★★★★, *Live Hypnobeat Live* (Upside 1987) ★★★, *Wooden Foot Cops On the Highway* (Rough Trade 1988) ★★★★.

## WORKING WEEK

The soul jazz band was formed in 1983 around the nucleus of Simon Booth (b. 12 March 1956; guitar) and Larry Stabbins (b. 9 September 1949; saxophone) as an offshoot of the soft jazz-influenced group Weekend. Adopting a harder jazz/Latin direction, Working Week commanded much music press attention and, in particular, 'style' magazines (*Blitz* and *The Face*), who latched on to the band's connection with the London jazz dance teams. Their radical image was strengthened by Booth and Stabbins left-wing allegiances, borne out on their 1984 debut single on Paladin/Virgin Records, 'Venceremos (We Will Win)'. The song, dedicated to the Chilean protest singer Víctor Jara, included guest vocals from Tracey Thorn, Robert Wyatt and Claudia Figueroa. The follow-up, 'Storm Of Light' featured Julie Tippetts on lead vocals. In time, the group recruited a permanent lead vocalist in Juliet Roberts. After her departure in 1988, Working Week reverted to the system of guest vocalists until the addition of a new vocalist in Yvonne Waite for 1991's *Black And Gold*. Although Working Week centred around Booth and Stabbins for recordings and live appearances, they employed a vast array of respected UK jazz musicians who, on various occasions, included: Harry Beckett (trumpet), Keith Tippett (piano), Kim Burton (piano), Cleveland Watkiss (vocals), Mike Carr (organ), Richard Edwards and Paul Spong (brass), Dave Bitelli (reeds), Annie Whitehead (trombone) and Nic France (drums). The group continued to work into the mid-90s, turning out quality recordings, although the initial wave of interest and impetus had by then somewhat subsided.
● ALBUMS: *Working Nights* (Virgin 1985) ★★★,

*Companeros* (Virgin 1986) ★★★, *Knocking On Your Door* (Virgin 1987) ★★★, *Fire In The Mountain* (10 1989) ★★★, *Black And Gold* (10 1991) ★★★.
● COMPILATIONS: *Payday* (Venture 1988) ★★★.

## WRATHCHILD

Formed in 1980 in Evesham, Worcestershire, England, as a Black Sabbath-influenced band, it was another two years before Wrathchild emerged at the forefront of the new glam rock scene. Original members Rocky Shads (vocals) and Marc Angel (bass) were joined by ex-Medusa personnel Lance Rocket (guitar) and Eddie Starr (drums). They subsequently released an EP on Bullet Records and toured heavily to promote it. By 1983 they had developed a melodramatic live show and perfected their Kiss/Angel influences, while retaining an 'English' quality. A year later their hard work paid off with a deal with Heavy Metal Records, but a bad choice of producer (Robin George) led to a slick but flat sound that was not at all representative. Soon afterwards they entered into a long-running legal battle with the company, which almost killed off the group. During this time indie label Dojo released a compilation of early material that was far superior to the official album – it also contained the definitive version of live favourite and title track, 'Trash Queens'. In 1988, they made their comeback with the aptly titled *The Bizz Suxx*. 'Nukklear Rokket' was also released and was followed with a tour that lacked the early aggression and visual drama. The follow-up album in 1989 fared badly against the more established glam rock bands such as Mötley Crüe, and the band once again entered a legal battle, this time to stop an American thrash metal band using their moniker. They won, and their namesakes appended America to their tag. However, they disappeared from view shortly thereafter.
● ALBUMS: *Stakk Attakk* (Heavy Metal 1984) ★★, *Trash Queens* (Dojo 1985) ★★★, *The Bizz Suxx* (FM Revolver 1988) ★★★, *Delirium* (FM Revolver 1989) ★★.
● VIDEOS: *War Machine* (Hendring Video/Castle Communications 1988).

## WRECKLESS ERIC

b. Eric Goulden, May 1954, Newhaven, Sussex, England. Launched by Stiff Records in the heyday of punk, Wreckless Eric, as his name suggested, specialized in chaotic, pub rock and roots-influenced rock. His often tuneless vocals belied some excellent musical backing, most notably by producer Nick Lowe. Wreckless Eric's eccentric single, 'Whole Wide World'/'Semaphore Signals', has often been acclaimed as one of the minor classics of the punk era. During 1977/8, he was promoted via the famous Stiff live revues where he gained notoriety off-stage for his drinking. For his second album, *The Wonderful World Of Wreckless Eric*, the artist offered a more engaging work, but increasingly suffered from comparison with the other stars on his fashionable record label. His commercial standing saw little improvement despite an attempt to produce a more commercial work, the ironically titled *Big Smash*. Effectively retiring from recording for the first half of

the 80s, Wreckless returned with *A Roomful Of Monkeys*, credited to the Captains Of Industry, and featuring members of Ian Dury's Blockheads. He then formed the Len Bright Combo with ex-Milkshakes members Russ Wilkins (bass) and Bruce Brand (drums), who released two albums and found nothing more than a small cult following on the pub/club circuit. The eventual dissolution of that band led to the formation of Le Beat Group Électrique with Catfish Truton (drums) and André Barreau (bass), and later the Hitsville House Band. Now resident in France, and a more sober personality, Goulden has found an appreciative audience.
● ALBUMS: *Wreckless Eric* (Stiff 1978) ★★, *The Wonderful World Of Wreckless Eric* (Stiff 1978) ★★★, *Big Smash!* (Stiff 1980) ★★, as Captains Of Industry *A Roomful Of Monkeys* (Go! Discs 1984) ★★, *Le Beat Group Électrique* (New Rose 1989) ★★★, *At The Shop!* mini-album (New Rose 1990) ★★, *The Donovan Of Trash* (Hangman/Sympathy For The Record Industry 1993) ★★★, as Hitsville House Band *12 O'Clock Stereo* (Humbug/Casino 1994) ★★★, as Eric Goulden *Karaoke* mini-album (Silo 1997) ★★★.
● COMPILATIONS: *The Whole Wide World* (Stiff 1979) ★★★, *Greatest Stiffs* (Metro 2001) ★★★.

## WYATT, ROBERT

b. 28 January 1945, Bristol, Avon, England. As the drummer, vocalist and guiding spirit of the original Soft Machine, Robert Wyatt established a style that merged the *avant garde* with English eccentricity. His first solo album, 1970's *The End Of An Ear*, presaged his departure from the above group, although its radical content resulted in a muted reception. Wyatt's next venture, the excellent Matching Mole, was bedevilled by internal dissent, but a planned relaunch was forcibly abandoned following a tragic fall from a window, which left him paralysed and confined to a wheelchair. *Rock Bottom*, the artist's next release, was composed while Wyatt lay in hospital. This heartfelt, deeply personal collection was marked by an aching vulnerability that successfully avoided any hint of self-pity. This exceptional album was succeeded by an unlikely UK hit single in the shape of an idiosyncratic reading of the Monkees hit 'I'm A Believer'. *Ruth Is Stranger Than Richard*, released in 1975, was a more open collection, and balanced original pieces with outside material, including a spirited reading of jazz bass player Charlie Haden's 'Song For Che'. Although Wyatt, a committed Marxist, would make frequent guest appearances, his own career was shelved until 1980 when a single comprised of two South American songs of liberation became the first in a series of politically motivated releases undertaken for Rough Trade Records. These performances were subsequently compiled on *Nothing Can Stop Us*, which was then enhanced by the addition of 'Shipbuilding', a haunting anti-Falklands War composition, specifically written for Wyatt by Elvis Costello, which was a minor chart entry in 1983.
Wyatt's fluctuating health has undermined his recording ambitions, but his commitment remains undiminished. He issued singles in aid of Namibia

and the British Miners' Hardship Fund, and contributed a compassionate soundtrack to 1982's harrowing *Animals*. Wyatt's subsequent recordings, *Old Rotten Hat*, *Dondestan*, and the mini-album *A Short Break*, proved to be as compelling as his impressive 70s oeuvre. Now relocated in Lincolnshire, after a number of years in post-Franco Spain, Wyatt returned to music in 1997 with one of his best ever albums. *Shleep* was as brilliantly idiosyncratic as anything he has recorded. Surrounded by musicians he genuinely respected, the feeling of the album is one of mutual accord. Brian Eno's production enhances Wyatt's beautifully frail vocals. Highlights include 'The Duchess', a poignant and honest song for his wife Alfie, who co-writes with him and whose gentle illustrations grace many of his album covers. Other noteworthy tracks are the wandering 'Maryan', the deeply logical 'Free Will And Testament' and the lightly mocking paean to 'Bob Dylan's 115th Dream', 'Blues In Bob Minor'. *Shleep* is a treasure, by a man treasured by all who possess a conscience and a heart. Wyatt's music is celebrated in a series of 1999 shows by a hand picked group of musicians led by the trombonist Annie Whitehead. A spin-off tour was inaugurated the following year.

● ALBUMS: *The End Of An Ear* (Columbia 1970) ★★★, *Rock Bottom* (Virgin 1974) ★★★★, *Ruth Is Stranger Than Richard* (Virgin 1975) ★★★, *Nothing Can Stop Us* (Rough Trade 1982) ★★★★, *Animals* film soundtrack (Rough Trade 1984) ★★★, *Old Rotten Hat* (Rough Trade 1985) ★★★, *Dondestan* (Rough Trade 1991) ★★★, *A Short Break* mini-album (Rough Trade 1992) ★★★, *Shleep* (Hannibal/Thirsty Ear 1997) ★★★★, *Dondestan Revisited* (Hannibal 1998) ★★★.

● COMPILATIONS: *Going Back A Bit: A Little History Of Robert Wyatt* (Virgin Universal 1994) ★★★★, *Flotsam Jetsam* (Rough Trade 1994) ★★★, various artists *Soupsongs: The Music Of Robert Wyatt* (Voiceprint 2000) ★★★★.

● FURTHER READING: *Wrong Movements: A Robert Wyatt History*, Michael King.

**X**

Formed in Los Angeles, California, USA, in 1977, X originally comprised Exene Cervenka (b. Christine Cervenka, 1 February 1956, Chicago, Illinois, USA; vocals), Billy Zoom (b. Tyson Kindale, Savannah, Illinois, USA; guitar), John Doe (b. John Nommensen Duchac, 25 February 1954, Decatur, Illinois, USA; bass) and Mick Basher (drums), although the last-named was quickly replaced by D.J. (Don) Bonebrake (b. North Hollywood, California, USA). The quartet made its debut with 'Adult Books'/'We're Desperate' (1978), and achieved a considerable live reputation for their imaginative blend of punk, rockabilly and blues. Major labels were initially wary of the band, but Slash, a leading independent, signed them in 1979. Former Doors organist Ray Manzarek produced *Los Angeles* and *Wild Gift*, the latter of which established X as a major talent. Both the *New York Times* and the *Los Angeles Times* voted it Album Of The Year and such acclaim inspired a major label recording contract with Elektra Records. *Under The Big Black Sun* was another fine selection, although reception for *More Fun In The New World* was more muted, with several commentators deeming it 'over-commercial' (Manzarek produced both albums).

In the meantime, X members were pursuing outside projects. *Adulterers Anonymous*, a poetry collection by Cervenka and Lydia Lunch, was published in 1982, while the singer joined Doe, Bonebrake, Dave Alvin (the Blasters), upright bass player Jonny Ray Bartel and accordionist Martin Lund in a part-time country outfit, the Knitters, releasing *Poor Little Critter On The Road* on the Slash label in 1985. Alvin replaced Billy Zoom following the release of *Ain't Love Grand* and X was subsequently augmented by guitarist Tony Gilkyson. However, Alvin left for a solo career on the completion of *See How We Are*. Despite the release of *Live At The Whiskey A Go-Go On The Fabulous Sunset Strip*, X were clearly losing momentum and the band was dissolved.

Doe and Cervenka continued recording as solo acts, with the latter also releasing spoken-word albums. They reunited with Bonebrake and Gilkyson in 1993 with a new recording contract for *Hey Zeus!*, although their unplugged album two years later was a more worthwhile comeback. Zoom rejoined the band for a series of concerts in 1998, and the original quartet recorded a cover version of the Doors' 'The Crystal Ship' for *The X-Files* soundtrack.

● ALBUMS: *Los Angeles* (Slash 1980) ★★★, *Wild Gift* (Slash 1981) ★★★★, *Under The Big Black Sun* (Elektra 1982) ★★★, *More Fun In The New World* (Elektra 1983) ★★, *Ain't Love Grand* (Elektra 1986) ★★★, *See How We Are* (Elektra 1987) ★★, *Live At The Whiskey A Go-Go On The Fabulous Sunset Strip* (Elektra 1988) ★★★, *Hey Zeus!* (Big Life/Mercury 1993) ★★,

*Unclogged* (Infidelity 1995) ★★★.
● COMPILATIONS: *Beyond & Back: The X Anthology* (Elektra 1997) ★★★★.

## XMAL DEUTSCHLAND

This experimental and atmospheric rock band formed in the autumn of 1980 and were based in Hamburg, Germany. With no previous musical experience, the essential components were Anja Huwe (vocals), Manuela Rickers (guitar) and Fiona Sangster (keyboards). Original members Rita Simon and Caro May were replaced by Wolfgang Ellerbrock (bass) and Manuela Zwingmann (drums). Insisting on singing in their mother tongue and refusing to be visually promoted as a 'female' band (Ellerbrock was the 'token' male), they continued to plough a singular, and largely lonely, furrow, releasing an obscure 7-inch single on the Zick Zack label. They first came to England in 1982 to support the Cocteau Twins, joining 4AD Records soon afterwards. The debut *Fetisch* highlighted a sound that tied them firmly to both their Germanic ancestry and the hallmark spectral musicianship of their new label. Huwe's voice in particular, was used as a fifth instrument, making the cultural barrier redundant. After the release of two well-received singles, 'Qual' and 'Incubus Succubus II', they lost drummer Zwingmann who wished to remain in England. Her replacement was Peter Bellendir who joined in time for rehearsals for the second album. The band signed to Phonogram Records, and after the release of *Viva* shortened their name to X-Mal. Scaled down to a trio of Huwe, Ellerbrock and new guitarist Frank Z and released the more mainstream *Devils* to little acclaim. They continued to play the occasional live show but disbanded after sessions for a fifth album were scrapped in summer 1990.
● ALBUMS: *Fetisch* (4AD 1983) ★★★, *Tocsin* (4AD 1984) ★★★, *Viva* (Phonogram 1987) ★★, as X-Mal *Devils* (Phonogram Germany 1989) ★★.

## XTC

Formed in Wiltshire, England, in 1972 as Star Park (Rats Krap backwards) this widely beloved UK pop unit became the Helium Kidz in 1973 with the addition of bass player Colin Moulding (b. 17 August 1955, Swindon, Wiltshire, England), drummer Terry Chambers (b. 16 July 1955, Swindon, Wiltshire, England) and a second guitarist Dave Cartner (b. Swindon, Wiltshire, England), to the nucleus of Andy Partridge (b. Andrew John Partridge, 11 November 1953; guitar, vocals). The Helium Kidz were heavily influenced by the MC5 and Alice Cooper. In 1975, Partridge toyed with two new names for the band, the Dukes Of Stratosphear and XTC. At this time singer Steve Hutchins passed through the ranks and in 1976 Johnny Perkins (keyboards) joined Moulding, Partridge and Chambers. Following auditions with Pye Records, Decca Records and CBS Records they signed with Virgin Records – at which time they were joined by new keyboard player Barry Andrews (b. 12 September 1956, West Norwood, London, England). The band's sparkling 1978 debut, *White Music*, revealed a keener hearing for pop than the energetic new wave sound with which they were often aligned.

The album reached number 38 in the UK charts and critics marked their name for further attention. Shortly after the release of *Go 2*, Andrews departed, eventually to resurface in Shriekback. Andrews and Partridge had clashed too many times in the recording studio. With Andrews replaced by another Swindon musician, Dave Gregory (b. 21 September 1952, Swindon, Wiltshire, England), both *Go 2* and the following *Drums And Wires* were commercial successes. The latter album was a major step forward from the pure pop of the first two albums. The refreshingly hypnotic hit single 'Making Plans For Nigel' (UK number 17) exposed them to a new and eager audience. Singles were regularly taken from their subsequent albums and they continued reaching the UK charts with high-quality pop songs, including 'Sgt. Rock (Is Going To Help Me)' and the magnificently constructed 'Senses Working Overtime', which reached the UK Top 10. The main songwriter, Partridge, was able to put his sharp observations and nursery rhyme influences to paper in a way that made his compositions vital while eschewing any note of pretension. The excellent double set *English Settlement* reached number 5 on the UK album charts in 1982, but with Chambers opting to leave the band it was the final album to feature a full-time drummer (although he contributed to two songs on the subsequent *Mummer*).

Partridge subsequently fell ill through exhaustion and nervous breakdowns, and announced that XTC would continue only as recording artists, including promotional videos but avoiding the main source of his woes, the stage. Subsequent albums found only limited success, with those of the Dukes Of Stratosphear, their psychedelic pop alter ego, reputedly selling more copies. *Mummer*, *The Big Express* and the highly underrated Todd Rundgren-produced *Skylarking* were all mature, enchanting works, but failed to set any charts alight. *Oranges & Lemons* captured the atmosphere of the late 60s perfectly, but this excellent album also offered a further, perplexing commercial mystery. While it sold 500,000 copies in the USA, it barely scraped into the UK Top 30. The highly commercial 'The Mayor Of Simpleton' found similar fortunes, at a desultory number 46. The lyric from follow-up single 'Chalkhills And Children' states: 'Chalkhills and children anchor my feet/Chalkhills and children, bringing me back to earth eternally and ever Ermine Street.'

In 1992 *Nonsuch* entered the UK album charts and two weeks later promptly disappeared. 'The Disappointed', taken from that album, was nominated for an Ivor Novello songwriters award in 1993, but could just as easily have acted as a personal epitaph. In 1995 the Crash Test Dummies recorded 'The Ballad Of Peter Pumpkinhead' for the movie *Dumb And Dumber* and in turn reminded the world of Partridge's talent. Quite what he and his colleagues in the band, and Virgin Records, had to do to sell records remained uncertain. Partridge once joked that Virgin retained them only as a tax loss. It is debatable that if Partridge had not suffered from stage fright and a loathing of touring, XTC would have been one of the major bands of the 80s and would have sold millions

---

of records. Those who are sensitive to the strengths of the band would rightly argue that this would have severely distracted Partridge and Moulding from their craft as songwriters.

After almost showing a profit the band decided to go on strike in 1992, they were finally released from their Virgin contract in 1996 and signed with the UK's Cooking Vinyl Records in late 1997. Following the departure of Gregory, who had tendered his resignation from the team, Partridge and Moulding broke their recording silence in 1999 with *Apple Venus Volume 1*. This proved to be their most successful record in many years, well reviewed and lapped up by their loyal fans. Their familiar guitar-based pop sound was augmented by some sumptuous orchestral arrangements. Sadly, these songs, like their earlier classics, are never likely to be performed on stage in front of an audience. The following year's *Wasp Star (Apple Venus Volume 2)* was even better. This beautifully produced record (by Nick Davis) shares the sumptuous sound of albums such as *Skylarking*. All of the band's influences coalesce like never before, from the riff-laden 'Playground' to the Beach Boys' simplicity of 'In Another Life' and 'My Brown Guitar'.

XTC remain one of the most original pop bands of the era and Partridge's lyrics place him alongside Ray Davies as one of the UK's most imaginative songwriters of all time. Moulding, although much less prolific, is the vital lung to Partridge's ever-pumping heart.

● ALBUMS: *White Music* (Virgin 1978) ★★★, *Go 2* (Virgin 1978) ★★★, *Drums And Wires* (Virgin 1979) ★★★★, *Black Sea* (Virgin/RSO 1980) ★★★, *English Settlement* (Virgin/Epic 1982) ★★★, *Mummer* (Virgin/Geffen 1983) ★★★, *The Big Express* (Virgin/Geffen 1984) ★★★, *Skylarking* (Virgin/Geffen 1986) ★★★★, *Oranges & Lemons* (Virgin/Geffen 1989) ★★★★, *Nonsuch* (Virgin/Geffen 1992) ★★★★, *Live In Concert* 1980 recording (Windsong 1992) ★★★, *Apple Venus Volume 1* (Cooking Vinyl/TVT 1999) ★★★★, *Homespun (The Apple Venus Volume 1 Home Demos)* (Cooking Vinyl/TVT 1999) ★★★, *Wasp Star (Apple Venus Volume 2)* (Cooking Vinyl/TVT 2000) ★★★★, *Homegrown (The Wasp Star Home Demos)* (Idea/TVT 2001) ★★★.
● COMPILATIONS: *Waxworks: Some Singles 1977–1982* (Virgin 1982) ★★★, *Beeswax: Some B-Sides 1977–1982* (Virgin 1982) ★★, *The Compact XTC: The Singles 1978–85* (Virgin 1987) ★★★★, *Explode Together: The Dub Experiments 78–80* (Virgin 1990) ★★★, *Rag & Bone Buffet: Rare Cuts & Leftovers* (Virgin/Geffen 1990) ★★★, *Drums And Wireless: BBC Radio Sessions 77–89* (Nighttracks 1994) ★★★, *Fossil Fuel: The XTC Singles 1977–92* (Virgin 1996) ★★★★, *Upsy Daisy Assortment* (Geffen 1997) ★★★★, *Transistor Blast: The Best Of The BBC Sessions* 4-CD box set (Cooking Vinyl/TVT 1998) ★★★, *Coat Of Many Cupboards* 4-CD box set (Virgin/Caroline 2002) ★★★★.
● VIDEOS: *Look Look: A Video Compilation* (Virgin Video 1982).
● FURTHER READING: *XTC: Chalkhills And Children – The Definitive Biography*, Chris Twomey. *XTC: Song Stories – The Exclusive Authorized Story Behind The Music*, XTC and Neville Farmer.

## Y&T

This San Francisco, California, USA-based band formed in 1972 as Yesterday And Today, but David Meniketti (vocals, lead guitar), Joey Alves (rhythm guitar), Phil Kennemore (bass, vocals) and Leonard Haze (drums) failed to make any real impact until they released *Earthshaker* as Y&T. *Earthshaker* was a classic hard rock record built on a blistering guitar barrage, Haze's thunderous rhythms and a superb collection of songs, catapulting the band into the public eye, but it also proved to be something of an albatross around the collective Y&T neck. *Black Tiger* was excellent, but subsequent records failed to maintain the standards set on *Earthshaker*. The *Open Fire* live set stopped the rot, and *Down For The Count* signalled a return to form, albeit in a more commercial direction. 'Summertime Girls' was picked up by US radio, but a disenchanted Y&T split with both their record label and drummer, feeling that Haze's image left a lot to be desired. Jimmy DeGrasso made his drumming debut on *Contagious* and Stef Burns replaced Alves for *Ten*, which were both credible hard rock albums, but the band's fortunes were waning and Y&T split in late 1990, with Burns moving on to Alice Cooper's band, DeGrasso joining White Lion and then Suicidal Tendencies, and Meniketti working with Peter Frampton. A brief Y&T reunion led to two new studio albums. Meniketti then embarked on a solo career, releasing *On The Blue Side* in 1999.
● ALBUMS: as Yesterday And Today *Yesterday And Today* (London 1976) ★★, as Yesterday And Today *Struck Down* (London 1978) ★★, *Earthshaker* (A&M 1981) ★★★★, *Black Tiger* (A&M 1983) ★★★, *Mean Streak* (A&M 1983) ★★, *In Rock We Trust* (A&M 1984) ★★, *Open Fire (Live)* (A&M 1985) ★★★, *Down For The Count* (A&M 1985) ★★★, *Contagious* (Geffen 1987) ★★★, *Ten* (Geffen 1990) ★★★, *Yesterday & Today Live* (Metal Blade 1991) ★★, *Musically Incorrect* (Music For Nations 1995) ★★, *Endangered Species* (Music For Nations 1997) ★★, *Live On The Friday Rock Show* 1984 recording (Strange Fruit 1998) ★★★.
● COMPILATIONS: *Forever* (A&M 1987) ★★★, *Anthology* (Castle 1989) ★★★, *Best Of '81 To '85* (A&M 1990) ★★★★, *Ultimate Collection* (Hip-O 2001) ★★★.

## YANKOVIC, 'WEIRD AL'

b. Alfred Matthew Yankovic, 23 October 1959, Lynwood, California, USA. Yankovic achieved popularity during the 80s and 90s by creating parodies of popular songs and accompanying himself with an accordion. He first found renown in 1979 with a parody of the Knack's hit 'My Sharona', retitled 'My Bologna'. The song was recorded in a bathroom at a college he attended in San Luis Obispo, California, USA, and played on the syndicated Dr. Demento radio programme. It subsequently appeared on a Rhino Records sampler album, *Dementia Royale*, which led to further appearances on the Demento show. 'Another One Rides The Bus', Yankovic's version of Queen's 'Another One Bites The Dust', became the most requested song in the 10-year history of the radio programme and was issued as a single on TK Records.

In 1983 Yankovic signed to Rock 'n' Roll Records, a division of CBS Records, and released his self-titled debut album, produced by Rick Derringer. It included the Knack and Queen parodies as well as 'Ricky', a parody of the Toni Basil hit 'Mickey' which doubled as a salute to the *I Love Lucy* television programme. *In 3-D*, also produced by Derringer (as were all of Yankovic's albums through the 80s) was released in 1984 and reached number 17 in the USA, with the single 'Eat It', a take-off of Michael Jackson's 'Beat It', reaching number 12. All of his record releases were accompanied by videos that received heavy play on MTV, furthering Yankovic's appeal. With his Hawaiian shirts and crazed appearance, Yankovic was a natural for the video age, as a post-modern version of early 60s parodist Allan Sherman who was an inspiration to him. Although he included original material on his albums, all of it humorous in nature and much of it set to polka-like rhythms, Yankovic's biggest hits remained his song parodies. 'King Of Suede', a 1984 spoof of the Police's 'King Of Pain', was followed by 'I Lost On Jeopardy', a parody of Greg Kihn's 'Jeopardy' which changed the focus to that of the US television game show *Jeopardy*. In 1985, Yankovic took on Madonna, changing her 'Like A Virgin' into 'Like A Surgeon'. His final chart single of the 80s was 'Fat', which returned to Michael Jackson for inspiration, this time skewering his 'Bad'. The jacket of the attendant *Even Worse* was itself a parody of Jackson's *Bad*. The following year, Yankovic co-wrote and appeared in the movie *UHF*.

Yankovic continued to issue popular albums into the 90s. His bestselling release, *Bad Hair Day*, included 'Amish Paradise' (which parodied both Stevie Wonder's original song and the Coolio rewrite), and skits of TLC, Soul Asylum, Presidents Of The United States Of America and U2. *Running With Scissors* featured a re-working of John Williams new *Star Wars* theme, set to the tune of Don McLean's 'American Pie'.

● ALBUMS: *'Weird Al' Yankovic* (Rock 'n' Roll 1983) ★★, *In 3-D* (Rock 'n' Roll 1984) ★★, *Dare To Be Stupid* (Rock 'n' Roll 1985) ★★, *Polka Party!* (Rock 'n' Roll 1986) ★★, *Even Worse* (Rock 'n' Roll 1988) ★★, with Wendy Carlos *Peter & The Wolf* (CBS 1988) ★★, *UHF/Original Motion Picture Soundtrack And Other Stuff* film soundtrack (Rock 'n' Roll 1989) ★★, *Off The Deep End* (Scotti Bros 1992) ★★, *Alapalooza* (Scotti Bros 1993) ★★, *Bad Hair Day* (Rock 'n' Roll 1996) ★★, *Running With Scissors* (Volcano 1999) ★★.

● COMPILATIONS: *'Weird Al' Yankovic's Greatest Hits* (Scotti Bros 1988) ★★★, *The Food Album* (Scotti Bros 1993) ★★, *Permanent Record: Al In The Box* 4-CD box set (Scotti Bros 1994) ★★, *Greatest Hits Volume II* (Scotti Bros 1994) ★★★, *The TV Album* (Scotti Bros

1995) ★★.
● VIDEOS: *The Compleat Al* (CBS-Fox 1985), *The 'Weird Al' Yankovic Video Library: His Greatest Hits* (Scotti Bros 1992), *Alapalooza: The Videos* (Scotti Bros 1994), *Bad Hair Day: The Videos* (Scotti Bros 1996), *Live!* (Volcano 1999).
● FURTHER READING: *The Authorized Al*, 'Weird Al' Yankovic with Tino Insana.
● FILMS: *Naked Gun: From The Files Of Police Squad!* (1988), *Tapeheads* (1988), *UHF* (1989), *Naked Gun 2 1/2: The Smell Of Fear* (1991), *Naked Gun 33 1/3: The Final Insult* (1994), *Spy Hard* (1996), *Nothing Sacred* (1997), *Desperation Boulevard* (1998).

## YARGO

Formed in the mid-80s, UK's Yargo fused jazz, soul, blues and reggae forms so uniquely that the music proved too distinctive to break them commercially. However, within the annals of rock history, this Manchester quartet will reside as major innovators in black music. While vocalist Basil Clarke injected a penetrating, yearning quality into his voice, occasionally reminiscent of an urgent Marvin Gaye, the rhythm section of drummer Phil Kirby and enigmatic bass player Paddy Steer created a minimal but infectious backing akin to Sly And Robbie, alongside guitarist Tony Burnside.

Primarily a live outfit at first, Yargo issued three promising singles – 'Get High' on the local Skysaw label in 1986, 'Carrying Mine' on Racket Manufacture the following February, and 'Help' on their own Bodybeat label, and attracted sizeable interest when they appeared on the UK Channel 4 television programme *The Tube*. However, it was *Bodybeat* that garnered the most praise, combining the singles with a hypnotic title track to create a sparse but mesmerizing soundtrack, set against tales of urban Manchester. In August 1989, the band's theme for Independent television's *The Other Side Of Midnight* was released, drawn from the long-awaited *Communicate*, issued in October. Smoother and fuller than *Bodybeat*, this should have established Yargo as a major commercial act, but it was sadly ignored by a nation seemingly obsessed with house music, and, as a result, it was not long before the band fragmented. Steer later worked with the musical collective, Homelife.
● ALBUMS: *Bodybeat* (Bodybeat 1987) ★★★★, *Communicate* (Bodybeat 1989) ★★★.

## YAZ
(see Yazoo)

## YAZOO

This UK electro-pop group was formed at the beginning of 1982 by former Depeche Mode keyboard player Vince Clarke (b. 3 July 1960, South Woodford, London, England) and vocalist Alison Moyet (b. Genevieve Alison-Jane Moyet, 18 June 1961, Basildon, Essex, England). Their debut single, 'Only You', climbed to number 2 in the UK charts in May and its appeal was endorsed by the success of the Flying Pickets' a cappella cover version, which topped the UK chart the following year. Yazoo enjoyed an almost equally successful follow-up with

'Don't Go', which climbed to number 3 in July. A tour of the USA saw the duo change their name to Yaz in order not to conflict with an American record company of the same name, although their highest US chart entry was a lowly 67 for 'Only You'. Meanwhile, their album *Upstairs At Eric's* was widely acclaimed for its strong melodies and Moyet's expressive vocals. Yazoo enjoyed further UK hits with 'The Other Side Of Love' (number 13) and 'Nobody's Diary' (number 3) before completing one more album, *You And Me Both*.

Despite their continuing success, the duo parted in 1983. Moyet enjoyed considerable success as a solo singer, while Clarke maintained his high profile with the Assembly and particularly, Erasure. Yazoo graced the UK charts on two further occasions, with François Kevorkian's remix of 'Situation' reaching number 14 in 1990, and a new mix of 'Only You' scraping into the Top 40 in 1999.

● ALBUMS: *Upstairs At Eric's* (Mute/Sire 1982) ★★★★, *You And Me Both* (Mute/Sire 1983) ★★★.
● COMPILATIONS: *Only Yazoo: The Best Of* (UK) *The Best Of Yaz* (US) (Mute 1999) ★★★.

## YAZZ

b. Yasmin Evans, 19 May 1963, Shepherd's Bush, London, England. Dance-pop singer who began her career in the music business as part of a quickly forgotten act, the Biz. After becoming a catwalk model and working as George Michael's stylist, she laid plans for a return to recording work. When she did so, she found rewards immediately, joining with DJs Coldcut on the February 1988 Top 10 hit 'Doctorin' The House'. In its wake her revamped version of Otis Clay's 'The Only Way Is Up' soared to the top of the UK charts in August, while 'Stand Up For Your Love Rights' reached the number 2 spot. Both of the latter were credited to Yazz And The Plastic Population. After three further Top 20 hits and tours Yazz took time out to have her first baby. She returned alongside Aswad in 1993 for 'How Long', but this failed to break the Top 30. A new solo single, 'Have Mercy' and the attendant *One On One* were further evidence of her attempts to re-establish herself via a contract with Polydor Records. Yazz recorded 1997's *The Natural Life* at UB40 frontman Ali Campbell's Kuff Studios. This pleasant reggae-inflected album proved to be her final release of the decade.

● ALBUMS: *Wanted* (Big Life 1988) ★★★, *One On One* (Polydor 1994) ★★★, *The Natural Life* (East West 1997) ★★★.
● COMPILATIONS: *The Wanted Remixes* (Big Life 1989) ★★, *At Her Very Best: Yazz And All The Greatest Hits* (Universal 2001) ★★★.
● VIDEOS: *The Compilation* (Big Life 1989), *Live At The Hammersmith Odeon* (Big Life 1989).

## YELLO

This Swiss electronic band is led by Dieter Meier (b. 4 March 1945, Zurich, Switzerland), the son of a millionaire banker, sometime professional gambler, performance artist, and member of the Switzerland national golf team. Meier provides the concepts whilst his partner Boris Blank (b. 2 October 1938,

Switzerland) writes the music. Previously Meier had been a member of Periphery Perfume band Fresh Color and had released two solo singles. Teaming up with Blank and tape manipulator Carlos Peron to form Yello, the trio released the 'I.T. Splash' single on Periphery Perfume before signing a recording contract with Ralph Records in San Francisco, a label supported by the enigmatic Residents. Yello debuted with 'Bimbo' and the album *Solid Pleasure* in 1980. In the UK they signed to the Do It label, launching their career with 'Bostich', a track which had already become an underground club classic in America. The trio proved popular with the Futurist and New Romantic crowds, but their most lasting influence would be on the nascent dance music scene.

Chart success in the UK began after a move to Stiff Records in 1983 where they released two singles, an EP and *You Gotta Say Yes To Another Excess*, the last album to feature Peron. A brief sojourn with Elektra Records preceded a move to Mercury Records in the mid-80s, where they released the highly popular albums *Stella* and *One Second*. On the latter they worked closely with Shirley Bassey and Billy MacKenzie (the Associates). 'Oh Yeah' provided the duo with their sole US chart entry, thanks to its inclusion on the soundtrack of the movies *Ferris Bueller's Day Off* and *The Secret Of My Success*. Meier and Blank enjoyed major success with the UK Top 10 single, 'The Race' (from 1988's *Flag*). Accompanied by a stunning video – Meier saw visual entertainment as crucial to their work – 'The Race' easily transgressed the pop and dance markets in the wake of the acid house phenomenon. The Yello blueprint, on which Meier mumbled his bizarrely imaginative lyrics over Blank's inventive electronic beats, proved highly popular in London clubs when spun alongside Chicago house tracks.

By the early 90s the duo's albums had begun to move into the realm of self-parody, and both Meier and Blank subsequently became more and more embroiled in cinema. Their soundtrack work includes *Nuns On The Run*, *The Adventures Of Ford Fairlaine*, *Senseless*, and the Polish-filmed *Snowball*, a fairytale whose creative impetus is entirely down to Yello. Meier and Blank also run Solid Pleasure, the innovative Swiss dance label, and their most recent works has shown a willingness to take on board developments in dance music by introducing contemporary techno and trance rhythms. In 1995, a 'tribute' album, *Hands On Yello*, was released by Polydor Records, with Yello's music played by various artists including the Grid, Carl Craig, the Orb and Moby.

● ALBUMS: *Solid Pleasure* (Ralph/Do It 1980) ★★★, *Claro Que Si* (Ralph/Do It 1981) ★★★, *You Gotta Say Yes To Another Excess* (Elektra/Stiff 1983) ★★★★, *Stella* (Elektra 1985) ★★★, *One Second* (Mercury 1987) ★★, *Flag* (Mercury 1988) ★★★, *Baby* (Mercury 1991) ★★, *Zebra* (Mercury/4th & Broadway 1994) ★★★, *Pocket Universe* (Mercury 1997) ★★★, *Motion Picture* (Mercury 1999) ★★★.
● COMPILATIONS: *Yello 1980–1985: The New Mix In One Go* (Mercury 1986) ★★★, *Essential* (Smash/Mercury 1992) ★★★★, various artists *Hands On Yello: The Remixes* (Polydor 1995) ★★★, *Eccentric*

*Remixes* (Mercury 1999) ★★★.

● VIDEOS: *The Video Race* (Mercury 1988), *Yello Live At The Roxy N.Y. Dec '83* (Mercury 1989), *Essential Video* (Mercury 1992).

## YELLOW MAGIC ORCHESTRA

Pioneers in electronic music, the influence of Yellow Magic Orchestra in this field is surpassed only by Kraftwerk. The massive commercial profile in their native country was the first example of the Orient grafting Western musical traditions into their own culture – and with Japan the birthplace of the world's technological boom in the late 70s, it was no surprise that the medium chosen was electronic.

Session keyboard player Ryûichi Sakamoto met drummer Yukihiro Takahashi while recording his debut solo album. Takahashi had already released solo work, in addition to being a member of the Sadistic Mika Band (an art-rock conglomeration whose three progressive albums were released in the UK for Harvest Records). He had also played in a subsidiary outfit, the Sadistics. The final member of Yellow Magic Orchestra was recruited when the pair met a further established musician, bass player and producer Haruomi Hosono (as well as playing he would produce the unit's first six albums). Having performed with two earlier recorded Japanese outfits, his was the most advanced solo career (he was on his fourth collection when he encountered Takahashi and Sakamoto).

Although the trio's 1978 debut was inauspicious, consisting largely of unconnected electronic pulses and flashes, the following year's *Solid State Survivor* established a sound and pattern. With English lyrics by Chris Mosdell, the tracks now had evolved structures and a sense of purpose, and were occasionally deeply affecting. *X∞ Multiplies*, however, was a strange collection, comprising comedy skits and no less than two attempts at Archie Bell And The Drells' 'Tighten Up'. The UK issue of the same title added excerpts from the debut album (confusingly, a US version was also available, comprising tracks from *Solid State Survivor* in the main). There were elements of both on *BGM* and *Technodelic* which predicted the beautiful synth pop produced by later solo careers, but neither were the albums cohesive or unduly attractive on their own account. More skits, again in Japanese, appeared on *Service*, masking the quality of several strong songs, leaving the same year's *Naughty Boys* to prove itself Yellow Magic Orchestra's second great album. *Naughty Boys* arrived with English lyrics now furnished by Peter Barakan (later a Takahashi solo collaborator). Accessible and less angular, the songs were no less enduring or ambitious.

The Yellow Magic Orchestra eventually sundered in the early 80s, with Sakamoto going on to solo and film soundtrack fame. His former collaborators would also return to their own pursuits, with Hosono enjoying success in production (Sandii And The Sunsetz, Sheena And The Rokkets) and Takahashi earning critical plaudits for his prolific and diverse solo output. News filtered through in 1993 that, on the back of interest generated by a number of dance music artists name-checking or simply sampling

their wares, Yellow Magic Orchestra were to re-form. The resultant *Technodon* was completed in March before the trio went their separate ways once again.

● ALBUMS: *Yellow Magic Orchestra* (Alfa 1978) ★★, *Yellow Magic Orchestra* US mix (A&M 1979) ★★, *Solid State Survivor* (Alfa 1979) ★★★, *Public Pressure* (Alfa 1980) ★★★, *X∞ Multiplies* (Alfa 1980) ★★, *BGM* (Alfa 1981) ★★★, *Technodelic* (Alfa 1981) ★★★, *Naughty Boys* (Alfa 1983) ★★★★, *Naughty Boys Instrumental* (Alfa 1983) ★★★, *Service* (Alfa 1983) ★★★, *After Service* (Alfa 1984) ★★★, *Faker Holic* (Alca 1991) ★★★, *Technodon* (Alca 1993) ★★★, *Live At Budokan 1980* (Alca 1993) ★★★, *Live At Kinokuni-Ya Hall 1978* (Alca 1993) ★★, *Greek Theater Live 1979* (Toshiba EMI 1997) ★★★.

● COMPILATIONS: *Sealed* 4-CD box set (Alfa 1985) ★★★, *Y.M.O. History* (Alfa 1987) ★★★★, various artists *Hi-Tech/No Crime: Yellow Magic Orchestra Reconstructed* (Planet Earth 1992) ★★★★, *Kyoretsu Na Rhythm (Best Of)* (Alfa/Restless 1992) ★★★★, *Techno Bible* 5-CD set (Alfa 1992) ★★★, *Go Home! The Complete Best Of The Yellow Magic Orchestra* (Toshiba/EMI 1999) ★★★★, various artists *YMO Remixes: Technopolis 2000–01* (JVC 2001) ★★★.

● VIDEOS: *YMO Giga Clip (Yellow Magic Orchestra History)* (Toshiba 1998), *Clips: History Of YMO* (Toshiba 2000).

## YELLOWJACKETS

Over three decades, the Yellowjackets have achieved a formidable reputation for their live performances and critical and commercial success with their recordings of electric pop jazz. The members of the band are accomplished musicians in their own right and perhaps this accounts for the Yellowjackets' two Grammys and six nominations.

The formative line-up was assembled in 1977 by Robben Ford (b. Robben Lee Ford, 16 December 1951, Woodlake, California, USA; guitar) to help record his *The Inside Story*. Joining Ford in the embryonic Yellowjackets were Russell Ferrante (keyboards), Ricky Lawson (drums) and Jimmy Haslip (b. James Robert Haslip, 31 December 1951, New York City, New York, USA; bass). The Yellowjackets self-titled 1981 debut featured Ferrante, Haslip, Lawson and Ford, with musical assistance from Bobby Lyle (piano) and Lenny Castro (percussion) among others. By the time of 1983's *Mirage À Trois*, Ford's presence was declining. Saxophonist Marc Russo featured prominently on *Samurai Samba* (1985) and *Shades* in 1986 rewarded the band's steady touring with a Grammy and six-figure sales. Drummer William Kennedy was the next addition to the line-up and this prompted the band to explore some new territory on *Four Corners*. The relaxed *Politics* (1988) was another Grammy winner and hinted at the Yellowjackets' future direction. Their next project, *The Spin* was recorded in Oslo, Norway with well-known engineer, Jan Erik Konshaug, and was a more acoustic, resolutely jazz album.

The Yellowjackets' debut for GRP Records, *Greenhouse*, featured saxophonist Bob Mintzer (b. 27 January 1953, New Rochelle, Westchester, New York, USA), replacing Russo who had departed to work with Kenny Loggins. *Live Wires*, their 1992 release, successfully demonstrated the multifaceted approach the Yellowjackets like to adopt. Indeed, the simplicity of the band's sound belies the diversity of their influences: 'We spend hours experimenting, studying and listening to music from all over the world. You can't be afraid to take chances. That's what it takes to continue to grow!'. The Ferrante/Haslip/Kennedy/Mintzer line-up continued with GRP throughout the decade, releasing a series of well-received and musically adventurous albums. *Club Nocturne* was something of a departure from their traditional sound, featuring vocal contributions from Kurt Elling, Brenda Russell and Jonathan Butler. Kennedy departed in 1999 to become more involved in gospel music. He was briefly replaced by Peter Erskine. Ferrante, Haslip and Mintzer were joined by new drummer Marcus Baylor on 2001's *Mint Jam*.

● ALBUMS: *Yellowjackets* (Warners 1981) ★★★, *Mirage À Trois* (Warners 1983) ★★★, *Samurai Samba* (Warners 1985) ★★★, *Shades* (MCA 1986) ★★★, *Four Corners* (MCA 1987) ★★★, *Politics* (MCA 1988) ★★★★, *The Spin* (MCA 1989) ★★★, *Greenhouse* (GRP 1991) ★★★, *Live Wires* (GRP 1992) ★★★, *Like A River* (GRP 1993) ★★★, *Run For Your Life* (GRP 1994) ★★★, *Dreamland* (Warners 1995) ★★★, *Blue Hats* (Warners 1997) ★★★, *Club Nocturne* (Warners 1998) ★★, *Mint Jam* (Yellowjackets Enterprise 2001) ★★★.

● COMPILATIONS: *Collection* (GRP 1995) ★★★★, *Priceless Jazz* (Universal 1998) ★★★, *The Best Of Yellowjackets* (Warners 1999) ★★★★.

## YELLOWMAN

b. Winston Foster, 1959, Kingston, Jamaica, West Indies. Yellowman was the DJing sensation of the early 80s and he achieved this status with a fair amount of talent and inventive and amusing lyrics. He built his early career around the fact that he was an albino and his success has to be viewed within its initial Jamaican context. The albino or 'dundus' is virtually an outcast in Jamaican society and Foster's early years were incredibly difficult. Against all the odds, he used this background to his advantage and, like King Stitt, who had previously traded on his physical deformities, Foster paraded himself in the Kingston dancehalls as 'Yellowman', a DJ with endless lyrics about how sexy, attractive and appealing he was to the opposite sex. Within a matter of months, he went from social pariah to headlining act at Jamaican stage shows and his popularity rocketed; the irony of his act was not lost on his audiences. He performed with fellow DJ Fathead at the Aces discotheque in St. Thomas where the duo built a solid reputation. Yellowman's words of wisdom were punctuated by Fathead chanting 'ribbit' and 'oink' sounds at the end of each line, which became *en vogue* in the early 80s. Yellowman and Fathead's records with producer Henry 'Junjo' Lawes were both witty and relevant, 'Soldier Take Over' being a fine example. Yellowman was also the first to release a live album - not of a stage show but recorded live on a sound system - *Yellowman And Fathead Live At Aces* included

performances from Jah Reubal and Little Harry alongside the DJ duo. The album captured Yellowman at the height of his powers and in full control of his 'fans'; none of the excitement is lost in the transition from dancehall to record.

Yellowman's records sold well and he toured the USA and UK to ecstatic crowds - his first sell-out London shows caused traffic jams and roadblocks around the venue. It seemed that he could do no wrong, and even his version of 'I'm Getting Married In The Morning' sold well. He was soon signed to a major contract with CBS Records and was King Yellow to everyone in the reggae business. However, this did not last, and by the mid-80s it had become difficult to sell his records to the fickle reggae market. Nevertheless, by this time he had been adopted by pop audiences all over the world as a novelty act and while he has never become a major star, he is still very popular and his records sell in vast quantities in many countries. He has released more records than a great many other reggae acts - no mean feat in a business dominated by excess. Having become both rich and successful through his DJing work, it is mainly his ability to laugh at himself and encourage others to share the joke that has endeared him to so many.

● ALBUMS: *Them A Mad Over Me* (Channel 1 1981) ★★★, *Mister Yellowman* (Greensleeves 1982) ★★★★, *Yellowman And Fathead Live At Aces* (VP 1982) ★★★★, with Fathead *Bad Boy Skanking* (Greensleeves 1982) ★★★, *Has Arrived With Toyan* (Joe Gibbs 1982) ★, *Live At Sunsplash* (Sunsplash 1982) ★★★★, with Purple Man, Sister Nancy *The Yellow, The Purple, And The Nancy* (Greensleeves 1982) ★★★★, with Fathead *For Your Eyes Only* aka *Divorced!* (Arrival/Burning Sounds 1983) ★★★, *Zungguzungguguzungguzeng!* (Greensleeves 1983) ★★★, with Josey Wales *Two Giants Clash* (Greensleeves 1984) ★★★★, with Charlie Chaplin *Slackness Vs Pure Culture* (Arrival 1984) ★★★★, *Nobody Move, Nobody Get Hurt* (Greensleeves 1984) ★★★, *King Yellowman* (CBS 1984) ★★, *Galong Galong Galong* (Greensleeves 1985) ★★★, *Going To The Chapel* (Greensleeves 1986) ★★, *Rambo* (Moving Target 1986) ★★★, *Yellow Like Cheese* (RAS 1987) ★★, *Don't Burn It Down* (Shanachie/Greensleeves 1987) ★★, *Blueberry Hill* (Greensleeves/Rohit 1987) ★★★, with General Trees *A Reggae Calypso Encounter* (Rohit 1987) ★★, *King Of The Dancehall* (Rohit 1988) ★★, with Chaplin *The Negril Chill* (ROIR 1988) ★★★, *Sings The Blues* (Rohit 1988) ★★, *Rides Again* (RAS 1988) ★★★, *One In A Million* (Shanachie 1988) ★★, *Badness* (La/Unicorn 1990) ★★★, *Thief* (Mixing Lab 1990) ★★★, *A Feast Of Yellow Dub Cooked By The Mad Professor* (RAS 1990) ★★★, *Mi Hot* (Pow Wow 1991) ★★, *Party* (RAS 1991) ★★★, *Reggae On The Move* (RAS 1992) ★★, *Live In England* (Greensleeves 1992) ★★, *In Bed With Yellowman* (Greensleeves 1993) ★★, *Reggae On Top* (Pow Wow 1993) ★★, *Prayer* (RAS 1994) ★★★, *Freedom Of Speech* (RAS 1995) ★★★, *Message To The World* (RAS 1995) ★★, *A Very, Very Yellow Christmas* (RAS 1998) ★★, *Yellow Fever* (Artists Only! 1999) ★★★, *Live In San Francisco* (2b1 II 2002) ★★★.

● COMPILATIONS: *20 Super Hits* (Sonic Sounds

1990) ★★★★, *Best Of Yellowman* (Celluloid 1996) ★★★, *Portraits* (RAS 1997) ★★★★, *Operation Radication*. (Reactive 1998) ★★★★, *Just Cool* (Culture Press 1999) ★★★, *Look How Me Sexy: Reggae Anthology* (VP 2001) ★★★, *Yellow Gold* (Artists Only! 2002) ★★.
● VIDEOS: *Raw And Rough (Live At Dollars Lawn)* (Jetstar 1989).

## YOAKAM, DWIGHT

b. Dwight David Yoakam, 23 October 1956, Pikeville, Kentucky, USA. Much of Yoakam's hip honky tonk music paved the way for rock audiences accepting country music in the 90s. A singer-songwriter with an early love of the honky-tonk country music of Buck Owens and Lefty Frizzell, he has always shown a distinct antipathy towards the Nashville pop/country scene.

Yoakam, the eldest of three children, moved with his family to Columbus, Ohio, when he was two. After an abortive spell studying philosophy and history at Ohio State University, he briefly sought Nashville success in the mid-70s, but his music was rated too country even for the *Grand Ole Opry*. He relocated to Los Angeles in 1978 and worked the clubs, playing with various bands including Los Lobos, but for several years he worked as a truck driver. In 1984, the release of a self-financed mini-album on the Oak Records label led to him signing for Reprise Records. Two years later, following the release of an expanded version of the mini-album (also called *Guitars, Cadillacs, Etc. Etc.*), he registered Top 5 US country chart hits with Johnny Horton's 'Honky Tonk Man' and his own 'Guitars, Cadillacs'. His driving honky-tonk music made him a popular visitor to Britain and brought him some success in the USA, although his outspoken views denied him the wider fame with the mainstream country audience of his contemporary Randy Travis. Nevertheless, in 1987 Yoakam enjoyed chart success with his cover version of the old Elvis Presley pop hit 'Little Sister'. He followed it in 1988 with a US country number 9 hit with his idol Lefty Frizzell's classic 'Always Late With Your Kisses'. He would also make the top of the country charts with 'Streets Of Bakersfield', duetting with veteran 60s superstar Buck Owens, and with the self-penned 'I Sang Dixie'. Yoakam played several concerts with Owens, after being instrumental in persuading him to come out of retirement and record again for Capitol Records.

Yoakam's straight country style is his most effective work, a point made clear when he attempted to cross over into the mainstream rock market in the early 90s with the European release *La Croix D'Amour*. During this period he also turned his hand to acting, appearing in a Los Angeles stage production, *Southern Rapture*, directed by Peter Fonda (by the end of the decade Yoakam had established himself as a film star of some note.) Yoakam returned to his roots in 1993 with the hardcore country of *This Time*. The album included the number 2 country hits 'Ain't That Lonely Yet', which won a Grammy Award for Best Country Vocal Performance, 'A Thousand Miles From Nowhere' and 'Fast As You'. *Dwight Live*, recorded at San Francisco's Warfield Theatre,

captured the fervour of his concert performances. Yoakam enjoyed his biggest hit for over five years with a cover version of Queen's 'Crazy Little Thing Called Love', featured on 1999's compilation set. The following year's *dwightyoakamacoustic.net* reworked his back catalogue in an acoustic format. *Tomorrow Sounds Today* included three further collaborations with Owens and a cover version of Cheap Trick's 'I Want You To Want Me'.

After almost 20 years of commercial success, Yoakam has firmly established his staying power as one of the leading artists of the new era of country music. There seems little doubt that his songwriting talents and singing style will ensure further major success. To quote *Rolling Stone*, 'Neither safe nor tame, Yoakam has adopted Elvis' devastating hip swagger, Hank Williams' crazy-ass stare and Merle Haggard's brooding solitude into one lethal package. Yoakam is a cowgirl's secret darkest dream.'

● ALBUMS: *Guitars, Cadillacs, Etc, Etc* mini-album (Oak 1984) ★★★, *Guitars, Cadillacs, Etc, Etc* (Reprise 1986) ★★★★, *Hillbilly Deluxe* (Reprise 1987) ★★★★, *Buenas Noches From A Lonely Room* (Reprise 1988) ★★★★, *If There Was A Way* (Reprise 1990) ★★★★, *La Croix D'Amour* (Reprise 1992) ★★★, *This Time* (Reprise 1993) ★★★★, *Dwight Live* (Reprise 1995) ★★★, *Gone* (Reprise 1995) ★★★, *Under The Covers* (Reprise 1997) ★★★, *Come On Christmas* (Reprise 1997) ★★, *A Long Way Home* (Reprise 1998) ★★★★, *dwightyyoakamacoustic.net* (Reprise 2000) ★★★★, *Tomorrow's Sounds Today* (Reprise 2000) ★★★, *South Of Heaven West Of Hell* film soundtrack (Warners 2001) ★★★.
● COMPILATIONS: *Just Lookin' For A Hit* (Reprise 1989) ★★★★, *Last Chance For A Thousand Years: Dwight Yoakam's Greatest Hits From The 90s* (Reprise 1999) ★★★★.
● VIDEOS: *Dwight Yoakam, Just Lookin' For A Hit* (Reprise 1989), *Fast As You* (Reprise 1993), *Pieces Of Time* (Reprise 1994), *Live On Stage* (Magnum Video 1997).
● FURTHER READING: *A Long Way Home (12 Years Of Words)*, Dwight Yoakam.
● FILMS: *Red Rock West* (1992), *The Little Death* (1995), *Sling Blade* aka *Reckoning* (1996), *Painted Hero* aka *Shadow Of The Past* (1996), *The Newton Boys* (1998), *Ozzie And Harriet: The Adventures Of America's Favorite Family* (1998), *The Minus Man* (1999), *South Of Heaven, West Of Hell* (2000), *Panic Room* (2002).

## YOUNG FRESH FELLOWS

Operating out of Seattle, Washington, USA, since the early 80s, the Young Fresh Fellows have released a body of rough-hewn, understated pop gems. Formed in 1982 by Scott McCaughey (bass, vocals), Chuck Carroll (guitar) and Tad Hutchinson (drums), their debut album was recorded in 1983 and released a year later. *Fabulous Sounds Of The Pacific Northwest* picked up immediate plaudits, *Rolling Stone* going so far as to describe it as 'perfect'. Joined by Jim Sangster (bass), they become a fully fledged offbeat new wave act, the dry humour and acute observations of their lyrics attracting a large college following. Their stylistic fraternity with the higher-profile Replacements was confirmed by their joint tours, both bands sharing what *Billboard* magazine described as 'a certain deliberate crudity of execution'.

After the mini-album *Refreshments* the Young Fresh Fellows moved to Frontier Records for 1988's *Totally Lost*. Despite being dogged by a 'joke band' reputation, brought about by an aptitude for satirizing high-school traumas, the band's critical reaction was once more highly favourable. However, Carroll played his last gig for the band in winter 1989 in Washington. He was replaced by the Fastbacks' guitarist Kurt Bloch (who continued with both bands). Their most polished album yet, 1989's *This One's For The Ladies* highlighted McCaughey's successful adaptation of the spirit of the Kinks, while Bloch's guitar melodies fitted in seamlessly. With the Young Fresh Fellows winding down during the mid-90s, McCaughey toured as second guitarist with R.E.M. in 1995 and worked with his side project the Minus 5, featuring a revolving cast of Seattle-based musicians. The Young Fresh Fellows remained active as a live act into the new millennium, with the occasional foray into the recording studio.

● ALBUMS: *Fabulous Sounds Of The Pacific Northwest* (PopLlama 1984) ★★★, *Topsy Turvy* (PopLlama 1985) ★★★, *The Men Who Loved Music* (PopLlama 1987) ★★★★, *Refreshments* mini-album (PopLlama 1987) ★★, *Totally Lost* (Frontier 1988) ★★★, *Beans And Intolerance* (No Label 1989) ★★, *This One's For The Ladies* (Frontier 1989) ★★★, *Electric Bird Digest* (Frontier 1991) ★★★, *Gleich Jetzt* (1 + 2 1992) ★★, *It's Low Beat Time* (Frontier 1992) ★★★, *Temptation On Saturday* mini-album (PopLlama/Munster 1993) ★★★, *Take It Like A Matador (Live In Spain)* (Impossible 1993) ★★, *A Tribute To Music* (Rock & Roll Inc. 1997) ★★★, split with the Minus 5 *Because We Hate You* (Hollywood 2001) ★★★.

● COMPILATIONS: *Includes A Helmet* mini-album (Utility 1990) ★★, *Somos Los Mejores!* (Munster 1991) ★★★.

## YOUNG MARBLE GIANTS

Formed in November 1978 as 'a desperate last-ditch attempt at doing something with my life' by Stuart Moxham (guitar, organ), this seminal, yet short-lived, trio from Cardiff, Wales, comprised the latter as the band's main songwriter, his brother Philip Moxham (bass) and Alison Statton (b. March 1958, Cardiff, Wales; vocals). Together they made their debut on *Is The War Over?*, a compilation of Cardiff acts, released in 1979. Their contribution reached the ears of Geoff Travis at Rough Trade Records who promptly invited them to record an album. Playing within minimalist musical landscapes the band utilized the superb, lyrical bass playing of Philip Moxham. The combination of Stuart's twangy/scratchy guitar and reedy organ with Statton's clear diction was evident on tracks such as 'Searching For Mr. Right', 'Credit In The Straight World' and 'Wurlitzer Jukebox' from *Colossal Youth*. This highly acclaimed album was followed the next year by the impressive *Testcard* EP, which reached number 3 in the UK independent charts, by which time the band had amicably split. The Moxham brothers noted that

recording separately would be the only way to maintain a healthy sibling relationship.

Stuart Moxham established the Gist, recording *Embrace The Herd* in 1983. This included the gorgeous 'Love At First Sight', which reached the UK Independent Top 20. Stuart's producing talents were called upon to oversee the recording of the Marine Girls' second album, *Lazy Ways*. Other projects in the 90s included work with Beat Happening, the 6ths and Etienne Daho, and several solo albums credited to Stuart Moxham And The Original Artists, including *Signal Path*, *Random Rules* and *Fine Tuning*. In later years his other profession, that of animation painter, gave him a credit on the movie *Who Framed Roger Rabbit?*. Phil Moxham found work sessioning for both Weekend and the Gist, while Statton formed Weekend for two jazz-inspired albums, before joining Ian Devine (ex-Ludus) in Devine And Statton and then former Weekend associate Spike in Alison Statton And Spike.

● ALBUMS: *Colossal Youth* (Rough Trade 1980) ★★★★.

● COMPILATIONS: with Weekend, the Gist *Nipped In The Bud* (Rough Trade 1984) ★★★, *Salad Days* (Vinyl Japan 2000) ★★★.

● VIDEOS: *Live At The Hurrah!* (Visionary 1994).

## YOUNG, PAUL

b. Paul Anthony Young, 17 January 1956, Luton, Bedfordshire, England. Prior to his major success as a solo artist, Young was a former member of Streetband, who made the UK charts in 1978 with the novelty record 'Toast'. He was then part of the much-loved Q-Tips, a band that did much to preserve an interest in 60s soul and R&B. As the Q-Tips collapsed from exhaustion and lack of finance, Young signed as a solo artist with CBS Records. Following two flop singles ('Iron Out The Rough Spots' and 'Love Of The Common People'), his smooth soul voice captured the public's imagination with 1983's superb chart-topping cover version of Marvin Gaye's 'Wherever I Lay My Hat (That's My Home)'. The following *No Parlez* was a phenomenally triumphant debut, reaching number 1 in the UK and staying in the charts for well over two years. Now, having sold several million copies, this album remains his finest work. It was a blend of carefully chosen and brilliantly interpreted covers including 'Love Will Tear Us Apart' (Joy Division), the aforementioned 'Love Of The Common People' (Four Preps/Nicky Thomas) and 'Come Back And Stay' (Jack Lee). After touring to support the album, Young experienced a recurring problem with his voice which would continue to plague his career. It was two years before he was able to record *The Secret Of Association*, but the quality of material was intact. This album also topped the UK chart and produced three top 10 singles, cover versions of Ann Peebles' 'I'm Gonna Tear Your Playhouse Down' and Daryl Hall's 'Every Time You Go Away' and 'Everything Must Change'. 'Every Time You Go Away' provided Young with his US breakthrough, reaching the top of the *Billboard* singles chart in summer 1985. He appeared at Live Aid, duetting with Alison Moyet, although it was obvious that his voice was once again troublesome. *Between Two Fires* was a below-par album, although his fans still made it a UK Top 5 hit. Little was heard from Young for over a year, and while it was assumed that his voice was continuing to cause him problems, the singer was merely re-assessing his life. He made an encouraging return singing Crowded House's 'Don't Dream Its Over' at the Nelson Mandela Concert at Wembley in 1988, after which Young went into hibernation until 1990; this time by his own admission he was 'decorating his house'. He returned with the Top 5 album *Other Voices* and embarked on an accompanying tour. Once again the choice of material was tasteful and included cover versions of Free's 'Little Bit Of Love' and Bobby Womack's 'Stop On By', while his reading of the Chi-Lites' 'Oh Girl' returned the singer to the US Top 10. The following year Young reached the UK Top 5, duetting with Italian singer Zucchero on 'Senza Una Donna (Without A Woman)'. His was one of the better performances at the Freddie Mercury tribute concert at Wembley Stadium in May 1992.

Young seemed destined for continuing success during the 90s, having proved that even with a sparse recorded output his sizeable following remained loyal and patient. Although his voice lacked the power and bite of old he was able to inject passion and warmth into his studio albums. This was apparent on the 1993 hit 'Now I Know What Made Otis Blue' and his reading of several soul classics on *Reflections*, which demonstrated the area of music where he has the closest affinity. Versions of 'Until You Come Back To Me', 'Ain't No Sunshine' and 'Reach Out, I'll Be There' highlighted a man who truly has soul even though his voice is leaving him. Following the relative commercial failure of his self-titled 1997 release, Young was dropped by East West Records. Two years later he embarked on the well-received Intimate tour, playing at small venues throughout the UK.

● ALBUMS: *No Parlez* (CBS 1983) ★★★★, *The Secret Of Association* (CBS 1985) ★★★, *Between Two Fires* (CBS 1986) ★★, *Other Voices* (CBS 1990) ★★★, *The Crossing* (Columbia 1993) ★★, *Reflections* (Vision 1994) ★★★, *Acoustic Paul Young* mini-album (Columbia 1994) ★★★★, *Paul Young* (East West 1997) ★★.

● COMPILATIONS: *From Time To Time: The Singles Collection* (Columbia 1991) ★★★★, *Best Ballads* (Sony 1995) ★★★, *Love Songs* (Columbia 1997) ★★★, *Super Hits* (Sony 1998) ★★★, *Simply The Best* (Sony 2000) ★★★.

● VIDEOS: *Video Singles* (CBS Video 1986).

## YOUTH BRIGADE

Formed in Los Angeles, California, USA, in the late 70s from the ashes of the Extremes, Youth Brigade initially comprised the Toronto, Canada born Stern brothers, Shawn (guitar, vocals), Adam (bass, vocals) and Mark (drums, ex-No Crisis; Sado Nation), and Greg Louis Gutierrez (guitar). One of Los Angeles' finest hardcore bands of the period, they also formed the BYO (the Better Youth Organization) label as a direct response to the Ellis Lodge riot of 1979 when bands including the Go-Go's played at a gig that was violently curtailed by riot police. BYO was housed at Skinhead Manor, an eight-bedroomed mansion in the heart of Hollywood, rented by an assortment of mavericks intent on creating an alternative media base (including fanzines, pirate radio, live shows, etc.). It was named in honour of the visiting Sham 69. Youth Brigade had started out as part of the Skinhead Manor collective, originally as a six-piece group with two singers. They soon crystallized into a line-up made up solely of the Stern brothers. Another band of the same name was born in Washington, DC, at the same time (playing the same type of aggressive punk music), but luckily this group faded from view before too much confusion arose.

Often compared to the Ruts because of their integration of reggae with punk pop, Youth Brigade's debut album was easily one of the most accessible of the 'So-Cal Hardcore' scene. Barely 1,000 copies of the original version of *Sound And Fury* were ever printed due to the band's dissatisfaction with the album's mastering. They decided to re-record the album, and replace many of the original tracks with new songs (the first version of the album was eventually re-released as *Out Of Print* in 1998). *Sound And Fury* demonstrated the band's potential with a wide variety of music employed even at this early stage in their career. 'Men In Blue', for example, included a rap, and the band also tackled the doo-wop classic 'Duke Of Earl'. They embarked on a major tour playing at over 100 venues in 1983 and 1984, covering much of the USA, Europe and Canada, but always using non-mainstream outlets to book the shows.

Following the departure of Adam Stern to art school, the remaining members shortened their title to Brigade to accommodate 'a further progression in style'. The new line-up featured bass player Bob Gnarly, formerly of Plain Wrap (Gutierrez had long since joined Salvation Army and then the Three O'Clock). Their first album as the Brigade, *The Dividing Line*, featured a cameo appearance from Jane Wiedlin on 'The Hardest Part' (in the character of a dizzy blonde actress called Candy). Stern's lyrics were evolving and taking in matters spiritual and emotional as well as social, but Brigade never took themselves too seriously, raps and breakdancing continuing to be a feature of their live shows. However, their previous audience remained unimpressed by what they saw as Brigade's conversion to conventional hard rock. The group disbanded, with Stern subsequently forming That's It! with Tony Withers, formerly of UK punk band the Stupids.

The Stern brothers reunited in the mid-90s, reactivating the Youth Brigade name and releasing a string of albums on their still operational BYO label.

● ALBUMS: *Sound And Fury* (BYO 1982) ★★★★, *Sink With Kalifornia* (BYO 1984) ★★★, as the Brigade *The Dividing Line* (BYO 1987) ★★, *Happy Hour* (BYO 1994) ★★, *To Sell The Truth* (BYO 1996) ★★★, *Out Of Print* 1982 recording (BYO 1998) ★★★★.

● COMPILATIONS: *A Best Of Youth Brigade* (Golf 2002) ★★★★.

# Z

**ZAPP**

Funk group based in Hamilton, Ohio, USA who, for a period during the 80s, rivalled major stars of the genre such as the Gap Band and Kool And The Gang. Zapp was formed by several members of the Troutman family, including brothers Roger Troutman (b. 29 November 1951, Hamilton, Ohio, USA, d. 25 April 1999, Dayton, Ohio, USA; vocals, guitar), Lester (drums), Larry (b. *c*.1945, d. 25 April 1999; percussion) and Tony. The latter recorded the minor R&B hit single 'I Truly Love You' for Gram-O-Phon Records in 1976. Zapp were heavily influenced by local heroes the Ohio Players, but soon generated a local following of their own, attracted by the unit's flamboyant showmanship and highly danceable music. Various other band members included backing vocalists Bobby Glover and Jannetta Boyce, keyboard players Greg Jackson and Sherman Fleetwood, and horn players Eddie Barber, Jerome Derrickson and Mike Warren. Support slots with kindred spirit George Clinton and his Parliament and Funkadelic outfits helped secure a recording deal with Warner Brothers Records in the late 70s.

Clinton's resident bass player Bootsy Collins contributed to Zapp's 1980 US Top 20 debut album, which contained their signature tune 'More Bounce To The Ounce – Part 1'. This song laid down the definitive Zapp sound, with funky bass and choppy rhythm guitars providing the backing for Roger Troutman's vocoderized vocals (generated through a talk box, a gadget previously used by Peter Frampton and Jeff Beck). Released as a single, 'More Bounce To The Ounce – Part 1' reached number 2 on the US R&B chart, and was subsequently sampled by rap artists including Ice Cube, Snoop Doggy Dogg and EPMD. In 1981 Roger Troutman worked on Funkadelic's brilliant *The Electric Spanking Of War Babies* and released his solo debut (as Roger). He would subsequently balance a successful solo career and production work with his continued involvement in Zapp. *Zapp II* included the highly addictive 'Dance Floor (Part 1)', an R&B number 1 in 1982. *Zapp III* was not as popular as the first two albums, although 'I Can Make You Dance (Part 1)' was a number 4 R&B hit.

Various members of the band worked with Roger on albums by artists affiliated to the Zapp family, including Dick Smith, Human Body, Bobby Glover, Lynch, New Horizons and Shirley Murdock. The latter, an exciting gospel/soul vocalist, appeared on 1985's *The New Zapp IV U*. Further excellent singles included 'It Doesn't Really Matter' (1985) and 'Computer Love Part 1' (number 8 R&B, 1986), but the band's commercial fortunes had declined by the end of the decade. Their 1993 compilation album, featuring several remixes and medleys, went platinum.

Zapp's influence on electro and hip-hop should not be underestimated, and Roger Troutman remained an in-demand session musician/vocalist and producer with urban R&B and hip-hop artists (including a high profile performance on Dr. Dre and 2Pac's 1996 hit single, 'California Love'). The Zapp story ended in tragedy on 25 April 1999, when Larry shot Roger before turning the gun on himself.

● ALBUMS: *Zapp* (Warners 1980) ★★★★, *Zapp II* (Warners 1982) ★★★, *Zapp III* (Warners 1983) ★★★★, *The New Zapp IV U* (Warners 1985) ★★★, *Zapp V* (Reprise 1989) ★★★.

● COMPILATIONS: as Roger And Zapp *All The Greatest Hits* (Reprise 1993) ★★★★, as Roger And Zapp *Compilation: Greatest Hits 2 And More* (Reprise 1996) ★★★, as Zapp And Roger *We Can Make You Dance: Anthology* (Rhino 2002) ★★★★.

**ZIMMER, HANS**

b. 12 September 1957, Frankfurt, Germany. Apparently, from the age of six, Zimmer wanted to be a composer, although he had no formal musical education. When he was 16 he went to school in England, and during the 70s spent some time at Air-Edel, writing jingles for television commercials. Following brief spells with synth-pop bands Buggles and Ultravox, Zimmer collaborated with the established movie composer Stanley Myers, to write the score for Nicolas Roeg's *Eureka*, and several other British films during the 80s, including *Moonlighting*, *Success Is The Best Revenge*, and *Insignificance*. His solo credits around that time included movies with themes such as apartheid (*A World Apart*), a psychological thriller (*Paperhouse*), a couple of eccentric comedies (*Twister* and *Driving Miss Daisy*), a tough Michael Douglas detective yarn (*Black Rain*), and a 'stiflingly old-fashioned' version of a Stefan Zweig short story, *Burning Secret* (1988). In that year Zimmer provided the music for 14 films in the UK and abroad, including the blockbuster, *Rain Man*, starring Dustin Hoffman and Tom Cruise. *Rain Man* earned Zimmer a nomination for an Academy Award ('When they found out that I was only 30, I didn't get it!'). He continued apace in the following years with scores for *Bird On A Wire*; *Days Of Thunder*, *Chicago Joe And The Showgirl* (written with Shirley Walker), *Pacific Heights*, *Green Card* (starring Gérard Depardieu in his English-language debut), *Thelma And Louise* ('a twanging, shimmering score'), *Backdraft*, *Regarding Henry*, *K2* (a crashing, electro-Mahlerian score), *Radio Flyer*, *The Power Of One*, *A League Of Their Own*, *Toys* (with Trevor Horn), *Where Sleeping Dogs Lie* (with Mark Mancina), *Point Of No Return*, *Calendar Girl*, *True Romance*, *Cool Runnings*, *The House Of The Spirits*, *Younger And Younger*, *I'll Do Anything*, *Africa: The Serengeti*, *Renaissance Man*, *The Lion King* (1994, Academy and Golden Globe Awards), *Drop Zone*, *Crimson Tide* (another Academy Award), *Beyond Rangoon*, *Nine Months*, *Something To Talk About*, *Two Deaths*, *Broken Arrow*, *Muppet Treasure Island*, *The Fan*, *The Whole Wide World*, *The Preacher's Wife*, *Smilla's Sense Of Snow*, *The Peacemaker*, *Scream 2*, *As Good As It Gets*, *The Last Days*, *The Prince Of Egypt*, *The Thin Red Line*, *The Road To El Dorado*, *Gladiator*, *Mission: Impossible II*,

*The Pledge, Hannibal, Pearl Harbor, Black Hawk Down*, and *Spirit: Stallion Of The Cimarron*.

In 1992, Zimmer composed the music for 'one of the most bizarre television re-creations to date', the 10-hour series, *Millennium*. His other work for the small screen includes the popular *First Born* (1988), *Space Rangers* (1993), *The Critic* (1994, series theme), and *High Incident* (1996, series theme). Zimmer is most certainly a major figure in music; his accomplishments in the film world for such a comparatively young man are already awesome.

● ALBUMS: *The Wings Of A Film: The Music Of Hans Zimmer* (PolyGram 2001) ★★★.

## ZTT RECORDS

Formed in January 1983 by producer Trevor Horn, a former member of the Buggles and Yes, together with his wife Jill Sinclair, Paul Morley, and Gary Langan. ZTT was one of the most innovative UK labels of the early 80s. Horn employed the sharp marketing skills of former *New Musical Express* journalist Morley, whose obtuse style and interest in unearthing obscure talent was allied to a love of ephemeral pop. ZTT was an abbreviation of Zang Tuum Tumb, a phrase used by the Italian futurist Russulo to describe the sound of machine-gun fire. The artistic notions of the label were emphasized through elaborate artwork and a release policy that encouraged the use of multi-format pressings. The label was distributed by Island Records until 1986, after which it pursued the independent route.

Among the early signings to the label were the Art Of Noise and Propaganda, both of whom enjoyed chart success and enhanced the label's *avant garde* reputation. The key act, however, was undoubtedly Frankie Goes To Hollywood, who conjured up a trilogy of spectacular UK number 1 hits in 1984 with 'Relax', 'Two Tribes' and 'The Power Of Love'. The release of 14 different mixes of 'Relax' also established ZTT and Horn as pioneering forces in the remix market. Frankie Goes To Hollywood's double album *Welcome To The Pleasure Dome* was quintessential ZTT, with arresting artwork, political slogans, and mock merchandising ideas included on the sleeve. The Frankie Goes To Hollywood flame burned brightly until the second album, *Liverpool*, which proved expensive and time-consuming and sold far fewer copies than expected. The label continued its search for original talent, but all too often signed notably obscure acts who failed to find success in the mainstream. Among the artists who joined ZTT were Act, Anne Pigalle, Insignificance, Nasty Rox Inc. and Das Psych-Oh Rangers. Roy Orbison was also signed for a brief period and Grace Jones provided a formidable hit with 'Slave To The Rhythm'. ZTT suffered its most serious setback at the hands of former Frankie Goes To Hollywood singer Holly Johnson, who successfully took the label to the High Court in 1988 and won substantial damages after the band's contract was declared void, unenforceable and an unreasonable restraint of trade.

The label then operated a joint venture with Warner Brothers Records for 10 years, enjoying major success with Seal and 808 State, before separating from the conglomerate in 1998. Their new roster of artists included heavy metal band Raging Speedhorn.

## ZZ TOP

Formed in Houston, Texas, USA, in 1970, ZZ Top evolved out of the city's psychedelic scene and consist of Billy Gibbons (b. 16 December 1949, Houston, Texas, USA; guitar, vocals, ex-Moving Sidewalks), Dusty Hill (b. Joe Hill, 19 May 1949, Dallas, Texas, USA; bass, vocals) and Frank Beard (b. 11 June 1949, Frankston, Texas, USA; drums), the last two both ex-American Blues. ZZ Top's original line-up – Gibbons, Lanier Greig (bass) and Dan Mitchell (drums) – was also the final version of the Moving Sidewalks. This initial trio completed ZZ Top's debut single, 'Salt Lick', before Greig was fired. He was replaced by Bill Ethridge. Mitchell was then replaced by Frank Beard while Dusty Hill subsequently joined in place of Ethridge. Initially ZZ Top joined a growing swell of southern boogie bands and started a constant round of touring, building up a strong following. Their debut album, while betraying a healthy interest in blues, was firmly within this genre, but *Rio Grande Mud* indicated a greater flexibility. It included the rousing 'Francene' which, although indebted to the Rolling Stones, gave the trio their first hit and introduced them to a much wider audience.

Their third album, *Tres Hombres*, was a powerful, exciting set that drew from delta music and high-energy rock. It featured the band's first national Top 50 hit with 'La Grange' and was their first platinum album. The trio's natural ease was highly affecting and Gibbons' startling guitar work was rarely bettered during these times. In 1974, the band's first annual 'Texas-Size Rompin' Barndance And Bar-B-Q' was held at the Memorial Stadium at the University Of Texas. 85,000 people attended: the crowds were so large that the University declined to hold any rock concerts, and it was another 20 years before they resumed. However, successive album releases failed to attain the same high standard and ZZ Top took an extended vacation following their expansive 1976/7 tour. After non-stop touring for a number of years the band needed a rest. Other reasons, however, were not solely artistic, as the trio now wished to secure a more beneficial recording contract.

They resumed their career in 1979 with the superb *Deguello*, by which time both Gibbons and Hill had grown lengthy beards (without each other knowing!). Revitalized by their break, the trio offered a series of pulsating original songs on *Deguello* as well as inspired recreations of Sam And Dave's 'I Thank You' and Elmore James' 'Dust My Broom'. The transitional *El Loco* followed in 1981 and although it lacked the punch of its predecessor, preferring the surreal to the celebratory, the set introduced the growing love of technology that marked the trio's subsequent releases. *Eliminator* deservedly became ZZ Top's bestselling album (10 million copies in the USA by 1996). Fuelled by a series of memorable, tongue-in-cheek videos, it provided several international hit singles, including the million-selling 'Gimme All Your Lovin'. 'Sharp Dressed Man' and 'Legs' were also gloriously simple yet enormously infectious songs. The trio skilfully wedded computer-age technology to their barrelhouse R&B to create a truly memorable set that established them as one of the world's leading live attractions. The follow-up, *Afterburner*, was another strong album, although it could not match the sales of the former. It did feature some excellent individual moments in 'Sleeping Bag' and 'Rough Boy', and the cleverly titled 'Velcro Fly'. ZZ Top undertook another lengthy break before returning with the impressive *Recycler*. Other notable appearances in 1990 included a cameo, playing themselves, in *Back To The Future III*. In 1991 a greatest hits compilation was issued and a new recording contract was signed the following year, with BMG Records. The band's studio work during this decade failed to match the commercial and critical success of the 80s, although 1996's *Rhythmeen* demonstrated a willingness to experiment with their trademark sound. The trio celebrated three decades playing music together on 1999's *XXX*. The following year Hill was diagnosed with hepatitis C, forcing the band to cancel a planned tour.

Over the years, one of ZZ Top's greatest strengths has been their consistently high-standard live presentation and performance on numerous record-breaking (financially) tours in the USA. One of rock's maverick attractions, Gibbons, Hill and Beard have retained their eccentric, colourful image, dark glasses and Stetson hats, complete with an almost casual musical dexterity that has won over hardened cynics and carping critics. In addition to having produced a fine (but sparse) canon of work, they will also stay in the record books as having the longest beards in musical history (although one member, the inappropriately named Frank Beard, is clean-shaven). Whether by design or chance, they are doomed to end every music encyclopedia.

● ALBUMS: *ZZ Top's First Album* (London 1970) ★★★, *Rio Grande Mud* (London 1972) ★★★, *Tres Hombres* (London 1973) ★★★★, *Fandango!* (London 1975) ★★, *Tejas* (London 1976) ★★, *Deguello* (Warners 1979) ★★★, *El Loco* (Warners 1981) ★★★, *Eliminator* (Warners 1983) ★★★★, *Afterburner* (Warners 1985) ★★★★, *Recycler* (Warners 1990) ★★★, *Antenna* (RCA 1994) ★★★, *Rhythmeen* (RCA 1996) ★★★, *XXX* (RCA 1999) ★★.

● COMPILATIONS: *The Best Of ZZ Top* (London 1977) ★★★, *Greatest Hits* (Warners 1992) ★★★★, *One Foot In The Blues* (Warners 1994) ★★★.

● VIDEOS: *Greatest Hits Video Collection* (Warner Music Video 1992).

● FURTHER READING: *Everything You Wanted To Know About ... ZZ Top*, Robert Draper. *Elimination: The ZZ Top Story*, Dave Thomas. *ZZ Top: Bad And Worldwide*, Deborah Frost. *Sharp Dressed Men: ZZ Top Behind The Scenes From Blues To Boogie To Beards*, David Blayney.

# INDEX

# D